D0959458

South Pacific

Rowan McKinnon
Brett Atkinson, Celeste Brash, Jean-Bernard Carillet,
Peter Dragicevich, Jocelyn Harewood, Nana Luckham,
Craig McLachlan, Dean Starnes

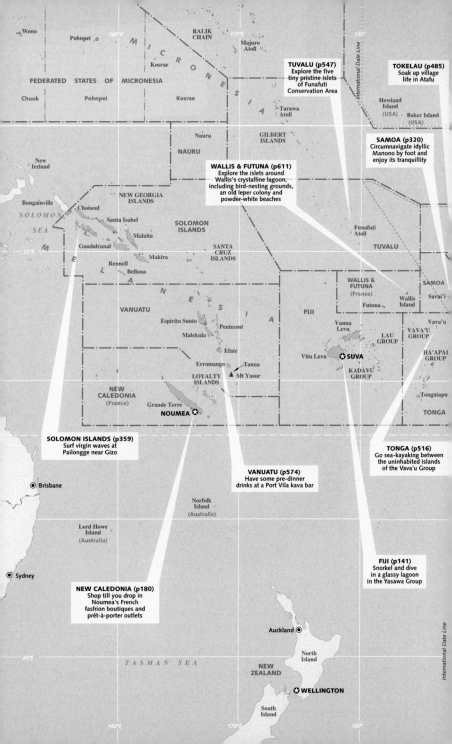

TUVALU (p547)
Explore the five tiny pristine islets of Funafuti Conservation Area

TOKELAU (p485)
Soak up village life in Atafu

SAMOA (p320)
Circumnavigate idyllic Manono by foot and enjoy its tranquillity

WALLIS & FUTUNA (p611)
Explore the islets around Wallis's crystalline lagoon, including bird-nesting grounds, an old leper colony and powder-white beaches

SOLOMON ISLANDS (p359)
Surf virgin waves at Pailongge near Gizo

VANUATU (p574)
Have some pre-dinner drinks at a Port Vila kava bar

TONGA (p516)
Go sea-kayaking between the uninhabited islands of the Vava'u Group

FIJI (p141)
Snorkel and dive in a glassy lagoon in the Yasawa Group

NEW CALEDONIA (p180)
Shop till you drop in Noumea's French fashion boutiques and prêt-à-porter outlets

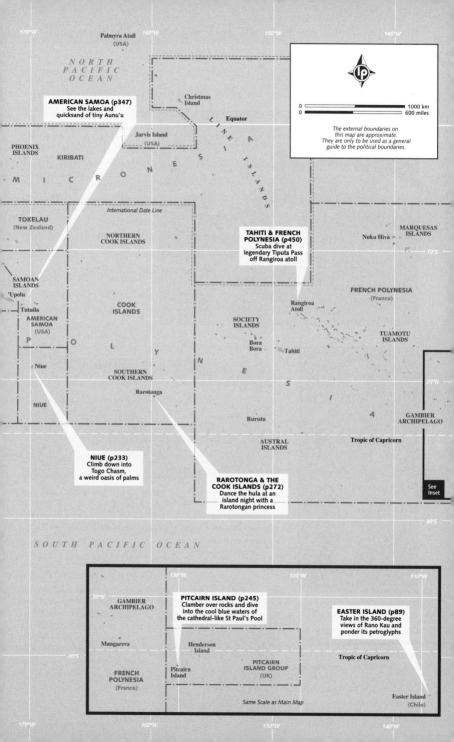

NORTH
PACIFIC
OCEAN

Palmyra Atoll
(USA)

Christmas
Island

Equator

Jarvis Island
(USA)

PHOENIX
ISLANDS

KIRIBATI

M I C R O N E S I A

TOKELAU
(New Zealand)

International Date Line

NORTHERN
COOK ISLANDS

SAMOAN
ISLANDS

'Upolu

Tutuila

AMERICAN
SAMOA
(USA)

COOK
ISLANDS

P   O   L   Y   N   E   S   I   A

Niue

SOUTHERN
COOK ISLANDS

NIUE

Rarotonga

SOCIETY
ISLANDS

Bora
Bora

Tahiti

Rangiroa
Atoll

FRENCH POLYNESIA
(France)

MARQUESAS
ISLANDS

Nuku Hiva

10°S

TUAMOTU
ISLANDS

20°N

GAMBIER
ARCHIPELAGO

Rurutu

Tropic of Capricorn

AUSTRAL
ISLANDS

See
Inset

30°S

SOUTH   PACIFIC   OCEAN

AMERICAN SAMOA (p347)
See the lakes and
quicksand of tiny Aunu'u

**TAHITI & FRENCH
POLYNESIA (p450)**
Scuba dive at
legendary Tiputa Pass
off Rangiroa atoll

NIUE (p233)
Climb down into
Togo Chasm,
a weird oasis of palms

**RAROTONGA & THE
COOK ISLANDS (p272)**
Dance the hula at an
island night with a
Rarotongan princess

The external boundaries on
this map are approximate.
They are only to be used as a general
guide to the political boundaries.

0   1000 km
0   600 miles

20°N

GAMBIER
ARCHIPELAGO

Mangareva

FRENCH
POLYNESIA
(France)

Henderson
Island

Pitcairn
Island

PITCAIRN
ISLAND GROUP
(UK)

Tropic of Capricorn

Easter Island
(Chile)

40°S

Same Scale as Main Map

PITCAIRN ISLAND (p245)
Clamber over rocks and dive
into the cool blue waters of
the cathedral-like St Paul's Pool

EASTER ISLAND (p89)
Take in the 360-degree
views of Rano Kau and
ponder its petroglyphs

170°W   160°W   150°W   140°W

130°W   120°W   110°W

170°W   160°W   150°W   140°W

On the Road

ROWAN McKINNON
Coordinating Author
That's me on the left with the dodgy leg in the cast – I broke my fibula bone before I left for the Cook Islands and dragged this thing all over the Cooks like a guy with a club foot. The pilot was the same guy who flew me every where. Somehow our planets aligned and he was on duty every time I hobbled up those steps.

BRETT ATKINSON I'd just scrambled out of the Matapa reef pool after coming face to face with a small shark. Now I'm trying to spot the sleek beastie again from above. I still don't know how it made it in to the pool from beyond the reef – possibly through a narrow tunnel in the coral.

JEAN-BERNARD CARILLET
There are lots of archaeological sites hidden in the jungle in the Marquesas, and it's a shame that they are largely underrated. This site on 'Ua Huka has three *tiki* (statues). I can hold on to this one, because it has lost its *mana* (spiritual power).

CELESTE BRASH Here I am at port with Captain Matt Jolly in Mangareva, French Polynesia, just before departing on our 36-hour voyage to Pitcairn Island aboard the M/V *Braveheart*. Once at sea, I suffered in my bunk till our sunrise arrival at Pitcairn – spectacular! The island was well-worth the seasickness.

NANA LUCKHAM We hired a boat from the town council to take us to tiny Funafula Islet, which has perfect desert island surroundings. Testing the warm waters was top of the list, but bathing suits are frowned upon in modest Tuvalu, so we had to do so fully clothed.

PETER DRAGICEVICH Flying to the gorgeous island of 'Ofu (Tonga) is a thrilling experience – not least because the airstrip has water at either end of it. That's me with Deb, the airport manager/air traffic controller/bookings agent/hostess/check-in clerk/luggage handler. She also looks after guests at the lodge next door.

CRAIG McLACHLAN Uninhabited Pau is about as idyllic as an island can get! Low tide reveals a ribbon of sand linking it to neighbouring Ngau. When I paddled there and held my camera at arms length to snap my own photo, it occurred that perhaps this paradise shouldn't be revealed to anyone else!

JOCELYN HAREWOOD Mele Cascades are a glorious spread of falls and pools, with rope ladders, slippery little tracks and hundreds of steps for you to make your way to the top. This day I was coaxed into abseilling back down the cascade. I made it into the bottom pool, waterlogged and totally exhillarated.

DEAN STARNES Starting as good clean fun, like most who visit the Sabeto Hot Springs, the temptation to get down and dirty in the mud proved irresistible. Watch your fellow wallowers carefully. The moment they start to whisper, be prepared for attack. Of course, mud slinging with impunity is unheard of and, armed with a fistful of ooze, I soon had my revenge.

For full author biographies see p657.

SOUTH PACIFIC EXPERIENCE

The Pacific Ocean is huge, taking up a third of the planet's surface. It's also incredibly varied, from the primitive regions of the remote Solomon Islands to the chic urban spaces of Noumea and Pape'ete. Many people travel to the region for rest and relaxation, to flop in a banana chair with a book on the beach, and idle a while over a reef with a mask and snorkel. But it's a tropical playground for active travellers too. Jean-Bernard Carillet, our resident Lonely Planet scuba junkie, has compiled a guide to diving in the South Pacific on p73. Surfers, hikers and and cavers will also find plenty of ways to stay busy.

Volcanoes, Mountains & Lakes

The islands of the Pacific are not all pancake-flat coral atolls. The region is very volcanically active, which has created impressive high islands with rugged mountainous interiors and uplifted coral reefs on others. Some islands are collapsed volcanic calderas that have lake systems in their sunken interiors. The South Pacific offers wonderful opportunities for hikers.

① Lake Te'Nggano (Rennell Island), Solomon Islands

The South Pacific's most famous lake is Lake Te'Nggano (p387) – a World Heritage site on Rennell Island, the remote Polynesian outlier.

② Mont Panié, New Caledonia

Mont Panié (1629m; p206) is New Caledonia's highest peak and a challenging two-day hike.

③ Mt Yasur (Tanna), Vanuatu

Vanuatu's vulcanology showpiece, Mt Yasur (p581), is one of the region's most active and most accessible volcanoes.

④ Des Voeux Peak (Taveuni), Fiji

Taveuni offers good trekking to the peak of 1195m Des Voeux Peak (p159) with majestic views over the Lau Group.

⑤ Tofua & Kao, Tonga

Cone-shaped 1109m Kao and 507m Tofua (p516) are in the Ha'apai islands – Kao is dormant while Tofua, Tonga's most active volcano, still bellows smoke.

⑥ Lake Lanoto'o ('Upolu) Samoa

'Upolu's Lake Lanoto'o (p315) is a crater lake in the remote central highlands – it's pea green and eerie.

⑦ Aunu'u, American Samoa

Tiny Aunu'u (p347) is a volcanic cone and at its northern end is fiery-red Pala Lake, an expanse of quicksand; and Red Lake, in its core, glows at dusk.

⑧ The Needle, Cook Islands

Rarotonga's popular half-day Cross-Island Track (p264) that runs from the north to south coasts goes past the Needle, a dramatic pinnacle 413m above sea level.

⑨ 'Ua Pou, French Polynesia

'Ua Pou (p463) has 12 basalt pinnacles that were once the cores of volcanoes – the signature landscape of the Marquesan postcards.

Surfing

Polynesians invented surfing and yet, apart from Tahiti, Samoa and Fiji, the South Pacific remains largely unexplored by surfers. Intrepid board riders are making inroads into other Pacific islands and finding brilliant uncrowded waves in warm, crystal-clear tropical waters. In some places the swell is seasonall: the cyclone season from late October to April brings waves from the north; and during wintertime (May to August) low-pressure systems in the Southern Ocean and Tasman Sea bring big swells to islands with exposed southern coastlines.

1 Gizo, Solomon Islands

The Solomons get great waves in the October-to-April monsoon season. Near Gizo, in Western Province, there are breaks at Pailongge, Titiana and Makuti Island (see p382).

2 Îlot Ténia, New Caledonia

The south side of Grande Terre gets big swells from the Tasman Sea and Antarctic Ocean in the May-to-August period. Perhaps the best wave in New Caledonia is on the long barrier reef – Îlot Ténia (p197).

3 Port Villa, Vanuatu

The surf in Vanuatu doesn't ever get huge but there are 1m waves very close to Port Villa at Pango Point and Erakor Point, and around Mele Bay at Devil's Point (p569).

4 Cloudbreak, Fiji

Fiji's most famous break is Cloudbreak (p137), off Tavarua in the Mamanuca Group.

5 Ha'atafu Beach, Tonga

Ha'atafu Beach (p509) is the centre of Tonga's fledgling surf scene.

6 'Upolu, Samoa

'Upolu is well and truly on the world surfing map and gets year-round swells and powerful wintertime waves. The island has a few specialist surfers' resorts where operators use boats to access some of the offshore breaks, including Salani Surf Resort (p318)

7 Tutuila, American Samoa

There's brilliant surfing in American Samoa, though not much of a surf scene. The south side of Tutuila gets solid 2m waves at Fagneanea and Sliding Rock (p355)

8 Rarotonga, Cook Islands

Rarotonga has the only surf scene in the Cooks, though there's surf off the perimeter reefs of most of the islands. Bodyboarding is popular in Rarotonga but there's just a tiny community of boardriders. The best surf comes with the November-to-April cyclone season, when there are fast and fierce waves off the Rarotongan Beach Resort (p268).

9 Teahupoo (Tahiti), French Polynesia

Tahiti hosts the Billabong Pro at legendary Teahupoo (p412), one of the world's great surfing breaks that can strike fear into even the most seasoned surfers.

10 Mataveri, Easter Island (Rapa Nui)

Rapa Nui is in the middle of nowhere and gets buffeted by surf from all directions. Mataveri (p93), on the southwest coast is a long point break and can be deadly – for advanced surfers only.

Caving

Volcanic activity has caused the limestone reefs that encircle many islands to lift, resulting in dramatic *makatea* that's riddled with caves and chambers. Amateur speleologists can visit many of the caves of South Pacific islands either on their own or with a guide. Many of the region's caverns served as sacred burial grounds and some still contain human remains. Many of the largest cave systems are not yet properly explored.

❶ Mataniko Falls, Solomon Islands

A two-hour walk east from Honiara brings you to the spectacular Mataniko Falls (p374), which thunders down a cliff. Higher up, the river passes through a vast cave full of stalagmites, swallows and bats. This cave was used by WWII Japanese trying to evade capture by the Americans.

❷ Grotte de Lindéralique, New Caledonia

About 2km south of the picturesque village of Hienghène, on Grande Terre's northeast coast, is the huge dome of Grotte de Lindéralique (p204). The limestone coast around this region has many caves and weird rock formations.

❸ Valeva Cave, Vanuatu

You can explore parts of Valeva Cave (p576) and its chambers, tunnels and beautiful underground lake in a kayak. There are strange footprints engraved in the rock floor.

❹ Sawa-i-Lau, Fiji

The ethereal Sawa-i-Lau caves and swimming pools (p146) were used by Brooke Shields in *The Blue Lagoon* and you can swim through an underwater passage into other chambers. The limestone walls have ancient carvings and inscriptions.

❺ 'Anahulu Cave, Tonga

'Anahulu (p509), Tonga's most famous cave, is a little overloved – burning fagot torches and foot traffic have blackened its stalactites and stalagmites – but it's still eerie. The pool is a popular swimming spot.

❻ Piula Cave Pool, Samoa

Piula Cave Pool (p315), east of Apia, has two wonderful cave pools connected by a 3m underwater passage that you can swim through.

❼ Vaikona Chasm, Niue

Vaikona Chasm (p233) is a vast chamber with long swimming pools that leads on and on into the darkness.

❽ Anatakitaki, Cook Islands

The endangered *kopeka* bird lives in 'Atiu's Anatakitaki cave (p280) and nowhere else.

❾ Ana Aeo Cave, French Polynesia

Speleologists should make for the *makatea* island of Rurutu in the Australs – the huge Ana Aeo Cave (p470), abundant in stalactites and stalagmites, is the showpiece of Rurutu's many caverns.

❿ Ana Kai Tangata, Easter Island (Rapa Nui)

The northern loop of the Parque Nacional Rapa Nui (p87) contains many caves and lava tubes. The remnants of birdmen rock-art paintings can be seen in Ana Kai Tangata.

Solace Of Solitude

The South Pacific is renowned for its wide open spaces, and while for people-per-sq-km it hardly rivals Macau or Hong Kong, you might be surprised to learn that several South Pacific countries rank right up there among the world's densest populations. Did you know that Tuvalu comes in at number 24 and Tonga 76? Getting far from the madding crowd can be harder than you might imagine.

⑥ Tokelau

You could be the only visitor on Tokelau (p485). Just getting there's a challenge as none of its three atolls have airstrips and only occasional cargo freighters and yachties drop by. Wade your way to one of the tiny islands ringing the country's 165 sq km of lagoon for a true desert-island experience.

① Hienghène & Pouébo, New Caledonia

The regions of Grand Terre's northeast from Hienghène to Pouébo (p204) are a world away from glitzy Noumea, with rivers and waterfalls, rainforest and dramatic coasts.

② Caqalai island, Fiji

Tiny Caqalai island (p150), just south of Ovalau in the Lomaiviti Group, is Fiji's antidote to the hubbub of the Mamanucas and Yasawas. There's a rustic resort run by Methodists and the beaches are heavenly.

③ Niulakita, Tuvalu

Only 30-odd of Tuvalu's 12,000 people call tiny Niulakita (p551) home. There's no formal accommodation but the beaches on this atoll are sublime.

④ Alofi, Wallis & Futuna

Get lost in this oft-forgotten French territory. Alofi (p231) has no permanent population, but there's solar-powered *fale* accommodation, shady trees and exquisite beaches.

⑤ Pau island, Tonga

Make for Pau island (p527), in the southern part of the Vava'u Group, for a deserted island experience. This uninhabited dream island is accessible by foot at low tide, when a slender ribbon of sand links Pau to Ngau.

⑦ Niue

The wilderness of Niue (p227), with its many caves in the uplifted coral *makatea* and superb snorkelling, more than makes up for what it lacks in idyllic beaches. Niue is the smallest independent country – 1300 people on an island of 269 sq km and lots of virgin rainforest.

⑧ Suwarrow, Cook Islands

Suwarrow (p290) was made famous by the hermit Tom Neale, who lived there for three long stints between 1952 and his death in 1977. His book *An Island to One's Self* is a classic. These days Suwarrow is the Cooks' only national park and its only residents are two part-time managers. You'll need a private yacht to get there.

⑨ Fatu Hiva (the Marquesas), French Polynesia

Fatu Hiva (p469) is the remotest of the Marquesas. With no airstrip and only occasionally serviced by boat, Fatu Hiva is an untouched paradise of towering mountains and virgin rainforest.

⑩ Pitcairn Island

Rugged little Pitcairn (p240) has punched well above its weight in Pacific history and today it's home to less than 50 people. There are plenty of *Bounty* relics to see and dramatic coastal and nature trails cliffs to explore.

17

Contents

Destination South Pacific

Slip on that sarong, listen for the lullaby of waves broken only by the satisfying 'thunk' of coconuts falling on golden sands and throw away your watch in preparation for 'island time'. The Pacific has a mindset all of its own. Its hugeness is big enough to hold all your dreams of snorkelling around idyllic coral atolls, slow-sunset evenings distilled with cocktails and beaches beautiful enough to send even the most stressed visitor into a catatonia of relaxation.

From tiny Tuvalu to controversial bad boy Fiji to uber-chic French Polynesia, the family of Pacific islands is a varied bunch. And you can choose how you'll acquaint yourself with this diverse crowd. Many opt for resorts in big centres like Fiji, the Cooks or Vanuatu, or plunge into another world diving among the dazzling coral and magical marine life that makes Nemo look like a pallid goldfish. But there's other ways to discover the Pacific. You could puzzle over lost civilisations amid the icons of Easter Island or see why Fletcher Christian hopped off the *Bounty* in favour of the remote paradise of Pitcairn Island. Why not get intrepid and seek out the live volcanoes or don your pith helmet to trek into lush forests? Then there's the shipwrecks to dive, bohemian capitals to explore and did we mention that a cocktail with at least a couple of tropical fruits in it is compulsory?

Of course in the vastness of the Pacific, it's not all kava and skittles. In bars across the Pacific you'll hear mumblings about Fiji and the Solomon Islands which, have both seen their share of unrest. The Solomons had the RAMSI (Regional Assistance Mission to the Solomon Islands) troops arrive in 2003 to police the nation, while coup-prone Fiji struggles to maintain diplomatic relations with other Pacific nations who don't seem to like the idea of skipping elections and military-based rule.

But while some cling to power there are also new freedoms in the islands. In 2008 French President Nicholas Sarkozy talked about his commitment to autonomy for New Caledonia, which has been a territory of France for decades with referendums to be held in the coming years. In Samoa with the death of the long-reigning King Malietoa Tanumafill II, the nation quietly overturned more than 40 years of monarchy by becoming a republic. The change means that Tonga is the Pacific's last remaining monarchy, which is based on the ancient rule of chiefs (p47).

Ex-colonies like Australia and New Zealand still exert considerable influence in the Pacific through their membership of the Pacific Islands Forum. New Zealand has been particularly vocal about removing Fiji from the forum because of its failure to host elections, which has seen Fiji respond by deporting NZ and Australian journalists. Australia continues to lobby for greater regionalism, whereby Pacific nations will act collectively on trade, fishing, waste management and air transport. Under the Forum's Pacific Plan the nations of the region would remove barriers to trade within the region and trade externally as a collective group. This could one day create a single currency in the Pacific and will certainly create favourable economies of scale.

Another interesting development has seen the experiment of a seasonal worker visa for workers from Kiribati, Tonga, Vanuatu and Papua New Guinea to fruit pick in the Australian horticulture industry. While some see this as offering employment opportunities to islanders and pumping money into their economies, human rights groups have identified it as open to exploitation in a form of 21st-century blackbirding (p44).

FAST FACTS

Most common unit of currency: US dollar (US$)

Total visitors: 1,206,632 (580,282 on holiday)

Estimated total population (including Micronesia): 9,504,445

Estimated number of islands in the Pacific: 25,000

Highest proportion covered of land covered by forest: 88.2% (Solomon Islands)

Highest proportion of women in national parliament: 14% Tokelau

Number of *Survivor TV* series filmed in the area: six (at 2009; more coming soon)

As old colonies change their roles in the Pacific, new powers are appearing. In 2006, China signed the catchily titled Action Plan of Economic Development and Cooperation with several Pacific nations offering trade and aid. Some diplomats have been critical of the move as an attempt to get a stake in fishing rights or keep a check on China's 'rogue state' Taiwan (which also has interests in the region). Still the Pacific – particularly Fiji and Tonga – are benefiting with building programmes, preferential loans and access to Chinese markets.

Japan has long been accused of vote-buying at the International Whaling Commission by offering aid to member nations such as the Solomon Islands to continue their whaling in the Pacific. In 2007 Japan further tried to increase its influence in the area by offering peacekeeping troops to the Solomons.

But there's one issue on which the Pacific won't compromise: global warming. Once it was only Tuvalu with its low-lying atolls who was speaking out, but at the 2008 UN Climate Change Conference in 2008 more than 40 island nations from around the world were lending their voices in protest. While small islands like Tuvalu and Tokelau are at risk of sinking, other environmental issues are a factor. Reduced land anywhere in the Pacific means less space for agriculture, and the precious corals of Fiji and French Polynesia are bleaching as water temperatures rise with the expanding hole in the ozone layer. General temperature increases could also multiply insect and bacteria populations and increase diseases such as malaria and typhoid. To see what you can do check the Greendex (p682) and read about responsible travel (p28).

But the Pacific dream has survived these nightmares and has preserved its fair share of isolated beaches, honeymoon escapes and sun-drenched resorts. In its vastness there's plenty of room to find your own Pacific by stretching out a towel, strapping on a snorkel and listening to the world's largest ocean lap at the shore.

'While small islands like Tuvalu and Tokelau are at risk of sinking, other environmental issues are a factor'

Getting Started

The South Pacific conjures up images of long white beaches, cool drinks with cocktail umbrellas and lazy days lying in the sun. While the region may seem like a dreamy tropical paradise it's certainly not all like that. Countries like French Polynesia and Fiji are used to the ways of tourists and have good tourism infrastructure, but other places like the Solomon Islands and Tuvalu don't get a lot of visitors and have few facilities for tourists. The region is home to some of the planet's most remote and isolated communities separated by vast distances, and studying domestic airline routes and schedules (and often booking flights) before you arrive is important if you want to see more than just one part of any South Pacific country.

Planning will help reduce costs too – some domestic routes can be done by boat, and the best places to stay aren't always the most expensive. Some islands are easily accessible while even getting to others can be a major challenge. The South Pacific is not a budget destination like Southeast Asia, but we've done our best to help you stretch your dollars, *pa'angas*, CFPs, talas and vatus.

WHEN TO GO

Weather is the most important factor when deciding when to travel. Most visitors travel outside the wet season. Tropical temperatures don't vary much – it's *always* hot – but during the wet things can be sticky and uncomfortable and places can be impossible to reach because of boggy roads. The wet season is also the time of cyclones. However, wet-season rains often fall in a single great deluge late in the afternoon or at night and can be spectacular to witness, and they freshen and cool the oppressive air.

See Climate Charts (p627) for more information

The wet season runs from November to April; the dry from May to October. However, many volcanic islands have tall mountains around which rising moist air condenses into clouds, and small micro-climates are common. For more on climate, see p64.

Many Pacific islanders live in Australia and New Zealand (NZ) and many children go to boarding school in these countries. Flights and inter-island boats are often fully booked at school-holiday times and around the Christmas–New Year period.

Prices are highest during peak tourist times, accommodation fully booked and planes packed. There are better deals in the shoulder seasons (either side of the dry season) in October and May. Read the Climate and When to Go sections in the country chapters and see the Climate Charts (p627).

Major local festivals and celebrations are always worth seeing. See the International Festivals & Events boxed text (p30) and the Festivals & Events sections in the country chapters.

Things can change quickly in the Pacific – a cyclone can knock out accommodation, roads, electricity and telephones, and local disputes can close off an area. It's best to have some flexibility about your travel plans and try to be adaptable. Islanders have a much more relaxed attitude towards time than people from Western cultures and there's no point getting frustrated when things don't go the way you expect them to – slow down and enjoy the sunshine.

Check for cyclones before you head off, particularly in or around the cyclone season. Try the **Central Pacific Hurricane Center** (www.prh.noaa.gov/hnl/cphc/) in Hawai'i or the **Fiji Meteorological Service** (www.met.gov.fj). For information on cyclones, see p65.

Travel advisories are published by some governments and provide updated warnings on countries considered unsafe, due to political unrest or natural

---

DON'T LEAVE HOME WITHOUT...

Travel light but pack carefully because you may not be able to buy what you left behind. Check visa requirements (p633) and vaccinations requirements (p644). Photocopy important documents – leave copies at home and take another set with you. Consider the weather conditions – the Cooks and the Solomons are too hot for trousers and sweaters but Vanuatu evenings can be cool. If you don't need bulky clothing leave it behind. Consider the following:

- travel insurance, noting emergency phone and policy numbers (see p630)
- anti-malarial prophylactics for countries where it's a problem (p648)
- basic first-aid kit (p644)
- international diving certificate
- hat, sunglasses, high-UV-protection sunscreen
- good footwear, lightweight trousers and long-sleeved shirt for protection against sunburn and mosquitos
- insect repellent and box-style mosquito net (p648)
- mask, snorkel, rash vest and reef shoes; C-card and logbook if you're diving
- umbrella or poncho-style raincoat that covers your backpack and opens into a groundsheet
- Swiss Army Knife
- torch (flashlight) for exploring caves and late-night village toilet expeditions
- good stash of books.

---

disasters. The Foreign Affairs departments in Australia (http://smartraveller .gov.au) and Canada (www.voyage.gc.ca/dest) both issue advisories, as does the **British Foreign & Commonwealth Office** (www.fco.gov.uk).

COSTS & MONEY

People are often surprised to learn that Pacific countries are generally not cheap to visit. Yes, they're mostly developing countries, but getting there and around, accommodation and food are all fairly expensive. There are two reasons for this: the Pacific has few tourists and there are huge expanses of water that separate these nations and their island groups. Planes and boats are the only modes of inter-island travel and on the islands roads are often poor so 4WDs are common. The cost of getting goods to such remote parts of the world is expensive. The cost of fuel is sky-rocketing and you need a lot of it in the Pacific. Food is mostly imported, as is pretty much everything else from car parts to crockery.

Despite this, travellers on all budgets find their way into the Pacific. Countries like French Polynesia and New Caledonia can be incredibly expensive, but you can get by on a lot less in places like Samoa and Fiji. Let go of your modern-world luxuries and you can live on next to nothing in a village or avoid the tourist hotels and stay in guest houses and dorms patronised by locals, church groups and aid workers.

Travel cheaply in Fiji or Tonga and you'll need at least US$40 per day, but even hard-nosed budget travellers who camp and self-cater in Tahiti will spend at least US$100 per day. Midrange travellers eating out and sleeping in hotels can expect a daily budget starting at US$100/300 in Fiji/Tahiti. Travellers opting for full-course restaurant meals and resort-style accommodation will be looking at US$200/600.

There are ways to stretch your money and planning will help cut costs – consider a round-the-world ticket (p636), an air pass (p636) or a package holiday (p640). Don't automatically discount package holidays as travel

CONDUCT IN THE SOUTH PACIFIC

Pacific islanders are pretty laid-back about most things including standards of dress, but dressing like a slob won't endear you to anyone. It's not appropriate for men to go bare-chested in town, and women's dress conventions are conservative. Casual attire is fine, but if you're attending a church service, place of worship or formal ceremony you'd better smarten up for the occasion – it would be disrespectful not to make some effort.

In many Pacific countries the display of women's thighs is considered sexually provocative, so skirts and shorts should be knee-length and your itsy bitsy bikini bottoms might cause consternation at the beach (wear board shorts instead). Topless bathing is accepted in a few countries, particularly those with ties to France, but it's usually restricted to resorts and certain beaches. Nude bathing is not on.

Public displays of affection between men and women, even two tourists, are often inappropriate, and flirting with locals can get you into a *lot* of trouble. Melanesians will often walk hand in hand – man with man and woman with woman – but this a simple expression of friendship. Melanesian countries are still generally intolerant of same-sex couples, though there is increasingly some gay pride expressed in the cities. Polynesia has a long tradition of trans-genderism and is more relaxed about homosexuality.

Avoid becoming visibly frustrated when things don't go your way and try not to cause people to lose face.

For information on tipping and bargaining, see p631.

While most islanders are happy about being photographed, some may be uncomfortable. Ask permission and always respect the answer.

See p57 for information about meeting locals.

agents – particularly those based in the country you're travelling to – can often get better rates with airlines and hotels, and tailor a package around your requirements. Accommodation is a major cost – see p623 for options. A place with a kitchen is one way to cut costs. Markets are the best way to buy fresh produce.

Hiring a bicycle or hitchhiking (p643) is worth considering. On some remote islands, hitching is the only option. Scuba diving will push up your costs, but if you bring a mask and snorkel you can enjoy the tropical underwater world for nothing.

See boxed text p69 for the Top 10 South Pacific conservation areas

Prices in this book are likely to change – they usually go up – but if the last tourist season was slow or the local economy crashes, they may be the same or even come down a bit. See p630 for more on handling money.

TRAVELLING RESPONSIBLY

As visitors, we all have responsibilities to local people and the environment. Learn about local customs and you'll find people much more accepting of you.

Certain fish species are becoming endangered – by eating swordfish, marlin, gemfish and southern bluefin tuna we exacerbate the problem (eating albacore tuna is fine).

Avoid buying souvenirs made from animal products – turtleshell, skins and bone. In many countries the importation of these products is illegal. Some of the same considerations apply for souvenirs made from coral and shells. Certain timbers are over-harvested and we should think carefully about what we purchase and how sustainable its production is. If you're buying handicrafts it's better to buy them from the maker than from a shop or emporium that's often owned by a foreign entrepreneur. This way the maker realises the full value of their work and you can contribute to what is sometimes a very marginal existence.

When in the wilderness, bury waste in holes 15cm deep and 100m from any watercourse. Don't use detergents or toothpaste in or near watercourses.

Bottled water is fast becoming an environmental scourge. There are vast amounts of energy vested in the production, filling and transportation of plastic bottles, and they're a major source of litter. It's far better to carry and refill your own water bottle. Where tap water is not potable it can be boiled or treated. Litter is a huge problem on Pacific islands – even if locals are blasé about rubbish, don't add to the problem by leaving your garbage behind.

For more on environmental issues, see p69. For more detailed information on responsible travel, see the boxed texts about diving (p77), yachting (p642) and conduct in the South Pacific (opposite).

TRAVEL LITERATURE

There are many excellent books that have been published about the Pacific. The Australian-based mail-order **Pacific Book House** (www.pacific bookhouse.com.au) specialises in new, used, out-of-print and rare books on the Pacific. Another good resource is US-based **Pacific Island Books** (www .pacificislandbooks.com). Fiji's **University Book Centre** (www.uspbookcentre.com) is also good. For more titles, see the Literature and Books sections in the country chapters.

Getting Stoned with Savages (J Maarten Troost) A funny and insightful story about a European couple living in Vanuatu and Fiji and the consumption of kava.

Vaka: Saga of a Polynesian Canoe (Sir Thomas Davis) The former Cook Islands Prime Minister tells a story of a canoe that sailed the ocean for 300 years – a fascinating exploration of Polynesian culture and history.

Song of the Solomons: Faultlines in the South Pacific (E Hunt Augustus) A fast-paced and excellent novel set against the WWII Battle of Guadalcanal.

30 Days in the South Pacific: True Stories of Escape to Paradise (edited by Sean O'Reilly et al) A lively anthology of travel writing in the Pacific isles.

Tales of the Pacific (Jack London) A collection of short stories from the author's time as a South Seas sailor.

Typee (Herman Melville) This and its sequel *Omoo* were Melville's first forays into the ripping yarns of South Seas whalers, and both much more successful in his lifetime than *Moby Dick*.

The Happy Isles of Oceania: Paddling the Pacific (Paul Theroux) A modern Pacific classic, although not everyone's a fan of Theroux's account of kayaking around the Pacific.

The Fatal Impact: The Invasion of the South Pacific 1767–1840 (Alan Moorehead) An acclaimed book on the impact of colonialism. Critically assesses the havoc wreaked by early European explorers.

Tales of the South Pacific, Rascals in Paradise and Return to Paradise (James Michener) Famous collection of short stories dealing with life in the South Pacific from WWII onward.

INTERNET RESOURCES

The internet is a powerful tool for travellers. For country-specific websites, see the Directory in the country chapters.

Lonely Planet (www.lonelyplanet.com) Summaries on travelling to most places on earth, postcards from other travellers and the Thorn Tree bulletin board.

Pacific Beat (www.abc.net.au/ra/pacbeat) Radio Australia's news and audio-streamed stories.

Pacific Magazine (www.pacificmagazine.net) News and reviews from the regional magazine.

Pacifica (www.pacifica.info) Good travel information.

South Pacific Organizer (www.southpacific.org) David Stanley of Moon Guides maintains this excellent website.

South Pacific Tourism Organisation (www.spto.org) Intergovernmental tourism organisation – good website with good regional and country-specific information.

Herman Melville, author of *Moby Dick*, spent nearly four years in the South Pacific aboard whaling ships. He deserted the *Acushnet* in July 1842 to spend three weeks with the Typee people of the Marquesas who were said to be cannibals, and romanced a Polynesian girl called Fayaway. His first two novels, *Typee* and *Omoo*, were based on these South Seas adventures. Queequeg, Ishmael's friend in *Moby Dick*, is a Polynesian cannibal turned whale harpooner.

TOP 10

FILMS

There are a couple of forgettable Blue Lagoon films shot in Fiji and three versions of the *Bounty* story (see p246), all of them excellent. **Ronin Films** (www.roninfilms.com.au) in Australia distributes some of the more obscure films and documentaries mentioned here.

1 **Since the Company Came** Excellent documentary about logging in the Solomons, land disputes and clan troubles.

2 **Pear Ta Ma 'on Maf (The Land Has Eyes)** Fiji's first feature film (2005) tells the tale of an island girl's struggle with poverty and prejudice and the strength she discovers in her island's mythology.

3 **Tongan Ninja** An NZ spoof of a Hong Kong kung fu movie – great fun!

4 **Tatau Samoa** German director Gisa Schleelein explores the life and work of Samoan tattoo master Paulo Sulu'ape.

5 **Wayfinders: A Pacific Odyssey** Documentary about traditional voyaging and the *Hokule'a* canoe.

6 **Return to Paradise** This 1953 film of James Michener's story starred Gary Cooper and remains a poignant story more than half a century later. It was filmed in Samoa.

7 **The Thin Red Line** This excellent war film set in Guadalcanal features some stunning scenery. The film was predominantly shot in Australia's Daintree rainforest.

8 **Rapa Nui** Co-produced by Kevin Costner in 1994, it's hardly essential viewing, but gives the feel of Easter Island's remote appeal.

9 **Castaway** Filmed on Fiji's remote Monruki Island, Tom Hanks survives a plane crash and befriends a volleyball called Wilson.

10 **The Other Side of Heaven** Based on a true story of an American Mormon missionary in Tonga in the 1950s.

INTERNATIONAL FESTIVALS & EVENTS

Festivals in South Pacific countries are always spectacular and often unusual. Regional celebrations and events are listed here. For other country-specific events, see Festivals & Events in the individual country directories.

1 **Rise of Palolo** (p332) It's not everywhere you get to celebrate worms rising at midnight. The celebrations are observed in Samoa and Fiji.

2 **Miss Galaxy Pageant** (p532) This international *fakaleiti* (transvestite) beauty pageant held in July in Nuku'alofa, Tonga, is riotous fun and always sells out.

3 **Festival of Pacific Arts** This vibrant festival (http://pacartsas.com) showcases traditional arts from around the Pacific and is held every four years in a different country. Next is Solomon Islands in 2012.

4 **Fest'Napuan** (p607) This annual four-day music festival in Port Vila, Vanuatu, in November showcases Pacific contemporary and traditional music (www.vanuatuculture.org).

5 **Hawaiki Nui Va'a** (p477) Canoes from many Pacific countries are raced between the islands of French Polynesia every November.

6 **Vaka Eiva** (p292) Held in November in Rarotonga, Vaka Eiva is the Cooks' biggest sporting event. Outrigger-canoe races are the feature of this week-long festival.

7 **South Pacific Games** In September 2011 New Caledonia hosts the South Pacific Games (www.southpacificgames.com), held every four years. Twenty-two Pacific nations take part in 32 sporting events – about 4000 athletes in all.

8 **Pacific Nations Cup** Fiji, Tonga and Samoa join Australia A, NZ Maori and Japan in play-offs for this annual prize in venues of all the participating teams (www.irb.com/pacificnationscup).

9 **Pacific Island Sevens Tournaments** Held annually in the Cook Islands, Fiji and Samoa, these games feature as much dance and celebration as rugby (www.oceaniarugby.com).

10 **Billabong Tahiti Pro** (p477) This event on the pro surfing world tour has surfers carving up waves at legendary Teahupoo in Tahiti in May.

Itineraries
CLASSIC ROUTES

LE GRANDE TOUR
One to Two Months/Fiji to the Cook Islands

Fly to Fiji and catch a boat to the **Yasawas** (p141) or **Mamanucas** (p135) where countless islets offer fantastic digs and brilliant beaches. Take a bus to the **Nausori Highlands** (p135) to experience traditional Fiji and then onto **Suva** (p125), where you can discover the best way to eat human at the **Fiji Museum** (p125; also see p132).

Join a **kava** (p575) session in one of Vanuatu's *nakamal* around Port Villa and see **Mt Yasur** (p581) glow in the dark on a night-time visit to one of the world's most accessible volcanoes.

Fly to **Noumea** (p180) where Pacific cultures are showcased at the wonderful **Tjibaou Cultural Centre** (p185).

Then head to French Polynesia, starting at vibrant **Pape'ete** (p409) before seeing idyllic **Mo'orea** (p420) and sublime **Bora Bora** (p438).

Enjoy the nightlife and restaurants of **Rarotonga** (p256) and unwind by **Aitutaki's** idyllic lagoon (p275).

Count the 12,000km moving east to west across the Pacific. This route takes in the region's most glorious lagoons and beaches from Melanesian Fiji, Vanuatu and New Caledonia to Polynesian Tahiti and Rarotonga.

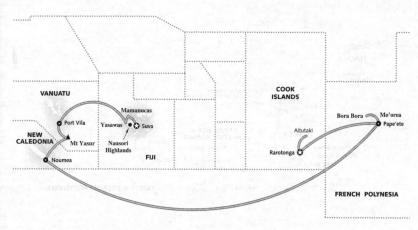

ROADS LESS TRAVELLED

POLYNESIAN ODYSSEY   One to Four Months/Tuvalu to French Polynesia

The tiny atolls of **Tuvalu** (p536) barely break the surface of the Pacific Ocean
(and won't for long if sea levels rise). The **Funafuti Conservation Area** (p547) is
a wonderland of uninhabited islets, reefs, seabirds, dolphins and turtles. In
Samoa's **Apia** (p305), go to the **Palolo Deep Marine Reserve** (p308), a shallow reef
rich in marine life, underwater caves and clams. The **Robert Louis Stevenson
Museum** (p314) is a highlight as is the eerie pea-green crater lake of **Lake
Lanoto'o** (p315). See the **Pulemelei Mound** (p328), Polynesia's largest ancient
monument, and Mt Matavanu's **lava fields** (p324).

This route takes in
most of Polynesia –
from the archaeo-
logical sites of
Samoa and Tonga
to cosmopolitan
Rarotonga and
Tahiti, and visiting
marine reserves
and ancient
burial caves
along the way.

Fly onto **Nuku'alofa** (p502) in the Kingdom of Tonga. See the **Royal Palace**
(not open to commoners; p502) on the way to lively **Talamahu Market** (p502).
Mu'a (Lapaha) (p508) is rich in archaeological ruins, and nearby is famous
'Anahulu Cave (p509). Head to the **Ha'apai Group** (p511) for simple beachside
living in a thatched *fale* or the **Vava'u Group** (p516) for more active adventures
where sea kayaking, surfing, caving and cycling are popular.

The Cooks' capital **Rarotonga** (p256) is a Polynesian princess. Walk the
Cross-Island Track (p264) and snorkel at sublime **Muri Beach** (p265). Catch a plane
to **Aitutaki** (p273) to see her exquisite **lagoon** (p275). Explore the caves of the
makatea islands of **'Atiu** (p279), **Mangaia** (p286) and **Ma'uke** (p282).

Fly to **Pape'ete** (p409), the chic capital of the French Pacific, and
squeeze in brilliant **Bora Bora** (p438) and **Mo'orea** (p420) before the money's
finally spent.

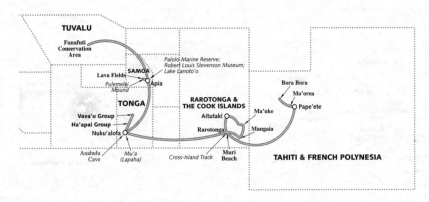

SOUTH PACIFIC OCEAN

MAKE LIKE A MELANESIAN   One to Four Months/Fiji to the Solomons

Start in **Nadi** (p108) and take a ferry out to the **Mamanucas** (p135) for a few days of blissful island hopping, partying and bedding down at beachside *bure* (thatched dwelling). Wend your way through the gorgeous **Yasawas** (p141) and dive or snorkel over the **Somosomo Strait** (p159). Get a boat back to cosmopolitan **Suva** (p125) and be measured for a sari and chow down at an Indo-Fijian curry house or Korean kimchi bar.

New Caledonia's capital **Noumea** (p180) blends Melanesia with French chic and comes with a hefty price tag. Classy restaurants and boutique shopping aside, don't miss the superb **Tjibaou Cultural Centre** (p185). Trek to the peak of **Mont Panié** (p206) and catch a boat to the exquisite **Île des Pins** (p216) and ride a *pirogue*.

Fly to Vanuatu and experience colourful **Port Vila** (p565) and the rich history of this former English/French colonial capital. Swim in the pools of **Mele-Maat Cascades** (p568) and have few shells of **kava** (p575) before trying some of Port Vila's restaurants and nightlife. Go to Tanna to see the active **Mt Yasur** (p581) volcano and take the two-day trek across Malekula's **Dog's Head** (p587) past the cannibal site, caves and traditional villages. On to **Pentecost** (p602) where yam farmers invented bungee jumping. Then **Espiritu Santo** (p593) for world-class diving and game fishing. Espiritu Santo's sleepy capital **Luganville** (p596) has many WWII remains, and nearby the **Matevulu Blue Hole** (p601) and **Millenium Cave** (p601) are highlights.

Ride a boat through the Solomon Islands stunning **Vonavona Lagoon** (p377), snorkel or dive off **Uepi Island** (p378) and chill out in **Gizo** (p381). Travel to **Malaita** (p383), one of the great repositories of traditional Melanesian culture where people summon sharks and live on artificial islands.

From the resort islands of Fiji and New Caledonia's chic boutiques to the kava bars and attractions of Vanuatu and onto the wilds of the rugged Solomons, this route showcases Melanesia in all its brilliant variety.

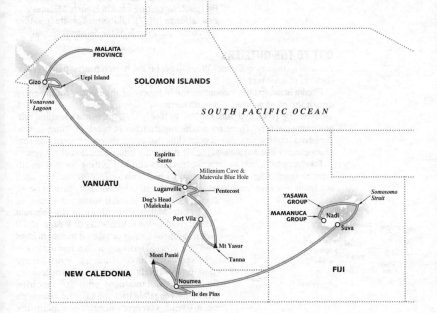

TAILORED TRIPS

SAILING THE SOUTH PACIFIC

The southeast trade wind makes the trip fairly predictable if sailed outside the December-to-March cyclone storm season, and the common cruising route from Panama to Torres Strait has earned the nickname the 'Milk Run'. Whether you arrive from the Panama Canal or the West Coast of the Americas, the **Marquesas Islands** (p457) are the targets after a stop at the Galapagos Islands.

If you got an early start from Panama, a side trip to **Easter Island** (p81) and **Pitcairn** (p240) before **French Polynesia** (p395) is a possibility, but it might be the longest side trip you ever did. After the majestic peaks of the Marquesas, the largest group of atolls in the world, the **Tuamotus** (p448), are next. This is the time to put down your daiquiri and pay attention, as this is known as the 'Dangerous Archipelago' and it has the wrecks on the many low unlit reefs to prove it.

Pape'ete (p409) in Tahiti becomes the natural hub to switch crew and stock up on Hinano beer, while pondering where to point your bow next. Leaving **Bora Bora** (p438), drop in on **Suwarrow** (p290) before deciding on **Samoa** (p296), **Rarotonga** (p256) or **Tonga** (p493) That is what makes South Pacific so great, in more ways than one.

The **Vava'u Group** (p516) in Tonga is hard to pass up, as is the tiny self-governing island of Niue with its moorings at **Alofi** (p231) with free wi-fi. Depending on your choice of hiding place during the cyclone season (Australia or NZ), the rest of the season could be spent in the islands of **Fiji** (p96), or casting off for French Melanesia at **New Caledonia** (p174), hiking on **Vanuatu** (p554) or the numerous islands of the **Solomons** (p359).

OUT TO THE OUTLIERS

Are you a country collector? Want to get off the beaten tourist path? Try on some of this for size.

Pitcairn Island (p240), famous as the hideaway of the *Bounty* mutineers, is one of the most isolated places on earth.

Fly via **Fiji** (p96) and **Samoa** (p296) to **Niue** (p227), the world's smallest self-governing country. There are no dreamy stretches of beach on Niue; instead the island has dramatic raised-coral cliffs that tower above the ocean and submarine caves like **Ana Mahaga** (p234) that bring international scuba divers.

Tokelau (p485) calls to intrepid travellers and just getting there is an adventure since there are no planes and a boat only once a fortnight or so. If sea levels rise (see boxed text, p489) Tokelau might simply cease to be, so it might be a case of see it while you can.

Dip into Melanesian culture in the **Solomons** (p359). Head to the wild reaches of **Malaita** (p383) with its artificial islands or take off to **Rennell Island** (p387), a World Heritage site that few explore.

If you still have time up your sleeve then go to **Tuvalu** (p536) and mingle with the 4500-odd Tuvaluans who are sardined onto tiny **Fongafale Islet** (p545), the country's main island. Overcrowding may explain the women's dance style during **fatele** (see boxed text, p541).

History

About 50,000 years ago the first people reached the Pacific islands, arriving in New Guinea from Southeast Asia via Indonesia. These people, now known as Papuans, share ancestry with Australia's Aborigines. Moving slowly east, the Papuans' progress halted in the northern Solomon Islands about 25,000 years ago, due to the lack of boats able to cross the increasingly wide stretches of ocean. Subsequent people, collectively known as Austronesians, moved into the area from the west, mingling with the Papuans and eventually becoming the highly diverse group of people known as 'Melanesians'. New Guinea and the Solomons were the only inhabited islands in the Pacific for many thousands of years.

For a definitive history of the region, grab yourself a copy of Ron Crocombe's *The South Pacific*, a solid look at the region's past and present now in its seventh edition.

The wider seas from the Solomons to Vanuatu were finally crossed in about 1500 BC. An Austronesian people now known as the Lapita (see the boxed text, p37) finally developed the technology and the skills to cross the open seas to New Caledonia. Heading east they quickly expanded through Fiji, Tonga and Samoa, where they developed the culture we now know as Polynesian.

The Melanesians of New Guinea and the Solomons mingled a little with the Lapita and followed them across the Pacific. Melanesians came to dominate New Guinea, the Solomons, Vanuatu, New Caledonia and Fiji.

THE STRANGE PACIFIC

Odd theories to explain where Polynesian people came from are nothing new. In 1864 zoologist Phillip L. Schlater couldn't work out how lemurs could still exist on Madagascar while their fossils were found in India. He speculated on a large continent called Lemuria which had joined India and Africa. Of course, once science discovered continental drift, the theory seemed to be debased, but that didn't stop less scientific supporters from taking on the idea.

Throughout the 1880s and 1890s, occultists speculated that Lemuria (sometimes abbreviated to Mu) was a lost civilisation. Author and cult founder Helena Blavatsky wrote that Lemuria was peopled by freakishly tall people who reproduced by laying eggs and led more spiritual lives than the rest of humanity possibly due to their isolation. The idea of Mu was later taken up by British acid house band, the KLF, who also called themselves the Justified Ancients of Mu Mu with an early record company called the Sound of Mu(sic).

While it sounds like an outlandish extension of the noble savage myth, sites like Easter Island's *moai* (p85) have brought much speculation as to the origins of Polynesian people. Other theories suggest that Polynesians are survivors from the sunken world of Atlantis or that they are descendants of aliens.

TIMELINE

50,000 years ago	1500 BC	200 BC
People first settle the Pacific in PNG and the Solomon Islands.	Long-distance seafaring begins in earnest in Vanuatu, New Caledonia, Fiji and central Polynesia.	Another wave of settlement: Polynesians spread east to the Society and Marquesas Islands (modern-day French Polynesia).

The Lapitas' Polynesian descendants waited on Samoa and Tonga for a thousand years or so, until more advanced ocean vessels and skills were developed. Some time around 200 BC they crossed the longer ocean stretches to the east to the Society and Marquesas island groups (in modern French Polynesia). From there, voyaging canoes travelled southwest to Rarotonga and the southern Cook Islands, southeast to Rapa Nui (Easter Island) in AD 300, north to Hawai'i around AD 400 and southwest past Rarotonga to Aotearoa (New Zealand) in AD 900.

The myriad islands and atolls of Micronesia, north of the Solomons and New Guinea, were populated by several groups of people over an extended period. Western Micronesia was reached by Asians island-hopping through the Philippines in about 1500 BC. Melanesians moved north into central Micronesia in 1000 BC, and eastern Micronesia was settled by Polynesians spreading northwards from their base in Fiji, Samoa and Tonga in the centuries up to AD 500.

Although the predominant direction of human movement was from west to east, population pressure and the occasional religious disagreement prompted constant movement of people across the oceans. So Polynesians can be found today in Melanesia's eastern islands, while the largely Melanesian Fiji is also home to many Polynesians and Micronesians.

Compared to the coast hugging of contemporary Europeans, the settlement of the Pacific Ocean was the most remarkable feat of ocean sailing up to that time. All but the furthest-flung islands of the massive Pacific were colonised by 200 BC. By contrast it was over 1000 years later that the Vikings crossed the (relatively small) Atlantic to make Europe's first cross-ocean settlement.

Melanesians embarked on regular trade and some war missions, but Polynesians travelled the broader stretches of open ocean (see boxed text, p38). Almost no Pacific islands were cut off entirely from other cultures, and the presence of the *kumara* (sweet potato) in the Pacific islands confirms that at least some journeys were made as far east as South America, probably from the Marquesas. Traditional stories also indicate exploratory journeys into Antarctic waters 'not seen by the sun'.

For further information about ancient Pacific cultures, see Arts (p52) and Religion (p51).

The discovery of the outrigger canoe, with its additional support, called *ama* in many Polynesian languages, allowed Austronesian people to journey vast distances across the Pacific.

EUROPEAN ARRIVAL

Like Pacific islanders, European explorers came in search of resources (gold and spices initially), driven by curiosity or national pride. Europeans were also inspired by one overpowering myth: the search for the great southern continent, Terra Australis.

Since the time of Ptolemy, scientists predicted the presence of a huge landmass in the southern hemisphere to counter the earth's northern con-

AD 300–400	1568	1768–79
The final major wave leaves the Societies and Marquesas: north to Hawai'i, southwest to the Cooks and southeast to Easter Island.	Don Alvaro de Mendaña y Neyra lands on Santa Isabel Island finding traces of gold and believes he has discovered King Solomon's Mines and names the islands the Solomons; subsequently dies of malaria.	Captain James Cook 'boldly goes' on three voyages through the Pacific, then gets killed in Hawai'i.

LAPITA

The ancient race of people known as the Lapita are thought to be responsible for the wide distribution of Polynesian culture and Austronesian languages in the Pacific. Coming from the Bismarck Archipelago in far-north Papua New Guinea (PNG) in around 1500 BC, they were the first to populate the islands from Vanuatu east to New Caledonia, Fiji, Tonga and Samoa. It was in Tonga and Samoa that the Lapita developed into the people we now call Polynesians.

The Lapita had an enormous influence from 1500 BC to 500 BC over a vast area of the Pacific, where their influence can been traced through the far-flung dispersal of their unique pottery. Lapita pottery has been found in PNG, New Caledonia, in parts of Micronesia and in Fiji, Tonga, Samoa and Futuna.

The Lapita were highly skilled sailors and navigators, able to cross hundreds of kilometres of open sea, and trade and settlement were important to their culture. They were also agriculturists and practised husbandry of dogs, pigs and fowls. Regarded as the first cultural complex in the Pacific, they were a highly organised people who traded obsidian (volcanic glass used in tool production) from New Britain (PNG) with people up to 2500km away in Tonga and Samoa.

Today you can see Lapita artefacts in the national museums of Vanuatu (p567) and Fiji (p125), and at Sigatoka (p119), also in Fiji.

---

tinents. Otherwise, it was believed, the globe would be top-heavy and fall over. Belief in this southern continent was unsubstantiated with explorers asked only to chart its existence, only to chart its coasts and parley with its people. In the absence of hard facts, Terra Australis was believed to be peopled with strange heathens and magical creatures, and rumoured to be rich in gold. The biblical tale of King Solomon had included vast gold mines in some unknown location. What could be a better spot than Terra Australis?

Spanish

In 1521 the Portuguese Ferdinand Magellan led a Spanish expedition that discovered, at the southern tip of the Americas, an entrance to the ocean he named Mar Pacifico – the Pacific Ocean – for its calmness. Magellan spotted only two small, uninhabited islands until he had sailed northwest across almost the entire ocean to Guam in Micronesia.

On Guam the first contact between Pacific islanders and Europeans followed a pattern that was to become all too familiar. The islander belief that all property was shared meant that Guam's islanders helped themselves to one of the expedition's small boats and Magellan retaliated – seven islanders were killed. Magellan himself was killed two months later while in the Philippines, but not before he became the first person to circumnavigate the globe (having previously visited the Philippines from the other direction).

1789	1812	1838
Fletcher Christian famously relieves Captain Bligh of his duties and then legs it to Pitcairn Island.	King Pomare II of Tahiti seeks conversion to Protestantism which leads to European support of his rule and allows him to centralise power.	After French Catholic missionaries were kicked off Tahiti, France sends in a gunboat which leads to the island being declared a French protectorate in 1842.

VOYAGING & NAVIGATION

Ancient Pacific islanders' voyages were motivated by war, trade, colonisation and the search for resources, or sometimes merely by curiosity and pride. The Tongans, known as the 'Vikings of the Pacific', ruled Samoa, Niue and eastern Fiji with an iron fist, and raided from Tuvalu to the Solomon Islands, 2700km to the west!

At the time of European contact, prodigious feats of navigation and voyaging still occurred, although not on as grand a scale as previously. The navigator-priest Tupaia, who boarded Cook's *Endeavour* in Tahiti, could name around 100 islands between the Marquesas and Fiji, and he directed Cook's search for islands west of Tahiti. For the entire circuitous journey to Java in Indonesia, Tupaia could always point in the direction of his homeland.

Canoes

The term 'canoe' (*vaka* or *va'a*) is misleading. The same word describes small dugouts used for river navigation, giant war vessels accommodating hundreds of men and 25m-long ocean-voyaging craft. Ocean-voyaging craft, either double canoes or single canoes with outriggers, carried one (or more) masts and sails of woven pandanus. Captain James Cook and contemporary observers estimated that Pacific canoes were capable of speeds greater than their own ships; probably 150km to 250km per day, so that trips of 5000km could be comfortably achieved with available provisions.

Navigation Techniques

Initial exploratory journeys would often follow the migratory flights of birds. Once a new land had been discovered, the method of rediscovery was remembered and communicated mostly by way of which stars to follow. Fine-tuning of these directions was possible by observing the direction from which certain winds blew, the currents, wave fronts reflecting from islands and the flight of land birds.

European Theories

Many European explorers were unable to believe that a Stone Age culture without a written language or use of the compass could have accomplished such amazing feats of navigation.

Passing European seafarers reported Easter Island's famous *moai* had toppled over between 1722 and 1868 with oral stories pointing to a civil war that saw the statues pushed over to indicate defeat.

Spaniard Don Alvaro de Mendaña y Neyra sailed west across the Pacific in search of Terra Australis in 1567. On the Solomon Islands, conflict with the locals arose when islanders were unable to supply the resources Mendaña needed to resupply.

It took Mendaña nearly 30 years to gain approval for his disastrous second voyage during 1595. An estimated 200 islanders were killed in the Marquesas when conflict broke out; there was even more conflict with locals when they reached the Solomons, and fighting also spread to the crew. Mendaña himself died of malaria, and the expedition limped to Peru under the command of the more humane Pedro Fernández de Quirós. Quirós led another expedition to the Pacific in 1605, discovering the Tuamotu Islands and Vanuatu.

1841	1845	1864
Pierre Louis Marie Chanel becomes patron saint of the Pacific islands after knocking on one too many doors in Futuna.	Tonga's King George Tupou I unites the nation with a little help from his prime minister, Reverend Shirley Baker.	The first 'blackbirded' labourers from Vanuatu and the Solomons arrive in Fiji.

Some assumed that an earlier, more advanced culture must have existed. They proposed that islanders were the barbaric survivors of this ancient empire, living on the mountain tops of the sunken continent of Mu.

Once the continent of Mu was discounted, a wide range of possible origins for Pacific islanders was considered, including India, Israel and the Americas. Others proposed that the islands had been settled quite accidentally, as fishermen were blown off course and lost at sea.

The majority of evidence, however, points towards mostly deliberate west to east migration. This conclusion rests on linguistic, genetic, anthropological and archaeological studies, vegetation patterns, computer modelling of wind and currents, and a study of oral traditions.

Modern Voyaging

The voyaging skills of today's Pacific islanders may not match that of their ancestors, but the traditional knowledge of navigational methods is still being put to everyday use. Both small inter-island trips and long-distance voyages have been used to test many theories about ocean voyaging.

Probably the most famous such voyage was that of Thor Heyerdahl's *Kon Tiki* from South America to the Tuamotus in 1947. The journey attempted to prove that Polynesia could have been populated from South America. While that theory has since been disproven by genetic evidence, the 8,000km caused many historians to rethink their ideas about Polynesian ancient technology and their ability to sail between islands.

Modern voyages along traditional routes have refined theories about canoe construction and navigational methods. Among such journeys, the 25m-long outrigger canoe *Tarratai* was sailed from Kiribati 2500km south to Fiji in 1976. That same year the voyage of the 20m *Hokule'a*, which used traditional navigation methods for the 4250km trip from Hawai'i to Tahiti, sparked a resurgence of interest in traditional navigation.

Other voyaging canoes include the 21m *Hawaiki Nui*, which sailed 4000km from Tahiti to Aotearoa in 1985. In 1995 *Te Au o Tonga*, captained by the former prime minister of the Cook Islands, Sir Thomas Davis (Papa Tom), sailed from Rarotonga to Tahiti, on to Hawai'i and back to Rarotonga. Part of the cargo on the last leg was less than traditional: Papa Tom's new 1200cc Harley-Davidson. The *Hokule'a* and *Te Au o Tonga*, among other great *vaka*, continue to make long voyages.

Dutch

Jacob Le Maire and Willem Schouten's 1616 search for Terra Australis introduced Europe to the Tongan islands and Futuna. Jacob Roggeveen spotted Bora Bora in the Society Islands in 1722, and Tutuila and Upolu in Samoa. Abel Tasman became the most famous Dutch explorer after charting Tasmania and the east coast of New Zealand in 1642, then landing on the islands of Tonga and Fiji.

French

The most famous French explorer, Louis-Antoine de Bougainville, came upon Tahiti and claimed it for France in 1768. He went on to the Samoan islands,

1889–94	1890–1903	1914
'Here he lies where he longs to be' – Robert Louis Stevenson abandons the chilly moors of Scotland for the warm delights of Samoa.	French post-Impressionist Paul Gauguin retreats to Tahiti and the Marquesas to devote his life to art.	Concerned about the proximity of an enemy territory during WWI, New Zealand sends troops to occupy German territories in Samoa.

THE DISAPPEARANCE OF LA PEROUSE

French explorer Comte de La Pérouse set off on a mission in 1785 to explore the Pacific just as Captain Cook had done. With two ships under his command and a collection of scientists his expedition promised to be France's great contribution to science. The ships passed through Tonga, Samoa and even met the fledgling Australian colony at Botany Bay, where La Pérouse took the chance to send his journals back to France with a British ship. He promised to be back in France by June 1789 and was never heard of again.

A mission was sent in search of La Pérouse, but found no trace. Almost 30 years later, the mystery began to unfold when an Irish captain bought some swords from the locals of Tikopia, a remote island in the Solomons, who had found then on the island of Vanikoro. The swords had belonged to La Pérouse's crew, and investigations with islanders on Vanikoro confirmed that two ships were wrecked there and survivors had lived on the island for several months. After skirmishes with locals, the castaways built a smaller boat and attempted to sail to another port, but must have died at sea.

In 2005 a wreck was discovered and formally identified as one of La Pérouse's vessels, but the story passed into legend long ago when Jules Verne dedicated a chapter 'Vanikoro' to the incident in his fantasy novel, *Twenty Thousand Leagues Under the Sea*.

then continued on to Vanuatu and discovered Australia's Great Barrier Reef. Bougainville's impact was greater than dots on a map, however; his accounts of the South Pacific sparked massive interest in Europe and created the myth of a southern paradise.

In 1827 Dumont d'Urville sailed the Pacific searching for his lost countryman, the Comte de La Pérouse, whose boat had sunk near the Solomon Islands in 1788. D'Urville's writings of this and another journey (10 years later) were to establish the concept of the three great subdivisions of the Pacific: Melanesia, Micronesia and Polynesia.

The Cook Islands were originally called the Hervey Islands by the modest Captain Cook. It was only after his death in the 1820s that the new name appeared in his honour on a Russian naval chart.

English

In 1767 Samuel Wallis – *still* searching for Terra Australis – landed on Tahiti, but the greatest of the English explorers was James Cook. His three journeys into the region – the first in 1768 most famously 'discovered' Australia and New Zealand – saw detailed mapping and exploration that would later allow others to follow. His third and final journey was the first European visit to Hawai'i where Cook was killed in a skirmish. His legacy can be seen throughout the Pacific with his detailed maps used up until the 1990s and several places bearing his name, most notably the Cook Islands.

Following the most famous of maritime mutinies, Fletcher Christian captained the *Bounty* to discover Rarotonga in the southern Cook Islands in 1789 (see the boxed text, p246).

1918–19	1942–45	1947
Spanish influenza ravages Tonga, Fiji and Samoa.	WWII fighting in the Solomons, PNG and Micronesia; Fijian Corporal Sefania Sukanaivalu is awarded the Victoria Cross.	Thor Heyerdahl (rather pointlessly) sails the balsa raft *Kon Tiki* from Peru to the Tuamotus.

CAPTAIN JAMES COOK *Tony Horwitz*

If aliens ever visit earth, they may wonder what to make of the countless obelisks, faded plaques and graffiti-covered statues of a stiff, wigged figure gazing out to sea from Alaska to Australia, from NZ to North Yorkshire, from Siberia to the South Pacific. James Cook (1728–79) explored more of the earth's surface than anyone in history, and it's impossible to travel the Pacific without encountering the captain's image and his controversial legacy in the lands he opened to the West.

For a man who travelled so widely, and rose to such fame, Cook came from an extremely pinched and provincial background. The son of a day labourer in rural Yorkshire, he was born in a mud cottage, had little schooling, and seemed destined for farm work. Instead, Cook went to sea as a teenager, worked his way up from coal-ship servant to naval officer, and attracted notice for his exceptional charts of Canada. But Cook remained a little-known second lieutenant until, in 1768, the Royal Navy chose him to command a daring voyage to the South Seas.

In a converted coal ship called *Endeavour,* Cook sailed to Tahiti, and then became the first European to land at NZ and the east coast of Australia. Though the ship almost sank after striking the Great Barrier Reef, and 40% of the crew died from disease and accidents, the *Endeavour* limped home in 1771. On a return voyage (1772–75), Cook became the first navigator to pierce the Antarctic Circle and circled the globe near its southernmost latitude, demolishing the ancient myth that a vast, populous and fertile continent surrounded the South Pole. Cook also crisscrossed the Pacific from Easter Island to Melanesia. Though Maori killed and cooked 10 sailors, the captain remained sympathetic to islanders. 'Notwithstanding they are cannibals', he wrote, 'they are naturally of a good disposition.'

On Cook's final voyage (1776–79), in search of a northwest passage between the Atlantic and Pacific, he became the first European to visit Hawaii, and coasted America from Oregon to Alaska. Forced back by Arctic pack ice, Cook returned to Hawaii, where he was killed during a skirmish with islanders who had initially greeted him as a Polynesian god. In a single decade of discovery, Cook had filled in the map of the Pacific and, as one French navigator put it, 'left his successors with little to do but admire his exploits'.

But Cook's travels also spurred colonisation of the Pacific, and within decades of his death, missionaries, whalers, traders and settlers began transforming – and often devastating – island cultures. As a result, many indigenous people now revile Cook as an imperialist villain who introduced disease, dispossession and other ills to the Pacific (hence the frequent vandalising of Cook monuments). However, as islanders revive traditional crafts and practices, from tattooing to *tapa,* they have turned to the art and writing of Cook and his men as a resource for cultural renewal. For good and ill, a Yorkshire farm boy remains the single most significant figure in the shaping of the modern Pacific.

Tony Horwitz is a Pulitzer-winning reporter and nonfiction author. His latest book is A Voyage Long and Strange (2008), about European exploration of North America .

MISSIONARIES

After a few largely unsuccessful Spanish Catholic forays into Micronesia during the 17th century, the first major attempt to bring Christianity to the Pacific was by English Protestants. The newly formed London Missionary Society (LMS) outfitted missionary outposts on Tahiti and

1958	1962	1963
'Wash that man right out of my hair' – the dreadfully camp musical *South Pacific* is unleashed upon the world.	Western Samoa becomes the first Pacific nation to be given independence.	The first South Pacific Games (now called Pacific Games) was held in Suva, Fiji.

Tonga, and in the Marquesas in 1797. These first missions failed – within two years the Tongan and Marquesan missions were abandoned. The Tahitian mission survived but its success was limited. For a decade there were only a handful of islanders who were tempted to join the new religion.

Other Protestants soon joined the battle. The new players in the South Pacific were the Wesleyan Missionary Society (WMS), fresh from moderate success in New Zealand, and the American Board of Commissioners for Foreign Missions (ABCFM), following their christianising of Hawai'i. The WMS and ABCFM both floundered in the Marquesas, but fared better in Tonga.

In the 1830s French Catholic missions were established in the Marquesas and Tahiti. Catholic missionaries were often as pleased to convert a Protestant as a heathen, with the fierce rivalry between the different denominations extended to their islander converts. Religious conflicts fitted easily into the already complex political melee of Pacific society, and local chiefs manipulated the two Christian camps for their own purposes.

Despite the slow start, missionary success grew. By the 1820s missionary influence on Tahiti was enormous. The Bible was translated into Tahitian, a Protestant work ethic was instilled, tattooing discouraged, promiscuity guarded against by nightly 'moral police' and the most 'heathen' practices such as human sacrifice were forbidden. From Tahiti, Tonga and Hawai'i, Christianity spread throughout the Pacific.

The missionaries' success was due to three major factors. Clever politics played a part, particularly the conversion of influential Tongan chief Taufa'ahau and the Tahitian Pomare family. The perceived link between European wealth and Christianity also played a part: missionaries 'civilised' as well as christianised, and islanders obtained European tools and skills such as literacy. Finally, the message of afterlife salvation fell on attentive ears as European arrival coincided with the massive depopulation through the spread of disease.

Missionaries shielded islanders from the excesses of some traders, and it was missionary pressure that finally put an end to the blackbirding trade (see p44). Putting Pacific languages into written form, initially in translations of the Bible, was another major contribution. While many missionaries deliberately destroyed 'heathen' Pacific artefacts and beliefs, others diligently recorded myths and oral traditions that would otherwise have been lost. A substantial portion of our knowledge of Pacific history and traditional culture comes from the work of missionary-historians.

The church remains an important political player in many islands on the basis of its strong history. Ruling dynasties in Tonga, Tahiti and Fiji all owed their success to missionary backing – just as missionary success owed a lot to those dynasties.

When French Catholic missionaries were kicked off Tahiti in 1836, France sent a gunboat in 1838, which led to the island being declared a French protectorate in 1842.

1971	1978	1980
Establishment of the South Pacific Forum (now the Pacific Islands Forum).	Solomon Islands and Tuvalu become independent.	The islands known as the New Hebrides become independent with the new name of Vanuatu.

TRADE
Whaling
European whalers enthusiastically hunted in the Pacific from the late 18th century. Trade peaked in the mid-19th century, then declined as whale products were superseded by other materials. The effect on the Pacific's whale population was catastrophic, but the effect on Pacific islanders was complex. There were opportunities for lucrative trade as ships resupplied and many Pacific islanders, as always fond of travel, took the opportunity to travel on whaling ships. Some islanders, however, were effectively kidnapped and forced to travel without consent; whalers of the Pacific were not the most gentle of men.

Bêches-de-Mer
Also known as *trepang*, sea cucumbers or sea slugs, *bêche-de-mer* is a marine organism related to starfish and urchins. An Asian delicacy, Pacific *bêches-de-mer* were sought by early-19th-century Europeans to trade for Chinese tea. *Bêches-de-mer* were relatively abundant and important trading relations were forged with islanders. For the most part trade was mutually beneficial, with islanders trading eagerly for metal, cloth, tobacco and muskets. The trade in *bêches-de-mer* was largely nonviolent, in contrast with the sandalwood trade.

Sandalwood
Nineteenth-century Europeans trading with China found another valued Pacific resource in fragrant sandalwood, used in China for ornamental carving and cabinet-making, as well as incense. By the 1820s these traders had stripped the sandalwood forests of Hawai'i, and looked to islands to the south. Extensive sandalwood forests on Fiji, Vanuatu, the Solomons and New Caledonia became the focus for traders keen to satisfy the demands of the Chinese market.

On each new island, payment for sandalwood was initially low. A small piece of metal, a goat or a dog was sometimes sufficient to buy a boatload of the aromatic wood. But as the supply of slow-growing sandalwood dwindled, the price rose – islanders demanded guns, ammunition, tobacco or assistance in war as payment.

While the sandalwood trade in Fiji was fairly orderly under the supervision of local chiefs, spheres of chiefly influence in the Solomons, Vanuatu and New Caledonia were much smaller and traders had difficultly establishing lasting relationships with islanders. Sandalwood was the most violent of any trades in the Pacific, and Melanesia's savage reputation in Europe was not improved. There were many attacks on ships' crews, sometimes motivated by a greed for plunder, but these attacks were a response to previous white atrocities. Melanesians assumed that

'...payment for sandalwood was initially low. A small piece of metal, a goat or a dog was sometimes sufficient to buy a boatload of the aromatic wood.'

1987	1996	1999
The Fijian coups: Rabuka takes over government; Fiji is declared a republic and dismissed from the Commonwealth.	The end of nuclear testing in the Pacific: last bombs detonated at Mururoa Atoll.	Tuvalu laughs all the way to the bank when it begins selling its '.tv' internet domain name to television shows around the world.

all Europeans belonged to the one kin-group, and thus were accountable for another's crimes.

The sandalwood trade was far from sustainable. Island after island was stripped of its forests, and the trade petered out in the 1860s with the removal of the last accessible stands.

BLACKBIRDING

In the late 19th century, cheap labour was sought for various Pacific industries such as mines and plantations. Pacific islanders were also 're-cruited' to labour in Australia, Fiji, New Caledonia, Samoa and Peru. Satisfying the demand for labour was a major commercial activity from the 1860s.

In some cases islanders were keen to sign up, seeking to share the benefits of European wealth. Often, though, islanders were tricked into boarding ships, either being deceived about the length of time for which they were contracted, or sometimes enticed aboard by sailors dressed as priests. In many cases no pretence was attempted: islanders were simply herded onto slaving ships at gunpoint.

The populations of many small, barely viable islands were devastated by blackbirders (a term used for the co-opting and sometime kidnapping of Islanders) – Tokelau lost almost half its population to Peruvian slaving ships in 1863, while the Tongan island of 'Ata lost 40% of its population, and as a result is today uninhabited. People were also taken as slaves from Tuvalu, New Caledonia, Easter Island, Vanuatu and the Solomons.

'Once the people were on board they locked them up and sailed away. Two men escaped and swam back to shore, but the rest were never seen again.' Kelese Simona, from Nukulaelae (p550), recalls in *Time and Tide: The Islands of Tuvalu* his father's eyewitness account of the day in 1863 that blackbirders kidnapped 70% of the island's population.

Blackbirding was outlawed by the introduction of the Pacific Islanders' Protection Act in 1872 by Britain, largely due to persistent lobbying by missionaries. Their campaigns resulted in the banning of overseas-labour recruitment to Australia (in 1904), Samoa (in 1913) and Fiji (in 1916). The British government followed up the law with regular patrols of the region to prevent unscrupulous blackbirders, marking the beginning of a colonialist mentality of protection.

While some islanders returned to their homelands, others remained – such as the large Melanesian population in Australia's Queensland. In Fiji the large plantation economy looked elsewhere for cheap labour transporting indentured labourers from India, who remain an important part of Fiji today (see p101).

FLAG FOLLOWS TRADE

Once European traders were established in the Pacific, many began agitating for their home countries to intervene and protect their interests. Missionaries also lobbied for colonial takeover, hoping that European law would protect islanders from the lawless traders. European powers began

2000	2001–05	2002
George Speight heads a Fijian coup with hostages held in parliament for eight weeks; Speight is eventually jailed.	Australia negotiates its 'Pacific Solution', imprisoning asylum seekers in PNG and Nauru.	US reality series *Survivor* comes to French Polynesia with *Survivor Marquesas* – later seasons brought world attention to Fiji, Vanuatu and the Cook Islands.

following a policy of flag following trade by declaring protectorates and then by annexing Pacific states.

Between 1878 and 1899 Germany annexed the Marshall Islands, northern Solomons and Samoa. The latter treaty ceded American Samoa to the US, joining the Phoenix Islands (now in Kiribati), which the US and Britain had claimed in 1836. After annexing French Polynesia (1840s) and New Caledonia (1853), the French lost interest for a while before claiming Wallis & Futuna (1880s) and going into partnership with Britain in Vanuatu in 1906.

Contrary to popular opinion, Britain was a reluctant Pacific-empire builder. However, it ended up with the largest of all Pacific empires, after being forced by various lobby groups to assume responsibilities for the Phoenix Islands in 1836, then Fiji, Tokelau, the Cooks, the Gilbert and Ellice Islands (modern Kiribati and Tuvalu), the southern Solomons and Niue between 1874 and 1900, and finally Vanuatu in 1906. Between 1900 and 1925, Britain happily offloaded the Cooks, Niue and Tokelau to eager New Zealand.

Colonialism brought a peace between warring European powers but an increase in tensions with islanders. The arrival of settlers brought many diseases, which had been unknown in the Pacific or had been experienced only in limited contact with explorers or traders, which had a horrific toll on islanders. Cholera, measles, smallpox, influenza, pneumonia, scarlet fever, chickenpox, whooping cough, dysentery, venereal diseases and even the common cold all had devastating effects. Most Polynesian populations were halved, while Micronesia and Melanesia's populations suffered even more. Some islands of Vanuatu were among the worst hit, dropping to just 5% of their original populations.

WAR IN THE PACIFIC

WWI had little impact on the Pacific, though German colonial rulers in Micronesia, Samoa and Nauru were exchanged for Japanese, New Zealand, Australian and British rule. Germany, slightly preoccupied with events in Europe at the time, didn't resist these Pacific takeovers.

In contrast, the Pacific was a major arena of conflict during WWII. The war with Japan was fought through the Micronesian territories Japan had won from Germany in WWI, in PNG and in the Solomons.

Initially Japan expanded south from its Micronesian territories almost unhindered and captured the Solomons in 1942. They began building an airfield on Guadalcanal (which today is Henderson Airport), which would supply further advances south. Allied forces staged a huge offensive that saw over 60 ships sunk in the surrounding waters that became known as Iron Bottom Sound. From 1944 US and Australian forces pushed the stubbornly defending Japanese back, island by island. US bombers based in the Marianas punished Japanese cities for 10 months until 6 August 1945, when

Sobering reminders of WWII in the Pacific include diveable shipwrecks in Vanuatu (p596), aircraft wrecks on Tuvalu's Nanumea Atoll (p550), and the wreckage strewn across the Solomons' Western Province (p375), Guadalcanal (p366) and the 60-odd warships that lie on the floor of Iron Bottom Sound.

2006	2007	2008
Commodore Frank Bainimarama deposes the Fiji government, declaring himself acting president in another coup.	Samoa's King Malietoa Tanumafili II dies and the nation becomes a republic, electing Tuiatua Tupua Tamasese Efi as head of state. The Solomons are struck by a tsunami killing 54 and making many thousands homeless.	Tuvaluan Prime Minister Apisai Ielemia and other Pacific leaders advocate reducing greenhouse emissions at UN Climate Change Conference in Poland.

MILITARY PLAYGROUND

In 1946, a US military officer met the people of the tiny Bikini Atoll in the Marshall Islands and asked if they'd be prepared to leave their island for 'the good of mankind and to end all world wars'. Over 160 Bikinians left their home to make way for 42,000 US personnel who would begin nuclear testing on this remote island.

Along with Eniwetak and Kwajalein atolls, the area became known as the Pacific Proving Grounds where 105 atmospheric tests were conducted until 1962. The most disastrous test occurred in 1954, when a hydrogen bomb code-named Bravo was detonated in an intense 20-mile high fireball that stripped branches from trees on surrounding islands. It was the largest US test, with fallout washing over other Marshall Islands along with a Japanese fishing boat, *Daigo Fukuryu Maru* (Lucky Dragon No 5). It was a beacon that blazed around the world, and eventually, in 1963, the Partial Test Ban Treaty was signed.

Some nations, however, didn't sign up. France began nuclear testing in 1966 on Mururoa Atoll, an isolated part of French Polynesia. Over 40 tests were conducted until 1974 when international pressure pushed their testing literally underground. They abandoned testing on Mururoa and drilled into the island itself, detonating a further 147 nuclear devices here and later at Fangataufa. The tests began to crack the atolls themselves and there were concerns that nuclear material would leak into the open seas. Protests (including those by Greenpeace ship *Rainbow Warrior*, which was bombed by French intelligence agents in 1985) eventually brought international condemnation and the last test was conducted in 1996 when France signed the Comprehensive Nuclear Test Ban Treaty.

The impact of the testing in the area was huge. In 1968, the US declared Bikini Atoll habitable again and returned Bikinians to their homeland. They remained there for 10 years until a team of French scientists investigated reports of birth defects and cancer among Bikinians. A second evacuation followed and the US made a payment of US$150 million, which was spent removing and destroying the top half-metre of soil. Compensation claims are still being made today as Bikinians attempt to discover the half-life of US responsibility.

Enola Gay took off from Tinian (Northern Marianas) to drop an atomic bomb on Hiroshima. Days later another was dropped on Nagasaki and the Pacific war was over.

The suffering of islanders during the Pacific war was immense: Japanese forces in Micronesia forced the transport of large numbers of islanders between various islands, seemingly without motive. People were concentrated in areas without adequate food, thousands died from hunger and thousands more were executed by the Japanese as an Allied victory became apparent. It is difficult to establish the frequency of rape of islanders by Japanese forces.

Soldiers from Fiji, the Solomons, Samoa, Tonga, French Polynesia and New Caledonia served in the armed forces, seeing action in the Pacific, Africa and Europe. Their valour cemented relations with other allies.

WWII had a lasting effect on the region. Most obviously, Japan's Micronesian colonies were taken over by the US, becoming the Trust Territory of the Pacific islands. However, the war also left a legacy of more widespread and subtle effects. There was a huge improvement in roads and other infrastructure on many islands. There was also an input of money, food and other supplies that contributed towards the development of so-called 'cargo cults', whose devotees believed the goods were gifts from ancestral spirits.

WWII also hastened the end of traditional colonialism in the Pacific, the relative equality between white and black US soldiers prompting islanders to question why they were still subservient to the British and the French. Many independence leaders were influenced by wartime experiences.

To hop aboard the *Rainbow Warrior* as it journeyed through the Pacific protesting against nuclear testing, read NZ journalist David Robie's *Eyes of Fire: A Reminder of When Nuclear Wars Came to Town*.

POSTCOLONIAL PACIFIC

From Samoa in 1962 through to Vanuatu in 1980, most of the Pacific island states gained independence (or partial independence) from their former colonial rulers. This was a relatively bloodless transition, with colonial masters as keen to ditch their expensive responsibilities as islanders were to gain independence. It took longer for the US to dismantle its Trust Territory of Micronesia, slowed by their desire to maintain a military presence in the region.

Only a handful of Pacific territories remain in the hands of the US (American Samoa), France (New Caledonia), Chile (Easter Island) and New Zealand (Rarotonga and the Cook Islands), with some gradually returning power to islanders. Self-government has not always been easy for Pacific nations with Fiji and the Solomons offering bellicose examples. Tonga, which was never officially colonised, remains the last monarchy in the Pacific, though the king has begun relinquishing his power in favour of democracy. Today the Pacific's governments face new challenges (see Destination South Pacific, p24) including environmental problems like global warming, particularly for smaller islands such as Tuvalu and Kiribati, which are at great risk from these effects.

The Pacific Island Report (http://pidp.eastwest center.org/pireport) is an invaluable online resource for keeping up with what's happening in the Pacific islands today.

The Culture

Pacific culture is as diverse as the islands in this vast ocean from the Solomon Islands to Easter Island, each isolated enough to have evolved a distinctive lifestyle. This diversity means that every generalisation is paired with its own exception, and the more you try to define the Pacific, the more it wants to invite you to the kava bowl and tell you to relax.

The region breaks down into Polynesia (Greek for 'many islands'), the un-PC-named Melanesia ('black islands') and the oft-forgotten Micronesia ('small islands'). The Polynesian people of the Pacific share a common ancestry in the Lapita people (see the boxed text, p37), though from this shared history each nation has developed a unique culture.

THE PACIFIC PSYCHE

Ever since Europeans have been journeying to the Pacific, they've been idealising its islands as paradise on earth. Eighteenth-century French philosopher Jean-Jacques Rousseau fantasised that the islands were a return to the innocence of Eden, populated by angelic beings who knew no guilt, ambition or social strictures. He dubbed these people 'noble savages', believing their lifestyle was a panacea to the Industrial Revolution infecting Europe at the time. When almost a century later Rousseau's countryman Paul Gauguin returned from Tahiti and the Marquesas with images of idyllic islands and angelic women, the islands were confirmed an earthly paradise.

Ironically for people believed to be living in heaven on earth, islanders converted to Christianity in great numbers (see p51). While tourist brochures will echo that the Pacific is a paradise, its denizens are far more diverse than Rousseau's escapist fantasies suggested, and more complex than the cherubic faces Gauguin depicted. For a look at the individual societies read the Culture section for each country.

Contrary to Rousseau's idea of a simple life free from rules, most Pacific islands share the common notion of *tapu* (or taboo, as it became pronounced in English), which holds certain objects or practices as sacred. It remains one of the common beliefs passed on by the Lapita people, who many believe originally settled the islands (p37). You only need to see how seriously some islanders observe the Sabbath to lose your ideas about a carefree people.

Melanesian communities were generally small – less than a few hundred people – with a 'bigman' as ruler. Hereditary factors were important in selecting a Melanesian bigman, but the individual's ambition and nous in politics and war were equally important. Power was hereditary on the male side only in some Polynesian societies, with the most senior male serving as *ariki*, *ari'i* or *ali'i* (chief) and with subchiefs and commoners beneath them, and it was strictly hierarchical in the islands of Hawai'i, Tonga and Tahiti. Unsurprisingly, after the arrival of Europeans these societies became single-ruler 'countries', resembling traditional monarchies. In egalitarian Samoa, *matai* (chiefs) were selected on the grounds of political acumen and ability rather than lines of descent. The power of chiefs and monarchies has waned, with Tonga the only remaining kingdom. Elsewhere in the South Pacific, Fiji's Great Council of Chiefs, which was a crucial support in previous coups, was ignored by Frank Bainimarama's seizing of power in 2007.

The central role of reciprocity in Melanesian culture has created a reputation for generosity and friendliness. In the past, aid in the form of food or labour would be given out of a sense of duty, with the expectation of the favour being returned in the future. Today most Melanesians continue to

'...French philosopher Jean-Jacques Rousseau fantasised that the islands were a return to the innocence of Eden, populated by angelic beings who knew no guilt, ambition or social strictures.'

TOP WEBSITES

- http://cafepacific.blogspot.com – an insight into journalism in the Pacific from NZ-based journalist David Robie.
- www.thebritishmuseum.ac.uk/world/pacific/islands/islands.html – this excellent site has heaps of art objects and a searchable database.
- www.tautaipacific.com – a NZ-based trust that supports modern Pacific artists, founded by Samoan Fatu Feu'u.

---

operate on this loose sense of karma, though the methods of exchange have been made more simple by the introduction of currency.

Family is key to islanders' perceptions of themselves, even when migrating to other countries. In some parts of Melanesia, languages evolved around family groups, with common languages being spoken by a larger group. Ancestor worship took this reverence of kin to a spiritual level and many Pacific islanders still believe strongly in the family unit, often sending money or gifts home to family when they emigrate.

Similarly, Polynesians have a strong respect for the family. Their tribal groups were based on extended family and the introduction of Christianity strengthened these ties. Today many small businesses are run by families, with extended families serving as additional employees or affiliates; don't be surprised if a guest house owner's cousin offers tours or other complementary services.

LIFESTYLE

The family is a vital element of islander society, reflecting the traditional clan basis of many Pacific communities. You can expect to be asked about your own family on numerous occasions, and some visiting couples become annoyed by the ubiquitous question: 'When are you going to have children?' Raising children is a shared activity in many Pacific island countries, with children often invited to join in communal activities, and disciplining by other parents is not uncommon.

Many islanders are seeing their traditions challenged by globalisation as they become more urbanised. The struggle between *kastom* (custom) and capitalism continues and can be seen in the abandonment of traditional diet in favour of processed Western food, which has led to high rates of obesity and type 2 diabetes among islanders.

The role of women in the Pacific is improving, though it can still be disturbing to female travellers. Female visitors may encounter everyday sexism, such as being leered at while swimming or having the answers to their questions directed to male companions, but for Pacific women the effects are more far-reaching. They are less likely to be employed and are typically poorer paid; in fact, some studies estimate that less than a third of the female populations of Fiji and Tuvalu work outside of the home. A darker side of gender relations is that Melanesia is plagued by domestic violence.

The role of women in the Pacific is complex. Many cultures are matrilineal and women can wield considerable power in village affairs even if they're not highly visible. Typically village men are vociferous about their power and prestige while women who are powerful conduct themselves in a manner much more behind the scenes.

Attitudes to homosexuality in the Pacific vary considerably, and in some parts of the region it is technically illegal (see the Directory, p629). In more conservative areas, religious leaders work themselves into a lather about

For an insight into the Pacific diaspora and cultural change, the film *My Lost Kainga* (www .mylostkainga.com) follows the story of a Tongan-born woman who grew up in Australia but returns to Tonga when her grandmother is dying.

it, as witnessed in Fiji when 3000 Methodists took to the streets protesting 'ungodly acts' in 2005.

Elsewhere attitudes are more tolerant. Tahitian *mahu* (men who act like women; see the boxed text, p402), for example, are respected within their culture and are openly gay. Similarly, in Tonga the 'third-gendered' *fakaleiti* can be bisexual and their cross-dressing skills are celebrated in the Miss Galaxy Pageant (see p497). Their equivalent in Samoa are called *fa'afafine*.

ECONOMY

Island economies vary from aid-based subsistence economies, such as Niue which depends heavily on New Zealand (NZ) government aid, to small-scale successes based in tourism, including French Polynesia or short-term gains like Tuvalu's sale of its .tv web address. Fiji had a burgeoning textiles industry and a history of tobacco and sugar industries, but coups interrupt growth and worry international investors.

Fishing is a huge industry right across the Pacific, though it's often done by foreign companies who pay for fishing concessions. Similarly, logging – done by foreign companies – is huge in the Solomon Islands, Fiji, Vanuatu and New Caledonia – basically anywhere where there are large islands with significant forests. The logging issue is very controversial as much of it is done illegally or bribes are paid to government ministers in exchange for logging grants. Mining is also big – New Caledonia produces half the world's nickel and the rich gold-and-copper mine at Gold Ridge on Guadalcanal is operating again after it was abandoned during the Solomons' ethnic crisis. Copra and palm-oil plantations are big in the Solomons and Vanuatu.

Ongoing obstacles to trade such as isolation and transportation make it costly to do business in the more remote areas of the Pacific. The Pacific Plan implemented by the Pacific Islands Forum is looking at pan-Pacific solutions, including managing fishing and sustained economic growth. Unemployment remains a major problem with many islanders leaving to work as sailors or emigrating to NZ. In 2009 Australia will trial a system of seasonal work visas with Tonga, Vanuatu, Kiribati and Papua New Guinea, which will allow workers to fruit pick. Whether this will increase money coming into island economies or see more islanders leaving their homes remains to be seen.

POPULATION

The population of the South Pacific islands is around 1.9 million (1.4 million people in Melanesia and 500,000 in Polynesia). Increasingly, populations are becoming coastal, urbanised and often focused on a main island.

The Pacific islands have always experienced diaspora, with more than 15% of Pacific islanders living in other countries around the Pacific rim, particularly NZ (210,000), mainland US (154,000) and Australia (65,000). Islanders living abroad maintain their community, culture and language, particularly by making waves in the arts (see p52).

SPORT

The Pacific has made a name for itself based on the success of its rugby players, and on islands such as Fiji and Samoa prowess on the rugby field often translates into status or political power. Football of several varieties is played throughout the islands during winter but it is rugby union that is most popular, with teams from Tonga, Fiji and Samoa competing in the fiercely competitive Pacific Tri-Nations. In 2007 the inaugural Pacific Nations Cup saw the three Pacific nations take on Japan and Maori New Zealand. The Pacific's other rugby-obsessed countries include Vanuatu, Tahiti, Niue, the Cook Islands and Solomon Islands. American football holds sway in

Fiji has 80,000 registered rugby players from its total population of 950,000 – almost 12%.

American Samoa, with players like Tui Alailefaleula, Toniu Fonoti and Joe Salave'a all playing in the US-based National Football League (NFL).

In villages across the Pacific, Saturday is the day for inter-village (and sometimes inter-island) netball, with games focused in the winter season, though they can be played year-round. There's strong grassroots support in Samoa, Vanuatu, Tonga, Niue and the Solomon and Cook Islands, and the countries often fight it out on the netball court in the Pacific or Commonwealth Games. Traditional rivals Fiji and Samoa are rated among the top 10 teams in the world, with Fiji winning the 2007 Pacific Games. While netball provides an important way for women to keep up contact with other villages, it is also becoming popular among men, even in macho Samoa.

Cricket remains a summer colonial legacy and it's most popular in Fiji and the Cook Islands, though you'll also hear the cracking of willow in Tonga. In Samoa there's a pitch in almost every village but it's usually used for the local game, *kirikiti,* which has a lot in common with cricket but throws in an extra bowler and commonly features singing and dancing from the batting team (see the boxed text, p300). Tokelau's brand of cricket, *kilikiti,* uses a three-sided bat and has teams that include most of the village. In Tonga, *lanita* (a bat and ball game) is another variation on traditional cricket.

Not surprisingly, given the islands' shared maritime history, canoeing is another sport common to most Pacific nations. The sport is a great source of national pride at events such as the annual Hawaiki Nui *va'a* (canoe) race in French Polynesia and the Pacific Games. Set to be held in New Caledonia in 2011, the South Pacific Games is a multisport event that showcases the region's best athletes.

> For a tiny island Nauru has two very odd national sports: weightlifting and Australian Rules Football; the latter can be explained by many Naruans being educated in Australia in the country's heyday.

RELIGION

Before the Europeans arrived, ancestor worship and magic were common beliefs in Melanesia, while in Polynesia a variety of gods were worshipped.

Melanesia's ancestor worship and sorcery were essential to every aspect of daily life, with spells cast for success in war, fishing and health. Headhunting and cannibalism were practised as sacred rituals as late as the 1950s, and in the Solomons and Vanuatu *kastom* continues to preserve the sacredness of traditions that have remained the same for centuries and which it is forbidden to question.

Across Polynesia, religious beliefs were remarkably similar because of the islands' common ancestry. The Polynesian pantheon was ruled by Tangaroa (Tangaloa or Ta'aroa) and included several lesser gods who divvied up the duties for the seas, forests, war, crops and other important aspects of life. While there were many commonalities within Polynesia, each myth had a different interpretation or elaboration (see the boxed text, p52).

Existing as a separate class alongside Polynesian chiefs, and often sharing their power, the priests known as *tohunga (tohu'a* or *kahuna)* were the keepers of Polynesian religion. As well as having divine knowledge such as creation myths or rituals, these priests were also interpreters of the gods' wills for the village. They could act as vital checks to ambitious chiefs or form an alliance of considerable political power by joining with them.

Christianity arrived in various forms in the early 19th century, and the race to convert the Pacific was on. Many countries have several different faiths, such as the Solomons and French Polynesia, which both have Anglican and Catholic believers based on the effectiveness of missionaries. Elsewhere in the Pacific, the Mormon Church met with a degree of success due to the stress placed on family values, including the ability to baptise ancestors retrospectively.

Traditional beliefs were incorporated, but overall Christianity has come to dominate spiritual life in the Pacific today. The popularity of church

MAUI'S FISH *Errol Hunt*

A legend common to many Polynesian cultures features the demigod Maui – a trickster, fool, hero, Polynesian Prometheus and first-rate fisherman. In this traditional tale, Maui is said to have fished one or more of the islands in the group up out of the ocean depths, but each island has its variations on the story.

In Tokelau, Maui hauled up each of the three coral atolls in that group; while fishing up Rakahanga in the Cooks he baited his hook with coconuts and leaves; he used a fish-hook fashioned from the jawbone of his grandmother in Aotearoa (New Zealand) and baited it with blood from his own nose; and on various islands of French Polynesia his bait was either his own ear or sacred crimson feathers. Whichever way the hook was baited, it caught onto the largest fish ever seen.

Maui's struggles to land his leviathan were aided by various magical chants and spells – and his prize was a fish so large that it formed the island of Rakahanga or Tongatapu, or whichever island is appropriate to the teller of the tale.

Maui's other contributions to humanity included stealing fire from the gods, slowing the path of the sun and creating the first dog. One of his major appeals to Polynesian society seems to be the use of trickery to defeat force. No Hollywood-style hero, Maui is fondly remembered as being particularly ugly.

singing in both Micronesia and Polynesia is testament to the missionaries' early efforts. Only Fiji, with its large Hindu and Muslim Indo-Fijian population, has significant numbers of non-Christians, though there is some tension between the two groups (see p101).

ARTS
Architecture

Traditional architecture throughout the Pacific had to adapt to very different conditions and would often need to be rebuilt after storms or war. Traditional Samoan *fale* (houses) are constructed without walls, but with woven blinds that can be lowered for harsher weather, while Fijian *bure* have walls and roofs of reeds or woven palms. Modern building materials are used today, with only large ceremonial buildings being constructed in the traditional fashion.

In Polynesia the *marae* (or *malae*) was the village meeting point and was open to both men and women. Villages may have several *marae* dedicated to different gods or religious practices. In western Polynesia, *marae* were simply village greens, possibly walled off with matting, while in the east they became elaborate structures. In Easter Island, the Societies, Australs and Marquesas *marae* were impressive open-air, paved temples with altars, carved-stone seating, platforms and walls, though only ruins and petroglyphs remain. In the Marquesas the *me'ae* were constructed from basalt blocks and were venues for religious acts of sacrifice and cannibalism.

Men's houses are still widespread throughout Melanesia and are often a village's dominant building. Their design symbolises the female and fecundity, with intricate carvings, towering facades and detailed interiors. They often employ complex joinery to create sturdy structures without the benefit of a single nail or screw. Throughout Melanesia secret councils of men continue to convene in these houses to practise rituals and produce traditional crafts.

In terms of modern architecture one of the highlights is undeniably New Caledonia's Tjibaou Culture Centre (see p185), which draws on traditional village architecture and mythology. Despite being designed by an Italian architect, this truly distinctive building uses timbers and styles that look to the region's past. Elsewhere in the Pacific you can see the vestiges of colonial architecture, including Suva's crumbling Grand Pacific Hotel (p128) or Nuku'alofa's Royal Palace.

Cinema & TV

Film-makers have long been drawn to the locations of the Pacific, though many films only superficially explore its culture. Hollywood's take on James Michener's novels *Return to Paradise* (1953) and *South Pacific* (1958) have plenty of postcard images, even if the latter was filmed in Hawai'i, Malaysia and, ahem, Spain. The original *Blue Lagoon* (1949) and the Brooke Shields remake (1979) both feature the Yasawa Islands, while Tom Hanks was *Cast Away* (2001) on location in Fiji.

Increasingly directors are exploring beneath the postcard veneer and showing the world the real Pacific. The pioneering director Dennis O'Rourke filmed political documentaries such as *Yap – How Did You Know We Would Like TV* (1980), which records the arrival of television on the small island, and *Half Life* (1985), a testimony to the nuclear chill that the Cold War cast over the Pacific. Continuing this tradition is the Annual International Oceania Documentary Film Festival, held annually in Pape'ete's cultural centre, which features several films made by Pacific islanders. In 2008 films included *L'île Nickel* (2007), examining the conflict between New Caledonia's nickel mining and its environment, and *Dieu est américain* (2007), examining the cargo cults of Vanuatu. For a range of must-see movies with a Pacific island theme, see p30.

Pacific islanders themselves are becoming film-makers. One of the most successful is animated TV series *bro'Town*, a politically incorrect look at the life of Samoan boys growing up in South Auckland currently in its fifth series. Made by a troupe of Samoans and Nuieans calling themselves the Naked Samoans, the series has enjoyed considerable success internationally. Several of the Naked Samoans appear in the feature films *Sione's Wedding* (2006) and *Children of the Migration* (2004), which have different takes on Pacific islanders in NZ. In the US, Fijian Vilsoni Hereniko shows the real Pacific to Hollywood with his feature *Pear Ta Ma 'on Maf* (*The Land Has Eyes*; 2005).

But for many visitors the Pacific remains the land of the *Survivor* TV series, with several series made in the region: *Survivor Marquesas* (2002), *Survivor Vanuatu* (2004), *Survivor Palau* (2005), *Survivor Cooks Islands* (2006), *Survivor Fiji* (2007) and *Survivor Micronesia* (2008). After the reality TV onslaught Britain's Channel Four thought it was time to turn the tables with *Meet the Natives* (2007), a TV series that followed villages from Tanna in Vanuatu as they journeyed to the UK to meet their idol, Prince Phillip.

A US TV series that explores American and Australian military action during WWII in the region, called *The Pacific* (2009), including key battles such as Guadalcanal and Iwo Jima and was shot on location.

Literature

The distinctive writing culture of the Pacific remains healthy despite problems of distance and lack of publisher interest. Writers such as the influential Samoan Albert Wendt have found success in NZ and based themselves there. Other Pacific writers were born in NZ but have drawn on their Pacific heritage in their work. Tusiata Avia's first book of poetry, *Wild Dog Under My Skirt*, takes a humorous look at her Samoan roots, while the Samoan novelist Sia Fiegel received such praise for her debut title *Where We Once Belonged* that she has become the first lady of Pacific literature and regularly tours her work throughout Australia, Europe and the US. Maori-language publisher Huia (www.huia.co.nz) also publishes islander books including *Island of Shattered Dreams* by Tahitian Chantal Spitz and the excellent anthology *Niu Voices*.

Much like NZ, Hawai'i is another powerhouse of Pacific literature, with small presses like Tin Fish Press (www.tinfishpress.com) publishing and championing Pacific writers. One international success story is Fijian Vilsoni Hereniko, a playwright who immigrated to Hawai'i and has begun making

---

TOP READS

- *Where We Once Belonged* (Sia Fiegel) – scoring the Commonwealth Prize for Best Novel, this rich evocation of a Samoan girl's rite of passage expertly meanders through several stories.

- *Leaves of the Banyan Tree* (Albert Wendt) – by another Samoan writer, this three-generation epic is an insight into the *'aiga* (family).

- *Tales of the Tikongs* (Epeli Hau'Ofa) – a cheeky romp on a fictional island that pokes fun at politics and love, and has been hailed as the South Pacific *Under Milk Wood*.

- *Treasure Islands* (Pamela Stephenson) – to get over her midlife crisis the gifted comedian-turned-psychologist buys a 112ft clipper and decides to retrace Fanny and Robert Louis Stevenson's trip through the Pacific.

- *My Samoan Chief* (Fay G Calkins) – an American woman marries a Samoan exchange student and returns to live with him in the Pacific in a classic cross-cultural romance.

For other Pacific-oriented titles, see p29.

---

feature films about the Pacific, including *Pear Ta Ma 'on Maf (The Land Has Eyes)*. The University of Hawai'i Press has always been an excellent supporter of Pacific writers.

Of course, Europeans have been scribbling about the Pacific for centuries, from Jack London to James Michener and Paul Theroux. Some authors settled in the Pacific paradise: Robert Louis Stevenson relocated to Samoa, while Herman Melville based his *Typee* on four months' desertion from a whaling boat on the Marquesas Islands. Other authors just breezed though, including Joseph Conrad who used his merchant naval career as research for *Victory*.

Music & Dance

Diversity is the byword for Pacific music, with enough variety to put the wind up any stereotyped grass-skirt preconceptions you might have had. Group dancing is a part of many rituals across the islands, and with the arrival of Christianity, church singing became popular with many islanders.

Siva, the traditional Samoan dance, has a Hawaiian feel with slow hand movements that often relate a narrative. Fijian *meke* act as melodic oral histories, telling the stories of battle, appointments of chiefs or gossip, with spears and fans as props. In the Cook Islands the rhythmic *hura* dance resembles the Hawaiian hula and is rivalled only by the Tahitian *tamure* as the most seductive dance of the Pacific.

Contemporary music often draws on traditional sound, as you can hear in the tunes of the Tokelauan band Te Vaka or Fiji's acoustic guitar group Somai Serenaders, who play *sigi drigi* (sitting and drinking) usually surrounding a kava bowl. In Vanuatu popular bands include OK! Ryos, Edou and Gurejele, who play Kaneka music, which fuses traditional with pop sounds. But increasingly islanders are nodding their heads to reggae (see the boxed text, opposite) or tuning into hip hop. The NZ music scene has benefited from Pacific migration to such a degree that NZ-based band Nesian Mystic coined the term *Polysaturated* as an album title that could describe NZ's recording industry, which includes Che Fu and Scribe, who have Samoan heritage. Internationally Samoans such as King Kapisi or the US-based, Samoan-descended Boo-Yaa T.R.I.B.E have inspired local rappers. Small production studios are appearing in the Pacific allowing for recording by the likes of Niuean MC Kava and a burgeoning gangsta scene in Suva that includes Sammy G and Mr Grin.

Check out the rhymes 'straight outta Suva' by tuning into Underdawg Production's YouTube channel (www.youtube.com/user/udawgfiji).

EDMOND VIRA, LEAD SINGER 26 ROOTS

Vanuatu-based band 26 Roots won the 2008 Radio Australia Pacific Break competition (www .abc.net.au/ra/pacificbreak/). Their prize included recording their song 'Broken Promises' and performing at Fest'Napuan music festival (p607). Lead singer, Edmond Vira, talks about music in the Pacific.

What was it like competing and winning Pacific Break? Competing was hard work – we spent two weeks recording in a tiny studio, it was the first time we'd recorded an electronic band. When we heard we'd won, it was a big surprise, we were all really excited.

How would you describe the music of 26 Roots to people who haven't heard it before? Our music is heavy roots reggae. We hope to give our music more of a local flavour in future – so far we are using a traditional *tamtam* (a wooden slit-gong) in some of our songs, but we plan to introduce new ideas as we continue to develop our music.

Why do you think reggae is so popular in the Pacific? Because it's black man's music, so it's easy for us to understand, and it comes from small islands which are like our islands. You'll find lots of island people can identify with reggae.

Your winning song is called 'Broken Promises' – what is it about? Our song is about corruption – we'd like our political leaders to listen to it and understand they need to stop corruption, stop jabbering away about promises they can't keep, and start developing the country.

How did you guys get together as a band? On 26 December 2005, a group of us from the Sapi 2 area of Luganville town on Santo built a little shack near a banyan tree and called it '26 Ghetto'. We used 26 Ghetto as a meeting place where the boys could 'story' and play music using a guitar and a ukulele. We started the band with a couple of acoustic guitars, a borrowed keyboard and a drum set made of old paint tins, buckets and lawnmower parts. Just occasionally we managed to raise enough money to practise in a studio using electronic instruments.

In 2007, older people from the area, including our families, set up a committee to help the band. In that year too, 26 Roots performed in public for the first time at La Fete de la Musique and the Independence celebrations in Santo. And we managed to acquire our first instruments and a very small sound system.

What other Pacific island bands do you listen to? Who are your favourites? We like hearing other bands that play reggae. Our favourites are Naio and CrossRoads from Vanuatu and Pacific Unity from New Zealand.

What was it like playing at Fest'Napuan? Does it help to have a crowd behind you? It was a wonderful feeling because we'd never before played on a big stage with a really good sound system. And it was great to know there was this crowd watching and enjoying our music. It also helped us to develop our skills by watching and learning from the other groups who were there.

What next for 26 Roots? Will you record an album? We need to develop more original songs before we are ready to record an album – before too long, we hope!

Tapa

No art form is as characteristic of the Pacific as the beating of mulberry bark to create the fibrous cloth *tapa*. Whether it's called *siapo* in Samoa, *mahute* on Easter Island or *masi* in Fiji, this is much more than an everyday fabric used to make clothing, baskets or mats. Fijian *masi* is essential to almost every stage of life: newborn babies are swaddled in it, coffins are covered with it and brides' mothers covet top pieces for their girls' wedding garb. In Tahiti it was made in huge sheets 3m wide and hundreds of metres in length, and signified the power of a chief. Great storehouses were built for a chief's *tapa*, and even in death tapa would be wrapped around a chief's mausoleum to signify his power in the next life. Tonga's Queen Salote honoured the making of tapa so highly that she once observed 'Our history is written in our mats'.

When making *tapa* the custom was to strip the bark from the mulberry (or sometimes the breadfruit) tree and then beat it into sheets on a special-ised anvil. The thin sheets would then be glued together using a natural substance such as manioc root. In some communities it was believed that *tapa* was devalued if patterns were applied, and the more culturally valued forms were fine, simple and undecorated. In Fiji the cloth was smoked over a sugar-cane fire to produce a tan colour.

The real value of *tapa* was based on the ritual surrounding its creation and the community that produced it, for *tapa* was more than an object. It was exclusively produced by women in a communal ritual that revealed the strength of a tribe more powerfully than battle. Throughout Melanesia and Polynesia it served as a diplomatic tool; when given to another tribal group it placed the group in debt to the giver, and the receiver would have to honour this debt. Far from being a simple financial exchange, the giving of tapa established an inviolable moral agreement that was sealed by ancestral spirits and gods. To break the relationship of receiving tapa meant that ancestors would be defiled and gods could become vengeful. Some tapa objects were given more value than others in these exchanges, with baskets and mats holding particular significance.

In the 19th century European visitors to the Pacific collected little tapa, perhaps dismissing it as 'women's craft' and failing to appreciate its simple beauty. With the arrival of calico and accompanying European values, the making of tapa declined. Tapa's legacy remains on several islands, though it is not made in the great quantities it once was. In Fiji, the island of Vatuelele is still renowned for its *masi,* while modern designers are inspired by the traditional art form; for example, former Miss Cook Islands Ellena Tavioni-Pitman uses block-printing patterns that are inspired by tapa decoration on her swimwear and clothing, which is exported to the US, UK and Europe.

> Used in tapa across the Pacific, paper mulberry trees *(Broussonetia papyrifera)* were one of the first imports into the region, and are believed to have been brought from China as early as 600 BC.

Tattoos

The journals of European explorers such as Joseph Banks and Captain Cook are full of references to tattoos *(tatau)*. Pacific islanders of both sexes were tattooed from the age of 14 to mark the onset of puberty and arrival into adulthood, and later to signify status within their tribal groups.

The apotheosis of the art was on the flesh of Marquesan warriors who 'wore' a full-body armour of toughened tattoos, including on their eyelids and tongues. In Tahiti, Samoa and Tonga tattoos were elaborate designs worn on the buttocks and hips, the natural pigments burrowed under the skin with tools of bone or shell. In Melanesia, scarring of the body was a popular alternative to tattooing, although tattoos also bestowed status.

While tattoos became popular with passing European seamen in the 19th century (even Joseph Banks came home with one as a souvenir), Christian missionaries began to discourage tattooing as they believed it had satanic associations. Fijian tattooing (with its strong links to sexuality) became virtually extinct, and in more remote areas like Palau it survived until the Japanese invasion.

> *The Tattooist* (2007) is a NZ horror movie that follows a man learning the *tatau,* the Samoan tradition of tattooing, which goes gorily wrong – though it features impressive images of traditional tattooing.

Samoan *tofuga* (tattooists) remain strongly traditional (see the boxed text, p354) and in Tahiti tattoos are a powerful link to precolonial cultures. The tattoo revival has seen full arm and leg designs becoming popular and even the full-body patterns are en vogue, particularly among Tahiti's traditional dancers. Tongans' *tatatau* (tattoos) were thought to be almost extinct, until a revival in 2003 by Samoan artist Su'a Sulu'ape Petelo.

Sculpture & Carving

Whether in wood, stone, coral or bone, sculpture is a universal form of expression across the Pacific. Given the abundance of ocean and the isolation of several atolls, the carving of war canoes was easily the most common form of sculpture. A canoe's prow acted as an ambassador for many journeying islanders,

TIPS ON MEETING LOCALS

Want to get chatting with the locals? A good conversation starter is often sports such as rugby or netball: 'Can Fiji/Samoa/Tonga knock over the Kiwis at the next Commonwealth Games?' Given that many islanders travel around the world, they may want to talk about where you're from and they're almost guaranteed to have a relative who moved to Auckland, Sydney or Wisconsin.

Observe these simple rules when visiting traditional villages:

■ Remove your shoes when entering a home.

■ Sit cross-legged on the floor, rather than with your feet pointing out.

■ Avoid entering a house during prayers.

■ Avoid walking between two people in conversation.

■ Try to remain on a lower level than a chief to show respect.

For more information on responsible travel, see p28..

the stylised front of the vessel clearly revealing the passengers' spiritual beliefs to those on land. On war canoes the depiction of gods of battle and death would have explicitly declared the intentions of visitors, giving them the psychological advantage of fear. In the Marquesas wooden carvings on the prow of a *tiki vaka* (canoe) depicted ancestors to protect against the dangers of the sea. Other objects, such as bailers, paddles and splash guards, were inlaid with symbolic motifs to act as protection or to bring prosperity in fishing or conflict.

Weapons and objects of war were crafted not only as martial tools but with considerable aesthetic and cultural value. Marquesan *u'u* (war clubs) are still prized by collectors for the fine-relief carvings of war gods that are depicted on two sides of the hardwood weapons. In Polynesia, woven or wooden shields often depicted protection deities, though Tongan nobles fought with whalebone shields that offered excellent protection.

One of the more popular and most misunderstood artworks were the masks and headgear that were made across the region. Most masks were never meant to be worn but were portrait-like depictions of a human face. Sometimes they were created to be destroyed in funeral pyres, or were preserved for hundreds of years and used in ongoing rituals. Other effigies and masks were built for long-dead ancestors to inhabit and watch over the clan, being given pride of place in a home or temple with much *tapu* associated with them.

In the Solomons headhunting created other ritual artefacts, with skulls used in consecration ceremonies or to mourn a chief's passing. Vanuatu was famous for its over-modelling of skulls, with clay, fibres or other materials being added to the bones to create elaborate effigies with eyes, teeth and hair, sometimes including earrings or other ornamentation. The crafting of these kinds of artefacts was the secret business of men's councils, particularly in Melanesia.

The most recognisable icons of Pacific art are the enormous *moai* which look stoically over Easter Island (see the boxed text, p88). *Moai* are similar to other eastern Polynesian statues, particularly the large stone *tiki* of the Marquesas and Tuamotu Islands. Tongans and Fijians crafted their figures from the bones and teeth of whales, which have a deep orange colour if well maintained. Tongan noblewomen wore small necklaces of whale ivory with designs that resemble Maori *tiki*.

Many wooden sculptures of the Pacific did not survive, either being burnt by missionaries as idols or looted by souvenir-hunting Europeans. Many examples of the Pacific's most impressive artworks are held in North American or European museums, such as the Marquesas collection at New York's Museum of Metropolitan Art or the pan-Pacific holdings of the British Museum.

'Weapons and objects of war were crafted not only as martial tools but with considerable aesthetic and cultural value.'

Food & Drink

The food of the South Pacific is as sturdy, jovial and inviting as the people who cook it. It's fulfilling comfort fare, so don't worry about consuming thousands of extra calories or piling your plate too high – the more you eat, the more the islanders will love you for it. One of the most important priorities in life on these warm, convivial islands is that there is enough food for all to sit down and enjoy a nourishing meal in good company.

While staples were once dictated by what the ancient navigating peoples brought in their canoes, each island nation now has a distinctive culinary style, which has been influenced by French, English and US colonisation and the presence of Chinese and Indian labourers. Root tubers, fish and pork now share a plate with pasta, rice and a smorgasbord of canned foods from corned beef to foie gras. Although visitors to the South Pacific will find traditional food less available, they will encounter a delicious mingling of cultures.

The sweet potato (which hails from South America) was first introduced to the Marquesas Island around AD 300, approximately 1300 years before the first European explorers.

STAPLES & SPECIALITIES

Starch, meat and fish make up the bulk of the Pacific diet. Vegetables have never played much of a part in traditional cuisines, although foreign influences have added some colourful touches incorporating a wider variety of ingredients.

Breadfruit

Breadfruit is typically eaten unripe and roasted till charred on an open fire; the flavour of the steaming starchy flesh is somewhere between a potato and a chestnut. It can also be fried into chips, boiled or baked in the oven. The addition of coconut cream kneaded into the cooked flesh makes a sweet, doughy paste that can be eaten as is or wrapped in leaves and baked to create a starchy pudding.

Find out everything you've ever wanted to know about breadfruit but were afraid to ask at www.hort.purdue .edu/newcrop/morton /breadfruit.html.

Many traditional cultures fermented breadfruit, both as a preservation technique and to add flavour to an otherwise bland diet (the fermented fruit develops a strong, sour taste). There have been stories of century-old fermented breadfruit being still edible. Breadfruit is also dried for preservation, particularly in the Solomon Islands and Samoa, but the fruit is now nearly always eaten fresh.

Taro

There are several varieties of taro, all producing an oblong root tuber that is boiled in water or steamed in a traditional earthen pit oven. It's a firm, starchy, potato-like food that has a slightly gooey exterior when cooked just right. Covered with coconut milk it exudes a hearty, gotta-be-good-for-you quality and makes a satisfying accompaniment to a meal.

TRAVEL YOUR TASTEBUDS

Pacific cuisines have been heavily influenced by other cultures and nowadays you won't find too many totally traditional dishes on the menu. Here are a few modern specialities that are found throughout the Pacific:

Sashimi Japanese-style raw fish, thinly sliced and served with rice and a sauce.

Raw fish in coconut milk Thin chunks of fish marinated in lemon juice, tossed in with various regional veggies and spices and doused in coconut milk.

WE DARE YOU!

If you've got the guts, give these regional favourites a try:

Fafaru (French Polynesia) Raw fish marinated in rotting fish-infused sea water; it smells like roadkill but the texture is divine.

Palolo (Vanuatu and Samoa) Collected from coral reefs, *palolo* looks like blue worms and is quite salty and served on toast.

Sea (sea slug innards – Samoa) This incredibly salty, oyster-like delicacy leaves a metallic aftertaste.

The leaves of certain species of taro can also be eaten, usually mixed in savoury stews or eaten with coconut milk. They resemble spinach when cooked, and are the only traditional leafy green in Polynesia.

Coconut

Nothing invokes the flavours of the South Pacific more than the versatile coconut. It's an all-in-one food: meat, sugar, oil and water, all conveniently presented in its own bowl and cup. Each of the nut's four growth stages provides a different form of food or drink. The first stage is ideal for drinking because there's no flesh inside, except for a tasty jelly-like substance. The best eating stage is the second, when the flesh inside is firm but thin and succulent. After this, the flesh becomes thick and hard – ideal for drying into copra. At its fourth stage the milk inside goes spongy, making what is sometimes known as 'coconut ice cream'.

> A single coconut has about as much protein as one-eighth of a kilogram of beef.

> The water inside a coconut is sterile and can be used in medical procedures.

Fruit

While the Polynesian islands are generally dripping in fresh fruit (think mangoes, papayas, pineapples, giant grapefruit and the world's sweetest bananas), some parts of Melanesia are less well endowed but you will still find tropical fruit as well as avocados and tomatoes. A few varieties of plantains and regular bananas are often cooked and served as a side dish, sometimes topped with coconut cream (delicious!). Most locals source fruit from their own trees or from family and friends, so it can sometimes be surprisingly hard to buy local fruit throughout the Pacific. When possible, the best and cheapest places to buy it are markets and roadside stalls.

Fish & Meat

Fresh fish and shellfish are found on nearly every restaurant menu and, as a rule, are fabulous. Surprisingly, pigs were traditionally more highly valued than seafood, and the preparation of pork played a key role in celebrations and events. Dog was once widely eaten but it's now a rare occurrence.

Regional meats include flying foxes (fruit bats) in eastern Polynesia and Melanesia, venison in New Caledonia and goat in the Marquesas Islands. High-quality lamb and beef imported from New Zealand (NZ) is often available, as are low-quality frozen chicken legs from the US.

> Archaeological remains discovered in Chile in 2008 confirmed that chickens were brought to South America from Polynesia around 100 years before European explorers.

Canned Influences

Ever-popular canned meat is cheap, easy and tasty; unfortunately, it's also full of fat, nitrites and empty calories. The effect of this and other imports such as soft drinks and fast food on the weight and health of native Pacific peoples is devastating. Heart problems, hypertension and diabetes are rife throughout the region.

Tinned food was introduced by soldiers posted in the islands during WWII. In some islands the locals actually prefer tinned fish to fresh because it's a sign of wealth.

DRINKS

Nothing is better on a hot Pacific day than an ice-cold coconut. It's slightly sweet, chock-full of electrolytes and comes in the world's best, most ecological cup: its own husk. Fresh juices can be difficult to find, and you'll often have to choose a bottle or can of juice that has been imported from somewhere far less appealing. If you can't find a coconut, your best choice for healthy rehydration is bottled water – stay away from the tap water unless you've been assured by a reliable source that it's OK (see p651).

Coffee is found everywhere, but the further you get from the major towns, the more likely it will be instant coffee.

Kava is the most important drink on many Pacific islands, both for ceremonial and mind-calming reasons (see the boxed text, opposite)

For in-depth info about the mysterious and powerful kava root, go to www.kavaroot.com.

Alcoholic Drinks

Attitudes to alcohol vary across the region. Having witnessed the detrimental effects of alcohol, such as domestic violence, some communities have banned alcohol completely, but in most countries it's freely available. Those nations with their own breweries – such as Tahiti (Hinano Beer), Tonga (Ikale Beer), Samoa (Vailima Beer), Cook Islands (Matutu) and the Solomon Islands (Solbrew) – produce excellent beers, and Australian, NZ and US beers are also widely available. There aren't too many happening bars or nightspots on most islands, but at swank hotels and resorts you'll find all the tropical, coconut and pineapple cocktails you could dream of imbibing. The French colonies offer a surprising selection of fine French wines.

Kava, the Pacific Elixir by Vincent Lebot, Mark Merlin and Lamont Lindstrom is an exhaustive study of the South Pacific beverage from a New Age perspective.

CELEBRATIONS

Traditionally, celebrations meant feasts prepared in traditional earthen ovens and the size of a feast was a way for chiefs to show off their power and wealth as well as to share it with their people. Today, throughout the Pacific, a celebration still usually means that delicious food will be prepared in an *umu* (*ahima'a* in French Polynesia, *lovo* in Fiji), but nowadays anyone can throw a party. In general, Christian holidays, birthdays and weddings are the main reason to celebrate.

Every island has its own method of preparing the feast, but the common theme is that a variety of food, ranging from meat and fish to taro and cabbage, is neatly wrapped in leaves or a wet cloth and cooked in a stone-lined, wood-fired pit covered with earth. The flavours and juices mingle for several hours and the resulting meal is steamy, tender and delectable.

In most island groups there are tourist-oriented local feasts of earthen cooked food (called 'Island Nights' in the Cook Islands, *fiafia* in Samoa, *meke* in Fiji, *laplap* in Vanuatu, *ma'a tahiti* in French Polynesia or *bougna* in New Caledonia) that usually involve dance performances and make for a great night out.

Cocktails in Tahiti by Richard Bondurant is a fun, picture-filled drink recipe book that can help you re-create paradise via a martini glass once you get back home.

WHERE TO EAT & DRINK

In most cases Pacific islanders do not have the ready cash to patronise restaurants, so eating establishments mostly serve the tourist or expat population and are concentrated in highly touristed areas. Bars aren't overly common, although some restaurants double as watering holes.

Restaurants in the French territories can be superb, but they are very expensive. In Fiji there are sumptuous, reasonably priced Indian restaurants and most islands have at least a handful of Western and Chinese places.

Opening hours vary from country to country in the South Pacific, but in general restaurants are open for lunch from around 11.30am to

KAVA

The drinking of kava remains a strong social tradition in many Pacific cultures, and is practised throughout almost all of Polynesia and much of Melanesia. As well as a form of welcome, it's used to seal alliances, start chiefly conferences and to commemorate births, deaths and marriages. To decline kava when it is offered is to decline friendship – so even though it may taste disgusting to you, you've got to gulp it down and appear impressed.

In many countries kava has helped retain ancient customs. Many people attribute a low crime rate to the calming, sedative effects of the drink, which, unlike alcohol, does not produce aggressive behaviour.

Ceremony

In more traditional areas, kava root is prepared by chewing it into a mush and spitting the hard bits onto leaves. Water is added to the mush, then it's all filtered through coconut fibres. This method produces a more potent brew as saliva triggers the root's active ingredients. Modern techniques involve pounding the kava root in a bucket, and it can even be prepared from a commercially produced powder.

Kava is served in a coconut-shell cup and usually the chief and honoured guests drink first. Some cultures expect drinkers to down the kava in a single gulp, any remaining liquid being poured on the ground. In Samoa a small amount is tipped out of the bowl before drinking. Sometimes kava is drunk in silence, but some cultures prefer a great deal of slurping to show appreciation. Sometimes your companions will clap while you drink, but other noises and conversation are generally kept to a minimum.

In some areas, particularly the more touristy ones where customs have become more lenient, both men and women drink kava. In most places, though, it is an exclusively male activity – some say the original kava plant sprang from the loins of a woman, hence the *tapu* (taboo).

Kava makes the drinker's eyes sensitive to glare, so any strong lights, especially flashbulbs, are very intrusive.

Experiential Effects

Kava has a pungent, muddy taste and you'll begin to feel its effects within 10 to 25 minutes. If it's a strong brew, it'll make your lips go numb and cold like you've had a Novocaine injection, then your limbs will get heavy and your speech will slow. If it's really strong, you might get double vision and want to go to sleep. Even from the mildest form of the drink, you will feel slightly sedated and have a general sense of wellbeing. Some islanders claim to have repeated religious experiences after drinking kava.

Medicinal Uses

Broken down, kava is a cocktail of up to 14 analgesics and anaesthetics that work as natural pain and appetite suppressants. The root also has antibacterial, relaxant, diuretic and decongestant properties, and has been recommended for cancer, asthma and stomach upsets. Studies showing that kava can combat depression, reduce anxiety and even lower blood pressure led to a short-lived kava boom in Western countries during the 1990s. Another study, although later discredited, claimed the root could potentially cause liver damage, which resulted in bans or warnings on kava beyond the South Pacific.

2pm or 3pm, and dinner is served from 6.30pm to around 9pm. In restaurants that are also drinking spots, the dinner hours might extend until 2am or later. Look for the authors' Best Eats boxed texts in each destination chapter.

There is inevitably some form of shopping outlet in all but the smallest of villages. Depending on the level of isolation, the choice may be limited and the goods expensive. Markets are the source of the freshest and cheapest foodstuffs, while shops often rely on canned goods.

DOS & DON'TS

■ Do make sure you try at least one meal cooked in a traditional earthen oven.

■ Do wash your hands before a meal; you might be eating with your fingers.

■ Do check regional chapters for the tipping protocols of countries you are visiting.

■ Don't eat turtle: it's endangered and you'll be promoting illegal business.

■ Don't just dig in: the Pacific is very religious and many people say grace before a meal.

VEGETARIANS & VEGANS

Fish, pork and chicken form the basis of most Pacific dishes, so vegetarians will have to either pick through their food or get creative with self-catering. The exception to this is Fiji, which has a large Indian population and great vegetarian options.

EATING WITH KIDS

Find over 150 recipes from all over Polynesia plus great discussions about outside influences in *Sam Choy's Polynesian Kitchen* by Sam Choy.

Kids can happily munch on fresh fish and fruit, chicken and coconut. Most places in the region have kid-pleaser items such as hamburgers, pastas and rice dishes on their menus, and the local cuisine is often soft enough for most children to be able to try new foods such as taro and breadfruit. Baby supplies are available in all but the most remote places.

Ice cream is frequently available, and it's a real treat in the hot weather.

HABITS & CUSTOMS

A Taste of the Pacific by Susan Parkinson, Peggy Stacy and Adrian Mattison is a culinary guide to the region and includes 200 island-inspired recipes.

Ways of eating in the Pacific islands vary according to the fare: Chinese and Japanese food is eaten with chopsticks; you should use your hands when eating traditional Pacific fare and some Indian specialities; and you can finally pick up a knife and fork for Western food. It's not as confusing as it sounds and, for the most part, no-one will ever complain if you fork through everything.

While many islanders eat copious breakfasts of fish, meat and staples such as rice, breadfruit or taro, visitors in hotels are more likely to encounter light breakfast fare like breads, coffee and sometimes fruit.

Lunch and dinner are often similar to each other, with plenty of fish and meat dishes available.

If you get invited to someone's home for dinner or a BBQ it's not uncommon for the hosts to wait to eat until their gusts have finished – so don't be shy, dig in.

Environment

The Pacific Ocean is enormous. At 165,250,000 sq km, it covers a third of the earth's surface – more than all the landmasses combined. The land area covers just 1,300,000 sq km and New Guinea, New Zealand and Hawai'i account for almost all of that (1,100,000 sq km).

We owe the divisions of the Pacific to the French explorer Dumont d'Urville who divided the region into three major subdivisions, along racial and cultural grounds. The names of these regions persist today more than 300 years after his death: Melanesia (Greek for 'black islands') composed of New Guinea, the Solomons, Vanuatu, New Caledonia and Fiji in the southern hemisphere; Micronesia ('small islands'), comprised the atolls and small islands to the north and northeast of New Guinea and the Solomons that extend across the equator; and Polynesia ('many islands'), the huge triangle of ocean and islands bounded by Hawai'i in the north, Easter Island (Rapa Nui) in the west and New Zealand (NZ) in the south. D'Urville's divisions were somewhat contrived though they continue to be a useful way of partitioning the Pacific.

The Pacific also has three types of islands: continental, high and low. Melanesia and NZ have the only large continental islands. Of the smaller islands, the 'high' ones are mostly the peaks of volcanoes, extinct or active, and 'low' islands, or atolls, are formed by coral growth on sunken submarine volcanoes (see p539 and the boxed text, p64).

GEOLOGY

Seven large tectonic plates and several smaller ones cover the surface of the earth which float on the planet's molten mantle. Oceanic plates are heavy and float lower in this mantle than continental plates do. The Pacific Ocean floor is mostly comprised of one enormous oceanic plate – the Pacific Plate. The Nazca Plate is much smaller and forms the sea floor of the Pacific's southeastern corner.

The boundary between these two plates is an 8000km line of submarine volcanoes called a constructive fault (or divergent boundary), running roughly north–south at the longitude of Easter Island. Basalt ejected from these volcanoes adds to the two plates and pushes them apart about 17cm per year. The Pacific Plate moves northwest, while the Nazca Plate moves southeast.

Where the Pacific's plates meet neighbouring continental plates, a destructive fault (convergent boundary) forms: the heavier oceanic plates are subducted – forced hundreds of kilometres down into the earth's molten magma and deep trenches are formed along the seams. Molten, mineral-rich material is released from the diving plate and rises to form lines of volcanic

---

NATURAL ENVIRONMENTALISTS?

It's wrong to think that pre-European Polynesians lived in harmony with the environment. As Ron Crocombe points out in his superb book *The South Pacific*, in the first 600 years of Maori settlement in NZ they'd hunted to extinction half the native species of birdlife, and the numbers of seals and sea lions were critically low. By the time of European arrival NZ Maoris were eating mainly fern roots. A Tongan cave unearthed human remains 3000 years old along with the bones of birds – pigeons, megapodes, herons – all long-since extinct. Hawai'i and the Marquesas show similar evidence, and the Cook Islanders of Mangaia hunted to extinction 10 endemic bird species and overexploited the island's marine resources. Easter Island was covered in rainforest until Polynesian settlers laid it bare.

CORAL ATOLLS

The ocean floor has many submerged volcanoes. Some rise above the sea's surface to become islands and corals begin to grow around the edges. If subsequent plate movement causes the volcano to sink, the coral continues to grow in order to stay close to sunlight. As the central island sinks, a fringing lagoon forms between the island and reef. A coral atoll is formed when the island finally sinks completely, leaving a ring of coral encircling an empty lagoon. Charles Darwin was the first person to recognise this phenomenon (see the boxed text, p539).

The long conversion of these coral islets to inhabitable islands begins when coral sitting above the sea's surface is broken up by waves, eventually forming a coarse, infertile soil. Seeds blown along by the wind, carried by the sea or redistributed in bird droppings can then take root. Initially, only the most hardy of plants, such as coconut palms, can survive in this barren environment. Once the pioneering coconuts have established a foothold, rotting vegetative matter forms a more hospitable soil for other plants.

The people of the Pacific islands have learned how to eke out an existence from even the smallest of coral atolls. Vegetables brought from other islands, such as taro and *kumara*, supplement what grows naturally, and fish from the sea and the lagoon provide protein. However, atoll populations live a precarious existence as resources are scarce and the atolls are vulnerable to droughts, storms and tsunamis.

A coral atoll lifted entirely above the water's surface by geological activity is known as a *makatea,* after one such island in French Polynesia.

archipelagos. You can see where the Pacific Plate meets the continental Indo-Australian Plate in the long chain of islands that stretches from Tonga and Samoa and goes northwest through Fiji, Vanuatu and the Solomons to the northern islands off New Guinea. This is an active volcanic region – Mt Tuvurvur erupted and destroyed Rabaul on the New Britain island in Papua New Guinea (PNG) in 1994 and continues to bellow smoke and ash. Vanuatu's volcanoes can get very angry shooting magma into the air and the night sky above glows fiery red – with the last major eruption in 2005. There's an active underwater volcano in Marovo Lagoon in the Solomons.

The Pacific has several parallel island chains. These are 'hot spot' volcano chains, formed where hot spots exist in the earth's mantle. As the ocean floor moves away to the northwest, the volcanoes become extinct, often sinking beneath the sea. In the Pacific's hot-spot island chains, the youngest, still-active volcanoes are always in the southeast and the older, extinct submarine mountains or coral atolls are in the northwest. The Australs in French Polynesia are classic examples of hot-spot island chains.

When two oceanic plates collide one is subducted under the other and the upper lip can form a chain of islands as sediments accumulate. The Mariana Islands in Micronesia – where the Pacific Plate is subducted under the Philippine Plate – is an example, and the adjacent Mariana Trench is the deepest part of the world's oceans.

Seismic activity can also cause earthquakes, such as the one that hit Guam in 1993, and tsunamis – huge walls of water propelled by underwater earthquakes. Tsunamis can do massive damage to low-lying islands and coastal towns. More than 2200 people were killed by the tsunami that hit Aitape, PNG, in 1998. Another struck Gizo in the Solomons killing 56 people in 2007.

Mt Yasur (p581) in Vanuatu is one of the Pacific's most accessible active volcanos. You'll also see evidence of recent eruptions in the lava flows of Savai'i, Samoa (p324).

CLIMATE

The tropical climate of the Pacific islands is generally warm to hot and humid. If you're coming from outside the region, the climate can take some days to get used to, but the evenness of temperatures and dense steamy air are

---

EL NIÑO

The prevailing easterly trade winds tend to send warmer surface water towards the western Pacific, resulting in more rainfall in that region (Melanesia, Australia and NZ) than in the east.

An El Niño (more correctly 'El Niño Southern Oscillation', or ENSO) event occurs when the annual Christmas-period reversal in wind direction combines with high air pressure in the western Pacific and low air pressure in the east. The warm surface water is then blown back towards the eastern Pacific, carrying rain along with it: western Pacific countries experience droughts at this time, while eastern islands suffer unusually heavy rains or cyclones.

While El Niño ('the Boy') develops in the Pacific, its effects on weather are felt worldwide. Although only recently understood, El Niño is no recent development. Evidence shows that El Niños have occurred for at least hundreds of years, and probably thousands. El Niños are often followed by a weaker related event called La Niña ('the Girl'), which reverses El Niño – bringing storms to the western Pacific and droughts to the east.

Upwelling of deep-sea water along the west coast of South America is reduced during El Niño events. This water is rich in nutrients that support marine food chains and, in turn, seabirds.

El Niños usually last for about a year and recur irregularly every four or five years – they are currently impossible to predict.

---

lovely once you've acclimatised. Air temperatures vary throughout the year from about 21°C to 28°C. The wet season is November to April and the dry season is May to October. Most Pacific islands get substantial rain, but some regions can experience long droughts. Coral atolls have no rivers and little ground water, and are particularly vulnerable to droughts.

The earth's rotation deflects air that flows toward the equator to the west and the result is trade winds. These winds blow from the southeast in the southern hemisphere and from the northeast in the northern hemisphere. The climate of the islands that face these cool, rain-carrying trade winds changes from one side of the island to the other – there's lots of rain in Suva while Nadi remains relatively arid. About Christmas time each year the prevailing easterlies of the trade winds weaken, then reverse for a time and blow from the west.

Warm moist air rises up tall volcanic islands to condense as clouds. This can cause localised rain events and even small electrical storms over tall islands on an otherwise blue-sky day – a brilliant sight from afar in a boat on a lagoon.

Tropical Cyclones

Tropical cyclones are massive systems of winds rotating around a centre of low atmospheric pressure. The resulting torrential rains, high waves and winds, which can reach as high as 200km/h, present a hazard to shipping and can cause extensive damage to crops and buildings.

Cyclones can occur at any time but are most common during the wet season (November to April). In general, only the west Pacific experiences cyclones; however, patterns change with El Niño and La Niña events, and may be affected by global warming.

A rose is a rose by any other name: cyclones are called hurricanes in the Atlantic and typhoons in the western Pacific.

WILDLIFE

The New Guinea island is rich in wildlife but as we go east in the Pacific it becomes more spartan. The higher islands – Samoa and the Melanesia isles – have the greatest diversity in flora and fauna, while smaller coral atolls and low islands can be almost desolate. Like human colonisers, most species moved across the ocean from west to east, and so western islands such as the Solomons are far more diverse in flora and fauna than the eastern Society Islands. This process continues as the Solomons' saltwater crocodiles are turning up in Vanuatu's far northern islands (possibly losing their way during cyclones).

Plant species spread across the Pacific as seeds and fruits borne across the sea by winds, in bird droppings and by ocean currents. But certain plants like kava, coconut, breadfruit and taro, as well as animals like pigs and dogs, were deliberately introduced by early Pacific settlers.

Animals

The only marsupial found in the region is the possum (cuscus) in the Solomons (PNG has possums and elusive tree kangaroos). Otherwise the fruit bat, or flying fox, is the only land mammal to have made its own way to the Pacific islands. Stowaways on voyaging canoes included rats and geckos (small lizards) that are now common. Land reptiles take the form of a few (non-venomous) snakes and monitor lizards in western Melanesia. Frogs are many in number and variety. The Solomons also have saltwater and freshwater crocodiles. Adult saltwater crocs can exceed 4m in length and can be dangerous to humans.

Insects thrive in the tropics, and centipedes and spiders can come in alarming sizes (thankfully all benign).

Birdlife is abundant and dominated by migratory seabirds. Frigatebirds are common, as are herons and eagles.

DOMESTIC ANIMALS

Settlers moving through the Pacific brought domesticated dogs, chickens and pigs. As ready sources of protein, some of these animals probably did not survive the voyage, but enough arrived to spread the three species across the Pacific. Wild chickens still roam and forage throughout the Pacific islands, and pigs still hold an important role in many Melanesian rituals and are a sign of Melanesian prestige. Interbreeding and competition from European canines wiped out the original Pacific dog. Since European contact, other introduced animals have included cattle, horses, sheep and goats.

Introduced dogs and rats had a major environmental impact on the isolated islands. Birds that previously had no natural predators now had to contend with several, and many species became extinct. The later introduction of cats, very efficient killing machines, caused even more extinctions.

MARINE LIFE & CORAL

Many thousands of species of fish and marine life live in the Pacific Ocean. Even the most casual of snorkellers will be astonished at the colour, variety and abundance of creatures encountered under the water. See the boxed text on p650 for information on the few fish to be wary of.

'Coral both looks and behaves like a plant, but it's really a minuscule primitive carnivorous animal.'

Coral both looks and behaves like a plant, but it's really a minuscule primitive carnivorous animal. Coral draws calcium from the water and excretes it to form a hard shell as protection for its soft body. As coral polyps reproduce and die, new polyps attach themselves in successive layers to the empty skeletons, which have formed tiny rocklike limestone structures. Coral reefs are made up of millions of the coral skeletons, and in this way a coral reef grows by about 15cm per year. Only the outer layer of coral is alive and its brilliant colours are actually the hues of algae living in symbiosis within the coral tissue. Not only is it environmental vandalism to pluck vivid coral from the ocean, it's futile because it loses its colour when dead.

Coral requires a water temperature of between 21°C and 28°C and as the algae needs abundant sunlight, the water must be sediment-free and

---

FLORA & FAUNA OF THE PACIFIC

The following books are useful for travellers who want to learn a little more about Pacific wildlife:

■ Now out of print, but worth hunting for, Dick Watling's *Birds of Fiji, Tonga and Samoa* includes colour illustrations of the central Pacific's birdlife.

■ *Birds of Northern Melanesia: Speciation, Ecology and Biogeography,* by Ernst Mayr and Pulitzer-prize winner Jared Diamond (who wrote *Guns, Germs and Steel*), is the most comprehensive twitter's tome in recent years.

■ Ewald Lieske and Robert Myers' *Coral Reef Fishes* is a guide to shallow-water fish of the Indo-Pacific and Caribbean.

■ *Coral Reef Animals of the Indo-Pacific,* by Terrence Gosliner et al, is the definitive text on coral invertebrates.

---

relatively shallow. There are three ways that coral forms: a fringing reef close to land; a barrier reef separated from land by a stretch of water; and as a coral atoll. Countless species of fish and marine life depend on coral reefs – they are one of the planet's most biodiverse habitats and, naturally, are excellent areas for diving and snorkelling as well as for fishing.

Corals use stinging nematocysts (a specialised type of cell) to catch prey, and some varieties can give humans a painful sting when touched. Despite their seemingly robust nature, corals are fragile and can be damaged by the gentlest touch. Stay well back from coral growths when diving or snorkelling over reefs (see the boxed text, p77) and avoid reef walking.

MARINE MAMMALS

The Pacific Ocean was home to many whales until the arrival of 18th-century whaling fleets that decimated numbers and left some species on the brink of extinction. The worldwide recovery of whale populations has been slowed by continuing Japanese, Icelandic and Norwegian whaling activities. Attempts to establish a South Pacific whale sanctuary that would protect whales as they migrate through Pacific waters continue – see boxed text, p68. In many Pacific countries whale-watching tours are offered – see the Whale Encounters boxed text, p523.

Dolphins abound and follow boats in the Pacific with the same enthusiasm they show elsewhere in the world. The dugong or sea cow, the source of the mermaid myth, thrives in the western Pacific. You may be lucky enough to see a manta ray leap into the air and pirouette before it splashes down again – a brilliant sight.

In many Pacific countries, whale-watching tours are a viable long-term alternative to whaling. See the ones that got away in Tonga (p523), Rarotonga (p266), French Polynesia (p470), American Samoa (p346), Niue (p234), New Caledonia (p221) and Fiji (p147).

SEA REPTILES

Sea turtles, including species like hawksbills, green turtles and leatherbacks, inhabit Pacific waters. Turtles have been an important native food source for centuries, and they and their eggs are still occasionally eaten by locals, particularly on more remote islands.

Colourful sea snakes, highly venomous but nonaggressive, are common throughout the Pacific.

Pacific yellow-bellied sea snakes gather in swarms at breeding season. Large swarms can be over 100km in length!

Plants

Taro is the most important crop of many islands in the Pacific, and both its spinach-like leaves and starchy corns are used as staple foods. Plantain also features in the diet of many Pacific islanders – bananas are picked when green and cooked as a vegetable.

WHALING IN THE SOUTH PACIFIC

Australia and NZ have for years been trying to get enough support among member countries in the International Whaling Commission (IWC) to have a South Pacific whale sanctuary declared, but have failed to gain the required three-quarters majority. The IWC pronounced a moratorium on commercial whaling in 1986, although Japan was allowed to continue to hunt whales under an agreed scientific-research clause (which is heavily criticised by opponents of whaling as commercial whaling in disguise). Japan has tried to have the ban overturned, and won a vote on the 'eventual return of commercial whaling' by one vote in 2006; however, the ban was not lifted.

All three major players in the debate (Japan, Australia and NZ) are significant suppliers of foreign aid to Pacific nations, raising accusations of 'vote buying' at the IWC on both sides of the disagreement.

In the 2007–08 season Japan planned to catch 935 minke whales (the IWC is undecided on whether minkes are endangered or not), and 50 fin whales (endangered).

Twelve Pacific countries and territories protect whales within economic exclusion zones. This area of 12 million sq km between French Polynesia and Australia is a de facto whale sanctuary.

COCONUT

The coconut palm is emblematic of the Pacific. The plant *(Cocos nucifera)* originated in Southeast Asia. Its migration across the Pacific was most likely a mixture of natural processes (the fruit is husked, buoyant and travels on currents) and deliberate introduction by ancient settlers.

Without the coconut palm many small Pacific atolls and islands would never have become inhabitable. Coconut palms are tolerant of sandy soils and high salinity levels, and they are the only large tree that grows on sandy atolls without human assistance. The coconut palm is incredibly versatile. The coconuts historically provided drinking water for long ocean voyages, and the tree's wood was the main building material for voyaging canoes. On land, coconut palms were used for house and roofing materials, for rope, weaving and fire-making. The coconut is still economically important to many Pacific countries, providing income from crude oil, coconut cream and copra.

The oldest known fossils that resemble the coconut palm date back more than 15 million years and were found in Bangladesh.

KUMARA

While most Pacific vegetables and trees originated in the west and migrated east, the *kumara (kumala* or *'umala)* or sweet potato originated in South America. Peruvians know it as *kumar*.

The east-to-west movement of the *kumara* was a foundation of Thor Heyerdahl's alternative theory that the Pacific was settled from the Americas. Heyerdahl's famous *Kon-Tiki* voyage in 1947 – 8000km on raft from Peru to the Tuamotus – proved that it was possible for a balsa-wood raft to reach the Pacific islands from South America, but his theory was overwhelmed by the bulk of other evidence that supported the west-to-east settlement of the Pacific (see the boxed text, p38). It's thought that Polynesians, probably Marquesans, voyaging to South America returned with *kumara*. From the Marquesas it was carried westwards, reaching western Polynesia fairly quickly and Melanesia by the 16th century.

This ubiquitous staple is easy to grow and has had a profound effect on Pacific communities. These days we see sweet potato on menus of fancy first-world restaurants and listen to TV celebrity chefs extolling its virtues as the new fad cooking ingredient – not so new to the people of the Pacific.

NATIONAL PARKS

The individual country chapters in this book list national parks and reserves. There are three Unesco-listed World Heritage sites in the South Pacific: East Rennell Island in the Solomons (p387); Henderson Island near Pitcairn (p248); and the Parque Nacional Rapa Nui on Easter Island (p87). As Rennell Island was one of the stepping stones in the Lapita people's settlement of the Pacific, and Henderson and Easter Islands were among the last islands to be settled, these sites have important anthropological as well as ecological significance.

ENVIRONMENTAL ISSUES

The most severe ecological danger to the nations of the Pacific is attributed to the developed world. Waste management of litter, from both the islands themselves and rubbish drifting ashore, is another major concern. Rising sea levels due to global warming is a critical issue for Pacific islanders and low-lying coral atolls are especially vulnerable. King tides are already threatening Tuvalu's nine low-lying atolls and islanders from PNG's Carteret group have had to relocate to Bougainville – we may soon see whole Pacific populations on the move as climate-change refugees.

Mangroves are an important lynchpin in Pacific ecosystems and are also vulnerable to rising sea levels.

For more information on the World Wildlife Fund's activities in the South Pacific, see www.wwfpacific.org.fj.

For more information on environmental issues in the Pacific islands, see the websites of the South Pacific Environment Programme (www .sidsnet.org/pacific /sprep) and the United Nations Environment Programme (www.unep .ch/conventions).

Fishing

Commercial fishing fleets in the Pacific catch around half of the world's fish – an annual harvest that approaches 100 million tonnes. While many seem to believe that the ocean is an infinite resource because of its vast size, others claim this catch is unsustainable. The UN has found that most commercially

---

TOP 10 CONSERVATION AREAS

All Pacific countries have national parks or conservation areas to protect their natural environments – some of the world's most fragile ecosystems.

'Eua (p510) This park on 'Eua is Tonga's premier ecotourism destination – a 449-hectare region of offshore sea caves, dense rainforest and the endemic *koki* (red shining parrot).

Funafuti Conservation Area (p547) This 3300-hectare park is comprised of five uninhabited islets, lagoon, reef and ocean on the western side Tuvalu's main atoll.

Koroyanitu National Heritage Park (p134) Koroyanitu is in the highlands of Fiji's Viti Levu and offers excellent hiking through native Dakua forest to archaeological sites and waterfalls.

Mont Panié (p206) New Caledonia's Mont Panié is a 5000-hectare botanical reserve – the mountain rises to 1629m.

Mt Talau National Park (p519) Dramatic 131m Mt Talau is the centrepiece of this national Park in Tonga.

Suwarrow National Park (p290) The Cook Islands' remote northern atoll was once home to hermit Tom Neale and is now the country's only national park.

Takitumu Conservation Area (p266) This 155-hectare park in Rarotonga is home to the threatened *kakerori* bird.

Tetepare (p378) The South Pacific's largest uninhabited island in the Solomons is a nesting ground for turtles and dugongs.

Uafato Conservation Area (p315) Fourteen-thousand hectares of rugged terrain and rainforest with one Samoa's few remaining stands of trees.

Vatthe Conservation Area (p602) Vanuatu's 4500-hectare Vatthe Conservation Area is on Espiritu Santo.

CLIMATE CHANGE & GLOBAL WARMING *Saufatu Sopoanga*

Tuvalu began to voice its concern about climate change internationally in the late 1980s. Our key concern then, and now, is sea-level rise, which has the potential to submerge the islands we call home. Successive governments in Tuvalu have amplified warnings of this threat.

More than 35 years ago, scientists hinted that manmade emissions of carbon dioxide and other greenhouse gases may be raising the earth's atmospheric temperature, causing glaciers and polar ice to melt and sea levels to rise. Since then an impressive canon of scientific research has been published.

Thirty-five years later, is the sea rising? We think it is, and this view is supported by a broad scientific consensus. Estimates of sea-level rise in the southwest Pacific range between 1 and 2mm per year. This is what science tells us and anecdotal evidence here in Tuvalu – just south of the equator, and west of the international dateline – suggests the same.

What we see in Tuvalu is marginally higher (peak) sea levels when tides are highest. This means annual high tides are creeping further ashore. There is crop damage from previously unseen levels of saltwater intrusion, and a higher incidence of wave washover during storms or periods of strong tidal activity.

Some commentators, journalists and scientists have attributed these phenomena to construction too close to fragile lagoon foreshores or ocean fronts, or to the loss of natural coastal protection from cutting down shoreline trees and shoreline mining. Whether or not this is true is debatable. If the sea is rising no amount of natural or artificial coastal protection that is not prohibitively expensive will fend it off. So-called 'adaptation' measures, however beneficial, merely delay the inevitable. Unless, of course, the worldwide volume of greenhouse gas production is cut drastically, and cut fast.

Tuvalu's nine small atolls and reef islands are geographically flat, rising no more than 4m above sea level. We cannot move away from our coastlines as all the land we inhabit is coastline. We have no continental interior to which we can relocate; no high interior, as is found on a volcanic island.

Confronting the Issues

Successive governments in Tuvalu have adopted the concept of sustainable development. But however much we try to put this concept into action locally, we also know it will not solve the problem of rising sea levels. So what else can we do?

As much as we try to meet the expectations of the international community, which demands that we include sustainable development in our national policy, our efforts on the ground have been mostly unsuccessful. (Other developing countries around the world share the same experience.)

In the context of climate change, it has become obvious to us that sustainable development is clearly not a defence against sea-level rise, no matter how hard the international debate tries to connect the two. As the former chairman of the Association of Small Island States, Tuiloma Neroni Slade, said: 'It may be that we manage to get our sustainable development polices right. Yet we will still face the risk that all will be undermined by climate change.' This reality is the situation we face in the Pacific. Manmade climate change is not a Pacific invention, nor are rising sea levels our problem to fix. There is only this: Tuvalu and other Pacific island countries will be among the first to suffer the catastrophic consequences of sea-level rise.

exploited fisheries worldwide are being fished beyond their capacity to recover, and has stated that the industry is 'globally nonsustainable' and that 'major ecological and economic damage is already visible'.

It is not only fish caught for consumption that are endangered – fishing fleets worldwide claim a 'bycatch' of almost 30 million tonnes per year. These are unwanted species such as dolphins, sharks and turtles that are pulled up along with the target species and then dumped. The infamous drift nets, which are legally limited to 2.5km in length but are often much longer, claim a huge bycatch.

The only international mechanism to combat climate change is the Kyoto Protocol. In the absence of potentially better alternatives, we have appealed to the international community: support the provisions set out in Kyoto without reservation, and achieve its stated greenhouse-gas emission targets. What we fear is whether or not countries ratify Kyoto, greenhouse gas emissions will continue to grow, unless there is drastic change; for example, in how industrial countries, by far the largest emitters of greenhouse gases, use energy. Yet fossil-fuel consumption continues to grow.

Not Enough is Being Done

Policy measures and nontechnological fixes are important tools in the battle to lower greenhouse-gas emissions worldwide. Examples of these measures include energy conservation, the creation of vast new carbon sinks and emissions trading. But these efforts will not stop the sea from rising unless there is widespread replacement of existing energy technology that uses carbon-based fuels. Sadly, this prospect seems highly unlikely in the foreseeable future.

Since as far back as independence in 1978, Tuvalu has consistently advocated the use of renewable energy. We have had some success with solar power, using a sustainable technology (solar photovoltaic). But Tuvalu still relies predominantly on imported petroleum to meet its energy needs. Curtailing this dependence will require public or private investment from the international community to finance a large-scale shift to solar energy.

This large-scale renewable investment and commitment has not been forthcoming. Make no mistake, Tuvalu stands ready to enter into partnership with any industrial country or manufacturer of solar energy equipment to transform its energy sector – and to play our part, however small, in reducing greenhouse-gas emissions. We cannot do it alone. The Intergovernmental Panel on Climate Change – in thousands of pages of research documentation – has explained the threat posed by manmade atmospheric warming, yet the concentration of carbon dioxide and other greenhouse gases in the atmosphere is growing.

Paying the Price

The effects of global warming are being felt everywhere. The reason why powerful decision-makers in countries who can make a difference continue to downplay the threat posed by global warming is beyond our understanding. Isn't humankind's future at risk? The biggest emitters of manmade greenhouse gases are the world's largest countries, in North and South America, Europe, Africa and Asia. Two countries, which are also the world's two most populous, China and India, represent the world's biggest future greenhouse-gas emissions threat. By comparison, Tuvalu's greenhouse-gas emissions are next to zero.

It is likely that within the next 50 to 100 years the nine islands of Tuvalu will at best become uninhabitable, at worst they will vanish. The outlook is grim, but what can Tuvalu do? As one of my predecessors wrote: 'Tuvalu's voice in the climate change debate is small, rarely heard, and heeded not at all. Industrial countries, with all their wealth, may fret, but if atmospheric temperatures (continue to) rise, even by a few degrees, the price will be paid by the islands of Tuvalu and all low-lying land just like it.'

Saufatu Sopoanga served as Tuvalu's ninth prime minister from
2002 to 2004 and deputy prime minister from 2004 to 2006.

Remnants of drift nets are often found wrapped around dead whales that wash ashore. Nets and lines that have broken loose continue to drift through the oceans, catching and killing as they go. Longlines drifting loose on the surface of the South Pacific have decimated albatross populations, bringing some species near to extinction. Closer to the coast, blast fishing and cyanide fishing – both illegal – kill everything nearby including coral and shellfish rather than just their target species.

To resource-poor Pacific islands, selling licences to fish their relatively large Exclusive Economic Zones (EEZ) is one of their few economic options.

Deforestation

Easter Island led the world in its deforestation efforts a thousand years before Magellan sailed into the Pacific. The resources put into constructing the famous *moai* statues of Easter Island turned the island into a desolate wasteland.

In modern times, many South Pacific governments with few other economic options have embraced logging as a necessary evil. Logging is usually done by offshore companies and widely reported graft and corruption is often involved in the granting of logging concessions by Pacific governments. Foreign logging companies often have no long-term interests in Pacific countries beyond the harvesting of timber resources and sometimes operate at every edge of what's legal. Local people rarely see net benefits from their traditional lands laid to waste. Only larger Pacific islands like those in the Solomons, Vanuatu, New Caledonia, Fiji and Samoa have sufficient timber reserves to interest such companies. Solomons' timber is perilously overharvested – by some accounts accessible timber will be exhausted within the next decade. Much of this logging is illegal, run by well-organised international syndicates and this fuels corruption, exploitation and violence. In 2007 the Anglican Church of Melanesia reported on widespread child sexual exploitation associated with an Asian logging company around Arosi in Makira Province in the Solomons.

As well as loss of habitat for native birds and animals, deforestation leads to massive soil loss, which is particularly serious on small coral islands such as Niue, whose soil quality has never been good. Increased runoff from deforested land leads to pollution of waterways and muddying of coastal waters, which can severely retard the growth of coral.

Nuclear Issues

The Pacific Ocean has seen more than its fair share of nuclear explosions. In fact, in one respect it all started here: the world's only hostile uses of nuclear weapons, on Hiroshima and Nagasaki in 1945, were launched from the Northern Marianas. Subsequently, the US, UK and (most stubbornly) France have conducted nuclear testing here.

In 1971 the nuclear-testing issue loomed large at the first meeting of the South Pacific Forum (SPF, now Pacific Island Forum). In 1986 the SPF's Treaty of Rarotonga established the South Pacific Nuclear-Free Zone, banning nuclear weapons and the dumping of nuclear waste. This was ratified 10 years later by France, the US and the UK.

France's Pacific nuclear-testing program commenced with atmospheric tests in 1966 at Moruroa and Fangataufa in French Polynesia. Their early atmospheric tests caused measurable increases in radiation in several Pacific countries and as far away as Fiji, 4500km to the west. Atmospheric testing was abandoned in 1974 under severe international pressure, but underground tests (totalling 127 on Moruroa and 10 on Fangataufa) continued until 1996.

'The effects of US atmospheric nuclear testing, which ceased in 1970, have rendered Rongelap and Bikini uninhabitable...'

The effects of US atmospheric nuclear testing, which ceased in 1970, have rendered Rongelap and Bikini uninhabitable (although short-term visits are fine); their people live in unhappy exile on neighbouring islands.

Fragile coral atolls were always a questionable place to detonate underground nuclear weapons, and the French have confirmed the appearance of cracks in the coral structure of Moruroa and Fangataufa atolls, and leakage of plutonium into the sea from Moruroa. The effect of large amounts of radioactive material leaking into the Pacific Ocean would be catastrophic and far-reaching. Claims of high rates of birth defects and cancer on neighbouring islands of French Polynesia are denied by the French, but are impossible to confirm because of the secrecy attached to government health records.

South Pacific Diving Jean-Bernard Carillet

The South Pacific is as much a Garden of Eden below the waterline as on land. No doubt you'll impress your friends when you get home with stories of awesome walls, high-voltage drift dives, close encounters with sharks and manta rays, luscious soft and hard corals, iconic wrecks and gorgeous reefs replete with multihued tropical fish. As if that wasn't enough, visibility is excellent, waters are warm year round, most dive centres are first rate and conditions are magnificent at most times – think turquoise coral shallows, inky-blue seas and idyllic backdrops as you travel to and from the sites. Each island has its own personality and distinctive assets, which make for a seemingly endless diving repertoire.

For beginners, the South Pacific is a great place to learn to dive, with an abundance of easy sites and safe conditions. Whatever your abilities, you'll experience sensory overload while diving in the South Pacific and Micronesia.

Jean-Bernard Carillet is a die-hard South Pacific lover and a diving instructor. He has dived extensively in French Polynesia, New Caledonia, Easter Island, the Cook Islands, Fiji, Vanuatu and the Solomon Islands. He has also co-authored Lonely Planet's *Diving & Snorkeling the Red Sea* and *Diving & Snorkeling Tahiti & French Polynesia.*

DIVING CONDITIONS

Diving is possible year-round, although conditions vary according to the season and location. Visibility is reduced in the wet season as the water is muddied by sediments brought into the sea by the rivers, and areas that are exposed to currents might also become heavy with particles. On average, visibility ranges from 15m to 50m.

In most Pacific countries the water temperature peaks at a warm 29°C during the rainy season, but can drop to 20°C in some areas, including New Caledonia and Easter Island, at certain times of the year. Though it's possible to dive without a wetsuit, most divers wear at least a Lycra outsuit to protect themselves from abrasions. A 3mm tropical wetsuit is most appropriate.

For advice on diving hazards, see p650.

DIVE SITES
Cook Islands

There's nothing to boggle the mind in the Cook Islands but at least it offers relaxed diving for recreational divers in a safe environment. You've got a bit of everything, but on a small scale. A number of sites were battered by cyclones in 2005, and it will take time for the corals to regenerate. These days local dive shops tend to use the sites located on the south side of Rarotonga, where you'll enjoy some good dives in the passages and along the sloping reef. Rarotonga also has three wrecks that are regularly dived. See p264 for more information. There's good diving off Aitutaki as well; see p275.

Easter Island

Easter Island is still a secret, word-of-mouth diving destination that savvy divers will add to their itinerary. But don't look for throngs of pelagics (species that usually live in open oceans rather than waters adjacent to land or reefs) or psychedelic corals – they are rare. What's the pull, then? In a word: visibility. The lack of pollution, run-off, particles and plankton guarantees maximum water clarity – 40m is the norm, but it can reach a phenomenal 60m. Another highlight is the dramatic seascape, with numerous breathtaking drop-offs, chasms, caverns, arches and overhangs, giving the sites a peculiarly sculpted look and an eerie atmosphere.

With an unrivalled variety of atmospheres, textures and shapes, the South Pacific is the Holy Grail of bubble-makers.

If you're prone to seasickness, take note: since the Easter Island waters are devoid of any protective barrier reef, be prepared to cope with sometimes difficult conditions to get to the sites, especially from June to September. When the sea is too choppy, diving trips are cancelled.

Most sites are scattered along the western and northern coasts. A few favourites include Motu Nui, which features a truly magical drop-off wreathed with coral; Motu Kau Kau, another bijou site which looks like a giant *moai* (statue) rising from the sea bed at 55m; and La Cathédrales, which refers to an underwater lavatube broken up by numerous faults; and the scenic La Pyramide, featuring a lava seamount festooned with corals and broken up by arches.

Most sites are suitable for all levels. See also p92.

Fiji

Fiji has achieved cult status among diving connoisseurs, and justifiably so. Where else in the world can you join a hair-raising shark feed, then drift with the currents along walls festooned with colourful soft corals, all in the same area?

VITI LEVU

If you're after the thrill of a lifetime, you could register for a shark-feeding session in Beqa Lagoon, off Viti Levu. Here you're certain to go nose-to-nose with dozens of sharks. Up to eight types of shark take part in the handfeeding, including ponderous-looking bull sharks and even the heavyweight of them all – tiger sharks. The feeders distribute about 250kg of dead fish during each dive, which gives you an idea of the orgy. These dives are conducted in a very professional way by experienced guides who know their job, but whether or not these artificial encounters are a good idea is subject to debate. See p123 for more information.

For less intimidating sites, head to the north shore of Viti Levu, off Nananu-i-Ra island. This area is a good balance of scenic seascapes, elaborate reef systems and dense marine life. Dream Maker and Breath Taker rank among the best sites in this area, featuring large pristine clumps of corals surrounded by neon-coloured fish. See also p133.

TAVEUNI

Taveuni has gained international recognition in the diving community. The Somosomo Strait, a narrow stretch of ocean that is funnelled between Taveuni and Vanua Levu, offers exhilarating drift dives in nutrient-filled waters and steep drop-offs mantled with healthy soft corals. Purple Wall, Great White Wall, Rainbow Passage, Vuna Reef and Annie's Bommies are the perennial faves in this area. See also p158.

KADAVU

Kadavu's highlight is Great Astrolabe Reef, a 100km-long barrier reef that hugs the southern and eastern coasts of the island. This reef acts as a magnet for countless species. The seascape is a mind-boggling combination of canyons, crevices and arches. The best dive spots include Broken Stone, Split Rock and Naiqoro Passage. See also p164.

THE MAMANUCAS

Diving in the Mamanucas is probably less spectacular, but it's still very rewarding, especially for novice divers. Prominent sites include the Supermarket and Gotham City, but we found them a bit overhyped – it's better to ask about lesser-known sites. See also p136.

Easter Island claims the best visibility of all Pacific dive sites, boasting up to an incredible 60m.

Fiji has rightly been dubbed 'the soft-coral capital of the world'.

The rundown in this chapter is by no means exhaustive. For more information, see Lonely Planet's *Diving & Snorkeling Fiji*, *Diving & Snorkeling Tahiti & French Polynesia*, *Diving & Snorkeling Guam & Yap* and *Diving & Snorkeling Chuuk Lagoon, Pohnpei & Kosrae*.

DIVING & FLYING

Most divers to the South Pacific and Micronesia get there by plane. While it's fine to dive soon *after* flying, it's important to remember that your last dive should be completed at least 12 hours (some experts advise 24 hours) before your flight to minimise the risk of residual nitrogen in the blood, which can cause decompression injury. Careful attention to flight times is necessary in this region because so much of the inter-island transportation is by air.

BLIGH WATER AREA & THE LOMAIVITI GROUP

If you have the chance to embark on a live-aboard, you'll probably dive the Bligh Water area and the Lomaiviti Group. Two seamounts rising from the abyss to just below the surface include E6 and Mt Mutiny – both act as magnets for a wide assortment of pelagics and reef species. See also p148. Off Gau island, Nigali Passage is an adrenaline-packed drift dive.

French Polynesia

Consistently billed as one of the world's great diving destinations, French Polynesia provides enthralling diving for the experienced and novices alike. From Tahiti in the Society Islands to Hiva Oa in the Marquesas and Rangiroa in the Tuamotus, the options are countless. One proviso: don't expect healthy corals in the Society Islands because several waves of the destructive crown-of-thorns starfish have caused extensive damage to many coral reefs.

SOCIETY ISLANDS

You could start your diving trip in Mo'orea (see also p422). The Tiki features gangs of black-tip, grey and lemon sharks. Opunohu Canyons/Eden Park is famous for the many bulky lemon sharks (up to seven individuals) that regularly patrol the area, in about 20m. In Ra'iatea, be sure to log Teavapiti Pass, which has lots of fish action (see also p433). In Bora Bora, Tapu, Toopua and Muri Muri never fail to impress, with frequent sightings of grey reef and blacktip sharks and eagle rays, and nicely shaped sloping reefs. See p439 for more information. From Bora Bora, you could fly to Maupiti, which has been gaining in popularity since the first dive centre opened in 2008. Maupiti's signature dives include the aptly named Manta Point, in the lagoon. This cleaning station is visited by manta rays; small fish come out of the coral heads to scour the mantas of parasites, in less than 6m. See also p447.

Manta rays commonly range in size from 2m to 4m. They are harmless filter feeders, eating mainly plankton. They have tails, but no barb as stingrays do.

THE TUAMOTUS

For the thrill of a lifetime, dive Tiputa Pass in Rangiroa (see also p451). The stuff of legend, this magical site is usually done as a drift dive. Divers descend at the edge of the drop-off and let themselves be sucked into the lagoon through the pass with the incoming current, amid a swirl of grey sharks and reef species. Fakarava shares similar characteristics. Garuae Pass and Tumakohua Pass are high-voltage drift dives that will leave you awestruck. Daytrips to nearby Toau, which is wilderness at its best, are also available from Fakarava.

For fans of manta rays, we suggest you head to the atolls of Manihi and Tikehau, which both claim a manta cleaning station in the lagoon. It's very easy and accessible – novice divers will love it.

THE MARQUESAS

For something different, visit Hiva Oa in the Marquesas. Most dive sites are located along the bottom of basaltic cliffs, at the southwestern part of the island. Since the Marquesas are devoid of any protective barrier reefs,

SCUBA SENSATIONS FOR EVERYONE

The dive menu is so eclectic in the South Pacific that it's hard for divers to decide where to go. Here is a brief summary of the types of dives on offer to help you select your slice of underwater heaven.

Wreck diving Vanuatu, Solomon Islands
Wall diving French Polynesia, Fiji
Drift diving French Polynesia, Fiji, New Caledonia
Muck diving Solomon Islands
Cave diving Niue, Tonga
Crystal-clear diving Niue, Easter Island, Tonga
Shark diving French Polynesia, Fiji, Solomon Islands
Manta diving French Polynesia, New Caledonia
Soft corals Fiji
Beginners All places!

the water is thick with plankton and visibility doesn't exceed 10m to 15m. Hiva Oa's iconic dive, Le Rabot, is an underwater archaeological site that was discovered in 2006, with dozens of old stone anchors lying on the sea floor, all encrusted with coral. The local dive centre also organises trips to Tahuata, across the Bordelais Canal. See also p467.

New Caledonia

New Caledonia's main claim to fame is its lagoon – supposedly one of the largest in the world. Off Nouméa, an excellent site well worth bookmarking is Passe de Boulari. Coral is not the strong point of the dive, but for fish action it's unbeatable. Another exciting pass is Passe de Dumbéa, which plays home to schools of groupers from October to December. In Hienghène you can't help but be impressed by Tidwan, Cathédrale and Récif de Kaun, all boasting an outstanding topography comprising canyons, chasms and fissures, plus prolific marine life.

The area off Poindimié is more renowned for reef life, soft corals and nudibranches. Most dive sites are located in Grande Passe de Payes and in Passe de la Fourmi.

Île des Pins features some stunning sites. Vallée des Gorgones, off Gadji's reef, is a killer, with an excellent drop-off adorned with a profusion of graceful sea fans and a dense array of reef fish. Récif de Kasmira is another superb site, featuring a coral mound ranging from 3m to 17m. If you're after something unusual, try Grotte de la Troisième (Cave of the Third). About 8km north of Kuto, it features an inland cave filled with crystal-clear fresh water. You'll navigate inside the cave, at about 6m, wending your way among stalactites and stalagmites. Beware of silt build-up, though.

The sites in the Loyalty Islands are also well worth bookmarking. Lifou's signature dives are Gorgones Reef and Shoji Reef, with delicate sea fans wafting in the current the main attraction. Keep your eyes peeled for pelagic sightings, including tuna, sharks, rays and barracudas. Ouvéa offers pristine sites south of the atoll.

See also p220.

Niue

Tiny Niue cannot really compete with its neighbouring heavyweights, but it boasts excellent diving nonetheless. No streams, no run-off, no pollution and no fringing reef equal gin-clear visibility (up to 50m). Apart from this, the main highlight is the dramatic seascape. The coral flats surrounding the island are honeycombed with caves, gullies and chasms. If you enjoy diving

The lagoon in New Caledonia is so large that getting to most sites on the barrier reef involves a boat trip – some journeys last as long as 45 minutes. On the plus side, most sites are uncrowded.

RESPONSIBLE DIVING

The Pacific islands and atolls are ecologically vulnerable. By following these guidelines while diving, you can help preserve the ecology and beauty of the reefs:

- Encourage dive operators in their efforts to establish permanent moorings at appropriate dive sites.
- Practise and maintain proper buoyancy control.
- Avoid touching living marine organisms with your body and equipment.
- Take great care in underwater caves as your air bubbles can damage fragile organisms.
- Minimise your disturbance of marine animals.
- Take home all your trash and any litter you may find as well.
- Never stand on corals, even if they look solid and robust.

---

in atmospheric caverns, you'll love Ana Mahaga (Twin Caves), a humungous coral structure riddled with swimthroughs, tunnels and arches. There are also a couple of great sites off Tamakautoga Reef. The Dome is another great cave system that extends about 30m back under the island. Egypt is almost as atmospheric – you'll meander among boulders in narrow channels bounded by high walls. Niue's iconic dive is Snake Gully, where divers are rewarded with the very unusual vision of dozens of sea snakes – some winding along the bottom, some seemingly knotted up together.

Niue's weak point is the lack of healthy coral. A cyclone in 2004 battered most coral structures, and they will take time to regenerate. Marine life is also poor in comparison with other South Pacific destinations due to the lack of nutrients.

See also p234.

> Niue offers great visibility (up to 50m), an underwater labyrinth of caves and chasms, and if you're brave, swarms of sea snakes.

Samoa

Samoa is certainly not a hardcore diver's destination, but that doesn't mean you should give it a wide berth. Off Savai'i, Tialipi's Heaven features a pleasant architecture – wend your way around pinnacles, swim-throughs and canyons in less than 25m. If you need to refresh your skills, Lelepa Bay is ideal, with countless juvenile fish in the shallows. At Coral Gardens you can weave around the coral structures and marvel at the colourful fauna fluttering about. You might also want to explore the *Juno*, a three-mast vessel that sank in 1881 in 25m of water. It's nothing spectacular, but it's scenic.

Off 'Upolu, you'll probably dive Anganoa Wall on the south coast, as well as Eagle Ray Gully. It's easy and comfortable.

See also p330.

> Samoan dive sites don't disappoint if they are taken for what they are: relaxed and easy.

Solomon Islands

Wrecks galore, reefs, drop-offs – the variety of sites is staggering in the Solomons, as are the quality of the diving and the sense of exploration.

GUADALCANAL

The obvious place to start your diving adventures is Guadalcanal, which has a number of world-class sunken WWII vessels lying close to the shore. Most sites can be reached by car from Honiara, the capital. A few favourites include *Bonegi I & II*, about 12km west of Honiara. *Bonegi I*, a giant-sized Japanese merchant transport ship, also known as the *Hirokawa Maru*, lies in 3m of water descending to 55m, just a few finstrokes offshore. About 500m further west, the upper works of *Bonegi II*, also known as *Kinugawa Maru*, break the surface, a towel's throw from the beach. East of Honiara, you'll

> Penetration of wrecks is a skilled speciality and should not be attempted without proper training.

DO YOU 'MUCK DIVE'?

Growing weary of sharks, manta rays and all the big stuff? Well, it's time to 'muck dive'. Don't feel offended – this simply means that you concentrate on tiny, small and unusual critters, such as ghost pipefish, pygmy seahorses, manta shrimps, nudibranches, flatworms and sand-dwelling species. The Solomons are a good place to get an education in this domain. All you need is a keen eye!

---

find the *Searpens*, a big ship that lies upside down, and the *John Penn*, a large US troopship that was sunk about 4km offshore.

See also p371.

TULAGI

Easily accessible from Honiara, Tulagi, in the Central Province, is another must for wreck enthusiasts (see also p375). It has superb sunken WWII shipwrecks, including the monster-sized USS *Kanawha*, a 150m-long oil tanker which sits upright, and the USS *Aaron Ward*, a 106m-long US Navy destroyer that's noted for its extensive arsenal of big guns. The catch? They lie deep, very deep (the *Kanawha* lies in 45m and the *Aaron Ward* in 65m), and are accessible to experienced divers only. Visibility is not the strong point here: expect 10m to 15m on average. There are also awesome reef dives, such as Twin Tunnels, which features two chimneys that start on the top of a reef in about 12m. Another signature dive, Sandfly Passage is an exhilarating wall drift dive. And there's Manta Passage, near Maravagi, one of the Solomons' best-kept secrets, with regular sightings of huge manta rays.

The Solomons are still synonymous with adventure, seclusion and mystery.

NEW GEORGIA

While Munda offers a good balance of wreck and reef dives, *the* hotspot is Marovo Lagoon. South Marovo rewards divers with a host of very scenic sites off a cluster of three islands – Kicha, Mbulo and Male Male Islands – that are accessible by a 15- to 30-minute boat ride from the village of Peava. North Marovo Lagoon has a vibrant assemblage of dramatic walls (on the ocean side), exhilarating passages (especially Charapoana Passage, just on the resort's doorstep) and uncomplicated reef dives, all within close reach of Uepi Island Resort, where the local dive centre is based. It's also a good place to learn to dive. See p378 for more information.

Another not-to-be-missed area is Ghizo Island, further west. Here again the diving is superlative, with a stunning mix of WWII wrecks (bookmark the *Toa Maru*, a virtually intact Japanese freighter that ran aground during WWII), superb offshore reefs ablaze with marine life, and plummeting walls. On the minus side, the 2007 earthquake/tsunami did wreak havoc on a few charismatic sites (particularly Grand Central Station, north of Gizo, and Hotspot, east of Gizo, where huge coral fields were battered), but overall it's not *too* bad in other places. Just off Fatboys, Kennedy Island is a lovely spot to learn to dive, with a parade of reef fish to be observed on the sprawling reef. See p382 for more information.

Tonga

Whale-watching is so popular in Tonga that it has stolen the show. While Tongan waters will never be mistaken for those of, say, French Polynesia, there's some excellent diving off Ha'apai (p512) and Vava'u (p521). The reefs are peppered with numerous caves that make for atmospheric playgrounds and eerie ambience. In some places you'll feel as though you're swimming in an underwater cathedral. Off Ha'apai, some sites well worth logging include the Arch, Foa Caves, Hot Spring Cave or Ha'ano Castle. Off Vava'u, it's more

Tonga's best selling point is its contoured underwater terrain.

or less the same story below the waterline. Swallows Cave is a must-see, as are Shark Tooth and Hunga Magic. The wreck of the *Clan MacWilliam* adds a touch of variety.

Vanuatu

A few finstrokes from the shore, the legendary USS *President Coolidge* is trumpeted as the best wreck dive in the world. The sheer proportions of this behemoth are overwhelming: resting on its side in 21m to 67m of water off Luganville (Santo), the *Coolidge* is 200m long and 25m wide. It's shrouded with a palpable aura, and much has been written about its history. Amazingly, more than 50 years after its demise it's still in very good shape. It's not heavily overgrown with marine life, so you will see numerous fittings and artefacts, including weaponry, gas masks, trenching tools, trucks, rows of toilets, a porcelain statue (the 'Lady'), a pool, personal belongings abandoned by 5000 soldiers, and all the fixtures of a luxury cruise liner. A minimum of five dives is recommended to get a glimpse of the whole vessel. Although nearly all dives on the *Coolidge* are deep (more than 30m), she is suitable for novice divers. You'll start at shallower depths (about 25m) and go progressively deeper as you become more familiar with the diving. See also p598.

The only downside is that the *Coolidge* has overshadowed other dive sites in Vanuatu. In Santo, other wrecks worthy of exploration include the *Tui Tewate* and the USS *Tucker*.

If you need a break from wreck dives, don't miss the opportunity to sample some truly excellent reef dives off Santo, including Cindy's Reef and Tutuba Point. That said, Santo's prominent dive site is Million Dollar Point, where thousands of tonnes of military paraphernalia were discarded by the US Navy when they left the country. Divers swim among the tangle of cranes, bulldozers, trucks and other construction hardware in less than 30m and finish their dive exploring a small shipwreck in the shallows. See p596 for more on Million Dollar Point.

And what about the diving in Efate? It can't really compete with Santo, but we found Hat Island, about 5km off the north side of Efate, as well as Paul's Rock, also off the north side of Efate, pretty appealing. The seascape is top notch, and you'll see a smorgasbord of reef fish. For experienced divers, the Corsair – a WWII fighter plane – rests in 30m of water near Pele Island. In the same area, local operators also recommend Gorgonia Forest, which is done as a drift dive. See p569 for more on diving in Efate.

DIVE CENTRES

In most cases, the standards of diving facilities are high in the South Pacific. You'll find professional and reliable dive centres staffed with qualified instructors catering to divers of all levels. The majority of dive centres are affiliated with an internationally recognised diving organisation – eg PADI, SSI, NAUI and CMAS. They are mostly hotel based, but they welcome walk-in guests. The staff members usually speak English.

Centres are open year-round, most of them every day, but it's best to reserve your dive a day in advance. Depending on the area, centres typically offer two-tank dives (usually in the morning) or single dives (one in the morning and one in the afternoon). Many sites are offshore and involve a boat ride.

Be aware that even if common standards apply, each dive centre has its own personality and style. It's a good idea to visit the place first to get the feel of the operation.

Diving in the South Pacific is expensive in comparison to most destinations in Asia, the Caribbean or the Red Sea. Set dive packages (eg five or

The USS *President Coolidge* was a luxury cruise liner converted to a troop carrier during WWII. In 1942, while entering what the captain thought were safe waters in Vanuatu's Espiritu Santo harbour, the ship struck two mines and sank very close to the shore. Visit www.michaelmcfadyen scuba.info for details on the history of the *Coolidge*.

HOW MUCH?

Two-tank dive: US$110 (without gear), US$130 (gear included)

Introductory dive: about US$95

Open-water certification: about US$500

THE FIRST TIME

The South Pacific provides ideal and safe conditions for beginners, with its warm, crystalline waters and prolific marine life. Arrange an introductory dive with a dive centre to give you a feel for what it's like to swim underwater. It will begin on dry land, where the instructor will run through basic safety procedures and show you the equipment.

The dive itself takes place in a safe location and lasts between 20 and 40 minutes under the guidance of the instructor.

You'll practise breathing with the regulator above the surface before going underwater. Then the instructor will hold your hand if need be and guide your movements at a depth of between 3m and 10m. Some centres start the instruction in waist-high water in a hotel swimming pool or on the beach.

There is no formal procedure, but you shouldn't dive if you have a medical condition – such as acute ear, nose and throat problems; epilepsy or heart disease (such as infarction); if you have a cold or sinusitis; or if you are pregnant.

If you enjoy your introductory dive, you might want to follow a four- to five-day course to get first-level certification. This will allow you to dive anywhere in the world – it's like a driving licence. The South Pacific is an excellent area in which to do the certification course.

---

10 dives) are usually cheaper. All types of courses are available. Gear hire may or may not be included in the price of the dive, so it's not a bad idea to bring your own equipment if you plan to dive a lot.

Check out www.vanuatu tourism.com/dive for more information on Van-uatu's dive operators.

See Dive Shops in the Activities sections of the individual country chapters for details of operators in those countries.

Required Documents

If you're a certified diver, don't forget to bring your C-card and logbook with you. Dive centres welcome divers regardless of their training background, provided they can produce a certificate from an internationally recognised agency.

Easter Island (Rapa Nui)

Somewhere you've seen that classic photo, beloved of brochures, of a row of *moai* (statues), either at sunset or with the indigo-blue waters of the Pacific as a backdrop. Now it's time to check out the real thing. Truth is, you'll never forget your first encounter with these strikingly enigmatic statues standing on stone platforms, like colossal puppets on a supernatural stage. They *do* emanate mystical vibes. The fact that they are scattered amid an eerie landscape adds to the thrill.

When the *moai* have finished working their magic on you, there's a startling variety (for such a small island) of adventure options available. Diving, snorkelling and surfing are fabulous (promise you won't tell *too* many people). On land, there's no better ecofriendly way to experience the island's savage beauty than on foot, from a bike saddle or on horseback. But if all you want to do is recharge the batteries, a couple of Bounty-licious expanses of white sand beckon.

Although it's world famous, Easter Island has managed to hold on to that slow-down-it's-the-South-Pacific feeling. There's only one road and few cars. The atmosphere is chilled out to the max. There are no showy resorts, just a smattering of family-run pensions, which ensures your money goes straight into local pockets, and a handful of luxurious options that blend unobtrusively into the environment. Although visitors are on the increase, everything remains small and personable, and that's the beauty of it.

Punctuate all this with the hugely popular Tapati Rapa Nui festival, featuring an incredibly vibrant programme of music, dance and traditional cultural events, and the South Pacific couldn't offer up a better finale.

HIGHLIGHTS

- Hoist a drink, hear live music or get hypnotised by the furious and sensual dance performance of a Rapa Nui group in **Hanga Roa** (p92)

- Climb to the top of the extinct volcano **Maunga Terevaka** (p87) or **Península Poike** (p88) for fabulous panoramic views

- Hear yourself scream 'Awesome!' at the **Orongo Ceremonial Village** (p89), dramatically perched on the edge of **Rano Kau** (p89)

- Get wet! Take a **surfing course** (p93), dive **La Cathédrale** (p92) or snorkel in crystal-clear waters off **Motu Nui** (p92)

- Ponder over the island's enigmatic past at **Rano Raraku** (p88), then to **Anakena** (p88) for a snooze under the swaying palms

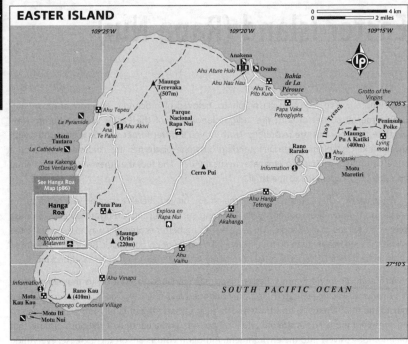

EASTER ISLAND

Anakena
Ahu Ature Huki
Ovahe
Ahu Nau Nau
Bahía de La Pérouse
Maunga Terevaka (507m)
Ahu Te Pito Kura
Grotto of the Virgins
Papa Vaka Petroglyphs
Ahu Tepeu
Parque Nacional Rapa Nui
La Pyramide
Ana Te Pahu
Ahu Akivi
Península Poike
Motu Tautara
La Cathédrale
Maunga Pu A Katiki (400m)
Lying moai
Ana Kakenga (Dos Ventanas)
Rano Raraku
Ahu Tongariki
See Hanga Roa Map (p86)
Cerro Pui
Information
Motu Marotiri
Hanga Roa
Puna Pau
Ahu Hanga Tetenga
Explora en Rapa Nui
Ahu Akahanga
Aeropuerto Mataveri
Maunga Orito (220m)
Ahu Vaihu
Ahu Vinapu
SOUTH PACIFIC OCEAN
Information
Rano Kau (410m)
Motu Kau Kau
Orongo Ceremonial Village
Motu Iti
Motu Nui

CLIMATE & WHEN TO GO

Just south of the Tropic of Capricorn, Easter Island has a mild climate with average daily temperatures around 20°C to 25°C. The island is hottest in January and February and coolest (but still relatively warm) in July and August. In summer tropical humidity can make the temperatures feel higher. July and August might be a bit chilly for some tastes, but are an ideal time for hiking. Downpours can occur during any season.

Any time is a good time to visit Easter Island, but the peak holiday season typically runs from late December to late February, and at this time hotel prices are highest.

COSTS & MONEY

If you come here from mainland Chile, be prepared for a shock. You'll find accommodation and restaurants on Easter Island fairly pricey for what you get. If you come from Tahiti, you'll heave a sigh of relief and will find the island fairly good value...

We've placed accommodation costing less than CH$30,000 a night for a double in the budget category, CH$30,000 to

---

EASTER ISLAND FACTS

Capital city Hanga Roa
Population 4800
Land area 117 sq km
International telephone code ☎ 56 32
Currency Chilean peso (CH$)
Languages Spanish and Rapa Nui
Greeting *Hola* (Spanish); *Iorana* (Rapa Nui)
Website www.netaxs.com/trance/rapanui.html

CH$60,000 in the midrange category and over CH$60,000 in the top end.

Note that prices are listed in pesos but a number of establishments also quote their prices in US$.

There are significant seasonal price variations, with rates rising during the summer months (December to March). In this chapter prices are for high season.

HISTORY

Although Thor Heyerdahl's 1947 *Kon-Tiki* expedition proved it was possible to cross to the Pacific islands from South America on balsa-wood rafts, the most accepted answer now is that the first islanders arrived either from the Marquesas, the Mangarevas, the Cooks or Pitcairn Island between the 4th and 8th centuries.

In 2007 Jose Miguel Ramirez Aliaga, an archaeologist from Valparaíso University, put forth the hypothesis that Polynesians, by sailing eastwards, might have continued on to central or southern Chile after discovering Rapa Nui.

The Rapa Nui developed a unique civilisation, characterised by the construction of the ceremonial stone platforms called *ahu* and the famous Easter Island statues called *moai* (see boxed text, p88). The population probably peaked at around 15,000 in the 17th century. Conflict over land and resources erupted in intertribal warfare by the late 17th century, only shortly before the arrival of Europeans, and the population started to decline. More recent dissension between different clans led to bloody wars and cannibalism, and many *moai* were toppled from their *ahu*. Natural disasters – earthquakes and tsunamis – may have also contributed to the destruction. The only *moai* standing today were restored during the last century.

European Arrival

When the Dutch admiral Jacob Roggeveen arrived on Easter Sunday 1722, many of the great *moai* were still standing, but there was no sign of any modern implements, suggesting the islanders did not trade with the outside world.

In 1774 the celebrated English navigator James Cook led the next European expedition to land on Rapa Nui. Cook, familiar with the Society Islands, Tonga and New Zealand (NZ), concluded that the inhabitants of Rapa Nui belonged to the same general lineage. His account is the first to mention that many *moai* had been damaged, apparently as a result of intertribal wars.

Fourteen years later French explorer La Pérouse found the people prosperous and calm, suggesting a quick recovery. In 1804 a Russian visitor reported more than 20 standing *moai*, but later accounts suggest further disruption.

European Takeover

Contact with outsiders nearly annihilated the Rapa Nui people. A raid by Peruvian blackbirders (slavers) in 1862 took 1000 islanders away to work the guano deposits of Peru's Chincha islands. After intense pressure from the Catholic Church, some survivors were returned to Easter Island, but disease and hard labour had already killed about 90% of them. The knowledge and culture lost has never been fully regained.

A brief period of French-led missionary activity saw most of the surviving islanders converted to Catholicism in the 1860s. Commercial exploitation of the island began in 1870, when French adventurer Jean-Baptiste Dutroux-Bornier introduced the wool trade to Rapa Nui and sent many islanders to work on plantations in Tahiti. Conflicts arose with the missionaries, who were at the same time deporting islanders to missions on Mangareva (in the Gambier Archipelago). Dutroux-Bornier was assassinated by an islander in 1877.

Annexation by Chile

Chile officially annexed the island in 1888 during a period of expansion that included the acquisition of territory from Peru and Bolivia after the War of the Pacific (1879–84).

By 1897 Rapa Nui had fallen under the control of a single wool company, which became the island's de facto government, continuing the wool trade until the middle of the 20th century.

In 1953 the Chilean government took charge of the island, continuing the imperial rule to which islanders had been subject for nearly a century. With limited rights, including travel restrictions and ineligibility to vote, the islanders felt they were treated like second-class citizens. In 1967 the establishment of a regular commercial air link between Santiago and Tahiti, with Rapa Nui as a refuelling stop, opened up the island to the world and brought many benefits to Rapa Nui people.

Easter Island Today

As of 2008 Easter Island became a *territoria especial* (special territory) within Chile, which means greater autonomy for the islanders. The main claim is for the return of native lands, and the new status should help settle these matters in the forthcoming years.

The Rapa Nui are also concerned about the development and control of the tourism industry. The rising number of visitors – approximately 50,000 tourists come to the

---

A FRAGILE HERITAGE

Easter Island is a superb open-air museum, but it's under threat. The case of a Finnish tourist, who broke off the ear of a *moai* (statue) to take home as a souvenir in March 2008, makes this issue all the more sensitive. We spoke to Enrique Tucki, director of Parque Nacional Rapa Nui (p87).

What should travellers be aware of when visiting Easter Island? Visitors mustn't walk on the *ahu* (ceremonial stone platforms), as they are revered by locals as burial sites. It's also illegal to remove or relocate rocks from any of the archaeological structures. Visitors should also resist the temptation to touch petroglyphs, as they're very fragile. And please, carry out all litter!

Do travellers have access to all areas on the island? Yes, provided they stay on designated paths to limit erosion. Also take note that motor vehicles are not allowed on Península Poike or Maunga Terevaka, and that camping is forbidden in the national park.

Are there any plans to reinforce the protection of the sites? We have only a few rangers in the national park, so it's crucial that visitors behave properly. Not following the rules could result in restricted access to certain sites in forthcoming years.

---

island each year – has an impact on the environment. New measures and regulations will probably be introduced to better protect the heritage sites.

THE CULTURE
The National Psyche
Rapa Nui people are generally very easygoing, but it's worth keeping in mind that it's a fairly conservative society and that marriage, family life and children still play a central role in everyday life, as does religion.

The most striking cultural feature is the intriguing blend of Polynesian and Chilean customs – you'll hear an *iorana* followed by a stream of Spanish, or an *hola* followed by Rapa Nui. Although Rapa Nui people identify more as Pacific islanders than Latin Americans, they have one foot in South America and one foot in Polynesia.

Lifestyle
Despite its unique language and history, contemporary Rapa Nui does not appear to be a 'traditional' society – its continuity was shattered by the near extinction of the population in the last century. However, although they have largely adapted to a Westernised lifestyle, Rapa Nui people are fiercely proud of their history and culture, and they strive to keep their traditions alive. These disparate forces, rather than clashing, exert a fascinating appeal. A civil servant is likely to attend the Sunday morning Mass dressed in a suit but may turn into a fierce warrior with an all-plumed costume during the Tapati Rapa Nui festival (see boxed text, p90).

Population
The population of 4800 includes a third non-Rapa Nui people who are from the Chilean mainland and a substantial number of Rapa Nui who live, permanently or temporarily, off the island.

ARTS
As in Tahiti, traditional dancing is not a mere tourist attraction but one of the most vibrant forms of expression of traditional Polynesian culture. A couple of talented dance groups perform regularly at various hotels. Tattooing is another aspect of Polynesian culture, and has enjoyed a revival among the young generation since the late 1980s.

If you're into woodcarving, you'll find some elaborate pieces in Hanga Roa.

LANGUAGE
Spanish is the official language, but the indigenous language is Rapa Nui, an eastern Polynesian dialect closely related to the languages of French Polynesia and Hawai'i. Some people in the tourist business speak English.

EASTER ISLAND BASICS

English	Spanish	Rapa Nui
Hello.	*Hola.*	*'Iorana.*
Goodbye.	*Adiós.*	*'Iorana.*
How are you?	*Cómo estás?*	*Pehe koe?*
I'm well (thanks).	*Bien (gracias).*	*Rivaria.*
Please.	*Por favor.*	*Maururu.*
Thanks.	*Gracias.*	*Maururu.*
Yes.	*Sí.*	*E-è.*
No.	*No.*	*'Ina.*

ENVIRONMENT
Geography
Easter Island is roughly triangular in shape, with an extinct volcanic cone in each corner – Maunga (Mt) Terevaka, in the northwest corner, is the highest point at 507m. The island's maximum length is just 24km, and it is only 12km across at its widest point. Much of the interior of Easter Island is grassland, with cultivable soil interspersed with rugged lava fields. Wave erosion has created steep cliffs around much of the coast, and Anakena, on the north shore, is the only broad sandy beach.

Ecology
Erosion, exacerbated by overgrazing and deforestation, is the island's most serious problem. In the most dramatic cases, the ground has slumped, leaving eroded landslides of brownish soil. To counteract the effects of erosion, a small-scale replanting programme is currently under way on Península Poike and at Ovahe. Only plants native to Oceania, such as Albizzia, *purau* (*Hibiscus tiliaceus*) or *aito* (ironwood), have been introduced.

HANGA ROA

pop 4400

The only settlement on the island, Hanga Roa isn't the most architecturally distinguished capital in the South Pacific. But lift the town's skin and the place will start to grow on you. Not only does Hanga Roa have all the services you need, but it also offers a couple of archaeological sites, two cute fishing harbours, a couple of modest beaches and surf spots, a few bars and discos where you can let your hair down, a bevy of crafts and souvenir shops, and a handful of excellent restaurants – not to mention the best ice creams this side of the dateline! Not too bad at all for a town this size.

ORIENTATION
Most services are on or around Av Atamu Tekena and Av Te Pito o Te Henua, the two main drags. Outside this main area, the irregular dirt roads are rarely marked and street signs are nonexistent. Fortunately, the place is so small that you'll find your way around in a day or so.

INFORMATION
For international calls and calls to mainland Chile, head to any internet café – they all double as call centres.

Banco del Estado (☎ 210 0221; off Tu'u Maheke s/n; ☽ 8am-1pm Mon-Fri) Changes US dollars and euros. Charges a CH$1500 commission on travellers cheques. There's also an ATM but it only accepts MasterCard. Visa holders can get cash advances at the counter during opening hours (bring your passport).

Hare Taui Moni (☎ 210 0265; Av Atamu Tekena s/n; ☽ 9am-3pm Mon-Fri, to 1pm Sat) The exchange office charges a 15% commission on MasterCard or Visa cash advances and a US$8 commission on travellers cheques (in US dollars only).

Hospital Hanga Roa (☎ 210 0215; Av Simon Paoa s/n)

Omotohi Cybercafé (Av Te Pito o Te Henua s/n; per hr CH$1500; ☽ 9am-10pm) Internet access and call centre.

Post office (Av Te Pito o Te Henua s/n; ☽ 9am-1pm & 2.30-6pm Mon-Fri, to 12.30pm Sat)

Puna Vai (Av Hotu Matua; ☽ 8.30am-1pm & 3-9pm Mon-Sat, 9am-2pm Sun) This petrol station also doubles as an exchange office. Much more convenient than the bank (no queues, better rates, longer opening hours, no commission on travellers checks). There's an ATM inside (MasterCard only).

Sernatur (☎ 210 0255; ipascua@sernatur.cl; Tu'u Maheke s/n; ☽ 8.30am-5.30pm Mon-Fri) Has various brochures and maps on the island.

Taim@net (Av Atamu Tekena s/n; per hr CH$1500; ☽ 10am-10pm) Internet café and call centre.

TRANSPORT
Everything revolves around Hanga Roa. For details on transport to/from and around the island, see p94.

SIGHTS
Hanga Roa
A must-see for anyone interested in Easter Island's ancient past, the well-organised **Museo Antropológico Sebastián Englert** (☎ 255 1020; www.museorapanui.cl; Sector Tahai; admission CH$1000; ☽ 9.30am-12.30pm & 2-5.30pm Tue-Fri, to 12.30pm Sat & Sun) makes for a perfect introduction to the island's history and culture. In the vicinity of the museum, the highly photogenic **Ahu Tahai** contains three restored *ahu*. Continue further north along the coast and you'll soon come across **Ahu Akapu**, with its solitary *moai*.

EASTER ISLAND (RAPA NUI)

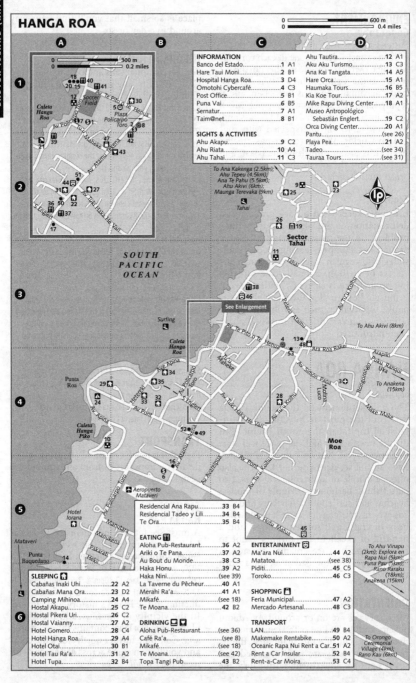

HANGA ROA

0 ———— 600 m
0 ———— 0.4 miles

INFORMATION
Banco del Estado.................1 A1
Hare Taui Moni.....................2 B1
Hospital Hanga Roa.............3 D4
Omotohi Cybercafé.............4 C3
Post Office............................5 B1
Puna Vai................................6 B5
Sernatur................................7 A1
Taim@net..............................8 B1

SIGHTS & ACTIVITIES
Ahu Akapu............................9 C2
Ahu Riata............................10 A4
Ahu Tahai............................11 C3

Ahu Tautira.........................12 A1
Aku Aku Turismo................13 C3
Ana Kai Tangata.................14 A5
Hare Orca............................15 A1
Haumaka Tours...................16 B5
Kia Koe Tour.......................17 A2
Mike Rapu Diving Center....18 A1
Museo Antropológico
   Sebastián Englert.............19 C2
Orca Diving Center.............20 A1
Pantu.............................(see 26)
Playa Pea............................21 A2
Tadeo............................(see 34)
Tauraa Tours..................(see 31)

SOUTH PACIFIC OCEAN

Sector Tahai

See Enlargement

To Ana Kakenga (2.5km);
Ahu Tepeu (4.5km);
Ana Te Pahu (5.5km);
Ahu Akivi (6km);
Maunga Terevaka (9km)

Tahai

To Ahu Akivi (8km)
To Anakena (15km)

Moe Roa

To Ahu Vinapu (2km); Explora en Rapa Nui (5km); Puna Pau (5km); Rano Raraku (18km); Anakena (15km)

To Orongo Ceremonial Village (4km); Rano Kau (6km)

SLEEPING
Cabañas Inaki Uhi............22 A2
Cabañas Mana Ora............23 D2
Camping Mihinoa.............24 A4
Hostal Akapu...................25 C2
Hostal Pikera Uri..............26 C2
Hostal Vaianny................27 A2
Hotel Gomero..................28 C4
Hotel Hanga Roa.............29 A4
Hotel Otai.......................30 B1
Hotel Tau Ra'a................31 A2
Hotel Tupa......................32 B4

Residencial Ana Rapu.......33 B4
Residencial Tadeo y Lili....34 B4
Te Ora............................35 B4

EATING
Aloha Pub-Restaurant.......36 A2
Ariki o Te Pana................37 A2
Au Bout du Monde...........38 C3
Haka Honu......................39 A2
Haka Nini...................(see 39)
La Taverne du Pêcheur......40 A1
Merahi Ra'a....................41 A1
Mikafé.......................(see 18)
Te Moana.......................42 B2

DRINKING
Aloha Pub-Restaurant...(see 36)
Café Ra'a....................(see 8)
Mikafé......................(see 18)
Te Moana..................(see 42)
Topa Tangi Pub..............43 B2

ENTERTAINMENT
Ma'ara Nui.....................44 A2
Matatoa...................(see 38)
Piditi............................45 C5
Toroko..........................46 C3

SHOPPING
Feria Municipal................47 A2
Mercado Artesanal..........48 C3

TRANSPORT
LAN..............................49 B4
Makemake Rentabike.......50 A2
Oceanic Rapa Nui Rent a Car..51 A2
Rent a Car Insular............52 B4
Rent-a-Car Moira.............53 C4

EASTER ISLAND IN...

Four days

Start the first day by visiting the **Museo Antropológico Sebastián Englert** (p85) for some historical background. Next, take a half-day tour to **Rano Kau** (p89) and then **Orongo Ceremonial Village** (p89) and soak up the lofty views. At night treat yourself to a proper feed at **Au Bout du Monde** (p91). On day two take a full-day tour to marvel at **Rano Raraku** (p88) and **Ahu Tongariki** (p88). On your return to Hanga Roa head straight to an atmosphere-laden bar (p92) on Av Atamu Tekena for the night vibe. Day three is all about Hanga Roa. Hit the **Mercado Artesanal** (p92) to put a dent in the wallet and then amble down Av Te Pito o Te Henua to enjoy the sunset at **Ahu Tautira** (below). Be sure to attend a traditional **dance show** (p92) later in the evening.

Day four should see you lazing the day away at **Anakena beach** (p88). Suitably rejuvenated, you can find a dance partner at **Piditi** (p92).

One Week

Follow the four-day agenda then make the most of the island's outdoor adventures. Book a **horse-riding excursion** (p93) along the north coast, spend a day diving off **Motu Nui** (p92), scramble up and down **Maunga Terevaka** (p93), and explore **Península Poike** (p88).

One Month

One month? Chances are you've fallen in love with a local. Rent a house in Hanga Roa and enjoy the romance!

Ahu Tautira overlooks **Caleta Hanga Roa**, the fishing port in Hanga Roa at the foot of Av Te Pito o Te Henua. It has two superb *moai*. Another impressive *moai* can be found on **Ahu Riata**, facing **Caleta Hanga Piko**, a smaller fishing harbour further south.

For a little dip, the tiny beach at **Playa Pea**, on the south side of Caleta Hanga Roa, fits the bill.

Around Hanga Roa

PARQUE NACIONAL RAPA NUI

Since 1935 much of Easter Island's land and all the archaeological sites have been grouped together as **Parque Nacional Rapa Nui** (Map p82; admission non-Chileans CH$5000). Admission is payable at Orongo Ceremonial Village (p89) and is valid for the whole park for the length of one's stay. Spending the extra cash on a guided tour or an islander who can explain what you are seeing is a very worthwhile investment.

There are ranger information stations at Orongo, Anakena and Rano Raraku.

Northern Loop

North of Ahu Tahai, the road is rough but passable if you drive slowly. Your best bet is to explore the area on foot, on horseback or by mountain bike, but there were no signs marking the sites at the time of writing.

About 2km north of Tahai is **Ana Kakenga**, or Dos Ventanas. This site comprises two caves opening onto the ocean (bring a torch). Continue about 2km north and you'll come across **Ahu Tepeu**. This large *ahu* has several fallen *moai* and a village site with foundations of *hare paenga* (elliptical houses) and the walls of several round houses. Off the dirt road to Akivi, **Ana Te Pahu** is a former cave dwelling with an overgrown garden of sweet potatoes, taro and bananas.

Unusual for its inland location, **Ahu Akivi**, restored in 1960, sports seven restored *moai*. They are the only ones that face towards the sea, but, like all *moai*, they overlook the site of a village, traces of which can still be seen.

To the northeast rises **Maunga Terevaka**, the island's highest point (507m). This barren hill is accessible only on foot or on horseback (see p93).

Continue to the south along the dirt track until you reach the turn-off to the volcanic **Puna Pau** quarry, which was used to make the reddish, cylindrical *pukao* (topknots) that were placed on many *moai*.

EASTER ISLAND (RAPA NUI)

NORTHEAST CIRCUIT

Beach bums in search of a place to wallow will make a beeline for the picture postcard white-sand **Anakena** beach. It also forms a perfect backdrop for **Ahu Nau Nau**, which comprises seven *moai*, some with topknots. A 1979 excavation and restoration revealed that the *moai* were not 'blind' but had inlaid coral and rock eyes.

On a rise south of the beach stands **Ahu Ature Huki** and its lone *moai*. Heyerdahl and a dozen islanders took almost 20 days to lever up this statue with wooden poles and ropes.

Nearby **Ovahe** beach offers more seclusion for wannabe Robinson Crusoes. Further east, beside Bahía de La Pérouse, a nearly 10m-long *moai* lies face down with its neck broken; the **Ahu Te Pito Kura** is the largest *moai* moved from Rano Raraku and erected on an *ahu*.

About 100m off the coastal road (look for the sign), you'll find **Papa Vaka Petroglyphs**, which features a massive basaltic slab decorated with prolific carvings.

And now, **Península Poike**, Rapa Nui's forgotten corner. At the eastern end of the island, this high plateau is crowned by the extinct volcano **Maunga Pu A Katiki** (400m) and bound in by steep cliffs. The landscape is stark, with huge fields of grass, free-roaming horses and intimidating cows. The best way to soak up the primordial rawness of Península Poike is to take a two-day horseback excursion from Hanga Roa, or

a day hike from the main road. Ask your guide to show you a series of small *moai* that lie face down, hidden amid the grass, as well as the **Grotto of the Virgins** (Ana O Keke), carved into the cliffs.

The monumental **Ahu Tongariki** has plenty to set your camera's flash popping, with 15 imposing statues, the largest *ahu* ever built. The statues gaze over a large, level village site, with ruined remnants scattered about and some petroglyphs nearby.

The volcano of **Rano Raraku** is a poignant archaeological site. Known as 'the nursery', it is the quarry for the hard tuff from which the *moai* were cut. You'll feel as though you're stepping back into early Polynesian times, wandering among *moai* in all stages of progress studded on the southern slopes of the volcano. Groups of *moai* are partly buried, their heads sticking out from the grassy slopes.

A trail leads over the rim into the crater. At the top the 360-degree view is truly awesome. Within the crater are a small, glistening lake and about 20 standing *moai*, a number of fallen ones and others only partly finished.

Rano Raraku is about 18km from Hanga Roa. There are several ruined *ahu* along the coastal road to Hanga Roa.

Southwest Trail

Past the Hotel Iorana in Hanga Roa, a sign points the way to **Ana Kai Tangata**, a vast cave

---

ARCHAEOLOGY IN EASTER ISLAND – LEARN YOUR AHU FROM YOUR MOAI

You don't need to have a university degree to appreciate the archaeological remains in Easter Island. The following explanations should suffice.

Ahu

Ahu were village burial sites and ceremonial centres and are thought to derive from altars in French Polynesia. Some 350 of these stone platforms are dotted around the coast. *Ahu* are paved on the upper surface with more or less flat stones, and they have a vertical wall on the seaward side and at each end.

Moai

Easter Island's most pervasive image, the enigmatic *moai* are massive carved figures that probably represent clan ancestors. From 2m to 10m tall, these stony-faced statues stood with their backs to the Pacific Ocean. Some *moai* have been completely restored, while others have been re-erected but are eroded. Many more lie on the ground, toppled over – usually face down – near an *ahu*.

Pukao

Archaeologists believe that the reddish cylindrical *pukao* (topknots) that crown many *moai* reflect a male hairstyle once common on Rapa Nui. Quarried from the small crater at Puna Pau, the volcanic scoria from which *pukao* are made is relatively soft and easily worked.

MOAI ON THE MOVE

How were the *moai* moved from where they were carved at Rano Raraku volcano to their *ahu* around the coast? Until recently most experts thought they were dragged on a kind of wooden sledge or on rollers, but in late 2005 Sergio Rapu, one of the island's most respected archaeologists, came to the conclusion that the *moai* were not dragged horizontally but moved in a vertical position. This theory would tally with oral history, which says that the *moai* 'walked' to their *ahu*. We asked him about his latest works. 'I have recently found that the *moai* had a small "tail" at the back of the base, which would ensure more stability on the platform. And thus, the statues could look over the village, like guardians.' Rapu also debunks the widely accepted theory of the toppling of the *moai*, suggesting that they were not toppled by enemies but instead by the owners of the *moai* (the chiefs, or the priests), who simply wanted to replace them – it was a way to keep the population under control by providing work.

As you'll soon realise, it's a never-ending debate. Never mind; it adds to the sense of mystery.

---

carved into black cliffs, which sports beautiful rock paintings.

Then comes what we think is one of the most memorable natural sights in the South Pacific: **Rano Kau**. Nearly covered in a bog of floating *totora* (reedlike plant), this crater lake resembles a giant witch's cauldron – awesome! Perched 400m above, on the edge of the crater wall on one side and abutting a vertical drop plunging down to the cobalt-blue ocean on the other side, **Orongo Ceremonial Village** (admission CH$5000) boasts one of the South Pacific's most dramatic landscapes. It overlooks several small *motu* (offshore islands), including Motu Nui, Motu Iti and Motu Kau Kau. Built into the side of the slope, the houses have walls of horizontally overlapping stone slabs, with an earth-covered arched roof of similar materials, making them appear partly subterranean. Orongo was the focus of an island-wide bird cult linked to the god Makemake in the 18th and 19th centuries. Birdman petroglyphs are visible on a cluster of boulders between the cliff top and the edge of the crater.

Orongo is either a steepish 2km climb or a short scenic drive from Hanga Roa.

Beyond the eastern end of the airport runway, a road heads south past some large oil tanks to **Ahu Vinapu**, with several toppled *moai*.

ACTIVITIES

For details of activities on Easter Island, see p92.

EASTER ISLAND FOR CHILDREN

Easter Island is not as attractive as Disneyland, mainly due to a lack of age-appropriate sights, although Rapa Nui are well disposed towards children. Some things to try are a visit to **Rano Raraku** (opposite), which can be a lot of fun (it's a bit like a theme park, after all!); a **horse-riding excursion** (p93) around Hanga Roa; and a splash at **Anakena** (opposite).

TOURS

We recommend joining an organised tour, since you get the benefit of an English-speaking guide who can explain the cultural significance of the archaeological sites. After your guided tour, you can explore at your leisure.

Plenty of operators do tours of the sites, typically charging CH$20,000 to CH$25,000 for a full day and CH$15,000 for a half-day. Entrance fees to Parque Nacional Rapa Nui (CH$5000) aren't included.

A few outfits offering a reliable service:
Aku Aku Turismo (☎ 210 0770; www.akuakuturismo.cl; Av Tu'u Koihu s/n)
Haumaka Tours (☎ 210 0274; www.haumakatours.com; cnr Avs Atamu Tekena & Hotu Matua) Offers customised tours.
Kia Koe Tour (☎ 210 0852; www.kiakoetour.cl; Av Atamu Tekena s/n)
Tauraa Tours (☎ 210 0463; www.tauraahotel.cl; Av Atamu Tekena s/n) At Hotel Tau Ra'a.

SLEEPING
Budget

Camping Mihinoa (☎ 255 1593; www.mihinoa.com; Av Pont s/n; campsites per person CH$4000, dm CH$7000, d without bathroom CH$8000, d CH$18,000-20,000) Cheap and cheerful, this backpacker crash pad is a popular spot for budgeters. Pitch your tent on the grassy plot, or choose one of the rooms in the main house. The five-bed dorm is cramped but serviceable. Perks include bike, car and tent hire (CH$1000), wi-fi access and laundry service. And you're just a pebble's throw from the seashore.

EASTER ISLAND (RAPA NUI)

TAPATI RAPA NUI: WHEN THE ISLAND GOES WILD

One word: unforgettable! Easter Island's premier festival, the **Tapati Rapa Nui**, lasts about two weeks in the first half of February and is so impressive that it's almost worth timing your trip around it (contact the tourist office for exact dates). Expect a series of music, dance, cultural and sporting contests between two clans that put up two candidates who stand for the title of Queen of the Festival.

The pinnacle of the festival is certainly the spectacle of Haka Pei, which takes place on the grassy flanks of the Cerro Pui, an extinct volcano in the middle of the island. A dozen male contestants run downhill on a makeshift sled made of banana tree logs tied together, at speeds that can reach 70km/h – hair-raising! No less awesome are the horse races, along a coastal track in Vaihu, where bareback riders tear along the racetrack several times. Equally heart-pumping (and our favourite) is the Taua Rapa Nui. This triathlon unfolds in the magical setting of the Rano Raraku volcano crater. The first stage consists of paddling across the lake on a *totora* (reedlike plant) boat. Then the contestants race around the lake carrying banana bunches on their shoulders. The last leg consists of swimming across the lake using a *totora* raft as a board.

Every evening dancing contests take place on a purpose-built stage in a vast field by the seashore in Sector Tahai.

On the last day the parade throughout Hanga Roa is the culmination of the festival, with floats and costumed figures.

The Tapati is your top chance to immerse yourself in traditional Rapa Nui culture. As one organiser told us, '*La esencia se ha mantenido y no se ha perdido el espíritu*' (We've kept the essence of the festival and its spirit has not been lost). Don't miss it!

Residencial Ana Rapu (☎ 210 0540; www.anarapu.cl; Av Hetereki s/n; s/d without bathroom CH$8000/15,000, with bathroom CH$15,000/20,000, cabañas CH$50,000-60,000; 🖳) You're not going to be writing about the cell-like rooms with shared bathroom, but at these prices you didn't expect the red carpet, right? Upgrade to a room with private bathroom or, if you're cashed up, a cabaña, with plenty of natural light pouring in and wonderful sea views. Pluses include laundry and a kitchen for guests' use.

Hostal Vaianny (☎ 210 0650; www.vaianny.com; Av Tuki Haka He Vari; s/d CH$10,000/20,000) Colourful, well priced, laid-back and secure – not only does it tick all the boxes for a good hostel stay, it's also within hollering distance of some of the town's best bars and restaurants. Rooms are itty-bitty, though.

Cabañas Inaki Uhi (☎ 255 1160; www.inaki-uhi.cl; Av Atamu Tekena; s/d CH$15,000/30,000) Here the 16 hospital-tidy rooms occupy two rows of low-slung buildings conveniently located on the main drag. They feel sterile, but it's squeaky clean and there are five shared kitchens. Wi-fi available.

Midrange

our pick **Te Ora** (☎ 255 1038; www.rapanuiteora.com; Av Apina s/n; r CH$35,000-55,000) Repeat visitors already book up the three snug rooms because they've learnt what you'll know after reading this review: Te Ora is Hanga Roa's mellowest place to stay for the price. All three rooms mix hardwoods and volcanic stones, but the Teora Ora, with sweeping views over the ocean, is a firm favourite. Your Canadian host, Sharon, can be counted on to be provide meticulous info about the area. There's a communal kitchen and wi-fi available.

Hostal Akapu (☎ 210 0954; www.hostalakapurapanui .cl; Sector Tahai s/n; s CH$25,000-30,000, d CH$40,000-60,000) These simple digs boast a location that your average luxury hotel would kill for. Not only that but also the setting is appealingly serene – there's nothing around but the rugged coastline. Though none of the three detached bungalows and six tiny rooms gets the view face on, you're within earshot of the sea. The kitchen in the dining room is available for guests.

Residencial Tadeo y Lili (☎ 210 0422; www.tadeolili .com; Av Apina s/n; s/d CH$45,000/60,000) This B&B's recipe for success has served it well over the years: keep your standards high and be attentive to your guests. This is reflected in the well-maintained bungalows. The knock-out ocean views from the terrace make a sundowner all the sweeter.

Hostal Pikera Uri (☎ 210 0577; www.pantupikerauri.cl; Sector Tahai s/n; s CH$40,000-46,000, d CH$51,000-60,000) A relaxing place, with a clutch of bungalows dotted on a grassy plot, within earshot of the sea. Aside from the boxy (and rather sombre) unit adjoining the dining room, they are commodious and beautifully attired.

Hotel Gomero (☎ 210 0313; www.hotelgomero.com; Av Tu'u Koihu s/n; s CH$45,000-55,000, d CH$55,000-65,000; ⊠ ⓢ) Water babies rejoice! The Gomero has a well-tended little pool nestled in lush gardens, which makes this place a restful spot in summer. Ask for a room in the new wing, which will set you back a few thousand extra pesos, but is much, much friendlier on the eyes.

our pick **Cabañas Mana Ora** (☎ 210 0769; www.manaora.cl; Sector Tahai; cabañas CH$60,000) Close your eyes and picture an adorable nest: an attractively decorated cottage perched scenically on a gentle slope overlooking the ocean. Well, it does exist. It includes a handy kitchenette and a terrace with seaviews. It's a bit of a schlep from the town centre (you'll need a bike), but there's nothing to disturb your dreams in this neck of the woods. Two more bungalows are planned.

Top End

Hotel Otai (☎ 210 0250; www.hotelotai.com; Av Te Pito o Te Henua s/n; s CH$45,000-55,000, d CH$60,000-75,000; ⊠ ⓛ ⓢ) A good base if you opt for the 'superior' rooms (especially Nos 138, 139 and 140, in a more recent wing).

Hotel Tau Ra'a (☎ 210 0463; www.tauraahotel.cl; Av Atamu Tekena s/n; s/d CH$70,000/80,000; ⓛ) A solid option. The 10 rooms are immaculate and flooded with natural light, and come equipped with firm beds and functional bathrooms. Alas, no sea views. Bill, the Aussie owner, is a treasure trove of local information.

Explora en Rapa Nui (☎ in Santiago 395 2703; www.explora.com; 3-night all-inclusive packages from s/d US$3350/4560; ⊠ ⓛ ⓢ) Ouch, the prices! But wow, the design! This ultraluxurious and green property blends unobtrusively into a small forested patch of volcanic-singed countryside. Rooms, all overlooking the roaring Pacific and fiery sunsets, feature indigenous materials in abundance. Prices include excursions. One downside: it feels a bit cut off from the rest of the island (it's about 6km away from Hanga Roa).

Other options:

Hotel Hanga Roa (☎ 210 0299; www.hotelhangaroa.cl; Av Pont s/n; d CH$120,000; ⊠ ⓛ) This sprawling establishment was undergoing an ample refurbishment when we dropped by and will feature a spa and 75 luxurious rooms (see its website).

Hotel Tupa (☎ 210 0225; www.tupahotel.com; off He_tereki s/n; d CH$180,000; ⊠ ⓛ) This ecoresort was under construction at the time of research and should be completed by 2010.

EATING

There are enough options to please most palates and suit every wallet.

our pick **Mikafé** (☎ 255 1059; Caleta Hanga Roa s/n; ice creams CH$1500-2500, sandwiches & cakes CH$1800-3000; ⓧ 9am-8pm) We confess having committed the sin of gluttony at this buzzy café. Hmm, the *helados artesanales* (home-made ice creams)! Oh, the damn addictive banana cake!

Aloha Pub-Restaurant (☎ 255 1383; Av Atamu Tekena; mains CH$6000-11,000; ⓧ dinner Tue-Sun) The moodily lit interior fits the bill for a *moment à deux*. The menu runs the gamut from seafood to meat dishes and salads to tacos.

Merahi Ra'a (☎ 255 1125; Av Te Pito o Te Henua s/n; mains CH$7000-9000; ⓧ lunch & dinner) The Merahi Ra'a has a wide assortment of fish delivered daily from the harbour, including tuna and *mahi mahi* (dorado). Order it grilled, raw, sashimi- or carpaccio-style.

Te Moana (☎ 255 1578; Av Atamu Tekena; CH$9000-15,000; ⓧ lunch & dinner Mon-Sat) Buzzy café-bar on the main drag. Its satisfying burgers will get the cholesterol oozing through your veins, or you can devour salads, fish and meat dishes.

our pick **Au Bout du Monde** (☎ 255 2060; Av Policarpo Toro s/n; mains CH$9000-15,000; ⓧ lunch & dinner Wed-Mon) In this agreeable venue run by a Rapanui–Belgian couple, every visitor ought to try the tuna in vanilla sauce or the duck

---

BEST EATS

The following establishments left us in a drooling mess.

- **Mikafé** (above) Dangerously addictive ice creams and sinful banana cakes.
- **Au Bout du Monde** (above) Imaginative cuisine in appealing surrounds.
- **La Taverne du Pêcheur** (p92) Excellent French fare and superb lobster.

foie gras. Leave room for dessert – the Belgian chocolate mousse is... Stop, we're drooling on the keyboard!

La Taverne du Pêcheur (☎ 210 0619; Av Te Pito o Te Henua s/n; mains CH$10,000-47,000; ☽ lunch & dinner Mon-Sat) After having two dinners in this French-run institution, all we can say is: *très bon* (very good). Standouts include *entrecôte d'Argentine* (beefsteak from Argentina), prepared with various sauces, lobster and a criminally unctuous crème brûlée. A good spot to hold hands and whisper by candlelight.

For self-caterers, there are a couple of supermarkets on Av Atamu Tekena.

Other options:

Haka Honu (Av Policarpo Toro s/n; mains CH$8000-12,000; ☽ lunch & dinner Tue-Sun) This buzzy eatery on the seafront features an eclectic menu and good ocean views.

Haka Nini (☎ 210 0918; Av Policarpo Toro s/n; mains CH$6000-8000; ☽ lunch & dinner Mon-Sat) A carbon copy of Haka Honu: same location, same dishes and same setting.

Ariki o Te Pana (☎ 210 0171; Av Atamu Tekena s/n; mains CH$1200-8000; ☽ lunch & dinner Mon-Sat) Surrender to some melt-in-your-mouth empanadas prepared mamma-style in this no-frills den.

DRINKING

Av Atamu Tekena has a smattering of pleasant bars featuring live music most evenings, including **Te Moana** (Av Atamu Tekena s/n; ☽ 11am-late Mon-Sat) and **Topa Tangi Pub** (Av Atamu Tekena s/n; ☽ 6pm-late Wed-Sat). Further south, **Aloha Pub-Restaurant** (Av Atamu Tekena s/n; ☽ 6pm-late Mon-Sat) is another hang-out of choice, with a loungy feel.

In search of a real espresso? **Mikafé** (☎ 255 1059; Caleta Hanga Roa s/n; ☽ 9am-8pm) is your answer, while **Café Ra'a** (☎ 255 1530; Av Atamu Tekena s/n; ☽ 9am-10pm) offers great people-watching opportunities.

ENTERTAINMENT

If there's one thing you absolutely *have* to check out while you're on Easter Island, it's a traditional dance show. The elaborately costumed troupe Kari Kari performs four times a week at a venue called **Ma'ara Nui** (Av Atamu Tekena s/n; show CH$10,000). Another well-regarded group, **Matatoa** (☎ 255 1755; www.matatoa .com; Av Policarpo Toro s/n; show CH$10,000), ignites the scene three times a week at the Au Bout du Monde restaurant.

If all you need is to let off steam, head to **Toroko** (Av Policarpo Toro s/n; admission CH$1500; ☽ 11pm-4am Thu-Sat) or **Piditi** (Av Hotu Matua s/n; admission CH$1500; ☽ 11pm-4am Thu-Sat), both with a mix of modern tunes and island pop.

SHOPPING

Hanga Roa has numerous souvenir shops, mostly on Avs Atamu Tekena and Te Pito o Te Henua. The best prices are at the open-air **Feria Municipal** (cnr Avs Atamu Tekena & Tu'u Maheke; ☽ Mon-Sat). The **Mercado Artesanal** (cnr Avs Tu'u Koihu & Ara Roa Rakei; ☽ Mon-Sat), across from the church, has more choices.

EASTER ISLAND DIRECTORY

ACCOMMODATION

All accommodation options are located in Hanga Roa except the Explora en Rapa Nui. *Residenciales* (homestays) form the bedrock of accommodation on the island, but there's a growing number of luxury options. At the other end of the scale, there's also a camping ground.

Air-con is still scarce, but fans are provided in the hottest months.

Upon arrival at the airport, you'll find *residencial* proprietors waiting there. Transfers are included.

Unless otherwise stated, most places come equipped with private bathroom, and breakfast is included.

ACTIVITIES
Cycling

Cycling is a superb way of seeing the island at your leisure, provided you're ready to come to grips with the steep and winding roads around the southern parts.

Makemake Rentabike (☎ 210 0580, 255 2030; www .makemakerapanui.com; Av Atamu Tekena; ☽ 9am-1pm & 4-8pm) hires out mountain bikes in tip-top condition. An easy loop is from Hanga Roa up to Ahu Tepeu, then east to Ahu Akivi and back to Hanga Roa (about 17km). The dirt track from Hanga Roa to Orongo Ceremonial Village is another stunner.

Diving & Snorkelling

There's excellent diving on Easter Island, with gin-clear visibility in excess of 40m and a dramatic seascape. However, don't expect swarms of fish.

It's diveable year-round. Water temperatures vary from as low as 21°C in winter to almost 27°C in summer.

Most sites are scattered along the west coast. A few favourites include Motu Nui and the very scenic La Cathédrale (the Cathedral) and La Pyramide (the Pyramid). For more information, see p73.

There are two diving centres in Easter Island. Prices start at CH$30,000 for a single dive. Both operators also offer snorkelling trips to Motu Nui.

Mike Rapu Diving Center (☎ 255 1055; www.mike rapu.cl; Caleta Hanga Roa s/n; ☯ Mon-Sat)

Orca Diving Center (☎ 255 0375; www.seemorca.cl; Caleta Hanga Roa s/n; ☯ Mon-Sat) Almost next door to Mike Rapu.

Hiking

You can take some fantastic trails through the island. A memorable walk is the way-marked Ruta Patrimonial, which runs from the museum up to Orongo Ceremonial Village (about four hours, 7km). Other recommended walks are the climb to Maunga Terevaka from near Ahu Akivi (about three hours) and the walk around Península Poike (one day). You can also follow the path along the northern coastline from Ahu Tahai to Anakena beach, then hitch back (should take about seven hours).

You can't get lost, but bring water and food and have a detailed map at hand.

Horse Riding

There's something romantic and adventurous about visiting the island on horseback. Several *residenciales*, hotels and tour agencies can provide horses or put together tailor-made excursions that take in sites near Hanga Roa or more remote places in the countryside.

Some reliable operators include **Piti Pont** (☎ 210 0664), **Pantu** (☎ 210 0577; www.pantupikerauri .cl; Sector Tahai s/n) and **Tadeo** (☎ 210 0422; Av Policarpo Toro s/n). Expect to pay about CH$25,000 for a half-day tour and CH$30,000 to CH$40,000 for a full-day tour with a guide.

Surfing

Easter Island is hit with powerful swells from all points of the compass throughout the year, offering irresistible lefts and rights – mostly lava-reef breaks, with waves up to 5m. The most popular spots are scattered along the west coast. Good news: it's uncrowded. For

---

PRACTICALITIES

- *Mercurio*, the national daily newspaper, can be purchased at various shops in Hanga Roa.

- Chilean programmes of the government-owned Television Nacional (TVN) are beamed to the island via satellite.

- Easter Island uses the NTSC system for videos.

- Electricity is supplied at 240V, 50 Hz AC.

- Easter Island follows the metric system. See the Quick Reference page inside this book's cover for a conversions table.

---

beginners, there are a couple of good waves off Caleta Hanga Roa. Seasoned surfers will take to Mataveri, to the southwest, or Tahai, to the northwest, where the waves are more challenging.

A handful of seasonal (usually from December to March) outfits based on the seafront offer surfing courses and also hire surfboards.

The shop **Hare Orca** (☎ 255 0375; Caleta Hanga Roa s/n), next to the Orca Diving Center, hires body boards and surfboards (per half-day CH$10,000).

BUSINESS HOURS

Offices are open from 9am to 5pm; some close for an hour at lunch time. Restaurants typically open until 9pm, though they may close early if business is slow.

EMBASSIES & CONSULATES
Chilean Embassies & Consulates

Australia Canberra (☎ 06-6286 2430); Melbourne (☎ 03-9654 4982); Sydney (☎ 02-9299 2533)

Canada Ottawa (☎ 613-235-4402); Toronto (☎ 416-924-0106); Vancouver (☎ 604-681-9162)

France (☎ 01 44 18 59 60; Paris)

New Zealand (☎ 04-471 6270; Wellington)

UK (☎ 020-7580-1023; London)

USA Los Angeles (☎ 310-785-0047); New York (☎ 212-980-3366)

Embassies & Consulates on Easter Island

There's no consulate on the island, but many countries have an embassy in Santiago, Chile.

HOW MUCH?

- **Half-day tour** CH$25,000

- **Admission to Parque Nacional Rapa Nui** CH$5000

- **Accommodation in a residencial** from CH$30,000

- **Fish dish in a restaurant** from CH$7000

- **1L petrol** CH$520

- **1L bottled water** CH$500

- **Glass of pisco** CH$1500

- **Woodcarving** depends on your bargaining skills

- **Empanada** CH$2000

FESTIVALS & EVENTS

In February the island goes wild during the colourful **Tapati Rapa Nui** festival (see boxed text, p90).

INTERNET RESOURCES

Easter Island Foundation (www.islandheritage.org) Information on history, travel, places to stay, culture, archaeology and more.

Easter Island home page (www.netaxs.com/trance /rapanui.html) Background facts and comprehensive links to information on everything from local politics to archaeology and tour operators.

MAPS

Tourist maps are distributed freely at Sernatur and tour agencies. More detailed maps, including the *Isla de Pascua Trekking Map* by JLM Mapas, are available at local shops.

MONEY

Easter Island uses the Chilean peso, but a number of businesses, especially lodgings and rental agencies, readily accept US dollars as cash (and euros, albeit at a pinch) and quote their prices in US dollars and in pesos. Travellers from Tahiti must bring US-dollar cash.

Many *residenciales*, hotels and tour agencies accept credit cards, but they usually charge a hefty commission for the service. In any case, don't rely solely on your credit card and make sure you keep some cash in reserve for the inevitable day when the ATM decides to throw a wobbly – there are only two in Hanga Roa. They only accept MasterCard.

For exchange rates, see the Quick Reference inside this book's front cover.

TELEPHONE

Easter Island's international telephone code is the same as Chile's (☎ 56), and the area code (☎ 32) covers the whole island. International calls (dial ☎ 00) start at around US$1 per minute. Mobile phones are also in use on the island.

TIME

Easter Island is six hours behind GMT, or five hours behind GMT in summer (daylight saving time). Thus, noon in Hanga Roa is 10am in Los Angeles, 6pm in London and 6am the next day in Auckland.

TOURIST INFORMATION

The primary source of tourist information is **Sernatur** (☎ 210 0255; ipascua@sernatur.cl; Tu'u Maheke, Hanga Roa). Any travel agency or hotel in Hanga Roa can also provide tourist information.

VISAS

Visa requirements are the same as for mainland Chile. Citizens of Canada, the UK, the US, Australia, NZ and most Western European countries need passports only. Upon arrival, visitors receive a tourist card and entry stamp that allows a stay of up to 90 days. Passports are obligatory. Check with a Chilean embassy for the latest information.

TRANSPORT IN EASTER ISLAND

GETTING THERE & AWAY
Air

The only airline serving Easter Island is **LAN** (☎ 210 0920; www.lan.com; Av Atamu Tekena s/n; ☼ 9am-4.30pm Mon-Fri, to 12.30pm Sat). It has four to seven flights per week to/from Santiago (Chile) depending on season and two per week to/from Pape'ete (Tahiti). A economy return fare from Santiago costs US$600 to US$900. From Pape'ete to Easter Island, flights start at US$600 return. From other South Pacific destinations, you'll have to stop in Tahiti. Easter Island can be included in round-the-world (RTW; see p636) or Circle Pacific (see p636) tickets with One World Alliance, which includes LAN.

Flights are often overbooked, so it is essential to reconfirm your ticket two days before departure.

Sea
Few passenger services go to Easter Island, but see p641 for more information. A few yachts stop here, mostly in January, February and March. Anchorages are not well sheltered.

GETTING AROUND
Outside Hanga Roa, nearly the entire east coast road and the road to Anakena are paved. Side roads to the archaeological sites are not paved, though most of these are in decent enough condition.

If you walk or ride a mountain bike or motorcycle around the island, carry extra food and water, since neither is available outside Hanga Roa.

To/From the Airport
The airport is just on the outskirts of Hanga Roa. *Residencial* proprietors wait at the airport and will shuttle you for free to your hotel or *residencial*.

Bicycle
Mountain bikes can be hired in Hanga Roa for about CH\$10,000 per day. Ask at your *residencial* or hotel.

Car & Motorcycle
Some hotels and agencies hire 4WDs for CH\$25,000 to CH\$45,000 per eight-hour day, and CH\$30,000 to CH\$60,000 for 24 hours depending on the vehicle. A word of warning: insurance is *not* available, so you're not covered should the vehicle get any damage. Don't leave valuables in your car.

Scooters and motorcycles can be hired for about CH\$25,000 to CH\$30,000 a day.

Contact the following outfits:

Oceanic Rapa Nui Rent a Car (☎ 210 0985; Av Atamu Tekena s/n)

Rent a Car Insular (☎ 210 0480; Av Atamu Tekena s/n)

Rent-a-Car Moira (☎ 210 0718; Av Te Pito o Te Henua s/n)

Taxi
Taxis cost a flat CH\$1500 for most trips around town. Longer trips around the island can be negotiated.

Fiji

FIJI

With alabaster beaches, cloudless skies and kaleidoscopic reefs, Fiji is the embodiment of the South Pacific dream. Most who head here want little more than to fall into a sun-induced coma under a shady palm, and with over 300 islands to choose from, the decision on where to unfurl your beach towel isn't easy. While some may find that anything more than two snorkelling excursions a day and half an hour on the volleyball court is not in keeping with Fiji's famously languid sense of time, there is more to these isles than can ever be seen from a deck chair or swim-up bar.

Beyond the beaches of the Mamanucas and Yasawas, a wonderland of lush mountains, hidden villages and a spirited capital await back on the mainland. Village life beyond the resorts is alive and kicking and, armed with a *sevu-sevu* (gift) of kava for the chief and a single word, '*bula!*', you'll be amazed at the friendliness and unaffected warmth of the locals. Furthermore, the beautiful Hindu temples and rich traditions of the large Indo-Fijian community add a vibrant splash of colour to the cultural soup.

As you would expect from 1100km of coral-fringed coastline, the Fijian waters offer some truly world-class diving and snorkelling. Spectacular coral gardens are often only a short waddle in flippers down the beach and there are plenty of dive shops on hand to whisk you out to fantastic drop-offs and swim throughs.

In a (coco)nut shell, Fiji is arguably the easiest place in the South Pacific to travel around. The population adopts you on arrival, and there's two robust cultures, a surprisingly diverse landscape and accommodation to suit most budgets.

HIGHLIGHTS

- Grab your favourite swim suit, slap on the factor 30 and wallow in the cobalt waters and somniferous sun of the **Mamanuca** (p135) and **Yasawa** (p141) islands

- Quell your knocking knees and remember to breathe when the first bull shark swims into view in the waters off **Pacific Harbour** (p122)

- Drink to the past at the old colonial pub in Fiji's first capital, **Levuka** (p148), or around the tanoa bowl at **Navala** (p135), Fiji's last traditional village

- Drop anchor with the yachties at **Savusavu Bay** (p151), Vanua Levu's prettiest town and first port of call for many touring boats

- Don a mask, fins and maybe even a tank to explore Taveuni's **Somosomo Strait** (p151) and Kadavu's **Great Astrolabe Reef** (p164)

CLIMATE & WHEN TO GO

Fiji has a mild, tropical maritime climate, with average temperatures of around 25°C throughout the year. Hot summer days can reach 31°C, but during the coolest months (July and August) the temperature can drop to between 18°C and 20°C. Humidity averages 70% to 80% in Suva year-round and 60% to 70% in Lautoka.

The wet season (summer) is November to April and coincides with Fiji's cyclone season when, although fairly rare (around 10 to 12 per decade), hurricanes are most likely to occur. The dry season (winter) lasts from May to October and is the best period to visit Fiji. The temperatures are cooler and humidity at this time sits a comfortable distance below stifling. November, February and March are also good as there are fewer tourists and you're more likely to find bargain accommodation. Conversely, dates that coincide with Australian and New Zealand school holidays are invariably busy and prices are high.

Diwali (p168) is held in late October or early November and this can be a fun, if manic, time to visit.

Although rainfall occurs throughout the year, you have the best chance for fine weather in the drier regions such as the Mamanuca and Yasawa groups. Suva gets significantly more rain than Lautoka. For general climate information and Suva's climate chart, see p627.

COSTS & MONEY

Although cheaper than many Pacific countries, Fiji is not a US$30-a-day destination and travellers are often surprised to find themselves paying more for accommodation and food than they would back home.

On average, budget travellers can expect to pay between F$90 and F$150 a day if they stay in dorms, travel on local buses and eat at cheap eateries or buy their food at produce markets.

Solo midrange travellers can expect to pay around F$190 per day, and couples can expect to pay around F$150 per person per day. These costs are based on using local transport, comfortable hotel accommodation and eating out three times a day. To reduce this, look out for accommodation with self-catering options and places where kids can stay free, and by avoiding island hopping and the expensive boat fares this entails.

Resorts usually include all meals and plenty of activities in their tariffs, and hover around F$300 to F$600 per night for a room suitable for a couple or a family of four. Top-end options can cost anywhere up to F$3000 a night for accommodation, food, alcohol and activities.

All rates quoted in this book are peak season rates, which tend to be 10% to 20% higher and include the 12.5% VAT (value-added tax) and new 5% hotel turnover tax.

HISTORY
Vitians

'Fiji' is actually the Tongan name for these islands, which was adopted by the Europeans. The inhabitants formerly called their home Viti.

Vitian culture was shaped by Polynesian, Melanesian and Micronesian peoples over 35 centuries of settlement. The Lapita people arrived from Vanuatu and the eastern Solomon Islands in about 1500 BC (see p37), and for about 1000 years they lived along the coasts and fished to their hearts' (and stomachs') content. Around 500 BC they became keen on agriculture and as a result the population shot up, tribal feuding got nasty and cannibalism became common.

European Arrival & Settlement

In the early 19th century Fiji was known to European whalers, sandalwood and *bêche-de-mer* traders. By the 1830s a small whaling and beachcomber settlement had been established at Levuka on Ovalau. It became one of the main ports of call in the South Pacific, and was the centre of the notorious blackbirding trade (see p44). Blackbirding originally encouraged the emigration of labourers from throughout the South Pacific (mainly the Solomons and Vanuatu) to work on Fijian plantations, but eventually the trade involved the kidnapping of islanders to work as labourers.

The introduction of firearms by the Europeans resulted in an increase in violent tribal warfare, particularly from the late 1840s to the early 1850s. The eventual victor, Ratu Seru Cakobau of Bau, became known to foreigners as Tui Viti (King of Fiji), despite having no real claim over most of Fiji.

By the mid-19th century London Missionary Society pastors and Wesleyan Methodist missionaries had found their way to Fiji, having entered the Southern Lau Group from Tahiti

FIJI

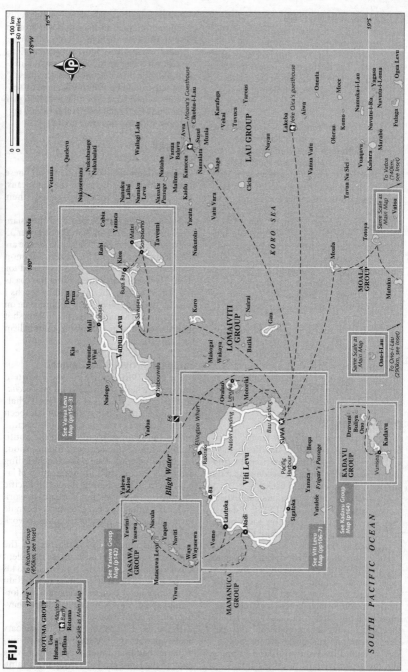

FIJI

0 ——— 100 km
0 ——— 60 miles

ROTUMA GROUP
Hatana • Uea
Hofliua • Rotuma
Macilo's
Barfly
Same Scale as Main Map

*To Rotuma Group
(450km, see Inset)*

Vetauua

Queleva

Nukusemanu
Nukubasaga
Nukubalati

Cikobia

Wailhagi Lala

Cobia
Yanuca
Rabi
Kioa
Matei
Sohosohmo

Nanuku
Lailai
Nanuku
Levu
Nanuku
Passage

Vanua Levu

Kia
Mali
Labasa
Drua Drua
Bua Bay

Macuata-
i-Wai
Nadogo
Labouwalu
Yadua

Kioa
Taveuni

*See Vanua Levu
Map (pp152-3)*

E6

Koro

Makogai
Wakaya

**LOMAIVITI
GROUP**

Batiki
Nairai
Gau

Naitaba
Vanua
Balavu
Malima
Kaido Kanacea
Namalata
Mago

Cicia

Nayau

Avea
Moana's Guesthouse
Cikobia-i-Lau
Sisui Munia
Vatu Vara
Nananu

LAU GROUP

Vekai
Tuvuca
Karafaga
Yarous
Oneata
Moce

Lakeba
Yeke Qica's guesthouse
Aiwa

Vanua Vatu
Oloraru
Komo

Namuka-i-Lau
Olgea Levu
Fulaga

*To Vatoa
(140km,
see Inset)*

*Same Scale as
Main Map*
Vatoa

Totoya

**MOALA
GROUP**

Moala

Matuku

Tavua Na Sici

Vuaqava
Kabara
Marabo
Navutu-i-Loma
Navutu-i-Ra

*Same Scale as
Main Map*
Ono-i-Lau

*To Ono-i-Lau
(290km, see Inset)*

KORO SEA

Ovalau
Levuka
Motoriki

Ellington Wharf
Rakiraki
Natovi Landing

Bau Landing
★ **SUVA**

Viti Levu

Beqa
Pacific
Harbour
Yanuca
Frigate's Passage
Vatulele

Ba
Lautoka
Nadi
Sigatoka

Vomo

*See Viti Levu
Map (pp106-7)*

**MAMANUCA
GROUP**

Viwa

**YASAWA
GROUP**

Yasawa
Yawini
Nacula
Yaqeta
Naviti
Matacawa Levu
Waya
Wayasawa

Yalewa
Kalou

Bligh Water

*See Yasawa Group
Map (p142)*

**KADAVU
GROUP**

Dravuni
Buliya
Ono
Vunisei
Kadavu

*See Kadavu
Group Map (p164)*

SOUTH PACIFIC OCEAN

177°E   178°E   180°   178°W   176°W

16°S   18°S

and Tonga in the 1830s. They gradually displaced the priests of the old religion and assumed privileged positions in island society, instilling a legacy of influence.

In 1849, when the home of a US commercial agent was accidentally destroyed by fire and not-so-accidentally looted, 'King' Cakobau was held responsible and presented with a bill for US$45,000. In 1862 Cakobau proposed that Britain should foot the bill to cover his debts, in exchange for cession of Fiji. The British consul declined, but the rumours caused a large influx of settlers to Levuka. Cakobau's huge debt was not cleared until 1868, when the Australian Polynesia Company agreed to pay it in exchange for land.

In 1871 Cakobau formed a Fiji-wide government but, unable to maintain peace, it quickly crumbled. Two years later Britain agreed to annex Fiji, citing blackbirding as its principal justification. Fiji was pronounced a British crown colony on 10 October 1874.

Colonial Period & Independence

Fiji's economy became depressed following the slump in the cotton market that occurred at the end of the US Civil War. Unrest and epidemics ensued, with measles wiping out a third of the indigenous population. Fearing a racial war, the colonial government sought the support of the chiefs in order to control the masses. The existing Fijian hierarchy was incorporated into the colonial administration and, in order to curb quibbling, the sale of land to foreigners was forbidden.

In 1882 the administrative capital was moved to Suva, as Levuka's geography hindered expansion. Under increasing pressure to make the Fijian economy self-sufficient, the colonial government turned to plantation crops, which demanded large pools of cheap labour. Indentured labour seemed the perfect solution, and between 1879 and 1916 over 60,000 Indians were transported to Fiji on five-year work contracts. Many came with hopes of escaping poverty, but were faced with heavy work allocations, low wages, unjust treatment and rationed food. The overcrowded accommodation forced people of different caste and religion to mix. Despite the hardship, the vast majority of *girmityas* (indentured labourers) decided to stay in Fiji once they had served their contract, and many brought their families across from India to join them. They were prohibited from buy-

FIJI FACTS

Capital city: Suva (Viti Levu)
Population: 861,000
Land area: 18,300 sq km
International telephone code: ☎ 679
Currency: Fijian dollar (F$)
Languages: English, Fijian and Hindi-Fijian
Greeting: *Bula* (Hello), Fijian; *Kaise* (Hello), Hindi-Fijian
Website: www.fijime.com

ing land and discouraged from interacting with Fijians.

On 10 October 1970 Fiji regained its independence after 96 years of colonial administration. The new constitution followed the British model, although political seats and parties were racially divided.

Fiji's first post-independence election was won by the indigenous Fijian Alliance Party (FAP), and Fijians were at first optimistic about their future. However, underlying racial tensions grew as the economy worsened. Most shops and transport services were (and still are) run by Indo-Fijian families, and a racial stereotype developed portraying Indo-Fijians as obsessed with making money. In reality, just like indigenous Fijians, the vast majority of Indo-Fijians belonged to poorer working classes and – unlike indigenous Fijians – they would never be able to have secure land tenure on their farming leases.

The Era of the Coups

Greater unity among workers led to the formation of the Fiji Labour Party (FLP), and in April 1987 an FLP government was elected in coalition with the National Federation Party (NFP). Despite having a Fijian prime minister and majority indigenous-Fijian cabinet, the new government was labelled 'Indian dominated' and racial tensions rose. On 14 May 1987, only a month after the elections, Lieutenant Colonel Sitiveni Rabuka took over the elected government in a bloodless coup and formed a civil interim government supported by the Great Council of Chiefs.

In September 1987 Rabuka again intervened with military force. The 1970 constitution was invalidated, Fiji was declared a republic and dismissed from the Commonwealth, and Rabuka proclaimed himself head of state.

The coups, which were supposed to benefit all indigenous Fijians, in fact caused immense hardship. The economy's two main sources of income, sugar and tourism, were seriously affected, overseas aid was suspended and about 50,000 people – mostly Indo-Fijian skilled tradespeople and professionals – emigrated.

In the elections of May 1999 the FLP formed a coalition with the Fijian Association Party. Indo-Fijian Mahendra Chaudhry became prime minister, and indigenous Fijians were far from pleased. Convinced that their traditional land rights were at stake, many refused to renew century-old leases to Indo-Fijian farmers. On 19 May 2000, armed men entered parliament in Suva and took 30 hostages, including Prime Minister Chaudhry. Failed businessman George Speight quickly became the face of the coup, claiming to represent indigenous Fijians. He demanded the resignation of both Chaudhry and President Ratu Sir Kamisese Mara and that a 1997 multi-ethnic constitution be abandoned.

Support for Speight's group was widespread, and Indo-Fijians suffered such harassment that many fled the country. Both Chaudhry and Mara eventually stepped down, the head of Fiji's military, Commander Frank Bainimarama, announced martial law and the 1997 constitution was revoked – but not for long.

In March 2001, the appeal court decided to uphold the 1997 constitution and ruled that Fiji be taken to the polls. Lasenia Qarase, heading the Fijian People's Party (SLD), won 32 of the 71 parliamentary seats in the August 2001 elections but defied the constitution by including no FLP members in his cabinet.

By 2004 the country was once again divided, this time by the Qarase government's draft *Promotion of Reconciliation, Tolerance and Unity (PRTU) Bill* whose opponents saw the amnesty provisions for those involved in the coup as untenable. Backed by the military, Commodore Frank Bainimarama presented a list of demands including dropping the PRTU and other controversial bills to the Qarase government with a December 4 deadline.

Although Qarase met several of the demands, it wasn't enough. On December 5, President Ratu Josefa Iloilo dissolved Parliament on Bainimarama's order and Qarase was put under house arrest. Several key groups, including the Methodist Church and the Great Council of Chiefs, did not approve of Bainimarama's coup and refused to meet without Qarase and President Iloilo (who Bainimarama had ousted in declaring a state of emergency) present. Taking matters into his own hands, Bainimarama dissolved the council and has acted as interim prime minister since.

To Be Continued…

Needless to say, international reaction was scornful. NZ Prime Minister Helen Clark compared Bainimarama to Zimbabwean dictator Robert Mugabe and refused to allow him to attend Pacific Islands Forum events in NZ. With international pressure mounting Iloilo was reinstated as president in 2007 but many speculate that this was only for appearance's sake and he has little influence.

On 6 August 2008, Bainimarama released the *People's Charter,* which he hoped would pave the way for more democratic elections and remove the racism and corruption he felt was systemic in the Qarase regime. Critics of the document have labelled it unconstitutional, pointing to key features that formalise the military's role in governing the country and brand it as the brainchild of a government in power through force.

To the condemnation of the UN Security Council, on April 11 2009 Josefa Iloilo overruled a court's decision that ruled Bainimarama came to power illegally in 2006. A state of emergency was declared, the judiciary was sacked and the constitution dissolved. Bainimarama was reappointed and were elections postponed to 2014. Meanwhile, police were ordered to enforce laws prohibiting the publishing of news that undermined the government. Stay tuned…

THE CULTURE
The National Psyche

If you've just read the foregoing brief summary of Fiji's history you might be hesitant to delve too deeply into the national psyche, which would be a shame. The Fijian people are the country's greatest asset. A smile goes a long way here, and Fijians of all backgrounds go to great lengths to make visitors feel welcome. Sometimes, however, these lengths can be too great. Not wishing to disappoint, a Fijian 'yes' might mean 'maybe' or 'no', which can be disconcerting if not confusing for visitors. Face-to-face confrontation is rare, but debate is a healthy component of daily life (just scan the readers' letters of any newspaper and you'll get the gist). The different challenges facing indigenous Fijians and Indo-Fijians remain key to a sense of national identity, and you're likely to

INDO-FIJIAN HISTORY & CULTURE Clement Paligaru

The majority of today's Indo-Fijians are the descendants of indentured labourers who were brought to Fiji up to 135 years ago to work on plantations. In 1919, when indentured labour was abolished, many leased land and established their own sugar cane, cotton, tobacco and rice farms. Others opened small stores or became public servants and, following a second wave of migrants in the 1930s, many have moved into commerce.

One legacy of the early plantation days is a laid-back culture. As indentured labourers, members of different castes were forced to share the same cramped quarters and compelled to dispense with many of the social mores and rigidities they had brought from India. Today the relative ease with which Indo-Fijians socialise is one of the characteristics that set them apart from other Indians.

India remains an important cultural beacon for Indo-Fijians, influencing rituals, culinary traditions, dress and entertainment. Most Indo-Fijians love homemade *roti* (traditional bread) served straight from the oven, steaming-hot curries, rice and *mithai* (traditional sweets). Tradition, pride and identity have also ensured that saris remain popular in Fiji and the Muslim- and Punjabi-influenced *salwaar kameez* is also de rigueur.

Entertainment and recreation continue to have a decidedly subcontinental flavour. Local cinemas provide a regular dose of Hindi-language Bollywood films and radios play an endless supply of Hindi pop.

Most aspects of Indo-Fijian lifestyle and culture have comfortably coexisted with the indigenous Fijian way of life, and large numbers of Indo-Fijians and indigenous Fijians live side by side, work together and go to the same schools. However, apart from attending some sports, entertainment and special occasions together, the two groups don't tend to engage socially. Their economic, educational, cultural and social priorities, including *tabu*, differ and these differences have proven rich fodder for political agitators.

Recently, however, mutual cultural exploration by Indo-Fijians and indigenous Fijians has seen a blurring of boundaries and increasing numbers from both communities speak each other's language. Indo-Fijian music and songs have even been recorded by indigenous Fijian artists; indigenous women are wearing Indian jewellery and using sari cloth for traditional outfits. Nightclubs are playing Bollywood DJ mixes and sports teams unwind with regular curry, beer and kava nights. Indo-Fijians are now even playing the indigenous Fijian-dominated rugby. But the most amazing transformation has been the elevation of Indian food in indigenous Fijian life and, in many homes, every second meal is a spicy curry.

The best chance a visitor has of experiencing Indo-Fijian culture is to attend a festival. Diwali (Festival of Lights) takes place across the nation around October or November. In Suva the South Indian fire-walking festival, held during July or August, takes place at the Mariamma Temple on Howell Rd. On Vanua Levu, the Ram Leela festival is held at the Mariamman Temple in Vunivau around October.

An Indo-Fijian, Clement Paligaru came to Australia in 1984. He has reported extensively on the Pacific region for the Australian Broadcasting Corporation.

hear both sides of the story in complete candour during any visit.

Multiculturalism

Fiji's population is the most multiracial in the South Pacific. Indigenous Fijians are predominantly of Melanesian origin, but there are Polynesian aspects in both their physical appearance and their culture. Most Indo-Fijians are descendants of indentured labourers. They constitute around 37% of the population, although large numbers continue to emigrate.

The government categorises people according to their racial origins, as you will notice on the immigration arrival card. 'Fijian' means indigenous Fijian, and while many Indo-Fijians have lived in Fiji for several generations they are still referred to as 'Indian', just as Chinese-Fijians are 'Chinese'. Fijians of other Pacific island descent are referred to by the nationality of their ancestors. Australians, Americans, New Zealanders – and Europeans – are referred to as 'Europeans'. Mixed Western and Fijian heritage makes a person officially 'part-European'.

HOME & HOSTED: VILLAGE ETIQUETTE

If you visit a village uninvited, ask to see the headman at once; it's not proper just to turn up and look around. Never wander around unaccompanied: beaches, reefs and gardens are all someone's private realm.

- Dress modestly; sleeves and *sulu* (traditional skirt of wrapped cloth) or sarongs are fine for both men and women.

- Take off your hat and sunglasses, and carry bags in your hands, not over your shoulder; it's considered rude to do otherwise.

- It is rare to see public displays of affection between men and women so curtail your passions in public to avoid embarrassing or offending locals.

- Bring *yaqona (kava)* with you. This is for your *sevusevu*, requesting permission to visit the village from the *turaga-ni-koro* (hereditary chief) and, in effect, the ancestral gods. He will welcome you in a small ceremony likely to develop into a *talanoa* (gossip session) around the *tanoa* (*yaqona* bowl) so be prepared to recount your life story.

- Check with your host if you can take photos and wait until after the *sevusevu* to start snapping.

- Stoop when entering a *bure* (thatched dwelling) and quietly sit cross-legged on the pandanus mat. It is polite to keep your head at a lower level than your host's. Fijians regard the head as sacred – never ever touch a person's head.

- If you're staying overnight, and had planned to camp but are offered a bed, accept it; it may embarrass your hosts if they think their *bure* is not good enough. If you'll be bathing in the river or at a shared tap, wear a *sulu* while you wash.

- Travel with thank-you gifts of tea, tinned meat, or sugar, or contribute some cash to cover costs.

- Sunday is for church and family so avoid visiting then.

Lifestyle

INDIGENOUS FIJIANS

Most indigenous Fijians live in villages in *mataqali* (extended family, or kinship, groups) and acknowledge a hereditary chief who is usually male. Each *mataqali* is allocated land for farming and also has communal obligations. Village life is supportive but also conservative; being different or too ambitious is seen to threaten the village's stability, and traditional gender roles are still very much in evidence.

Concepts such as *kerekere* (obligatory sharing) and *sevusevu* (a gift presented in exchange for an obligatory favour) are still strong, especially in remote areas. The consumption of *yaqona*, or kava, remains an important social ritual, and clans gather on special occasions for traditional *lovo* feasts and *meke* (dance and song performance that enacts stories and legends).

INDO-FIJIANS

Most of this group are fourth- or fifth- generation descendants of indentured labourers. The changes these labourers were forced to undergo, such as adapting to living communally with Indians from diverse backgrounds, created a relatively unrestricted, enterprising society distinct from the Indian cultures they left behind. This is the basis for the Indo-Fijian culture of today.

Extended families often live in the same house, and in rural areas it's common for girls to have arranged marriages at an early age. Many women wear traditional dress, although dress codes are more cosmopolitan in Suva. See the boxed text, p101, for more details.

Population

Fiji's population hovers around 860,000 and growth has virtually halved in the last 30 years, due in no small part to political disharmony since independence. About 25% of Fijians are school age, and around 60% of the population are urban dwellers. Almost half the entire population resides in Suva.

RELIGION

Religion is extremely important in all aspects of Fijian society. Of the country's 52% Christians, about 37% are Methodists. Hinduism is practised by 38% and Islam by about 8%.

MODERN PRESSURES

Fiji is becoming increasingly urbanised, and it is in the towns and cities that traditional values and the wisdom of elders are often less respected. Many young people travel to the cities for education, employment or to escape the restrictions of village life, but with increased freedom comes competition for jobs and a less supportive social structure. This urban drift has resulted in squatter settlements on the edges of many towns, and the high levels of deprivation in these communities have led to the presence of beggars, street kids, and an increase in crime.

To make matters worse, the simmering tension between indigenous and Indo-Fijians have led many indigenous landowners to refuse to renew their land leases with their Indo-Fijian tenants. Deprived of their sugar cane farms and suddenly homeless, whole families have been forced into these squatter-settlement camps, compounding the problems there. This estrangement between land-owning ethnic Fijians and entrepreneurial Indians is currently one of Fiji's hottest topics.

ARTS

Indigenous Fijian villagers practise traditional arts and crafts, such as woodcarving and pottery, dance and music, and making *masi* (see p104). Some arts remain an integral part of the culture, while others are practised solely to satisfy tourist demand. Indo-Fijians, Chinese Fijians and other cultural groups also retain many of their traditional arts.

Contemporary art includes fashion design, pottery and, though not common, painting and photography. The most likely place to see contemporary work displayed is Suva.

Dance

Visitors are often welcomed with an indigenous *meke*, a dance performance enacting stories and legends. They vary from touristy performances accompanied by a disco-Fijian soundtrack (common in resorts) to the traditional and low-key.

One of the best places to see contemporary dance in Fiji is the Oceania Centre for Arts and Culture (ask at the Fiji Visitors Bureau for performance times) at the USP Laucala Campus in Suva.

Literature

Fiji's small community of poets and writers produce gritty, realist literature. Joseph C Veramu's 1996 novel *Moving Through the Streets* is an eye-opener about disaffected youth in Suva. Daryl Tarte's historical saga *Fiji* and more recent novel *Stalker on the Beach* look at the influence of outsiders on the country.

Beyond Ceremony: An Anthology of Fiji Drama showcases some of Fiji's playwrights, including Vilsoni Hereniko, Sudesh Mishra, Jo Nacola, Raymond Pillai and Larry Thomas.

Since the 1970s Indo-Fijian writers have increasingly worked in English. Writers of note include Subramani, Satendra Nandan and poet Mohit Prasad (*Eating Mangoes*, 2001). The theme of the injustice of indenture rates highly in Indo-Fijian literature.

Collections of women writers' poetry include *Of Schizophrenic Voices* by Frances Koya and *Nei Nim Manoa* by Teresia Teaiwa.

Kava in the Blood (1999) by Peter Thomson is the evocative autobiography of a white Fijian who became a senior civil servant and was imprisoned by Rabuka during the 1987 coup.

Film

For a look at the indigenous Fijian diaspora, search out *No 2* (2006), an NZ film about a Fijian family living in Auckland and the breakdown of their traditional values and the resulting intergenerational conflict.

Music

Unsurprisingly, reggae has been a major influence on contemporary Fijian music, and you're likely to hear Bob Marley and his Fijian counterparts recycled continuously on popular radio stations. Even if you're not a reggae fan, there's something inimitably Fijian about wailing the latest reggae track out the window and waving comrade-like to locals on a road trip.

Popular acts include Seru Serevi, Lia Osborne and Daniel Rae Costello, and bands including Black Rose, the Bad Boys, Delai Sea and Voqa ni Delai Dokidoki. Young Fijians have embraced hip-hop with several new artists including rapper Sammy G, Mr Grin, up-and-coming Redchild and Tukaine. Music from Bollywood films and

Indian dance and pop music are understandably popular. It's not an entirely one-sided relationship – Indo-Fijian singer Aiysha a big hit in India.

Choral CDs are also extremely popular, thanks to the tradition of enthusiastic Sunday service attendance. Missing out on the rousing but dulcet tones of a Fijian mass would be a crime.

Bark Cloth

You'll most likely become acquainted with *tapa* (also known as *masi* or *malo*), the Fijian art of making bark cloth, during your first shopping expedition. The cloth is made from the inner bark of the paper mulberry bush, which has been soaked in water and scraped clean, then beaten and felted for hours into sheets of a fine, even texture. Intricate rust and brown patterns are printed either by hand or stencil, often carrying symbolic meaning. The paints are traditionally made from an infusion of candlenut and mangrove bark; pinker browns are made from red clays, and black from the soot of burnt *dakua* resin and charred candlenuts. For more information about *tapa*, see p55.

LANGUAGE

The majority of indigenous Fijians speak Fijian at home. Indo-Fijians speak Fijian-Hindi but English is the official language and spoken widely.

There are no equivalents for 'please' and 'thank you' in Fijian-Hindi. To be polite in making requests, people use the word *thoraa* (a little) and a special form of the verb ending in *naa*, eg *thoraa nimak denaa* (please pass the salt). For 'thanks', people often just say *achhaa* (good).

Fijian basics

Hello.	*Bula!*
Hello (response).	*Io, bula/Ia, bula* (more respectful).
Goodbye (if departing long-term).	*Moce.*
See you later.	*Au saa liu mada.*
How are you?	*Ni sa bula?*
Good, thanks.	*An sa bula vinaka.*
Thank you (very much).	*Vinaka (vakalevu).*
Yes.	*Io.*
No.	*Sega.*
My name is...	*O yau o...*

Fijian-Hindi basics

Hello. ('How are you?')	*kaise*
Fine (response).	*tik*
Farewell.	*fir milegaa*
Yes.	*ha*
No.	*nahi*
What's your name?	*aapke naam kaa hai?*
My name is...	*hamaar naam...*

ENVIRONMENT
Geography
The Fiji archipelago has about 332 islands, varying from mere bumps a few metres in diameter to Viti Levu ('Great Land') at 10,400 sq km. Only about a third are inhabited. The smaller islands are generally of coral or limestone formation, while the larger ones are of volcanic origin; hot springs continue to boil on Vanua Levu. Fiji's highest peak is Viti Levu's majestic Tomanivi (Mt Victoria) at 1323m.

Ecology
Fiji's tropical forests are home to some of the richest natural communities in the South Pacific. Unfortunately, economic progress and the wheels of industry have seen around 15% of these forests cleared since the 1960s. Logging remains a constant, but many villages are turning to ecotourism as an alternative means of income. However, while remote villages can benefit from the income brought by low-impact tourism, even sensitive developments bring additional pollution and rapid cultural change. Some resorts like to include the tag 'eco' in their moniker without actually following through with the whole idea.

Waste management is a national problem and marine pollution near Suva is severe. Overfishing and destructive fishing techniques are commonly employed and global warming has contributed to extensive coral bleaching.

Greenpeace and WWF have offices in Suva and they campaign regionally on issues including ocean fisheries and climate change.

VITI LEVU

pop 585,000 / area 10,400 sq km

Like a grand chief presiding over a tribal council, Viti Levu, the largest of the Fijian islands, is the pivotal point around which the wheels of industry, commerce and politics turn. The 'mainland's' beaches may run a distant second to those of the outer islands, but Viti Levu's lush interior and steamy highlands offer dramatic vistas and some of the country's best trekking. The hinterland is framed by the resort-rich Coral Coast on its southern side and by the less visited and more rugged Kings Road to the north. Befitting its status as the largest South Pacific city, Suva is a sultry hub of culture, cuisine and urban activity, and it offers an engaging glimpse into a nation far different from that depicted by Fiji's promotional adverts.

ORIENTATION
Suva, the country's capital, largest city and main port, is in the southeast. Most travellers arrive in the west of the island at Nadi International Airport, 9km north of central Nadi and 24km south of Lautoka.

Nadi and Suva are linked by the sealed Queens Rd that runs along the southern perimeter of Viti Levu (221km) and contains the scattering of villages and resorts known as the Coral Coast.

Heading north from Suva, the Kings Rd is mostly sealed and travels for 265km through Nausori (where Suva's airport is located), the eastern highlands, Rakiraki, Ba (on the north coast), and Lautoka. South of Rakiraki is Fiji's highest point – Tomanivi (Mt Victoria) at 1323m.

Three roads head up from the coast to the Nausori Highlands villages of Navala and Bukuya (via Ba, Nadi and Sigatoka).

DANGERS & ANNOYANCES
Travelling around Viti Levu is easy and safe, and most visitors will encounter a warm reception, particularly in rural areas. As with most urbanised centres, Nadi, Lautoka and Suva offer some dangers. Pickpockets roam, so keep your valuables out of sight, particularly in crowded areas. Walking around during daylight hours is a perfectly safe exercise; however, as soon as night begins to descend it's a no go. This is particularly pertinent in Suva – from dusk onwards locals will catch a taxi, even for a distance of 300m; you should as well.

There have been reports of muggings in Colo-i-Suva Forest Park (see p125), so head there in a group or pay the minimal fee for a guide.

TRANSPORT
Getting There & Away
Most travellers arrive in Fiji at Nadi International Airport. See p170 for details on international carriers. Nadi and Suva are both domestic transport hubs, with flights

FIJI

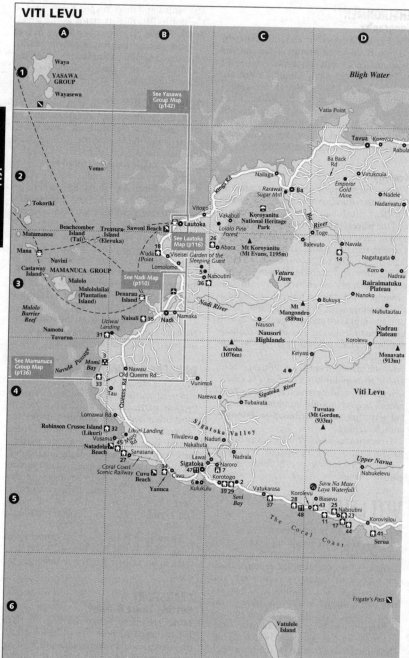

VITI LEVU

A   B   C   D

1

Waya

YASAWA GROUP

Wayasewa

See Yasawa Group Map (p142)

Bligh Water

Vatia Point

Tavua Korovou

Rabula

2

Vomo

Nailaga   Rarawai Sugar Mill   Ba   Ba Back Rd   Vatukoula

Emperor Gold Mine

Nadele

Nadarivatu

Tokoriki

Vitogo   Vakabuli   Koroyanitu National Heritage Park

River   Toge

Matamanoa

Beachcomber Island (Tai)   Treasure Island (Elevuka)   Saweni Beach   **Lautoka**

See Lautoka Map (p116)

26   Abaca   *Lololo Pine Forest*

Balevuto   Navala

Nagatagata

Mana

N'uda Point   Viseisei   Garden of the Sleeping Giant

Mt Koroyanitu (Mt Evans, 1195m)   18   14

Navini   MAMANUCA GROUP   Lomolomo

Koro   Nadrau

Castaway Island   Malolo

See Nadi Map (p110)

5   Naboutini   36   *Vaturu Dam*

Rairaimatuku Plateau

Bukuya   Nanoko   Nubutautau

Malololailai (Plantation Island)   Denarau Island

Nadi River

Mt Mangondro (889m)

Nadrau Plateau

Malolo Barrier Reef

Naisali   35   **Nadi**   Namaka

Nausori   **Nausori Highlands**

Korolevu   Monavatu (913m)

Namotu   Tavarua

Uciwai Landing   31

Koroba (1076m)   Keiyasi

See Mamanuca Group Map (p136)

3   Momi Bay   3

33   Nawau   Old Queens Rd

Tau   Vunimoli

Sigatoka River

Viti Levu

4

Lomawai Rd   Narewa   Tubairata

Tuvutau (Mt Gordon, (933m)

Robinson Crusoe Island (Likuri)   32   Likuri Landing

Sigatoka Valley

Vusama   45   Tilivalevu   Naduri

Natadola Beach   27   Sanasana   Nakabuta   Nadrala

Upper Navua

Nabukelevu

Coral Coast Scenic Railway   34   Cuvu Beach   Lawai   Sigatoka   47   Naroro

Savu Na Mate Laya Waterfall

Yanuca   Cuvu   6   2   Korotogo   Vatukarasa

5   Kulukulu   39 29   Korolevu   28   Biasevu   43   25   Naboutini

Sovi Bay   37   48   11   17   44   23

Korovisilou

Serua   41

The Coral Coast

6

Frigate's Pass

Vatulele Island

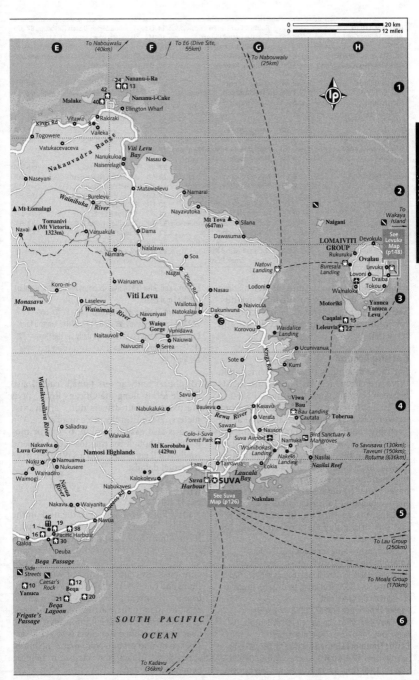

to many of the other islands, as well as boat services and cruises to offshore islands. See p171 and individual island chapters for information on interisland flights and ferry details.

Getting Around

For those in a hurry or after a scenic flight, there are cheap, regular light plane flights between Nadi and Suva for around F$160.

Viti Levu has a regular and cheap bus network. Express buses operated by Pacific Transport and Sunbeam Transport link the main centres of Lautoka, Nadi and Suva, along both the Queens and Kings Rds. Slower, local buses also operate throughout the island, and even remote inland villages have regular (though less frequent) services. Before heading to an isolated area, check that there is a return bus as sometimes the last bus of the day stays overnight at the final village.

Companies and services available:

Coral Sun Fiji (☎ 672 3105; www.coralsunfiji.com) Runs comfortable, air-conditioned coaches between Nadi's airport and Suva (F$20, four hours, twice daily), stopping at resorts on the Coral Coast.

Feejee Experience (☎ 672 3311; www.feejee experience.com) Offers hop-on-hop-off coach packages from F$396. See p173 for more information.

Pacific Transport Limited Lautoka (☎ 666 0499; Yasawa St) Nadi (☎ 670 0044) Sigatoka (☎ 650 0088) Suva (☎ 330 4366) About six express buses run daily between

Lautoka and Suva (F$14 five/six hours for express/regular) via the Coral Coast.

Sunbeam Transport Limited Lautoka (☎ 666 2822; Yasawa St) Suva (☎ 338 2122/2704) Around four Lautoka-Suva express services go daily via the Queens Rd (F$15, five hours). Also about six services daily travel via the Kings Rd.

Minibuses and carriers (small trucks) also shuttle locals along the Queens Road. Taxis are plentiful, but drivers don't always use meters, so confirm the price in advance. Viti Levu is also easy to explore by car or motorbike, although for the unsealed highland roads you'll generally need a 4WD. See p173 for rental details.

NADI
pop 31,400

Nadi is Fiji's revolving door, the neck in the hourglass through which everyone must pass. Its proximity to the airport and Port Denarau ensures a constant flow of travellers arriving and departing, and consequently this town-cum-business centre is littered with hotels, shops and eateries. While Nadi is a convenient base to organise trips around Viti Levu and to offshore islands, there are no real 'must-sees' in Nadi itself. The most common advice you'll hear from seasoned travellers is to get in, get stocked up and get out. Nadi makes no bones about this – in fact, it specialises in helping people do just that.

FIJI

VITI LEVU IN...

Four Days

In all likelihood you'll land in Nadi – Fiji's international air hub. Nadi is no great shakes but there are several exciting day trips to choose between. You may want to unwind with an excursion to **Robinson Crusoe Island** (p118) or, to see what lies beyond that tumbling ascent of hills, a tour to the Nausori Highlands (below).

On day two, get outta town and among the vivid orchids at the **Garden of the Sleeping Giant** (p111). Follow this up with a soak in the **Sabeto Hot Springs** (p111) and an evening meal at one of **Denarau's luxury resorts** (p114).

Day three is all about the coast. Start out with a morning horse ride along **Natadola Beach** (p118), Viti Levu's finest stretch of sand, and then make your way to a **Coral Coast resort** (p122) for views of the offshore reef and some healthy pampering.

On day four scramble up and down the **Sigatoka Sand Dunes** (p119) or, for something less energetic, mingle with the wildlife at **Kula Eco Park** (p120).

One Week

Continue your Viti Levu exploration with a dose of diving in **Beqa Lagoon** (p123) or a kayak tour up the **Navua River** (p123).

End the week with a day exploring Suva where you can meander through the **Fiji Museum** (p125), fuel up on a curry and kick off the night on the dance floor at **O'Reilly's** (p131).

Information

You won't have any trouble finding banks and ATMs in Nadi. ANZ, Westpac and Colonial National Bank all have branches along Main St, and there is an ANZ bank (with an ATM) at the airport. It opens for all international flights. Internet is also thick on the ground in Nadi and costs around F$3 per hour.

DSM Medical Centre (☎ 670 0240; www.dsmcentre fiji.com.fj; 2 Lodhia St; ☷ 8.30am-4.30pm Mon-Fri, till12.30pm Sat) Specialising in travel medicine with radiology and physiotherapy departments.

Fiji Visitors Bureau (FVB; ☎ 672 2433; www.fijime .com; Suite 107, Colonial Plaza, Namaka; ☷ 8am-4.30pm Mon-Thu, to 4pm Fri) Fiji's official tourism bureau has helpful staff with accurate advice.

Police (☎ emergency 917, 670 0222; Koroivolu Ave)

Post Office Airport (☎ 6722 045; Nadi International Airport) Downtown (☎ 670 0001; Sahu Kahn Rd, Nadi)

TRAVEL AGENCIES

The travel agents at the airport will find you before you've had time to hail a taxi. The major and more reputable companies have offices and representatives on the ground, while the 13 agencies upstairs are smaller local operators who take turns pouncing on anyone with a backpack. They can offer good deals but their advice isn't impartial.

Some agencies:

Great Sights Fiji (☎ 672 3311; enquiries@great sightsfiji.com; Nadi airport concourse) Specialising in 4WD day tours to Navala (F$179 per person), Nausori Highlands (F$99), Koroyanitu National Park (F$119) and Abaca (F$109).

Rosie Holidays (☎ 672 2755; www.rosiefiji.com; Nadi airport concourse) Organises multiday treks into the Central Highlands (six days F$1147 per person), the Sigatoka Valley (four days F$828) and day treks to the Nausori Highlands (F$115) as well as busloads of tours to Sigatoka Valley/Kula Eco Park, Viseisei Village/the Garden of the Sleeping Giant and Pacific Harbour. It is also the agent for Thrifty Car Rental.

Travel Fiji Holiday (☎ 670 3276; cnr Main St & Andrews Rd)

Sights

SRI SIVA SUBRAMANIYA SWAMI TEMPLE

Striking a vibrant pose against a dramatic mountainous backdrop, this peaceful Hindu **temple** (☎ 670 0016; admission F$3.50; ☷ 5.30am-7pm) leaves the hustle of Main St far in its wake. The temple itself is decorated with carved wooden deities that travelled all the way from India, along with the artists who painted the multihued exterior and vivid frescoes. It is one of the few places outside India where you can see traditional Dravidian architecture, and there is usually a temple custodian on hand to help answer those curly questions about Lord Shiva's various reincarnations.

FIJI

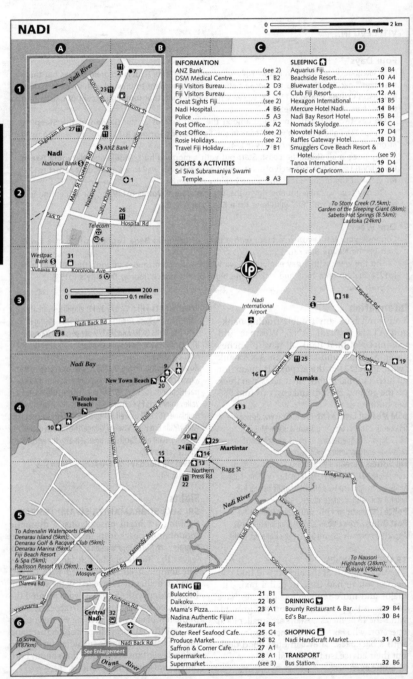

NADI

INFORMATION	
ANZ Bank	(see 2)
DSM Medical Centre	**1** B2
Fiji Visitors Bureau	**2** D3
Fiji Visitors Bureau	**3** C4
Great Sights Fiji	(see 2)
Nadi Hospital	**4** B6
Police	**5** A3
Post Office	**6** A2
Post Office	(see 2)
Rosie Holidays	(see 2)
Travel Fiji Holiday	**7** B1

SIGHTS & ACTIVITIES	
Sri Siva Subramaniya Swami Temple	**8** A3

SLEEPING	
Aquarius Fiji	**9** B4
Beachside Resort	**10** A4
Bluewater Lodge	**11** B4
Club Fiji Resort	**12** A4
Hexagon International	**13** B5
Mercure Hotel Nadi	**14** B4
Nadi Bay Resort Hotel	**15** B4
Nomads Skylodge	**16** C4
Novotel Nadi	**17** D4
Raffles Gateway Hotel	**18** D3
Smugglers Cove Beach Resort & Hotel	(see 9)
Tanoa International	**19** D4
Tropic of Capricorn	**20** B4

EATING	
Bulaccino	**21** B1
Daikoku	**22** B5
Mama's Pizza	**23** A1
Nadina Authentic Fijian Restaurant	**24** B4
Outer Reef Seafood Cafe	**25** C4
Produce Market	**26** B2
Saffron & Corner Cafe	**27** A1
Supermarket	**28** A1
Supermarket	(see 3)

DRINKING	
Bounty Restaurant & Bar	**29** B4
Ed's Bar	**30** B4

SHOPPING	
Nadi Handicraft Market	**31** A3

TRANSPORT	
Bus Station	**32** B6

Nadi River

Ashram Rd

Sukuna St

Sahayam Rd

Clay St

Nadi
National Bank

ANZ Bank

Main St / Queens Rd

Nadovu Rd

Satu Khan

Park St

Telecom

Hospital Rd

Westpac Bank

Vunavau Rd

Koroivolu Ave

Nadi Back Rd

To Story Creek (7.5km);
Garden of the Sleeping Giant (8km);
Sabeto Hot Springs (8.5km);
Lautoka (24km)

Legalega Rd

Votualevu Rd

Nadi
International
Airport

Queens Rd

Namaka

Nadi Back Rd

Nadi Bay

New Town Beach

Wailoaloa Beach

Nadi Bay Rd

Wailoaloa Rd

Martintar

Northern Press Rd

Ragg St

Nadi River

Nawson Highlands Rd

Miegunyah

To Nausori
Highlands (28km);
Bukuya (45km)

To Adrenalin Watersports (5km);
Denarau Island (5km);
Denarau Golf & Racquet Club (5km);
Denarau Marina (5km);
Fiji Beach Resort & Spa (5km);
Radisson Resort Fiji (5km)

Denarau Rd
(Narewa Rd)

Kennedy Ave

Solovu Rd

Mosque

Queens Rd

Andrews Rd

Yasusania

Central Nadi

See Enlargement

To Suva
(187km)

Nadi Back Rd

Oruna River

FIJI

HINDU SYMBOLISM

Tiny Hindu temples and shrines dot the Fijian countryside, each one symbolising the body or residence of the soul. For Hindus, union with God can be achieved through prayer and by ridding the body of impurities – hence no meat in the belly or shoes on the feet when entering a temple.

Inside the temples Hindus give symbolic offerings and blessings to their many gods. Water and flowers symbolise the Great Mother who personifies nature, while burning camphor represents the light of knowledge and understanding. Smashing a coconut denotes cracking humans' three weaknesses: egotism (the hard shell), delusion (the fibre) and material attachments (the outermost covering). The white kernel and sweet water represent the pure soul within.

Hindus believe that a body enslaved to the spirit and denied all comforts will become one with the Great Mother. Life is compared to walking on fire: a disciplined approach, like that required in the fire-walking ceremony, leads to balance, self-acceptance and the ability to see good in all.

Visitors are welcome as long as they're dressed modestly, leave their shoes at the entrance and take photos only from the outside.

GARDEN OF THE SLEEPING GIANT

This beautiful **garden** (Map pp106-7; ☎ 672 2701; Wailoko Rd; adult/child/family F$12/6/30; ☑ 9am-5pm Mon-Sat, 9am-noon Sun) is a tribute to the orchid, boasting dozens of varieties of the colourful flower amid a sea of tropical vegetation. Tucked beneath the foothills of the Sabeto mountain range, the garden offers visitors a network of walking tracks, lily ponds and perfect picnic spots. To get here, travel along the Queens Rd for about 6km north of Nadi airport and turn east onto Wailoko Rd for a further 2km. A taxi from Nadi will cost around F$13.

SABETO HOT SPRINGS

A few kilometres further inland from the Garden of the Sleeping Giant are the **Sabeto Hot Springs** (Map pp106-7; F$10; ☑ 9am-5pm Mon-Sat); a series of geothermal hot pools with floors of soft and silty, knee-deep mud. The pools are very informal – just a few ponds in a field – but they are fun. What starts as a few playful smears invariably turns into a full-on fight with mud slinging from all quarters.

Activities & Tours

Nadi is a good base to explore the west side of Viti Levu (check out p109 for a run-down on the tours offered by Nadi travel agents) and take day trips to the closer of the Mamanuca (p137) and Yasawa islands (p142).

Sleeping

The black-sand New Town and Wailoaloa Beaches will disappoint anyone with visions of white sands and aqua oceans but are quiet and peaceful and the best beaches Nadi has to offer. Closer to town, there's a scattering of hotels along Queens Rd that have easy access to buses in and out of downtown. Most accommodation offers free transfers from the airport if they know to expect you.

BUDGET
New Town Beach

Smugglers Cove Beach Resort & Hotel (Map pp106-7; ☎ 672 6578, www.smugglersbeachfiji.com; Wasawasa Rd; dm incl breakfast F$28, r F$98-185, f F$198; ☒ ☐ ☎) This recently opened resort straddles the backpacker–midrange market with clean and simple rooms for the latter and a dark, cavernous, 34-bed dormitory (partitioned into four-person cubicles) for the former. It's popular with the younger crowd who take advantage of the tour desk, restaurant, minimart, coin-operated laundry and free use of the Nadi Golf Course.

Tropic of Capricorn (☎ 672 3089; chopkins@bigpond.net.au; 11 Wasawasa Rd; dm F$15-27, d F$80-95; ☒ ☎) Warm-hearted 'Mama' has added a new, beachside, two-storey block to her older, fan-cooled dorms. Both options are good value but they oddly sandwich the pool and dining area between them. Guests here are welcomed like stray kittens into an orphanage with excellent home-cooked meals (mains F$10 to F$18).

Bluewater Lodge (☎ 672 8858; bluewaterfiji@connect.com.fj; New Town Beach; dm incl breakfast F$23, d incl breakfast F$90; ☒ ☒ ☎) This spic-and-span house has been converted into a trendy little backpackers. Each dorm has only three beds and there's a small pool in the garden. It's a 500m walk to the beach but, for those wanting a little peace and quiet, this is the pick of the bunch.

The wee restaurant (mains F$16 to F$25) and bar opens for dinner only.

Aquarius Fiji (☎ 672 6000; www.aquarius.com.fj; 17 Wasawasa Rd; dm incl breakfast F$26-30, d F$90-115; ☒ ☒ ⬜ ⬛) This professional set-up attracts backpackers by the planeload. There's a good restaurant, lively bar, and a beachside pool area with enough hammocks for the sun-starved masses. Doubles are cheerful and sunny, and those upstairs have balconies overlooking the beach. The cheaper dorms sleep 12 and are slightly airless and cramped when full.

Queens Road

Nomads Skylodge (☎ 672 2200; www.nomadsskylodge .com.fj; Queens Rd, Namaka; 8-/6-/4-bed dm F$25/28/31, tw & d F$78-128; ☒ ☒ ⬜ ⬛) Set well off the main road in a grassy compound, Nomads has enough space to accommodate a small army of holidaymakers. Like most accommodation at this price level, the dorms and basic singles and doubles are fairly spartan although, for a bit more, you can get air-conditioning, a private bathroom, phone and TV. Onsite facilities include a restaurant (mains F$10 to F$18), volleyball courts, a games' room, a tour desk and a large pool.

Nadi Bay Resort Hotel (☎ 672 3599; www.fijinadibay hotel.com; Wailoaloa Rd, Martintar; dm F$27-30, s/d without bathroom from F$71/84, s/d with bathroom from F$82/96; ☒ ☒ ⬜ ⬛) Perennially busy, the Nadi Bay is a one-stop backpacker hub with a range of dorms, doubles and suites, two excellent restaurants (mains F$11 to F$24), two bars, two palm-fringed pools and a small movie theatre. Some rooms are better value than others but generally the standard is fairly good. The tour desk here is a bit cheeky; they like to charge the 5% Hotel Turnover Tax on the tours they book, which isn't standard practice.

Hexagon International (☎ 672 0044; www.hexagon fiji.com; Queens Rd, Martintar; r F$66-97, apt F$159; ☒ ⬜ ⬛) This two-storey complex surrounds a central, tiled pool and, while the rooms are sparsely furnished, what they do have – essentially just a bed – is bright and perky. The pool area is a bit light on the greenery but makes up for it with wi-fi hotspots and a beauty spa next door.

Nadi Outskirts

Stoney Creek Resort (☎ 672 2206; www.stoneycreekfiji .net; Sabeto Rd; dm F$28, s/d shared bathroom F$50/64, r with bathroom F$80-110; ⬜ ⬛) Hidden at the base of

the highlands, this resort has a taste of the Wild West with cosy dorms in mock train carriages and doubles with sweeping views in cute and private *bure*. There's a saloon-style bar and restaurant (meals F$6 to F$10) and a good range of activities on offer. Rates include breakfast and free internet, and the resort also provides a free airport shuttle. There are regular 'Sabeto' buses from Nadi bus station (F$1.70, one every 1½ hours between 8am and 5.30pm).

MIDRANGE
Wailoaloa Beach

Beachside Resort (☎ 670 3488; www.beachsideresortfiji .com; Wailoaloa Beach Rd; s F$68-145, d F$76-153, tr F$138-149 incl breakfast; ☒ ☒ ⬜ ⬛) Actually it's not quite Beachside – it's more like Beach-near. This small and personal resort may have a cheeky moniker, but the appealing digs, helpful staff, tidy grounds and funky restaurant atone. Stylish and immaculate rooms with polished tiled floors and plenty of natural light are dressed in timber and Fijian prints. The more expensive versions have balconies overlooking the pool and an alfresco dining area, while cheaper (but no less classy) rooms are tucked behind the main complex. The resort's trendy Coriander Cafe (mains F$18 to F$30) dishes up inventive fare along the lines of Thai chicken pizza or coconut fish bites.

Club Fiji Resort (☎ 672 0150; www.clubfiji-resort .com; Wailoaloa Beach Rd; d F$94-188, f F$288; ☒ ☒ ⬛) Making the most of its beachside location, Club Fiji feels more like a resort and less like a transit stop than most other options around Nadi. Daily activities include excellent value fishing trips (F$30 to F$40 per person) and free nonmotorised water sports. In the accommodation stakes you can choose between Mediterranean style villas, ocean-view *bure* or smaller timber and thatched *bure*.

Queens Road

Raffles Gateway Hotel (☎ 672 2444; www.raffles gateway.com; Namaka; d & tw F$98-155, tr/f F$172/196; ☒ ☒ ⬜ ⬛) Directly opposite the airport, behind the mock colonial entrance, Raffles is a sound choice. Those with kids will appreciate the pool's waterslide and the fact that children under 16 stay free. Cheaper standard rooms are pinchy but cool and crisp, while the superior rooms are a leap in value with their lounge furniture, TVs and private patios. There's a poolside restaurant (mains F$13 to F$28) and a grassed central courtyard flanked by massive bougainvilleas that give an accurate idea of the age of this long-time favourite.

Mercure Hotel Nadi (☎ 672 2255 reservations@mercure nadi.com.fj; Queens Rd, Martintar; s F$149-169, d & tw F$179-209; ✕ ✕ ➋) Renovated and fancied up into a flashy haven of creature comforts, the Mercure offers large deluxe or modern superior rooms, all of which have bar fridges, TVs and sassy bathrooms. Families populate the grassy grounds, which include a sizeable pool and alfresco restaurant (mains F$20 to F$30, Saturday Mongolian BBQ F$35 per person).

TOP END
Near the Airport
Novotel Nadi (☎ 672 2000; reservations@novotelnadi .com.fj; Namaka; r F$158-198; ✕ ✕ ➌ ➋) The Novotel (formerly the Mocambo) underwent a major overhaul with the name change and now features the oh-so-modern, brown-on-beige colour scheme so popular with Fiji's hip hotels. The rooms aren't huge, but many enjoy mountain views and all come with flat-screen TVs and internet connections. In addition to the usual facilities you'd expect at a top hotel – like shops, business centre and swimming pool – there is also a nine-hole golf course and day spa. Children under 16 stay free and locals, or those who say they are, get discounts.

Tanoa International (☎ 672 0277; www.tanoa hotels.com; d F$220-280; ✕ ✕ ➌ ➋) The Tanoa International is the flagship of the Tanoa chain and by far its finest hotel. The 148-room, two-storey complex was built in 1965 and still boasts some of the best rooms this side of Denarau. Guests here enjoy tennis courts, a beauty spa, gym, lush gardens, swanky cafes and Saturday curry and Sunday roast buffets (F$28). Again, substantial discounts are given to those who phone ahead and ask for local rates. Kids 12 and below stay free.

Eating
Although small, Nadi caters to travellers' palates well with a decent variety of Indian, Chinese and Western cuisine. Most hotels and resorts, including those in the budget categories, have restaurants where nonguests are welcome.

RESTAURANTS
Mama's Pizza (☎ 670 0221; Main St, Nadi; mains F$8-22; ✕ lunch & dinner; ✕) Traditionalists may

want to stick to the proven crowd pleasers, but everyone else should check out the flip side of the menu for the gourmet varieties. This downtown store (they have a few shops around town) is rather dark and uninviting, although the wood-fired pizzas here are the best around.

Saffron & Corner Cafe (☎ 670 1233; Jacks Mall, Sagayam Rd, Nadi; mains F$15-25; ✕ lunch & dinner Mon-Sat, dinner Sun; ✕) This place has a split personality. On one side is a cafe serving regular light lunches and burgers while the other half is an upmarket Indian restaurant specialising in fine Indian cuisine. The trouble is that patrons don't always know where one ends and the other begins.

our pick **Nadina Authentic Fijian Restaurant** (☎ 672 7313; Queens Rd, Martintar; mains F$20-30; ✕ lunch & dinner) Nadina is perfect for sampling local specialities without overloading on starchy carbs. Traditional foods like cassava and *dalo* (a taro-like root vegetable) are served with delicious sauces, and the *kokoda* (raw fish marinated in lime juice, coconut milk and onions) is divinely tender. Bring a bottle of wine (and some mosquito repellent) and sit on the veranda or in your own mini-*bure* in the garden.

Daikoku (☎ 670 3622; cnr Queens Rd & Northern Press Rd; mains $26-52; ✕ lunch & dinner Mon-Sat) Perched around large square hot plates, patrons sip Asahi beer while their individual chef performs the sometimes gentle, sometimes energetic, but always entertaining art of *teppanyaki*. There is also delicate sushi or sashimi for starters.

CAFES & QUICK EATS
The bottom end of Main St in downtown Nadi has a number of cheap curry houses, all of which expend far more energy on the cheap nosh than on the dim surrounds. You can lunch there for around F$4.

Bulaccino (☎ 672 8638; Main St, Nadi; light meals & snacks F$4-16; ✕ breakfast & lunch; ✕ ➋) This place has the perfect antidote to shoppers' fatigue – riverside tables, strong coffee and scrummy cakes. Healthy options include salads, roti wraps, Bircher muesli and fresh tropical juices.

our pick **Outer Reef Seafood Cafe** (☎ 672 7201; Lot 2, Queens Rd, Namaka; sandwiches F$6-10, mains F$29-48; ✕ breakfast, lunch & dinner; ✕) Upfront the Outer Reef cafe doesn't look much beyond the ordinary, but out back it's a secret oasis of contemporary al fresco dining. The enclosed courtyard has a bar, raised gardens, sunshades and a large flat screen TV to watch the rugby on. The staff here are exceptionally friendly – even by Fijian standards – and a funky little band performs from Friday to Sunday.

SELF-CATERING
Nadi has a large **produce market** (Hospital Rd) with lots of fresh fruit and vegetables as well as several bakeries and large supermarkets on Main St.

Drinking
Most travellers seem content to drink at the hotel bars and restaurants, but to rub shoulders with locals head to either of these pubs in Martintar, on the way to the airport.

Bounty Restaurant & Bar (☎ 672 0840; 79 Queens Rd, Martintar) This convivial bar–restaurant is named after the local rum (and not the chocolate bar) and is thick with seafaring kitsch. Even though it hosts a solid drinking phase somewhere between dinner and the live music, most drunken sailors are well behaved.

Ed's Bar (☎ 672 4650; Lot 51, Queens Rd, Martintar) Ed's is the other long-time favourite and, like Bounty across the road, you'll need to get your beer boots on early if you want a table to rest your Fiji Bitter. On Friday and Saturday nights live bands often hit the boards; otherwise the music favours the jazz, hip-hop and rap genres.

Shopping
Nadi's Main St is a tribute to souvenir and duty-free shops, and their mass-produced products are aimed unashamedly at mass tourism. Some of the strong-arm tactics employed in the smaller shops can be a bit tiring, although nothing compared with Asia or India. The best chance of finding something unique is to head to the **Nadi Handicraft Market** (Koroivolu Ave) but it's wise to check the prices in the major shops beforehand.

Getting There & Around
Nadi International Airport is 9km north of downtown Nadi and there are frequent local buses just outside the airport that travel along the Queens Road to town (F$0.65). Buses depart from New Town Beach for downtown Nadi six times daily, Mondays to Saturdays

(F$0.75, 15 minutes, six daily, Monday to Saturday). See p108 for information on getting to and from Nadi by bus. Taxis are plentiful in Nadi, but they don't use meters; agree on a price before getting in.

Around Nadi
DENARAU ISLAND
Like a cruise ship docked at a port, Denarau Island (2.55 sq km) is an artificial enclave of fancy resorts, manicured gardens, heavenly pools and professionally run tourist facilities. Although it bears little resemblance to the rest of Fiji, it's a popular place to indulge in some pampering at one of the international resorts found here. Be warned – what the brochures and websites don't advertise is that Denarau is built on reclaimed mangrove mudflats, and the beach has dark-grey sand and murky water unsuitable for snorkelling.

Port Denarau Retail Centre (www.portdenarau.com.fj) is busy with the comings and goings of buses and ferries, dropping off and collecting those going to and from the Yasawa and Mamanuca islands. There's a growing selection of shops and restaurants here.

Activities
Adrenalin Watersports (☎ 675 1288; www.adrenalin fiji.com) has the licence to run the watersports shops at all of the Denarau Resorts and at Port Denarau Retail Centre. It specialises in Jet Ski tours to Beachcomber, Castaway or Malolo islands (F$386 solo riders, F$216 per person for tandem riders).

Denarau Golf & Racquet Club (☎ 675 9711; info@ denaraugolf.com.fj) This club has an immaculately groomed 18-hole golf course with bunkers in the shape of sea creatures. Green fees are F$125/85 for 18/nine holes.

Sleeping & Eating
Proving that money loves company, seven resorts have opened in Denarau and more are planned. They each have four or five restaurants and a bevy of bars, and welcome their competitors' guests with open arms. The free inter-resort 'bula' bus trundles between them (and the port) on a continuous circuit.

Radisson Resort Fiji (☎ 675 6677; www.radisson .com/fiji; r F$333-575; ❌ 🖳 ❌ 🈁) The Radisson has taken pool design to new heights. Faced with an unappealing beach, the architects have spared no expense with this mammoth free-form pool. Its waterfall can be seen from the reception, and it boasts lagoons, sandy beaches, a white water tunnel, adult areas and an island containing a day spa. The kids club here is F$20 per day and there are free kayaks, windsurfers and catamarans. There are 270 rooms and all suites are self-contained.

Fiji Beach Resort & Spa Managed by Hilton (☎ 675 6800; www.fijibeachresortbyhilton.com; r $389-889; ✕ ▣ ✕ ▣) A series of seven rectangular, interlocking pools surrounded by artistically simple day beds is a nice architectural change from the other resorts. The long beach front (the best Denarau has to offer) can be seen from all rooms (most with kitchens) and our favourite Denarau restaurant, Nuku (mains F$35 to F$56), is onsite. While the Hilton may top the dining list, it has the worst lobby and fails to impress when first arriving. The kids club here is free.

Westin Denarau Island (☎ 675 0000; www.westin .com/denarauresort; r F$435-865; ✕ ▣ ✕ ▣) The Westin is more adult oriented, although children are welcome (kids club available for a one-time F$55 fee) with its elegant lobby featuring a beautiful blend of dark timber, pale sandstone and alternating low and vaulted ceilings. The small artificial beach here is a nice spot to relax, and the signature 'Heavenly' day spa is arguably the nicest in Fiji. After some serious pampering, you can sit back and relax while taking in a firewalking demonstration (Wednesdays and Saturdays, F$85 including buffet meal).

Getting There & Away

West Bus Transport (☎ 675 0777) has six buses daily (less frequently on Sunday) from Nadi bus station to Denarau Island. A taxi from downtown costs F$12.

VISEISEI & VUDA POINT

About 12km north of Nadi is Viseisei village, which, according to local lore, is the oldest settlement in Fiji. The story goes that *mataqali* (kinship groups) here are descendants of the first ocean-going Melanesians who landed 1km north of here circa 1500.

The **Vuda Point Marina** (☎ 666 8214; www.vuda marina.com.fj) is a well-organised and thriving boaties lure. Facilities include free showers, an excellent notice board, coin-operated laundry, sail makers, berths, a general store and yacht repair specialists and chandlery.

First Landing Resort (☎ 666 6171; www.first landingfiji.com; r incl breakfast F$325-425; 2-bedroom villa incl breakfast F$820-920; ✕ ✕ ▣) Perched on the water's edge and dripping with palms and colourful foliage, this resort is made to order for those who enjoy package holidays. The *bure* and villas are like cheerful hotel rooms with bright, tiled bathrooms and mosquito-screened verandas. The more expensive villas have private plunge pools and, although the beach isn't great, there's an artificial island in the shape of a footprint. The restaurant serves excellent seafood (mains F$25 to F$38), timid pasta and wood-fired pizza.

SONAISALI ISLAND

There's plenty of white sand at **Sonaisali Island Resort** (Map pp106-7; ☎ 670 6011; www.sonaisali.com; r incl breakfast F$495-682, ste incl breakfast from F$891, ✕ ✕ ▣ ▣), but unfortunately none of it's on the beach. Like Denarau, Sonaisali is on the edge of mangroves, and the dark sand disappoints some. To compensate there is a large pool with a swim-up bar and an endless array of activities including a free kids club. The glossy brochures and slick website tend to really raise expectations beyond their ability to deliver, but it remains a popular destination for antipodean package tourists. The meal plan (adult/child F$70/35) is the way to go for big eaters, but bring plenty of duty-free booze – the drinks are pricey (cocktails F$22). The hotel rooms in the double-storey building are getting tired, whereas the semi-detached *bure* are far nicer, with spa baths built into the verandas.

Sonaisai is a 25-minute drive, followed by a three-minute boat shuttle (free for guests) from Nadi airport. A taxi from the airport costs F$32, the resort shuttle F$55.

UCIWAI LANDING

Uciwai Landing, used by surfers to access the Mamanuca surf breaks, is 18km southwest of Nadi. Surfing is really the only reason to head here. The only place to stay is **Rendezvous Beach Resort** (☎ 628 4427; www.surfdivefiji.com; camping per person F$20, dm F$30, s/d shared bathroom F$60/70, s/d private bathroom F$80/125, prices incl breakfast and internet; ▣ ✕ ▣), where the air is thick with the scent of board wax, sunblock and surfing lingo. It's fairly basic and the staff are as languid as the seasoned surfers who visit but will organise surf trips to Mamanuca breaks (p137). Resort transfers from Nadi/airport are F$40/60, or local buses to Uciwai from Nadi bus station (F$1.50) depart at 8am, 1.30pm and 5.30pm weekdays, and 7am, 1pm and 5pm Saturday.

LAUTOKA

pop 52,900

Sweet Lautoka is 'Sugar City' and its colonial history is entwined with the cane it's nicknamed after. The **Lautoka Sugar Mill** has been operating here since 1903 and the local economy still relies heavily on diminishing returns. During the cutting season, sugar trains putt along the main street and in September the city crowns a Sugar Queen at the annual Sugar Festival.

From a traveller's perspective, there's not much to do. If you wander the wide streets amid swaying saris and aromatic curry houses, stroll along the picturesque esplanade towards the sugar mill or take a peek at the small botanical gardens and the Hare Krishna **Sri Krishna Kaliya Temple** (☎ 666 4112; 5 Tavewa Ave; ☷ 8am-6pm), you have pretty much seen the best of the city. Banks and Internet access are plentiful.

Sleeping

Cathay Hotel (☎ 666 0566; www.fiji4less.com; Tavewa Ave; dm F$22-24 s & d F$55, tr F$74; ☒ ☲) Easy on the wallet and with a handy central location, the Cathay's dorms and simple rooms are good value. There are only four beds to a dorm and the spacious rooms come with air-con or fan-cooled, with or without private bathrooms options. The food, however, isn't one of their strong points.

Sea Breeze Hotel (☎ 666 0717; fax 666 6080; Bekana Lane; s F$52-68, d F$58-74; ☒ ☒ ☲) Sequestered

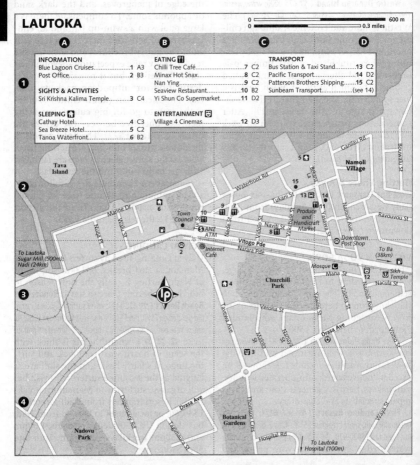

down an alley near the city centre, this hotel has piously austere rooms (embellished only by the bedside Bible) that provide a spotless and tranquil sanctuary. The more expensive sea-view rooms with air-con are the nicest. There's also a TV lounge where breakfast is available (F$4 to F$10).

Tanoa Waterfront (☎ 666 4777; www.tanoahotels .com; Marine Dr; r F$128-188; ✗ ⊠ ⬚ ⬚) Lautoka's top hotel has a top waterfront location. The cheapest rooms are spotlessly clean and have the ambience and trimmings of a midrange US hotel chain. The more expensive rooms have contemporary interiors, flat screen TVs and small balconies overlooking two pools. Onsite is a gym, coin-operated laundry, small children's playground, a bar and restaurant.

Eating

Lautoka has fewer restaurants than Nadi or Suva but lots of inexpensive lunchtime eateries.

Minax Hot Snax (☎ 666 1306; 56 Naviti St; meals F$5; ☾ breakfast & lunch) This unassuming family-run restaurant is the best place in town to sample authentic South Indian food. Meals are prepared using fresh ingredients including jackfruit, okra, *lauki* (a kind of gourd) and local spinach.

ourpick **Seaview Restaurant** (☎ 666 4592; cnr Naviti & Tui Sts; mains F$5-12; ☾ breakfast, lunch & dinner) This has been a long-time favourite with locals and travellers alike for good reason. The relaxed family atmosphere, pleasant bar, reasonable prices and delicious food served in huge portions leave little room for the competition to get a look in. You can order anything from roast chicken to *masala dosa*, and the family-sized pizza could feed a whole rugby team.

Chilli Tree Cafe (☎ 665 1824; 3 Tukani St; meals F$6-12; ☾ breakfast & lunch, Mon-Sat; ✗) This corner cafe is the best place to grab a paper and coffee, build a sandwich and settle into a chair behind the plate-glass window for some serious people-watching.

Nan Ying (☎ 665 2668; Nede St; mains F$13-30; ☾ lunch & dinner Mon-Sat, dinner Sun; ✗) Twinkly lights, backlit pictures and fake flowers give this place an air of Chinatown kitsch that would do San Francisco proud. Fragrant poultry and noodle dishes, sizzling seafood hotplates and fried rice specials demonstrate that these cooks know their way around their chopsticks.

Drinking & Entertainment

Lautoka has a limited number of pubs and clubs, which generally veer towards the seedier side. The best place for a relaxing drink with the locals is at the bar at Seaview Restaurant reviewed above.

Village 4 Cinemas (Namoli Ave) Hollywood and Bollywood are screened in harmony at Lautoka's main cinema. Tickets are F$4/5 for children/adults, except on Tuesday when they are F$1 cheaper.

Getting There & Around

Local buses shuttle between Lautoka and Nadi every 15 minutes (F$2.10). Sunbeam Transport and Pacific Transport also have frequent bus services to and from Nadi (F$2.80, one hour) and Suva (F$14.50, six hours) via both the Queens and Kings Rds (F$17, seven hours). Both companies have offices in Yasawa St, opposite the market, where you can pick up timetables. Taxis are plentiful but loathe to use their meters.

SOUTHERN VITI LEVU & THE CORAL COAST

Skirting the southern half of the mainland, the Queens Rd winds through cane fields and snakes over dry hills along the stretch of shore known as the Coral Coast. This region is peppered with small towns, all manner of accommodation options and some interesting local attractions. Despite the name, the Coral Coast doesn't offer particularly good snorkelling and the coral shelf is often exposed at low tide. Further east the weather turns more inclement, and the road near Pacific Harbour is flanked by waves of green hills on one side and a fringing reef that drops off dramatically into the deep blue of the ocean on the other.

Momi Bay

The first of the Coral Coast attractions are the **Momi Guns** (adult/child/family F$3/1/6; ☾ 9am-5pm), an evocative WWII battery built to defend Fiji against the Japanese Imperial Army; an army who had already swept through Papua New Guinea, the Solomon Islands and parts of what is now Vanuatu. A quick scan of the horizon will reveal why this spot was chosen for the installation. The guns (and now tourists) have unobstructed views to Malolo Barrier Reef, the Mamanuca islands and Navula Passage.

SLEEPING & EATING

Seashell@Momi (☎ 670 6100; www.seashellresort.com; dm incl meals F$86, s/d shared facilities incl breakfast F$47/70, r include breakfast F$158-190, apt incl breakfast F$231-315; ☒ ☒ ☐ ☒) Accommodation comes in all shapes and sizes at Seashell, from self-contained *bure* and apartments to spacious suites, inexpensive lodges and roomy dorms. Onsite facilities include a tennis court, two pools, a restaurant (mains F$10 to F$20), Nadi transfers, (F$25 per person), a dive operator (two-tank dive/PADI Open Water Course F$165/575) and boat access to the Mamanuca surf (p137).

GETTING THERE & AWAY

The turn-off to the Momi Guns is 18km from Nadi. A bus leaves Nadi for Momi Bay at 8am, 12.30pm, 2.30pm and 4pm and costs F$2. The 11.15am bus from Sigatoka costs F$3.80. Both buses pass the Momi Guns and the resort, but do not operate on Sundays.

Robinson Crusoe Island

Robinson Crusoe Island Resort (☎ 628 1999; www .robinsoncrusoeislandfiji.com; dm/s/d incl meals from F$86/103/206; ☒) is a hit with families. Every Tuesday, Thursday and Sunday the island becomes anything but deserted when it is besieged by visiting day-trippers (adult/child F$89/45 including Nadi and Coral Coast transfers). From start to finish, expect a fairly intense (and slightly tacky) entertainment programme loosely themed along cultural lines. The rest of the week is far quieter. The kitschy dorms and thatched *bure* are very basic, and shared facilities utilise cold water, bucket showers. The beautiful white-sand beach isn't great for snorkelling, although there is an onsite dive operator (two-tank dive/PADI Open Water Course F$120/450) who can get you to better reefs. Transport to and from Nadi costs F$79.

Natadola Beach

Natadola's wide stretch of sand is lauded throughout Fiji as the mainland's best beach. Unlike elsewhere, this beach isn't nearly as tidal, and the absence of coral allows for enough surf to satisfy beginners and body surfers. Rather persistent locals offer **horse riding** (F$10) along the beach to some nearby caves. It's a picturesque ride but be prepared to bargain hard. Natadola's tranquillity is set to change as, sometime in 2009, the massive

InterContinental Resort Fiji (www.natadolafiji.com) is set to open and with it will come a massive influx of tourists.

SLEEPING & EATING

Yatule Beach Resort (☎ 672 8004; reservation@ yatuleresort.com.fj; villa F$200-$320, fm villa F$530 ☒ ☐ ☒) Originally built to accommodate the executives involved in the building of the InterContinental, the Yatule has been remodelled into a very decent midrange resort. All the thatched-roof villas have mini-kitchens, bedrooms and separate lounges. The family villa has four separate bedrooms and is ideal for teenage kids who need privacy. The restaurant (mains F$18 to F$26) has a fantastic beachside location and is a great place for a beer.

Natadola Beach Resort (☎ 672 1001; www.natadola .com; r F$225, villa F$275; ☒) This adult-only resort injects a soft splash of Spain into Fiji and skips the mod cons in favour of spacious bathrooms, small private courtyards and tiled interiors. The archways and stucco walls give it a Mediterranean feel, although the lush gardens and meandering pool are Fijian tropical through and through. The restaurant-cum-bar (mains F$27 to F$32) is open to non-guests and it's a popular lunch stop with day-trippers.

GETTING THERE & AWAY

Paradise Transport buses head to and from Sigatoka (F$3, one hour, four daily Monday to Friday), although most travellers arrive on organised daytrips from Nadi or on the Coral Coast Scenic Railway (see below). Keen walkers could follow this track from Yanuca to Natadola Beach (about 3½ hours) and catch the train or bus back.

For those with a rental car, turn off Queens Rd onto Maro Rd 36km from Nadi.

Yanuca & Around

Past the turn-off to Natadola, the Queens Rd continues southeast, winding through hills and down to the coast at Cuvu Bay and Yanuca, about 50km from Nadi. Yanuca itself is a blink of a village, but it's home to a couple of good attractions.

It's impossible to miss the station for the **Coral Coast Scenic Railway** (☎ 652 0434; Queens Rd) near the causeway entrance to the Fijian Resort. An old sugar train makes the 14km, 1¼-hour run to Natadola Beach every

Tuesday, Thursday, Saturday and Sunday morning (adult/child F$91/45 including BBQ lunch). Chugging slowly past villages, forests and sugar plantations is a great introduction to the area and a hassle-free way to visit Natadola Beach. On Mondays, Wednesdays and Fridays the train creeps east for a Sigatoka shopping excursion (adult/child F$38/19).

Kalevu Cultural Centre (☎ 652 0200; admission 1hr/½ day guided tour F$20/55; ☽ 9am-4pm) This purpose-built centre is still recovering after an earlier fire in which many irreplaceable artefacts were destroyed. There are, however, demonstrations and small displays on Fijian culture and traditional ways of life.

Gecko's Resort (☎ 652 0200; www.fijiculturalcentre .com; tw shared bathroom F$58, d F$120, self-contained fm F$150-175, rates include breakfast; ✗ ▢ ✗ ▣) As this hotel forms part of the Kalevu Cultural Centre admission to the cultural village is sometimes included in the room tariff. The accommodation here has recently expanded to include 28 simple but nice hotel rooms, and the restaurant (mains $F12 to F$49) serves a decent steak.

Shangri-La's Fijian Resort (The Fijian; ☎ 652 0155; www.shangri-la.com; r incl breakfast from F$490; ✗ ▢ ✗ ▣) Occupying its own tiny island and linked to the mainland by a private causeway, this resort occupies one of the Coral Coast's prime spots. The recently upgraded 442 rooms come in a variety of configurations and packages – some of which include free breakfasts and children's meals. For big kids there's golf, a posh day spa, excellent restaurants, bars, tennis courts and wedding chapel. For little kids there's a kids club, three swimming pools, snorkelling and babysitters.

The Fijian Resort is about a 45-minute drive from Nadi and 11km west of Sigatoka.

Sigatoka & Around
pop 9500

Sigatoka is a neat and orderly town that serves as the commercial hub for the farming communities that live in the fertile Sigatoka Valley. It's also a popular day trip for tourists in the area and, while all its major attractions are a short taxi ride out of town, its riverside location, bustling produce market, supermarket, souvenir shops and local mosque mean that it's a pleasant place to while away a few hours. There are no great places to stay in Sigatoka town but options are plentiful at nearby Korotogo on the coast.

SIGHTS
Sigatoka Sand Dunes

Windswept and peppered with sheets of grey sand, these impressive **dunes** (adult/child/family F$8/3/20, children under 6 free; ☽ 8am-4.30pm) are one of Fiji's natural highlights. For millions of years, sediment brought down by the Sigatoka River has been washed ashore and blown inland by prevailing winds to form giant dunes. They now stand around 5km long, up to 1km wide and 10m to 60m high. A mahogany forest was planted in the 1960s to halt the dunes' slow expansion onto Queens Rd, and in 1989 the state-owned part of the area was declared a national park. Archaeological excavations suggest that this area has been occupied for thousands of years, and human skeletal remains and pottery shards suggest that concealed beneath the shifting sands is one of the largest burial sites in the Pacific.

Tavuni Hill Fort

This defensive **fort** (adult/child F$12/6; ☽ 8am-5pm Mon-Fri, 8.30am-1.30pm Sat) was built in the 18th century by Tongan chief Maile Latumai who was seeking to escape an era of political and social upheaval in his homeland. He and his entourage arrived in 1788 in a double-hulled canoe and, although it took some time, they were eventually accepted and given this land to build their fort. The steep limestone ridge here was an obvious strategic location because of its commanding views.

The site has been restored as a means of income for villagers and it's the most accessible fort of its kind in Fiji. The information centre, a number of grave sites, a *rara* (ceremonial grounds) and a *vatu ni bokola* (head-chopping stone) all help to provide an insight into the strong pre-colonial links between Tonga and Fiji. Its regular local buses pass Tavuni Hill ($0.75, seven a day on weekdays), heading for Mavua. A taxi costs F$8 one way.

Naihehe Cave

The **Naihehe cave**, about an hour's drive upriver from Sigatoka, was once used as a fortress by hill tribes and has the remains of a ritual platform and cannibal oven. Adventures in Paradise (see p120) offers guided tours here.

FIJI

A HAIRY SITUATION

For indigenous Fijians the head is *tabu*. In reverence to this sanctity, Fijians once spent entire days with the hairdresser. As a symbol of masculinity and social standing, men sported flamboyant, often massive hairdos, ranging from the relatively conventional giant puffball (up to 30cm tall) to more original shaggy or geometric shapes. Styles were stiffened into place with burnt lime juice and dyed grey, blue, orange, yellow and white, sometimes striped or multicoloured. Women, on the other hand, wore far more conservative hairdos – close-cropped with random tufts dyed rusty brown or yellow. A wife's hair could never outdo her husband's, and a husband's could not outdo the chief's.

People slept on uncomfortable-looking wooden pillows to keep their coiffure from being spoilt. The head was specially dressed for festive occasions with accessories like hair scratchers, ornamental combs, scarlet feathers, flowers and grated sandalwood. Shaving one's head was a profound sacrifice for a man and often done as a symbol of mourning or to appease a wrathful ancestral spirit.

Early Europeans were astonished by the variety of elaborate styles. After a missionary allegedly measured one hairdo at 5m in circumference, the custom was deliberately suppressed by Christians who regarded the practice as not suitable for the 'neat and industrious Christian convert'.

ACTIVITIES
Surfing
Sigatoka has Fiji's only beach break, over a large, submerged rock platform covered in sand and at the point break at the mouth of the Sigatoka River.

TOURS
Adventures in Paradise (☎ 652 0833; www.adventures inparadisefiji.com; tours per person including Coral Coast/ Nadi hotel transfers F$99/119, child 5-12 years half price) Offers day trips to Naihehe Cave and its large cathedral-like chamber.

Sigatoka River Safari (☎ 650 1721; www.sigatoka river.com; jet boat tours per person including Coral Coast/Nadi hotel transfers F$195/215, child 4-15 years F$89) The half-day jet-boating trips include a 45km whirl up the Sigatoka River, a village visit and lunch.

SLEEPING & EATING
Unless you're stuck, you're better off heading to the superior accommodation in nearby Korotogo.

True Blue Hotel & Restaurant (☎ 650 1530; Sigatoka Club Bldg, Queens Rd; dm F$20, s/d F$35/45, mains F$8-24; ☺ lunch & dinner; ⊠ ⊠) The draw here is the elevated position and lovely views from the cavernous, dancehall-like restaurant up the mangrove-lined Sigatoka River. The meals aren't quite in the same league as the view, and the rooms are a notch down in quality again. The saggy beds have seen more action than Rambo.

Vilisite's Seafood Restaurant (☎ 653 0054; Queens Rd; mains F$8-17; ☺ breakfast, lunch & dinner; ⊠) Tuck into fabulous seafood in kitschy tropicana surrounds at this popular Fijian eatery. The

extensive menu includes curries and Chinese dishes but you'd be nuts to bypass the shell-fish. Takeaway is also available.

Sigatoka Club (☎ 650 0026; mains F$8-24; ☺ lunch & dinner) Downstairs from the True Blue Restaurant, this club is the best drinking hole in town. Grab a seat in one of the waterfront booths or help prop up the horseshoe-shaped bar with the locals.

GETTING THERE & AROUND
Pacific Transport and Sunbeam Transport run several express buses a day between Nadi and Sigatoka (F$4.50, 1¼ hours) and between Sigatoka and Suva (F$8.50, 3 hours).

Korotogo & Korolevu
The Coral Coast begins its dazzling thread in earnest at the small village of Korotogo. From here the road winds along the shore, skirting clear blue bays and scaling progressively greener hills as it heads east. Unexpected glimpses of coral reefs and deserted beaches make this the most photogenic stretch of the Queens Rd highway. Villages are plentiful and each is announced by a series of judder bars designed to slow traffic and reduce accidents. East of Korolevu, the road turns away from the shore and climbs over the southern end of Viti Levu's dividing mountain range towards Pacific Harbour.

SIGHTS
Kula Eco Park
Supported by the National Trust for Fiji and several international parks and conservation bodies, this **wildlife sanctuary** (☎ 650 0505; www

.fijiwild.com; adult/child F$20/10; ⊙ 10am-4.30pm) is a must for fans of the furred, feathered and scaled. Wooden walkways traverse streams, Fijian flora and a menagerie of hawksbill sea turtles (hand fed at 11am, 1pm and 3.30pm daily), reptiles, birds (including Fiji's national bird, the kula parrot), fruit bats, tropical fish and live coral. The park has come a long way since 1997, when most of the birds here were either dead or dying, and today the park runs invaluable breeding programmes for Fiji's only remaining duck species, the Pacific black duck, and the crested and banded iguana.

DIVING
The Korolevu stretch of coast offers some spectacular diving, and most of the resorts in the area are serviced by **Dive Away Fiji** (☎ 650 1124; www.diveaway-fiji.com) or **South Pacific Adventure Divers** (☎ 653 0555 ext 609; www.spadfiji.com). Both will collect guests from any place that doesn't have an onsite concession, and both are similarly priced at around F$190/700 for a two-tank dive/PADI Open Water Course.

SLEEPING
Budget
Vakaviti (☎ 650 0526; www.vakaviti.com; Sunset Strip; dm F$20, r F$100-150; 🛋) Tumbling down a steep and densely vegetated embankment, Vakaviti is a bit of a mixed bag. The small, clean dormitory is quite dark and the bathroom has only cold water, whereas the split-level motel rooms are far nicer and overlook the pool.

Beachhouse (☎ 653 0500; www.fijibeachouse.com; camping per person incl breakfast F$23, dm incl breakfast F$30, d incl breakfast F$93; ✖ 🛋 🛋) Backpackers flock to this long-time favourite because of it's clean and simple digs and its easy access via public transport. Dorms are in two-storey timber houses and doubles are in colourful duplex bungalows. There's a pretty pool, cheap cafe and onsite cooking facilities. Activities include horse riding (F$20 per hour) and a recommended 'jungle trek' to a waterfall (F$8).

ourpick Mango Bay Resort (☎ 653 0069; www.mangobayresortfiji.com; dm incl breakfast F$36-45, d incl breakfast F$90-270, 4-person luxury tent incl breakfast F$189; ✖ 🛋 🛋) Mango fizzes with the sound of happy holiday-makers. It occupies its own slice of beachside heaven and has enough accommodation options – dorms, safari tents, lodges and *bure* – to keep everyone happy. Mango targets the 18- to 35-year-old set and is an overnight stop for the Feejee Experience

crowd. Snorkelling, diving and game fishing can all be arranged here and the restaurant does decent nosh. Let them know you are coming so you can be collected from the Queens Rd junction.

Also recommended:

Tubakula Beach Bungalows (☎ 650 0097; www.fiji4less.com/tuba.html; dm F$26, s/tw without bathroom F$58/63, ste F$115-164; ✖ 🛋) Clean dorms, singles, doubles and A-frame, self-contained chalets.

Namatakula Village Homestay (www.fijibure.com/namatakula/index.htm; per adult/child incl meals F$70/35) For simple accommodation, generous meals and an authentic window onto traditional village life.

Midrange
Bedarra Beach Inn (☎ 650 0476; www.bedarrafiji.com; Sunset Strip; r include breakfast F$167-180; ✖ 🛋) This place is a gem. It offers spacious, spotlessly clean rooms with tiled floors and plenty of natural light, genuinely friendly staff and just the right mix of resort-style comfort and do-it-yourself practicality. There's also an excellent restaurant (mains F$20 to $30) and a unique ripple-shaped lounge bar.

New Crow's Nest Resort (☎ 650 0230; www.crowsnestfiji.com; Sunset Strip; r F$135-145; ✖ ✖ 🛋 🛋) The hillside, split-level bungalows make the most of their elevated position with fine balconies facing ocean views. The whole place has undergone a recent facelift and is currently good value. Kids stay free and the rooms (some with kitchens) are large enough to accommodate families of four.

Tambua Sands Beach Resort (☎ 650 0399; www.tambuasandsfiji.com; d F$130-170; 🛋) This friendly resort will suit intrepid travellers looking to indulge. *Bure* are beachside or oceanview; the latter are pricier but dressed up like chic holiday flats and better value. The manicured lawns are littered with sun lounges and there's a good restaurant (mains F$15 to F$34) and plentiful activities.

Waidroka Surf & Dive Resort (☎ 330 4605; www.waidroka.com; dm incl meal package $195, d incl breakfast $240-295, ste incl breakfast $250; 🛋 🛋) Over a hilly dirt road, Waidroka caters to serious divers (a two-tank dive/PADI Open Water Course costs F$170 to F$195/750) and surfers with a small flotilla of boats to ferry guests to local breaks (F$45, nonguests F$55) and Frigate Passage (F$85, nonguests F$95). Guests stay either in the bright orange *bure* or in the adjoining terrace rooms; both are very smart. Taxis from Nadi cost F$140 but it is cheaper if you bus to Korovisilou village and ask to be collected from there (F$18 per car).

Top End

Crusoe's Retreat (☎ 650 0185; www.crusoesretreat.com; r incl breakfast F$240-370; 🖳 🖭) Tucked into a fold between two hills on the coast, Crusoe's remote location is emphasised (or exasperated) by the fact there are no TVs, radios or newspapers available. There are 28 fan-cooled *bure*, a fabulous restaurant and a resident dive operator (F$246/784 for a two-tank dive/PADI Open Water Course). Hotel transfers from Nadi airport are F$130 per person return. A taxi is around F$150 or F$15 if you bus to the Warwick first.

Naviti Resort (☎ 653 0444; www.navitiresort.com.fj; r incl breakfast/all inclusive F$299/508, ste incl breakfast/all inclusive $522/615; 🗶 😢 🖳 🖭) Heavy on the greenery and light on the concrete, the colossal Naviti has all the goodies – four restaurants, five bars, a nine-hole golf course, swim-up bar, health spa and kids club. But, unlike other resorts, the all-inclusive package includes beer, wine, Sigatoka shopping excursions, a sunset cruise and a choice between à la carte or buffet dining (although the food is average at both).

More top-end options:

Outrigger on the Lagoon (☎ 650 0044; www.out rigger.com/fiji; r from F$567; 🗶 😢 🖳 🖭) Stylish rooms and *bure*, superb views and excellent facilities in a five-star, four-storey shell.

Wellesley Resort (☎ Fiji 603 0664, New Zealand booking office +64 4 474 1308; www.wellesleyresort.com.fj; Man Friday Rd; d incl breakfast and Nadi transfers F$189-399; nais) Romantic boutique resort with 15 suites and a stunning, if somewhat isolated, location.

Warwick Fiji Resort & Spa (☎ 653 0555; www .warwickfiji.com; s & d incl breakfast $350-550, ste incl breakfast $740; 🗶 😢 🖳 🖭) Owned by the same crowd that owns Naviti, the Warwick is another feature-laden, activity-rich resort. Five restaurants, seven bars and lagoons with all-tide swimming areas.

EATING

All of the resorts above (with the exception of Vakaviti) have restaurants and bars – in some cases, multiple restaurants and bars – and they all welcome the opportunity to steal a few clients from their neighbours. The pricey **Wicked Walu** (☎ 653 0555; 🕑 dinner) at the Warwick (try saying that after a few beers) has particularly good steak and seafood (mains F$30 to F$50) and a prominent setting on its own island.

Mayshaars Cuisine (☎ 652 0584; Sunset Strip; mains F$8-15; 🕑 breakfast, lunch & dinner) No need to dress up for this place. Diners take their seats on wooden picnic tables in front of a small supermarket and, while its setting is hardly glamorous, the meals are tasty and excellent value.

Vilisite's Restaurant (☎ 650 1030; Queens Rd; mains F$12-38; 🕑 breakfast, lunch & dinner) If you have a Hawaiian shirt you'll feel right at home, as this place drips tropical garb. With its sweeping ocean views, it's the nicest restaurant in the area outside the flashy resorts.

Le Café (☎ 652 0877; Sunset Strip; mains F$10-20; 🕑 breakfast, lunch & dinner) Just west of the shops; Le Café has a Swiss chef who cooks European-style food – tasty pizzas are the speciality. There's also a daily happy hour from 5pm to 7pm.

GETTING THERE & AWAY

The Korotogo area is about 8km east of Sigatoka, and Korolevu village is 31km east of Sigatoka. Regular buses ply the Queens Rd and will drop guests off outside most resorts. For the more isolated resorts it is best to phone ahead and arrange collection or a taxi once you have reached the Coral Coast vicinity.

Pacific Harbour

The unseemly swamp that was once Pacific Harbour has been tamed, drained, subdivided and pedicured into a brochure-perfect housing development quite unlike the rest of Fiji. The wide cul-de-sac streets, flawless lawns and ordered river setting might seem incongruous to some but local residents love it. Recently Pacific Harbour has marketed itself as the 'Adventure Capital of Fiji' on the basis of a number of adrenalin-fuelled activities including shark diving in nearby Beqa (*ben-ga*) Lagoon and rafting and trekking in the Namosi Highlands.

SIGHTS

The **Arts Village** (☎ 345 0065; www.artsvillage.com; tours per adult/child from F$55/28; 🕑 9am-4pm Mon-Sat) endeavours to showcase some of Fiji's cultural heritage with demonstrations and performances by local actors dressed in traditional costumes. The mock battles and Disneyesque surrounds tend to make it more like an entertaining theme show than an educational experience, but those with families enjoy it thoroughly. For our money, the best of the tours is the fire-walking, *lovo* feast and *meke* show held every Tuesday, Thursday and Saturday (per adult/child F$75/37; 10.45am).

Attached to the Arts Village, the **Marketplace** is a congregation of eateries, supermarkets and souvenir shops and is a pleasant spot in which to kill an hour or so.

ACTIVITIES

The beach at Deuba is reasonable for swimming, and the **Pearl Championship Golf Course** (☎ 345 0905; 18-holes with/without club hire F$71/47, 9-holes with/without club hire $24/42) on the outskirts of town can provide a challenging game on a bunker-peppered course. For something a little faster, try swinging through the jungle with Zip Fiji (☎ 930 0545; www.zip-fiji.com; adult/child F$120/60; h8am-8pm).

Diving

There are more than 20 excellent dive sites near Pacific Harbour, mostly within **Beqa Lagoon**, but these are overshadowed by the opportunity to dive with 4m-long tiger sharks and massive, barrel-chested bull sharks without being caged (or sedated). The dives are well organised (they would have to be), and not nearly as intimidating as many imagine. The tigers don't always show but the bulls are regularly seen between February and early September.

Aqua-Trek Beqa (☎ 345 0324; www.aquatrek .com; Pearl South Pacific) and **Beqa Adventure Divers** (☎ 345 0911; www.fiji-sharks.com; Lagoon Resort) both specialise in this activity, and their prices average around F$190/230/650 a two-tank dive/two-tank shark-feeding dive/PADI Open Water Course.

TOURS

Rivers Fiji (☎ 345 0147; www.riversfiji.com; Pearl South Pacific; day tours per person from F$205) Rivers Fiji offers excellent kayaking and rafting trips through the scenic gorges of the Namosi Highlands and Upper Navua River.

Discover Fiji Tours (☎ 345 0180; www.discover fijitours.com) Based just outside Pacific Harbour at Navua, this outfit has several day tours (from F$115 per person) to the Navua River area, which include waterfall visits, 4WD trips and kayaking.

SLEEPING

Club Oceanus (☎ 3450 498; info@cluboceanus.com; 1 Atoll Pl, Pacific Harbour; dm/d/f F$25/85/120; ⊠ 🐾 🖭) This riverside resort has ten recently painted, self-contained flats in a long, compact block. It's good value and located in a convenient spot on the canal, and plans to open a cafe are well underway.

Tsulu Backpackers & Apartments (☎ 345 0065; www.tsulu.com; dm F$30-34, d F$150, 1-/2-/3-bedroom apt F$160/210/485; 🐾 🖳 🖭) This place is the kind of psychedelic trip that would give Austin Powers a head rush. Attached to the Arts Village, Tsulu has picked up the artistic gauntlet and really, and we mean really, run with it. The walls (and in some cases the ceilings) of the dorms, double rooms and self-contained apartments are painted in vibrant murals. One room is painted bright blue and features life-size fish, coral gardens and a snorkeller painted on the ceiling above.

our pick **Uprising Beach Resort** (☎ 345 2200; www .uprisingbeachresort.com; dm incl breakfast F$35, d incl breakfast F$160-180; 🖳 🖭) Just within walking distance from town, this recently opened resort has 12 spacious *bure* and a spotlessly clean dorm. The *bure* have trendy outdoor showers, bifold doors, thatched roofs and wood-panelled walls. The restaurant (mains F$14 to F$24) serves mainly Tex-Mex cuisine and, if the bar is not quite the hot spot it claims to be, there are enough barflies buzzing around to give it a cheery vibe.

Pearl South Pacific (☎ 345 0022; www.thepearlsouth pacific.com; Queens Rd, Pacific Harbour; r F$248-314, ste F$582-666; ⊠ 🐾 🖳 🖭) No expense has been spared during recent renovations at the Pearl and it is now one of Viti Levu's little treasures. Style gurus will overdose on the marble bathrooms, low-slung beds and private decked alcoves with cushioned sunloungers. The day spa, Sunday afternoon jazz and one of the best restaurants on the coast will keep those looking to splurge well fed and relaxed to the point of happy paralysis.

Also recommended:

Club Coral Coast (☎ 345 0421; clubcoralcoast@connect .com.fj; Lot 12 Belo Circle; d without/with bathroom F$40/90-120; 🖭) Seven rooms in two blocks, each with a kitchenette and bath.

Lagoon Resort (☎ 345 0100; www.lagoonresort.com; Fairway Pl, Pacific Harbour; r F$170-295, ste F$325; ⊠ 🐾 🖭) Grand, colonial-style estate with dignified rooms, restaurant and service.

FIJI

EATING

Water's Edge (☎ 345 0145; Arts Village Marketplace; mains F$8-28; ☺ breakfast & lunch daily, dinner Fri-Sun) The deck-side dining is surrounded by the water lily pond and is a great place for lunch. The menu is strong on pizza (available to take away), pasta and vino. Meals come with 30 minutes of complimentary internet.

Oasis Restaurant (☎ 345 0617; Arts Village Marketplace; mains F$16-36; ☺ breakfast, lunch & dinner; ☒ ▣) Unless you are a fan of bodice-ripping novellas, skip the second hand book shelves and stick to perusing the menu. The long list of burgers, sandwiches, tortillas, curries and seafood dishes make for good reading.

Sakura House (☎ 345 0256; River Dr; mains F$20-35; ☺ dinner) Although it features other Asian dishes, the Japanese *tempura, sashimi, shabu-shabu* and *teriyaki* are its speciality.

Mantarae Restaurant (☎ 345 0022; Pearl South Pacific; mains F$34-38; ☺ dinner Tue-Sat) This place is worth the splurge; the mouth-watering, contemporary, fusion-style cuisine has diners drooling their way from the main course to dessert. Sprawled out on a day bed, or sequestered behind the mirrored bar, it's fine dining all the way with a wine list to match.

GETTING THERE & AWAY

Pacific Harbour is about an hour's express bus ride from Suva (F$4.15) and around 3½ hours from Nadi (F$15). A taxi to Suva costs F$40.

Namosi Highlands

The steamy Namosi Highlands, north of Pacific Harbour, have Fiji's most spectacular scenery, complete with rainforests, steep ranges, deep river canyons and tall waterfalls. The simplest way to see these highlands is to sign up with one of the Pacific Harbour tour companies (p123) that specialise in this remote area or, if you have your own wheels (preferably 4WD), take a detour inland from Nabukavesi.

Offshore Islands

Offshore from Pacific Harbour, a 64km-long barrier reef encloses the exquisite **Beqa Lagoon**, world-famous for its dizzying dive sites including Side Streets and Caesar's Rocks. Divers are joined by avid surfers who test their mettle on the powerful left-hand breaks at **Frigate's Passage**. Anchored amid the lagoon are Beqa and Yanuca Islands, untouched except for a handful of inconspicuous resorts.

BEQA

area 36 sq km

The volcanic and rugged island of Beqa is best known for its villagers who practise traditional firewalking but the best place to see them isn't on Beqa; it's now performed chiefly for tourists at the Coral Coast resorts.

The cosy and relaxed **Lawaki Beach House** (☎ 992 1621, 368 4088; www.lawakibeachhouse.com; camping incl meals F$68, dm/s/tw incl meals F$78/96/192; ▣) comprises two double *bure* with en-suites and a six-bed dorm. There is good snorkelling off the secluded, pristine white-sand beach, as well as visits to the nearby village, diving and surfing (F$225 for the boat, plus F$15 per hour). Meals are served in the communal TV lounge, and the resort can organise boat transfers from Pacific Harbour for F$70 per person one way. Alternatively you can catch the small public ferry from the Navua Jetty. The ferry usually leaves between noon and 2.30pm from Monday to Saturday, and costs F$30 per person one way. It returns to Navua at 7am every day but Sunday.

Two other options:

Beqa Lagoon Resort (☎ 330 4042; www.beqalagoon resort.com; r F$200; ☒ ▣ ☎) Twenty-five *bure* with classy bathrooms and traditional interiors.

Lalati Resort (☎ 347 2033; www.lalati-fiji.com; r incl meals from s/d/tr F$600/880/1170; ☒ ☎) Intimate and lavish with only seven *bure*.

YANUCA

Compact and beautiful Yanuca is a mass of green hills, interrupted by a village and a couple of surf camps. The beaches here are lovely but it's Yanuca's proximity to the surf breaks of Frigate's Passage that lures travellers here.

Batiluva (☎ 345 1019, 992 0019; www.batliuva.com; dm/d incl meals F$175/350) Many a surfer hits this camp for a week only to wake a month later in a hammock wondering where the time went. Spotless and airy dorms and double rooms are let on a per person basis with couples getting dibs on the doubles. 'Gourmet jungle meals' are included in the tariff but, more importantly, so is the daily boat out to Frigates for the surf-til-you-drop clientele. Transfers from Pacific Harbour are F$50 return, per person.

Yanuca Island Resort (☎ 336 1281, 997 8958; www .frigatesreef.com; per person incl meals F$150). This simple camp is etched into a protected, grassy groove of the island. There is one dorm with solid timber bunks and mosquito nets, plus two cabins with private bathrooms attached.

Meals are served in an open-air dining area. Snorkelling straight off the tiny beach is good, but most guests head out to the reef on a daily basis. Daily boat transfers to Frigates Passage are included, but the return transfers from Pacific Harbour are F$50 per person.

SUVA
pop 194,300

Suva (pronounced soo-va) is more than just the Fijian capital; it is the largest city in the South Pacific, an important regional centre and a cosmopolitan milieu of cultures and influences. This is partly due to the University of the South Pacific, which is jointly owned by 12 Pacific nations and attracts a vibrant potpourri of island students. The compact downtown grid is equally diverse with grand colonial buildings, modern high-rises and shiny shopping plazas flanked by a breezy esplanade.

Beyond downtown Suva there is a string of pretty suburbs dribbled along the hills that crowd the capital's busy port. On the city outskirts lie the ballooning settlement camps of tin sheds and home to around half of Suva's inhabitants.

On a less serious but equally grey note, clouds tend to hover over Suva and frequently dump rain on the city (around 300mm each year), which accounts for the lush tropical plants and comparative lack of tourists.

Information

Internet access is cheap (F$3 per hour) and abundant in Suva, and many of the cyber cafes along Thomson St are open 24 hours. There are also plenty of banks, ATMs and Western Union–affiliated currency exchange shops scattered along the same street.

ATS Pacific Holiday Inn (☎ 330 1600); Tradewinds (☎ 336 4086) Books local tours and activities, including those at nearby Pacific Harbour.

Fiji Visitors Bureau (FVB; ☎ 330 2433; www.fijime .com; cnr Thomson & Scott Sts; ☯ 8am-4.30pm Mon-Fri, 8am-12pm Sat) Friendly, knowledgeable and unbiased staff can advise on local tours and accommodation options throughout Fiji.

Fintel (☎ 331 2933; 158 Victoria Pde; internet per hr $5; ☯ 8am-8pm Mon-Sat) This office has Fiji's only voice-over-internet telephones with international calls costing only F$0.20 per minute.

Maharaj Medical Centre (☎ 327 0164; Sports City Centre, Laucala Bay Rd, Laucala Bay; ☯ 9am-1pm, 2-6pm Mon-Fri, 9am-1pm Sat & Sun) Private medical centre.

Police (☎ 911/331 1222; Pratt St)

Post Fiji (☎ 321 8450; Thomson St)

USP Book Centre (☎ 323 2500; www.uspbookcentre .com; USP Laucala campus) stocks the country's best selection of local and international novels, Lonely Planet guides, and Pacific non-fiction.

Sights

FIJI MUSEUM & THURSTON GARDENS

Situated in the middle of **Thurston Gardens** this small but excellent **museum** (☎ 331 5944; www.fijimuseum.org.fj; Ratu Cakobau Rd; adult/child F$7/5; ☯ 9am-4.30pm Mon-Sat) delves into Fiji's archaeological, political, cultural and linguistic evolution. The museum features original examples of musical instruments, cooking apparatus, jewellery and a daunting array of Fijian war clubs. The section exhibiting cannibal utensils provides a vivid insight into traditional life. The massive Ratu Finau, Fiji's last *waqa tabus* (double-hulled canoe), is the museum's showpiece, although some of the smaller exhibits, like the well-chewed, but ultimately inedible, shoe of Thomas Baker (a Christian missionary eaten for his indiscretions in 1867), are just as interesting.

The gardens outside are all that remains of the original village of Suva and, although they have grown more haphazard with every passing coup, the stately fig trees are still a great spot to picnic beneath and ponder your new-found knowledge.

COLO-I-SUVA FOREST PARK

This lush rainforest **park** (☎ 332 0211; adult/child F$5/1; ☯ 8am-4pm Mon-Sun) is a cool and peaceful respite from downtown Suva. It is only 2.5 sq km in size but boasts 6.5km of walking trails that navigate clear, natural pools and gorgeous vistas. Many of the trails follow the Waisila Creek as it slips and slides its way towards the Waimanu River. The creek gives rise to natural swimming holes, some of which have rope swings and are guaranteed to bring out the Tarzan in anyone.

You can buy your ticket and pick up a map from the visitor information centre on the left side of the road as you approach from Suva. It's worth asking about the security situation and, if it is of concern, forking out extra to have a guard show you around the park.

To get here, take the Saweni bus from Suva bus station (F$1.30, 30 minutes, half-hourly).

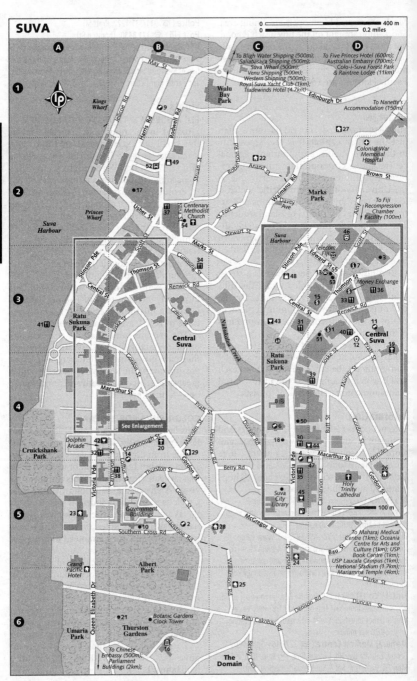

SUVA

0 ——— 400 m
0 ——— 0.2 miles

INFORMATION

ANZ Bank	1	D3
ATS Pacific	(see 23)	
British High Commission	2	B5
Dominion House Arcade	3	D3
Embassy of Nauru	4	C4
Embassy of Tuvalu	5	B5
European Union Representative	6	C4
Fiji Visitors Bureau	7	D3
Fintel	8	C4
French Embassy	(see 3)	
German Consulate	9	B1
Japanese Embassy	(see 3)	
Map Shop	10	B5
Netherlands Consulate	(see 51)	
New Zealand Embassy	11	D3
Police Station	12	D3
Post Fiji	13	D3
South Pacific Tourism Organisation	(see 42)	
US Embassy	14	B4
Westpac Bank	15	D3

SIGHTS & ACTIVITIES

Fiji Museum	16	B6
Municipal Market	17	B2
Old Town Hall	18	C4
Roman Catholic Cathedral	19	D3
St Andrew's Church	20	B4
Thurston Gardens	21	B6

SLEEPING

Colonial Lodge	22	C2
Holiday Inn	23	A5
Peninsula International Hotel	24	C5
South Seas Private Hotel	25	C6
Southern Cross Hotel	26	D5
Studio 6 Apartments	27	D1
Suva Motor Inn	28	C5
Tanoa Plaza	29	B4

EATING

Ashiyana	(see 18)	
Bad Dog Cafe	30	C4
Capital Palace	31	C3
Daikoku	32	A4
Esquires Coffee House	(see 42)	
Esquires Coffee House	33	D3
Govinda's Vegetarian Restaurant	34	B3
Maya Dhaba	35	C5
MHCC Department Store	36	D3
Morris Hedstrom Supermarket	37	B2
Old Mill Cottage	38	B5
Roma's Hook and Chook	39	D4
Shanghai Seafood House	40	D3
Tiko's Floating Restaurant	41	A3

DRINKING

Bar 66	42	A4
JJ's on the Park	43	C3
O'Reilly's	44	D4
Traps Bar	45	C5
Victoria Wines & Spirits	(see 44)	

ENTERTAINMENT

Village 6 Cinemas	46	D2

SHOPPING

Government Crafts Centre	47	D5
Suva Curio & Handicraft Centre	48	C3
Suva Flea Market	49	B2

TRANSPORT

Air Fiji	50	C4
Air New Zealand	51	D3
Air Pacific	(see 53)	
Bus Station	52	B2
Consort Shipping	(see 3)	
Pacific Sun	53	D3
Patterson Brothers Shipping	54	B2
Qantas	55	D3
Taxi Stand	(see 52)	

OTHER SIGHTS

The forebidding and handsome **government buildings** (1939 and 1967), at the end of Carnarvon St, are set on heavy foundations atop reclaimed land. Opened in 1992, the **parliament buildings** (☎ 330 5811; www.parliament.gov.fj; Battery Rd; admission free) are far more aesthetic and adorned with traditional Fijian *tapa* cloths and works of art. It's advisable to call ahead if you want to tour the grounds, but you can also obtain a visitor's pass from the guard at the main entrance.

Set in a breadth of breezy gardens, the University of the South Pacific's main **Laucala Campus** (USP; ☎ 331 3900; www.usp.ac.fj; Laucala Bay Rd) is a pleasant spot for a stroll and bout of people-watching. Students from islands throughout the Pacific attend the university, and the cultural diversity is a curio in itself.

The beating heart of Suva is the **Municipal Market** (Usher St; 6am-6pm Mon-Fri, 6am-4.30pm Sat) and it's a great place to spend an hour or so poking around with a camera. Besides the recognisable tomatoes, cabbages and chillies, look out for bitter gourds, kava, jackfruit, *dalo* (a taro-like root vegetable), *rourou* (*dalo* leaves) and sweet potatoes.

Activities

The **Royal Suva Yacht Club** (☎ 331 2921; rsyc@kidanet.net.fj; office 8am-5pm Mon-Fri, 9am-1pm Sat) is a popular watering hole for yachties and locals alike and the notice board here is a good place to find crewing positions. The marina has dockside fuel and water. Anchorage fees are F$8 per day or F$30 if you prefer to overnight in one of the six berths. There are laundry and shower facilities for those who have just arrived, and the office should be able to advise on immigration procedures.

Suva Walking Tour

Downtown Suva has a scattering of colonial buildings and places of interest, making it a pleasant place to wander around. Give yourself several hours for this tour.

Start your journey with that most Suvan of destinations – the **municipal market (1)**. Ogle as traders ply their kava, vegetables and fruit. Make your way down Rodwell Rd, turn left onto Usher St, right onto Thomson and then immerse yourself in **Cumming St (2)**. Suck in the scent of incense and curry and marvel at the stunning saris displayed in the shop windows. Turning right onto Renwick Rd, make a beeline for the water by going down Central St. Take a breather on Stinson Pde and snap up the dramatic views of **Suva Harbour** and **Joske's Thumb (3)**. Drop into the **Suva Curio & Handicraft Centre (4**; p132) and potter through the stalls of handmade arts and crafts. Turn left and follow the esplanade till you reach **Ratu Sukuna Park (5)**. Amble through this tree-littered plot to make

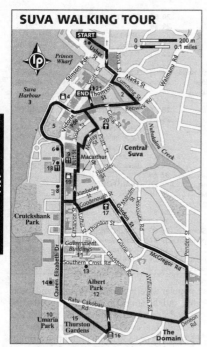

SUVA WALKING TOUR

WALK FACTS

Start Municipal Market
Finish Visitor Information Centre
Distance About 4km
Duration Three hours

your way back to Thomson St. Continue south down Victoria Pde, past the pale colonial 1926 **Fintel building (6)** and the 1904 **old town hall (7)**. Now home to several restaurants, the old town hall building was once used for dances, bazaars and performances. The stately 1909 **Suva City Library (8)** is also here. If you need a pick-me-up, duck across the road to **Bad Dog Cafe (9)** for a coffee or, better yet, a fruit smoothie and a slice of the best cake in town.

Continue down Victoria Pde and take a rest at **Umaria Park (10)**, teeming with kids scrambling over monkey bars and offering extensive water views in the background. On your right-hand side are the stately **government buildings (11)**. Presiding over the manicured green lawns are statues of Ratu Cakobau and Ratu Sukuna.

In the block south of the government buildings, you may catch a rugby union team in action in **Albert Park (12)**. On the northern edge of the park is the **Kingsford Smith Pavilion (13)**, named after the famous aviator who landed here. On the seaside, opposite the park, is the glorious old **Grand Pacific Hotel (14)**. Built in 1914 by the Union Steamship Company, its ship-style architecture is reminiscent of the luxury liners that once plied the seas. The hotel has been abandoned since 1992 but restoration plans are under way.

Once you've passed the hotel, cross the road, keeping Albert Park on your left. At the corner of Ratu Cakobau Rd and Queen Elizabeth Dve is the entrance to **Thurston Gardens (15**; p125). Meander through this balmy park and take a breather beneath one of the stately figs. Within the grounds is the **Fiji Museum (16**; p125).

Continue east along Ratu Cakobau Rd and ascend into the inner suburbs. Turn left at Pender St and left again at McGregor Rd. Amid the tranquil residential streets you'll have sweeping views of the city below. Continue along McGregor Rd, which turns into Gordon St and leads back to the city centre. Turn left at Goodenough St, with **St Andrew's Church (17)** on the corner. Follow Goodenough St and dogleg your way back to Victoria Pde for a well-earned Indo-Fijian curry at **Ashiyana (18**; p130).

Head back onto Carnarvon St to bypass the main drag. Stroll past the bars and clubs of this little back road and duck into the **Government Crafts Centre (19**; p132), a small outlet selling some of the finest crafts in Fiji. Continue walking north along Carnarvon St, crossing Gordon St to Murray St. At the corner of Murray and Pratt Sts is the 1902 **Roman Catholic Cathedral (20)**, built of sandstone imported from Sydney and one of Suva's most prominent landmarks. Turn left onto Pratt St, right onto Renwick Rd and left onto Pier St to end your journey at the **Fiji Visitor Bureau (21**; p125).

Sleeping
BUDGET

South Seas Private Hotel (☎ 331 2296; www.fiji 4less.com/south.htm; 6 Williamson Rd; dm/s/d/f shared bathroom F$19/35/46/54; s/d with bathroom F$58; ✗) The art deco sign out front sets the scene for this grand old dame of the Pacific. The sweeping interior veranda, classic white exterior, high ceilings and wide halls speak of the romance of a bygone era. This large colonial house and former girls-only hostel welcomes backpackers with the best dorms in walking distance of central Suva. The rooms are fan-cooled, simple and clean.

our pick Raintree Lodge (☎ 332 0113; www.raintreelodge.com; Princes Rd, Colo-i-Suva; dm F$25, d/tw shared bathroom F$65, bure F$165; ✗ 🖳 ⚏) Built around a rainforest-fringed lake that was once a rock quarry, this ecolodge is a popular stop on the Feejee Experience circuit. Three dormitories, a communal kitchen and double and twin room lodges can all be found tucked into this private pocket of forest. For those after a little more privacy there are five *bure* set in tranquil spots with plump beds, private decks and TV and DVD players (movies available). The lakeside bar and restaurant (mains F$15 to F$28) serves excellent food; the only drawback with staying here is the F$10, 11km taxi ride back to town. Fortunately, the Tacirua Transport bus to Sawani passes the Raintree Lodge (F$1.80, 30 minutes) half-hourly from Monday to Saturday.

Colonial Lodge (☎ 330 0655; www.coloniallodge.com .fj; 19 Anand St; dm incl breakfast F$30, s/d/tr shared bathroom, incl breakfast F$38/80/100; 🖳) Run by a friendly and boisterous family, this budget homestay is wrapped around a family home in a series of interconnected rooms and ad hoc additions. If you end up in one of the airless rooms with low ceilings you'll appreciate the homey lounge. Evening meals here cost F$12.

MIDRANGE

Studio 6 Apartments (☎ 330 7477; studio6@unwired .com.fj; 1-3 Walu St; s/d F$60/110; ✗ ⚏) The 105 motel rooms are starting to look shabby but are essentially clean and comfortable. There are six different room types (including many self-contained options) and it's seldom full, so ask to see a few before settling on one. The hillside location affords some terrific harbour views.

Nanette's Accommodation (☎ 331 6316; www .nanettes.com.fj; 56 Extension St; r incl breakfast F$89-125, apt incl breakfast F$150-175; ✗ 🖳 ⚏) This former residence is only a 10-minute walk to downtown Suva but set a world away in tranquil gardens. The four upstairs rooms of varying size share a communal TV lounge and kitchen, and all have bathrooms, some with enticingly large tubs. Downstairs are three homely apartments with their own spacious kitchens and bed-

rooms. The staff are so friendly you'll want to take them home with you.

Suva Motor Inn (☎ 331 3973; www.hexagonfiji.com; cnr Mitchell & Gorrie Sts; d F$117-183; ✗ ⚏) Fab for families, the Suva Motor Inn is a little humble with its title. The four-storey hotel (no lift) is shaped like a 'U' around a small pool into which snakes a waterslide. All rooms have balconies (the best with views to Albert Park) and the larger two-bedroom apartments sleep four and have kitchens. The rooms are large, but the TVs tiny – it's a solid midrange choice.

Five Princes Hotel (☎ 338 1575; www.fiveprinceshotel .com; 5 Princes Rd; d F$155, d self-contained F$185, villa F$300; 🖳 ✗ ⚏) The aged 1920s exterior belies the transformation that this one-time colonial villa has undergone on the inside. Solid teak furniture, polished timber floors, power showers, satellite television and broadband internet connections are all to be had in timelessly appointed rooms. The stand-alone cottages are similarly decorated but also include kitchenettes and private verandas.

There are many more midrange options to be found around Suva including:

Southern Cross Hotel (☎ 331 4233; southerncross1@ connect.com.fj; 63 Gordon St; r F$95-115; ✗ ⚏) Good value, modest rooms around courtyard pool.

Peninsula International Hotel (☎ 331 3711; www.peninsula.com.fj; cnr McGregor & Pender Sts; d/tr F$85/105; ✗ ✗ ⚏) Large hotel with snug rooms in a leafy residential area.

TOP END

Tanoa Plaza (☎ 331 2300; www.tanoahotels.com; cnr Gordon & Malcolm Sts; r F$159-178; ste F$323; ✗ ✗ 🖳 ⚏) The rooms are comfortable, functional and forgettable. It's sleek and sophisticated in that minibar, pamper products in the bathroom, kind of way. The views, though, are impressive and it's one of Suva's best.

Tradewinds Hotel (☎ 336 2450; www.tradewindssuva .com.fj; Queens Rd, Lami; d garden/ocean view F$210/236; ✗ ✗ ⚏) Now part of the Accor group, this one-time starlet was getting a long-overdue renovation at the time of research. Walk-in rates were 60% of the rack rates quoted above, but the unrefurbished rooms were fairly plain and devoid of personality. The great waterfront location and the views across Draunibota Bay require no improvement.

Holiday Inn (☎ 330 1600; reservations@holidayinn suva.com.fj; Victoria Pde; r F$290-590; ✗ ✗ 🖳 ⚏) Right on the harbour shore, opposite the government buildings and museum, the Holiday Inn has spacious, cool and comfortable rooms. The inn patently appeals to business travellers and those on coach tours, and it has the facilities to match.

Eating

For a compact city, Suva offers a relatively diverse array of eateries. Besides the restaurants listed here, you will find excellent hole-in-the-wall curry houses dotted all over town, late-night BBQ stands near Ratu Sukuna Park and a good selection of cheap eats in the shopping mall food courts.

WESTERN & FIJIAN

Old Mill Cottage (☎ 331 2134; 49 Carnarvon St; dishes F$5-12; hbreakfast & lunch, Mon-Sat) Officials and government aides from the nearby embassies cram the front veranda of this Suva institution to dabble in authentic Fijian fare. Exotic dishes including *palusami* (meat, onion and *lolo* – coconut milk – wrapped in *dalo* leaves and baked in a *lovo*) are displayed under the front counter alongside Indian curries and vegetarian dishes. The restaurant occupies two adjoining and somewhat dilapidated cottages. One serves breakfast, the other lunch.

our pick Bad Dog Cafe (☎ 330 4662; cnr Macarthur St & Victoria Pde; mains F$15-25; hbreakfast, lunch & dinner Mon-Sat, lunch & dinner Sun; ✕) This trendy drinking hole serves tasty bar snacks and crowd-pleasing mains. The cheery clink of wine glasses and the constant stream of food from the kitchen attest to its popularity. The Cajun chicken, Thai curries, squid rings and potato

wedges were all good, but it was the smoothies and pizza that made our toes curl.

Tiko's Floating Restaurant (☎ 331 3626; off Stinson Pde; mains F$25-40; ✟ lunch & dinner Mon-Fri, dinner Sat) The only way to be any more harbour-side would be to stand in the water. This permanently moored, former Blue Lagoon cruise ship, is best enjoyed when there's little motion in the ocean. The excellent surf-and-turf fare includes New Zealand steak, fresh local fish (*walu* and *pakapaka*) and an extensive wine list.

INDO-FIJIAN

Ashiyana (☎ 331 3000; Old Town Hall Bldg, Victoria Pde; mains F$8-16; ✟ lunch & dinner Tue-Sat, dinner Sun) This pint-sized restaurant is a longstanding Indian favourite with some of the best butter chicken in town and curries so spicy that even the taxi drivers consider them hot.

Maya Dhaba (☎ 331 0045; 281 Victoria Pde; F$8-17; ✟ lunch & dinner; ✕ ✕) Refined Maya Dhaba screens hip-gyrating, Bollywood musicals on flat-screen TVs in Suva's most urbane restaurant. The meals are excellent and you can wrap your naan around any number of Indian classics.

JAPANESE & CHINESE

Capital Palace (☎ 331 6088; 64 Victoria Pde; mains F$10; ✟ lunch & dinner; ✕) This place has become a Sunday *yum cha* institution, and the rather curt service does little to dampen the appetite of the happy diners. The menu offers plenty of Chinese classics and a few dishes straight out of *Fear Factor*. Try the stretched sea cucumber soup or the fish bones rice noodles soup.

MOVING TO THE BEAT OF A DIFFERENT DRUM

Dancers pay homage to the steady beat of the drums, seemingly oblivious to the spectators. The poorly lit room is crowded with both tourists and locals yelling '*Bula*' to one another over the din. As a big, indigenous Fijian man – who should be playing the chief in this scene – approaches with a flower behind his ear and a pitcher of beer on his tray, you don't need any reminding that this is no *meke*. This is Saturday night in Suva, when the country's urban youth let down their hair and pole-dance to pop music.

Fiji's urban youth face many of the same difficulties as young people around the globe: teenage parenthood, crime, drugs and skyrocketing unemployment (only one in eight school-leavers finds a job). However, these youths also find themselves straddling two opposing worlds – the traditional, conservative society of the villages many have left behind, where life was filled with cultural protocols, and the liberal, individualistic lifestyle of the modern and increasingly Westernised city.

The rising club and cafe culture is bringing together youths from indigenous and Indo-Fijian backgrounds, in the midst of a city filled with ethnic strife. Many face the near impossibility of surviving unemployment. Although it's not the Fiji of postcards, Fiji's rising urban youth culture is an intrinsic aspect of the country and an unexpected eye-opener.

Shanghai Seafood House (☎ 331 4865; 6 Thomson St; mains F$13-20; ☺ lunch & dinner Mon-Sun) In the heart of the shopping district, this first-floor restaurant is plush in a kitschy, fake-flower kind of way. The encyclopaedic menu and alfresco seating on the balcony induce long, lazy lunches.

Daikoku (☎ 330 8968; Victoria Pde; mains F$19-30; ☺ lunch & dinner Mon-Sat) Upstairs past the closet-sized bar, the acrobatic culinary skills of Daikoku's *teppanyaki* chefs are reason enough to spend an evening here. The seafood, chicken and beef seared on the sizzling *teppanyaki* plates compare with any Tokyo restaurant.

CAFES & QUICK EATS
Esquires Coffee House (☺ breakfast, lunch & dinner Mon-Sun; ✂ ✂) Dolphin Arcade (☎ 330 0333; Dolphin Arcade, Victoria Pde); Downtown (☎ 330 0828; Renwick Rd) Both outlets serve good coffee (F$3.50 to F$5.50) but only average cakes and sandwiches (F$3 to F$9). Based on the same fair trade and organic bean model as the New Zealand parent company, these cafes also offer free wi-fi access in air-conditioned comfort.

Roma's Hook and Chook (☎ 368 1071; Gordon St; meals $5-15; ☺ lunch & dinner) Traditional fish 'n chips and rotisserie chicken go upmarket in this take-away–cafe hybrid. The fish (from swordfish to parrot fish) comes with either regular or spicy batter or grilled, diced and threaded on skewers with veggies.

SELF-CATERING
Suva Municipal Market (Usher St) is the best place for fresh fish, fruit and vegetables. The best supermarket in town is Superfresh in the **MHCC Department Store** (Thomson St) where you can also pick up fresh bread and muffins from the bakery on the ground floor.

Drinking
Suva's drinking and dancing dens get happy and loaded on Friday and Saturday nights when Victoria Pde swarms with clubbers and bar hoppers. Happy hours last from 6pm to 8pm, and many clubs charge an entrance fee (no more than a few dollars) by 10pm. Dress standards aren't high but you won't be admitted wearing flip-flops and shorts. Watch out for pickpockets on the dance floor, and always take a taxi after dark.

If you're looking for something to wash down a picnic, try **Victoria Wines & Spirits** (☎ 331 2884; Victoria Pde; ☺ 11am-9pm Mon-Fri, till 2pm Sat).

ourpick O'Reilly's (☎ 331 2322; cnr Macarthur St & Victoria Pde) O'Reilly's kicks the evening off in relatively subdued fashion – relaxed punters playing pool or watching sport on the numerous TVs. But it brews quite a party as the hours tick by, and, come 11ish, the place is generally throbbing with a diverse crowd shaking their bits to Europop, soft metal, techno, peppy rock-pop…basically anything that keeps the crowd moving. It is one of the few pubs where a reasonably smart dress code prevails, so dig out your best threads. Aside from the name on the door and the token Guinness on tap, there is nothing particularly Irish about O'Reilly's other than it may have you seeing wee leprechauns by midnight.

Traps Bar (☎ 331 2922; Victoria Pde) Something of a subterranean saloon bar with a series of cave-like, dimly lit rooms. Take a seat in the pool room with wide-screen TV (yes, with sports) or join the happy din at the main bar. The crowd is generally young, trendy and dancing by 11pm. Live music is frequent (usually Thursdays), as are Bob Marley sing-alongs.

Bar 66 (☎ 330 8435; above Dolphin Arcade, Lotus St) This place is popular with jeans-clad uni students and one of the few places where both Fijians and Indo-Fijians socialise. The crowd is younger, the vibe cooler and everyone dances to the hip-hop, funk and rap skilfully mixed by the resident DJ.

JJ's on the Park (☎ 330 5005; Stinson Pde) This classy eatery also has a long bar, which is a nice place to sip a cocktail or glass of red. The atmosphere is refined and relaxed, and caters to an older crowd. There are views to the ship-studded harbour, service is attentive and a Fijian Belafonte often (Monday to Thursday) taps the ivory in the background.

Entertainment
Check out the entertainment section of the *Fiji Times* for upcoming events, cinema listings and what's on at nightclubs.

Village 6 Cinemas (☎ 330 6006; Scott St; admission adult/child F$5.50/4.50) Recently released Hollywood and Bollywood films battle it out at Suva's flashy cinema complex.

Fijians are fanatical about their rugby, and even if you aren't that keen on the game it's worth going to a match. The season lasts from April to September, and teams tough it out at the **National Stadium** (Laucala Bay Rd, Laucala). The atmosphere is huge. Ask at the

Fiji Visitors Bureau (p125) if there will be a match during your stay.

Shopping

There are a number of tourist-oriented shops along Victoria Pde and in the downtown shopping malls. They mostly stock mass-produced souvenirs so you have a better chance of finding something more distinctive at one of the local markets.

Government Crafts Centre (☎ 331 5869; Macarthur St) Although it's more expensive than elsewhere, this craft shop sells high-quality work by local artisans, and most money spent here goes directly to the rural artisans.

Suva Curio & Handicraft Centre (Stinson Pde) The endless stalls are thick with throwing clubs, masks, cannibal forks, *tanoa* bowls and *masi* (tapa cloth). If you know your stuff it is possible to get some excellent buys here, although you will have to bargain well to do so.

Suva Flea Market (Rodwell Rd) Less touristy than the handicraft market above, this is another great place to buy *masi* (tapa cloth) and traditional crafts. There is also a second-hand bookstall near the back that is worth checking out.

Getting There & Away

Suva is well connected to the rest of the country by air and inter-island ferries. These are detailed in the Getting Around section on p171.

Frequent local buses operate along Queens Rd and Kings Rd from Suva's **main bus station** (Rodwell Rd), although it's worth waiting for a **Sunbeam Transport** (☎ 382 122) or **Pacific Transport** (☎ 330 4366) express bus if you are going some distance. Sample adult fares include: Pacific Harbour (F$3.60), Korolevu (F$6.70), Sigatoka (F$8.50), Nadi (F$9.35) and Lautoka (F$14.20). The Coral Sun bus leaves the Holiday Inn at 7.30am and 3.50pm, calling at the major Coral Coast resorts as it travels to Nadi International Airport.

Nausori International Airport is 23km northeast of central Suva. Nausori Taxi & Bus Service (☎ 331 2185) has regular shuttle buses between the airport and the Holiday Inn hotel in Suva (F$10). Otherwise, a taxi from the airport to/from Suva costs a standard F$27

Getting Around

It is easy to get around central Suva on foot. Taxis are quite cheap for short trips and they actually use their meter.

VITI LEVU'S KINGS ROAD

While the Kings Rd may lack the coastal scenery of the faster and more popular Queens Rd, it makes amends with ribboning, highland ascents, gorgeous views over the Wainibuka River and, from Viti Levu Bay, a coast-skirting run to Lautoka past rugged cliffs and sugar cane fields. The price to be paid for this relatively untrammelled scenery is in the form

---

DINING ON THE DEAD

Fijians began feasting upon one another as far back as 2500 years ago. In traditional Fijian society dining on the enemy was considered the ultimate revenge, as a disrespectful death was a lasting insult to the enemy's family and the departed spirit. When missionaries brought cannibalism to a halt in the late 19th century, it had become a ritualised part of everyday life. Bodies were either consumed on the battlefield or brought back to the village spirit house, where they were butchered, baked and eaten on the local war god's behalf. In celebration of the event, men performed the *cibi* (death dance) and women the *dele* – a dance in which they sexually humiliated corpses. Captives were often forced to watch their own body parts being consumed or even to eat some themselves!

For cannibalistic feasts, men fed themselves with special long-pronged wooden forks. Considered sacred relics, these forks were kept in the spirit house away from women or children. Mementos were kept of the victims to prolong the victor's sense of vengeance. Necklaces, hairpins or earlobe ornaments were made from human bones and skulls were sometimes made into *tanoa* (kava drinking bowls). Flesh was smoked and preserved for snacks, and war clubs were inlaid with teeth. Viti Levu Highlanders placed the bones of victims in tree branches as trophies and rows of stones were used to tally the number of bodies eaten by the chief.

Early European visitors and settlers were understandably obsessed with cannibalism. Those who managed to keep their wits and limbs about them recorded gruesome, fascinating stories.

of a slow trip on a bumpy road. In the wet season a 4WD is recommended, particularly on the unsealed portion between Korovou and Dama, but buses ply this route no matter what the road's condition. Another road follows the coast to Natovi Landing (about a 20-minute drive), from where there are bus and ferry services to Labasa on Vanua Levu via Nabouwalu and Levuka on Ovalau (p172 and Levuka on Ovalau (p172).

Nausori
pop 25,000
On the eastern bank of the Rewa River, Nausori is a bustling service centre for the area's agricultural and industry workers. Its only draw for travellers is its airport – the country's second largest. The airport, about 3km southeast of Nausori, is a hub for Air Fiji and Sun Air domestic flights.

Vaileka, Rakiraki & Ellington Wharf
Northwest from Korovou, the road slides alongside Wainibuka River, past small villages, towards Viti Levu Bay. As you approach Rakiraki, keep an eye on the skyline; the imposing Nakauvadra Range is believed to be the home of the great snake-god Degei, creator of all the islands.

West of Rakiraki junction, there is a turn-off that leads past the sugar mill to the small service town of **Vaileka**. This is where buses arrive and depart from, and it's a good place to stock up on provisions before heading offshore. Town amenities include a supermarket, taxi rank, internet, produce market, Westpac and ANZ banks (both with ATM machines) and several greasy fast-food restaurants.

Heading out of Rakiraki towards Nadi, look out for **Udreudre's Tomb**, the resting place of Fiji's most notorious cannibal whose personal tally reached at least 872 corpses. It's about 100m west of the Vaileka turn-off, on the left and resembles a rectangular slab of concrete.

The turn-off to **Ellington Wharf** is about 5km east of Rakiraki junction, and it is here that resorts collect their guests for the short boat ride across to Nananu-i-Ra.

ACTIVITIES
The reefs of Rakiraki offer some excellent **scuba diving** with dense marine life and beautiful coral gardens. Dream Maker ranks as one of the best in the area with its bright mosaic

of sea fans and gorgonians. Both resorts have onsite dive shops and knowledgeable staff.

SLEEPING & EATING
Volivoli Beach (☎ 669 4511; www.volivoli.com; Volivoli Rd; dm/d shared bathroom F$26/105 villas F$336; ☜) Located on the northernmost point of Viti Levu, the 8-person dorms share a huge deck and come with two bathrooms apiece. Further up the hill is another lodge divided into four doubles that share a communal lounge and a wide hall that doubles as a kitchen. Far removed from the noisy backpackers and on the opposite side of the restaurant and bar (mains F$10 to F$18) are 13 self-contained, two-bedroom villas with sweeping ocean views and modern, crisp interiors. If you are disappointed by the mangrove-lined beach you'll be pleasantly surprised by the picturesque sand spit only a minute's walk around the corner.

Wananavu Beach Resort (☎ 669 4433; www.wananavu.com; garden/ocean/beachfront bure incl breakfast F$200/270/350-380, f incl breakfast F$450; ☒ ☜) The restaurant (mains F$32 to F$39) here has gorgeous views over the beautiful pool area and out to Nananu-i-Ra island. All the *bure* have timber floors, panelled walls, air-con and their own small decks surrounded by bougainvillea-filled gardens. The beach here is entirely artificial and, although the landscapers have done an excellent job with strategically placed palm trees, most guests end up swimming in the pool.

GETTING THERE & AWAY
Sunbeam has regular express buses along the Kings Rd from Suva (F$10.60, 4½ hours) and Nadi (F$9.50, 2¼ hours) that stop at Vaileka and the turn-off to Ellington Wharf. To avoid lugging groceries and gear 1.3km to the wharf, get off at Vaileka and catch a taxi (F$15) to the jetty.

Nananu-i-Ra
area 3.5 sq km
Tiny and perfectly formed, Nananu-i-Ra is only a hop and a skip from the mainland but quite different in character. There are no roads or villages, most residents are of European descent and cattle grazing has cleared much of the island's dense vegetation. The wide beaches and scalloped bays support a small enclave of wealthy holiday homes and basic backpacker cottages. Those who walk the grassy hills are rewarded with fine views

FIJI

across the water to the volcanic Nakauvadra mountain range on the mainland.

ACTIVITIES

Papoo Divers (☎ 944 4726; papoodivers@mobileemail .vodafone.com.fj) is the only dive shop based at Nananu-i-Ra, and the dive instructor has 19 years experience in these waters. They charge F$150 for a two-tank dive including equipment and F$500 for an open-water course.

The island's exposure to the southeast trade winds make it ideal for **windsurfing** and kitesurfing, especially from May to July when the winds are generally 10 knots or more. **Safari Island Lodge** (☎ 669 3333, 669 3700; www.safarilodge .com.fj) is the only place that has kite-boarding and windsurfing gear for hire (beginner/advanced equipment F$350/500 per week) and an experienced instructor.

SLEEPING & EATING

As there is no electricity on the island, power is available only in the early evenings when the generator is turned on. Most accommodation is fairly basic, there's no bank and some budget places do not accept credit cards so bring enough cash for the duration of your stay. Both Betham's and McDonald's Beach Cottages have outdoor cafes with limited menus and small stores selling the basics.

McDonald's Beach Cottages (☎ 628 3118; www .macsnananu.com; dm/tw F$27, tw/fm cottage F$89/131) McDonald's offers a scattering of super-tidy cabins on a nicely landscaped property right in front of the jetty. The cute blue and yellow cottages are self-contained, and it's popular with do-it-yourself types. The outdoor restaurant serves great pizza (F$17), which is probably the best food on the island (although it is a very small island).

Betham's Beach Cottages (☎ 669 4132; www .bethams.com.fj; dm/tw F$20/110 cottage F$130) These self-contained cottages are like upmarket caravan cabins. Each is fully furnished, and the spacious eight-bed dorm has its own kitchen, bathroom and veranda. The open-air restaurant (mains F$17 to 23) here serves hearty meals if you place your order by 1pm.

ourpick Bulavou Beach Bungalows (☎ 669 3755; www.bulavoubeachbungalowsfiji.com dm/d/tr/q F$30/150/150/150) This is by far the nicest accommodation on the island and, as it is no dearer than elsewhere, it's the logical place to stay. There are three newly constructed, double-storey chalets with a unit on each floor.

Each unit has two rooms furnished with a queen-sized bed, a set of bunks and two single beds. The units are let on a per-bed or per-room rate. Meal packages are available (F$55, breakfast and dinner).

GETTING THERE & AWAY

Nananu-i-Ra is a 15-minute boat ride from Ellington Wharf, and each resort runs its own transfers (around F$30 to F$40 per person return). Arrange your pick-up in advance.

Koroyanitu National Heritage Park

An hour's drive from Lautoka and deep within Viti Levu's interior, the Koroyanitu National Heritage Park is a world away from the Mamanucas and Yasawas (although both island chains are visible from the summit of Castle Rock). The area has beautiful nature walks through native Dakua forests and grasslands, birdwatching, archaeological sites, waterfalls and swimming. Contact the **Abaca Visitor Centre** (☎ 666 6644, after the beep dial 1234; admission F$8) for more information. Abaca (pronounced am-barth-a) village is at the base of **Mt Koroyanitu** (Mt Evans).

ACTIVITIES
Hiking
From Nase Lodge, a marked track leads its way up to **Castle Rock** and its impressive views. It takes about three hours (one way) up some steep inclines, so wear something grippy.

Mount Batilamu Trek (☎ 664 5747, 927 3592; fax 664 5547) organises 2½-day tours up the Sabeto Valley, including village visits and transfers from Nadi/Lautoka hotels for F$430. Scaled-down versions include an overnight trek to Mount Batilamu ($250 person) and a day trek to the summit ($150).

SLEEPING & EATING
Experience highland village culture with a **village stay** (per night incl meals F$45), which can be arranged through the Abaca Visitor Centre.

Nase Lodge (dm F$35) This old colonial lodge, about 400m uphill from the village, has 12 bunk beds and cooking facilities but neither electricity nor showers (wash in the river). The ladies in the village will cook meals on request but you should fortify these with your own supplies.

GETTING THERE & AWAY
There are currently no buses to Abaca, but if you contact the Abaca Visitor Centre, they

can advise if the local carrier has resumed running. Alternatively, they can arrange a car to collect you from Nadi (F$100 each way). A cheaper option would be to rent a car and drive yourself. If driving, turn inland off Queens Rd at Tavakubu Rd, then right at Abaca Rd. It's a further 10km of gravel road up to Abaca (4WD only).

Nausori Highlands
The grassy slopes of the Nausori Highlands snake their way into the mountainous interior, leaving the coastline and panoramic views in their wake. This region is one of the best places to experience traditional Fijian culture and hospitality and, although the region shares the same name as the airport town of Nausori near Suva, its small villages and scattered settlements are quite different. See p102 for guidelines on village etiquette.

SIGHTS
Navala
pop 800
On the banks of the Ba River, Navala is by far Fiji's most picturesque village. The houses here are all traditional *bure*, built with local materials using time-honoured techniques. Navala is a photographer's delight, but you need to get permission and pay the F$15 entrance fee before wandering around. If arriving independently, ask the first person you meet to take you to the *turaga-ni-koro* (the chief appointed headman who collects the entrance fee). A traditional *sevusevu* is not required, although all other village etiquette rules outlined on p102 apply.

SLEEPING & EATING
our pick **Bulou's Eco Lodge** (☎ 628 1224, 666 6644, after the beeps dial 2116; dm incl meals $65, bure per person incl meals $75) On the river's edge a kilometre south of Navala, retired couple Seresio and Bulou N Talili and their son Tui have established a grassroots ecolodge. There is a traditional *bure* in the garden and a 10-bed dorm attached to the house with cold-water showers and flush toilets but no electricity. Tui is an excellent guide and he accompanies guests around the village introducing them to his relatives and friends. His mother is an excellent cook and takes her responsibility of keeping guests well fed seriously.

GETTING THERE & AWAY
The local buses from Ba to Navala (F$2.60) leave Ba bus station at 12.30pm and 5.15pm Monday to Friday and at noon, 4.30pm and 5.15pm on Saturday. Buses return to Ba at 6am, 7.30am and 1.45pm Monday to Saturday. Ring Bulou's Lodge in advance and they will pick you up from Navala.

If driving from Ba, there are a couple of turns to watch out for: at the police post turn left, passing a shop on your right, and at the next fork in the road keep left. The road is rough and rocky, but usually passable.

MAMANUCA GROUP
Reliably sunny and basking in a lagoon cradled by the Malolo Barrier Reef, these 20 or so islands need little introduction. Their white-sand beaches and crystalline seas are trumpeted far and wide by the Fiji Visitors Bureau and have provided cinematic backdrops to such films as Tom Hanks' *Castaway* and the TV reality series, *Survivor.* Although they make little contribution to the national culture, the Mamanuca Group is a tourist magnet. Whether you prefer to spend your days poolside getting intimate with a Fiji Bitter or making the most of the world-class, snorkelling, diving and surfing, you'll find it all here.

Transport
GETTING THERE & AWAY
Thanks to their proximity to both Port Denarau and Nadi airport, the Mamanuca islands are easily reached by catamaran, speedboat, plane or helicopter. Most people arrive on one of the three high-speed catamarans departing from Port Denarau, and tickets include courtesy pick-up from hotels in the Nadi region. Prices are for one-way adult fares. Children aged five to 15 are half-price.

Awesome Adventures (☎ 675 0499; www.awesome fiji.com) The *Yasawa Flyer* calls at South Sea Island (F$68), Bounty (F$60), Beachcomber (F$68) and Vomo (F$135) on its way north to the Yasawas.

Malolo Cat I & II (☎ 672 2444, 672 2488, 675 0205) Fast catamarans to Malololailai (Musket Cove and Plantation Island Resorts) three times daily.

South Sea Cruises (☎ 675 0500; www.ssc.com.fj) Six daily catamaran transfers to: South Sea Island (F$50), Bounty Island (F$60), Beachcomber Island (F$68),

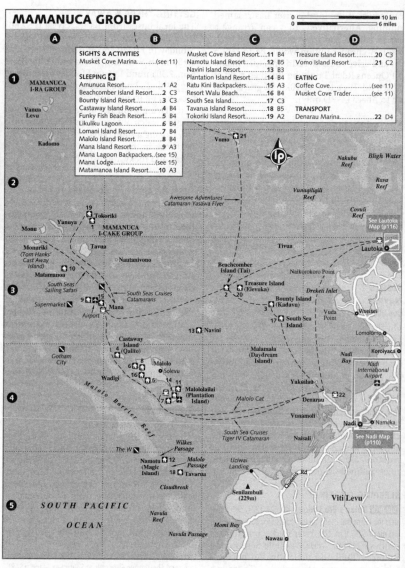

MAMANUCA GROUP

SIGHTS & ACTIVITIES	Musket Cove Island Resort....**11** B4	Treasure Island Resort.............**20** C3
Musket Cove Marina..........(see 11)	Namotu Island Resort..........**12** B5	Vomo Island Resort................**21** C2
	Navini Island Resort.............**13** B3	
SLEEPING	Plantation Island Resort........**14** B4	**EATING**
Amunuca Resort.....................**1** A2	Ratu Kini Backpackers...........**15** A3	Coffee Cove.......................(see 11)
Beachcomber Island Resort....**2** C3	Resort Walu Beach................**16** B4	Musket Cove Trader...........(see 11)
Bounty Island Resort.............**3** C3	South Sea Island..................**17** C3	
Castaway Island Resort..........**4** B4	Tavarua Island Resort...........**18** B5	**TRANSPORT**
Funky Fish Beach Resort.........**5** B4	Tokoriki Island Resort...........**19** A2	Denarau Marina..................**22** D4
Likuliku Lagoon....................**6** B4		
Lomani Island Resort.............**7** B4		
Malolo Island Resort.............**8** B4		
Mana Island Resort...............**9** A3		
Mana Lagoon Backpackers..(see 15)		
Mana Lodge........................(see 15)		
Matamanoa Island Resort......**10** A3		

Treasure Island (F$68), Mana (F$83), Matamanoa (F$105), Castaway Island (F$78), Malolo (F$78) and Tokoriki ($105).

Prices for quick, scenic flights are comparable to catamaran prices. **Pacific Sun** (☎ 330 4388; www.pacificsun.com.fj) has daily flights from Nadi to Mana (adult/child F$88/58 one way) and Malololailai (adult/child F$71/40).

Activities

DIVING

Mamanuca **diving** sites teem with fantastically gaudy fish circling impossibly psychedelic corals. The visibility here astounds first-time divers and you can see forever – well, 30m to 40m for much of the year. The companies listed below are the big fish in the diving pond, with multiple dive shops on multiple islands (Castaway and Plantation Island Resorts operate their own dive shops for similar prices).

Aqua-Trek (Vitu Water Sports ☎ 670 2413; www.viti watersports.com), is based at Mana Island Resort and Matamanoa Island Resort. A two-tank dive costs F$215 and a PADI Open Water Course costs F$780.

Reef Safari (☎ 675 0566; www.reefsafari.com.fj) has dive shops at South Sea Island, Bounty Island and Amunuca Island Resort. A two-tank dive/PADI Open Water Course costs F$200/575.

Subsurface Fiji (☎ 666 6738; www.subsurfacefiji.com) runs the dive shops at Beachcomber, Malolo, Musket Cove and Treasure Island. It also offers diving with free pick-ups for guests at Namotu, Navini, Tavarua, Resort Walu Beach, Funky Fish and Likuliku. A two-tank dive costs F$230 and a PADI Open Water Course is F$740.

SURFING

The reefs off the southern Mamanuca islands have some of the world's most formidable breaks, but currently two American-owned resorts, Tavarua Island Resort and Namotu Island Resort (see p141), lease these rights and only their guests get unrestricted access to legendary lefthanders **Cloudbreak** and **Restaurants** off Tavarua, and **Namotu Left** and **Swimming Pools** off Namotu. Others must put their name down, wax their board with uncertainty and pray they'll be allocated one of the 17 Saturday change-over spots.

The resorts on Malololailai and Malolo are good bases for surfers wishing to surf **Wilkes Passage's** fast right. Locals **Suju Tukutuku** (☎ 973 5885; sujisurf@yahoo.co.uk), **Jacob** (also known as Scobie) or **Small John** (☎ 930 2262) all make livings transferring thrill seekers to the breaks for F$40 per person.

Tours

Day cruises to the Mamanucas from Nadi are exceedingly popular and generally include transfers from Nadi hotels, lunch, nonmotorised water activities and as much sunburn as you can handle.

Captain Cook Cruises (Sailing Adventures Fiji; ☎ 670 1823; www.captaincook.com.au) offer a day cruise to Tivua, a tiny coral island, for F$139/70 per adult/child, a dinner cruise for F$99/50 per adult/child, and three-day, two-night cruise/camping trips to the Mamanucas and southern Yasawas.

Sail Adventures Fiji (☎ 623 2001; www.sailing adventuresfiji.com) target backpackers with a three-day sailing cruise to the Yasawas (F$415) on their 15m-long yacht, *Pelorus Jack*. Accommodation is in dormitory-style bunks.

Sunsail Fiji (☎ 670 5192; www.malamalaisland.com; Main St, Nadi) offer three cruises daily (half day/full day, adult F$89/99, children 4-14 half price) to Malamala, a small, uninhabited island.

Seaspray (☎ 675 0500; www.ssc.com.fj) Travel is by catamaran to Mana where the two-masted schooner *Seaspray* motors (the sails are seldom unfurled) to Monuriki.

South Sea Cruises (☎ 675 0500; www.ssc.com.fj) Apart from the catamaran transfers these boats are used to ferry day-trippers from Port Denarau to various islands. Prices per child/adult are: South Sea Island (F$59/110), Beachcomber (F$50/99), Mana Island Resort (F$70/130), Castaway Island (F$99/140), Treasure Island (F$70/130), Bounty (F$70/125), Malolo Island Resort (F$70/135), Amunuca (F$95/135). Half-day options are also available.

SOUTH SEA ISLAND

South Sea Island is the smallest of the island resorts and little more than a bump of sand with some trees on top. You can circumnavigate the whole island in three minutes, two if you hurry.

Many backpackers spend a night at **South Sea Island** (☎ 675 0500; www.ssc.com.fj/South_Sea_Island .aspx; dm F$89; 🏊) on their way to or from the Yasawas. The only accommodation is in the 32-bed dorm (which could do with a decent cleaning) above a communal lounge.

BOUNTY ISLAND
area 0.02 sq km

Twenty-hectare Bounty (Kadavu) is bigger than its immediate neighbours but still takes only 20 minutes to walk around or, if you don't stop to tease clown fish, 1½ hours to snorkel. The white-sand beach attracts both endangered hawksbill turtles and the all-too-common day-tripper (see South Sea Cruises on above for tour prices).

Bounty Island Resort (☎ 628 3387; www.fiji -bounty.com; dm incl meals F$85-90, d bure incl meals F$276; ❌ 🏊) is a notch above South Sea Island in terms of quality and a few decibels quieter than Beachcomber. The 12 *bure* with tiled floors, air-conditioning and attached bathrooms are fairly basic by Mamanuca standards but those returning from the Yasawas will appreciate the hot showers, fridges and round-the-clock electricity. The dorms are situated in a large, partitioned building located out the back.

BEACHCOMBER ISLAND
area 0.2 sq km

Tiny Beachcomber (Tai) has the reputation of being *the* Pacific party island, and tales of drunken debauchery are told far and wide. The truth? In recent years some of the shine has rubbed off Beachcomber's disco ball. None the less, the huge bar, live music and activities involving the inappropriate use of alcohol mean that this island isn't about to put away its boogie shoes anytime soon.

Beachcomber Island Resort (☎ 666 1500; www .beachcomberfiji.com; dm incl meals F$101, r s/d incl meals F$231/309, bure d incl meals F$400-446; ⊠ ☐ ☑) Accommodation options include rooms in a lodge, some clean but basic beach huts and a double-storey *bure* that sleeps 120. This may sound like dormitory hell but it is actually quite nice. The food at Beachcomber is excellent, particularly the buffet breakfasts, which are far better than you'll find elsewhere at comparable backpackers.

TREASURE ISLAND
area 0.06 sq km

Treasure Island (Elevuka) is another tiny island that takes mere minutes to walk around and is no more than a flyspeck on most maps. It's covered in tropical gardens and ringed by a white-sand beach.

Treasure Island Resort (☎ 666 6999; www.fiji-treasure .com; bure/duplex F$450/890; ⊠ ☐ ☑) caters for families. The new pool has plenty of sloping 'beaches' for toddlers, and the turtle-feeding and mini-putt course are ideal for older kids. It has 66 comfortable but tired air-conditioned units housed in 34 duplex *bure* with roofs that resemble witches' hats. Standards at Treasure have been slipping, and the quality of food and overall cleanliness has fallen below that of other Mamaunca resorts. Optional meal packages cost F$77/94 for two/three meals daily (half-price for kids under 12).

VOMO

This wedge-shaped 90-hectare island rises to a magnificent high ridge and has two lovely beaches (one or the other will be sheltered if it is windy) and some of the best snorkelling in the group.

Vomo Island Resort (☎ 666 7955; www.vomofiji.com; villa from F$1300; ⊠ ☐ ☑) The *bure* here feature stylish Pacificana touches, indigenous wooden floors and separate living areas. If money is no object, then the new 'private residence' has four bedrooms (all with private living areas) in three separate pavilions framing a private pool. Rates include divine meals – all of which are three-course – daily snorkelling trips, access to the 9-hole, 'pitch 'n put' golf course and nonmotorised water sports. Vomo is the only five-star resort to accept children.

NAVINI
area 0.25 sq km

Surrounded by a beautiful beach and a fringed by a reef, teeny Navini was once used for chiefly meetings until the landowners decided to lease it.

There are only 10 *bure* at the exquisite **Navini Island Resort** (☎ 666 2188; www.navinifiji.com.fj; bure F$545-695; ☐), all within 10m of the beach. The standard *bure* have two rooms, and the larger 'premier' *bure* (sleeping three) have verandas at either end. The honeymoon *bure* have a courtyard tiled with pebbles and a private spa. A three-meal plan of fresh and fabulous food costs F$98 and, as there are more staff than guests, the service can't be faulted.

Return transfers by resort speedboat (adult/child/family F$198/99/594) allows you to maximise your time on the island no matter what your flight schedule.

MALOLOLAILAI
area 2.4 sq km

Tranquil Malololailai is the second largest island of the Mamanuca Group and encompasses three resorts, a marina and an airstrip. The lagoon offers protected anchorage for yachties but the beach is extremely tidal and not ideal for swimmers.

MUSKET COVE MARINA
Musket Cove Marina (☎ 666 2215 ext 1279; VHF channel 68; mcyc@musketcovefiji.com) facilities include 26 moorings (F$15 per day), 25 marina berths (F$2 per metre, per day), dockside fuel and water, postal services, laundry, rubbish disposal, hot showers, book swap, noticeboard and limited repair services.

In September each year, the Musket Cove Yacht Club hosts **Fiji Regatta Week** and the Musket Cove to Port Vila yacht race. Traditional nautical sports such as wet T-shirt, hairy-chest and beer-drinking contests also feature in the programme. The **Musket Cove Trader** (General Store; ☎ 666 2215; ☷ 8am-7pm) is probably the best-stocked shop in the Mamanucas (but don't expect mainland prices) and runs a small cafe overlooking the marina called the **Coffee Cove** (lunch F$12.50; ⏰ 10am-6.30pm).

Sleeping & Eating

Musket Cove Island Resort (☎ 666 2215; www.musket covefiji.com; r F$275; d garden/lagoon/beachfront bure F$505/505/617, q villa F$758; 🖥 🍸) Musket Cove offers several types of accommodation, from hotel rooms to self-catering thatched *bure*. The newer Armstrong Island villas – clustered on an artificial island – have over-water verandas and a private pool.

Named after the owner, Dick's Place (mains F$26 to $37) often hosts theme nights including the popular 'pig-on-a-spit' (although this isn't so popular with the pig). The casual Ratu Nemani Island Bar is linked to the resort by a walkway and is the place for do-it-yourself barbeques, cold beers and salty banter with visiting yachties.

Plantation Island Resort (☎ 666 9333; www .plantationisland.com; d garden/beachfront F$281/413, studio/2-bedroom/beachfront bure F$413/522/606; 🌴 🖥 🍸) There are kids spilling out everywhere here; they're in the sea, in the pool, painting T-shirts, climbing plaster cows, egg-and-spoon racing, watching TV and eating chips in the free Club Coconut. Like Mana Island Resort, this place is huge (850 people can stay here) and has a slight holiday camp feel about it – you may have to line up for your buffet or set meal (adult/child full meal packages are F$68/40). The rooms come in a dizzying array of options. For starters there are hotel-style rooms that are either bright and cheerful or dated and passé depending on your fashion sense. Another option is the two-bedroom garden *bure* featuring twin beds in the front, a big lounge area and a master bedroom out the back.

Lomani Island Resort (☎ 666 8212; www.lomani island.com; r incl breakfast F$630, ste incl breakfast F$690; 🌴 🍸) Lomani is David to the Goliath next door. This small, adult-only resort has a huge pool, a classy colonial-style bar and a decent outdoor restaurant (meal plans F$80 per person). The blocks of rooms have a Mediterranean feel to them due to their stucco walls and arched doorways.

Getting There & Away

The *Malolo Cat* catamaran operates transfers from Denarau, and Sun Air has a shuttle service from Nadi. See p135 for details.

MALOLO

The daddy of the Mamanuca Group has two villages, four resorts, mangroves and coastal forest. The island's highest point, **Uluisolo** (218m), offers panoramic views of the Mamanucas and southern Yasawas.

Funky Fish Beach Resort (☎ 651 3180; www.funky fishresort.com; dm/d F$30/80, 1-bedroom bure F$120, 2-bedroom bure F$240; 🖥 🍸) Funky Fish is popular with surfers and is run by former rugby Fiji Coach and All Black, affable Brad Johnston. The excellent dorms here are modern, spotlessly clean and partitioned into groups of four. The 'rock lobster' *bure* are small with thatched roofs and outdoor showers, while the larger, beachside 'grand grouper' *bure* can accommodate four. Tasty meals (2/3 meal packages F$50/60) are served in an impressive hillside *bure* that enjoys panoramic views over the extremely tidal beach.

Resort Walu Beach (☎ 665 1777; www.walubeach .com; dm/s/d incl meals F$95 per person, bure incl meals F$140 per person; 🌴 🖥 🍸) Walu Beach was built for the cancelled Australian TV show, *The Resort*. While the owners figure out its future, Walu Beach is offering some fantastic deals. You get all the facilities of a three-star resort for only slightly more than backpacker rates. The resort's main restaurant–bar has Sky TV, and the included meal package features three-course evening meals.

Malolo Island Resort (☎ 672 0978; www.malolo island.com; oceanview/beachfront/f bure F$595/695/1120; nais) Malolo describes itself as having 'plantation style duplex accommodation reminiscent of the colonial era', which is a fairly accurate description of the 49 *bure* with their '90s bright blue detailing. If the rooms are slightly tired, the families who stay here don't seem to care and there is no faulting the white-sand beach or lush tropical gardens. There are three restaurants (mains F$25 to F$40), a day spa, an adults-only lounge, walking trails and dive shop. Optional meal packages cost adult/child F$85/42.50 per day.

Likuliku Lagoon (☎ 672 4275; www.likulikulagoon .com; garden/beachfront/deluxe beachfront/overwater bure F$1250/1500/1700/2100; 🌴 🌴 🖥 🍸) For couples with the cash to splash, the intimacy and privacy to be had here extend almost scrurilously far beyond a do-not-disturb sign on the door. The top-of-the-line over-the-water *bure* are the only ones of this kind in Fiji, and even Likuliku's second-tier accommodation boasts private plunge pools, thatched lounging

FIJI

pavilions, his and hers closets and inside and outside showers. As you would expect in this five-star-plus category, a gourmet chef prepares the food (the tiny canapés are ambrosial).

CASTAWAY ISLAND
area 0.7 sq km
Reef-fringed, 70-hectare Castaway Island is 27km west of Denarau island and just short of paradise.

OUR PICK **Castaway Island Resort** (☎ 666 1233; www.castawayfiji.com; island/oceanview/beach/f bure F$625/735/845/1690; 🖥 😮 🍸) The oldest and still one of the best family destinations. The 66 spacious *bure* have two rooms to accommodate those with children (kids stay free), small verandas and intricate *masi* ceilings. The rooms were last renovated in 2006, which accounts for their simple but stylish interiors. There's a swimming-pool bar, an open-air pizza shack and a great dining terrace overlooking the ocean where dinner costs F$30 to F$40. Alternatively pay F$105/53 adult/child per day for the unrestricted meal plan once you arrive. The excellent kids' club will take three- to 12-year-olds off your hands so that you can make use of the well-maintained and complimentary nonmotorised water sports.

MANA
Beautiful Mana has a good selection of beaches and a peppering of hills with spectacular views. Upmarket Mana Island Resort stretches for over 80 hectares between the north and south beaches while the three budget resorts are sewn into the folds of the island's only village. For an interesting snorkelling experience, check out the south beach pier where the fish go into a frenzy under the night lights.

Sleeping & Eating
A manned guard post and a high fence separate the three backpacker resorts from the Mana Island Resort and, like a mini Berlin Wall, divide the wealthy west from the ragged poor in the east. It was erected during a period of aggressive competition between the resorts but, although the boundary still stands, the mood has long since improved.

Ratu Kini Backpackers (☎ 672 1959; www.ratukini .com; dm incl meals F$53-65, d incl meals F$153-176; 🖥) No-fuss, no-frills dorms sharing cold water showers. The doubles are in a long block that's almost indistinguishable from the village. Ask

to see the 'deluxe' rooms, which are even further back from the water but considerably smarter. The lively bar here is the centre of backpacker nightlife, since (a) it overlooks the beach and (b) there is a TV.

Mana Island Resort (☎ 665 0423, 666 1455; www .manafiji.com; island/oceanfront/beachfront bure incl breakfast F$317/587/823, r incl breakfast F$470, ste incl breakfast $764; 😮 😮 🖥 🍸) One of the oldest and largest island resorts in Fiji, the 82 hotel rooms and 70 *bure* span the low-lying ground between the north and south beaches. Despite its size, it's not as impersonal as you might imagine, and the Fijian and Japanese staff are genuinely friendly. The rooms come in a variety of configurations and are constantly being refurbished. In 2008, the 'island' *bure*, had their turn and are currently good value. Even nicer are the 'ocean front' *bure* which were designed with couples in mind. There are also some hotel-like suites with a bedroom on a mezzanine floor.

There are three mediocre restaurants (buffets cost adult/child $34/free; meal plans available) and three bars, a circular pool, a horizon pool, a brand-new day spa, tennis courts and a great kids' club for three- to 12-year-olds.

Other budget options include:

Mana Lodge (☎ 620 7030, 921 4368; dm incl meals F$60, d incl meals F$150-180).

Mana Lagoon Backpackers (☎ 929 2337; dm/d incl meals F$55/130, tr/q shared bathroom, incl meals F$155/200)

Getting There & Away
Guests of Mana Lagoon Backpackers and Ratu Kini can use the resort's own *Mana Flyer* transfer boat (F$120 return). Mana is serviced by South Sea Cruises catamarans and airline Pacific Sun. See p135 for details.

MATAMANOA
Covered in dense vegetation, dotted with coconut palms and surrounded by white-sand beaches, Matamanoa is a secluded and hilly island just north of Mana.

The adults only **Matamanoa Island Resort** (☎ 672 3620; www.matamanoa.com; d unit/bure incl breakfast $386/622; 😮 🖥 🍸) has 20 *bure* overlooking a lovely, white-sand beach. All *bure* have a veranda and beach views (half facing sunrise, half sunset). There are also 14 good-value, but not nearly as nice, air-conditioned hotel-style units with garden views. Daily meal plans cost F$81.

MONURIKI

Tiny uninhabited Monuriki (and ironically not Castaway Island) featured in the 2001 Tom Hanks movie *Cast Away,* and every resort worth its cabanas and cocktails sells day trips to what is increasingly referred to as the **Tom Hanks Island**. The trips cost around F$40 to $70 depending on how far the boat has to travel to get there and what kind of lunch, if any, is included.

TOKORIKI

The small, hilly island of Tokoriki has a beautiful, fine white-sand beach facing west to the sunset and is the northernmost island in the Mamanuca group.

Amunuca Resort (☎ 664 0642; www.amunuca.com; bure rainforest/island/garden/beachfront F$252/381/487/605 fm F$487, ste $663; ✗ ☐ ☎) Dark timber floors, fashionably worn leather couches and a series of blindingly white pavilions overlook a co-balt sea. This newbie opened in 2007 and the architects have done a wonderful job splicing the white-washed, Greek island–like buildings with traditional thatched Fijian-style roofs. Rooms range wildly in quality from the adults-only, spilt-level suites domi-nated by a two-person spa bath to sparsely furnished *bure* with little more than beds and a TV. The beach is very nice, although the coral shelf is very high here and much of the reef is exposed at low tide.

Tokoriki Island Resort (☎ 672 5926; www.tokoriki .com; d bure F$862, d villa F$1150; ✗ ☐ ☎) This place is the ideal romantic get-away. The whole place drips with orchids, and there are queen-sized beds with old-fashioned mosquito net canopies and a gorgeous island-style wedding chapel of stone, wood and stained glass. The 30 beachfront *bure* have indoor and outdoor showers, and it's only a few steps past the hammock to the beach. The five newer villas have private plunge pools, beautiful interiors and large sandstone terraces. Lunch is served in the pleasant terrace and pool area while the gourmet candle-lit dinners (mains F$32 to F$43) are served in the restaurant.

TAVARUA & NAMOTU

These two small coral islands at the south-ern edge of the Malolo Barrier Reef have leased the exclusive rights to Fiji's best surfing breaks. Both are marketed in the US to American surfers and only rarely take walk-in clients.

Tavarua Island Resort (☎ 672 3513; www.tavarua .com; s/tw incl meals F$300/450) has accommodation in simple *bure* along the beach, and rates include daily surf trips and meals. Bookings need to be made well in advance through **Tavarua Island Tours** (☎ in the USA 805 686 4551; fax 805 683 6696), in California.

Namotu Island Resort (☎ 670 6439; www.namotu island.net; ✗ ☐ ☎) is a little bit of Bali in Fiji. Generally, guests are in groups and book in advance through **Waterways Surf Travel** (☎ in the USA 310-584-9900; waterways@waterways.com), in Malibu. No children under 12.

YASAWA GROUP

Washed in dazzling sunshine and strung along 90km of reef, these 20 volcanic is-lands represent Fiji at its picture postcard best. The Yasawas, rich in blue lagoons and alluring beaches, but devoid of banks, shops, cars or roads, is a forced sojourn from life's hectic pace. This island chain has long been a backpacker favourite, but a new tide of midrange and top-end accom-modation options are enticing an increas-ingly diverse crowd, and now tourism, along with agriculture, forms the backbone of the local economy.

Information

The Yasawas are still remote; electricity is in-termittent at best (usually only at night) and not many places accept credit cards. Some of the budget resorts offer their own, cheaper boat transfers to and from the mainland but be aware that the trip is quite long, across an exposed stretch of water, and weather condi-tions can change quickly. Dormitories are seldom full but it's worth pre-booking double rooms and private *bure*.

As there are no restaurants in the Yasawas, meals are always included in the tariff but the quality and quantity of food rises and falls like a tide. There is little fussy eaters can do to minimise this, other than work the grape-vine on the *Yasawa Flyer* and pack snacks.

Transport

GETTING THERE & AROUND

Half the fun of staying in the Yasawas is get-ting on and off the modern *Yasawa Flyer* as it works its way up the chain towards Nacula. The 25m catamaran is operated by **Awesome**

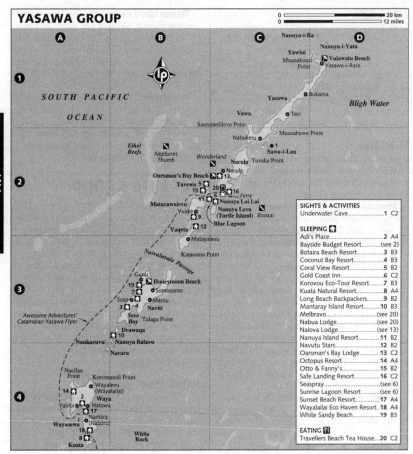

YASAWA GROUP

SOUTH PACIFIC OCEAN

Bligh Water

SIGHTS & ACTIVITIES	
Underwater Cave	1 C2

SLEEPING	
Adi's Place	2 A4
Bayside Budget Resort	(see 2)
Botaira Beach Resort	3 B3
Coconut Bay Resort	4 B3
Coral View Resort	5 B2
Gold Coast Inn	6 C2
Korovou Eco-Tour Resort	7 B3
Kuata Natural Resort	8 A4
Long Beach Backpackers	9 B2
Mantaray Island Resort	10 B3
Melbravo	(see 20)
Nabua Lodge	(see 20)
Nalova Lodge	(see 13)
Nanuya Island Resort	11 B2
Navutu Stars	12 B2
Oarsman's Bay Lodge	13 C2
Octopus Resort	14 A4
Otto & Fanny's	15 B2
Safe Landing Resort	16 C2
Seaspray	(see 6)
Sunrise Lagoon Resort	(see 6)
Sunset Beach Resort	17 A4
Wayalailai Eco Haven Resort	18 A4
White Sandy Beach	19 B3

EATING	
Travellers Beach Tea House	20 C2

Adventures Fiji (☎ 675 0499; www.awesomefiji.com), and with an accommodation booking desk on-board (credit cards accepted), island-hopping travellers are able to book their beds as they go. The boat departs Denarau Marina at 9.15am daily, calling into the Mamanuca islands of South Sea, Bounty, Beachcomber and Vomo before reaching the Yasawa Group. It takes about 1¾ hours to Kuata or Wayasewa (F$95 per person, one way), two hours to Waya (F$95), three hours to Naviti (F$105) and 4½ hours to the lagoon shared by Tavewa, Nanuya Lailai and Nacula (F$115). In the afternoon it follows the same route back to the mainland calling into all the resorts once more. A few resorts also charge F$10 to F$15 to collect guests from

the *Flyer*. Island-hoppers should consider a 'Bula Pass' (seven/14/21 days F$279/389/459) that enables unlimited travel but only one return to Denarau.

Awesome Adventures also offers five-/ six-night accommodation packages from F$500/639 per person, but if you're looking for flexibility you're better off booking your accommodation separately.

Turtle Airways (☎ 672 1888; www.turtleairways.com) has daily seaplanes from Nadi to Turtle Island Resort (US$888 per couple return).

Tours

CRUISES

Captain Cook Cruises (☎ 670 1823; www.captaincook .au; 15 Narewa Rd, Nadi) Has three-/four-/seven-night

Mamanuca and Yasawa cruises on board the 68m MV *Reef Escape* with a swimming pool, bars, lounges and air-con. Accommodation ranges from cabins with bunk beds up to deluxe staterooms. Prices per person, twin-share, for cabin/stateroom including all meals and activities (except diving) are F$1410/1758 (three nights) or F$3125/3896 (seven nights). Children up to 15 years pay F$480/840 for a three/seven-day trip, regardless of the type of accommodation.

Blue Lagoon Cruises (☎ 666 1662; www.bluelagoon cruises.com; 183 Vitogo Pde, Lautoka) Offers cruises aboard huge motor-yachts from F$1364/2810 for two/four nights per twin-share cabin. Seven-day Gold Club Cruises aboard the luxury MV *Mystique Princess* start at F$5342 for a twin-share cabin. A seven-day Luxury Dive Cruise aboard the *Fijian Princes* start at F$7691 per cabin if both occupants are diving. Children under 15 pay 11% to 15%, depending on the cruise. Transfers, cruise activities and food are included.

Awesome Adventures (☎ 675 0499; www.awesome fiji.com) Three-night cruises on the 27m *Wanna Taki* cost F$363/541 per person in either a dorm or a double. Rates include all meals, transfers and activities. The boat's dorm accommodates 27 people in bunks, and the three doubles are areas partitioned off by a curtain.

KAYAKING

Australian-operated **Southern Sea Ventures** (☎ 02-8901 3287; www.southernseaventures.com) and **World Expeditions** (☎ 02-8270 8400; www.world expeditions.com) both run eight-day kayaking safaris through the Yasawas from May to October. Trips cost from A$2150 per person.

SAILING SAFARI

Captain Cook Cruises (☎ 670 1823; www.captain cook.com.au) has sailing trips to the southern Yasawas aboard the tall-ship SV *Spirit of the Pacific*. Accommodation is in simple thatched *bure* ashore or canvas beds below deck. Snorkelling, fishing, village visits and *lovo* feasts are included. Prices per person, twin share, for a three-/four-day trip are F$510/680.

Robinson Crusoe Island Resort (☎ 628 1999; www .robinsoncrusoeislandfiji.com) offers a four-night sailing cruise on the 15m yacht *Pelorus Jack* for F$500 per person. It includes all meals and dormitory-style accommodation on the boat.

KUATA

Petite Kuata is the first Yasawa stop for the *Flyer* and, with its unusual volcanic rock formations, it makes a fine introductory impression. The best snorkelling is off the southern end of the island, and the summit can be conquered in a hot and sticky 20 minutes.

Sitting on a coarse sandy beach with Wayasewa hovering in the foreground, **Kuata Natural Resort** (☎ 620 3874; camp site per person/dm/ d incl meals F$45/60/150-180) appeals to unfussy backpackers with a 20-bed and 10-bed dorm and traditional en suite *bure* tightly arranged around the gardens. Standards are modest, and the price range quoted above reflects the age and subsequent quality of the *bure*.

WAYASEWA

Also known as Wayalailai (Little Waya), Wayasewa is dominated by Vatuvula, a volcanic rock plug that dramatically towers over the beaches below. The hike to the top is a fun scramble, and views take in the whole Yasawa Group. A 35-minute boat ride away is a local reef renowned for its **shark snorkelling** (F$15/25, without/with equipment). The sharks, which are mostly white tip reef sharks, are totally harmless, but their sleek looks and stealth-like appearance make a thrilling outing. The trips can be arranged through **Dive Trek Wayasewa** (☎ 628 3292; two-tank dives/PADI Open Water Courses F$150/550), which is based at the Wayalailai Eco Haven Resort.

Wayalailai Eco Haven Resort (☎ 628 3292; www .wayalailairesort.com; camp site per person/dm/d/fm incl meals F$45/60/150-180/170) is owned and operated entirely by villagers. This two-tiered budget resort is tucked squarely beneath Vatuvula's granite façade. There are bamboo and thatched *bure* overlooking the beach, and the ageing, ex-schoolhouse dorms of old have been superseded by a lighter and brighter lodge.

WAYA

With rugged hills, beautiful lagoons and a periphery of long sandy beaches, Waya is easy on the eyes. Walkers can tackle the summit of **Ului Nakauka** (three hours return from Octopus Resort) and snorkellers can explore the thick rim of coral that traces the island.

Sleeping & Eating

our pick Octopus Resort (☎ 666 6337; www.octopus resort.com; dm F$42-59, d F$169-290; ✗ ▣) The laid-back vibe, chilled tunes, cold beers, swaying

FIJI

hammocks and a wide sandy beach peppered with thatched sun huts make Octopus more than a few notches up the coconut tree in terms of quality. The compulsory meal package (F$45) includes excellent à-la-carte lunches and set dinners in a sand-floored restaurant. A multitude of activities are posted daily on the blackboard and there's a raft of accommodation options – two categories of immaculate dorms, simple but modern lodges with shared facilities and traditional *bure* with private outdoor showers. To dive at Octopus costs F$185/595 for a two-tank dive/PADI Open Water Course.

Sunset Beach Resort (☎ 666 6644, after the beep dial 6383; dm/d include meals $60/140) Sunset has one of the most beautiful settings in the Yasawas and this low-key backpacker camp overlooks the thin and photogenic sand bridge that connects Waya to Wayasewa. The thatched *bure* are large and simple and the 12-bed dorm is fairly rudimentary, but if the standards are basic, the staff here – including the dog – are very hospitable.

Looking like two hurricanes shy of being blown away completely, two more budget options are:

Adi's Place (☎ 665 0573, dm/d incl meals F$60/130-180)

Bayside Budget Resort (☎ 666 6644, after the beep dial 6383; dm include meals F$60).

NAVITI & AROUND
area 33 sq km

One of the largest and highest (up to 380m) of the Yasawa islands, Naviti has a rugged volcanic profile and a dazzling snorkelling site where you can swim with **manta rays**. The best time to see the giant rays is between June and August. All the resorts in the area offer snorkelling trips for around F$25 per person plus snorkel hire, but only Mantaray Island Resort employs spotters, sending the boat out only when they are assured of a successful encounter. **Reef Safari** (☎ 664 5301; www.reefsafari .com.fj) is based at Mantaray Island Resort but will pick up from anywhere in the Naviti area. A two-tank dive/PADI Open Water Course costs F$200/575 including equipment.

Korovou, Coconut Bay and White Sandy Beach resorts share a protected stretch of white-sand beach, but the swimming is only marginal here due to a bank of ugly, dead reef. Fortunately, a short track (around a 10-minute walk) provides access to the pretty and secluded Honeymoon Beach.

Sleeping & Eating

Korovou Eco-Tour Resort (☎ 651 3173; 603 0049; koro voultk@connect.com.fj; dm/d/villa incl meals F$70/180/350) As Korovou is the largest and most popular of the Natuvalo Bay options, activities here tend to be more reliably organised and the food of a better standard. It has 24-bed dorms, new stone and wooden villas and cheaper wooden lodges.

Mantaray Island Resort (☎ 664 0520; www .mantarayisland.com; sites per person incl meals F$85, dm incl meals F$90, d incl meals F$212-269; 🖳) Mantaray occupies its own wee island, spreading through and over a small hill between two pretty beaches. The modern dorm is divided into cubicles of four bunk beds, and each contains its own fan and light. The cheaper 'tree-house' *bure* share the self-composting toilets and hot showers with the dorm while the 'jungle' *bure* have private bathrooms.

Botaira Beach Resort (☎ 603 0200; www.botaira .com; dm/d incl meals $100/418) This resort extends over a long patch of secluded beach thick with palm trees. Guests enjoy plenty of privacy as there are only 11 *bure* here; nine new and stylish, two more basic and older (ask for a discount).

Also available at Natuvalo Bay:

White Sandy Beach (☎ 666 4066, 666 6644, after the beep dial 1360; dm/d incl meals F$65/150-200)

Coconut Bay Resort (☎ 666 6644, after the beep dial 1300; dm/d incl meals F$60/150)

TAVEWA
area 3 sq km

This small, low island houses some of the Yasawa Group's northernmost resorts. A pleasant beach unfurls itself on the southeastern coast but it's often plagued by buffeting trade winds (great for kite surfers). Head to Savutu Point, just around the bend for relief from the gales and some lovely snorkelling. An ambling ascent to the top of the central crest affords photogenic views of the Yasawas, particularly at sunset.

Based at Coral View, **Dive Yasawa Lagoon** (☎ 666 2648, marine VHF channel 72; www.diveyasawa lagoon.com) will also pick up from other resorts (transfer fees apply) on nearby islands. Every Saturday and Wednesday, Dive Yasawa operates a shark dive where you are likely to see two 4m lemon sharks and occasionally 2m grey reef sharks. A two-tank dive/ PADI Open Water Course costs F$175/650 including equipment.

Sleeping & Eating

Coral View Resort (☎ 922 2575; www.coralviewfiji.com; dm/d incl meals F$60/210; 🖳) This well-run, budget resort is often full to the brim with young Brits intent on drinking the island dry, and the nightly entertainment often features beach parties and bonfires. Accommodation options range from an older, cramped 18-bed dorm with a separate cold water shower block to good-value stone cottages with high-pitched roofs and *masi* (tapa cloth) and bamboo-lined interiors.

Otto & Fanny's (☎ 666 6481; www.ottoandfanny .com; dm/d incl meals F$100/210; 🖳) On a sprawling property, among a former copra plantation, this quiet, homely place has a small village of *bure* with private bathrooms and a spacious, 12-bed dorm. The flat, grassy grounds are in-undated with coconut trees that offer plenty of wide-open spaces. Otto and Fanny's is closest to Tavewa's best patch of beach. They charge F$20 return for *Yasawa Flyer* transfers.

NACULA

Blanketed with rugged hills and soft peaks, the interior of the third-largest island in the Yasawas is laced with well-trodden paths leading to villages and small coves. Beach devotees will be ecstatic to know that Nacula's Long Beach is ideal for swimming.

Sleeping & Eating

Safe Landing Resort (☎ 664 0031; slr@yahoo.com; camp sites per person incl meals $45, dm/d incl meals $60/185) This place had been closed since 2006 but was only weeks away from reopening when we called. From what we saw, Safe Landing promised to have some of the smartest dorms and *bure* in the area.

Oarsman's Bay Lodge (☎ 672 2921; www.oarsmans bay.com; dm/d incl meals $88/295; fm $264; 🗙 🖳) Boasting a prime slice of sandy real estate, Oarsman is one of Yasawas most popular resorts (book ahead). The *bure* are clean and crisp with modern bathrooms and private verandas, and several have interconnecting rooms ideal for families. Less appealing is the cramped dorm built directly above the restaurant in the apex of the second storey.

Nalova Lodge (☎ 672 8267; nalova_resort@yahoo .com d incl meals F$180-250) This teeny resort offers six homey *bure* of varying sizes, but only the more expensive options include private bathrooms. As there is no restaurant or central bar, meals are served on your *bure's* porch.

Simple accommodation is also offered at these slightly shambolic resorts:

Melbravo (☎ 924 6610, 978 0407; dm incl meals F$60, d with/without bathroom incl meals F$150/120).

Nabua Lodge (☎ 666 9173; nabualodgefiji@connect .com.fj; dm incl meals F$68, d with/without bathroom incl meals F$135/180)

NANUYA LAILAI

Ever since a young, bikini-clad Brooke Shields thrilled movie-goers in a remake of *The Blue Lagoon*, Nanuya Lailai's **Blue Lagoon** has been a magnet for snorkellers, divers, luxury cruise boat passengers and yachties – all keen to dabble in its gorgeous depths.

On the exposed eastern side of the island is the settlement of Enadala and several budget resorts. Connecting the Blue Lagoon and Enadala beaches is a well-trodden track. **Westside Watersports** (☎ 666 1462; www.fiji-dive.com), located at Nanuya Island Resort, is an experienced dive operation. It caters to guests at resorts on nearby islands, including the up-market Turtle Island Resort, as well as Blue Lagoon Cruise passengers. A two-tank dive/PADI Open Water Course costs F$165/635.

Sleeping & Eating

Gold Coast Inn (☎ 665 1580, 666 6644, after the beep dial 7777; dm/d incl meals F$60/150) Offering the highest standard of accommodation in this strip of budget resorts, the private timber *bure* have a double and single bed as well as their own bath-rooms. This resort is a smallish affair – there are only seven bungalows and a small dormitory – but it's run by a family with a big heart.

FAST FOOD

On 29 April 1789, Captain William Bligh and 18 loyal crew members were set adrift by mutineers of HMS *Bounty* in an open boat just 7m long and 3m wide. The epic journey that followed passed through treacherous water littered with shallow reefs and islands inhabited by cannibals. As they passed the Yasawas, two war canoes put to sea and began pursuit. Fortunately a squall swept in some much-needed wind to raise the mainsail and blew Bligh and his crew to the safety of the open sea. This body of water is known as Bligh Water today and, while the Yasawas remain considerably undeveloped, the locals are considerably friendlier.

Sunrise Lagoon Resort (☎ 666 6644, after the beep dial 9484; dm/d incl meals F$60/150) Camper than a row of pink tents and more fun than a bowl of kava, Sunrise is a hit with budget travellers if, for no other reason than that the two men who run the place, Queenie and Bridget, are so refreshingly unique. The pervading atmosphere is chatty and welcoming, although the accommodation and bathrooms are a little on the sloppy side and can only be charitably described as rustic.

ourpick **Nanuya Island Resort** (☎ 666 7633; www .nanuyafiji.com; d incl breakfast F$239-401; 🖵) A short walk, even in flippers, to the azure waters of the Blue Lagoon, this swish and understated resort is the kind of place you picture when you dream of indulgence, beachside cocktails and exquisite vistas. The *bure* are Fiji-nouveau; the roofs may be thatched but the interiors are chic and elegant. All are fan-cooled and have their own bathroom with solar-heated hot water. This place oozes romance and it's a favourite spot for couples (no children under seven), although the *bure* can accommodate families of up to four. The beachside restaurant is very atmospheric and the à-la-carte fare (F$24 to F$35) deliciously inventive.

MATACAWALEVU & YAQETA

Matacawalevu is a 4km-long hilly volcanic island protected by the large Nasomo Bay on its eastern side. Nanuya Levu (Turtle Island) is to the east, and to the south, across a protected lagoon used for seaweed farming, is Yaqeta.

Long Beach Backpackers (☎ 666 6644, after the beep dial 3032; camp site incl meals F$50, dm incl meals F$60, d incl meals F$150-200) At the time of research the whole place is being upgraded. There were several new *bure* (all with private bathrooms), a new 20-bed dorm and a large beachside restaurant in the pipeline. If only they remember to replace the sheets along with the buildings, Long Beach has the potential to become one of the best budget resorts in the Yasawas.

Navutu Stars (☎ 664 0553; www.navutustarsfiji.com; d F$587-998; ✗ 🖵 🖭) This boutique hotel specialises in opulent decadence Pacific style with petal-sprinkled baths, intimate sunset dining and complimentary massages on arrival. The white-washed villas have king-sized beds, exquisitely detailed 7m high roofs and fantastic views north from their private decks. Children below 14 are not permitted and the food is fabulous (meal packages available from F$100).

SAWA-I-LAU

At Sawa-i-Lau, underwater limestone rocks are thought to have formed a few hundred metres below the surface and then uplifted over time. Shafts of daylight enter the great dome-shaped **cave** (looming 15m above the water surface), where you can swim in the natural pool. With a guide, a torch and a bit of courage, you can also swim through an underwater passage into an adjoining chamber. The limestone walls have mysterious indecipherable carvings, paintings and inscriptions.

Most Yasawa budget resorts offer trips to the caves for around F$45 per person, but you should check whether this includes the F$10 entrance fee.

ROTUMA

pop 3000 / area 43 sq km

Far-flung and isolated, the tiny volcanic island of Rotuma drifts in the Pacific 636km northwest of Suva. The vast distance between its tiny frame and the mainland may be an accident of geography, but this divide has allowed Rotumans to evolve ethnically and linguistically independent of the mainland. The best time to visit is during *Fara*, an annual six-week festival beginning on 1 December that sees Rotumans toss aside their strong work ethic for dancing, parties and general revelry. There are no banks or shops here.

TRANSPORT
Getting There & Away

Air Fiji Suva (☎ 331 5055; www.airfiji.com.fj) flies from Suva to Rotuma on Wednesdays for F$375 one way.

Visiting yachts must obtain permission to anchor from the Ahau government station in Maka Bay, on the northern side of the island.

SLEEPING & EATING

The easiest way to stay on Rotuma is through a Rotuman contact (try www.rotuma.net). Alternatively, contact the Rotuman Island Council via the Fiji Visitors Bureau in Nadi or Suva.

Mojito's Barfly (☎ 889 1144; Motusa) has simple rooms with shared facilities, but they're generally reserved for government workers. Meals are also available, given plenty of notice.

OVALAU & THE LOMAIVITI GROUP

area 484 sq km.

Lomaiviti literally means 'Middle Fiji' and although the group is just off Viti Levu's east coast, it really does feel like the middle of nowhere. It is therefore hard to believe that this is where the Fijian nation was made, and picturesque Levuka, Ovalau's main town, was Fiji's earliest European settlement and the country's first capital. Today it's laid-back and the political machinations long departed, but with the right wind you may yet catch a whiff of the town's wild and immoral colonial days.

South of Ovalau, the tiny coral islands of Leleuvia and Caqalai have sandy beaches, good snorkelling and simple budget resorts. Hawksbill turtles visit to lay their eggs, and a pod of around 10 humpback whales passes the east coast of Ovalau on their annual migration between May and September.

Transport

GETTING THERE & AROUND

Air Fiji (☎ 344 0139; fax 344 0252; Beach St, Levuka) has twice daily flights between Suva and Ovalau (F$65). The airstrip is about a 40-minute drive from Levuka. Minibuses to the airport (F$5 per person) will pick you up from outside the Air Fiji office or from your hotel on request. A taxi costs about F$30.

Patterson Brothers Shipping (☎ 344 0125; Beach St) has a daily bus/ferry/bus service from Levuka to Suva via Natovi Landing (F$25, four hours). You can also opt to stay on the boat at Natovi and sail to Nabouwalu on Vanua Levu, and then continue by bus to Labasa (F$55).

Levuka is tiny and easy to get around on foot. There is a taxi stand opposite the Westpac bank, where carriers depart for Lovoni.

LEVUKA

pop 3750

Levuka is one of the most picturesque towns in the South Pacific. Remnants of its colonial past – timber pool halls, offices and stores – litter the streets like preserved props from an old western movie. But the sea and lush green mountains that contain the town are undeniably Fijian. It's an extremely friendly place and you'll be warmly welcomed by the mixture of indigenous Fijians, Indo-Fijians, Chinese Fijians, part-European Fijians and the odd, eccentric expats who inhabit this town. If you stay for a week, you'll be mates with them all.

Information

Levuka Hospital (☎ 344 0221; Beach St)
Ovalau Watersports (☎ 344 0166; www.owlfiji.com; Beach St; ☉ 8.30am-5pm Mon-Fri, 8.30am-1pm Sat) Dive shop, information centre, tour booking office and internet access.
Police Station (☎ 344 0222; Totoga La)
Post Office (Beach St) Cardphone outside.
Ovalau Tourist Information Centre (☎ 330 0356; Levuka Community Centre, Morris Hedstrom Bldg, Levuka; ☉ 8am-1pm & 2-4.30pm Mon-Fri, Sat till 1pm) Has an information board detailing Ovalau's accommodation and eating options and also organises Levuka town tours.
Westpac Bank (Beach St) Foreign exchange, cash advances on Visa or MasterCard and Lomaiviti's only ATM.

Sights

About 10 minutes' walk south of town is **Cession Site**, where the Deed of Cession was signed in 1874. Across the road the **Provincial Bure** sits like a loaf of wholemeal bread covered in straw. Prince Charles made his HQ here when he represented Her Majesty's Government during the transition to independence in 1970. The new meeting venue next door was built for a 2006 Great Council of Chiefs conference but that was cancelled due to the 2006 coup and it has yet to be used.

Downtown stands the **former Morris Hedstrom trading store** (1868), the first in Fiji. Behind its restored façade is a branch of the **Fiji Museum** (admission F$2; ☉ 8am-1pm & 2-4.30pm Mon-Fri, 9am-1pm Sat), which holds a small exhibition detailing the history of Levuka, including some wonderful old colonial photos.

Other buildings to keep an eye out for include the **Sacred Heart Church** (1858); Levuka's **original police station** (1874); the **Ovalau Club** (1904), Fiji's first private club; and the **former town hall** (1898). You'll also find the stone shell of the South Pacific's first **Masonic Lodge** (1875) and Levuka's only Romanesque building. It was burnt to a husk in the 2000 coup by villagers egged on by their church leaders. Local Methodists had long alleged that Masons were in league with the devil and that tunnels led from beneath the lodge through the centre of the world to Masonic HQ in Scotland. Surprisingly, this turned out not to be the case.

FIJI

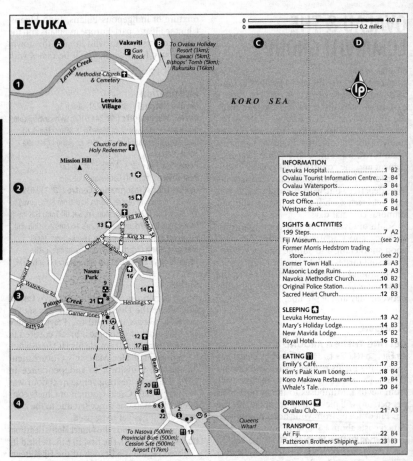

LEVUKA

KORO SEA

The **199 Steps of Mission Hill** are worth climbing for the fantastic view. The simple coral and stone Gothic-style **Navoka Methodist Church** (1864) near the foot of the steps is one of Fiji's oldest churches.

On Langham St, the **Royal Hotel** (1860s) is Fiji's oldest hotel, rebuilt in 1903. Check out the fantastic old snooker room, and play a game of hunt-the-Royal-Hotel-staff.

In **Cawaci**, north of the town, Fiji's first two Catholic bishops rest in the Gothic-style **Bishops' Tomb** (1922).

Activities

Cycling is a good way to explore Levuka and its surrounding area. The road to the south is fairly flat, and the north is OK until about Cawaci, after which it gets very hilly. Mountain bikes are available from Ovalau Watersports (p147), costing F$10/15 per half/full day.

Excellent **diving** sites in the Lomaiviti waters offer encounters with manta rays, hammerheads, turtles and reef sharks. To the west, Blue Ridge, off Wakaya Island, is famous for its bright blue ribbon eels. There is stunning soft coral at Snake Island and Shark Reef and excellent hard coral at Waitovu Passage. Ovalau Watersports offers two-tank dives/PADI Open Water Courses/reef snorkelling trips for F$150/650/40.

Levuka is a port of entry into Fiji for visiting **yachts**. Authorities don't always answer on radio Channel 16, so anchor near Levuka's

Queen's Wharf and make your way ashore. Formalities are usually simpler here than in Suva.

Tours

All of these tours (and more) can be booked through Ovalau Watersports (p147).

Epi's Midland Tour (☎ 602 1103, 923 6011; epitours@ hotmail.com; per person F$35, minimum 4; ◔ departs 10.30-11.30am Mon-Sat) takes you to Lovoni village in the crater of an extinct volcano. Transport is a combination of trekking and local carrier, the scenery is stunning and the storytelling is fantastic. The tour includes lunch in the village and a dip in the river.

Round Island 4WD Tours (per person F$35, minimum 4, ◔ departs 10am) takes you round the island in a 4WD, taking in the major historical sites around Levuka, the village of Lovoni, and the Solomon Islanders' settlement at Wainaloka.

Silana Village Tour (per person F$35, minimum 6) runs every Wednesday and includes a *meke* (traditional dance) and a *lovo* feast.

Ovalau Watersports can also arrange whale-watching trips in season (May to September) and day trips to Leleuvia or Caqalai (F$70 per person, including lunch).

Sleeping

New Mavida Lodge (☎ 344 0477; Beach St; dm/d F$25/80 inc breakfast) An imposing (by Levuka standards) cream building sitting behind a white picket fence. Pass through the gleaming floors and high ceilings of the lobby to find comfortable rooms with hot water bathrooms, TV and balconies, and a six-bed dorm.

Royal Hotel (☎ 344 0024; www.royallevuka.com; s/d/tw $29/43/43, cottages from $85; ✗ ▯ ☎) The Royal is the oldest hotel in Fiji, dating back to the 1860s. This proud timber building is thick with colonial atmosphere, from the creaking wooden floorboards to the hallways, plastered with black-and-white photographs. Upstairs each room is different, full of quirky old furniture, iron bedsteads, sloping floors and wonderful semi-enclosed private verandas complete with old-fashioned white cane chairs and wooden shutters. Recommended.

our pick **Levuka Homestay** (☎ 344 0777; www .levukahomestay.com; Church St; s/d incl breakfast F$126/148) A lovely neo-colonial house with great sea views and four large, comfortable, light-filled rooms with terraces, each one on its own level. The laid-back owners live on the highest level and regularly invite their guests

to share a drink with them on their enormous deck overlooking the harbour. The never-ending breakfast includes delicious doses of fruit, muesli, toast, banana pancakes, bacon and eggs.

Also available:

Ovalau Holiday Resort (☎ 344 0329; ohrfiji@connect .com.fj; camping per person F$10, dm/s/d F$12/15/28, s/d self-contained bungalow F$45/77; ☎) Roughly 4km outside Levuka, a few candy-coloured *bure* across from the beach.

Mary's Holiday Lodge (☎ 344 0013; Beach St; dm/s/d incl breakfast F$15/20/35) Rudimentary but friendly old hotel.

Eating & Drinking

Emily's Cafe (☎ 344 0382; lunch F$4, pizzas F$7; ◔ breakfast, lunch & dinner Mon-Sat, dinner Sun) Serves coffee and a selection of home-baked cakes and fresh bread as well as fast-food favourites like rotis and pies.

Whale's Tale (☎ 344 0235; breakfast $6, lunch sandwiches $8, mains $12; ◔ lunch & dinner Mon-Sat) Ask a local to recommend a place to eat and they'll probably send you here. This is a perennial favourite serving 'the best fish and chips in Fiji', as one local resident told us. There are excellent burgers, sandwiches and an astoundingly good-value F$17 set dinner menu.

Kim's Paak Kum Loong (☎ 344 0059; mains F$8; ◔ lunch & dinner) This is hands down the best place to get Chinese food in Levuka. There are two menus here – one with standard Chinese dishes, another with a mixture of Fijian-style fish and meat dishes and a selection of Thai curries. This place is usually busy, and there's a good street-side balcony for voyeurs. Sunday night is buffet night so come prepared to be stuffed.

Koro Makawa Restaurant (☎ 344 0429; pizzas from F$9; daily ◔ breakfast, lunch & dinner) You can get curries, fish and chips and other European meals here, but locals love it for their hit-or-miss pizza – 'one of the best you've ever tasted or a total disaster'. If you're willing to take the risk, go for one of the many fishy toppings – the tuna is the most fitting since the cannery's right on the doorstep.

Ovalau Club (◔ 4pm-9.30pm Mon-Thu, 2pm-midnight Fri, 10am-midnight Sat, 10am-9.30pm Sun) This grand colonial-style building is the main place in town to go for a drink. It was Fiji's first gentlemen's club, and it's extremely atmospheric. Local residents (mostly expats) get together for a drink at 6pm every Tuesday, and tourists are always welcome to join them.

FIJI

WHAT LIES BENEATH

If you head out to the islands south from Ovalau, your boat will likely travel through Qavo Passage, a break in the reef. Many indigenous Fijians believe that beneath these waters lies a sunken village where ancestral spirits continue to reside. Stories of fishermen hooking newly woven mats are whispered around Levuka. When passing over this *tabu* site, Fijians remove their hats and sunglasses and talk in hushed, reverent tones as it is believed that the spirits are capable of doling out nasty punishments to those who upset them. Whether or not you choose to believe the story, avoid offending and upsetting your hosts – respect their beliefs and follow suit. One tourist who refused to take off his baseball cap when we visited sent a Fijian woman into terrified hysterics.

CAQALAI

The gorgeous coral island of Caqalai comes close to the best a backpacker island can get. It's only a 15-minute walk around the island's beautiful white-sand beaches, which are fringed with palms and offer some great snorkelling.

The Methodist-run **Caqalai Island Resort** (☎ 343 0366; www.fijianholiday.com; camping/dm/bure incl meals per person F$35/45/55) is rustic and dry (but you're welcome to BYO). It has cold showers in shared bathrooms, and the food is delicious. Scuba diving, village visits, boat trips to tiny Honeymoon Island and Sunday church services fill the activity board.

One-way transfers to/from Levuka cost F$30 per person (arrange at Ovalau Watersports; see p147) or F$25 per person (minimum two people or F$50) to Ovalau's Bureta airstrip. From Suva, catch a bus heading down the Kings Rd and get off at Waidalice Landing, which is next to Waidalice bridge. You need to call ahead for a boat from Caqalai to pick you up here (F$30 per person).

LELEUVIA

area 0.17 sq km

Just south of Caqalai sits Leleuvia, another palm-fringed coral island with golden-sand beaches. Low tide is a good time to explore the island, when a vast area of sand, rock and tidal pools is exposed.

Leleuvia Island Resort (☎ 336 4008 or 359 5150; info@leleuvia.com; dm/bure F$40/50 per person including all meals) came under new management in 2007. A large, open sand-floored bar and restaurant, a gorgeous, wide stretch of beach and an assortment of pretty thatched *bure* (with electricity) mean things are looking great. The staff are very friendly and usually put on all kinds of entertainment (such as kava drinking and beach bonfires). While not on a par with Caqalai, the snorkelling is good here and you can hire equipment. Village trips and fishing excursions are also possible.

Boat transfers to/from Suva are F$30 each way (from Waidalice Landing). Transfers to/from Levuka cost F$30 each way. Call in advance for a pick up, or you can book via Ovalau Watersports Ovalau Watersports (p147).

VANUA LEVU

pop 139,514 / area 5587 sq km

Although Vanua Levu is Fiji's second-largest island and easily accessible, it's often overlooked in favour of its more publicised neighbours, and the north and west of the island are virtually untouristed. The island's largest town – Labasa – is a service centre for the predominantly Indo-Fijian sugar cane farmers, many of whom are descendants of the original indentured labourers brought to work on the plantations.

The southeast sees a trickle of visitors, particularly pretty Savusavu – a small town set in a sweeping bay that has proven to be an irresistible lure for expats and yachties. This area is predominantly indigenous Fijian and home to a gorgeous landscape chock-full of rainforests, coconut plantations and arresting views of the ocean. The irregular and deeply indented coastline provides some superb diving, snorkelling and kayaking opportunities.

Transport

GETTING THERE & AWAY

Air Fiji Labasa (☎ 881 1188) Savusavu (☎ 885 0538) has daily flights from both Suva and Nadi to Labasa (F$175/205) and Savusavu (F$140/185). **Pacific Sun** Labasa (☎ 885 0141) Savusavu (☎ 885 2214) also flies from Suva/Nadi to Labasa for the same price. Air Fiji also has daily flights between Savusavu and Taveuni island (F$225).

There are several boat services to and from Vanua Levu, but unless you've got plenty of time on your hands it's not really worth it – you won't save much money and the trip is significantly longer. The boats leave Suva, dock at Savusavu and then continue on to Taveuni. Buses transport those with a Labasa ticket from the dock at Savusavu.

Consort Shipping (☎ 330 2877; fax 330 3389, Suva) sails twice a week from Suva to Savusavu departing Suva at 5pm on Tuesday and Friday.

Bligh Water Shipping Suva (☎ 331 8247); Savusavu (☎ 885 3192); Labasa (☎ 881 8471) departs Suva at 6pm on Monday, Wednesday and Friday to Savusavu.

Grace Ferry Labasa (Gulam Nabi & Sons; ☎ 881 1152; Nasekula Rd); Savusavu (Country Kitchen; ☎ 927 1372) has a bus/boat trip from Taveuni to Savusavu and Labasa (F$20-F$25).

SAVUSAVU
pop 4970

Not long ago, Vanua Levu's second-largest centre was a small and dusty peninsular town, easily outclassed by its fabulous views across the bay to the western mountain range. The views haven't changed, but recent years have brought a property boom and the main street is now flush with good restaurants, lively bars and well-stocked shops. Savusavu is one of the most popular places in Fiji for visiting yachties to put down anchor – there are two excellent marinas here, and Savusavu Bay fills up with vessels during the high season. A new marina complex is planned on the waterfront east of town.

Savusavu Bay once saw a great deal of volcanic activity, and **hot springs** continue to bubble near the wharf and behind the playing field. Don't even think about bathing in them – they're literally boiling.

Information

All the major banks along the main road have ATMs and foreign exchange services, and give cash advances on major credit cards.

Curly Cruising & Internet (☎ 885 0122) Yachting information centre, tour office and internet access.

Customs (☎ 885 0727; ☽ 8am-1pm, 2-4pm Mon-Fri) West of the marinas.

Hospital/Ambulance (☎ 885 0444)

Police (☎ 885 0222)

Post Office At the eastern end of town near Buca Bay Rd.

Siloah Clinic (☎ 885 0721; ☽ 9am-5pm Mon-Fri) Behind Savusavu Wines and Spirits on the main road.

Sights

Savusavu is Vanua Levu's liveliest and prettiest settlement and, while there is a distinct lack of cultural shows and tourist sights, the sweeping bay, backed by sloping green hills and a main street dotted with decorative plant pots and flowers, is its biggest draw.

Dating back to 1880 and originally one of Fiji's first copra mills, the **Copra Shed Marina** (☎ 885 0457; fax 885 0989; coprashed@ connect.com.fj) has been rebuilt as Savusavu's service hub for tourists and expats. It encompasses a bevy of facilities as well as a small historical display. Moorings in the pretty harbour between Savusavu and Nawi Islet cost F$10/260 for a day/month in high season, F$8/210 for a day/month in low season.

Close by, **Waitui Marina** (☎ 885 0536; fax 885 0344; ☽ closed Sunday) is based at a beautiful restored boatshed, and facilities include showers and a private club. Moorings cost F$10/225 a day/month in high season.

Activities
DIVING

Savusavu has excellent dive sites in and around Savusavu Bay, as well as along the coast towards Taveuni. In some spots it is possible to see schools of barracuda, kingfish, tuna and sometimes hammerheads. The prices below include all gear.

KoroSun Dive (☎ 885 2452; www.korosundive.com) Has a dive shop on the jetty. Two-tank dives/PADI Open Water Course cost F$190/750.

L'Aventure Jean-Michel Cousteau (☎ 885 0188; laventurefiji@connect.com.fj) Based at the Jean-Michel Cousteau Resort (p154). Two-tank dives/PADI Open Water Course cost F$280/860.

Rock n' Down Under Divers (☎ 885 3447 or 932 8363; Waitui Marina) Two-tank dives/PADI Open Water Course cost F$195/600.

Tours

J Hunter Pearls (☎ 885 0821; www.pearlsfiji.com) offer snorkelling with a difference – among black pearls on a working pearl farm. Tours

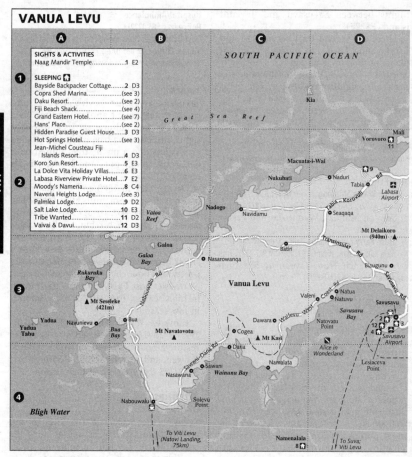

VANUA LEVU

SIGHTS & ACTIVITIES
Naag Mandir Temple................1 E2

SLEEPING
Bayside Backpacker Cottage........2 D3
Copra Shed Marina.................(see 3)
Daku Resort.......................(see 2)
Fiji Beach Shack..................(see 4)
Grand Eastern Hotel...............(see 7)
Hans' Place.......................(see 2)
Hidden Paradise Guest House.......3 D3
Hot Springs Hotel.................(see 3)
Jean-Michel Cousteau Fiji
   Islands Resort.................4 D3
Koro Sun Resort...................5 E3
La Dolce Vita Holiday Villas......6 E3
Labasa Riverview Private Hotel....7 E2
Moody's Namena....................8 C4
Naveria Heights Lodge.............(see 3)
Palmlea Lodge.....................9 D2
Salt Lake Lodge..................10 E3
Tribe Wanted.....................11 D2
Vaivai & Davui...................12 D3

SOUTH PACIFIC OCEAN

depart weekdays at 9.30am and 1.30pm (F$25). BYO snorkel.

Rock n' Down Under Divers (☎ 885 3447 or 932 8363; Waitui Marina) As well as diving, these guys offer village visits (F$60 per person) and cruises (F$40-F$70 per person). They also hire kayaks (F$40 a day) and bikes (F$35 a day).

Tui Tai Adventure Cruises (☎ 885 3032; www.tuitai.com) If you're put off the idea of cruising by visions of a cheesy behemoth, never fear. The *Tui Tai* – an elegant, motorised sailboat – is sexy as hell, and the small number of guests keeps the mood friendly and relaxed. A typical five-night itinerary includes Taveuni, Kioa and Rabi Islands and starts at F$5608/3738 per person single/double. All accommodation is in cabins with private bathroom and air-con.

More tours:

Trip n Tour (☎ 885 3154; tripntour@connect.com.fj; Copra Shed Marina) Offers include tours to a copra plantation, Labasa and fishing excursions.

Seahawk Yacht Charters (☎ 885 0787; www.seahawkfiji.com) Day cruises aboard a 16m yacht with captain, cook and crew. Per person from F$85.

Sleeping

The best sleeping options are out of town, either on Lesiaceva Point to the southwest or on the Hibiscus Hwy to the east. Buses and taxis service both these locations.

BUDGET

Hidden Paradise Guest House (☎ 885 0106; s/d incl breakfast F$25/50, with air-con F$30/60; ▨) This place

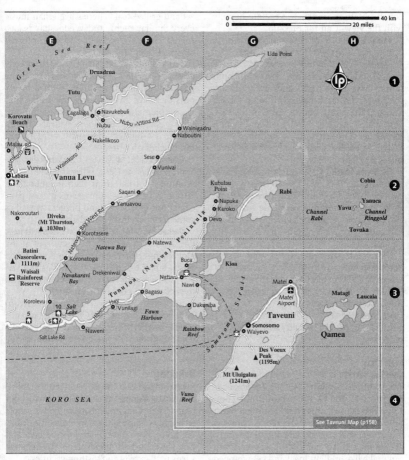

has the cheapest rooms in town and is the best place to meet other budget travellers. It's a no-frills deal, with spotless rooms sharing a bathroom and cold-water showers.

Bayside Backpacker Cottage (☎ 885 3154; tripntour@ connect.com.fj; Lesiaceva Rd; s/d F$40/50) Located 3km from town, this granny *bure* is a real bargain. There are two single beds, a decent kitchen and TV and DVD. Snorkelling at the pebble beach across the road is wonderful at high tide. The friendly Bowers will let you use their mountain bikes; otherwise, it's F$3 by taxi into town.

MIDRANGE
Daku Resort (☎ 885 0046; www.dakuresort.com; Lesiaceva Rd; budget rooms F$60, oceanview bure s/d F$140/150, 2-bedroom bure F$220; 4-bedroom pool house F$200, 3-bedroom beach house F$230; 💻 📺) At this resort cum self-improvement centre, guests participate in a surprisingly diverse array of courses, from gospel singing to watercolour painting to meditation and yoga. The sea-green and white tin-roofed *bure* have sweeping sea views, and there's top-notch fish viewing to be had at the pebble beach.

Naveria Heights Lodge (☎ 851 0157; justnaveria@ connect.com.fj; Naveria Pde; r incl breakfast F$140; ✗) Owned by a fitness instructor and a massage therapist, this lovely house combines breathtaking vistas with breathless activity. Fitness freaks are kept busy with mountain biking, hiking and exercise classes while couch potatoes are left to vegetate happily with the view. Call for pick-up.

Vaivai & Davui (☎ 885 3154; tripntour@connect.com .fj; Vaivai Nov-Apr/May-Oct F$1320/1495 per week, Davui Nov-Apr/May-Oct F$1150/1320 per week; ⌘) These two grand two-bedroom, two-bathroom homes have huge decks and extraordinary views over Savusavu Bay. With room for six, Vaivai is the larger and the pick of the two, with a lush garden, a baby cot and even a telescope. The kitchen is equipped with Fisher & Paykel whitegoods, and the reef offers fantastic snorkelling.

Fiji Beach Shack (☎ 885 1002; www.fijibeachshacks .com; day/week F$240/1580) This seriously glam two-level holiday home down by Lesiaceva Point boasts contemporary chic furniture, two bedrooms, a plunge pool and a fabulous bathroom complete with a sunken bath big enough for two.

More midrange options:

Hot Springs Hotel (☎ 885 0195; www.savusavufiji.com; Nakama Rd; dm F$36, r with fan/air-con incl breakfast F$80/125; ⌘ ☎) Great harbour views, majestic deck, average rooms and tired bathrooms.

Copra Shed Marina (☎ 885 0457; coprashed@connect .com.fj; r F$165; ✕ ⌘) Two luxury units with good marina views.

TOP END

Koro Sun Resort (☎ 885 0262; www.korosunresort.com; Hibiscus Hwy; s/d bure from F$460/560, 2-bedroom bure from F$600; ⌘ ☎) Facing a beautiful lagoon 13km east of town, this pretty resort has plush hillside and beachside *bure*, tennis courts, a nine-hole golf course, kayaks, bikes, kids' programme and a rainforest spa, where you can make like a Fijian meal and get wrapped in a banana leaf.

Jean-Michel Cousteau Fiji Islands Resort (☎ 885 0188; www.fijiresort.com; d bure from F$1000; ▯ ☎) This outstanding luxury ecoresort is owned by the son of Jacques Cousteau and, not surprisingly, it attracts divers from around the world. The *bure* are suitably luxe with handmade furnishing, large decks and private garden areas. The gourmet meals are included in the price, and children are welcome and are lavished with attention in their own Bula Club.

Eating

Bula Re Cafe (☎ 885 0377; meals from F$8; ☼ 10am-10pm daily; ▯) Sit inside or on a breezy plant-filled terrace overlooking the water. Food includes sandwiches, crepes, pasta, schnit-

zel and grilled fish. There's live Fijian music every Sunday night, and Wednesday is *lovo* night. There's free wi-fi and one internet terminal (F$8 an hour).

Surf and Turf (☎ 885 0511; Copra Shed Marina, lunch/ dinner meals from F$8/20; ☼ lunch & dinner) This is the poshest restaurant in town, with a lovely outside space overlooking the water that is complemented by a great wine list and tasty pasta, steak and lobster meals (F$40). Lunch is a lighter affair with burgers and sandwiches on offer.

Captain's Cafe (☎ 885 0511; Copra Shed Marina; pizza from F$15, lunch/dinner F$8/16; ☼ breakfast, lunch & dinner) A more informal affair than neighbouring Surf and Turf, this joint serves pizzas, pancakes, full-on fry-ups and burgers as well as some seriously tasty milkshakes.

Decked Out Cafe (☎ 885 0195; Hot Springs Hotel; meals F$19; ☼ breakfast & dinner) The restaurant at the Hot Springs Hotel has a menu of home-made pizza, Fijian fish dishes, quesadillas and salads. It's fairly quiet except at weekends and on the occasional pool barbeque night.

Savusavu also has a Morris Hedstrom Supermarket, a couple of Chinese restaurants, a daily market selling fruit and veggies and a **Hot Bread Kitchen** (☼ 6am-8pm Mon-Sat, 6am-1pm Sun) for fresh bread.

Drinking

Savusavu Yacht Club (☎ 885 0685; Copra Shed Marina) and **Waitui Marina** (☎ 885 0536) both consider tourists temporary members, and most people feel right at home at these friendly little drinking holes. Both have plenty of cold beer and fine views and are good places to exchange yarns with expats and visiting yachties.

Shopping

D Solanki (☎ 885 0025) Head to this tailors for beautifully made, double-stitched saris at bargain prices. They also sell traditional Fijian dress and Western clothes if you can't make the sari thing work for you.

Art Gallery (☎ 885 3054; Copra Shed Marina) and **Tako Handicraft** (☎ 885 3956; Copra Shed Marina) both sell jewellery, sculptures, postcards and handicrafts by local artists.

Getting There & Around

Air Fiji (☎ 885 0538) and **Pacific Sun** (☎ 885 2214) have offices in the Copra Shed Marina. Savusavu airstrip is a 3km, F$2 taxi ride, south of town.

Buses to Labasa (F$7, three hours, five daily) depart from 7.30am to 3.30pm. Some buses take the longer, scenic route from Savusavu to Labasa along Natewa Bay, departing at 9am (F$13, six hours).

Buses from Savusavu to Napuca (F$7, 4½ hours), at the tip of the Tunuloa Peninsula, depart at 10.30am, 1pm and 2.30pm daily.

There are buses from Savusavu to Lesiaceva Point (F$1, 15 minutes, five daily except on Sunday) between 6am and 5pm. For confirmation of bus timetables in the south, ring **Vishnu Holdings** (☎ 885 0276).

Carpenters Rental Cars can be booked through **Trip n Tour** (☎ 885 3154; tripntour@connect .com.fj; Copra Shed Marina); prices start at F$110 for a two-door 4WD. Bula Re Cafe (opposite) is an agent for **Budget Rent a Car** (☎ 881 1999), where prices start at about F$100 a day for a sedan and F$120 for a 4WD.

TUNULOA PENINSULA

The lush and scenic Tunuloa Peninsula is an excellent area to explore by 4WD. The area is prime for birdwatching and hiking but you'll need a local guide; ask your resort to arrange. The rough, bumpy Hibiscus Hwy passes copra plantations, old homesteads and waving villagers. The road becomes extremely slippery with rain so double-check the tyres before setting out and keep a firm grip on the steering wheel. There are no restaurants or shops along this route.

About 20km east of Savusavu, the Hibiscus Hwy veers right (south); the turn-off to the left (north) follows the western side of Natewa Bay, an alternative 4WD route to Labasa. At Buca Bay the highway turns north through the habitat of the endangered silktail bird.

If you turn south at Buca Bay, you'll head up over the mountain to the village of **Dakuniba**. The going is slow but you'll be rewarded with dazzling views. Just outside Dakuniba, mysterious petroglyphs are inscribed on large boulders; be sure to bring a sevusevu for the village chief if you plan to visit these.

Salt Lake Lodge (☎ 828 3005; www.saltlakelodgefiji .com; Hibiscus Hwy; 2/4 person bure F$70/90) At the centre of everything, Salt Lake offers two bungalows with a strong eco ethos. Built with local tropical timber, the bungalows sit on stilts at the edge of a lake with a beach bar, lounge and eating area between them and an outdoor kitchen. Other than lazing about there's tubing, snorkelling, biking, kayaking and fishing.

La Dolce Vita Holiday Villas (☎ 851 8023; ladolce vitafiji.com; Hibiscus Hwy; d villas incl meals F$350) La Dolce has gorgeous round wooden bure with vaulted ceilings, great decking, large, modern bathrooms and fabulous sea views. Golfers are kept happy with a six-hole course, and if that doesn't float your boat there's boules, horse-riding, jet skiing, bushwalking, snorkelling and trips with a 'dolphin caller' to see (and sometimes swim with) spinner dolphins. A taxi from Savusavu costs about F$25.The power is on from 5.30 to 11pm.

There are other accommodation options on the western edge of the Tunuloa Peninsula but they are best accessed by boat from Taveuni. See p160 for more information.

LABASA & AROUND
pop 24,095

In Vanua Levu's predominantly Indo-Fijian largest town, Bollywood tunes waft through an air already thick with heat and the smell of molasses. Sitting on the northwestern side of the island's mountain range, about 5km inland on the banks of the meandering Labasa River, Labasa is a sugar town, and crushed cane husks and sugar trains abound.

While Labasa is a bustling trade, service and administrative centre, it doesn't have a lot to offer tourists. Most shops and services can be found on Nasekula Rd, the main street. In an emergency, contact the police (☎ 881 1222; Nadawa St) or the **hospital** (☎ 881 1444; Butinikama-Siberia Rd).

Sights

About 2km south off Nasekula Rd, **Wasavula Ceremonial Site** (Vunimoli Rd) is the resting place of a sacred monolith that villagers believe grew from the ground. Behind the standing stone is the village cemetery and an area once used during cannibalistic ceremonies. Unless you are given a guided tour, it's easy to walk right past the flat vatu ni bokola (head-chopping stone) and the bowl-like stone in which the brain was placed for the chief.

Brightly painted red, yellow and blue, **Naag Mandir Temple** is built around the sacred **Cobra Rock**, the area's most interesting sight. About 3m in height, the rock's natural curved formation resembles a cobra poised to strike. Covered in colourful flower and tinsel garlands, the rock is beseeched with offerings of fruit, fire and coconut milk. Devotees swear that the rock grows in size and that the roof has been raised several times over the years to accommodate it. Remove your shoes before entering and circle the rock clockwise three or five times. Buses from Labasa to Natewa Bay pass the temple; a taxi costs about F$10.

Sleeping

Labasa Riverview Private Hotel (☎ 881 1367; fax 881 4337; Nadawa St; dm F$15, s/d with shared bathroom F$30/40, s/d with air-con & bathroom F$60/80; ☒) The five-bed dorm here is good value, with a clean, well-equipped kitchen and a balcony overlooking the river. The double rooms, however, are cramped and dark, although the bar is a tad more cheery.

Grand Eastern Hotel (☎ 881 1022; grest@connect .com.fj; Rosawa St; r standard/deluxe/executive F$77/103/128; ☒ ☒) This is the plushest, if slightly care-worn, hotel in Labasa and its pleasant colonial atmosphere is bolstered by halls lined with old black-and-white photos of the town in its heyday. Standard rooms have small porches facing the river, but it's worth paying the extra for the newer deluxe rooms, with large double beds and sofas that open out onto the court-yard swimming pool.

Tribe Wanted (☎ 992 0428; www.tribewanted .com) A 'unique community tourism project' founded by two young English entrepreneurs in 2006 when they signed a three-year lease on Vorovoro island. The idea is to create a virtual 'tribe' of up to 5000 members who could then pay to visit the island and, working with the local community, physically participate in the building of an ecovillage and a real-life tribe on Vorovoro. Seven days on Vorovoro (the minimum stay), including meals and pick-up and drop-off at Labasa, costs F$600 and includes a one-year membership of the tribe. While the current lease is due to expire on 1 September 2009, it will be up to the Vorovoro chief to decide what happens to the Tribe Wanted community and it looks likely that a new 10-year lease will be signed and the operation will continue.

Palmlea Lodge (☎ 828 2220; www.palmleafarms .com; Tabia/Naduri Rd; s/d from F$110 a) Just off the road that heads down to Savusavu, 15km out of town, this ecoresort overlooks the Great Sea Reef. Sitting on gentle green slopes leading down to the sea are a few spacious *bure* with vaulted ceilings and large verandas. They grow their own fruit and veg on an organic farm and make every effort to manage the resort in an ecofriendly fashion.

Eating

Labasa is full to the brim with basic cafes serving Labasa's three favourite cuisines – Indian, Chinese and Greasy. Eat early; most close by 7pm.

V Rana's Snack Bar (☎ 881 4351; Nasekula Rd; snacks F$0.70; ☒ 7am-6pm Mon-Fri, till 4pm Sat) This place is friendly and has comfortable booths where you can snack on bhajis, samosas and Indian sweets.

Jie Ning Cafe (Nasekula Rd; dishes F$8; ☒ breakfast, lunch & dinner) Chinese favourites such as chow mein and sweet and sour are dished up here in stomach-satisfying portions.

Oriental Bar & Restaurant (☎ 881 7321; Jaduram St; meals F$8; ☒ lunch & dinner Mon-Sat, dinner Sun; ☒) Although you wouldn't guess from the outside (look for the orange door and pink balcony), this is one of Labasa's most upmarket and at-mospheric restaurants, with a strong Chinese twist to its Fijian décor. The menu has a wide choice of tasty Chinese dishes, including plenty of veggie and a few Fijian options.

Grand Eastern Hotel (☎ 881 1022; Rosawa St; lunch/dinner F$15/25; ☒ breakfast, lunch & dinner) The res-taurant at the colonial Grand Eastern serves Western-style food such as steaks and burgers. You can also eat out on the patio overlooking the swimming pool.

Getting There & Around

For flights head to the office of **Air Fiji** (☎ 881 1188; Nasekula Rd) or **Air Pacific** (☎ 881 1454; Northern Travel Service office, Nasekula Rd). The airport is about 11km southwest of Labasa; catch the Waiqele bus (F$0.80, four times daily Monday to Saturday, as per flight schedule on Sunday). A taxi from Labasa costs F$12. See p171 for flight and ferry details to and from Labasa.

There are regular buses between Labasa and Savusavu (F$7, five times daily between 7am and 4.15pm, four on Sunday). A 9am bus takes the scenic route (F$13, six hours) to Savusavu along Natewa Bay. Buses to Nabouwalu depart three times daily (F$9, Monday to Saturday).

Taxis are plentiful, and the main stand is near the bus station. **Budget Rent a Car** (☎ 881 1999; Vakamaisuasua) is south of town.

NAMENALALA

The volcanic island of Namenalala rests on the Namena Barrier Reef, now a protected ma-rine reserve, 25km off the southeastern coast of Vanua Levu. From November to February, hawksbill and green turtles lay their eggs on

Namenalala beaches. There is an old **ring fortification**, but the village disappeared long ago. Today there's just one small, upmarket resort.

Moody's Namena (☎ 881 3764; www.moodysnamena fiji.com; five-night all-inclusive packages, incl transfers from Savusavu, cost from F$2650 per person sharing; ☯ closed March & April) has six bamboo-and-timber *bure* on a forested ridge. Free activities include windsurfing, fishing, snorkelling, reef excursions, barbecues, volleyball, and use of canoes and paddle boards while diving costs F$200 per two-tank dive. There is a five-night minimum stay and no children under 16 years old are permitted.

TAVEUNI

Kaleidoscopic above and beneath, this small island is a haven for divers, bushwalkers and nature lovers. Up top, a carpet of green palms, tropical wildflowers and a dense, prehistoric rainforest attracts an array of colourful bird life. Down below, particularly around the reefs of Somosomo Strait, underwater gardens of dazzling corals and improbable sea creatures are as impressive as their terrestrial counterparts.

Taveuni boasts some of Fiji's highest mountains, including Des Voeux Peak (1195m) and the cloud-shrouded Mt Uluigalau (1241m), the country's second-highest summit. The black sand beaches that dot the coast are proof of these mountains' volcanic origins, and only the villages of Lavena and Matei can claim white sandy shorelines.

Those seeking to escape the beaten track will find plenty of opportunities in Taveuni to do so, although adventuring is best tackled with an umbrella – it rains often.

Transport

GETTING THERE & AWAY

Flying over the gorgeous reefs between Taveuni and Viti Levu is stunning. At Matei airport, **Pacific Sun** (☎ 6720 888) has two flights a day to/from Nadi (F$170 one-way) and **Air Fiji** (☎ 888 0062) has one to two flights daily to/from Nadi (F$255 one way) and Suva (F$185 one-way). Both routes are often heavily booked. Once repairs to Savusavu runway are finished, daily flights between Taveuni and Savusavu will recommence.

The Wairiki Wharf for large vessels such as the MV *Suilven* is about 1km south of Waiyevo.

Smaller boats depart from the Korean Wharf, about 2km north. **Consort Shipping and Bligh Water Shipping** (☎ 888 0261 or 331 8247 in Suva) have regular Suva–Savusavu–Taveuni ferries. Bligh Water is the more comfortable and reliable service (see p172 for details). **Grace Ferry** (☎ 888 0320; Naqara) runs a bus/boat trip to Savusavu and Labasa (F$20 to F$25). The boat departs from the Korean Wharf at 8.45am. The booking office is in Naqara.

GETTING AROUND

Getting around Taveuni involves a bit of planning due to the length of time between buses. You can rent 4WDs in Naqara, although it's far cheaper to rent a taxi for the day.

From Matei airport expect to pay about F$20 to Waiyevo, and F$60 to Vuna (about one hour) in a taxi. Most upmarket resorts provide transfers for guests.

Bus

Taveuni's bus schedule is very lax, and buses may show up an hour early or late. Be sure to double-check return bus times when you board, just to make sure there is one.

Pacific Transport (☎ 888 0278) runs buses from Wairiki to Bouma at 8.30am, 11.30am and 4.20pm. The last bus continues to Lavena, where the first bus of each morning starts out at 5.45am. On Tuesday and Thursday all buses go as far as Lavena. On Sunday there is one bus at 3.30pm from Wairiki to Lavena and one from Lavena to Wairiki at 6.45am.

From Naqara, buses run to Navakawau at 9am, 11.30am and 4.45pm Monday to Saturday. There is only one bus on Sunday. From Matei, buses run to Wairiki at 11.30am Monday to Saturday, with additional services during school term.

Car

Budget Rent a Car (☎ 888 0291; gardenstate@connect .com.fj; Garden State Price Point; Naqara) has 4WDs for F$135 to F$185 per day.

Taxi

Taxis are readily available in the Matei and Waiyevo areas – it may be wise to book ahead on Sunday. Hiring a taxi for a day to tour the island should cost around F$150. For destinations such as Lavena you can go by bus and return by taxi, but you must arrange this before you go.

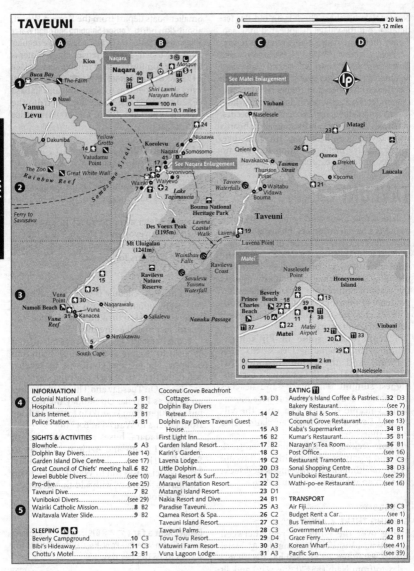

Activities

DIVING & SNORKELLING

Taveuni has achieved near-mythical status among divers. The Somosomo Strait reveals a gazillion fish, sharks, turtles, fantastic coral and, in November, pilot whales. The most famous of the vibrant soft-coral sites is Rainbow Reef, which fringes the southwest corner of Vanua Levu but is most easily accessed from Taveuni. In January and February, water clarity is reduced due to plankton blooms and northerly winds from the equator.

There is plenty for snorkellers, too. The three small islands immediately offshore from Naselesele Point in Matei have good snorkelling (known as the local 'Honeymoon Island').

You can also snorkel happily at Prince Charles Beach or Beverly Beach.

There are numerous dive operations in Waiyevo, southern Taveuni, Matei and the offshore island resorts. On average, a two-tank dive costs around F$225 and a PADI Open Water Course F$650, including equipment. Respected operators include:

Garden Island Dive Centre (☎ 345 0324; www .gardenislandresort.com) Opening at the Garden Island Resort (p160) in early 2009.

Dolphin Bay Divers (☎ 992 4001, 828 3001; www .dolphinbaydivers.com) Operates from Dolphin Bay Divers Retreat (see p160).

Pro-dive (☎ 888 0125; www.paradiseinfiji.com) Based at Paradise Taveuni (see p161)

Jewel Bubble Divers (☎ 888 0586; www.jeweldivers .com), Near Beverly Beach in Matei; provides high-quality gear and is locally owned and run.

Taveuni Dive (☎ 828 1063, 888 0063; www.taveuni dive.com), Good, professional set-up located in Wairiki and Taveuni Estates.

Vunibokoi Divers (Dive Taveuni; ☎ 888 0560; www .tovutovu.com) Popular divemaster Tyrone Valentine has logged an incredible 14,000 dives and does everything possible to avoid damaging local eco-systems. Based at Tovu Tovu Resort (p161)

BIRDWATCHING

Taveuni is one of Fiji's best locations for birdwatching, with over 100 species of birds to be found. Try Des Voeux Peak (p159) at dawn for a chance to see the rare orange dove and silktail. Along the Lavena Coastal Walk (p163), keep your eyes peeled for parrots, fantails, flame doves, the Fiji goshawk and wattled honeyeater. Avid birdwatchers also recommend the Vidawa rainforest hike in the Bouma National Heritage Park (see p162).

WAIYEVO, SOMOSOMO & AROUND

Waiyevo is unlikely to win any beauty prizes but it's the administrative centre of the island and home to the hospital, police station, some ferry links and a resort. About 2.5km north of Waiyevo is Naqara, Taveuni's metropolis – if you take metropolis to mean a few supermarkets, a budget hotel, internet cafe and a bank. To the north of the river is Somosomo, the largest village on Taveuni and headquarters for the *Tui Cakau* – high chief of Taveuni. The **Great Council of Chiefs'** **meeting hall** *(bure bose)* was built here in 1986 for the gathering of chiefs from all over Fiji.

About 2km south of Waiyevo is Wairiki village, with a general store and a beautiful old hilltop mission.

Information

The larger supermarkets and top-end resorts may accept credit cards for a fee.

Colonial National Bank (☎ 888 0433; Naqara; ☯ 9.30am-4pm Mon, 9am-4pm Tue-Fri) The only bank on the island will exchange currency and travellers cheques and has an ATM.

Hospital (☎ 888 0444; Waiyevo)

Lanis Internet (Naqara; per min $0.20; ☯ 8am-8pm Mon-Sat) Next to Chottu's Motel.

Police (☎ 888 0222; Waiyevo) There is also a police station in Naqara.

Post Office (☎ 888 0027; Waiyevo) Beneath the First Light Inn in Waiyevo.

Sights & Activities

Although the International Date Line officially doglegs Fiji, the **180-degree meridian** cuts straight through Taveuni, about a 10-minute walk south of Waiyevo. A red survey beacon marks the spot along the water and there's an info board on the field above.

Peering over the Somosomo Strait, the **Wairiki Catholic Mission** is best visited during the 7am, 9am or 11am Sunday Mass. Join the congregation sitting cross-legged on the floor beneath an impressive beam ceiling and stained-glass windows (reputedly from France) as they belt out a few hymns. In the presbytery, there's a painting of a famous battle in which a Catholic missionary helped Taveuni's warriors develop a strategy to defeat their Tongan attackers.

Before sliding down the natural rock chutes of the **Waitavala Water Slide**, ask a local kid for a demo first and study their technique with care. Locals warn that unless you have a death wish do not even consider starting from the top, and be prepared to be dumped unceremoniously in the small pool with at least a couple of bruises. To get here, head north from Waiyevo, take the first right at the bus stop, take another right at the branch in the road, pass a shed and then go left down a hill. You'll see a 'waterfall' sign. This is private property so if you pass anyone, ask permission.

On a clear day the views from **Des Voeux Peak** (1195m) are fantastic – it's possible to see Lake Tagimaucia and perhaps even the

Lau Group. Allow three to four hours to walk the steep and arduous 6km ascent and at least two to return. From Waiyevo, take the inland track just before Wairiki Catholic Mission. Alternatively, arrange for a lift up and then walk back at your leisure.

In the mountains above Somosomo, **Lake Tagimaucia** rests in an old volcanic crater some 823m above sea level. Fiji's national flower, the rare *tagimaucia*, grows on the lake's shores and blooms from late September to late December. The hike is overgrown and muddy; start from Somosomo where you need to present the chief with a *sevusevu* and ask permission. Take lunch and preferably a guide; allow eight hours for the round trip.

Sleeping

Chottu's Motel (☎ 888 0233; Naqara; s/d/tr budget F$40/50/60, deluxe s/d F$59/71) Chottu's has two types of room: budget, which are basic and share cold water bathrooms, and deluxe, which are still pretty bare-bones but have small TVs, private facilities and kitchenettes.

First Light Inn (☎ 888 0339; firstlight@connect.com.fj; Waiyevo; r with fan/air-con & bathroom F$56/66; 🌐) Convenient for the ferries, this is a relaxed and friendly place with a spotless self-catering kitchen for guests and a satellite TV. Try to ring before you turn up as it is not always staffed.

Garden Island Resort (☎ 888 0286; www.garden islandresort.com; s/d/tr F$240/270/330; 🌐 🖵 🌐) Revamped rooms and a new dive shop were due to open here in early 2009. It's the only resort in the area and has great views over to the Somosomo Strait and Vanua Levu and beyond.

Nakia Resort and Dive (☎ 888 1111; www.nakiafiji.com; bure from F$340/530) Four homely yet luxurious *bure* sit on a grassy hillside looking out to sea at this raved-about ecoresort. These guys use alternative energy wherever possible and vegetables from their organic garden in their restaurant.

Eating & Drinking

Kumar's Restaurant (☎ 888 1005; Naqara; breakfast $2, meals $4; 🕐 breakfast, lunch & dinner before 7pm Mon-Sat) Cute little blue shed-like place serving cheap omelettes for breakfast and good curries.

Narayan's Tea Room (Naqara; snacks $3-5; 🕐 8am-6pm Mon-Sat) Next to the bus station, this simple but good cafe offers cakes, snacks and the odd curry.

Wathi-po-ee Restaurant (☎ 888 0382; Waiyevo; meals F$4-7; 🕐 breakfast, lunch & dinner Mon-Fri, breakfast & lunch Sat & Sun) A basic place that serves big plates of chow mein, curries and Fijian dishes as well as eggs, bacon and toast for breakfast. The sign for the old Cannibal Cafe, and its notorious slogan, 'We'd love to have you for dinner', is still at the back.

The Bakery Restaurant (Wairiki; lunch/dinner F$10/15; 🕐 breakfast, lunch & dinner) This new place next to Taveuni Dive serves good breakfasts, burgers and coffee.

For self-caterers, **Kaba's Supermarket** (☎ 888 0088; Naqara; 🕐 8am-5pm Mon-Fri, till 1pm Sat & Sun) is fully stocked. There is also a large MH Supermarket in Somosomo (which sells alcohol, but not on Saturday afternoon or Sunday) or the Wairiki supermarket, which is open on Sundays. For fresh fruit and vegetables try the stalls along the main street of Naqara.

SOUTHERN TAVEUNI

The road south from Waiyevo winds along the rugged coast through beautiful rainforest, *dalo* and coconut plantations to Vuna and Kanacea villages. Check out the **blowhole** on the dramatic, windswept South Cape. As swells crash into the rocky coast, geysers of sea spray are forced skyward through vents in the stone.

Diving and snorkelling on Vuna Reef and nearby Rainbow Reef are excellent. See p158 for details on dive operators.

Sleeping & Eating

BUDGET & MIDRANGE

Dolphin Bay Divers Retreat (☎ 828 3001, 926 0145; www.dolphinbaydivers.com; Vanaira Bay, Vanua Levu; tent sites per person F$15, safari tent/bure F$50/90; 🖵) Just a bay over from Almost Paradise on Vanua Levu, this is a friendly place with simple *bure* (new ones are under construction), space for camping and some permanent safari tents. A big hit with divers, the food here is good, plentiful and eaten family style (meal plans are F$60 per day). Transfers from Matei cost $60 one-way. Dolphin Bay cannot be contacted from Buca Bay on Vanua Levu due to lack of mobile reception; turning up unannounced might leave you stranded.

Almost Paradise (☎ 828 3000, 992 6782; www.almostparadisefiji.com; Vanua Levu; s/d F$155/195; 🖵) This place is in a sheltered bay on Vanua Levu, but is most easily accessed by boat from Taveuni. There are just a few en suite wooden bungalows here with rainwater showers, solar power and teeny kitchenettes. There's no beach, but there's good snorkelling at the house reef and you can hire kayaks and paddle up a small river in the mangroves. Transfers from Taveuni cost F$45. It was closed for renovation at the time of research.

Further budget options:

Dolphin Bay Divers Taveuni Guest House (☎ 888 0531; www.dolphinbaydivers.com; dm/d F$15/55) Large, spotless house with two double bedrooms and a shared bathroom.

Vuna Lagoon Lodge (☎ /fax 888 0627; dm/s/d F$22/48/65) Somewhat of a cross between a homestay and a private rental, this simple wooden house is a few steps from the beach near the village of Vuna. Call ahead.

TOP END

Paradise Taveuni (☎ 888 0125; www.paradiseinfiji.com; s/d/from F$400/500 incl all meals; 🖳) Set in a former plantation on an elevated piece of land, the *bure* here are luxury all the way. Expect large decks, day beds, separate living and sleeping quarters, huge bathrooms (some with outdoor Jacuzzis and rock showers) and plenty of daily activities. The place is run with military precision and any problems are fixed with startling efficiency.

Vatuwiri Farm Resort (☎ 888 0316; vatuwirifiji.com; cottages d incl meals F$500) One of the last working estates in the South Pacific and Taveuni's biggest cattle farm, Vatuwiri has two small cottages perched on a lawn on the water's edge. Both have gorgeous views and there's fabulous swimming and snorkelling to be done here.

MATEI & AROUND

Matei is a residential area on Taveuni's northern point. Much of the freehold land has been bought by foreigners searching for a piece of tropical paradise. A five-minute stroll from the tiny airport brings you to a long stretch of road and a number of places to stay, eat and organise dive trips with.

Sleeping

BUDGET

Beverly Campground (☎ 888 0381; sites per person F$10, permanent tent F$15, dorm F$15) A 15-minute walk west of the airport, this is one of those magical spots where everybody makes friends easily and camping isn't a chore. The campsite has a white-sand beach and is set beneath huge, poison-fish trees. It has very basic facilities including a sheltered area for cooking and dining.

Bibi's Hideaway (☎ 888 0443; sites per person F$15, family bure F$100, s/d bure F$70-90, honeymoon bure F$110) A rambling five-acre hillside plot hides a selection of *bure* in varying sizes among the fruit and palm trees. There are self-catering facilities here and plenty of room for pitching tents. They are extremely friendly and the prices are always up for negotiation.

Tovu Tovu Resort (☎ 888 0560; www.tovutovu.com; bure with/without bure F$85/100, f bure F$130) Steeped in history, this resort is based on a subdivided copra estate and is still owned by the Petersen family who once ran the plantation. It's the best budget place in town and has a selection of wooden *bure* with little wooden verandas, kitchenettes, hot-water bathrooms and fans. Tovu Tovu is a 20-minute walk southeast of Matei airport.

Little Dolphin (☎ 888 0130; www.littledolphintaveuni .com; d cottage F$100) This tiny, two-storey, top-heavy cottage has a breezy bedroom and a veranda overlooking the ocean. Besides a kitchen and hot-water bathroom, there are a couple of shelves of books, and snorkels and kayaks can be borrowed for free.

MIDRANGE

Coconut Grove Beachfront Cottages (☎ 888 0328; www.coconutgrovefiji.com; bure F$300-390) A stone path studded with fish mosaics leads to three calm and comfortable cottages and a quiet slice of golden, sandy beach. Two of the *bure* have rock showers with sea views, and the restaurant here is one of the best on the island.

Karin's Garden (☎ 888 0511; www.karinsgarden fiji.com; cottage from F$320) A lovingly cared-for two-bedroom cottage with a kitchen, sitting room, veranda and bird's-eye view of the reef. The rooms are big and cosy and the owners affable and relaxed. There is a two-night minimum stay.

TOP END

Maravu Plantation Resort (☎ 332 4303; www.maravu .net; s/d/tr standard bure from F$310/450/520, deluxe bure F$380/580/700, s/d/t ocean-view villa F$590/1000/1180; 🏊 🖳) A former copra plantation across the road from the beach, this isn't as swish as the other luxury resorts, but some of the *bure* do have nice ocean views and the more expensive have outdoor Jacuzzis and showers. Free activities include horse riding, mountain biking and kayaking. Meal plans offer two/three meals per day for F$30/50.

Taveuni Island Resort (☎ 888 0441; www.taveuni islandresort.com; bure F$680-750 per person; honeymoon villa F$2500; 🖳 🖭) Popular with honeymoon-ers and divers on package vacations, these dozen hillside *bure* offer complete privacy, polished wood floors, wicker furniture and romantic outdoor showers. Rates include the mouth-watering meals that are served on the beach, by the pool or in your *bure*. No children under 15.

Taveuni Palms (☎ 888 0032; www.taveunipalms fiji.com; d villa F$2000, per extra person/child F$440/260; 🔀 🖳 🖭) Breathtakingly beautiful, com-pletely tasteful and directly on the beach, Taveuni Palms boasts two villas, each on their own private half-acre with private beach, spa, swimming pool as well as private staff (includ-ing a personal chef who prepares five-course meals every night).

Eating & Drinking

There are several good choices in Matei. If you're here on a Wednesday, try the *lovo* or buffet complete with entertainment at Naselesele village (your accommodation will be able to arrange this for you). Profits go to the local school.

our pick **Audrey's Island Coffee & Pastries** (☎ 888 0039; coffee & cake F$10; 🕙 10am-6pm) You can sit on the deck of US-born Audrey's house and enjoy some fabulous, freshly baked cakes with coffee while looking down the sweeping coast road and out to sea. If you're lucky she may share the recipe.

Coconut Grove Restaurant (☎ 888 0328; lunch F$7-22, dinner F$14-35; 🕙 breakfast, lunch & dinner) Take off your shoes and enjoy the sea views from the deck of this guesthouse's lovely restaurant. The menu includes wonderfully fresh vegetar-ian dishes, homemade pasta, soups, salads and fish. You can just turn up for breakfast or lunch but you'll have to add your name to the list pinned on the door if you're coming for dinner.

Vunibokoi Restaurant (☎ 888 0560; dinner mains F$18; 🕙 breakfast, lunch & dinner) Tovu Tovu Resort's restaurant has large windows over-looking the island of Viubani. At lunch there are burgers and sandwiches, and the evening dinner board may include such delights as crab curry, stir-fried prawns and *rourou* (dalo leaf) soup. On Friday, there's a good-value buffet for F$20.

Restaurant Tramonto (☎ 888 2224; pizza from F$25, meals F$20-25; 🕙 lunch & dinner) If you're in the market for a pizza the size of a small child then Tramonto won't disappoint. If cheesi-ness leaves you cold then there are a couple of other well-prepared dishes available daily, including fish and chips and lamb shanks. On Sunday there's a buffet dinner (F$25) and on Wednesday there's a barbecue (F$20). Reservations required.

Local supermarkets include **Bhula Bhai & Sons** (☎ 888 0462) and **Sonal Shopping Centre** (☎ 888 0431).

EASTERN TAVEUNI

Eastern Taveuni's beautiful wild coast and lush rainforest are in good hands, with local landowners rejecting logging in favour of ecotourism and other sustainable practices. Scenes for the 1991 movie, *Return to the Blue Lagoon*, were filmed at Bouma National Heritage Park.

Bouma National Heritage Park

Taveuni still retains large amounts of pristine forest and the **national park** (admission $12; www .bnho.org) protects around 80% of this and cov-ers about 150sq km of coastal forest and rain-forest. Within are several kilometres of bush walks and three beautiful **Tavoro Waterfalls**. The walking track begins opposite the reception *bure*, south of the river in Bouma.

The first waterfall is only 10 minutes' walk along a flat path and is a great place for a dip. The second waterfall, a further 30 or 40 minutes along, is smaller but also has a good swimming pool. The track is steep in places, with a river crossing, but has steps, handrails and lookout spots to rest. The 30-minute hike to the third and smallest fall is less well main-tained and often muddy. It has a great swim-ming pool and, if you bring your snorkelling gear, you'll be able to see the hundreds of prawns in the water.

If you are a keen walker, try the **Vidawa Rainforest Trail**. Beginning at Vidawa village, it passes through the historic fortified vil-lage site of Navuga and cuts through tropical rainforests rich with birds before linking with the Tavoro Waterfalls described above. You can only do this walk with a guide and need to book in advance. The trip runs Monday to Saturday and can take a maximum of eight people (F$40). The price includes guides, lunch, afternoon tea and park admission fee. Book through **Tavoro Waterfalls Visitor Centre** (☎ 888 0390; 🕙 9am-4pm).

Waitabu Marine Park

This area offers excellent snorkelling off a white-sand beach. You can visit the park only with a guide. The village of Waitabu has set up a half-day tour (☎ 888 0451; per person F$40/35 for 1/4 or more), which includes a guided snorkel, *bilibili* ride and morning and afternoon tea in the village. There's also a backpackers' tour with guided snorkelling and boat transfers (F$20 per person).

Lavena Coastal Walk

The 5km Lavena Coastal Walk is well worth the effort. The trail follows the forest edge along the beach, past peaceful villages and then climbs up through the tropical rainforest to a gushing waterfall. There's some good snorkelling and kayaking here and Lavena Point is fine for swimming.

The path is clearly marked and well maintained. To reach the falls at the end of the trail you have to clamber over rocks and swim a short distance through two deep pools. If you're visiting in the rainy season, the rocks near the falls can be slippery, if not flooded. It can be difficult and dangerous to reach the falls at this time.

The park is managed through Lavena Lodge. Park entrance is F$12 or F$15 with a guide. Kayaks can be hired for F$40 per day, and guided kayak tours are available.

Run by friendly informative staff, **Lavena Lodge** (☎ 888 0116; tw per person F$30 inc fees) has basic, clean rooms, a shared kitchen and bathroom. There's electricity in the evening for a maximum of eight people. Next to a beach, this is a great place to relax after a hard day's hike, and meals are available (F$7/10 breakfast/lunch or dinner). There's a tiny shop in the village, but if you're planning to cook, bring your own supplies.

OFFSHORE ISLANDS

Matagi
area 1 sq km

Horseshoe-shaped Matagi (aka Matangi), formed by a submerged volcanic crater, is 10km off Taveuni's coast and just north of Qamea. Its steep rainforest sides rise to 130m.

The deluxe *bure* at **Matangi Private Island Resort** (☎ 888 0260; www.matangiisland.com; d standard island bure US$525, d beachfront bure US$690, d treehouse US$900, 2-bedroom villa US$1050; 🖳 🖳) are roomy enough to turn cartwheels in, and it's romance run amok in the 'treehouses' that are perched 5m up in the canopy. Rates include meals, most activities (although not scuba diving) and Taveuni transfers. This is an adults only resort.

Qamea
area 34 sq km

Only 2.5km east from Taveuni, Qamea is a green and hilly island skirted by bays with white-sand beaches. The island is rich in birdlife and notable for the *lairo*, the annual migration of land crabs.

Maqai Resort & Surf (☎ 9907 900; www.maqai.com; dm/s/d/tw F$30/40/80/80) is a brand-new surf resort situated on a beautiful stretch of beach overlooking three surf breaks. Accommodation is basic, in safari tents and a dorm.

Qamea Resort & Spa (☎ 888 0220; www.qamea.com; d/tr bure F$1250/1540, d premium villa F$1910; 🖳 🖳) Another adults only affair, the magnificently thatched *bure* are dotted along a stretch of beautiful white-sand beach. Refurbished in 2007, the huge, air-conditioned *bure* are decorated with Fijian art, and some feature plunge pools, spa baths and rock showers. Rates here include meals and transfers to and from Taveuni. Activities including snorkelling, diving, windsurfing, sailing, outrigger canoeing, village visits and fishing trips can all be arranged here.

KADAVU

pop 12,000 / area 450 sq km

About 100km south of Viti Levu, this untamed group of islands forms a hilly and verdant backdrop against the empty sea. The absence of roads and infrastructure helps to maintain a prehistoric façade, and Kadavu's 72 villages still rely largely on subsistence agriculture. Tourism is expanding at a slow creep, enough to beckon travellers without greatly affecting the existing culture.

The only town on the island is petite Vunisea. There's not much here to interest tourists but it's the group's administrative centre, where you'll find the police station, post office, hospital (all on the top of the hill) and airstrip.

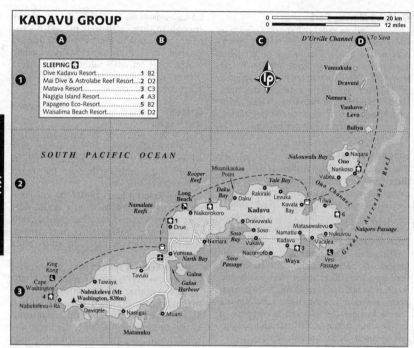

KADAVU GROUP

0 ————————— 20 km
0 ————————— 12 miles

SLEEPING 🏠
Dive Kadavu Resort................................1 B2
Mai Dive & Astrolabe Reef Resort....2 D2
Matava Resort.......................................3 C3
Nagigia Island Resort...........................4 A3
Papageno Eco-Resort...........................5 B2
Waisalima Beach Resort.......................6 D2

SOUTH PACIFIC OCEAN

The magnificent Great Astrolabe Reef is Kadavu's main lure. Cutting a vivid swathe around the group's base, it rewards visitors with some of the finest diving in the Pacific. But the interior is just as colourful and the lush rainforests, especially on the eastern side, are home to a wide variety of birdlife, including the celebrated Kadavu musk parrot.

ACTIVITIES

The mountains have rainforest, numerous waterfalls and **hiking** trails. Ask locals about current conditions before setting out. The isolated villagers are very traditional, so when visiting a village, ask to speak to the *turaga-ni-koro* – the village headman – first, remove your hat and don't carry things on your shoulders (see p102 for further advice).

Kadavu has excellent **diving**, with the famous Astrolabe Reef skirting the eastern side of the group. Expect to see brilliantly coloured corals, vertical drop-offs and a wonderful array of marine life. Unfortunately, the weather often dictates which sites are available, as visibility can range from 15m to 70m. Most resorts have dive outfits.

The best **surfing** in Kadavu is found around Cape Washington, at the southernmost end of Kadavu.

Tamarillo Sea Kayaking (☎ in New Zealand 04-239 9885; www.tamarillo.co.nz/fiji; per person F$2400; ✹ May-Sep) offers interesting seven-day kayak tours around Kadavu with meals and accommodation in budget resorts and villages. All the resorts have two-person ocean kayaks for hire.

TRANSPORT
Getting There & Around

Flying is a quicker and safer option than the ferry trip between Kadavu and Suva, which can be rough and whose timetable is erratic. The small boats used for transfers to and from the airstrip often don't have life jackets or radios.

Air Fiji (☎ 331 3666; suvasales@airfiji.com.fj) has daily return flights from Suva to Kadavu (F$220). **Pacific Sun** (☎ 672 0888; www.pacificsun .com.fj) has daily flights to Kadavu from Nadi (F$220 return).

Venu Shipping (☎ 339 5000; 330 7349; Rona St, Walu Bay, Suva) operates the largely irregular and unreliable MV *Sinu-i-Wasa* between Suva and

Kadavu (F$55/75, seat/berth one way). It's mostly for cargo and local use and can take anything from four hours to two days.

Kadavu's few roads are restricted to the Vunisea area, except for one rough, unsealed road to Nabukelevu-i-Ra around the southern end of Kadavu. Small boats are the group's principal mode of transport. Each resort has its own boat and will pick up guests from Vunisea airstrip; be sure to make arrangements in advance.

SLEEPING

Waisalima Beach Resort (☎ 331 7281; www.waisa limafiji.com; camping per person F$10, dm F$25, s/d without bathroom F$75 per person, s/d with bathroom F$100/150 per person) Waisalima is all about simple pleasures. The thatch *bure* are far from glamorous but the beds are comfy, and there are plenty of hammocks on a long beach. The meal plans (F$50 per day) includes plenty of fruit, home-baked pastries, fresh fish and vegetables from the garden. Return boat transfers from Vunisea airstrip cost F$100 per adult. Viti Water Sports charge F$185/650 for a two-tank dive/PADI Open Water Course here.

Mai Dive & Astrolabe Reef Resort (☎ 603 0842; www.maidive.com; camping per person F$75, s/d F$180/270) Located on Ono island, the pretty pale-green wooden bungalows line the beach at this brand-new resort. All have wooden verandas and open-air showers so you can wash under the stars. Meals are included in the tariff. Return airport transfers are F$140 per adult. Children under 16 free if with two or more adults. A two-tank dive/PADI Open Water Course costs $180/580.

Matava Resort (☎ 333 6222; www.matava.com; d without/with bathroom F$120-220 pp; ✗) Matava wins glowing reviews from travellers for its well-considered mix of budget and midrange accommodation. Rustic, airy thatch and timber *bure* clamber up the neat hillside grounds, framed by wide decks looking out to sea. Meals, using vegetables and herbs from the organic garden, are eaten communally in the lantern-lit restaurant–bar *bure*. While the resort doesn't have a sunbather-friendly strip of beach, there are suitable spots a short kayak away. One-hour boat transfers from Vunisea airstrip cost F$50 per person. Budget travellers can opt to share a *bure* with other single travellers for F$30 a night and buy their meals separately. The recommended Mad Fish

Dive Centre is based here. Two-tank dives/ PADI Open Water Courses cost F$200/610 including equipment.

Nagigia Island Resort (☎ 603 0454; www.fiji surf.com; dm $115, s/d/t from $263/206/160 pp; ✗) Nagigia's home is a remote and staggeringly photogenic island on the far western side of the island group, near Cape Washington. *Bure* and dorms capture dramatic reef, surf and mountain views, and hang so close to the water they're practically dipping their toes in the sea. There's no beach to speak of, but there are sufficient spots for sunbathing and lots of little wooden platforms with steps leading into the water. Nagigia is known as a surfer resort and has a choice of five breaks that produce rideable waves all year round. Meal plans are an additional F$60 per person. Return boat transfers from Vunisea airstrip are F$70 per person.

Papageno Eco-Resort (☎ 603 0466; www.papageno ecoresort.com; s/d from $300/$420; ✗) Ecologically friendly and embedded in a thick tropical garden, Papageno is the quintessential island sanctuary. Cool garden rooms include futon-style beds and furniture made from local materials. Larger *bure* have plenty of space and privacy. The food is excellent, and kava ceremonies, sea kayaking and hiking are all free. A two-tank dive/PADI Open Water Course costs F$160/620.

Dive Kadavu Resort (☎ 368 3502; www.divekadavu .com; s/d/t/f $320/560/780/980; ✗) This appealing resort has unfussy *bure* with comfortable beds, verandas, hot water and tidy bathrooms. Most of the visitors are here on dive packages, from the United States. Sheltered from the prevailing southeasterly winds, it boasts an excellent beach where the snorkelling and swimming is wonderful regardless of the tide. Rates include meals and airport transfers. A two-tank dive/PADI Open Water Course costs F$150/650.

LAU GROUP

Fiji's final frontier, the 57 Lau islands are strewn across the southwest corner of Fiji's vast archipelago like a rash of green spots on the skin of the Pacific. Few visit here, but those who do report of countless bays, deserted, reef-rimmed atolls and sparsely populated islands with hilly interiors.

Lau islanders are known for their wood-carving and *masi* (bark cloth) crafts, and have been greatly influenced by neighbouring Polynesian cultures. Although the climate here is drier than most parts of Fiji, storms can be fierce and some of the bays are used as hurricane shelters by visiting yachts.

Transport

GETTING THERE & AWAY

Air Fiji (☎ 331 5055; www.airfiji.com.fj) flies Suva–Vanua Balavu (F$170 one way) on Fridays and between Suva and Lakeba (F$170 one way) on Mondays.

If you have plenty of time and a masochistic streak you can also reach the Lau Group by cargo/passenger boats (see p172).

Yachties wishing to visit Lau need to clear customs and immigration first (see p171), and then apply for permission from the Ministry for Fijian Affairs.

VANUA BALAVU

area 53 sq km

This beautiful island, averaging about 2km wide, has lots of sandy beaches and rugged limestone hills. The celebrated **Bay of Islands**, also known as Qilaqila, sits in the northwest pocket and is a spectacular site for diving, kayaking and swimming. **Lomaloma**, the largest village, was Fiji's first port, regularly visited by

---

KNOW BEFORE YOU GO

■ The Lau are Fiji's wild frontier. There are no hotels, bars, restaurants, dive shops, banks or tourist shops. Only two islands, Vanua Balavu and Lakeba, have guest houses. Neither accepts credit cards.

■ Meals will be mostly whatever the locals can catch or grow. Expect plenty of fresh seafood, local fruits and starchy vegetables.

■ Book flights well in advance and confirm your reservation. Flights are infrequent, sometimes rescheduled and generally full. If it rains and the grass on the landing strip is dangerously slippery, the plane will return to Suva.

■ Boats can run weeks behind their published timetables and, if they do, the local shops will run out of goods. BYO snacks.

---

sailing ships trading in the Pacific. Today the people of Vanua Balavu rely largely on copra and *bêche-de-mer* for their income.

Now that Nawanawa Estate has closed, there is only one place to stay in Vanua Balavu.

Moana's Guesthouse (☎ 822 1148, 820 1357; www.moanasguesthouses.com; r per person incl meals F$75, children under 12 F$50; ✕ ▣) Moana's covers all the basics with beach *bure* and guesthouse options. The three simple *bure* are a 1km walk from Sawana village and mere metres from a tidal beach. The *bure* are simple, thatched affairs with mosquito nets, solar power, private bathrooms and mats laid over concrete floors. Back in Sawana they offer homestay-style accommodation in a Tongan-style cottage. Moana's can arrange boat, snorkelling and fishing trips and collects travellers from the airstrip for F$40 return. They have internet, but it's slow and not always working.

FIJI DIRECTORY

ACCOMMODATION

Fiji has a good range of accommodation including five-star hotels, B&Bs, hostels, motels, resorts, treehouses, bungalows on the beach and village homestays.

Budget travellers can expect to pay F$25 to F$35 for a dorm bed and between F$70 to F$135 for a double with shared facilities. Dedicated single rooms are rare. Many backpacker resorts in Nadi, Viti Levu's Coral Coast and the Mamanucas have excellent facilities, but some of the *bure* on the outer islands are only a hurricane or two away from total collapse.

There is virtually no organised camping in Fiji, and it's vital to seek permission before setting up camp anywhere. Most of Fiji's land, even in seemingly remote areas, is owned by the local *mataqali* (family groups) or villages. If you are invited to camp in a village, be sure to read up on village etiquette (p102) and take a *sevusevu*.

The bulk of accommodation in Fiji falls under the midrange banner. Options include hotels, motels and resorts ranging from F$130 to F$250 for a room, regardless of whether occupied by one or two adults. Guests can expect bathrooms, TVs and bar fridges in hotels, and many lodges and resorts offer self-contained

---

PRACTICALITIES

■ *Fiji Times*, *The Daily Post* and the *Fiji Sun* are the national daily newspapers. *Fiji Magic* (www
.fijilive.com/fijimagic) is a monthly publication detailing the prices of accommodation, restaurants, activities and tours.

■ The government-sponsored Fiji Broadcasting Commission has stations in English (Radio Fiji 3 and 104FM), Fijian (Radio Fiji 1) and Fiji-Hindi (Radio Fiji 2 and 98FM). Bula 100 plays an eclectic mix of pop, rock, reggae, dance, folk, country and local music. Fiji has one television station, and some resorts and bars have Sky satellite TV.

■ The video and DVD systems used in Fiji are PAL, which is the same as Australia, NZ, Europe, the UK and most of Asia and the Pacific.

■ Electricity is supplied at 240V, 50Hz AC. Outlets use flat two- or three-pin plugs like those in Australia and NZ.

■ Fiji follows the metric system of measurement. See the Quick Reference page for conversions.

---

units. Top-end options generally include five-star chains and resorts, with prices ranging from F$280 to F$2000 per room.

The term 'resort' is used very loosely in Fiji and can refer to any accommodation near the sea, ranging from backpacker-style to pure luxury.

Rates quoted in this book include Fiji's 12.5% value-added tax (VAT) and the 5% hotel turnover tax.

ACTIVITIES
Diving & Snorkelling
Fiji offers some spectacular snorkelling. Among the best spots are Nananu-i-Ra off Viti Levu's northern coast, as well as islands in the Mamanuca and Yasawa groups. Reefs are often very close to the coasts but in many places you can swim only at high tide, and channels can be dangerous.

Fiji is also a diver's mecca, with magnificent reefs and a raft of operators, so getting to some premium sites is dead – no pun intended – easy. Most dive shops charge between F$190 and F$230 for a two-tank dive and from F$575 to F$780 for a PADI Open Water Certification. See p74 for further information on diving.

Hiking
Viti Levu and Taveuni are the best islands for hiking. Suva's Colo-i-Suva Forest Park (p125) and Taveuni's Lavena Coastal Walk (p163) have marked trails that don't require guides or permission. Hiking hot spots in the Viti Levu Highlands include Mt Batilamu and Koroyanitu National Heritage Park (p134).

Kayaking
Sea-kayaking tours are available during the drier months (between May and November), and combine paddling with hiking, snorkelling, fishing and village visits. Two prime areas for kayaking safaris are the Yasawa (p143) and Kadavu (p164) groups.

Surfing
Surfing usually requires boat trips as the majority of breaks are on offshore reefs. The best spots are in barrier-reef passages along southern Viti Levu (Frigate's Passage p124) and in the southern Mamanucas (Cloudbreak, Namotu Left and Wilkes Passage, p137). These should be tackled only by experienced surfers. The dry season (May to October) is the best time to surf due to low pressures bringing in big waves.

BUSINESS HOURS
Most businesses open weekdays from 8am to 5pm, and some from 8am to 1pm on Saturday. Government offices are open from 8am to 4.30pm weekdays (to 4pm on Friday). Many places close for lunch from 1pm to 2pm and practically nothing happens on Sunday. Restaurants generally open for lunch (11am to 2pm) and dinner (6pm to 9pm) from Monday to Saturday, as well as dinner on Sunday.

CHILDREN
Fiji is a major family destination and very child-friendly. Many resorts cater specifically for children, with baby-sitting, cots and high chairs, organised activities, children's pools and kids' clubs. In many resorts children stay, and in some cases eat, free.

FIJI

EMBASSIES & CONSULATES
Fijian Embassies & Consulates
Fiji has diplomatic representation in the following countries.

Australia (☎ 02-6260 5115; www.fijihighcom.com)
China (☎ 10-6532 7305; www.fijiembassy.org.cn)
Japan (☎ 03-3587 2038; www.fijiembassy.jp)
New Zealand (☎ 04-473 5401; www.fiji.org.nz;)
UK (☎ 020-7584 3661; www.fijihighcommission.org.uk)
USA (☎ 202-337 8320; www.fijiembassydc.com)

Embassies & Consulates in Fiji
Australia (☎ 338 2211; 37 Princes Rd, Tamavua, Suva)
Canada (Consulate; ☎ /fax 972 2400; Nadi airport)
China (☎ 330 0251; 147 Queen Elizabeth Dr, Suva)
European Union (☎ 331 3633; 4th fl, Fiji Development Bank Centre, Victoria Pde, Suva)
Federated States of Micronesia (☎ 330 4566; 37 Loftus St, Suva)
France (☎ 331 2233; 7th fl, Dominion House, Thomson St, Suva)
Germany (☎ 331 2927; 82 Harris Rd, Suva)
Japan (☎ 330 4633; 2nd fl, Dominion House, Thomson St, Suva)
Korea (☎ 330 0977; 8th fl, Vanua House, Victoria Pde, Suva)
Nauru (☎ 331 3566; 7th fl, Ratu Sukuna House, Suva)
Netherlands (☎ 330 1499; 1st fl, Crompton Solicitors Suite, 10 Victoria Arcade, Suva)
New Zealand (☎ 331 1422; 10th fl, Reserve Bank Bldg, Pratt St, Suva)
Tuvalu (☎ 330 1355; 16 Gorrie St, Suva)
UK (☎ 322 9100; Victoria House, 47 Gladstone Rd, Suva)
USA (☎ 331 4466; 31 Loftus St, Suva)

FESTIVALS & EVENTS
See p629 for regional public holidays.

February/March
Hindu Holi (Festival of Colours) People squirt coloured water at each other; best seen in Lautoka.

March/April
Ram Naumi (Birth of Lord Rama) Hindu religious festival in Suva Bay. Worshippers wade into the water and throw flowers.

July
Bula Festival One of Fiji's biggest festivals – held in Nadi with rides, music, shows and the crowning of 'Miss Bula'.

August
Hibiscus Festival (www.hibiscusfiji.com) Held in Suva, with floats, food stalls, fair rides and the crowning of 'Miss Hibiscus'.

Hindu Ritual Fire Walking Performed by southern Indians in many temples, including Suva's Mariamma Temple.

September
Sugar Festival Lautoka's streets come alive with parades and fun fairs.
Fiji Regatta Week (www.musketcovefiji.com) Annual international regatta held at Muscat Cove in the Mamanucas.

October/November
Diwali Festival (Festival of Lights) Hindus worship Lakshmi, houses are decorated, business is settled, and candles and lanterns are set on doorsteps to light the way of the god.
Ram Leela (Play of Rama) Hindus celebrate through theatrical performances the life of god-king Rama and his return from exile.

INTERNET ACCESS
Internet cafes are fairly prolific in Suva, Lautoka and Nadi, and competition means that you can jump online with broadband access for as little as F$3 per hour. Access outside urban centres is more limited and pricier (up to F$8 per hour).

Wireless internet access is a recent phenomenon to Fiji thanks to **Unwired Fiji** (☎ 327 5040; www.unwired.com.fj); you'll need to purchase a special modem from them.

INTERNET RESOURCES
Fiji Government (www.fiji.gov.fj) Contains press releases, news and immigration updates.
Fiji Times (www.fijitimes.com.fj) Fiji's daily newspaper online.
Fiji Village (www.fijivillage.com) Geared to overseas Fijians, this site is updated with daily news and has excellent links to local events.
Fiji Visitors Bureau (www.fijime.com) Fiji's official tourism site, offering information on accommodation, activities and getting around, with links and an email directory.
Fijilive (www.fijilive.com) Live updates on Fijian news.

MAPS
The best place to buy maps of the Fiji islands is the Map Shop (Map p126; ☎ 321 1395; Rm 10, Department of Lands & Surveys, Government Bldgs) in Suva. It sells big (1:50,000) and detailed topographic maps of each island or island group, as well as maps of Suva. The front of the telephone book has a series of excellent city and town maps. The Hema map of *Fiji* is the most useful for tourists.

INTO THE FIRE

Hindu fire walking is part of a religious festival and the culmination of a 10-day period of absti-nence, meditation and worship. During this time it is believed that the participants are cleansed of all physical and spiritual impurities. On the final day, devotees bathe in the ocean and have their tongues, cheeks and bodies pierced with three-pronged skewers. In an almost trance-like state they then dance to the temple where, in front of a statue of the goddess Maha Devi, they walk across a pit of charred wood raked over glowing coals.

The day after the festival, and seemingly none the worse for their ordeal, I met a few of these extraordinary men.

Is this the first time that you have participated in the festival? This is my fourth time. I didn't walk over the ash on my first year – it came slowly to me. I walked at first because my mother and uncle wanted me to but now the rewards outweigh the sacrifices.

What is the most difficult aspect of fire walking? The preparation is the most difficult. You must give up many things – meat, cigarettes, kava, alcohol, sex and all impure thoughts. As for the pain – if you have the blessing of the goddess, the piecing of the skewers feel like the bites of small ants.

Why do you walk? I walk to show my devotion and I take vows for my wishes to be granted. I hope for business success; others pray for their illness to be cured, success in exams or for a child.

What is the secret to fire walking? Why is it that you don't get burned? There is no secret. Anyone with a true heart and who has meditated with their teacher and abstained from meat and sex will not be hurt. If it happens that your mind is upset or if you think of your girlfriend or wife instead of remaining focused on the goddess, then you might be burnt.

MONEY

The local currency is the Fiji dollar (F$); it's fairly stable relative to Australian and New Zealand dollars. The dollar is broken down into 100 cents. Bank notes come in denomi-nations of $50, $20, $10, $5 and $2. There are coins to the value of $1, $0.50, $0.20, $0.10, $0.05, $0.02 and $0.01. See the inside front cover for exchange rates.

ATMs

ATMs are common in urban areas and most accept the main international debit cards, including Cirrus and Maestro, as well as Visa and MasterCard. Before you head out to remote parts of Fiji, check in the appro-priate chapter to find out if you will be able to access money, exchange currency or cash travellers cheques.

Taxes

All prices quoted in this chapter are inclusive of VAT (value-added tax), a 12.5% sales tax on goods and services and, for accommodation listings, the 5% hotel turnover tax.

TELEPHONE

The international telephone code for Fiji is ☎ 679. There are no area codes.

The easiest way to make local calls within Fiji is to buy a Transtel Tele Card, available in denominations from F$3 to F$50. Dial 101 and follow the automated instructions (in English). For international calls, the cheapest calling cards are Call the World for Cheap cards, available from shops in urban centres.

Mobile Phones

Vodafone (www.vodafone.com.fj) is the only mobile phone company in Fiji. It operates a GSM digital service and has roaming agreements with Vodafone in Australia, NZ and the UK, as well as Optus in Australia. Cheap mobile phones are readily available in urban areas from F$20 and SIM cards start at F$10.

TIME

Fiji is 12 hours ahead of GMT. When it's noon in Suva it's midnight the previous day in London, 5pm the previous day in Los Angeles, noon the same day in Auckland and 10am the same day in Sydney.

TOURIST INFORMATION IN FIJI

The head office of the **Fiji Visitors Bureau** (☎ 672 2433; www.fijime.com; Suite 107, Colonial Plaza, Namaka) is in Nadi. There is also an office in Suva (☎ 330 2433).

HOW MUCH?

- Taxi in Nadi or Suva: F$5-12
- Snorkel hire: F$10-20
- Local bus ride: 65c
- Coffee: F$3
- Cocktail: F$10
- 1L petrol: F$2
- 1L bottled water: F$2.50
- Stubbie of Fiji Bitter: F$5-8
- Souvenir T-shirt: F$30
- Samosa: 50c

The **South Pacific Tourism Organisation** (☎ 330 4177; www.spto.org; 3rd fl, Dolphin Plaza, cnr Loftus St & Victoria Pde, Suva; ☼ 9am-4pm Mon-Fri) is a useful source for regional information.

VISAS

A free tourist visa for four months is granted on arrival to citizens of more than 100 countries, which includes most countries belonging to the British Commonwealth, North America, much of South America and Western Europe, India, Israel, Japan and South Korea. You can check www.fiji.gov.fj/publish/fiji_faqs .shtml for a full list. You are required to have an onward ticket and a passport valid for at least three months longer than your intended stay.

Nationalities from countries excluded from this list will have to apply for visas through a Fijian embassy prior to arrival.

Tourist visas can be extended for up to six months by applying through the Department of Immigration. You will need to show an onward ticket and proof of sufficient funds, and your passport must be valid for three months after your proposed departure. You will need to apply at the **Immigration Department** (☎ 331 2672; Government Bldg, Suva).

Those entering Fiji by boat are subject to the same visa requirements as those arriving by plane. Yachts can enter only through the designated ports of Suva, Lautoka, Savusavu and Levuka. Yachts have to be cleared by immigration and customs, and are prohibited from visiting any outer islands before doing so.

TRANSPORT IN FIJI

GETTING THERE & AWAY
Air

Most international flights to Fiji arrive at Nadi International Airport, with a few flights landing at Nausori International Airport near Suva.

As you enter the arrivals area in Nadi, you will be greeted by serenading guitar and a sea of smiling faces, mostly representatives of local accommodation and the many travel agencies.

Nausori International Airport, about 23km northeast of downtown Suva, is principally used for domestic flights by Pacific Sun and Air Fiji.

Code-sharing arrangements mean that Qantas ticket holders are carried on Air Pacific planes and United Airlines passengers are carried by Air New Zealand. See p636 for details of air passes that include Fiji.

The following international airlines fly to and from Fiji:

Aircalin (☎ 672 2145; www.aircalin.nc)
Air Fiji (☎ 331 5055, 672 2521; www.airfiji.com.fj)
Air New Zealand (☎ 331 3100; www.airnewzealand.co.nz)
Air Pacific (☎ 672 0888, 330 4388; www.airpacific.com)
Air Vanuatu (☎ 672 2521, 331 5055; www.airvanuatu.com)
Korean Air (☎ 672 1043; www.koreanair.com.au)
Pacific Blue (☎ 672 0777; www.flypacificblue.com)
Qantas Airways (☎ 672 2880, 331 3888/1833; www .qantas.com.au).
Solomon Airlines (☎ 672 2831; www.flysolomons.com)
United Airlines (☎ in Australia 131 777; www.united.com)

Fares from Sydney or Brisbane are typically A$700/1350 return low/high season. From Auckland to Fiji costs about NZ$600/1200 low/high season. Fares from the USA vary greatly in price, depending on season and ticket restrictions. Los Angeles–Nadi with Air New Zealand is about US$1200/1800 low/high season. A return ticket from London to Nadi costs about £850/1600 low/high season.

DEPARTURE TAX

Fijian departure tax is incorporated into your ticket, so there is no need to pay it at the airport.

Sea

Travelling to Fiji by sea is difficult unless you're on a cruise ship or yacht.

Yachts need to head for the designated ports of entry at Suva, Lautoka, Levuka or Savusavu, to clear customs, immigration and quarantine. Present a certificate of clearance from the previous port of call, a crew list and passports.

Yachties need to apply to the **Ministry for Fijian Affairs** (www.fiji.gov.fj/publish/m_fijian_affairs .shtml) for special written authorisation to visit the outer islands. Before departing, you'll again need to complete clearance formalities (within 24 hours), providing inbound clearance papers, your vessel's details and your next port of call. Customs must be cleared before immigration, and you must have paid all port dues and health fees.

Yacht Help (☎ 675 0911, VHF Marine channel 16; www.yachthelp.com; Shop 5, Port Denarau, Nadi) is an extremely efficient aid to skippers. They can arrange Lau cruising permits, assemble provision orders and contact tradesmen, and they publish the *Fiji Marine Guide*.

GETTING AROUND

By using local buses, carriers and ferries, you can get around Fiji's main islands relatively cheaply and easily. If you'd like more comfort, or are short of time, you can use air-conditioned express buses, rental vehicles, charter boats and small planes.

Air

AIRLINES IN FIJI

Air Fiji and Pacific Sun have regular inter-island flights by light plane. Most Air Fiji services operate out of Nausori, while Pacific Sun is based in Nadi. Pacific Sun often transports passengers' luggage in a separate plane, and arriving before or after your possessions is a common occurrence.

Air Fiji (☎ 331 5055; www.airfiji.com.fj) operates flights from Suva to Nadi (F$145), Kadavu (F$120), Koro (F$135), Labasa (F$175), Lakeba (F$175), Levuka (F$80), Moala (F$160), Rotuma (F$375), Savusavu (F$140), Taveuni (F$170), Vanua Balavu (F$170), Cica (F$165) and Gau (F$105). From Nadi, there are flights to Suva (F$145), Labasa (F$205), Savusavu (F$185) and Taveuni (F$225). There is also a flight between Savusavu and Taveuni (F$225). On Mondays and Fridays, Air Fiji flies its only two international routes to Tonga and Tuvalu.

Pacific Sun (☎ 330 4388; www.pacificsun.com.fj) domestic routes are from Suva to Nadi (F$145), Labasa (F$175) and Taveuni (F$175), and from Nadi to Suva (F$145), Kadavu (F$145), Labasa (F$205), Malololailai (F$83), Mana (F$96) and Taveuni (F$225).

CHARTER SERVICES

Charter services are most commonly used by those wishing to maximise their time at island resorts.

Island Hoppers (☎ 675 0670; www.helicopters.com.fj) Helicopter transfers to most of the Mamanuca resort islands. A flight to Vomo, Castaway, Waidigi and Tokoriki resorts by helicopter costs $294 one way per person.

Turtle Airways (☎ 672 1888; www.turtleairways .com) Turtle Airways also charters a five-seater Cessna and a seven-seater de Havilland Canadian Beaver. Contact them for rates.

Pacific Island Seaplanes (☎ 672 5644; www.fijisea planes.com) also offers transfers to islands in the Mamanuca, Yasawa and Lau Groups.

AIR PASSES

Air Fiji has a 30-day air pass that is sold only outside Fiji. It costs US$270 for those living in the USA and F$517 for everyone else. The pass includes four flights but you can have additional legs for F$100 per sector. Children under 12 get a 25% discount, and infants are charged 10% of an adult fare.

Boat

With the exception of the upmarket resort islands, often the only means of transport to and between islands is by small local boats. Life jackets are rarely provided; if the weather looks ominous or the boat is overcrowded, seriously consider postponing the trip!

FERRY

High-speed and comfortable catamarans link Viti Levu to the Yasawa and Mamanuca groups. Less reliable services link the mainland to Vanua Levu, Taveuni and Ovalau. Irregular boats also take passengers from Suva to the Lau Group, Rotuma and Kadavu. The fast catamarans aside, ferry timetables are notorious for changing frequently, and there is often a long wait at stopovers. Toilets can become filthy, so take your own toilet paper.

Note that most car-rental agencies won't let you take their car on board.

FIJI

NADI-MAMANUCAS
South Sea Cruises (☎ 675 0500; www.ssc.com.fj) and **Malolo Cat** (☎ 672 2444, 672 2488, 675 0205) have catamarans shuttling daily between Denarau Marina and the Mamanuca islands. See p137 for more information.

NADI-YASAWAS
Awesome Adventures (☎ 675 0499; www.awesomefiji .com) runs a large yellow catamaran called the *Yasawa Flyer* to all of the Yasawa Group islands, plus several of the Mamanuca islands daily. See p142 for more information.

SUVA-KORO-SAVUSAVU-(LABASA)-TAVEUNI
Consort Shipping (☎ 330 2877; fax 330 3389; consort ship@connect.com.fj; Ground fl, Dominion House Arcade, Thomson St, Suva) sails twice a week from Suva to Savusavu (F$90/60 for cabin/seat) via Koro (F$85/55 for cabin/seat). It takes 12 hours to reach Savusavu and another four hours on to Taveuni (F$110/70 from Suva for cabin/seat). For those bound for Labasa, a bus meets them at Savusavu and transports them from there. A Suva to Labasa fare including the bus costs cabin/seat F$110/70.

SUVA-SAVUSAVU-(LABASA)-TAVEUNI
Bligh Water Shipping Suva (☎ 331 8247; www.bligh watershipping.com.fj; 1-2 Matua St, Walu Bay); Lautoka (☎ 666 8229; Shop 3, Nede St); Savusavu (☎ 885 3192; 1st fl, Water Front Bld); Labasa (☎ 881 8471; Shop 4, Sangam Complex); Taveuni Agents – Tima Ltd (☎ 888 0261) Departs Suva at 6pm on Monday, Wednesday and Friday to Savusavu. For those bound for Labasa a bus meets the boat at the wharf. MV *Suilven* then departs Savusavu at 6am on Tuesdays, Thursdays and Saturdays arriving at Taveuni at 10.30am. Adult fares from Suva to Savusavu/Taveuni/Labasa are F$67/78/73. A fare for the Savusavu to Taveuni leg costs F$45.

Grace Ferry Labasa (Gulam Nabi & Sons; ☎ 881 1152; Nasekula Rd); Savusavu (Country Kitchen; ☎ 927 1372) has a bus/boat trip from Taveuni to Savusavu and Labasa (F$20 to F$25).

(SUVA)-NATOVI-LEVUKA-NABOUWALU (VANUA LEVU)
Patterson Brothers Shipping operates a daily service (F$25 one way), which involves a bus ride (1½ hours) from Suva (Western Bus Terminal, Rodwell Rd) to Natovi Landing, followed by a ferry to Buresala Landing

(one hour) and another bus to Levuka (one hour).

It is possible to travel on to Nabouwalu on Vanua Levu where you can continue by bus to Labasa (F$55).

SUVA-KADAVU
Venu Shipping (☎ 339 5000; Rona St, Walu Bay, Suva) has once weekly passenger services on MV *Sinu-i-wasa* (see p164).

SUVA-LAU GROUP
Saliabasaga Shipping (☎ 331 7484; dark-green shipping container on Muaiwalu Wharf, Suva) has monthly trips aboard MV *Tunatuki* to Lakeba, Nayau, Cicia, Tuvuca, Vanua Balavu and occasionally Kome, Namaku-i-Lau, Moce and Oneata.

Western Shipping (☎ 331 7484; yellow shipping container on Naryan Jetty, Suva) operates the *Cagi Mai Ba* to the islands in the Southern Lau group and Northern Lau groups.

SUVA-MOALA GROUP
Saliabasaga Shipping (☎ 331 7484; dark-green shipping container on Muaiwalu Wharf, Suva) MV *Tunatuki* runs monthly trips to Moala, Matuke and Totoya in the Moala group.

SUVA-ROTUMA
Western Shipping (☎ 331 7484; yellow shipping container on Muaiwalu Wharf, Suva) operates the *Cagi Mai Ba* to Rotuma once a month.

LAUTOKA-SAVUSAVU
Bligh Water Shipping Suva (☎ 331 8247; 1-2 Matua St, Walu Bay); Lautoka (☎ 666 8229; Shop 3, Nede St); Savusavu (☎ 885 3192; 1st fl, Water Front Bld); Labasa (☎ 881 8471; Shop 4, Sangam Complex); Taveuni Agents – Tima Ltd (☎ 888 0261) Departs Lautoka every Monday, Wednesday and Friday at 4pm and arrives between 3am and 4am, but passengers can stay aboard until it gets light. The boat MV *Westerland* departs Savusavu for Lautoka on Tuesdays, Thursdays and Sundays at 9pm arriving around 9am. Fares cost F$64 one way.

Bus
Catching a local bus on Fiji's larger islands is an inexpensive and fun way of getting around. While they can be fairly noisy and smoky, they are perfect for the tropics, with unglazed windows and pull-down tarpaulins for when it rains. There are bus stops but you can often just hail buses, especially in rural areas.

Sunbeam Transport and Pacific Transport are the main carriers on Viti Levu (see p108); the latter also operates services on Taveuni (see p157). Local companies operate buses on Vanua Levu; see p154 for services in Savusavu and p156 for Labasa.

Reservations are not necessary for local buses. If you are on a tight schedule or have an appointment, it may be a good idea to buy your ticket in advance, especially for coach trips over longer distances (eg Suva to Nadi). Pacific Transport and Sunbeam issue timetables from their offices in Lautoka.

Car & Motorcycle

Ninety per cent of Fiji's 5100km of roads are on Viti Levu and Vanua Levu (about a fifth are sealed). Both islands are fun to explore by car.

DRIVING LICENCE

If you hold a current driving licence from an English-speaking country, you are entitled to drive in Fiji. Otherwise, you will need an international driving permit, which should be obtained in your home country before travelling.

HIRE

Rental cars are relatively expensive in Fiji. Despite this, it is a good way to explore the larger islands, especially if you can split the cost with others. The shorter the hire period, the higher the rate; a week or more with an international company will cost around F$85 per day, excluding tax, but the same car can cost twice as much for one or two days' hire. It's usual to pay a deposit by credit card. If you don't have one, you'll need to leave a hefty cash bond. Generally, the larger, well-known companies have better cars and support, but are more expensive.

A valid overseas or international driving licence is required. The minimum age requirement is 21 or, in some cases, 25.

Avis Rent a Car (www.avis.com.fj) Nadi airport (☎ 672 2233); Nausori airport (☎ 337 8361); Suva (☎ 337 8361); Korolevu (☎ 653 0833); Korotogo (☎ 652 0144)

Budget Rent a Car (www.budget.com.fj) Labasa (☎ 881 1999); Nadi airport (☎ 672 2636); Nausori airport (☎ 347 9299); Savusavu (☎ 881 1999); Sigatoka (☎ 650 0986); Suva (☎ 331 5899); Taveuni (☎ 888 0291)

Hertz (www.hertzfiji.net) Nadi airport (☎ 672 3466); Suva (☎ 338 0981)
Thrifty Car Rental (www.thrifty.com) Nadi airport (☎ 672 2935); Suva (☎ 331 4436)

INSURANCE

Third-party insurance is compulsory, and all car-rental companies add it onto the daily rental rate (count on F$22 to F$30 depending on the size of the vehicle). Personal accident insurance is highly recommended if you are not already covered by travel insurance. Renters are liable for the first F$500 damage. Common exclusions, or problems that won't be paid for by the insurance company, include tyre damage, underbody and overhead damage, windscreen damage and theft of the vehicle.

ROAD RULES

Driving is on the left-hand side of the road. The speed limit is 80km/h, which drops to 20km/h in towns. Many villages have speed humps to force drivers to respect the village pace. Seat belts are compulsory for front-seat passengers. Should you pick up a parking fine in Suva it's likely to be around F$2.

Tours

Fiji has many companies providing tours within the country, including hiking, kayaking, diving, bus and 4WD tours. Cruises to the outer islands such as the Mamanucas and Yasawas are extremely popular.

Popular with the under 35-year-olds are the tours run by Nadi-based **Feejee Experience** (☎ 672 3311; www.feejeeexperience.com). These tours allow you to hop on and off as you like within six months. Tours start at F$396 for the four-day 'Hula Loop'. The price includes sandboarding down the Sigatoka Dunes, tubing on the Navua River, visiting Suva nightclubs, *bilibili* (bamboo raft) trips, the mud pools at Sabeto, kayaking and snorkelling at Volivoli (Rakiraki). It does not include accommodation or food. Feejee Experience has a stellar reputation, and those who sign up for a tour generally rave about it, although before you book, it's worth keeping in mind that a perfectly comfortable, air-conditioned Sunbeam Bus will also take you around the island for F$31.50.

FIJI

New Caledonia

Dazzling – yes, New Caledonia is dazzling. Its lagoon surrounds it with every colour of blue. So the light and the space delight your senses. The 2008 prestigious listing of the lagoon as a World Heritage site has brought the people together to celebrate and protect from village level through to government.

Moreover, New Caledonia isn't just a tropical playground. There's a charming mix of French and Melanesian: warm hospitality sitting beside European elegance, gourmet food beneath palm trees, designer clothing next to woven mats, resorts, bungalows, concrete, bamboo. Wander past colonial-era buildings and through museums, soaking up the cultures of these joint owners of the land. But most of all, have fun, because there are long gorgeous beaches backed by cafes and bars, with horizons that display tiny islets to attract day-trippers. Be lured into helicopters, kayak, rock-climb, sail, dive into a world of corals, canyons, caves and heritage shipwrecks, go whale-watching or relax on the warm sand of a deserted isle. Natural wonders and manmade delights at your fingertips.

South of the capital, expanses of red earth and olive scrub, sparkling bays and waterfalls surround Kanak settlements, all of which remind you how to live at one with the earth. The north is compelling, with dramatic rock formations, stunning coastlines, silent mountains, dusty country towns and wide white fly-fishing territory. Ferry across to Île des Pins to feel the magic of pencil-thin araucaria pines, watching dreamily as you laze by the diamond-blue lagoon or snorkel in a natural aquarium. Gather your things for a jaunt to the Loyalty Islands, richly steeped in Kanak culture, and wonder how you'll ever leave this delightful country.

HIGHLIGHTS

- Get your Pass to Culture & Nature in **Noumea** (p185) to admire Napoleon at the **Aquarium des Lagons** (p185), marvel at the architecture at the **Tjibaou Cultural Centre** (p185), dream about days past at **Musée de la Ville de Noumea** (p183).

- Drive north on a geo-adventure to **La Roche Percée** (p198), **La Coeur de Voh** (p201) and the towering black jagged **Lindéralique rocks** (p204) at Hienghène

- Absorb the silence in the drowned forest, the solitary bush or on a deserted little islet, all in the **Far South** (p192)

- Glide across Baie d'Upi on **Île des Pins** (p216) in a *pirogue* (outrigger canoe) and then feast on grilled lobster under the pines.

- Scuba dive and snorkel, check out the shark nursery and watch the whales passing on the gorgeous **Loyalty Islands** (p206).

Hienghène ★
Loyalty Islands
La Coeur de Voh ★
La Roche Percée ★
Noumea ★   ★ Far South
★ Île des Pins

NEW CALEDONIA

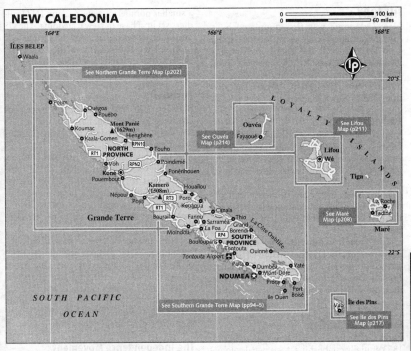

CLIMATE & WHEN TO GO

New Caledonia has a temperate climate with two main seasons: cold (June to August) and hot (mid-November to mid-April). Water temperatures drop to 21°C in the cold season, and average air temperatures are around 24°C during the day and 15°C at night. Travellers wanting to laze around on the beach should avoid these months, but for hikers this is an ideal time to visit New Caledonia. In the hot season, average maximum temperatures vary between 26°C and 30°C. The cyclone season occurs during the hottest months, January to March.

NEW CALEDONIA FAST FACTS

Capital city (and island) Noumea (Grande Terre)
Population 300,000
Land area 18,575 sq km
International telephone code ☎ 687
Currency Cour de Franc Pacifique (CFP)
Languages French and Kanak
Greeting *Bonjour* (Hello)
Website www.office-tourisme.nc

Overall, the best time to visit New Caledonia is from September to December, when the days are not too hot and sticky, and there's less likelihood of rain.

For Noumea's climate chart, see p627.

COSTS & MONEY

It's said that New Caledonia costs an arm and a leg, but it's so beautiful you'll hardly miss your limbs. A budget holiday generally means camping, but you'll need to bring a tent or buy one here. You can also stay in a *case* (a large thatched hut with mattresses on the floor). These options range from 1000 CFP to 2500 CFP. Homestays and gîtes cost up to 6000 CFP per person.

All other accommodation offers only a double rate, which makes it almost worth bringing your secret friend. Bungalows and budget hotels cost up to 14,000 CFP a double. Midrange hotels run up to 22,000 CFP a night and top-end hotels go up from there. Accommodation may be cheaper if you buy a package deal; for example, Air Caledonie packages to the Loyalty Islands are great value.

Another expense is the cost of transfers as petrol is shipped in.

HISTORY

New Caledonia was first populated by a hunter-gatherer people known as the Lapita, who arrived from the islands of Vanuatu around 1500 BC; see p37 for more on Lapita. From about the 11th century AD until the 18th century, groups of Polynesians also migrated to New Caledonia.

Early Europeans

English explorer James Cook spotted Grande Terre in 1774, naming it New Caledonia because the terrain reminded him of the highlands of Scotland (which was called Caledonia by the Romans).

During the 19th century British and US whalers, followed by sandalwood traders, were the first commercial Westerners to land on the islands.

The first missionaries, two Protestant Samoans from the London Missionary Society, arrived on Île des Pins in 1841. A little later, French Catholic missionaries established a mission at Balade on the northeast coast of Grande Terre in 1843.

French Colonisation

France officially claimed New Caledonia in 1853, initially establishing it as a penal colony. The first shiploads of convicts arrived at Port-de-France (present-day Noumea) in 1864. In 1871 they were joined by political prisoners from the Paris Commune uprising and the Arab revolt of 1870 against the French colonial government in Algeria.

Having served their sentences, many former convicts were given concessions to farm and a shipload of orphans was dispatched to be their wives. They landed at Baie de l'Orphelinat, hence its name. As more settlers arrived an increasing amount of Melanesian land was taken over. This resulted in the revolt of 1878, led by chief Ataï, which lasted several months and was eventually quashed by the French, aided by allied clans.

WWI & WWII

During WWI male Caldoches (New Caledonia's European inhabitants) and Kanaks (the indigenous Melanesians) were recruited to fight on the French and Turkish fronts.

During WWII New Caledonian soldiers fought for the allied forces in North Africa, Italy and France. Meanwhile, 40,000 US and a smaller number of New Zealand (NZ) soldiers set up a base in New Caledonia. The US headquarters was what's now La Promenade in Anse Vata. The influence of the US soldiers in particular ushered New Caledonia into the modern era.

Postwar

Between 1946 and 1956 Kanaks were progressively given the right to vote, and in 1953 the first political party involving Kanaks was formed.

A nickel boom in the 1960s and '70s saw many New Caledonians abandoning their professions to work in the nickel industry. The boom brought a large number of French migrants, seen as opportunists by the locals. After the boom a lot of people were left unemployed.

Independence became an increasingly important issue for Kanaks, and the majority of Kanak parties joined to form the Front Indépendentiste (Independence Front) in 1979. In 1977 Jacques Lafleur established the loyalist Rassemblement pour la Calédonie dans la République (RPCR), the main adversary of the pro-independence movement.

The Independence Movement

In 1984 other pro-independence parties joined the Front Indépendentiste to form the Front de Libération National Kanak et Socialiste (FLNKS), with Jean-Marie Tjibaou as its leader.

In that same year, mounting political tensions resulted in Les Événements (the Troubles), a period of violent confrontation between pro-independence Kanaks and loyalist supporters.

In 1986 the UN General Assembly voted in favour of adding New Caledonia to its decolonisation list.

Conflict & Resolution

In January 1987 the French National Assembly approved a new plan for the territory and an election was called for 24 April 1988, the same day as the first round of voting for the French presidency. Pro-independence supporters demanded that the date be changed, and ended up boycotting the election. The disagreement led to the Ouvéa hostage drama (p213).

The presidential elections saw the Socialists returned to power and a concerted effort was made to end the bloodshed in New Caledonia.

Newly elected Prime Minister Michel Rocard brokered the Matignon Accords, a historic peace agreement signed by the two New Caledonian leaders, Jean-Marie Tjibaou and Jacques Lafleur.

Under the accords it was agreed that New Caledonia would be divided into three regions: the Southern, Northern and Loyalty Islands provinces. It was assumed that the latter two would come under Kanak control in an election. The accords also stated that a referendum on self-determination would be held in 1998, with all New Caledonians eligible to vote.

In May 1989 Jean-Marie Tjibaou and his second-in-command, Yeiwene Yeiwene, were assassinated (see p213). Their party split and lost power. Kanaks were discouraged. President Mitterand brought the French army home and brokered another deal which included education opportunities and economic benefits, and a clear path towards independence.

A Common Destiny

The new agreement between the FLNKS, RPCR and French government was signed in Noumea in 1998. The Noumea Accord outlines a 15- to 20-year period of growth and development. It also calls for the establishment of a common destiny for New Caledonians, including symbols of national identity such as an anthem and flag. Three governing bodies in Parliament, the elected representatives of the three provinces, means there has to be consensus through discussion and understanding. Working together has become a theme for both political and racial harmony. Where, 20 years ago, there were two societies, these days European and Melanesian people socialise more readily, Kanak youth attend university and interracial marriages are totally acceptable in many circles.

THE CULTURE
The National Psyche

New Caledonia is a mix of Western efficiency and Pacific casualness with an unmistakable Frenchness. Noumea is where many French, Caldoches and people of Asian origin have made their fortunes in business, and they love displaying that wealth with shiny cars and flash houses. Noumeans are also very sporty: you'll see them cycling, jogging and walking along the city's picturesque southern bays.

Outside the capital, rural Caldoches are called Broussards (people from the bush). They are great storytellers, while rural Kanaks may be shy at first. However, the one thing all rural New Caledonians have in common is their generosity and warm hospitality.

Lifestyle

The lifestyles enjoyed by Kanaks and Caldoches are similar in many ways as both groups are family oriented and enjoy being outdoors in their leisure time. What sets them apart are cultural differences such as *la coutume,* the essential component of Kanak society.

La coutume is a code for living that encompasses rites, rituals and social interaction between and within clans. During important events such as birth, marriage and mourning, symbolic offerings are made and discussions are held.

Population

New Caledonia's population of around 300,000 includes 45% indigenous Kanaks, 35% Europeans, plus Polynesians, Asians and other minority groups. Two-thirds of the population live in the greater Noumea region.

All New Caledonians are French citizens, but are divided into various groups.

Kanaks, the indigenous Melanesians, belong to clan communities known as *tribus,* and though many move to Noumea for education and employment, they maintain strong ties with their *tribus,* returning for holidays and cultural and family celebrations.

New Caledonia's European population has two distinct groups: the Caldoches and the Métros. Caldoches were born in New Caledonia and have ancestral ties to the penal colony or the early French settlers. Many Broussards are cattle breeders who have forged a culture of their own, similar to that of outback Australia.

The term Métro comes from Métropolitain, as in metropolitan France, and refers to those who were born in France and migrated.

There is a large Polynesian population in New Caledonia, mainly from the French territory of Wallis and Futuna. In fact, more Wallisians live in New Caledonia than in their homeland and they make up 12% of the population.

People of Asian origin, including Indonesians, Vietnamese and Chinese, began arriving in New Caledonia in the early 20th century. Today they are mainly involved in the trade sector.

SPORT

Pétanque, a game inherited from the French and sometimes called boules, is played mainly by men on a *boulodrome*, a smooth, hard pitch. Soccer, volleyball and a local version of cricket are also popular.

ARTS

Wood sculpture is a popular form of artistic expression in New Caledonia, particularly in Kanak culture. Île des Pins is famous for its sculpted wooden posts. A few workshops on Lifou are open to the public. Soapstone sculpture is popular on the northeast coast of Grande Terre around Pouébo.

Several art galleries in Noumea sell paintings by local artists; for an overview of Kanak arts, visit the Tjibaou Cultural Centre (p185).

Dance

Many dance styles are popular in New Caledonia, including *pilou* (traditional Kanak dance), Tahitian, Vietnamese and Indonesian. Performances are held regularly at festivals and public events such as the Jeudis du Centre Ville (p182) in Noumea.

Literature

New Caledonia has a dynamic literary scene made up of several publishers and many authors.

Déwé Gorodey is a Kanak politician and writer who evokes the struggle for independence in her writing and gives a feminist view of Kanak culture. *The Kanak Apple Season* is a collection of short stories, exploring Kanak political and cultural issues.

Pierre Gope is another Kanak writer whose works include poetry and plays. Caledonian Nicolas Kurtovitch writes poetry, short stories and plays. *Les Dieux sont borgnes* is a play co-written by Gope and Kurtovitch. The first half is set in the 18th century at the arrival of Captain James Cook. The second half is set in contemporary New Caledonia. Bernard Berger, also Caledonian, is a cartoonist whose *Brousse en Folie* comic-book series is immensely popular.

Louis-José Barbançon, a Caledonian historian, has written books on the penal-colony history and the difficult political climate of the 1980s. *L'Archipel des Forçats* looks at the convict history of New Caledonia.

Music

In addition to popular Western music and hip-hop, reggae has a huge following in New Caledonia, along with music from Tahiti, Vanuatu and Fiji. The immensely popular local music known as Kaneka is a mixture of reggae and traditional Kanak rhythms.

Dick and Natr Buama have both produced solo albums. Edou, leader of the band Mexem from Lifou, produces albums, both solo and with his band. Gulaan, former lead singer of OK! Ryos, sings beautiful melodies in his clear, mellow voice. Tim Semeke and his cultural dance troupe We Ce Ca have produced several albums and perform at the Tjibaou Cultural Centre (2.30pm Tuesday and Thursday).

Watch out for groups N.Guraya and Umargue on weekends, or Vertigo and Shotgun at music festivals like November Rock Fest when they appear at Bodega, Le Muzz' Bar and Bout du Monde.

LANGUAGE

There are more than 30 Kanak languages. French is the official language.

New Caledonian basics

Hello/Good morning.	Bonjour.
Good evening.	Bonsoir.
Goodbye.	Au revoir or Tata (Kanak farewell).
Yes.	Oui.
No.	Non.
Thank you (very much).	Merci (beaucoup).
Please.	S'il vous plaît.
Excuse me.	Excusez-moi.
I'm sorry.	Pardon.
How are you?	Comment allez-vous?
I'm fine (thanks).	Je vais bien (merci).
I don't understand.	Je ne comprends pas.

ENVIRONMENT

Despite its small size, New Caledonia has a rich endemic biodiversity. The main threats to its natural environment are mining, deforestation, cattle farming, deer and wildfires. The barrier reef that surrounds New Caledonia is 1600km long and ranges from 200m to 1km in width. Inside the reef, the lagoon is seldom more than 25m deep and provides the country with a fabulous aquatic-based lifestyle. The ocean is 1km deep outside the reef.

BEST EATS

New Caledonia's restaurants offer a range of cuisines, all with stylish presentation, accomplished service, a fine touch of herb and spice to flavour every bite, and a gourmet blend of local produce. Explore every possible dining option, absorb every view and relax with the warm hospitality. You are being pampered by expert foodies. You'll find that lunchtime three-course menus are way cheaper than the same repast in the evening, so splurge at midday and then you can go shopping for French wine, cheeses, terrines and baguettes for a lovely picnic by any of the idyllic bays at sunset.

- Walk down to Le Roof (p190) at the end of the pier at Anse Vata for a gastronomic experience.
- Be entertained by a Melanesian dance troupe in the open bar at Hôtel Oure on Île des Pins and then move into the restaurant (p219) for local fish prepared with the finest touch.
- Tuck into one of those famous *bougnas* while you look out over Hienghène marina, at Gîte Ka Waboana (p205).
- Take it easy, with a tasty *plat du jour* on the veranda at Hôtel Banu (p198).
- Chat to the locals whose turn it is to cook for you at Snack Fassy (p215) on Ouvéa.
- Join other guests around the table for a delicious three-course meal at Kanua Tera Ecolodge (p196).

Geography

The territory is an archipelago that comprises the Grande Terre (16,500 sq km); Île des Pins (152 sq km); the Loyalty Islands (1980 sq km); and the tiny Îles Belep. Scattered around at considerable distances are various minuscule and uninhabited dependencies.

Grande Terre is 450km long with 400km of central ranges dividing the lush, mountainous east coast from the dry west coast and its savannah plains. It is rich in minerals and has one of the biggest nickel reserves in the world. The opencast mining used to extract nickel has left scarred mountains, blocked rivers, farmland turned to swamp and damaging run-offs into the lagoon. Thirty years after legislation was introduced to stop the environmental impact, the slow-growing endemic plants still haven't covered the gouged areas.

The Loyalty Islands and Île des Pins are uplifted, flat coral islands. New Caledonia has 1600km of reef enclosing a magnificent 23,500 sq km turquoise lagoon.

Ecology

New Caledonia's flora and fauna originated in eastern Gondwanaland, evolving in isolation when Grande Terre became separated 80 million years ago. As a result there are many unique plants and animals, especially birds, and per square kilometre New Caledonia boasts the world's richest diversity. Of the 3250 flowering plant species, 80% are native.

There's an estimated 68 species of land birds, about 20 of which are indigenous. The most renowned indigenous species is the endangered *cagou (Rhynochetus jubatus)*, New Caledonia's unofficial national bird (see p186). Of the few land mammals, only *roussettes* (members of the fruit-bat family), a traditional Kanak food source, are indigenous. Introduced mammals include rusa deer, which are causing major damage to native plants and the environment (see them on Caldoche farms on the west coast). Venison is served in local restaurants.

New Caledonia's waters are home to around 2000 species of fish. Humpback whales visit between July and September. New Caledonia's 14 species of sea snakes are often sighted on the water's surface or on land. The most commonly seen is the amphibious *tricot rayé* (banded sea krait). They are highly venomous but not aggressive and bites are extremely rare.

Parks & Reserves

There are many land and marine parks and reserves in New Caledonia. In the Far South, Parc Provincial de la Rivière Bleue (p192) and Chutes de la Madeleine (p193) are easily accessible. The ascent of Mont Panié (p206), at 1629m New Caledonia's highest peak, is suitable for fit hikers.

NOUMEA

pop 92,000

With its cheerful multi-ethnic community, New Caledonia's cosmopolitan capital is both sophisticated and uncomplicated, classy and casual. The relaxed city sits on a large peninsula, surrounded by picturesque bays, and offers visitors a variety of experiences. Diners have the choice of eating out at sassy French restaurants or humble establishments in Chinatown, while shopaholics can blow their savings on the latest Paris fashions or go bargain hunting for imported Asian textiles.

ORIENTATION

Central Noumea revolves around Place des Cocotiers, a large, shady square with landscaped gardens, a couple of blocks in from the waterfront. The main leisure area where locals and tourists hang out lies south of the city centre at Baie des Citrons and Anse Vata, with beaches, restaurants, bars and nightclubs. The domestic airport at Magenta is 4km to the east of the city centre.

Maps

Bookshops sell IGN maps with scales ranging from 1:50,000 to 1:500,000. These have the most geographical detail but they're about 15 years old. The Office du Tourisme (right) has free maps of Noumea and New Caledonia.

INFORMATION
Bookshops

Librairie Calédo Livres (Map p184; ☎ 273 811; 21 rue Jean Jaurès) Specialises in books on New Caledonia and the Pacific.
Librairie Montaigne (Map p184; ☎ 273 488; 23 rue de Sébastopol) Has a selection of books and travel guides in English.

Internet Access

Cyber BD Citron (Map p182; ☎ 241 169; cyber-bdc@live.fr; 35 promenade Roger Laroque; per 30min 400 CFP) In the Baie des Citrons complex.
Cyber Noumea Centre (Map p184; ☎ 262 698; tetnet@mls.nc; Galerie Noumea Centre; per 30min 400 CFP)

Medical Services

Pharmacies, identified by a green cross, are dotted all over Noumea. On Saturday afternoons and Sundays, only one emergency pharmacy is open, according to a rotating schedule.
Decompression Chamber (Map p184; ☎ 264 526) A Comex 1800 decompression chamber, next to the hospital, is available 24/7, accessible by land, sea or air.
Hôpital Gaston Bourret (Map p184; ☎ 256 666, emergencies 256 767; 7 rue Paul Doumer) Noumea's main hospital.

Money

ATMs are outside most banks, and they accept most major credit cards. There are several banks on av de la Victoire/Henry Lafleur.
Banque BNP Paribas (Map p182; ☎ 262 103; 111 promenade Roger Laroque) At the Anse Vata shops.
Banque Calédonienne d'Investissement (BCI; Map p184; ☎ 242 060; 20 rue Anatole France)
Banque Société Générale (Map p184; ☎ 256 300; 44 rue de l'Alma & 56 av de la Victoire/Henry Lafleur) Western Union representative.

Post

Main post office (Map p184; ☎ 268 400; 7 rue Eugène Porcheron) The main office of the Office des Postes et Télécommunications (OPT) has a poste restante and fax service, and there's an ATM outside the building. There's also a post office on route de Anse Vata, on the way to the beach.

Tourist Information

First, pick up the free *Weekly* from airports, tourist sites, hotels, Office du Tourisme etc. It is spot on, with everything to do that week including the theme for Thursday's festivities. Also get the monthly entertainment guide *NC Pocket* (www.sortir.nc) for the month's festivals, exhibitions, concerts and Jeudis du Centre Ville themes.

Next collect a fantastic range of information, plus maps, brochures, booklets and DVDs for the entire country from the following offices:
Office du Tourisme (Map p184; ☎ 287 580, free call 057 580; www.office-tourisme.nc, www.visitnewcaledonia .com; Place des Cocotiers; ⏱ 8am-5.30pm Mon-Fri, 8am-noon Sat) The very friendly staff offer practical information in English or French, make bookings for you, and have walls layered with pamphlets about every activity and service.
Office du Tourisme, Anse Vata (Map p182; ☎ 277 359; 113 promenade Roger Laroque; ⏱ 9am-5pm) It's a little smaller than the office in the city centre, but the service is just as good.

Travel Agencies

Companies that organise transport, tours and accommodation within New Caledonia include the following:

NOUMEA IN...

One Day
Head out to the **Tjibaou Cultural Centre** (p185) on **le petit train** (p185), then into town for a picnic at **Place des Cocotiers** (p189) or a three-course lunch at **La Chaumière** (p189). Spend the afternoon at the **beach** in Anse Vata or Baie des Citrons (p186), taking time out for a drink across the road. In the evening, amble down to **Le Bout du Monde** (p189) to watch the boats against the sunset while you dine, then check out the music at **Le Muzz' Bar** (p191).

Two Days
Follow the itinerary above on your first day, and on the second day do the Noumea **walking tour** (p187), starting with breakfast at the **market** (p183). Visit the **aquarium** (p185) before catching a taxi boat to **Île aux Canards** (p186) to snorkel. Back on terra firma, head to the **Baie des Citrons** (p190) for dinner, then check out the nightlife at one of Anse Vata's **bars** (p191).

Air Calédonie (Map p184; ☎ 287 888; 39 rue de Verdun)
Alpha International (Map p182; ☎ 272 420; www.alpha-tourisme.com; 143 rte de l'Anse Vata)
Arc en Ciel Voyages (Map p184; ☎ 271 980; www.arcenciel-voyages.nc; 59 av du Maréchal Foch)
New Caledonia Hotels (www.newcaledoniahotels.travel) Itineraries, flights, tours and accommodation online.

GETTING THERE & AWAY
Air
Air Calédonie (Map p184; ☎ 287 888; www.air-caledonie.nc; 39 rue de Verdun; ⏱ 7.30am-5pm Mon-Fri, to 11am Sat) is the domestic airline, with flights to northern Grande Terre, Île des Pins and the Loyalty Islands. It also has a **ticket office** (☎ 252 177) at the domestic airport in Magenta.

Boat
The friendly and efficient **Capitainerie** (Harbour Master's Office; Map p184; ☎ 277 197; port.moselle@sodemo.nc) is at Port Moselle's southern end. Noumea is connected to the Loyalty Islands and Île des Pins by the fast *Betico* ferry and the *Havannah*, a slower cargo boat (see p225).

GETTING AROUND
To/From the Airport
Tontouta International Airport is 45km northwest of Noumea. Public buses operated by **Carsud** (☎ 251 615; 400 CFP) run there from the corner of rues Georges Clémenceau and Paul Doumer. Several private companies, including **Philo Tours** (☎ 289 957; philo@canl.nc) and **Arc en Ciel Voyages** (p226), run airport transfers (one-way 3000 CFP). **Taxis** (☎ 283 512) into Noumea cost 11,000 CFP (shared).

Magenta domestic airport is serviced by Blue-line Karuia buses (200 CFP) and a taxi to the city or beaches costs around 1700 CFP (shared).

Bus
Red-and-white buses (200 CFP) operate around the city from 6am to 7pm. The ticket office is at Place des Cocotiers, and the routes are colour coded.
Bleue (Blue) Tjibaou Cultural Centre–Magenta–city centre.
Jaune (Yellow) Faubourg Blanchot–city centre–Gare de Montravel.
Orange (Orange) Val Plaisance–Anse Vata–city centre.
Verte (Green) Kuendu–city centre–Baie de L'Orphelinat–Baie des Citrons–Anse Vata.
Violette (Purple) Magenta–Vallée des Colons–city centre.

The hop-on, hop-off **Noumea Explorer** (☎ 271 980; day pass 1000 CFP; ⏱ 7am-6pm Tue-Sun) does an hourly circuit from Anse Vata into the city via Baie des Citrons and then on to the Maritime Museum in Nouville, the Parc Zoologique et Forestier and the Tjibaou Cultural Centre before returning to Anse Vata.

Car & Scooter
The Office du Tourisme has a comprehensive list of car- and scooter-hire companies; also see p226 for some suggestions. Car rental costs from 5000 CFP per day, including free 150km per day.

Taxi
Noumea's taxis are operated by **Radio Taxis de Noumea** (☎ 283 512). The main taxi rank (Map p184) is on rue d'Austerlitz, adjacent to the Galerie Noumea Centre.

NEW CALEDONIA

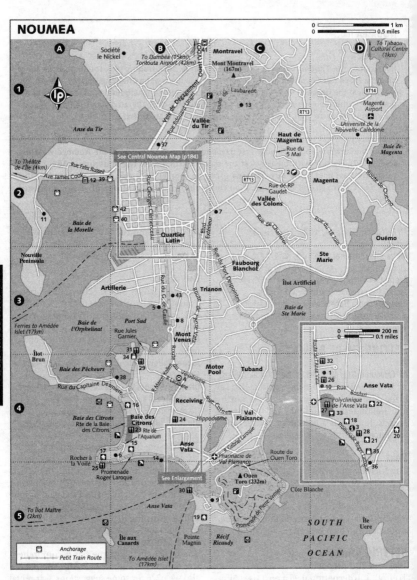

NOUMEA

SIGHTS
Place des Cocotiers

This is the heart of the city. The square (Map p184) slopes gently from east to west and at the top is a band rotunda, a famous landmark dating back to the late 1800s, where teenagers meet in the afternoon to show off their hip-hop dance moves. Place des Cocotiers is the

perfect spot to watch the world go by. Near the band rotunda there's a popular *pétanque* pitch and a giant chess board. Down the other end it's like a lush botanical garden, with palms and large spreading trees.

Regular concerts and street markets are held in Place des Cocotiers. The popular **Jeudis du Centre Ville** (Thu evenings Apr–Nov) street market has a different theme each week, outlined in *NC Pocket*, free at the Office du Tourisme. Stalls sell arts and crafts, fresh produce, cakes and local dishes, and entertainment includes live music and traditional dance.

Musée de la Ville de Noumea

The beautiful colonial-style **Musée de la Ville de Noumea** (Noumea Museum; Map p184; ☎ 262 805; rue Jean Jaurès; admission 100 CFP; 9am-4.45pm Mon-Sat), dwarfed by towering palm trees, overlooks Place des Cocotiers. It features temporary and permanent displays on the early history of Noumea.

Cathédrale St Joseph

The **cathedral** (Map p184; ☎ 273 288; 3 rue Frédéric Surleau) was built in 1888 by convict labour and is one of Noumea's landmarks. It has beautiful stained-glass windows and an elaborately carved pulpit, altar panels and confessional. The main entrance is generally locked, but you should find the side doors open.

Musée de Nouvelle-Calédonie

The **Musée de Nouvelle-Calédonie** (Museum of New Caledonia; Map p184; ☎ 272 342; smp@gouv.nc; 42 av du Maréchal Foch; adult/child 200/50 CFP; 9-11.30am & 12.15-4.30pm Wed-Mon) provides an excellent introduction to traditional Kanak and regional Pacific culture. Local exhibits are displayed on the ground floor and regional artefacts on the mezzanine level.

Mwâ Ka

The magnificent Mwâ Ka (Map p184) is erected in a landscaped square opposite Musée de Nouvelle-Calédonie. The 12m totem pole is topped by a *grande case* (chief's hut), complete with *flèche faîtière* (carved rooftop spear), and its carvings represent the eight customary regions of New Caledonia. The Mwâ Ka is mounted as the mast on a concrete double-hulled *pirogue*, steered by a wooden helmsman, and celebrates Kanak identity as well as the multi-ethnic reality of New Caledonia.

Le Marché

The colourful multi-hexagonal-shaped **market** (Map p184; 5-11am) is beside the marina at Port Moselle. Fishermen unload their catch; trucks offload fruit, vegetables and flowers; and there's fresh-baked bread and cakes, plus delights like terrines and olives. The arts and crafts section includes a central cafe. On Saturday and Sunday a local string band keeps shoppers entertained. The market is at its busiest early in the morning.

Musée de l'Histoire Maritime

The **Musée de l'Histoire Maritime** (Maritime Museum; Map p182; ☎ 263 443; 11 av James Cook; adult/child 400/200 CFP; 10am-5pm Tue-Sun) has bits of boats and exhibitions on early seafaring days in New Caledonia and the Pacific.

NEW CALEDONIA

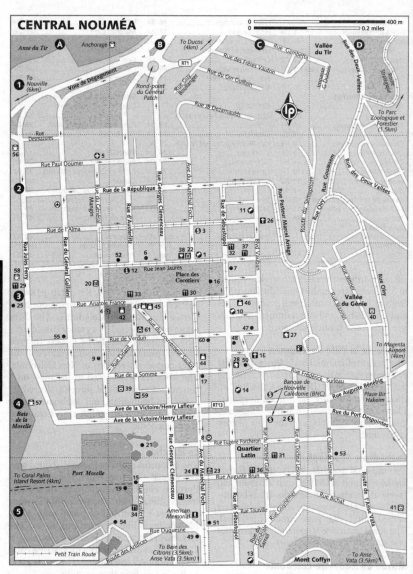

Parc Zoologique et Forestier

Wander along a network of paths through gardens of native shrubs and trees, cactus and forest with a changing backdrop of sea views in the distance and native species such as the flightless *cagou*, *roussette*, *notou* pigeon and various parakeets right in front of you. The **Parc Zoologique et Forestier** (Zoological and Botanical Gardens; Map p182; ☎ 278 951; Rte de Laubarède; adult/child 400 CFP/free; ☾ 10.15am-5.45pm Tue-Sun, to 5pm May-Aug) also has a cafe, a playground and an enclosure with farm animals for children to pet.

Le petit train (opposite) and Noumea Explorer buses (p181) run here from the city centre, or it's a quick taxi ride out.

ONE PASS, SIX PLACES

On your first visit to a Noumea museum or site, ask about buying the 'Pass to Nature & Culture'. It costs 1700 CFP but it gives you entry to three museums, the aquarium, the Tjibaou Cultural Centre and the zoo and botanical gardens. However, those aged over 60 get much better individual entry discounts. Get to all the places on the hop-on, hop-off Noumea Explorer (p181).

Tjibaou Cultural Centre

The **cultural centre** (☎ 414 545; www.adck.nc; Rue des Accords de Matignon; adult/child 500 CFP/free, guided tours 1500 CFP; ☷ 9am-5pm Tue-Sun) is a tribute to a remarkable man, pro-independence Kanak leader Tjibaou who was assassinated in 1989. It sits in a peaceful woodland and mangrove setting on Tina Peninsula. Displays include sculpture, paintings and photographs representing Kanak culture, as well as other cultures from around the Pacific. The main buildings are a series of tall, curved wooden structures which rise majestically above the trees. The harmony between this contemporary architecture (designed by Italian architect Renzo Piano, who also designed

Paris' Pompidou Centre) and the surrounding landscape is amazing. Behind the main building are traditional *grandes cases*; traditional Kanak dance shows by We Ce Ca are held every Tuesday and Thursday at 2.30pm. Amenities include a multimedia library, theatre, shop and cafe. Blue-line city buses and the Noumea Explorer bus (p181) run regularly to the centre.

Aquarium des Lagons

This **aquarium** (Map p182; ☎ 262 731; www .aquarium.nc; rte de l'Aquarium; adult/child/student/senior 650/115/210/300 CFP; ☷ 10am-4.45pm, closed Mon) is stunning. Species found in New Caledonian waters, including nautilus, sea snakes, stone fish, turtles and sting rays, have realistic surroundings in their huge tanks. Living coral displays are surprising but don't miss the emperor of coral reefs: Napoleon fish. How cute are these? In the meantime, follow the progress of 46 tagged loggerhead turtles on the aquarium website.

Le Petit Train

Yes, that was a train you saw. It's very cute and entertaining, and a big photo opportunity. **Le Petit Train Touristique de Noumea** (☎ 778 073; transcar@lagoon.nc; adult/child 1200/600 CFP) makes

THE CAGOU

The *cagou (Rhynochetos jubatus)* is a much-loved New Caledonian bird and an unofficial national symbol. It is about 50cm tall with soft grey plumage and crest, red eyes and an orange beak. Its call sounds like a dog barking; ironically, dogs are its main predator as the *cagou* cannot fly. It mates for life and females have one baby a year.

two large loops a day (except Sunday) leaving Palm Beach at 9.30am and 1pm, passing through Baie de Citron, the city centre and out to Parc Zoologique et Forestier, offering grand views as you return inland to Palm Beach. Purchase tickets from the driver.

Beaches

The two most popular beaches are at **Anse Vata** (Map p182) and **Baie des Citrons** (Map p182). On a breezy day at Anse Vata, you can watch the colourful kite- and wind-surfers skimming up and down the bay. The best thing: as they face different directions one of these beaches is always free of wind for the sun loungers.

Islets

The waters around Noumea are sprinkled with beautiful islets. Most are marine reserves and the clear waters surrounding them are great for snorkelling.

ÎLE AUX CANARDS & ÎLOT MAÎTRE

Île aux Canards (Map p182) and Îlot Maître are the cutest postcard-perfect poppets of islets. You can see them just a swim out from Anse Vata. Pick up a map of the underwater walkway on Île aux Canards, or buy a waterproof one at the kiosk.

Plages Loisirs (Map p182; ☎ 269 000; plageloisirs@mls .nc; 110 promenade Roger Laroque) runs taxi boats to Île aux Canards (1000 CFP) and Îlot Maître (2400 CFP) from a kiosk at Anse Vata. Snorkel hire is 600 CFP.

Go out in a glass-bottom taxi boat (1800 CFP per 45 minutes) with **Colleen Excursions** (Map p182; ☎ 795 929; cruellas@offratel.nc; 56 promenade Roger Laroque), located at Fun Beach. Or head for the islets (with/without a stop 1000/800 CFP), watching the sea life on the way. Rent snorkel gear and wet suits (500 CFP) or go reef fishing (three hours 6200 CFP).

Dumbéa River

The RT1 crosses Dumbéa River at **Parc Fayard**, 16km north of Noumea. It's a popular spot during the hot summer months as the shady park is a good picnic area, the river offers good swimming here, and there's plenty of hiking tracks along two branches of the river: north takes you to a canyon, south to a dam.
Terra Incognita (☎ 253 993, 789 446; terincognita@canl .nc) hires canoes and kayaks, and runs full-moon kayaking trips down the river (two hours, 3000 CFP).

Yala Ranch (☎ 774 623, 848 534; mikesaint pol@caramail.com; rte du Golf; 1hr 2000 CFP) has an equestrian centre and pony club. Ride your horse through the river for a fun summer activity.

ACTIVITIES
Diving

Noumea dive clubs **Alizé Diving** (Map p182; ☎ 26 25 85; www.alizedive.com; Nouvata Park Hôtel) and **Amédée Diving Club** (☎ 264 029; www.amedee .sponline.com, www.amedeediving.nc; 28 rue du Général Mangin) charge 11,000 CFP for an intro dive along with a day trip and lunch at Phare Amédée, a marine reserve with plenty of marine life including sharks and rays and healthy coral. A two-dive package is 14,500 CFP. Other dives include the *Dieppoise* and *Toho V* wrecks; see p220 for details of the 'Plongée' discount card.

Abyss Plongée (Map p182; ☎ 791 509; www.abyssnc .com; Marina Port du Sud, Baie de l'Orphelinat) dives at many sites around Grande Terre and charges 7200 CFP for an intro dive and 11,000 CFP for a double dive, plus transport costs. Dive clubs all offer PADI courses.

Other Water Activities

On the beach at Anse Vata under the large hut, **Plages Loisirs** (Map p182; ☎ 269 000; plageloisirs@mls.nc; 110 promenade Roger Laroque; ◔ 7.30am-5.30pm) hires equipment like kayaks (per hour 1500 CFP), windsurfers (per hour 1800 CFP) and hobby cats (per hour 4000 CFP), along with **Vata Plaisirs** (Map p182; ☎ 781 300, 765 909; www.mdplaisirs .com), which offers introductory lessons (1500 CFP). Ask about the MD Plaisirs Card, which gives you 40% discount (eg catamaran 2100 CFP, kayak 950 CFP) and is usable here, in Poé and in Koumac.

Locajet (Map p182; ☎ 262 613, 777 979; www.locajet .info; half-day 1/2 riders 18,000/12,000 CFP each), in Nouville on the western side of Baie de la

Moselle, rents jet skis. Do a circular whiz from Baie de la Moselle to Île aux Canards, Îlot Maitre, a few more islets and back to the northern side of the Nouville peninsula. Check out the helicopter package.

Bernard at **Aquanature** (Map p184; ☎ 264 008, 78 36 66; quanature@canl.nc; Pacific Charter Kiosk; morning/afternoon/full-day 5000/4000/7000 CFP) takes you out from Port Moselle to snorkel on the reef; he finds the best spots and you get coffee and cakes as well.

See p221 for information on boats to hire, or get a full list of companies from the Office du Tourisme. See opposite for taxi-boat or glass-bottom boat trips.

Land-based Activities

You'll find all your favourite sporting activities are available in Noumea, or around Grande Terre: golf, squash, clay-pigeon shooting; just ask at the Office du Tourisme.

Noumea Fun Ride (Map p184; ☎ 269 626; noumeafunride.org@canl.nc; Gare Maritime; scootcars 1/2hr 4500/6000 CFP) rents fun movable vehicles including miniature cars (5000/8000 CFP per one/two hours) if you're over 16 years of age. There's also mountain and beach bikes (1100/1300 CFP per hour/half-day), helmets, racks, child seats, roller blades and scooters for kids (2300/2700 CFP per hour/half-day).

The Office du Tourisme produces a folder, *Randonnées en Nouvelle-Calédonie*, of helpful brochures describing many small or grand walks, cycling trips and climbs across islands, through forests and up many creeks.

Le Circuit Historique, a lovely booklet produced by the **Hôtel de Ville** (Town Hall; ☎ 273 115; www.ville-noumea.nc; 16 rue du Général Mangin), takes you on a fascinating history tour past Noumea's old buildings (from 1856 on).

NOUMEA WALKING TOUR

Wake up early and head to Port Moselle for a breakfast of coffee and croissants at the **market** (1; p183). Go across to the square to admire the amazing **Mwâ Ka** (2; p183), then walk down av du Maréchal Foch to the corner of rue de la Somme to see the **Bibliothèque Bernheim** (3; ☎ 242 090; 41 av du Maréchal Foch; ☯ 1-5.30pm Tue, Thu & Fri, 9am-5.30pm Wed, to 4pm Sat), the attractive colonial-style public library with its old chandeliers and curved wooden staircases.

Turn right into rue de la Somme and walk along to the steps at the top of the street, which

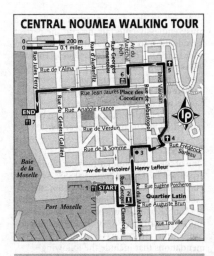

CENTRAL NOUMEA WALKING TOUR

lead up the side of a building to rue Frédéric Surleau and **Cathédrale St Joseph** (4; p183). From the cathedral, head north along blvd Vauban to the attractive old stone **Temple Protestant (5)** at the top of rue de l'Alma. Then head down to the charming **Musée de la Ville de Noumea** (6; p183), opposite Place des Cocotiers. From there, head down to the waterfront and along to attractive Gare Maritime. If a cruise ship is docked, there'll be a spread of stalls crammed with souvenirs upstairs, or have a coffee downstairs at **Café de la Gare** (7; ☯ 7am-4pm Mon-Sat).

NOUMEA FOR CHILDREN

Face it, the children want to stay on the beach, swimming and building sand castles at **Anse Vata** or **Baie des Citrons** beaches (opposite). But if anything will drag them away, it's a ride on **le petit train** (p185).

There are shady **playgrounds** (Map p182) at Baie de l'Orphelinat off rue du Générale de Gaulle, and next to the public swimming pool at Ouen Toro near Anse Vata. Or head to **Le Marché** (p183). There's a buzz of activity, plenty of things to buy, and opposite, in the car park, children's **fair rides** (200 CFP; ☯ from 3pm Mon-Sun).

NEW CALEDONIA

A visit to the new **aquarium** (p185) is a must: endlessly entertaining and the perfect introduction to a trip out in a glass-bottom boat (p186). The **Parc Zoologique et Forestier** (p184) offers stacks of running space. And when Thursday evening comes around, go by **Place des Cocotiers** (p182), where traditional dances will entrance them, there's Liese's famous face-painting stall, an ice-cream bar and candyfloss for the ultimate sugar fix.

TOURS

One of the most popular tours of Noumea is organised by *le petit train* (p185). Aventure Pulsion and Caledonia Tours (p195) run day excursions to the Far South. There are tours to Monts Koghis, tours on the deep blue and tours up north. See p226 for a few ideas, or contact the Office du Tourisme for recommendations that include the following:

Alpha International (Map p182; ☎ 272 420; www .alpha-tourisme.com; 143 rte de l'Anse Vata) Catamaran trips to islets.

Mary D (Map p182; ☎ 263 131; www.amedee.ws; Galerie Palm Beach, Anse Vata; ☺ 9am Mon-Sat) A grand day on one of *Mary D*'s launches out to Amédèe Islet (p186); 12,900 CFP). Visit the lighthouse, snorkel off-shore or from the glass-bottom boat, feed sharks on the reef, indulge in a luscious three-course buffet lunch and see fun dance and cultural shows.

SLEEPING

Noumea has few budget options but some hotels have grouped together and offer more relaxed tariffs. Many offer very good deals on their websites. Almost all of the hotels offer free wi-fi; return transfers to Tontouta airport are 6000 CFP by bus.

Budget

our pick **Auberge de Jeunesse** (Map p184; ☎ 275 879; www.yhanoumea.lagoon.nc; 51bis rue Pasteur Marcel Ariège; dm/d 1700/3700 CFP; ☐) This sparkling-clean hostel, behind St Joseph's Cathedral, has a fantastic view of the city and Baie de la Moselle. The energy here is exciting. It's an extra 200 CFP for HI nonmembers; wi-fi or computer use is 300 CFP an hour. Linen is provided. You'll get stacks of tourist info. The quickest way to get there from the centre of town on foot is up the 103 steps at the top of rue Jean Jaurès. Advance bookings are recommended.

Lantana Beach Hôtel (Map p182; ☎ 262 212; www .hotel-lantana.nc; 113 promenade Roger Laroque; r 7600 CFP) It's looking its age but still kicking, just across the

road from the beach at Anse Vata. Great value, free wi-fi, fridges and coffee-making facilities. Ask about the discount for staying a week.

Motel Anse Vata (Map p182; ☎ 262 212; www .motelansevata.com; 19 rue Gabriel Laroque; r 8000 CFP) It's looking orange, retro, and simply plain but it's just up the road from Palm Beach mall and you get your own little bit of balcony and your own front door key. There's a small, very clean kitchen for guests to share, and a happy atmosphere.

Midrange

Hôtel Beaurivage (Map p182; ☎ 262 055; www .grands-hotels.nc; 7 promenade Roger Laroque; standard/seaview 9200/10,200 CFP; ☒ ☒) Talk about position. This rather faded retro hotel is just across the road from the beach at Baie des Citrons and a quick step away from the restaurant strip. Yet it's a quiet spot and rooms are airy.

Hôtel Le Surf (Map p182; ☎ 286 688; www.grands -hotels.nc; Rocher à la Voile; r 9800; ☒ ☒) Two large hotel sections with a network of private balconies bridge together across an access road with a casino and restaurant below. All rooms have stunning views, meals are reliably good, and it's an easy stroll to either Anse Vata beachfront or Baie de Citrons. The breakfast buffet is 1800 CFP, dinner mains cost from 1600 CFP.

Hôtel Le Paris (Map p184; ☎ 281 700; www.best western-leparishotel.com; 45 rue de Sébastopol; s/d/f 10,500/12,000/15,500 CFP) It's good to be in the centre of Noumea, a short stroll into the French atmosphere of Place des Cocotiers. The staff are delightful, making it a bit of a home away from home.

Le Pacifique (Map p182; ☎ 262 200; www.nc hotels.nc; 123 promenade Roger Laroque; r pool/ocean view 14,400/16,400 CFP; ☒ ☒) It doesn't look much, but it opens onto top-end Nouvata Park Hôtel's spreading swimming pools, shops and restaurant, which are yours to use.

Casa del Sole (Map p182; ☎ 258 700; www.casadelsole .nc; 10 rte de l'Aquarium; 1-/2-bedroom apt 16,500/18,300 CFP) These spacious stunning apartments have bright kitchenettes, comfy furnishings and a private terrace filled with views. It's a couple of minutes' walk from the beach, shops and restaurants.

Top End

Nouvata Park Hôtel (Map p182; ☎ 262 200; www.nc hotels.nc; 123 promenade Roger Laroque; r garden/beach view 18,900/22,900 CFP; ☒ ☒) This grand hotel in the middle of the tourist atmosphere at Anse Vata has all the facilities you could possibly need. It also offers deluxe rooms and suites (from 27,900 CFP). The lounging areas, pool area and restaurants are welcoming, making for good places to meet other guests.

Ramada Plaza (Map p182; ☎ 239 000; www.ramada plaza-noumea.nc; Rue Boulari; studio 19,900 CFP, ste deluxe/executive 36,900/46,900 CFP) The rooms and suites at the twin-towered Ramada Plaza are tastefully decorated in contemporary Pacific style. Rooms have racecourse or sea views and facilities include a kids' club and spa. The revolving restaurant features fine dining with fine views (dishes from 2500 CFP, set lunch menu 3900 CFP). There are amazing deals on the website, like three nights all inclusive out of Sydney. Take a look.

our pick **Coral Palms Island Resort** (☎ 260 512; www.nchotels.nc; Îlot Maître; B&B garden-/beach-view bungalows 34,900/41,900 CFP, over-water bungalows 69,000 CFP; ✷ 🏊) An idyllic hotel on Îlot Maître with bungalows in an island garden and luxury over-water accommodation where you snorkel off your own deck into a coral garden. The pool has a swim-up bar, the activities kiosk has a range of water-sport equipment and in case you're interested, there's a charming wedding chapel. Transfers on the Coral Palms launch are 2400 CFP.

Le Méridien Noumea (Map p182; ☎ 265 000; www .lemeridien.com; Pointe Magnin; classic/superior/executive B&B 36,000/41,000/44,000 CFP; ✷ 🏊) This stunning hotel by Anse Vata beach has landscaped grounds, an hypnotic pool area and several restaurants. You have transport to all sites and activities, should you ever wish to drag yourself off the premises. Check out the special deals on the website.

EATING

Noumea has fabulous restaurants specialising in French and international cuisine as well as seafood. The hotels all have excellent restaurants as well. Many places are closed on Sunday or Monday.

City Centre

You'll see numerous small *snacks* (eateries) in Chinatown but prices are sometimes better, and the surroundings definitely better, in the restaurants.

Coco Glacé (Map p184; ☎ 249 989; Place des Cocotiers; lunch 350-550 CFP; ✷ 7am-6pm Mon-Sat) Smell cooking waffles, see shaded outdoor tables, think

what diet? There are also ice creams, sorbets and crêpes at this kiosk.

Best Cafe (Map p184; ☎ 251 010; 47 rue de Sébastopol; mains 1250-2950 CFP; ✷ 6.30am-11pm) It looks a bit ordinary, but the food is delicious. The chef edges the prawns with a salt that makes them burst with flavour, and the *plat du jour* is often a roast.

L'Annexe (Map p184; ☎ 253 315; Place des Cocotiers; lunch 1550-1950 CFP; ✷ 7am-6pm Mon-Sat) Sit by a pond while you enjoy an excellent meal, like Hawaiian fish salad. And the front servery sells mouthwatering sandwiches, quiche, pizza and cakes (350 CFP to 550 CFP).

Zanzibar (Map p184; ☎ 252 800; 51 rue Jean Jaurès; mains 1900-2700 CFP; ✷ lunch Mon-Fri, dinner Mon-Sat) It's all atmospheric timber and cloth, with a tiny upstairs veranda and a range of dishes like duck with lavender. It's famous for its desserts. A three-course menu is 2600 CFP.

La Kasbah (Map p184; ☎ 278 861; 15 rue de Sébastopol; mains 1900-3700 CFP; ✷ lunch Tue-Sun, dinner Mon-Sun) Enter another universe in this fascinating spot, where the *tajines* are large and full of glorious flavours that almost match the exotic decor. Sharing a *tajine* is totally acceptable.

Quartier Latin & Port Moselle

Snack Loan (Map p184; ☎ 271 351; rue August Brun; dishes 550 CFP; ✷ lunch Mon-Fri, dinner Mon-Sat) This takeaway *snack* specialises in Asian food, including mouthwatering samosas, spring rolls and rice and noodle dishes. It's in a colonial house with a red roof.

Roulottes (Map p184; rue Georges Clémenceau; dishes around 600 CFP; ✷ dinner) These food vans in the large car park opposite the market serve great takeaway meals.

Le Bout du Monde (Map p184; ☎ 277 728; 4 rue de la Frégate Nivôse; mains 1600-2900 CFP; ✷ 7am-11pm) This relaxed bar and restaurant that spills out towards the marina at Port Moselle serves a lunchtime salad buffet (1200 CFP) on weekdays, but you can also order à la carte. So try an ostrich fillet.

La Chaumière (Map p184; ☎ 272 462; 13 rue du Docteur Guégan; menus lunch/dinner 2300/3400 CFP; ✷ lunch Mon-Fri, dinner Mon-Sat) The atmosphere is warm and uncluttered in this old colonial building where fabulous fine dining makes it very popular. French favourites like fish soup or confit of duck come with traditional accompaniments it's hard to find elsewhere. Come for lunch, share the menu, whatever, just don't miss out.

IT ALL TASTES GREAT

New Caledonian restaurants are famous for their fine dining. But it's at the *snacks* (eateries), cafes and country pubs that you really appreciate the flare and flavour of French cuisine: everything is prepared with sauces and marinades you could die for. Take the simple sandwich. It's a very long delicious crusty baguette with leg ham dripping out the sides, or perhaps a homemade terrine stacked inside. If a restaurant serves Pacific cuisine, the meal will be simple but elegant, fish in lemon say, using local produce.

Buffets look good and cost a bomb. But a seafood buffet is wonderfully indulgent. Then there's the 'menu', designed to stretch your waist and shrink your wallet. Many places let you share them. If you're on a tour that includes lunch, wow. Magnificent. And you thought you'd get blackened sausages.

The Melanesian specialty is *bougna*: yam, sweet potato, taro, other vegetables and meat, fish or seafood covered in coconut milk, wrapped in banana leaves and cooked on hot stones in an earth oven for two hours. Most Melanesian-run gîtes can prepare a *bougna* but you must order 24 hours in advance. Lobster *bougna* is the most expensive option and perhaps not the best way to treat something as special as the local lobsters; they so fresh and sweet.

On the islands a lot of your food, and all your drinks, arrive by boat, so don't be surprised if your choice isn't available. And if all the fishermen are off to a wedding, there'll be no seafood that day. It happens.

Baie de l'Orphelinat

Le Galapagos (Map p182; ☎ 262 218; 21 rue Jules Garnier; mains 1900-2500 CFP; ☺ lunch & dinner Mon-Sat) The Galapagos serves food cooked to perfection, with sauces you keep remembering. A two-/three-course lunch menu is 2200/3200 CFP. At night it's tapas (800 CFP), with a fantastic cheese buffet (1900 CFP) on Thursday night and live music Saturday night. Book in for a game of squash while you're here.

Galerie Port Plaisance has pleasant cafes serving tasty meals at reasonable prices (like veal scallopine for 1200 CFP) in attractive open settings. **Snack** (☎ 797 697; mains 650-1350 CFP; ☺ 7am-6pm Mon-Fri, 8am-2pm Sat), across the driveway in Cercle des Nageurs Caledoniens, is a popular terrace with sandwiches from 400 CFP and filling mains.

Baie des Citrons

The electric strip at Baie des Citrons has some neat shops tucked between an amazing line of restaurants clamouring to be noticed: Italian, seafood, steak, Mexican, salad, fusion, Basque. Wander along, join all the other people enjoying the atmosphere and having a drink or two, then pick your spot, but be good and leave the ice-cream bar till last. Main meals cost between 1500 CFP and 3300 CFP.

Anse Vata

Snack Ulysse (Map p182; ☎ 286 928; rte de l'Anse Vata; sandwiches 450-750 CFP; ☺ lunch & dinner) A popular *snack* that serves generously filled hot or cold sandwiches, burgers, chips and rice dishes. Eat in or take away.

Casa Italia (Map p182; ☎ 259 258; 113 rte de l'Anse Vata; small/large pizzas 1500/2400 CFP; ☺ lunch & dinner Mon-Sat) This Italian restaurant is famous for its authentic pizzas and pasta dishes and warm atmosphere. Everything is homemade; try the grappa if you dare.

L'Amédée (Map p182; ☎ 261 035; rte de l'Anse Vata; mains 1900-5500 CFP; ☺ lunch Mon-Fri, dinner Mon-Sat) It's a cosy restaurant for lovers of seafood. The menu has pictures of the fish, so you know what you're ordering; the crab d'Amédée comes piled high, the sauces are rich as.

Le Roof (Map p182; ☎ 250 700; 134 promenade Roger Laroque; mains 2500-3500 CFP; ☺ lunch & dinner) Out on the pier, spacious and open, Le Roof has a large central backlit hole so that you can see ocean, fish and perhaps even a turtle. Add two large aquariums, delicate white china, majestic wine glasses, delicious fish dishes and its like fine dining for mermaids.

La Sorbetière (Map p182; ☎ 262 803; sandwich/crepe/croque 400/350/450 CFP; ☺ 8am-6pm) serves indulgent ice creams, waffles and crepes. Up the other end, **Fun Beach Restaurant & Grill** (Map p182; ☎ 26 3132; mains 1300-2800 CFP; ☺ 11am-2pm & 6-11pm) is all Western-style pasta, fish and steak, served on a deck by the bay. And it's a pleasant spot for a drink in the evening.

There are two little curved malls: Palm Beach has several eating options serving meals costing from 680 CFP; at the western end, La Promenade has Vietnamese, Chinese, Thai, Australian (meals from 1200 CFP to 5500 CFP). Wonton soup (700 CFP) at the Vietnamese is magnificent.

DRINKING
Bars

Everywhere, your drinks are served with a bowl of peanuts or marinated olives. So nice. The bars along the Baie des Citrons strip where everyone gathers include **Malecon Café** (Map p182; ☎ 282 805; ⏰ to 11pm), which offers quiche and pizza (650 CFP) to help you drink more, and the microbrewery, **Les 3 Brasseurs** (Map p182; ☎ 241 516; ⏰ till midnight Sun-Thu, till 2am Fri & Sat), where you can choose your poison, blonde, amber or brown, from the stainless-steel brewing equipment. Its upstairs restaurant serves a Plat de Saison (2500 CFP). Both bars have live music on Friday, Saturday and Sunday nights. Ask for their monthly concert brochure.

In Anse Vata, **Bodega Del Mar** (Map p182; ☎ 261 153; 134 promenade Roger Laroque) is a trendy bar on the pier that features kegs for tables and ragged posters. It really buzzes with 30ish-aged casual types. Tapas costs 700 CFP to 900 CFP. **Le Bilboquet Plage** (Map p182; ☎ 264 660; Palm Beach; ⏰ 11am-2pm & 6.30pm-1am), an upstairs French brasserie that serves tasty meals and snacks (from 650 CFP), has a spacious veranda that's a relaxing place for a drink amidst plenty of potted palms (well, green stuff).

Back in the city, **Le Bilboquet Village** (Map p184; ☎ 264 330; 45 av du Maréchal Foch; ⏰ 9am-11pm Mon-Sat) serves drinks and meals in the charming courtyard of an old court house at Le Village.

If you prefer to drink in a classy bar with comfy lounge chairs and mood music, the friendly staff make stylish **L'Etrave** (Map p182; ☎ 259 440; promenade Roger Laroque; ⏰ 9am-midnight) both casual and fun.

In the city centre, **Le Bout du Monde** (Map p184; ☎ 277 728; 4 rue de la Frégate Nivôse) at the Port Moselle marina is a pleasant place for a drink as well as a meal (see p189). And check out **Le Muzz' Bar** (Map p184; ☎ 277 930; 37 rue Jean Jaurès; ⏰ 6pm-late Tue-Sun), new and inviting, oozing atmosphere, it features popular live music (from 9pm Thursday to Saturday) and some nights the owners play jazz, beautifully. There's tapas (Thursday to Sunday, 600 CFP) and skewers barbecued in the beer garden.

For a South Pacific experience, head out to Dumbéa where **Nakamal du Col** (Dumbéa; kava

---

> **ALCOHOL & WATER**
>
> An alcohol licence may allow beer to be sold only while food is being served. Other places may have a 24-hour licence. You can only buy alcoholic drinks at special bottle shops from Friday evening till Sunday evening. Sadly, or suspiciously, you can buy a bottle of wine in a supermarket for, say, 850 CFP yet pay 650 CFP for a small glass of wine at a restaurant. Perhaps have your drink after dinner, on your balcony with that view to die for. Just a thought.
>
> The country's water supply is managed by the same company that manages Sydney water. Of course if you come from Melbourne that won't impress. But nevertheless, tap water is excellent quality everywhere.

per shell 100 CFP; ⏰ 3.30-10pm Mon-Fri, 3.30pm-midnight Sat & Sun), a kava house on the RT1, has small *farés* on a terraced hillside with panoramic views over Noumea and its bays. Don't miss the sunset.

ENTERTAINMENT

The Office du Tourisme publishes the *NC Pocket* (www.sortir.nc) entertainment guide.

The nightlife mostly happens naturally: the buzz along Baie des Citrons as young people and music fill the bars and spill across to the beach; the slightly older group that park their cars along the Anse Vata foreshore and make the most of the heavenly nights and music drifting or beating across the bay.

On weekends, towards midnight, the Anse Vata crowds might head to **L'Acropole** (Map p182; ☎ 241 938; 119 promenade Roger Laroque), **Mister Swing** (Map p182; ☎ 240 393; 115 promenade Roger Laroque) or **Cort'o Maltese** (Map p182; ☎ 262 725; 134 promenade Roger Laroque), on the small pier at the eastern end of the bay.

There are always sporting activities, markets, fairs and animations happening somewhere. Check them out on www.newcaledoniatourism-south.com/calendar/index.cfm.

Cinemas & Theatres

Ciné City (Map p184; ☎ 292 020; 18 rue de la Somme; admission 950 CFP) Ten theatres screen a large range of movies in French. During La Foa Film Festival (June/July) movies are screened, both here and at La Foa's Cinéma Jean-Pierre Jeunet, in their original language.

NEW CALEDONIA

The ugly **entertainment centre** (Salle de Spectacles, FOL; Map p184; ☎ 272 140; 51 rue Olry) and lovely old theatres **Théâtre de Poche** (☎ 250 750; 6 blvd Extérieur) and **Théâtre de l'Île** (☎ 255 050) have local groups, amateur theatre and stand-up comedy nights. Ask for the programmes at Office du Tourisme or visit www.sor tir.nc.

SHOPPING

You'll find shops selling French designer labels as well as prêt-à-porter outlets along rue de Sébastopol, rue de l'Alma and rue Jean Jaurès. There are also duty-free shops in this area. Two shops selling local clothing brands are **Teeprint Boutique** (Map p184; 48 rue Anatole France) and **Tricot Rayé** (Map p182; Galerie Commercial Port Plaisance).

Galerie Commercial Port Plaisance (Map p182) and Galerie Noumea Centre (Map p184) are attractive, bustling malls; tiny Palm Beach mall (Map p182) has 24 boutiques and cafes and Le Village (Map p184) has a few gift shops around a lovely courtyard.

L'Atelier des Femmes de Nouvelle-Calédonie (Map p184; cnr rue du Gouverneur Sautot & rue Anatole France) sells local crafts and **L'Association des Sculpteurs de Nouvelle-Calédonie** (Map p184; ☎ 775 124; rue Anatole France), next door, sells Kanak sculptures.

GRANDE TERRE

pop 210,000 / area 16,500 sq km

A chain of mountains sweeps down the middle of Grande Terre, and the wide plains that stretch along its west coast are dotted with country towns where cattle breeders stroll down the street in Stetsons and cowboy boots. On the east coast the mountains descend to the sea, their lush vegetation meeting the steep and sinuous coastline. Waterfalls rush down the mountainsides into deep pools and out into the famously colourful lagoon, where the islands' inhabitants spend much of their leisure time fishing, boating and enjoying other water sports. Grande Terre is not only New Caledonia's major island, but also the third-largest island in the Pacific after Papua New Guinea and NZ.

THE FAR SOUTH

The Far South feels like a remote wilderness. The vast, empty region is characterised by its hardy scrub vegetation and red soil, and

offers a wide range of activities including hiking, kayaking, abseiling and mountain biking. If you are looking for a bit of action and adventure, head to the Far South. If you're looking for a peaceful, isolated spot by a river, head to the Far South. Sadly, the controversial pipe carrying waste from the nickel processing plant will dump into the ocean, almost alongside the South's specially protected Merlet Marine Reserve.

Orientation & Information

To get to the Far South, head east out of Noumea towards Mont-Dore. The easiest route is to follow the Voie Express out of Noumea to the RP1. The road forks when it reaches the mountain at La Coulée: take either the RP3 across to Yaté or continue along the RP1 south to Prony and Port Boisé, then the two routes eventually meet at the Chutes de la Madeleine. Ask about road conditions before you start as they can be blocked or pretty bad due to the construction of the nickel processing plant.

A small **visitor information centre** (☎ 433 344; ☾ 8am-4pm Mon-Fri, 8am-noon Sat & Sun) beside the RP1 at Boulari has information on accommodation and activities, including several walking-track brochures.

Getting There & Around

You'll need to hire a car to explore the Far South; see p226 for car-rental agents in Noumea. It's about a 1½ hour drive to Yaté from Noumea. Buses to Yaté (600 CFP, two hours) leave from Noumea's Gare Routière at 11.30am Monday to Saturday but don't connect with a return service. Tours which include a commentary plus lunch are always a good option (see p195).

Sights
PARC PROVINCIAL DE LA RIVIÈRE BLEUE

Spacious protected Blue River Park is a reserve for many bird species, including the *cagou*. The landscape is a mixture of the Far South's typical scrub vegetation and dense rainforest and includes gigantic kaori trees, at least 1000 years old and with trunks up to 2.7m across. Take the RP3 from La Coulée to get to the western end of the hydroelectric dam, **Lac de Yaté**, where you enter lovely **Parc Provincial de la Rivière Bleue** (☎ 436 124; adult/student 400/50 CFP; ☾ 7am-5pm Tue-Sun, entry closes 2pm).

NEW CALEDONIA

There is a visitor information centre by the entrance gate which has good displays in English and French on the park's flora and fauna. At the entrance you will also find free maps that outline the park's many walks.

One of the park's famous features is a drowned kaori forest, the trunks reaching, ghostlike, out of the clear blue water. Go on a moonlight paddle to become part of it.

To the west and northwest of the park are the Rivière Blanche and Rivière Bleue, Lac de Yaté's main tributaries. You can drive along the banks of Rivière Blanche to the end of the road, walk or bike along the Rivière Bleue side, or kayak up the river.

CHUTES DE LA MADELEINE

This ladylike **waterfall** (☎ 469 247; adult/child 400/200 CFP; ☒ 8am-5pm), with its wide apron of tinkling water, sits in a botanic reserve in the middle of a vast plain. Swimming is forbidden at the waterfall, but it is permitted where the road runs beside the river between the waterfall and **Site de Netcha** (☎ 469 247; day entry adult/child 1000/500 CFP). Here, there are wooden diving platforms over the river and shelters and tables overlooking the water where you can picnic. Best of all, there's a kid's playground and you can rent kayaks.

To get to the waterfall from the RP3, take the signposted road turning towards the eastern end of the Lac de Yaté; it is 11km to the waterfall. This road joins the road connecting Prony and Port Boisé a few kilometres further on.

YATÉ & CASCADE DE WADIANA

From the eastern end of Lac de Yaté, the RP3 winds to the top of a mountain and then drops steeply to the sea. If you turn right at the bottom of the escarpment and cross a small bridge, the road leads past Wao to tourist gîtes and campsites. If you continue, the road veers left to Yaté village, where there's a small shop and petrol pump.

South of Wao you come to Touaourou and then Goro. At Goro the road passes beside **Wadiana falls**, which cascade down a rocky slope into a natural pool where you can swim. From Goro you can go on, past the rusting remnants of an iron-mining operation, to Port Boisé and round past Prony back to Noumea.

PORT BOISÉ

Port Boisé is an isolated bay surrounded by a forest of Cook Pines, 6.5km from the turn-off on the main road. The ecolodge here makes a good base for the walking tracks along the coast and to a lookout point. It's also a top spot for lunch.

PRONY

Once a convict centre, Prony sits in a lush hollow surrounded by forest beside Baie de Prony. No cars are allowed. A stream runs through the village of corrugated-iron cottages and overgrown stone ruins. It's a charming place to wander through or enjoy a picnic beside the sea. A plaque tells about Capitaine Sebert landing here in 1887. He found rosewood, wanted in Europe for walking sticks, pipes and clogs, ebony, koup and kaori. Across the stream a banyan has sculpted its roots to the edge of the cliff. Look for the little purple mushrooms and brilliant orange fungi.

Baie de Prony is a good place for yachts to hide from the Westerlies. **Casy Express** (☎ 793 260; casyexpress@lagoon.nc; 2500 CFP) runs taxi boats out to islands from here, whale-watching trips leave from here between July and September, and there's hot springs to be visited. The GR1 walking track also starts about 500m south of the village at Baie de la Somme, which is part of the larger Baie de Prony.

Activities

There's a great range of activities waiting in the Far South: canoeing, kayaking, mountain biking, walking, abseiling, hunting, sitting by a stream. During the whale-watching season (July to September), there are dozens of local men with boats, ready to take you out **whale-watching** (adult per day 8500 CFP). The Office du Tourisme has a list of companies in the **Syndicat des Activités Nautiques et Touristiques** (www.nouvelle-caledonie-nautisme.nc) that adhere to its Whale-Watching Quality charter:

Aventure Pulsion (Map p182; ☎ 262 748; www.aventure-pulsion.nc/sorties.htm; kayaks half-/full day 2500/4500 CFP) Rent your kayak in Noumea (carried on your own car) or take a guided sea-kayak tour to a hot spring, a moonlight paddle over the drowned forest or a river or lake kayak (4200 CFP, see the website for dates).

Koghi Decouverte/Sud Loisirs (☎ 778 143; koghi decouverte@hotmail.com, sudloisir@lagoon.nc) Hire a mountain bike (2200 CFP) on weekends, in Parc Provincial de la Rivière Bleue. Ask the ranger at the park entrance for directions to the kiosk.

Pacific Free Ride (☎ 792 202; www.pfr.nc) Go abseiling down the falls at Goro or Yaté (8000 CFP), or canoe in Baie de Prony and Baie des Pirogues (half-day 5000 CFP).

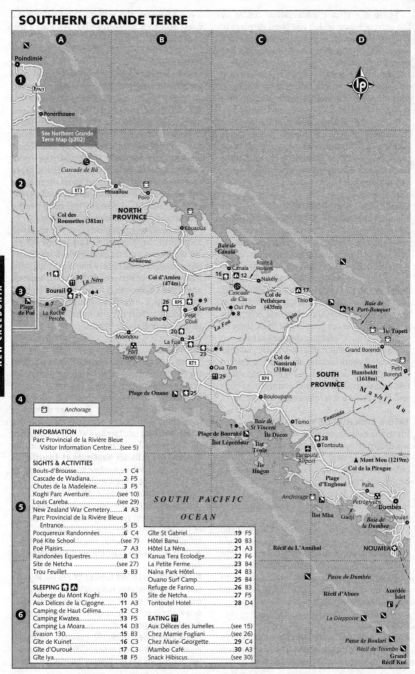

SOUTHERN GRANDE TERRE

NEW CALEDONIA

INFORMATION
Parc Provincial de la Rivière Bleue
  Visitor Information Centre.....(see 5)

SIGHTS & ACTIVITIES
Bouts-d'Brousse............................1 C4
Cascade de Wadiana.......................2 F5
Chutes de la Madeleine....................3 F5
Koghi Parc Aventure....................(see 10)
Louis Careba.............................(see 29)
New Zealand War Cemetery..............4 A3
Parc Provincial de la Rivière Bleue
  Entrance...............................5 E5
Pocquereux Randonnées..................6 C4
Poé Kite School..........................(see 7)
Poé Plaisirs...............................7 A3
Randonées Equestres.....................8 C3
Site de Netcha ....(see 27)
Trou Feuillet.............................9 B3

SLEEPING
Auberge du Mont Koghi..................10 E5
Aux Delices de la Cigogne...............11 A3
Camping de Haut Gélima.................12 C3
Camping Kwatea.........................13 F5
Camping La Moara.......................14 D3
Évasion 130.............................15 B3
Gîte de Kuinet...........................16 C3
Gîte d'Ouroué...........................17 C3
Gîte Iya.................................18 F5

Gîte St Gabriel..........................19 F5
Hôtel Banu..............................20 B3
Hôtel La Néra...........................21 A3
Kanua Tera Ecolodge.....................22 F6
La Petite Ferme..........................23 B4
Naïna Park Hôtel.........................24 B3
Ouano Surf Camp........................25 B4
Refuge de Farino.........................26 B3
Site de Netcha...........................27 F5
Tontoutel Hotel..........................28 D4

EATING
Aux Délices des Jumelles.............(see 15)
Chez Mamie Fogliani................(see 26)
Chez Marie-Georgette....................29 C4
Mambo Café.............................30 A3
Snack Hibiscus......................(see 30)

Poindimié
Ponérihouen
See Northern Grande
Terre Map (p202)
Cascade de Bâ
Houaïlou
Poro
Col des
Roussettes (381m)
NORTH
PROVINCE
Kouaoua
Kouaoua
Baie de
Canala
Col d'Amieu
(474m)
Canala
Nakéty
Route à
Horaires
Cascade
de Ciu
Col de
Péthécara
(435m)
Thio
Baie de
Port-Bouquet
La Néra
Bourail
La Roche
Percée
Plage
de Poé
Farino
Sarraméa
Oui Poin
Petit
Couli
Moindou
La Foa
La Foa
Fort
Teremba
Oua Tom
Col de
Nassirah
(318m)
SOUTH
PROVINCE
Grand Borendi
Petit
Borendi
Mont
Humboldt
(1618m)
Île Tupeti
Plage de Ouano
Plage de Bouraké
Îlot Léprédour
Bouloupari
Baie de
St Vincent
Île Ducos
Île
Ténia
Île
Hugon
Tomo
Tontouta
Tontouta
Tontouta
Airport
Mont Mou (1219m)
Col de la Pirogue
Plage
d'Enghoué
Païta
Anchorage
Îlot Mba
Gadji
Petroglyphs
Dumbéa
Baie de
la Dumbéa
Boulari
NOUMÉA
SOUTH PACIFIC
OCEAN
Récif de l'Annibal
Passe de Dumbéa
Récif d'Abore
Amédée
Islet
La Dieppoise
Passe de Boulari
Récif de Toombo
Grand
Récif Kué
Anchorage

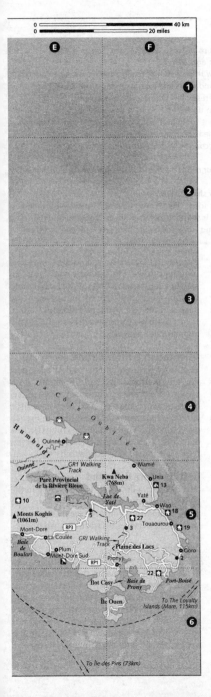

Terra Incognita (☎ 789 446; www.terincognita.com)
Kayak rental at Parc Provincial de la Rivière Bleue (5500
CFP). Full moon kayaking (4200 CFP); park nature tour by
foot, bike, kayak and 4WD (11,000 CFP).

GR1 WALKING TRACK

The **GR1** (Grande Randonnée 1; www.trekking-gr-sud
-nc.com) is a five-day (123.4km) walk (Great
Walk) between Prony through Parc Provincial
de la Rivière Bleue and on north to Dumbéa.
Trek from the sea through plains, forests,
hills and streams, along mule tracks and
into pond or marsh. The air might be moist,
acrid or crisply alpine; the views are always
magnificent. Bunk down in a hut along the
way; download the route and hut details from
the website. Drop-offs or pick-ups need to
be arranged either through the office at **Site
de Netcha** (☎ 469 247) or **Aventure Pulsion** (www
.aventure-pulsion.nc/taxi.htm) has a taxi service to
and from the different legs of the walk (from
10,000 CFP for up to eight people).

Tours

The following tours of the Far South are based
on a minimum of two adults:

Aventure Pulsion (Map p182; ☎ 262 748; www.aventure
-pulsion.nc; 4WD per adult per day 16,000 CFP) A grand
adventure in a 4WD, visiting waterfalls, tribal villages, bays
and mountain tops. Lunch is a three-course feast and you'll
learn heaps from your driver/guide. Tours leave at 8am.
Other tours, like the one-/two-day kayak tours, cost from
5800/10,000 CFP.

Caledonia Tours (☎ 259 424; caledoniatours@lagoon
.nc; adult/child 11,500/7500 CFP) Specialise in day tours
through the Blue River Park. Swim, walk through rainforest, bird-watch and listen to a rich commentary about
geology, botany, wildlife and history. Lunch is a BBQ by the
river. Tours leave at 8.15am.

Sleeping & Eating

Accommodation places serve meals to non-
guests but you must book in advance.

Site de Netcha (☎ 469 247; camping 1200 CFP) Cute
little roofed campsites are set by the river.
Camp fires, tables and benches sit between
the bushes, the toilet is swish and there's a
shower and basin. There's no electricity and
you must take drinking water.

Gîte Iya (☎ 469 080; camping 1500 CFP, bungalows
5000 CFP) The rustic but comfortable bungalows
are in a coconut grove beside a small private
beach. Set menus cost 2200 CFP (closed for
dinner on Sunday), or 3600 CFP for lobster.
You can snorkel along the fringing reef not

FLORENT LIMENTO, AVENTUR PULSION

Florent is a part-time tour guide. He takes groups of six to eight on day trips in a 4WD.

You came to Noumea from France five years ago. Why?

I was dreaming about a tropical island and I saw there were not much people on New Caledonia and also the size of the island with mountains and rivers and that made my destination. I had no real idea of what to expect but I was most interested in discovering this big land.

Are you pleased to be bringing your children up here?

Yes, yes. It is quite safe. No cars, pollution is not too bad. I feel safe, you won't get an allergy. And the Melanesian way of life, you're not worried about money, the future. For me it is a dream to grow a kid in a place that was my dream, a country that is part of me now.

You obviously love the South. Why?

For me it is a place of freedom. You can find your own little river and camp there. You're allowed to make a fire camp and you see nobody.

You take tourists to the South. What do you show them?

You know there's the views, the waterfalls, the tribal villages. You have this special vegetation; some come from the dinosaur era. The reef here is still alive, put your line in the water and there's fish, take a boat to a small island and your island is for yourself. Where else can you find that?

---

far from the beach. There's a signpost to the gîte, just south of Wao.

Gîte St Gabriel (☎ 464 277; camping 1000 CFP, bungalows 13,000 CFP) You can see St Gabriel's lawns sweeping down to the beach from the main road, about 3km south of Touaourou. It's a peaceful spot and you can go for long walks along the beach. The bungalows are crisply modern; Marie-jo serves seafood platters, *bougna* and other local dishes (set menu from 2400 CFP, order in advance) in the open restaurant. Canoes and bikes can be hired for 500 CFP per half-day.

Kanua Tera Ecolodge (☎ 469 000; www.tera.nc; d/f 12,600/15,600) Port Boisé seems so isolated, on the edge of a magical forest of Cook Pines. Then you come down a narrow road into a lovely garden with nestled bungalows and a spectacular restaurant that floats out from the cliff. The beach is shallow but you can snorkel on the edge of the fringing reef. It re-opened in 2009, shiny new but the meals are as delicious as ever (tropical breakfast 1900 CFP).

Camping Kwatea (☎ 966 182; faré s/d 1500/2000 CFP) Four *farés* are in a market garden of sweet potato, taro, papaya and coconut. All have ocean views and shared facilities. Idyllic actually. Your hosts, Marie and Bonaventure, produce a range of *bougnas* (1000 CFP), adding quails or fish to your liking. Tours to Unia tribal village, hiking and demonstrations of traditional farming or boating practice are on offer.

CENTRAL GRANDE TERRE

Not far from the bustling cosmopolitan capital, Central Grande Terre offers enrich-

ing cultural experiences, coastal scenery and mountain treks. On the west coast you can stay in a Kanak *tribu* or a Caldoche farm and explore the countryside by foot or on horse back. On the east coast, in Thio and Canala, there are simple campsites in beautiful coastal and riverside settings.

Orientation & Information

The west-coast settlements of Bourail and La Foa are the main towns in the region. Both have a *gendarmerie*, pharmacy, post office, bank and supermarket. And both have little cinemas that screen the latest films in French on Wednesday and weekend evenings (tickets 800 CFP). West of Bourail is La Roche Percée, New Caledonia's only surf beach.

Getting There & Around

Several buses a day from Noumea stop in the west-coast towns. There is a daily bus to Thio and Canala from Noumea (see p226), but no connecting services between the two towns.

Amédée Islet

This islet (Map pp194–5), about 20km south of Noumea, is famous for its tall white lighthouse, **Phare Amédée** (admission 200 CFP), that was built in France, shipped out in pieces, and assembled on the postcard island in 1865. Climb up its spiral staircase to a narrow shelf with 360-degree views. The lighthouse marks one of only three natural breaks in the barrier reef that allow boats access to the mainland.

There's a snack bar and curio shop for visitors who come here on a day trip on the *Mary D* (p188), which leaves from Port Moselle. It's also a popular spot for scuba divers and snorkellers.

Monts Koghis

Monts Koghis (Map pp194–5) are clad in rainforest and rich native flora, and they have several walking trails; the Direction des Ressources Naturelles (p221) publishes a free walking map. Or take a treetop trail on swinging bridges and rope walks with **Koghi Parc Aventure** (Map pp194-5; ☎ 430 252, 821 485; talon@mls .nc; trail 2000 CFP; ☺ 10am-4pm Sat & Sun, by reservation Mon-Fri), behind the *auberge* (p198). Fun. The turn-off to these mountains is on the RT1, 14km north of central Noumea.

Caltours (p226) runs half-day tours to Monts Koghis.

Boulouparis

Just north of Tontouta airport is Boulouparis, where a turn-off to Bouraké beach takes you to the departure point for trips to **Îlot Ténia**, a beautiful sandy islet surrounded by clear waters near the barrier reef. The islet is a popular surfing, diving and snorkelling spot.

Bouts-d'Brousse (☎ 432 962; www.ilot-tenia.com; half-/full-day boat trips 4600/6800 CFP) organises trips to the island which include dolphin watching; great fun, especially for children. Take your own picnic lunch. Trips depart at 9am. Scuba diving (intro dive 7800 CFP) includes exploring a magnificent coral massif that rises from the reef face.

La Foa & Around

La Foa is a neat little town 1½ hours from Noumea. The friendly and efficient staff at **La Foa Tourisme** (☎ 416 911; www.lafoatourisme.asso .nc; ☺ 8am-5.30pm Mon-Fri, 9am-5pm Sat, 9am-noon Sun), the visitors information centre, can advise on accommodation and activities in La Foa, Farino and Sarraméa. A major event on New Caledonia's social calendar is the June/July film festival where international films, screened in their own language, are shown at La Foa's **Cinéma Jean-Pierre Jeunet** (☎ 416 911). Each year, the festival is presided over by a famous person from the film industry.

The **sculpture garden** (☺ 8am-8pm Sep-Apr, to 6pm May-Aug) behind La Foa Tourisme features wonderful sculptures by artists from throughout New Caledonia. The garden is a pleasant place for a picnic, with a children's playground and public toilets.

Sarraméa, 15 minutes' drive north of La Foa, sits in a lush valley surrounded by mountains. At the end of the road a path continues through a farm gate to **Trou Feuillet**, also known as *la cuve*, a refreshing rock pool in a mountain stream. On the main road, just past the Sarraméa turn-off, is **tribu de Petit Couli**, where a beautiful old *grande case* stands at the end of a row of tall araucaria pines.

Farino is a mountain village in primary tropical forest, known for its produce and craft markets held every second Sunday of the month. The real crowd puller is its Vers de Bancoule market day in September, which culminates in a contest to see who can eat the most fat, wriggling white grubs.

ACTIVITIES

The **Refuge de Farino** (☎ 443 761) organises quadbike tours (one/two hours 5000/6000 CFP) in the forest around Farino, and walks to waterfalls, and Parc Grande Fougeres (big fern trees). The turn-off to Farino is on the road to Sarraméa.

Jayak Surfari (☎ 782 103, 797 374; www.jayaksurfari .com; day trips 5000 CFP) takes you out to surf or fish or walk about an islet.

There are many walks and horse treks in the La Foa region. Most places offer half- or full-day treks and some offer overnight treks:

Louis Careba (☎ 443 817; 1hr walks/horse treks 1500/3500 CFP) Louis offers historical and botanical walking and horse treks in *tribu* de Oua Tom. The turn-off is 13km south of La Foa.

Pocquereux Randonnées (☎ 773 254; 1hr/half-/full-day trek 3000/6000/12,000 CFP) The turn-off is 3km south of La Foa (on the road to La Petite Ferme). Mario Mediara also offers camping/*case* accommodation for 500/1000 CFP and meals for 1800 CFP.

Randonnées Equestres (☎ 417 281, 354 522; guided walk 2000 CFP, half-/full-day horse trek 5000/8000 CFP) In the mountains 25km northeast of La Foa. Overnight walks or horse treks to Canala can also be arranged.

SLEEPING & EATING

Refuge de Farino (☎ 443 761; refuge.farino@lagoon.nc; camping 700 CFP, bungalows 7400 CFP) On a hillside in Farino's forest, Sabine's timber bungalows have a kitchenette and magnificent views from their decks. There's BBQs, a hot tub, a playground and breakfast (750 CFP). Just lovely. BYO food, or eat at Mamie's, 1km back down the road.

NEW CALEDONIA

IT'S NOT LIKE THEY'RE BLOWFLIES

You never know, do you. Take deer: Bambies, cute as. They were introduced into New Caledonia and have become an ecological disaster. There are more deer than people now, they ringbark forest trees, and even greenies agree they're a pest. So hunting has become an intrinsic part of local life. If you're interested in the venison, it can go back overseas with you, you just need an invoice saying it's been through proper channels. Or hold one big spit roast before you leave. If you're after a trophy head, you should come in the rutting season (July and August). After that the antlers fall off. Your trophy must be stuffed by a taxidermist, and the meat is inedible.

It's difficult to bring your own gun. Contact Hôtel Banu and Hôtel La Nero for advice, then you'll need a hunting licence to borrow a gun and a ration of ammunition.

La Petite Ferme (☎ 443 405; lafoatourisme@canl.nc; camping 1000 CFP, bungalows 4000 CFP) These pre-fab bungalows make a base to go hunting; your host, Jean Louis, runs 4WD night spins to see the deer. Meals (five-courses with drinks 4000 CFP) are served in the garden, but book 48 hours ahead (six days ahead if you're a large group wanting cassoulet).

Ouano Surf Camp (☎ 469 090; www.ouano surf.com; camping 1050 CFP, bungalows with/without bathroom 7000/6600 CFP) New in town and just what was needed for surfers and others, there's everything here, including a laundry, modern but basic bungalows and great meals. It's a 20-minute boat ride out to surf the reef breaks.

Tontoutel Hotel (☎ 351 111; ecotel@canl.nc; s/d/family 6700/8200 CFP/12,300 CFP; ☒) It's five minutes from Tontoutel International Airport, so it's perfect if you're catching an early morning flight. Ecotel Association for Hotel and Catering Training trains students there. Rooms are large and comfortable and there's a pleasant restaurant.

Hôtel Banu (☎ 443 119; fax 443 550; s/d/f 4400/5200/7600 CFP, bungalows s/d 6400/7200 CFP; ☒ ☒) Looking quaint, in the middle of La Foa, but the accommodation behind the hotel is excellent. The restaurant is open for all meals except Sunday dinner, and the cheerful staff serve the best *plat du jour* (1300 CFP) and other delicious meals (1300 CFP to 6500 CFP) using local produce. Or have a gourmet sandwich on the porch (550 CFP) then try counting the 4700 caps on the bar's ceiling.

Auberge du Mont Koghi (☎ 412 929; koghi land@offratel.nc; Dumbéa; chalet/half-board 7500/15,000 CFP) Overlooking Noumea and its bays, 476m above sea level, the *auberge* has chalets and more remote huts about a 10-minute walk into the forest. The restaurant is open for all meals. It has a fireplace, warm timber interior, and specialises in melted-cheese *raclette* (3900 CFP).

Naïna Park Hôtel (☎ 443 540; www.nainaparkhotel .com; bungalows B&B 8900 CFP; ☒ ☒) These bungalows are quite delightful, set amidst shady tropical trees at the entrance to La Foa. There's a relaxing pool area and a grand restaurant (dishes 2300 CFP to 3800 CFP, closed Monday).

Évasion 130 (☎ 445 577; www.hotel-evasion.com; B&B r/bungalow 9900/17,500 CFP; ☒ ☒) Smart modern bungalows with little verandas overlook a stream at the end of the road in Sarraméa. Or stay in a spacious room in the hotel. Évasion's top chef offers fine dining and elegant buffets (meals 2500 CFP to 4500 CFP) in the spacious restaurant.

Chez Mamie Fogliani (☎ 432 314; meals 2500-3500 CFP) Mamie's table d'hôte is very popular. Enjoy filling Caldoche cuisine including venison, wild pig, fish and duck dishes. It's 3km from the Farino *mairie* (town hall).

Aux Délices des Jumelles (☎ 434 665; set menus from 3000 CFP; ☒ lunch Tue-Sun) In a gorgeous garden near the chapel in Sarraméa, Bernadette serves four courses of Kanak cuisine that delight her guests. Try her special coffee with coconut jam (*mamarènü*). Book 24 hours ahead and dinner is available by arrangement (BYO drinks).

Chez Marie-Georgette (☎ 443 817; set menu 3000-3500 CFP) This table d'hôte adjacent to the *tribu de Oua Tom* serves Kanak cuisine including *bougna*, and chicken or prawn dishes. Book 24 hours in advance and take your tent so you can stay the night (camping 1000 CFP).

Bourail & Around

With a rural atmosphere and strong Caldoche community, Bourail is the next biggest town on Grande Terre after Noumea. The main road crosses the Néra river bridge at the southern end of town, and the turn-off to La Roche Percée and Poé beach is immediately after the bridge.

An old stone building 500m south of the centre houses the **Musée de Bourail** (☎ 441 218; adult/student 250/100 CFP; ☺ 8-11am & 1-5pm Mon-Fri, to 4pm Sat, to 3pm Sun). Its displays include objects relating to the presence of US and NZ troops in Bourail during WWII and a guillotine complete with the basket where the decapitated head was placed. The guillotine was brought to New Caledonia in 1867. Behind the museum there's a *case*.

Bourail holds a hugely popular **country fair** (☎ 412 104; admission 500 CFP) over the weekend closest to August 15: farm animals on display; produce, arts and crafts for sale; children's rides; food stalls; and, the highlight, a rodeo. Campsites are available, 25,000 people are expected; there's contests, races, demonstrations. One grand weekend.

About 9.5km east of Bourail is the well-tended **New Zealand War Cemetery**, where over 200 NZ soldiers killed in the Pacific during WWII are buried. NZ troops set up a hospital in the area during the war, and many locals received free medical care there. A ceremony is held at the cemetery on the Saturday closest to Anzac Day (25 April) and local children place a flower on each grave.

La Roche Percée has two famous rock formations: **La Roche Percée** (pierced rock) and **Le Bonhomme**, a rock shaped like a tubby man. A walking track begins at the base of the cliff near the rocks and follows the coast for 4km past Baie des Tortues (Turtle Bay) to Baie des Amoureux (Lover's Bay).

There's a panoramic viewing point above Le Bonhomme where you can often spot turtles in Baie des Tortues below. With its bent araucarias and wide beach, Baie des Tortues is a beautiful spot but beware of the strong currents. To get there, follow the main road round to the right instead of turning left to La Roche Percée. As you ascend the hill, turn onto the dirt road to the left.

ACTIVITIES

The surf at La Roche Percée is caused by a break in the fringing reef, so you don't have to go out to the reef to catch a wave. The best spot is at the mouth of the Néra river. When you've conquered the shore breaks, Nëkwéta (right) offers trips to the barrier reef to surf (four hours for 5300 CFP), snorkel (half-day 5500 CFP) or explore Île Vert (3100 CFP).

The dive club **Bourail Sub Loisirs** (☎ 442 065, 782 065; butterfly.diving@lagoon.nc; 2-dive package 12,000 CFP), also at the Néra river mouth, will take you to see magnificent corals along vertical drops and canyons with abundant sharks, rays and Napoleon fish. Surfing trips to the barrier reef and boat trips (from 3000 CFP) can be arranged.

Plage de Poé is a beautiful, long white-sand beach 9km north of La Roche Percée. It's all happening on the beach at Poé:

Glass-bottom boat tours (1800 CFP)

Poe Kite School (☎ 776 059; www.poekiteschool.com; 1½hr 6000 CFP) Teaches kitesurfing.

Poe Plaisirs (☎ 750 001; www.mdplaisirs.com) Hires kayaks (1600 CFP per hour), windsurfers (beginners/intermediate 1000/2700 CFP per hour) and funboards (6700 CFP per day). Ask about the MD Plaisirs discount card.

SLEEPING & EATING

our pick Nëkwéta (☎ 419 081; www.nekweta.com; case adult/child 3000/1500 CFP) The attractive campsite is like a small botanic garden with areas to sit and discuss the breaks. It's at La Roche Percée, one block back from the beach.

Aux Delices de la Cigogne (☎ 442 552; s/d 4500/6300 CFP) A traditional Alsace table d'hôte which features crane in its menu (three-course meal with wine 3200 CFP). It's highly recommended by the locals who like to stay the night in the newly renovated rooms – basic but with ensuite. Book in advance; it's 4km north of Bourail on the main road.

El Kantara (☎ 441 322; el.kantara@lagoon.nc; d fan/aircon 5700/6500 CFP; ☒ ☒) It's very orange, with motel-type rooms in lines, but the pool's a drawcard and it's a short walk through to La Roche Percée beach. The large dining room is open for all meals (1750 CFP to 2450 CFP) and there's a shady deck for lounging, table tennis, *pétanque* and canoe hire.

Chez Catherine et Pascal (☎ 439 806, 795 782; d/tr 6000/7000 CFP) Another sweet tropical garden in La Roche Percée with attractive pre-fab bungalows, lots of private space and charming hosts who'll cook for you if you ask (breakfast 700 CFP, three-course dinner with wine 3000 CFP).

Hôtel La Néra (☎ 441 644; s/d 6700/7700 CFP; ☒ ☒) This Bavarian-style hotel with a river view is by the Néra river bridge. Dishes like veal provencial cost between 1900 CFP and 2300 CFP at the hotel's cosy restaurant (breakfast is 800 CFP). Try your hand at clay pigeon shooting here (25 shots for 2500 CFP).

NEW CALEDONIA

RICK ANEX, RICK'S PLACE, LA ROCHE PERCÉE

Owner of Rick's Place (see below)

New Caledonia's reef has been granted World Heritage status. What was the listing based on?

It fulfils all the criteria. It has exceptional natural beauty and is of universal value. It is the only place in the world that has all the components of a reef and associated eco-systems in one place. The mangroves, giant lagoon, river deltas, wet lands, coral plateaus, sea grass, internal fringing reef. And it's almost unbroken barrier reef surrounds a spectacular number of species of all forms of marine life.

How will protecting New Caledonia's reef benefit the rest of the globe?

This reef has the chance of being saved. With its geographical position and isolation, there's been less coral bleaching than on other major reefs, showing it has a greater potential to survive global warming. Plus there's less effluent from agriculture and general pollution. So it could be the world's best chance of preserving a reef ecosystem.

But New Caledonia has major industries. Do they not cause a problem?

For sure. Industrial development is anathema to the reef. In fact we requested World Heritage status for the entire reef, but political issues, driven by industrial requirements, meant only six areas were finally included, areas where there was no mining or industrial sites.

You played a big role in the request.

Yes, I was inspired by the efforts of Tasmanian Greens to get Franklin River inscribed on the World Heritage list. It is essential that we do everything possible to protect our environment against development without concern for the consequences.

Rick's Place (☎ 442 281; www.rochepercee.com; chalet weekday/weekend 8000/11,000) A rustic romantic cubby for two in La Roche Percée, up some steps and over the river, with a large kitchenette and sitting area, bedroom, front deck, and carved chairs and door handles. If Rick's at home (next door), listen to his stories about local history and the early days of surfing. He has bikes, kayaks and coffee he roasts himself.

Gîte du Cap (Map p202; ☎ 469 009, 766 617; gites ducap@tropik.nc; maisonnette/chalet B&B 10,000/5800) A further 24km up the RT1 from Bourail, turn at the sign on col du Cap and it's 8km down towards the sea to Gîte du Cap. The well-equipped maisonnettes sleep five, the chalets three, on this 70 hectare farm that stretches down to the ocean. Germaine cooks traditional meals (3800 CFP) using local produce while Yann takes you around the farm, or to fish, canoe and hike.

Snack Hibiscus (☎ 441 217; dishes 1400 CFP, snacks 450-600 CFP; ☽ 7am-6pm) Yes it's hibiscus pink, busy and serves good paninis, toasted sandwiches and burgers, or copious fish or chicken dishes.

Mambo Café (☎ 442 930; dishes 1500-2300 CFP; ☽ 7am-1pm & 5.30-8pm) This cafe in the centre of town specialises in Asian dishes with prawns or beef, and pizzas (from 1500 CFP).

Thio & Canala

These two east-coast towns are in the heart of mining country, where the mountains are scarred by the destructive mining practices of the past. Don't be put off, though, as the rest of the landscape is beautiful. There are a couple of lovely beaches in Thio where you can camp. Thio also has a small **mining museum** (☎ 445 177; adult/child 200 CFP/free; ☽ 8am-3pm Tue-Fri, to noon Sat & Sun).

A scenic coastal drive from Thio heads 30km south to Petit Borendi. The starkly contrasting red, green and blue of the earth, vegetation, sea and sky are amazing.

Beware the *Route à Horaires* (schedule road), a 13km goat track called a road between Thio and Canala. If you arrive outside the schedule, you have to wait for two hours because cars can only depart at odd hours from the Thio end, between 5am and 5pm, and at even hours from the Canala end, between 6am and 6pm. Plus, you can only enter the road in the first 20 minutes of your hour. After dark, traffic becomes two-way. Don't try to think why.

The views from the valley looking up at the 60m **Cascade de Ciu** are spectacular. The turn-off to the waterfalls, a sealed road beside a green corrugated-iron shop, is 2km south of Canala.

SLEEPING & EATING

Contact **Canala Information Centre** (☎ 426 061) or **Thio Tourism Information Desk** (☎ 442 504) for information on camping in the area.

Gîte d'Ouroué (☎ 445 085; camping 1100 CFP) North of Thio, in a coconut grove beside a remote beach, with a long shady stretch of lawn. Half-day kayak hire costs 500 CFP.

Camping de Haut Gélima (☎ 786 490; camping 1100 CFP) A tranquil campsite beside a river, 1.5km from the main road about 3km south of Canala; the turn-off is signposted.

Gîte de Kuinet (☎ 428 442; camping 1100 CFP, case 3600 CFP) In *tribu* de Kuinet, on the road to Cascade de Ciu, these *cases* are a modern version of the traditional structures. Meals are 2800 CFP.

Camping La Moara (☎ 445 184; camping 1500 CFP) This grassy campsite sits by a white-sand beach curved around a small bay. It's 11km southeast of Thio.

NORTHWEST COAST

Much of the northwest coast and its rolling plains are taken up by cattle ranches. The coast is not great for swimming, as it has mangrove swamps and shallow bays, so it makes more sense to head inland for horse trekking or staying on a Caldoche farm or in a Kanak homestay.

Getting There & Around

Air Calédonie flies twice weekly from Noumea to Koné (☎ agency 472 113) and Koumac (☎ agency 475 390); see p225. There are daily buses from Noumea (see p225). The **gare routière** (bus station; Rue Roger Trouillot), 300m from the roundabout in Koumac, has schedules for buses going north to Poum and northeast to Ouegoa and Pouébo.

Koné & Around

Koné, the Northern Province capital, has a post office, *gendarmerie,* clinic, pharmacy, supermarkets and banks with ATMs. It is noted for its excellent horse-trekking opportunities. Pouembout, 8km south of Koné, is in many ways an extension of the capital.

North of Koné, in Voh, there's a mangrove swamp which has developed some unusual natural designs. The most intriguing is a perfect heart shape, **La Coeur de Voh**, which is on the cover of *Earth from Above,* the book of aerial photography by famous photographer Yann Arthus-Bertrand. There's a track up to

a viewing point on a mountain but the heart is best seen from the air. **Alain Nouard** (☎ 472 593; 30min flight 6000 CFP) or **Pierre Couget** (☎ 473 287; 60min flight 10,000 CFP) from the ultra-light club in Koné take microlight flights on weekends. Book well in advance.

Places that organise guided horse treks into the foothills or to the summits of the central mountain range include:

Centre d'accueil d'Atéou (☎ 472 613; per 2/4hr 2000/3000 CFP) In *tribu* d'Atéou, 20km from Koné. It's signposted from behind the post office.

Patrick Ardimanni (☎ 422 151; Koné) Near Hôtel Koniambo, Patrick takes 7-day treks to Hienghène (23,000 CFP).

SLEEPING & EATING

It's a good idea to book your accommodation as early as possible as places are booked by people associated with the mining complex being developed in the Koniambo mountains.

Camping d'Atéou (☎ 472 613; camping/cabin 1000/1500 CFP) Visitors and trekkers can stay in a wooden cabin which has wonderful views down the mountain to the coast, or camp under shady trees. Meals cost 1500 CFP.

Hôtel Le Bougainville (☎ 472 060; www.hotel-bougainville.nc; r/bungalow d 7300/8300 CFP; ✷ ☲) In the centre of Pouembout, happily colourful bungalows are set in a quiet garden. The restaurant (meals 2000 CFP to 2600 CFP, closed Sunday dinner) is in a stunning *case* where you'll enjoy excellent meals (the beef fillet is especially good).

Hôtel Hibiscus (☎ 472 261; www.hibiscushotel.net .nc; r std/luxury 7800/8800 CFP; ☲) This modern hotel at the southern end of Koné has attractive cool rooms and a white airy restaurant (dinner menu 3900 CFP) opening onto a paved pool area.

ourpick Paddock de La Boutana (☎ 471 617; paddockboutana@mls.nc; adult/child 8000/4500 CFP) Marie-Claude is your host at this peaceful farmstay 20km inland from Pouembout. The rates include breakfast and dinner, tours of the farm and deer-spotting trips. Go hiking, swim in the rivers and creeks. It's lovely. Marie-Claude can't take children under seven.

Hôtel Koniambo (☎ 473 940; www.grands-hotels.nc; r 11,800 CFP; ☲) Named after the mountain range behind it and recently rebuilt, this makes a very comfortable base to explore the surrounding 'stockman's country'. The restaurant's buffet features regional dishes, such as venison, and international cuisine.

NEW CALEDONIA

NEW CALEDONIA

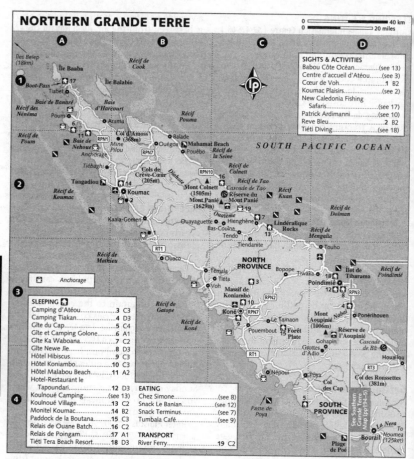

NORTHERN GRANDE TERRE

0   40 km
0   20 miles

SIGHTS & ACTIVITIES
Babou Côte Océan	(see 13)
Centre d'accueil d'Atéou	(see 3)
Cœur de Voh	1 B2
Koumac Plaisirs	(see 2)
New Caledonia Fishing Safaris	(see 17)
Patrick Ardimanni	(see 10)
Reve Bleu	2 B2
Tiéti Diving	(see 18)

Tumbala Café (☎ 424 439; snacks 450-650 CFP, mains 1500-2400 CFP; ☼ 6am-11pm Mon-Fri) The bright and popular Tumbala Café is the best place to eat in Koné. It serves light snacks, fish and meat dishes like veal escalope and chicken with caramel.

Koumac

Koumac, further north than Koné, is quite big. Like Koné, it has a post office, *gendarmerie*, clinic, pharmacy, supermarkets and banks with ATMs. **Koumac Tourisme** (☎ 427 842; www.koumac-tourisme.com; ☼ 9am-noon & 1-4pm Mon-Fri, 9am-noon Sat), the information centre, is at the northern end of town opposite the post office. Elise will give you lots of local advice.

Located near the roundabout, eye-catching **Église Ste Jeanne d'Arc** was constructed in 1950

out of a WWII aircraft hangar. Take a peek inside at its stained-glass windows and traditionally inspired wood carvings.

Head to Koumac's lovely marina, La Marina de Pandop, where the new dive club, **Reve Bleu** (☎ 424 564; www.revebleucaledonie.com), is geared up to provide a grand professional experience. It's a 15-minute boat ride to the reef with your PADI divemaster. Intro dives are 7000 CFP, double explorative dives 13,000 CFP.

Koumac Plaisirs (☎ 790 791; www.mdplaisirs.com) hires windsurfers (one hour 1000 CFP, 600 CFP with the MD Plaisirs Card). Intro lessons (one hour) cost 1500 CFP.

Monitel Koumac (☎ 476 666; monitelkoumac@lagoon .nc; bungalows s/d 8500/9500 CFP, chalets s/d 10,500/11,500 CFP; ☒) has sweet stone bungalows or Western-style units that are timber-lined and well-equipped. They look out on the pool with its inviting deck chairs. The restaurant features a central buffet (set menu from 2300 CFP).

THE FAR NORTH

The remote region north of Koumac is known as the Far North. Up here, fishermen wade around the endless white with their lines and nets, thinking they're in heaven. The area is considered one of the world's top five for fly-fishing; the world record is from here. Richard Bertin of **New Caledonia Fishing Safaris** (☎ 251 940; www.fishinpeace.com) organises sportfishing tours to Poingam. Don't worry: it's catch, tag and release. You can also go big-game fishing in Richard's Boston Whaler, deer hunting (see p198) or birdwatching. A package out of Tontouta, all-inclusive, staying in a luxurious safari tent is 50,000 CFP a day.

SLEEPING & EATING

Stock up on supplies before heading to the Far North as there's not much available in the tiny town of Poum.

ourpick **Relais de Poingam** (☎ 479 212; camping 1000 CFP, bungalows 9400 CFP, safari tent 13,500 CFP; ⚊) On a long beach at the northern tip of Grande Terre are these comfortable bungalows that everybody loves. The private bathrooms are cutely outside and the restaurant serves delectable crab, fish, wild pig or venison meals (from 2800 CFP). The shallow lagoon is not great for swimming, but the saltwater pool is. The safari tent is total luxury for those who love the creature comforts. From the turn-off south of Poum, it's 23km to Poingam. The first 6km are sealed; the rest is packed earth but quite good.

Gîte et Camping Golone (☎ 479 078, 472 000; camping 1200 CFP, bungalows 6000 CFP) A tranquil and isolated place on a small peninsula where you can hire a tent (700 CFP). Breakfast is 800 CFP, and dinner is 2200 CFP to 4600 CFP, depending on what seafood delights you request. The turn-off is about 400m north of Hôtel Malabou Beach. Take your mosquito repellent.

Hôtel Malabou Beach (☎ 476 060; www.grands -hotels.nc; d/tr bungalows 11,900/15,000 CFP, 6-person ste 22,900 CFP; ⚊ ⚊) Along a white-sand beach in Baie de Néhoué are these well-equipped bungalows with separate bedrooms and private terraces. The restaurant's grand buffet (3700 CFP) specialises in seafood straight from the lagoon. There's kayaks, treks, tennis, minigolf –

no end of activities. The hotel is signposted on the main road (transfers from Koumac airport are 5000 CFP return).

NORTHEAST COAST

The stunning coastline here is edged by foot-hills covered in lush vegetation, gentle rivers, fascinating rock formations, waterfalls and deserted beaches. Visitors can experience traditional Kanak life in a *tribu* plus there's nature trails to suit all levels of fitness, from 20-minute walks to hikes lasting several days. Keen hikers can climb Mont Panié (1629m), New Caledonia's highest peak.

Orientation

Poindimié and Hienghène are the two main towns on the northeast coast. Both have grocery stores, a post office, clinic, pharmacy, bank and ATM, and *gendarmerie*. The airfield at Touho is halfway between Poindimié and Hienghène.

Getting There & Around

Air Calédonie flies two to four times weekly to Touho (☎ agency 428 787); see p225. **ALV** (☎ /fax 425 800; Poindimié; car hire per day from 5000 CFP) can meet you at the airport with a hire car.

Buses from Noumea run daily to Poindimié and six times weekly to Hienghène; see p225. Buses run from Koumac to Pouébo four times a week.

If you're driving, it's best to come up the west coast and then cross the island at Bourail, Koné or Koumac. If you cross south of Bourail the road between Kouaoua, north of Canala, and Houaïlou winds through the mines and can seem very long.

Driving on the RT3 across from Bourail, the road veers north at the roundabout in Houaïlou, and then crosses the long Houaïlou bridge. Another 13.5km north, turn down the gravel track immediately after the bridge at *tribu* de Bâ to a lovely picnic spot at a waterfall, **Cascade de Bâ** (car/adult 100/50 CFP), beside a large pool that's perfect for a swim.

However, the drive not to be missed is from Koné via the scenic Koné–Tiwaka road (RPN2) that winds through the mountains over high river bridges and past forested slopes, to the Tiwaka river mouth, 14km north of Poindimié. Halfway through the mountains you can detour via **tribu de Bopope**, with its charming bark-and-thatch *cases* perched on the edge of steep slopes.

> **DOUBLE IDENTITY**
>
> Many *tribus* and towns on the northeast coast have more than one name or are spelt differently. Road signs show two variations.

Poindimié

The largest town on the coast, Poindimié has a picturesque coastline and, stretching inland, the peaceful valleys of Ina, Napoémien and Amoa river, where you can admire the lush vegetation and magnificent treeferns of the natural bush or pretty *tribu* gardens. These valleys are delightful places for a walk or a scenic drive. Ina valley is at the southern end of town. To get to Napoémien, turn inland at the *mairie*. In Amoa valley, turn at the bridge just before the church at Tié Mission.

Poindimié overlooks **Îlot de Tibarama**, an islet just offshore. **Tiéti Diving** (☎ 424 205; www.tieti-diving.com; 2-dive package 12,000 CFP) is run by a friendly instructor who also offers transfers to Îlot de Tibarama (per person 1500 CFP), a great spot to relax, snorkel and swim.

SLEEPING & EATING

Camping Tiakan (☎ 428 514; camping 500 CFP) A peaceful campsite, 22km south of Ponérihouen, with a little thatched shelter alongside each site and hot water. A half-day of fishing costs 2000 CFP.

Gîte Newe Jïe (☎ 427 074; bungalows 4800 CFP, case s/d 2500/5000 CFP) This gîte in Vallée d'Ina offers comfortable and impeccably clean accommodation, with a large, well-equipped kitchen and dining area. It's hard to find; take the Vallée d'Ina turning 2km south of Poindimié and follow the signposts illustrated with a hut.

Hotel-Restaurant le Tapoundari (☎ 427 111; letapoundari@hotmail.com; s/d 6800/7800 CFP) Look for the pink place behind the bridge. Its basic rooms sit along open corridors, but they're perfectly adequate and have ensuites. The restaurant, however, is fabulous and open for all meals during the week. The locals eat here, enjoying terrines, seafood and steaks (meals 1700 CFP to 2400 CFP). Take advantage of the small helping for 1100 CFP deal.

Tiéti Tera Beach Resort (☎ 426 400; www.tieti.tera.nc; r/ste 12,600/26,300 CFP; ✱ ▨) Reputed to be the best resort up north, it is indeed splendid and spacious, and features stacks of timber beams and carvings for a rich atmosphere. Plus you're an easy walk away from charming Poindimie. Breakfast is 1300 CFP and dinner dishes like red snapper with eggplant and goat cheese cannelloni, cost from 2100 CFP to 2799 CFP. Or choose a three-course menu (lunch/dinner 3200/4100 CFP).

Snack Le Banian (☎ 866 481; dishes 1100-1700 CFP; ✆ 7am-5pm Mon-Fri, 7am-3pm Sat) Two large banyan trees watch over this friendly place where an excellent chef oversees the paninis and toasted sandwiches, then cooks tasty veal, fish or chicken dishes. Or enjoy his salads, and the fun range of coffees.

Chez Simone (☎ 427 484; ppswc@lagoon.nc; dishes from 1900 CFP) You may like to book in for the night (single/double 3500/6500 CFP) after your feast of home-cooked Kanak cuisine. Dishes are based around wild deer, pig or fish. The turn-off is 4km south of Poindimié and it's another 3.5km to Simone's in *tribu* de Nessapoé.

Hienghène

This serene village with its fairy-tale buildings is tucked into the foothills on the shores of Baie de Hienghène, at the mouth of the Hienghène River. The area has fascinating rock formations, and it is also important historically as it was the home of Jean-Marie Tjibaou, New Caledonia's pro-independence leader. People speak of Tjibaou with great respect, and he is buried in Tiendanite, a *tribu* 20km up the Hienghène valley.

Hienghène's renowned **Poule Couveuse** (Brooding Hen) rock formation sits on one side of the entrance to Baie de Hienghène, facing the sphinx on the other. You can view these two rock formations from the signposted lookout, 2km south of the village. There's a better profile of the sphinx about 1.5km north of the village.

The **Lindéralique rocks** are towering black limestone rocks with jagged edges, which begin about 10km south of Hienghène.

The **visitor information centre** (☎ 424 357; hienghen-tourism@mls.nc; Hienghène; ✆ 8am-noon & 1-5pm Mon-Fri, 8am-3pm Sat) looks over the Hienghène marina (which is also the bus terminal (see p226). Sylvana and her colleague in the centre can book accommodation in *tribus*, help you contact **Association Dayu Biik** (☎ 428 777; dayubiik@lagoon.nc; ✆ 8.30am-5.30pm Mon-Fri) for trekking in the area (see opposite), and arrange traditional meals and dances in local table d'hôtes.

ACTIVITIES

There are dozens of excellent local guides in Hienghène, waiting to take you on the hike of your life, through and over this stunning region of mountain, forest, river, waterfall, beach, lagoon and extraordinary rock formation. Email hienghen-tourism@mls.nc and choose your adventure.

At Lindéralique village, about 4km south of Hienghène, you can kayak beneath the overhanging rocks. There is also a large cave, **Grotte de Lindéralique** (adult/child 200/100 CFP), which you can visit. To get there follow the signposted turn-off 2.5km south of Hienghène.

Hienghène's small **Centre Culturel Goa Ma Bwarhat** (☎ /fax 428 074; culturehienghene@mls.nc; museum adult/child 150 CFP/free; ☒ 8am-5pm Mon-Thu, to 4pm Fri & Sat, 9am-noon Sun) has exhibitions, a museum and a sculptor's workshop. It organises jazz, choral and classical concerts at Grotte de Lindéralique once a month.

Go diving with **Babou Côté Océan** (☎ 428 359; www.babou-plongee.com) around unique cliff faces of gorgonia and sheltered coral massifs (intro/double dives cost 8000/10,600 CFP), on island trips which include snorkelling (2500 CFP), or on a river walk (3500 CFP). It's based at Koulnoué Camping.

SLEEPING & EATING

In the Hienghène valley there are many *accueil en tribu* (per person around 1000 CFP), traditional homestays with Kanak families. Visitors usually take part in everyday activities and meals (breakfast 400 CFP, dinner 1200 CFP, *bougna* 1500 CFP). Book through Hienghène's visitor information centre at least three days in advance.

our pick Koulnoué Camping (☎ 428 359; camping per person 400 CFP, tent hire 1000 CFP) Just past Koulnoué Village is this pretty campsite on its own tiny bay where you can swim and picnic for 100 CFP. Sleep beneath the towering rock formations. The Babou Côté Océan dive club (above) is based here.

Gîte Ka Waboana (☎ 424 703; r/bungalow 4500/8400 CFP) These colourful bungalows with kitchenettes perch on a hill opposite the marina, with views of the bay. Breakfast (1050 CFP) and the daily menu (2420 CFP) are served in a rustic little eating area which is often booked out.

Koulnoué Village (☎ 428 166; bungalow 12,500 CFP, 4-person case 12,500 CFP; ☒ ☒) Feel young again at this ex–Club Med establishment that still has plenty of good vibes. The bungalows are spacious, well-equipped and have private porches out to the beach. The traditional *case* is along the beach. Play tennis, canoe, go horse riding. There's a tiny supermarket 8km down the road if you find the buffet thing impossible (breakfast 1800 CFP, dinner 3500 CFP). The turn-off is 8.5km south of Hienghène; transfers from Touho are 5000 CFP return.

Snack Terminus (☎ 957 001; meals 1200-1500 CFP; ☒ 6am-5pm) Overlooking the marina is this bright and shiny little place, selling snacks and drinks and home-cooked lunches.

North of Hienghène

This is the wildest and most stunning stretch of the northeast coast. It's covered in tropical vegetation, and waterfalls and streams rush down the mountains to join the sea.

New Caledonia's last surviving **river ferry**, a quaint old timber pontoon, carries vehicles across the wide Ouaïème River, 17km northwest of Hienghène. It's free and runs 24 hours a day. The ferry's uniqueness makes the crossing one of the highlights of the journey.

The rugged coastal scenery changes to rolling hills, plains and mangrove swamps at **Pouébo**. Inside Pouébo's large Catholic church there's a marble **mausoleum** where the remains of Bishop Douarre, who set up New Caledonia's first Catholic mission, are interred. The first Europeans arrived in New Caledonia at Balade and Bishop Douarre arrived in 1843. The stained-glass windows in the small church here tell the story from the first Catholic mass. In 1853 France officially laid claim to New Caledonia at Balade, the same year in which Douarre died.

An altar beneath an enormous banyan at **Mahamat beach** commemorates that first Catholic mass on Christmas Day 1843. The turn-off to the altar is 1.5km north of the church.

ACTIVITIES

The area north of Hienghène is an amazing drawcard for trekking enthusiasts and nature lovers. However, all activities require a guide and authorisation for you to enter tribal territories. Guides and permissions are arranged by **Association Dayu Biik** (☎ 428 777; dayubiik@lagoon .nc; ☒ 8.30am-5.30pm Mon-Fri), including authorisation from the **Direction du Développement Economique et de L'Environnement** (DDEE; ☎ 427 252; Poindimié). It takes one to two weeks for arrangements to be finalised, so get your requests in as early as possible.

Mont Panié includes about 5000 hectares of botanical reserve. Its peak is New Caledonia's highest and the climb to the top is a magical two-day hike (19,000 CFP, maximum four people) out of Tao, passing giant kaoris, mountain araucarias, magnificent coloured rocks, waterfalls and creeks. Other guided walks cost around 12,900 CFP for one day.

You can also go on a half-day adventure around the **Cascade de Tao** (3/12 people 4200/7350 CFP), which plummets down a mountainside 7km north of the Ouaïème River ferry. A path leads to the bottom of the falls starting at the cottage just after Tao bridge (200 CFP). If you're a thrill seeker, you can **abseil** (per person 10,000 CFP) down the waterfall; check with Association Dayu Biik.

SLEEPING & EATING

There are a couple of **campsites** (camping 1000 CFP) north of the Tao river ferry where you can simply turn up. Stock up on groceries before you go.

Run by a friendly family, **Relais de Ouane Batch** (☎ 424 792; ouanebatch@lagoon.nc; camping 800 CFP, bungalows without bathroom 4700 CFP) is located 16km north of the river ferry. The bungalows have communal bathrooms with hot showers. There's also a table d'hôte that serves very good meals (2700 CFP); book 24 hours in advance. Activities include canoe hire (half-/full-day 600/1000 CFP) and fishing trips (10,000 CFP).

LOYALTY ISLANDS

pop 22060 / area 1980 sq km

Maré, Lifou and Ouvéa. Such fairy-tale names for fairy-tale islands, each with their own characteristics: Maré is known for its deep rock holes, rugged coastal scenery and serene beaches; Lifou for its breathtaking cliff-top views and small secret beaches; Ouvéa for its unending beach and tranquil lagoon stretching endlessly to the horizon. They're all sparsely populated with secluded beaches, hidden caves and deep holes. They all have large tracts of impenetrable bush, but their roads are so good that driving around is a dream. Loyalty Islands? Captain Cook named them that, perhaps because the people are so friendly.

The locals blend traditional and modern lifestyles with ease, offering tourists a charming experience. You'll need to take cash (although each island has a bank with an ATM). You must book meals 24 hours in advance; seafood is a speciality and most places offer lobster or crab platters.

You'll find a shop with limited groceries in each village. Most places offer camping but only a couple have tents for hire.

Getting There & Away

Air Calédonie flies at least twice a day between Noumea and each island (p225). There are fabulous flight-and-hotel packages (from 24,000 CFP); or visit all three for 32,300 CFP with the air pass (p225).

The *Betico* and *Havannah* sail from Noumea to the islands, and between the islands, once or twice a week; see p225.

Getting Around

The islands don't have public transport and only Lifou has a taxi (two actually). Your accommodation can arrange transfers, but it's best to hire a car and have it waiting for you, especially if you're on a day trip. Car-rental companies drop off vehicles at the airport, wharf or accommodation places for free.

Hitchhiking is common everywhere but it can take a while for a car to come along.

MARÉ

pop 7400 / area 641 sq km

With its scenic coastline of stunning beaches and rugged coral cliffs and an interior that hides impressive sunken pools and a mysterious ancient rock edifice, it is small wonder that Maré's geographical features have inspired legends.

Orientation & Information

The small coastal town of Tadine is Maré's main centre; if you're travelling by ferry you'll arrive or leave from the wharf there. Tadine has shops, a petrol station, a pharmacy and a market on Tuesday and Friday.
Air Calédonie (☼ 8-11am & 2-5pm Mon-Fri) airport (☎ 455 510) Tuo (☎ 454 277) Has an office in Tuo on the main road between La Roche and Tadine.
BCI bank (☎ 454 062; ☼ 7.15am-noon & 1.15-4pm Mon-Fri)
post office (☎ 454 105; ☼ 7.45-11.15am & 12.15-3pm Mon-Fri)

KANAK GRANDE CASE

The *grande case* (big hut) is one of the strongest symbols of the Kanak community. It was traditionally home to the chief. Nowadays the *grande case* is the political centre of the district where the chief, who inherits his position, gathers with the village representatives to discuss the running of the community and affairs they want discussed in parliament.

Where possible, the *grande case* is built on a knoll above the rest of the village. The central pillar, an immense tree trunk, is erected first. It will support the entire *case* and symbolises the chief. A stone hearth is laid between the central pillar and the entrance which is via a low doorway flanked by carved posts.

Inside, the walls and ceiling are lined with wooden posts or beams, lashed to the frame with strong vines, all of which lean against the central pillar to symbolise the clan's close link to the chief. Finally, the roof is topped with a *flèche faîtière,* a carved wooden spear that becomes home to ancestral spirits.

A *grande case* is always surrounded by large spiked tree-trunk fences. Only enter these areas with a guide and ask permission before taking photos.

Sights

TADINE & WESTERN MARÉ

The main road runs beside the coast for almost the entire length of western Maré. It's a picturesque drive, taking you past beaches, cliffs, *tribus* and forests.

The southwest coast has several gorgeous **beaches** where you can swim or snorkel during the day and watch the glorious sunsets in the evening. The small beach at Eni is the southernmost beach where you might spot **humpbacked whales** between July and September. Further north between Cengéité and Wabao, there's a fabulous beach beside a small enclosed lagoon whose water is an exquisite turquoise.

Keep going to the long white beach at Hôtel Nengone Village (p209) or continue to la plage de Pede, a sheltered beach protected by the headland at Cap Wabao. A path to the beach leads through a gate from the main road at the sharp bend where it joins the coast.

Between these two beaches is the village of Medu. Just north of Medu there is a *trou bleu* (deep rock pool) near the road known as **La Grotte de Pethoen**, where you can see the dark shapes of eels swimming beneath an overhanging rock wall. Ask permission from anyone in Medu to go there.

Inland from Medu there is another *trou bleu* known as **Le Bone de la Léproserie**; there was once a leper hospital nearby which explains the name. This enormous hole in the limestone rock, hidden by thick vegetation, drops vertically to a pool of still water. It's one of the largest drowned cavities in the world. Ask if you need permission to visit, and what

condition the track is in after you turn at the signposted turn-off. The *trou bleu* is 1.5km down the track beside some solar panels.

About 3km south of Tadine is a large **Aquarium Naturelle**, a rock pool sunk in the cliffs and linked to the sea by an underground channel. Watch for Napoleon fish, perroquettes, picods and sometimes turtles swimming in the translucent water (take bread so that they come quickly). It is signposted by a parking area beside the main road.

Yeiwene Yeiwene's grave sits facing the sea beside the road about 2km south of Tadine. Yeiwene Yeiwene is the FLNKS leader, who was assassinated with Jean-Marie Tjibaou in 1989. Ask permission before approaching the grave.

About 3km off the La Roche–Tadine Road, on the road to Thogone, is **Trou de Bone**, a deep rock cavity which drops to a lush tropical garden and a pool. It's on the right-hand side of the road as you're heading to Thogone, about 1.5km from the turn-off. It isn't signposted, so look out for a metal guardrail beside the road. Yell out to let off some steam and hear your echo.

LA ROCHE & EASTERN MARÉ

Paths lead through the forest to the coast in the northeast of Maré; you can inquire about them at the various *tribus*. Maré's southeastern coastline is rugged and windswept.

There is a small exhibition of Kanak artefacts at **Centre Culturel Yeiwene Yeiwene** (☎ 454 479; ⊙ 7.30-11.30am & 1-4pm Mon-Fri), about 2km out of La Roche. Behind it, and more interesting because of their mysterious nature, are the stone ruins known as the **Hnaenedr wall**. This

NEW CALEDONIA

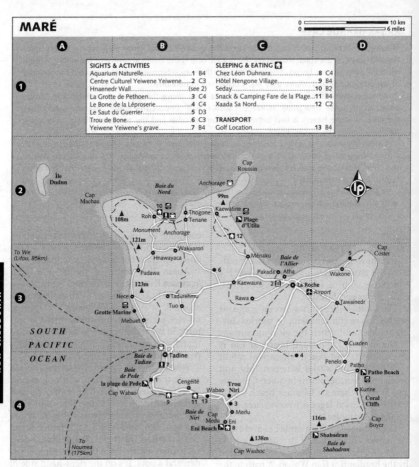

MARÉ

SIGHTS & ACTIVITIES	
Aquarium Naturelle	1 B4
Centre Culturel Yeiwene Yeiwene	2 C3
Hnaenedr Wall	(see 2)
La Grotte de Pethoen	3 C4
Le Bone de la Léproserie	4 C4
Le Saut du Guerrier	5 D3
Trou de Bone	6 C3
Yeiwene Yeiwene's grave	7 B4

SLEEPING & EATING	
Chez Léon Duhnara	8 C4
Hôtel Nengone Village	9 B4
Seday	10 B2
Snack & Camping Fare de la Plage	11 B4
Xaada Sa Nord	12 C2

TRANSPORT	
Golf Location	13 B4

ancient rock fortification dates back to AD 250. The origins of the people who built the wall and its purpose are not entirely clear but legend tells of two warring tribes who agreed to construct walls for protection.

A huge limestone rock covered in vegetation near the coast gives the surrounding area of **La Roche** (the Rock) its name. The rock, known locally as Titi, rises above an attractive Catholic church with a red steeple. You can climb to the top of the rock with a local guide. Make inquiries in the *tribu*.

East of La Roche is **Le Saut du Guerrier** (Warrior's Leap). It is a gap in the cliffs, 5m wide and 30m above the pounding surf. Legend tells of a warrior who escaped his enemies by leaping across the abyss. Try to

imagine the jump as you look down at the rocks and waves below.

Shabadran is an isolated, sheltered spot at the very south of Maré surrounded by cliffs and forest. The curved sandy beach is cut off from the sea by a reef, where waves crash and send foaming water cascading over coral terraces into a small sparkling lagoon.

Activities

Follow the pleasant 6km **coastal walk** that links the beach at the northern end of Hôtel Nengone Village with that at Pede. It is mostly flat and shady as the path follows the shoreline through the trees. Near Cap Wabao, it veers inland and meanders through a forest beneath a small cliff. Turn

---

BONIFACE WAHAGA

Boniface Wahaga works in maintenance for Hôtel Nengone Village

You're a Maré local?

Yes. All the family has stayed here, father, grandfather. Great grandfather lived on the other side of the island. People here and there, hence family everywhere from marrying. Used to be, when they get married they have to marry from Tadine. Now it's different. I have married to a lady from Lifou. My adopted mother is from Ouvéa. One man here married to white people from Fiji. Other man to Wallis islander. Used to be, only marry Melanesian. Now it's different.

Do you mind having tourists on your island?

No, no. Before, no hotel. Just work in garden. Now there's a choice. I have family in *tribu* Singate. Mostly people from *tribus* around hotel work there, because the chief is chief of the land of the hotel. I never went outside this area to find a job.

The government offers scholarships to 400 Kanak people each year. Do you know people that this has helped.

It helps everyone. Local people push their kids now, must go to class, must study. No money but get a scholarship. There's training by hotel and government. People go to Canada, New Zealand, then get jobs in reception, kitchen. It's good for young generation.

---

left at the end of the cliff and follow the wide path straight ahead through a wooded paddock to Baie de Pede.

Possibly the best walk on the islands is the coastal walk to Shabadran. Of course, Shabadran's beauty is enhanced by the effort of clambering along steep cliffs. But the views are amazing, and after a two-hour walk you descend to the exquisite beach: take plenty of water, a picnic lunch and wear sturdy footwear. You must have a **guide** (☎ 450 596; 1/2 days 3700/12,600 CFP), so contact Damas in Kurine, the last *tribu* before the end of the road. Book in advance; you need to be relatively fit.

Tours

The hotels and gîtes organise tours of the island for around 3000 CFP per person. Local entrepreneurs include the following:

Boniface Wahaga (☎ 454 500) Runs guided snorkelling excursions to the coral beds up north.

Emile Lakoredine (☎ 454 244, 454 500) Offers glass-bottom boat tours (three hours for 2100 CFP).

Kaloï Cawidrone (☎ 454 501) Leads tours of his vanilla plantation for 500 CFP.

Lakoredine Transport (☎ 454 244, 454 500) Ernest Lakoredine takes round-island tours (2800 CFP) and rents scooters (4200 CFP a day).

Sleeping & Eating

Seday (☎ 450 225; camping 1100 CFP, case per person 2000 CFP) Up north, in the quiet *tribu* of Roh, is a little honeymoon bungalow (3700 CFP) set on a rock in the water, plus three bungalows along the rocky coast. Sit on the wooden platform

over the water, or slither between the rocks where it's great to snorkel. The restaurant serves excellent meals (1600 CFP to 1900 CFP) based on fish and home-grown vegetables. Jacques, the owner, is a sculptor and runs workshops; other activities include fishing and walks. Transfers are 2900 CFP.

Xaada Sa Nord (☎ 454 385; http://wiako.ifrance.com; camping 1100 CFP, r 6900 CFP) Spacious motel-style rooms by the main road are painted cheery colours. Jacques will arrange boat or beach trips, but it's a 45-minute walk if you just want a swim. He has cars for hire from 6300 CFP, airport/wharf transfers are 2900/4200 CFP, meals are 1800 CFP, breakfast 600 CFP.

Chez Léon Duhnara (☎ 454 370; camping 1100 CFP, case 2100 CFP) This homestay in a coconut grove has two *cases*, two toilet blocks and camping across from the rocky shoreline of Baie de Niri, a short stroll from white-sand Eni beach. Dinner mains are 1900 CFP, airport and wharf transfers 3800 CFP and island tours are 3300 CFP.

our pick **Snack & Camping Fare de la Plage** (☎ 454 224; camping 1200 CFP, case per person 1600 CFP) Down south, on idyllic Wabao beach, there is a *case* with beds for eight, and grassy spots for campers. Delicious meals (from 1200 CFP to 3000 CFP) are served at covered tables on the beach, every lunch and dinner (except Sunday lunch). So romantic and there's no need to book. Airport/wharf transfers cost 2800/1700 CFP, there's kayaks for hire (per hour 380 CFP) and island tours are 2900 CFP.

Hôtel Nengone Village (☎ 454 500; nengone@ canl.nc; bungalow/ste 13,000/23,000 CFP; 🔅 🖭) All

NEW CALEDONIA

brand-new redesigned bungalows sit along a boardwalk looking quaint and tropical, yet modern, featuring local timbers. An infinity pool flows below the restaurant, there's some coral a few steps out from the shore and kayaks are available. This is Maré's top accommodation option. Meals (breakfast 1700 CFP, dinner mains 1200 CFP to 2600 CFP) are served in a pleasant room overlooking the ocean; airport/wharf transfers cost 2600/1400 CFP.

Getting Around

You can try cycling around the island if you are fit but roads are long, straight and monotonous. Nengone Village hires bicycles (half-/full-day 650/1100 CFP).

The best way to get around Maré is by car. Car hire companies include the following:

Golf Location (☎ 450 942; Wabao; per day from 5300 CFP)
K3000 (☎ 450 044, 950 220; s.boulange@lagoon.nc; per day from 6300 CFP)

LIFOU

pop 10,320 / area 1207 sq km

Lifou is home to magnificent cliff-top views, sheltered bays with coral shelfs teeming with colourful tropical fish, secluded beaches, fascinating caves and a rich traditional culture. Water is pumped from underground, electricity is mainly wind-generated; in fact, the island is unpolluted except for household rubbish, which is collected twice-weekly.

Orientation & Information

The main centre in Lifou is Wé, where the Loyalty Island's provincial offices are based. Wé stretches for about 2km along the main road beside Baie de Châteaubriand. You can people-watch or relax on the white and aqua beach, there's a market Wednesdays and Fridays, a good supermarket, little gift shops, a beauty salon and an interesting marina.

Air Calédonie (🕒 7.30-11.30am & 12.30-5.15pm Mon-Fri, 8-11.30am Sat) airport (☎ 455 520) Wé (☎ 455 550) An office in Wé and a desk at the airport.
BCI bank (☎ 451 332; 🕒 7.20am-noon & 1-3.45pm Mon-Fri) On the main road opposite Air Calédonie. It has an ATM (DAB).
Cyber@ (☎ 450 904; internet per 30min 400 CFP; 🕒 8.30am-noon & 1-7pm Mon-Fri, 8.30am-noon & 2.30-5.30pm Sat, 8.30am-noon Sun) Opposite the provincial offices.
Laverie (per bag-full 1500 CFP) There are two laundries in Wé.

Marina (☎ 451 062; dae@loyalty.nc; 🕒 6am-6pm Mon-Fri) Customs and immigration clearance.
Post office (☎ 451 100; 🕒 7.45am-3pm Mon-Fri) Behind the provincial offices.
Visitor information centre (CEMAID; ☎ 450 032; cemaid@lagoon.nc; 🕒 7.30-11.30am & 12.30-4.30pm Mon-Fri) Next to the *mairie*. There's also a CEMAID booth at the airport with maps and stacks of info.

Sights

Jokin, Lifou's northernmost *tribu*, sits on the cliff tops overlooking a vast bay with brilliant sunset views; the footpath to the left of the church here leads to a cove where you can snorkel among the coral formations. Between the church and the cliffs is a large attractive *case*. Ask permission before taking photos.

The road from Jokin to Easo winds through a cool green forest past Mucaweng, a *tribu* known for its **vanilla plantations**. Félix Bolé shows visitors around his plantation for a small fee; sample vanilla tea or coffee and buy beans (200 CFP each). The farm is down the track next to the white water tower in Mucaweng.

At the large white cross at Easo, a sealed road turns off to a parking area on the Easo peninsula beneath the small **Chapelle Notre Dame de Lourdes** that's topped by a statue of the Virgin Mary. Steps lead up the hill to the chapel from where there are fantastic views of Baie de Jinek to the west and Baie du Santal to the east and south. The chapel was built in 1898 to commemorate the arrival of the first Catholic missionaries in 1858.

About 200m before the chapel a road heads off to **Baie de Jinek**, where steps from a wooden platform built above sharp coral rocks lead down to the water. It's a great place for snorkelling as the bay's clear and the water teems with small tropical fish.

Northeast of the airport, near *tribu* de Tingeting, you can visit **Grotte du Diable** (Devil's Cave); turn right after the church in Tingeting and follow the signposts to the house of **Adrien Trohmae** (☎ 451793; tour per adult/child 800/400 CFP, filming 500 CFP), who runs guided tours of the cave.

Stop off at the little *tribu* of **Hnathalo**, about 3km southeast of the airport. It's home of the chief of Wetr, one of Lifou's three districts. There's a splendid *grande case* behind the chief's house that you're welcome to visit with a guide. Just ask in the *tribu*.

Don't miss the blissful and secluded beach at **Peng** on Baie du Santal, 3.5km off the Wé–Drueulu Road; turn off at the *tribu*

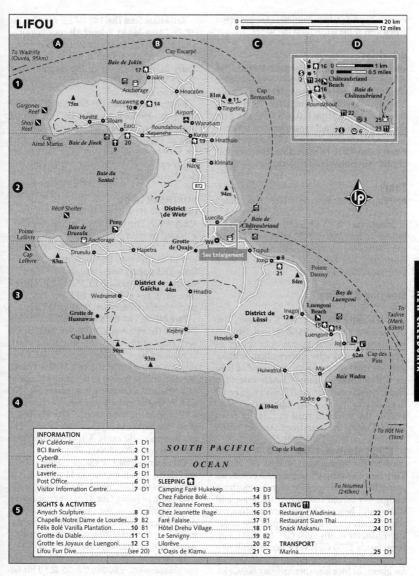

LIFOU

NEW CALEDONIA

SOUTH PACIFIC OCEAN

INFORMATION	
Air Calédonie	1 D1
BCI Bank	2 C1
Cyber@	3 D1
Laverie	4 D1
Laverie	5 D1
Post Office	6 D1
Visitor Information Centre	7 D1

SIGHTS & ACTIVITIES	
Anyach Sculpture	8 C3
Chapelle Notre Dame de Lourdes	9 B2
Félix Bolé Vanilla Plantation	10 B1
Grotte du Diable	11 C1
Grotte les Joyaux de Luengoni	12 C3
Lifou Fun Dive	(see 20)

SLEEPING	
Camping Faré Hukekep	13 D3
Chez Fabrice Bolé	14 B1
Chez Jeanne Forrest	15 D3
Chez Jeannette Ihage	16 D1
Chez Jeannette Ihage	17 B1
Faré Falaise	17 B1
Hôtel Drehu Village	18 D1
Le Servigny	19 B2
Lilorève	20 B2
L'Oasis de Kiamu	21 C3

EATING	
Restaurant Madinina	22 D1
Restaurant Siam Thai	23 D1
Snack Makanu	24 D1

TRANSPORT	
Marina	25 D1

Hapetra. Further down, **Drueulu** is the home of the chief of Gaïcha district. The *grande case* sits by the beach.

On the east coast, at Jozip, you can visit a sculptor's workshop, where Dick Ukewed and his wife Jacqueline, Lifou's first woman sculptor, run **Anyach Sculpture** (☎ 451 479; 7-11am & 1-4pm Mon-Fri, 7-11am Sat & Sun).

Luengoni beach is a stretch of fine white sand bordering a stunning lagoon. Locals boast that it is New Caledonia's most beautiful beach. The sheltered bay is a renowned turtle haunt. Just before Luengoni beach is **Grotte les Joyaux de Luengoni** (the Jewels of Luengoni). These limestone caves are both above and below ground; the underground caves have beautiful deep rock pools which shimmer emerald green when you shine a torch on the water.

Activities

Lifou Fun Dive (☎ 450 275; www.lifoufundive.com; 2-dive package 12,900 CFP), based at Easo, organises dive trips to the sheltered Shoji and Gorgones reefs. The club also offers night dives (7500 CFP), full-day sailing trips (10,000 CFP per person) and whale-watching excursions between July and September (10,000 CFP per person). Lifou's dive sites have an abundance of soft corals, gorgonians and tropical fish.

Tours

Noël Pia (☎ 932 649; per person 1600 CFP) takes guided treks to the Grotte les Joyaux de Luengoni.

Someltrans (☎ 451 478; someltrans@cyberdidact.net; half-/full-day tours 2700/4800 CFP) takes you around the island; the company also runs transfers from gîtes and hotels, to Luengoni or Peng beaches (2000 CFP).

Sleeping & Eating

WÉ

Chez Jeannette Ihage (☎ 838 154; camping 1100 CFP, bungalow d/family 4600/5300 CFP, case 1900 CFP) Jeannette's homestay buzzes with energy as backpackers and adventurers organise their day. It's right on the beach at the end of Baie de Châteaubriand. Jeannette only caters for house guests (meals from 2100 CFP), so you'll need to stay to enjoy her famous crab dish. Follow the unsealed road in front of *tribu* Luecilla along the waterfront. Airport/wharf transfers are 2600/1300 CFP.

Hôtel Drehu Village (☎ 450 270; www.drehu .grands-hotels.cc; bungalow/ste 13,200/21,000 CFP; 🖳 🛋) Turn down towards Châteaubriand beach and you're in this lovely garden where comfortable bungalows spread through to the grass and white-sand beach. The restaurant tables are romantically situated around a pool and under a *faré* (dinner mains 1900 CFP to 3400 CFP). Breakfast is 1700 CFP. It's a gentle stroll to a group of shops; there's canoeing and kayaking for guests, or bike hire (per half-day 600 CFP). Airport/wharf transfers are 2200/800 CFP.

Snack Makanu (☎ 833 532; dishes 600-1000 CFP; 🕑 7.30am-7pm Mon-Fri, 8am-2pm Sat) You know the food's good when everyone wants to eat there. It's outside Korail Alimentation and offers a choice of meals with rice, slices of quiche and light snacks, served at tables on its small veranda.

Restaurant Siam Thai (☎ 457 266; mains 850-1100 CFP; 🕑 7.30am-2pm & 5.30-10pm) All your favourite Thai dishes, like fried rice and chicken in coconut curry, are served at this low-key spot. Sadly there's no view of the marina; Siam Thai's veranda faces a quarry. Still, the food makes up for it.

Restaurant Madinina (☎ 450 188; mains 1100-1800 CFP; 🕑 9am-3pm & 6.30-11pm Mon-Sat) This relaxed waterfront restaurant serves generous helpings of West Indian food and you must try the French–Caribbean very spicy chicken. It's lovely eating on the veranda overlooking Baie de Châteaubriand.

NORTHERN LIFOU

Lilorève (☎ 451 423; camping 1000 CFP, bungalows s/d 4700/5400 CFP) Three thatched bungalows sit on a grassy property sloping down to Baie du Santal, with a wide view over the bay and a private sandy cove. There's mattresses on the floor and a sparkling-clean shower block. A set menu is 2000 CFP to 3500 CFP. There's bike/car hire (1700/6600 CFP per day); airport/wharf transfers are 2400/3400 CFP.

Faré Falaise (☎ 450 201; camping 1100 CFP, r/case 2100/2100 CFP, bungalows 5000 CFP) Perched on the very edge of the cliffs at Jokin, these rustic bungalows have wooden decks to see magnificent sunsets and the best views. Guests can also stay in rooms in the family house or in a *case*, and a set menu is available for 1800 CFP. Activities include bike hire (per day 1500 CFP) and island tours (3900 CFP). The beach is via 200 steps, but it's great snorkelling. The gîte accepts credit cards. Airport/wharf return transfers cost 1700/2000 CFP.

Chez Fabrice Bolé (☎ 450 769; camping 1100 CFP, case 2100 CFP) This homestay in Mucaweng is in a vanilla plantation, beside the winding forest road south of Jokin. Guests can sample homemade vanilla jams for breakfast (650 CFP; dinner menu 1900 CFP) and tour the plantation to see the interesting pollination process. Airport/wharf transfers are 1500/3200 CFP.

Le Servigny (☎ 451 244; www.hotel-servigny.nc; case/r/bungalow 4200/6900/8900 CFP; 🖳 🛋) This fab place is actually only five minutes from the beach at Easo. It has a large swimming pool in a pleasant garden, so don't be put off by its position. The two-bedroom bungalows are spacious, with plenty of mod cons. M Albert cooks French cuisine to die for (breakfast 1200 CFP, dinner mains from 750 CFP, set menu 2700 CFP). An island tour with picnic (6000

CFP) includes the mysterious west coast. Cars/
bikes can be hired for 5000/1700 CFP a day.
Airport/harbour transfers are 320/2100 CFP.

SOUTHERN LIFOU

Chez Jeanne Forrest (☎ 451 656; camping 1100 CFP,
case/bungalow 2100/4200) Bungalows squat around
the spacious lawns that run down to magnificent Luengoni beach. Jeanne is charming
and cooks tasty local dishes (from 2500 CFP),
but don't forget to book. Jeanne also arranges
hikes to cliffs and caves.

Camping Faré Hukekep (☎ 451 434; camping 1100
CFP, paillote without bathroom 4700 CFP) At the end
of Luengoni beach, away from the main
road, this gorgeous place is oh so peaceful, the breeze whispering between the
coconut palms. The *paillotes* (huts) have
both beds and mattresses; bathrooms are
shared. There's a kitchen, or meals cost
1200 CFP (breakfast 600 CFP). Turn left
down the sealed road opposite the monument with a cross. Airport/wharf transfers
are 3200/2100 CFP (shared).

L'Oasis de Kiamu (☎ 451 500; www.oasis-de-kiamu
.com; d/tr/family 9700/11,800/15,800 CFP; 🏊 🖺) New
owner Dicher Grava has big plans for this
charming spot in a large garden beneath a cliff.
The pool is going to be bigger and the restaurant will be grand indeed. In the meantime, it's
lovely as it is: there's tennis and table tennis,
dinner mains are 1800 CFP, or 4000 CFP for
lobster, and the family room has a kitchenette.
Airport/wharf transfers are 2600/1400 CFP.

Getting Around

The best way to get around is by car. Short
bike excursions can be enjoyable but the island is too big to tour entirely by bike. Car
rental companies include the following:

Aéro Location (☎ 450 494; contact@aeroloc.nc; per day
from 7400 CFP)

Loca V (☎ 450 777; locav@lagoon.nc; per day from 4700 CFP)

OUVÉA

pop 4360 / area 132 sq km

Think 25km of long perfect white beach backed
with grass and wild tropical flowers. Look further out, over an exquisite lagoon stretching as
far as you can see. Add a chain of tiny islets, the
Pléiades. Sound unreal? Nope. It's just Ouvéa.

Orientation & Information

Ouvéa is a thin sliver of land with administrative centres at Wadrilla and Fayaoué.

However, the facilities in these villages are
so spread out that nowhere can really be
described as a centre. There's a clinic near
the airport.

Air Calédonie (🕑 7.30-11am & 1.30-4pm Mon-Fri)
Airport (☎ 455 530) Office (☎ 457 022) Has an office in
Wadrilla and a desk at the airport in Houloup.

BCI bank (☎ 457 131; Wadrilla; 🕑 7.20am-noon Mon-
Fri, plus 1-3pm Wed)

Post office (☎ 457 100; Fayaoué; 🕑 7.45-11.15am &
12.15-3pm Mon-Fri)

Sights

The **Grotte de Kong Houloup** cave is in the bush
behind the airport at Houloup. Drive or walk
to the bottom of the cliff where the cave is set
in the cliff wall. Chez Jedyjah (☎ 459 095; 865 936;
per person 1100 CFP) takes guided tours to the cave
and provides interesting commentary on local
legends, history and flora.

The large white **memorial** in Wadrilla is a
tribute to 19 Kanaks who died in 1988, when
French military personnel stormed a cave to
free French *gendarmes* being held hostage by
the pro-independence movement. Tragically,
pro-independence leaders Jean-Marie Tjibaou
and Yeiwene Yeiwene were assassinated opposite the memorial at the first-year memorial
ceremony. Their perpetrator believed they had
ceded too much to France.

A bit further north you can see the **desalination plant** that produces 400,000L of water a
day to be trucked all over the island. Past that
is the **Coconut Oil Distillery & Soap Factory** (admission
free; 🕑 7.30-11am Mon-Fri), a fascinating mix of
vats and distillery apparatus. Local leaves are
used to perfume the soap.

The deep, scary **Trou Bleu d'Anawa** is sunk
in the coral rock and connected to the sea
underground. You can see fish and turtles
in the blue water. Turn left along a track just
past the Anawa shop, where the road curves
sharply away from the coast. The pool is behind the house, where you can ask permission.
If you fall in, they say there's a rope down
there (yeah, sure).

Heading south from the airport, you reach
a long, narrow bay that stretches from **Humen**
to **Lékiny**. Two small channels at the Lékiny
end let in water from the open sea and cliffs
rise above the bay to the east. There's a cave
around from the edge of the cliff where locals
go for church services, especially at Christmas.
See the cliffs from a beautiful spot, reached via
the Humen turn-off.

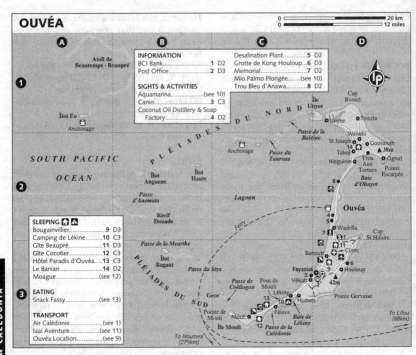

OUVÉA

The island's only bridge is **Pont de Mouli** at Lékiny, where Ouvéa's southern tip is cut off by a wide channel that flows out of Baie de Lékiny into the lagoon. From the bridge, the display of dazzling white sand and different shades of blue is broken by outlines of sharks, rays, turtles and fish swimming beneath you.

At the very south of Ouvéa is **tribu de Mouli**, a peaceful settlement spread along the waterfront. An avenue of araucaria pines leads up from the beach to the Catholic church, and the road continues past the *tribu* to the tip of the island. When the weather is calm, it is a good place to snorkel, over a coral plateau, but be careful of the strong currents.

Activities

The interesting new building on the beach in Fayaoué is the sailing club **Canio** (☎ 457 101; 8-11.30am & 1-4.30pm Mon-Sat). Canio rents per one/two hours windsurfers (1500/2500 CFP), hobby cats (from 2000/2500 CFP) and kayaks (1000/1700 CFP).

It is prohibited to swim in Lékiny Bay so you must go with a guide if you wish to wade

across to visit the cave in the cliffs or snorkel over the abundant coral; contact Félix at **Camping de Lékine** (☎ 925 512; guide per 2hr 800 CFP; Mon, Tue, Fri & Sat).

Aquamarina (☎ 450 067; aquamarina-ouvea@yahoo.fr) organises glass-bottom boat trips around Baie de Lékiny (adult/child 1750/1000 CFP). If you cannot go snorkelling, this is your chance to see the wonderful marine life of the bay up close.

Shark-watching is possible near Unyee in the north and Lékiny Bay in the south late each year, when large sharks give birth in the warm shallow waters. Their hormones kick in, making them quiet (so they don't eat their offspring), and not dangerous to tourists. Ask for a guide at Weneki or Lékiny, or go with **Randonée Pedestre** (☎ 987 205; St Joseph; 2000 CFP) – Antoine Omei takes northern discovery walks around the very old primary forest and to Nimek where it's a magical 6km walk to see the shark nursery (BYO lunch). Walks leave from in front of St Joseph Church.

Mio Palmo Plongée (☎ 450 067; aquamarina-ouvea@yahoo.fr; 2-dive package 11,600 CFP) is a friendly scuba-diving club based at Camping de Lékine. Take an intro dive for 6500 CFP, or an open-water PADI course for 40,000 CFP.

Tours

To get to the Pléiades du Nord contact **Le Banian** (☎ 457 063; 4-person trip 20,000 CFP), a homestay near St Joseph. For Pléiades du Sud contact **Koïo Drany** (☎ 457 287; per person 6000 CFP), based in Fayaoué.

Charly Aema (☎ 450 760; adult/child 5000/2500 CFP; ☺ Mon-Sat) organises sea expeditions on the lagoon and to Pléiades du Sud where you can snorkel and fish and enjoy a picnic. See Moague, below.

You can also visit Pléiades du Sud on a diving trip with Mio Palmo Plongée.

Sleeping & Eating

There is a grocery shop in each *tribu*, although the best-stocked is Chez Fella in Fayaoué, near the *gendarmerie*. Most places to stay can prepare lobster or coconut crab (around 3000 CFP).

Gîte Cocotier (☎ 457 040; camping 1000 CFP, case per person 2000 CFP, paillotes d/tr 3500/4000 CFP, bungalows s/d 4500/5000 CFP) Sammy is your host at this homestay about 500m north of the church in Mouli. It's across the road from the beach, but you can pitch your tent on the beachfront. Hire bikes for 2000 CFP a day, or take a four-hour island tour for 3500 CFP. A set menu is 2200 CFP. Airport/wharf transfers cost 2000/3000 CFP.

Bougainvillier (☎ 457 220; camping 1100 CFP, s/d 3900/4600 CFP) Walk down a track from the beach to this homestay in Fayaoué. There's three attractive thatched bungalows in a dense garden. Breakfast is 650 CFP and the set menu is 2400 CFP. Return airport/wharf transfers cost 1100/3200 CFP.

Moague (☎ 450 760; camping 1100 CFP, paillotes s/d 5000/5700 CFP) This friendly homestay is about 5km south of the bridge, before the church. It's run by Charly Aema, who is famous for his boat excursions. There's a set menu for 1200 CFP, and coconut crabs, lobster or *bougna* on request for around 3000 CFP per person. Airport/wharf transfers are 3000 CFP.

Camping de Lékine (☎ 450 067, 425 512; camping 1600 CFP, hut 3700 CFP) This is a delightful spot beside Baie de Lékiny, near the bridge. You can hire a tent with mattress for 700 CFP, a bike/scooter for 1500/4200 CFP a day, there's a kitchen and you're next to the scuba-diving club. All good. Airport/wharf transfers are 3000/2000 CFP.

Le Banian (☎ 457 063; case s/d 4000/4700 CFP) Up north, near St Joseph, with its signpost down a side road (unhelpful!), this homestay is like a Spanish hacienda: white stone courtyard, tropical plants, three *cases* looking cool, each with three beds. Have *bougna* (1600 CFP) or lobster (3200 CFP) if you order in advance; a set menu costs 2100 CFP. Airport or harbour transfers are 1400 CFP.

Gîte Beaupré (☎ 457 132; bungalows d/tr 10,400/11,000 CFP, studios 5800 CFP) Three bright wooden bungalows in a large garden are across the road from the beach. The basic studio rooms are airy and have shared bathrooms. The restaurant is open to anyone, but you must book (breakfast 850 CFP, main meals from 1600 CFP, lobster 3800 CFP). Airport/wharf transfers are 1000/1500 CFP. The owner, Willy, hires cars and scooters (from 7000 CFP and 5000 CFP a day) and takes guests on tours with/without a crab lunch for 7500/3500 CFP.

our pick **Hôtel Paradis d'Ouvéa** (☎ 455 400; www .hotelparadis.com; cottage 52,500 CFP, 2-/4-/6-person villa 34,700/52,500/76,700 CFP; 🏊) Step out of your luxurious spacious cottage onto a stunning white-sand beach, or lay on your private deck and think about swimming in the azure sea. The tropical restaurant with soaring ceilings serves delicious meals (mains 3300 CFP or set menu 4500 CFP) although it's tempting to keep ordering the thin-sliced fish (oh yum). Hire bikes for 2000 CFP per four hours. Airport return transfers are 2000 CFP and around-island tours 3700 CFP.

Snack Fassy (chicken or fish main 750 CFP; ☺ 7am-8pm) A fun place with tables set under a thatched roof. Nine local tribes take week-long turns to run the *snack*, and obviously enjoy it. Order in advance for specials, like lobster or lagoon crab (2100 CFP).

Getting Around

Car-hire companies include:

Julau Location (☎ 454 530; per day from 5000 CFP)
Ouvéa Location (☎ 457 377; per day from 7400 CFP)

There's one **private bus** (☎ 457 077; 250 CFP; ☺ Mon-Sat) that leaves St Joseph at 6.30am, passes through Fayaoué at 7.30am, arrives at Mouli at 9am, then returns to Fayaoué by 10.30am and St Joseph by 11.30am. The driver stops anywhere along the route if you flag him down.

Iaai Aventure (☎ 453 512; per day 1900 CFP), 200m south of Gîte Beaupré in Fayaoue, rents bikes.

NEW CALEDONIA

ÎLE DES PINS

pop 1900 / area 152 sq km

A tranquil paradise of turquoise bays, white-sand beaches and tropical vegetation, Île des Pins (Isle of Pines) is also a haunting place where dark caves hide in the forest and the bush invades the crumbling ruins of a convict prison. The Kuniés, as the island's inhabitants are known, have kept alive the tradition of sailing *pirogues*, and you'll see these ancient craft gliding elegantly across the calm lagoon. Île des Pins' *escargots* (snails) are a local speciality and most places serve them. Seafood, in particular lobster, is another popular dish. All restaurants attached to gîtes or hotels accept nonguests, but you must book in advance. Restaurants can also prepare sandwiches if you'd like a picnic.

Orientation & Information

Vao is the main administrative centre. Kuto is the main tourist area, although hotels and gîtes are all around the island; most organise car rental and island or lagoon excursions. The Office du Tourisme in Noumea (p180) can also book accommodation, car rental and activities.

BCI bank (☎ 461 045; Vao; ⏱ 8am-noon & 1-3.30pm Mon & Fri, 8am-noon Tue & Wed, 1-3pm Thu) Opposite the red-roofed market, with an ATM inside.

Post office (☎ 461 100; ⏱ 7.45-11.15am & 12.15-3pm Mon-Fri) It also has a public telephone; there are other phones at the airport and wharf.

Visitor information centre (☎ 461 027; Vao; www.ile-des-pins.com; ⏱ 8-11.30am & 2-4pm Mon-Fri, 8.30-11.30am Sat) Opposite the market. There's an information desk (☎ 461 400) at the airport which opens for flights.

Dangers & Annoyances

Do not climb the taboo rock in Baie de Kanuméra (Le Rocher). This is the large vegetation-covered rock with wooden stairs up the side that is separated from the beach at high tide. It is OK to swim around it or sit on the sand beneath it.

It's forbidden to kite-surf near Île des Pins, or for yachts to sail through St Joseph, Upi and Koroxu bays.

Getting There & Away

Air Calédonie (⏱ 7.30-11am & 2-5pm Mon-Fri, 7.30-11.30am Sat) airport (☎ 448 840) Kuto (☎ 448 850) flies to Île des Pins from Noumea at least twice daily (see p225).

The *Betico* sails from Noumea at 7am most Wednesdays, Saturdays and Sundays, docking at the wharf in beautiful Baie de Kuto. It returns to Noumea at 5pm (9400 CFP).

Getting Around

It is important to arrange a hire car, transfer or tour in advance, so you're not stranded at the airport or wharf, especially if you're on a day trip:

Jean-Marie Vakie (☎ 867 435) Can take you to a destination, or collect you. If you're staying overnight, your host will arrange transfers.

Taxis (☎ 791 926, 768 450) Have to be booked well in advance.

Some rental companies that drop your car where you want it include the following:

Kuto Services (☎ 461 147; per day from 7800 CFP)

NC-First (☎ 461 090; ncfirstresa@lagoon.nc; per day from 7500 CFP)

Oure, Kou-Bugny and Kodjeue hotels, and Gîte Nataiwatch hire cars (per day from 7500 CFP).

Other rental options are:

Bikes Gîte Nataiwatch and Hôtel Kodjeue (per half-/full-day 1000/1500 CFP). Cycling is excellent: not many steep climbs and short distances between places.

Boats Hôtel Oure and Le Méridien (per half-/full-day 50,000/80,000 CFP).

Electric Bikes Hôtel Kodjeue (half-/full day 1500/2500 CFP).

Kayaks Hôtel Kodjeue (half-/full day 750/1500 CFP).

Pirogues Hôtel Oure (per half-/full-day 5700/7300 CFP).

Scoot cars Kunié Loca Fun (☎ 435 480; Kuto; per half-/full-day 5000/7000 CFP) You must be over 16 but a driver's licence isn't necessary.

Scooters Hôtel Kou-Bugny (per half-/full-day 4000/5500 CFP).

VAO

Île des Pins' main village, Vao, is a serene place with several interesting sights and activities in the town and the surrounding area.

The attractive 19th-century **Catholic church** dominates Vao. It was established by the Marist priest Father Goujon, who managed to convert most of the island's population in just over 30 years following his arrival in 1848. A path behind the church leads up to a small chapel from where you can admire the view over the village to the lagoon.

The **Statue de St Maurice** at (signposted) Baie de St Maurice commemorates the arrival of

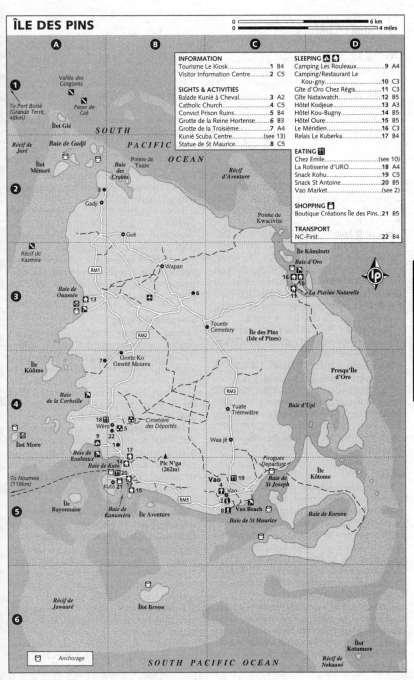

ÎLE DES PINS

0 _____ 6 km
0 _____ 4 miles

To Port Boisé
(Grande Terre,
48km)

Vallée des
Gorgones

Passe de
Gié

Îlot Gié

SOUTH

PACIFIC

OCEAN

Récif de
Jaré

Baie de Gadji

Îlot
Ménoré

Pointe de
Tuure

Baie
des
Crabes

Récif
d'Aventure

Gadji

Gué

Pointe de
Kwacivita

Récif de
Kasmira

Baie de
Ouaméo

Wapan

Île Kônubutr
Baie d'Oro

La Piscine Naturelle

Île
Kûûmo

Grotte Ko
Gnwëë Meureu

Touete
Cemetery

Île des Pins
(Isle of Pines)

Presqu'Île
d'Oro

Baie
de la Corbeille

Île Moro

Wêrö

Cimetière
des Déportés

Yuate
Trémwâtre

Baie d'Upi

Waa jê

Baie de
Rouleaux
Baie de Kuto

Kuto

Pic N'ga
(262m)

Pirogues
Departure

Baie de
St Joseph

Île
Kôtomo

To Noumea
(118km)

Île
Bayonnaise

Baie de
Kanuméra

Île Aventure

Vao
Vao

Vao Beach

Baie de St Maurice

Baie de Koroxu

Récif de
Jawaaré

Îlot Brosse

Îlot
Kotumere

Anchorage

SOUTH PACIFIC OCEAN

Récif de
Nekaawi

NEW CALEDONIA

PIROGUE EXCURSION

Its scenery aside, Île des Pins' most famous attraction is its wooden *pirogues* with their triangular sails that glide you softly over the deep blue. *Pirogues* leave Baie de St Joseph at 8am, heading for Baie d'Oro where a path leads through the forest to magical *la piscine naturelle* (natural pool, opposite). Laze on the sand around the pool or snorkel above a kaleidoscope of fish in its clear waters. Bring your picnic lunch or indulge your senses further by booking into one of Baie d'Oro's wonderful eating options, all just a five-minute stroll along the waterway (see p220).

Organised *pirogue* excursions, including transfers to Baie de St Joseph and from Baie d'Oro, cost around 3800 CFP. Or just turn up before 8am (sail 1800 CFP) and arrange your lift back from Baie d'Oro.

---

the first missionaries on the island and is also a war memorial. You don't need permission to photograph the solemn circle of wooden totem poles guarding a statue of Christ, just above the beach.

Baie de St Joseph, 2km east of Vao, is also referred to as Baie des Pirogues. Early morning, when the *pirogues* are out on the water, is the best time to visit. Later in the day you can watch sailors building their *pirogues* on the beach under the coconut palms. A trip on one of these crafts is a must if you're visiting Île des Pins; see the boxed text, above.

The **market** (6-11am Wed & Sat) sells local produce. It's opposite the visitors centre 100m south of the church.

Snack Kohu (461 023; dishes 750-1200 CFP; 8.30am-4pm Mon & Wed-Fri, to 3pm Sat) is a pleasant place to stop, with tables under thatched shelters and everyone very friendly. Meals include chicken or steak and chips, sandwiches (from 350 CFP) and a *plat du jour* (1300 CFP). It's in a garden on the road heading north from Vao.

KUTO

Kuto has two gorgeous aquamarine bays, separated by the narrow neck of Kuto peninsula. **Baie de Kuto** is the perfect place to lie on the beach or swim in the calm sea. Leafy trees grow to the edge of the beach, so you're always guaranteed some shade. For snorkelling go to **Baie de Kanuméra**, where coral grows not far from the shore. Transfers to your accommodation around Kuto are airport/wharf 2000/600 CFP.

Just north of Baie de Kuto, beside the main road, are the crumbling, overgrown ruins of an old **convict prison** built in the late 19th century. Île des Pins was initially used as a place of exile for convicts, including Paris Communards and Algerian deportees in the 1870s.

Opposite is the **Tourisme Le Kiosk** (9am-11pm & 2-6pm Mon-Sat), grocery shop and boutique selling Crocs.

Feeling energetic? Take a 45-minute climb up **Pic N'ga** (262m), the island's highest point. The path is mostly exposed, so it's best to go early morning or late afternoon. From the summit there are fantastic views over the entire island and its turquoise bays. The signposted path begins from the main road 200m south of Relais Le Kuberka.

Sleeping & Eating

Camping Les Rouleaux (461 116; camping 1100 CFP) A popular spot for board riders and kite surfers, this large, shady campsite has happy locals attending to your needs. It fronts on to the sandy beach at Baie des Rouleaux; heading north, turn left at the information kiosk (look for the green crocodile), then take the right fork and follow the power lines for 1km.

Relais Le Kuberka (461 118; camping 1600 CFP, s/d 6500/8400 CFP, bungalows d/tr/q 10,400/13,100/15,800 CFP) A short walk from the beach is this home-away-from-home. Rooms and bungalows are set around a small tidy garden and pool. The restaurant serves an excellent range of meals (dishes 2000 CFP).

Gîte Nataiwatch (461 113; www.nataiwatch .com; camping 1800 CFP, traditional bungalows s/d without bathroom 8500/9200 CFP, B&B modern s/d 8700/9900 CFP) A relaxed and popular gîte in a wooded area towards the eastern end of Baie de Kanuméra. Modern concrete bungalows have bathrooms, traditional ones have kitchens but share bathrooms. Meals cost 1600 CFP.

Hôtel Kou-Bugny (461 800; www.kou-bugny .com; std/deluxe bungalows 22,600/25,600 CFP;) Kou-Bugny spreads across the quiet road from Kuto beach: traditional-inspired bungalows under spreading branches of trees by a small pool; restaurant and boutique all glass and

NEW CALEDONIA

modern on the beachfront. Breakfast is 2400 CFP; and for dinner, chef Mickael produces elegant dishes (mains 2100 CFP to 2900 CFP) that include bouillabaisse.

our pick **Hôtel Oure** (☎ 431 315; www.tera.nc; garden/lagoon/beach bungalows 32,000/48,000/56,000 CFP; ⛄ 🖵 🛋) This is so delightful. Step off your wide veranda, across the grass, to amazing Baie de Kanuméra, closed in by pine-covered islands so you're in your own aquamarine paradise with coral gardens a flipper-kick from the sand. The open bar and dining room (mains 2200 CFP to 2600 CFP) open on to a curving pool area. Enjoy friendly service every day and Melanesian dancing on Saturday night.

Snack St Antoine (☎ 434 710; papiidp@live.fr; meals 1500-3500 CFP; ☺ 9am-late) This tiny place with the big beach bar by the wharf is run by Yves, who serves a mean beer. Sandwiches are 550 CFP and meals include lobster if you order in advance. He offers wi-fi, safe anchorage for yachties, bathroom and laundry facilities, and sells basic groceries. St Antoine closes at 7pm on Saturday and Wednesday.

Shopping
Boutique Créations Île des Pins (☎ 461 268; ☺ 9-11.30am & 2.30-5.30pm) Near the wharf in Kuto, this shop sells Île des Pins souvenirs, including coffee-table books (in English), postcards, and hand-painted tops and *pareus* (sarongs). A DVD (3950 CFP) featuring Île des Pins underwater and island scenes is also on sale. Several of the books about the island were written by the boutique's owner, Hilary Roots.

THE WEST COAST
As you travel north there's open areas and patches of forest. A couple of roads lead to beaches. About 8km from Kuto a signposted turn-off leads down a dirt track to the sunken **Grotte de la Troisième**. Stop when you come to a clearing where cars can turn around; the cave is 30m down a path. If you climb into the cave's wide opening, you can peer into its depth. With a torch and a sense of adventure, you can go down the steep slippery floor of the cave to the bottom, which is filled with fresh water. Experienced divers can venture even further into the underground caves.

Activities
Kunié Scuba Centre (☎ 461 122; www.kunie-scuba.com; intro/2-dive from 7000/12,500 CFP, boat trip 8500 CFP), based

at Hôtel Kodjeue, organises dives to the caves and sites off the northern tip of the island, especially Vallée des Gorgones, to see soft and hard corals, eagle rays and leopard sharks (ask about the accommodation-and-dive packages). Boat excursions include snorkelling gear and picnic lunch. Fishing trips can also be arranged for 8500 CFP per person.

Balade Kunié à Cheval (☎ 499 307; horse treks per hr/half-day 2500/6000 CFP) at the northern tip of the island, organises horse treks along the beach, through the forest or up to the plateau. Turn down a dirt road at the 'ranch' signpost on the road to Gadji.

Sleeping & Eating
Hôtel Kodjeue (☎ 461 142; www.hotelkodjeue.com; B&B bungalows std/deluxe 16,000/29,000 CFP; 🛋) Into sunsets? This is your dream then, on calm Baie de Ouaméo. Different-sized bright bungalows on a wide lawn offer choices: kitchenette, overwater, garden view, simple, family? They're all good. The hotel has a small grocery store, but the restaurant meals are tempting (mains 1900 CFP to 3500 CFP). Airport or wharf transfers cost 600 CFP.

La Rotisserie d'URO (☎ 779 074; mains 700-1200 CFP; ☺ 8.30am-2.30pm Tue-Sun) will set you up with a BBQ chicken meal, or chicken sandwich (500 CFP) for a beach picnic.

BAIE D'ORO & AROUND
North of Vao the road climbs gradually towards the central plateau, where you have views over the dense forests of the east coast to the sea. Turn east opposite a small cemetery to beautiful secluded **Baie d'Oro**, its long white-sand beach enclosed on one side by a reef and on the other by tall araucaria pines. The area is best known for **la piscine naturelle**, a pool of exquisite turquoise water sheltered behind the reef. It is part of a waterway leading from the open sea to Baie d'Oro: follow the sandy waterway from Le Méridien or Chez Regis. Another waterway leads north back to Baie d'Oro, coming out near Chez Emile and Camping/Restaurant Le Kou-gny.

Just north of the airport road turning is **Grotte de la Reine Hortense** (admission 200 CFP), an impressive cave which tunnels into a limestone cliff. A path leads through a beautiful wild tropical garden to the wide entrance. This cave was where Queen Hortense, wife of a local chief, is believed to have taken refuge for several months during intertribal conflict in 1855; there's a smooth rock ledge where she slept. The friendly lady who maintains the cave can tell you its history and that of the island in general.

The cave's earth floor is slippery; take a torch if you have one. The sealed road down to the cave is signposted.

Sleeping & Eating

Camping/Restaurant Le Kou-gny (☎ 469 545; camping 1200 CFP) This rustic campsite and restaurant has an excellent reputation for its lobster meals (4300 CFP) and fish menu (2200 CFP). Tables are set under the trees on the beach overlooking a dreamy lagoon.

Gîte d'Oro Chez Régis (☎ 434 555; www.gitedoro -iledespins.com; camping 1500 CFP, bungalows 10,000 CFP) Estelle will look after you at this shady campsite, where four bungalows sit along the waterway leading to *la piscine naturelle*. The open-thatched restaurant is famous for its *bougnas* (chicken/lobster 2500/4000 CFP); order a day in advance. If you arrive around 10am, you can watch the ladies preparing them. Airport/wharf transfers cost 1200/1600 CFP.

Le Méridien (☎ 461 515; meridienidp@meridien .nc; B&B r/ste/bungalow 60,000 CFP/70,000/80,000 CFP; 🖭) Tropical luxury: cool timber floors flowing through to private decks, idyllic forest all round, views across Baie d'Oro to araucarias silhouetted against the sky, a swimming pool that seems to flow into the lagoon. Central lounge, bar and restaurant areas invite you to relax, enjoy. Transfers are 2200 CFP. Dinner mains like tajine lamb (luscious) are 2900 CFP to 3500 CFP. Plus there's a full range of tours and activities on offer.

Chez Emile (☎ 791 319; menu 3500-4000 CFP) Between the Riviere de Sable waterway leading to *la piscine naturelle* and Le Kou-gny is a casual little spot where fish, chicken and escargots are barbecued to perfection. Camping (1200 CFP) is available.

NEW CALEDONIA DIRECTORY

ACCOMMODATION

Hotels everywhere have glorious garden and ocean views. Prices start around 7000/14,000/22,000 CFP per night for a room

in a basic/midrange/top-end hotel for a single or double.

Bungalow prices range from 6000 CFP to 11,000 CFP. It's another 1000 CFP for a third person. Bungalows usually have private bathrooms, a communal kitchen or an on-site restaurant.

There are homestays (*accueil en tribu*), gîtes and campsites everywhere, except in Noumea. Campsites have toilets and showers of varying degrees of cleanliness and cost from 1100 CFP per tent. Homestays and farmstays are usually in a Melanesian family compound and have *cases* (with mattresses on the floor) or bungalows (with beds). They cost from 1000 CFP to 6000 CFP per person. All places have towels and soap for 300 CFP; meals are extra.

All transfers quoted are return rates.

ACTIVITIES
Abseiling

New Caledonia has many waterfalls and rock formations which are ideal for abseiling. The **Gecko Club** (☎ 783 258; www.gecko-club.com) has information about the various areas. **Pacific Free Ride** (☎ 792 202; www.pfr.nc) arranges abseiling in the south of Grande Terre, and **Association Dayu Biik** (p204) organises abseiling in the north.

Diving

Scuba diving is big here, with many dive sites, most of which are reached by boat. Prices reflect this, but a two-dive package costs from 10,000 CFP. Out on the barrier reef there are many shipwrecks and, closer, several intentionally sunk ships.

Nouvelle-Calédonie Plongée (www.nouvelle caledonieplongee.com) offers 'Plongée' cards which give a 15% discount on dives. Cards (5000 CFP and valid for one year) can be purchased at member clubs; check the website for clubs and contact details.

Fishing

Air Mer Loisir and Pacific Charter (see opposite) in Noumea rent fishing boats. **New Caledonia Fishing Safaris** (☎ 251 940; www.newcaledoniafishing safaris.nc), also based in Noumea, runs sportfishing safaris around Poum and other spots.

Hiking

New Caledonia has diverse landscapes that are great for hiking, best done during the cooler mid-year months. Popular hiking areas and

---

PRACTICALITIES

■ *Les Nouvelles Calédoniennes* (www.lnc.nc) is the only daily newspaper. *Les Infos* is a weekly current affairs papers and the *New Caledonia Weekly* is a free weekly paper published by the Office du Tourisme with what's on and helpful details for tourists.

■ There's one public television station, Télé Nouvelle-Calédonie, part of the French territories broadcasting service (RFO). All programmes are in French. Canal Satellite, a network of pay channels, has more choice.

■ Radio Nouvelle-Calédonie (RNC) is the national radio service. Other radio stations include Radio Djiido; Radio Rythme Bleu (RRB); NRJ, mainly music for young people; and Radio Océane.

■ Videos are usually based on the PAL system.

■ Plugs have two round pins (220-240V, 50Hz AC).

■ New Caledonia follows the metric system. See the Quick Reference page for conversions.

---

tracks around Noumea include Monts Koghis (p197), Parc Provincial de la Rivière Bleue (p192) and the GR1 walking track (p195).

Association Dayu Biik (p204) organises guided walks in the Hienghène region.

The **Office du Tourisme** (www.office-tourisme.nc, www.trekking-gr-sud-nc.com) has fantastic brochures and maps detailing a selection of hikes. Or visit the **Direction des Ressources Naturelles** (Map p184; ☎ 243 260; env@province-sud.nc; 19 av du Maréchal Foch) in Noumea.

Horse Riding
Many ranches and *tribus* on Grande Terre offer one- or multiple-day horse-riding trips into the central mountain ranges; check the Dumbéa, La Foa and Koné sections.

Sailing & Boating
The Cercle Nautique Calédonien (yacht club; p224) is a good place to inquire about yachting and sailing.

Air Mer Loisir (Map p184; ☎ 282 901; www.aml.nc; Port Moselle, Noumea) Skippered or bare-boat 12m catamarans and monohulls from 77,000 CFP and 62,000 CFP a day on 'the best lagoon in the world'.

Pacific Charter (Map p184; ☎ /fax 261 055; www.pacificcharter.nc) Hires out a range of motor boats, from a 5.5m flyer, departing from Port Moselle (per half-/full day from 19,000/29,000 CFP).

Scenic Flights
Helicopters fly a maximum of three people over Noumea's bays, the islets sprinkled across the lagoon, shipwrecks and the barrier reef. A longer flight takes in the incredible inlets of

the Far South. The honeymoon flight (42,000 CFP) includes a 30-minute champagne stop on an island. Operators:

Helicocean (☎ 253 949; helicocean@mls.nc; 30-min flight 30,400 CFP)

Hélisud (☎ 269 662; helitourisme@mls.nc; 30-min flight 31,500 CFP)

Water Sports
The best spots for **snorkelling** are the reefs around the Loyalty Islands and Île des Pins. Bring your own gear and watch out for strong currents. In Noumea, take a boat to the Île aux Canards, Îlot Maître or Amédée Islet (p186) marine sanctuaries.

Windsurfing and **kite-surfing** are extremely popular on Noumea's bays. Equipment can be rented at Anse Vata from Plages Loisirs (p186).

Glisse Attitude (Map p182-3; ☎ 782 769; glisseattitude@lagoon.nc; per hr/half-day 4500/9000 CFP) in Noumea organises kite-surfing trips and courses.

MD Plaisirs (p186) has water-sports equipment at Anse Vata, Poé and Koumak plus introductory lessons (from 1500 CFP per hour). Get an MD Plaisirs card for up to 40% discount.

Surfing trips to the reef are run by Nëkwéta (p199) in Bourail and Bouts-d'Brousse (p197) in Boulouparis.

Whale-Watching
Humpback whales cause a flurry of whale-watching excursions off Grande Terre's south coast (p193) and Lifou (p212) between July and September. You may even sight them from the beach in Maré.

BUSINESS HOURS

Government offices and most private businesses are open Monday to Friday from 7.30am or 8am to 4pm or 5pm, closing between 11.30am and 1.30pm. However, banks in Noumea and most post offices around New Caledonia remain open at lunchtime.

Shops are open weekdays from 7.30am to 11am and 2pm to 6pm, and Saturday from 8am to noon. Some supermarkets don't close for lunch and are open all day Saturday and Sunday morning.

Sunday is extremely quiet throughout New Caledonia.

CHILDREN

If you're travelling in Noumea with children, see p187 and check out Lonely Planet's *Travel with Children*. Infants under three years stay free at most places. Children under 12 pay half the adult rate for accommodation and activities.

It's handy to travel with a fold-out change bag, and in Noumea or on Île des Pins car-hire companies can provide a safety seat.

DANGERS & ANNOYANCES

In general, New Caledonia is very safe for travellers. Always check that you're not walking or swimming in a taboo area, or on somebody's property.

EMBASSIES & CONSULATES

Australia (Map p184; ☎ 272 414; 19 av du Maréchal Foch, Noumea)
Japan (Map p182; ☎ 253 729; 45 rue du 5-Mai, Noumea)
Netherlands (Map p184; ☎ 284 858; 1st fl, 33 rue de Sébastopol, Noumea)
New Zealand (Map p184; ☎ 272 543; 2nd fl, 4 blvd Vauban, Noumea)
UK (Map p184; ☎ 282 153; 14 rue Générale Sarrail, Noumea)
Vanuatu (Map p184; ☎ 277 621; 1st fl, 53 rue de Sébastopol, Noumea)

FESTIVALS & EVENTS

See p629 for details of regional holidays. The Office du Tourisme website (www.office -tourisme.nc) has a calendar of events.
Festival of the Yam (March) Kanak festival marking the beginning of the harvest.
Giant Omelette Festival (April) At Dumbéa, a dozen chefs, 7000 eggs and many hands make a

---

COUNTRY FAIRS & RODEOS

Country fairs are popular and colourful events enjoyed by rural folk and townies alike. As well as livestock and produce contests, there are craft and food stalls, and children's rides. The highlight is the rodeo, when stockmen compete in bulldogging or flap about like rag dolls on the backs of bucking bulls. The crowd delights in the action and also gets to see a lot of horseless (or bull-less) riders carried out of the arena on stretchers.

Don't miss Païta's famous 'Fête du Boeuf' or Bourail's 'Foire de Bourail' and Koumac's 'Foire de Koumac'.

---

free-for-all 3.5m-diameter omelette. Held close to Easter at Parc Fayard.
Avocado Festival (May) Held in Nece, Maré. It's the island's biggest fair, celebrating the end of the harvest.
La Foa Film Festival (late June) A week celebrating film in La Foa and Noumea.
Bastille Day (14 July) France's national day. Fireworks on the 13th and a military parade in Noumea on the 14th.
Noumea Contemporary Art Biennale (July/August) Held every two years.
Marathon Internationale de Noumea (July/August) Held annually, attracts top athletes from all over the world.
Live en Août (August) Noumea's annual music festival featuring foreign and local bands.
Foire de Bourail (August/September) Three-day fair featuring a rodeo, cattle show, horse racing and a beauty pageant.
Équinoxe (October) Held in Noumea. Biennial festival of contemporary theatre, dance and music.
Fête du Bœuf (October/November) Païta's popular fair and rodeo.
Sound & Light Show (October/November) Impressive light shows staged at Fort Teremba, near La Foa, over a fortnight.

INTERNET ACCESS

All hotels offer free wi-fi access, sometimes in guests' rooms but usually in the lobby. Internet cafes are few and far between.

INTERNET RESOURCES

Kaori (www.kaori.nc) Contains links to other New Caledonian websites, and information on news and upcoming events.
New Caledonia Holidays (www.newcaledonia.com.au) Loads of holiday suggestions.
New Caledonia Online (www.kaledonie.com) A portal to numerous New Caledonian websites.

New Caledonia Tourism (www.visitnewcaledonia.com) A fun site (in several languages) determined to captivate you.
Office du Tourisme (www.office-tourisme.nc) The official site (in French, English and Japanese) for New Caledonia's tourism.

MAPS

The Office du Tourisme in Noumea (p180) and Anse Vata has good free maps of New Caledonia and detailed maps of specific regions.

Charts can be consulted at the CNC (p224); or you can buy them at **Marine Corail** (Map p184; ☎ 275 848; 28 rue du Général Mangin, Noumea), along with excellent mariners' maps produced by the Service Hydrographique et Océanographique de la Marine (SHOM).

MONEY

New Caledonia doesn't have to be too expensive. Try a drive-and-camp holiday (BYO tent), cheap eateries provide delicious meals (from 1200 CFP) and a lunchtime sandwich is a splendid thing. Supermarkets sell Number One beer (120 CFP), terrine (350 CFP), Roquefort cheese (330 CFP) and baguettes (120 CFP). What more does one need?

The 5% services tax is usually included in displayed prices. Banks in Noumea and some of the main centres change travellers cheques. For exchange rates, see the Quick Reference page. Tipping is not expected.

ATMs

Most banks have ATMs which accept major credit cards. There are ATMs around Noumea and other major towns and villages. Some post offices also have ATMs.

HOW MUCH?

- **Filled baguette:** 450 CFP
- **Cup of coffee:** 300 CFP
- **Music CD:** 3000 CFP
- **Short taxi ride:** 1100 CFP
- **Cinema admission:** 950 CFP
- **1L petrol:** 170 CFP
- **1L bottled water:** 180 CFP
- **Number One beer:** 350 CFP
- **Souvenir T-shirt:** 1800 CFP
- **Croissant:** 200 CFP

Credit Cards

Credit cards are accepted by hotels, restaurants, big shops and airline offices in Noumea, but not at budget places outside the capital.

TELEPHONE

New Caledonia's international telephone code is ☎ 687.

You can dial ☎ 19 for a cheaper call to certain destinations, including France (33 CFP per minute), Australia and NZ (38 CFP), the UK (70 CFP) and Japan (60 CFP). To make a reverse-charge call (en PCV), you'll need to dial ☎ 1050.

Mobile Phones

Mobile-phone numbers begin with '7', '8' or '9'. To use your mobile phone in New Caledonia it needs to be compatible with the network (GSM 900/1800). Beware: a local SIM card costs 6190 CFP and includes only 3000 CFP credit. For assistance dial ☎ 1014 free call.

Phonecards

To use a public phone, you need a télécarte (25/80/140 units cost 1000/3000/5000 CFP). For a fixed phone you can use IZI cards (1040/3120/5200 CFP). Both cards are available at post offices and some tobacconists' shops in Noumea.

TIME

New Caledonia is 11 hours ahead of GMT. It's one hour ahead of Australian Eastern Standard Time (Sydney, Brisbane and Melbourne) and one hour behind NZ and Fiji.

TOURIST INFORMATION

The visitor information centre is the **Office du Tourisme** (☎ 287 580; www.office-tourisme.nc; place des Cocotiers, Noumea).

VISAS

European Union, Swiss, Australian and NZ citizens are allowed entry into New Caledonia for three months without a visa. Some visitors, including citizens of Japan, Canada and the US, are allowed entry for one month without a visa. To verify the latest visa requirements, check the French government website for New Caledonia at www.et at.nc.

TRANSPORT IN NEW CALEDONIA

GETTING THERE & AWAY
Air

AIRPORTS & AIRLINES
All international flights land at Tontouta International Airport, 45km northwest of Noumea. For details on travelling between Tontouta and Noumea, see p181.

The following airlines fly into New Caledonia. Air France flies code-share with Aircalin (Air Calédonie International). Departure tax is included in your flight tickets.

Air France (Map p184; ☎ 258 888; www.airfrance.com; 41 rue de Sébastopol, Noumea)

Air New Zealand (Map p184; ☎ 286 677; www.airnewzealand.com; Axxess Travel, 22 rue Duquesne, Noumea)

Air Vanuatu (Map p184; ☎ 286 677; www.airvanuatu.com; Axxess Travel, 22 rue Duquesne, Noumea)

Aircalin (Map p184; ☎ 265 500; www.aircalin.com; 8 rue Frédéric Surleau, Noumea)

Qantas (Map p184; ☎ 286 546; www.qantas.com; 35 av du Maréchal Foch, Noumea) Access from rue de Verdun.

ASIA
Aircalin has three flights a week from Osaka and five a week from Tokyo (US$1400 return).

AUSTRALASIA
Qantas and Aircalin flights leave from Brisbane four times a week and Sydney daily. A return fare from Sydney/Brisbane starts at US$850/900.

There are four flights per week between Auckland and Noumea, either with Air New Zealand or Aircalin, starting from US$700.

EUROPE
Aircalin, code-sharing with KLM/Air France/Cathay Pacific/Singapore Airlines, flies via Japan for around US$2600. Qantas has three flights weekly via Singapore (US$2800).

NORTH AMERICA
The main gateway is from Los Angeles or New York via Pape'ete (French Polynesia): fly with Air France or Air Tahiti Nui to Pape'ete (US$2400), and connect with an Aircalin flight to Noumea. Air New Zealand flies via Auckland or Qantas via Sydney (US$2400).

Another option is to fly with Air Pacific from Los Angeles to Noumea via Nadi. The price is in the same range.

PACIFIC
Aircalin offers a South Pacific Air Pass for people residing outside the region. It allows, for example, a one-way pass from Pape'ete (US$340), Sydney (US$220) or Port Vila (US$160). Before you rush to buy them, these don't include any taxes (visit www.aircalin.com for details).

Aircalin flies to Nadi (Fiji) once or twice a week (US$700 return) and to Pape'ete once a week (US$1200 return).

You can fly between Port Vila (Vanuatu) and Noumea several times a week (from US$360 return) with Aircalin or Air Vanuatu.

SOUTH AMERICA
Use an Aircalin flight to Pape'ete and connect with a LAN flight to Santiago, via Easter Island. Or fly with Qantas via Sydney (around US$2700).

Sea
BOAT
The passenger and cargo boat **Havannah** (☎ 270 405; cmisa@lagoon.nc; one way 10,850 CFP) sails to Vanuatu (Port Vila, Malekula and Espiritu Santo) every six weeks.

CRUISE SHIP
Like floating white cities, 75 cruise ships visit New Caledonia each year, and all dock at Noumea's Gare Maritime where **Office du Tourisme** (www.office-tourisme.nc) opens a booth for them. The ships also drop anchor at other spots around New Caledonia.

Pacific Sun, Pacific Star and *Pacific Princess* (www.pocruises.com.au/html) are the most regular visitors. In Noumea, contact **CMA-CGM** (Map p184; ☎ 270 183; nma.scristofoli@cma-cgm.com; 32 rue du Général Galliéni, Noumea).

YACHT
New Caledonia welcomes about a thousand yachties every year. There are marinas and customs/immigration clearing services in Noumea, Koumac, Hienghène and Lifou. One hour before arriving in Noumea, use VHF 67 to contact the **Capitainerie** (harbour

master's office; Map p184; ☎ 277 197; port.moselle@ sodemo.nc; ⏱ 8am-4pm Mon-Fri, to 11am Sat, to 10am Sun), who'll call in Quarantine, Immigration and Customs. There's berthing assistance, fuel, laundry and many services available. Rates for berthing at the marina start at 1500 CFP a day (live aboard), or use the facilities from 1400 CFP for three days.

The **Cercle Nautique Calédonien** (Map p182; CNC; ☎ 262 727; informations@cnc.asso.nc; VHF Channel 68; 2 rue du Capitaine Desmier, Noumea) yacht club at Baie des Pêcheurs is a good source of information about yachting and sailing.

Cruising New Caledonia & Vanuatu, by Alan Lucas, gives details on many natural harbours and out-of-the-way anchorages. The *Cruising Guide to New Caledonia,* by Joël Marc, Ross Blackman and Marc Rambeau, is a general yachting guide that also provides an exhaustive list of possible anchorages around the islands. See p223 for information on purchasing marine charts.

GETTING AROUND

Air

New Caledonia's domestic airline is **Air Calédonie** (Map p184; ☎ 287 888; www.air-caledonie.nc; 39 rue de Verdun, Noumea; ⏱ 7.30am-5pm Mon-Fri, to 11am Sat), which flies out of Magenta airport in Noumea to airports at the following destinations:

- Koné, Touho and Koumac twice a week (from 25,000 CFP return)
- each of the Loyalty Islands two to four times daily (23,500 CFP return); there are flights between islands three to four times a week (transit in Noumea).
- Île des Pins two to four times daily (16,400 CFP return).

The website has flight schedules, Air Pass (below) details and booking facilities. There are Air Calédonie agencies at all flight destinations, and a **ticket office** (☎ 252 177) at Magenta airport.

AIR PASS

For international travellers, the Air Calédonie Pass (32,300/6950 CFP per four-flight coupon/extra coupon) offers roughly half-price domestic flights. This pass is sold through the Air Calédonie office in Noumea. You need to fax them your passport and international ticket to qualify.

Bicycle

You have to be pretty eager to cycle round 400km-long Grande Terre. However, Ouvéa and Île des Pins are ideal for cycling. Bikes can be transported on the *Betico* and *Havannah* ferries.

There are few bike lanes in Noumea, and drivers both in the capital and elsewhere are not necessarily courteous to cyclists, so you need to be vigilant.

Boat

The *Betico,* a fast passenger ferry, sails from Noumea to Île des Pins (2½ hours) at 7am most Wednesdays, Saturdays and Sundays. It returns to Noumea at 5pm (9400 CFP return).

For the Loyalty Islands, on Monday the *Betico* sails Noumea–Maré–Lifou–Noumea; on Thursday or Friday, it sails Noumea–Lifou–Ouvéa–Lifou–Noumea (13,800 CFP return). Crossings take 3½/4½/5½ hours to Maré/Lifou/Ouvèa.

A return economy ticket from Noumea to Île des Pins costs 9400 CFP, and to a Loyalty Island costs 13,800 CFP. Tickets can be bought at the **Gare Maritime des Îles** (Map p184; ☎ 260 100; commercial.betico@mls.nc; Ferry Terminal, 1 av James Cook, Noumea; ⏱ 7.30am-5.30pm Mon-Fri, 6-10am Sat) on the way to Nouville.

The *Havannah,* a cargo boat, runs on Monday between Noumea and Maré and Lifou (return 8000 CFP). It is operated by **Compagnie Maritime des Îles** (☎ 273 673; cmisa@ lagoon.nc; Ferry Terminal), which has an office at 2 av Henri Lafleur, Quai des Caboteurs.

For details on boat charters, see p221).

Bus

Nearly every town on Grande Terre is connected to the capital by bus, all leaving from Noumea's old **gare routière** (bus station; Map p184; ☎ 249 026; 36 rue d'Austerlitz, Noumea; ⏱ 7.30am-noon & 1.30-4pm), next to Ciné City. It is best to book in advance, especially if you are travelling on Friday or Sunday.

Carsud (Map p182; ☎ 251 615; Gare de Montravel, rue Edouard Unger, Noumea) operates buses between Noumea and the greater Noumea region between 6am and 6pm. They go as far north as Tontouta (400 CFP), passing through Dumbéa (320 CFP) and Païta (360 CFP), and south to Plum in Mont-Dore (400 CFP).

On the other islands there are practically no buses. It's essential to prearrange transport (or hitchhike).

NEW CALEDONIA

AROUND GRANDE TERRE BY BUS

The following schedules are for services departing from Noumea. Fares range from 600 CFP to 2000 CFP.

Destination	Duration	Frequency
Bourail	2½hr	Mon-Sat
Canala	3½hr	daily
Hienghène	6½hr	Mon-Sat
Koné	4hr	daily
Koumac	5½hr	daily
La Foa	1¾hr	Mon-Sat
Poindimié	5hr	daily
Pouébo	6½hr	Wed & Fri
Thio	2hr	daily
Yaté	2hr	Mon-Sat

Car, Scooter & Campervan

Touring New Caledonia by car or campervan allows you to explore places off the beaten track which aren't easy to reach by bus. Car-hire rates are reasonable. New Caledonia's major roads and most of its minor ones are sealed and in good condition. Road signs are sometimes missing or placed down the turn-off where they can't be seen, so a good map is essential.

DRIVING LICENCE

A valid licence from your own country will suffice to drive in New Caledonia.

HIRE

Car-rental companies abound in Noumea and the larger ones have desks at the airport. The Office du Tourisme (p180) has a list of companies. Most companies rent small sedans from 4000 CFP including 150km per day. Per extra kilometre costs from 23 CFP. With unlimited kilometres it costs from 7000 CFP per day. Look for deals such as one-week's all-inclusive rental from 28,000 CFP.

In the Loyalty Islands and Île des Pins, prices start at 7500 CFP per day with unlimited kilometres.

Reliable car- and camper-rental companies include the follwing:

Budget-Pacific Car Rentals (Map p182; ☎ 276 060; www.agence-budget.com; 2 promenade Roger Laroque, Anse Vata)

Caltours Caravanes et Loisirs (Map p182; ☎ 411 092, 968 181; marysecaltours@hotmail.com; 43 rue Unger, Vallée du Tir; per day from 5500 CFP) Prices depend on the campervan model.

Point Rouge (Map p182; www.pointrouge.nc; ☎ 285 920; 96 rue du Général de Gaulle, Orphelinat) Also rents scooters for 1800 CFP a day.

INSURANCE

No extra insurance is required when hiring a car. Some companies charge a security deposit of 100,000 CFP.

ROAD RULES

Driving in New Caledonia is on the right-hand side of the road. The speed limit on a main road is 110km/h and in residential areas 50km/h. Seat belts are compulsory.

The maximum permissible blood alcohol concentration is 0.05%, and random breath testing is carried out.

Taxi

Taxis are confined to Noumea, the larger towns on Grande Terre and a couple of islands. They run on a meter.

Tours

Tour operators in Noumea organise tours and activities in and around the city, as well as throughout New Caledonia. The Office du Tourisme has details.

Arc en Ciel Voyages (Map p184; ☎ 271 980; www.arcenciel-voyages.nc; 59 av du Maréchal Foch, Noumea) Arranges tickets for travelling or touring anywhere, including day trips to the islands.

Aventure Pulsion (Map p182; ☎ 262 748; aventure@canl.nc) Organises off-the-beaten-track tours by 4WD in the Far South (see p193).

Caledonia Tours (☎ 259 424; caledoniatours@lagoon.nc) Runs tours to Blue River Park (see p195).

Caltours (Map p184; ☎ 411 092, 812 001; 7 rue Charles de Verneuilh, Noumea; tours from 5000 CFP) Organises half-day tours to Monts Koghis, full-day tours to Bourail or the Far South, and a week-long tour of Grande Terre.

Terraventure (☎ 778 819; www.terraventurenc.org/ 1/2/4 days 5900/16,600/45,000 CFP) Local adventures, discovery weekends: kayak on the Forgotten Coast, splodge in a hot pool out of Prony, check out Canala.

VIP Tours (☎ 435 308, 792 789; j.brighton@lagoon.nc) A day trip called the Once-upon-a-time Tour. It includes lots of jokes and banter.

Outside Noumea, many places offering accommodation run tours such as guided walks or horse treks, usually on private or customary land.

Niue

Niue (*new*-ay) may be the world's smallest independent nation, but the Pacific island known as the 'Rock of Polynesia' packs in plenty of surprises for the intrepid traveller. Don't expect any palm-fringed beaches and languid lagoons, but look forward to a rugged landscape of limestone caverns, hidden sea caves, and a rocky, untamed coast. Ditch the deck chair and airport novel, and pack a pair of rugged walking shoes and a sense of adventure instead.

Once you've explored Niue's robust exterior, don mask and snorkel and investigate the coral communities and pools fringing Niue's reef. From June to September get face to face with humpback whales nursing their calves in the safe haven of Niue's warm waters. Descend further to the indigo depths for some of the best diving in the Pacific.

And after all this honest exercise, chill out with the friendly locals at cliff-top cafes and beach-front bars. The tiny population of Niueans and *palagi* (European) expats is very friendly, so be prepared to trade waves with *everyone* as you drive (slowly) around the island.

On 5 January 2004 Niue was devastated by Cyclone Heta, one of the biggest storms ever recorded in the Pacific. But now the tiny nation is bouncing back. Getting to Niue is more affordable and easier than ever, and there are several new eco-friendly and low-key ways to explore the island.

Alone in the planet's biggest ocean, Niue remains defiantly and dramatically different.

NIUE

HIGHLIGHTS

- Dive with tangles of sea snakes at **Snake Gully** (p234) or negotiate twin underwater chimneys at **Ana Mahaga** (p234)

- Float calmly as a **humpback whale** (p234) and her calf swim beneath you

- Experience the Pacific Ocean's power at **Togo Chasm** (p233) and **Talava Arches** (p232)

- Explore the fish-laden **reef pools** (p232) near Matapa Chasm

- Get friendly with Niue's movers and shakers with an essential visit to the **Washaway Café** (p235), the Pacific's only self-service Bar

Talava Arches ★
Ana Mahaga ★ Matapa Chasm

★ Togo Chasm

Snake ★ ★ Washaway Café
Gully

CLIMATE & WHEN TO GO

Niue is best from May to October, when temperatures are lower and there's less rain. The average daytime temperature is 27°C from May to October and 30°C from November to April. December to March is the cyclone season.

November to June is the low season, when you'll find accommodation discounts. The Christmas–New Year period is very busy

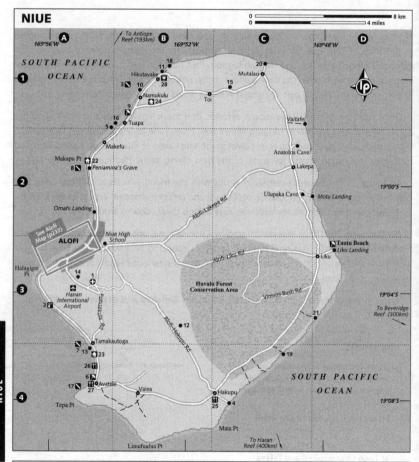

INFORMATION	
Hospital	1 A3
SIGHTS & ACTIVITIES	
Ana Ana Lookout	2 A3
Ana Mahaga	3 B1
Anapala Chasm	4 C4
Avaiki Cave	5 A1
Avatele Beach	6 A4
Channeling	7 A4
Dome	8 A2
Hio Beach	9 B1
Limu Pools	10 B1
Matapa Chasm	11 B1

Misa Kulatea's Nature Walks	12 B3
Niue Dive	13 A4
Niue Golf & Sports Club	14 A3
Niue's Highest Point	15 C1
Palaha Cave	16 B1
Snake Gully	17 A4
Talava Arches	18 B1
Togo Chasm	19 C4
Uluvehi Landing	20 C1
Vaikona Chasm	21 D3

SLEEPING	
Coral Gardens Motel	22 A2
Golden Age Pacific	(see 6)

Matavai Resort	23 A4
Namukulu Motel	24 B1
EATING	
Hakupu Fiafia	
Night	25 C4
Israel Mart	26 A4
Matavai Resort	
Restaurant	(see 23)
Washaway Café	27 A4
DRINKING	
Matapa Bar	28 B1
Sails Bar	(see 22)

with holidaying Niueans returning from New Zealand (NZ), and flights and accommodation should be booked well in advance. Flights and accommodation are also tight during the Constitution Celebrations (see p237) around 19 October.

COSTS & MONEY

New Zealand dollars are used in Niue; stock up before you leave Auckland as there are no ATMs.

Niue is not a budget destination, but it also lacks expensive high-end accommodation. Staying in a guesthouse with shared bathroom facilities and cooking your own meals costs around NZ$80 per day. Motel accommodation with a few restaurant meals will set you back around NZ$160. Staying at the Matavai Resort and dining out all the time is around NZ$300.

HISTORY

Niue's first settlers arrived about 1000 years ago from Samoa and Tonga. European contact began in 1774 when James Cook attempted to land on the island during his second Pacific voyage. Cook left after trying to land three times, and the rebuffed explorer dubbed Niue 'Savage Island'. Niueans insist the islanders' unfriendly reception was simply a robust traditional 'challenge', but the name 'Savage Island' scared off visitors for many years.

In 1846 the London Missionary Society (LMS) secured a Christian presence on Niue through Peniamina, a Niuean who converted to Christianity in Samoa.

In 1900 Niue became a British colony and in 1901 was handed over to NZ. The islanders were not consulted on this imperial mandate, and protested when NZ proposed incorporating Niue with the Cook Islands.

Pressure for self-government began after WWII, but as the island's economy was dependent on NZ aid and family remittances, the Niueans were in no rush to go it alone. In 1974 Niue achieved self-government in 'free association' with NZ, and every three years Niue elects a 20-member legislative assembly. Niue has the dubious record of the world's highest per capita number of politicians – around one MP for every 60 people.

Niueans have held NZ citizenship since 1974 and opportunities offshore have seen the population decline from a 1966 high of 5200. The government claims the current popu-

lation is around 1700. According to islanders, about 1100 is more realistic, down from around 1300 in 2005.

The most serious threat to Niue's survival as an independent state came on 5 January 2004 when Cyclone Heta devastated the island with winds up to 300km/h and sent 30m waves crashing over Niue's cliffs. Many people left Niue permanently after the cyclone, but the island's remaining population is now rebuilding the country through a combination of tourism and low-level agriculture, including the production of *noni* juice and vanilla.

Niue remains heavily dependent on overseas aid, with NZ providing an estimated NZ$20 million per year. Other major donors include Australia and the European Union (EU).

In recent decades, Niue's government has drawn the attention of get-rich-quick investors and other borderline con artists. Wild plans to generate revenue have included quarantining llamas en route from South America to NZ, and welcoming quasi-religious sects from the United States, Malaysian clear-felling logging companies and Chinese resort developers.

In August 2008, local businessman Toke Talagi was elected premier, and at the time of writing was pledging tax reform and an overhaul of Niue's massive 450-person public works employee force.

More than a few locals remain defiantly cynical, and keep an eye on the endless Pacific horizon for the next get-rich-quick snake oil salesman to wash ashore.

THE CULTURE
National Psyche & Lifestyle

Traditional Polynesian values are followed by Niueans. Sunday is a day of rest, and many Niueans go to church both morning and afternoon. Boating is prohibited between

4am and 9pm on a Sunday, ruling out diving or fishing.

Your best bet after a friendly church service is a siesta, a good book or a relaxing swim.

Population

The resident population of around 1100 is complemented by 20,000 Niueans in NZ and 3000 in Australia.

ARTS

Traditionally, Niuean arts are expressed in weaving, and Niuean hats are renowned across the Pacific. The best examples of hat weaving can be seen at the show days held by Niue's 14 villages during the year or during the Constitution Celebrations. Visitors are usually welcome at the weaving mornings held by women in local villages. Enquire at the visitor information centre about what's on.

The Niuean diaspora has produced several well-known identities. Musicians with Niuean ancestry include Che Fu and *How Bizarre* hitmaker Pauly Fuemana from OMC. Niuean-born actor Shimpal Lelisi starred in the NZ film *Sione's Wedding,* and voices the character of Valea in *bro'Town,* an animated TV series he also co-writes.

The best-known artist on Niue is originally from NZ. Mark Cross moved to Niue in 1978 with his wife's family, and his hyper-real paintings capture the edgy beauty of the island. You can see Mark's work online (www .markcross.nu), in the lobby of the Matavai Resort (p235), and at Tahiono Arts (Map p232) in the Commercial Centre in Alofi. Tahiono Arts also showcases work from other local artists, including intricate *tapa* (bark cloth) designed by Kenneth Green.

Literature

Niue, the Island and Its People by S Percy Smith was first published in 1902 and then reprinted in 1983 with the inclusion of period photographs.

Niue's **library** (Map p232; ⏲ 8am-4pm Mon-Fri) is located up a long driveway behind the Niue Primary School in Alofi. Visitors are welcome. Ask for *My Heart is Crying a Little* by Margaret Pointer, the poignant story of the ill-fated decision to incorporate Niuean soldiers into NZ's Maori contingent during WWI, and *Would a Good Man Die?* by Dick Scott, which recounts the 1953

murder of NZ Resident Commissioner Hector Larsen.

Niuean artist John Pule's novels include *The Shark that Ate the Sun* and *Burn My Head in Heaven.*

LANGUAGE

The Niuean language is similar to Tongan, with influences from Samoan and Pukapuka in the Cook Islands. The letter 'g' is pronounced 'ng' as in Samoan. Most people speak English as a second language.

Niuean basics

Hello.	Fakaalofa atu.
Goodbye.	Koe Kia (to one person), Mutolu Kia (two or more people).
How are you?	Malolo nakai a koe?
I'm well (thanks).	Malolo (fakaaue).
Please.	Fakamolemole.
Thank you.	Fakaaue lahi.
Good luck.	Kia monuina.
Eat.	Kai.
Drink.	Inu.
Be careful of *ugas* (coconut crabs) when driving at night.	Fakaholo fakasekiseki he po neke mapela e tau uga.
What time is rush hour?	Hola fiha e tula lavelave?
Yes.	E.
No.	Nakai.

ENVIRONMENT
Geography

Niue is one of the world's largest raised coral atolls, or *makatea*. There are few beaches, no rivers and the coastline is studded with spectacular caves, chasms and ravines. Rainfall percolates easily into the island's porous limestone interior, and an adequate water supply is guaranteed by the huge subterranean water lens.

Niue fringes the Tonga Trench and the ocean drops away rapidly just 50m from the coast. Three reefs are included in Niue's territorial waters – Beveridge, Antiope and Haran.

Wildlife

Birdlife includes *veka* (woodhens), parakeets and white-tailed terns, and native mammals include rats and fruit bats. The two major challenges to native wildlife are feral cats and the devastation caused by Cyclone Heta to the island's trees. Following the cyclone, islanders took to feeding birds and bats tinned

---

BEST EATS

This Pacific social whirl was current at the time of writing, but check with the visitor information centre for the current state of play. For traditional Niuean food, your best bet is Jenna's buffet on a Tuesday night (see below).

- Saturday – Dive into the Matavai Resort's (p236) good-value weekend buffet (NZ$28) from 7pm. Bookings are essential. Get there early for a sunset beer in the Dolphin Bar and spy the resident spinner dolphins and turtles on the reef below.

- Sunday – Drinks at Washaway Café (p235) begin around 4pm. After a focaccia fish sandwich (NZ$12), stop for an ice cream at nearby Israel Mart (p236).

- Tuesday – The Niuean buffet (NZ$28) at Jenna's (p236) starts at 7.30pm. Booking ahead by Monday morning is essential.

- Wednesday – Have a cheap and cheerful curry at Gill's Indian Restaurant (p236) before kicking on for dancing at the Matapa Bar (p236) from 9.30pm.

- Friday – It's Fish & Chips night, and there's the choice of a 6pm start at Jenna's (p236) or a 7pm kick-off at the Matavai Resort (p236).

---

peaches after the trees had been stripped bare by the Grade 5 storm. Vegetation is slowly recovering, but the damage from Cyclone Heta is still evident.

The cyclone also damaged coral reefs, and marine life is now regenerating to normal levels. You'll see tropical fish and striped *katuali* (sea krait) in the waters. These sea snakes are extremely venomous but non-aggressive – you'd basically need to shove a finger down a sea snake's throat for it to bite you.

Small spinner dolphins and whales are found along the coast, and humpback whales migrate north from the Antarctic between June and October to breed in Niue's warm waters.

Ecology

The fisheries of the coastal waters are protected by legislation, and no marine creatures can be taken using scuba equipment. From January to May the *kaloama* (juvenile goatfish) and *atule* (big-eye scad) spawning seasons close certain fishing and swimming spots. Signs are posted.

In the east the Huvalu Forest Conservation Area protects imposing trees, beautiful wildflowers and Niue's enormous coconut crabs, *uga* (oong-a). It's estimated that around 2000 *uga* survive. To preserve their numbers, the export of *uga* is specifically banned when Niuean expats return to NZ during Christmas and New Year. Be careful not run over *uga* on the road when you're driving at night.

ALOFI

Niue's capital stretches languidly for several kilometres along the west coast. Alofi's southern area was badly damaged during Cyclone Heta and abandoned structures punctuate the cliff top.

In central Alofi is **Opaahi Landing** where James Cook attempted, unsuccessfully, to come ashore in 1774. Opposite the police station, the **Utuko sea track** leads to a postcard-sized beach with good snorkelling.

Located further north, opposite the Commercial Centre, is **Tomb Point**, where the graves of two island kings – Tuitoga (r 1867–87) and Fataaiki (r 1888–96) – look out on the island's wharf. Also situated at Tomb Point, Niue's *palagi* history is marked by the 19th-century graves of settlers from the LMS, and the resting place of NZ Resident Commissioner Hector Larsen, who was murdered by escaped prisoners in 1953.

AROUND THE ISLAND

You will need to walk, climb and sometimes swim to see the attractions hugging Niue's perimeter. Rent a car or motorcycle and get exploring. The distances and destinations provided below are in a clockwise direction from the police station in Alofi, taking the 60km coast road. It's a good idea to bring sturdy hiking boots for Niue's sharp coral terrain.

NIUE

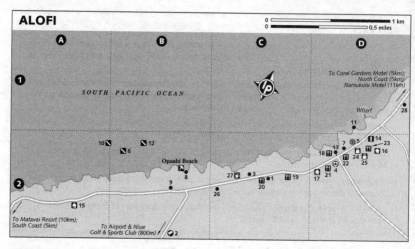

ALOFI

0 ____ 1 km
0 ____ 0.5 miles

SOUTH PACIFIC OCEAN

To Coral Gardens Motel (5km);
North Coast (5km);
Namukulu Motel (11km)

Wharf

Opaahi Beach

To Matavai Resort (10km);
South Coast (5km)

To Airport & Niue
Golf & Sports Club (800m)

Avaiki Cave (7km) is named after the legendary Polynesian homeland and was where Niue's first settlers landed. A narrow gorge leads to a coastal cavern cradling a heavenly rock pool. Swimming is forbidden at Avaiki on a Sunday and when the *kaloama* spawn. **Palaha Cave**, with stalagmites and stalactites, is a further 200m.

At low tide on **Hio Beach** (9.9km) you can walk across the reef about 100m north to a perfect natural aquarium, where a winding chasm features small overhangs and caves. Larger fish are usually in the deeper canyon nearer the reef. Hio is also a popular spot for surfcasting.

At the **Limu Pools** (10.5km) a blurring effect is created with the mixing of cooler spring water and warmer sea water. Unfortunately, the coral was damaged by Cyclone Heta, but marine life is slowly returning, especially in Limu's second pool to the north. There are a few tables and it's a nice place for a picnic.

A turn-off another 1.2km north (11.7km) leads to two attractions. Walk for 15 minutes (approximately 1km) down the right fork to the **Talava Arches**, a labyrinth of caves that were used as covert lookouts to warn of raiders in earlier times. The arches are best visited at low tide; a torch is useful and the caves can be slippery.

It's a steamy trek through exposed coral terraces to the arches, so refresh yourself five minutes down the left fork in the **Matapa Chasm**, the favourite swimming spot of Niue's kings of yesteryear. The chasm is cool and shady, protected from the sun by imposing walls.

Just before the tracks to Talava Arches and Matapa Chasm, a path leads from the village green at Hikutavake down the cliffs to a couple of **reef pools** situated right beside the crashing Pacific. The snorkelling is superb – with occasional sightings of turtles – but don't forget to keep a very close eye on the incoming tide.

NIUE

From Hikutavake follow the road inland past **Niue's highest point** (68m) to Mutalau (18.6km). A sea track leads to the **Uluvehi Landing**, where slave traders kidnapped many Niueans in 1860 to work in the guano mines of Chile. None ever returned.

It's another 15km south along the coast road from Mutalau to the turn-off for **Vaikona Chasm** (33.7km).

Keep an eye out for red trail arrows as you trek for 20 minutes (1km) through the forest and a maze of coral pinnacles to Vaikona Chasm. Descend into the darkness through a sloping cave to the chasm floor. At the near end is a small freshwater pool and further in is a larger pool. Green ferns fringe the pools and an oval of sky peeks through above. It's a magical swim under a wall to the end of the long pool, surfacing in a large dark cave. The brave can continue on through more caves. A mask, snorkel and underwater light are essential.

Walk on to the coast after leaving the chasm but be prudent – the red arrows stop. Identify where you emerge on the cliffs as the landscape looks very similar (see the boxed text, above).

A local guide is essential for exploring Vaikona Chasm. Ring **Willy Saniteli** (☎ 4392) at Fishaway Charters, or see

him at the Washaway Café (p235) on a Sunday afternoon.

The final stretch of the 20-minute walk from the coast road to **Togo Chasm** (36.5km) is through a jagged grove of indigo coral pinnacles. Traverse a long ladder to a compact oasis dotted with palms. Togo (pronounced tong-oh) is like a Middle Eastern dream, but the spell is broken by waves crashing through concealed sea caves.

At Hakupu (40.7km), drive along the sea track and walk a few minutes to **Anapala Chasm**. An uneven series of steps traverses a slim ravine to a freshwater pool. Keep your eyes peeled for *uga* scurrying into the nooks and crannies.

The coast road drops steeply to the sheltered beach at **Avatele** (pronounced ava-sally; 48.6km), where there is good kayaking and swimming. Complete your circuit at **Ana Ana Lookout** (54.3km) for sweeping views along Niue's west coast.

ACTIVITIES

Catch the local *palagi* perspective on the **Hash House Harriers** walk/run on Monday afternoons from 5pm. Ring **Namukulu Motel** (☎ 3001) or ask at the visitor information centre for the week's

---

LOST ON NIUE Tony Wheeler

'What's the most dangerous thing that's ever happened to you?' It's a question I'm frequently asked and, sadly, I have to admit that apart from a few crazy taxi drivers I've never felt my life was in mortal danger. Although there was an occasion on Niue, when a series of dumb decisions got me in real trouble.

I'd parked my car by the roadside and set off to follow the trail past the Vaikona Chasm to the cliffs which drop precipitously into the sea. I was only planning to be gone for half an hour but stupid action number one was not to put my water bottle in my day pack. The trail, marked with red arrows for most of the way, led me to the coast and I clambered along the cliff tops for a couple of hundred metres south.

Dumb decision number two was not to mark where the trail emerged on the coast, for when I came to return I couldn't find it. Rocky cliffs, dramatic sea views, razor-sharp *makatea*, tangled vegetation – it all looked the same. I walked back and forth along the coast trying various likely looking trails back towards the road, but all of them petered out. Eventually I decided the only option was to follow the most likely looking trail as far as it went and then press on until I hit the marked trail or, eventually, the road. I soon found myself clambering up and down jagged gullies and ravines, fighting my way through tangled undergrowth, scratching my legs and arms and getting thirstier by the moment.

An hour later I'd travelled perhaps a hundred metres and had begun to ponder what would happen if I were to fall and break an ankle or leg. Eventually my car would be found and I'd be searched for, but how long would it take to find me? On this knife-edged terrain I began to have visions of bleeding to death before I died of dehydration. Of course, I did eventually find my way out, although back at the hotel I tossed my shoes straight in the bin – they'd been cut to ribbons on the jagged rocks.

location. Visitors are also welcome at the **Niue Golf & Sports Club** (Map p228), which has a compact nine-hole golf course and tennis courts.

Try **mountain biking** on Niue's forest tracks. The Rally of the Rock is an annual mountain bike rally held in early May. See www.mark cross.nu for details.

Diving

Niue Dive (Map p228; ☎ 4311; www.dive.nu) runs two-dive trips for NZ$140. Renting a complete set of up-to-date and well-maintained equipment pushes the cost to NZ$170. A four-day open-water course is NZ$650. There is no decompression chamber on Niue, and you'll need to schedule dives to fit in with your return flight to Auckland on a Saturday night.

See p76 for details of Niue's diving highlights, including the **Dome** under-island cave system (Map p228), **Ana Mahaga** (Twin Caves; Map p228), the combination dives of **Egypt** (Map p232) and **Tunnel Vision** (Map p232), and **The Chimney** (Map p232). Expect visibility up to 50m, especially during the May to October dry season. The water temperature is warm, peaking at 29°C in January and falling to 25°C in August.

Channeling (Map p228) is the place to see tropical fish, starting at brain coral 30m deep and meandering through winding channels to the shallows. Off Avatele is **Snake Gully** (Map p228), filled with a writhing mass of sea snakes. The surface of the water is punctuated by snakes poking through to breathe. Painted crayfish fill a nearby cavern, and morays, turtles and porcupine puffer fish are also sighted.

Snorkelling

The lagoon at **Avatele** (Map p228) has excellent marine life and is best on a calm day with an incoming tide. Beyond the lagoon the channel is dangerous. Beginners will enjoy the **Utuko Reef** (Map p232) in Alofi and the delightful reef pools at **Hio Beach** (p232). Further north at **Matapa** (p232) a pair of giant natural pools are uncovered at low tide on the edge of the reef. Be careful, as the Pacific breakers crash metres away. Since Cyclone Heta there is less marine life at **Limu Pools** (p232) but the coral is slowly regenerating.

Around the island there are places to snorkel outside the reef, but they should only be attempted by confident swimmers. Always seek local advice about entry points and

water conditions before venturing offshore. **Niue Dive** (Map p228; ☎ 4311; www.dive.nu) operates snorkelling trips (adult/child NZ$40/25) to sites around the island, including Snake Gully. You can also swim and snorkel with spinner dolphins (adult/child NZ$50/35; open April to December) and humpback whales (adult/child NZ$90/70; open June to October).

Fishing

Wahoo, tuna and *mahimahi* (dolphin fish) are abundant. **Nu Tours** (☎ 4365; nutours@niue.nu; 4hr trips NZ$280) operates fishing trips for one to two people with all safety and fishing gear provided. Fish with **Fishaway Charters** (☎ 4392; sarah@niue.nu; 4hr trips NZ$250) and you can personally barbecue your catch at the Washaway Café (opposite).

Kayaking

Explore beyond Niue's reef with **Kayak Niue** (☎ 4224, after hours 4097; www.kayakniue.nu; 3hr guided tours NZ$60). Guide-yourself 'freedom rentals' are NZ$20 per hour. Ask for Meshu at the visitor information centre. Kayaking is limited to travellers 16 years and older.

NIUE FOR CHILDREN

Niue is the Pacific's best action-packed solution to getting the kids away from a computer. Mountain biking on the sea tracks is spectacular, and biking in the forest and through the villages is an easygoing alternative. There is safe snorkelling in the natural aquariums at **Limu Pools** (p232) and **Matapa Chasm** (p232), and fans of fantasy novels can fire their imagination as they clamber through the caverns at **Talava Arches** (p232) and **Vaikona Chasm** (p233).

As the climbing can be quite rugged, Niue is best suited to older children with a good sense of balance and adventure. Sturdy footwear is essential. Check out the **tours** (below) offered by Misa Kulatea (nature walks) and Herman Tagaloailuga (reef walks). Note that Misa's tour is not recommended for children aged under eight. Kids of all ages will enjoy an outing in a glass-bottom boat.

A pleasant **playground** (Map p232) in memory of a mother and son killed during Cyclone Heta sits atop the cliffs in Alofi South.

TOURS

Herman Tagaloailuga (☎ 3016) is Niue's leading conchologist, or shell expert, and takes visitors on reef walks (NZ$45). **Misa Kulatea** (Map p228; ☎ 4381) conducts nature walks in the forest, explaining traditional Niuean customs. Misa's tours can be booked through the visitor information centre. They require a minimum of two people and cost NZ$45 for adults. Children aged 16 and under pay NZ$1 per year of age. On demand Misa can also guide explorations of Niue's many cave systems.

Hunting at night for *uga* is a lot of rugged fun amid the sharp coral of the forest. Contact **Willy Saniteli** (☎ 4392; sarah@niue.nu), owner of the Washaway Café, to organise late-night *uga* hunting and baiting deep in the forest. Willy's also the man to see if you're looking to explore the challenging Vaikona Chasm (p233).

For a more leisurely *uga* experience, contact **Ane** (☎ 3503; per person NZ$25; ☼ 4pm Mon-Fri by arrangement) in the village of Liku.

Alofi Rentals (Map p232; ☎ 4017; www.alofirentals .nu) offers two-hour glass-bottom boat trips (adult/child NZ$45/25). For a round-the-island experience by road, **Island Style Tours** (☎ 4246; 3hr tour NZ$55) runs the Circle Island Tour. **Nu Tours** (☎ 4365; nutours@niue.nu) operates two-hour reef cruises (NZ$120).

Bookings for all tours can be made at the visitor information centre.

SLEEPING

Niue's accommodation options are divided by geography. The upmarket Matavai Resort sits in the southwest above one of Niue's best reefs. Budget and midrange guesthouses cluster in Alofi. Sunset-friendly motels fringe the northwest coast. Apart from the Matavai Resort, accommodation includes kitchen facilities, often on a shared basis in the cheaper places. See www.niueisland.com for details of special packages combining accommodation and flights.

Following the 2008 Pacific Islands Leaders Forum, several renovated local houses are now available for rent. See www.niueisland.com.

Kololi's Guesthouse (Map p232; ☎ 4258; rupina@niue .nu; s/d NZ$40/50, d with bathroom NZ$65, 2-bedroom units NZ$110; ☒ ☐) Centrally located in the heart of Alofi, Kololi's is clustered around a spacious and private lawn. There's a communal kitchen and laundry, a TV and DVD room, and newly installed wi-fi access.

Peleni's Guesthouse (Map p232; ☎ 4153; pelenis guesthouse@niue.nu; s/d NZ$50/60, house NZ$170; ☒) Take one room with shared facilities, or go

island crazy and rent the whole house. It's a short early-morning stroll to market on a Tuesday or Friday, and Alofi's restaurants are nearby, so family-run Peleni's is good if you lack private transport.

Golden Age Pacific (Map p232 & Map p228; www.gold enagepacific.co.nz; units NZ$110) Two refurbished local houses have all mod cons including wi-fi and DVD players. The house near Avatele is good for couples, while the larger complex near Alofi is ideal for groups and families.

Coral Gardens Motel (Map p228; ☎ 4235; www.coral gardens.nu; units NZ$120; ☒ ☐) Five self-contained units shrouded in shady glades skirt the cliff top 5km north of Alofi. It's a handy place for sunsets, whale-watching and discovering essential local gossip at Sails Bar. Negotiate a ladder to swim in a spectacular natural pool at the base of the property.

our pick Namukulu Motel (Map p228; ☎ 3001; www.namukulu-motel.nu; units NZ$130; ☒) Cyclone Heta forced friendly Kiwis Robyn and Joe Wright to relocate up the hill to a shady mango grove with great views along Niue's west coast. Three spacious bungalows, each with a double bed, two single beds and fully equipped kitchen, cluster near a swimming pool with picnic tables and a barbecue. Take a chilled beer to their cliff-top eyrie and look for humpback whales cruising by.

Matavai Resort (Map p228; ☎ 4360; matavai@niue .nu; r with ceiling fan/air-con NZ$188/232; ☒ ☒ ☐ ☒) Niue's premier resort has a restaurant, two bars and two swimming pools cascading to a reef with turtles and dolphins. All rooms have a veranda and include a fridge and ISD phone. Use of mountain bikes and golf clubs is free.

EATING & DRINKING

Niue's limited dining scene is relatively expensive. From Monday to Friday a few places open for lunch. At the weekend, especially on Sunday, options are more restricted. Booking ahead is strongly recommended, especially in the evening and during the low season from November to June. In recent times, restaurants have been working together to ensure at least one place is open most nights. See p231 for the Best Eats.

our pick Washaway Café (Map p228; ☎ 4822; meals NZ$12; ☼ from 11am Sun) Share a beer with the New Zealand High Commissioner, the Niuean police chief and assorted yachties at this relaxed spot right on Avatele Beach. It's the self-proclaimed only 'self-service bar in the Pacific', so help yourself to drinks and settle the bill with owner Willy at the end of the night. Don't forget to order a tasty fish focaccia sandwich or one of the biggest burgers either side of the International Date Line. Washaway is open until the last customer reluctantly leaves.

Gill's Indian Restaurant (Map p232; ☎ 4180; meals NZ$16; ⏰ 11am-9pm Mon-Fri, 5-9pm Sat & Sun) The back-to-basics Gill's is great for indecisive diners. Beef, chicken or lamb curry? With roti or rice? Grab a cold beer – an easy decision – and you're sorted. Gill's is also a popular takeaway option.

Crazy Uga Café (Map p232; ☎ 1277; meals NZ$10-20; ⏰ 9am-2pm Mon-Fri & 9am-noon Sat) Perched above the tide surging onto Utuko Reef, the Crazy Uga offers the best start to a new day; choose between 'the Big Uga' and 'the Little Uga' breakfast. Throughout the rest of the day a friendly team turns out panini sandwiches, tasty homemade pies and Niue's best coffee.

Jenna's Café (Map p232; ☎ 4316; meals NZ$16-28; ⏰ 6-9pm Fri-Sat, buffet from 7.30pm Tue) Originally an all-day café, Jenna's now focuses on Fish & Chips night on Friday and Saturday, and a popular Niuean Buffet ($28) on Tuesday night. Maybe get fish and chips to go and cross the road to admire the sea views. Booking ahead for the Tuesday buffet is essential.

Falala Fa (Map p232; ☎ 4697; meals NZ$20-30; ⏰ 11am-2pm & 6-9pm Tue, Wed & Fri, 5-10pm Sat) Literally meaning 'Four Sisters', Falala Fa is a buzzy venue with a well-stocked bar and a great line in local fish. Opening hours can be haphazard, so always phone to make a dinner booking. Service can be aloof and slow, but the food is (eventually) the island's best.

Matavai Resort Restaurant (Map p228; ☎ 4360; meals NZ$20-30; ⏰ noon-9pm) The Matavai has a Fish & Chips night on Friday, a good-value Niuean barbecue buffet on Saturday and OK à la carte servings for the rest of the week. Park yourself outside with a cold one to watch sunset on the world's biggest horizon. Bookings are essential.

Hakupu Fiafia Night (Map p228; ☎ 4381; per person NZ$40) At the time of writing, a weekly village *fiafia* (dance) night was being planned for the village of Hakupu, with food including island specialities such as *ota* (marinated raw fish) and *uga*. Ask at the visitor information centre for the current state of play.

Israel Mart (Map p228; ☎ 4844; ⏰ 2-9pm Mon-Fri, 4-9pm Sun) Israeli owner Avi serves Niue's best

range of ice cream (16 flavours). He also has more than 4000 rental DVDs, including surprisingly up-to-date new releases.

Many visitors choose self-catering, but don't bring fresh food to Niue as it will be subject to quarantine regulations. Alofi's **supermarket** (Map p232; ☎ 4306; ⏰ 8am-5pm Mon-Fri) has a moderate range of canned goods and basic groceries. Fruit and vegetables are best obtained at the weekly **market** (Map p232; ⏰ 6-11am Tue & Fri) or an expanding range of places selling organic produce. There are usually fresh lettuces and tomatoes available at the **Central Services petrol station** (Map p232; Alofi South).

In season, most accommodation owners provide fresh fruit for breakfast, including papaya, mango and bananas.

Buy fresh spices, meats and cheeses at the **Double M Butchery** (Map p232; ☎ 4139; ⏰ 8.30am-4.30pm Mon-Fri, 4-7.30pm Sat) in Alofi's Commercial Centre. For fresh fish, including tuna and *mahimahi*, give Avi a call at Israel Mart (see left). To buy fresh or cooked *uga*, contact **Ane** (☎ 3503). Niue's huge crabs are available by order on Tuesday and Wednesday afternoons. Expect to pay around NZ$40 per crab.

In the evenings, quench your Pacific thirst at local hangouts, the **Pacific Way Bar** (Map p232; Alofi South) or the **Matapa Bar** (Map p228; Matapa Chasm), or head to **Sails Bar** (Map p228; Coral Gardens Motel) for a *palagi* perspective. Wednesday is the busiest night at Sails, when the guitars and old songs usually come out about 6.30pm.

Visitors can purchase duty-free beer, wine and spirits up to four working days after arriving on Niue at the Customs & Bond Store, behind the Commercial Centre in Alofi. If you're bringing duty-free beer or liquor from NZ, note that for recycling reasons, only canned beer is allowed into Niue.

NIUE DIRECTORY

BUSINESS HOURS

Shops open from 9am to 4pm Monday to Friday. At weekends some smaller village shops open for basic groceries, usually for a three-hour period in the morning and afternoon.

FESTIVALS & EVENTS

The Constitution Celebrations around 19 October mark Niue's independence. Visitors are often invited to the premier's cocktail party at the Matavai Resort. The celebrations include singing, dancing, sports events and handicraft displays. The Monday of the celebrations is Peniamina Day, celebrating the arrival of Christianity in 1846.

Each of Niue's 14 villages usually has a show day during the year. In recent years, the island's population decline has seen some smaller villages cancel their annual shindigs.

See www.niueisland.com for show day timing and p629 for details of regional public holidays.

INTERNET ACCESS

Niue has a progressive Internet policy with free wi-fi access. Coverage is still patchy and the speed can be slow, so park yourself at the Crazy Uga Café (opposite) with your laptop and a coffee. Yachties can usually access the wi-fi network if moored near Alofi. Internet access is available at **RockET Systems** (Map p232; per 30min NZ$4.50; ✆ 9am-3pm Mon-Fri) opposite the Commercial Centre. In 2008, the government supplied low-cost laptops to all school children, a countrywide world first.

INTERNET RESOURCES

Connecting Niueans (www.niuean.com) Community portal to link Niueans across the globe – check out the busy online chat rooms to tap into current issues.
Mark Cross (www.markcross.nu) The homepage for artist Mark Cross includes quirky journals detailing life on 'The Rock'.

Niue Tourism Office (www.niueisland.com) Comprehensive resource for pre-trip planning. Also includes online booking for accommodation.

Niue's .nu domain is used by 160,000 Internet users internationally, including a high percentage in Sweden where 'nu' translates to 'now'.

MAPS

The free Jasons South Pacific Passport map of Niue is available at the airport and at the visitor information centre in Alofi.

MEDICAL SERVICES

Niue's new **hospital** (Map p228; ✆ 4100; ✆ 8am-4pm Mon-Fri, 9-10am & 7-8pm Sat & Sun) opened in 2006 near the airport.

MONEY

NZ dollars are used on Niue (for exchange rates, see the Quick Reference page). **Bank South Pacific** (Map p232; ✆ 4221; Commercial Centre; ✆ 9am-3pm Mon-Fri) changes travellers cheques and exchanges foreign currency, but stock up on NZ dollars before you leave Auckland. Cash advances are available on Visa only for a 3.5% commission and a NZ$10 fee. Avoid visiting the bank on a Tuesday as this is the regular payday for Niue's significant government workforce. There is a Western Union office in the bank.

Note that at the time of writing, only Visa credit cards could be used at more expensive accommodation, car-rental agencies and at Niue Dive. Check online at www.niueisland.com to see if Mastercard and American Express have been reinstated for use on Niue.

HOW MUCH?

- **Organic vanilla pods at Alofi market:** NZ$5

- **Snorkelling gear rental:** NZ$5 per day

- **Mountain bike rental:** NZ$10 per day

- **Can of beer at the Matavai Resort:** NZ$5

- **Can of beer at the Customs & Bond Store:** NZ$2

- **1L petrol:** NZ$2.30

- **600mL bottled water:** NZ$3

- **Can of Steinlager beer:** NZ$3

- **Souvenir T-shirt:** NZ$30

- **Coconut porridge from Alofi market:** NZ$3

Cash is vital at all other businesses and there are no ATMs on the island.

POST

Niue's post office is in Alofi's Commercial Centre. Niuean stamps and handmade postcards and greeting cards are available.

TELEPHONE

Niue's **Telecom office** (⊙ 24hr) is in the Commercial Centre. Peak-rate calls cost NZ$1.60 per minute to NZ, NZ$2.30 to Australia, and NZ$4.20 to North America or Europe. The international access code is ☎ 00. Phonecards are not available and there is no mobile phone service on Niue. Relaxing never came so mandatory.

TIME

Niue is 11 hours behind GMT. When it is noon in Niue it is 3pm in Los Angeles, 11pm in London and 11am in Auckland the following day. Daylight saving time is not adopted.

TOURIST INFORMATION

The **Niue Visitor Information Centre** (Map p232; ☎ 4224; www.niueisland.com; Alofi Commercial Centre; PO Box 42, Alofi) is in Alofi.

Overseas offices:

Australia (☎ 1300 136 483; niuetourism@bigpond.com .au; Level 3/313 Burwood Rd, Hawthorn 3122)

NZ (☎ 09-585 1493; niuetourism@clear.net.nz; PO Box 68716, Newton, Auckland)

TRAVEL AGENCIES

Peleni's Travel Agency (Map p232; ☎ 4317; pelenis travel@niue.nu; Alofi South)

VISAS

There are no visa requirements for stays of less than 30 days, as long as you have 'sufficient funds' and an onward ticket.

TRANSPORT IN NIUE

GETTING THERE & AWAY
Air

Air New Zealand (www.airnewzealand.com) operates a direct flight, departing from Auckland on Sunday morning, and arriving in Niue on Saturday afternoon after crossing the International Date Line. Return flights leave Niue one hour after landing and arrive back in Auckland on Saturday night. Book online or through Peleni's Travel Agency (above). Return fares begin at around NZ$620, but increase sharply with demand. Try and book as early as possible.

If you are planning to travel in the Christmas–New Year period, book well ahead as Niueans living in NZ return en masse for the holiday season.

Sea

No regular passenger ships service Niue, but several cruise ships visit annually.

Most yachts visit from April to December, away from the cyclone season. There is no accessible pier on the island, but the **Niue Yacht Club** (☎ 4017; www.niueyachtclub.com) has 14 well-maintained moorings available. Harbour fees are NZ$10 per day per yacht. Yachts should aim to arrive on weekdays.

GETTING AROUND
To/From the Airport

Hanan International Airport (Map p228) is 2km southeast of Alofi. Accommodation places usually include free airport transfers at no charge. A taxi is around NZ$20.

DEPARTURE TAX

A departure tax of NZ$30 is charged for all travellers 12 years and older. Yachties are also subject to the departure tax.

Bicycle

Niue's gentle roads and forest tracks are ideal for cycling. Mountain bikes are available for hire from most accommodation places or Alofi Rentals (below) for around NZ$10 per day.

Car & Motorcycle

Niue has no public transport system. Hire a vehicle with two wheels or four wheels from **Alofi Rentals** (Map p232; ☎ 4017; www.alofirentals.nu) or **Niue Rentals** (Map p232; ☎ 4216; www.niuerentals.nu). Plenty are available, but book ahead for Christmas/New Year or the Constitution Celebrations. Weekly rates are around NZ$250 per week for cars and NZ$150 for motorcycles.

Driving is conservative. Your biggest worry will be straining your fingers as you acknowledge *every* oncoming vehicle with a little wave. Driving is on the left-hand side of the road; the speed limit is 40km/h in the villages and 60km/h out of town. Present your regular driver's licence to the police in Alofi, and for NZ$10 you'll receive a colourful palm tree–covered local licence.

Note that the Niuean police are serious about enforcing drink driving laws and that insurance for rental cars is not available on the island.

Taxi

Taxis are available from **Alofi Rentals** (☎ 4017).

Pitcairn Island

What's rarely mentioned about Pitcairn Island, between the infamous *Bounty* story and the 2004 sex trials gossip, is that it's a place of incredible natural beauty. The island's 4.5 sq km surface is almost entirely sloped and has a varied landscape – from desolate rock cliffs that look over an infinite expanse of sea to lush hillsides bursting in tropical plenty. As one of the most remote destinations on the planet, as well as the smallest territory in the world, the island feels both claustrophobic and wildly exhilarating. After a few days of hiking, exploring and meeting the local characters, it's not hard to understand why the islanders love it here and have been through so many hardships (from extreme isolation to scalding worldwide press) to stay here.

The nearest inhabited island to Pitcairn Island is Mangareva in French Polynesia which is 480km, about a 36-hour boat ride, away. Besides a few hundred cruise ship passengers per year (who often only spend an hour or two on Pitcairn when the ship passes), the only visitors are a few yachts, occasional groups of boat-chartering birders and a handful of ham radio enthusiasts.

The archipelago consists of two low-lying atolls, Oeno and Ducie, World Heritage–listed Henderson Island – a *makatea* (raised coral island) with a virtually untouched environment and endemic birdlife – and Pitcairn itself, which is the only inhabited island.

HIGHLIGHTS

- Taking a cool dip in the electric blue, glass-clear waters of **St Paul's Pool** (p245)
- Climbing up the precipice to **Christian's Cave** (p245) and imagining what must have gone through the mutineer's head as he sat there hundreds of years ago
- Mingling with the locals on Friday nights at **Christian's Café** (p246)
- Watching a flightless Henderson rail trundle by as you relax on the mosquito-free shores of **Henderson Island** (p248)
- Descending the cliff at Down Rope to fish off Pitcairn's only beach and inspect the **petroglyphs** (p245), reminders of Pitcairn's pre-European history

Henderson Island
★

★ Pitcairn Island

PITCAIRN ISLAND GROUP

0 ⊏⊏⊏⊏⊏ 200 km
0 ⊏⊏⊏⊏⊏ 120 miles

130°W   *SOUTH PACIFIC*   126°W

OCEAN

Oeno
Island

To Mangareva
(450km)

See Henderson
Island Map (p249)

25°S   See Pitcairn
Island Map (p244)

Ducie
Atoll

PITCAIRN ISLAND FACTS

Capital city (and island) Adamstown (Pitcairn)
Population 50
Land area 4.5 sq km
Number of islands four
International telephone code ☎ 64
Currency NZ dollar (NZ$; official); US dollar (US$;
for tourist goods and services)
Languages English and Pitkern
Greeting Wat a way
Website www.government.pn & visitpitcairn.gov.pn

CLIMATE & WHEN TO GO

Pitcairn's climate is mild and equable, with mean monthly temperatures varying from 19°C in August to 24°C in February. The lowest temperature ever recorded was 10°C; the highest, 34°C. Annual rainfall (around 2000mm) is spread unevenly, but July and August are usually the driest months and November the wettest.

HISTORY

The islands of the Pitcairn group have always had a close connection with Mangareva in the Gambier Archipelago (p472), and at one time a Polynesian trading triangle operated between Mangareva, Pitcairn and Henderson. Pitcairn had the only quarry in this part of Polynesia where flakes could be chipped off the sharp-edged stones to make adzes and other tools. Inhospitable Henderson Island's small population supplied red tropicbird feathers, green turtles and other 'luxury' goods.

Overpopulation devastated Mangareva, and deforestation removed the trees used for making the great seagoing canoes. In a classic example of the flow-on effect of ecological disasters, the downfall of Mangareva led to the abandonment of both Henderson and Pitcairn.

When the explorer Pedro Fernández de Quirós chanced upon Henderson Island in 1606 it was uninhabited, which was presumably the case for Pitcairn Island also.

The four Pitcairn islands would probably have been annexed by the French, along with the Tuamotu and Gambier islands, were it not for the British settlement founded by the *Bounty* mutineers. For more on Pitcairn Island's history, see p243; for Henderson Island's history, see p248.

The Pitcairn Island group is Britain's last overseas territory in the Pacific. The governor, who is also the British high commissioner to New Zealand (NZ), lives in Wellington.

Prior to the sex trial (see p242), the island was governed at arm's length. The governor now has a representative in residence. At a local level, the Island Council consists of a mayor plus appointed and elected members, and tends to local matters including island maintenance, shipping arrivals, communications and medical services.

THE CULTURE

Pitcairn's families are descendants of the original *Bounty* mutineers and their Tahitian companions, plus other arrivals over the years. The island's extraordinarily remote nature means Pitcairners have forged a distinct language and culture. The isolated community is extremely close-knit and its gossipy and clan-like nature has been called 'claustrophobically intimate' by Kathy Marks in her 2008 book *Pitcairn: A Paradise Lost*, and was even more criticised by Dea Burkett in her 1997 travel memoir *Serpent in Paradise*. After all the bad press, the islanders have become very protective of their unusual way of life and generally do not welcome journalists. With a population that hovers around 50 – about half the number considered necessary to remain viable – it's been questioned by outsiders if the culture will survive.

Self-reliance is a way of life on Pitcairn, so when the longboats (see p247) crash through the waves from Bounty Bay to rendezvous with visiting ships, everyone's at quayside to help unload. It's not somewhere you can go it alone – community spirit is all-important. It's only by sticking together that Pitcairners have survived on this isolated outpost for so long.

Farming, fishing and shooting breadfruit from trees are everyday activities for much of the community, as are fixing machinery

PITCAIRN ISLAND

PITCAIRN'S FUTURE

Tiny Pitcairn hit world headlines due to the drama of seven men charged with a string of sex offences, including rape and indecent assault, on young girls. Beyond the seven men charged, nearly all the men on the island (going back as far as three generations) were implicated and some of the charges (later dropped) involved girls as young as three years old.

During trials held from October 2004, six of the men, which included most of the heads of the community, were found guilty. The convicted received sentences ranging from community service to six years' jail. However, jail sentences (which were in a comfortable Pitcairn building that the convicts built themselves) were soon reduced to home detention, and by the end of 2008 the only remaining prisoner was expected to be put on house arrest as well. Because of the shortage of manpower on the island, all of the convicts are called on when there is work to be done (that requires their skills) – so essentially very little prison time is served. Most of the convicted have not admitted to or apologised for their alleged crimes.

In the meantime, life on Pitcairn has changed irrevocably. Deep within the closest-knit society imaginable, sisters, daughters and wives were pitted against uncles, fathers and brothers and, just as often, each other. Pitcairn's women overwhelmingly sided with their men and the family members who did testify are generally considered traitors to their island. Many Pitcairners argue that sex around age 12 was normal and consensual for girls on the island, thus no crimes were actually committed.

The silver lining to these fissures is that centuries of sexual abuse may have stopped. Jaqui Christian who testified in the trials and has now bravely moved back to the island in the hope of helping her homeland get back on its feet says, 'The main thing that's changed is that people now know that crime will be punished'. While the convicted sex offenders weren't given strict sentences, the island itself, with the eyes of the world looking critically upon it, has felt the repercussions.

Another huge change is that the UK government has sent over a whole crew of non-locals to aid the community, including a family community advisor, a doctor, the UK Governor's representative, a community constable and a school teacher. Outsiders inundated the island during the trials, outnumbering the local adult population for the first time in Pitcairn's history. The new arrivals aren't as self-sufficient as the locals and need to buy food and services. As a result a few locals are starting businesses such as a hair salon and a bakery, and there's now a fortnightly market where everyone can sell their specialty foodstuffs as well as a hotch potch of goods. Jaqui Christian plans on opening a cafe. She says: 'The future of Pitcairn is in specialisation. Where families used to be self-sufficient the community is evolving to have jobs and businesses, and not everyone will have time to farm'. Some islanders are worried about the changes that all the outsiders could bring but most welcome whatever it takes that will allow them to continue living on their island. Pitcairn Commissioner Leslie Jacques has stated that the aim is to lift the population to 100. Islanders hope the population gap will be filled by expat Pitcairners lured back home by new opportunities.

Since 2000, financial aid from the British Government has amounted to around NZ$50 million, which will see to the building of a new jetty on the opposite side of the island from Bounty Bay and a sealed road from it to Adamstown. There's now a pristine museum, a renovated landing at Bounty Bay and the island's main access road has been sealed. Funding has been approved to establish wind power to provide 24-hour electricity; at present, the island's generator is turned on for just 10 hours per day. Satellite connections are in place and there's inexpensive telephone, internet and TV in nearly every home. Apiculture (bee keeping) has been under way for quite some time, and the island's honey is revered as one of the world's purest. The plan is to boost annual production to 20,000 jars. The island has a new medical centre and even a dentist's chair. The jail, when no longer in use, may well become an eco-tourist lodge. There was talk of an airstrip, but it's been deemed non-cost effective.

Small jobs (70 in all and divided between about 35 able bodies), such as managing the store, working at the post office or manning the meteorological station, are all subsidised by the UK and allow folks to have a small but regular income. Essential trips to NZ (mostly for medical procedures) are also paid for and fuel, health and other essentials are all subsidised. While rumours circulate around the island that the British Government would like nothing more than to be rid of this tiny speck of an expensive place, the islanders are not going to give it up any time soon.

and homes. Most islanders hold government jobs (see opposite), though most income is derived from producing woodcarvings, woven baskets, honey and the island's famous stamps to sell to passengers on passing ships (and by mail order at www.lareau.org/pitc mall.html or through islander's individual websites found on http://groups.yahoo.com /group/FRIENDSofPITCAIRN). Furthermore, it's domain name (.pn) has provided a good income generator for the island.

RELIGION

In 1887 a Seventh-Day Adventist missionary from the US converted the whole island, so Saturday is observed as the Sabbath. Nowadays very few people follow the other 'rules', and shellfish and all edible kinds of fish are eaten and nearly everyone drinks alcohol (although you need a US$25 per year permit to do so). On average Adamstown's Saturday **church** service draws in a crowd of five or six people, about 10% of the population. Unlike most of Polynesia there are no pigs on the island due to Seventh-Day Adventism prohibiting its followers from eating pork.

LANGUAGE

Pitcairners communicate quite happily in English, but among themselves they lapse into Pitkern (18th-century seafaring English spiced with Polynesian words). So if someone asks their neighbour to dinner, they'd say 'yourley come eit a weckle?' and you might get asked 'bout yu gwen?' (where are you going?). In either English or Pitkern they love to curse but contain themselves politely with new visitors.

ENVIRONMENT

The four islands of the Pitcairn group, essentially outliers of the Tuamotu and Gambier islands of French Polynesia, comprise 43 sq km of land scattered over a vast tract of ocean; it's more than 600km from Oeno Island in the west to Ducie Atoll in the east.

Tiny Pitcairn is a high island – the tip of a mountain rising out of the sea – with hardly any fringing reef. This very fertile lump of rock has only one rocky beach, but what it lacks in sand it more than makes up for with dramatic cliffs which have been the down-

fall of more than one islander (see the boxed text, p248).

Oeno and Ducie are classic atolls, a scattering of low-lying sandy islets on a coral reef fringing a central lagoon. Henderson, the largest island in the group, is a *makatea* island, an ancient coral reef pushed up above sea level by geological forces.

PITCAIRN ISLAND

pop 50 / 4.5 sq km

Visitors to Pitcairn aren't asked by islanders what they've seen or done on the island, they're asked who they've met. While the precarious landscape of volcanic rock and fertile red earth surrounded by the indigo sea is enough to make any jaw drop, it's the people and their odd English–Polynesian culture who have stolen the show since they arrived back in the late 18th century. Go see Carol and Jay Warren if you're interested in flora and fauna, Betty Christian bakes the best cakes and Brenda Christian likes to take folks fishing at Down Rope, the island's only beach. Len Brown is the most respected carver on the island and Pawl Warren keeps tabs on Mrs T, the resident Galapagos tortoise, and can usually help you find her. If you want a stiff drink, hip music and maybe a movie on a plasma-screen TV, go see Andrew Christian up on the ridge. Anywhere you go, you're told, just walk on in, everybody does.

Just arriving to the island is an adventure where, after a day and a half or more at sea, you're met by a longboat usually filled with about half the population to greet you. If the sea is rough you'll have to literally dive off the side of your boat and into the arms of some pirate-looking local in the longboat. Then it's off to Bounty Bay's newly restored jetty. Next hop on a quad bike up the accurately named Hill of Difficulty, the steep trail that leads up to the island's only settlement, Adamstown; in 2005 this mud track made history by becoming Pitcairn's first paved road. Adamstown is perched 120m above the sea on the Edge. Houses here are either 'upside' or 'downside' of the main road through the small settlement.

HISTORY

It is believed there was a Polynesian settlement on the island between the 12th and 15th centuries, and perhaps an earlier settlement as many as 2000 years before that. As the mutineers

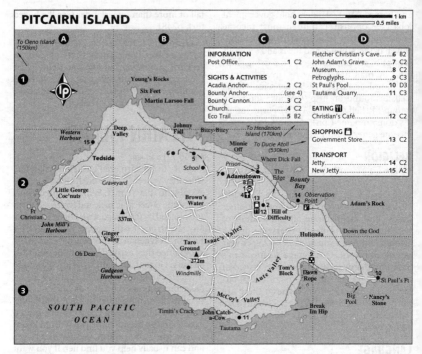

PITCAIRN ISLAND

0 _____ 1 km
0 _____ 0.5 miles

INFORMATION
Post Office...........................1 C2

SIGHTS & ACTIVITIES
Acadia Anchor.....................2 C2
Bounty Anchor.................(see 4)
Bounty Cannon...................3 C2
Church................................4 C2
Eco Trail.............................5 B2

Fletcher Christian's Cave......6 B2
John Adam's Grave...............7 C2
Museum...............................8 C2
Petroglyphs..........................9 C3
St Paul's Pool......................10 D3
Tautama Quarry..................11 C3

EATING
Christian's Café...................12 C2

SHOPPING
Government Store................13 C2

TRANSPORT
Jetty..................................14 C2
New Jetty...........................15 A2

To Oeno Island (150km)

Young's Rocks
Six Feet
Martin Larsoo Fall

Western Harbour
Deep Valley
Johnny Fall
Bitey-Bitey
To Henderson Island (170km)

Minnie Off
To Ducie Atoll (530km)
Where Dick Fall

Tedside
School
Prison
Adamstown
The Edge
Bounty Bay

Graveyard
Little George Coc'nuts
Brown's Water
Observation Point
Adam's Rock

Pt Christian
John Mill's Harbour
337m
Hill of Difficulty
Down the God

Ginger Valley
Oh Dear
Taro Ground
272m
Isaac's Valley
Hollanda

Gudgeon Harbour
Windmills
Aute Valley
Tom's Block
Dawn Rope
St Paul's Pt

SOUTH PACIFIC OCEAN
Timiti's Crack
McCoy's Valley
John Catch-a-Cow
Tautama
Break Im Hip
Big Pool
Nancy's Stone

were to prove, small though it was, Pitcairn provided all the basic necessities of life.

In 1767 Philip Carteret sailed by on HMS *Swallow* and named the island after Major Pitcairn of the marines. Finding it was one thing – Carteret was unable to land and his mischarting of the island by 300km made relocating it a problem.

In January 1790 the *Bounty* mutineers arrived on inhospitable Pitcairn after a long search for a remote hideaway, far from the long arm of British naval justice and almost certain death at the gallows. Led by Fletcher Christian, the party was made up of eight other mutineers, six Tahitian men, 12 Tahitian women and a child. Once they were settled on the island the *Bounty* was burnt (both to prevent escape and to avoid detection), but their island community proved to be anything but a safe haven. Chaos and bloodshed ruled the first years, largely due to the English mutineers' slavelike treatment of the Polynesian men. Things escalated when a mutineer demanded that one of the Tahitians give up his wife, following the death of the mutineer's partner in a fall. A cycle

of murder and revenge commenced, and by 1794 all six Tahitian men and five of the nine mutineers, including Fletcher Christian, had been killed. Only Young, Adams, Quintal and McCoy survived.

The few peaceful years that followed were brought to an end when McCoy discovered how to produce a killer spirit from the roots of the *ti* plant. By 1799, under the influence of the drink, McCoy had thrown himself into the sea with a rock tied around his neck and Quintal had become so crazed under the drink's influence that Adams and Young killed him in self-defence. A year later Young died of asthma, leaving John Adams as the sole survivor of the 15 men who had arrived a decade earlier.

Populated by Adams (who had recently discovered religion), 10 women and 23 children, Adamstown was a neat little settlement of God-fearing Christians when American Captain Mayhew Folger rediscovered Pitcairn Island in 1809, solving the 19-year mystery of what had happened to Christian and the *Bounty* after the mutiny. By this time British attention was focused on the struggle with Napoleon and there was no interest in the mutineer who was guilty of a crime that was now decades old.

Ship visits became more frequent, and by the time Adams died in 1829 there was concern that the island would become overpopulated. In 1831 the British Government relocated the islanders to Tahiti, but within months 10 of the Pitcairners, lacking immunity to a variety of diseases, had died – including Thursday October Christian, the son of Fletcher Christian and the first child to be born on Pitcairn. By the year's end, the 65 survivors were all back on Pitcairn.

The island became a British colony in 1838, but there were again fears of overpopulation. This time the entire population of 194, was moved to Norfolk Island, an uninhabited former Australian prison island situated between Australia and NZ. Not all the settlers were content with their well-equipped new home, and in 1858, two years after being relocated, 16 Pitcairners returned to their isolated outpost, just in time to prevent the French annexing Pitcairn to their Polynesian colony. More families returned over the years, raising the population to 43.

Right up to the mid-1870s, Pitcairners were followers of the Church of England. However, the arrival of a box of Seventh-Day Adventist literature from the US in 1876 saw the beginnings of change. A decade later, the arrival of a Seventh-Day Adventist missionary heralded real conversion from the teachings of Pastor Simon Young. A mission ship was sent out from the US in 1890 and the happy proselytes were baptised with a dousing in one of the island's rock pools, and the local pigs were swiftly killed to remove the temptation of pork.

Although Pitcairn's population grew to 223 just before WWII, depopulation rather than overpopulation has become the major concern. With British funds being poured into the island for development since the 2004 sex trials, a few ex-islanders are being lured back home. The presence of British officials and government workers has raised the current population to around 60, although only about 50 of those could be considered permanent residents. For more on Pitcairn's recent history, see the boxed text, p242.

SIGHTS & ACTIVITIES

Jaqui Christian, the head of Pitcairn Tourism, can arrange full tours of the island by ATV for US$40.

Reminders of the island's *Bounty* origins are kept in a **museum** (admission US$2), which was opened in 2005. The most famous item is what is possibly the **Bounty bible**, kept under glass. It was actually sold in 1839 and was apparently returned to the island in 1949, but there are conflicting reports about whether this is the true *Bounty* bible or not. Pitcairners hope that many more items will eventually find their way back to the island.

The **Bounty anchor**, salvaged by Irving Johnson in 1957, stands between the courthouse and post office, and there's a **Bounty cannon** further along the road. The **anchor** from the *Acadia,* wrecked on Ducie Atoll (p249), is displayed on the Edge, overlooking Bounty Bay.

The large **petroglyphs** on the rock face at the bottom of Down Rope are reminders of Pitcairn Island's pre-*Bounty* Polynesian habitation. The island's important Polynesian stone **quarry** is at Tautama, 1km west around the coast and if you search around in the bush you can still find stone shards from the tool making that went on here. The road to Down Rope continues to **St Paul's Pool**, a stunning cathedral-like natural pool fed and drained by the sea where you can swim when the sea isn't too rough. The island's **Galapagos tortoise** is the survivor of a pair left here by a visiting yacht in the 1940s. Until recently the tortoise was called Mr T, but a visiting specialist discovered he was a she, so it's now Mrs T. She lives (gated off from people's veggie gardens) on Tedside, the other side of the island from Adamstown where the new jetty will be built. A few islanders visit her on the weekend to feed her bananas.

The island's other new attraction is a beautifully tended **eco trail**, developed in conjunction with Trinity College in Ireland. There are a handful of stops with excellent explanatory notes about endemic plant species, fauna and the island's history. The highlight is the proliferating yellow fatu (*Abutilon pitcairnense*) plant, native only to Pitcairn Island and considered to be one of the world's most rare flowers. The eco trail leads seamlessly to the steep and prickly hill climb to **Fletcher Christian's cave**, overlooking the settlement, where the leading mutineer is said to have hidden, either to watch for pursuing ships or to evade the killings that swept the island in the settlement's early years. On 23 January each year, the *Bounty*'s

MUTINY ON THE BOUNTY

On 28 April 1789 Captain William Bligh and 18 crewmen of the HMS *Bounty* were involuntarily relieved of their duties and set adrift in an open boat off the island of Tofua in Tonga, with a minimum of supplies. The most famous naval mutiny in history, the incident made the *Bounty* a household name. The event also inspired several Hollywood extravaganzas and a plethora of books.

The *Bounty*'s mission was to fetch breadfruit from Tahiti to feed England's African slave population in the Caribbean. Under the command of Bligh, an expert navigator who had trained under Captain James Cook, the expedition arrived in Tahiti in September 1788 after a particularly arduous 10-month journey. The breadfruit season was over and they had to wait six months in Tahiti before returning. Three weeks into the return journey, the crew, led by the master's mate Fletcher Christian, mutinied.

Traditionally, Bligh has been painted as the brutal villain in the incident, taken to violent outbursts and fond of floggings. Christian, on the other hand, was seen as the crew's saviour, and so became a literary romantic hero. In more recent times, attempts have been made to turn these reputations around, to the extent that Bligh is seen in some circles as a kindly captain while Christian is regarded as a mad drug addict. Whatever their characters – a topic that will probably remain moot for years to come – it's likely that the mutineers were not motivated by Bligh alone. Six months in Tahiti, and the Tahitian brides taken by many of the crew, would also have had something to do with it.

Bligh

Whatever problems Bligh had with people skills, he was a brilliant navigator. Against the odds, he managed to get the longboat, and most of his loyal crew, 7000km from Tonga to Timor in the Dutch East Indies (modern-day Indonesia).

Sailing west, they were the first Europeans to sight Fiji, and they also charted several unknown islands in Vanuatu.

They finally reached Timor in the Dutch East Indies on 14 June 1789. Determined to get that breadfruit, Bligh returned to Tahiti in 1792 but with 19 marines – in case of further morale problems. Bligh's career also took him to Australia, and in 1806 he was governor of New South Wales when the so-called 'rum rebellion' overturned his government. Bligh was exonerated from blame – again.

The Mutineers

Under Christian's command the mutineers returned to Tahiti, then attempted to settle on Tubai in the Austral Islands. Meeting local resistance, they split into two groups: Fletcher took a group of sailors and Tahitians off in search of Pitcairn Island, while a second group of 16 sailors stayed behind on Tahiti.

demise is commemorated by towing a burning model of the ship across Bounty Bay.

The only **mutineer's grave** is that of John Adams, in Adamstown.

SLEEPING & EATING

There's no hotel on the island, but visitors are accommodated with islanders and pay US$70 per night for room and full-board. The **Island Council** (☎ 9 3660186; admin@pitcairn.gov .pn) advertises the need for lodging when visa applications are lodged, and volunteer families are picked on a semi-rotating scale.

Every Friday night Olive Christian and her family open up **Christian's Café** (meals NZ$12; beer or wine NZ$2 per glass), a surprisingly classy place with sea views, in their home at 'Big Fence'. Order a day in advance for your choice of meat or fish. Portions are huge, the food is fresh and fabulous, and about half the island shows up for the party.

SHOPPING

The islanders do a busy trade turning out curios for visiting ships, including the signature woven round pandanus baskets, the famous models of the *Bounty* and a variety of *miro* wood carvings. On average, 10 cruise ships stop per year and provide the bulk of the locals' income. Honey (NZ$11 for a small pot on-island) and Pitcairn Island stamps are also specialities.

Limited food supplies are available from the **Government Store** in Adamstown, which opens three times a week for a few hours or on request.

The Pursuit

After Bligh returned to England, Captain Edward Edwards (a tyrant who made Bligh look like a saint) was sent in the *Pandora* to search for the mutineers.

Edwards sailed past Ducie Atoll in the Pitcairn group, but he didn't see the larger island 470km to the west where Christian's small troupe had settled. However, Edwards did find and capture 14 of the 16 mutineers who had remained on Tahiti, and he stuffed them into a cage on the *Pandora*'s deck before heading back for England. Unfortunately, Edward's sailing skills were not up to Bligh's standards and he ended up sinking the *Pandora* on the Great Barrier Reef off Australia's northeast coast. Of the surviving prisoners, three were ultimately hanged for the mutiny.

Books

The American duo of Nordhoff and Hall wrote three books on the *Bounty* mutiny and its aftermath in 1934. The first of the three, *Mutiny on the Bounty*, provided the plot line for the first two Hollywood versions of the story (see later). *Men Against the Sea* follows Bligh's epic open-boat voyage, while *Pitcairn Island* follows Fletcher Christian and his band to Pitcairn.

Two other sources are Richard Hough's *Captain Bligh and Mr Christian* (1973) and Greg Dening's *Mr Bligh's Bad Language* (1992).

More recently, *Fragile Paradise*, by Glynn Christian (Fletcher's great-great-great-great-grandson), is a well-researched, if a little speculative, investigation of the mutiny and the story of the mutineers on Pitcairn.

The newest title to take on this tale is *The Bounty – The True Story of the Mutiny on the Bounty* (2003) by Caroline Alexander. It focuses on the 10 mutineers who were captured in Tahiti and their subsequent fate, and brings a fresh perspective to the story by casting Bligh in a good light.

Films

The *Bounty* story has been made into a handful of motion pictures. The first, *In the Wake of the Bounty* (1933), was memorable only for being Errol Flynn's first film (he was cast as a noble Fletcher Christian). Simultaneously, Hollywood was making *Mutiny on the Bounty* (1935) with Clark Gable in the same role – neither film was too concerned with historical accuracy. The 1962 remake of *Mutiny on the Bounty*, starring Marlon Brando as Christian and filmed in Tahiti, was slightly less inaccurate.

The Bounty (1984), based on Hough's book, is a surprisingly good re-enactment of the tale, with magnificent scenes of Mo'orea in French Polynesia. While Anthony Hopkins plays a more likeable and complex Captain Bligh, Mel Gibson plays a handsome Fletcher Christian.

GETTING AROUND

Tin, *Tub* and *Moss* are 13m-long open boats that are used for transport between Bounty Bay and boats anchored offshore, and for occasional trips to Oeno and Henderson islands. These longboats are Pitcairn's lifeline. Everything but everything comes ashore via them, and it's no mean feat for the island men to load them in monster Pacific swells as they pitch alongside huge ocean-going cargo vessels.

Three- and four-wheeled fat-tyred motorcycles, otherwise known as ATVs, are the usual means of transport used to get around the island. The island's six or so kilometres of steep dirt roads turn to sticky mud when it rains, but otherwise it's great for hiking or running.

OTHER ISLANDS

It's pretty phenomenal that an island as remote as Pitcairn Island has a population at all. The rest of the islands in the archipelago are even less hospital and are thus uninhabited.

OENO ISLAND

Two narrow passes enter Oeno's outrageously blue and healthy central lagoon. The outer reef is 4km across, with a palm-covered island a few kilometres long on the western side, pointing towards a smaller sandbank islet.

Captain James Henderson, who gave his name to Henderson Island, came across Oeno Island in 1819, but it was an American whaling ship which gave Oeno its name in 1824.

PITCAIRN ISLAND

PITCAIRN ISLAND

READING THE LAND

There's a straightforward, down-to-earth approach to everything Pitcairnese, and the island's place names are no exception – they're simple, descriptive and rather worrying. Over the years, islanders appear to have had a disturbing propensity for falling right off Pitcairn, many of them tumbling down a sheer cliff face while gathering birds' eggs, chasing goats or fishing. Heathen idols were found and cast into the sea at Down the God, and the intriguingly named 'Little George Coc'nuts' was a coconut grove owned by George Young, son of mutineer Ned Young. Northwest of Adamstown, below Fletcher Christian's Cave, the cliffs must be particularly dangerous since the map lists the following: 'Where Dick Fall', Johnny Fall' and the succinct 'Minnie Off'. It's no better on the South Coast where you'll find 'Break Im Hip', or the north coast, 'Martin Larsoo Fall'. But the south coast has the most enigmatic and worrying warning of all – 'Oh Dear'.

The *Bowden* was wrecked on Oeno in 1893, and the captain and crew made their way to Pitcairn in the ship's boat. The Pitcairn islanders made four salvage trips to the *Bowden*, resulting in one of the islanders contracting typhoid fever from the filthy bilge water. Back on Pitcairn, the infection raced through the islanders, killing 13 people.

You might be able to talk the *Braveheart* or *Bounty Bay* ships (see p250) into stopping for a quick visit to or from Pitcairn if the conditions are right. Otherwise Pitcairners fit out two of their longboats with essential supplies and swap everyday life on Pitcairn for a fortnight's summer holiday on Oeno when possible. The 120km journey is a 10-hour overnight trip from Pitcairn Island.

HENDERSON ISLAND

This classic example of a *makatea* island, 168km northeast of Pitcairn, is the largest island of the Pitcairn group. Measuring 9.6km long by 5.1km wide, the island is believed to have been uplifted by three undersea volcanoes – Adams, Young and Bounty – to the southeast of Pitcairn.

A fringing reef has grown up around two-thirds of the island's 26km coastline. The sheer 15m-high cliffs run all the way around the island and are difficult to climb. Henderson's interior rises to a 30m flatland with a central depression, which was once the lagoon inside the old reef. The sharp, crumbling ground in the interior is carpeted in a dense thicket of *pisonia* brush and stands of the fine *miro* wood, which Pitcairners occasionally harvest for woodcarving.

The island is populated by Polynesian rats and four species of endemic land birds – the flightless Henderson rail, the colourful Stephen's lorikeet, the territorial Henderson fruit dove and the Henderson warbler. Nine seabird species and the occasional green sea turtle nest here. There are no mosquitos.

The usual landing spot is long North Beach, which is littered with flotsam and jetsam. During certain tides there is sometimes a freshwater spring in a cave at the north of the island.

Because of its pristine condition and rare birdlife, Henderson Island was declared a Unesco World Heritage site in 1988. Visitors require a licence to visit, which is dependent on approval by the Pitcairn Island Council. The ship *Bounty Bay* (see p250) sometimes visits Henderson Island.

History

Polynesians settled on Henderson between the 12th and 15th centuries, and there may have been earlier inhabitants between 900 BC and 350 BC. Limited freshwater supplies, lack of soil for agriculture and dangerous reef entries made Henderson a difficult place to live.

The island was uninhabited when Portuguese explorer Quirós, sailing under the Spanish flag, visited in 1606. The island was rediscovered by the *Bounty* mutineers in 1790, en route to their new home on Pitcairn, and again in 1819 by Captain James Henderson of the British merchant ship *Hercules*.

The wrecking of the whaling ship *Essex* on the island in 1820, after a charge by a sperm whale near the Marquesas, is believed to have provided the inspiration for Herman Melville's *Moby Dick*.

In the early 1980s American, Arthur M 'Smiley' Ratcliffe (or Ratliff), had plans to buy or lease the island, flatten the vegetation, turn it into a cattle ranch and build a home and airstrip. This was a major factor in the island's subsequent World Heritage listing.

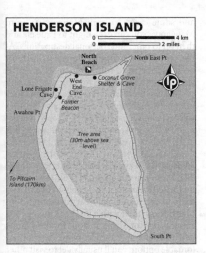

HENDERSON ISLAND

Over the years, various investigations into the island's natural history and archaeology have been conducted.

DUCIE ATOLL

This coral atoll is composed of the 100m-wide main *motu* (island), Acadia Island, stretching for over 3km around the lagoon, and three smaller islands. The lagoon is inaccessible, but on its eastern side gentle whirlpools drain water straight out to sea. There are no palm trees and the vegetation is limited to just two hardy types. Polynesian rats, lizards and tens of thousands of seabirds inhabit the island. It's the least visited and remote island in the archipelago and is 540km east from Pitcairn Island.

Ducie was discovered by Quirós in 1606 and named Encarnacion. It was rediscovered by Edward Edwards on the *Pandora* in 1791, during his *Bounty* hunt, and named after his patron, Lord Ducie. After the British *Acadia* was shipwrecked here in 1881, the crew made a nightmare 13-day voyage to Pitcairn in the ship's boat. Two of them married Pitcairners, and until recently Coffin was a familiar Pitcairn family name (from the shipwrecked sailor, Phillip Coffin). In February 2008 a group of ham radio enthusiasts made a record 183,686 contacts from this remote location,

The usual landing point on Acadia Island is marked by a **memorial**, which notes the recovery of the *Acadia*'s main anchor in 1990. The anchor can now be seen on Pitcairn (see p245). The wreck of the ship is directly offshore from the monument in about 10m of water.

PITCAIRN ISLAND DIRECTORY

ACCOMMODATION

See p246 for information on Pitcairn's limited sleeping options.

INTERNET RESOURCES

Many Pitcairners have their own websites from which they sell Pitcairn goods shippable from the island. A few also have up-to-date news and some great photography.

Friends of Pitcairn (http://groups.yahoo.com/group/FRIENDSofPITCAIRN) A web group that posts all of the islander's individual websites on its home page.

Henderson Island (www.winthrop.dk/hender.html) Info and accounts of this World Heritage-listed island.

Pitcairn Islands Government (www.government.pn) Informative site that is also the official Pitcairn government portal.

Pitcairn Islands Study Center (http://library.puc.edu/pitcairn) California-based centre with shipping schedules and Pitcairn history.

Pitcairn Islands Tourism (www.visitpitcairn.pn) The official tourism site for Pitcairn promises the most up-to-date info on how to travel to the island and what to expect when you get there.

Pitcairn Today (www.onlinepitcairn.com/pitcairn_today.htm) Relatively recent local news.

MONEY

New Zealand dollars (for exchange rates see the Quick Reference page) are the official currency of Pitcairn Island, although US dollars are used for everything tourist related; and in actuality, any major currency as well as French Polynesian CFP are readily accepted. Budget on at least US$490 per week.

POST OFFICE

The post office is in Adamstown and opens from 8.30am to whenever there are no more customers on Sunday, Tuesday and Thursday, or right before the mail can leave on a ship.

TELEPHONE & FAX

Pitcairn Island now has very affordable phone rates and most homes have a private telephone. Service is based in Auckland, New Zealand and

PITCAIRN ISLAND

the rates are identical to those in this city. Calls to Auckland are free, and those to/from New Zealand are about NZ$0.15 per minute. Most people will let you use their phone if you pay them the cost of the call.

There's just one public telephone on the island: its number is ☎ 76233-7766; the fax number is 7767. Pitcairn phonecards are available if you need to use this phone.

TIME

Pitcairn is 8½ hours behind GMT (9½ during daylight saving).

VISAS

There's a $30 fee for a two-week visa or a yacht landing fee, and a US$150 fee for a six month visa. All stays must be approved by the island council. If you want to drink alcohol you'll need to purchase a US$25 liquor license.

Visa applications are processed by the **Pitcairn Islands Administration** (☎ 64-9-366 0186; admin@pitcairn.gov.pn; PO Box 105 696, Auckland, NZ). Think up a good reason for your stay (not all applications are approved) and allow two weeks for the application to be considered.

TRANSPORT IN PITCAIRN ISLAND

GETTING THERE & AWAY

Pitcairn is remote with a capital 'R'. There's no airstrip and no way of getting here except across the seemingly endless blue ocean.

Landings on Pitcairn are notoriously difficult: it's not unknown to travel all the way to the island and then be unable to set foot on land due to rough seas. All this could become easier in the near future, as EU and DFID (UK Department of International Development) funding has been allocated to build a new jetty on the opposite side of the island from Bounty Bay – the idea is that at least one side of the island will always be protected from rough seas.

Cargo Ship & Charter Vessel

The most comfortable and reliable but expensive way to get to Pitcairn is by hopping on the NZ-based **M/V Braveheart** (www.braveheart.pn; round-trip US$5000), a 39m 'remote location support and research vessel' that is chartered by the British Government to transport Pitcairners

and some cargo to/from Mangareva. From Mangareva you can get a flight to Pape'ete and then on to other international destinations. At the time of research, the *Braveheart* had just been contracted to run a regular service of at least eight trips per year, four for supplies and passengers direct from New Zealand and four more between Mangareva and Pitcairn. Services will begin in August 2009 and it's hoped that demand will be great enough to keep running this many boats per year. Contact the *Braveheart* for the schedule. Otherwise, the Cook Islands-based **R/V Bounty Bay** (www.pacific-expeditions.com; round-trip from US$2900), an alarmingly small (16m) but sturdy motorised catamaran, makes about five charter tours to the islands per year (departing from Mangareva), each with a different theme (one cultural, one for diving and one for flora, fauna and birdwatching). Besides being the most affordable option, you'll usually get to visit other islands in the archipelago as well.

At the time of research, the only cargo ship servicing Pitcairn was the *Taporo VIII* out of Pape'ete (p409), French Polynesia via Mangareva (though it does not take passengers). Get in touch with **Pitcairn Islands Tourism** (www.visitpitcairn.pn) for up-to-date info.

Cruise Ship

About 10 cruise ships call at Pitcairn every year. Like cargo vessels, they anchor well offshore and, seas permitting, passengers are ferried to Bounty Bay aboard the ship's rubber inflatable or its tender, or alternatively on the Pitcairn longboats. While cruise ships will take Pitcairners as passengers to/from the next port of call, non-islanders are required to take the full cruise package. Andrew Christian (www.andrew.christian.pn) lists the cruise ship schedule on his website.

Yacht

Mangareva (p472) in French Polynesia is the best place to try your luck for a place on a Pitcairn-bound yacht. Visiting yachties should come well equipped – Pitcairners are happy to sell fresh fruit and supply fresh water, but other supplies generally have to be imported from NZ and may be in short supply. There is no sheltered anchorage at Pitcairn and boats must be moved when the winds change.

GETTING AROUND

For further details on getting around the islands, see p247.

Rarotonga & the Cook Islands

Fifteen tiny flecks of land cast across 2 million sq km of sea, the Cook Islands is a South Pacific paradise that's at once remote and accessible, modern and traditional. The Cooks are about as close to the mid-Pacific as you can get (without being in the water) and far removed from the frenetic outside world. Swaying coconut palms shade beaches of dazzling white sand, cerulean-blue lagoons teem with tropical fish, while thundering surf crashes against perimeter reefs.

The Cook Islands, named after Captain James Cook himself, have long been a refuge for runaways, hermits and wannabe Robinson Crusoes drawn by a heady mix of warm South Seas air, pristine beaches and azure lagoons, and abundant fresh fish and tropical fruit.

Modern Rarotonga has its feet firmly planted in the 21st century, with a groovy café culture, fine restaurants, boutiques and funky nightlife. It's a cosmopolitan place that's deadly good-looking. Yet Rarotonga's contemporary appearance is predicated on a traditional Polynesian character that looks both to the future and to a past that is steeped in legends and oral history. The sublime lagoon of Aitutaki, ringed with tiny deserted islands, is one of the jewels of the Pacific and a must-see Cook Islands destination.

The outer islands display their Polynesian traditions much nearer the surface. Here you can drink home-brew at a traditional 'Atiuan *tumunu* (bush-beer drinking club), explore the ancient *makatea* (raised-coral cliffs) and taro fields of Mangaia and swim in the underground cave pools of Mitiaro and Ma'uke. The opportunities for walkers and cavers are rich and many. For the most intrepid travellers the remote Northern Group – with its coral atolls and huge crystal-clear lagoons – provides an incredible South Seas experience that too few ever get to see.

The Cooks are seductive, beautiful and alluring – some who come never manage to leave.

HIGHLIGHTS

- Swim in the pristine azure waters of Rarotonga's **lagoon** (p265)
- Trek along Rarotonga's **cross-island track**, **inland trails** and **valley walks** (p264)
- Explore Aitutaki's stunning **lagoon** (p275) on a hired kayak and find your own desert island
- Spend some time on **'Atiu** (p279) exploring its caves, coffee plantations and unique birdlife
- Learn about Mangaia's ancient ways and explore its mysterious limestone **burial caves** (p288)

Aitutaki

'Atiu

Rarotonga's Inland Trails & Valley Walks
Rarotonga's Lagoon

Mangaia

RAROTONGA & THE COOK ISLANDS FACTS

Capital city (and island) Avarua (Rarotonga)
Population 21,000
Land area 241 sq km
Number of islands 15
International telephone code ☎ 682
Currency NZ dollar (NZ$)
Languages Cook Islands Maori and English
Greeting *Kia orana* (Hello)
Website www.cook-islands.com

CLIMATE & WHEN TO GO

Any time of the year is a good time to visit the Cook Islands. It's warm and sunny all year round; the hottest, wettest months are during the cyclone season between November and March. High/low temperatures are 29°C/23°C in February, dipping to 25°C/18°C from June to September. See p627 for Avarua's climate chart.

Historically, a severe cyclone has hit the Cooks once every 20 years – but in 2005 the islands were battered by five major cyclones in five weeks.

Book flights well ahead for December, when many Cook Islanders return home from overseas for the Christmas holidays.

COSTS & MONEY

The Cook Islands uses the New Zealand (NZ) currency, though you'll get some Cook Islands coins in change. Spend them before you leave as they cannot be exchanged outside the Cooks.

Budget travellers can expect to pay about NZ$20 for a dorm bed and from about NZ$45/60 for singles/doubles. The midrange space is broad and singles cost from about NZ$90 up to NZ$250 or more, although many rooms and bungalows are designed for double occupancy and cost the same for one. Those with money to burn will be looking at upwards of NZ$350 per night, and NZ$1000 or more is not uncommon.

Evening main dishes in restaurants cost from about NZ$18, though there are many good cafés and takeaway options.

HISTORY

Cook Islanders are Maori people closely related to native New Zealanders and French Polynesians. The Maori had no written his-

tory, but historians believe that Polynesian migrations from the Society Islands in French Polynesia to the Cooks began around the 5th century AD – oral histories speak of around 1400 years of Polynesian activity on Rarotonga. A *marae* (religious meeting ground) on tiny Motutapu in Rarotonga's Muri Lagoon is estimated to be around 1500 years old. In the 14th century great ocean-going *vaka* (canoes) departed from Rarotonga for Aotearoa (New Zealand) – the settlers were ancestors of present-day New Zealand Maori.

During his disastrous second voyage from Spanish-occupied Peru, Don Alvaro de Mendaña y Neyra came upon Pukapuka on 20 August 1595 – he would die just months later in the Solomon Islands. Eleven years later Mendaña's chief pilot Pedro Fernández de Quirós led another Pacific expedition, stopping at Rakahanga. James Cook explored the Cooks in 1773 and 1779. Only ever setting foot on Palmerston and never finding Rarotonga, Cook named the group the Hervey Islands in honour of a British Lord of the Admiralty. In his 1835 *Atlas de l'Océan Pacifique*, Russian explorer and cartographer Admiral Adam Johann von Krusenstern renamed them in honour of Captain Cook.

Reverend John Williams of the London Missionary Society (LMS) arrived on Aitutaki in 1821. In 1823 Papeiha, a convert from Ra'iatea in the Societies, moved to Rarotonga and set about converting the islands to Christianity. Though many *marae* were destroyed and sacred artefacts were carted off to British museums, much of the island's culture survived, including the traditional titles of *ariki* (chief) and *mataiapo* (subchief), the land-inheritance system and the indigenous language. The missionaries imposed a catalogue of strict rules and doctrines (known as the 'Blue Laws') and brought deadly diseases such as whooping cough, measles, smallpox and influenza, leading to a long-term decline in population numbers.

The Cook Islands became a British protectorate in 1888, in response to fears of French colonisation. In 1901 the islands were annexed to NZ, and the Southern and Northern Groups together became known as the Cook Islands.

During WWII the US built airstrips on Penrhyn and Aitutaki, but the Cooks escaped the war largely unscathed, unlike

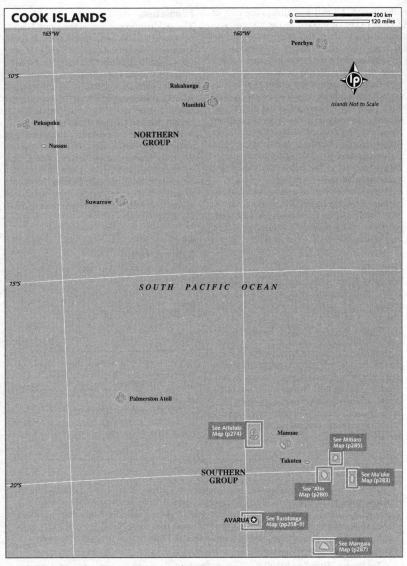

COOK ISLANDS

0 ⊏━━━━━━━━ 200 km
0 ⊏┅┅┅┅┅┅┅ 120 miles

165°W

160°W

Penrhyn

10°S

Rakahanga

Manihiki

Islands Not to Scale

Pukapuka

NORTHERN
GROUP

Nassau

Suwarrow

15°S   SOUTH   PACIFIC   OCEAN

Palmerston Atoll

See Aitutaki
Map (p274)

Manuae

See Mitiaro
Map (p285)

Takutea

See Ma'uke
Map (p283)

SOUTHERN
GROUP

See 'Atiu
Map (p280)

20°S

AVARUA ✪   See Rarotonga
             Map (pp258-9)

See Mangaia
Map (p287)

many of their South Pacific neighbours. In 1965 the Cook Islands became internally self-governing in free association with NZ.

THE CULTURE
The National Psyche

Cook Islanders carry NZ passports, which allow them to live and work in NZ and, by extension (courtesy of the Special Category Visa), to live and work in Australia. This means that many Cook Islanders are well-travelled, modern people. Rarotonga is a cosmopolitan and sophisticated place, yet beneath this Westernised veneer many Maori traditions remain, including traditional titles, family structure and the system of land inheritance. All native islanders are part of a family clan connected to the ancient system of *ariki*. Many still refer to themselves as from their 'home island' – Mangaian or Aitutakian. But there's a continuing exodus from the outer islands to Rarotonga, NZ and Australia, and some claim that Cooks Islands' nationhood is undermined by that Kiwi passport – when the going gets tough the islanders move away to Auckland or Melbourne. Tourism is the Cooks' only major industry, but few tourists go beyond Rarotonga and Aitutaki. The outer islands have a fraction of the populations they had a few decades ago.

Politics, sport, dance, music, land and inheritance remain important, as do community, family and traditional values. Christian religion, in its various flavours, is taken very seriously.

Lifestyle

Islanders from Rarotonga are thoroughly 21st-century people, with modern houses, regular jobs and reasonable salaries. Elsewhere in the Cook Islands, however, people live a much more traditional lifestyle – fishing, growing crops, and practising traditional arts and crafts. Family and the church are perhaps the two most influential elements in most islanders' lives, but they remain relaxed and informal about most aspects of day-to-day living. Like elsewhere in the Pacific, Cook Islanders are especially relaxed about time-keeping – things will happen when they do.

Population

The resident population of the Cook Islands is around 21,000, but around 80% of Cook Islanders live overseas. More than 50,000 Cook Islanders live in NZ, half that number in Australia, and several thousand more in French Polynesia, the Americas, Europe and Asia. Of those who do live in their country of origin, more than 90% live in the Southern Group, with 60% living on Rarotonga.

Like many Pacific islands, the Cooks are struggling with a long-term population drain, as islanders move overseas in search of higher wages. More than 90% of the population is Polynesian, though the people of some of the Northern Group islands are more closely related to Samoans than to other Cook Islanders.

ARTS
Dance & Music

Cook Islanders love to dance and they're reputed to be the best dancers in Polynesia. You can see them strut and swagger – women and men – at island night performances, which combine a traditional meal with music and dance. Traditional dance forms include the *karakia* (prayer dance), *pe'e ura pa'u* (drumbeat dance), *ate* (choral song) and *kaparima* (action song). Men stamp, gesture and knock their knees together, while women shake and gyrate their hips in an unmistakeably suggestive manner.

The islanders are also great singers and musicians. The multi-part harmony singing at a Cook Islands church service is truly beauti-

---

BEST EATS

Gourmands rejoice – Rarotonga has some outstanding places to eat, and Aitutaki has a few hidden gems too. There are few formal restaurants on the outer islands, and self-catering is the only option. There's not much local food on restaurant menus, apart from *ika mata* (marinated raw fish in coconut cream), but you can try traditional cooking at Punanga Nui Market's food stalls (p271), at an island night (see the boxed text, p272) or *umukai* (traditional feast cooked in an underground oven).

- The famous Flame Tree (p270) is still going strong, serving some of Rarotonga's finest cuisine.
- Vaima Restaurant & Bar (p270) serves sublime food in a memorable beachfront setting.
- Sue Carruthers, Rarotonga's best chef, cooks up a storm at Tamarind House (p270).
- Tauono's (p278), on Aitutaki, is a feast for all the senses with fresh organic ingredients from the on-site garden.
- Aitutaki's Café Tupuna (p278) offers superb à la carte cuisine in a lovely garden dining room.

I DO

Many couples come to the Cook Islands to get married. It's easy to see why – the Cooks are *très romantique*. Most hotels and resorts offer wedding packages, and there are also several specialist wedding companies – an internet search will turn up many. Cook Islands marriages are legally binding worldwide. You need a copy of your birth certificate and passport. If you've been married before you will need your divorce papers or a death certificate. The Marriage Registrar requires a minimum of four days before the wedding day to issue a marriage licence (otherwise a NZ$45 extra fee is incurred). You may now kiss.

---

ful, but pop music is popular too. Polynesian stringbands, featuring guitars and ukuleles, often perform at local restaurants and hotels.

Arts & Crafts

Traditional woodcarving and woven handicrafts (pandanus mats, baskets, purses and fans) are still popular in the Cooks. You'll see women going to church wearing finely woven *rito* (coconut-fibre) hats, mainly made on the Northern Group islands. Ceremonial adzes, stone taro pounders and *pupu ei* (snail-shell necklaces) are produced on Mangaia, and the best place to see traditional *tivaevae* (appliqué work, used for bedspreads, cushion covers and home decoration) is at the Fibre Arts Studio on 'Atiu. Black pearls are grown in the Northern Group and are an important export – you'll see plenty of black-pearl and pearl-shell jewellery around (see p272). 'Ei (floral necklaces) and 'ei katu (tiaras) are customarily given to friends and honoured guests – you're bound to receive a few during your time in the Cooks, especially if you visit the outer islands.

Literature

You should be able to pick up most of these titles around Avarua's main bookshops (see p257).

An Island to Oneself by Tom Neale is the classic desert-island read, written by a New Zealander who lived as a virtual hermit on Suwarrow during the 1950s and 1960s.

Robert Dean Frisbie ran a trading outpost on Pukapuka in the 1920s and wrote two evocative memoirs, *The Book of Pukapuka* and *The Island of Desire*.

Sir Tom Davis (Pa Tuterangi Ariki) was – among many things including medical doctor and NASA scientist – the Cook Islands' prime minister for most of the 1980s (he died in 2007). His autobiography is called *Island Boy*.

If you're after local legends, pick up *Cook Islands Legends* and *The Ghost at Tokatarava and Other Stories from the Cook Islands*, both by the notable Cook Islands author Jon Tikivanotau Jonassen. Pukapukan poet Kauraka Kauraka has published several books of poems including *Ta 'Akatauira: My Morning Star*.

Akono'anga Maori: Cooks Islands Culture, edited by Ron and Marjorie Tua'inekore Crocombe, is an excellent book that looks at culture manifested in traditional Polynesian tattooing, poetry, art, sport and governance.

Guide to Cook Islands Birds by DT Holyoak is a useful guide to the islands' native birds, with colour photos and tips for identification.

LANGUAGE

Cook Islands Maori (Rarotongan) is a Polynesian language similar to New Zealand Maori and Marquesan (from French Polynesia). There are some small dialectical differences between many of the islands, and some northern islands have their own languages. English is spoken as a second (or third) language by virtually everyone.

In Rarotongan, the glottal stop replaces the 'h' of similar Polynesian languages; for example, the Tahitian word for 'one', *tahi* (ta-hee), is *ta'i* (ta-ee) in Rarotongan.

Rarotongan basics

Hello.	Kia orana.
Goodbye.	Aere ra.
How are you?	Pe'ea koe?
Please.	Ine.
Thanks (very much).	Meitaki (ma'ata).
Yes.	Ae.
No.	Kare.
Cheers!	Kia manuia!

ENVIRONMENT

The Cook Islands' small land mass (just 241 sq km) is scattered over 2 million sq km of ocean, midway between American Samoa and Tahiti.

The 15 islands are divided into Northern and Southern Groups. Most of the Southern Group are younger volcanic islands, although Mangaia is the Pacific's oldest island. The Northern Group are coral atolls that have formed on top of ancient sunken volcanoes (see the boxed text, p64). 'Atiu, Ma'uke, Mitiaro and Mangaia are 'raised islands' characterised by *makatea* – rocky coastal areas formed by uplifted coral reefs. All the Northern Group islands are low coral atolls, with an outer reef encircling a lagoon.

Waste management is a major issue in the Cook Islands. Glass, plastic and aluminium are collected for recycling, but there's still a huge surplus of rubbish. Water supply is also a major concern.

Rising sea levels associated with global warming are a huge threat to the Cooks. Many of the islands of the Northern Group are low-lying and could be uninhabitable within the next 100 years (see the boxed text, p70). Climate scientists predict that severe cyclones are likely to become much more common.

Wildlife

Rarotonga's mountainous centre is covered with a dense jungle of ferns, creepers and towering trees, providing habitat for the island's rich birdlife. Coconut palms and spectacular tropical flowers grow almost everywhere in the Cook Islands, though the once-common pandanus trees are now rare on Rarotonga and 'Atiu.

The only native mammal is the Pacific fruit bat (flying fox), found on Mangaia and Rarotonga. Pigs, chickens and goats were introduced by the first Polynesian settlers, along with rats, which devastated the islands' endemic wildlife, especially native birds. The *kakerori* (Rarotongan flycatcher) was almost wiped out, but is now recovering thanks to the establishment of the Takitumu Conservation Area on Rarotonga. Other native birds include the cave-dwelling *kopeka* ('Atiu swiftlet) on 'Atiu, the *tanga'eo* (Mangaian kingfisher) and the *kukupa* (Cook Islands fruit dove).

RAROTONGA

pop 10,500 / area 67.2 sq km

The capital of the Cook Islands is stunning in its natural beauty and physical drama. A broad band of flame-orange coral reef encircles the island – the floor of a brilliant sapphire-blue lagoon backed by long stretches of sparkling white beach. Beyond the reef, breakers foam and crash like distant thunder. Rarotonga's settlements and villages are mostly nestled on the flatlands near the coast, but behind here the island rises spectacularly through lush fields and rural farmland to the rugged and thickly forested mountains of the island's interior – these silent, brooding peaks dominate the island's landscape from every angle.

Rarotonga has plenty of history, too, with ancient *marae* and monuments to explore and some of the best-preserved coral churches in the South Pacific. With great hotels and resorts, boutique shopping and fine restaurants, Rarotonga is a seductive mix of creature comfort and South Seas beauty – most visitors never venture further than this Polynesian princess.

HISTORY

Legend tells that Rarotonga was discovered by Io Tangaroa who arrived about 1400 years ago from Nuku Hiva in the Marquesas (French Polynesia). In the early 13th century two great warrior chiefs, Tangi'ia from Tahiti and Karika from Samoa, arrived in *vaka* (ocean-going canoes) to conquer the island, and rule Rarotonga as joint kings. The land was divided among six tribes, each headed by an *ariki*. The first recorded European visitor was Philip Goodenough, captain of the *Cumberland,* who came in 1814 and spent three bloody months looking for sandalwood. In 1823 missionaries John Williams and Papeiha set out to convert the Rarotongans, and in little more than a year Christianity had taken a firm hold.

ORIENTATION

Though Rarotonga is the largest of the Cook Islands, it's compact and accessible, circumnavigated by a 32km coastal road known as the Ara Tapu (Sacred Road). Inland is a second road, the Ara Metua (Ancient Road), built in the 11th century. The Ara Metua passes through farmland, taro plantations and rambling homesteads in the foothills of Rarotonga's mountainous centre. The island's rugged interior can be crossed only on foot. There are no private beaches on Rarotonga, but take care not to cross private land in order to access the shoreline.

INFORMATION
Bookshops
Bounty Bookshop (Map pp262-3; ☎ 26660; Avarua) The island's main bookshop is near the post office.
CITC Shopping Centre (Map pp262-3; ☎ 22000; Ara Maire Nui, Avarua)
Cook Islands Library & Museum Society (Map pp262-3; ☎ 28468; Makea Tinirau Rd, Avarua)
University of the South Pacific (USP; Map pp262-3; ☎ 29415; Makea Tinirau Rd, Avarua) The best (and cheapest) place for books on Cook Islands history, politics and culture.

Internet Access
Internet access is widely available on Rarotonga, and the average charge is about NZ$9 an hour. There are wi-fi hotspots all around the island, including most of the major resorts. Telecom sells pre-paid wi-fi cards in denominations of NZ$15 (50MB), NZ$36 (150MB), NZ$50 (250MB) and NZ$64 (400MB).
Click Internet Lounge (Map pp262-3; ☎ 23885; Cooks Corner Arcade, Avarua)
Deli-licious Café (Map pp258-9; ☎ 20858; Muri; ☺ 7am-5pm)
Internet Shop (Map pp262-3; ☎ 20727; Avarua; ☺ 9am-5pm Mon-Fri, 9am-1pm Sat)
Kavera Central (Map pp258-9; ☎ 20012; Kavera)
Telecom (Map pp262-3; ☎ 29680; Tutakimoa Rd, Avarua; ☺ 24hr) Open all hours with wi-fi access.
Telepost (Map pp262-3; ☎ 29940; CITC Shopping Centre, Ara Maire Nui, Avarua) Wi-fi access.

Medical Services
Hospital (Map pp258-9; ☎ 22664; 24hr emergency service) On a steep hill up behind the golf course.
Outpatient clinic (Map pp258-9; ☎ 20065) About 1km east of Avarua.
CITC Pharmacy (Map pp262–3; ☎ 22000, Ara Maire Nui, Avarua) Part of the CITC department store.

Money
ANZ (Map pp262-3; ☎ 21750; www.anz.com/cook islands; ☺ 9am-3pm Mon-Thu, 9am-4pm Sat) There are ATMs at the main branch in Avarua, at Wigmore's Superstore (Vaimaanga) and at the Suprette grocery store opposite Dive Rarotonga ('Arorangi).
Westpac (Map pp262-3; ☎ 22014; www.westpac.co.ck; ☺ 9am-3pm Mon-Fri, 9-11am Sat) The main branch is beside the Foodland supermarket in Avarua, and another airport branch opens for international flights – both have ATMs. Westpac ATMs also at Oasis Service Centre (Nikao) and JMC Store (Muri).

Post
Post office (Map pp262-3; ☎ 29940; ☺ 8am-4pm Mon-Fri, 8am-noon Sat)

Tourist Information
Cook Islands Tourist Authority (Map pp262-3; ☎ 29435; www.cook-islands.com; Avarua; ☺ 8am-4pm Mon-Fri) The main tourist office can help with everything from accommodation and nightspots to inter-island flights and shipping services.

Travel Agencies
There are two main travel agencies on Rarotonga. They often have good airfare-and-accommodation packages and deals to the outer islands.
Island Hopper Vacations (Map pp258-9; ☎ 22576; www.islandhoppervacations.com; Turama House, Nika'o)
Jetsave Travel (Map pp262-3; ☎ 27707; www.jetsave.co.ck; Ara Maire Nui, Avarua)

TRANSPORT
Getting There & Away
Unless you're travelling by private yacht, you'll arrive by plane from Los Angeles (LA), Auckland or Pape'ete. Air New Zealand, Pacific Blue and Air Tahiti are the only international carriers that fly through the islands. See p294 for information on getting to and from Rarotonga.

Getting Around
TO/FROM THE AIRPORT
Most hotels and hostels provide transfers from the airport. **Raro Tours** (Map pp258-9; ☎ 25325; coaches@rarotours.co.ck) operates an airport shuttle service (NZ$10 one way to anywhere on the island).

BUS
Circle-island buses run around the coast road in both directions, departing from Cook's Corner Arcade in Avarua. Daytime buses going clockwise depart hourly 7am to 4pm Monday to Friday, 1pm to 4pm on Saturday, and 8am to noon and 2pm to 4pm Sunday. Buses going anticlockwise depart at 25 minutes past the hour, 8.25am to 4.25pm Monday to Friday only. A night bus service runs clockwise Monday to Saturday from 6pm to 10pm, with extra hourly buses on Friday night from midnight to 2am.

The bus adult/child fare is NZ$4/3 for one ride, NZ$7/4 for a return trip (two rides) or NZ$25/13 for a 10-ride ticket. A family pass, valid for two adults and two kids, costs

RAROTONGA & THE COOK ISLANDS

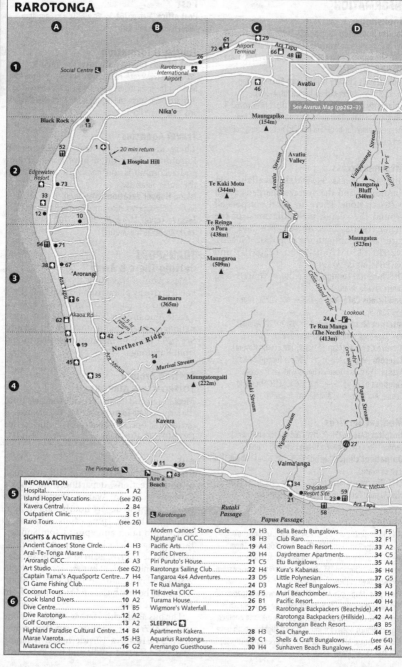

RAROTONGA

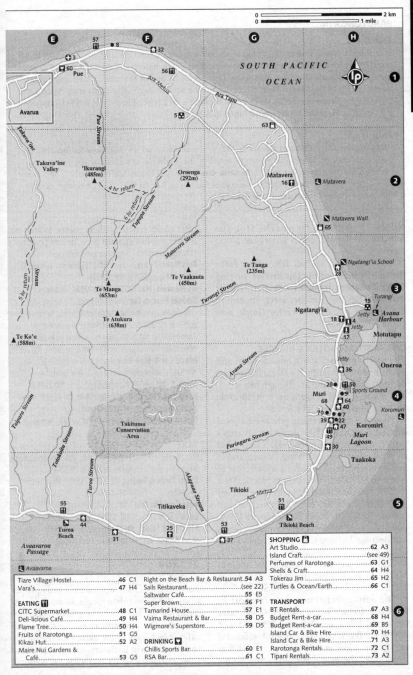

0 — 2 km
0 — 1 mile

SOUTH PACIFIC
OCEAN

Avarua

Takuva'ine
Valley

Takuva'ine
Valley

'Ikurangi
(485m)

Oroenga
(292m)

Matavera

Matavera

Matavera Wall

Te Tanga
(235m)

Te Vaakauta
(450m)

Te Manga
(653m)

Ngatangi'ia School

Turangi

Te Atukura
(638m)

Ngatangi'ia

Avana
Harbour

Te Ko'u
(588m)

Motutapu

Oneroa

Muri

Sports Ground

Koromuri

Takitumu
Conservation
Area

Koromiri

Muri
Lagoon

Taakoka

Tikioki

Titikaveka

Tikioki Beach

Turoa
Beach

Avaavaroa
Passage

Avaavaroa

Tiare Village Hostel	46	C1	
Vara's	47	H4	
EATING			
CITC Supermarket	48	C1	
Deli-licious Café	49	H4	
Flame Tree	50	H4	
Fruits of Rarotonga	51	G5	
Kikau Hut	52	A2	
Maire Nui Gardens & Café	53	G5	

Right on the Beach Bar & Restaurant	54	A3	
Sails Restaurant	(see 22)		
Saltwater Café	55	E5	
Super Brown	56	F1	
Tamarind House	57	E1	
Vaima Restaurant & Bar	58	D5	
Wigmore's Superstore	59	D5	
DRINKING			
Chillis Sports Bar	60	E1	
RSA Bar	61	C1	

SHOPPING			
Art Studio	62	A3	
Island Craft	(see 49)		
Perfumes of Rarotonga	63	G1	
Shells & Craft	64	H4	
Tokerau Jim	65	H2	
Turtles & Ocean/Earth	66	C1	
TRANSPORT			
BT Rentals	67	A3	
Budget Rent-a-car	68	H4	
Budget Rent-a-car	69	B5	
Island Car & Bike Hire	70	H4	
Island Car & Bike Hire	71	A3	
Rarotonga Rentals	72	C1	
Tipani Rentals	73	A2	

RAROTONGA IN...

Two Days

Take a **circle-island tour** (p266) or hire a scooter and buzz around the back roads (below) to get acquainted with the island. Factor in some snorkelling and swimming around sublime **Muri Lagoon** (p262) or **Aro'a Beach** (p262), and enjoy fine cuisine at one of the island's best restaurants – **Vaima** (p270) or the **Flame Tree** (p270). Spend the second day exploring **Avarua** (below) and browsing for **souvenirs** (p272). Work up an appetite with a spot of swimming in the lagoon, and then head straight out for an **island night** (p272).

Four Days

Highland Paradise Cultural Centre (p262) is the place to go on day three for insights into traditional culture. Spend the evening exploring the **nightlife** of Avarua where you can walk between the **Whatever Bar** (p271), **Banana Court Bar** (p271) and **Staircase** (p271) and shake your groove thang at **Rehab** (p271). Keep your fourth day free for the island's hidden highlight – the unforgettable **Cross-Island Track** (p264).

NZ$26. There's also a day pass (NZ$16). The bus can be flagged down anywhere along its route.

You can pick up bus timetables from the tourist office or the bus drivers, or ring **Cook's Passenger Transport** (☎ 25512, after hr ☎ 20349). Several free booklets, including the Jasons *Cook Islands Visitor Guide*, also contain timetables.

CAR, MOTORSCOOTER & BICYCLE

The speed limit is 50km/h outside town and 30km/h around Avarua. It's illegal for motorcyclists to ride two abreast (though many do), and if you exceed 40km/h on a motorcycle without a helmet you'll be fined.

To rent a motor vehicle you need a local driving licence (NZ$20) issued at Avarua's police station (Map pp262–3). You'll need to show your home driving licence and if you're not licensed to drive a motorcycle at home you'll have to take a short practical test (NZ$5; once around the block). You can get your licence any day from 8am to 3pm, but turn up early – the police station issues 150 to 200 licences to tourists every day and queues can be long. Driving is on the left-hand side of the road.

Cars and jeeps are available for around NZ$55 to NZ$70 per day. Mountain bikes are around NZ$6/40 per day/week.

The quintessential mode of transport in the Cook Islands is the scooter. Good rates for rental bikes are around NZ$20/85 per day/week. But if you shop around, scooters/cars go for as low as NZ$12/33 per day. Local firms offer the best deals and some hotels offer cheap rentals to their guests. Watch out for the red-hot exhaust pipe, unless you fancy taking home a 'Rarotongan tattoo'.

Avis Rental Cars Airport (☎ 21039; www.avis.co.ck); Avarua (Map pp262-3; ☎ 22833)

BT Rentals (Map pp258-9; ☎ 23586; 'Arorangi)

Budget Rent-a-Car (www.budget.co.ck); Airport (☎ 21039; open only for international flights); Avarua (Map pp262-3; ☎ 20895; 2 St Joseph Rd); downtown Avarua (Map pp262-3; ☎ 26895); Edgewater Resort (Map pp258-9; ☎ 21026); Rarotongan Beach Resort (Map pp258-9; ☎ 20838)

Island Car & Bike Hire (Map pp258-9; ☎ 22632; www.islandcarhire.co.ck; Ara Tapu); Avarua (Map pp262-3; ☎ 24632); Muri (Map pp258-9; ☎ 21632)

Rarotonga Rentals (Map pp258-9; ☎ 22326; www .rarotongarentals.co.ck) At the airport.

Tipani Rentals (Map pp258-9; ☎ 22382; 'Arorangi)

TAXI

Rates are about NZ$2.50 per kilometre; from Muri to the airport will cost NZ$40.

Areiti Taxis & Tours (☎ 23012, 55752; Muri Beach; ☼ 24hr)

Aroa Taxi Shuttle (☎ 28144; 'Arorangi)

Doro's Taxi (☎ 21400, 52355; Avana; ☼ 24hr)

Kia Orana Taxis (☎ 20203, 50721; ☼ 24hr)

Muri Beach Taxis (☎ 21625; Muri Beach)

AVARUA

Avarua, fronting a pretty bay on Rarotonga's north coast, is the Cook Islands' only proper town. Hardly an urban jungle, Avarua's largest buildings are barely the height of a coconut tree, and the atmosphere of the shops and cafés is laid-back in the extreme. Avarua has the island's twin harbours, main market and some intriguing sights, including the National

Culture Centre, the ruined Para O Tane Palace and the old Banana Court – once one of the most notorious bars in the South Pacific.

Orientation & Information

There's one main road, the Ara Maire Nui, which starts from the main traffic circle near Avarua Harbour and runs right through town. The commercial centre is west of the traffic circle. Past the shops at the western end of town is Punanga Nui Market and Avatiu Harbour, where the inter-island passenger freighter ships and Port Authority are based. The airport is 1km further west.

Sights

Near the traffic circle is the **Philatelic Bureau** (Map pp262-3; ☎ 29336), where you can purchase Cook Islands coins and stamps.

On the inland side of the main road, half a block east of the traffic circle, are the **Para O Tane Palace** (Map pp262-3) and its surrounding area, **Taputapuatea**. The palace is where Makea Takau, the paramount *ariki* of the area, signed the treaty accepting the Cook Islands' status as a British protectorate in 1888. The building is now a picturesque ruin, and it's closed to the public, although officially it's still one of the island's main seats of power.

Further east is the historic **Beachcomber Gallery** (Map pp262-3; ☎ 21939; Ara Tapu) building that was once an LMS missionary school. These days it houses Avarua's trendiest shops. On the opposite side of the road is Avarua's white-washed **Cook Islands Christian Church** (CICC; Map pp262-3; Makea Tinirau Rd), built in 1853. The **graveyard** contains the graves of the author Robert Dean Frisbie (p255) and Albert Henry, the first prime min-

ister of the Cook Islands. The main church service is at 10am on Sunday.

Inland behind the Para O Tane Palace, the **Cook Islands Library & Museum Society** (Map pp262-3; ☎ 28468; Makea Tinirau Rd; admission NZ$2; ☺ 9am-1pm Mon-Sat, 4-8pm Tue) houses a collection of Pacific literature and a small museum, with intriguing exhibits including an old whaling pot, spears and the island's first printing press. Nearby, at the junction of Are Metua and Takuva'ine Rd, is the Papeiha Stone. This marks the spot where Tahitian preacher Papeiha preached the gospel in Rarotonga for the first time.

The **National Museum** (Map pp262-3; ☎ 20725; Victoria Rd; admission by donation; ☺ 8am-4pm Mon-Fri) inside the National Culture Centre has a selection of Cook Islands and South Pacific artefacts, and it sometimes hosts temporary exhibitions. The **National Library** (Map pp262-3; ☎ 20725) is nearby.

AROUND THE ISLAND

The sights listed here are anticlockwise from Avarua, and are all near the main coast road.

Black Rock

On the coast just beyond the golf course is Black Rock (Turou), traditionally believed to be where the spirits of the dead commenced their voyage to 'Avaiki (the afterworld). It's also one of the island's best **snorkelling** spots. Look out for the sign to the Rarotonga Hospital from where there are commanding views of the island's west coast.

'Arorangi

On Rarotonga's west coast, 'Arorangi was the first missionary-built village, conceived as a model for other villages on the island.

SADDLE SORE?

We're not sure how many registered motor-scooters there are in the Cooks, but we reckon – counting every man, woman and child – there'd be enough for about three or four each. This egalitarian form of transport is everywhere you look. To see a minister dressed in his flowing best white finery aboard his trusty Honda on the way to Sunday-morning church is a visionary sight indeed. People smoke and chat riding two-abreast, talk on the phone and maybe chew a sandwich at the same time. We saw one gentleman riding with a 100L esky under one arm and another with a large extension ladder. Enormous Polynesian mamas visibly ooze over each side while tiny children cling on behind.

Locals prefer the manual 110cc 'postie bike' but the scooters hired to tourists are usually the automatic type. They're easy to ride – a cooling breeze up your Bermuda shorts – with push-button ignitions, brakes and throttle, and rent for around NZ$25 per day. Even if you've never ridden a motorcycle before, after 10 minutes you're riding like a pro and after a few days you'll be walking like a cowhand.

RAROTONGA & THE COOK ISLANDS

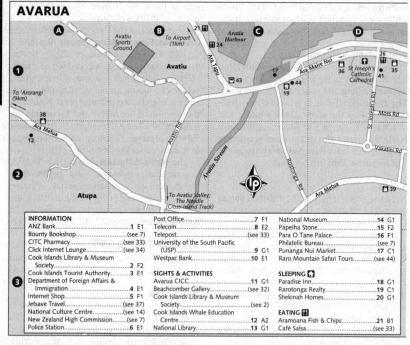

AVARUA

INFORMATION
ANZ Bank	1 E1
Bounty Bookshop	(see 7)
CITC Pharmacy	(see 33)
Click Internet Lounge	(see 34)
Cook Islands Library & Museum Society	2 F2
Cook Islands Tourist Authority	3 E1
Department of Foreign Affairs & Immigration	4 E1
Internet Shop	5 F1
Jetsave Travel	(see 37)
National Culture Centre	(see 14)
New Zealand High Commission	(see 7)
Police Station	6 E1
Post Office	7 F1
Telecom	8 E2
Telepost	(see 33)
University of the South Pacific (USP)	9 G1
Westpac Bank	10 E1

SIGHTS & ACTIVITIES
Avarua CICC	11 G1
Beachcomber Gallery	(see 32)
Cook Islands Library & Museum Society	(see 2)
Cook Islands Whale Education Centre	12 A2
National Library	13 G1
National Museum	14 G1
Papeiha Stone	15 F2
Para O Tane Palace	16 F1
Philatelic Bureau	(see 7)
Punanga Nui Market	17 C1
Raro Mountain Safari Tours	(see 44)

SLEEPING
Paradise Inn	18 G1
Rarotonga Realty	19 C1
Shekinah Homes	20 G1

EATING
Aramoana Fish & Chips	21 B1
Café Salsa	(see 33)

The missionary Papeiha is buried at the 1849 **CICC** (Map pp258-9).

There are several interesting art galleries in 'Arorangi, including **Pacific Arts** (Map pp258-9; ☎ 20200; merkens@oyster.net.ck; Ara Tapu) and the **Art Studio** (Map pp258-9; ☎ 22510; ikgeorge@oyster.net.ck).

Highland Paradise Cultural Centre

High above 'Arorangi, **Highland Paradise** (Map pp258-9; ☎ 21924; www.highlandparadise.co.ck; tours adult/child 6-12 yr/under 6 yr NZ$60/30/free) stands on the site of the old Tinomana village with panoramic views over the west and south coasts. Members of the Pirangi family, descendants of Tinomana Ariki, take visitors on a two-hour tour of the site, including gardens, *marae*, chief's throne and old lookout. Transport is included. On Wednesday there's a fabulous NZ$79 sunset island night.

South Coast

The south coast of Rarotonga has the island's best **beaches**. The best snorkelling is at Aro'a, Titikaveka and Tikioki. On the eastern edge of the abandoned Sheraton resort site, a road leads inland to **Wigmore's Waterfall** (Map pp258-9),

a lovely cascade dropping into a fresh, cool swimming pool.

Muri

Muri (Map pp258-9), with its four *motu* (islets), is the most beautiful section of Rarotonga's encircling lagoon. The water – with vivid hues of brilliant blue – is packed with tropical fish, especially around the *motu* (Taakoka, Koromiri, Oneroa and Motutapu) and out towards the reef. Taakoka is volcanic while the others are sand cays. The swimming is wonderful here over sparkling-white sand. Water-sports equipment (p265) and lagoon cruises are available from Muri through Captain Tama's and Reef to See (p265).

MURI WALKING TOUR

Start at the northern end of Muri Beach at **Avana Harbour**, one of the only deepwater passages into Rarotonga's lagoon. The great ocean-going *vaka* set off from here in the 14th century to settle NZ – the so-called 'Great Migration'. Walk a little north onto the small promontory to see **Marae Vaerota**, the traditional *marae* of the Kainuku Ariki, where

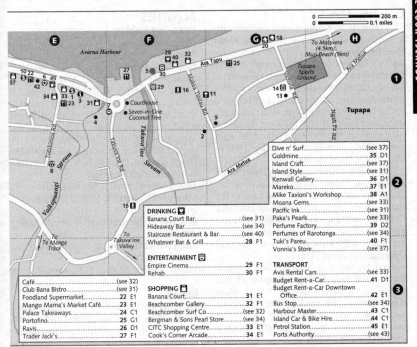

DRINKING 🍸
Banana Court Bar.............................(see 31)
Hideaway Bar..................................(see 34)
Staircase Restaurant & Bar.............(see 40)
Whatever Bar & Grill.........................28 F1

ENTERTAINMENT 🎭
Empire Cinema.................................29 F1
Rehab..30 F1

SHOPPING 🛍
Banana Court...................................31 E1
Beachcomber Gallery.......................32 F1
Beachcomber Surf Co.....................(see 32)
Bergman & Sons Pearl Store..........(see 34)
CITC Shopping Centre.....................33 E1
Cook's Corner Arcade......................34 E1

Dive n' Surf....................................(see 37)
Goldmine...35 D1
Island Craft....................................(see 37)
Island Style....................................(see 31)
Kenwall Gallery................................36 D1
Mareko..37 E1
Mike Tavioni's Workshop..................38 A1
Moana Gems...................................(see 33)
Pacific Ink.......................................(see 31)
Paka's Pearls..................................(see 33)
Perfume Factory...............................39 D2
Perfumes of Rarotonga....................(see 34)
Tuki's Pareu.....................................40 F1
Vonnia's Store.................................(see 37)

TRANSPORT
Avis Rental Cars.............................(see 33)
Budget Rent-a-Car............................41 D1
Budget Rent-a-Car Downtown
Office..42 E1
Bus Stop..(see 34)
Harbour Master................................43 C1
Island Car & Bike Hire......................44 C1
Petrol Station...................................45 E1
Ports Authority...............................(see 43)

Café..(see 32)
Club Bana Bistro.............................(see 31)
Foodland Supermarket.....................22 E1
Mango Mama's Market Café.............23 E1
Palace Takeaways............................24 C1
Portofino...25 G1
Ravis...26 D1
Trader Jack's...................................27 F1

WALK FACTS

Start Avana Harbour
Finish Muri Village
Distance 2km
Duration Two hours

---

the canoes were blessed and human sacrifices were made to the gods.

Head south and look out for the picturesque **Ngatangi'ia CICC**, where you'll find some interesting headstones. Opposite in the park there's the **ancient canoes' stone circle** and a plaque commemorating the seven canoes that completed the journey to NZ: *Takitumu, Tokomaru, Kurahaupo, Aotea, Tainui, Te Arawa* and *Mataatua*. There's a **modern stone circle** further south that commemorates the arrival of traditional Polynesian canoes during the sixth Festival of Pacific Arts in 1992.

Glorious **Muri Beach** is south of here, one of the island's best snorkelling areas. It's a lovely walk along the shoreline with views over the four palm-covered **motu** in the lagoon – Motutapu is the furthest north, with Oneroa,

Koromiri and little Taakoka to the south. The remains of one of Rarotonga's oldest **marae** are on Motutapu, but you'll need to hire a kayak to get out there. Pick up some light refreshment at **Sails Restaurant** (p270) or the **Barefoot Bar** at the Pacific Resort (p268), then amble down the main road to **Shells & Craft** (Map pp258-9; ☎ 22275) to see some spectacular conch and clam shells.

Matavera

The old **CICC** (Map pp258-9) is lovely at night when the outside is lit up. **Perfumes of Rarotonga** (see p272) concocts perfumes, liqueurs and colognes, and there's a pottery shop at the rear.

Arai-Te-Tonga

A small sign points off the road to the island's most important marae site, **Arai-Te-Tonga** (Map pp258-9). Situated just off the Ara Metua there's a stone-marked *koutu* (ancient open-air royal courtyard) site in front of you. This whole area was a gathering place, and the remains of the *marae*, the *koutu* and other meeting grounds are still visible.

Cross-Island Track

This three- to four-hour hike, from the north to south coasts via the 413m **Te Rua Manga** (Needle; Map pp258–9), is the most popular walk on Rarotonga, passing through some of the island's most impressive natural scenery. You shouldn't try to do the walk in a north–south direction, as the chances of taking a wrong turn are much greater. Wear adequate shoes, take plenty of drinking water and lather on the mosquito repellent. Parts of the walk get extremely slippery in wet weather – you're likely to get muddy and sweaty.

The tourist office recommends walkers join a guided tour (p266), but it's perfectly possible to do the walk on your own. The road to the starting point starts south of the Avatiu Harbour. Continue on the road up the valley by Avatiu Stream until you reach a sign announcing the beginning of the walk. A private vehicle road continues for about 1km.

From the end of the vehicle road a footpath leads off and after 10 minutes drops down and crosses a small stream. Don't follow the white plastic power-cable track up the valley, but instead pick up the track beside the massive boulder on the ridge to your left, after the stream crossing.

From here, the track climbs steeply up to the Needle (about 45 minutes). At the first sight of the Needle there's a boulder in the middle of the path – a nice place for a rest. A little further on is a T-junction; the Needle is a 10-minute walk to the right. Don't try to climb up to the Needle itself, as there have been several recent rockfalls and landslides, and there's a long, probably fatal drop on either side of the trail. Follow the track round to the left instead, and you'll begin the long, slippery descent towards the south coast.

After 30 minutes the track meets the Papua Stream and follows it downhill, zigzagging back and forth across the stream. After about 45 minutes, the track emerges into fernland. Be sure to stick to the main track; there are several places where minor tracks seem to take off towards the stream but these end at dangerous spots upstream from the waterfall. Another 15 minutes further on, the main track turns back towards the stream, bringing you to the bottom of **Wigmore's Waterfall** (Map pp258-9). A dirt road leads from the south coast up to the waterfall. It's about a 15-minute walk to the coast road, where you can flag down the circle-island bus or cool off in the nearby lagoon.

ACTIVITIES
Deep-Sea Fishing

Deep-sea fishing is popular in the Cook Islands, with catches of *mahimahi* fish and tuna (from October to May), wahoo and barracuda (April to October), and sailfish and marlin (November to March). All of the following operators have safety gear – contact them by telephone or down at the Avatiu wharf where the boats tie up. A five-hour tour, including lunch and refreshments, costs around NZ$160 per person. The **CI Game Fishing Club** (Map pp258-9; ☎ 22230), just west of Avarua, is where anglers swap yarns.

Akura Charters (☎ 54355; fish@akura.co.ck)

Fisher's Fishin' Tourz (☎ 23356, 55154; bafisher@oyster.net.ck)

Hook Fishing Charters (☎ 54475; hookfish@pacific motors.co.ck)

Pacific Marine Charters (☎ 21237; www.pacific marinecharters.co.ck)

Seafari Charters (☎ 20328, 55096; www.seafari.co.ck)

Diving

Diving is fantastic outside the reef, especially around the passages along the island's southern side. There are canyons, caves and tunnels to explore, and outside the lagoon the island drops off to around 4000m, although most diving is between 3m and 30m.

Rarotonga has several well-preserved shipwrecks, including SS *Maitai* off the northern shore. Other well-known diving spots include Black Rock in the north; Sandriver and Matavera Wall on the island's east side; and the Avaavaroa, Papua and Rutaki passages in the south (see p73).

Rarotonga has four accredited diving operators, all offering twice-daily boat trips. Single-tank dives cost NZ$70 to NZ$75 and two-tank dives are about NZ$125, including gear. Introductory dives are available and four-day open-water courses cost around NZ$420.

Cook Island Divers (Map pp258-9; ☎ 22483; www .cookislandsdivers.com; 'Arorangi)

Dive Centre (Map pp258-9; ☎ 20238; www.thedive centre-rarotonga.com; Aro'a Beach)

Dive Rarotonga (Map pp258-9; ☎ 21873; www.dive rarotonga.com; 'Arorangi)

Pacific Divers (Map pp258-9; ☎ 22450; www.pacific divers.co.ck; Muri Beach)

Hiking

The island's mountainous centre is crisscrossed by some stunning walking tracks and trails. The top walk is the **Cross-Island Track** (opposite), but there are lots of others to discover. The best guide is *Rarotonga's Mountain Tracks and Plants* by Gerald McCormack and Judith Künzlé, also authors of *Rarotonga's Cross-Island Walk*.

Wear light, breathable clothing and sturdy boots, and check the weather forecast before you go. Tell someone where you're headed and when you expect to return.

Sailing & Water Sports

Muri Lagoon and the island's south coast are the best places for swimming, windsurfing, sailing and kayaking. Sailing races start at Muri Beach every Saturday and Sunday afternoon from around 1pm. Kayaks are readily available, and many hotels provide them for guests' use. They're easy to handle, great fun and ideal for exploring the deserted *motu* on Muri Lagoon.

The **Rarotonga Sailing Club** (Map pp258–9; ☎ 27349; Muri Beach) rents out kayaks (NZ$7/12 for one/three hours) and small sailing boats (NZ$35/100 for one/three hours).

The 38ft trimaran **Hotel California** (☎ 23577; www.paradise-sailing.co.ck; adult/child NZ$75/35) does three-hour afternoon cruises including refreshments. Sunset cruises are also offered.

Captain Tama's AquaSportz Centre (Map pp258–9; ☎ 27350; www.captaintamas.com; Muri Beach), beside the Rarotonga Sailing Club, rents out kayaks (singles/doubles NZ$7/10 per hour) and sailboards (NZ$25 per hour).

Swimming & Snorkelling

Rarotonga's spectacular lagoon is fantastic for snorkelling and swimming – it's crystal-clear, warm and packed with technicolour fish and coral. The beaches along the island's southern and western sides are all good for swimming, but the northern and upper-eastern sides are not as good. The best snorkelling is around Muri Lagoon, Aro'a Beach, Titikaveka and Tikioki in the south of the island, and Black Rock in the northwest. Many of these areas are protected by *ra'ui* (traditional conservation areas).

Snorkelling gear is available from the island's diving operators (see opposite); some hotels also provide free gear for guests' use. **Dive n' Surf** (Map pp262–3; ☎ 27122; Ara Maire Nui, Avarua) sells good-quality fins, masks and snorkels. **Captain Tama's AquaSportz Centre** (Map pp258–9; ☎ 27350; Muri Beach), beside the Rarotonga Sailing Club, has snorkelling gear for hire.

Reef to See (☎ 22212; reef2see@oyster.net.ck) offers twice-daily snorkelling trips at 9am and 2pm (adult/child NZ$65/40). It's best to call ahead to book your place.

Surfing

Surfing is in its infancy on Rarotonga. Bodyboarding is popular but local board-riders are few and it's not the place to come to learn – the reef-breaks are steep and fast, and the water is shallow. Raro surfing is dangerous – for intermediates and experts only – and too fast for longboarders. The island's north gets swells in the November-to-March cyclone season while the south works best during the May-to-August 'winter'. There are breaks at **Social Centre** in the northwest, off the **Rarotongan Beach Resort**, **Avaavaroa** and **Papua** on the south coast, and **Koromiri**, **Turangi** and **Matavera** on the east side. Since the waves break outside the lagoon it's a long paddle to the action. For local advice talk to Paka Worthington, of Paka's Pearls (p272), and the guys at Chillis Sports Bar (p271) – forget the surfwear stores. BYO surfboards and a measure of courage.

Other Sports

Volleyball is often played on Muri Beach or at the Rarotongan Beach Resort (p268). **Tennis** courts are available at Edgewater Resort (Map pp258–9; ☎ 25435) and Rarotongan Beach Resort.

Rarotonga's nine-hole **golf course** (Map pp258–9; ☎ 20621; www.rarotonga.nzgolf.net; ☼ 8am-2pm Mon-Fri, members only Sat) is near the airport.

RAROTONGA FOR CHILDREN

Always check with the place you're staying about their policy on children, as many don't cater for kids under 12. For really little ones, you can hire strollers, car seats, porta-cots and the like from **Coco Tots** (☎ 56986; www.cocototots.com).

The top draw for kids is the island's colourful lagoon and the spectacular beach that stretches around the island. Good spots for snorkelling are **Muri**, **Tikioki** and **Aro'a Beach** – smoothies and ice creams are never far away at **Fruits of Rarotonga** (p269) and the **Saltwater Café** (p269). For an in-depth look at the island's underwater inhabitants, kids will adore Captain Tama's **glass-bottom boat** (p266), which chugs around Muri Lagoon – they might spot humpback whales between July and October.

THE COCONUT KING

He zips up coconut trees, conjures fire from dry twigs and cooks up island feasts. He is **Piri Puruto III** (Map pp258-9; ☎ 20309), Rarotonga's best-known showman, and well into his sixties. The show costs NZ$15 and runs several nights a week. There's also a traditional *umukai* on Sunday that you can help prepare (NZ$49). Children get in to all Piri's activities for half price.

Active kids will love exploring the island's jungle-covered interior, especially in the company of **Pa Teuraa** (below), the Cook Islands equivalent of Indiana Jones. Pa offers informative nature walks as well as guided tours across the island. A jeep-ride around the island with **Tangaroa 4x4 Adventures** (right) will be sure to please, or you can buckle them in for a spin with **Coconut Tours** (right). Sunday's must-do is a traditional *umukai* with the venerable **Piri Puruto III** (above) and his world-famous coconut show.

TOURS
Glass-Bottom Boat
Captain Tama's AquaSportz Centre (Map pp258-9; ☎ 27350; Muri Beach) operates glass-bottom boat tours (adult/child NZ$70/35), including snorkelling and a barbecue lunch, on Koromiri. The tours run from 11am to 3pm Monday to Saturday.

Scenic Flights
Air Rarotonga (☎ 22888; www.airraro.com) offers 20-minute scenic flights (minimum two, maximum three; adult/child NZ$90/50), complete with onboard commentary. Flights take place from 8.30am to 4pm daily.

Walking Tours
Pa's Mountain Walk (☎ 21079; adult/child NZ$55/25) is a guided trek over the cross-island track run by dreadlocked Pa Teuraa – herbalist, botanist and traditional healer. Pa's cross-island walk runs on Monday, Wednesday and Friday (weather permitting), and he conducts nature walks on Tuesdays and Thursdays.

The **Takitumu Conservation Area** (TCA; Map pp258-9; ☎ 29906; kakerori@tca.co.ck; Ara Tapu, Avarua) is a private forest reserve in Rarotonga's southeast corner. There are guided tours around the reserve (adult/child NZ$50/30)

where you might see the endangered *kakerori* (Rarotongan flycatcher).

Whale Watching
Humpback whales visit the Cook Islands from July to October. Most dive operators and fishing charters offer whale-watching trips in season. The **Cook Islands Whale Education Centre** (Map pp262-3; ☎ 21666; www.whale research.org; Ara Metua, Atupa) has plenty of information about whales, including the best time to see them.

Vehicle Tours
A round-the-island tour is a great way to see the island, especially if you're only here for a few days. **Raro Tours** (Map pp258-9; ☎ 25325; coaches@rarotours.co.ck) does an Island Discovery Tour twice daily Monday to Friday, including pick-up and drop-off at your hotel, for NZ$60 per person.

Mr T's Tropical Tours (☎ 73915) does circle-island tours, including pick-up and drop-off, for NZ$50.

Raro Mountain Safari Tours (Map pp262-3; ☎ 23629; www.rarosafaritours.co.ck; opposite Punanga Nui Market) runs three-hour expeditions (adult/child 6-11 years NZ$75/35) around the island's rugged mountains, inland valleys and historical points of interest in safari-style jeeps. Transfers and a fresh-fish beach barbeque lunch are included. Tours run Monday to Friday at 9am and 1.30pm, and at noon on Sunday.

Tangaroa 4x4 Adventures (Map pp258-9; ☎ 22200; www.tangaroa4x4.co.ck; Ara Tapu, Vaima'anga) runs a tour of the island's main attractions, including the inland road, Avana Harbour, eastern heights, *marae*, library, power station and even the Rarotongan prison. The three-hour tour, which includes lunch and transfers, runs Monday to Saturday and Sunday afternoon (adult/child NZ$60/30).

Coconut Tours (Map pp258-9; ☎ 24004; www.coconut tours.co.ck; per person 1-/2.5-hr ride NZ$100/150, two people in buggy per person NZ$55/95) leads a convoy of excited wannabe rally drivers in quad-bikes (single seaters) and buggies (seat two people) through the mud, backroads and streams of the island's rugged interior. Tours run twice daily, rain or shine.

SLEEPING
Rarotonga has accommodation options to suit all budgets, although postcard-perfect views come at a premium. For more options,

try **Rarotonga Accommodation** (http://rarotonga accommodation.com), **Cook Islands Resorts & Accommodation** (www.rarotonga.islands-resorts.com), **Cook Islands A to Z** (www.cookislandsatoz.com) and **Jetsave Travel** (www.jetsa ve.co.ck).

Budget

Rarotonga has several run-down motels with some self-contained rooms, but budget travellers are much better served at the backpacker establishments, which have high visitor turnover and strong competition. Shared kitchen and bathroom facilities are generally good and there are often discounted activities and vehicle hire.

Rarotonga Backpackers (Map pp258-9; ☎ 21590; www .rarotongabackpackers.com; hillside/beachside dm NZ$18/20, s NZ$35/40, tw NZ$38/48, d from NZ$42/48, self-contained bungalows from NZ$69, beachfront d & q $80-150; ☎ ☐) The pick of the bunch in the backpacker market, with a beachfront site and a quirky hillside site both offering various room types from dorms to fully self-contained suites and a beachfront house. At both sites, dorms and rooms are set around a central pool, and there are self-contained units with private verandas and fabulous views. There are deals on scooter and car hire and activities. When we visited, Rarotonga Backpackers was purchasing a new site on Aitutaki, so ask about packages.

Tiare Village Hostel (Map pp258-9; ☎ 23466; www.tiare village.co.ck; dm/s/d/poolside units NZ$20/25/45/70; ☐ ☎) Near Avarua, behind the airport, this hostel is a good choice for budget travellers, groups and families. Small dorm rooms inside the large main house share a kitchen, bathroom and comfortable lounge. Outside there are three tiny self-contained A-frame chalets and several roomy self-contained poolside units.

Vara's (Map pp258-9; ☎ 23156; www.varas.co.ck; dm NZ$20-25, s NZ$38-44, d NZ$50-75, units NZ$120-140; ☐) Vara's, on Muri Beach, is popular with the young party set. It's cheap, in a perfect location and, with all sorts of room configurations, it's always busy. Vara's has a reputation for late-night revelry and organised pub crawls – those seeking South Seas tranquillity should look elsewhere. The beachside accommodation can be cramped but the hillside lodge offers more room, better value and great views.

Aquarius Rarotonga (Map pp258-9; ☎ 21003; www .aquariusrarotonga.com; dm NZ$30, s & d NZ$150; ☒ ☐ ☎) This new property, on the beachfront next to the airport, offers ocean-view self-contained doubles and a large dorm area. A good choice for families, Aquarius is spotlessly clean and good value, with 24-hour reception, TV lounge and swimming pool, and is conveniently located within walking distance to the Avarua shops and restaurants.

Aremango Guesthouse (Map pp258-9; ☎ 24362; www .aremango.co.ck; s/d from NZ$35/60) Aremango is a large purpose-built facility with a mix of shared and private fan-cooled rooms arranged along a central hallway. The common lounge, bathroom and kitchens are clean, comfortable and well fitted out. Muri Beach is a short walk away. They don't care for post-10pm noise at Aremango, so you're either tucking into bed or heading offsite to drink and make merriment.

Etu Bungalows (Map pp258-9; ☎ 25588; www.etubunga lows.com; d bungalows NZ$90, extra persons NZ$35) These simple garden bungalows, on Rarotonga's sunset side, are a good option for couples or small families on a budget. With roomy open-plan interiors, high ceilings and plenty of light, each bungalow has a kitchen, small bathroom and shady veranda. They're good value and just a short walk across the road to the beach. The owners have a similar set-up on Aitutaki called Esma Villas (see p277).

Shells & Craft Bungalows (Map pp258-9; ☎ 22275; www.shellbungalows.co.ck; d/q NZ$120/140, flat NZ$100) In a great location 100m from Muri Beach behind Terry's Shells & Craft shop, these two large self-contained bungalows with full kitchens are great value. One has a mezzanine level that sleeps an extra two, and next to the shop there's a huge flat (not so prettied up) that sleeps four.

Midrange

Paradise Inn (Map pp262-3; ☎ 20544; www.paradiseinn rarotonga.com; s NZ$69-93, d/tr/f NZ$116/135/149) Paradise Inn was once Rarotonga's largest and liveliest dance hall but has been refitted to provide simple, good-value self-contained accommodation with kitchen facilities. The location, a few minutes' walk to Avarua's shops and restaurants, is terrific. The old building is packed with character, with a huge lounge, polished-wood floors, nautical knick-knacks, an honesty bar and a fine sea-view veranda.

Kura's Kabanas (Map pp258-9; ☎ 27010; www.kkabanas .co.ck; cottage NZ$120, studios NZ$200, cabanas NZ$200; ☒ ☐) Shady palms, lagoon views and a glorious china-white beach are just steps from the doors of Kura's four airy timber-framed cabanas. They're well appointed with broad verandas and tasteful furniture. Two larger 1st-floor family studios can sleep four (children under 12 free). Fully-equipped kitchens, queen beds, TVs and a great location make this hard to beat in the price range. Kura also has the self-contained 'Luv Nest' high in the hills, snug enough for two.

Daydreamer Apartments (Map pp258-9; ☎ 25965; www.daydreamer.co.ck; 1-/2-bedroom apt NZ$140/195) These five large, light and airy apartments offer excellent value, with the smaller comfortably sleeping three and the larger five. Though not directly on the beach, they're a short walk to the sea. The modern units have separate dining, lounge and bedroom areas, each with a small patio area. The apartments are well set up for self-catering families, and children are welcome.

Club Raro (Map pp258-9; ☎ 22415; www.clubraro .co.ck; d NZ$140-210; ✷ 🖳 🐾) Club Raro has comfortable motel rooms strewn along a pebbly beachfront and around a central pool. The walkways are tiled and there's not the lush garden we see at other properties, but the 2½-acre facility caters well to its visitors with bars and a restaurant, wi-fi, scooter hire, pool table and organised activities. Free breakfast daily.

Sunhaven Beach Bungalows (Map pp258-9; ☎ 28465; www.mysunhaven.com; studios NZ$195-260, bungalows NZ$230-300; ✷ 🐾) A top choice. Sunhaven offers great value in some of the largest self-contained rooms on the island, set around a beachfront swimming pool on a quiet stretch of west-coast beach. The nine bungalows are sparkling clean and simply finished, with white-tile floors, cane furniture and functional fixtures. Not especially Polynesian but a million-dollar location.

Bella Beach Bungalows (Map pp258-9; ☎ 26004; www .ck/bellabeach; bungalows NZ$200) With the waves all but licking the stilts of these four simple, functional units at Titikaveka on the island's south side, they're about as close to the beach as you can get and they boast glorious ocean views. Inside there are tiled floors, kitchens, small bathrooms and comfortable king-sized beds, while outside there are large sundecks overlooking the beach.

Muri Beachcomber (Map pp258-9; ☎ 21022; www .beachcomber.co.ck; per double units NZ$255-355; ✷ 🖳 🐾) With a choice of garden and seaview units and luxury villas overlooking lovely grounds and a tropical lily pond, the Muri Beachcomber has a relaxed family-friendly village feel. The accommodation is modern – clean lines and tasteful appointments – and on-site facilities include guest lounge, laundry, pétanque court, free kayak use and snorkelling gear. There are 22 units on the 2½-acre property but plenty of space in between and the location is terrific.

Magic Reef Bungalows (Map pp258-9; ☎ 27404; www .magicreef.co.nz; s & d NZ$295-395; ✷ 🖳 🐾) On a golden stretch of sand on the sunset side of the island, the brand-new Magic Reef gets rave reviews. The large thatched bungalows have tasteful décor with four-poster beds, fans and aircon, galley kitchens, private outdoor showers and bathtubs, separate bathrooms and TV/DVD. Airport transfers are complimentary, as is the first morning's breakfast. There's a pétanque course and huge BBQ for guests' use, though the weird pirate-ship-shaped swimming pool is a touch too Disneyland for our tastes.

Top End

Rarotongan Beach Resort (Map pp258-9; ☎ 25800; www .therarotongan.com; garden/beachfront r NZ$270/370, ste NZ$445-730, honeymoon bungalow NZ$680; ✷ 🖳 🐾) As big and busy as it is, the Rarotongan offers excellent accommodation and amenities at a reasonable price. Popular with families, honeymooners and wedding parties, it has a prime location right on Aro'a Beach. It's all suitably Polynesian with Tangaroa statues, floral designs and Cook Islands motifs everywhere, and the rooms continue the tropical theme. Ask after package deals to its sister Aitutaki Beach Resort.

Pacific Resort (Map pp258-9; ☎ 20427; www.pacific resort.com; villas NZ$370-1200; ✷ 🖳 🐾) Though not as impressive as its sister Pacific Resort Aitutaki, the larger Pacific Resort Rarotonga is nonetheless excellent. Right on Muri Beach and shaded by overhanging palm trees, the 64 self-contained units are smart, elegant and unfussy, with some deference paid to local materials and traditional building styles – the best have sitting rooms and private verandas. There are all the amenities you'd expect as well as two eateries, the beachfront Barefoot Bar and the open-air Sandals Restaurant.

Apartments Kakera (Map pp258-9; ☎ 20532; www .apartmentskakera.com; apt NZ$380-600; ✷ 🖳 🐾) With three huge modern apartments that blend sleek modern décor with some lovely

Polynesian touches, Kakera also boasts a long list of eco-credentials. The split-level apartments have high ceilings, private courtyard gardens with plunge pools, full kitchens and flat-panel TV/DVD and entertainment systems. This new family-friendly option is also popular for weddings and honeymooners. Enquire about deals and specials.

Crown Beach Resort (Map pp258-9; ☎ 23953; www .crownbeach.com; 1-/2-bedroom villas NZ$500/725, beachfront NZ$700-750; ☒ ☐ ☒) Crown Beach manages to keep the best of the old and the new, the small and the large. Too big to be boutique, yet retaining much of what we admire most in Rarotonga's best small hotels, the Crown Beach has individually finished thatched bungalows, each with private garden, blonde timber, wicker furniture and local artwork. Bars, restaurants, a gym, day spa, function centre, gift shop and wi-fi are all bundled up in a not-so-small package.

Sea Change (Map pp258-9; ☎ 22532; www.sea-change -rarotonga.com; villas NZ$500-1050; ☒ ☐ ☒) Many of Rarotonga's boutique hotels look to this place as a benchmark. The impeccably appointed free-standing thatched villas have interiors that are fabulously appointed with luxury king-size four-poster beds, home entertainment systems, flat-screen TVs and private outdoor pools. The open-plan villas are finished in earthy tones and traditional materials that offset the contemporary design elements.

our pick **Little Polynesian** (Map pp258-9; ☎ 24280; www.littlepolynesian.com; villas NZ$550-950; ☒ ☐ ☒) The 10 beachfront and four garden villas at Little Polynesian are a superb blend of traditional Polynesian design (with traditional Mangaian sennit binding) and modern architecture, and the uninterrupted lagoon view from the foyer and pool and each of the king beds is sublime. The décor is simple, elegant, uncluttered and unerringly beautiful, and the appointments – from the private decks and daybeds to the outdoor showers and lime-washed timbers – are just right.

Long-Term Rental

Renting a house is often the best-value way to visit the island, especially for families. Fully furnished two-bedroom houses cost around NZ$250 to NZ$400 per week.

Jetsave Travel (Map pp262-3; ☎ 27707; www.jetsave .co.ck; Ara Maire Nui, Avarua)

Nikao Holiday Homes (☎ /fax 20168; aretai@oyster .net.ck)

Rarotonga Realty (Map pp262-3; ☎ /fax 26664; www .rarorealty.co.ck; Ara Tapu, Avarua)

Shekinah Homes (Map pp262-3; ☎ /fax 26004; www .shekinah.co.ck; Ara Tapu, Avarua)

EATING
Cafés & Quick Eats

Fruits of Rarotonga (Map pp258-9; ☎ 21509; breakfasts NZ$3-5; ☒ Mon-Sat) Homemade jams and tropical-flavoured chutneys (from NZ$3.60) are divine at this little shop opposite Tikioki beach, but it's good for smoothies, cakes and fruit juices too.

Aramoana Fish & Chips (Map pp262-3; ☎ 21250; meals NZ$7-10; ☒ lunch & dinner) Fresh fish and chips beside Avatiu Harbour. Aramoana also sells fresh and smoked fish for your self-catering pleasure.

Saltwater Café (Map pp258-9; ☎ 20020; meals NZ$8-22; ☒ breakfast & lunch Mon-Fri, dinner Tue-Thu) This colourful roadside fibro shack, on the south coast at Titikaveka, is a great place for an inexpensive lunch or cold drink. The eclectic menu includes tempura prawns and Mexican enchiladas. Ex-Sydneysider Carey Winterflood runs the joint and is a friendly conversationalist – he'll mind your bag while you swim at the beach opposite. A top spot.

Café (Map pp262-3; ☎ 21283; Ara Tapu; cakes & muffins NZ$2-5, lunch from NZ$8; ☒ breakfast & lunch Mon-Sat) Café shifted premises recently into the brilliantly refurbished Beachcomber building and hasn't missed a beat. Customers take their first-class coffees and light meals in the shaded central atrium that's bathed in muted sunlight, and idly turn pages of the morning paper or Café's current arty magazines.

Maire Nui Gardens & Café (Map pp258-9; ☎ 22796; lunch NZ$7-15; ☒ Mon-Fri) A glorious café on the southern side of the island, with a thatched terrace offering views over botanical grounds and tranquil lily ponds. Owner Hinano MacQuarie's homemade cakes and afternoon teas are well known all over the island, and afterwards you can take a relaxing stroll around the gardens (NZ$3).

Deli-licious Café (Map pp258-9; ☎ 20858; www.deli licious.net; lunch NZ$8-16; ☒ breakfast & lunch; ☐) Right in the heart of the Muri beach community is Deli-licious. It's a class act serving up cooked breakfasts and salads, sandwiches, pies and toasted pidés for lunch. Excellent 'Atiu coffee is served along with shakes and smoothies. This place is always buzzing, and has half a dozen internet terminals, a couch and shady outdoors eating area.

Palace Takeaways (Map pp262-3; ☎ 21438; Avatiu Harbour; burgers NZ$4-8, meals NZ$10-13; ⓨ lunch & dinner Mon-Sat) Ever-popular Palace does a roaring trade serving massive burgers and fast-food fare from a roadside stall beside Avatiu Harbour.

Mango Mama's Market Café (Map pp262-3; ☎ 20284; breakfast NZ$7-18, lunch NZ$10-20; ⓨ breakfast & lunch Mon-Sat; 🖳) This is the new incarnation of Mama's Café, which served Avarua townsfolk for nearly 20 years, though they've upped the ante with a sleek fit-out of the new bright and airy self-service canteen across the road from Cook's Corner. The food's also good, with hearty cooked breakfasts and light lunchtime vittles such as sweetcorn fritters and Mango Mama's chowder.

Café Salsa (Map pp262-3; ☎ 22215; mains NZ$8-25; ⓨ breakfast & lunch daily) This trendy café/restaurant is more Auckland-chic than Polynesian, and one of Avarua's hottest spots for lunch. There's a varied menu and huge specials board; dishes range from spinach, feta and pawpaw salads and Cajun-style chicken to wood-fired pizzas.

Club Bana Bistro (Map pp262-3; ☎ 21476; breakfast NZ$8-17, lunch NZ$12-22; ⓨ breakfast & lunch) The ice-cold fruit smoothies here are a tonic on a hot day. This colourful open-air café-bar in the Banana Court Building serves fresh 'Atiu coffee and all-day breakfasts. The eclectic menu features Caesar salad, burgers, curries and open sandwiches, and daily-changing specials.

Restaurants

Raviz (Map pp262-3; ☎ 22297; mains NZ$16-20; ⓨ lunch & dinner) Rarotonga's only Indian restaurant is the real deal, popular with locals and visitors alike. Have your Madras fish curry, chicken tikka or lamb korma done just the way you like it. On Monday and Tuesday all mains are NZ$13.

Sails Restaurant (Map pp258-9; ☎ 27349; www.sailsrestaurant.co.ck; mains NZ$16-30; ⓨ lunch & dinner) In a great location overlooking the sands and sea of Muri Lagoon, breezy Sails is a lovely open-air bistro-bar serving light lunchtime fare and heartier evening meals. With Rarotonga's yacht club next door there's an interesting mix of yachties and beach bums who come to enjoy well-prepared but unpretentious food.

Trader Jack's (Map pp262-3; ☎ 26464; www.traderjackscookislands.com; mains NZ$18-32, platters NZ$50) This long-time favourite of Rarotonga's smart set took a caning in the 2005 cyclones. But Trader Jack's seized the opportunity for a re-build and the faithful returned. The maritime theme (with some interesting old photos), panoramic sea views and fine food make for a pleasant and memorable place to eat. The front bar has simple pub food while the restaurant is more classy.

Right on the Beach Bar & Restaurant (Map pp258-9; ☎ 22461; www.manuia.co.ck; mains NZ$18-34; ⓨ lunch & dinner) Huddled under a thatched canopy, this beachfront restaurant at the Manuia Beach Boutique Hotel offers the intoxicating mix of fine dining, brilliant South Seas sunsets and the feel of sand between your toes. The twice-weekly island night and buffet is popular – book ahead.

Kikau Hut (Map pp258-9; ☎ 26860; mains NZ$22-28; ⓨ dinner Mon-Sat) Candles and dim lighting make this circular restaurant in 'Arorangi a great place for an evening meal. The international cuisine is well prepared and the hosts are friendly and convivial. There's regular live music and a breezy relaxed atmosphere – come as you are.

Vaima Restaurant & Bar (Map pp258-9; ☎ 26123; www.vaimarestaurant.com; mains NZ$24-36; ⓨ dinner Mon-Sat) This family-run restaurant, in the island's south, is one of Rarotonga's best and well worth making a booking. The dining room has a tasteful island décor that features local artworks, a beachfront patio and breezy outside terrace. An evening meal here, with the sunset, a chilled NZ sauvignon blanc and sumptuous Pacific cuisine, is a memorable Rarotongan experience.

Flame Tree (Map pp258-9; ☎ 25123; www.flametreerestaurant.com; mains NZ$24-38; ⓨ dinner) The new owners of Flame Tree, at Muri Beach, had quite some shoes to fill after founder Sue Carruthers moved on to open Tamarind House, and they're doing a heck of a job of it. It's still one of the island's best restaurants with an attractive outside courtyard and a more formal dining room inside. The International cuisine is first class and always popular, with an inventive mix of local ingredients and European flair.

our pick Tamarind House (Map pp258-9; ☎ 26487; www.tamarind.co.ck; mains NZ$25-35; ⓨ breakfast, lunch & dinner) Sue Carruthers, Rarotonga's top chef, made her reputation with the Flame Tree, but has since fitted out this sweeping colonial-style building on the island's north shore. Book a table on the grand veranda and enjoy the cool evening breeze and some outstanding food – an inspired fusion of European, Asian and islander flavours. There's a good wine list, smart professional service and an elegant South Seas atmosphere.

Portofino (Map pp262-3; ☎ 26480; Ara Tapu; mains NZ$25-35; ☺ dinner Mon-Sat) There's a surprising number of Italian restaurants in Rarotonga, but Portofino is the original and still the best. Traditional pastas and Raro's best wood-fired pizzas are served in the relaxed, pastel-coloured dining room, or you can have takeaways delivered.

Self-Catering

Foodland (Map pp262-3; ☎ 23378; Ara Maire Nui; ☺ 8am-6pm Mon-Fri, 8am-2pm Sat) The best all-round supermarket is in the middle of Avarua's main shopping strip, with fresh bread, fruit and vegetables, packaged goods and a deli counter.

CITC Supermarket (Map pp258-9; ☎ 22000; Ara Tapu; ☺ 8am-6pm Mon-Fri, 8am-4pm Sat) Halfway to the airport from Avarua, the huge CITC Supermarket is great for tinned and packaged produce, but lousy for fresh food. There's a liquor store attached.

Wigmore's Superstore (Map pp258-9; ☎ 20206; ☺ 6am-9pm) The south coast's only proper grocery store is more expensive than Avarua's supermarkets. It's the only large supermarket that trades on Sunday and has a small liquor store.

Super Brown (Map pp258-9; ☎ 20140; Tupapa; ☺ 24hr) Super Brown is Raro's only all-night convenience store and petrol station, with a fair selection of groceries and takeaway food.

Early on Saturday mornings head to **Punanga Nui Market** (Map pp262-3) for an excellent variety of fresh fruit and vegetables, fish and seafood, barbecued snacks, and stalls selling fresh bread and traditional Polynesian food.

DRINKING & ENTERTAINMENT
Bars & Nightclubs

The main after-dark action is centred around Avarua. Raro's big night out is Friday, but Saturday is quickly catching up in popularity…and Wednesday and Thursday. On Friday most places stay open till around 2am, but doors are bolted shut at midnight on Saturday out of respect for the Sabbath. Most restaurants double as bars, and resort bars are open to nonguests.

There are several organised pub-crawls, including the **Friday Night Life Tour** (☎ 25435)

at the Edgewater Resort and the **Nitelife Tour** (☎ 25800) at the Rarotongan Beach Resort, which come complete with minibus and stone-cold sober driver. Several hostels, including **Aremango Guesthouse** (☎ 24362) and **Backpackers International Hostel** (☎ 21847), run less-organised (less genteel) Friday-night tours.

Whatever Bar & Grill (Map pp262-3; ☎ 22299) Who'd have thought – an open-air bar on a disused rooftop? Perched just off the main road out of Avarua, this is a great place that attracts trendy young things and gets lively on Friday and Saturday nights. There are DJs and the Whatever Stringband is always fun on Wednesdays. The night-time views across town and the harbour are brilliant, and the atmosphere is relaxed and welcoming.

Staircase Restaurant & Bar (Map pp262-3; ☎ 22254; ☺ Mon-Sat) Upstairs behind the Topshape Health & Fitness Centre building, the Staircase is always popular. The bar's decked out with atmospheric island decor and has regular live bands and DJs, as well as good-value island nights on Thursday and Friday.

RSA Bar (Map pp258-9; ☎ 20590; Avatiu) Opposite the airport, the dog-eared bar at the Returned Servicemen's Association is a cheap, cheerful place that gets busy for Monday's 'Tattoo Night' (a potent local tipple flavoured with cranberry).

Hideaway Bar (Map pp262-3; ☎ 22224; Cook's Corner Arcade) As its name suggests, the Hideaway is tucked away and is pretty small. On busy weekend nights everyone crams in to check out the live bands, and there are usually DJs a couple of nights a week.

Banana Court Bar (Map pp262-3; ☎ 23397) Once one of the most notorious drinking holes in the Pacific, the cavernous Banana Court is much tamer now. It's a good place for a drink, and has late-night discos on Friday and Saturday. Gay-friendly.

Chillis Sports Bar (Map pp258-9; ☎ 26240; Ara Tapu) There's an interesting mix of people at Chillis, where a rooftop satellite dish beams in sports events from all over the world.

Rehab (Map pp262-3; ☎ 25717; ☺ late Tue-Sat) Rehab is the 'fun clinic' – dance and trance-techno grooves thump' n' bump under ultra-violet and stroboscopic lights. For clubbers who like to move it, move it.

Cinema

Empire Cinema (Map pp262-3; ☎ 23189; Ara Tapu; adult/child NZ$8/4) Nightly new-release films.

ISLAND NIGHTS

Rarotonga's traditional form of evening entertainment is the island night – a spectacular showcase combining traditional dance and music (karioi) with a lavish buffet of local food (kai). Dancing, drumming and singing are always on show, but fire-juggling, acrobatics and storytelling are often thrown into the mix.

Island nights are held regularly at the large resorts, and every night except Sunday you can catch a show somewhere on the island. Extravagant affairs are featured at the **Pacific Resort** (p268), **Edgewater Resort** (Map pp258–9; ☎ 25435), **Crown Beach Resort** (p269) and the **Rarotongan Beach Resort** (p268). You'll pay between NZ$10 and NZ$25 for the show on its own, or NZ$55 to NZ$65 for the show and buffet. On Wednesday night **Highland Paradise** (p262) has a NZ$79 show that includes transport, a cocktail and an umu feast. On Thursday and Friday nights the **Staircase Restaurant & Bar** (p271) features a show costing just NZ$35 including food (show only NZ$5) – it's one of the island's best. If you want the full shebang we recommend the **Rarotongan Beach Resort** (p268). Ask at the tourist office for island night timetables.

SHOPPING
Arts & Crafts

There are shops around Avarua selling local basketwork, shell jewellery, necklaces, carvings and musical instruments. Many islands have their own speciality handicrafts, including rito (coconut-fibre) fans and hats from the Northern Group and pupu ei necklaces from Mangaia. Beware of cheap Asian imports.

Mike Tavioni (Map pp262-3; ☎ 24003; Ara Metua, Atupa) You can visit the workshop of Rarotonga's most renowned sculptor and carver, on the back road near Avarua. See his stone carvings at the Punanga Nui Market and the National Culture Centre.

Art Studio (Map pp258-9; ☎ 27788; ⏰ 10am-5pm Tue-Fri, 10am-1pm Sat) Two large carved wooden heads guard the entrance to this interesting gallery in 'Arorangi. Local artists are showcased and many works are for sale.

Kenwall Gallery (Map pp262-3; ☎ 25526) This gallery in Avarua features local art.

Island Craft (Avarua Map pp262-3; ☎ 22009; Ara Maire Nui; Muri Map pp258-9; ☎ 28011) The best-stocked souvenir shop is in Avarua, though some of its stuff is pretty tacky. The smaller Muri Beach store, next to Deli-licious Café, has a more select range. **Punanga Nui Market**, the **Beachcomber Gallery** (Map pp262-3; ☎ 21939; Ara Tapu, Avarua) and **Island Style** (Map pp262-3; ☎ 21901; Banana Court) have the best selections of local craftwork.

Black Pearls & Jewellery

Only the Cooks and French Polynesia produce black pearls, which are much rarer than their cream-coloured cousins. A single pearl could cost you anything from NZ$5 to well over NZ$2000. The largest retailers include **Bergman & Sons Pearl Store** (Map pp262-3; ☎ 21902; www.icon .net.nz; Tutakimoa Rd); **Beachcomber Gallery** (Map pp262-3; ☎ 21939; Ara Tapu); **Goldmine** (Map pp262-3; ☎ 24823) on Avarua's main road; and **Paka's Pearls** (Map pp262-3; ☎ 26064; www.pakas-pearls.com) and **Moana Gems** (Map pp262-3; ☎ 22312; www.moanagems .co.ck) in the CITC Shopping Centre.

Tokerau Jim (Map pp258-9; ☎ 24305; www.tokerau jim.com) With a small store and workshop in Matavera, Tokerau Jim does beautiful and incredibly fine carvings on pearls and pearl shell.

Pareu & Other Clothing

Printed pareu (sarongs) cost around NZ$10 to NZ$15, while handmade ones cost NZ$25 to NZ$35. The same stores around Avarua sell ultra-vivid Hawai'ian floral shirts (NZ$30 to NZ$95) that turn the volume way up – check out **Vonnia's Store** (Map pp262-3; ☎ 20927; Ara Maire Nui), **Tuki's Pareu** (Map pp262-3; ☎ 25537; Ara Maire Nui) and **Mareko** (Map pp262-3; ☎ 20548; Ara Maire Nui).

Great local T-shirts are sold at surfwear shops including **Turtles & Ocean/Earth** (Map pp258-9; ☎ 27113; Avatiu), **Dive n' Surf** (Map pp262-3; ☎ 27122; Ara Maire Nui, Avarua) and **Beachcomber Surf Co** (Map pp262-3; ☎ 27130; Ara Tapu).

Perfumes, Soaps & Coconut Oil

Perfumes of Rarotonga (Map pp258-9; ☎ 26238) On the main road in Matavera, this place makes its own perfumes, soaps, liqueurs and scented oils. Handmade coconut soap costs around NZ$4 while a bottle of perfume starts at around NZ$15. There's another **outlet** (Map pp262-3; Cooks Corner Arcade) in Avarua, or you can buy the products at the **Perfume Factory** (Map pp262-3; Ara Metua).

Stamps & Coins

Philatelic Bureau (Map pp262-3; ☎ 29336) Cook Islands coins and bank notes are sold here, plus sets of Cook Islands stamps (highly prized by philatelists). The unique $3 Cook Islands note is available in two designs.

Tattoos

Pacific Ink (Map pp262-3; no phone; stormykara@hotmail .com; ☒ 10am-3pm Mon-Fri) For the souvenir that lasts and lasts, try Pacific Ink, where you can choose from many traditional designs.

AITUTAKI

pop 2200 / area 18.3 sq km

Aitutaki, the Cooks' second-most-visited island, curls gently around one of the South Pacific's most stunning lagoons. The many hues of its pure aqua-blue water, the foaming breakers around the perimeter reef and the broad sandy beaches of its many small deserted islets make for a glorious scene. This is the Pacific island people imagine – swaying coconut palms and blindingly white beaches. Whether from the air or the water, Aitutaki will take your breath away. It's just 45 minutes by air from Rarotonga but feels like another world. Although there are some impressive plush resorts, this island is slower and much less commercialised. Sunday is solemnly observed as the day of prayer and rest. Whether or not you're a believer, take the opportunity to see a local church service – the singing is delightful.

Sunday flights from Rarotonga were recently introduced to howls of protest from elements of the religious community. Despite this, Aitutaki has an oversupply of accommodation, and many smaller family tourism operators are doing it hard – visitor numbers are falling, and those who do visit are coming on Air Rarotonga's day tour (see p275) or opting for the upmarket resorts.

HISTORY

Legend tells that Ru from 'Avaiki (Ra'iatea in French Polynesia) arrived at Aitutaki by *vaka* (canoe). He came with four wives, four brothers and their wives, and 20 royal maidens at the Akitua *motu* (now the Aitutaki Lagoon Resort).

Aitutaki's first European visitor was Captain William Bligh, who arrived on the *Bounty* on 11 April 1789 (17 days before the famous mutiny). In 1821 John Williams left Papeiha and Vahapata here to convert the islanders to Christianity. Charles Darwin called in on the 1835 *Beagle* voyage, and in the 1850s Aitutaki become a favourite port of call for whaling ships. During WWII American soldiers arrived to build two long runways, and in the 1950s the lagoon was used as a refuelling stopover for the Tasman Empire Air Line's (TEAL; Air New Zealand's predecessor) luxurious 'coral route' across the Pacific flown by Solent flying boats. John Wayne and Cary Grant were just two of the celebrities who spent some time on Akaiami *motu* while their Solent was refuelled.

ORIENTATION

Aitutaki is shaped like a curved fishhook: at the point you'll find O'otu Beach and the private Aitutaki Lagoon Resort, and the airstrip is slightly to the north. On the west side are most of the hotels and Arutanga, the island's main town. On the east coast are the small villages of Tautu, Vaipae and Vaipeka. The *motu* around the edge of Aitutaki's lagoon are uninhabited.

INFORMATION

Ask at your hotel if you should boil the water before drinking it. Many places get their drinking water from separate rain tanks.

There aren't any dogs on Aitutaki (the island's canine population was blamed for a leprosy outbreak) but there are plenty of roosters – bring earplugs if you're planning on sleeping in.

The main police station is behind the Orongo Centre near the wharf in Arutanga.

Aitutaki Tourism (www.aitutakitourism.com)

ANZ Bank agent (☎ 31418; ☒ 8am-3pm Mon-Fri) Inside Mango Trading, ATM outside.

Hospital (☎ 31002; ☒ 24hr) On the hill behind Arutanga.

Post office & Telecom (☎ 31470; ☒ 8am-4pm Mon-Fri) In the Administration Centre in Arutanga.

SpiderCo Internet Lounge (☎ 31780; lounge@ aitutaki.net.ck; per min NZ$0.50)

Visitor information centre (☎ 31767; retire-tourism@ aitutaki.net.ck; ☒ 8am-noon & 1-4pm Mon-Fri)

Westpac (☎ 31714; ☒ 9.30am-3pm Mon-Thu) In the Administration Centre in Arutanga with an ATM.

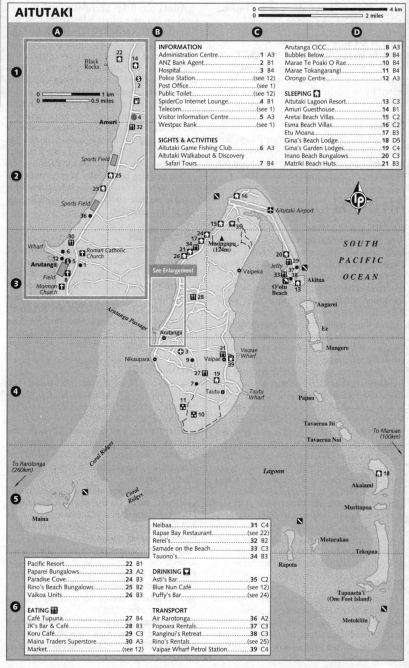

AITUTAKI

TRANSPORT
Getting There & Away

Air Rarotonga (www.airraro.com; Arutanga ☎ 31888; Rarotonga ☎ 22888) operates several flights to Aitutaki from Rarotonga Monday to Saturday, and one flight on Sunday. Regular one-way adult/child fares cost from NZ$206/155. There's also a direct flight from Aitutaki to 'Atiu every Wednesday (NZ$178/134).

Air Rarotonga runs Aitutaki Day Tours from Monday to Saturday, leaving Rarotonga at 8am and returning at 5.30pm. The cost is NZ$499/375 per adult/child, including hotel transfers, flights, a lagoon cruise with snorkelling gear and lunch.

Cargo ships travelling to the Northern Group occasionally stop at Aitutaki (see p295).

Getting Around

Island Tours (☎ 31379) offers a minibus transfer service that costs NZ$10 to and from the airport. Make arrangements with Willy at the airport. The larger resorts provide transfers for their guests.

Various places rent out bicycles (NZ$5 per day), scooters (NZ$25), cars and jeeps (NZ$70 to NZ$100). Try **Popoara Rentals** (☎ 31739; www .popoara.com; O'otu Beach), **Ranginui's Retreat** (☎ 31657; O'otu Beach) or, for the best range, **Rino's Beach Bungalows & Rentals** (☎ 31197; Arutanga).

AROUND THE ISLAND
Arutanga

After you've been to Rarotonga, Arutanga, Aitutaki's only town, seems astonishingly quiet with few signs of life even on weekdays when the shops are open. The island's main harbour is by the Orongo Centre. The lovely weather-beaten **CICC** church near the Administration Centre was built in 1828, making it the oldest in the Cooks. It has lovely stained-glass windows, fine carved wood panelling and an old anchor precariously suspended from the ceiling.

Marae

Aitutaki's *marae* are notable for their large stones. Orongo *marae* used to sit where the Blue Nun Café is today, in Arutanga. The main road goes through a large *marae*, and on the inland road between Nikaupara and Tautu there are some of the most magnificent *marae* on the island – including **Tokangarangi** and **Te Poaki O Rae** – mostly reclaimed by the jungle.

Maungapu

The 30-minute hike to the top of Maungapu (124m), Aitutaki's highest peak, provides splendid views over the entire atoll and the sapphire-blue lagoon. The track starts off pretty gently opposite the bungalows of Paradise Cove, but gets more challenging towards the summit.

Aitutaki Lagoon

Aitutaki's stunning lagoon, brimming with marine life and ringed by 15 palm-covered *motu*, is one of the treasures of the South Pacific. **Maina** (Little Girl) offers some of the best snorkelling spots and is home to the red-tailed tropicbird, once prized for its crimson feathers; the wreck of the cargo freighter *Alexander*, run aground in the 1930s, is nearby. **Akaiami** is where the old TEAL flying boats landed to refuel on the trans-Pacific 'Coral Route' between Fiji, Samoa and Tahiti – the remnants of the old jetty can still be seen. **Tapuaeta'i** (One Foot Island) is the best-known *motu*, fringed by white beaches and divided from its neighbour, Tekopua, by a deepwater channel that's teeming with tropical fish.

ACTIVITIES
Swimming & Snorkelling

The best swimming, snorkelling and beaches are around the *motu*, especially near **Maina**, accessible by boat (see p276). The folks at **Matriki Beach Huts** (p276) offer the only snorkelling trips outside the perimeter reef where the marine life is much more abundant. Just south of Black Rocks you can walk out to the outer reef on a coral causeway that starts 50m from the shore. The nicest swimming beaches on the main island are **O'otu Beach** and the wharves at **Vaipae** and **Tautu**. The island's east coast is mainly shallow mud and mangrove swamp.

Diving

Scuba diving is fantastic in Aitutaki. The visibility is great, and features include dropoffs, multilevels, wall dives and cave systems. Many divers ask to dive on the wreck of the *Alexander*, but it sits in a mere metre of water and is just as suitable for snorkellers.

There are a couple of diving operators on the island, with **Bubbles Below** (☎ 31537; www .diveaitutaki.com; 1/2 dives NZ$95/170, PADI discover/open-water course NZ$160/450) being recommended. Talk to the entertaining manager Onu (Turtle) Hewett.

TOURS

Most of the tour operators on Aitutaki don't have offices. Arrange a cruise by calling the operator or ask the people you're staying with to arrange it. The operator will collect you from your hotel.

Fishing

Find out about the fishing scene at **Aitutaki Game Fishing Club** (☎ 31379), by the wharf in Arutanga. Prices for fishing trips range from NZ$90 to NZ$180.

Aitutaki Sea Charter (☎ 31281)

Baxter's Fishing Charters (☎ 31025; baxter@aitutaki.net.ck)

Vaikore Bone Fishing Charters (☎ 31292)

Lagoon Cruises

For many, an Aitutaki lagoon cruise is a highlight. There are several operators who cruise around the *motu* and snorkelling spots. All provide snorkelling gear, a barbecue fish lunch and a stop at Tapuaeta'i (One Foot Island) – remember to take your passport to get it stamped at the One Foot Island 'post office'. Lagoon cruises generally cost NZ$65 (children NZ$32.50).

Aitutaki Adventures (☎ 31171; ◷ cruises Sun-Fri) Lagoon cruises include snorkelling, fish-feeding and a barbecue lunch on Tapuaeta'i.

Aitutaki Glass Bottom Boat (☎ 31790; story@aitutaki.net.ck; adult/child NZ$37/37.50) Aitutaki's only glass-bottomed boat cruises outside the barrier reef to see turtles and the rich marine life.

Bishop's Lagoon Cruises (☎ 31009; bishopcruz@aitutaki.net.ck; ◷ tours Mon-Sat) Tours visit Maina, Moturakau and Tapuaeta'l; there's a tour to Akaiami and Tapuaeta'i (NZ$35), as well as sunset, honeymoon cruises and *motu* drop-offs.

Kia-Orana Cruises (☎ 31442; kcruise@aitutaki.net.ck; ◷ Sun-Fri) The main tour visits Maina, Moturakau, Honeymoon Island and Tapuaeta'i.

Paradise Islands Lagoon Tours (☎ 31248; titiai tonga@aitutaki.net.ck) Cruises are on a Polynesian-style catamaran, the *Titi Ai Tonga* (Wind from the South), which has a roof and onboard bar.

Teking (☎ 31582; teking@aitutaki.net.ck) Offers a main 'Four Island' cruise to Akaiami, Tapuaeta'i, Honeymoon Island and Maina.

Other Tours

Aitutaki Walkabout & Discovery Safari Tours (☎ 31757; safari@aitutaki.net.ck) offers a walkabout tour (adult/child NZ$45/10) concentrating on the island's flora and fauna, and a 'discovery safari' (adult/child NZ$55/10) that visits the island's main historical sites in a yellow Jeep. Both tours run twice daily from Sunday to Friday. During crab season, there's a nighttime crab hunt (adult/child NZ$45/10).

Chloe & Nane's Tropicool Tour (☎ 31248) runs minibus tours to the villages and *marae* of Aitutaki (NZ$30) Monday to Saturday, and a popular sunset tour to see Aitutaki's rare blue lorikeet.

SLEEPING
Budget

Amuri Guesthouse (☎ 31231; www.ck/aitutaki/amuri; s/d/tr NZ$40/70/90) Amuri has six double bedrooms and two shared bathrooms with a large dining and kitchen area in the owner's house. Very clean, friendly and excellent value.

Matriki Beach Huts (☎ 31564; www.matrikibeach huts.com; s NZ$55-66, d NZ$75-80) Three knocked-up beachfront fibro shacks with mural painted walls and one self-contained garden unit comprise this most delightfully ramshackle place to stay. The split-level huts share toilet facilities but are otherwise self-contained with kitchenettes and showers and the most brilliant location. Matriki runs snorkelling trips outside the lagoon reef and offers fishing charters and activities.

Vaikoa Units (☎ /fax 31145; s/d NZ$65/75, beachfront bungalows NZ$110-120) The two self-contained beachfront bungalows are large and light with kitchens and sundecks, but they're a little dowdy and need a freshen-up. The older motel units at the rear are dark, but clean and good value if you're just bunking down. The location is the saving grace – the pearly white beach is priceless.

Gina's Garden Lodges (☎ 31058; www.ginasaitutaki desire.com; s/d/tr NZ$75/120/150; ⊛) Set among a peaceful garden of fruit trees and flowers in Tautu, these four large family-friendly lodges are the best value on Aitutaki. Queen Manarangi Tutai, one of Aitutaki's three *ariki* (high chiefs), is the proprietor here and one of the island's most gracious and charming hosts. The self-contained lodges have high ceilings and large verandas overlooking the gardens and decked swimming pool, and each has beds in a small loft that are perfect for kids. Gina's is in Tautu, a few kilometres from town, so you'll need transport. Queen Tutai also runs **Gina's Beach Lodge** (s/d/tr NZ$180/300/375 including transfers) on

Akaiami Island, and guests can choose to spend a while at each.

Midrange

Inano Beach Bungalows (☎ 31758; www.inanobeach .com; lagoon-view/beachfront bungalows NZ$130/160) Offering excellent value for money, Inano Beach Bungalows have been built using largely local materials and traditional methods. There are woven pandanus walls, ironwood balconies and mahogany tabletops. Near the end of the airport fronting a nice stretch of beach, Inano's self-contained bungalows are large with good kitchen facilities.

Rino's Beach Bungalows (☎ 31197; rinos@aitutaki .net.ck; s/d/tr from NZ$120/180/240, beachfront bungalows NZ$240-300; ☒) Rino's is the only motel-style accommodation on Aitutaki. In a great beachfront location, it's clean and serviceable, with large apartments near the beach and several rooms in the twin-storey buildings nearer the road. They have no Polynesian character – more a riot of dag kitsch – but they're good value and most have kitchenettes and sea views. Patrons get discounted scooter and vehicle hire at Rino's Rentals across the road.

Paradise Cove (☎ 31218; www.paradisecove.co.ck; bungalows NZ$180) Paradise Cove has really lifted its act since we were here last, retiring its tiny beach huts and making over the beachfront bungalows. It's on a glorious beach shaded by coconut palms, and the thatched polehouse bungalows offer uninterrupted views across the lagoon from private verandas. Inside the A-frame bungalows are king-size beds, kitchenettes with fridge, bathrooms and ceiling fans. They're not huge, but the two largest can sleep three (children under 10 stay free).

Esma Beach Villas (☎ 31836; www.esmavillas.com; d NZ$190) This is the small-scale sister operation to Etu Villas on Rarotonga's west coast, though here the beachfront location is superior on the quiet northern tip of the island near the airport and golf course. The three fan-cooled self-contained villas are simple with large verandas, queen beds and basic kitchen facilities. You'll need transport.

Paparei Bungalows (☎ 31837; www.papareibunga lows.com; d NZ$225) Paparei offers two modern self-contained beachfront bungalows near the centre of town. They're large, clean and well equipped, and nicely decorated in an unfussy way. Owners Vicki and Peter Petero are lovely hosts.

Aretai Beach Villas (☎ 31645; www.aretaibeachvillas .com; bungalows NZ$300; ☒ 🖳) The lovely two-bedroom villas at Aretai are the largest on the island, and definitely the best presented and best value for money in this price range. Halfway between Arutanga and the airport, with wonderful sea views and outstanding facilities – including full kitchens, dining areas, gorgeous décor and furniture, and huge patios – these villas are ideal for families or groups who want a little style in their lifestyle. In her early eighties, Mama Tatui is the matriarch and genial host at Aretai – just don't ask her about the website.

Top End

our pick Etu Moana (☎ 31458; www.etumoana.com; villas from NZ$425; ☒ ☒ 🖳) These boutique beach villas have thatched roofs and luxurious furnishings – gleaming Tasmanian oak floors, lofty ceilings, king-sized beds with private outdoor showers and teak sundecks. The design and décor are superb and very classy, and there's a tear-drop pool complete with rock garden, sun-shaded tables and a deluxe honesty bar. If you prefer your luxe resort a little downsized and understated, then this is the place. Children under 12 are not welcome.

Aitutaki Lagoon Resort (☎ 31201; www.aitutaki lagoonresort.com; garden/beachfront/over-water bungalows NZ$450/600/1235; ☒ 🖳 🏊) Aitutaki Lagoon Resort, ensconced on its own Akitua Island, has everything the finicky glam jetset patron would expect. It's truly beautiful, with great expanses of glistening white beach and a private ferryman to shunt you to and from the mainland. There are bars and restaurants, a pool and day-spa facility. The thatched garden and beachfront villas are large, light and comfortable, but the over-water bungalows are exquisite. Non-guests are welcome – drop in for a visit. The resort offers packages and discounts for extended stays – see the website.

Pacific Resort (☎ 31720; www.pacificresort.com; beachfront bungalows/ste/villas NZ$1220/1610/2310; ☒ 🖳 🏊) Like its sister resort in Rarotonga, Pacific Resort Aitutaki is a benchmark in luxury Polynesian. From the Oriental lily ponds and enormous carved-timber reception desk of its sumptuous foyer to the rough-rendered walls and timber floors, décor and views of the split-level restaurant, the Pacific Resort is breathtaking. The rooms are superb, with commanding views, huge private beach decks and private garden bathrooms with outdoor showers. The whole facility is impressive, with

coiffured gardens and pathways and an in-
genious tiered use of a steep site. Naturally,
there's wi-fi throughout. Come and enjoy the
restaurant, even if you can't afford to stay.

EATING

Samade on the Beach (☎ 31526; O'otu Beach; lunch
NZ$8-12, dinner NZ$15-26; ☽ lunch & dinner) This is
a brilliant place for a beer or lunch by the
lagoon, or an evening meal watching the sun
go down. The cool sand floor – delicious between your toes – and thatched roof add to
the atmosphere. The food is simple – fish,
burgers, pizzas, salads – and done without
flair or fanfare, but the view is serene and the
staff and customers are convivial and relaxed.
Samade has regular island nights and a great
Sunday barbecue.

Kuro Café (☎ 31110; meals NZ$10-18; ☽ breakfast
& lunch; ▣) Kuro's arrival has put some flair
into café fare. All-day cooked breakfasts and
lunches (including Caesar salad, Thai chicken
curry, BLT, pastas and calamari) are done just
right. When we dropped in, wi-fi internet was
coming soon.

Tauono's (☎ 31562; cakes NZ$3-6, lunch NZ$12-19;
☽ lunch & afternoon tea Mon, Wed & Fri, dinner by appointment) Tauono's is a delight – a tiny garden café
run by one-time Austrian Sonja and Tauono,
her philosophical Aitutakian husband.
Renowned for its coconut cake and afternoon
teas, Tauono's offers brilliant home-cooked
cuisine served alfresco. The food is prepared
according to what's been freshly picked from
their on-site organic garden. Tauono, a sometimes woodcarver with a bone-dry sense of
humour, might regale you with some ponder-
ings. Stop by for a homemade cake and fresh
fruit and veg from Sonja's shop (open 10am
to 5pm Monday to Friday).

The restaurants attached to the upmarket
resorts all offer fine dining to non-guests,
and the standard is excellent.

Rapae Bay Restaurant (☎ 31720; lunch from NZ$10,
mains NZ$27-55; ☽ lunch & dinner) Perhaps the
standout resort restaurant is in the Pacific
Resort. It offers superb Pacific fusion cuisine
in a brilliant split-level patio setting – the
views and surrounds are fabulous.

JK's Café & Bar (☎ 31052; mains NZ$14-25; ☽ lunch
daily, dinner Mon-Sat) JK's, in a terrific hilltop setting above Amuri, is popular with locals and
visitors alike. The varied menu offers burgers and seafood platters, but also curries, ri-
sottos, pasta and traditional dishes such as

ika mata. Patrons dine on informal benches
under a breezy veranda. JK's bar kicks on
after dinner – it's a great place to mingle
with Aititukians.

our pick **Café Tupuna** (☎ 31678; Tautu; mains NZ$26-
30; ☽ dinner) This is the only independent restaurant on Aitutaki offering fine dining. It's in a
lovely rural setting in the hills behind Arutanga.
The menu features fresh local fish and seafood
cooked with island flavours and exotic spices.
The lush garden setting makes for a relaxed
atmosphere and there's a good wine list.

Self-caterers can stock up at Aitutaki's **market** (Orongo Centre; ☽ 7am-3pm Mon-Sat) where early
birds will get the best of the fresh fish and
vegetables. **Maina Traders Superstore** (☎ 31055;
☽ 6am-8pm Mon-Sat) in Arutanga and **Rerei's**
(☎ 31358; ☽ 6am-8pm Mon-Sat) in Amuri (with
the Heineken sign) are the main places to
pick up groceries. On the island's east side,
Neibaa (☎ 31655; ☽ 8am-9pm Mon-Fri, 6-9pm Sat, 7am-
9pm Sun), in Vaipae, is the only trader that opens
Sunday. There are a few good takeaway places
around the island.

DRINKING & ENTERTAINMENT

Asti's Bar (☎ 31283; ☽ dinner & drinks Wed-Sun) The
old Coconut Crusher Bar has been rebirthed
as Asti's, and it's worth a look if only for the
improbable building that it is – bits of corrugated iron and plyboard, and a wall made
of stacked-up bottles.

Blue Nun Café (☎ 31604; Orongo Centre; ☽ dinner
& drinks Tue-Sun) Aitutaki's old banana-packing
plant, at the waterside end of the market enclosure, is now home to the Blue Nun Café.
There's a vast concrete dance floor where
weekend discos and island nights – some
of the Cooks' best – kick into action, and a
large bar and breezy informal dining area that
serves sandwiches and burgers.

Puffy's Bar (☎ 31317; ☽ dinner & drinks Mon-Sat)
Puffy's is a tiny bar popular with locals and
backpackers from nearby Paradise Cove.
Simple meals and cheap booze are served,
and there's also a weekly island night.

PALMERSTON

pop 52 / area 2.1 sq km

Palmerston, 55km northwest of Rarotonga, is
the Southern Group's only true atoll, halfway
towards the Cooks' Northern Group. The
lineage of all Palmerston Islanders can be

traced to just one man – prolific Englishman William Masters, a ship's carpenter, who arrived from Manuae with two Polynesian wives in 1863. Having quickly added a third wife, over the next 36 years Masters created his own island dynasty. William Masters came from Gloucester and his progeny spoke excellent English with a thick Gloucester accent. Today, there are three main families on Palmerston (who spell their name Marsters), and you'll find Marsterses scattered throughout the Cooks and the rest of Australasia – the total number of William's descendants is now well into triple figures.

There's no organised accommodation on Palmerston, but if you're planning on travelling there, contact the island secretary **Tere Marsters** (☎ 37684, 54660; palmerstonisland@ hotmail.com). The only way to reach the island is by inter-island freighter or private yacht (see p295).

'ATIU

pop 570 / area 27 sq km

In pre-European times 'Atiu was an important seat of regional power – its warriors were renowned for ferocious fighting and ruthlessness. By contrast, the rocky, reef-fringed island is now better known for gentler pursuits. It's the Cooks' eco-capital and a haven for naturalists and bird-lovers. It also attracts adventurous travellers in search of an island with a more traditional edge. Its five main villages (Areora, Tengatangi, Mapumai, Te'enui and Ngatiarua) are clustered together on the island's central plateau, surrounded by a band of fertile swampland and lush taro plantations. The *makatea* – the dramatic ring of upthrust rock that's rich in marine fossils and was once the island's exterior reef – is just one of 'Atiu's natural features. The island is also covered with forest and honeycombed with limestone caves. 'Atiu's most famous cave is Anatakitaki Cave, the only known home of the *kopeka* ('Atiuan swiftlet).

HISTORY

'Land of Birds' or 'Land of Insects' is the translation of 'Atiu's traditional name 'Enua Manu. Along with its neighbours Ma'uke and Mitiaro, 'Atiu makes up the Nga Pu Toru (Three Roots). In the recent pre-European

times, 'Atiuan *ariki* overlorded smaller Ma'uke and Mitiaro. 'Atiuan warriors also made incursions on Rarotonga and Aitutaki, but without success. James Cook was the first European to land on 'Atiu on 3 April 1777. Reverend John Williams landed on 19 July 1823. Rongomatane, the leading 'Atiuan chief, was converted to Christianity after Williams' missionaries ate sugarcane from Rongomatane's sacred grove – he subsequently ordered all the idols on the island to be burnt. The arrival of missionaries Williams and Tahitian Papeiha is celebrated on Gospel Day (19 July).

INFORMATION

ADC Shop (☎ 33028; Areora) Provides cash advances on credit cards.
'Atiu Tourism Society (☎ 33031; www.atiutourism.com)
Centre Store (☎ 33773; Te'enui) Travellers cheques (NZ dollars only) can be cashed here.
Post & Telecom (☎ 33680; fax 33683; ☖ 8am-4pm Mon-Fri) In the same building, north of Mapumai village.
www.atiu.info Excellent information resource on 'Atiu.

TRANSPORT

Air Rarotonga (☎ 33888; www.airraro.com) flies between Rarotonga and 'Atiu Monday to Saturday. Return fares cost from NZ$356/267 for adults/children. On Wednesday you can fly direct Aitutaki–'Atiu from NZ$197/148 for adults/children (one way). See p295 for information on inter-island shipping services.

You'll need transport to get around 'Atiu. The circle-island road is fun for exploring by motorbike – walking tracks lead down to the dramatic beach. Accommodation places can provide motorbikes (NZ$25 per day), and **T & J Rentals** (☎ 33271; Areora) also has bicycles.

Are Manuiri (☎ 33031) rents out a 4WD car for NZ$65 per day, and **Atiu Villas** (☎ 33777) has a soft-top Jeep for NZ$60 a day, as well as a few bicycles.

SIGHTS
Caves

Deep limestone caves, hidden away deep in the bush-covered *makatea*, are the most famous feature of 'Atiu. A torch and sturdy walking shoes are essential – the coral is razor-sharp. The main caves are on private land and you'll need a guide to visit them (see p281). Many caves were used for burials – it's *tapu* (taboo) to disturb the bones, so unless you fancy taking home a curse…

RAROTONGA &
THE COOK ISLANDS

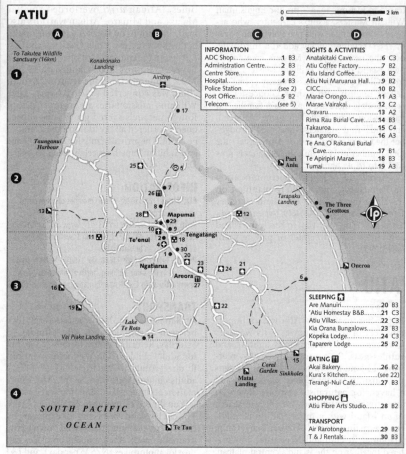

'ATIU

0 ——— 2 km
0 ——— 1 mile

To Takutea Wildlife
Sanctuary (16km)

Konakonako
Landing

Airstrip

Taunganui
Harbour

Pari
Aniu

Tarapaku
Landing

The Three
Grottoes

Oneroa

Mapumai

Tengatangi

Te'enui

Ngatiarua

Areora

Lake
Te Roto

Vai Piake Landing

Coral
Garden Sinkholes

Matai
Landing

SOUTH PACIFIC
OCEAN

Te Tau

INFORMATION
ADC Shop...........................1 B3
Administration Centre.........2 B3
Centre Store.......................3 B3
Hospital..............................4 B3
Police Station................(see 2)
Post Office.........................5 B2
Telecom..........................(see 5)

SIGHTS & ACTIVITIES
Anatakitaki Cave................6 C3
Atiu Coffee Factory............7 B2
Atiu Island Coffee..............8 B2
Atiu Nui Maruarua Hall.......9 B2
CICC.................................10 B2
Marae Orongo...................11 A3
Marae Vairakai..................12 C2
Oravaru............................13 A2
Rima Rau Burial Cave........14 B3
Takauroa..........................15 C4
Taungaroro.......................16 A3
Te Ana O Rakanui Burial
  Cave..............................17 B1
Te Apiripiri Marae.............18 B3
Tumai...............................19 A3

SLEEPING
Are Manuiri......................20 B3
'Atiu Homestay B&B..........21 C3
Atiu Villas........................22 C3
Kia Orana Bungalows........23 B3
Kopeka Lodge...................24 C3
Taparere Lodge.................25 B2

EATING
Akai Bakery......................26 B2
Kura's Kitchen.............(see 22)
Terangi-Nui Café...............27 B2

SHOPPING
Atiu Fibre Arts Studio........28 B2

TRANSPORT
Air Rarotonga...................29 B2
T & J Rentals....................30 B3

Eerie **Anatakitaki** is 'Atiu's most spectacular cave, a multichambered cavern surrounded by banyan roots and thick jungle. It's also home to the rare *kopeka*, or 'Atiuan swiftlet – listen for its distinctive echo-locating clicks.

Te Ana O Rakanui and **Rima Rau** are both burial caves. Rima Rau is reached by a vertical pot-hole, and both are packed with musty old skulls and skeletal remains. They're a tight squeeze inside – claustrophobics be warned. **Lake Te Roto** is noted for its *itiki* (eels), a popular island delicacy. On the western side of the lake, a cave leads right through the *makatea* to the sea.

Beaches

'Atiu's barrier reef is close to shore; the sur-rounding lagoon is rarely more than 50m wide

and its waters quite shallow. **Taunganui Harbour**, on the west coast where the water is clear and deep, is the best spot for swimming. About 1km south is **Oravaru Beach** where Captain Cook's party made its landing. Further south, **Taungaroro** and **Tumai** are two of the most popular swimming beaches.

You can swim in the three lovely sinkholes west of **Takauroa beach** only at low tide. Between Takauroa Beach and Matai Landing, the fall-ing tide empties through the sinkholes and fish become trapped in a fascinating natural aquarium known as the **Coral Garden**.

Coffee Plantations

Coffee was introduced to 'Atiu by early 19th-century traders and became a thriving export

---

TUMUNU

Christian missionaries took to eradicating kava drinking among Cook Islanders so 'Atiuans developed home-brewed alcohol and the *tumunu* (bush-beer drinking clubs) were born. Men would retreat into the bush and imbibe 'orange beer'. *Tumunu* are still held regularly on 'Atiu; the *tumunu* is the hollowed-out stump of a coconut palm traditionally used for brewing beer. *Tumunus* retain some of the old kava-drinking ceremonies, but these days the vessel is likely to be plastic. Technically, bush-beer drinking sessions are still illegal.

The annual 'Atiu Tumunu Tutaka is held each December. Ten or more judges are selected from the island visitors to judge the best *tumunu* of 'Atiu – an award of great prestige. Most locals and hotel owners can arrange a *tumunu* visit. Traditionally, it's for men only, but the rules relax for tourists, and males and females are welcome. Be warned – 'orange beer' can be pretty potent stuff.

---

industry. By the 1980s, however, the coffee trade had declined and the plantations were fallow. German-born Juergen Manske-Eimke moved to 'Atiu in the 1980s and re-established coffee production. Juergen's **Atiu Coffee** (☎ 33031; www.adc.co.ck/coffee) is machine-roasted in the coffee factory in Mapumai village. Mata Arai, whose family had grown coffee in the 1950s, returned to 'Atiu in the 1990s and resumed production. Her **Atiu Island Coffee** (☎ 33088) is hand-picked, hand-dried and hand-roasted, using coconut cream to give the coffee its flavour. Both growers offer tours (NZ$10), which include plenty of opportunities to taste the local brew.

Marae

Marae Orongo, near Oravaru Beach, was once 'Atiu's most sacred *marae*, and it's still a powerfully atmospheric place – many locals are reluctant to go near it. You'll need a guide as it's on private land (see Tours, below).

Marae Vairakai, along a walking track north of Kopeka Lodge, is surrounded by 47 large limestone slabs, six of which have curious projections cut into their top edges.

Te Apiripiri Marae is where the Tahitian preacher Papeiha first spoke the words of the Gospel in 1823. There's not much left of the marae to see, but a stone commemorates the site.

TOURS

Atiu Tours (☎ 33041; www.atiutoursaccommodation .com), run by affable Englishman Marshall Humphreys, offers an informative 3½-hour circle-island tour (NZ$40) visiting *marae*, beaches and other historical points of interest. There's also an excellent 2½-hour tour

to Anatakitaki (NZ$25) and Rima Rau burial cave ($20).

George Mateariki (☎ 33047), or Birdman George as he's commonly known, is 'Atiu's resident ornithologist and a local celebrity thanks to his highly entertaining ecotour ($50). George oversaw the release of the endangered *kakerori* (Rarotongan flycatcher) here from Rarotonga, and with luck you'll meet his favourite pair of birds (named George and Mildred after the 1970s UK sitcom).

Andrew Matapakia (☎ 33111) offers lagoon fishing tours (NZ$25), and **Ngere Tariu** (☎ 33011) takes anglers on deep-sea fishing cruises ($100).

Paiere Mokoroa (☎ 33034) at Taparere Lodge and **Man Unuia** (☎ 33283) of Kopeka Lodge both offer historical island tours, based on personal research, for NZ$25.

SLEEPING

Are Manuiri (☎ 33031; www.adc.co.ck; Areora; dm per person NZ$30, s & d NZ$60, tr NZ$75) 'Atiu's only budget accommodation is this three-bedroom house in the centre of Areora village. There's a clean shared kitchen, living room and bathroom, but not much in the way of private space.

Taparere Lodge (☎ /fax 33034 or 55377; info@ atiutourims.com; dm/s/d NZ$40/70/90, extra person NZ$20) With two large breeze-block units and a larger dorm room, Taparere is bright, airy and cheerfully decorated. Accommodation is self-contained with kitchen facilities and (sometimes) hot-water showers – shady verandas overlook a pleasant valley. Per-person return airport transfers are NZ$20.

Atiu Homestay B&B (☎ 33041; www.atiutoursaccomm odation.com; r per person NZ$45; 🖵) Tour provider Marshall Humphries rents out rooms in his large comfortable family home near Areora.

A double and a twin comprise the accommodation (with shared bathrooms), and guests have the run of the house. A tropical breakfast is complimentary, and evening meals can be arranged.

Kia Orana Bungalows (☎ 33013; boaza@kia_orana .co.ck; d NZ$80) Except for some gingerbread trim you'd reckon these dinky timber bungalows belonged to a Romanian gypsy caravan train. The chalets inside are tiny, with a diminutive kitchen-and-bedroom area, but have nice views across a jungle valley from rear verandas. The bungalows are looking a little dog-eared but offer great value for money.

Kopeka Lodge (☎ 33283; stay@kopekalodge-atiu.com; s/d NZ$90/130) Three rustic plywood chalets sit in rural grounds southeast of Areora village, with one single and two double units complete with self-contained kitchen. The stained-wood and pale-green colour scheme is simple, but the units are quite comfortable.

our pick Atiu Villas (☎ 33777; www.atiuvillas.com; bungalows s & d NZ$160-180, extra persons NZ$20; ▫ ▫) The extra money goes a long way at Atiu Villas, which was built from local materials 25 years ago by Roger Malcolm (one-time Doctor of Physics and island mayor) and his 'Atiuan wife Kura. Nearing three decades on, it's the best address on the island. Six delightful villas are arrayed around a shady garden and have decks from where you can take in the valley views. There's a pool, tennis courts and a large bar-restaurant. Complimentary wi-fi is provided, as is internet access on resident computers. Prepaid bookings made 12 weeks in advance earn a 15% discount.

EATING & DRINKING

Self-catering from the slim pickings at the grocery stores – largely tinned and frozen food – is the most reliable eating option. 'Atiu has a couple of restaurants, but they're closed unless there are a few tourists on the island.

Kura's Kitchen (☎ 33777; Atiu Villas; dinner NZ$25) Kura, at Atiu Villas, cooks up evening vittles whenever there's a quorum, and sometimes there's an informal island night that kicks off in the thatched restaurant-bar area (NZ$35 with food, or NZ$10 for the show).

Terangi-Nui Café (☎ 33101; Areora; dinner NZ$25; ☺ 7.30am-9.30pm) The lovely Parua Tavioni runs this café-restaurant serving breakfast, lunch and dinner (depending…). If the gates

are open she's willing so try some delightful 'Atiuan hospitality.

Akai Bakery (☎ 33207; Mapumai) Fresh-baked bread is ready for the milling crowd by about 11am each day. Saturday is the Seventh-Day Adventist Sabbath and the baking doesn't begin until dusk – at 11.30pm there's that milling crowd again.

SHOPPING

Atiu Fibre Arts Studio (☎ 33031; www.adc.co.ck/art; Te'enui; ☺ 8am-3pm Mon-Fri, 1am-1pm Sat) The studio specialises in *tivaevae* (appliqué work) and traditional textile arts. Machine-sewn double- to queen-size *tivaevae* cost NZ$600 to NZ$1100. Hand-sewn *tivaevae*, taking countless hours of work, cost upwards of NZ$1500. There's an on-site gallery.

Terangi-Nui Café (☎ 33101; Areora) A small shop inside Parua Tavioni's café sells pareu, gifts and clothing.

MA'UKE

pop 390 / area 18.4 sq km

Although much flatter than 'Atiu and only slightly larger than Mitiaro, Ma'uke is also characterised by its *makatea* and thick coastal forest. Ma'uke is a sleepy and quietly charming island, traditional in its ways and circled by a rough coastal track. It's pockmarked with many underground caverns, including Motuanga, a network of limestone chambers said to stretch right out underneath the reef. Known as the Garden Island, Ma'uke is one of the Cooks' main exporters of tropical flowers, which means your goodbye *'ei* is likely to be particularly impressive.

INFORMATION

Hospital (☎ 35664; ☺ 8am-noon & 1-4pm Mon-Fri)
Police station (☎ 35086) Between the Administration Centre and the wharf.
Post office & Telecom office (☺ 8am-noon & 1-4pm Mon-Fri) There's a 24-hour Kiaorana cardphone (☎ 35685) outside and Internet access (per 30min NZ$10.50).
Wendy's Store (☎ 35102) ANZ agent, near the Divided Church in Areora; changes some currencies.

TRANSPORT

Air Rarotonga (www.airraro.com; airport ☎ 35120 Kimiangatau ☎ 35888) flies Monday, Wednesday and Friday between Rarotonga and Ma'uke

MA'UKE

0 ————— 1 km
0 ————— 0.5 miles

A   **B**

INFORMATION
Administration
Centre...................**1** A4
Hospital.................**2** A3
Police Station........(see 1)
Post Office...........**3** A4
Telecom................(see 3)
Wendy's Store......**4** A4

SIGHTS & ACTIVITIES
Divided Church......**5** A4
Kea's Grave...........**6** B5
Marae
  Puarakura........(see 18)
Marae
  Rangimanuka......**7** B4
Motuanga Cave......**8** B5
Vai Ma'u...............**9** A5
Vai Moraro.........**10** B4
Vai Moti.............**11** B5
Vai Ou...............**12** B4

Vai Tango............**13** A4
Vai Tukume..........**14** A5

SLEEPING
Ri's Retreat (Airport).**15** A3
Ri's Retreat
  (Anaraura).........**16** B5
Tiare Cottages.......**17** A4

EATING
Aretoa Store..........**18** A4
Ariki Store...........(see 18)
Kato's Store.........**19** B4
Ma'uke Market......(see 1)
Tua Trading..........**20** B4

DRINKING
Tura's Bar...........**21** A4

TRANSPORT
Air Rarotonga........**22** A3

SOUTH PACIFIC
OCEAN

'Angataura

Airstrip
Kimiangatau
Taunganui
Landing
(Wharf)
Oiretumu
Kopupooki
(Stomach Rock)
Beach
Anaputa
Ngatiarua
Areora
Reservoir
Uriaata
One'unga
Swamp
Arapaea
A'anga
Anaiti
Anaraura
Tukume
Teoneroa
Utu
Rererua
Anaokae

from NZ$578/358 return for adults/children. There are occasionally unscheduled flights between Ma'uke and Mitiaro. See p295 for details of travelling by cargo ship.

You can organise scooter hire for NZ$25 per day from Tiare Cottages and Ri's Retreat (see p284). Tiare also rents out bicycles. Transfers to/from the airport cost NZ$10.

SIGHTS
Caves
Like its sister islands, 'Atiu and Mitiaro, Ma'uke's raised-coral *makatea* is riddled with caves, many filled with cool freshwater pools. **Vai Tango** is the best cave for swimming, a short walk from Ngatiarua village. Schoolkids often head there at weekends and afternoons after school and they can show you where to find it. Other interesting caves in the island's north, reached by old coral pathways across the *makatea,* include **Vai Ou, Vai Tukume, Vai Moraro, Vai Ma'u** and **Vai Moti.**

Motuanga (the 'Cave of 100 Rooms') is a complex of tunnels and caverns in the island's southeast that's said to extend all the way under the reef and out to sea. Seismic activity is slowly causing the chambers to close up, and nowadays you can explore only eight of them. The cave was used as a hiding place from 'Atiuan war parties.

Beaches
An 18km-long circle-island road takes you past Ma'uke's many secluded coves and beaches, which are one of the island's main attractions. One of the nicest is **One'unga**, on the east side, and **Teoneroa** and **Tukume** on the island's southwestern side are also delightful. Other beaches, such as **Anaraura** and **Teoneroa**, have sheltered picnic areas that are popular with the island's pigs. **Kea's Grave** is on the cliffs above Anaiti where the wife of Paikea (the Whale Rider) is said to have perished while waiting for her husband's return.

South of Tiare Cottages is **Kopupooki (Stomach Rock) beach**, with a beautiful fish-filled cave that becomes accessible at low tide.

Marae
Marae Rangimanuka, the *marae* of Uke, is one of Ma'uke's many *marae* that are now overgrown, but you can still find it with a guide. **Marae Puarakura** is a modern *marae,* still used for ceremonial functions, complete with stone seats for the *ariki, mataiapo* and *rangatira* (subchief).

TOURS
Guided cave tours are offered by **Pi Tua** (☎ 35033), a sprightly 60-something who leaps around the *makatea* like a teenager. Also try **Tangata Ateriano** (☎ 35270), who's based at Tiare Cottages.

> ### THE DIVIDED CHURCH
>
> Ma'uke's CICC was built by two villages, Areora and Ngatiarua, in 1882. When the outside was completed, there was disagreement between the villages about how the inside should be decorated so they built a wall down the middle. The wall has since been removed, though the interior is decorated in markedly different styles. Each village has its own entrance, sits at its own side and takes turns singing the hymns. The minister stands astride the dividing line down the middle of the pulpit.

SLEEPING

Tiare Cottages (☎ 35192; www.mauke.com; budget bungalows s/d NZ$70/75, self-contained lodge s/d NZ$80/90, beachfront house NZ$150) The old tin-roofed budget lodges are a little basic, with a main sleeping area and a simple kitchen, toilet and shower tacked on the end. The newer self-contained lodge is more comfortable, with a better equipped kitchen and an airy and cheerily furnished bedroom. There's also a brilliant house with panoramic sea views from its cliff-top perch – it's self-contained and excellent value. Dinner costs $25 per person.

Ri's Retreat (☎ 35181; keta-ttn@oyster.net.ck; bungalows NZ$115) Ri's Retreat has a bunch of bungalows located near Anaraura Beach and a few more located near the airport. The bungalows are all sparkling clean and brightly decorated, with large beds, modern bathrooms and verandas. Opt for the seaside bungalows, built on stilts beside the beach – the better choice.

EATING & DRINKING

Guests at Tiare Cottages have the option of home-cooked dinners for NZ$25 per meal. The best of Ma'uke's grocery stores is Tua Trading near the Divided Church – shelves at Aretoa Store and Ariki Store can be pretty bare. Kato's Store is the island's only bakery.

From 8.30am on Friday morning you can buy fresh produce at Ma'uke's market, near the wharf.

Liquid refreshment is available at **Tura's Bar** (☎ 35023; ☒ Fri) opposite Ma'uke College.

MITIARO

pop 230 / area 22.3 sq km

The tourism juggernaut that churns through Rarotonga and Aitutaki is a world away from sleepy Mitiaro. Here people live much the same way as their ancestors have for hundreds of years (except for electricity and motor-scooters). Mitiaro may not be classically beautiful in the traditional South Pacific sense – the beaches are small, and where the land's not covered with boggy swamp it's mainly black craggy rock. Yet Mitiaro is an interesting slice of traditional Polynesian life and makes for a rewarding place to spend a few days. Like on 'Atiu and Ma'uke, the *maketea* of Mitiaro has many deep and mysterious caves, including the brilliant underground pools of Vai Nauri and Vai Marere. Mitiaro also has the remains of the Cook Island's only fort. The islanders on Mitiaro are great craftspeople, and you'll discover that the weaving, woodcarving and traditional outrigger canoes are all beautifully made.

INFORMATION

Electricity is supplied daily from 5am to midnight and 24 hours on Friday, Saturday and Sunday. It's difficult to change money on the island so bring plenty of cash. Don't drink the tap water, and watch out for the island's vicious mosquitoes.

The Administration Centre, located near the wharf, houses the **post office** (☒ 9am-4pm Mon-Fri), **Telecom** (☎ 36680; ☒ 8-10am & 1-3pm), **police station** (☎ 36110, 36124), **island secretary** (☎ 36157, 36108) and the mayor. **Julian Aupuni** (☎ 36180), Mitiaro's tourism officer, is also based at the Administration Centre.

TRANSPORT

Air Rarotonga (☎ 36888; www.airraro.com) flies to Mitiaro on Monday, Wednesday and Friday. The adult/child return cost is NZ$578/358. For information on inter-island ships, see p295.

SIGHTS
Beaches, Caves & Pools

The Cook Islands' only sulphur pool is **Vai Marere**, a 10-minute walk from Mangarei village on the Takaue road. From the main

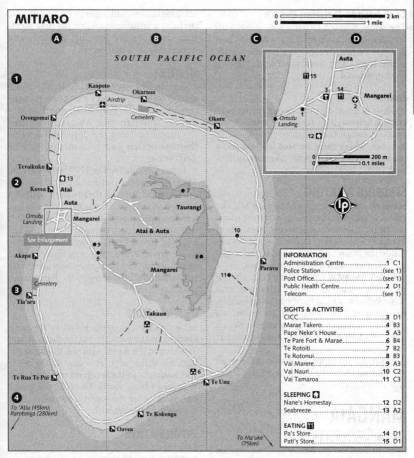

MITIARO

INFORMATION
Administration Centre..................1 C1
Police Station...........................(see 1)
Post Office...............................(see 1)
Public Health Centre.................2 D1
Telecom.................................(see 1)

SIGHTS & ACTIVITIES
CICC.......................................3 D1
Marae Takero............................4 B3
Pape Neke's House.....................5 A3
Te Pare Fort & Marae.................6 B4
Te Rotoiti................................7 B2
Te Rotonui...............................8 B3
Vai Marere...............................9 A3
Vai Nauri...............................10 C2
Vai Tamaroa...........................11 C3

SLEEPING
Nane's Homestay.....................12 D2
Seabreeze..............................13 A2

EATING
Pa's Store..............................14 D1
Pati's Store............................15 D1

road it's barely visible and easy to miss, but as you duck into the cave it broadens out into a gloomy cavern covered with stalactites. According to locals, the water here has healing properties.

Fifteen minutes' walk, across the sharp *makatea* from the coast, is **Vai Tamaroa**. The real highlight is the deep sparkling-blue **Vai Nauri**, Mitiaro's 'natural swimming pool'. Local women hold gatherings known as *terevai* at both Vai Tamaroa and Vai Nauri, where they gather to swim and sing the bawdy songs of their ancestors.

Marae & Te Pare Fort

The *marae* of Mitiaro are largely consumed by jungle, but you are still able to see the stone seat of the *ariki* and several graves at **Marae Takero**, located near the abandoned Takaue village. The remains of **Te Pare Fort**, set deep in the *makatea*, are Mitiaro's most impressive ancient ruin. It was built as a defence against 'Atiuan raiders. In times of danger people would assemble in the underground shelter, while above was a lookout tower from which approaching canoes could be seen.

The only tour guide to Te Pare Fort is Mitiaro's tourism officer, **Julian Aupuni** (☎ 36180), who has permission to visit the site from its owner Po Tetava Ariki. Papa Neke leads tours around the island's other historical sites; he can be contacted through **Seabreeze** (☎ 36153).

Cook Islands Christian Church

The white-painted CICC is a fine sight, with its blue trim, stained-glass windows and parquet ceiling decorated with black-and-white stars. The Sunday church singing is inspirational.

Lakes

Mitiaro is unique in the Cooks for its twin lakes, Te Rotonui (Big Lake) and Te Rotoiti (Small Lake). A rough track leads to the edge of Te Rotonui, where there's a boat landing and a pleasant picnic spot. Both lakes are stuffed with *itiki*, a local delicacy.

SLEEPING & EATING

Seabreeze (☎ 36153; r per person incl meals NZ$75) The only real visitor accommodation on the island is run by a local family on the outskirts of Mangeri. There are a couple of simple rooms inside the main one-storey house and a spacious self-contained unit out the back.

Nane's Homestay (☎ 36107; s/d NZ$35/45) The only other place to stay on Mitiaro is with Nane Pokoati, a local *mataiapo* and a bubbly, friendly host. There are no private rooms, just beds in a communal sleeping area in Nane's large, modern house. Meals are included at extra cost.

Limited food supplies are sold at the small village food shops, Pa's Store and Pati's Store, and at Seabreeze.

MANGAIA

pop 560 / area 51.8 sq km

Next to Rarotonga, Mangaia (pronounced mung-EYE-ah) is the Cooks' most geographically dramatic island. The second largest of the islands, it's only slightly smaller than Rarotonga, with a towering circlet of black two-tiered raised-coral *makatea* (three-tiered in the island's north) concealing a huge sunken volcanic caldera that falls away on each side of the 169m Rangimotia ridge, the island's central spine. This sunken interior is swampland planted with taro fields and vegetables.

Mangaia is the Pacific's oldest island – at once craggy and lushly vegetated – and riddled with limestone caves that once served as sacred burial grounds and havens during tribal fighting. There are lakes in the island's centre, dramatic cliffs and many spectacular lookout points. Mangaians have a reputation

for haughtiness and superiority, and they're perhaps a little less voluble on first meetings, but they are friendly, gracious and impeccably well mannered.

HISTORY

Mangaian legend tells that the island was not settled by voyagers on canoes but that the three sons of the Polynesian god Rongo – Rangi, Mokoaro and Akatauira – lifted the island up from the deep, and became the first settlers and ancestors of the Nga Ariki tribe.

James Cook landed in 1777 but found the Mangaians were hostile and quickly moved on. Cannibalism had already been outlawed by Mangaian chief Mautara 100 years before the first missionaries arrived. John Williams was the first missionary to land in 1823 but, like James Cook, he was not welcome. Subsequent Polynesian missionaries had more success – the Mangaians were eventually converted to Christianity by the Rarotongan preacher Maretu.

ORIENTATION

Mangaia's three main villages are on the coast: Oneroa in the west, Ivirua in the east and Tamarua in the south. Oneroa, the main village, has three parts: Tava'enga to the north and Kaumata to the south on the coast, and Temakatea high above the second *makatea* tier overlooking the ocean. The airstrip is in the north of the island.

INFORMATION

Babe's Store (☎ 34092; Oneroa) The island's ANZ agent.
Post & Telecom (☎ 34680; Internet access per 30min NZ$10.50; 🕑 7.30am-4pm Mon-Fri) On the hill above Oneroa.
Visitor information centre (☎ 34289) In the Administration Centre at the bottom of the Temakatea road cutting.

TRANSPORT

Air Rarotonga (☎ 34888; www.airraro.com) flies between Rarotonga and Mangaia four times a week from NZ$270 return. See p295 for details on shipping services from Rarotonga to Mangaia.

You need a motorbike to get around Mangaia. There are some very rough sections of road in the island's south, and the cross-island roads are muddy and perilous after rains. Moana Rentals (☎ 34307) hires out motorcycles for NZ$25 per day.

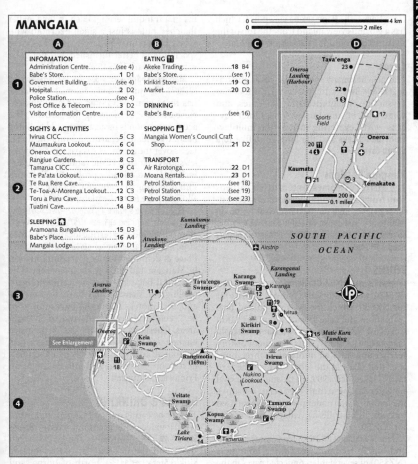

MANGAIA

INFORMATION		EATING 🍴	
Administration Centre.............(see 4)		Akeke Trading.....................18 B4	
Babe's Store.............................1 D1		Babe's Store........................(see 1)	
Government Building...............(see 4)		Kirikiri Store.......................19 C3	
Hospital.....................................2 D2		Market..............................20 D2	
Police Station.........................(see 4)			
Post Office & Telecom...............3 D2		DRINKING	
Visitor Information Centre..........4 D2		Babe's Bar..........................(see 16)	

SIGHTS & ACTIVITIES		SHOPPING 🛍	
Ivirua CICC...............................5 C3		Mangaia Women's Council Craft	
Maumaukura Lookout...............6 C4		Shop.................................21 D2	
Oneroa CICC.............................7 D2			
Rangiue Gardens.......................8 C3		TRANSPORT	
Tamarua CICC............................9 C4		Air Rarotonga.....................22 D1	
Te Pa'ata Lookout..................10 B3		Moana Rentals....................23 D1	
Te Rua Rere Cave....................11 B3		Petrol Station.....................(see 18)	
Te-Toa-A-Morenga Lookout....12 C3		Petrol Station.....................(see 19)	
Toru a Puru Cave....................13 C3		Petrol Station.....................(see 23)	
Tuatini Cave............................14 B4			

SLEEPING 🛏	
Aramoana Bungalows...............15 D3	
Babe's Place............................16 A4	
Mangaia Lodge........................17 D1	

SIGHTS
Avarua Landing

Fishermen return from their morning's exploits around 8am or 9am in tiny outrigger canoes with several huge wahoo and tuna. Hang around for the cleaning and gutting because there are three giant green turtles that come to feed on the entrails and offcuts that are cast into the water.

Whales pass just beyond the reef in the July-to-October season.

Churches & Marae

Mangaia has some of the finest old CICCs in the Cooks. **Tamarua CICC** is especially beautiful, and still has its original roof beams, woodcarved interiors and sennit-rope binding. The interiors of the Oneroa and Ivirua churches were once even more impressive, but were sadly mostly removed in the 1980s.

Mangaia has 24 premissionary *marae,* but you'll need a guide to find them since they have been mostly overtaken by bush.

Rangimotia & Inland Roads

At 169m, Rangimotia is the highest point on the island with stunning coastal views. From the Oneroa side, a dirt road leads to the top. The island's interior is cross-hatched by tracks and dirt roads, which are great for walking, but they can get very muddy after heavy rain.

There are several stunning viewpoints including **Te-Toa-A-Morenga** lookout, just inland from Ivirua; the **Maumaukura** viewpoint, which has a glorious view inland from the top of the *makatea* cliff; and **Te Pa'ata** above Oneroa.

Caves

Mangaia has many spectacular caves, including **Te Rua Rere**, a huge burial cave that has crystalline stalagmites and stalactites, and some ancient human skeletons. Other caverns worth exploring include the multileveled **Tuatini Cave** and the long, mazelike **Toru a Poru Cave**.

Rangiue Gardens

Lyn Martin welcomes visitors to her gardens with fruit trees, tropical flowers and spectacular sea views, high on the *makatea* at Ivirua on Mangaia's east coast. She also teaches visitors to dye their own *pareu*. Book at **Mangaia Airport Shop** (☎ 34388).

TOURS

Doreen Tangatakino & Ura Herrmann (c/- Babe's Place ☎ 34092) take visitors on a full-day island tour for NZ$50, which includes the inland taro plantations and Lake Tiriara. Tours to Tuatini Cave cost NZ$30. Doreen's husband **Moekapiti Tangatakino** (c/- Babe's Place) is the school history teacher and does an informative three-hour tour that takes in the lookouts over the taro farms, lakes, the 1909 wreck site of the coal freighter *Saragossa* (only the anchor remains), the human *umu* (underground pit-oven used to cook human flesh), villages and *marae* for NZ$50.

Tere Tauakume (☎ 34223) leads a fascinating and highly recommended three-hour tour (NZ$50) of several interconnected caves in the Ivirua area. **Maui Peraua** (☎ 34388) leads tours to his family cave of Toru a Poru (NZ$35) and popular traditional pole-fishing tours on the reef (NZ$25) – you can have your catch cooked on the beach.

SLEEPING

When we visited, several deluxe beachfront villas (to be called Mangaia Villas) were nearing completion near the wharf. Owned by Rarotongan motor-traders the **Pickering family** (☎ 23888), they'll raise the stakes in the tourist-accommodation scene.

Aramoana Bungalows (☎ 34278; www.aramoana .com; Ivirua; s & d NZ$40, bungalow s/d NZ$60/80, larger bungalow s/d NZ$115/135) Aramoana, on the island's eastern side, has simple free-standing cab-

ins in a tranquil setting. Each of the smaller thatched huts is just a small bedroom with a tiny bathroom. The larger units are more spacious and better furnished, but not great value. Meals are NZ$45 extra.

Mangaia Lodge (☎ 34324; fax 34239; Oneroa; s/d NZ$40/70) This tumbledown colonial-style lodge has three plain bedrooms and a sunny, enclosed terrace overlooking the gardens. The accommodation is basic, but the old building has a dilapidated charm and million-dollar views over the ocean. The separate shared toilet/shower block is rustic (at best). Meals are included, and friendly proprietor Torotoro Piiti is looking to renovate the lodge pending a longer lease from the island council.

our pick **Babe's Place** (☎ 34092; www.babesplace .co.ck; Oneroa; s/d/tr incl all meals NZ$75/120/150) With all meals included, a terrific location and four large comfortable motel-style rooms, Babe's Place is definitely the best accommodation in Mangaia and good value for money. The delightful Babe is the island's entrepreneur, owning the island's main store, liveliest bar and this motel. The units have mosquito nets, colourful bedspreads and small patio areas. Guests have 24-hour use of the main kitchen – with a fridge, tea and coffee – and the lounge area with a TV. Lively Babe's Bar, next door, parties on well into the night on Friday and Saturday.

EATING & DRINKING

There's no eating out on Mangaia, but meals are provided with accommodation. **Babe's Store** (☎ 34092; Tava'enga) is the best-stocked shop, and the few smaller places include **Kirikiri Store** (☎ 34133), north of Ivirua, and **Akeke Trading** (☎ 34206), inland from Oneroa. A weekly Friday-morning market kicks off at 8am beside the Oneroa post office. **Babe's Bar** (☎ 34092; www.babesplace.co.ck; Oneroa) opens Friday and Saturday nights.

SHOPPING

Basketwork, tie-dyed *pareu*, stone pounders and *pupu ei* are Mangaia's most famous handicrafts. Expat Australian Lyn Martin runs the tiny **Mangaia Airport Shop** (☎ 34388), which opens for incoming flights. The opening hours of the Mangaia Women's Council **craft shop** (🕒 8am-1pm Mon-Wed), just south of Oneroa, can be erratic, but the island **Administration Centre** (☎ 34289) will tell you when it's next open. The market often has some traditional crafts for sale.

NORTHERN GROUP

The sparsely populated tropical idylls of the Northern Group are breathtaking in their beauty and remoteness. It was this that inspired writers Tom Neale and Robert Dean Frisbie (p255) who both lived out their desert-island dreams as castaways on these far-flung coral atolls, among the crystal-clear lagoons, diamond-white beaches and technicolour sunsets. Only the hardiest and most intrepid of travellers ever make it out to the Northern Group – flights are few and mind-bogglingly expensive, but if you can surmount the logistical challenges the rewards are sublime.

TRANSPORT

Air Rarotonga (☎ 22888; www.airraro.com) flies from Rarotonga to Manihiki once a week, and Pukapuka occasionally. Flights take about 3½ hours, and the return adult/child fare is a staggering NZ$2700/2020! Penrhyn is occasionally serviced for a return adult/child fare of (wait for it…) NZ$3440/2580. Bad weather, limited fuel supplies and too few bookings can cause the flights to be cancelled at short notice.

The only other regular transport to the Northern Group islands is on the Taio Shipping cargo ship. To reach Rakahanga, you must fly to Manihiki and then take a boat. Some boats travel between Pukapuka and Samoa. For more information on inter-island cargo shipping, see p295.

Suwarrow is accessible only by private yacht, although you can get passage on the research vessel **Bounty Bay** (☎ 23513, 52400; www.pacific-expeditions.com), which visits a few times a year.

MANIHIKI
pop 350 / area 5.4 sq km
Manihiki, 1046km from Rarotonga, is where most of the Cooks' black pearls are farmed. It has a magnificent lagoon – one of the South Pacific's finest – and is a highlight of the Northern Group. Nearly 40 tiny *motu* (islets) encircle the enclosed lagoon, which is 4km wide at its broadest point. The island is the summit of a 4000m underwater mountain. The US ship *Good Hope* made the first European discovery in 1822, and Manihiki was a US territory until it was ceded in 1980.

Tauhunu is the main village, and the airstrip is at Tukao on this island's northern point. Black pearls are the island's economic mainstay, and they're harvested from September to December. The lung-busting abilities of the island's pearl divers are legendary – they can dive to great depths and stay submerged for minutes at a time.

Manihiki Lagoon Villas (☎ 43123; www.manihiki lagoonvillas.com; s/d incl all meals NZ$110/200), a beachside retreat, offers bungalows built on the water's edge of the lagoon. The accommodation is simple but the location is deluxe.

RAKAHANGA
pop 140 / area 4.1 sq km
With two major islands and many smaller *motu* dotted in a turquoise lagoon, Rakahanga is another idyllic island. The lagoon here is unsuitable for pearl-farming, and the few families who live here are concentrated in Nivano village in the southwestern corner. The only export is copra, although the island is still renowned for its fine *rito* hats, which are mostly sold on Rarotonga.

PENRHYN
pop 250 / area 9.8 sq km
Penrhyn is the northernmost of the Cook Islands, and boasts one of the largest lagoons in the country – so huge that the twin islands on opposite sides of the lagoon are barely visible from each other. Penrhyn has three deepwater passages that make excellent harbours, a fact that attracted whalers and traders in the 19th century. Peruvian blackbirders (slave-traders) also visited the island in the 1860s. Penrhyn is another centre for black-pearl production, and some interesting shell jewellery is produced on the island. The remains of a crashed B17 bomber are reminders of the WWII US servicemen who were stationed here and built the airstrip.

Soa's Guesthouse (☎ 42018; fax 42105; Omoka village; r NZ$95) is run by Soa Tini, a local fisherman and pearl farmer, who has a three-bedroom family house in the centre of Omoka village.

PUKAPUKA
pop 510 / area 5.1 sq km
Well known for both its sensuous dancers and beautiful girls, remote Pukapuka

is in many ways closer to Samoa than to the rest of the Cook Islands. Pukapuka's most famous resident was the American travel writer Robert Dean Frisbie, who lived here in the 1920s and wrote several evocative accounts of his life on the islands. Pukapuka sustained severe damage during the 2005 cyclones.

Contact the **island secretary** (☎ /fax 41712) or the **island council** (☎ 41034) to arrange home-stay accommodation.

SUWARROW

pop 2 / area 0.4 sq km

The Cook Islands' only national park is a nature-lovers' paradise, home to huge colonies of seabirds and some of the country's richest marine life. Two atoll managers live here six months of the year to oversee the park. During cyclone season they head back to Rarotonga. Suwarrow is best known as the home of Tom Neale, who lived here for three long stints between 1952 and his death in 1977. You can relive his adventures in his classic book *An Island to Oneself*, and visit his old house on Anchorage Island – one room is still furnished just as it was when he lived here. The only way you're likely to be able to visit Suwarrow is by private yacht.

RAROTONGA & THE COOK ISLANDS DIRECTORY

ACCOMMODATION

Officially, visitors are required to have booked accommodation before arriving in the Cook Islands, although you can usually arrange a hotel when you arrive at the airport. However, the many places to stay on Rarotonga are booked up well in advance, and you might find there's nothing available in your budget range, so it pays to plan ahead.

Rarotonga has loads of accommodation, including hostels, motel-style units, self-contained bungalows and some expensive top-end hotels and large-scale resorts. All the major Southern Group islands have organised accommodation. For families, rent-ing a house (p269) can be a good way to cut costs. Practically everywhere provides self-catering facilities.

Manihiki and Penrhyn are the only Northern Group islands with guesthouses.

ACTIVITIES

The Cook Islands make for the perfect place to kick back and relax, but if you're the energetic type you will find that there's plenty of activities to keep you occupied. Rarotonga is an excellent place for hiking, and there are several trails in the region for you to explore. Aitutaki's backcountry roads and deserted beaches also have plenty of great opportunities for walking and exploring. 'Atiu, Ma'uke, Mitiaro and Mangaia all have countless trails winding through the *makatea*. History and archaeology enthusiasts will enjoy visiting the historic *marae* on most of the islands. Many of these traditional religious meeting grounds are still used today for formal ceremonies, such as the investiture of a new *ariki* or *mataiapo*.

Water Sports

The sheltered lagoons and beaches on Rarotonga and Aitutaki are great for swimming and snorkelling. Diving is also excellent, with good visibility and lots of marine life, from sea turtles and tropical fish to reef sharks and eagle rays. See p73 for more diving information. You can hire snorkelling gear on Aitutaki and Rarotonga, as well as kayaks, sailboards and other water-sports equipment.

Raro has just a handful of resident surfers, but there are serious waves outside Rarotonga's perimeter reef and a budding community of bodyboard riders (see p265).

Kite surfers have only recently discovered the charms of Aitutaki's glorious lagoon (see p275).

Glass-bottomed boats operate from Muri Beach, and there are several lagoon cruise operators in Aitutaki. Deep-sea fishing boats can be chartered on Rarotonga and Aitutaki. From July to October, whale-watching trips are available.

Caving

The Cook Islands has some extraordinary caves to explore including Anatakitaki and

PRACTICALITIES

- Rarotonga's *Cook Islands News* (www.cinews.co.ck), published daily except Sunday, and the *Cook Islands Herald*, published on Wednesday, provide coverage of local news and international events.

- Radio Cook Islands (630 kHz AM; www.radio.co.ck) reaches most of the islands and broadcasts local programs, as well as Radio New Zealand news and Radio Australia's world news service. The smaller KC-FM (103.8 MHz FM) station can be received only on Rarotonga. There is one (very low-budget) national television station, CITV, and cable channels are available at some hotels.

- The PAL system is used in the Cooks. Video tapes and DVDs can be hired all over Rarotonga.

- Electricity is 240V AC, 50Hz, as in Australia and NZ, using Australian-style three-blade plugs. Power is available 24 hours a day throughout the Southern Group except on Mitiaro, where it runs from 5am to midnight Monday to Thursday and 24 hours a day Friday to Sunday.

- The Cook Islands uses the metric system. See the Quick Reference page for conversions.

Rima Rau on 'Atiu (p279), Motuanga on Ma'uke (p283), Vai Nauri on Mitiaro (p285) and Te Rua Rere on Mangaia (p288)

BUSINESS HOURS

The business week is 9am to 4pm Monday to Friday, and most shops are open on Saturday morning until noon. Small grocery stores keep longer hours, from 6am or 7am until 8pm or 9pm. The banks are open till 3pm on weekdays, but only Avarua's Westpac is open on Saturday morning.

CHILDREN

Travelling with kids presents no special problems in the Cook Islands, although many smaller hotels and bungalows don't accept children aged under 12 – ask about their policy before booking.

CUSTOMS

The following restrictions apply: 2L of spirits or wine or 4.5L of beer, plus 200 cigarettes or 50 cigars or 250g of tobacco. Quarantine laws are strictly enforced, and plants, animals or any related products are prohibited. Firearms, weapons and drugs are also prohibited.

DANGERS & ANNOYANCES

Swimming is very safe in the sheltered lagoons but be wary around reef passages, where currents are especially strong. Rarotonga's main passages are at Avana Harbour, Avaroa, Papua and Rutaki; they exist on other islands as well, often opposite streams.

Mosquitoes can be a real nuisance in the Cooks, particularly during the rainy season (around mid-December to mid-April). Use repellent; mosquito coils are available everywhere.

EMBASSIES & CONSULATES
Cook Islands Consulates
Cook Islands' overseas consulates:
Australia (☎ 02-9907 6567; fax 9949 6664; Sir Ian Graham Turbott, 8/8 Lauderdale Ave, Fairlight, NSW 2094)
Belgium (☎ 32-25431 1000; fax 2543 1001; Mr Todd McClay, 10 Rue Berckmans, 1060 Brussels)
New Zealand Auckland (☎ 09-366 1100; fax 309 1876; Mrs Rima Ngatoa, 1st fl, 127 Symonds St, PO Box 37-391); Wellington (☎ 04-472 5126; fax 472 5121; Mr Tepure Tapaitau, 56 Mulgrave St, PO Box 12-242, Thorndon)
USA California (☎ 805-987 0620; mets@gte.net; Metua Ngarupe, 1000 San Clemente Way, Camarillo 93010); Hawai'i (☎ 808-842 8999; fax 842 3520; Robert Worthington, Kamehameha Schools, c/o 144 Ke Ala Ola Rd, Honolulu 96817)

Consulates in the Cook Islands
New Zealand (☎ 22201, 55201; nzhc@oyster.net.ck; New Zealand High Commission, PO Box 21, Avarua; above the Philatelic Bureau) is the only country that has diplomatic representation in the Cook Islands. Citizens from other countries seeking consular advice should talk to the Secretary of the **Department of Foreign Affairs & Immigration** (Mike Mitchell; ☎ 29347; mitchell@mfai.gov .ck) on the 3rd floor of the Trustnet building in Avarua.

FESTIVALS & EVENTS

April
Dancer of the Year Dance displays are held throughout April, culminating in the hotly contested Dancer of the Year competition.

July
Gospel Day 20 July on 'Atiu, 21 July on Mitiaro, 25 July on Rarotonga, and elsewhere on 26 October. The arrival of the gospel to the Cook Islands is celebrated with *nuku* (religious plays).

August
Constitution Celebration (Te Maire Nui) Celebrates the 1965 declaration of independence and is the major festival of the year in the Cook Islands.
Tiare (Floral) Festival Week Celebrated with floral float parades and the Miss Tiare beauty pageant.

November
Vaka Eiva This week-long canoe festival celebrates the great Maori migration from Rarotonga to NZ. There are many race events and celebrations of Cooks culture.

HOLIDAYS

The Cook Islands has a multitude of public holidays. The celebrations are often accompanied by music, dancing and general high-jinks.
New Year's Day 1 January
Good Friday & Easter Monday March/April
Anzac Day 25 April
Queen's Birthday First Monday in June
Gospel Day (Rarotonga only) 25 July
Constitution/Flag-Raising Day 4 August
Gospel Day (Cook Islands) 26 October
Christmas Day 25 December
Boxing Day 26 December

INTERNET ACCESS

Rarotonga is rapidly moving into the information age with many public places where people can get online (see p257) and many businesses having websites. Aitutaki had just one internet café when we visited (p273), but at least one more was on the way (p278). Most of the Telecom offices on the outer islands have small cyberbooths, though the connection is very slow and pricey. Wi-fi access is available at the main internet cafés on Rarotonga and many of the main resorts and hotels.

INTERNET RESOURCES

Cook Islands Government Online (www.cook-islands.gov.ck) Who's who in Cabinet and ministries and departments.

Cook Islands News (www.cinews.co.ck) Online edition of the daily Cook Islands newspaper.
Cook Islands Herald (www.ciherald.co.ck) Online edition of the popular weekly newspaper.
Cook Islands Tourism Authority (www.cook-islands.com) Central information site for the main tourist office.
Cook Islands Website (www.ck) Local business details, including tourist operations.
Oyster Internet (www.oyster.net.ck) The Cooks internet provider with good information and links.
Telecom Cook Islands (www.telecom.co.ck) Searchable telephone directories.
www.the-cook-islands.com Some good basic travel and accommodation information.
www.cookislands.org.uk Hosted out of the UK, this is the only non-commercial website covering the Cooks.
Reserve Cook Islands (www.reservecookislands.com) One of several accommodation booking engines.

MONEY

With Cirrus, Maestro and Visa-enabled ATMs, these days it's often simpler to withdraw money from your home bank or credit account than carry travellers cheques and wads of cash. But cards can get lost or stolen and it pays to be prudent – you might want to use a mix of hard currency, travellers cheques and plastic. Outside Rarotonga and Aitutaki, changing currency and travellers cheques and using credit cards is all but impossible.

Cash

On Rarotonga there are ANZ ATMs in Avarua and at Wigmore's Superstore and at the Suprette grocery store ('Arorangi). Westpac has ATMs in Avarua, the airport, at Oasis Service Centre (Nikao) and JMC Store (Muri). The airport branch opens for international flights. You can change money at the Westpac and ANZ banks in Avarua and at some hotels for a fee.

There are just two ATMs on Aitutaki, but you can change money and travellers cheques at the Administration Centre. On the other islands you'll need to take a supply of cash with you.

Credit Cards

Visa, MasterCard and Bankcard are accepted at most places on Rarotonga. The Westpac and ANZ banks in Avarua give cash advances on all three cards. Amex and Diners Club cards are accepted at upmarket hotels and restaurants. Credit cards are accepted at the larger hotels on Aitutaki and at some places on 'Atiu. Elsewhere, it's cold hard cash or nothing.

HOW MUCH?

- **Bus ticket:** NZ$4
- **Internet access per hour:** NZ$9
- **Island night and buffet:** NZ$35-65
- **Guided tour:** NZ$50-70
- **Midrange private villa with sundeck on Rarotonga:** NZ$250 per night
- **1L petrol on Rarotonga:** NZ$2.80
- **1L bottled water:** NZ$3.50
- **Stubbie of Matutu beer:** NZ$5
- **Souvenir T-shirt:** NZ$25-35
- **Ika mata:** NZ$8
- **Single black pearl:** NZ$5-2000

Currency

NZ dollars are used in the Cook Islands. For exchange rates, see the Quick Reference page. You'll probably get a few Cook Islands coins in change (in denominations of 5c, 10c, 20c, 50c, $1, $2 and $5), but make sure to spend them before you leave, as Cook Islands currency cannot be exchanged anywhere in the world. The Cook Islands prints a $3 note that's quite collectable and available at the Philatelic Bureau in Avarua.

Taxes

A 12.5% VAT (value-added tax) is included in the price of most goods and services. All prices quoted in the text include VAT. A departure tax of NZ$30 (children NZ$10) applies when leaving the Cook Islands.

Tipping

While tipping is not customary in the Cook Islands, neither is it frowned upon. Haggling over prices is considered rude.

Travellers Cheques

You'll receive a better exchange rate for travellers cheques than for cash; all brands of travellers cheques are cashed at banks. Many of the outer islands have nowhere to change travellers cheques, so get them cashed before you leave Rarotonga.

PHOTOGRAPHY & VIDEO

Traditional print film and digital processing are available on Rarotonga. High-speed film is use-

ful in the densely forested interior of Rarotonga, and in the *makatea* of 'Atiu and Ma'uke. Bring a flash for photographing inside caves.

POST

Poste-restante mail is held for 30 days at post offices on most islands. To collect mail at the post office in Avarua it should be addressed to you c/o Poste Restante, Avarua, Rarotonga, Cook Islands. There's no home postal delivery in the Cooks – everyone uses post office boxes.

TELEPHONE

All the islands, with the exception of Nassau, are connected to the country's modern telephone system. Each island has a Telecom office, which also has a fax machine.

The country code for the Cook Islands is ☎ 682, and there are no local area codes. Dial ☎ 00 for direct international calls and ☎ 017 for international directory service. The local directory operator is ☎ 010. You can make collect calls from any phone by dialling ☎ 015.

Prepaid Kiaorana cards are available in NZ$5, NZ$10, NZ$20 and NZ$50 denominations from the post office, Telecom, Telepost and many shops and hotels. They can be used for local, inter-island and international phone calls and work from both public and home telephones.

Many mobile phone (cellphone) carriers have global-roaming facilities, so your home handset will work in the Cooks provided **Cook Islands Telecom** (☎ 29680; www.telecom.co.ck) has an agreement with your provider. However, you can get a local number by buying a Kokanet SIM card for NZ$25 at the main Telecom office in Avarua. There is mobile reception in Rarotonga and Aitutaki, but nowhere else.

TIME

The Cook Islands are east of the International Date Line, 10 hours behind Greenwich Mean Time (GMT). The country has no daylight-saving time. When it's noon in the Cooks it's 10pm in London, noon in Tahiti and Hawai'i, 2pm in LA, 10am the next day in Fiji and NZ, and 8am the next day in Sydney.

TOURIST INFORMATION

The **Cook Islands Tourism Corporation** (CITC; ☎ 29435; www.cook-islands.com; PO Box 14, Avarua) is in the centre of Avarua on Rarotonga.

Overseas offices:

Asia (☎ 66-2 652 0507; asiamanager@cook-islands.com; c/o Pacific Leisure Group, 8/F Maneeya Centre, 518/5 Ploenchit Rd, Bangkok 10330, Thailand)

Australia (☎ 02-9211 6590; ausmanager@cook-islands .com; Level 6, 69 Reservoir St, Surry Hills, NSW 2010)

Canada (☎ 1-888 994 2665; canadamanager@cook -islands.com; 1133-160A St, White Rock, British Columbia V4A 7G9)

Continental Europe (☎ 49-30 4225 6026; europe manager@cook-islands.com; Karl-Marx-Allee 91A, 10243 Berlin, Germany)

New Zealand (☎ 09-366 1106; nzmanager@cook -islands.com; Level 1, 127 Symonds St, Parnell, Auckland)

UK (☎ 44-20 7367 0928; ukmanager@cook-islands.com; Colechurch House, 1 London Bridge Walk, London SE1 2SX)

USA (☎ 310-545 4200; usamanager@cook-islands.com; 1334 Parkview Ave, Suite 300, Manhattan Beach, California 90266)

VISAS

No visa is required to visit the Cooks. A visitor permit, good for 31 days, is granted on arrival with a valid passport, an onward or return airline ticket and a confirmed hotel booking (see p290). Visitor permits can be extended up to six months at the **Department of Foreign Affairs & Immigration** (☎ 29347) in Avarua.

TRANSPORT ON RAROTONGA & THE COOK ISLANDS

GETTING THERE & AWAY
Air

The Cook Islands can be included as a stopover between the US and NZ, Australia or French Polynesia. See p636 for round-the-world tickets and Pacific air passes.

Low-season travel to the Cooks is from mid-April to late August, and the high season runs from December to February. There's heavy demand from NZ to the Cooks in December, and in the other direction in January. Fares quoted in this section exclude airport taxes and charges.

AIRLINES

Air New Zealand (www.airnewzealand.com), **Pacific Blue** (www.flypacificblue.com) and **Air Tahiti** (www.airtahiti .aero) are the only international carriers that fly to the Cook Islands. Air New Zealand oper-

ates at least one daily flight from Rarotonga to Auckland as well as a weekly Saturday flight to/from LA. From Auckland you can catch regular Air New Zealand flights to cities in Australia, NZ and Asia, and from LA there are frequent flights to Europe and the rest of the US.

Pacific Blue (part of the Virgin group) operates two weekly flights from Brisbane, Sydney and Melbourne to Rarotonga via Auckland.

ASIA
Air New Zealand's connections to/from Tokyo go through Auckland. The basic return fare starts from around ¥220,000 including taxes and charges.

AUSTRALASIA
Air New Zealand has daily scheduled flights between Auckland and Rarotonga, with extra flights a couple of days a week. Standard low-season fares to Auckland start at NZ$480 and double that for return flights.

Flights from Australia to Rarotonga (and back) go via Auckland. With **Air New Zealand** (☎ 132476; www.airnewzealand.com.au) return adult low/high season fares from Sydney and Brisbane are from A$850/1350, and from Melbourne they cost from A$750/1250. **Pacific Blue** (☎ 131645; www .flypacificblue.com) flies to Rarotonga twice weekly via Auckland with return fares from Sydney, Brisbane and Melbourne starting at around A$700/1100 for low/high season, although some of these flights stop at several capital cities on Australia's east coast.

NORTH AMERICA
Air New Zealand's flights from the US to the Pacific depart from LA. There's just one weekly flight (currently Saturday). Return fares start from US$835/1160 in the low/high season. All Air New Zealand flights from the US follow the LA–Cook Islands–Auckland route. Interestingly, the LA–Rarotonga route is not economic and the Cook Islands government subsidises Air New Zealand, paying for every empty seat – about NZ$3 million per annum.

Travel options from Canada are similar to those from the US. From Vancouver, **Air New Zealand** (☎ 800-663-5494; www.airnewzealand.ca) return fares to Rarotonga (via LA) start from around C$1500/1950 in the low/high season.

PACIFIC
Apart from NZ, the only Pacific island with direct flight connections to Rarotonga is Tahiti.

Air Tahiti (www.airtahiti.aero) flies to Rarotonga Tuesdays and some Saturdays; fares start from 62,000 CFP return.

Sea

It's not uncommon to see hundreds (even thousands) of people ferried into Avarua from a giant cruise ship anchored outside the harbour. Rarotonga is a favourite port of call for South Pacific cruise ships but they don't take on passengers, typically arriving in the morning and departing in the afternoon after quick island tours and souvenir shopping.

YACHT

The Cooks are popular with yachties except during the November-to-March cyclone season. Once you arrive at Rarotonga, fly your Q flag and visit the **Harbour Master** (☎ 28814; Avatiu Harbour, Rarotonga). There are other official ports of entry at Aitutaki, Penrhyn and Pukapuka, which have good anchorages. Virtually uninhabited, Suwarrow Atoll is a trophy destination for cruising yachties, but isn't an official entry.

There's a slim chance of catching a crewing berth on a yacht from the Cook Islands to Tonga, Samoa, Fiji, French Polynesia or NZ. You can ask at Rarotonga's **Ports Authority** (Map pp262-3; Avatiu Harbour), where yachties leave messages if they are looking for crew.

GETTING AROUND

Unless you're sailing your own yacht, travel between the Cook Islands is limited to one passenger ship and Air Rarotonga flights. Flights to the Northern Group islands are expensive (see p289) and only Manihiki, Penrhyn and Pukapuka have airstrips.

Air

Air Rarotonga (☎ 22888; www.airraro.com) is the only domestic airline in the Cook Islands. There are several daily flights to Aitutaki, and several weekly flights between Rarotonga and the rest of the Southern Group. Other than the high-traffic Rarotonga–Aitutaki route, Air Rarotonga will cancel or move flights to consolidate passengers if there are too many empty seats.

Flights to the Northern Group are more erratic – there's a scheduled weekly Tuesday flight to Manihiki, and flights to Penrhyn are flown only when there's sufficient demand.

The baggage allowance for the Southern Group is 16kg (excess NZ$3 per kilogram), for the Northern Group it's 10kg (excess NZ$6.50 per kilogram). Passengers are allowed one piece of hand luggage not exceeding 3kg.

Boat

Shipping schedules are notoriously unpredictable – weather, breakdowns and unexpected route changes can all put a kink in your travel plans. Ships stop off at each island for just a few hours, and only Rarotonga and Penrhyn have decent harbours; at all the other islands you go ashore by lighter or barge.

Taio Shipping (☎ 24905, 24912; taio@oyster.net.ck; Avatiu Wharf) is the only inter-island shipping company and its vessels are far from luxury cruise liners: there's limited cabin space, and some ships have no cabins at all. Showers and toilets are available to all passengers.

It takes a day for ships to get from Rarotonga to the Southern Group. Each island costs NZ$85; the Rarotonga–Mangaia–Ma'uke–Mitiaro–'Atiu–Rarotonga round trip takes four days (NZ$250). It's four days to reach the Northern Group. The monthly Rarotonga–Manihiki–Rakahanga–Penrhyn–Rarotonga service takes 10 to 12 days (NZ$600 to NZ$1200 return), and every two months a ship travels to Palmerston and Pukapuka.

The private research vessel **Bounty Bay** (☎ 23513, 52400; www.pacific-expeditions.com), based on Rarotonga, runs ecotrips around many of the more remote islands of the Cooks, including Palmerston, Takutea and Manuae.

Local Transport

All the islands are good for cycling. Rarotonga has a regular circle-island bus service, taxis and bicycles, motorcycles and cars for hire. Aitutaki has a taxi service and bicycles, motorcycles and cars for hire. 'Atiu has a taxi service, rental motorcycles and a couple of Jeeps. Ma'uke has rental motorcycles.

Hitchhiking is legal, and if you're walking along an empty stretch of road someone will stop and offer you a lift before too long.

Tours

Circle-island tours on Rarotonga (see p266) offer a good introduction to the island's history, geography and traditional culture. Guided tours are also offered on Aitutaki, 'Atiu, Ma'uke and Mangaia.

Rarotongan travel agencies (see p257) can organise single-island or multi-island package tours. Day trips from Rarotonga to Aitutaki are available (see p275).

Samoa

Anchored at the heart of the Polynesian world, Samoa rises languidly from the sea, draped in tenacious tropical foliage and surrounded by iridescent lagoons.

This tiny nation has a proud history, spanning over 3000 years. The first Polynesians to reclaim their independence following European colonisation, the Samoans have held on to their traditional way of life and the control of their own lands to a degree that their Hawaiian or Maori cousins can only dream of. Village life is still the norm here, and traditional forms of governance and communal ownership carry much legal weight. For the enquiring traveller, this makes Samoa a fascinating place.

If your ideal for a South Pacific holiday is to lie around a five-star resort all day while impeccably efficient staff deliver cocktails on silver trays, Samoa may not be for you. There are a few nice resorts, but some of the other Pacific islands do that kind of thing much better. What Samoa excels in is affordable, unpretentious beachside accommodation, friendly people and a relaxed pace of life. It's supremely easy to get around, everyone speaks English and political stability is almost guaranteed.

You'll have no trouble filling your days snorkelling around turquoise lagoons and lazing on white-sand beaches. The more intrepid can hack their way through the rainforest to stare into the overgrown maws of extinct craters, clamber into lava tubes, explore ancient sites or plunge into idyllic swimming holes at the bottom of secluded waterfalls.

Then, at the end of each day, perhaps as you finally order that cocktail, the steamy climate is sure to lull you into 'Island time' – that unhurried state of mind that is the mark of a successful Samoan sojourn.

HIGHLIGHTS

- Soak up the village vibe while strolling around the island of **Manono** (p320)
- Step off the beach and snorkel the coral jungles of **Aleipata's beaches** (p315)
- Party with the locals in the bars and nightclubs of dinky **Apia** (p313)
- Have a lost-world moment, standing atop the mysterious **Pulemelei Mound** (p328)
- Bathe in the idyllic isolation of the **To Sua Ocean Trench** (p316)
- Admire the sunset from the edge of the world at coral-ringed **Cape Mulinu'u** (p327)

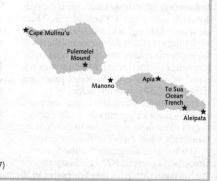

SAMOA FACTS

Capital city (and island) Apia ('Upolu)
Population 179,200
Land area 2934 sq km
International telephone code ☎ 685
Currency Samoan tala (ST)
Languages Samoan, English
Greetings talofa; malo (informal)
Website www.visitsamoa.ws

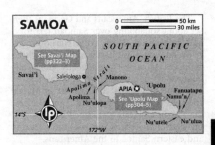

CLIMATE & WHEN TO GO

The most comfortable time to visit is between May and October, during the dry season. The major festivals are also held around this time. During the wet season (November to April), the islands tend to squelch underfoot and receive the occasional battering from tropical cyclones. Huge numbers of Samoans jet in from New Zealand (NZ), Australia and the USA during the December–January holiday period, when you may have trouble booking flights.

The average annual temperature is 26.5°C in coastal areas, with a decrease in temperature as the land rises inland, while humidity averages around 80%. For more climatic information, see p627.

HISTORY
Prehistory

The oldest evidence of human occupation in Samoa is Lapita village, partially submerged in the lagoon at Mulifanua on the island of 'Upolu. Carbon tests date the site at 1000 BC. For more on Lapita, see boxed text, p37.

Archaeologists have discovered over a hundred star-shaped stone platforms across the islands. It's believed that these platforms, dubbed 'star mounds' (see boxed text, p345), were used to snare wild pigeons, which was once a favoured pastime of *matai* (chiefs). Savai'i's Pulemelei Mound is the largest ancient structure in the Pacific.

Around AD 950 warriors from Tonga established their rule on Savai'i, and then moved on to 'Upolu. They were eventually repelled by Malietoa Savea, a Samoan chief whose title, *Malie toa* (Brave warrior), was derived from the shouted tributes of the retreating Tongans. There was also contact with Fiji, from where legends say two girls brought the art of tattooing. The Samoans never really trusted their neighbours – *togafiti* (tonga fiji) means 'a trick'.

European Contact

Whalers, pirates and escaped convicts apparently introduced themselves to Samoa well before the first officially recorded European arrival in the region. This was the Dutchman Jacob Roggeveen, who approached the Manu'a Islands in American Samoa in 1722. Other visitors followed in his wake and over the next 100 years numerous Europeans settled in. The settlers established a society in Apia and a minimal code of law in order to govern their affairs, all with the consent of 'Upolu chiefs who maintained sovereignty in their own villages. Along with technological expertise, the *palagi* (Europeans) also brought with them diseases to which the islanders had no immunity.

Missionaries

In August 1830 missionaries John Williams and Charles Barff of the London Missionary Society (LMS) arrived at Sapapali'i on Savai'i's eastern coast. They were followed by Methodist and Catholic missionaries, and in 1888 Mormons added to the competition for souls. Samoans were quite willing to accept Christianity due to the similarity of Christian creation beliefs to Samoan legend, and because of a prophecy by war goddess Nafanua that a new religion would take root in the islands. Although interdistrict warfare was not abolished until the start of the 20th century, schools and education were eagerly adopted.

Squabbling Powers

There were (and still are) four paramount titles relating to four 'aiga (extended families), equivalent to royal dynasties, in what is now Samoa: Malietoa, Tupua Tamasese, Mata'afa and Tu'imaleali'ifano. During the 1870s a civil dispute broke out between two of these families, dividing Samoa. Much land was sold to Europeans by Samoans seeking to acquire armaments to settle the matter.

The British, Americans and Germans then set about squabbling over Samoan territory, and by the late 1880s Apia Harbour was crowded with naval hardware from all three countries. Most of it subsequently sunk – not because of enemy firepower, but because of a cyclone that struck the harbour in March 1889. After several attempted compromises, the Tripartite Treaty was signed in 1899, giving control of western Samoa to the Germans and eastern Samoa to the Americans.

Foreign Administration

In February 1900 Dr Wilhelm Solf was appointed governor, and the German trading company DHPG began to import thousands of Melanesians and Chinese to work on its huge plantations. But although the Germans had agreed to rule 'according to Samoan custom', they didn't keep their word. In 1908, three years after the eruption of Savai'i's Mt Matavanu, there was an eruption of human discontent with the organisation of the Mau a Pule (Mau Movement) by Namulau'ulu Lauaki Mamoe. In January 1909 Namulau'ulu and his chief supporters were sent into exile.

In 1914, at the outbreak of WWI, Britain persuaded NZ to seize German Samoa. Preoccupation with affairs on the home front prevented Germany from resisting. Under the NZ administration, Samoa suffered a devastating (and preventable) outbreak of influenza in 1919; more than 7000 people (one-fifth of the population) died, further fuelling anger with the foreign rulers. Increasing calls for independence by the Mau Movement culminated in the authorities opening fire on a demonstration at the courthouse in Apia in 1929. Eleven Samoans, including the Mau leader Tupua Tamasese Lealofi III, were killed.

Following a change of government (and policy) in NZ, Western Samoa's independence was acknowledged as inevitable and even desirable, and in 1959 Prime Minister Fiame Mata'afa was appointed. The following year a formal constitution was adopted and, on 1 January 1962, independence was finally achieved.

Since Independence

The Human Rights Protection Party (HRPP) has been in power for most of the period since independence. Economic development has been excruciatingly slow or nonexistent, far below population growth, but at least the country has been politically stable.

'Upolu and Savai'i have been battered by several huge tropical storms over the past two decades: beginning with cyclone Ofa in February 1990 and cyclone Val in December 1991.

In 2009 a storm was brewing over an unpopular government decision to switch from driving on the right-hand side of the road to the left. The rationale was to allow access to cheap second-hand vehicle imports from NZ.

THE CULTURE

Many visitors correctly sense that below the surface of the outwardly friendly and casual Samoan people lies a complex code of traditional etiquette. Beneath the light-heartedness, the strict and demanding fa'a Samoa (Samoan way) is rigorously upheld.

The National Psyche

'Aiga, or extended family groupings, are at the heart of the fa'a Samoa. The larger an 'aiga, the more powerful it is, and to be part of a powerful 'aiga is the goal of all tradition-minded Samoans. Each 'aiga is headed by a matai, who represents the family on the fono (village council). Matai are elected by all adult members of the 'aiga and can be male or female, but over 90% of current matai are male.

The fono consists of the matai of all of the 'aiga associated with the village. The ali'i (high chief of the village) sits at the head of the fono. In addition, each village has one pulenu'u (a combination of mayor and police chief) and one or more tulafale (orators or talking chiefs). The pulenu'u acts as an intermediary between the village and the national government, while the tulafale liaises between the ali'i and outside entities, carries out ceremonial duties and engages in ritual debates.

'Ava (kava) is a drink derived from the ground root of the pepper plant. The 'ava ceremony is a ritual in Samoa, and every government and matai meeting is preceded by one.

Beneath the matai, members of a village are divided into four categories. The society of untitled men, the aumaga, is responsible for growing food. The aualuma, the society of unmarried, widowed or separated women, provides hospitality and produces various goods such as *siapo* (decorated bark cloth) and the *ie toga* (fine mats) that are an important part of *fa'alavelave* ceremonies (see boxed text, p339). Married women are called *faletua ma tausi*. Their role revolves around serving their husband and his family. The final group is the *tamaiti* (children). Close social interaction is generally restricted to members of one's own group.

Individuals are subordinate to the extended family. There is no 'I', only 'we'. The incapable are looked after by their family rather than by taxpayers, and with such onerous family (plus village and church) obligations, it's a struggle for any individual to become wealthy. Life is not about individual advancement or achievement, but about serving and improving the status of your *'aiga*. The communal ownership of land and lack of reward for individual effort tend to stymie Western-style economic development, but has kept control of most of Samoa's resources in Samoan hands.

Lifestyle

Parents and other relatives treat babies with great affection, but at the age of three the children are made the responsibility of an older sibling or cousin. *Fa'aaloalo* is respect for elders, the most crucial aspect of the *fa'a* Samoa, and children are expected to obey not just their immediate relatives, but all the *matai* and adults in the village as well as older siblings. Parents rarely hug or praise their children, so the youth often suffer from low self-esteem and lack confidence and ambition. Parents also routinely resort to violence to punish their children.

Fun family activities are few and far between; a rare exception is White Sunday in October, when children eat first, star in church services, and are bought new clothes and toys. Some teenagers resort to *musu* (refusing to speak to anybody) as a form of protest.

Overriding all else in Samoa is Christianity. Every village has at least one large church, ideally a larger one than in neighbouring villages. These operate as the village social centre, the place where almost everyone makes an appearance on Sunday, dressed up in their formal best. Sunday morning church services are inevitably followed by *to'onai* (Sunday lunch), when families put on banquets fit for royalty.

Sa, which means 'sacred', is the nightly vespers, though it's not applied strictly throughout all villages. Sometime between 6pm and 7pm a gong sounds, signifying that the village should prepare for *sa*. When the second gong is sounded, *sa* has begun. All activity should come to a halt. If you're caught in a village during *sa*, stop what you're doing, sit down and quietly wait for the third gong, about 10 or 15 minutes later, when it's over.

A rigid approach to Christianity has led to conservative attitudes on many social issues, including homosexuality, but this is tempered by a generally tolerant attitude to *fa'afafine* – men who dress and behave like women. The name *fa'afafine* means 'like a woman' and has no obvious parallel in Western society. *Fa'afafine* fulfil an important role in the social fabric, often helping out with the children and looking after their parents in old age. A *fa'afafine* may have

---

BEST EATS

Samoa's best restaurants combine local favourites – such as *oka* (raw fish in lime juice and coconut milk), *palusami* (taro leaves cooked with coconut cream), baked breadfruit and taro – with the flavours of Italy, France, India, China and Japan.

- Deserving its reputation as the country's best restaurant, Bistro Tatau (p312) continues to develop its own style of Samoan fusion.

- Proving that Apia doesn't hold the monopoly on interesting restaurants, Seabreeze Restaurant (p317) combines memorable food with an unforgettable setting.

- Wildfire (p312) excels in bringing traditional tastes to the table.

- Savai'i's best-eating option, CC's Restaurant (p324) serves a varied menu with considerable Filipino flair.

- Outside of Sunday lunch with a village pastor, the buffet at Aggie Grey's culture performance (p313) is the best place to gorge yourself to bursting on authentic Samoan specialities.

IT'S JUST NOT CRICKET

One of the primary requirements for any serious *kirikiti* player is the ability to dance and play cricket at the same time. *Kirikiti* is a unique South Pacific version of the English game of cricket, and is a great example of how an imported measure of civilisation has been adapted to suit Samoan needs. The willow bat became a three-sided club of a size that would make any warlord happy, and the ball was fashioned out of rubber – all the better to be catapulted into the local lagoon. This is a colourful game, too – Samoans keep their whites for church on Sunday; the runs are made in *lava-lava* (wraparound sarong) and sandals.

And the rules? Well, it's just not cricket. There can be any number of players in a Samoan team, which means a game can continue for days, sometimes weeks, at a time. But there's none of that 'stand and watch the grass grow' stuff about this game either. As the batsman swings at every ball, the leader of the opposite team jumps up and down and blows his whistle incessantly in a kind of syncopated rhythm. The rest of the team also gyrates, clapping hands in rhythmic harmony, at the same time watching for an opportunity to catch out the rival. Only when all the batsmen of the opposing team have been dismissed does the other team get its chance.

It's energetic, exuberant and lots of fun. From June to September you'll see it in every village just before sunset.

---

a relationship with a man, but this isn't seen as homosexual. Neither are they seen as women, per se. Many are born entertainers, taking on a role akin to a satirical jester or a Western-style drag queen.

Population

The population of Samoa is nearly 180,000, the vast majority of whom are Polynesian Samoans. Three-quarters of them live on the island of 'Upolu. The urban area of Apia houses around 21% of the nation's population, with the rest sprinkled around the small villages that mainly cling to the coastline. Minorities include both expat and Samoan-born Europeans (called *palagi*, in Samoan) and a small number of Chinese; both minorities are centred on Apia.

SPORT

Sport in Samoa is a community event, which might explain why this tiny nation turns out a disproportionate number of great sports-people. Drive through any village in the late afternoon and you'll see people of all ages gathering on the *malae* (village green) to play rugby, volleyball and *kirikiti* (see boxed text, above). *Fautasi* (45-person canoe) races are held on special occasions. Samoa's main obsession is rugby union and the national team, Manu Samoa, are local heroes – as are the many Samoan players who fill the ranks of rugby union, rugby league and netball teams in NZ, Australia, the UK and France.

ARTS

Architecture

Traditional (not to mention highly practical) Samoan architecture is exemplified by the *fale*, an oval structure with wooden posts but no walls, thus allowing natural airflow. It's traditionally built on a stone or coral foundation and thatched with woven palm or sago leaves. Woven coconut-leaf blinds can be pulled down to protect against rain or prying eyes, but in truth, privacy in such a building is practically impossible.

Palagi-style square homes with walls, louvre windows and doors, though uncomfortably hot and requiring fans, have more status than traditional *fale* and are becoming more common in Samoa.

Fiafia

Originally, the *fiafia* was a village play or musical presentation in which participants would dress in costume and accept money or other donations. These days the term '*fiafia* night' usually refers to a lavish presentation of Samoan fire- and slap-dancing and singing, accompanied by a buffet dinner. But traditional *fiafia* are still performed during weddings, birthdays, title-conferring ceremonies and at the opening of churches and schools.

Drummers keep the beat while dancers sing traditional songs illustrated by coordinated hand gestures. A *fiafia* traditionally ends with the *siva,* a slow and fluid dance performed by the village *taupou* (usually the daughter of a high chief), dressed in *siapo* with her body oiled.

Literature

Towering over Samoan literature is Albert Wendt, a novelist, poet, academic and latterly visual artist, now resident in NZ. Many of his novels deal with the *fa'a* Samoa bumping against *palagi* ideas and attitudes, and the loss of Samoa's pre-christian spirituality; try *Leaves of the Banyan Tree* (1979), *Ola* (1995) or *The Mango's Kiss* (2003). Perhaps some of the prose is too risqué for the Methodists who run most of Samoa's bookshops, as copies are hard to track down in Samoa – you'll have better luck overseas or online.

The Beach at Falesa by Robert Louis Stevenson is a brilliant short story set in Samoa by a master stylist with inside knowledge of the South Pacific. Stevenson spent the last four years of his life in Samoa; for details, see p314.

Music

Music is a big part of everyday life in Samoa, whether it be the exuberant drumming that accompanies *fiafia* nights (opposite), the soaring harmonies of church choirs, the tinny local pop blaring out of taxis or the stirring German marches that the Police Brass Band play every weekday at 7.45am, when they march from their station along Apia's Beach Rd to hoist the national flag in front of the government offices.

Traditionally, action songs and chants were accompanied by drums and body slaps, but guitars, ukuleles and Western-style melodies are now a firm part of the *fiafia* repertoire. Songs were once written to tell stories or commemorate events and this practice continues today. Love songs are the most popular, followed by patriotic songs extolling local virtues. *We are Samoa* by Jerome Grey is Samoa's unofficial national anthem.

MOOD-SETTING READS

- *Palagi Tafaovale* – Bob Rankin (2008): A lively and perceptive memoir from a long-term resident.

- *His Best Pacific Writings* – Robert Louis Stevenson (2004): Cherry-picks his late-19th-century output.

- *The Mango's Kiss* – Albert Wendt (2003): A riveting novel following the fortunes of a Savai'ian family in the early 20th century.

- *Where We Once Belonged* – Sia Figiel (1996): An exuberant story of a young girl growing up and searching for identity in a traditional Samoan village.

- *My Samoan Chief* – Fay G Calkins (1962): Entertaining memoir about marrying into the *fa'a* Samoa.

Contemporary artists include the reggae-influenced Ben Vai and hip-hopper Mr Tee, both of whom write in Samoan and perform regularly around Apia. However, it's offshore that Samoan artists are hitting the big time, especially the new breed of NZ-based rappers such as King Kapisi, Scribe and Savage (see boxed text below).

Siapo & Ie Toga

The bark cloth known as *siapo* is made from the inner bark of the *u'a* (paper mulberry tree) and provides a medium for some of the loveliest artwork in Samoa.

The fine mat called *ie toga* is woven from pandanus fibres split into widths of just a couple of millimetres and can involve years of painstaking work. *Ie toga,* along with *siapo,*

A SAMOANS-HITTING-THE-BIG-TIME PLAYLIST

- *Nesian 101* – Nesian Mystik (2008): Ukulele, rap and disco blend in this NZ number one from a band featuring mixed Samoan, Maori, Tongan and Cook Island ancestry.

- *Swing* – Savage (2005): After featuring in the movie *Knocked Up,* this song entered the US and Australian charts; it had already been number one in NZ.

- *Screems from the Old Plantation* – King Kapisi (2004): From an opening ukulele strum and Samoan chant, Kapisi kicks into a contagious rap celebrating his homeland; it was voted one of the Top 50 NZ songs of all time.

- *Not Many* – Scribe (2003): Scribe's strident statement of intent hit the Top 30 in Australia and spent 10 weeks at number one in NZ.

make up 'the gifts of the women' that must be exchanged at formal ceremonies. Agricultural products comprise 'the gifts of the men'.

Tattooing

Samoa is the last of the Polynesian nations where traditional tattooing is still widely practised (albeit against the wishes of some religious leaders). The traditional *pe'a* (male tattoo) covers the man's body from the waist to the knees. Women can elect to receive a *malu* (female tattoo), but their designs cover only the thighs.

The skills and tools of the *tufuga pe'a* (tattoo artist) were traditionally passed down from father to son, and sharpened shark teeth or boar tusks were used to carve the intricate designs into the skin. It was believed that the man being tattooed must not be left alone in case the *aitu* (spirits) took him. In most cases the procedure takes at least a fortnight. Noncompletion would cause shame to the subject and his *'aiga*.

LANGUAGE

Samoan is the main language spoken, although most people also speak English. In Samoan, the 's' replaces the 'h' of many other Polynesian languages, 'l' replaces 'r' and a glottal stop replaces 'k'. Therefore, the Tahitian word for 'one', *tahi*, is *tasi* in Samoan, *rua* (two) is *lua*, and *ika* (Rarotongan for 'fish') is *i'a*. The soft 'ng' sound in Samoan is written as a 'g' (*palagi*, for example, is pronounced 'pah-lah-ngee').

Samoan basics

Hello.	Talofa or Malo.
Goodbye.	Tofa.
How are you?	O a mai 'oe?
I'm well (thanks).	Manuia (fa'afetai).
Please.	Fa'amolemole.
Thanks (very much).	Fa'afetai (tele).
Yes.	Ioe.
No.	Leai.
Two beers, please.	E lua pia fa'amolemole.

ENVIRONMENT
Geography

Samoa lies in the heart of the vast South Pacific, 3700km southwest of Hawai'i. Tonga lies to the south, Fiji to the southwest, Tuvalu to the northwest and Tokelau to the north, while to the southeast are the Cook Islands.

The country has a total land area of 2934 sq km and is composed primarily of high,

eroded volcanic islands with narrow coastal plains. It has two large islands: Savai'i (1700 sq km) and 'Upolu (1115 sq km). The nation's highest peak, Mt Silisili on Savai'i, rises to 1866m. The small islands of Manono and Apolima lie in the 22km-wide Apolima Strait that separates 'Upolu and Savai'i. A few other tiny, uninhabited rocky islets and outcrops lie southeast of 'Upolu.

Ecology

On the heights of Savai'i and 'Upolu is temperate forest vegetation: tree ferns, grasses, wild coleus and epiphytic plants. The magnificent *aoa* (banyan tree) dominates the higher landscapes, while other areas are characterised by scrublands, marshes, pandanus forests and mangrove swamps. The rainforests of Samoa are a natural apothecary, home to some 75 known medicinal plant species.

Because Samoa is relatively remote, few animal species have managed to colonise it. The Lapita brought with them domestic pigs, dogs and chickens, as well as the ubiquitous Polynesian rat. But apart from two species of fruit bat (protected throughout the islands after being hunted close to extinction) and the small, sheath-tailed bat, mammals not introduced by humans are limited to the marine varieties. Whales, dolphins and porpoises migrate north and south through the islands, depending on the season.

Pili (skinks) and *mo'o* (geckos) can be seen everywhere, and various types of turtles visit the islands. The only land creature to beware of (besides the unloved and unlovely dogs) is the giant centipede, which packs a surprisingly nasty bite.

'UPOLU

pop 136,000 / area 1115 sq km

'Upolu may be the smaller of Samoa's two main islands, but it certainly doesn't suffer from an inferiority complex. When it comes to population, development and tourist infrastructure, it's well on top.

If your first experience of Samoa is the 35km drive from the airport to Apia, you'll already have passed the bulk of the island's population who live in the procession of tidy northwest coast villages that gradually join together to form the capital. The rest of

'Upolu has a charmingly rural feel. The main roads pass through small villages where pedestrians wave cheerful greetings and cars are forced to make way for livestock.

The island is roughly four times longer than it is wide, stretching west to east like a giant humpback whale. The volcanic interior is draped in dense greenery that modestly shrouds secretive lakes and waterfalls.

Most visitors devote themselves to the dazzling strips of sand that skirt 'Upolu's southern shoreline, with regular forays into the pristine offshore lagoons to poke their noses into coral groves and schools of fish. But you can also hike into tangled rainforest, visit rough coastal cliffs formed by the cooling of lava rivers, adopt an old-world manner in a colonial manor, and enjoy the company and cultural teachings of congenial locals. Divers, experienced surfers and golfers will find plenty to keep themselves busy. The urban attractions of Apia shouldn't be neglected either – not if you fancy the odd boogie, movie, or a choice of eating and drinking establishments.

Whether your vision of Polynesian paradise is lying around a resort, cocktail in hand and nose buried in a Dan Brown novel, or whether it's shooting pool with the locals in a ramshackle pub, 'Upolu's got the options.

Getting Around
TO/FROM THE AIRPORT
Faleolo Airport is on the coast, 35km west of Apia. It's worth checking whether your hotel or resort offers free airport transfers – many

---

'UPOLU FOR CHILDREN
Most of 'Upolu is protected from the surf by a reef and many of the beaches are shallow, but you'll still need to watch out for strong currents and keep the kids well supervised. Piula Cave Pool (p315) and Togitogiga Recreation Reserve (p317) are both good for a freshwater splash, while Papase'ea Sliding Rocks (p314) adds more thrill for older kids. *Fiafia* nights (p313) are a guaranteed winner for any age group.

---

of the larger ones have minivans for the task. Otherwise there's always an armada of taxis ready to ferry arrivals to the city or other 'Upolo destinations. The fare to Apia is around ST50 to ST60.

If you're travelling alone, it's cheaper to catch an airport shuttle. It pays to prebook, but you'll usually spot them waiting across from the terminal for all of the major international flights (they don't bother meeting the small planes from Pago Pago). Both **Samoa Scenic Tours** (☎ 26981) and **Go See Samoa** (☎ 44136) have shuttles that stop at any of Apia's hotels (both per person ST25) and take around 45 minutes.

Many of the international flights arrive and depart at ungodly hours, but if you're lucky enough to have one at a reasonable time, buses may be an option. Walk out to the main road and hail any bus approaching from your right to get to Apia. To get to Faleolo Airport from Apia (ST3.10), take any bus marked 'Pasi o le Va'a', 'Manono-uta', 'Falelatai' or 'Faleolo'.

SAMOA

'UPOLU IN...

Two Days
Spend a day exploring Apia (p305), making sure to visit **Palolo Deep Marine Reserve** (p308) and the **Robert Louis Stevenson Museum** (p314). That night, catch a **fiafia** (p313) or head out for dinner at **Bistro Tatau** (p312) and a **drink** at the **Apia Yacht Club** (p313). The following day take a loop of the eastern end of the island and return to Apia via The Cross Island Rd. Stop on the way to splash around the **Pilua Cave Pool** (p315), **Lalomanu** (p315) and **To Sua Ocean Trench** (p316).

Four Days
Start as above, but stop for the night at **Lalomanu** (p315) to allow plenty of time to laze around the beach. Rather than taking The Cross Island Rd back to Apia, continue around the entire island, stopping at one of the south-coast resorts, such as **Virgin Cove** (p318), for your third night. After dragging yourself off the beach, continue to loop back to Apia for a final night's feasting at **Wildfire** (p312) and partying at **I Spy** (p313).

SAMOA

'UPOLU

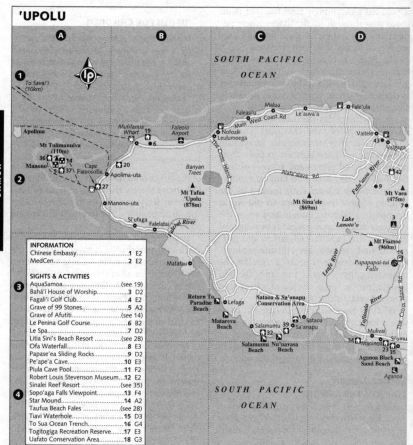

SOUTH PACIFIC
OCEAN

To Savai'i
(10km)

Apolima

Mt Tulimanuiva
(110m)
Manono
Cape
Fatuosofia

Manono-uta

Si'ufaga
Falelatai

Mulifanua
Wharf

Faleolo
Airport

Nofoalii
Leulumoega

Faleasi'u
Malua
West Coast Rd
Le'auva'a
Fale'ula

Vaitele

Valgaga

Banyan
Trees

Mt Tafua
'Upolu
(878m)

Alafa'alava Rd

Mt Sina'ele
(869m)

Mt Vaea
(475m)

Lake
Lanoto'o

Mt Fiamoe
(960m)

Papapapai-tai
Falls

Matafau

Return To
Paradise
Beach

Lefaga

Matareva
Beach

Salamumu

Salamumu
Beach

Sataoa & Sa'anapu
Conservation Area

Sataoa
Sa'anapu

Nu'uavasa
Beach

Leife River

Mulivai

Si'umu

Aganon Black
Sand Beach

Aganoa

SOUTH PACIFIC
OCEAN

INFORMATION

BUS

Buses connecting Apia with almost every other part of 'Upolu leave from both Maketi Fou (the main market) and from behind the Flea Market. Drivers circle between the two until the bus is full (this can take up to an hour) and are liable to veer off route to deposit locals at their front doors. There are set bus stops on the coastal road, but if you hail the driver they'll stop almost anywhere. Pay as you leave the bus. Buses begin running early in the morning and stop in the early afternoon.

A bus schedule for 'Upolu that includes fare information is available from the **Samoa Tourism Authority** (☎ 63500; www.samoa.travel; Beach Rd; ☽ 9am-5pm Mon-Fri, to noon Sat).

To reach the Aleipata district at the eastern end of the island, catch the Lalomanu bus. To head east along the north coast, take the Falefa, Fagaloa or Lotofaga bus. For any point along The Cross Island Rd, take either the Si'umu or Salani bus. For Togitogiga and O Le Pupu-Pu'e National Park, take the Falealili or Salani bus.

CAR

The main roads in 'Upolu are excellent – so good, in fact, that frequent speed humps have been placed in front of villages to slow the traffic down. The sealed Main Coast Rd winds its way around 'Upolu, while three roads cross over the island's east–west central ridge and divide it roughly into quarters. The central one

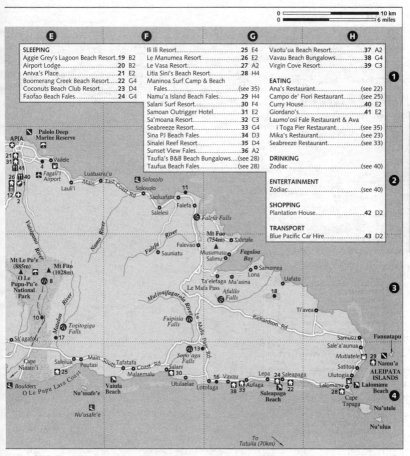

begins in Apia as Faleālili St before becoming The Cross Island Rd further south, where it passes close to 'Upolu's highest peak, Mt Fito (1028m). There's another Cross Island Rd to the west and the steeper, picturesque Le Mafa Pass Rd in the east.

A high-clearance 2WD vehicle should be adequate for all but the road to Uafato and to Aganoa Black Sand Beach, where a 4WD is a necessity. Outside of Apia and the road between the city and the airport, petrol stations are in short supply.

APIA
pop 37,240

Few people come to a Pacific paradise to hang around in a small city with not much in the way of beaches. That's a shame as Apia can be a lot of fun – and its position near the centre of the island makes it a handy base to explore all parts of 'Upolu. It's the only place in Samoa big enough to have a decent selection of eateries, bars and entertainment, but it's still small enough that within a week you'll be recognising people on the street.

The only town of any note in Samoa, Apia has grown from a small harbourside settlement to sprawl along the coast and up the slopes of Mt Vaea, swallowing up about 50 villages in the process. These villages still retain their own traditional forms of governance, but significant parcels of freehold land are also available for those wishing to escape the strictures of village life. This includes a significant

SAMOA

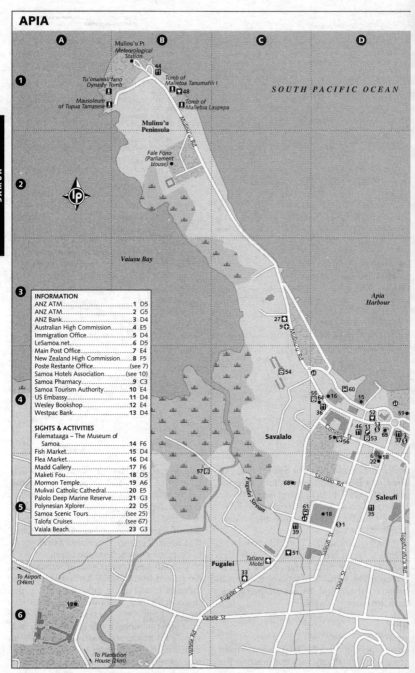

APIA

INFORMATION
ANZ ATM	1 D5
ANZ ATM	2 G5
ANZ Bank	3 D4
Australian High Commission	4 E5
Immigration Office	5 D4
LeSamoa.net	6 D5
Main Post Office	7 E4
New Zealand High Commission	8 F5
Poste Restante Office	(see 7)
Samoa Hotels Association	(see 10)
Samoa Pharmacy	9 C3
Samoa Tourism Authority	10 E4
US Embassy	11 D4
Wesley Bookshop	12 E4
Westpac Bank	13 D4

SIGHTS & ACTIVITIES
Falemataaga – The Museum of Samoa	14 F6
Fish Market	15 D4
Flea Market	16 D4
Madd Gallery	17 F6
Maketi Fou	18 D5
Mormon Temple	19 A6
Mulivai Catholic Cathedral	20 E5
Palolo Deep Marine Reserve	21 G3
Polynesian Xplorer	22 D5
Samoa Scenic Tours	(see 25)
Talofa Cruises	(see 67)
Vaiala Beach	23 G3

Mulinu'u Pt
Meteorological Station

Tu'imaleali'ifano Dynasty Tomb

Mausoleum of Tupua Tamasese

Tomb of Malietoa Tanumafili I

Tomb of Malietoa Laupepa

Mulinu'u Peninsula

Fale Fono (Parliament House)

Vaiusu Bay

SOUTH PACIFIC OCEAN

Apia Harbour

Savalalo

Saleufi

Fugalei Stream

Savalalo Rd

Convent St

Fugalei

Tatiana Motel

Fugalei St

Vaitele St

To Airport (34km)

To Plantation House (2km)

Vaitele Rd

Saleufi St

Vaea St

Togafuafua Rd

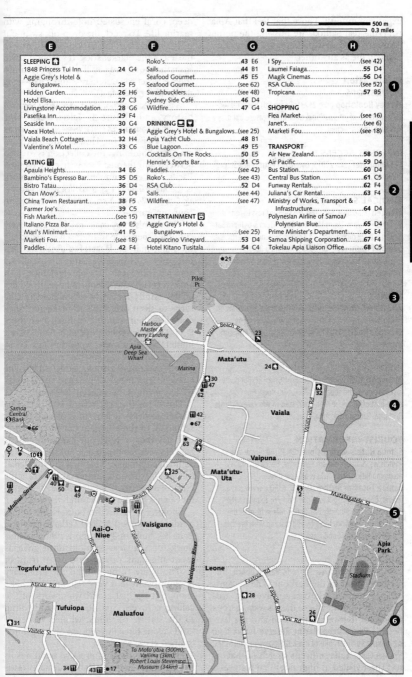

SLEEPING
1848 Princess Tui Inn	**24** G4
Aggie Grey's Hotel & Bungalows	**25** F5
Hidden Garden	**26** H6
Hotel Elisa	**27** C3
Livingstone Accommodation	**28** G6
Pasefika Inn	**29** F4
Seaside Inn	**30** G4
Vaea Hotel	**31** E6
Vaiala Beach Cottages	**32** H4
Valentine's Motel	**33** C6

EATING
Apaula Heights	**34** E6
Bambino's Espresso Bar	**35** D5
Bistro Tatau	**36** D4
Chan Mow's	**37** D4
China Town Restaurant	**38** F5
Farmer Joe's	**39** C5
Fish Market	(see 15)
Italiano Pizza Bar	**40** E5
Mari's Minimart	**41** F5
Marketi Fou	(see 18)
Paddles	**42** F4

Roko's	**43** E6
Sails	**44** B1
Seafood Gourmet	**45** E5
Seafood Gourmet	(see 62)
Swashbucklers	(see 48)
Sydney Side Café	**46** D4
Wildfire	**47** G4

DRINKING
Aggie Grey's Hotel & Bungalows	(see 25)
Apia Yacht Club	**48** B1
Blue Lagoon	**49** E5
Cocktails On The Rocks	**50** E5
Hennie's Sports Bar	**51** C5
Paddles	(see 42)
Roko's	(see 43)
RSA Club	**52** D4
Sails	(see 44)
Wildfire	(see 47)

ENTERTAINMENT
Aggie Grey's Hotel & Bungalows	(see 25)
Cappuccino Vineyard	**53** D4
Hotel Kitano Tusitala	**54** C4

I Spy	(see 42)
Laumei Faiaga	**55** D4
Magik Cinemas	**56** D4
RSA Club	(see 52)
Tropicana	**57** B5

SHOPPING
Flea Market	(see 16)
Janet's	(see 6)
Marketi Fou	(see 18)

TRANSPORT
Air New Zealand	**58** D5
Air Pacific	**59** D4
Bus Station	**60** D4
Central Bus Station	**61** C5
Funway Rentals	**62** F4
Juliana's Car Rental	**63** F4
Ministry of Works, Transport & Infrastructure	**64** D4
Polynesian Airline of Samoa/ Polynesian Blue	**65** D4
Prime Minister's Department	**66** E4
Samoa Shipping Corporation	**67** F4
Tokelau Apia Liaison Office	**68** C5

SAMOA

expat community. Those that feel that Apia isn't 'the real Samoa' are missing the point. This is as valid an expression of 21st-century Samoan life as any other.

Information

BOOKSHOPS

Wesley Bookshop (☎ 24231; Beach Rd) Has a reasonable selection of international trash and treasure but only a limited Samoan section.

INTERNET ACCESS

LeSamoa.net (☎ 21016; Lotemau Centre, Vaea St; per 10min ST2)

MEDICAL SERVICES

MedCen (Map pp304–5; ☎ 26519; The Cross Island Rd, Vailima; ☽ 9am-10pm Mon-Fri, 10am-1pm & 6-10pm Sat & Sun) Private clinic with a 24-hour emergency department.
Samoa Pharmacy (☎ 20355; Mulinu'u Rd; ☽ 8.30am-12.30pm, 1.30-4.30pm & 6-9pm Mon-Fri, 8am-noon & 6-9pm Sat, 6-9pm Sun)

MONEY

ANZ Bank (☎ 69999; Beach Rd) There are also ATMs on Vaiala-Vini Rd and on Saleufi St opposite Maketi Fou.
Westpac Bank (☎ 20000; Beach Rd) Has an ATM out the front.

POST

Main post office (☎ 27640; Post Office St) For poste restante, go to the separate office, two doors from the main post office. Have mail addressed to you care of: Poste Restante, Samoa Post, Apia, Samoa.

TOURIST INFORMATION

Samoa Hotels Association (☎ 30160; www.samoa -hotels.ws; Samoa Tourism Authority, Beach Rd) Books accommodation, ferry tickets and car hire.
Samoa Tourism Authority (☎ 63500; www.samoa .travel; Beach Rd; ☽ 9am-5pm Mon-Fri, to noon Sat) Occupying a prominently positioned *fale* in front of the government building. Usually well stocked with brochures, but the service is hit and miss.

Sights

The closest beach to Apia is **Vaiala Beach**, immediately east of the harbour. The currents can be strong, so take care and avoid the area marked by buoys where there's a dangerous whirlpool. Between the beach and the harbour is **Palolo Deep Marine Reserve** (Vaiala Beach Rd; adult/child ST3/1, hire of mask & flippers/snorkel ST5/3; ☽ 8am-6pm), a magnificent stretch of shallow reef (best visited at high tide) that features a

deep, coral-encrusted hole thronging with marine life. To reach the drop-off, swim out from the beach to the dark patch of water to the left of the marker stick. It's around 100m from the shore, and you'll need flippers and a snorkel to get you out there without damaging the coral (or your feet).

A good starting point for exploring Samoa's history and culture is **Falemataaga – The Museum of Samoa** (☎ 21911; Vaitele St; admission free; ☽ 10am-4.30pm Mon-Fri). Housed in a German-era school building, the collection is divided between four themed rooms: history, culture, Pacific and environment. In the same block is the **Madd Gallery** (☎ 26051; Ifiifi St; admission free; ☽ 9am-3pm Mon-Fri), a small space focusing on contemporary art.

The town's three main markets are a lively cultural experience in themselves, especially the main market, **Maketi Fou** (Fugalei St). This dirty, noisy, 24-hour bazaar is almost always jammed with locals lugging vegetables, meat and groceries, and devouring deep-fried delights. Family members of stallholders take turns to sleep overnight to make sure they don't lose their spot. Pretty much everything is sold here, from hair dye to bananas. Craft hunters will find *siapo*, woodcarvings, coconut-shell jewellery, *kirikiti* bats and balls, *lava-lava* (wraparound sarongs) and T-shirts. The ambience is somewhat enlivened by the fume-ridden chaos of the adjacent bus station.

Down on the waterfront is Apia's **Flea Market** (Beach Rd), a labyrinth of small stalls selling all of the aforementioned craftwork. Don't bother to test your bargaining skills here, however, as haggling is not an element of Samoan commerce. Nearby is the **Fish Market** (off Beach Rd), where a scramble takes place at the crack of dawn every Sunday to snag the freshest catches for the post-church *to'onai*.

Looking over the harbour is the white, Madonna-topped **Mulivai Catholic Cathedral** (Beach Rd), built in 1905 and a reliable landmark for sea-weary sailors until government and bank offices rose up in front of it. The white tiling around the sanctuary is reminiscent of a very religious butcher's shop, but the patterned woodwork of the ceiling is lovely. Sparkly fabric adds bling to the statues of saints, while splashes of lurid colour filter through the spray-painted 'stained glass' windows.

One of the most impressive buildings in Samoa is the massive **Mormon Temple** (Vaitele

St) taking up 1736 sq m on the western approach to town. Completed in 2005 after a fire destroyed the previous building, the white granite edifice has an elegant Art Deco sensibility and is capped by a golden angel.

Activities

Fagali'i Golf Club (Map pp304-5; ☎ 20120; Royal Samoa Country Club, Plantation Rd, Fagali'i; per 9/18 holes ST10/20; ☺ 6am-6.30pm) has an 18-hole, par 70 course. Club hire is ST20 (with a ST50 deposit).

If you're after a less active pursuit, **Le Spa** (Map pp304-5; ☎ 38601; off The Cross Island Rd, Vaoala, massage per 90min ST150) is a haven of tranquillity, where you can pamper yourself with a beauty treatment or therapeutic massage, including the traditional Samoan *fofo* style. It also hosts yoga and guided meditation classes. You'll find it signposted from The Cross Island Rd opposite the large Shrine of Three Hearts.

Walking Tour

Start from **Aggie Grey's Hotel & Bungalows** (**1**; p311), Samoa's most famous address. Founded in 1933, it became a popular haunt of American servicemen during WWII. The late

Aggie Grey is said to have been the inspiration for the character of Bloody Mary in James Michener's novel *Tales of the South Pacific*.

Cross the road and walk west along the sea wall to the **John Williams monument (2)**. It celebrates an early missionary who was killed and eaten in 1839 while evangelising in Vanuatu. His bones were recovered and buried under the church across the road. A little further along you'll pass the genteel wooden colonial-style **Supreme Court (3)**.

As you continue along Beach Rd, gaze up at the recessed statues and twin turrets of the **Mulivai Catholic Cathedral** (**4**; opposite) on your left and then the *fale*-style **Samoa Tourism Authority office** (**5**; opposite) on your right. This and the large government buildings behind it were built on reclaimed land. Originally the

WALK FACTS

Start Aggie Grey's Hotel & Bungalows
Finish Independence Memorial
Distance 3.5km
Duration 1½ hours

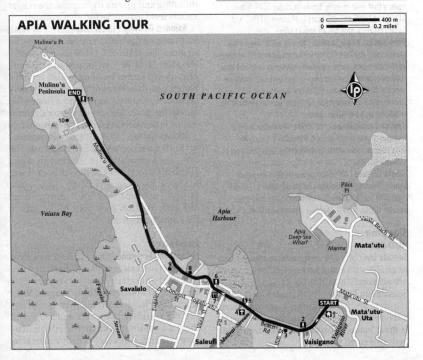

APIA WALKING TOUR

clock tower (6), constructed in memory of those who fought and were killed in WWI, stood near the water's edge. Across the road are the elegant arches of the Spanish Mission-style Chan Mow's building (7).

From the clock tower, take the smaller road heading behind the library to check out the Fish Market (8; p308) and then the Flea Market (9; p308).

Now amble north through the pretty park beside the sea wall that buttresses the eastern shore of Mulinu'u Peninsula until you reach the large peach-hued bowler hat that is Samoa's parliament house, the Fale Fono (10). In case you had any doubts about Samoa's Christian leanings, cross the road to read the Independence Memorial (11). It was built to celebrate the independence of Western Samoa on 1 January 1962 and bears the inscription 'Samoa is founded on God', with lengthy thanks paid to each person of the Holy Trinity.

Tours & Cruises

Polynesian Xplorer (☎ 26940; www.polynesian xplorer.com; Lotemau Centre, Vaea St) Full-service travel agency that runs tours in 'Upolu (half-day ST79, full-day ST179 to ST199) and day tours to Manono (ST180) and Savai'i (ST269). Also has an airport office.

Raw Shakti Yoga Samoa (☎ 779 6400; www.yoga samoa.com; day tour ST250, minimum 2 people) Combines adventure travel, yoga, gourmet vegetarian food and local cultural experiences in its one- to two-week all-inclusive retreats. It also offers day tours that include two hours of customised yoga instruction, an active pursuit (snorkelling or hiking) and a delicious lunch.

Samoa Scenic Tours (☎ 26981; www.samoascenic tours.ws; Aggie Grey's Hotel & Bungalows, Beach Rd) Runs tours around 'Upolu (half-/full day ST85/150) and to Manono (ST180).

Talofa Cruises (☎ 26695; www.talofacruises.com; Samoa Shipping Corporation, Beach Rd; adult ST220-320, child ST145-210) Offers four different cruise itineraries around 'Upolu, Savai'i, Manono, Apolima and Namu'a.

Sleeping

BUDGET

Seaside Inn (☎ 22578; www.seasideinnsamoa.ws; Beach Rd; dm ST39, s/d/tr without bathroom ST85/100/120, s/d/tr/f with bathroom ST110/135/150/195; 🌐 💻) Laid-back Seaside Inn has simple but clean rooms opening on to an airy communal area with a guest kitchen and a convivial cafe-bar. The 'dorm' is great value, consisting of only two single beds in a small room.

Hotel Elisa (☎ 21116; www.hotelelisa.ws; Mulinu'u Rd; budget wing s ST50-60, d ST65-135, main building r ST280-420; 🌐 💻 🌐) The main face of the Hotel Elisa is a three-storey modern block with large upmarket rooms, the front ones offering wonderful sea views. Hidden away at the back is an older two-storey wooden wing where the budget rooms share bathroom and kitchen facilities. The same high standard of housekeeping is maintained throughout.

Valentine's Motel (☎ 22158; valentine@samoa.ws; Fugalei St; s/d from ST60/80; 🌐 💻) This friendly place has the feel of a big family home, a perception reinforced by the prominent tomb of a family member on the back lawn. Air-conditioned rooms with private bathroom and kitchenette are available for ST135.

1848 Princess Tui Inn (☎ 23342; www.princesstui .ws; 1 Vaiala Beach Rd; dm ST60, s ST130-195, d ST165-230, tr ST200-240, q ST240-270; 🌐 💻) Directly opposite Vaiala Beach this dowager princess has lots of atmosphere, occupying a gracious Victorian villa and a more modern cottage next door. The single-sex dorms have bunk beds, sleeping eight. Even with the addition of air-conditioning and private bathrooms, the pricier rooms seem expensive for what's offered.

Samoan Outrigger Hotel (Map pp304-5; ☎ 20042; www.samoanoutriggerhotel.com; Falealili St, Moto'otua; fale per person ST60, s ST130-170, d ST150-200, tr ST180-200, f ST230-300; 🌐 💻 🌐) Set in a high-ceilinged, century-old timber building hidden behind a high hedge, this charming place offers smartly decorated midrange rooms and a row of *fale* facing the pool. The newer air-conditioned rooms downstairs are a little claustrophic.

Hidden Garden (☎ 31252; gardenvi@lesamoa.net; Vini Rd; fale s/d/tr/q incl breakfast ST70/100/150/200) The only accommodation of its kind in Apia, Hidden Garden, on the outskirts of town, has basic *fale* in an appealingly tropical plot of land populated by a small army of dogs and cats. You can cook your own meals in the communal kitchen.

MIDRANGE

Livingstone Accommodation (☎ 30350; www.aliving stone.ws; Fa'atoia Lane; s/d ST100/130) Each of these cute gold-and-green cottages is named after an Australian National Rugby League (NRL) team. Each has its own toilet and small living room furnished with a TV and fridge, and there's a communal kitchen available. The long-term rates are exceptionally reasonable.

Book your stay at lonelyplanet.com/hotels

'UPOLU •• Apia **311**

SAMOA

LOCAL TIPS

After a decade working in top hotel spas in London, former Miss Samoa Ivy Warner returned home to start up Le Spa (p309) in the hills above Apia. We asked her to share some of her favourite Samoan spots.

- **Faofao Beach Fales** (p316) 'You can enjoy the beach from natural *fales* under big trees. There's a real family feel to it.'
- **Fafa O Sauai'i** (p327) 'There's a nice lagoon to swim in and it really feels like it's at the end of the world.'
- **I Spy** (p313) 'I love to dress up and go dancing here. It's the closest we've got to an overseas nightclub.'
- **Paddles** (p312) 'The food is excellent, but the best thing is the lovely Rossi family who run it.'
- **Tiavi waterhole** (p315) 'A serene place with fresh cold water, perfect on a hot day.'

our pick Aniva's Place (Map pp304-5; ☎ 23431; anivas@lesamoa.net; off Falealili St, Moto'otua; s ST110-150, d ST130-170, tr ST170-190, q ST190-210, all incl breakfast; 🎨 🛜) Owned by a wonderfully hospitable Samoan-Scottish family, this two-storey suburban dwelling offers a homey atmosphere with clean, comfortable rooms, an honesty bar and a small pool. All but the cheapest rooms have private bathrooms. An extended family of return travellers make this their Apian home away from home.

Pasefika Inn (☎ 20971; www.pasefikainn.ws; Matafagatele St; s ST140-160, d ST160-180, tr/q ST200/220; 🎨 🛜) This humble inn has a casual, airy feel enhanced by a spacious communal lounge, guest kitchen and swimming pool. You'll pay more for rooms with balconies, but they are considerably bigger.

Vaea Hotel (☎ 22714; www.vaeahotel.com; Togafu'afu'a Rd; r ST150-250; 🎨) So new it wasn't quite finished at the time of research, the 14-room Vaea promises to be a handsome property with modern, well-equipped rooms. Roughly hewn logs support the entrance and line the balconies on the 1st floor.

Vaiala Beach Cottages (☎ 22202; www.vaialabeach.com/vaiala/; Vaiala-vini Rd; s/d/tr US$50/75/85) Only a short stroll from the ocean, this grouping of humble but comfortable self-contained cottages are set among gardens brimming with frangipani, multicoloured hibiscus, ginger flowers and breadfruit. Lower rates are offered for longer stays.

TOP END

Le Manumea Resort (Map pp304-5; ☎ 27755; www.manumearesort.com; The Cross Island Rd, Vailima; r ST350; 🎨 🛜 🖥) Le Manumea inhabits the slightly cooler climes of the slopes above Apia. Despite being near the road, the large restaurant-bar *fale*, resort-style pool and attractive gardens bring plenty of island charm to this upmarket complex of six two-unit bungalows.

Aggie Grey's Hotel & Bungalows (☎ 22880; www.aggiegreys.com; Beach Rd; s US$120-165, d & tw US$130-175, ste US$350-900; 🎨 🖥 🛜) There's a 1950s charm to this iconic hotel. Tiki carvings, painted rock exteriors and tropical flowers lend the central pool area a Disney feel. It wouldn't take much to picture famous former guests such as James Michener, William Holden or Marlon Brando swaggering into view. The best rooms are the *fale*-inspired garden bungalows, followed by the standard rooms facing the pool. They're larger and quieter than the more expensive rooms in the ocean-view wing.

Eating

Apia is the only place in Samoa where you won't be held hostage to the culinary abilities (or lack thereof) of your accommodation provider. There's a decent selection of eateries scattered around town, with most of the upmarket ones lining the waterfront.

RESTAURANTS

Curry House (Map pp304-5; ☎ 777 4301; The Cross Island Rd, Vailima; mains ST7-20; 🕑 lunch & dinner Mon-Sat) Drop by this small eatery for delicious Indian fare before catching a band at neighbouring Zodiac.

Roko's (☎ 20992; Ifiifi St; mains ST13-54; 🕑 breakfast, lunch & dinner) Roko's terrace tables gaze over a lush gully – it's a great spot for a cocktail, but you'll need mosquito repellent, day or night. The menu lurches between Thai, Japanese, Samoan, French and Italian, but has a lightness of touch missing from many of its peers.

Swashbucklers (☎ 28584; Mulinu'u Rd; mains ST16-47; ☺ dinner Tue-Sat) Although you need to order at the counter, the restaurant at the Apia Yacht Club takes advantage of million-dollar views with tables practically on the sea wall itself. The food's a crowd-pleasing mix of fish and chips, steaks, Mexican dishes and salads.

China Town Restaurant (☎ 26177; Falealili St; dishes ST16-80; lunch & dinner) A favourite with local Chinese (always a good sign), China Town offers a big range of delicious dishes, many of which will feed two with a side order of rice. The décor may be humble, but the salt and pepper lobster (ST80) is world class.

Wildfire (Map pp304-5; ☎ 28790; Beach Rd; lunch ST16-24, dinner ST22-45; ☺ breakfast, lunch & dinner Mon-Sat) The best place to sample Samoan specialities mixed into a modern restaurant menu, Wildfire's food is excellent, although the timing and service can be haphazard. The varieties of shellfish in 'Samoa On The Reef' are so exotic that even our Samoan friends found it difficult to identify them.

Giordano's (Map pp304-5; ☎ 25985; off Falealili St, Moto'otua; mains ST19-40; ☺ dinner Tue-Sun) Sit in the back courtyard with its Italian murals and thatched *fale*-style roof, and tuck into delicious pizza featuring such exotic (for Samoa) toppings as olives, blue cheese, parmesan, pepperoni and anchovies.

Apaula Heights (☎ 20836; off Vaitele St; mains ST20-75; dinner Mon-Sat) The restaurant of choice for locals with a special occasion to celebrate, high-altitude Apaula Heights's signature dishes include tuna steaks, garlic prawns and chilli bugs (that's crustaceans, not insects). Look for the sign pointing up a small unnamed road from Vaitele St.

Sails (☎ 20628; Mulinu'u Rd; mains ST26-48; ☺ lunch & dinner Mon-Sat, dinner Sun) Canvas sails provide shelter at this upmarket waterside restaurant and bar. The menu is a mixture of Italian, Indian and Island influences, with seafood to the fore.

Paddles (☎ 21819; Beach Rd; mains ST28-53; ☺ lunch Mon-Fri, dinner Mon-Sat) A delightful Italian-Samoan family serve delicious home cooking and ready conviviality at this attractive terrace restaurant. Pasta and seafood dominate.

our pick Bistro Tatau (☎ 22727; Beach Rd; mains ST48-65; ☺ lunch Mon-Fri, dinner Mon-Sat; ☒ Ⓥ) You'd be hard-pressed to find another menu as innovative as Tatau's in Samoa, fusing

local favourites such as *palusami* into soufflé and ravioli. Polished floorboards, white tablecloths, vibrant local art, tropical floral arrangements and efficient barefoot waiters in *lava-lavas* complete the experience.

CAFES & QUICK EATS

Seafood Gourmet (mains ST6-22; ☺ breakfast, lunch & dinner Mon-Sat) Mulivai (☎ 24625; Togafu'afu'a Rd); Mata'utu-tai (☎ 25962; Beach Rd) There are two branches of this local institution, favoured by Samoans and expats alike for its no-frills but tasty seafood meals and burgers. Both have open-sided dining areas and the Mata'utu-tai branch has the advantage of marina views.

Fish Market (off Beach Rd; fish & chips ST7.50; ☺ 7am-3pm Mon-Fri, to noon Sat) Locally rated as the best fish and chips, and you can be assured of freshness.

Sydney Side Cafe (☎ 24368; Convent St; mains ST10-29; ☺ breakfast & lunch;) If the quality of your morning coffee affects how you cope with your day, head here for a wake-up call. The on-to-it staff serve it up good and strong, along with delicious breakfasts and sandwiches. The couscous salad is delicious.

Bambino's Espresso Bar (☎ 24364; Vaea St; mains ST12-25; ☺ breakfast & lunch Mon-Fri; ☒) Bambino's is the air-conditioned little baby brother of Sydney Side, offering a similar selection of omelettes, wraps, sandwiches and salads, along with excellent coffee.

Italiano Pizza Bar (☎ 24330; Beach Rd; small pizzas ST18-24; ☺ lunch & dinner Mon-Sat, dinner Sun) Locals and travellers converge on this humble waterfront pizzeria to talk, drink jugs of lurid alcoholic mixtures and add their scrawl to the graffiti on the walls. And yes, the pizzas are great.

SELF-CATERING

There's an abundance of fresh produce at **Maketi Fou** (Fugalei St; ☺ 24hr) and the **Fish Market** (off Beach Rd; ☺ 7am-3pm Mon-Fri, to noon Sat). Central supermarkets with reasonable selections include **Chan Mow's** (☎ 22616; Beach Rd; ☺ 8am-4.30pm Mon-Fri, to 12.30pm Sat), **Farmer Joe's** (Fugalei St; ☺ 6am-9pm) and **Mari's Minimart** (☎ 23163; Beach Rd; ☺ 6am-7pm).

Drinking

Apia's waterfront is well supplied with drinking options, though few open their doors on a Sunday and some of the dodgier pool halls aren't pleasant places to be at closing. All of them shut their doors promptly at midnight, when the party spills out on to the seawall. Other options include the bars at the following restaurants and hotels: **Paddles** (☎ 21819; Beach Rd; ☙ lunch Mon-Fri, dinner Mon-Sat), **Wildfire** (Map pp304-5; ☎ 28790; Beach Rd; ☙ breakfast, lunch & dinner Mon-Sat), **Sails** (☎ 20628; Mulinu'u Rd; ☙ lunch & dinner Mon-Sat, dinner Sun), **Roko's** (☎ 20992; Ifiifi St; ☙ breakfast, lunch & dinner), **Zodiac** (Map pp304-5; ☎ 7515112; The Cross Island Rd, Vailima; ☙ 11am-11pm) and **Aggie Grey's Hotel & Bungalows** (☎ 22880; www .aggiegreys.com; Beach Rd).

Apia Yacht Club (☎ 21313; Mulinu'u Rd; ☙ 5-11pm Tue-Sun) Its private club status makes it one of the few sure-fire places for a drink on a Sunday evening. The sea views merely reinforce the relaxing effects of a cold Vailima beer.

Blue Lagoon (Beach Rd) Head upstairs for sea views and ice-cold beers. Later in the evening the dance floor fills up with the young and horny, both Samoan and *palagi* alike.

Cocktails on the Rocks (☎ 20736; Beach Rd; ☙ 3pm-midnight Mon-Sat) Known as 'Cocks on the Rocks', this small bar is a favourite haunt of expats, newly arrived *palagi* and their sometimes suspiciously friendly admirers.

Hennie's Sports Bar (☎ 22221; Fugalei St; ☙ 7am-midnight Mon-Sat) Football jerseys adorn the walls and live 'sport' takes place on the pool table and darts board. There are no pretensions here, just a boisterous crowd of drinkers who all seem to know each other and are more than happy to welcome newcomers.

RSA Club (Returned Services Association; ☎ 20171; Beach Rd) Nicknamed 'the Rosa', this lively place is anything but flowery: the standard drink is a 750mL Vailima beer, the floor has possibly the oldest, most scarred linoleum on the planet and you don't want to be here if a fight breaks out (it's best to avoid the pool tables at closing time).

Entertainment

By Samoan standards, Apia is spoiled for choice when it comes to entertainment. If you've had enough of beachside peace and quiet, here's the place to catch a flick, see a show or boogie the night away – at least until midnight.

FIAFIA

Fiafia cultural performances are popular, so it's best to book ahead and get in early for a good seat.

Aggie Grey's Hotel & Bungalows (☎ 22880; www .aggiegreys.com; Beach Rd; dinner & show ST65) Aggie Grey's stages arguably the best show accompanied by a sumptuous buffet every Wednesday at 6.45pm. Aggie Grey Jnr carries on the tradition of her famous grandmother by dancing the final *siva*, and the evening is capped off by a spectacular fire dance where the pool is set alight.

Laumei Faiaga (☎ 26128; Mulinu'u Rd; dinner & show ST55) Laumei Faiaga has a commitment to training young performers, especially in fire dancing. It hosts an exclusively Samoan show on Tuesdays and a broader Polynesian show on Fridays (buffet from 7.30pm, show 8.30pm).

Hotel Kitano Tusitala (☎ 21122; Mulinu'u Rd; adult/child ST60/30) A *fiafia* is performed here on Thursday nights at 7pm.

Zodiac (Map pp304-5; ☎ 751 5112; The Cross Island Rd, Vailima) On Fridays Zodiac hosts an *'ava* ceremony.

LIVE MUSIC

Laumei Faiaga (☎ 26128; Mulinu'u Rd) Hosts live music Monday to Saturday. 'Musician's Monday' is its regular jam night.

RSA Club (Returned Services Association; ☎ 20171; Beach Rd) The RSA often stages bands on weekends.

Cappuccino Vineyard (☎ 22049; Convent St) Several evenings a week, this casual cafe spreads its tables across a pedestrian mall and local musicians serenade patrons with easy-listening numbers.

Zodiac (Map pp304-5; ☎ 751 5112; The Cross Island Rd, Vailima; ☙ 11am-11pm) A tropical beer garden is the big attraction of this tiny bar, decorated with classic Aussie album covers. Accomplished live musicians entertain on Tuesday and Saturday nights.

NIGHTCLUBS

I Spy (☎ 20194; Beach Rd; admission Wed & Thu free, Fri & Sat ST7-10; ☙ 6pm-midnight Wed-Sat) Apia's premier spot to see, be seen and shake your booty to soulful house and R'n'B. It gets packed to the rafters with well-dressed young things on weekends.

Tropicana (☎ 32332; Fugalei; admission ST5; ☙ 6pm-midnight Wed-Sat) Tucked down a dubious-looking road, Tropicana offers a genuine slice of local nightlife. A wide age group comes to party in this pretension-free zone, either to a live band or DJ. Saturday nights see the fabulous Blondie and her *fa'afafine* friends mixing up traditional *siva* dances with fierce Shirley Bassey lip-synch numbers. Heading from town on Fugalei St, turn right at the first road after the bridge (before Tatiana Motel) and veer left at the first intersection.

Blue Lagoon is also recommended; see p313.

CINEMAS
Magik Cinemas (☎ 28126; Convent St; adult/child ST6/4; ☯ Thu-Sun) Big Hollywood blockbusters often hit the screens here before they reach Australia or NZ and for a fraction of the price.

Shopping
Memorable souvenirs can be bought at various shops around Apia, including *siapo, ie toga* and finely made, multi-legged *'ava* bowls. A treasure trove of such crafts is available from **Maketi Fou** (Fugalei St; ☯ 24hr) and the **Flea Market** (Beach Rd); for details, see p308 and p308.

Plantation House (Map pp304-5; ☎ 22839; Lotopa Rd, Alafua) The best place for high-quality, locally made craft and gifts, including beautiful hand-blocked fabric, *lava-lava*, prints, tailored shirts, bedding sets and jewellery. It's situated at the southern end of the same road as the Mormon Temple.

Janet's (☎ 23371; upstairs, Lotemau Centre, Vaea St) Not all of its stock is locally made, but there's a large range of wood carvings, *siapo* and gifts.

Getting Around
Apia has an extraordinary number of taxis and the fares are cheap. You shouldn't be charged more than ST5 for a ride within town, though it pays to check the fare before you get in. At the time of research there was a plan to introduce meters to all taxis.

Recommended companies include:
City Central Taxis (☎ 23600)
Malo Fou Taxis (☎ 27861)

AROUND APIA
Papase'ea Sliding Rocks
Kids and adults alike have a great time skimming down the waterfalls into cool rock pools at **Papase'ea Sliding Rocks** (off Maugafolau Rd; adult/child ST2/1; ☯ 7am-6pm). If you visit during the dry season, check that the water level is deep enough to be safe.

The site is 6km from central Apia, well signposted from the road past the Mormon

Temple. Take the Se'ese'e bus (ST2.20) from Maketi Fou and ask to be dropped off at the turn-off for Papase'ea.

Robert Louis Stevenson Museum & Mt Vaea Scenic Reserve
This interesting **museum** (☎ 20798; www.rlsmuseum .com; The Cross Island Rd, Vailima; adult/child ST15/5; ☯ 9am-4pm Mon-Fri, to noon Sat) occupies the Scottish author's former residence. Stevenson had the mansion built in 1890 after deciding that the tropical climate of 'Upolu might ameliorate his tuberculosis, but he died there a mere four years later. In that short time the Samoan people adopted him as one of their favourite sons, affectionately calling him Tusitala (Teller of Tales).

The estate is an enchanting place with a centrepiece lawn and perfectly manicured gardens. The house, substantially destroyed in the cyclones of 1991 and 1992, was lovingly rebuilt and opened as a museum in 1994 on the centenary of Stevenson's death. Access is by a half-hour tour that leads through rooms filled with antiques and sepia family photographs.

Stevenson is buried in the adjacent **Mt Vaea Scenic Reserve** (admission free). Look for the badly angled signs for the path to the tomb. At the first unmarked fork, turn left. After a short climb this path forks again: the right-hand trail (30 minutes) is steeper but shorter; the left-hand trail (45 minutes) is gentler but still involves a final slippery section. At the top you'll be greeted by a wonderful view of Apia, a stately Victorian tomb under a rain of yellow flowers, and clouds of vicious mosquitoes.

A taxi from Apia to the museum costs ST7, or take the Vaoala or Siumu bus (ST1.80) from Maketi Fou.

Bahá'í House of Worship
The architecturally interesting **Bahá'í House of Worship** (The Cross Island Rd, Tiapapata; ☯ 6am-6pm) sits in formal gardens near the highest point of The Cross Island Rd and is one of only eight such structures in the world – all are different except for being domed and having nine sides and entrances, reflecting the faith's central tenet of a basic unity of religions and peoples. Designed by Canadian Husayn Amanat and dedicated in 1984, its elegant white dome reaches 28m. Attendants in the adjoining information centre will happily answer any questions about the faith, which originated in Persia in 1844.

A taxi from Apia costs around ST22 or you can catch the Siumu bus (ST3.90) from Maketi Fou.

Lake Lanoto'o

The pea-green crater of **Lake Lanoto'o** is about as removed from human habitation as you can get on 'Upolu. Its remote central highlands location and alternating warm and cold currents lend it an eerie nature. It's also known as Goldfish Lake as it's full of wild goldfish.

The steep trail leading to the lake from the car park (located 3km along a very rough side road) is overgrown and forks repeatedly. Consequently, a number of hikers (including locals) have gotten lost. You would be foolish to attempt it without a guide. A dependable outfit is **SamoaOnFoot** (☎ 31252, 759 4199; gardenvi@ lesamoa.net), which organises trips to the lake (one to two people ST140, three or more per person ST60), including gumboot hire for the 40-minute (each way) hike and plenty of time for a swim.

Papapapai-tai Falls

About 3.5km south of the Bahá'í House of Worship is the lookout for **Papapapai-tai Falls** (The Cross Island Rd; viewing free), a 100m waterfall that plunges into a forested gorge. Roughly 100m before the lookout, an unmarked track leads to the **Tiavi waterhole**, a blissful place to cool off on a hot day.

EASTERN 'UPOLU

The pointy end of 'Upolu is blessed with Samoa's best beaches, offering the winning combination of white sand, clear waters and excellent snorkelling. Heading east from Apia there's a succession of sleepy villages along the surf-battered shoreline. The road turns sharply inland not far past Pilua Cave Pool and skirts rainforest and plantations before hitting the glorious Aleipata coast. While the tight rows of beach *fales* at Lalomanu may not be to everyone's taste, it's this containment of tourism that enables the surrounding villages to preserve their chilled out traditional way of life while still enjoying the benefits of foreign cash.

The road hugs the shore as you round the corner onto the south coast. Saleapaga is rockier than Lalomanu but still has nice stretches of sand. Hidden just off the road, Vavau is one of Samoa's loveliest beaches, offering the requisite juxtaposition of snow-like sand, palm trees and crystalline waters along with a picturesque island within wading distance.

Sights

PIULA CAVE POOL

Secreted beneath the campus of Piula Methodist Theological College, **Piula Cave Pool** (Main East Coast Rd; adult/child ST5/3; ☷ 8am-4pm Mon-Sat) consists of two enchanting fish-filled freshwater grottoes side by side, only metres from the sea. The brave can swim between them via a 3m underwater passage, although it's difficult to find in the darkness at the rear of the caves.

From Apia, take the Falefa or Lalomanu bus (ST3.10).

UAFATO CONSERVATION AREA

The 14 sq km of wild and rugged terrain that comprises the **Uafato Conservation Area** boasts untouched rainforest that marches down from 'Upolu's northeastern hills to dip its toes in the ocean. Flora lovers can track down a rare stand of *ifilele* (the tree used for carving *'ava* bowls), while fauna lovers can observe numerous bird and bat species going about their aerial business. Uafato village is known for its traditional carvers, who are usually willing to demonstrate their art to visitors.

Uafato can be reached via a rough road that winds around Fagaloa Bay from the turn-off at Falefa Falls. This route offers beautiful views, but don't go past Saletele without a high-clearance vehicle. Another option is the road (4WD only; 10km) signposted off Le Mafa Pass Rd to the village of Ta'elefaga.

SamoaOnFoot (☎ 31252, 759 4199; gardenvi@lesamoa .net) offers 15km guided walks along Fagaloa Bay (per person ST95).

ALEIPATA BEACHES & REEFS

At the southeastern end of 'Upolu, Aleipata district has a reef system that remains relatively unscarred by starfish infestations and destructive human practices, such as dynamite fishing. Familiarise yourself with its submerged beauty by just walking in off the fabulous beach at **Lalomanu**, or by venturing offshore to the islands of **Nu'utele**, **Nu'ulua** and **Namu'a** – the first two are part of a conservation area that protects sea bird nesting grounds. If you're lucky, you might spot a turtle, but beware of potentially deadly varieties of cone shells and strong currents.

SAMOA

The bus from Apia to Lalomanu (ST5.70) takes up to 90 minutes. The family that runs Namu'a Island Beach Fales (right) provides day access to the island (including the return boat trip) for ST20 per person.

TO SUA OCEAN TRENCH

The word 'trench' doesn't conjure any of the magic of this marvellous place. **To Sua Ocean Trench** (Main South Coast Rd; adult/child ST10/5; ⏰ 7am-6pm) is actually a large sunken waterhole with almost sheer rock walls decorated in greenery, accessed by a sturdy wooden ladder. Once you've descended the 20-odd metres into the crystalline waters of this fairy grotto, there's a most serene sense of being removed from the world. You can swim under a broad arch of rock, serenaded by droplets of water hitting the surface, to another large opening to the sky. The pool is fed by the waves surging through an underwater passageway – don't attempt to swim through it.

When you've had your fill of this enchanted waterhole, take the short track to the wave-battered cliffs. The well-groomed garden is a great spot for a picnic.

SOPO'AGA FALLS

The 54m-high **Sopo'aga Falls** (Le Mafa Pass Rd; adult/child ST3/free) empty themselves into an enormous gorge close to where the Main South Coast Rd meets Le Mafa Pass Rd. The well-signposted lookout is quite a distance from the falls, but the owners make an effort to give value for the entrance fee by touring visitors around their well-labelled kitchen garden. Traditional artefacts are also displayed, including drums and an *umukuka* (cooking house).

Activities

You can hire snorkelling gear (ST20) from **Litia Sini's Beach Resort** (☎ 41050; www.litiasinibeach.ws; Main South Coast Rd, Lalomanu) and **Taufua Beach Fales** (☎ 41051; www.samoabeachfales.com; Main South Coast Rd, Lalomanu). Tafua also hires volley balls (ST10), kayaks (single/double per hour ST20/30), life jackets (per hour ST15) and mountain bikes (per half-/full-day ST30/50).

On Thursdays Litia Sini's offers a three-hour tour of Lalomanu village where you can meet the *matai*, try your hand at basket-weaving and cook up a feast in an *umu* (earthen oven; minimum four people, per person ST30).

Sleeping

NAMU'A & LALOMANU

Taufia's B&B Beach Bungalows (☎ 47179; www.samoabeachbungalows.ws; Main South Coast Rd, Lalomanu; fale per person incl breakfast ST55) One of the most basic budget options at Lalomanu, friendly Taufia's offers six simple open *fale* with pull-down plastic sheets for privacy.

Taufua Beach Fales (☎ 41051; www.samoabeach fales.com; Main South Coast Rd, Lalomanu; open fale s/d/tr ST90/140/210, enclosed fale ST100/160/240, all incl breakfast & dinner; 🖳) Taufua has an extensive range of *fale*. Choose between open and enclosed *fale* and then add ST10 per person for a proper bed rather than a mattress, an additional ST10 for a porch and another ST10 for private bathroom. At its centre is an attractive dining *fale* where a *fiafia* is held on Wednesday and Saturday nights.

our pick **Namu'a Island Beach Fales** (☎ 751 0231; namuaisland@hotmail.com; Namu'a; fale per person ST90) Namu'a is only a short boat ride from Mutiatele, but once you're on this tiny island you'll feel like 'Upolu is light years away. Do an early morning circumnavigation of the shoreline, clamber up the steep central peak and snorkel the surrounding reef. Ask for a west-facing *fale*, as those facing north bear the brunt of incoming wind. Prices include two meals and the return boat trip.

Litia Sini's Beach Resort (☎ 41050; www.litiasinibeach .ws; Main South Coast Rd, Lalomanu; fale s/d incl breakfast & dinner ST130/200) From the small raised decks of the enclosed wooden *fale*, it's only a short dash into Lalomanu's turquoise lagoon. The prices are steep for *fale*, but you do get a ceiling fan, electric light, lockable door and a night security guard to watch your car. The well-maintained toilet block is just across the road.

SALEAPAGA

Faofao Beach Fales (☎ 41067; Main South Coast Rd, Saleapaga; open/enclosed fale per person ST30/40) Faofao treats guests like family. Mealtimes often feel more like social events, and the Saturday night *fiafia* (guests/nonguests free/ST30) is just one cause for celebration. There's a separate charge for meals (breakfast/lunch/dinner ST10/15/15), but when you tote it all up it's still a reasonable rate for food and a thatched roof over your head.

Boomerang Creek Beach Resort (☎ 40358; boomerang@samoa.ws; Main South Coast Rd, Saleapaga; fale incl breakfast s/d/tr ST60/100/150) 'Resort' is an overly grand description for this fairly simple collection of *fale*, although it does have a restaurant-bar attached (Ana's Restaurant, below). The *fale* on the hillside terraces are cheaper (and feel more private) than those anchored on the beach. Add ST20 to the price for a room with private bathroom.

AUFAGA & VAVAU
Vavau Beach Bungalows (☎ 41306; Main South Coast Rd, Vavau; r ST180) At the time of research, plans were afoot to build a luxury resort on this beautiful beach, but until then make the most of the relative isolation of these six large wooden bungalows, each with a double and a single bed, a kitchenette and patio.

Seabreeze Resort (☎ 41391; www.seabreezesamoa .com; off Main South Coast Rd, Aufaga; s/d/tr ST380/400/460, q ST580-660, all incl breakfast; ☒ ▣) Like the cocktail of the same name, you could easily become intoxicated by Seabreeze's cool, tropical charms. Set in a picturesque bay lined with palm trees and scattered with tiny islands, this small resort offers comfortable bungalows decorated with Gauguin prints and fresh flowers. Kayaks are available (single/double per hour ST15/25). Its excellent restaurant and bar (below) will take care of your dining needs – including seabreezes.

Eating
Ana's Restaurant (☎ 40358; Main South Coast Rd, Saleapaga; mains ST10-27; ⏱ 7am-9.30pm) Attached to Boomerang Creek Beach Resort (opposite), Ana's serves solid standbys, such as omelettes, French toast and pancakes for breakfast, and burgers, stir-fries and fish and chips for dinner. There's a bar attached, and when the resort's full it runs *fiafia* nights.

Seabreeze Restaurant (☎ 41391; off Main South Coast Rd, Aufaga; mains ST30-70; ⏱ breakfast, lunch & dinner) Beautifully decorated and idyllically situated on the edge of the bay, Seabreeze Resort's restaurant offers the best food by far on this end of the island. The chef's Fijian Indian, so a recommended 'curry of the day' (served with roti, dhal and rice) finds a place on the menu alongside seared wasabi tuna and imported NZ steak.

SOUTH COAST
The fact that Samoa's swankiest resorts are clumped on this stretch of coastline says much about its beauty. It's a delight to drive through

the villages, the bright houses painted with the same stridency of colour as the native flora (Samoa doesn't do wallflowers), which is particularly lush and tropical on this side of the island. You'll also find Samoa's only national park.

Many of the beaches are a bumpy drive from the main road, giving welcome seclusion after the road-hugging bays of Aleipata.

Sights
TOGITOGIGA RECREATION RESERVE
The **Togitogiga Recreation Reserve** is a tropical oasis centred on a series of gentle waterfalls. Unless you visit on a Saturday, you'll probably have the sheltered swimming holes between the falls to yourself – although you won't get much of a swim if the weather's been particularly dry. To get here, take the access road for O Le Pupu-Pu'e National Park and stop at the parking area.

O LE PUPU-PU'E NATIONAL PARK
The 29 sq km **O Le Pupu-Pu'e National Park** stretches 'from the coast to the mountaintop', which is what the park's name means. Experienced hikers can pick up a trail near the Togitogiga Recreation Reserve car park, which leads through thick rainforest to **Pe'ape'a Cave** (six hours return), a large lava tube inhabited by *pe'ape'a* (swiftlets); bring a torch. From here you can continue along a heavily overgrown trail to **Ofa Waterfall** (three days return). A guide, such as Eti from **SamoaOnFoot** (☎ 31252, 759 4199; gardenvi@lesamoa .net), is essential.

At the park's western boundary, a bumpy 3km unsealed access road (open 7am to 4pm) leads to the magnificently rugged **O Le Pupu Lava Coast**, where a rocky coastal trail leads along lava cliffs, the bases of which are constantly harassed by enormous waves.

SOUTH COAST BEACHES & REEFS
The south coast of 'Upolu hosts numerous secluded beaches where you can play castaway amid leaning coconut palms and surf-lapped sand.

To the east of O Le Pupu-Pu'e National Park, there's a decent surfing spot at **Vaiula Beach**, accessed from Tafatafa village. West of the park is **Aganoa Black Sand Beach** (admission per 4WD ST10, surf fee ST10), where the water is deep enough for swimming but there's no reef to protect you. There's a popular surf break called **Boulders** here, just off Cape Niuato'i. The very rough 3km track to Aganoa is 150m east of the one-lane stone bridge in Sa'agafou – don't attempt it without a 4WD. The beach is a 10-minute walk to the east.

Near the bottom of The Cross Island Rd, there are several lovely beaches attached to resorts. Further on, **Salamumu** (admission per car ST5) is a beautiful set of beaches reached by a pot-holed 5.5km track. The approach to **Matareva** (admission per car ST10) is only slightly better, leading to a series of delightful coves with shallow snorkelling areas and lots of rock pools.

At Lefaga village is **Return to Paradise Beach** (☎ 777 4986; admission per car ST10; ♻ Mon-Sat), which had a starring role in the 1951 Gary Cooper film *Return to Paradise*. This particular paradise is a little rough on swimmers, however, due to submerged boulders and heavy surf. From here, a narrow road lined by dozing villages heads west to Falelatai.

Activities

At **Sinalei Reef Resort** (☎ 25191; www.sinalei.com; Main South Coast Rd, Maninoa) nonguests can hire kayaks (per hour/two hour/half-day ST15/25/40), masks and snorkels (per hour/half-day ST5/10) and fins (per hour/half-day ST7/15) from its water sports centre. The resort (opposite) also offers various boat trips (1½ to four hours ST40 to ST175).

For surfing and diving operators, see p330.

Sleeping

BUDGET

Sina PJ Beach Fales (☎ 775 783; sinapjfales@gmail.com; Tafitoala; fale per person incl breakfast ST40) A slice of village life, these simple semi-enclosed *fales* line the water's edge in quiet Tafitoala. There are good surf breaks nearby.

Maninoa Surf Camp & Beach Fales (☎ 31200; maninoa .beachsurf@lesamoa.net; Main South Coast Rd, Maninoa; open/enclosed fale per person ST50/60) Squeezed between two luxury resorts, this humble collection of beach *fales* looks more ramshackle than it actually is. There's a chilled-out communal area where you can shoot pool, watch TV or raid the library. Surfers can add an extra ST30 for a daily boat trip to the breaks.

MIDRANGE

our pick **Virgin Cove Resort** (☎ 27085; www.virgin-cove .ws; Sa'anapu; fale s ST210-210, d ST160-250, tr ST240-360, q ST320, bungalow s ST250-380, d ST300-450, tr ST410-620, all

incl breakfast) This is what Pacific Island dreams are made of – blindingly white sandy coves and picturesque *fale* poking out of lush tropical foliage. Accommodation ranges from traditional *fale* with lockers and electricity, to thatched-roof stilt bungalows with proper beds and private bathroom. All are well-spaced out for privacy's sake and children under 12 aren't allowed. The stone-walled, open-air showers (cold water only) are charming. The only downsides are the ever-present mosquitoes, flip-flop–stealing crabs, the extremely rough access road (only just doable in a high-clearance 2WD) and variable meals (mains ST20 to ST45). To reach it, head to Sa'anapu (access fee per car ST5) and turn right.

Salani Surf Resort (☎ 41069; www.surfsamoa .com; Salani; d ST150, nonsurfer/surfer package per person US$135/165; 💻) Located at the mouth of the Fupisia River, Salani caters primarily to experienced surfers with packages that include transfers, accommodation, meals, tours, guided surfing, and use of kayaking and snorkelling gear. Numbers are limited to a total of 16 guests at any one time. Accommodation is in wooden huts on stilts with decks and proper beds. There's a separate ablutions block with solar-powered showers.

TOP END

Ili Ili Resort (☎ 41808; www.iliiliresort.com; Saleilua; r ST350; ❄) Reached by a bumpy coastal road leaving the Main South Coast Rd at Saleilua, Ili Ili has four spacious bungalows with some nice design touches, such as washbasins fashioned from 'ava bowls. It was still fairly new when we visited, so the gardens were looking a little barren, but it does have the advantage of being on the doorstep of lush O Le Pupu-Pu'e National Park.

Sa'moana Resort (☎ 28880; www.samoanaresort.com; Salamumu; r AU$220-500; ❄ 🍴) Lovely Salamumu Beach is the secluded setting of this small surfer- and child-friendly resort. The Aussie owners can point you to nearby breaks and arrange guided surfing expeditions (ST120). Accommodation is in seven humbly furnished A-frame bungalows; the largest have a mezzanine and sleep up to six. Some have waterless composting toilets or lava-walled open-air bathrooms. When you're not splashing around the sublime infinity-lipped seawater pool by the water's edge, you can shoot pool, watch DVDs or dine at the restaurant (lunch ST17 to ST25, dinner ST28 to ST60).

Coconuts Beach Club Resort (☎ 24849; www .coconutsbeachclub.com; Main South Coast Rd, Maninoa; d US$270-460, villas US$460-1950; ❷ ☐ ☯) This large resort has hotel suites, beachside bungalows, over-the-water *fales* and balcony-equipped 'tree houses'. The snorkelling isn't great, but you can hire a kayak or content yourself with lazing around the pool and swimming up to the bar.

Sinalei Reef Resort (☎ 25191; www.sinalei.com; Main South Coast Rd, Maninoa; d US$260-530, tr US$340-460, ste US$680-1100; ❷ ☐ ☯) If you like to laze around the pool and be handed cocktails by charming waiters, Sinalei's the best place in Samoa to do it. This large, beautifully landscaped plot by the ocean offers well-appointed, stand-alone, TV-free units, along with two restaurants, tennis courts, a golf course, water sports centre and good snorkelling around an ocean spring. Some of the suites have their own pools and private beach. The staff are delightful, but the service isn't always commensurate with the hefty prices charged.

Eating
Campo de' Fiori Restaurant (☎ 41808; Ili Ili Resort, Saleilua; mains ST22-55; ☯ lunch & dinner) The expat Roman owner serves up a handful of different dishes each day in Ili Ili Resort's breezy dining *fale*, including gnocchi, pasta and fresh seafood. The daily-baked bread shouldn't be missed.

Laumo'osi Fale Restaurant & Ava i Toga Pier Restaurant (☎ 25191; Sinalei Reef Resort, Main South Coast Rd, Maninoa; mains ST25-60; ☯ 8am-9pm) Sinalei alternates evening meals between its two restaurants. The pier restaurant is the pick of the two, offering an eclectic menu of Samoan dishes, Japanese noodles, pasta dishes, salad and grills in a romantic waterside setting. Themed buffet dinners are served in the *fale* restaurant. Saturday night is Asian night (ST60) – you can eat as much as you like, but the food is lacklustre given the price. For ST10 more you get entertainment with your buffet at the Wednesday night *fiafia* (6.30pm).

Mika's Restaurant (☎ 24849; Coconuts Beach Club, Main South Coast Rd, Maninoa; lunch ST28-39, dinner ST50-55; ☯ breakfast, lunch & dinner) The main restaurant at Coconuts travels the globe for inspiration, serving delicious Italian, French and Samoan dishes and a wonderful Hawaiian *ahi poke* salad (raw fish with sesame oil and chilli).

NORTHWESTERN 'UPOLU
The least attractive part of 'Upolu, the main reason for staying here is to be near the airport, the ferries to Savai'i and the boats to the Apolima Strait islands. The coastline is quite built-up, particularly between Apia and the airport, and the brilliantly coloured lagoon is too shallow for a satisfying swim.

Information
You'll find ATMs at Faleola Airport, along with currency exchange bureaux. The Go Mobile shop at the airport offers internet access (per 15 minutes ST5).

Activities
Based at Aggie Grey's Lagoon Beach Resort, **AquaSamoa** (☎ 45611; www.aggiegreys.com; Main West Coast Rd) offers a large variety of aquatic pursuits, including diving, snorkelling expeditions (per person ST50 to ST90), water-skiing, wake-boarding, knee-boarding or tubing (all ST75 per run), jet-skiing (per 15 minutes ST100), fishing (first hour ST95, then ST60 per hour) and kite-boarding instruction (per four hours ST400). You can also hire kite-boarding equipment (per hour ST200), catamarans (per hour ST50), canoes, pedal boats and water bikes (all ST30 per hour).

In front of Aggie's is the trim greenery of the par-72 **Le Penina Golf Course** (☎ 770 4653; Main West Coast Rd; green fees per 9/18 holes ST81/135, equipment hire per 9/18 holes ST50/90; ☯ 8am-5pm Mon-Sat, noon-5pm Sun).

Sleeping & Eating
Airport Lodge (☎ 45584; airportlodge@lesamoa.net; Main West Coast Rd; s ST135-270, d & tw ST155-320, tr & q ST170-320; ❷ ☯) The simple bungalows at Airport Lodge are handy to the airport and Savai'i ferry. You'll pay extra for the uninspiring food (breakfast ST20, dinner ST40 to ST50).

Le Vasa Resort (☎ 46028; www.levasaresort.com; Main West Coast Rd; r US$180-600; ❷ ☯) A millennia ago the Tongans were booted out of Samoa at this grassy headland, but you can expect a warmer welcome. This personable little resort offers spacious ocean-facing bungalows, some sleeping up to six. Kayaks and bikes are free, but meals aren't included (mains ST45 to ST60).

Aggie Grey's Lagoon Beach Resort (☎ 45611; www.aggiegreys.com; Main West Coast Rd; s/d/tr/q

SAMOA

US$190/200/210/240; 🔀 💻 🍸) Lacking the period charm of its famous Apia sister, the best things about this vast sprawling resort are its large pool, spacious grounds and proximity to the airport. For these prices you might expect a little more luxury and design verve than the luridly painted concrete-block accommodation wings. And the lacklustre but expensive meals and cocktails wouldn't be quite so bad if you weren't trapped so far from alternatives. There's a dedicated kid's club and a scintillating *fiafia* every Thursday night.

MANONO
pop 1090 / area 3 sq km

If you'd like to temporarily escape engine noise and fractious village dogs, the small island of Manono offers a tranquil option. Canines and cars have been banished, and the only things that might snap you out of a tropical reverie are occasional blasts from stereos and the tour groups that periodically clog the island's main trail.

It's obligatory for visitors to do the 1½-hour circumnavigation of the island via the path that wends its way between the ocean and people's houses. They're friendly sorts here, so expect to be greeted with a cheery *'malo'* a dozen or so times.

The trail winds through Lepuia'i, where you'll see the two-tiered **Grave of 99 Stones**. It's dedicated to high chief Vaovasa, who was killed after an unsuccessful attempt to abduct his 100th wife from 'Upolu. The most beautiful section is Manono's less-populated northern edge, where little bays offer terrific views of Apolima. Apai village has the island's best beach.

If you follow the path behind the women's committee building in Salua, you'll eventually end up on top of Mt Tulimanuiva (110m) where there's a large **star mound** (see boxed text, p345). Nearby is the **grave of Afutiti**, who was buried standing up to keep watch over the island. Allow 90 minutes to two hours for this side trip.

Sleeping

Vaotu'ua Beach Resort (☎ 7245500; Faleu; fale per person incl breakfast & dinner ST90) As resorts go, this is a low-key affair comprising a small, shady compound with a half-dozen simple *fales*. Prices don't include boat transfers.

Sunset View Fales (☎ 45640; Lepuia'i; fale per person without/with bathroom ST100/130) Rustic but bright beach shacks are offered here, along with a daily boat trip out to the edge of the reef for memorable snorkelling stints. Price includes all meals and boat transfers, making this the better of the island's two options.

Getting There & Away

Both **Samoa Scenic Tours** (☎ 26981; www.samoascenic tours.ws; Aggie Grey's Hotel & Bungalows, Beach Rd, Apia) and **Polynesian Xplorer** (☎ 26940; www.polynesian xplorer.com; Lotemau Centre, Vaea St, Apia) in Apia offer day tours of Manono; for details, see p310.

If you'd rather go it alone, head for the jetty just south of Le Vasa Resort. Buses marked either 'Manono-uta' or 'Falelatai' (ST3.90) will get you here from Apia (allow 90 minutes). The boats leave when they feel like it, which is usually when there's a tourist willing to pay the inflated fare – about ST30 to ST40 each way. Although the boats are small, Manono is inside the reef so the 20-minute trip isn't usually rough.

APOLIMA
pop 80 / area 1 sq km

Few travellers make the trip out to minuscule but ruggedly beautiful Apolima. From a distance, its steep walls look completely inaccessible. When you get closer you can spy the narrow gap in the northern cliffs, through which small boats can enter the crater and land on a sandy beach. The small settlement consists of a handful of buildings interspersed with pig pens, jungly foliage and (naturally) a large church. A mellifluous choir practises here on Saturday night before singing with even more conviction during Sunday morning services; dress up for the occasion. To get an overview of the island, climb up to the small **lighthouse** perched high on the crater's northern rim.

Getting to Apolima isn't easy. To start with, you'll need an invitation to stay with a local family. Leota, the *matai* from Sunset View Fales (above) may be able to arrange this, along with a boat to come and collect you. As such arrangements are done on an ad hoc basis, you'll need to negotiate a fee you're happy with and make sure that it includes the return boat journey, accommodation and food. Sourcing a boat on a Sunday isn't an option.

SAVAI'I

pop 43,100 / area 1700 sq km

If 'Upolu is shaped like a humpback whale, Savai'i is a giant turtle with its head forming the Falealupo Peninsula in the northwest. A spectacular combination of plantations, lush jungle, sea-smashed cliffs, pristine waterfalls and ragged volcanic cones (around 450 of them) form its shell. The volcanic nature of the largest island in Polynesia outside NZ and Hawai'i has resulted in some gargantuan lava overflows in Savai'i's northern reaches. The island has a leading role in Samoan mythology, its rough landscape yielding numerous legendary formations and enigmatic archaeological sites.

Savai'i is 'Upolu's laidback cousin. In this less developed, sparsely populated paradise, the *fa'a* Samoa remains strong. Scattered around the coastline are breezy villages, where children sit atop the tombs of ancestors, men wander the roadside cheerfully swinging bush knives and weather-beaten churches resound with the melodies of Sunday services.

Getting There & Away

AIR

At the time of research there were no flights to Savai'i, but there was talk of reopening Fagali'i Airport on the outskirts of Apia. If that happens, it's possible that regular flights between Fagali'i and Ma'ota Airport, 5km west of Salelologa, will recommence.

BOAT

Two car ferries tackle the 22km Apolima Strait between 'Upolu and Savai'i daily (per passenger ST9, car plus driver ST50 to ST65). The larger of the two is the more comfortable. It departs from Mulifanua Wharf on 'Upolu at 8am, midday and 4pm, and from Salelologa Wharf on Savai'i at 6am, 10am and 2pm. The smaller ferry departs at the same times but from the opposite wharves. On Tuesdays the larger ferry has only one sailing in each direction, leaving Salelologa at 6am and returning at 4pm. On Sundays the sailing times are 10am, midday, 2pm and 4pm from Salelologa (alternating large then small), and 6am, midday, 2pm and 4pm from Mulifanua (small then large).

Vehicles should be prebooked through the **Samoa Shipping Corporation** (☎ in Apia 20935, in Salelologa 51477). Before putting your car on

the ferry at Mulifanua Wharf, you must have its underside cleaned (free) at the spraying station 100m before the boat terminal. This is done to prevent the spread of the Giant African Snail.

Getting Around

BUS

Salelologa's market is the main terminal for Savai'i's colourful, crowded buses. For the east-coast beaches take the Pu'apu'a bus or to continue on to Fagamalo, take the Lava Field Express. To carry on to Manase, take the Manase or Sasina bus. The Falealupo bus will take you around the Falealupo Peninsula, while the Salega or Fagafau buses trundle past the Alofaaga Blowholes and Satuiatua Beach. The most you'll pay for a ride is ST9.80 (to Asau). Buses to out-of-the-way destinations are timed with the ferries.

CAR

It's a joy to drive the sealed Main Coast Rd that circles the island, but keep an eye out for stray children, pigs, dogs and chickens. Off the main road you'll encounter a few bumpy tracks where at the very least you'll need a high-clearance 2WD (if not a 4WD if there's been heavy rain). This includes the steep, rocky climb up Mt Matavanu.

There are several petrol stations around Salelologa but only a few others scattered around the island.

Cars can be hired from here, but as there's more competition in 'Upolu it sometimes works out cheaper and easier to bring a car over on the ferry.

TAXI

A small army of taxis congregates around the Salelologa Market and greets every boat that arrives.

SALELOLOGA & THE EAST COAST

Ragtag Salelologa stretches up from the ferry terminal, offering little of interest except for a bustling **market** (☒ early-late Mon-Sat), selling everything from groceries to colourful reef fish laid out on slabs. It's as close as Savai'i gets to a proper town, making it a useful place to stock up on supplies and cash before heading further afield.

Heading north you'll pass a tight series of villages fronting a shallow lagoon. It's only once you round the point at Tuasivi that

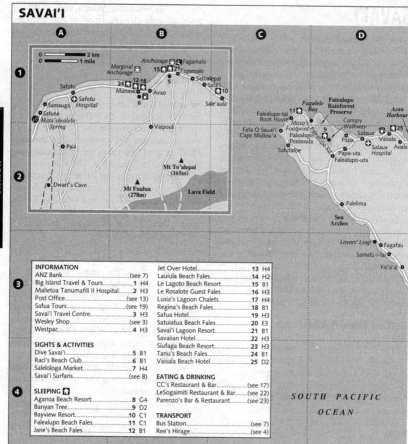

SAVAI'I

INFORMATION
ANZ Bank....................................(see 7)
Big Island Travel & Tours...............**1** H4
Malietoa Tanumafili II Hospital.......**2** H3
Post Office................................(see 13)
Safua Tours..............................(see 19)
Savai'i Travel Centre....................**3** H3
Wesley Shop..............................(see 3)
Westpac...................................**4** H3

SIGHTS & ACTIVITIES
Dive Savai'i...............................**5** B1
Raci's Beach Club........................**6** B1
Salelologa Market........................**7** H4
Savai'i Surfaris..........................(see 8)

SLEEPING
Aganoa Beach Resort....................**8** G4
Banyan Tree..............................**9** D2
Bayview Resort..........................**10** C1
Falealupo Beach Fales..................**11** C1
Jane's Beach Fales......................**12** B1

Jet Over Hotel..........................**13** H4
Lauiula Beach Fales.....................**14** H2
Le Lagoto Beach Resort................**15** B1
Le Rosalote Guest Fales................**16** H3
Lusia's Lagoon Chalets.................**17** H4
Regina's Beach Fales....................**18** B1
Safua Hotel.............................**19** H3
Satuiatua Beach Fales..................**20** E3
Savai'i Lagoon Resort..................**21** B1
Savaiian Hotel.........................**22** H3
Siufaga Beach Resort..................**23** H3
Tanu's Beach Fales.....................**24** B1
Vaisala Beach Hotel....................**25** D2

EATING & DRINKING
CC's Restaurant & Bar.................(see 17)
LeSogaimiti Restaurant & Bar.........(see 22)
Parenzo's Bar & Restaurant..........(see 23)

TRANSPORT
Bus Station.............................(see 7)
Ree's Hirage............................(see 4)

things get exciting, as long white-sand beaches come into view, outlining the vivid aquamarine lagoon. The best of them, **Siufaga** and **Lano**, are among Savai'i's finest. The area also has numerous freshwater pools and springs for bathing.

Information
BOOKSHOP
Wesley Shop (☎ 51244; Salelologa) Small selection.

INTERNET ACCESS & TOURS
Big Island Travel & Tours (☎ 51970; sianics@ yahoo.com; Salelologa; per 30min/hr ST5/9) Turn left when leaving the ferry to find this travel agent that runs tours of the island (half-/full-day ST280/350) and offers internet access.

Safua Tours (☎ 51271; Lalomalava) Based at the Safua Hotel (p324), this outfit conducts knowledgeable day tours (per person ST120) and can organise village stays.
Savai'i Travel Centre (☎ 51206; savaiitravelcentre@ lesamoa.net; Salelologa; per 15/30/60min ST5/8/14) This multitasker organises travel around the island, books international flights, offers internet access and sells petrol.

MEDICAL SERVICES
Malietoa Tanumafili II Hospital (☎ 53511; Main North Coast Rd, Tuasivi) Has on-call doctors and a pharmacy. Other basic hospitals are at Safotu, Sataua and Satuiatua.

MONEY
ANZ Bank (☎ 51213; Salelologa; ☺ 8.30am-3pm Mon-Fri, to noon Sat) Beside the market.

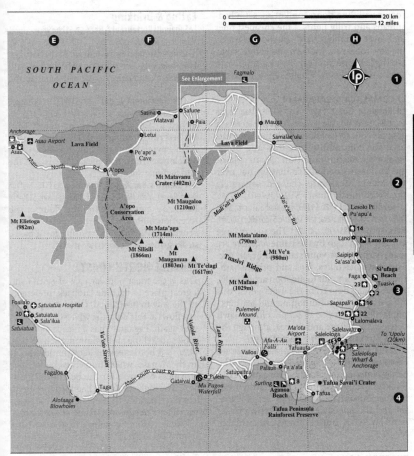

Westpac Bank (☎ 51208; Salelologa; ☹ 9am-3pm Mon-Wed, to 4pm Thu-Fri)

POST
Post office (Blue Bird Mall, Salelologa; ☹ 8.30-noon & 1-4pm Mon-Fri) Has telephones.

Sleeping
There are several places to stay in Salelologa, but it's only once you head out of town that you really start to experience the restful charms of Savai'i.

SALELOLOGA
Lusia's Lagoon Chalets (☎ 51487; www.lusiaslagoon chalets.ws; fale per person ST55-65, unit d ST210-270, tr ST250-310; ☢) Lusia's most basic options are

simple plywood *fale* among the trees or rough wooden *fale* on stilts over the lagoon. Although the latter are seemingly cobbled together out of driftwood and have mattresses on the floor rather than beds, the cute sea-gazing decks make them the better option. The self-contained units are a large jump up in comfort, offering private bathroom, hot water and air-conditioning. Kayaks can be hired for ST20 and there's deep enough water for a proper swim off the pier.

Jet Over Hotel (☎ 51565; www.jetoverhotel.ws; fale ST70, r ST110-180; ☢ ⚛) You'll find this curious hotel at the back of the Blue Bird Mall in central Salelologa, midway through the process of changing from a dated motel into something resembling a resort. The old wing has large rooms with lino floors, pink trim, satin bed-spreads and frilly lights – the cheapest ones look over a lumber yard. Facing the water, the new rooms are modern and comfortable. On the lawn are possibly the smartest *fale* in Samoa – brand new, with louvre windows.

LALOMALAVA & SAPAPALI'I

Le Rosalote Guest Fales (☎ 53568; Main North Coast Rd, Sapapali'i; fale per person ST60) There's a genuine village feel here, with the large *fale* used for community meetings and bingo sessions. Accommodation is in pleasant enclosed wooden *fale* that jut out over the water. Meals are charged separately (breakfast/lunch/dinner ST20/30/40).

Savaiian Hotel (☎ 51296; savaiianhotel.com; Main North Coast Rd, Lalomalava; fale s/d/tr/q ST65/100/150/200, unit s/d/tr ST155/185/220; ✷ ☒) The snazzy large bungalows that go by the name *fale* here are many steps above your standard beach *fale*. They have balconies, fans and private bathrooms for a start, not to mention actual walls, windows and doors. For the units, add to this TVs, fridges, air-conditioning and tea-making facilities. They're all set on a lovely lawn between the village and the sea, although the water's too shallow for a decent swim.

Safua Hotel (☎ 51271; safuahotel@lesamoa.net; Lalomalava; s/d ST90/150, incl breakfast ST110/150) The Safua Hotel is not as attractive as it was in its heyday and it's situated well away from the oceanfront, but the staff are delightful and the *fale*-style cottages have private bathrooms. A buffet dinner is available for ST30.

TUASIVI & LANO

Lauiula Beach Fales (☎ 53897; www.lauiulabeachfales.com; Main North Coast Rd, Lano; fale per person incl breakfast & dinner ST80) Long, languid Lano Beach easily rates as one of the best strips of sand on Savai'i, making these beachside *fale* an extremely attractive proposition. Breakfast and dinner are served in a gorgeous carved dining *fale*.

Siufaga Beach Resort (☎ 53518; www.siufaga.com; Main North Coast Rd, Tuasivi; s US$145-290, d US$155-310, tr US$170-330, q US$180-340; ✷ ☒) Siufaga Beach is just as beautiful as Lano Beach, and the resort set-up across the road from the palm trees and turquoise water is well positioned to capitalise on it. These large, luxurious units hooked around a lushly landscaped pool are the most upmarket in Savai'i.

Eating & Drinking

LeSogaimiti Restaurant & Bar (☎ 51296; Savaiian Hotel, Main North Rd, Lalomalava; lunch ST13-15, dinner ST15-40) The handsome new restaurant at the Savaiian Hotel serves ever-popular fish/chicken/sausages/steak and chips, along with Samoan and Thai dishes.

CC's Restaurant & Bar (☎ 51487; Lusia's Lagoon Chalets, Saleloga; mains ST15-45) Although it's attached to a backpackers' hang-out, CC's is the best restaurant in Savai'i. While that isn't really saying a lot, the Filipino chefs serve delicious curries, fish meals, salads and the odd Samoan speciality.

Parenzo's Bar & Restaurant (☎ 53518; Siufaga Beach Resort, Main North Coast Rd, Tuasivi; mains ST20-60) Parenzo's commands the top floor of the reception building at Siufaga Beach Resort, providing a memorable setting for a pasta, steak, grilled fish or lobster meal.

CENTRAL NORTH COAST

This is the most popular part of Savai'i and a great place to become laidback, preferably all the way to horizontal. Once you pass the lava flows at Sale'aula, the white-sand beaches start again. Fagamalo has a nice lagoon with good snorkelling and swimming at high tide. There's a bottleneck of accommodation at lovely Manase, where numerous budget *fale* providers compete for the beachfront business. The high chief here had the foresight to ban dogs, making this one of the most pleasant villages to explore outside of Manono.

The bus from Salelologa to Manase costs about ST6.

Sights

LAVA FIELD

The Mt Matavanu eruptions between 1905 and 1911 created a moonscape in Savai'i's northeastern corner as a flow of lava 10m to 150m thick rolled through plantations and villages. The Main North Coast Rd crosses this dark, fractured lava field and provides access to several interesting sites.

The modern, iron-roofed *fale* of the village of **Mauga** encircle a shallow, almost perfectly circular crater populated by banana palms. The access road is guarded by an enormous Catholic church. Approach a villager if you'd like to be shown around.

In Sale'aula, 5km north of Mauga, are several **lava-ruined churches** (tour adult/child ST5/3). On the western side of the 'information *fale*' is a

CLOSE ENCOUNTERS OF THE TURTLEY KIND

Samoa's endangered turtles are wonderful creatures and it's certainly a thrill to catch a glimpse of one. Unfortunately if you're snorkelling, they'll usually hear you and swim off long before you see them. Divers have much better odds – experienced operators can take you to sites where the turtles barely look up as you gurgle past.

For those not fortunate enough to spot one in the wild, a turtle enclosure near Satoalepai has a dozen or so captive turtles on display and offers the chance to swim with them for ST5. This is not a conservation effort and neither is it a zoo. There's no expert on hand to ensure the creatures are fed a healthy diet, looked after when sick, or to carry out an effective breeding programme. The shallow ponds and papaya diet are a far cry from the saltwater depths and jellyfish feasts that these creatures are used to. If you venture here, you'll notice that most of them don't use their back flippers much at all.

It's hard to blame villagers for wanting to make a few tala, but travellers should at least be aware of what they're supporting.

trail leading to the **LMS Church**, where 2m of lava flowed through the front door and was eerily imprinted by corrugated iron when the roof collapsed. Behind it a short trail leads over an expanse of twisted black rock stretching to the sea. North of the church is the **Virgin's Grave**, which purportedly marks the burial place of a girl so pure that the lava flowed around her grave, leaving it untouched.

MT MATAVANU CRATER & DWARF'S CAVE

A visit to the volcano responsible for the devastation visited upon northeastern Savai'i a century ago is worth the price of admission if only to meet 'Da World Famous Craterman', the larger-than-life Seu Api Utumapu who maintains the **crater track** (☎ 724 5146; admission ST20; ☻ 9am-4pm Mon-Sat) and collects the fee on behalf of his village.

From Safotu take the turn-off to Paia village and from there the signposted track up the mountain; you can walk the 8km route from Paia, or drive up in a high-clearance 2WD (though a 4WD is recommended). After a lengthy stint of bouncing over the old lava flow, you'll reach the *fale* that serves as Da Craterman's headquarters. If he's not around, just keep heading up and you'll doubtless find him. From here there's an even bumpier 2km to the car park, where a 10-minute trail leads to the crater's edge. Keep the kids tight at hand as there's a vertiginous drop into the lush greenness below. The whole route is lined with cheesy signs in Da Craterman's peculiar style of Pidgin English, representing the visitors from 110-and-counting countries who have made the trek.

From Paia, you can also visit the **Dwarf's Cave** (guide per group ST20; ☻ 9am-5pm Mon-Sat), an intriguing subterranean lava tube. It's said that no one's reached the end of it and your guides will keep leading you through its prodigious depths, crossed by subterranean rivers, until you tell them to turn around. It's signposted off the Main North Coast Rd, just west of the Mt Matavanu turn-off. In Paia, look for the faded signpost on the right and wait outside the blue *fale* at this intersection; someone should appear to guide you to the cave. Bring your own torch and reliable footwear.

MATA'OLEALELO SPRING

One of many that have been used by villagers along the coast for centuries, this **freshwater spring** (Safune; admission ST2; ☻ 7am-5pm Mon-Sat) offers a refreshing swim in a pool-like environment.

PE'APE'A CAVE

This **cave** (Main North Coast Rd; adult/child ST5/2; ☻ 8am-5pm) sits beside the coast road just south of Letui. A guided exploration of this small lava tube takes only 10 minutes, but you'll see white-rumped Polynesian swiftlets and their nests up close. Bring your own torch.

Activities

The lovely folks at **Dive Savai'i** (☎ 54172; www.divesavaii.com; Main North Coast Rd, Fagamalo) offer a family-friendly half-day snorkelling tour (adult/child under 12 years ST60/30, snorkelling gear ST20) stopping at three different sites. They also hire snorkelling equipment on a casual basis (full set per 24 hours ST30).

As well as having the only internet cafe in the area (first five minutes ST5, each subsequent minute ST0.50), **Raci's Beach Club** (☎ 54003; www.rbcltd.ws; Main North Coast Rd, Manase) hires snorkelling gear (full set per half-/full-day ST20/30), kayaks (single per one-/two-/three-hour/half-day/full-day ST20/30/35/40/50), rubber boats (per half-/full-day ST20/30) and bikes (per half-/full-day ST25/40). It operates out of two locations: one by the petrol station and the other at its beachside bar. A range of snorkelling and kayaking tours are offered (ST30 to ST50).

Sleeping & Eating

All of the following options are on the Main North Coast Rd and they all include breakfast in the rates. Those in Manase throw in lunch and dinner as well.

SALE'AULA

Bayview Resort (☎ 54170; www.bayviewresort.ws; r ST150-200; ⛄) If you're a lava lover, this resort is perched on the solid river of rock. The 10 sweet cottages are nicely furnished with comfy beds and decks. Escape from the heat of the black rocks in a freshwater pool by the lagoon or borrow a kayak to explore the area.

FAGAMALO

Savai'i Lagoon Resort (☎ 54168; www.savaiilagoon .co.nz; d/tr/q ST320/410/500) These large, self-contained, modern units are comfortable and clean, but perhaps a little overpriced for the simplicity of the furnishings and lack of air-conditioning. Use of volleyball and pétanque courts, kayaks and dinghies are free, along with UV-filtered drinking water, which the resort provides free of charge to the local village.

Le Lagoto Beach Resort (☎ 58189; www.lelagoto .ws; d US$200-250, tr US$230-280; ⛄ 🖵) The wooden bungalows at this boutique resort are well equipped and wonderfully atmospheric. A cheaper apartment is available for groups, but it's quite run down. The restaurant (mains ST20 to ST75) doesn't always get it right, but it's the best option on the north coast and open daily for nonguests; it would be tempting to eat the surprisingly reasonably priced lobster every day.

MANASE

Tanu's Beach Fales (☎ 54050; tanubeach@samoa -experience.com; fale per person ST50, s/d ST90/160) Long-standing Tanu's is the biggest of the Manase operators, which is only fitting as it's owned by the village's *ali'i* (high chief; the man to be thanked for the dog ban). There are dozens of simple traditional *fales* dotting the nicest part of Manase beach. If you'd prefer a proper bed and solid walls, an accommodation block has been set up across the road offering simple, clean rooms with shared but well-kept bathrooms.

Regina's Beach Fales (☎ 54054; fale per person ST55) It's nice to know that there are still small, welcoming, family-run operations like Regina's that don't charge the earth. The *fale* are of the traditional variety with woven blinds and mattresses on the floor, but they do have electric lights. Meals are more like low-key social events, with the substantial local dishes such as roast breadfruit and taro served up at a communal dining table.

Jane's Beach Fales (☎ 54066; www.janesbeach.ws; fale per person ST70) Pretty pink-and-yellow Jane's is another well-rated, convivial accommodation provider on the crowded Manase strip. The *fales* are lockable and have double beds and small decks. There's also a small shop and bar, and canoes can be hired.

NORTHWESTERN SAVAI'I

Jutting out from the western end of Savai'i is the beautiful Falealupo Peninsula, rich with sites associated with significant Samoan legends. The peninsula's remoteness and protected tracts of rainforest lend it an almost unnerving calm.

In past years, burglars have targeted tourists in this area, so make sure you lock your car and don't leave anything of value in it or in your *fale*.

Sights

A'OPO CONSERVATION AREA & MT SILISILI

The two- to three-day return trip to the summit of Mt Silisili (1866m), the highest point in Samoa, traverses some wonderful rainforested sections of the A'opo Conservation Area and Savai'i's mountainous backbone. To organise a guide speak to the *pulenu'u* of A'opo (ask in the town's small shop for directions). You'll pay in the vicinity of ST40 per person per day and will need to supply food and water and all the requisite camping and hiking equipment.

FALEALUPO RAINFOREST PRESERVE

In 1989 the 1200-hectare area of lowland rainforest on the peninsula's northern side became the first customary-owned conservation area in Samoa. This was achieved thanks to the assistance of Dr Paul Alan Cox, an American ethnobotanist who was working with indigenous healers in Falealupo when he discovered that the area's *matai* had reluctantly signed a contract with a Japanese logging firm in order to pay for the construction of a primary school. After watching the whole village weeping over the loss of their sacred rainforest, Dr Cox personally guaranteed the money for the school. Upon learning this, chief Fuiono Senio ran 9km through the forest to stop the bulldozers.

A sign marked **Canopy Walkway** (Falealupo Rd; admission ST10; 🕑 7am-6pm) leads to a *fale* beside a school, which is where you purchase your entry ticket (hold on to it as it also covers you for Moso's Footprint and the Rock House). At the time of research the walkway itself (a 24m jerry-built bridge strung 9m above the rainforest floor between two large trees) was closed for renovation. However, you can still climb via a sturdy wooden ladder to the top of the magical nearly 230-year-old banyan tree that forms one end of it. Samoan's traditionally believed that *aitu* (spirits) made their home in such places. You can check out that theory by spending the night here (see right).

MOSO'S FOOTPRINT

The ancient 1m by 3m rock depression called **Moso's Footprint** (Falealupo Rd; admission incl in Canopy Walkway ticket; 🕑 7am-6pm) is decidedly unremarkable apart from the legend that surrounds it. The story goes that the giant Moso made the footprint when he stepped from Fiji to Samoa. You'll find it well signposted in front of a tidy *fale*.

FALEALUPO RUINS & ROCK HOUSE

Cyclones Ofa and Val struck the peninsula in 1990 and 1991, completely destroying the village of Falealupo. The decision was made to rebuild the village further inland and the ruined village was left in tatters – until recently when some families have begun to move back. The ruins of the **Catholic church** (Falealupo Rd) are particularly enigmatic.

> ### GATEWAY TO THE UNDERWORLD
> The natural beauty of the Falealupo Peninsula befits its spiritual significance. In pre-Christian times it was believed to be the gateway for souls into the next world. According to tradition, there are two entrances to the underworld: one for chiefs and another for commoners. One entrance is through a cave near Cape Mulinu'u and the other is on the trail made by the setting sun over the sea.

About 300m southwest of the ruins is the partly collapsed lava tube known as the **Rock House** (Falealupo Rd; admission incl in Canopy Walkway ticket; 🕑 7am-6pm). Legend says that it's the result of a house-building competition between Falealupo's men and women, a contest the women won. During the cyclones, whole families sheltered here. Like Moso's Footprint, the story is more interesting than the actual cave, and it's quite an effort to find – you'll probably have to pay to get one of the local kids to lead you to it (ST5 is plenty).

FAFA O SAUAI'I

At Cape Mulinu'u you'll find **Fafa O Sauai'i** (Falealupo Rd; 🕑 8.30am-5pm Mon-Sat), where you can stand at the western end of the earth and look into tomorrow. It's particularly wonderful at sunset. In pre-Christian times this was considered one of Samoa's most sacred spots (see boxed text, above). Don't pass up a swim in the large rock pool, where you don't even have to enter the water to watch fish dart around the colourful corals at the base of the rocks.

When we pulled up an elderly man requested a ST20 admission fee, which may be acceptable if there's a group of you or you're planning to stay the whole day, but for a short visit it's beyond extortionate. When we made to leave the price was quickly reduced to ST10.

Sleeping & Eating

Banyan Tree (Falealupo Rd; price on application) Samoa's most unusual accommodation is offered on a platform set high in a banyan tree in the Falealupo Rainforest Preserve (left). This roofless treehouse sleeps up to six people, with mattresses and mosquito nets provided. There's no telephone number for bookings;

if you're interested, just turn up and negotiate a price.

Falealupo Beach Fales (☎ 774 7420; www.falealupo beachfales.ws; Falealupo Rd, Falealupo; fale per person incl breakfast & dinner ST60) Surrounded by a high lava-stone wall, presumably to protect it from burglary, this set of well-kept but simple *fale* sits alongside a pretty white-sand beach.

Vaisala Beach Hotel (☎ 58016; www.vaisala beachresort.ws; off Main North Coast Rd, Vaisala; s/d/tr/q/f ST100/120/140/160/180; ⊠) The Vaisala faces its own beautiful deep-enough-for-a-decent-swim beach. The rooms are dated but comfortable; if you're lucky, you might get a shifting-image holy picture on the wall. All rooms have terraces and an extra ST20 will buy you air-conditioning. The hotel's restaurant also has an outdoor deck and serves filling set-menu dinners (ST45) regularly attended by local musicians.

SOUTH COAST

With less reef to protect it, Savai'i's south coast witnesses some dramatic confrontations between land and sea, resulting in blustering blowholes and some great surfing spots. If you thought the rest of Savai'i was chilled out, wait to you hit this sparsely populated stretch.

Sights
ALOFAAGA BLOWHOLES

Blasting sea water tens of metres into the air, these **blowholes** (Taga; admission ST5; ⊙ 7am-6pm) are at their most dramatic at high tide. Their full power is demonstrated on stormy days, when waves crash into the rocky coast and water surges through the narrow lava chasms before being vented upwards. Pay admission at the first *fale* and park your car at the second *fale*, near the main blowhole; if you drive into the accommodation compound, you'll be charged ST5 to park there. Don't get too close to the blowholes as freak waves occasionally break over the rocks.

There's often someone at hand to perform the nifty trick of throwing coconuts into the blowhole at just the right time to have them shoot up with the water. To prevent being accosted for money retrospectively, agree a price in advance or make it clear upfront that you're not going to pay for the spectacle. When we visited, an enterprising old man started throwing in coconuts unbidden and then asked for ST20 for his efforts. If you have any problems, complain to the village *pulenu'u* or whoever's taking money at the entrance.

From here you can follow a track around the coast to the now deserted village of Fagaloa (three to four hours return).

PULEMELEI MOUND

Polynesia's largest ancient structure is the intriguing, pyramidal Pulemelei Mound, marked on some maps as Tia Seu Ancient Mound. It measures 61m by 50m at its base and rises to a height of more than 12m. It's a stirring place, with views from its stony summit both to the ocean and into thick, primordial jungle. On sunny days, colourful butterflies swarm across it and birds swoop overhead. For more information as to its possible purpose, see boxed text, p345.

Unlike neighbouring Afu-A-Au Falls, which has a well-displayed sign on the main road outlining the admission fee and opening hours, this sight seems to have fallen off the radar. Admission used to be included with a visit to the falls, but the people collecting the entry fee there when we visited didn't seem to know anything about it. We weren't approached at the mound, but that's not to say that there isn't a charge as it's certainly private property. This ambiguity leaves the door open for unscrupulous sorts to capitalise on; in any case, if you're approached by an official-seeming person, don't hand over more than ST5.

To get here, head down the road flanked by iron poles that starts about 300m beyond the iron-girder bridge on the opposite side of the river from the falls (there's no signage). Before long you'll reach a reasonably deep ford over a stream – not worth risking unless you've got a 4WD or a grunty, high-clearance 2WD. If you park here, there's an easy but exposed 2km walk along this plantation road to the short track leading to the mound. A couple of hand-drawn signs quite a distance down the road will confirm you're on the correct path (veer left if you're ever in doubt). Shortly after crossing a culvert you'll see a place to park your 4WD and another rough sign on your left marking the start of the track. From here it's a 15-minute trek through a coconut grove and then a virtual processional way of bright pink and blue flowers.

As both parking areas are secluded, don't leave any valuables in your car. After your efforts you can reward yourself with a cooling dip at Afu-A-Au Falls.

AFU-A-AU FALLS

Gorgeous **Afu-A-Au Falls** (off Main South Coast Rd; adult/child ST5/2; ☺ 8am-5pm Mon-Sat, 11am-5pm Sun), also known as Olemoe Falls, offer visitors dreamy tropical seclusion and a refreshing swim in a 8m-deep waterhole. The waters are spring fed to remain cool, green and deep even during the dry season. They're well signposted from the main road; pay admission at the *fale* near the entrance.

TAFUA PENINSULA RAINFOREST PRESERVE

This **preserve** (admission ST5) contains superb stands of rainforest and rugged stretches of lava coast studded with cliffs and sea arches. A highlight is the **Tafua Savai'i crater**: its sheer, deep walls are choked with vegetation, giving it a lost-world feel. You may catch glimpses of flying foxes napping in the trees far below.

To get here, take the side road signposted to Tafua opposite the now defunct Ma'ota Airport and pay the custom fee about 50m along. It's reasonably difficult to find the crater, so it's worth taking the services of a guide; however, be sure to agree on a price beforehand (the young man who collected our custom fee and insisted on showing us around went on to ask for a further ST20 at the end of the tour; ST10 is a fairer price for an hour's work).

If you decide to go it alone, follow the road for 2.6km and park at the beginning of the gated road on your left (if you reach the Tafua village sign, you've gone too far). After about 650m of flat road leading past taro and banana plantations, look for a small thatched *fale* on your right. The path to the crater is hard to discern in the long vegetation but it starts between this *fale* and a large dead tree, its white trunk blackened at the bottom. The rocky path becomes clearer as you head into the rainforest towards the crater's precipitous lip. Follow it around to the left for better views into the volcanic bowl and over the centre of the island.

Activities

At the western end of Fa'a'ala village, a track leads to lovely **Aganoa Beach** (per person/surfer ST5/20). There are strong currents here, so swim with care. Pay the fee at Aganoa Beach Resort. This is the base for **Savai'i Surfaris** (☎ 50180; savaiisurfaris@samoa.ws; Aganoa Beach Resort, Fa'a'ala), which runs surf tours around the island; for details, see Aganoa Beach Resort (right).

Surfers will also find an excellent left-hand surf break at **Satuiatua** (per person ST10); the fee is used to support the local school.

Sleeping

Satuiatua Beach Fales (☎ 56026; sbr@lesamoa.net; Main South Coast Rd, Satuiatua; fale per person incl breakfast & dinner ST55) Self-sufficient surfers love this friendly place and there's some good snorkelling here too, although the broad lagoon starts out quite shallow. Futon-style beds make a nice change from the usual mattress on the floor, especially at this price. The restaurant (lunch ST7 to ST20) is set up on a spacious outdoor deck and serves decent dinners.

Aganoa Beach Resort (☎ 50180; savaiisurfaris@samoa.ws; Fa'a'ala; fale without/with bathroom ST100/150, all incl breakfast & dinner) This resort exploits the beauty of a fine little beach and some excellent associated surf breaks on the western edge of Tafua Peninsula. Nonsurfers can snuggle down in the bed-equipped *fale* after a long day of inactivity. Meals are served at the resort's Kahuna Bar & Grill (mains ST10 to ST25). Surfers' packages start at ST200 per day, including transfers to surf spots around the island.

SAMOA DIRECTORY

ACCOMMODATION

It's fair to say that accommodation options in Samoa are limited. There's little budget accommodation outside the ubiquitous *fale*; and at the other end of the scale, only a handful of resorts qualify as truly luxurious. At both ends of the scale, many properties are overpriced given the quality offered. That said, much of the country's accommodation occupies idyllic settings on the beautiful sands that fringe the islands – this meets the minimum requirements for most visitors.

The accommodation in this chapter is listed according to price, ordered based on the cheapest option offered at each property. In Samoa, we generally treat any place that charges up to ST100 as budget accommodation. Midrange places usually cost ST100 to ST250, while we regard anywhere charging over ST250 as top-end accommodation.

An excellent source of accommodation information is the **Samoa Hotels Association** (Map pp306-7; ☎ 30160; www.samoa-hotels.ws; Samoa Tourism

SAMOA

Authority, Beach Rd, Apia). It also acts as a booking agent, taking its fee from the provider not the guest.

The simple structures called *fales* come in a variety of styles. At their most simple and traditional, they're just a wooden platform with poles supporting a thatched roof, surrounded by woven blinds that can be pulled down for privacy. Woven sleeping mats are laid on the floor, topped by a mattress with sheets and a mosquito net. From this basic model various degrees of luxury can be added: electric lights, ceiling fans, proper beds, wooden walls (often with some trellis work to let a breeze flow through), lockable doors and decks. Avoid those with plastic-sheeting walls as these tend to flap around in the wind without letting much air through. Bathroom facilities are usually a communal block, with cold water being the norm. The price usually includes breakfast and often a set lunch and dinner as well.

Fales are usually priced per person, ranging from a reasonable ST50 (including meals) to well over ST100. As a result, couples or larger groups may find themselves paying much more for what is basically one step up from camping on the beach than they would for a midrange hotel.

Hotel, motel and resort accommodation ranges from rooms in slightly dilapidated buildings with cold-water showers to well-maintained rooms with all the mod cons. There's sometimes access to a shared kitchen. Resorts tend to offer bungalow-style accommodation (sometimes called *fales* to sound exotic), with the bigger ones having swim-up cocktail bars and multiple restaurants.

Stays with families in local villages can be organised through **Safua Tours** (Map pp322-3; ☎ 51271; Safua Hotel, Lalomalava, Savai'i); for details, see p322.

ACTIVITIES

Visiting Samoa is less about seeing sights as doing stuff – particularly things that involve tropical beaches. Snorkelling and swimming will be big on the daily checklist for most visitors, but especially hyperactive sorts can fill their holiday with diving, surfing, kayaking and hiking. See the destination sections for further information on place-specific pursuits, as well as where to indulge in that other popular activity – ordering cocktails from the bar.

PRACTICALITIES

- Samoa's main newspaper is the *Samoa Observer* (ST2.50), published (mainly in English) on weekdays, with the *Weekend Observer* published on Saturdays.

- Apia has several radio stations, playing everything from local pop and hip-hop to international hits. Radio Australia has interesting English-language content and news on 102FM. In the east of 'Upolu, 104.1FM has the best reception; tune in for bible-bashing in Samoan and some pleasant church choirs.

- The video format used is NTSC.

- Use Australian-style three-blade plugs to access Samoan electricity (240V, 50Hz AC).

- Samoa uses the standard metric system. See the Quick Reference inside this book's front cover for conversions.

Diving

While Samoa's reefs are more damaged than those of some of its neighbours, there are still some fantastic dive sites to explore, providing access to a multitude of tropical fish and larger marine creatures, such as turtles and dolphins. There are good diving operators on both main islands and many travellers use Samoa as a place to gain their certification. See p77 for information on the main dive sites.

Prices are fairly consistent between the dive operators. An introductory dive costs ST300, two-tank dives start from ST260 and PADI open-water courses are ST1200. The main dive centres on each island are:

AquaSamoa (Map pp304-5; ☎ 45662; www.aquasamoa .com; Aggie Grey's Lagoon Beach Resort, Main West Coast Rd, 'Upolu)

Dive Savai'i (Map pp322-3; ☎ 54172; www.divesavaii .com; Main North Coast Rd, Fagamalo, Savai'i)

Fishing

Samoan reefs and their fishing rights are owned by villagers, so you can't just drop a line anywhere; seek permission first. If you'd like to go fishing with locals, inquire at your hotel or beach *fale*, or speak to the *pulenu'u* of the village concerned.

Game fishing is becoming increasingly popular in the islands – in fact, Samoa has been rated one of the top 10 game fishing destinations in the world. The **Samoa International Game Fishing Tournament** (www.fishing.ws) heads out from Apia Harbour in early May.

Hiking

Samoa's rugged coastal areas, sandy beaches, lush rainforests and volcanoes all invite explorations on foot. However, trails can quickly become obscured because of the lush tropical environment and half-hearted track maintenance. Combine this with the effects of heavy rain and there's often a good chance of getting lost (or at the very least covering yourself in mud). For more remote treks, it pays to take a guide with you.

Guiding costs vary enormously. Sometimes villagers will be happy to accompany you for nothing; at other times, they'll be seeking goods as a reward (like cigarettes), but mostly they'll be interested in cash.

SamoaOnFoot (☎ 31252, 759 4199; gardenvi@lesamoa .net) is based in Apia, but offers expert guided hikes anywhere in Samoa, including Lake Lanoto'o (p315), Uafato Conservation Area (p315) and O Le Pupu-Pu'e National Park (p317). On Savai'i, Mt Silisili (p326) offers a challenging multiday trek.

Shorter tracks that don't require a guide include the short but steep walk to Robert Louis Stevenson's grave near the summit of Mt Vaea (p314), the Mt Matavanu crater walk (p325) and the stride across what was once Savai'i's biggest plantation to Pulemelei Mound (p328).

Even on short walks, the sun and the almost perpetually hot and humid conditions can take their toll. Be sure to carry insect repellent to ward off mosquitoes, antihistamines to counter wasp stings if you're allergic to them, and sufficient water and salty snacks to replenish body elements lost to heavy sweating, and always protect yourself from the sun with a hat and sunblock. Good walking shoes are also essential.

Kayaking

Kayaks are perfect for pottering around the lagoons and several accommodation providers have them available to be borrowed and hired.

Island Explorer Kayak Samoa (☎ 777 1814; www.island explorer.ws) caters to everyone from beginners to experienced paddlers, offering day trips, overnight two-day tours to Namu'a and four-day south-coast expeditions (all ST180 per day, with accommodation and meals extra).

Snorkelling & Swimming

The novice snorkeller will find Samoa's waters fascinating and filled with life, but those who have travelled to other parts of the Pacific might find that it compares unfavourably. In places the reef has been damaged by cyclones and human contact, but in mostly a short walk straight out from the beach will still reveal live corals and an abundance of colourful fish. Some particularly good and accessible spots are Lalomanu (p315), Namu'a (p315) and Palolo Deep (p308). More and more places are hiring out snorkelling gear, but it's still well worth bringing your own mask and snorkel with you.

The majority of Samoan beaches are great for splashing about in but too shallow for satisfying swimming. Always ask permission from local villagers before using their beach.

Surfing

Powerful conditions, sharp reefs and offshore breaks that are difficult to access mean that surfing in Samoa is challenging, to say the very least, and probably one of the worst places in the world to learn the sport! While the surf can be unbelievable at times, offering waves of a lifetime in glorious surroundings, conditions are generally difficult to assess, with some very dangerous situations awaiting the inexperienced or reckless. Despite all this, the islands have become an increasingly popular destination for experienced surfers. The wet season (November to April) brings swells from the north; the dry season (May to November) brings big swells from the south.

It's best to hook up with a surfing outfit. They know all the best spots and provide boat transport to them and, perhaps more importantly, they have established relationships with local villagers and understand the culture – they know where it is and isn't OK to surf. Operators include Salani Surf Resort (p318), Maninoa Surf Camp (p318), Sa'moana Resort (p318) and Savai'i Surfaris (p329) at Aganoa Beach Resort.

BUSINESS HOURS

Banks are usually open from 9am to 3pm Monday to Friday (some branches open on Saturday between 8.30am and 12.30pm). Shops usually operate from 8am to 4.30pm

---

THE RISE OF THE BLUE WORMS

In one of those bizarre quirks of nature that seem almost unbelievable, a humble worm initiates an annual ritual with such precision that you could almost set your clock by it. On the seventh day after the full moon in October or November (or sometimes both, depending on when in the month it falls), the palolo reefworm (a polychaete worm of the *Eunicidae* family, *Eunice viridis*), emerges from the coral reefs to mate. The blue-green vermicelli-shaped worms, rich in calcium, iron and protein, are a prized delicacy. This salty treat is said to be a great aphrodisiac. Parties take place on beaches at the best spots, waiting for the big event. When the worms finally appear at around midnight, crowds carrying nets and lanterns hurriedly wade into the sea to scoop them up.

---

on weekdays and from 8am to noon on Saturday, though kiosks and convenience stores keep longer hours. Eateries serve breakfast and lunch between 8am and 4pm, and dinner from 6pm to around 9pm. Bars in the main towns often open for drinking around lunchtime and point patrons to the front door at midnight. Government offices open from 8am to 4.30pm.

On Sunday almost everything is closed, although ripples of activity appear in the evening. Markets normally get underway by about 6am; Maketi Fou in Apia is active more or less 24 hours a day.

We don't give opening hours for establishments mentioned in the text unless they differ greatly from the standard hours outlined above.

For information about Samoan public holidays, see p629.

CHILDREN

The Samoan climate (except the long periods of heavy rain or the odd cyclone of course), warm waters and dearth of poisonous creatures make the islands a paradise for children. You'll find that Samoans tend to lavish attention on very young children, which means that foreign toddlers will not be starved for attention or affection while visiting the islands.

Never leave your child unsupervised near beaches, reefs or on walking tracks, particularly those running along coastal cliffs (these are never fenced). Lonely Planet's *Travel With Children* has useful advice on family travel. Typically only the upmarket resorts provide cots, and bigger car-rental agencies have car seats, so it may pay to bring your own.

For favoured childish activities on 'Upolu, see boxed text, p303. For details of the practicalities concerning children visiting the South Pacific, see p627.

EMBASSIES & CONSULATES

Following is a list of countries with diplomatic missions based in Apia:

Australia (Map pp306–7; ☎ 23411; www.embassy.gov .au/ws.html; Beach Rd; ☺ 8.30am-4pm Mon-Fri) Canadian consular services are also provided here.

China (Map pp304–5; ☎ 777 2479; The Cross Island Rd, Vailima; ☺ 8.30am-noon & 2-4.30pm)

New Zealand (Map pp306–7; ☎ 21711; Beach Rd; ☺ 8am-4pm Mon-Fri)

USA (Map pp306–7; ☎ 21631; 5th fl, ACC Bldg, Apia; ☺ 9.30am-noon & 1-4pm Mon-Wed & Fri, 9.30am-noon Thu)

FESTIVALS & EVENTS

The main causes of celebration across Samoa include the country's **independence** festivities over the first three days of June: namely the **Teuila Festival** in Apia in September, when Samoa's capital reels in the tourists with canoe races, food and craft stalls, traditional dancing and a beauty pageant; and **White Sunday**, the day that Samoan children rule the roost, which is held on the second Sunday in October.

Another event to look out for is the **Palolo Rise** celebrations in October/November; see the boxed text, above.

INTERNET ACCESS

It's usually only top-end hotels and resorts that can help those who have brought their own computers to Samoa and want to connect to the internet. Otherwise, your only option for accessing the Web (assuming your accommodation provider doesn't have any terminals for guests' use) is an internet cafe. Note that Web connections can drop out with frustrating frequency on these remote islands. There are several internet cafes scattered around Apia. On Savai'i, the only places to get connected are in Salelologa and Manase. Expect to pay anywhere between ST10 and ST30 for an hour's access.

INTERNET RESOURCES

Samoa Observer (www.samoaobserver.ws) The website of the country's main newspaper is a good resource for news and current affairs relating to Samoa, as well as the Pacific region as a whole.

Samoa Tourism Authority (www.visitsamoa.ws) A comprehensive website for independent Samoa, with an up-to-date events calendar and easy-to-browse information on activities, attractions and useful organisations.

Samoan Hotels Association (www.samoahotels.ws) An extensive, regularly updated listing of Samoan places to stay, including photos of many of the properties.

Samoan Sensation (www.samoa.co.uk) It hasn't been updated for a while, but this website still has some interesting background information on Samoan culture.

MAPS

The free Jasons *Samoa Visitor Map* is updated annually and is widely available. It's reasonably basic but should suit most visitors' needs. The more detailed 1:200,000 *Samoa* map published by Hema (ST17.50) can be purchased from various places in Apia, including Janet's (p314).

MONEY

The tala (dollar), divided into 100 sene (cents), is the unit of currency in use in Samoa. In this book, unless otherwise stated, all prices given are in tala. See the Quick Reference inside this book's front cover for exchange rates.

ATMs

Several branches of the ANZ and Westpac banks are equipped with ATMs. Be aware that ATMs can be prone to running out of bills at the start of the weekend. Take plenty of cash with you (in small denominations) when you're heading outside the bigger settlements.

Tipping

Tipping is not expected or encouraged in Samoa. It is, however, deemed acceptable for exceptional service at finer restaurants.

TELEPHONE

State-owned SamoaTel is the main telecommunications provider. Collect and credit-card international calls can be made from public phones by dialling ☎ 956 from Apia, ☎ 957 from the rest of 'Upolu, ☎ 958 from Savaii and ☎ 959 from the airport.

HOW MUCH?

- **Main course in a fine-dining restaurant:** from about ST25
- **Fale accommodation:** from ST50 per night
- **Admission to Afu-A-Au Falls:** ST5 per person
- **Day tour of 'Upolu:** from ST150
- **Car hire:** about ST150 per day
- **1L of unleaded petrol:** ST2.91
- **1L of bottled water:** ST5.30
- **355mL bottle of beer:** ST3 to ST4
- **Souvenir T-shirt:** ST35 to 45
- **Panikeke (Samoan pancake) from market:** ST0.10

Mobile Phones

Since converting to GSM technology, mobile phone providers and outlets have mushroomed throughout Samoa. The big names are Digicel, SamoaTel and Go Mobile. They'll test whether your phone is compatible before selling you a SIM card for around ST30 (usually including ST5 to ST10 worth of free minutes). Prepay top-up scratch cards can be purchased from dozens of shops around both islands. Reception is generally very good, especially on Digicel.

Phone Codes

The country code for Samoa is ☎ 685. The nation does not use area codes.

Phonecards

Phonecards are available from Go Mobile outlets in denominations of ST5, ST10, ST20 and ST50, and can be used in around 150 public payphones around 'Upolu and Savai'i. A local call to a landline costs ST0.03 per minute and other national calls cost ST0.21 per minute. The most you'll pay for an international call is ST2.69 per minute.

TIME

Samoa is just east of the International Date Line, which means its dates are the same as those of North America. Local time is Greenwich Mean Time/Coordinated Universal Time (GMT/UTC) minus 11 hours. Therefore,

SAMOA

when it's noon in Samoa, it's 11pm the same day in London, 3pm the same day in Los Angeles, 9am the following day in Sydney and 11am the following day in Auckland.

You'd be surprised how many people forget about the date difference, especially when making the relatively short journey from Fiji or Auckland. Make sure you double check your accommodation bookings or you may find yourself arriving a day before you're expected.

Samoa recently decided to adopt daylight saving time. In early October the clocks go forward (to GMT/UTC minus 10 hours), returning to normal in late March.

VISAS

A free, 60-day visitor permit is granted to all visitors on arrival in Samoa – except for American Samoans who must obtain a 30-day single entry or multiple-entry permit – provided they have an onward ticket and a passport valid for at least another six months. You'll also be required to provide a contact address within the country, so have the name of a hotel ready upon arrival.

Samoan visitor permits may be extended by several weeks at a time by the country's **Immigration Office** (Map pp306-7; ☎ 20291; www .samoaimmigration.gov.ws; Convent St, Apia; ☽ 8am-4pm Mon-Fri). Take along your passport, wallet and two passport-sized photos and don't make any other plans for the rest of the day. You may also need to have proof of hotel accommodation, onward transport and sufficient funds for your requested period of stay.

TRANSPORT IN SAMOA

GETTING THERE & AWAY
Air

All flights to Samoa arrive at **Faleolo Airport** (airport code APW; Map pp304-5; ☎ 21675; Main West Coast Rd, 'Upolu), 35km west of Apia. Many of the current flights arrive and depart in the early hours of the morning, but airport transfer and accommodation providers are well used to this. At the time of research there was some talk of reopening Fagali'i Airport (Map pp304-5), on Apia's eastern outskirts, for American Samoan services.

Direct flights head to Samoa from American Samoa, Tonga, Fiji, Auckland, Brisbane,

> **DEPARTURE TAX**
>
> An international departure tax of ST40 is payable when flying out of Samoa.

Sydney and Los Angeles. If you're flying from the northern hemisphere, the Air New Zealand flights via Los Angeles are likely to be the most straightforward, with plenty of potential codeshare options available through the airline's **Star Alliance** (www.staralliance.com) partners. Samoa is often a stopover or cheap 'optional extra' on tickets between Europe/North America and New Zealand and on round-the-world fares. Unfortunately, at the time of research Air New Zealand was considering dropping its LA–Samoa–Tonga–Auckland services, asking for large subsidies from the Samoan and Tongan governments to guarantee their continuation.

Airlines that service Samoa include the following (all phone numbers mentioned here are for dialling from within Samoa, unless otherwise indicated):

Air New Zealand (airline code NZ; Map pp306-7; ☎ 20825; www.airnz.com; cnr Convent & Vaea Sts, Apia; ☽ 8.30-4.30 Mon-Fri, 9am-noon Sat) Flights from Auckland, Los Angeles and Tonga.

Air Pacific (airline code FJ; Map pp306-7; ☎ 22172; www.airpacific.com; 5th fl, Central Bank Bldg, Beach Rd, Apia; ☽ 8.30am-5pm Mon-Fri, 8am-noon Sat) Flies from Nadi twice weekly.

Inter Island Airways (airline code IIA; ☎ 42580; www .interislandair.com; Faleolo Airport) Two daily flights to American Samoa; return fares from ST355.

Polynesian Airline of Samoa (airline code PH; Map pp306-7; ☎ 21261; www.polynesianairlines.com; Beach Rd, Apia) The state carrier flies to American Samoa three to five times daily.

Polynesian Blue (airline code DJ; www.polynesianblue .com) A joint venture between Virgin Blue and the Samoan Government, 'Poly Blue' flies from Auckland, Brisbane and Sydney. Samoan bookings are handled by Polynesian Airline of Samoa.

South Pacific Express (airline code SPEX; ☎ 1-684-699 9900; rhuffla@southpacificexpress.as) Little SPEX flies two to three times daily from American Samoa.

Sea
SHIP

The **Samoa Shipping Corporation** (Map pp306-7; ☎ 20935; www.samoashipping.com; Beach Rd, Apia) runs a car ferry/cargo ship called *MV Lady Naomi* between Apia and Pago Pago (American Samoa) once a week. It departs from Apia on Tuesday at midnight and Pago Pago on Thursday at 4pm. The trip takes seven hours each way. Return deck fares are ST160/100 per adult/child; return cabin fares are ST190/120. Note that American passport holders can only buy one-way tickets from Apia.

Cargo ships sail between Apia and remote Tokelau about three times a month. Bookings for the 24- to 26-hour trip can be made in Apia at the **Tokelau Apia Liaison Office** (Map pp306-7; ☎ 20822; Fugalei St, Apia; ⏱ 8am-5pm Mon-Fri). You must obtain a Tokelau visa before booking. Return deck fares are NZ$286/143 per adult/child; return cabin fares are NZ$528/266.

YACHT

Between May and October (outside the cyclone season), the harbours of the South Pacific swarm with yachts from around the world, many following the favourable winds west from the Americas, while others head north from NZ. Apia serves as the official entry point for private yacht owners visiting Samoa. In Savai'i, there are also anchorages at Fagamalo, Salelologa Wharf and Asau Harbour.

Visiting yachts must apply for clearance from the **Prime Minister's Department** (Map pp306-7; ☎ 21339; 5th fl, Government Office Bldg, Beach Rd) in Apia; bear left as you exit the elevator and take the unmarked door straight through the archway. The captain will need to present crew passports and the boat's registration papers.

GETTING AROUND

Air

There have been no scheduled domestic flights in Samoa since Fagali'i Airport (Map pp304–5), near Apia, was closed in 2004. As we've previously noted, there's talk of reopening this airport, which means that Polynesian Airline (opposite) may recommence flights to Savai'i at some point in the future.

Bicycle

Touring 'Upolu and Savai'i by bicycle is a scenic, reasonably relaxed option – we say 'reasonably' because aggressive dogs are a prevalent problem. The roads are generally in good condition and traffic is minimal. The major roads encircling the islands are sealed and relatively flat, but you'd need a sturdy mountain bike to tackle most of the trails to beaches and other coastal attractions. You can transport a bike between Samoa's two main islands on the ferry (see p321).

A big challenge for cyclists is the heat. Even during the coolest months of the year (July, August and September), afternoon temperatures will still be high. Plan to avoid cycling long stretches in the heat of the day. Also bear in mind that buses are unlikely to be able to accommodate bicycles should you run out of leg power.

Bikes are a common form of local transport in Samoa, so it shouldn't be hard to track down a bike repairer if you really need one. But it's obviously best to bring your own comprehensive bike repair kit, a decent lock and heavy-duty panniers. Some accommodation providers offer bike hire, but these are for day touring, not long-distance rides.

Boat

The ferry from Mulifanua Wharf is the only option for travel between 'Upolu and Savai'i (p321). Small boats leave from Cape Fatusofia for Manono (p320). The Samoa Shipping Corporation operates scenic cruises out of Apia (p310).

The **Apia Yacht Club** (Map pp306-7; ☎ 21313; Mulinu'u Rd, Apia; ⏱ 5-11pm Tue-Sun) is a good place to share information on sailing around the islands over a cold beer (see p313).

Bus

Travelling by public bus in Samoa is an experience that shouldn't be missed. The buses are vibrantly painted (look out for the Bon Jovi–themed one), wooden-seated vehicles (prepare yourself for hard jolts) that blast Samoan pop music at deafening volumes (prepare yourself for endless reggaefied Christmas carols from October on). The drivers are often as unique as the vehicles and services operate completely at their whim. If a driver feels like knocking off at 1pm, he does, and passengers counting on the service are left stranded. Never rely on catching a bus after about 2pm. Buses are also scarce on Saturday afternoon and often only cater to church services on Sunday.

All buses prominently display the name of their destination in the front window. To stop a bus, wave your hand and arm, palm down, as the bus approaches. To signal that you'd like to get off the bus, either knock on the ceiling or clap loudly. Fares are paid to the driver – try to have as near to the exact change as possible.

Although most visitors don't notice it at first, there is a seating hierarchy on Samoan buses.

SAMOA

Unmarried women normally sit together, while foreigners and older people must have a seat and sit near the front of the bus. Don't worry about arranging this yourself – the locals will see to it that everything is sorted out. The way in which Samoans stack themselves on top of each other on crowded buses without losing any dignity is akin to a social miracle.

Details about specific routes and fares are provided at the start of the 'Upolu (p304) and Savai'i (p321) sections.

Car

Getting around by car in Samoa is quite straightforward. The coastal roads on both main islands are sealed and the general condition of most other main roads is also pretty good. A 4WD will make trips down rough, unsealed side roads much more comfortable, but nearly all of these side routes can be tackled in a high-clearance 2WD. After heavy rain, however, some roads will be inaccessible to 2WD vehicles.

DRIVING LICENCE

Visitors to Samoa need to obtain a temporary driving licence. Most car-hire companies can issue these, or you can call into the **Ministry of Works, Transport & Infrastructure** (Map pp306-7; ☎ 21611; Beach Rd; license per 1/2 months ST12/24; ⊙ 9am-5pm Mon-Fri) in Apia. You'll need to present a valid overseas driving licence.

HIRE

There are literally dozens of car-hire agencies in Samoa and, on top of this, some of the larger accommodation providers also hire vehicles. Most of the agencies are in or around Apia and the airport, and the prices can be quite competitive. Note that you can usually take hire cars from 'Upolu over to Savai'i and back, but cars hired on Savai'i cannot be taken to 'Upolu. It's sometimes cheaper to hire in 'Upolu even given the ferry fee, especially if you obtain a discount for a longer booking.

When hiring a vehicle, check for any damage or scratches and note everything on the rental agreement, lest you be liable for damage when the car is returned. Furthermore, fend off requests to leave your passport or a cash deposit against possible damages. Many places will require a credit card pre-authorisation by way of a deposit and it's usual to pay in advance.

Apia has numerous car-hire agencies. Prices start at around ST120 per day, with discounts offered for longer-term rentals. Hire cars are subject to a ST1000 to ST2000 insurance excess in the event of any accident.

Recommended companies include:

Blue Pacific Car Hire (Map pp304-5; ☎ 22668; www .bluepacific.ws; Main West Coast Rd, Vaigaga, 'Upolu; ⊙ 8am-4.30pm)

Discovery Rentals (☎ 29230; www.discovery-rentals .com; Faleolo Airport, Main West Coast Rd, 'Upolu; ⊙ 8am-5pm) Free pick-up from the airport during opening hours; it also hires out mopeds.

Funway Rentals (Map pp306-7; ☎ 22045; www .funwayrentals.ws; Beach Rd, Apia)

Juliana's Car Rental (Map pp306-7; ☎ 23009; Mata'utu St; Apia)

Ree's Hirage (Map pp322-3; ☎ 51678; Salelologa, Savai'i) Car hire from about ST130 per day.

INSURANCE

It's essential to have your hire car covered by insurance as repair costs are extremely high in Samoa. Insurance costs aren't always included in the price of a quote, so always double-check this. Hire cars are subject to a ST1000 to ST2000 insurance excess (nonreduceable).

ROAD RULES

Despite opposition the Samoan Government has decided to change the law from driving on the right-hand side of the road to the left-hand side. Unless public opposition escalates, it's likely that this change will have been made by the time you read this. Either way, don't be surprised to see a mixture of left-hand and right-hand drive vehicles on the road and some confused motorists. The speed limit within central Apia and through adjacent villages is 40km/h; outside populated areas it's 55km/h.

Local Transport

On 'Upolu, taxis can be a useful transport option for day-tripping (for price details, see p314); however, the same can't be said for taxis on Savai'i, which are only convenient for short trips. However, the impending move towards installing meters may even this out – but may also increase the rates. It always pays to have the correct change as drivers can be (perhaps too conveniently) relied upon not to have any.

If you find a driver you hit it off well with early on, it can be worth getting their telephone number and using their service during your stay. You may be able to negotiate a decent day rate that compares favourably with a hire car.

American Samoa

Jutting out of the Pacific like the jagged outline of a shark's smile, American Samoa's small set of islands has natural beauty in profusion. The best bits, such as extravagantly handsome Ofu, rate among the world's finest islandscapes and beaches. Ofu is the sort of island that bored office workers all over the world daydream about: white sands, clear waters, abundant marine life and a majestic rainforest backdrop. Yet few will ever venture here – which, let's be honest, is part of its charm.

American Samoa isn't the easiest South Pacific destination to get to. You can only fly here from Samoa or Hawai'i and the best spots require an additional flight to the outlying islands. All of this takes time and money – enough to put most people off.

Comparisons to its close sibling, independent Samoa, are inevitable. They both share the same language, culture, gene pool and (until 1900) history. The impact of American culture on this island group is fascinating. Everything is bigger in American Samoa: the cars, the houses (traditional *fale* are a rarity) and certainly the people. Perhaps the most striking difference for the traveller is that the comparative wealth of American Samoa has resulted in less reliance on the tourist dollar and, as a result, less things for tourists to do.

However, American Samoa is still the prettier sister. Setting foot on one of the virtually untouched strips of sand in the outlying Manu'a Islands, you might find yourself so seduced by her natural charms that you never want to leave.

AMERICAN SAMOA

HIGHLIGHTS

- Catching an eyeful of rainforest-clad mountains and startling white sands as you lift your head out of the crystalline waters of **Ofu Beach** (p351)

- Circling the plantations and crater lakes on the diminutive island of **Aunu'u** (p347)

- Cooling off in a rainforest glade under the bracing waters of **Nu'uuli Falls** (p344)

- Alternating snorkelling and whale-watching in **Fagatele Bay National Marine Sanctuary** (p346)

- Watching the waves pound into the cliff at the mythic **Turtle & Shark site** (p345)

Nu'uuli Falls ★
★ Aunu'u
★★ Turtle & Shark site
Fagatele Bay National Marine Sanctuary

Ofu Beach ★

AMERICAN SAMOA FACTS

Capital city (and island) Pago Pago (Tutuila)
Population 63,500
Land area 197 sq km
International telephone code ☎ 1-684
Currency US dollar (US$)
Languages Samoan, English
Greetings *Talofa; malo* (informal)
Website www.ashpo.org

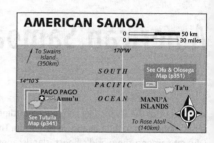

CLIMATE & WHEN TO GO

The best time to visit American Samoa is during the dry season from May to October. During the wet season (November to April), most rainfall occurs at night and the main discomfort (excepting the odd cyclone) is caused by higher levels of humidity. The exception is Pago Pago harbour in Tutuila, where Rainmaker Mountain ensures that the surrounding area receives over 5000mm of precipitation annually. For more climate information, turn to p627.

If you intend visiting around December–January, remember that this is the peak holiday period for Samoan expats living in the US, Australia and New Zealand (NZ). Book flights well in advance.

HISTORY

Prehistory

Archaeological finds near the villages of Tula and Aoa at the eastern tip of Tutuila, and at To'aga on Ofu, reveal that the islands have been inhabited for more than 3000 years. Traditionally Samoans believed that the Manu'a Islands were the first land to emerge at the hands of the god Tagaloa. The Tu'i Manu'a (paramount chief of the islands) was held in high esteem by Samoans. Although various conflicts ultimately split the islands, the paramount chief was still a proud and powerful figure at the time of cession to the US at the beginning of the 20th century.

European Contact

In 1722 Dutchman Jacob Roggeveen sighted the Manu'a Islands but sailed on without landing. In May 1768 French explorer Captain Louis-Antoine de Bougainville bartered with the inhabitants of Manu'a, but merely sighted Tutuila. The first expedition to set foot on Tutuila was headed by Frenchman Jean-

François de Galaup, comte de la Pérouse, who landed at Fagasa in 1787. The encounter had a tragic finish, with the French and the Samoans fighting each other at A'asu: 12 sailors and 39 villagers were killed, and A'asu was christened Massacre Bay (see p346).

US Military Rule

A Samoan civil war in the 1870s and 1880s was co-opted by the US, Britain and Germany into an argument over which foreign power should rule the islands. By the time the dust had settled, control of western Samoa had been granted to Germany and, by 1900, the islands of eastern Samoa had been formally annexed to the US by a deed of cession signed by all local chiefs. Eastern Samoa became a naval station under the jurisdiction of the US Department of the Navy. In exchange, the US agreed to protect the traditional rights of indigenous Samoans. The inhabitants acquired the status of US nationals but were denied a vote or representation in Washington.

In 1905 the military commander of Tutuila was given the title of governor and the territory officially became known as American Samoa.

Increasing Democracy

Until the 1960s American Samoa retained its traditional social structure and subsistence economy. But under the orders of President Kennedy, American Samoa was swiftly modernised, with European-style homes replacing traditional *fale* (houses with thatched roofs and open sides), electrification and the construction of an international airport and tuna canneries.

Through the 1960s and 1970s a series of referenda resulted in the adoption of a constitution, a democratically elected governorship and a two-chamber legislature. In 1980 American Samoans were allowed, for the first time, to elect a delegate to serve in the US House of Representatives. However, this delegate doesn't have any voting rights in the house.

Recent Decades

In January 1987 the territory was hit by cyclone Tusi, one of the worst storms in recorded history. The Manu'a Islands were particularly hard hit. To compound matters, cyclones Ofa and Val ploughed through the area in early 1990 and late 1991. Then, in late 2005, the eye of the massive tropical storm Olaf passed right over the islands.

While American Samoa relies heavily on funding from the US Government, the relationship isn't as one-sided as it seems. Many a US sports team would be in a much poorer state without their Samoan players. American Samoans are very loyal to the US and many serve in the US military.

THE CULTURE

More than most Polynesian peoples, Samoans have maintained their traditional way of life in their sauna of a climate, and still closely follow the social hierarchies, customs and courtesies established long before the arrival of Europeans.

For a profile of the Samoan psyche and a description of the Samoan lifestyle, see the cultural detail provided in the Samoa chapter (p298).

Population

Most of the 63,500-strong population live on the main island of Tutuila. The birth rate is high but this is offset by emigration to Hawai'i and the US mainland. Some 1500 foreigners reside in American Samoa, most of whom are Koreans or Chinese involved in the tuna or garment industries. About one-third are *palagi* (Westerners), many of whom hold government jobs, usually in the teaching or health fields.

ARTS

American Samoa shares its artistic traditions with Samoa, from the energetic song-and-dance routines called *fiafia* and the satirisation of their elders by village youth in the skit-based *Faleaitu* (meaning 'House of Spirits'), to the breezy architecture of the *fale*, intricate tattoos (p354), and the lovely *siapo* (bark cloth) and *ie toga* (fine mats) used in customary gift exchanges (see below). For more on these, see the Arts section of the Samoa chapter (p300).

LANGUAGE

For an overview of the pronunciation of the Samoan language, and some introductory words and phrases, see the Language section of the Samoa chapter (p302).

ENVIRONMENT
Geography

American Samoa has a total land area of 197 sq km. The main island, Tutuila, is 30km long and up to 6km wide. The Manu'a group, 100km east of Tutuila, consists of the islands of Ta'u, Ofu and Olosega, all wildly steep volcanic remnants.

FA'ALAVELAVE Martin Robinson

Fa'alavelave (lavish gift-exchange ceremonies) are a fundamental part of the *fa'a* Samoa (Samoan way). It could be a wedding, funeral, title-installation or the opening of a new school or church; the basics are the same and can last all day. Everyone dresses up in dazzling colours as the *'aiga* (extended family), village or church shows off their wealth and status. This is measured in terms of *ie toga* (fine mats) and money gifts, as well as the feast of pork, taro, chop suey and cakes. An *'ava* (kava) ceremony involves the *matai* (family chiefs) and honoured guests. Then the *tulafale* (orators) make long, poetic speeches, and generous gifts of *ie toga*, food and money are exchanged by different groups. A careful note is made of all these exchanges and everything is done with a flourish. Afterwards, youth groups may put on a *fiafia* (a village play or traditional dance-and-song performance).

It takes months to raise the money and weeks of hard work to organise these events. In American Samoa major ceremonies involve thousands of kilos of food, thousands of *ie toga* and tens of thousands of dollars. The large remittances sent back to their *'aiga* on the islands by Samoans abroad are another burdensome *fa'alavelave*, often made at the expense of their own immediate families.

BEST EATS

American Samoa has such an obvious fondness for artery-clogging US-style fast food like burgers and pancakes that you'll be hard-pressed to find any traditional dishes on most menus. A welcome dose of variety comes courtesy of the Chinese, Korean and Japanese expat communities.

■ If you've an urge to sample traditional *umu*-cooked specialities, you'll do no better than the Wednesday night feast at Tisa's Barefoot Bar (p349).

■ Goat Island Cafe (p349) offers an interesting menu and light touch.

■ Japanese, Korean and Chinese influences combine with the freshest seafood at Manuia (p349).

■ If you're going to gamble with heart disease, you may as well do it somewhere as tasty as Mom's Place (p349).

The easternmost part of the territory is tiny Rose Atoll, two minuscule specks of land (plus a surrounding reef) which were declared a Marine National Monument in 2009. This special recognition by the US Government helps to protect the green turtle, as well as the extremely rare hawksbill turtle. Only scientific research expeditions are currently allowed to visit the atoll.

Equally tiny Swains Island is situated 350km north-northwest of Tutuila and consists of a 3.25 sq km ring of land surrounding a brackish lagoon. Both culturally and geographically it belongs to Tokelau (p485), but in 1925 the island's owner, the Jennings family, persuaded the US to annex it.

Ecology

The wild inhabitants of American Samoa includes two species of flying fox, *pili* (skinks), *mo'o* (geckos) and the harmless *gata* (Pacific boa), which is found only on Ta'u. The surrounding waters are home to pilot whales, dolphins and porpoises, while hawksbill turtles occasionally breed on remote beaches. Bird species include the nearly flightless banded rail, the barn owl and the superb *sega* (blue-crowned lory). While walking in rainforests, listen for the haunting calls of the rare multi-coloured fruit doves (only 50 survive on

Tutuila) and the beautiful green-and-white Pacific pigeons.

Tutuila is characterised by its broadleaf evergreen rainforest. Ofu, Olosega and Ta'u host temperate forest vegetation such as tree ferns, grasses, wild coleus and epiphytic plants.

TUTUILA

pop 62,000 / area 132 sq km

Tutuila is a mass of sharp edges and pointy bits, softened somewhat by its heavy padding of rainforest. It's little wonder that the island's radio jocks insist on referring to it as 'The Rock'. It makes for a dramatic first impression, whether arriving by sea or air. The second impression is an inevitable disappointment as you leave the airport and drive through what appears to be a drab LA suburb. Thankfully, colourful local buses await to spirit you with chaotic aplomb from one end of the island to the other. At Tutuila's spiky extremities you'll find shallow turquoise waters and white sands, all backed by those craggy green peaks.

ORIENTATION

Tutuila's one main road follows the twisty coastline from Fagamalo in the island's northwest to Onenoa in the far northeast, a distance of 50km. Deep Pago Pago Harbor nearly divides the island in half. Heading southwest from here along the coastal road, you soon reach Nu'uuli, a loosely defined commercial area. South of Nu'uuli is another commercial area called Tafuna. The island's highest point is Matafao Peak (653m).

INFORMATION
Bookshops
Iupeli Siliva Wesley Bookshop (Map p344; ☎ 633 2201; Fagatogo) Has some Samoan titles, plus mass-market paperbacks.

Internet Access
DDW (Don't Drink the Water; Map p344; ☎ 633 5297; Pago Pago; per 15/30/60 min US$3/5/10; 🕑 6.30am-2pm Mon-Fri, 7am-2pm Sat) Free internet access if you buy a meal.
Feleti Barstow Public Library (Map p344; ☎ 633 5816; Utulei; per day US$5; 🕑 9am-5pm Mon-Fri)

AMERICAN SAMOA

AMERICAN SAMOA

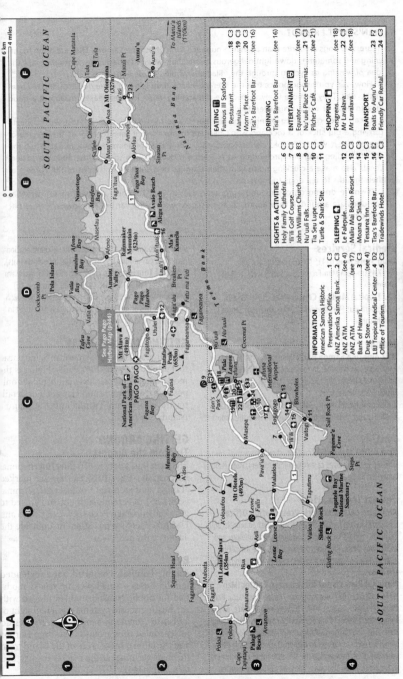

TUTUILA

INFORMATION

American Samoa Historic		
Preservation Office.	**1**	C3
ANZ Amerika Samoa Bank.	**2**	C3
ANZ ATM.	(see 17)	
ANZ ATM.	**3**	C3
Bank of Hawai'i.		
Drug Store.	(see 4)	
LBJ Tropical Medical Center.	**4**	D2
Office of Tourism.	**5**	C3

SIGHTS & ACTIVITIES

Holy Family Cathedral.	**6**	C3
'Ili'ili Golf Course.	**7**	C3
John Williams Church.	**8**	B3
Nu'uuli Falls.	**9**	C2
Tia Seu Lupe.	**10**	C3
Turtle & Shark Site.	**11**	C4

SLEEPING

Le Falepule.	**12**	D2
Mailu Mai Beach Resort.	**13**	C3
Moana O Sina.	**14**	C3
Tessarea Inn.	**15**	C3
Tisa's Barefoot Bar.	**16**	E2
Tradewinds Hotel.	**17**	C3

EATING

Famous III Seafood	(see 16)	
Restaurant.	**18**	C3
Manula.	**19**	C3
Mom's Place.	**20**	C3
Tisa's Barefoot Bar.	(see 16)	

DRINKING

Tisa's Barefoot Bar.	(see 16)	

ENTERTAINMENT

Equator.	(see 17)	
Nu'uuli Place Cinemas.	**21**	C3
Pilcher's Café.	(see 21)	

SHOPPING

Forsgrens.	(see 18)	
Mr Lavalava.	**22**	C3
Mr Lavalava.	(see 18)	

TRANSPORT

Boats to Aunu'u.	**23**	F2
Friendly Car Rental.	**24**	C3

MAN'S BEST FRIEND?

Aggressive dogs are more than a passing nuisance throughout the Samoas. They are often frightening and sometimes downright dangerous, particularly when in a pack. They certainly make the idea of walking or cycling through the villages a whole lot less appealing.

However, you'll soon notice that the average village mutt is much more docile during the heat of the day. They're more likely to become threatening when the heat eases, making it a good idea to drive or catch taxis after dark.

Locals offer conflicting opinions on the best tactic to protect yourself. Most will advocate carrying a big stick or a rock and won't hesitate to use them if threatened – as the heroine of one of Albert Wendt's books claims, Samoans are only fond of animals they can eat. Often the act of bending over and pretending to pick up a rock is enough to send the dogs scarpering. Locals also make a clucking noise with their tongues or a shhhing noise out of the corners of their mouths to tell dogs to move on.

If you're driving onto someone's property, wait in your car for a moment to see whether any dogs are around. If they approach aggressively, wait in the car until the owner comes out to greet you.

Medical Services

Drug Store (Map p341; ☎ 633 4630; Faga'alu; ☽ 7.45am-5pm Mon-Fri, to 2pm Sat) A well-stocked pharmacy.

LBJ Tropical Medical Center (Map p341; ☎ 633 1222; Faga'alu; ☽ emergency 24hr) American Samoa's only hospital.

Money

ANZ Amerika Samoa Bank (Map p344; ☎ 633 1151; Fagatogo) Has branches in Fagatogo and Tafuna and additional ATMs at the airport, the hospital, Pago Plaza and inside Tradewinds Hotel.

Bank of Hawai'i (Map p344; ☎ 633 4226; Utulei) Has a second branch in Tafuna, on the main road from the airport.

Post

Post office (Map p344) Travellers should have mail addressed to themselves care of General Delivery, Pago Pago, American Samoa 96799.

Tourist Information

American Samoa Historic Preservation Office (Ashpo; Map p341; ☎ 699 2316; www.ashpo.org; Nu'uuli) Excellent contact for history, sociology, anthropology and archeology buffs. Produces the excellent, free *A Walking Tour of Historic Fagatogo* booklet; available here and from the museum.

National Park Visitor Information Center (Map p344; ☎ 633 7082; www.nps.gov/npsa; Pago Plaza, Pago Pago; ☽ 8am-4.30pm Mon-Fri) Very helpful place, with info on the National Park of American Samoa and walking trails. The NPS (National Park Service) arranges for traditional weavers or carvers to demonstrate their skills every weekday, both here and in the fale in front of the museum in Fagatogo. They also run a homestay program, putting

visitors in touch with villagers who offer accommodation (expect to pay around US$50 to US$100 including meals).

Office of Tourism (Map p341; ☎ 699 9411; www.am samoa.com; Tasi St, Tafuna; ☽ 7.30am-4pm Mon-Fri) Getting information to tourists doesn't seem to be a high priority for this office, tucked away down a side street in Tafuna in a building with no signage.

GETTING THERE & AWAY

All flights and boats to American Samoa hea to Tutuila; see p357 for details. Flying is th most popular and painless option, but it's onl possible from Samoa and Hawai'i. For detail on travel between Tutuila and the Manu' Islands, see p357.

GETTING AROUND
To/From the Airport

Frequent buses between Tafuna Internationa Airport and Pago Pago Harbor are marke 'Tafuna' and stop right outside the termina (US$1.25). If arriving at night you'll need t get a cab into Pago Pago (between US$15 an US$20). There's a taxi stand just outside th airport entrance.

Bus

Riding Tutuila's colourful *'aiga* (extende family) buses – small pick-up trucks modi fied for public transport and equipped wit ear-busting sound systems – is a highlight o a visit to American Samoa. These buses d unscheduled runs around Pago Pago Harbo and the more remote areas of the island from the main terminal at the market in Fagatog (see Map p344).

AMERICAN SAMOA IN...

Two Days

Begin with breakfast at **DDW** (p349) and then spend the day exploring the eastern end of Tutuila. Stop for a swim at **Alega Beach** (p347) and lunch at **Tisa's** (p349) before catching the ferry to **Aunu'u** (p347) for the afternoon. Head back to Pago Pago Harbor for dinner at **Goat Island Cafe** (p349). Start the next day at **Mom's Place** (p349) and hit the west of the island, including **Tia Seu Lupe** (p345), **Holy Family Cathedral** (p345), the **Turtle & Shark site** (p345) and a drive along the **western beaches** (p346). Cool off in **Nu'uuli Falls** (p344) and head to **Manuia** (p349) for dinner.

Four Days

Head straight to **Ofu** (p351) and spend the first two days snorkelling, lying around the beach and exploring **Olosega** (p351) by foot. Head back to Tutuila and fill your last two days as above.

Buses regularly head east to Aua (US$1) nd Tula (US$1.50), and west to Tafuna US$1.25) and Leone (US$1.50). Less equently, buses go to Fagasa (US$1), 'oloaufou on the central ridge (US$1.50), manave (US$1.50) and Fagamalo in the ɪr northwest (US$2); a trip to the north- est villages often means disembarking at eone and catching another bus from there. uses also head over Rainmaker Pass to 'atia (US$1.75).

ɪr

2WD is fine for motoring around Tutuila. ⸦ar-hire agencies charge between US$60 and JS$100 per day. For insurance information, ee p358.

The following are recommended ompanies:

vis Car Rental (☎ 699 2746; res@avissamoa.com; ﬧfuna International Airport)

ʳiendly Car Rental (Map p341; ☎ 699 7186; reser ⊿tions@friendlycarrental.com; Tafuna)

ﬧr Amos Car Rental (☎ 699 4554; siramosrental@ ɑhoo.com; Tafuna International Airport)

ɑxi

ɑxis are plentiful and convenient in Pago ⸥ago, Nu'uuli and Tafuna, but are prohibi- ɪvely expensive for island touring.

⸥AGO PAGO

⸥op 6400

⸥ot so much a town as a collection of villages et around the harbour of the same name, ⸥ago Pago walks a fine line between beauty ɪnd beastliness. The attractive side comes ʳourtesy of its stunning natural setting – ⸦ deep bowl of water overlooked by mag-

nificent mountain ridges and peaks. This is counterbalanced by a motley collection of industrial buildings lining the water's edge, a steady flow of pick-up trucks on the coastal road, the pungent aroma of the tuna canneries on the northern shores and the inhabitants' rather carefree approach to garbage disposal.

Confusingly, Pago Pago (pronounced *pung-o pung-o*, and often shortened to the singular) is used to describe the small village the far end of the harbour, the harbour itself, the 'town' and, often, the whole island of Tutuila or even the whole of American Samoa. The most built-up parts of the Pago Pago urban area are Utulei and Fagatogo, which are both situated to the southeast of the harbour.

Utulei is edged by a **beach** lined with day *fale*, where you can shelter from the sun between swims. Fagatogo is the adminis- trative centre and contains the **Fono** (Map p344), the traditionally inspired building that houses American Samoa's Senate and House of Representatives.

Nearby, the **Museum of American Samoa** (Map p344; ☎ 633 4347; admission free; ⊙ 8am-4pm Mon-Fri) has a small but interesting dis- play of Samoan artefacts, including *va'a* (bonito canoes), *alia* (war canoes), coco- nut-shell combs, pigs' tusk armlets and na- tive pharmacopoeia, plus information on traditional tattooing.

Fagatogo market (Map p344) was in the process of being rebuilt at the time of research, but when it reopens it should once again become the town's social cen- tre on a Friday night. Locals come here to gossip, ransack food stalls and browse

AMERICAN SAMOA

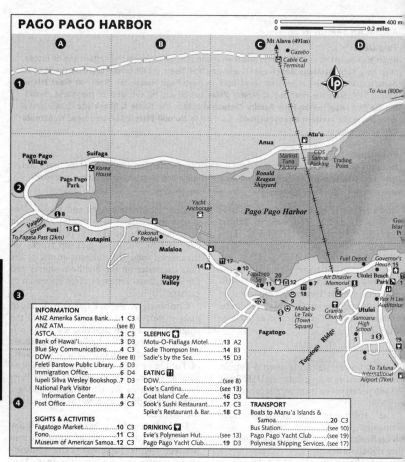

PAGO PAGO HARBOR

INFORMATION
ANZ Amerika Samoa Bank......1 C3
ANZ ATM...........................(see 8)
ASTCA.............................2 C3
Bank of Hawai'i..................3 D3
Blue Sky Communications......4 C3
DDW.............................(see 8)
Feleti Barstow Public Library....5 D3
Immigration Office...............6 D4
Iupeli Siliva Wesley Bookshop..7 D3
National Park Visitor
Information Center............8 A2
Post Office.......................9 C3

SIGHTS & ACTIVITIES
Fagatogo Market................10 C3
Fono............................11 C3
Museum of American Samoa..12 C3

SLEEPING
Motu-O-Fiafiaga Motel........13 A2
Sadie Thompson Inn.............14 B3
Sadie's by the Sea...............15 D3

EATING
DDW.............................(see 8)
Evie's Cantina.................(see 13)
Goat Island Cafe................16 D3
Sook's Sushi Restaurant........17 C3
Spike's Restaurant & Bar........18 C3

DRINKING
Evie's Polynesian Hut..........(see 13)
Pago Pago Yacht Club..........19 D3

TRANSPORT
Boats to Manu'a Islands &
Samoa............................20 C3
Bus Station.....................(see 10)
Pago Pago Yacht Club ....(see 19)
Polynesia Shipping Services..(see 17)

freshly arrived coconuts, breadfruit and other produce. By Saturday, all the good stuff is gone and the market is hushed for another week.

WESTERN TUTUILA

Most of the western end of Tutuila is taken up by the ruggedly beautiful, rainforest-wreathed mountains that line the northern coast. The bulk of the population inhabits the flat plains to the south, particularly the Los Angeles–lite strip-mall suburbs of Tafuna and Nu'uuli. However, once you pass Leone, a succession of cute villages lining pretty white-sand beaches reminds you that you're in a Polynesian paradise after all.

Nu'uuli Falls

Standing in stark relief to Nu'uili's nonde script strip of restaurants and convenienc stores, this secluded **waterfall** (Map p341; Nu'uul with a deliciously cool swimming hole a its base seems even more magical. Th surrounding rainforest muffles the soun of the water cascading down 20m of jag ged black lava rocks, which are strangel redolent of the sort of geometric sculptur that you might find in the plaza of a date 1970s skyscraper.

This is a local secret: there are no sign posts and it's a little hard to find. Comin along the main road from the west, turn le at the Nu'uuli Family Mart and follow thi side road, veering left when you see the pi

STAR MOUNDS

More than 140 distinctive stone or earthen mounds dating back to late prehistoric times have been found scattered across the Samoan archipelago. Dubbed star mounds, the structures range from 6m to 30m in length, are up to 3m high and have from one to 11 raylike projections radiating from their base. Forty of these star mounds have been discovered (though not yet excavated) in Tuiula's east on the road between Amouli and Aoa.

The main theory regarding the star mounds is that they were used for pigeon-snaring, an extremely important sport of chiefs that was traditionally pursued from June through September. Villagers would follow their *matai* (chiefs) into the forest to observe and support competitions.

However, American archaeologists David Herdrich and Jeffrey Clark believe star mounds also served a much more complex function in Samoan society, including being sites for rituals related to marriage, healing and warfare. The archaeologists also believe the star mounds came to reflect the position of the *matai* and the notion of *mana* (supernatural power).

arm. At the end, park on the grass to the left you'll see a pink house downhill on your right) and look for the start of the track in front of you. If you see anyone outside the house it would be polite to ask their permission to continue on, but you shouldn't have to pay any money.

The track is quite narrow and rough but should only take about 15 minutes. At the first juncture, veer to the left and continue until the trail reaches the stream. Stop here and look for the path leading steeply up the hill on the other side before wading across.

Tia Seu Lupe

The most accessible of American Samoa's fascinating star mounds (see above) is secreted behind a statue of St Mary near the Catholic Cathedral – a fitting symbol, perhaps, of the loss of ancient practices following the arrival of Christianity. **Tia Seu Lupe** (Map p341; Tafuna) has a viewing platform where you get a good look at the two distinct tiers of the structure, without disturbing the ancient site. The name literally means 'earthen mound to catch pigeons'.

To find it, head towards the Tradewinds Hotel and take the second road to the right; park by the statue at the very end of this road.

Holy Family Cathedral

The real beauty of this imposing Catholic **cathedral** (Map p341; ☎ 699 2209; Tafuna), with its space-age bell tower and dissected dome, lies inside. Remarkably restrained for a Samoan church, light streams into the simple interior where traditional Catholic and Samoan imagery is blended together in a wonderful set of carved wooden statues and stained-glass windows.

Above the altar a larger-than-life-sized Samoan Christ offers an *'ava* cup with outstretched hands, while a traditionally garbed man and woman sit cross-legged looking on. Stained-glass images of the Holy Family top each transept, with a *puletasi*-wearing Madonna with child at one end, and a muscular St Joseph and infant Jesus taking a break from their wood-carving at the other. Outside a life-sized nativity scene swaps the stable for a *fale* and the manger for an *'ava* bowl. In the foyer, Duffy Sheridan's large canvas entitled *The Holy Family* pictures an idyllic Samoan village scene with the mother opening a coconut while the father carves a canoe.

Turtle & Shark Site

The most famous of Tutuila's legends is set at this dramatic cliff-top **site** (Map p341; Vaitogi; access fee US$2; ◷ Mon-Sat). According to just one of the myriad versions of this legend, an old blind lady and her granddaughter jumped into the sea after being turned out of their village during a time of famine. When their family learned what they'd done, they went to the shore, guilt-ridden, and called the pair by name. A turtle and shark appeared, and the family knew that their relatives had been miraculously transformed in the water and were OK.

Even if the turtle and shark have taken the day off, you'll enjoy the rugged character of the place, with its black lava cliffs, heavy surf and blowholes. Don't swim here though, as this is a sacred site; also, the currents are treacherous.

Fagatele Bay National Marine Sanctuary

Fagatele Bay (Map p341; ☎ 633 7354; www.fagatele bay.noaa.gov), a submerged volcanic crater, is fringed by Tutuila's last remaining stretch of coastal rainforest and its cliffside depths contain more than 140 species of coral. It's also visited by numerous turtle species and, between August and November, by migrating southern humpback whales. With these marvellous natural assets, it's little wonder that the bay was designated a marine sanctuary in 1986.

It's best to call the office number to check the latest situation regarding access to the bay. Usually you can drive part of the way on the access road and then walk the remainder.

Leone

The village of Leone welcomed the first missionary to Tutuila in 1832. John Williams subsequently erected the island's first **church** (Map p341), garnishing it with three towers, some stunning woodwork and stained glass. Try to attend a service here on Sunday morning, when villagers congregate in their best whites to sing hymns before heading home for a lunchtime banquet.

Between the church and the sea is a monument to Williams.

Cape Taputapu

Cape Taputapu is Tutuila's westernmost point and received its name (*taputapu* means 'forbidden') after imaginatively fearful tales about it were spread around by locals who wanted the cape's valuable grove of paper mulberry trees all to themselves. No such taboos prevent modern-day visitors from enjoying the cape's beautiful location.

Just past Amanave is a lovely white-sand beach known as **Palagi Beach** (Map p341); ask for directions in the village store. Beyond Amanave, the road winds around valleys and over ridges to the small villages of Poloa, Fagali'i, Maloata and Fagamalo, revealing spectacular views of the coastline along the way.

Massacre Bay

A marvellous 4km **hiking trail** (four hours return) leads from the scenic village of A'oloaufou, high up on the rocky spine of Tutuila, down to A'asu on Massacre Bay (Map p341). Massacre Bay's foreboding name is due to a skirmish between French sailors and

Samoan villagers that occurred there in 1787 leaving 51 people dead.

The track begins near the community garden in A'oloaufou and is apparently maintained (or not, as the case may be) by the sole family residing in A'asu. It's often overgrown, extremely muddy and difficult to navigate, particularly on the climb back up. Hikers should seriously consider hiring a guide in A'oloaufou (costs between US$5 and US$10).

Matafao Peak

Keen climbers will want to tackle the island's highest point, 653m-high Matafao Peak (Map p341). The narrow, unrelentingly steep and very rough trail (three to four hours one way) starts opposite the beginning of the Mt Alava walk; look for the metal ladder. Needless to say, only very experienced hikers/climbers should attempt this trail. It's highly recommended that you organise a guide in Fagasa village.

EASTERN TUTUILA

The east of The Rock is free of the American suburban/industrial feel that mars some of the other parts. *Fale* may have given way to clunky concrete-block houses, but otherwise the small villages cling to the shoreline as they've done for centuries.

Rainmaker Mountain

Also known as Mt Pioa, 523m-high Rainmaker Mountain (Map p341) is the culprit that traps rain clouds and gives Pago Pago Harbor the highest annual rainfall of any harbour in the world. From afar it looks like a single, large peak, but a drive up Rainmaker Pass for close up views reveals that the summit is actually three-pronged. The mountain and its base area are designated a national landmark site due to the pristine nature of the tropical vegetation on the slopes.

National Park of American Samoa

Created in 1988, the territory's sole national park protects pristine landscapes and marine environments on Tutuila, Ofu (see p351) and Ta'u (see p352). The 1000-hectare Tutuila section (Map p341) follows the north coast between the villages of Fagasa and Afono.

From Aua, a surfaced road switchbacks steeply up over Rainmaker Pass and down to Afono and Vatia. Between these two villages

s the beautiful, secluded **Amalau Valley**, home
o many forest bird species and to two rare
pecies of flying fox. Stop at the lookout point
ust past the western side of Amalau Bay for
ome wonderful views.

Vatia is a peaceful village situated on a lovely,
oral-fringed bay. Guarding the mouth of the
ay, tiny **Pola Island** has magnificent, sheer,
.20m-high cliffs populated by seabirds. For
close-up of soaring rocks and birds, head
hrough the village and park at the school,
hen walk 300m to reach the wonderfully iso-
ated beach at the base of the cliffs.

The NPS hiking trail that leads up **Mt Alava**
491m) and then down to the coast presents
a wonderful way to experience the park's
owland and montane rainforests, its thriving
birdlife and the peacefulness that permeates
t. On Mt Alava, a metal stairway leads up
o a TV transmission tower and the rusted
remains of a cable-car terminal that once ran
.8km across Pago Pago Harbor to Solo Hill.
The 5.5km ridge trail (1½ to two hours one
way) starts from Fagasa Pass. Behind the rest
'ale at the end of this section, a very steep
trail (including ladders in places) leads 2km
down to Vatia; allow an additional two hours
for the descent.

The National Park Visitor Information
Center (p342) in Pago Pago is an invaluable
source of information about all three sections
of the park.

Eastern Beaches

Alega Beach (Map p341), a short drive east of
Pago Pago, is a lovely stretch of sand that
gets crowded with Samoan bodies on the
weekend. It's not only a great place to swim
and snorkel (check currents and conditions
with locals first), but is also overlooked by
Tisa's Barefoot Bar (p350), the perfect spot
for a cold drink. You can waive the access
fee for the beach (US$5) by simply buying
a drink at Tisa's.

Just east of Alega Beach is well-looked-
after **Avaio Beach** (Map p341; access fee US$2; ⏰ 7am-
6pm), which is also known as '$2 Beach', for
obvious reasons. The water's shallow but it's
a good spot for snorkelling and there's a little green island just offshore.

Masefau & Sa'ilele

A cross-island road leads from the village
of Faga'itua up over a pass before winding
slowly down to Masefau (Map p341), one

of those villages that look too idyllic to be
anything but a mirage.

Back at the pass, a turn-off takes you down a
narrow, potholed road to Sa'ilele (Map p341),
which has one of the island's loveliest beaches:
coconut palms are anchored into the sand by
mounds of rocks and coral fragments, and
the water is placid. The sandy area below the
large rock outcrop at the beach's western end
provides an excellent place for a picnic.

AUNU'U

pop 476 / area 3 sq km

The tiny, tangled confines of Aunu'u (Map
p341) are perfect for a half-day of roaming
and exploring on foot. Actually, there's no
other choice as the island only has a handful
of vehicles. The walking tracks are pretty good
but you might still want to consider arranging
a guide when you get off the ferry (US$8 is a
reasonable fee for a tour of the island).

At the north end of the island is **Pala Lake**,
a deadly looking expanse of quicksand whose
fiery red hue is best appreciated at low tide.
Within Aunu'u's central volcanic crater lies
Red Lake, filled with eels and suffused by a
preternatural glow at dusk. On the island's
eastern shore is rough-and-tumble **Ma'ama'a
Cove**, a rocky bowl constantly pounded by
large waves. Legend says that this is the site
of Sina ma Tigila'u (Sina and Tigila'u), two
lovers who were shipwrecked here. You can
make out bits of crossed 'rope' and broken
'planks' embedded in the rocks.

Below the western slope of Aunu'u's crater are the **Taufusitele Taro Marshes**, which are
planted Hawaiian-style with swamp taro. The
safest place to swim on the island is in the little
harbour, where the water's so clear that you
can see the coral from the breakwater.

Small launches head to Aunu'u from the
dock at Au'asi. If you catch a boat with other
villagers, you pay US$1 each way. If you have
to charter a boat, be prepared to pay around
US$10 for the return trip. Boats don't run
on Sunday.

TUTUILA FOR CHILDREN

Kids will love Tutuila's tropical climate and the
reef-sheltered, shallow waters of the eastern
beaches (left) where they can give snorkelling
a whirl. They'll also get a kick out of the *fiafia*
at Equator restaurant at Tradewinds Hotel
(p348). If they're old enough for a short but
rough trek through the rainforest, take them

to Nu'uuli Falls (p344) for a splash about. If the weather turns nasty, the movies are a good backstop (p350).

Babysitters are virtually impossible to find. Quiz your accommodation provider about child-minding options.

SLEEPING

If you needed any more evidence of American Samoa's reliance on government support rather than tourism, you need only look at the limited accommodation choice on Tutuila. Most places seem to set their rates based on the official government per diem allowance (about US$120), whether they're worth it or not. There are surprisingly few waterside options.

Pago Pago

Motu-0-Fiafiaga Motel (Evalani's; Map p344; ☎ 633 7777; Pago Pago; r without bathroom US$60; ☒) Better known as Evalani's, this idiosyncratic and friendly budget motel has decor which could best be described as brothel-chic. Head down the scarlet-carpeted corridors, lined with 1980s-style mirrors embossed with roses and scantily clad women, and you'll find that the rooms are actually very comfortable for the price – although they do tend to shake when trucks rumble past on the main road which runs alongside. We'd recommend flip-flops for the communal showers.

ourpick Le Falepule (Map p341; ☎ 633 5264; isabel@ blueskynet.as; Faga'alu; s/d US$135/145; ☒ 🖳) Sitting on the terrace of this luxury boutique B&B, sipping a beverage you've poured for yourself from the honesty bar and gazing over the most sublime ocean views, you may never want to leave. Falepule ticks all the boxes – the staff are delightful, the breakfasts deliciously tropical, the rooms elegantly and comfortably furnished (with a gentle Samoan theme), and the location quiet and private but close to both Pago Pago and the airport. There's even a free laundry service and wireless internet. You'll find it at the end of a steep driveway 200m north of the hospital turn-off.

Sadie Thompson Inn (Map p344; ☎ 633 5981; www .sadiethompsoninn.com; Malaloa; r US$135-150, apt US$175-195; ☒) Debate continues over whether this wooden inn edged with elegant white verandas was where the original Sadie Thompson (immortalised in Somerset Maugham's novel *Rain*) set up her red light. Regardless, the dozen or so rooms here are large and com-

fortable, and there's a restaurant and ba on site.

Sadie's by the Sea (Map p344; ☎ 633 5900; ww .sadieshotels.com; Utulei; r US$149; ☒ 🖳 🏊) The 'b the sea' bit is the big drawcard here. It's on of the few places with a swimable beach a its doorstep – but if you have qualms abou bathing in Pago Pago Harbor, there's als a bat-shaped pool. Hidden behind a hibis cus hedge at the edge of town, this vaguel *fale*-styled block has 47 recently refurbished large rooms.

Western Tutuila

Maliu Mai Beach Resort (Map p341; ☎ 699 7232; mali mai@blueskynet.as; Fogagogo; s/d US$65/85; ☒) It call itself a resort, but Maliu Mai is more like a motel with a large entertaining area where bands and other events are staged. The room are simple and clean, but the best thing abou this place is its location on a stormy littl beach with a sheltered waterhole.

Tessarea Inn (Map p341; ☎ 699 7793; fax 699 7790 Vaitogi; r US$95-125, apt US$140-180; ☒ 🏊) Seclude down a quiet street near the golf course, thi friendly place has a selection of clean room ranging from standards (with en suites, TVs fridges and air-conditioning) to two-bedroom self-contained apartments. It's a great place for families – it has the feel of a big suburban house and the kids will love the pool.

ourpick Moana O Sina (Map p341; ☎ 699 8517; isobel@ blueskynet.as; Fogagogo; s/d US$135/145; ☒ 🖳) The seaside version of Le Falepule (left), Moana O Sina shares the same owners and excellent standards. Beautiful lawns slope down to a lovely natural rock pool, where you can cool off in the shallow water while tropical fish dart around and waves crash against the cliffs below.

Tradewinds Hotel (Map p341; ☎ 699 1000; www .tradewinds.as; Main Ottoville Rd, Tafuna; r/ste from US$149/240; ☒ 🖳 🏊) Tradewinds has all the bells and whistles you'd expect from such a large, pricy hotel – including an enticing re-sort pool, day spa, restaurant, internet room and an ATM in the high-ceilinged lobby – and like many such hotels it's opted for a bland, generic look for its spacious rooms and broad corridors. The location is handy to the airport not by the sea.

Eastern Tutuila

You may be able to arrange an overnight stay in Vatia through the National Park of

American Samoa's homestay program; see p342.

Tisa's Barefoot Bar (Map p341; ☎ 622 7447; www .tisasbarefootbar.com; Alega Beach; fale per person US$50) Unlike their cousins to the west, American Samoans have enthusiastically traded *fale*-life for the joys of concrete block construction. Tisa's is the only place that offers travellers the traditional option, but even then the comfort is ratcheted up a notch. There are no mattresses on the floor in these babies, just comfy beds and decks for endless ocean-gazing.

EATING

American Samoa's reputation for fatty fried foods is not generally contradicted by the eateries on Tutuila (steak and eggs with a side order of spam, anyone?). The main road leading from the airport is a tribute to America's fast-food giants and a testimony to the high esteem they hold in the Polynesian palate. A scattering of Asian restaurants (mainly Chinese, Korean and Japanese) provides a lighter alternative,

Cafes & Quick Eats

Mom's Place (Map p341; ☎ 699 9494; Tafuna; mains US$4-8; ⊗ breakfast & lunch Mon-Sat; ✗) Mom's rich, diner-style cooking won't help keep your waistline under control, but to hell with it. Try your luck at getting through a plate of *panikeke* (the round doughnuts which Samoans call pancakes), or go island-style with corned beef hash or spam and eggs.

Spike's Restaurant & Bar (Map p344; ☎ 633 7177; Fagatogo; mains US$5-13; ⊗ breakfast & lunch) Homer Simpson would love this diner. We could barely move after one of Spike's delicious hot cakes – three come with the 'small' stack. The truly gluttonous should hold out for the Friday buffet breakfast (US$7.95).

DDW (Don't Drink the Water; Map p344; ☎ 633 5297; Pago Plaza, Pago Pago; mains US$6-16; ⊗ breakfast & lunch Mon-Sat) This relaxed cafe gets superbusy at breakfast and lunchtime, when local workers stampede through the door to tuck into well-cooked burgers, omelettes, steaks and tasty cakes.

Restaurants

Evie's Cantina (Map p344; ☎ 633 7781; Pago Pago; mains US$5-13; ⊗ lunch Tue-Fri, dinner Tue-Sun) Late at night this Mexican restaurant morphs into a nightclub, but until then it serves big, tasty burritos, enchiladas and other cheesy treats. Grab a booth and watch your stomach bulge once the food arrives.

Manuia (Map p341; ☎ 699 9927; Tafuna; meals US$7-24; ⊗ 11am-10pm Mon-Sat) Tucked away in a Tafuna backstreet, this local eatery is well worth hunting out for its tasty selection of Korean, Japanese and Chinese dishes. Try the sashimi tuna and vegetables mixed in the chef's own chilli and red pepper sauce, served with kimchi and rice. It's nearly as good as the zany mural of a giant squid and semiclad women adorning the walls.

Famous III Seafood Restaurant (Map p344; ☎ 699 8555; opposite Laufou Shopping Center, Nu'uuli; mains US$8-27; ⊗ 10am-10pm Mon-Sat; ✗) 'Famous' might be overstating it, but the Nu'uuli branch of this small Tutuila chain does serve excellent Chinese dishes in portions large enough to strain even an American Samoan waistline. A single serve of its sublime hot-and-sour soup is enough to refill your bowl eight times over. Its Famous predecessors can be found in Pago Pago and Faga'alu.

Sook's Sushi Restaurant (Map p344; ☎ 633 5525; GHC Reid Bldg, Malaloa; mains US$10-20; ⊗ lunch & dinner Mon-Sat) This one-room Japanese restaurant offers a rainforest ambience albeit entirely constructed out of plastic vegetation and twinkling fairy lights. Try the generous sushi, sashimi and tempura dishes, or the Korean *kalbi* (ribs).

Tisa's Barefoot Bar (Map p341; ☎ 622 7447; Alega Beach; meals US$12-18) The food at this beachside institution is superb, with vegetarians well catered for. The opening hours can be sporadic, so it pays to call ahead. On Wednesday nights it fires up the *umu* (stone oven) for their legendary Samoan feast (US$40), where traditional fare is given an international twist.

our pick Goat Island Cafe (Map p344; ☎ 633 5900; Sadie's by the Sea, Utulei; mains US$12-28; ⊗ breakfast, lunch & dinner) If it's a reasonably healthy and comparatively inventive menu you're after, this resort restaurant is your best option. Plus it has the added bonus of offering waterside tables. Try the 'island-style' curried prawns, served with rice and vegetables.

DRINKING

Evie's Polynesian Hut (Map p344; ☎ 633 7781; Pago Pago; admission free Tue-Thu, US$3 Fri & Sat) Sporting more aliases than your average mobster (Evie's Cantina, Evalani's, Motu-O-Fiafiaga Motel), this Pago Pago mainstay comes into its own on the weekends when DJs hit the decks. Its Halloween parties are legendary.

AMERICAN SAMOA

Pago Pago Yacht Club (Map p344; ☎ 633 2465; Utulei) From the outside deck of the yacht club, there's a magnificent sea-level view of Rainmaker Mountain. If you're seated out there just as water-swollen clouds blow in from the northeast, you'll actually see the rain drops marching across the surface of the harbour and climbing up the foreshore to smack down on the yacht club roof. Yachties love to gather here and gab while clutching cold beers.

Tisa's Barefoot Bar (Map p341; ☎ 622 7447; Alega Beach) Tisa's driftwood bar is the perfect place to rest your elbows and wash your throat while gazing out over some typical Polynesian beachfront beauty.

ENTERTAINMENT

For an all-singing, all-dancing, thigh-slapping, Samoan *fiafia*, head to the Equator restaurant at Tradewinds Hotel (p348) on a Friday night. A buffet dinner is included in the price (US$21).

If local TV isn't floating your *bonito* canoe, you can always head to **Nu'uuli Place Cinemas** (Map p341; ☎ 699 9334; Nu'uuli; adult/child US$6.75/4) for some smash-'em-up Hollywood action.

A handful of bars and cafes host local musicians, including Tisa's (above) and **Pilcher's Café** (Map p341; ☎ 699 7191; Nu'uuli) on a Friday and Saturday night.

SHOPPING

Don't expect Armani but most of your more humble purchasing requirements can be fulfilled in the shopping centres and strip malls of Tafuna, Nu'uuli and Pago Pago. If it's souvenirs you're after, stock up on cheap *lava-lava* (wraparound sarongs) and patterned shirts at **Forsgrens** (Map p341; ☎ 699 4269; Laufou Shopping Center, Nu'uuli) or the wonderfully named **Mr Lavalava** Nu'uuli (Map p341; ☎ 699 7707; Laufou Shopping Center) Tafuna (Map p341; ☎ 699 1570).

MANU'A ISLANDS

pop 1500 / area 65 sq km

Sometimes the best things in life require a bit of effort, and that's certainly true of Manu'a. These three islands, anchored about 100km to the east of Tutuila, are some of the most remote and beautiful you could hope

to encounter in the Pacific. Although the rest of your stay may suffer in comparison, plan to visit them near the beginning of your trip as any disruption in the weather could keep you here longer than you intended. That's hardly likely to be a hardship, as Ofu is the undisputed highlight of any visit to American Samoa.

Ofu, Olosega and Ta'u may be separate islands, but they all share the same marvellous natural characteristics: enormous cliffs sheltering seabird colonies; expired volcanic cones; undisturbed beaches that flow into lagoons stocked with a brilliant array of coral; and a sense of timelessness that makes watches completely redundant. The Manu'a Islands make the laid-back environs of Tutuila seem just about chaotic by comparison, so when you visit, pack plenty of extra reading material and a willingness to fall asleep in the middle of the day.

INFORMATION

Ofu village has a bank near the wharf and a basic medical clinic. The only post office on Ofu–Olosega is in Olosega village.

The sleepy village of Fiti'uta on Ta'u has several stores selling basic supplies, as well as a post office and a bank.

GETTING THERE & AWAY

AIR

Ofu's airport is a 500m surfaced strip at Va'oto, squeezed in between the sea and mountains. On Ta'u, there's an airport at Fiti'uta.

For details of Inter-Island Airways flights between the Manu'a Islands and Tutuila, see p357.

BOAT

For information on the boat service between the Manu'a Islands and Tutuila, see p357.

GETTING AROUND

There are no established plane or boat services between individual Manu'a islands. Ofu and Olosega are joined by a bridge, but to get from either of them to Ta'u requires a flight to Tutuila and back. A **charter boat** (☎ 655 1104; hire US$150) can be arranged but it's no cheaper and the crossing can be rough.

Getting around on the islands themselves involves walking or sticking your thumb out. There are only a handful of vehicles on the islands but few drivers will pass a walker without offering a lift. Vaoto Lodge (p352) hires out a truck for US$50 per day, including petrol.

OFU & OLOSEGA

pop 290 (Ofu), 220 (Olosega) / area 5.2 sq km (Ofu), 3 sq km (Olosega)

These twin islands, separated by a deep channel but linked by a bridge, are as close to paradise as anywhere you'll find on this blue planet. Ofu has its sole village at its western end, leaving the rest of the island delightfully unpopulated. Taking up its southern shoreline, **Ofu Beach** is 4km of shining, palm-fringed white sand, flanked by ridiculously picturesque jagged peaks that rise behind it like a giant shark's tooth.

This, along with 140 hectares of offshore waters, comprises the Ofu section of the **National Park of American Samoa** (see p346). The reef here is considered to be one of the healthiest in all the Samoas. The water's wonderfully clear and the coral forms giant mushroom shapes only metres from the shoreline. Multitudes of coloured fish dart around, occasionally pursued by reef sharks (they're harmless fellows, to humans at least, but a little freaky for a novice snorkeller).

Behind Ofu Beach is the **To'aga site**, where in 1987 archaeologists found an unprecedented array of artefacts ranging in age from the earliest times of Samoan prehistory to modern day. The excavations have been filled, so there's nothing to actually see here. Samoans believe the area of bush between the road and

the beach is infested with devilish *aitu* (spirits or ghosts). The upshot of this is that you're likely to have one of the world's best beaches all to yourself.

The 5.5km-long, often indistinct track (five hours return) to the summit of **Mt Tumutumu** (494m) begins just north of Ofu village wharf and twists up to the TV relay tower atop the mountain, where a large rock provides a handy viewpoint. You'll need sensible shoes, long trousers (to protect from cutting plants), heavy-duty mosquito repellent and a bush knife to hack through the foliage.

Olosega shares the same marvellous encircling reef system as Ofu. The two islands look conjoined, but are separated from each other by the 137m-wide Asaga Strait. From the cyclone-proof **bridge**, the water is impossibly clear. Local kids regularly jump off, letting the current carry them to shore. This isn't advised to travellers – if you get the wrong tides you could just as easily be carried straight out to sea.

The 1.5km walk from Olosega village up to **Maga Point** on the island's southern tip is a highlight of a visit. The point's steep cliffs, the reefs marching out from the shore, and the view of distant Ta'u and the Pacific horizon are simply unforgettable. To avoid local dogs, veer around Olosega village on the beach. After passing the rubbish tip, pick your way along the coral-strewn beach and look for the narrow trail that climbs up the hillside.

AMERICAN SAMOA

OFU & OLOSEGA

Sleeping & Eating

our pick **Vaoto Lodge** (☎ 655 1120; www.vaotolodge
.com; s/d/tr/f US$75/85/95/110) Hop off the light air-
craft and wander 50m across the lawn and
you've arrived at this little slice of paradise.
Drop off your bags and head straight into the
water for sensational snorkelling. The units
are simple but clean and comfy, each with a
bathroom and firm beds. The friendly family
that runs the place provides bikes, snorkelling gear, board games and a book and DVD
library (only the family cabin has a TV and
the one in the lounge only gets one channel) and dishes up delicious meals (US$35
for three meals). Beer and other drinks are
available. Bring plenty of insect repellent as
the mosquitoes are vicious.

Both Ofu and Olosega villages have basic
stores where you can stock up on provisions.

TA'U

pop 800 / area 39 sq km

On the dramatic south coast of this remote,
sparsely populated island, some of the highest
sea cliffs in the world rise 966m to Mt Lata,
the territory's highest point. Much of Ta'u is
covered in dense rainforest and dotted with
inactive cones and craters. If you do venture
out here, you'll invariably have the island's
marvellous forests, volcanic remnants and
numerous bird species mostly to yourself.

The main settlement on Ta'u consists of
the villages of Ta'u, Luma and Si'ufaga in the
island's northwest. From Ta'u village there's
a good walk south to secluded **Fagamalo Cove**.
It was in Luma that the young Margaret
Mead researched her classic anthropological work, *Coming of Age in Samoa*, in 1925.
Despite the permissive impression you may
have gained from that text, visitors should
be aware that Ta'u is the most conservative part of American Samoa. Bikinis are a
definite no-no.

The Ta'u segment of the **National Park of
American Samoa** (see p346) occupies 2160 hectares of land and 400 hectares of offshore
waters. Its lowland and montane rainforests
are home to flying foxes and numerous native birds, including black noddies, white
terns, multicoloured fruit doves and the revered *lupe* (Pacific pigeon). Ta'u is also the
only habitat of the Pacific boa.

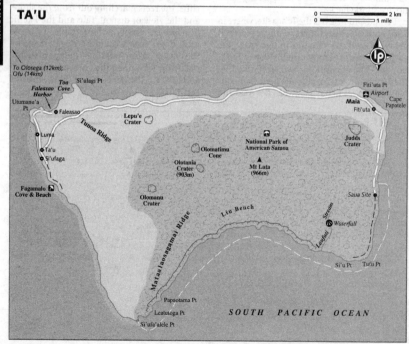

TA'U

0 ————— 2 km
0 ————— 1 mile

To Olosega (12km);
Ofu (14km)

Si'ulagi Pt

*Toa
Cove*

*Faleasao
Harbor*

Utumanu'a
Pt

Fiti'uta Pt
Airport

Cape
Papatele

Maia

Fiti'uta

Faleasao

Lepu'e
Crater

Tunoa Ridge

Luma

Ta'u

Si'ufaga

Olomatimu
Cone

National Park of
American Samoa

Judds
Crater

Olotania
Crater
(903m)

Mt Lata
(966m)

Fagamalo
Cove & Beach

Olomanu
Crater

Mataalaasagamai Ridge

Liu Bench

*Laufuti
Stream*

Saua Site

Waterfall

Si'u Pt

Tufu Pt

Papaotama Pt

Leatutóga Pt

SOUTH   PACIFIC   OCEAN

Si'ufa'alele Pt

AMERICAN SAMOA

AND GOD CREATED SAMOA

Samoans claim their land is the 'cradle of Polynesia', a place created by the sky god Tagaloa (Tangaroa). Before the sea, earth, sky, plants or people existed, Tagaloa lived in the expanse of empty space. He created a rock, commanding it to split into clay, coral, cliffs and stones. As the rock broke apart, the earth, sea and sky came into being. From a bit of the rock emerged a spring of fresh water.

Next, at Saua in the Manu'a Islands, Tagaloa created man and woman, whom he named Fatu and 'Ele'ele ('Heart' and 'Earth'). He sent them to the region of fresh water and commanded them to people the area. He ordered the sky, which was called Tu'ite'elagi, to prop itself up above the earth.

Tagaloa then created Po and Ao ('Night' and 'Day'), which bore the 'eyes of the sky' – the sun and the moon. At the same time he made the nine regions of heaven, inhabited by various gods.

In the meantime, Fatu and 'Ele'ele were 'peopling the area'. Reckoning that all these people needed some form of government, Tagaloa sent Manu'a, a son of Po and Ao, to be the people's chief. The Manu'a Islands were named after this chief, and from that time on, Samoan kings were called Tu'i Manu'a tele ma Samoa 'atoa (King of Manu'a and all of Samoa).

Next, the countries were divided into islands or groups of islands. The world now consisted of Manu'a, Viti (Fiji), Tonga and Savai'i. Tagaloa then went to Manu'a and noticed that a void existed between it and Savai'i. Up popped 'Upolu and then Tutuila.

Tagaloa's final command was: 'Always respect Manu'a; anyone who fails to do so will be overtaken by catastrophe.' Thus, Manu'a became the spiritual centre of the Samoan islands and, to some extent, of all Polynesia.

About 2.5km from Fiti'uta is the legendary **Saua site**, where Tagaloa is said to have created the first humans before sending them out to Polynesia (see the boxed text, above). This sacred place is an atmospheric landscape of volcanic boulders, wild surf and windswept beach. Short trails lead to the main archaeological area and three *fale* have been erected for shelter. Keen hikers can continue via a rough track to Tufu Point. If you've arranged a guide you could plug on for another 2km to a waterfall on the **Laufuti Stream**.

Only very experienced, intrepid and/or foolhardy hikers tackle the island's jungly interior – and only the certifiable would do so without a guide. You should be able to hack your way to **Judds Crater** in Ta'u's northeast in about three hours from the road near Fiti'ua. A recent expedition to Mt Lata was forced to turn back after two days.

Sleeping & Eating

You may be able to arrange village-stay accommodation on Ta'u through the National Park of American Samoa (see p342). **Sunrise Homestay** (☎ 677 3414; Fiti'uta; r US$75) offers simple rooms without hot water in a house near the airport. It also provides meals (breakfast and lunch US$7.50 each, dinner US$10).

AMERICAN SAMOA DIRECTORY

ACCOMMODATION

Fale accommodation for tourists has never quite caught on in American Samoa. Instead, beds are almost all found in generic motels, hotels and a handful of B&Bs – most of which are overpriced.

The sleeping options in this chapter are listed according to cost, ordered based on the cheapest option offered at each property. In American Samoa, budget accommodation peaks at US$70, midrange places charge between US$70 and US$130, and top-end facilities levy over US$130.

The National Park of American Samoa operates a village homestay program; for details, see p342.

ACTIVITIES

When you've got as much money coming from Uncle Sam as American Samoa has, the incentive to turn on things for tourists is lessened considerably. Unlike Samoa, American Samoa doesn't offer a lot of organised activities. If you've got a particular interest, you'll need to bring your own gear and make your own fun.

ILLUSTRATING SAMOA

The full-bodied *pe'a* (male tattoo), which extends from the waist to just below the knees, is a prized status symbol in Samoa. It can take weeks to complete and is a very painful process. Thus, anyone who undergoes the ritual is considered to be extremely brave. Any adult member can, in effect, receive a *pe'a* if the *'aiga, tufuga* (tattoo artist) and village leaders agree that it is suitable. The *tufuga* is usually paid with traditional gifts of *ie toga* and food.

Tattooing was discouraged when the missionaries came, but as young Pacific islanders take more pride in their cultural heritage, there has been a revival of interest in the traditional designs, though with a modern twist.

The contemporary tattoo sported by many young, more Westernised Samoans, comes without social and cultural restrictions. But the designs may signify a person's *'aiga*, ancestors, reference to nature or something very personal. The wrist and armband tattoos may have been originally developed for tourists, but they are now a popular Samoan fashion and many young Samoans sport a wrist, arm or ankle tattoo of their own design. They can be made with the modern machine or by the traditional comb.

Diving

There are no commercial diving operators in American Samoa, which is a shame as the northern and western ends of the island are said to have excellent visibility and walls of coral that are over 18m deep. If you've brought your own gear you should investigate plumbing the depths of the Fagatele Bay National Marine Sanctuary (p346).

Fishing

Pago Pago Yacht Club (p350) serves as the headquarters for the local game-fishing association. Inquire here about fishing charters.

Golf

Tutuila's **'Ili'ili Golf Course** (Map p341; ☎ 699 2995; 'Iii'ili) is a 'very forgiving' 72-par course with dramatic mountain peaks overlooking it to the north and a view of the Pacific to the east. Green fees for nine/18 holes are US$3/5 on weekdays and US$4/7 on weekends. Club hire costs US$10 and carts are US$14.

Hiking

The high rocky ridges and cliffs that are the most prominent feature of American Samoa's islands afford some spectacular hiking. However, only a couple of trails on Tutuila are regularly maintained. The condition of the rest depends on the severity of recent storms and whether any villagers have bothered to clear a way through. Even on the smallest islands, hikers have gotten lost in the tenacious undergrowth. For these reasons, local guides are highly recommended; on Ta'u in the Manu'a group, they're a necessity and tend to nominate a high fee with this knowledge in mind.

Wear long trousers due to the trailside thorns and sharp grasses that will slice unprotected skin. Sturdy walking shoes are also essential. A big stick is another useful piece of hiking gear, used to dissuade village dogs. Also carry plenty of insect repellent, sunblock, water and snacks.

Snorkelling & Swimming

It may come as a surprise that large parts of American Samoa aren't suitable for swimming due to shallow reefs, pounding surf and swift currents sucking out through breaks in the reefs. Always seek local advice on the best places to swim, and never swim or snorkel alone.

The best beach is on Ofu, which also offers the best snorkelling. You can download a wonderful resource on all the Ofu–Olosega snorkelling spots at www.vaotolodge.com /snorkel.html. On Tutuila, snorkellers should head to the Fagatele Bay National Marine Sanctuary (p346) – and bring all their own gear with them.

Aunu'u's tiny harbour is one of the best places in American Samoa for a decent deep swim. In most other spots the water is too shallow for anything other than snorkelling and splashing about. On Tutuila, try Alega and Avaio in the east (p347) and the little bays lining the island's western tip (p346). Some charge a fee, but in every case the beach belongs to the village and you should ask permission before swimming. In some places it's forbidden to swim on a Sunday. Utulei Beach (p343) is popular with the locals, but being in Pago Pago Harbor it could hardly rate as the cleanest option.

Surfing

The surfing situation in American Samoa is the same as the diving situation – some great spots, but no operators. According to those in the know, the surf here is (or was) one of the best-kept secrets of the South Pacific. Powerful 2m waves breaking in very shallow water over very sharp coral, however, make it an activity only for the very experienced. Bring all your own surfing gear to American Samoa.

Some of the best surfing is found just beyond the reef near Faganeanea, south of Pago Pago, but if the trade winds are blowing and the tides aren't right, surfing will be impossible. Other breaks worth investigating include those at Poloa and Amanave around Cape Taputapu, and at Sliding Rock in Tutuila's southwest.

BUSINESS HOURS

Banks open from 8.30am to 4pm Monday to Friday (some branches have a drive-through service on a Saturday between 8.30am and 12.30pm). Shops operate from 8am to 4.30pm on weekdays and from 8am to noon on Saturday, though village stores keep longer hours. Eateries serve breakfast and lunch be-

tween 8am and 4pm, and dinner from 6pm to 10pm. Bars in the main towns often open for drinking around lunchtime and often close at midnight. Government offices open from 9am to 5pm.

We don't give opening hours for establishments mentioned in the text unless they differ greatly from the standard hours outlined in this section.

For details about Samoan public holidays, see p629.

CHILDREN

The sunny tropical climate enjoyed for much of the year by American Samoa – with the possible exception of rain-harassed Pago Pago – emboldens children to make the most of the islands' warm waters. There are few natural threats to the health of children here, but note that walking trails and beaches are entirely unsupervised.

See Lonely Planet's *Travel With Children* for advice on family travel.

See the Tutuila for Children section (p347) for suggestions on how to keep kids occupied during your visit. For details of the practicalities concerning children visiting the South Pacific, see p627.

EMBASSIES & CONSULATES

All American Samoan diplomatic affairs are handled by the US. There are no consulates or embassies in American Samoa and no places that are able to issue visas for the US.

FESTIVALS & EVENTS

American Samoa's main public holiday is Flag Day (17 April), which commemorates the raising of the US flag over the islands in 1900 with an arts festival and much traditional fanfare. In May there's National Tourism Week, which aims to attract international visitors to the islands. Far more vivacious is Tisa's Tattoo Festival in October, the inaugural version of which took place in 2005 at Tisa's Barefoot Bar on Tutuila. Also in October (on the second Sunday of the month) is White Sunday, when kids get to celebrate being kids.

INTERNET ACCESS

Only a handful of top-end hotels and guesthouses offer internet access and there are very few internet cafes. See p340 for the best-value connection options.

PRACTICALITIES

- American Samoa's main newspaper is the *Samoa News*, published daily Monday to Saturday.

- The main radio stations are Radio KHJ (93FM) and Radio KSBS (FM 92.1).

- The government-owned TV station, KVZK, broadcasts Channel 2 (local programs, noncommercial US fare) and Channel 4 and 5 (commercial US programs). Privately owned KHJ-TV is a NBC affiliate.

- The video format used is NTSC.

- US-style plugs are used in American Samoa (110V, 60Hz AC).

- American Samoa uses the American version of the imperial system. See the Quick Reference page for conversions.

INTERNET RESOURCES

American Samoa Historic Preservation Office
(www.ashpo.org) This site includes information on Samoa's history and a good walking tour.

National Park of American Samoa (www.nps.gov /npsa) This excellent site has information on the park's homestay program, and local flora and fauna.

Office of Tourism (www.amsamoa.com) .

Samoa News (www.samoanews.com) For the latest American Samoan news.

MAPS

The maps in this book should be sufficient for navigating around the islands. The Tourism and National Park offices (p342) both produce free brochures with maps included, but they're not much more detailed.

The University of Hawai'i's *Islands of Samoa* map (US$4) has good topographic detail of both American Samoa and Samoa, but dates from 1990. You can usually pick up a copu from the Iupeli Siliva Wesley Bookshop (p340).

MONEY

The US dollar, divided into 100 cents, is the unit of currency in use in American Samoa. For exchange rates, refer to the Quick Reference page. In this chapter, unless otherwise stated, all prices given are in US dollars.

ATMs

Automated teller machines are provided by the ANZ Amerika Samoa Bank and the Bank of Hawai'i on Tutuila in both Pago Pago and Tafuna.

HOW MUCH?

- **Main course in a restaurant:** from US$7
- **Night in a midrange hotel:** from US$95
- **Nine holes of golf in Tutuila:** from US$3
- **Ferry ride to Aunu'u:** US$1
- **Car hire:** from US$60 per day
- **Gallon of unleaded petrol:** US$2.50
- **1L of bottled water:** US$2
- **355mL bottle of Vailima beer:** US$3
- **Souvenir T-shirt:** US$6 to US$8
- **Huge serve of Samoan pancakes:** US$4.85

Tipping

Tipping is not expected or encouraged in American Samoa. It is, however, deemed acceptable for exceptional service at finer restaurants.

TELEPHONE

It is **ASTCA** (American Samoa Telecommunications Authority; Map p344; ☎ 633 1121; Fagatogo) rather than the post office which runs the territory's telephone services. It has a large office in Pago Pago with banks of phones available. It sells phonecards in units of US$5, US$10 and US$20, though cardphones are virtually nonexistent outside of Pago Pago, Tafuna and Nu'uuli.

A cheaper option for international calls is the Toa Com prepay cards (available in the same denominations) which allow you to call from any landline (local call rates apply) via an internet-based service. Toa Com charges 7c per minute to the US and 10c per minute to the UK or NZ.

Mobile Phones

You can hire phones or buy SIM cards for use in GSM 900-compatible phones from **Blue Sky Communications** (Map p344; ☎ 699 2759; Fagatogo Sq; ⊗ 8am-5pm Mon-Fri, 9am-2pm Sat). However, these SIMs are of no use in the Manu'a Islands. If you're planning to travel there, you're better off getting a SIM from ASTCA.

Phone Codes

The country code for American Samoa is ☎ 1-684. The territory has no area codes.

TIME

The local time in American Samoa is Greenwich Mean Time/Coordinated Universal Time (GMT/UTC) minus 11 hours. Therefore, when it's noon in American Samoa, it's 11pm the same day in London, 3pm the same day in Los Angeles, and 9am the following day in Sydney.

VISAS

US citizens equipped with a valid passport and an onward ticket can visit American Samoa visa-free. Nationals of the following countries equipped with a passport (valid for at least 60 days) and an onward ticket will receive a free one-month visa on arrival: Andorra, Australia, Austria, Belgium, Brunei, Canada, Denmark, Federated States of Micronesia, Finland,

France, Germany, Iceland, Ireland, Italy, Japan, Liechtenstein, Luxembourg, Monaco, the Netherlands, NZ, Norway, Portugal, San Marino, Singapore, Slovenia, Spain, Sweden, Switzerland and the UK. Nationals of all other countries must apply in advance for their one-month visa (US$40).

Visa extensions are handled by the **Immigration Office** (Map p344; ☎ 633 4203; www.asg-gov .net/legal%20affairs.htm; ground fl, Executive Office Bldg, Utulei; ✆ 8am-4pm Mon-Fri), located within the government building in Pago Pago. Visas can only be extended by one month; the fee for this varies depending on what country you hail from.

TRANSPORT IN AMERICAN SAMOA

GETTING THERE & AWAY
Air
There's no better illustration of the physical isolation of American Samoa than the fact that you can only fly directly to Tutuila from Samoa and Hawai'i. It's for this reason that many visitors tie a trip to this far-flung US territory to an exploration of Samoa and/or other South Pacific destinations.

All flights land in Tafuna International Airport, 15km southwest of Pago Pago Harbor. Following are the airlines that service American Samoa (telephone numbers listed here are for dialling from within American Samoa). They all have offices at the airport.

Hawaiian Airlines (airline code HA; ☎ 699 1875; www.hawaiianair.com) Flies twice a week from Honolulu; return fare from US$1373.

Inter Island Airways (airline code IIA; ☎ 699 7100; www.interislandair.com) Two daily flights to Samoa; return fares from US$182.

Polynesian Airline of Samoa (airline code PH; ☎ 699 9126; www.polynesianairlines.com) Flies to Samoa three to five times a day.

South Pacific Express (SPEX; ☎ 699 9900; rhuffla@ southpacificexpress.as) SPEX flies two to three times daily from Samoa.

Sea
FERRY
A car ferry/cargo ship called MV *Lady Naomi* runs between Pago Pago and Apia once a week. It departs Pago Pago each Thursday at 4pm for the seven-hour trip. Return deck fares

are US$110; return cabin fares are US$130. Tickets must be purchased at least one day in advance from **Polynesia Shipping Services** (Map p344; ☎ 633 1211; Pago Pago).

YACHT
During the region's dry (and cyclone-free) season between May and October, yachts cruise all around the South Pacific. Pago Pago's deep, spectacular harbour serves as the official entry point for private yacht owners.

Yachts should be granted free anchorage in the harbour for the first week of their stay, but are liable for a monthly rate after that. Vessels arriving from Hawai'i will need to present a US customs clearance document from Honolulu.

GETTING AROUND
Air
Inter Island Airways (☎ in Tutuila 699 7100, in Ofu 655 7100, in Ta'u 677 7100; www.interislandair.com) flies the 30-minute air route from Tutuila to Ofu and from Tutuila to Ta'u (both US$155 return). There are services most days but they're frequently cancelled due to unsafe cross-winds at the Manu'a airstrips. It's possible you'll get stuck out there for a couple of days more than you intended, so it's always safest to schedule a Manu'a visit at the beginning of your American Samoan holiday and be a bit flexible with your dates.

There are no flights between Ofu and Ta'u.

Bicycle
Tutuila is not very conducive to a cycling tour. The island is mountainous, traffic can be heavy, and a complete circuit is impossible since there are no roads across the rugged north coast. Dogs can also be a major hassle here. You could conceivably take a bike over to the Manu'a Islands by boat, but the minimalist road networks of these islands make this a rather dubious plan.

Cyclists heading to American Samoa should come prepared for the almost incessant heat and humidity, and should bring their own repair kits, spares, a good lock and heavy-duty panniers.

Boat
The **MV Sili** (☎ 633 5532, 633 4160) chugs between Pago Pago and the Manu'a group. It departs Tutuila every second Thursday at 10pm and one-way tickets cost US$35 (plus US$3 per

AMERICAN SAMOA

piece of luggage); tickets are sold between 8am and 4pm on the day of departure. The journey takes 12 hours and stops are made at both Ofu and Ta'u. This boat doesn't enter Manu'a harbours – rather, you transfer to a smaller boat at the harbour entrance.

Pago Pago Yacht Club (p350) is where yachties hang out and share information, usually out on the deck with a Vailima beer in one hand and a cigarette in the other.

Bus

Villages and towns on the island of Tutuila are serviced by 'aiga-owned buses. The vehicles – modified pick-up trucks with deadly sound systems – theoretically run until early evening, but don't try to test this theory out after 2pm on Saturday, or on Sunday after church services are finished. All buses display the name of their final destination in the front window. To stop a bus, wave your hand and arm, palm down, as the bus approaches. To signal that you'd like to get off the bus, either knock on the ceiling or clap loudly. Pay the fare to the driver; try to have the exact fare.

Details of routes and fares are given on p342.

Car

Hiring a car allows you to explore Tutuila quickly and comfortably via the island's good sealed roads. That said, complete reliance on a hire car will rob you of the unique cultural experiences that can be gained on public transport.

At the time of writing, motorcycles were not available for hire in American Samoa.

DRIVING LICENCE

A valid foreign driving licence should allow you to drive in American Samoa, though you can always get yourself an international driving licence to be absolutely certain.

HIRE

When hiring a vehicle, check for any damage or scratches before you get into the car and note everything on the rental agreement, lest you be held liable for damage when the car is returned.

For details of car-hire firms on Tutuila, see p343.

INSURANCE

It's essential to have your hire car covered by insurance as repair costs are extremely high. Several local car-hire firms offer contracts where there's no option of accepting a CDW (collision/damage waiver). The lack of a CDW technically means that the car hirer is liable for *all* costs resulting from an accident, regardless of whose fault it is, so sign such contracts at your peril. You should insist on a CDW, for which you pay an extra fee of around US$10 per day.

ROAD RULES

Vehicles drive on the right-hand side of the road. The speed limit is 32km/h (20mph) through villages and 55km/h (35mph) outside populated areas.

Local Transport

TAXI

Taxis on Tutuila are expensive and are only convenient for short trips.

Solomon Islands

Maybe you've already read about the Solomon Islands. This was probably in a crumpled *National Geographic* in some dentist's waiting room. Now it's time to unleash your inner adventurer and uncover all the hidden delights of these islands.

For those seeking an authentic Melanesian experience or 'something completely different' (the slogan used by the tourist office), the Solomons are hard to beat. From WWII relics to skull shrines shrouded with a palpable historical aura, and challenging hikes to village visits, there's so much on offer, far from the crowds. Then there's the visual appeal, with scenery reminiscent of a Discovery Channel documentary: volcanic islands that jut up dramatically from the cobalt blue ocean, croc-infested mangroves, huge lagoons, tropical islets, emerald forests and forgotten valleys cloaked in greenery.

Don't expect sweeping white-sand beaches, ritzy resorts and Cancun-style nightlife – the Solomons are not a beach holiday destination. With only a smattering of traditional guest houses in leaf-hut villages and a few comfortable and romantic, vaguely safari-style hideaways, it's tailor-made for ecotourists.

For outdoorsy types, the Solomons are heaven on earth, with lots of action-packed experiences that can easily be organised. Climb an extinct volcano on Kolombangara, slog through jungle paths to reach secluded waterfalls on Guadalcanal, surf the uncrowded waves off Ghizo, snorkel pristine reefs or kayak across Marovo Lagoon. Beneath the surface, an unbeatable repertoire of diving adventures awaits, with awesome WWII shipwrecks, shoals of colourful fish and dizzying drop-offs.

After several years of civil unrest, this last frontier is currently considered safe for independent travellers, so you have no excuse but to squeeze it in to your South Pacific odyssey.

HIGHLIGHTS

- Assist rangers in tagging marine turtles, on ecofriendly **Tetepare Island** (p378)
- Drift off to sleep at an intimate lodge at **Langa Langa Lagoon** (p386)
- Chill out at a laid-back resort on **Mbabanga Island** (p382)
- Don a mask, fins and a tank and flipper-kick into the **wreck of a WWII Japanese ship** off Guadalcanal (p373) or **Tulagi** (p375)
- Spend the day spotting rusty **WWII relics** around Honiara (p373)

CLIMATE & WHEN TO GO

From late May until early December (the dry season), southeasterly winds produce pleasantly mild weather. Rainfall is light and rain periods are usually several days apart.

From mid-December to mid-May, monsoon winds come from the west or northwest bringing the wet season – a time of higher temperatures, humidity and rainfall. Short, sharp, torrential rains are followed by bright sunshine. Cyclones can blow up between January and April.

Daytime coastal temperatures vary through the year from 27°C to 32°C. At night the temperature falls to around 19°C. The humidity can be oppressive and is highest in the morning.

The most comfortable time to visit the Solomons is between June and September, although humidity levels are lowest from October to December. The surfing season is from October to April.

COSTS & MONEY

Prices have soared over the last few years, especially domestic flights and hotels.

Where there is enough accommodation to warrant it, we've divided our reviews into budget (less than S$250 a night for a double room), midrange (between S$250 and S$800) and top-end (over S$800) categories. There is a 10% value-added tax (VAT), and all prices in this book are inclusive of tax.

Most hotels and resorts, and all resthouses, quote their rates in Solomon Islands dollars, although a few high-end places will usually also list the prices in Australian dollars.

There aren't seasonal price variations. Credit cards transactions usually incur a 5% commission.

HISTORY

Papuan-speaking hunter-gatherers from New Guinea were settling the southern and eastern Solomon Islands by 25,000 BC. They were the only inhabitants for thousands of years, until Austronesian-speaking proto-Melanesians began moving in around 4000 BC. The Lapita people (see boxed text, p37) appeared between 2000 and 1600 BC.

Polynesians from the east settled the outer islands such as Rennell, Bellona and Ontong Java between AD 1200 and 1600, and their settlements suffered raids from Tongans between the 14th and 18th centuries.

Spanish Exploration

Spaniard Don Alvaro de Mendaña y Neyra left Peru with two ships in November 1567. On 7 February 1568 he saw and named Santa Isabel, and settled there. On 11 August, after six months of conflict, the voyagers set sail for Peru.

Mendaña returned almost 30 years later in 1595 with four ships and 450 would-be colonists. He came upon and named Santa Cruz, and established a settlement dying there of malaria. After two months the settlement was abandoned and the survivors limped back to Peru.

Mendaña's chief pilot from 1595 was the Portuguese Pedro Fernández de Quirós, who left Peru with three small ships on 21 December 1605 and reached the Duff Islands early in 1606.

Further Exploration & Early Trading

There was almost no further contact with Europeans until 1767, when the British Captain Philip Carteret came upon Santa Cruz and Malaita.

British, French and American explorers all followed, and whalers also began arriving in 1798. Sandalwood traders visited from the 1840s to late 1860s, buying pigs, turtle shell, pearl shell and bêches-de-mer (bottom-dwelling sea creatures). The sandalwood traders were known as being notoriously cruel (see p43) and from the 1860s firearms traded with sailors produced an explosive growth in both head-hunting and slave raids; the diseases the Europeans carried also resulted in thousands of deaths. At this time missionaries were active elsewhere throughout the South Pacific, but they moved cautiously in the Solomon Islands, which became known as the most dangerous place in the South Pacific.

SOLOMON ISLANDS FACTS

Capital city (and island) Honiara (Guadalcanal)
Population 538,000
Land area 27,540 sq km
International telephone code ☎ 677
Currency Solomon Islands dollar (S$)
Languages 74 indigenous languages, plus Solomons Pijin (English is widely spoken)
Greeting Halo (Hello)
Website www.visitsolomons.com.sb

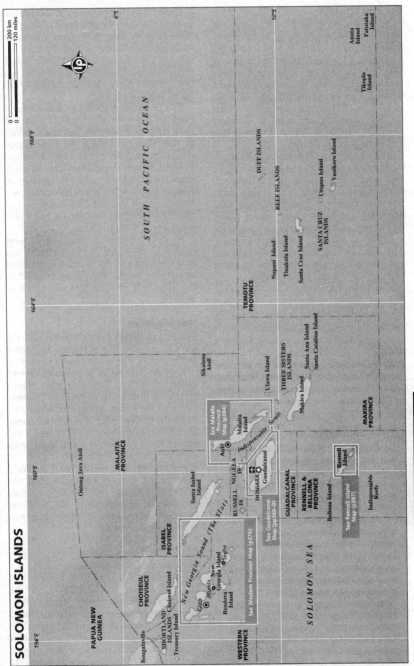

SOLOMON ISLANDS

0 ——— 200 km
0 ——— 120 miles

SOUTH PACIFIC OCEAN

SOLOMON SEA

PAPUA NEW GUINEA

Bougainville

CHOISEUL PROVINCE

SHORTLAND ISLANDS Choiseul Island
Treasury Island

WESTERN PROVINCE

Gizo Munda New Georgia Island
Rendova Island Seghe
New Georgia Sound (The Slot)

See Western Province Map (p376)

ISABEL PROVINCE

Santa Isabel Island

Ontong Java Atoll

MALAITA PROVINCE

Sikaiana Atoll

RUSSELL NGGELA IS
IS

See Malaita Province Map (p384)
Auki
Malaita Island

HONIARA Guadalcanal

See Guadalcanal Map (pp368-9)

GUADALCANAL PROVINCE

RENNELL & BELLONA PROVINCE

Bellona Island

Rennell Island See Rennell Island Map (p387)

Indispensable Reefs

Indispensable Strait

Ulawa Island

THREE SISTERS ISLANDS

Makira Island Santa Ana Island
Santa Catalina Island

MAKIRA PROVINCE

TEMOTU PROVINCE

Nupani Island REEF ISLANDS

DUFF ISLANDS

Tinakula Island
Santa Cruz Island

SANTA CRUZ ISLANDS

Utupua Island Vanikoro Island

Anuta Island
Fatutaka Island

Tikopia Island

SOLOMON ISLANDS

The Protectorate

In the 1890s about 50 British traders and missionaries were present in the Solomons, and Germany was active in New Guinea, the Shortlands, Choiseul, Santa Isabel and Ontong Java. On 6 October 1893 Britain proclaimed a protectorate over the archipelago's southern islands, which was extended in 1897 and again in 1898. In 1899 Britain relinquished claims to Western Samoa, and in return Germany ceded the Shortlands, Choiseul, Ontong Java and Santa Isabel to Britain.

Missionaries sought to eradicate local culture, declaring customs and ceremonies to be evil. Sorcery and head-hunting diminished, but islanders continued to die in huge numbers from European diseases. Between 1871 and 1903 blackbirders (slave traders) took 30,000 men from the Solomons to work in the cane fields of northern Australia and Fiji (see p44). Blackbirding was eventually outlawed and some islanders returned to the Solomons years later, bringing cloth and rifles.

The Kwaio Rebellion on Malaita in 1927 was a rejection of European values (see below). In 1928 several Kwaio rebels were hanged in the then-capital, Tulagi.

WWII

In April 1942 the Japanese seized the Shortland Islands. Three weeks later Tulagi was taken and the Japanese began building an airstrip on Guadalcanal.

THE KWAIO REBELLION

On 4 October 1927 District Officer William Bell was in Kwaio territory (Malaita) to collect tax and confiscate rifles. With him were 14 Malaitan constables. A Kwaio called Basiana killed Bell, and in the ensuing melee all but one of the constables were killed.

The reaction in Tulagi, the capital, was immediate – and excessive. The cruiser HMAS *Adelaide*, dispatched from Sydney, shelled all the villages it could find, gardens were poisoned, and sacred objects were destroyed. The Kwaio claimed that more than a thousand people were killed.

Six Kwaio (including Basiana) were later hanged in Tulagi and 30 others died in jail. This ruthless action subdued the Kwaio but left a long legacy of ill feeling towards government and Europeans.

United States troops landed on Guadalcanal in August 1942. In the early hours of 9 August, while landings were in progress, a Japanese naval force left Rabaul in New Guinea to attack the US transports at Red Beach before they unloaded. This, the Battle of Savo, was one of the US Navy's heaviest defeats – 1270 Allied sailors were lost.

The US forces gradually gained the upper hand, but at a tremendous cost of life on both sides. After six months the Japanese withdrew to New Georgia. During the Guadalcanal campaign, six naval battles were fought and 67 warships and transports sunk – so many ships were sunk off the northern coast of Guadalcanal that this area is now called Iron Bottom Sound. Around 7000 American and 30,000 Japanese lives were lost on land and at sea, many of them to disease.

As 1943 progressed, more islands were retaken by the Allies, and by the year's end only Choiseul and the Shortlands remained in Japanese hands. These were returned to the Allies only after the Japanese surrender in 1945.

Independence

Tulagi was gutted during the war and the Quonset-hut township of Honiara replaced it as the capital. The economy was in ruins.

A proto-nationalist postwar movement called Marching Rule (Ma'asina Ruru) sprang up in Malaita, opposed to cooperation with the British authorities, whose rule had been restored after WWII. Mass arrests by British authorities in 1947 and 1948 caused the movement to wane, and it died out after US forces left in 1950.

Britain began to see the need for local government, and a governing council was elected in 1970. The British Solomon Islands Protectorate was renamed the Solomon Islands five years later and independence was granted on 7 July 1978.

A Troubled Young Nation

For years the Gwale people resented the fact that their traditional land was being settled by migrants from Malaita. Early in 1999 the Guadalcanal Revolutionary Army (GRA) began to terrorise and kill rural Malaitans who were forced to flee to the capital or back to their home island. The Malaitan Eagle Force (MEF) was formed to protect the interests of Malaitans and soon gained the upper hand. Hundreds died in the fighting. Following mediation by Australia and New Zealand, the Townsville Peace Agreement was signed in October 2000. A general amnesty was declared and many weapons were handed in.

However, what began as ethnic tension descended into general lawlessness, thuggery and intimidation. Though the conflict was confined to Guadalcanal, 'events' started happening elsewhere, including in the Western Province. The whole country was crippled and traumatised, and the fragile economy collapsed. Pacific neighbours feared that the Solomons would become a failed state.

On 24 July 2003 the RAMSI, an Australian-led coalition of police from Pacific island states, was deployed throughout the whole country to restore law and order. Security was quickly re-established.

This was too good to be true. In April 2006 the election of controversial Snyder Rini as prime minister resulted in two days of rioting and anarchy in the streets of Honiara, in which the historic Chinatown and huge Pacific Casino Hotel were razed (despite the presence of RAMSI). Australia flew in reinforcements for the RAMSI personnel. After a no-confidence vote, Rini resigned just eight days after the election. The subsequent ascension of Manasseh Sogavare as prime minister brought calm to the Solomons' capital.

Solomon Islands Today

RAMSI remains in an ongoing capacity while the country slowly rebuilds, and it doesn't look like the personnel will be leaving anytime soon.

Due to highly unstable parliamentary coalitions, changes of government are frequent occurence in the Solomon Islands. On 13 December 2007, Manasseh Sogavare lost a no-confidence motion, and one week later the Member for North East Guadalcanal, Derek Sikua, was elected as the 13th prime minister of the Solomon Islands. He seems committed to ensuring peace, social harmony and reconciliation. On 10 January 2009, he made a public apology to the Malaitans for the offences that were committed against them during the ethnic tension.

With restored security and increased stability, economic prospects are positive. Thanks to better air connections from Australia, tourism is on the rise, and the Gold Ridge Mine, 40km southeast of Honiara, which was closed in 2000 due to civil unrest, should recommence commercial operations in 2010.

In early April 2007, a tsunami struck Western and Choiseul provinces. Gizo, the Solomons' second-largest city, was at the centre of the disaster.

THE CULTURE

Solomon Islanders' obligations to their clan and village bigman (chief) are permanent and enduring, whether they live in the same village all their lives or move to another country. As in most Melanesian cultures, the *wantok* system is observed (see p364).

BEST EATING

The dining scene is still fairly limited in the Solomons, but if you're after fresh food cooked to perfection, you'll be in seventh heaven. And the winners are...

- Great coffees, superb fruit salad with yoghurt and a spiffing waterfront setting – Raintree Café (p372) is not to be missed.

- A fab terrace overlooking the turquoise lagoon, with Kolombangara island in the distance – we can't think of a more atmospheric location to devour fish 'n' chips than at Fatboys (p383).

- Capitana Restaurant (p372) offers superb Japanese specialities, including a devilish sashimi.

- The superb three-course meals served at Uepi Island Resort (p380) in Marovo will keep everyone happy except your personal trainer.

- The chef is French at Club Havanah (p373), which bodes well. Sophisticated French fare with a Melanesian twist – a winning alchemy.

- Ah, the lobster Mornay served at Agnes Lodge (p377)... Stop, we're drooling!

THE WANTOK SYSTEM

Fundamental to the Solomons' culture and common to many Melanesian societies is the idea of *wantok*. In Pijin, *wantok* simply means 'one talk', and your *wantok* are those who speak your language – your clan and family. All islanders are born with a set of obligations to their *wantok*, but they're also endowed with privileges that only *wantok* receive.

Within the village, each person is entitled to land and food, and to share in the community assets. Any clans people, whether in Honiara or Hanoi, are expected to accommodate and feed their *wantok* until they can make more permanent arrangements.

For most Melanesian villagers it's an egalitarian way of sharing the community assets. There's no social security system and very few people are in paid employment, but the clan provides economic support and a strong sense of identity.

The *wantok* system affects everything: if you are tendering out a construction project and a *wantok* bids, you give the contract to the *wantok*. If your bus driver is a *wantok*, you won't have to pay. And if you have a *wantok* in the judiciary, maybe you won't go to jail.

In the political and public-affairs arenas, the *wantok* system can translate as nepotism and corruption. In the Solomons it has undermined democratic institutions and hampered the country's development.

The National Psyche

There's an enormous sense of relief that things have 'normalised' after the ethnic tension. People are coming back to the Solomons – business and trade are doing better. People are participating in good faith in the reconciliation process and want to get on with things after years of having to put everything on hold.

Lifestyle

Beliefs, ceremonies, totems and traditional valuables vary between communities, but the Solomon Islands are quintessentially Melanesian (except for a few Polynesian outliers). Melanesian culture is deeply rooted in ancestor worship, magic and oral traditions. Villagers often refer to their traditional ways, beliefs and land ownership as *kastom*; it's bound up in the Melanesian systems of lore and culture (see p48). In Malaita the spirit of a dead person can live in a shark; the shark is thus offered gifts and worshipped.

Population

The Solomons' 2005 population was estimated at 538,000. Melanesians represent 94% and Polynesians 4%. The large Micronesian communities who were resettled from Kiribati by the British in the 1960s are still called Gilbertese. The remainder of the population is made up of Chinese and expats, mainly Aussies, Kiwis, Brits and Yanks.

The Solomons' population density of 14.5 people per sq km is one of the Pacific's lowest.

Most of the population lives in rural villages. Urban drift caused Honiara's population to grow by 7% per year until the ethnic tension of the late 1990s.

Most Solomon Islanders live in coastal villages close to freshwater springs. Each family has a few scattered vegetable plots.

RELIGION

About 96% of the population is Christian. Of these, 35% are members of the Anglican-affiliated Church of Melanesia and 20% are Roman Catholics.

Islanders still practise pre-Christian religions in a few remote areas, particularly on Malaita; in other places traditional beliefs are observed alongside Christianity.

NGUZUNGUZU

The *nguzunguzu* (pronounced noo-zoo-noo-zoo) once adorned canoe prows to ward off water spirits, guide the craft through jagged reefs and protect the warriors aboard. The figurehead rests its chin either on two clenched fists (for war), a human head (head-hunting) or on a dove (peace). The best carvings are made of ebony and inlaid with nautilus shell, which make a striking contrast with the smooth, jet-black timber.

Although native to Western Province, the *nguzunguzu* has been taken up as a national symbol and is embossed on the S$1 coin.

ARTS

Literature

Ples Blong Iumi – The Solomon Islands: the Past Four Thousand Years, by Sam Alasia, contains contributions by 14 Solomon Islanders. *Zoleveke: A Man from Choiseul*, by Gideon Zoleveke, recounts the story of a Choiseul man who became a cabinet minister.

From Pig-Theft to Parliament: My Life Between Two Worlds, by Jonathan Fifi'i, tells of the author's childhood in Malaita, the Marching Rule movement and parliamentary life.

James Jones' classic *The Thin Red Line* (1963) was made into the 1998 film starring Sean Penn, George Clooney and Nick Nolte. This grim WWII story is fictional but set in Guadalcanal.

Often very funny and sometimes insightful, *Solomon Time* by Will Randall (2003) tells of a disenchanted English school teacher who spends a year trying to establish a chicken farming business on Rendova.

Hector Hothouse's *White Headhunter: The Extraordinary True Story of a White Man's Life among Headhunters of the Solomon Islands* tells the story of the Scotsman John Renton who lived in Malaita from 1868 to 1875.

Lightning Meets the West Wind: The Malaita Massacre, by Roger Keesing and Peter Corris, is the story of William Bell, the Kwaio Rebellion and the brutal reprisals exacted on the Malaitan people by the British afterwards.

Books on the Solomons' experience in WWII include Eric Feldt's *The Coast Watchers*, Richard F Newcomb's *Savo* and *Guadalcanal Diary* by Richard Tregaskis. *The Big Death: Solomon Islanders Remember WWII*, by Geoffrey M White and others, is a collection of islanders' own stories.

Happy Isles in Crisis by Clive Moore (2005) is the first comprehensive study of the events in Guadalcanal and the ensuing period of ethnic tension that paralysed the country. Moore discovers many deep historical roots to the problem.

Music

Solomon Islanders are incredibly musical people – it's a must to go to a local church service to listen to the singing. The local music scene is in its infancy, but a few artists are making names for themselves around the Pacific, including Sharzy, a boy soul singer from Malaita.

> **RECOMMENDED LISTENING**
>
> Tipa's album *Maiae* (2005) is a classic example of breezy islander sounds fused with modern music and strong multipart vocal harmonies. Traditional string-band elements and percussion are layered with keys, guitars, drums and bass, and fantastic vocal arrangements. The songs are strong with catchy melodies.

The Malaitan pipe bands (or bamboo bands) are amazing. In ensembles of 12 or so members, the band plays bamboo pipes in all sizes bundled together with bushvine. They're played as panpipe and flutes, and as long tubes whose openings are struck with rubber thongs to make an unusual plinketty-plonk sound. Drums and tea-chest basses are sometimes incorporated, as are traditional costumes and energetic dancing. You can see them performing in Honiara's hotels.

Narasirato mix classic Malaitan panpipe music with contemporary beats.

Carving

There are strong carving and artefact-making traditions in the Solomons. Once more widespread, pottery is now produced only in northwestern Choiseul.

Carvings incorporate human, bird, fish and other animal motifs, often in combination, and they frequently represent deities and spirits. Woodcarvings are inlaid with nautilus or trochus shell. Carvings of *nguzunguzu* (canoe figureheads, also carved in miniature; see opposite) and animals are produced from kerosene wood and rare and expensive ebony. Decorated bowls and masks are widely available, as are stone replicas of traditional shell money. 'Riverstone' carvings are popular too.

Weaving

Bukaware baskets, trays, table mats and coasters are made in many parts of the Solomons and are woven from the very tough *asa* vine. Gilbertese make sturdy brown sleeping mats out of the pandanus leaf. Finely woven shoulder bags are produced on Rennell and Bellona.

Tattoos

Tattoos are a traditional art form and their motifs or designs can be indicative of a person's age and social position –

SOLOMON ISLANDS

for example whether a boy has been initiated. Tattooing is more common among fairer-skinned peoples.

Facial engraving is practised on Malaita; a grooved, unpigmented design is made using a scraper bone against the skin. In northern Malaita men are tattooed below the eye and women decorate their breasts.

Chests are tattooed on the islands of Rennell and Bellona.

Currency

Kastom mani (custom money) is used for paying bride price and other special transactions. Shell money is used in Malaita, while in the Temotu Islands red-feather coils are still used.

LANGUAGE

There are 74 mutually unintelligible indigenous languages in the Solomon Islands, and it's common for people from villages only a few kilometres apart to be unable to understand each other. As a result, islanders who aren't *wantok* communicate in Pijin. Educated people generally speak English so you can get by without learning any Pijin. However, if you try a few words in Pijin you'll find that people lose their shyness.

Lonely Planet's *Pidgin* phrasebook has a large section on Solomon Islands Pijin.

Solomon Islands Pijin basics

Hello.	*Halo.*
Goodbye.	*Lukim iu (bihaen).*
How are you?	*Iu stap oraet nomoa?*
I'm well (thanks).	*Mi stap gudfala (tanggio tumas).*
Please.	*Plis.*
Thanks.	*Tanggio (tumas).*
Yes.	*Ies.*
No.	*Nomoa.*

ENVIRONMENT

The Solomons has more than 4500 plant species, including 230 varieties of orchid. Tropical rainforest covers the islands, although much of it has been degraded by logging operations.

The spectacular marine environment is home to a rich variety of fish, corals, anemones and many other creatures, including eight species of venomous sea snakes. Several islands are breeding grounds for green and hawksbill turtles.

The Solomons has 173 bird species, 40 of them endemic. Some, such as the Rennell fantail and the slaty flycatcher of Vanikoro, ar found only on one island.

Four rat species are larger than domestic cats, and other land mammals include the cuscus and flying fox (fruit bat).

Among the lizards are the 1.5m-long monitor lizard, freshwater crocodiles and the very dangerous saltwater crocodile, which can exceed 5m in length.

More than 130 butterfly species are found locally, and 35 are endemic. The two largest forms, the Queen Victoria birdwing and the blue mountain birdwing, have wing spans over 25cm.

Geography

The islands of the Solomons form a scattered double chain that extends 1667km southeast from Bougainville in Papua New Guinea. The Solomon Islands are the third-largest archipelago in the entire South Pacific.

Of the 992 islands, 347 are populated. The largest islands are Guadalcanal (5336 sq km), Malaita (3840 sq km), Santa Isabel (3380 sq km), Choiseul (3200 sq km), Makira (3188 sq km) and New Georgia (2145 sq km). The country's highest peak, Mt Makarakombu (2447m), is located on Guadalcanal. There are active volcanoes, and earthquakes here are common.

The majority of the islands of the Solomons are fringed with coral reefs and sheltered lagoons; many have formed around volcanic cones, while others, such as Rennell, are former reefs that have been uplifted by volcanic activity.

GUADALCANAL

pop 104,000 / area 5336 sq km

The largest island in the Solomon group, Guadalcanal hosts the national capital, Honiara. Outside Honiara, the island is largely untamed and raw – a place to live out your Indiana Jones fantasies, blazing a trail amid wild jungles. The adventure starts by looking for WWII relics around Honiara and plunging into the wreck-strewn waters of Iron Bottom Sound. Then you could explore the rugged beauty of the Weathercoast or escape to a far-flung resort on eastern Guadalcanal.

RIENTATION

uadalcanal is oriented vaguely east–west, ith Honiara on the northern coast over-oking Iron Bottom Sound, the famous -aveyard of WWII's Battle of Guadalcanal. he hills that are located behind Honiara ventually become a mighty mountain nge reaching 2400m that separates the Veathercoast people from those on the orthern coast.

ANGERS & ANNOYANCES

he presence of RAMSI personnel ensures at law and order are enforced, and there's o reason to be paranoid in Honiara or in uadalcanal. Be sure to use your common ense and avoid walking alone in deserted treets. Beware of pickpockets at the mar-et and in crowded areas. At night, take taxi.

RANSPORT

etting There & Away

IR

nternational flights land at Honiara's Ienderson Airport, and all domestic routes egin and end in Honiara. See p393 for details f international flights.

Guadalcanal Travel Services (GTS; ☎ 22586; uadtrav@solomon.com.sb; Mendana Ave; ⏱ 8am-4.30pm Ion-Fri, 9am-noon Sat) represents most inter-ational and regional airlines, including olomon Airlines, SkyAirWorld, Pacific irlines (☎ 20031; www.flysolomons.com; Mendana Ave; ⏱ 8am-4pm Mon-Fri, 8.30-11.30am Sat) main office is n the centre of town.

OAT

'or passenger boats to/from Honiara, see 394.

etting Around

O/FROM THE AIRPORT

The standard taxi fare into town is S$80.

AR

Rental car can be arranged through the Pacific Casino Hotel.

MINIBUS

Honiara's minibuses are cheap, frequent (in daylight hours) and safe. The flat fare around own is S$3.

TAXI

There are taxis everywhere in Honiara. They don't have meters, so agree on a fare before hopping in – S$8 per kilometre is reasonable.

HONIARA

pop 57,000

A dusty place with lots of decrepit build-ings, no real architectural highlights and a rather mediocre seafront setting (no beach), Honiara can leave you wondering if you took a wrong turn at Brisbane airport. Don't de-spair! Among Honiara's rewards are pleas-ing botanical gardens, well-stocked souvenir shops, a bustling wharf, an atmospheric mar-ket, a museum and a few high-quality restau-rants and bars. And fantastic diving, right on its doorstep.

It's also the optimal launching pad for ex-ploring the various WWII battlefields around the city.

Orientation

Honiara's central area, from the Mendana Hotel to Chinatown, can be covered in a 30-minute walk along Mendana Ave, the town's main strip. In this area are the central market, the port complex, shops, embassies, banks, ho-tels and restaurants. The 11km urban sprawl along the coast has the settlements of Rove and White River to the west, while eastwards are Chinatown and Mataniko.

Information

You'll find a few internet cafés in the NPF Plaza building in Honiara. Rates average S$20 per hour. The Pacific Casino Hotel and the Solomon Kitano Mendana also offer internet access, with longer opening hours, and most hotels have wi-fi.

Internet Cafe Zone (NPF Plaza, Mendana Ave; ⏱ 8.30am-5pm Mon-Fri) Upstairs.

Solosoft (NPF Plaza, Mendana Ave; ⏱ 8am-7pm Mon-Fri, 8am-3pm Sat) Upstairs.

MEDICAL SERVICES

National Referral Hospital (☎ 23600; Kukum)

Point Cruz Chemist (☎ 22911; Mendana Ave; ⏱ 8am-5pm Mon-Fri, 8am-1pm Sat) A well-stocked pharmacy.

MONEY

There are four 24-hour ATMs in the centre. ANZ and Westpac have one each; you'll find two more booths (also owned by ANZ and Westpac) outside the post office. They accept

GUADALCANAL

Visa and MasterCard. Note that there is also an ANZ-operated ATM and a small bureau de change at the airport.

ANZ (☎ 21111; Mendana Ave; ⏰ 9am-4pm Mon-Fri) Changes all major currencies and travellers cheques. Expect long queues.

Bank South Pacific (☎ 21874; Mendana Ave; ⏰ 8.30am-3pm Mon-Fri) Changes all major currencies and travellers cheques.

Westpac (☎ 21222; Mendana Ave; ⏰ 9am-4pm Mon-Fri) Changes all major currencies (cash and travellers cheques) except euros.

POST

Solomon post (Mendana Ave; ⏰ 8am-4.30pm Mon-Fri, 8am-noon Sat) Sells stamps, envelopes and postcards. It also houses a Western Union counter.

TELEPHONE

Telekom Haus (Mendana Ave; ⏰ 8.30am-4.30pm Mon-Fri, 9am-noon Sat) Next to the post office. Sells prepaid phonecards, Bumblebee cards (for wi-fi access) and Breeze cards (prepaid mobile phone card). Also has Internet access.

TOURIST INFORMATION

Solomon Islands Visitors Bureau (SIVB; ☎ 22442; www.visitsolomons.com.sb; Mendana Ave; ⏰ 8am-4.30pm Mon-Fri) There's little printed material but staff can provide advice and contact isolated lodges and villages (by two-way radio) to make bookings. Also sells useful maps.

TRAVEL AGENCIES

Guadalcanal Travel Services (GTS; ☎ 22586; guadtrav@solomon.com.sb; Mendana Ave; ⏰ 8am-4.30pm Mon-Fri, 9am-noon Sat) Can arrange flight

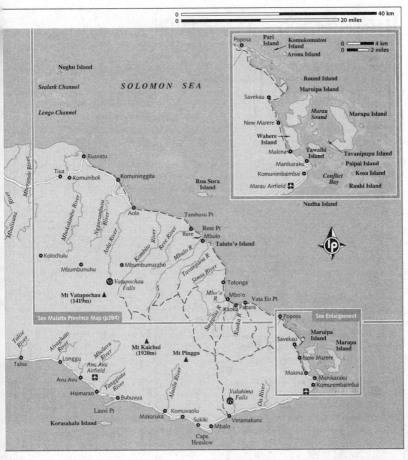

See Malaita Province Map (p384)

See Enlargement

(domestic and international) bookings and make reservations for major resorts in the Solomons.

Sights

Be prepared for a sensory overload at the bubbling **Central Market** (Mendana Ave; ☽ dawn-dusk Mon-Sat), the country's principal food market. It has a huge selection of fresh produce as well as souvenir shells and jewellery.

The modest **National Museum & Cultural Centre** (☎ 24896; Mendana Ave; admission by donation; ☽ 9am-4pm Mon-Fri, 9am-2pm Sat) features interesting displays. Behind it are nine traditionally constructed houses as well as a few boldly carved wooden statues.

The conical-shaped concrete building that's perched on the hill above Hibiscus Ave is the **National Parliament**. Inside, the dome boasts a rich tapestry of traditional art, including arching frescoes.

Skyline Dr has commanding views over the town and leads to the **US War Memorial**, a steep 30-minute walk up from Mendana Ave. The compound has marble slabs bearing detailed descriptions of battles fought during the Guadalcanal campaign.

Expand your knowledge on local flora or simply picnic and relax at the **Botanical Gardens** (☎ 22832; Lenggakiki; admission by donation; ☽ 8am-5pm). These lovely grounds on the hills located above the city provide a green haven for nature lovers. Various short walks are signposted, and there's a little cultural village.

HONIARA

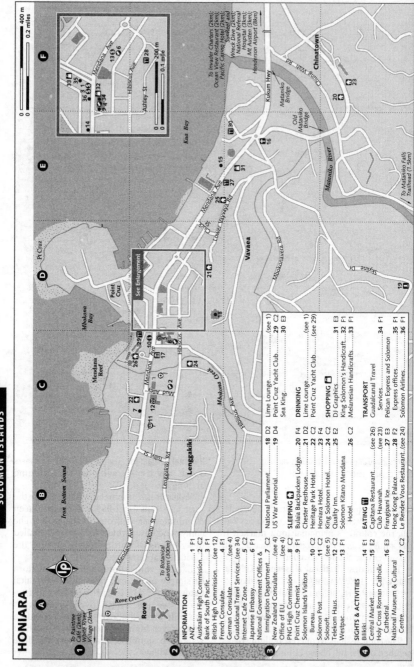

SOLOMON ISLANDS

HONIARA IN...

Two Days

Start your day with muesli and a cappuccino at the **Lime Lounge** (p372) before getting some cultural sustenance at the **National Museum & Cultural Centre** (p369). Then take a taxi up to the **Botanical Gardens** (p369) and enjoy the cool, verdant surrounds. Feeling peckish? Head to the **Raintree Café** (p372) and devour the daily special. Suitably re-energised, squeeze your way into the **Central Market** (p369) for some hectic browsing. Sunset is perfect for a cold Solbrew beer at **Point Cruz Yacht Club** (p372), followed by a flavoursome sashimi at nearby **Capitana Restaurant** (p372).

The next morning, take a day tour to visit the **WWII battlefields** (p373 & p373) around the capital or tackle the **Mataniko Falls** (p374) if you're in the mood for a refreshing dip. If you're a diver, be sure to dive the sensational WWII wrecks at **Bonegi** (below). Back in Honiara, enjoy French cuisine at **Club Havanah** (p373).

Activities

Diving is Honiara's trump card, with a fantastic collection of WWII wrecks lying offshore in Iron Bottom Sound, including Bonegi I & II to the west, and the *John Penn* to the east. See p77 for more information on diving. Contact the following dive shops:

Coastwatchers (☎ 21255, 73672; www.coastwatchers .com.sb)

Invader Charters (☎ 23085; www.invadercharters .com.au) Based at the Pacific Casino Hotel.

SunReef and Wreck Dive (☎ 23659, 73137; www .sunreefdive.com) Based at the Pacific Casino Hotel.

Tours

The following outfits can arrange half-/full day tours around Honiara, taking in the WWII battlefields, waterfalls and other sights. They can also organise trips to Savo and Tulagi. Prices vary according to the party size:

Coastwatchers (☎ 21255, 73672; www.coastwatchers .com.sb)

Destination Solomons Travel & Tours (☎ 23444; destsolo@solomon.com.sb)

Guadalcanal Foundation Tours (☎ 38338; technisyst@solomon.com.sb)

Island Connection (☎ 88123; thaprimitive@gmail.com)

Tourism Solomons (☎ 27772, 21150; toursol@ solomon.com.sb)

Sleeping

BUDGET

Budget really isn't part of the vernacular in Honiara, but there are a couple of acceptable options in the centre. Both places have shared facilities and fan-cooled twin rooms.

Bulaia Backpackers Lodge (☎ 28819; Chinatown; per bed S$100) Rooms are crude and the shared bathrooms leave something to be desired, but it's manageable for a night or two. Be positive – the smart Honiara Hotel is just across the street (read: you can make use of its restaurant and pool). It's a 10-minute walk to the central market.

Chester Resthouse (☎ 26355; mbhches@solomon .com.sb; Lower Vayvaya Rd; r S$200) This budget set-up is popular with travellers and local families because it's betel nut-spitting distance from the action. Rooms are petite and lack privacy but are in good nick, there's a relaxed mood, the communal areas are homey and the shared bathrooms won't make you squirm. There's a broad balcony facing the harbour – just perfect for dipping into a novel or two. It's also a safe choice for women travellers.

MIDRANGE

Honiara Hotel (☎ 21737; www.honiarahotel.com.sb; Chinatown; d S$250-1000; 🖳 🖳) While it's not exactly city central, this place has a genuine ace up its sleeve – a large pool. Other pluses include a bar, a gym and two good restaurants. Accommodation-wise, plump for the more recent rooms, which are well equipped, elegant and fresh. The rooms in the older wings aren't such a good deal. The view over Iron Bottom Sound is great for gushy types, although the walk up to the highest units may leave smokers and oldies short of breath. Wi-fi.

Quality Inn (☎ 25150; qualityinn.solomon@yahoo .com; Lower Vayvaya Rd; d from S$280; 🖳) The rooms are spartan (make that 'dank' for the cheaper ones) and the furnishings scream: 'Dump me at the flea market', but it's all about the supreme location – on a hill overlooking the central market and Iron Bottom Sound, a

SOLOMON ISLANDS

stone's throw from the centre. An acceptable fallback if the others are full.

our pick **Raintree Café** (☎ 22086; www.raintree honiara.com; White River; s/d incl breakfast S$400/500) This cute café-cum-B&B, right by the seashore, about 3km west of the centre just past the White River market, is an appealing option, despite the fact that the Orchid and the Frangipani rooms face a concrete wall. The moral of the story: try for the aptly named Ocean View, within earshot of the sea. Excellent bedding, elegant furniture, polished floorboards and dollops of atmosphere. And good breakfasts. It's safe for women travellers, provided you don't walk outside at night (the road is unlit); take a taxi. During the day, numerous vans ply the route between the White River market and the city centre. Wi-fi.

TOP END

Pacific Casino Hotel (☎ 25009; www.solomon-hotel .com; Kukum; d S$600-1400; ✲ ❑ ☎) You certainly won't fall in love with this large waterfront hotel complex at the eastern end of town (the neon-lit corridors are a bit oppressive) but it's efficiently run and a convenient base, with loads of amenities, including an internet café, a restaurant, two tennis courts, a dive shop and a bar. Aim for a room with a sea view.

our pick **King Solomon Hotel** (☎ 21205; www.solo monislandsresorts.com; Hibiscus Ave; d S$800-1300; ✲ ☎) This is a longstanding venture with all the usual upscale touches, yet it somehow retains a more laid-back feel than its competitors. Maybe it's the traditional carvings that adorn the entrance, or the gaggle of expats and locals who congregate at the bar. Anchored on a steep hill with a kinky funicular that shunts people between the rooms and the reception area, it features a variety of comfortable units scattered amid beautifully landscaped grounds and boasts a stress-melting swimming-pool built into the hill. Wi-fi.

Solomon Kitano Mendana Hotel (☎ 20071; kitano@ mendana.com.sb; Mendana Ave; d S$1000-1600; ✲ ❑ ☎) The Mendana scores high on amenities, with two restaurants, a bar, an airy foyer and a souvenir shop, but the pool is a sad joke. While the rooms in the older blocks are a bit long in the tooth, the new wing showcases stylish, chocolate-and-cream interiors, and affords sea views. Wi-fi.

Heritage Park Hotel (Mendana Ave) As we write, the people behind the Heritage Park Hotel are building what promises to be a top-notch hotel with a boutique feel. It will feature 48 suites and 20 apartments and a wide range of amenities, including a restaurant, a bar and a disco. It should be completed by the time you read this.

Eating

Lime Lounge (☎ 23064; off Mendana Ave; mains S$40-60; ✆ 7am-5pm Mon-Fri, 8am-3pm Sat, 9am-3pm Sun) Perfect for breakfast, lunch or a snack attack any time of the day, funky little Lime Lounge is *the* meeting place for expats. Soak up the atmosphere over a newspaper or a magazine or check out your emails (wi-fi is available with the Bumblebee card; see p391).

Raintree Café (☎ 22086; White River; mains S$40-120 ✆ 7am-9.30pm) The mellowest spot in Honiara. Picture a lovely waterfront location, ample views of Savo, tropical décor and excellent organic food, with vegetarian options. Munch on the crunchy 'garden salad', tuck into a pizza (from 4pm), devour homemade cakes or sample the delicious fruit salad with honey and yoghurt. Lovely tea, coffee and juices, too. It's a shame the service is so slow. It's in White River, about 3km west of the centre.

Point Cruz Yacht Club (☎ 22500; Mendana Ave; mains S$40-80; ✆ lunch & dinner) A hot summer's night, a balmy sea breeze, a cold Solbrew and well-prepared fish 'n' chips – what better way to top off an active day on Guadalcanal? It's nothing fancy (think plastic chairs rather than teak furniture) and the choice is limited, but sizzling hot value for what you get.

Le Rendez Vous Restaurant (☎ 21205; King Solomon Hotel, Hibiscus Ave; mains S$90-120; ✆ breakfast, lunch & dinner) Beside the reception at King Solomon Hotel, the Rendez Vous serves good food in pleasant surrounds, with wooden tables and chairs under a thatched roof. From burgers to seafood and daily specials, the menu covers enough territory to suit most palates.

Capitana Restaurant (☎ 20071; Solomon Kitano Mendana Hotel, Mendana Ave; mains S$80-200; ✆ breakfast, lunch & dinner) If you have a sashimi or a yakitori craving that must be met while in the Solomons, head to the Capitana for authentic Japanese food. Next door, the Raratana Terrace Café serves classic Western dishes and boasts a terrace overlooking the sea.

Ocean View Restaurant (☎ 25009; Pacific Casino Hotel, Kukum; mains S$100-200; ✆ breakfast, lunch & dinner) The big dining room lacks character but the seafront terrace is inviting, with great views north over the Nggela Islands. Pizzas, meat dishes and seafood feature prominently on the menu.

ourpick Club Havanah (☎ 21737; Honiara Hotel, Chinatown; mains S$180-250; ☽ dinner) The G-spot for local gourmands. Georges, the adept French chef, is a true alchemist, judging from the ambitious *canette braisée à l'orange* (braised duckling with orange sauce). Leave room for the decadent *marquise aux deux chocolats* (white and black chocolate mousse). Good choice of Australian and French tipples, too. Next to the pool, a cheaper alternative is the Oasis Restaurant, open for breakfast, lunch and dinner.

For good Chinese fare, head to the pagoda-like **Hong Kong Palace** (☎ 23338; Hibiscus Ave; mains S$50-200; ☽ lunch & dinner). If you have a seafood fetish – crab, lobster, shellfish all prepared with a variety of sauces – opt for the stadium-sized **Sea King** (☎ 23678; off Mendana Ave; mains S$70-200; ☽ lunch & dinner Mon-Sat), near the central market.

You didn't think we would forget the ice cream addicts? If, like us, you think life is unbearable without a scoop of chocolate or vanilla, bookmark **Frangipani Ice** (Mendana Ave; ☽ 8am-4pm).

Drinking & Entertainment

If you've just arrived in the Solomon Islands, you'll find the bar scene pretty dull in Honiara. But those who've just arrived from several weeks in the provinces will feel like they're in Ibiza!

Check out the bars at Honiara's top-end hotels, which are popular and often offer live entertainment several times a week – bamboo bands, Micronesian hula dancers and karaoke. For a cold beer, nothing beats Point Cruz Yacht Club (opposite). For a fruit juice or a cuppa, head to Lime Lounge (opposite) and Raintree Café (opposite).

Shopping

There are a few prominent stores with better-than-average crafts on and around the main drag, including **Melanesian Handicrafts** (☎ 22189; Point Cruz) and **King Solomon's Handicraft** (Mendana Ave). It's also worth considering the gift shops at top-end hotels as well as the shop at the National Museum (p369).

For shell jewellery, head to the central market (p369). For CDs of local music, **DJ Graphics** (Mendana Ave) is the best bet.

EAST OF HONIARA

This side of Honiara is more built-up than the western side, with much development along the coastal road, but once you get inland to the central foothills you'll get a back-to-nature feel. Most of the WWII battlefields are in the vicinity of Henderson airport.

One of the star attractions east of Honiara includes **Mataniko Falls**, which feature a spectacular thundering of water down a cliff straight into a canyon below. They're accessible on foot only (see p374).

At **Mt Austen** (410m), a dirt track leads to a former **Japanese Observation Point**. Americans in WWII dubbed this spot Grassy Knoll. There's a plaque that explains the strategic importance of Mt Austen during WWII.

About 6.5km from Honiara is the turnoff south to the **Betikama SDA Mission**. The sprawling property comprises a large handicraft shop and a small museum with an outdoor collection of WWII debris.

A memorial at **Henderson Airport** honours US forces and their Pacific islander allies. About 100m to the west of the terminal is the scaffold-style **US WWII control tower**.

About 4.5km past the airport, a road heads inland and follows the west bank of the Tenaru River. After 1.5km there's Marine Hospital No 8, the first wartime hospital in Guadalcanal, in **Tenaru Village**. Tenaru is the launching pad for the **Tenaru Waterfalls** (see p374).

Back on the main road, continue west to **Tetere**. A few metres before reaching the shore of **Tetere Beach**, a dirt track to the west leads to 30 or more abandoned **amtracks** (amphibious troop carrier).

WEST OF HONIARA

Diving, a few beaches and WWII relics – this is what you'll find west of Honiara, up and around to Lambi Bay. The seas between Guadalcanal's northwestern coast and Savo Island were the site of constant naval battles between August 1942 and February 1943. By the time the Japanese finally withdrew, so many ships had been sunk it became known as Iron Bottom Sound. As a result, it's now a fantastic playground for divers. For more information on diving, see p371 and p77.

In **Poha**, take a peek at a **Japanese memorial**, with three marble slabs. There's also a rusty tank behind the memorial.

Mamara Beach has black sand and is OK for swimming and bathing.

TAKE A DIP!

Short of dreamy expanses of white sand on Guadalcanal, you can take a dip in lovely natural pools. But you've gotta earn these treats, as they are accessible on foot only. A guide is required for both. Your best bet is to go through a tour operator (see p371) in Honiara.

Mataniko Waterfalls

If you need to cool off, these little cascades beckon. The hike starts in Lelei village with a steep ascent to a ridge, followed by an easier stretch amid mildly undulating hills. Then you'll tackle a gruelling descent on a slippery muddy path to reach the floor of the little canyon where the Mataniko flows. You can float all the way back to Lelei if there's enough water – it can be a lot of fun.

It takes roughly two hours return to do this walk.

Tenaru Waterfalls

The gorgeous Tenaru Waterfalls reward visitors with a dreamy tropical seclusion and a refreshing swim in a snug natural pool. It's a fairly easy four-hour walk (return) from a tiny settlement about 2km south of Tenaru Village. The path follows the floor of the river valley and cuts across the river's many bends.

Bonegi, about 12km from Honiara, is famous for its **diving**, with two large Japanese wrecks lying just offshore. They are best known as Bonegi I and Bonegi II. There's also a black-sand **beach** that is suitable for a picnic. There's a *kastom* fee of S$25 per person.

Just past the Bonegi II site, at Tasivarongo Point, there's a bush track that heads inland and runs about 400m to a well-preserved **US Sherman tank**.

Another place synonymous with great **diving** is **Ruaniu** (also known as Bonegi III), about 4.5km west from Bonegi II. There's a 6500-tonne Japanese transport ship that just lies offshore.

About 25km from Honiara, a turn to the south from the coastal road brings you within 1km of the **Vilu Open-Air Museum** (S$25; ☽ dawn-dusk), which features US and Japanese memorials, Japanese field guns and the remains of several US aircraft.

Continue about 1km to **Ndoma**, another reputable **diving** area. Backtrack to the coastal road, then turn left for about 500m. The wreck of a US B-17 Flying Fortress bomber lies 100m off the dark-grey sand beach.

EASTERN GUADALCANAL

If you read this section, you've probably decided to wind down a few gears at **Tavanipupu Island Resort** (☎ 22586 in Honiara; www.tavanipupu .com; Tavanipupu Island; s incl 3 meals A$275). Run by an American woman, this quirky place (see the 'test' on the website) lies on a small island

off Guadalcanal's eastern tip. You're going to love this: six tastefully decorated, spacious bungalows scattered in a lovely coconut grove that overlooks the beach. There's no electricity, but kerosene lamps are provided. Food is a definite plus, with super fresh ingredients. Apart from snorkelling (gear provided), there aren't many things to do, but that's exactly why you want to stay here. Bookings are made through Guadalcanal Travel Services (p368) in Honiara. Rates include boat transfers from Marau airstrip (about 20 minutes).

Getting there is a bit tricky, as Solomon Airlines operates flights to Marau on a charter basis only (about S$1300 per person return).

THE WEATHERCOAST

Fast-flowing creeks tumble down the steep sides of tall, jagged mountains, some in a continuous chain of small cascades. Ridges covered in thick, emerald bush fall abruptly to the shore. And a sprinkling of sparsely populated villages dotted along the coast seem lost in time.

To visit this area, you'll have to blaze your own trail – literally – on foot or by boat, or combining both. There's no formal accommodation, only village stays. A guide is mandatory and can be arranged in villages.

The best source of information on hiking in the Weathercoast is *Treks and Adventures in the Solomon Islands*, which can be downloaded from the SIVB website (www.visitsolo mons.com.sb).

CENTRAL PROVINCE

Another world awaits just a two-hour boat ride from Honiara, either in the Nggela (Florida) group or on Savo. If you're serious about diving and snorkelling, bookmark the Nggela group. If you're more into hiking and cultural experiences, make a beeline for Savo. Better yet, combine the two!

Central Province also comprises the Russel Islands, but there's no tourist infrastructure.

NGGELA ISLANDS

pop 21,600 / area 1000 sq km

The Nggelas' main draws? Diving, snorkelling and an ultra-chilled atmosphere. The two main islands are Tulagi and Nggela Sule. They have rugged interiors, convoluted coastlines, long white-sand beaches and mangrove swamps.

Transport

Small cargo boats take two hours to ply between Tulagi and Honiara, charging about S$90 one way. In Honiara, they leave from the little beach next to Point Cruz Yacht Club.

Mangalonga (Mana)

Honiara's expats come to this small island near the northern end of the Nggela group to decompress at **Maravagi Resort** (☎/fax 29065; www.maravagiresort.com.sb; r A$60), and it's easy to understand why – the location is stunning, with gorgeous coral pinnacles that extend just off the dining room. The rustic leafhouse bungalows feature private bathrooms, breezy terraces, mozzie nets and electricity. Avoid the six charmless adjoining rooms at the back. Food (meals A$50 per day) is tasty. Village visits and snorkelling trips can be arranged. There are talks of opening a dive centre here – stay tuned. Boat transfers can be arranged from Honiara (from A$190). Credit cards are accepted.

Tulagi

In the middle of the Nggelas, Tulagi was the Solomons' former capital; it was also a Japanese base during WWII. This laid-back town has a few useful services for travellers, including a post office, an ANZ ATM (but bring cash in case it gets wobbly), a Telekom office and a couple of places to stay.

There's fabulous **diving** off Tulagi, including world-class wrecks (see p78) – think a destroyer, an oil tanker and a corvette. Based at Vanita Motel, **Tulagi Dive** (☎ 32131, 32052; www.tulagidive.com.sb) is a highly professional dive shop run by Australian Neil Yates. Prices start at S$400 for a reef dive, excluding gear. Transfers from Honiara can be arranged.

Most divers stay at the no-frills but well-kept **Vanita Motel** (☎ 32074; fax 32186; r without bathroom S$200, r with bathroom from S$250), next door to Tulagi Dive.

SAVO

pop 3500 / area 31 sq km

It's hard not to fall for the laid-back tempo and wild scenery of Savo. Though lying just 14km north of Guadalcanal, it's a world away from the capital. Imagine an active volcano with a pair of dormant craters, coconut groves, a narrow strip of grey-sand beach, a few hot springs that are accessible by foot, as well as a megapode field where hundreds of female birds lay their eggs in holes scratched into the hot sand.

Savo is also one of the most dependable locations in the Solomons to spot pods of dolphins, which usually congregate off the west coast.

Sunset Lodge (☎ 21213 in Honiara; Kuila; s incl 3 meals S$250), in Kuila village, features 20 tidy rooms, some with private bathrooms, in a fairly bland concrete building on a hillside (ask for a sea-facing room upstairs). The setting is enchanting, with the added appeal of tasty meals (hmm, will it be fresh fish or megapode eggs today?); transfers can be arranged from Honiara.

WESTERN PROVINCE

pop 68,000 / area 5330 sq km

You're heading to the Western Province? Lucky you! It has everything in spades, from sensational diving to historical sites and hiking to village visits. It's a definite highlight of a Solomon Islands trip, offering the whole palette of impressive landscapes and panoramas – pristine lagoons, tropical islets, tall volcanic islands, lush jungles, white-sand bars and beaches and turquoise coral shallows. Those looking for some creature comforts will find good tourist infrastructure (by Solomon Islands' standards), with soothing ecolodges and resorts where you can drink in the majestic scenery from a tranquil sundeck.

SOLOMON ISLANDS

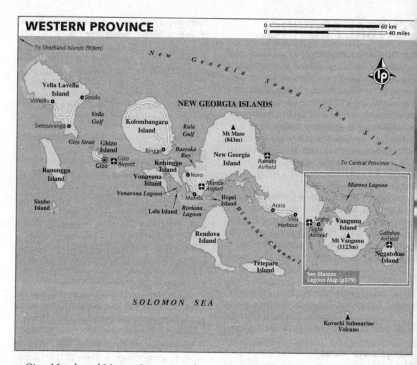

Gizo, Munda and Marovo Lagoon are the three unmissable destinations in 'the West'. Thanks to reliable inter-island boat and plane services, they can easily be combined and toured at a leisurely pace.

WEST NEW GEORGIA

pop 22,000 / area 2145 sq km

The island of New Georgia, the biggest of the Western Province, and its neighbours, including Vonavona, Kohinggo and Tetepare, have been gaining in popularity over the last few years. Ghizo and Marovo, watch your backs! West New Georgia has its fair share of attractions as well as reliable accommodation options, a hatful of historic sights and thrilling dive sites. And there's Tetepare. Ah, Tetepare...

Munda

New Georgia's largest settlement (though we're hardly talking Manhattan), on New Georgia itself, makes a suitable base for exploring this part of the province. It has the airport terminal, a police station and a well-equipped hospital. The

post office (��� 8.30am-noon, 1-3.30pm) is in the centre, as is the **Bank South Pacific** (☎ 62177; ����� 8.30am-3pm Mon-Fri), where you can change cash and travellers cheques. The ANZ branch, in a building close to the post office, has an ATM. Check your emails at **Telekom** (per hr S$48; ☉ 8am-noon & 1-4.30pm Mon-Fri).

SIGHTS

Apart from the tiny market, sights are scarce in Munda, and there's no beach. History buffs will consider the three small private **museums** of WWII relics, though 'museum' is an optimistic description – expect leafhut houses. The one closest to Agnes Lodge is run by Gordon Beti (no sign; ask for exact location); the second, and most interesting, is further east along the road, just behind the soccer field, a 20-minute walk from Agnes Lodge. Run by Alphy Barney Paulson, who speaks good English, it features lots of utensils, ammunition, machine guns, shells, crockery, helmets, shavers and knives, among other things, all left behind by the Japanese and the Americans. The third one, a further 10-minute walk on the same road, is operated by Bolton Lasu. *Kastom* fees are S$25 each.

Text on left margin: **SOLOMON ISLANDS**

To get to the museums from Agnes Lodge, go to the main road, walk about 200m to the east and take the dirt road to the left (just before the 'EC Trading' sign).

ACTIVITIES

On the **diving** scene, Munda seems to play second fiddle to the better-marketed Ghizo island or Marovo Lagoon. But after having checked out five dive sites here, we say: injustice! New Georgia has an exciting selection of wrecks, drop-offs, reefs and underwater caves. Based at Agnes Lodge, **Dive Munda** (☎ 62156; www.munda dive.com) is owned by a friendly British couple, and the office is run by lovely Ahi. Sunga, the divemaster, is very knowledgeable about diving in the Western Province. Two morning boat dives costs A$160 with tank and weights, or A$190 with all equipment. At most dive sites, snorkelling (A$50) is possible.

TOURS

The easiest way to get a broad look at the delights around West New Georgia is to take a half- or one-day tour. Based at Agnes Lodge (below), **Go West Tours** (☎ 62180; 🕑 7am-5pm Mon-Fri, 8am-4pm Sat) offers a wide range of excursions into Roviana and Vonavona Lagoons (including Skull Island), to Holupuru Falls, and various WWII sites (especially the relics at Enoghae, Baeroko Bay, Kohinggo and Vila Point) and river trips. Prices start at S$500 for two people (half a day). You can also ask to be left on Hopei Island, a ten-minute boat ride from Agnes Lodge. Hopei Island has a nice little arc of white sand, good snorkelling and lots of shade – the perfect place to play Robinson Crusoe.

SLEEPING & EATING

Agnes Lodge (☎ 62133; www.agneslodge.com.sb; dm A$18-25, d A$65-130, ste A$170; 🖼) A traveller favourite for years, Agnes Lodge is very well run, with an ethical twist: it's locally owned and staff are shareholders. Accommodation-wise, 'there's something for everybody', says New Zealander and manager Don Croft, who ensures the place is kept shipshape. On a budget? Opt for a room with shared facilities in the Tatangala or Zazala wings. Want a few more creature comforts? The renovated rooms in the Naru wing are your answer. In search of more privacy? Upgrade to one of the eight Ibibu cottages, which are large and comfy, with air-con, or to a seafront suite. The place isn't luxurious but is in top nick, the

vibe in the adjacent bar fun and casual and the lobster Mornay served at the on-site restaurant legendary. It's right on the waterfront (no beach, alas), a short walk from the airstrip. Credit cards are accepted. Wi-fi.

GETTING THERE & AWAY

The minuscule airport terminal has a **Solomon Airlines** (☎ 62152) counter.

Solomon Airlines connects Munda with Honiara (from S$1070, daily), Gizo (from S$625, daily) and Seghe (from S$625, six times a week). Flights go twice-weekly to Ramata (from S$625).

Go West Tours (☎ 62180) has a shuttle service to Gizo (S$200, two hours, three weekly) stopping at Noro and Ringgi on Kolombangara en route. It departs Munda at 7.30am and returns the same day. **MV Pelican Express** (☎ 28104 in Honiara) doesn't pull into Munda on its Sunday Honiara–Gizo route, but does stop at Noro (from Honiara S$400), from where you can organise transport to Agnes Lodge (reservations necessary). **MV Solomon Express** (☎ 28064 in Honiara) does the same route on Friday for the same fares.

Around New Georgia

If you want to dunk yourself in a natural pool, head to the 10m **Holupuru Falls**, east of Munda. Outdoorsy types will tackle **Mt Bau**, about 9km inland. You'll need a guide (ask at Agnes Lodge, left).

There's no reason to stop in **Noro**, 16km northwest of Munda up the Diamond Narrows, which is home to the large government-owned Soltai fish cannery.

In Baeroko Bay you'll see the *Casi Maru*, a **sunken Japanese freighter** near the shore (and a dive site). **Enoghae**, at the jutting northern lip of the bay, has several large **Japanese WWII anti-aircraft guns** still hidden in the scrub.

Roviana Lagoon

Extending 52km eastwards from Munda, **Roviana Lagoon** has many small idyllic islets formed from coral shoals. The best way to enjoy them is to join a lagoon tour. Contact Go West Tours (left) in Munda or Zipolo Habu Resort (p378) on Lola Island.

Vonavona Lagoon

This beautiful lagoon extends for 28km between the tiny islets of Blackett Strait islets and the long, sandy island of Nusaghele.

A truly spooky sight, **Skull Island** is the final resting place for the skulls of countless vanquished warriors, as well as a shrine for the skulls of Rendovan chiefs.

On **Lola Island**, about 20 minutes by boat from Munda, **Zipolo Habu Resort** (☎ 62178; www.zipolohabu.com.sb; bungalows A$130-200) attracts Ernest Hemingway fans, surfies and divers. The four standard all-wood bungalows are large but fairly basic and share facilities, while the more expensive deluxe unit boasts a private bathroom with hot shower, 24-hour electricity and lagoon views. The owners plan to renovate and build another deluxe unit, but the defining factor is the atmosphere, which is relaxed and uncomplicated. The meal package costs A$80 per day. Zipolo Habu offers village tours, sportfishing and surf charters. Return boat transfer to Munda costs A$120 per boatload. Divers can be picked up at the resort by Dive Munda. Yachties are welcome – for a drink, a meal, or just to relax (VHF 68).

Tetepare Island

If snorkelling with dolphins, swimming with dugongs, spotting crocodiles and tagging turtles has you dashing for your jungle apparel, then Tetepare Island could be your place. This large rainforest island is one of the Solomons' conservation jewels and feels like a piece of Eden. It's ranked as a fantastic place to chill out and watch wildlife.

The **Tetepare Descendants' Association** (☎ 62163 in Munda; www.tetepare.org; s incl 3 meals S$350), which manages this heaven for ecotourists, welcomes visitors in its two simple yet genuinely ecofriendly leafhouses (solar power, shared facilities, no air-con) that rise just metres from the ethereal green forest. What makes this place extra special is the host of environmentally friendly activities available. These are at an extra cost, but you'll be accompanied by trained guides. Food is fresh, copious and organic. Minuses: the duration and cost of transfers (two hours from Munda, S$1600 per boatload one-way).

MAROVO LAGOON

On New Georgia's eastern side, Marovo Lagoon is the world's finest double barrier-enclosed lagoon, bordered by the large New Georgia and Vangunu Islands on one side and a double line of long barrier islands on the other. It contains hundreds of beautiful small islands,

most of which are covered by coconut palms and rainforest and surrounded by coral.

Here you can visit laid-back villages and explore *tambu* (sacred) sites, picnic on deserted islands, take a lagoon tour or a fishing trip, hear the myths and legends of the islanders, meet master carvers, dive in fish soup, kayak across the lagoon or take a walk across rainforest or up awesome summits.

Don't expect paradise on earth, though. Marovo lagoon is *not* a beach holiday destination – truly idyllic stretches of sand are almost nonexistent – and years of intense logging have left their scars, literally. After rain, run-off discolours the lagoon water, which changes from a brilliant aqua to a bluey-brown. Because of contentious logging issues, Marovo Lagoon was not listed as a World Heritage site.

Information

There are no phones in the Marovo Lagoon area, but bookings for resorts and lodges can be made through SIVB (p393) or the main tour operators in Honiara (p371). There's no bank; bring a stash of cash.

Transport

GETTING THERE & AWAY

Air

There are two main gateways to Marovo: Seghe (for North Marovo Lagoon) and Nggatokae Island (for South Marovo Lagoon). Flights connect Seghe to Honiara (S$950), Munda (S$623) and Gizo (S$730) about six days a week.

Nggatokae is serviced from Honiara (from S$950, twice weekly) and Seghe (or Munda, twice weekly).

Boat

Both **MV Pelican Express** (☎ 28104 in Honiara) and **MV Solomon Express** (☎ 28064 in Honiara) stop at Mbunikalo (S$300, 20 minutes from Nggatokae), Nggasini (in central Marovo; S$350) and Seghe (S$440) on their way to Gizo. *MV Pelican Express* plies this route on Sunday (return on Monday) while *MV Solomon Express* runs on Friday (return on Sunday).

Activities

For **diving** fiends, a trip to Marovo Lagoon is a life goal, but there's plenty of exhilarating dives for both experts and novices. Here's

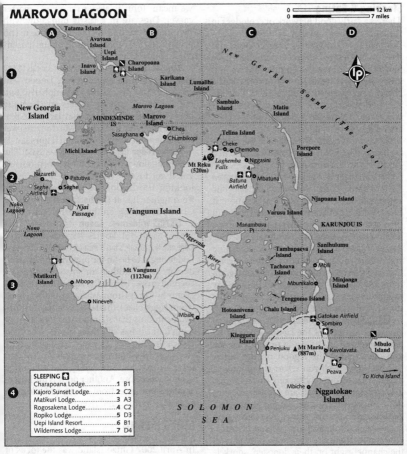

MAROVO LAGOON

SLEEPING
Charapoana Lodge	1 B1
Kajoro Sunset Lodge	2 C2
Matikuri Lodge	3 A3
Rogosakena Lodge	4 C2
Ropiko Lodge	5 D3
Uepi Island Resort	6 B1
Wilderness Lodge	7 D4

the menu: channels, caves, drop-offs, coral gardens, bommies, clouds of technicolour fish (and yes, sharks are part of the package) and a few wrecks thrown in for good measure. See the diving chapter (p78) for more information.

Marovo Lagoon has two state-of-the-art dive centres.

Solomon Dive Adventures (satellite ☎ 8816 315 63887; www.solomondiveadventures.com; Peava) Based in South Marovo Lagoon, a 10-minute walk from Wilderness Lodge (p380). Fun dives cost from US$40 to US$60, and gear rental is an extra US$55.

Uepi Island Resort (in Australia ☎ +61 3 9787 7904; www.uepi.com; Uepi Island) Offers stunning dives (from A$65) throughout North Marovo Lagoon. Caters mainly to resort guests.

With hundreds of lovely sites scattered throughout the lagoon, **snorkelling** is equally impressive. Lodges can organise lagoon tours and snorkelling trips, which cost anything from S$30 to S$150 per person depending on distance and duration.

Kayaking is probably the most entrancing way to explore Marovo Lagoon – and the most environmentally sound as well. Uepi Island Resort can arrange multiday kayaking trips.

If you've got itchy feet, don't forget your **walking** shoes. Consider scaling Mt Mariu (887m) on Nggatokae (two days), climbing the hill that lords over Chea Village on Marovo island (two hours) or tackling Mt Reku (520m) on Vangunu (half a day).

Sleeping & Eating

There's a fairly good network of ecolodges in the lagoon. These low-key, family-run establishments are great places to meet locals and have an authentic cultural experience. Brace yourself for thin walls, lumpy pillows and a few creepy-crawlies, but lap up the rustic charm and interesting discussions that are part and parcel of the 'lodge' experience. If you want to pamper yourself, opt for Uepi Island Resort or Wilderness Lodge.

Most places overlook the lagoon but there's no beach. The following places are listed in a clockwise order, from west to east.

Matikuri Lodge (Matikuri Island; s S$100, per bungalow S$130) Matikuri Lodge's drawcard is its bucolic authenticity and soothing sense of isolation, at the western arc of Marovo Lagoon. Digs are in three island-style bungalows that face the sea; the four rooms in the main house are more ordinary. Added to this is the over-water dining area where you can recline amid lush vegetation in perfect serenity. Guided walks, lagoon tours and visits to Seghe's market on Tuesday can be organised. Boat transfers to Seghe airstrip (20 minutes) are S$70 plus fuel.

our pick Uepi Island Resort (Uepi; www.uepi.com) Anchored on one of the lagoon's barrier islands, exposed on one side to the open sea and overlooking the lagoon on the other, this extremely well run resort is the kind of haven stressed-out city slickers dream about. The spacious bungalows are comfortable, but not flash, and are scattered amid lovely bush gardens and coconut palms. The ethos here is laid-back, ecological and activity-oriented. Divers rave about the sensational dive sites in the channel right on their doorstep, snorkellers make the most of the stunning house reef and kayakers explore the lagoon. Perks include a bar, a breezy dining room with excellent meals, a dive shop and village tours. It's terrific for honeymooners and families, too.

Charapoana Lodge (Charapoana; s incl 3 meals S$330) The owners of this well-regarded ecolodge sadly passed away in 2008, and it was due to be taken over by the family when we visited. It's just across the passage from Uepi Island, so you can dive at Uepi Island Resort if space is available.

Kajoro Sunset Lodge (Vangunu; s incl 3 meals S$250) John Wein, the loquacious owner, is something of a character in Marovo. Launch into the contentious issue of the wrongdoings of local logging companies and you'll see what

we mean. John is also a renowned master carver. Digs are in a rustic bungalow with two simple rooms facing the lagoon (no beach). Various tours can be organised, including a trek up to Mt Reku.

Rogosakena Lodge (Vangunu; s incl 3 meals S$300) Here the veranda overlooks the lagoon – so soothing. The two rooms are simply laid out, but welcoming and the owners are charming hosts. Ask for the room that faces the sea. They'll take you by boat to Mbatuna market if you happen to be there on a Thursday.

Ropiko Lodge (Nggatokae; s incl 3 meals S$350) The two bungalows here are a bit worn out, so you'll get to stay in the main house overlooking the lagoon. A wrecked Japanese Zero fighter lies at the back of the property. Good snorkelling on the nearby reef.

our pick Wilderness Lodge (☎ satellite in the Solomon Islands +61 145 125 948; www.thewilderness lodge.org; Nggatokae; s incl 3 meals A$130) Wilderness Lodge ought to be on the prescription list of all doctors as an antidote for stress. Nestled in a coconut grove right by the lagoon and run efficiently by Corey (from Australia) and Waelinah (from Nggatokae), this large leafhouse features two bedrooms that share a bathroom. Luxury it ain't, but it has charm in spades. The food is healthy, there's 24-hour solar-generated electricity, the house reef is magnificent and there are excellent snorkelling and swimming spots just offshore. Another draw is the host of activities available, from diving and hiking to crocodile-spotting and river trips.

GHIZO ISLAND

pop 6000 / area 37 sq km

In April 2007 Ghizo Island was the focus of international media when it was severely hit by a tsunami caused by an underwater earthquake. The island has since recovered and has regained its status as the Solomons 'tourist epicentre', but this is not saying much.

Little Ghizo island is a dwarf next to its neighbours, but it has the Solomons' second-biggest 'city', Gizo (pronounced the same, spelt differently) – the most developed area outside the capital.

Transport

GETTING THERE & AWAY

Air

The **Solomon Airlines** (☎ 60173; Middenway Rd; ☒ 8.30am-4.30pm Mon-Fri, according to flight departures and arrivals on weekends) office in Gizo is near the police station and the airfield is on Nusatupe Island; the five-minute boat trip between the airfield and town costs S$50. Up to three daily flights link Gizo to Honiara (from S$1250). There are also four weekly flights between Gizo and Munda (S$650), and three weekly flights between Gizo and Seghe (S$710). From Gizo, other flights go to Choiseul and Shortland (both S$780, three weekly).

Boat
The passenger boats **MV Pelican Express** (☎ 28104) and **MV Solomon Express** (☎ 28064) are an excellent alternative to flying. They do a Honiara–Gizo route taking in Mbunikalo, Gasini and Seghe in Marovo Lagoon; and Noro en route. The 12-hour Honiara–Gizo trip costs S$500 (S$550 1st class upstairs). *MV Pelican Express* plies this route on Sunday (return on Monday) while *MV Solomon Express* runs on Friday (return on Sunday).

Go West Tours (☎ 62180; Agnes Lodge, Munda) runs a three-weekly shuttle boat connecting Munda to Gizo (and vice versa) via Noro (S$200, two hours).

Gizo
pop 4500
Apart from a few churches and the bustling market on the waterfront, there's little to see in Gizo. The architecture is charmless, with a smattering of buildings gently rusting away under the sun. The main reason to come here is for the diving and, increasingly, surfing.

The 2007 tsunami did give Gizo a good licking, but the town fared better than the rest of the island and has benefited from the presence of international aid organisations.

INFORMATION
Credit cards are accepted by tour operators and better hotels (expect a 5% surcharge). The Gizo Hotel (p383) and PT 109 (p383) have wi-fi access.

ANZ Bank (☎ 60262; Middenway Rd; ☻ 9am-4pm Mon-Fri) Has an ATM (Visa and MasterCard)

Antech Computer Ltd (Middenway Rd; per hr S$50; ☻ 8.30am-5pm Mon-Thu, 8.30am-4.30pm Fri) Fairly good connections

Bank South Pacific (Middenway Rd; ☻ 8.30am-3pm Mon-Fri) Changes cash and travellers cheques

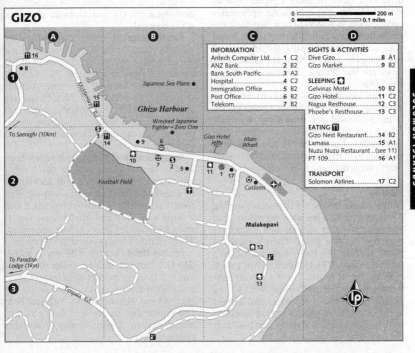

Hospital (☎ 60224; Middenway Rd)

Immigration Office (☼ 8am-noon & 1-4.30pm Mon-Fri) Behind ANZ Bank. Can issue a visitor's permit if you proceed from Bougainville (PNG) and the Shortlands.

Telekom (Middenway Rd; per hr S$48; ☼ 8.30am-noon & 1-4.30pm) Sells phonecards, prepaid mobile phone cards and Bumblebee (wi-fi) cards. Internet access is available too.

ACTIVITIES
Diving & Snorkelling

Let's get one question out of the way: what was the impact on the marine ecosystem of the tsunami that hit the Gizo area in 2007? Well, large tracts of reefs were battered and a smattering of iconic sites, including Hotspot and Grand Central Station, lost much of their appeal, but overall the level of destruction was relatively low. See p78 for more information on dive sites.

Danny and Kerrie Kennedy have run **Dive Gizo** (☎ 60253; www.divegizo.com; Middenway Rd), a reputable dive outfit at the western end of town, since 1985. They will probably meet you at the airport or wharf and drive you to your digs. You'll pay A$150 for a two-tank dive, which also includes a picnic (add an extra A$30 for gear rental). An open-water certification is A$630. Their two-tank organisation is a winning formula: you spend your surface interval on a secluded island or having lunch at Fatboys (opposite). Most dives are less than a 20-minute boat ride from Gizo.

Sanbis Resort (opposite) has its own little dive shop, which caters for the resort's guests.

In the mood for **snorkelling**? Kennedy Island, just off Fatboys, is your answer. Take the shuttle to Fatboys (S$90), hire snorkelling gear (S$70) at the resort and snorkel to your heart's content.

Surfing

Ghizo Island is still a fairly secret surfing Nirvana, despite a few glowing reports that were published in various surf magazines over the last few years. There's excellent point surfing off Pailongge, on Ghizo's southern coast. The October-to-April swell rises to 2m or more. There's a great left-hander nearer Titiana village, with a long paddle out to the reef's edge, and a right at Pailongge. Dive Gizo is a good source of information and had plans to rent boards at the time of research.

Hiking

Climbing up to the crater's rim on Kolombangara (the big island facing Gizo) is an exhilarating two-day/one-night hike. We met an Australian couple at the Gizo Hotel who had just completed the climb, and we quote: 'This was the most arduous hike in our lives. It's wet and muddy all the way up, it's steep, there are lots of mosquitoes and the path is irregular. But the atmosphere and views are truly awesome. We wouldn't do it twice, but we'll never forget the experience.'

You'll need guides and porters. Dive Gizo (left) can arrange logistics (about S$1000 per person, including transfers from Gizo).

SLEEPING
In Gizo

Phoebe's Resthouse (☎ 60161; per person S$100) Phoebe's, we can't blame you for your foam mattresses and spartan rooms with shared facilities because there are stunning ocean views from the veranda and the place is super-quiet. Plus the large airy common area with kitchen is a good place to socialise with medical students from the UK and Australia who work at the hospital.

Paradise Lodge (☎ 60024; dm/d with private facilities S$110/265, q S$390) At Paradise Lodge you've got the advantage of commanding views of the ocean and absolute quietness. But it's a 15-minute walk to town (or a 30-minute tedious slog uphill, or a S$20 taxi ride). Dorms are clean but feel a bit claustrophobic; upgrade to the bigger rooms upstairs. If you don't fancy cooking, you can order breakfast (S$45) and evening meals (S$110).

Nagua Guesthouse (☎ 60012; r with shared bathroom S$220, self-contained air-con s & d S$330; ☒) A coconut's throw from Phoebe's, this homely little guesthouse has a series of wood-panelled rooms interestingly laid-out (rooms 8 and 9 boast a balcony and lovely ocean views) and a few ordinary three- to four-bed rooms. There's a functional communal kitchen too.

Gelvinas Motel (☎ 60276; Middenway Rd; d S$450; ☒) Gelvinas couldn't be closer to the action – it faces the market stalls (expect some noise in the morning). Rooms are simple but spacious and well turned out, with firm beds and immaculate sheets, and there's a communal kitchen. A good-quality, if not very exciting, choice.

SOLOMON ISLANDS

Gizo Hotel (☎ 60199; www.gizohotel.com; Middenway Rd; r S$850-1000; ✕ ☀) This full-service hotel is Gizo's best, right on the main drag. Relatively pricey but worth it; the neat grounds include a reputable restaurant and bar, plus a lovely pool amid lush vegetation at the back – very relaxing. Some rooms have sea views, others open onto the garden and the pool, and they're all comfortable and well equipped. Wi-fi.

Mbabanga Island

our pick **Fatboys** (☎ 60095; www.fatboysgizo.com; bungalows A$190) This exquisite property had just changed ownership when we passed through – it now belongs to Gizo Hotel (which is still good news). The five bungalows blend tropical hardwoods, traditional leaf, rich textiles and elegant furniture. The narrow beach is average but the snorkelling is sensational. The defining factor, however, is the lovely bar and restaurant directly over the exquisite waters of Vonavona Lagoon. A good place to throw away your Blackberry and tune into island time.

Sanbis Resort (☎ 66313; www.solomonwatersport .com; per bungalow incl 3 meals A$420) Sweeeet! This delightful place with green credentials (all waste is recycled, the lighting is solar-powered) has six beachside bungalows all tastefully designed, blending blond-wood and dark-wood materials, and come equipped with quality furnishings. Enjoy a sundowner in the overwater bar area, snorkel over healthy reefs and a recently sunk shipwreck just offshore and treat yourself to a healthy meal. The catch? The atmosphere is a bit staid. Wi-fi.

EATING & DRINKING

Lamasa (Middenway Rd; mains S$30-40; ✓ lunch Mon-Fri) This little den on the main drag has brilliant value fish 'n' chips.

Gizo Nest Restaurant (Middenway Rd; mains S$30-70; ✓ breakfast, lunch & dinner Mon-Sat) You wouldn't guess it from the unprepossessing surrounds, but this place serves decent Chinese dishes. Pity about the slow service.

PT 109 (Middenway Rd; mains S$60-100; ✓ lunch Mon-Fri) Named after John F Kennedy's WWII patrol boat, which was sunk off Gizo, and in a great waterfront location, this place has relaxed vibes. A blackboard displays a few simple dishes, such as local fish, chicken or fish 'n' chips. You can drop by for a cooling drink in the afternoon. Sometimes it's open for dinner.

Fatboys (☎ 60095; Mbanga Island; mains S$50-120; ✓ lunch & dinner) What a view! The dining room is on a pier that hovers over the turquoise waters of Vonavona Lagoon. Tuck into crayfish or fish 'n' chips, then don a mask, a snorkel and fins (S$50) and swim over sandy shallows that extend onto Kennedy Island. Fatboys is accessible only by boat from Gizo; take the daily shuttle at 11am (S$100 one-way).

Nuzu Nuzu Restaurant (☎ 60199; Gizo Hotel, Middenway Rd; mains S$80-150; ✓ breakfast, lunch & dinner) The nexus of pretty much everything in Gizo, Nuzu Nuzu Restaurant offers well-prepared food along with zero pretension and laid-back, quirky service. No culinary extravaganza, but tasty seafood (hmm, lobster!), fresh fish and giant meat dishes. The menu changes daily, as displayed on a handwritten blackboard. Excellent breakfasts, too. Entertainment is offered at weekends when a Gilbertese group puts a dance show.

ISLANDS AROUND GHIZO

War debris and natural attractions are the main drawcards of the islands surrounding Ghizo. Also known as Nduke, **Kolombangara** features a classic cone-shaped volcano that rises to 1770m; it's a two-day hike to the top and back. **Simbo** has two active volcanic cones in the south. **Vila Point** was an important WWII Japanese base, and you can still see guns in the bush.

Mountainous **Vella Lavella** is dominated by the dormant volcano Mt Tambisala, and it is noted for its bird life.

MALAITA PROVINCE

pop 123,000 / area 4300 sq km

Despite its huge potential, tourism has yet to take off in this fascinating province that sees only a small stream of adventure travellers. In the main destinations (Auki, Malu'u and Langa Langa Lagoon) there's enough infrastructure to travel safely on your own. Elsewhere it's virtually uncharted territory.

MALAITA ISLAND

pop 90,000 / area 3840 sq km

Easily reached from Guadalcanal, Malaita is a secretive island with narrow coastal

SOLOMON ISLANDS

plains, deep valleys, sharp ridges and a rugged island interior that rises to 1303m at Mt Kolovrat. It's a great place to 'get lost' in.

Malaitan people have long migrated to other parts of the Solomon Islands, particularly to Guadalcanal. Even today, they are very well represented in Solomons business, politics and power. It was resentment towards these successes and incursions that led to the ethnic tensions of the late 1990s (see p362). They are a dynamic people with deep traditions, rich culture and a history of anti-authoritarianism that manifested itself in the Kwaio Rebellion (see p362) and the postwar Marching Rule movement (p362).

Malaita has artificial islands that support whole communities. It has sacred caves and rivers, and strong traditions in carving and seafaring. Animist and ancestor worship is also widespread. The crowded artificial islands in Langa Langa and Lau Lagoons (see below) are highlights.

Transport
GETTING THERE & AWAY
Solomon Airlines (☎ 40173; Auki) flies from Honiara to Auki (from S$700, once to twice daily). The Solomon Airlines office is based at Auki Motel.

On Friday **MV Pelican Express** (☎ 28104 in Honiara, 38165 in Malaita Island) runs from Honiara to Auki (S$200) and returns on Saturday. **MV**

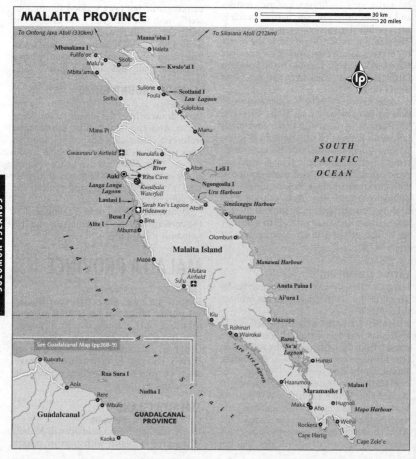

Solomon Express (☎ 28064 in Honiara) runs from Honiara to Auki (S$160) on Tuesday, and onwards to Afio near Malaita's southern tip (S$260), returning on Wednesday.

GETTING AROUND

Auki's Gwaunaru'u airfield is 10km from town. A ride into town costs S$20 on the Solomon Airlines bus that meets every flight.

Very few vehicles travel Malaita's 325km of pot-holed roads outside Auki. The roads are appalling. Trucks carrying people and goods up the 'north road' towards Malu'u leave from the wharfs in the early morning. Others leave for Foula, Atori and Atoifi across the island.

Auki

pop 4500

Auki is an intriguing hodgepodge of ramshackle shops, modern administrative buildings and houses on stilts that are curled around a wonderfully shaped bay, at the foot of jungle-clad hills. Wandering its quiet streets, you wouldn't guess it's the Solomons' third-largest town; everything moves slowly except at the lively market and the bustling wharf.

An **ANZ** (☎ 40160; off Loboi Ave; ☒ 9am-4pm Mon-Fri) with an ATM (Visa and MasterCard) and a **Bank South Pacific** (☎ 40484; off Loboi Ave; ☒ 8.30am-3pm Mon-Fri) are in the town centre and change major currencies and travellers cheques. There's also a little **post office** (☒ 8am-noon & 1-4.30pm Mon-Fri). Get online at **Telekom** (per hr S$48; ☒ 8.30am-noon & 1-4pm Mon-Fri).

SIGHTS

One definite must-see is the friendly fishing village of **Lilisiana**, about 1.5km from the centre. With its traditional-style houses raised on stilts over the shore, it's photogenic to boot. An hour's walk east of Auki is **Riba Cave**, with stalagmites, several large subterranean chambers and an underground river.

If you need to refresh yourself, nothing can beat **Kwaibala Waterfall**, about 3km from the centre.

SLEEPING & EATING

Auki Motel (☎ 40014; fax 40059; Loboi Ave; r S$130-450; ☒) This little number has the best facilities in town, bathrooms are in good nick, and it features a range of rooms to suit all budgets. Downstairs rooms are a tad cramped but have private bathrooms and shared air-con (the air-con unit is in the corridor). Pity about the flimsy mattresses in the cheaper, three-bed rooms upstairs, but you'll survive if you pile up two mattresses. The menu at the **restaurant** (mains from S$40; ☒ breakfast, lunch & dinner) varies according to what's available. No alcohol is allowed on the premises.

Auki Lodge (☎ 40079; Batabu Rd; s/d S$340/440; ☒) 'Lodge' sounds pretentious for what you get. Think uninspired architecture and rooms with very ordinary interiors.

Rarasu (☎ 40280; off Maasina Rulu Pde; mains from S$40; ☒ lunch & dinner Mon-Sat, dinner Sun) The only independent restaurant in town is a nice surprise. Choice is very limited, but the dishes are fresh and generous. Rarasu has rooms for rent next door (from S$200).

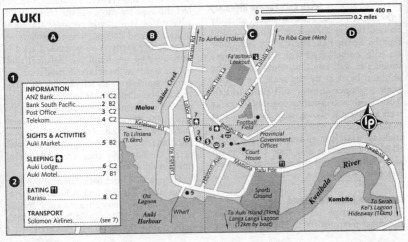

AUKI

0 ____ 400 m
0 ____ 0.2 miles

INFORMATION
ANZ Bank.....................1 C2
Bank South Pacific........2 B2
Post Office...................3 C2
Telekom......................4 C2

SIGHTS & ACTIVITIES
Auki Market.................5 B2

SLEEPING
Auki Lodge..................6 C2
Auki Motel...................7 B1

EATING
Rarasu........................8 C2

TRANSPORT
Solomon Airlines..........(see 7)

To Airfield (10km)
To Riba Cave (4km)
Fa'asitoro Lookout
Sikiea Creek
Rarasu Rd
Cotton Tree La
Lofafa Rd
Lokafa La
Molou
Kelakwai Rd
Loboi Ave
To Lilisiana (1.6km)
Laitaba Rd
Batabu Rd
Football Field
Provincial Government Offices
Court House
Maasina Rulu Pde
Hibiscus Ave
Osi Lagoon
Sports Ground
Kwaibala River
Kwaibala Rd
Kombito
To Serah Kei's Lagoon Hideaway (16km)
Wharf
Auki Harbour
To Auki Island (1km) Langa Langa Lagoon (12km by boat)

ARTIFICIAL ISLANDS

Malaita has a large number of artificial islands, particularly in Langa Langa and Lau Lagoons. Some of these date from the 1550s and new ones are built each year. They were originally built as a defence against head-hunters and tribal war.

Stones from the lagoon floor are collected and piled on a sandbar or reef until they reach around 2m above the high-tide mark. Sand is spread around, houses are built and coconuts palms are planted.

The largest islands exceed 1 sq km in size and tend to be very crowded; some are surrounded by a coral wall. Most, however, are very small and have room for only a few houses.

Langa Langa Lagoon

If there's one not-to-be-missed place on Malaita, it has to be Langa Langa Lagoon. Extending from seven to 32km south of Auki, the lagoon is famous for its artificial islands, particularly Laulasi and Busu. Langa Langa Lagoon is a strong centre for traditional activities, especially shell-money making. It's also renowned for shipbuilding.

Caveat: 'lagoon' is not necessarily synonymous with 'turquoise', as you'll quickly realise. Waters here are more chocolatey than sapphire, and you also won't find stunning beaches to sun yourself on. Instead you come here for the laid-back tempo. And not to forget the magical setting. And the supremely relaxing **Serah Kei's Lagoon Hideaway** (☎ 40344, 72344; s incl 3 meals S$160-200), an aptly named retreat that's run with grace and flair by Serah Kei. There's one bungalow on stilts embellished with a few feminine touches as well as a four-room house. The ablution block is tip-top with, joy of joys, both a proper shower and flush toilets. Your host will arrange lagoon tours as well as cultural shows, such as grass-skirt making, a demonstration of shell-money making and leaf sawing (costing from S$200). There are also nice carvings on sale. Call Serah and she will arrange transfers from Auki.

Northern Malaita Island

The 'north road' leaves Auki and follows the coast from Sisifiu to Sisolo, providing lovely sea views. The welcoming subprovincial headquarters of **Malu'u** is an obvious stop between Auki (four hours over 82km of passable road) and Lau Lagoon at the 'head road' two hours away. You can spend the night at **Malu'u Lodge** (s S$120), which has fan-cooled rooms, a kitchen and shared facilities.

And now, **Lau Lagoon**. This 35km-long lagoon contains more than 60 artificial islands. There's no formal accommodation, but you can arrange your stay in a village; ask the chief.

Central & Eastern Malaita Island

There's a road across the mountainous interior to the east coast around Atori that is washed out in the mid-year wet season.

It's possible to visit the traditional Kwaio people who inhabit the rugged east-central part of Malaita and worship sharks. Shark-calling rituals climax with a boy sitting astride a shark and riding it around the lagoon. The Kwaio stronghold is between Uru Harbour and Olomburi. Check with SIVB in Honiara (p368), which can give advice on guides and other matters.

RENNELL & BELLONA PROVINCE

pop 2400 / area 629 sq km

If, after visiting Malaita, Guadalcanal and the Central and Western Provinces, you still feel the urge for more off-the-beaten-track adventures, you should consider travelling to Rennell and Bellona, where travellers are an absolute rarity. You will need a bit of DIY spirit to surmount the logistical challenges (such as basic accommodation, no public transport, no telephones etc), but you will be amply rewarded because life in this region is so different from that in the rest of the Solomon Islands. Both Rennell and Bellona islands are Polynesian outliers, sharing similar languages and cultures. Geologically they are both rocky, uplifted-coral atolls.

Though still rural backwaters at the time of research, Rennell and Bellona will embrace modernity some time soon – mobile phones and an ATM should have made their mark during the lifetime of this book.

RENNELL ISLAND

pop 1400 / area 276 sq km

Surrounded by high cliffs, Rennell is a fine example of a raised coral atoll and a Shangri-la for both ecotourists and twitchers. At 130 sq km, World Heritage-listed **Lake Te'Nggano**, located in the southeast, is the South Pacific's largest expanse of fresh water and feels like an untouched paradise. The lake is the old lagoon floor and the tall cliffs that surround it are the old reef. Its western end has 200-odd coral islets and swamps. Four villages lie along the shore, including Te'Nggano, the subprovincial headquarters. It's famous for both its abundant bird and marine life, including tilapia, giant eels, sea snakes, frigate birds and cormorants. Though unfortunately Lake Te'Nggano is not a suitable place to get wet, as there is no beach and the waters here are murky.

Several bird species are endemic to Rennell, including the Rennell fantail and the rare Rennell white spoonbill.

Guest houses at Lake Te'Nggano can organise excursions on the lake. Regular stops include Octopus Cave, a spooky cave on the north shore, and a visit to Bird Island, where hundreds of cormorants, boobies and frigates nest year-round.

Sleeping & Eating

Rennell Island has a few simple resthouses, which can be booked through Solomon Islands Visitors Bureau which is situated in Honiara (p368). A good tip is to base yourself at Lake Te'Nggano. The only good reason to stay in Tinggoa, which is situated 50km west of Lake Te'Nggano, is if you are departing on an early flight. Lake excursions can be arranged through your guest house. Plan on S$500 for two persons, fuel included.

Moreno Guesthouse (Tinggoa; r without bathrooms S$150, meals per day S$130) A clean place with 17 bare rooms near the airstrip.

Neitasi Lodge (Lake Te'Nggano; s incl 3 meals S$160) Just beside the 'head road', at the entrance of the lake. A rustic yet atmospheric house on stilts, entirely built from natural materials, directly over the water.

Kiakoe Lakeside Lodge (Lake Te'Nggano; s incl 3 meals S$290) Located on the northern shore, which is a

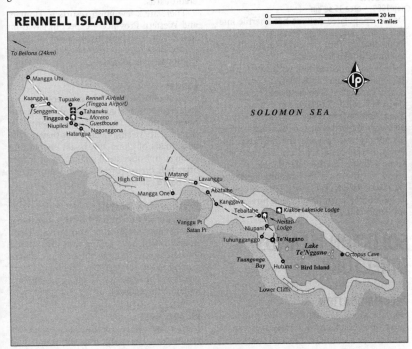

RENNELL ISLAND

0 — 20 km
0 — 12 miles

To Bellona (24km)

Mangga Utu

Kaanggua   Tupuake   Rennell Airfield (Tinggoa Airport)
Senggeria   Tahanuku
Tinggoa   Moreno
Niupilesi   Guesthouse
Hatangua   Nggonggona

SOLOMON SEA

High Cliffs   Matangi   Lavanggu
Mangga One   Abataihe
Kanggava
Tebaitahe   Kiakoe Lakeside Lodge
Vanggu Pt   Niupani   Neitasi Lodge
Satan Pt
Tuhungganggo   Te'Nggano
Lake Te'Nggano   Octopus Cave
Tuangonga Bay   Hutuna   Bird Island
Lower Cliffs

SOLOMON ISLANDS

short boat ride away from the head road, this 'lodge' is the best organised of the lot. Digs are in a house perched on a hillside or in two bungalows. Canoe transfers can be arranged (S$80 one way, five minutes).

Getting There & Away

From Honiara, Solomon Airlines (p394) flies to Rennell (S$900, three weekly) via Bellona or vice versa. The Bellona–Rennell sector costs S$625. Rennell airfield is in Tinggoa, on the west of the island. Moreno Guesthouse acts as the Solomon Airlines agent.

Getting Around

Getting to Lake Te'Nggano is a bit of a chore. The 50km of poor road between the Tinggoa airport and the lake runs through rainforest and takes at least three hours by 4WD, longer by truck.

The only 'regular' transfer service is organised by the people from Kiakoe Lakeside Lodge (p387), who meet most flights to collect cargo, and charge S$150 if it's a shared ride.

BELLONA

pop 1000 / area 15 sq km

Densely populated Bellona has a fertile interior and is encircled by forest-covered cliffs rising 30m to 70m. The cliffs are mostly easy to climb, unlike Rennell's.

Bellona is pockmarked with caves, where ancient rituals once took place.

You can stay at **Suani Resthouse** (Tangakitonga; s incl 3 meals S$200). Located on Bellona's east coast, **Aotaha Cave Lodge** (☎ 27796 in Honiara; s incl 3 meals S$250) has an enchanting setting. It's set around caves at the cliffbase, and some of the beds are in the cave itself! Some expats on the island also recommend the more recent **Tawahiti Guesthouse** (☎ 75122 in Honiara; s incl 3 meals S$250). All places in Bellona can arrange bicycle hire, hiking and snorkelling trips.

SOLOMON ISLANDS DIRECTORY

ACCOMMODATION

Honiara, Gizo, Munda and Auki provide a range of options, and the standards can be quite good. Elsewhere, most of the tourist accommodation comprises small, traditional-style lodges. Booking your accommodation ahead will enable your host to meet you at the airfield or port – useful where there's no public transport.

Camping

Don't even think of camping – pitching a tent flies in the face of traditional Melanesian hospitality, and villagers will be offended if you turn down their offer to sleep in a dwelling provided.

Hotels & Resorts

Tourist-class hotels are confined to Honiara, Gizo, Munda and Auki – expect to pay from S$400 for a fan-cooled room with private facilities in Honiara, a bit less on the outer islands. Although basic by international standards, these hotels generally have rooms with or without private shower and air-con, depending on what you're prepared to pay. A telephone, TV and tea-and-coffee-making facilities may be provided. Most have restaurants and bars, offer wi-fi service (or internet facilities) and take credit cards.

There are a few plush resorts in Honiara and Western Province – expect to pay from S$900 for a deluxe twin room at these places. Elsewhere accommodation is in basic leafhouse-style lodges.

Lodges

Typical of Marovo, 'lodges' refers to local-style bungalows, which usually have a quaint homemade feel to them. Bathrooms are shared. They're simply built but they usually have loads of character, boast enchanting settings and offer local colour. Most lodges offer half board (breakfast and dinner) or full board (all meals).

Resthouses & Hostels

These comprise church hostels, provincial government resthouses and private resthouses. Most have ceiling fans and shared kitchen and washing facilities. They charge around S$100 per person per night and most guests will be islanders. Alcohol and smoking are often forbidden.

Village Stays

Most villages have a leafhouse set aside for visitors' use. The charge is usually nominal. If

PRACTICALITIES

- The country's only newspaper is the daily *Solomons Star* (S$5), offering lively and independent commentary on Solomons affairs. It can be read online at www.solomonstarnews.com. The Solomons also has two twice-weekly newspapers – the *National Express* and the *Island Sun*. The Solomon Times Online (www.solomontimes.com) is a web-only news service.

- Local radio (SIBC) broadcasts programmes in English and Pijin on MW (1035kHz) and SW (5020kHz), with local and overseas features and news. The Australian Broadcasting Corporation (ABC) is at 630kHz MW.

- The national TV is One News. It broadcasts 7am to 8am and 9pm to 10pm in English in Honiara and Auki. Hotels with satellite TV can pick up CNN, BBC World and Australian programmes.

- The Solomons uses the PAL video system.

- Where electricity exists (often delivered by generator), the Solomons uses 240V, 50Hz AC and Australian-style three-pin plugs.

- The Solomons uses the metric system of measurement. See the Quick Reference page for conversions.

there isn't a leafhouse, you may be able to bed down in the local school or clinic.

Villages rarely have electricity, and the water supply often comes from a stream or communal tap. The toilet is a hole in the ground, or a reserved place in the bush or over the reef. Bring enough food to share around – tinned meat or tuna, tea, coffee and sugar are useful.

Village stays can be arranged with locals who have an idea of what tourists want and expect. Visiting on this basis is highly recommended – it is a wonderful experience for the traveller and it puts money into local communities.

Contact the visitor information centre in Honiara (p368) if you want to stay in a village or a lodge. Staff can make suggestions and organise bookings.

ACTIVITIES

The Solomon Islands offer a range of outdoor activities, including hiking, kayaking, scuba diving, snorkelling, swimming, surfing, fishing, birdwatching and caving. There are also numerous archaeological and WWII sites to visit.

Diving

Wrecks, wrecks, wrecks. And what wrecks: hundreds of sunken WWII metal giants – ships and aircraft. Many of these are accessible and, having been undisturbed for 60 years, have a wealth of objects *in situ*; underwater visibility is usually good to around 30m. No wonder that the Solomons is consistently

ranked among the best destinations on Planet Scuba; see p77 for an overview.

The extensive coral life is also superb, though the 2007 tsunami has taken its toll on some sections of the reefs in Western Province. Fish life is no less impressive, with the whole spectrum of reef species and the occasional pelagics, including manta rays and sharks.

You'll find dive operators in Honiara, Tulagi, Munda, Marovo and Gizo. They employ professional staff and their facilities are usually top-notch (which usually comes at a surprise for many divers, given the lack of infrastructures in the country). The Solomons is also a great place to learn diving.

Two highly reputable live-aboard dive boats operate in the Solomons and are under the same management: **MV Bilikiki** and **MV Spirit of Solomons** (www.bilikiki.com). Both offer regular cruises around the Russell Islands and Marovo Lagoon.

Dive operators rent all equipment and you must carry your certification.

Water temperatures in the Solomons are perfectly comfortable without a wetsuit – they can reach 30°C in January – but be sure that you wear a rash vest or other form of upper-body protection from sunburn and skin grazes.

PREARRANGED DIVE HOLIDAYS

Many divers prearrange their stay in the Solomons. Australian-based specialist companies offering package dive tours include the following:

SOLOMON ISLANDS

Allways Dive Expeditions (☎ 03-9885 8863, toll free 1800 338 239; www.allwaysdive.com.au) In Melbourne's Ashburton.

Dive Adventures (☎ 02-9299 4633, 03-9646 5945; www.diveadventures.com.au) In Sydney and Melbourne.

Diversion Dive Travel (☎ 07-4039 0200, toll free 1800 607 913; www.diversionoz.com) Based near Cairns, Queensland.

Fishing

Most resorts and lodges can arrange fishing trips, and several tour operators specialise in fishing. Zipolo Habu Resort (p378) is a specialist fishing resort. Sailfish, marlin, shark, tuna, kingfish, Spanish mackerel, barracuda and wahoo are common. Always ask permission before casting off from the shore into the sea or a river.

Hiking

The cooler mid-year months are most suitable for hiking. Most of the resorts and lodges offer walks up many of the nearby volcanoes as well as bushwalks. Climbing either Mt Mariu (p379) or Kolombangara (p382) involves a two-day hike, but their summits offer magnificent views. Serious hikers could also trek the Weathercoast (p374), on Guadalcanal.

Snorkelling

Snorkelling in the Solomons is excellent. The warm, clear water of the lagoons and the countless colourful fish and corals make it a real treat. It's a good idea to bring your own gear, although most dive shops have rental equipment. Dive operators typically charge around A$40 for snorkelling trips.

Surfing

Surfing is taking off in the Solomons and new breaks are being discovered all the time. The swell runs from October to April and can reach 2m or more at Pailongge on Ghizo, Lola Island in Vonavona Lagoon, at Poro on Santa Isabel and Tawarogha on Makira. The reef-breaks tend to be a long paddle from the shore, but the conditions can be excellent. Zipolo Habu Resort (p378) on Lola Island in Western Province offers surf charters, and Dive Gizo (p382) is well clued up on surfing at Ghizo.

ECOSURFING

Surfing in the Solomon Islands is so cool. The tropical water is warm and crystal clear, the breaks are powerful and consistent. There's absolutely no surf rage, no crowds and no stoner-guys bongin' on in the Kombi in the carpark. Here you feel like a pioneer. Tony Jansen, who's been based in the Solomons for 15 years, and is a surfer himself, pushed the frontiers even further and launched **Surf Solomons** (www.surfsolomons.com), an exciting concept that combines surfing, ecotourism and sustainable travel.

What's the idea behind Surf Solomons? I organise surfing expeditions in Malaita and Guadalcanal. Given the lack of infrastructure, you can't really travel on your own on these islands. We take only small groups.

What are the benefits for the local communities? We ensure that villagers are involved in the process. We motivate them to build and run small surf camps. Surfers stay in leafhuts within the communities, so that they can genuinely interact with the locals. And there's not only surfing. Traditional dance shows, feasts and village tours are also part of the trip. Food is locally produced. It's a significant amount of money that flows in the community. We provide them with soft loans and training. And of course, as locals have a fantastic knowledge of the waves, they take surfers in canoes to the breaks. It's a win-win situation.

How did the local communities react? There was some kind of suspicion at the beginning, but now locals are genuinely excited. My wife, who's from Malaita, and I, met with chiefs and elders. Truth is, villagers couldn't figure that foreigners could be interested in their culture.

What's the next step? I'm about to launch surfing trips to Makira and Isabel, which are really the ultimate, with perfectly shaped breaks.

As told to Jean-Bernard Carillet

If you really want to feel like a pioneer, contact **Surf Solomons** (www.surfsolomons.com) in Honiara. This ecofriendly operator organises guided surfing expeditions to Malaita, Santa Isabel and Makira islands – it's really unique.

Surfers should seek permission at the nearest village before entering the water. Bring your own boards.

BUSINESS HOURS

Banking hours in Honiara are from 8.30am to 3pm Monday to Friday. Government offices open from 8am to noon and 1pm to 4pm Monday to Friday. Private businesses close half an hour later and operate on Saturday until midday.

Most shops in town open from 8.30am to 5pm Monday to Friday and until noon on Saturday – some open longer, including on Sunday.

CHILDREN

The Solomons is a great place to travel with children, though keep in mind that there's malaria. Kids are an ever-present part of village life, and foreign kids are quickly absorbed into the local activities. Don't be surprised to see your two-year-old being carried around on the hip of a local seven-year-old girl – child-rearing is a communal responsibility in the Solomons.

DANGERS & ANNOYANCES

After several years of bloody fighting between the Guadalcanal Islanders and Malaitans, and riots in April 2006 (see p362), how safe is the country? The good news is that, with the help of foreign aid, the Solomons are bouncing back and visitors will feel more than *welkam*. The whole country is now safe and you can now travel wherever you wish. There's malaria, so take prophylactics.

EMBASSIES & CONSULATES
Solomon Islands Embassies & Consulates

Australia High Commission (☎ 02-6282 7030; info@solomonemb.org.au; Suite 3, 18 Napier Close, Deakin, ACT 2600); Consulate (☎ 02-9361 5866; consul@solomedic.net; 5th fl, 376 Victoria St, Darlinghurst, NSW 2010); Consulate (☎ 03-9722 1761; reghconsult@aol.com; Carinya Homestead Rd, Wonga Park, Victoria 3115)

EU (☎ 02-732 7085; siembassy@compurservecom; Ave Edouard Lacomblé 17, 1040 Brussels, Belgium)
PNG (☎ 323 4333; GB House, Unit 3, Kunai St, Port Moresby)

Embassies & Consulates in the Solomon Islands

Australia (☎ 21561; fax 23691; www.solomonislands.embassy.gov.au; Mud Alley, Honiara)
EU (☎ 22765; ecsol@solomon.com.sb; City Centre Bldg, Mendana Ave, Honiara)
France & Germany (☎ 22588; tradco@solomon.com.sb; Tradco Office, City Centre Bldg, Honiara)
Japan (☎ 22953; fax 21006; NPF Bldg, Honiara)
NZ (☎ 21502/21503; nzhicom@solomon.com.sb; City Centre Bldg, Honiara)
PNG (☎ 20561; fax 20562; Anthony Saru Bldg, Honiara)
UK (☎ 21705; bhc@solomon.com.sb; Telekom Haus, Honiara)

FESTIVALS & EVENTS

Independence Day is the Solomon Islands' most important annual festival, with celebrations held all around the country. Annual holidays in the Solomons include New Year's Day, Easter, Whit Monday and Christmas; see p629 for details of regional holidays.
Queen's Birthday First Monday in June
Independence Day 7 July
National Thanksgiving Day 26 December

INTERNET ACCESS

Broadband is finally being rolled out to the Solomons. You'll find internet cafés in Honiara and in Gizo. **Solomon Telekom** (www.solomon.com.sb) has public email facilities in Honiara, Gizo, Munda and Auki – wherever there is a provincial Telekom office. It costs about S$20 to S$48 per hour.

Some top-end hotels have a computer you can use to get online.

Wi-fi is also available at the better hotels and at a few cafés in Honiara, Munda and Gizo thanks to the Bumblebee card, which was launched by Solomon Telekom in 2006. You buy a prepaid card (S$50 for two hours or S$250 for seven days), available in some shops or at Solomon Telekom offices, and you can get online at designated wireless areas.

INTERNET RESOURCES

Most of the resorts and dive operators have websites or at least an advertising presence on the web.

SOLOMON ISLANDS

Solomon Islands Department of Commerce (www
.commerce.gov.sb) The country's official website has a
number of useful links.
Solomon Islands Visitors Bureau (www.visitsolomons
.com.sb) The Solomons' official tourism promotion organisation has a comprehensive website.

MAPS
Hema produces a map (1:1,200,000) of the
Solomons that's available in gift shops and
at the tourist office in Honiara.

MONEY
ATMs & Credit Cards
There are ATMs at the ANZ and Westpac
banks in Honiara's main strip, as well as
Auki, Tulagi, Munda, Gizo and Noro.

The main tourist-oriented businesses, including travel agents, the Honiara branch of
Solomon Airlines, a few dive shops and most
upmarket hotels and resorts accept credit
cards, but elsewhere it's strictly cash. Take
note that most outfits apply a 5% surcharge
per transaction if you pay with plastic.

Currency
The local currency is the Solomon Islands'
dollar (S$). For exchange rates, see the Quick
Reference page.

A supply of coins and small-denomination
notes will come in handy in rural areas, at
markets, and for bus and boat rides.

Moneychangers
The Bank South Pacific, Westpac and ANZ will
change money in most major currencies. The
Bank South Pacific has a network of branches
and agencies around the country; only the
branches will change travellers cheques.

Taxes
There's a 10% government tax on hotel and
restaurant charges, but more basic places often
don't include it. It's worth asking your hotel
whether this is included in the quoted rate,
as quite often it's not. All prices given in this
book are inclusive of tax.

Tipping & Bargaining
Tipping and bargaining are not traditionally
part of Melanesian culture, but it's becoming
increasingly acceptable to ask a carver for a
'second price' (often they'll tell you both prices
at the outset). Haggling is considered rude.

HOW MUCH?

- **Newspaper:** S$5
- **Bottle of soft drink:** S$5
- **Coffee:** S$10 to S$15
- **Single-tank scuba dive:** S$500
- **Evening-meal course** S$100 to S$200
- **1L petrol:** S$13
- **1L bottled water:** S$10 to S$13
- **Stubbie of Solbrew beer:** S$15 to S$20
- **Souvenir T-shirt:** S$40 to S$70
- **Sausage in a but:** S$10

Travellers Cheques
Stick to the name brands: Visa, Amex
and Thomas Cook. Travellers cheques in
Australian dollars can be readily exchanged
at hotel desks.

TELEPHONE
The Solomons' IDD is ☎ 677; there are no
area codes.

Solomon Telekom (www.telekom.com.sb) operates
the country's telephone system; a teleradio
(radio telephone) network connects isolated communities. Public phones are reasonably common in the larger centres and
phonecards are widely available – the local
Telekom office is the place that you'll need
to go for all your telephone requirements.
The cheapest way to make an international
telephone call is from a public telephone with
a prepaid phonecard. You can purchase the
phonecards in denominations of S$22, S$55
and S$110.

Solomon Telekom offers GSM mobile
phone service in Honiara, Munda, Noro,
Seghe, Gizo and Auki (Rennell and Bellona
should get a mobile signal by the time you
read this). Prepaid SIM cards from Solomon
Telekom, called 'Breeze cards', are available
for purchase and come in denominations of
S$20, S$50 and S$100.

Solomon Telekom has international
roaming agreements with Australia's Telstra
and Optus.

At the time of writing, Digicel was planning to start operating in the Solomons,
which would end Solomon Telekom's monopoly on the mobile phone market in
the country.

TIME

Time in the Solomons is officially 11 hours ahead of Greenwich Mean Time. Local time is the same as in Vanuatu, one hour ahead of Australian Eastern Standard Time, and one hour behind Fiji and NZ. There's no daylight saving. When it's noon in the Solomons it's 1am in London, 5pm the previous day in Los Angeles, 1pm in Auckland and 11am in Sydney (summer time notwithstanding).

TOURIST INFORMATION IN THE SOLOMON ISLANDS

The **Solomon Islands Visitors Bureau** (SIVB; ☎ 22442; www.visitsolomons.com.sb; Mendana Ave, Honiara) has information about the whole of the Solomon Islands, and has helpful staff if not much in the way of printed material. They can contact isolated lodges and villages to make bookings.

VISAS

Citizens from most Western countries don't need a visa to enter the Solomon Islands, just a valid passport, an onward ticket, and sufficient funds for their stay. On arrival at the airport, you will be given a visitor's visa for up to three months, depending on the departure date printed on your onward ticket.

Visitors permits can be extended for a further three months at the **immigration office** (☎ 22179; Mendana Ave, Honiara). It takes 24 hours and costs S$50 (one month) or S$150 (three months).

WOMEN TRAVELLERS

It's not usual for local young women to be out at night by themselves. Exercise normal caution in Honiara – after dark, take a taxi and stay in busy areas. Female tourists swimming or sunbathing alone at isolated beaches might attract unwanted attention.

Foreign women travelling solo around remote villages are very rare. In villages male travellers are sometimes accommodated in structures that are *tabu* for women, so it might not be possible for couples to sleep together. There may be other areas that women are not allowed to see, and this should be respected.

Melanesians are very sensitive about the show of female thighs so shorts and skirts should be knee-length and swimwear should incorporate boardshorts rather than bikini bottoms.

TRANSPORT IN THE SOLOMON ISLANDS

GETTING THERE & AWAY

Air

The Solomons' only international airport is Henderson Airport (code HIR), 11km east of Honiara.

Brisbane, Nadi, Vila, Nauru and Port Moresby have services to Honiara. See p636 for details of air passes.

The following airlines have regular scheduled flights to Solomon Airlines.

Air Pacific (www.airpacific.com)
Air Niugini (www.airniugini.com.pg)
Our Airline (www.ourairline.com.au)
Pacific Blue (www.flypacificblue.com)
SkyAirWorld (www.skyairworld.com)
Solomon Airlines (☎ 20031; www.flysolomons.com; Mendana Ave, Honiara)

Guadalcanal Travel Services in Honiara (p368) is a sales agent for all airlines.

Solomon Airlines, the national carrier, no longer has any aircraft other than its small domestic fleet but leases aircraft from Air Vanuatu and Our Airline (ex-Air Nauru).

ASIA

The most direct route to/from Asia is via Port Moresby in PNG (p394) but it's simpler and cheaper (and connections may be more frequent) via Brisbane.

AUSTRALIA

Honiara is well serviced from Brisbane. At the time of writing, three airlines were offering regular flights between the two cities. They include Solomon Airlines (four weekly flights), SkyAirWorld (three weekly flights) and Pacific Blue (two weekly flights). Prices start at A$650 return.

FIJI

Air Pacific connects Honiara with Nadi once a week. Air Niugini connects Honiara with Nadi twice a week. The return fare starts at S$3200.

NAURU

Our Airline operates from Nauru to Honiara (and on to Brisbane) twice weekly. Prices start at A$600 return.

SOLOMON ISLANDS

DEPARTURE TAX

An airport tax of S$100 is charged for passengers boarding international flights leaving Honiara.

PAPUA NEW GUINEA
Air Niugini flies from Port Moresby to Honiara twice a week. Return fares are about S$2800 including tax.

VANUATU
Air Pacific connects Honiara with Port Vila once a week. Return fares are S$3500 including tax.

Sea
YACHT
The Solomons is a favourite spot for yachties who take refuge in the lagoons during cyclone season. Along with Honiara, Korovou (Shortland Islands), Gizo, Ringgi, Yandina, Tulagi Island and Graciosa Bay are official ports of entry where you can clear customs and immigration.

'Crew wanted' notices are sometimes posted at the **Point Cruz Yacht Club** (☎ 22500; VHF 16) in Honiara. See also the excellent (but not completely up-to-date) www.gizoyachtclub.com.sb and www.noonsite.com. See p641 for more about yachting in the Pacific.

GETTING AROUND
Air
Solomon Airlines (☎ 20031; www.flysolomons.com; Mendana Ave, Honiara) services the country's 20-odd airstrips with its De Havilland Twin Otters, Britton Norman Islanders and Bombardier Dash 8s. The main tourist gateways, including Gizo, Seghe (for North Marovo Lagoon), Munda and Auki are serviced daily from Honiara, but be sure to confirm your flight at least 24 hours before your departure because flights are often delayed.

Baggage allowance is set at 20kg per passenger. Domestic airfares in this chapter include taxes.

Boat
DINGHIES
Outboard-powered dinghies are the most common means of transport in the Solomons, supplying goods to stores all over the country. People pay a fare to travel a sector. Charters cost around S$1500 per day for the boat and a driver; fuel is often not included (S$20 per litre in remote areas).

PASSENGER BOATS
Both MV *Pelican Express* and MV *Solomon Express* offer a reliable service between Honiara, Western Province (including Marovo Lagoon and Gizo) and Malaita. In Western Province Go West Tours (p377) offers a three-weekly shuttle between Munda and Gizo.

Bus
Public minibuses are found only in Honiara. The flat S$3 fare will take you anywhere on the route, which is written on a placard behind the windscreen of the bus. Elsewhere, people pile into open-backed trucks or tractor-drawn trailers.

Car & Motorcycle
The country has around 1300km of generally dreadful roads. International driving permits are accepted, as are most driving licences. Driving is on the left side of the road.

Hire cars are available only in Honiara. Contact Pacific Casino Hotel (p372).

Hitching
If you want a ride through the countryside, flag down a passing vehicle and ask the driver the cost of a lift. In rural areas most vehicles double as public transport.

Local Transport
TAXI
Taxis are plentiful in Honiara and there are small fleets in Gizo and Auki. They don't have meters, so agree on the price before you set off. The fare to the airport from Honiara was S$80 at the time of writing.

Tahiti & French Polynesia

Just the name Tahiti conjures up centuries of legend and lifetimes of daydreams. Its 18th-century reputation as a wanton playground of flower-bedecked Polynesians in an Eden-like setting has effortlessly morphed into a 21st century image of a chic and sexy holiday haven for the jet set. And yes, French Polynesia is seductively tranquil and lushly gorgeous, but there's much more to the country than cocktails on the beach and flashing the platinum card.

When you're not idling in the scent of gardenias, warm damp breezes and ukulele riffs by starlight, try hiking up a waterfall valley, paddling out on a surfboard or diving through sharky passes. While tours are available for everything, it's just as fun to head out on your own to explore that enticing coral head with a mask and snorkel or rent a bike. While the resorts make headlines, the country's unsung heroes are the impressive collection of family *pensions* that range from rickety rooms in someone's home to luxurious boutique style bungalows on private islets. Staying at these places not only saves money, but also allows you to meet locals and have a more authentic experience.

From the vast lagoons of the Tuamotu atolls, to the culturally intense Marquesas Islands and the cool climate of the Austral Archipelago, French Polynesia's 117 islands are spread over a marine area the size of Europe, providing enough diversity and surprises to last several voyages. If you can forgo a few frills you'll find that French Polynesia can be considerably less expensive than most major cities in Europe. For this calibre of adventure and sublime setting, we think it's worth it.

HIGHLIGHTS

- Wandering through jungle-clad archaeological sites before reaching **Mo'orea's** (p420) magnificent belvedere viewpoint perched between mountains and bays.

- Learning to love sharks in the wild and diving in the fauna-rich Tiputa Pass of **Rangiroa** (p450) in the Tuamotus.

- Watching the best of the best wiggle their hips and waggle their knees at Tahiti's **Heiva Festival** (p477) dance competitions.

- Strapping on your boots and exploring the wild green yonder of **Nuku Hiva's** (p458) wild and rugged ridges and valleys.

- Pampering yourself on ultra gorgeous and over-the-top luxurious **Bora Bora** (p438), a temple to high-octane hedonism.

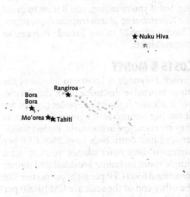

★ Nuku Hiva

Rangiroa ★
Bora
Bora ★
Mo'orea ★★ Tahiti

TAHITI & FRENCH POLYNESIA

TAHITI & FRENCH POLYNESIA FACTS

Capital city (and island) Pape'ete (Tahiti)
Population 245,405
Land area 3500 sq km
Number of islands 118
International telephone code ☎ 689
Currency Cour de Franc Pacifique (CFP)
Languages Tahitian and French
Greeting *La ora na* (Tahitian), *Bonjour* (French)
Website www.tahiti-tourisme.com

CLIMATE & WHEN TO GO

The dry winter period from May to October is the best time to visit: the weather is cooler and there is much less rainfall. Temperatures rise during the November to April summer rainy season when it's humid, cloudy and *very* wet. Three-quarters of the annual rainfall occurs during this period, generally in the form of brief, violent storms, although torrential rains lasting several days are not uncommon.

French Polynesia is south of the equator, but school holidays fall in line with those of the northern hemisphere. This means the peak tourist season is July and August, and during this period it's no mean feat getting flights and accommodation. Christmas to early January, late February and early March, the Easter period, early May and early October are also quite busy times. The peak July–August season coincides with the Heiva Festival (see p477), held throughout July, when the region comes to life.

Diving is popular year-round, as is surfing, but if you're sailing, you'll want to avoid the November to March tropical depressions. Check out p627 to see French Polynesian climate charts.

COSTS & MONEY

French Polynesia is known to be one of the most expensive destinations in the Pacific, but if it's any consolation, prices (except for at the big resorts) aren't going up as fast as they are elsewhere in the world. Budget travellers can find dorm beds from 2500 CFP per night: on some outer islands, you can get a simple room including breakfast and dinner for around 6500 CFP per night per person. On the other end of the scale are US$10,000 per night bungalows and restaurants that don't even bother to list the prices on the menu (if you need to know you can't afford it). In this chapter 'budget' lodging is anything up to 10,000 CFP per night, 'midrange' is from 10,000 CFP to 20,000 CFP and the sky is the limit for 'top-end'. For eating, 'budget' goes up to 1200 CFP and 'midrange' is from 1200 CFP to 2500 CFP.

HISTORY

No one really knows why early peoples migrated here or even where they came from. Modern theories have Polynesian voyages originating from the Philippines or Taiwan, spurred on by territorial disputes or overpopulation. Whatever the reason, ancient Polynesians packed up their outriggers with coconuts, *uru* (breadfruit), taro, sugar cane, dogs, pigs and chickens and headed out into the blue. These were feats of maritime prowess, not to be matched by Europeans for more than 1000 years.

European Arrival

European explorers first ventured into the region in 1595, although major expeditions didn't really get underway until the late 18th century. Lacking the navigation methods that Polynesians had developed over millennia of Pacific travel, the Europeans searched for islands in the Pacific by means of a rather random needle-in-a-haystack method.

MENDAÑA & QUIRÓS

Don Alvaro de Mendaña y Neyra came upon the Marquesas Islands in 1595 on his second search for Terra Australis Incognita, the nonexistent great southern continent. Mendaña named the islands after his patron, Marquesas de Mendoza, but his visit resulted in open warfare and 200 islanders were killed.

Mendaña's pilot, Pedro Fernández de Quirós, returned in 1606 and discovered the Tuamotus before sailing to Vanuatu.

WALLIS

The *Dolphin* anchored at Matavai Bay in Tahiti's lagoon in late June of 1767. A quarter of the crew was down with scurvy and Samuel Wallis himself was incapacitated during most of his visit. Initially, the arrival was greeted with fascination as hundreds of canoes surrounded the ship, including canoes carrying young women 'who played a great many droll wanton tricks'. When the locals' fascination turned to fear, Wallis began by firing grapeshot at the Tahitians and finished

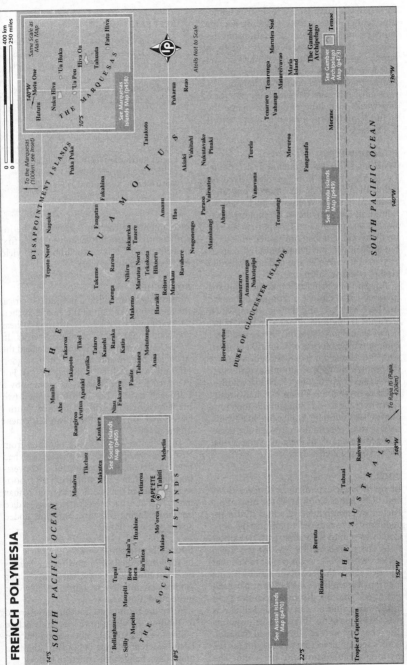

FRENCH POLYNESIA

0   400 km
0   250 miles

SOUTH PACIFIC OCEAN

T H E M A R Q U E S A S

Same Scale as Main Map

140°W   Motu One
Hatutu   Nuku Hiva   'Ua Huka
   'Ua Pou   Hiva Oa   Fatu Hiva
    Tahuata

See Marquesas Islands Map (p458)

To the Marquesas (100km: see inset)

D I S A P P O I N T M E N T I S L A N D S

Tepoto Nord   Napuka
Puka Puka

Fakahina

T U A M O T U

Pukarua   Reao

Fangatau

Manihi
Ahe   Takaroa
Takapoto   Tikei
Rangiroa   Aratua   Apataki   Takume   Raroia
   Toau   Kauehi   Nihiru   Rekareka
Makatea   Niau   Faaite   Raraka   Marutea Nord   Tauere
Tikehau   Fakarava   Katiu   Tekokota   Tatakoto
   Tahanea   Hikueru
Kaukura   Motutunga   Haraiki
  Anaa   Reitoru
See Society Islands   Marokau
Map (p405)   Amanu

Mataiva   Ravahere
  Akiaki
  Hao   Vahitahi
   Nengonengo   Nukutavake
   Paraoa   Pinaki
   Marutea   Vairaatea
  Manuhangi   Turéia
  Ahunui
Hereheretue   Vanavana

Tenararo   Tenarunga   Marutea Sud
Vahanga   Matureivavao
Maria   Island

The Gambier Archipelago   Temoe

See Gambier Archipelago Map (p473)

Tematangi
Morane

Atolls Not to Scale

136°W

140°W

Mehetia

T H E S O C I E T Y I S L A N D S

Bellinghausen   Tupai
Scilly   Maupiti   Bora   Taha'a
  Mopelia   Bora   Huahine
   Ra'iatea
   Maiao   Mo'orea
   Tetiaroa
  PAPEETE ⊙ Tahiti

DUKE OF GLOUCESTER ISLANDS

Anuanuraro
Anuanurunga
Nukutepipi

SOUTH PACIFIC OCEAN

Fangataufa
Moruroa

See Tuamotu Islands Map (p449)

Rurutu

T H E A U S T R A L S

Raivavae
Tubuai

Rimatara   Rapa

To Rapa Iti (Rapa) 420km

See Austral Islands Map (p470)

148°W

Tropic of Capricorn

152°W

14°S

16°S

18°S

22°S

by sending a party ashore to destroy homes and canoes. The natives suddenly became more friendly and a trade relationship developed: the crew was desperate for fresh supplies and the Tahitians, who had not yet discovered metals, were delighted to receive knives, hatchets and nails in exchange.

Wallis only stayed in Matavai Bay for a few weeks, just long enough to name the island King George's Land and to claim it for Britain.

BOUGAINVILLE

With his ships *La Boudeuse* and *L'Étoile*, Louis-Antoine de Bougainville arrived on Tahiti in April 1768, less than a year after Wallis. At this time Wallis was still homeward bound, so Bougainville was completely unaware he was not the first European to set eyes on the island. His visit only lasted nine days, but Bougainville was a more cultured, considered man than Wallis and had no unfriendly clashes with the Tahitians.

Bougainville explained that the Tahitians 'pressed us to choose a woman and come on shore with her; and their gestures, which were not ambiguous, denoted in what manner we should form an acquaintance with her'. Bougainville's reports of Venuslike women with 'the celestial form of that goddess', and of the people's uninhibited attitude towards matters sexual, swept through Paris like wildfire.

Unaware that the Union Jack had already flown over the island, Bougainville took time out to claim Tahiti for France but, like Wallis, he was soon overshadowed when the greatest Pacific explorer of them all, James Cook, arrived on the scene.

COOK

In three great expeditions between 1769 and 1779, James Cook filled the map of the Pacific so comprehensively that future expeditions were reduced to joining the dots. Cook was sent to the Pacific with two ambitious tasks. One, which was for the Royal Society, was to observe the transit of Venus as it passed across the face of the sun. By timing the transit from three very distant places, it was hoped that the distance from the earth to the sun could be calculated. Tahiti was selected as one of the three measuring points (the other two were in Norway and Canada). Cook's second objective was to hunt for the mythical great continent of the south. The

instruments of the time proved to be insufficiently accurate to achieve Cook's first objective, but Cook's expeditions did yield impressive scientific work.

BOENECHEA

Already firmly established in South America, the Spanish looked upon the Pacific as their backyard and were less than happy to hear about other European navigators' visits. In 1772 Don Domingo de Boenechea sailed the *Aguilla* from Peru and anchored in the lagoon off Tautira on Tahiti Iti (Small Tahiti). For the third time, the island was claimed by a European nation. Boenechea installed two inept missionaries and established Tautira as the first long-term European settlement on the island.

In 1775 the *Aguilla* again returned from Peru. The two Spanish missionaries, who had been spectacularly unsuccessful at converting 'the heathen', and who from all reports were terrified of the islanders, were more than happy to scuttle back to Peru. Boenechea died on Tahiti during this visit, and thus ended Spanish rule on Tahiti.

Bounty Mutineers

In 1789 the infamous mutiny on the *Bounty* occurred after Bligh's crew had spent six long comfortable months on Tahiti. See p246 for more about the *Bounty*.

After the mutiny the mutineers returned to Tahiti and Tubuai in the Australs before sailing to a more remote hideaway on Pitcairn Island. Sixteen stayed behind on Tahiti, a move that changed the course of history.

Before the Europeans arrived, power had been a local affair. No ruler was strong enough to control more than a patch of land, and Tahiti was divided into a number of squabbling groups. However, once they realised the persuasive power of European weaponry, Tahitians pressed the *Bounty* mutineers to take sides in local conflicts. The mutineers became mercenaries to the highest bidder, the Pomare family.

That deal was the beginning of the Pomares' metamorphosis into a ruling dynasty. Pomare I, known as Tu, controlled most of Tahiti by the time he died in 1803; his son Pomare II took over, a trend which was to continue through the century.

Whalers, Missionaries & Depopulation

The London Missionary Society (LMS) landed at Tahiti's Point Vénus in March 1797 and did its best to rid the islanders of their wicked ways. Dancing, 'indecent' songs, tattoos, nudity, indiscriminate sex and even wearing flowers in the hair were banned once the missionaries got their patron, Pomare II, on their side.

Whalers and traders arrived in Polynesia in the 1790s, spreading diseases, encouraging prostitution and introducing alcohol and more weapons.

Plagued by diseases against which they had no natural immunity, the population plummeted. When Cook first visited, Tahiti's population was about 40,000. In 1800 it was less than 20,000 and by the 1820s it was down to around 6000. In the Marquesas the situation was even worse – the population dropped from 80,000 to only 2000 in one century.

Pomares & the Missionaries

After 1815 the Pomares ruled Tahiti, with Protestant missionaries advising them on government and laws, and trying to keep whalers and Australian traders at arm's length. Pomare II died in 1821, leaving his son Pomare III to rule until his death six years later in 1827, at which point the young Queen Pomare IV assumed the throne.

The queen's missionary advisers, seeing her only as an interim ruler until the next king arrived, turned a blind eye to some of her youthful excesses. She wasn't averse to a little singing and dancing, and even visited passing ships. Queen Pomare IV made the most of her leeway and ruled Tahiti for 50 years.

English Protestant missionaries were the major advisers to chiefs in the Society, Austral and Tuamotu Islands. But in the Gambier Archipelago and the Marquesas Islands, French Catholic missionaries were in control. In 1836 two French missionaries, Laval and Caret, visiting Pape'ete from the Gambier Archipelago, were caught up in this rivalry when the British promptly arrested and deported them.

French Takeover

The French saw the deportation of Laval and Caret as a national insult. Demands, claims, counterclaims, payments and apologies shuttled back and forth. In 1842 Admiral Dupetit-Thouars settled matters by turning up in *La Reine Blanche* and pointing the ship's guns at Pape'ete, forcing Queen Pomare to yield. French soldiers promptly landed, along with Catholic missionaries.

The French arrested and deported George Pritchard, the British missionary who was the queen's consul and unofficial chief adviser. Queen Pomare, still hoping for British intervention, fled to Ra'iatea in 1844 and a guerrilla rebellion broke out on several islands. The rebels were subdued and by 1846 France controlled Tahiti and Mo'orea. The queen returned to Tahiti in 1847 as a mere figurehead.

Queen Pomare died in 1877; her son, Pomare V, had little interest in the position and abdicated in 1881. French power extended to include most of the other Society Islands in 1888, although rebellions continued to rumble on Ra'iatea until almost the end of the century. The Gambier Archipelago was annexed in 1881 and the Austral Islands in 1900–01.

20th Century

Soon after the turn of the century an economic boom attracted colonists, mostly French. By 1911 there were about 3500 Europeans in the islands, adding to Chinese immigration, which had begun in 1864 with cotton production at Atimaono on Tahiti. The foundations of a multiethnic society were in place.

French Polynesia was directly involved in both world wars. In WWI almost 1000 Tahitian soldiers fought in Europe, and on 22 September 1914 two German cruisers patrolling the Pacific sank the French cruiser *Zélée* and shelled the Pape'ete market. In WWII, 5000 US soldiers were based on Bora Bora, and a 2km runway was built in 1943. Tahitian volunteers in the Pacific Battalion fought in North Africa and Europe.

In 1946, the islands became an overseas territory within the French Republic, sparking agitation for independence. A political party, the Rassemblement Démocratique des Populations Tahitiennes (RDPT; Democratic Assembly of Tahitian Populations) took centre stage on the political scene for about 10 years.

On 22 July 1957, the territory officially became French Polynesia. The 1960s were a real turning point. In 1961, Faa'a airport was built, opening French Polynesia to the world. Shortly after, the filming of *Mutiny on the Bounty* on Tahiti poured millions of dollars into the economy. In 1963, the nuclear-testing Centre Expérimental du Pacifique (CEP; Pacific Experimentation Centre) was established at Moruroa and Fangataufa.

From 1977 to 1996, French Polynesia took over internal management and autonomy from France. The nuclear testing of the era shook Polynesia physically, socially and economically: violent protests rocked Pape'ete in 1987 and 1995 and the CEP made French Polynesia economically dependent on France. The end to nuclear testing in 1996 also meant the end of the prosperity of the previous 30 years.

French Polynesia Today

Over the last few decades, French Polynesia's control over its own government and resources has been widened. Although independence from France is a possibility in the future, it is unlikely to happen anytime soon. Funds sent from France to help French Polynesia develop its own industries to work towards economic independence have been mostly squandered by the local government. Long time president Gaston Flosse was voted out of office in 2004 and over the next four years the government changed seven times.

At the beginning of 2009 Oscar Temaru was once again elected president after Gaston Tong Song was forced to resign after too many of his party members stopped supporting him.

The standard of living in the region is relatively high, but French Polynesia is in a vulnerable economic situation, with very few natural resources to draw upon and a system based on imports. Funding to French Overseas Territories has become sharply scrutinised by

French President Nicholas Sarkozy and cutbacks, that will greatly traumatise the French Polynesian economy, were starting to be put into place by France at the end of 2008.

THE CULTURE
The National Psyche

If French Polynesia had a national slogan it might be *'haere maru'* (take it slow), words that often fall off the lips of Tahitians when addressing their busy French and Chinese cohabitants. It's hard not to take it slow in the islands. With one road encircling the main island of Tahiti, it's easy to get caught driving behind an old pick-up truck at 40km/h with no chance of passing; national holidays seem to close up the shops and banks once every week or so; and getting served in a restaurant can take an eternity. This can be frustrating to anyone in a hurry, but somehow it all works out: you make it to wherever you were going even if it did take twice as long, the bank can wait till tomorrow and your food arrives once you are really, really hungry. The Tahitian people know this and always seem slightly amused by anyone who tries to break the rhythm of calm.

Regardless of 'Tahiti time', Pape'ete manages to move at a pace fitting for a capital: there are traffic jams, everyone is on a mobile phone and the nightlife shakes on till 5am. The modern world is quickly infiltrating the slow pace of life and this is most evident in the younger generations.

Lifestyle

The traditional Tahitian family is an open-armed force that is the country's backbone. Although modern girls are increasingly less likely to stay home and have baby after baby, an accidental pregnancy is considered more of a blessing than a hindrance and babies are passed along to another eager, infant-loving family member. *Faamu* (adopted children) are not thought of as different from blood brothers and sisters to either the parents or siblings – although the real mother, and occasionally the father, sometimes remain a peripheral part of the child's life.

This family web is vitally important to an individual. When people first meet, the conversation usually starts with questions about family and most people are able to find a common relative within minutes. This accomplished, they are 'cousins' and fast friends.

TOP PICKS

Best Over-the-Top Lux Resorts

If you're going to really splurge, French Polynesia just might be the best place in the world to do it. The following places are the best of the best.

- Intercontinental Resort & Thalasso Spa (p444), Bora Bora
- Le Taha'a Private Island & Spa (p437), Taha'a
- Tikehau Pearl Beach Resort (p455), Tuamotus
- Saint Régis Resort (p444), Bora Bora
- Le Méridien Bora Bora (p444), Bora Bora
- Te Tiare Beach Outrigger Resort (p429), Huahine
- Legends Resort (p424), Mo'orea

Best-Value Accommodation

The following are our top picks for good value – they are not necessarily the cheapest places, they simply have the best cost-to-worth ratio.

- Sofitel Maeva Beach (p414), Tahiti
- Taaroa Lodge (p414), Tahiti
- Raiatea Lodge (p435), Raiatea
- Pension Motu Iti (p423), Moorea
- Novotel Bora Bora Beach Resort (p443), Bora Bora
- Maupiti Residence (p448), Maupiti
- Paahatea Nui (p461), Nuku Hiva
- Pension Ariiheevai (p456), Mataiva
- Pension Meherio (p429), Huahine
- Pension Bounty (p452), Rangiroa

The flip side is many new couples find out too late they are *tapu* (taboo), too closely related for the family to accept.

It's not all roses in what appears to be such a warm, fuzzy family framework. Domestic violence and incest are prevalent. This is closely connected with high rates of alcoholism. The government has launched numerous programs addressing these issues but little progress has been made.

Despite these domestic problems, women do hold a strong position in French Polynesian society. Wallis' first encounter, with whom he believed to be a Tahitian chief, was a woman. Today, Nicole Bouteau, one of Tahiti's newest political stars, has started her own centrist political party that is rapidly gaining popularity. In the household, women are most often the homemakers, but they don't wear this hat lightly. They radiate a strength and dignity that sees them in charge of everything domestic and sometimes more. Men (particularly those who don't drink) often share in the chores of cooking, cleaning and baby rearing; it's not uncommon to see massive, muscular, tattooed men nuzzling with an infant or holding hands with a toddler to cross the road.

Although religion has been teaching people to think otherwise, homosexuality is generally viewed as a natural part of human existence. This tolerance is displayed most strongly by the presence of *mahu* (or the more flamboyant, transvestite-like *raerae*), effeminate men who live their lives as women (see boxed text, p402). Lesbians are more rare but are generally accepted.

Pakalolo (marijuana) and the Bob Marley lifestyle have been thoroughly embraced in French Polynesia, but harder drugs are rare. The exception is Ice, a highly addictive meta-amphetamine that has rapidly gained popularity in the upper classes of Pape'ete.

> **GENDER BENDER**
>
> You'll find that some women serving food in restaurants working at hotels or in boutiques aren't actually women at all. *Mahu*, males who are raised as girls and continue to live their lives as women, were present when the first Europeans arrived in the islands. Although the missionaries did their hardest to halt this 'unnatural crime', *mahu* are still an accepted part of the community today.
>
> It remains unclear, however, whether this practice has a sexual or a social origin, but it is generally assumed to be the latter as *mahu* don't necessarily have sex with men. Even so, anyone seeking the mythical notion of a sexually free Tahiti should note that most of French Polynesia's modern-day prostitutes are (very convincing) transvestites.

The government has responded with an impressive effort, with publicity campaigns and heavier customs security at the airport that will hopefully curb the problem before it becomes too serious.

Population

Paralleling worldwide patterns of urbanisation, French Polynesia's people have migrated towards the city and main island: 69% of the population currently make their home on Tahiti and 75% of those on Tahiti live in Pape'ete or its suburbs. While a few atolls in the Tuamotus manage to keep residents for work in the Tahitian pearl industry, most islands in the Tuamotus, Gambier, Marquesas and the Australs have dismal growth rates below 1%. The Society Islands' Leeward Islands – especially ones with a bigger tourist industry such as Bora Bora, Huahine and Ra'iatea – are growing at the same steady rate as the Windward Islands (which include Tahiti and Mo'orea). Island birth rates are dropping steadily, although they are still relatively high at 17.7 per 1000 (it's around 13 per 1000 in Australia and France).

On all the islands the majority of the population lives in coastal zones. The rugged interior is virtually uninhabited, but archaeological evidence indicates that this wasn't always the case. Only in the Marquesas do people live mostly in the valleys; this is a habit left over from times when living near the beach left them more vulnerable to warring neighbouring tribes.

ARTS

The zealous missionaries endeavoured to wipe out all forms of 'primitive' Polynesian art and culture. They destroyed temples and carvings, banned tattooing and dancing, and generally took a lot of the joy out of life. Fortunately some traditions survived this period of cultural censorship, and in recent years there has been a revival of Polynesian culture, particularly in music, dance and tattooing.

Cinema

Tahiti's role as a movie backdrop is almost exclusively tied up with the film *Mutiny on the Bounty*. The story has been told three times on the silver screen. Starring Anthony Hopkins and Mel Gibson, the 1980s third remake was filmed almost entirely on Mo'orea. Anthony Hopkins plays the not-quite-so-bad-and-mad Bligh and Mel Gibson is the more-handsome-than-ever Christian.

James Michener's *South Pacific* may have been about Polynesia, but it certainly wasn't filmed there (rather Tioman Island in Malaysia). *Tabu,* released in 1931, was filmed on Bora Bora. This work of fiction explores the notions of *tapu,* and when one of the directors was killed in an accident shortly after finishing filming, there was plenty of speculation that his death may have been the result of including taboo parts of the island in the film.

In 1979, a big-budget remake of *Hurricane,* the 1937 classic based on a Nordhoff & Hall novel, was filmed on Bora Bora. The film was a major flop, despite an all-star cast; for TV it was retitled *Forbidden Paradise.*

Dance

The dances that visitors see in French Polynesia are not created for tourists: they are authentic performances and play a major part in spreading the influence of Tahitian culture. In this land of oral traditions, dance is not merely an aesthetic medium but also a way to preserve the memory of the past.

The luxury hotels offer quality dance shows about twice a week. On Tahiti and Mo'orea they are performed by semiprofessional groups, but on other islands the companies are more amateur. These shows come with a buffet (costing around 8000 CFP) and are open to all. If you only wish to attend the show, enquire about the hotel's policy. The best dance performances are held at the annual Heiva Festival in July (p477).

The most common forms of dance are the Otea, with fast gyrating hip action for the women and scissor-like leg movements for the men; and the Aparima, a free-flowing and graceful dance that tells a story using hand movements and song.

Literature

Polynesia has been getting the Western pen flowing since the first European explorers returned with accounts of paradise islands and beautiful people. But oral recitation was the first fountain pen of the Pacific, and the written word only came into being after the missionaries began producing texts in Tahitian in the 19th century. This dependence on the spoken word has meant that Polynesia's history has been recreated out of European observations, and also means that literature written by Polynesians has only recently begun to grace the bookshelves.

There are a number of interesting Polynesian writers who are slowly changing the literary landscape, but few have been translated into English. If you read French, writers such as Henri Hiro, Turo Raapoto, Michou Chaze, Chantal Spitz and Louise Peltzer are all interesting.

The Materena Series by Celestine Hitiura Vaite, a Tahitian living in Australia, are three novels set in contemporary Tahiti; the first book of the series Breadfruit (2000) is the most widely read book in French Polynesia.

Music

Traditional Polynesian music, usually performed as an accompaniment to dance, is heard reverberating through the islands.

Ukuleles and percussion instruments dominate this style of music, which is structured by a hypnotic and an often quite complex drum beat. Song, both traditional and religious, is also popular and important.

Modern Polynesian music (see p365) by local artists is the blaring soundtrack to everyday life, whether it's in a bus, at a cafe or on the radio. Some groups also perform in hotels and bars.

Painting & Sculpture

Even today, well over a 100 years after his arrival on Tahiti, painting in the South Pacific is synonymous with Paul Gauguin, the French post-Impressionist painter. Gauguin spent much of his later life in Polynesia, and presented Europe with images of the islands that moulded the way Europeans viewed (and, arguably, continue to view) Polynesia. In his wake a number of predominantly European artists – working in media ranging from watercolour to line drawing – have also sought inspiration in the region.

Henri Matisse made a short visit to Tahiti in 1930, but his Polynesian work is eclipsed by the work of Jacques Boullaire. Boullaire, a French artist who first travelled to Tahiti in the 1930s, produced many magnificent watercolours; reproductions of his work are readily available today.

Traditionally the best sculpture and woodcarvings have come out of the Marquesas, where fine tiki (sacred statues), bowls, mortars and pestles, spears and clubs are carved from rosewood, tou wood or in stone.

RECOMMENDED LISTENING

- **Angelo Neuffer** Highly political and poetic lyrics have made Angelo one of the most popular Tahitian artists of all time. One of his best albums is Te Nuna'a no Ananahi.

- **Bobby** Very listenable, almost dreamy Polynesian music. His album with Angelo, titled Bobby and Angelo, is one of the most listened to albums in Tahiti.

- **Ester Tefana** For old-fashioned, ukulele-accompanied, Tahitian mood music, Ester is your best bet.

- **Fenua** Bringing Tahitian music into the future, this group fuses the traditional with techno for an explosive sound.

- **Tapuarii Laughlin** Most modern classics are written by 'Tapu' who mixes surfer-cool with traditional.

- **Te Ava Piti** This is your classic Polynesian music with plenty of fast ukulele riffs.

- **Trio Kikiriri** Perhaps a bit cheesy to Western ears, this syntho/ukelele group is an all-time favourite for weddings and parties where people dance the Tahitian foxtrot.

Tattoos

Since the early 1980s, tattooing has enjoyed a strong revival, becoming one of the most expressive and vibrant vehicles of Polynesian culture. With encouragement from the great Samoan masters, young Tahitians have delved into their ancient traditions and have brought this ancestral form of bodily adornment, with its undisputed artistic qualities, completely up to date. Today many Polynesian men and women sport magnificent tattoos as symbols of their identity.

Modern tattooing is completely for the sake of style or beautification; in ancient times it was a highly socially significant and sophisticated art. First, it was a symbol of community or clan membership and geographic origin. Each island group had their own style of tattoo: the Tuamotu islands used simple, geometric shapes; the Marquesans' designs were the most intricate and elaborately designed and are the inspiration for contemporary tattoos. Second, it was an initiation rite: in the Marquesas, the onset of adulthood was marked by a ceremony during which young men would display their tattoos as symbols of bravery; women were not allowed to help with the cooking until they passed a rite of having their hands tattooed. Third, social status was displayed through tattooing: as people progressed through different stages of life, they covered their bodies with more tattoos. This aesthetic adornment played a part in the seduction process as well. Finally, tattooing served to intimidate: in the Marquesas, warriors tattooed their faces to make themselves look terrifying to enemies.

LANGUAGE

Tahitian and French are the official languages of French Polynesia, although much of the tourist industry uses English. If you venture to the more remote and less touristy islands, it's useful to know some French. On all islands, at least trying a few words in French, and even more so, Tahitian, will win you friends – fortunately, bad French is readily accepted.

Tahitian, known as reo Maohi, is a Polynesian language very similar to Hawaiian and Cook Islands Maori. Other languages in the islands include Austral, Marquesan and Tuamotuan.

In Tahitian, a glottal stop replaces the consonants 'k' and 'ng'. The Polynesian word

vaka (canoe) is *va'a* in Tahitian. It's important to use the glottal stop as the break can change the meaning of the word. For example, the Tahitian word *hoe* means 'paddle' or 'row', but *ho'e* is the word for 'one'.

Tahitian basics

Hello.	La ora na, nana.
Goodbye.	Parahi, nana.
Welcome.	Maeva, manava.
How are you?	E aha te huru?
Thanks.	Mauruuru roa.
Yes.	E, 'oia.
No.	Aita.
My name is…	To'u i'oa 'o…
I don't understand.	Aita i ta'a ia'u.

ENVIRONMENT

The environmental repercussions of French nuclear testing are still hotly debated. The view that Moruroa and Fangataufa were fissured by tests and that radioactivity had leaked was confirmed in 1999, when the French government admitted for the first time that cracks existed in the atolls' coral cones.

Atolls are ecologically fragile places, but French Polynesia has been slow to do much to protect them. It's a catch-22: the islands' mainstay, tourism, depends on the idyll of an unspoilt natural environment, but increased development is tarnishing that image.

Geography

French Polynesia is a vast, scattered collection of 118 islands and atolls that stretch across five million sq km of ocean. However, most of these volcanic blips are small and the five archipelagos have a total land area of barely 3500 sq km.

The Society Islands, the westernmost archipelago, have mountains and lagoons protected by barrier reefs, sometimes dotted with small fringing islets known as *motu*. Subdivided into the Windward and Leeward Islands, the Societies are home to more than three-quarters of French Polynesia's population. Polynesia's administrative capital, Pape'ete, is on Tahiti.

The Tuamotus, east of the Society Islands, are classic low-lying coral atolls. The remote Marquesas, north of the Tuamotus and not far from the equator, are rugged high islands but lack barrier reefs or lagoons. Finally, there are the even more remote and scattered Australs, also high islands, and the tiny Gambier Archipelago.

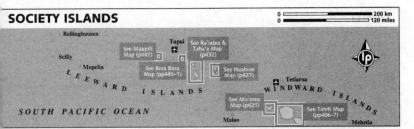

Ecology

Basically, anything that couldn't swim, float or fly to French Polynesia has been introduced; therefore the flora and fauna is limited compared with that of the west Pacific. There are no snakes but plenty of insects and about 100 species of *manu* (birds). Seabirds include terns, petrels, noddies, frigate birds and boobies.

Any dismay about the lack of animal diversity on land is quickly made up for by the quantity of underwater species – it's all here. The coral reefs provide a rich environment for sea creatures including *rori* (sea cucumber), sharks, *ono* (barracuda), manta rays, moray eels, dolphins and the endangered *honu* (turtle). In Nuku Hiva, in the Marquesas, electra dolphins, also known as pygmy orcas or melon-headed whales, gather in their hundreds in a unique phenomenon; while on Rurutu, Tahiti and Mo'orea it's possible to swim with humpback whales.

Ancient Polynesian navigators brought plants and fruits that flourished. In the 19th century missionaries and settlers imported other ornamental and commercial plants. Vegetation varies significantly from one archipelago to another. On the atolls, where the soil is poor and winds constant, bushy vegetation and coconut palms predominate. On the high islands, plant cover is more diverse and changes according to the altitude.

TAHITI

pop 178,083 / area 1045 sq km

Tahiti might have a scant collection of white beaches and vistas over turquoise lagoons, but it's the undisputable centre of modern French Polynesian culture; plus the nightlife and outdoor adventures available make it the most action-packed island in the country. The near vertical, waterfall-laden mountains are as inviting as ever and are becoming increasingly popular for lush day hikes and canyoning (rappelling down waterfalls). The surf pumps year-round and locals are friendly enough to share their breaks; Pape'ete's clubs rock on till 4am and the best dance performances in the country take place at the annual Heiva Festival (p477) and at the big resorts. It's not a Gauguin painting, but Tahiti is a myth-busting version of Polynesia that would be a shame to miss.

ORIENTATION

The *pointe kilométrique* (PK; kilometre point) markers start at zero in Pape'ete and increase in both a clockwise and an anticlockwise direction around Tahiti Nui until they meet at Taravao, the town at the isthmus that connects Tahiti Nui with Tahiti Iti. Taravao is 54km from Pape'ete clockwise (via the east coast) and 60km anticlockwise (via the west coast). The counting starts again on Tahiti Iti, where the markers only go as far as the sealed road – remarkably, there's no road along the easternmost coast.

INFORMATION

The tourist office, main post office, the majority of the banks and the best bookshops are all clustered in Pape'ete.

Bookshops

Pape'ete has a few good bookshops, but the range in English is always poor.

La Maison de la Presse (Map pp416-17; Blvd Pomare) This is the best choice in town for mags and news in English.
Odyssey (Map p416; ☎ 50 13 15; 9 Place de la Cathédrale) It's huge but has only a small English section.

Emergency
Ambulance (☎ 15)
Police (☎ 17)

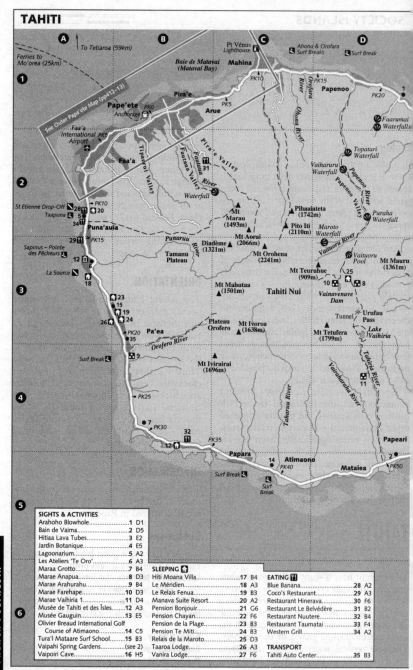

TAHITI

To Tetiaroa (59km)

Ferries to Mo'orea (25km)

Baie de Matavai (Matavai Bay)

Pt Vénus Lighthouse

Ahonu & Orofara Surf Breaks

Surf Break

Mahina

PK10

Orofara River

Ohonu River

PK15

Papenoo

PK20

1

Faarumai Waterfalls

Topatari Waterfall

Vaiharuru Waterfall

Papenoo River

Papenoo Valley

Pira'e

PK5

See Outer Pape'ete Map (pp412-13)

Pape'ete

PK0

Anchorage

Arue

Pira'e Valley

Pirae Valley

Fautaua Valley

Fautaua River

Waterfall

31

Faa'a International Airport

PK5

Faa'a

Tipaerui Valley

Tipaerui River

Mt Marau (1493m)

Pihaaiateta (1742m)

Pito Iti (2110m)

Maroto

Maroto Waterfall

Puraha Waterfall

St Etienne Drop-Off

28 20

Taapuna 5

34

Puna'auia

PK10

Mt Aorai (2066m)

Mt Orohena (2241m)

Vaihuru River

Vaituoru Pool

Vaituoru

Mt Mauru (1361m)

29 PK15

Sapinus – Pointe des Pêcheurs

12 6

La Source

18

Punaruu River

Diadème (1321m)

Tamanu Plateau

Mt Teuruhue (909m)

10 25 8

Tahiti Nui

Vainavenave Dam

23

15

19 24

26 35

Pa'ea

PK20

Plateau Orofero

Oropero River

Mt Ivoroa (1638m)

Mt Mahutaa (1501m)

Tunnel

Urufau Pass

Lake Vaihiria

Mt Tetufera (1799m)

Surf Break 9

Mt Iyirairai (1696m)

Taharuu River

Vaitehararahia River

Tahiria River

11

PK25

7 PK30

32

17 PK35

Papara

14 PK40

Atimaono

Papeari

2 PK50

Mataiea

Surf Break

Surf Break

SIGHTS & ACTIVITIES
Arahoho Blowhole	1 D1
Bain de Vaima	2 D5
Hitiaa Lava Tubes	3 E2
Jardin Botanique	4 E5
Lagoonarium	5 A2
Les Ateliers 'Te Oro'	6 A3
Maraa Grotto	7 B4
Marae Anapua	8 D3
Marae Araharuhu	9 B4
Marae Farehape	10 D3
Marae Vaihiria 1	11 D4
Musée de Tahiti et des Îsles	12 A3
Musée Gauguin	13 E5
Olivier Breaud International Golf Course of Atimaono	14 C5
Tura'I Mataare Surf School	15 B3
Vaipahi Spring Gardens	(see 2)
Vaipoiri Cave	16 H5

SLEEPING
Hiti Moana Villa	17 B4
Le Méridien	18 A3
Le Relais Fenua	19 B3
Manava Suite Resort	20 A2
Pension Bonjouir	21 G6
Pension Chayan	22 F6
Pension de la Plage	23 B3
Pension Te Miti	24 B3
Relais de la Maroto	25 D3
Taaroa Lodge	26 A3
Vanira Lodge	27 F6

EATING
Blue Banana	28 A2
Coco's Restaurant	29 A3
Restaurant Hinerava	30 F6
Restaurant Le Belvédère	31 B2
Restaurant Nuutere	32 B4
Restaurant Taumatai	33 F4
Western Grill	34 A2

TRANSPORT
Tahiti Auto Center	35 B3

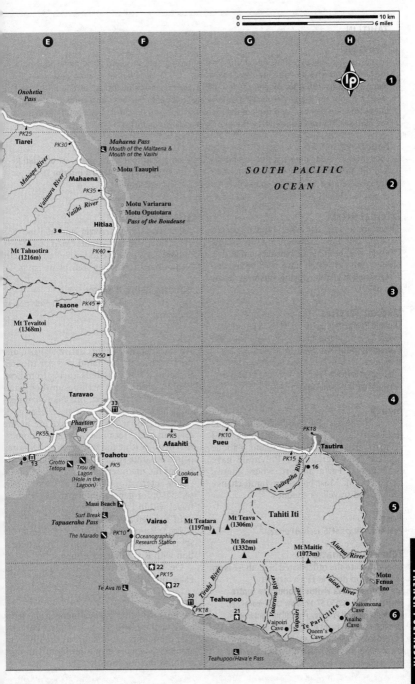

TAHITI IN...

Two Days

Spend the first day exploring colourful Pape'ete, making sure to spend some time shopping at the famous **Marché de Pape'ete** (Pape'ete Market; (p415). Have dinner at a chic restaurant like **Mango Café** (p415). After dinner, catch a dance performance and cocktail at one of the posh resorts, or opt for a night of dancing in Pape'ete's cacophonous **bars and clubs** (p419). Head out of town on day two, and explore the island on your own or with a tour. Spend the night at the fantastic **Vanira Lodge** (p415), the most creative *pension* in Tahiti.

Four Days

Follow the two-day itinerary, then spend day three on a boat tour along the coast of Tahiti Iti and the **Te Pari** (p412). On day four take a hiking excursion to the **island's interior** (p412) or just plop yourself on a beach somewhere with mask, fins and a snorkel.

Internet Access

There are at least 10 cyber cafes in central Pape'ete but few elsewhere on the island. Outside of Pape'ete your best bets are at post offices, most of which have wi-fi access and a terminal available during business hours (see p477).

Medical Services

Clinique Paofai (Map pp416-17; ☎ 46 18 18; cnr Blvd Pomare & Rue du Lieutenant Varney; ☽ 24hr) Private clinic.
Mamao Hospital (Map pp412-13; ☎ 46 62 62, 24hr emergencies 42 01 01; Ave Georges Clémenceau) The biggest hospital in French Polynesia, with good facilities and a range of medical specialities.

Money

There are banks (Banque Socredo, Banque de Tahiti and Banque de Polynésie) and ATMs scattered around the island. Banque Socredo and Banque de Polynésie have branches at Faa'a airport, where there's also an ATM. Most banks on Tahiti change money and travellers cheques.

Post

Post office (Map pp416-17; Blvd Pomare)

Tourist Information

In addition to the office listed here, there is an information desk at Faa'a airport.
Gie Tahiti Manava visitor information centre (Map pp416-17; ☎ 50 57 12; www.tahiti-manava.pf; Fare Manihini, Blvd Pomare; ☽ 7.30am-5pm Mon-Fri, 8am-noon Sat) Has heaps of information on all of French Polynesia. Although Mo'orea and Bora Bora have helpful tourist offices, the more remote islands don't, so if you have any queries, ask here.

TRANSPORT

All international arrivals land at Pape'ete's Faa'a International Airport (Map pp412–13), although it's possible to head almost directly to another island after your plane lands.

Getting There & Away

Pape'ete is the hub of all French Polynesian transport.

AIR

All international flights arrive at Faa'a airport, with both Air Tahiti and Air Moorea flights to the other islands leaving from here. Flights within each archipelago hop from one island to the next, but many connections between archipelagos are via Faa'a.

International check-in desks are at the east end of the terminal. Air Tahiti's domestic check-in is at the west end; Air Moorea is in a separate small terminal slightly to the east of the main terminal.

For international flights to/from Tahiti, see p480; for general information about air travel within French Polynesia, see p481.

In Pape'ete, **Air Tahiti** (Map pp416-17; ☎ 86 42 42; Rue du Maréchal Foch; ☽ 7am-5pm Mon-Fri, 8-11am Sat) is both at the airport and at the intersection with Rue Edouard Ahnne.

On Tahiti, **Air Moorea** (☎ 86 41 41) is based at Faa'a airport.

BOAT

All boats to other islands moor at the ferry quay at the northern end of Blvd Pomare. The numerous cargo ships to the different archipelagos work from the Motu Uta port zone, to the north of the city.

See p482 for general information on inter-island ships, and the individual island chapters or sections for specific information on travel to/from those destinations.

Getting Around

Public transport in Tahiti is limited so you're best off renting a car.

TO/FROM THE AIRPORT

Taxis are expensive in French Polynesia, so if your hotel offers to collect you from the airport, jump at the chance. Otherwise the taxi drive to central Pape'ete will set you back 2000 CFP during the day and 2500 CFP at night (8pm to 6am).

If you arrive at a reasonable time of the day, you'll be able to catch any bus going towards town from the airport, which will take you straight to the centre of Pape'ete in about 15 minutes for a flat fare of 130 CFP during the day and 250 CFP after 6pm (children cost 65 CFP; it's an extra 100 CFP for your baggage). Walk straight across the car park outside the airport, up the steps to street level and across the road to hail a city-bound bus. From Pape'ete to the airport, take a bus heading to Faa'a and Outumaoro – the destination will be clearly posted on the front – from along Rue du Général de Gaulle.

Bus

Weekdays, buses around Pape'ete and along the west and north coasts operate roughly every 15 minutes from dawn until about 5.30pm except for the Pape'ete–Faa'a–Outumaoro line, which supposedly operates 24 hours but in reality gets very quiet after 10pm. Services are less frequent on weekends. Fares start from 130 CFP (80 CFP for children and students), and getting to Tahiti Iti costs 400 CFP.

Tahiti's buses have their route number and the final destination clearly marked. There are official bus stops but drivers will stop if you hail them.

Car

Driving in Tahiti is quite straightforward and, although accident statistics are not encouraging, the traffic is fairly light once you get away from Pape'ete. Apart from the freeway out of Pape'ete to the west, the traffic saunters along at an island pace.

Many of the following car-rental agencies also have desks at the big hotels.

Avis Faa'a airport (Map pp412-13; ☎ 85 02 84); Rue des Remparts (Map pp416-17; ☎ 54 10 10; cnr Rue des Remparts & Ave Georges Clémenceau)

Daniel Rent-a-Car (Map pp412-13; ☎ 82 30 04; Faa'a airport)

Europcar Faa'a airport (Map pp412-13; ☎ 86 60 61); Pape'ete (Map pp416-17; ☎ 45 24 24; cnr Ave du Prince Hinoi & Rue des Remparts)

Hertz (Map pp412-13; ☎ 82 55 86; Faa'a airport)

Tahiti Auto Center (Map pp406-7; ☎ 82 33 33; www .tahitiautocenter.pf; PK20.2, Pa'ea) Had the cheapest published rates at the time of writing.

Tahiti Rent-a-Car (Map pp412-13; ☎ 81 94 00; Faa'a airport)

Hitching

Hitching in Tahiti is relatively easy and usually quite safe, but solo women could encounter problems and should use common sense (ie don't get in a car full of men). Avoid hitching on Friday and Saturday nights, when the roads are filled with alarmingly intoxicated drivers.

TAXI

Taxis are so expensive that most visitors choose to ignore them (except when arriving at the airport late at night). All the big hotels have taxi ranks, and there are plenty of taxis in central Pape'ete.

PAPE'ETE

With Polynesian smiles, French-style sidewalk cafes and the occasional guy on the kerb strumming a ukulele, Pape'ete does feel exotic despite its lack of beaches and blue water. Yeah, the edges are grimy and it's a little seedy, but the waterfront's new palm-fringed promenade has made the town prettier and the busy streets and lanes are dripping with fabulous restaurants. If you're looking for a night out, this is the country's best stop but beyond boogying, there's really not more than a day or two worth of sights to keep you busy. For anything resembling a holiday brochure, get out of town.

Between Rue du 22 Septembre and Rue F Cardella is the colourful and oh-so Polynesian **Marché de Pape'ete** (Map pp416-17; ☷ 6am-6pm) that's bursting with flowers, food, tropical fruit, pâtisseries, art and souvenirs. The food is downstairs and the rest, upstairs.

The bustling **waterfront** is another big attraction; although beyond watching the yachts, cargo ships and inter-island ferries toing and froing with their cargos of people and goods there's not much to see. By mid-2009 a man-made beach just northeast of To'ata Square should be completed, but we'd advise against swimming in the polluted port waters.

Towards the outer edge of Pape'ete's urban sprawl in Arue is a replica of *Mutiny on the Bounty* co-author **James Norman Hall's house** (Map pp412-13; admission adult/child 600 CFP/free; ⊗ 9am-4pm Mon-Sat). The house is in a shady garden and is decorated with Hall's original circa-1920s furniture, plus heaps of photos and memorabilia.

Walking Tour

It's easy to get lost in Pape'ete and dumping the map and throwing caution to the trade winds is the best way to explore the town. Fortunately, the centre is so small that it's equally as easy to find your way home again. This route makes a good base from which to branch out on your own.

Start from the west along the four-lane Blvd Pomare, shaded by overhanging trees. **To'ata Square** (1; above) is spacious, paved and a lovely place for strolling as long as it's not mid-day – there's not a speck of shade.

You can't miss Central Pape'ete's imposing pink church, the **Temple Paofai** (2); the missionaries would be rapt to see how busy the church is on a Sunday morning.

On the inland side of the road is the **Robert Wan Museé de la Perle** (3) where you can bask in the air-con before warming up again in the shady, green haven of **Parc Bougainville** (4) further down the road.

Continue along Blvd Pomare till you reach **Vaima Centre** (5), with shops, a few restaurants, internet cafe and most of the airline offices. Stop here for a drink at the iconic, yet pricey **Le Rétro** (6; p419), great for people-watching.

Continue along the waterfront and then turn right into Rue du 22 Septembre to the **Marché de Pape'ete** (7; p409). If it's lunchtime, head upstairs to see if the local band is playing.

WALK FACTS

Start To'ata Sq
Finish Place Vaiete
Distance 2km
Duration Two hours

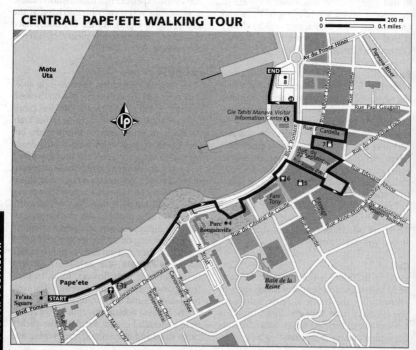

CENTRAL PAPE'ETE WALKING TOUR

If you stroll back towards Blvd Pomare, on the harbour side is the **Place Vaiete** (8), which is home to multiple *roulottes* (food vans) and occasional live music at night but is quite peaceful during the day. There are plenty of public benches along here where you can sit and watch the world go by.

Sights

It's another world outside of Pape'ete: the sea is a deep blue, the jagged, green mountains frame the sky and cars putter along at 50km/h.

AROUND TAHITI NUI
Coast Road

The following is a 114km clockwise circuit around Tahiti Nui.

The **Baie de Matavai** (Matavai Bay; Map pp412-13) was the favourite locale of early European explorers. **Point Vénus** (Map pp412-13; PK10), the promontory that marks the bay's eastern end, was the site of Cook's observatory, built to record the transit of Venus across the face of the sun to try to calculate the distance between the sun and the earth. Today it's a popular, shaded black-sand beach overlooked by an impressive lighthouse. It's unsigned; just turn off at Venus Star Supermarket at PK10.

In the right swell the **Arahoho Blowhole** (Map pp406-7; PK22), just before Tiarei, puts on a good show. Just 100m past the blowhole, a sign-posted road heads inland to the trailhead for the three exceedingly high **Faarumai waterfalls** (Map pp406-7; PK22).

Once you reach **Taravao** (Map pp406-7; PK54) you're at the narrow isthmus where Tahiti Nui joins Tahiti Iti. If you're not going to Tahiti Iti (right), continue along the road and you'll come to the **Jardin Botanique** (Botanic Gardens; Map pp406-7; PK51.2; admission 500 CFP; 9am-5pm), where walking paths wend their way through 137 hectares of ponds, palms and a superb *mape* (chestnut) forest. Nearby is the interesting **Musée Gauguin** (Gauguin Museum; Map pp406-7; admission 600 CFP; 9am-5pm). Don't expect too many original works but do wander the gardens.

From the **Bain de Vaima** (Vaima Pool; Map pp406-7; PK49) it's a short hop to **Vaipahi Spring Gardens** (Map pp406-7), which rivals the beauty of the Botanical Gardens and has an impressive natural waterfall. A number of short walks start from the gardens and lead to more falls; a two-hour loop is the longest but it's not well-marked.

At PK28.5 wander the manicured path that runs beside the road and through **Maraa**

Grotto (Map pp406-7), a series of overhung, ferny caverns with crystal-clear pools set in a fairytale park.

In the Pa'ea district tranquil **Marae Arahurahu** (Map pp406-7; PK22.5) is the best-looking *marae* (traditional temple) on the island. The **Orofero River** (Map pp406-7; PK20) is a popular surfing break.

The excellent **Musée de Tahiti et des Îles** (Museum of Tahiti & its Islands; Map pp406-7; ☎ 58 34 76; PK15.1; admission 1000 CFP; 9.30am-5.30pm Tue-Sun) in Puna'auia has one of the best collections in the Pacific, including dioramas about island geology, archaeological finds and ancient art. Outside is one of Tahiti's most popular surf breaks.

Inland

It's a wonderful but rugged 39km road across Tahiti from Papenoo in the north to Mataiea in the south, via the Relais de la Maroto hotel and Lake Vaihiria. Unfortunately the road is closed between the lake and the hotel, so you can only see half of the route in one day.

From Papenoo the track follows the wide **Papenoo Valley** (Map pp406-7), the only valley to cut right through the ancient crater, passing waterfalls and pools before finally reaching the Relais de la Maroto.

From here tracks fan out to several *marae*, including the extensive **Marae Farehape** (Map pp406-7) and the beautifully restored **Marae Anapua** (Map pp406-7). There are some fine natural swimming pools and striking waterfalls nearby.

If starting the route from the south coast at PK47.5, the track follows the river to a catchment lake and the extensive remains of **Marae Vaihiria I** (Map pp406-7). From here the road climbs quickly to **Lake Vaihiria** (Map pp406-7).

You can walk inland from Pape'ete to the **Fautaua Valley trail** (Map pp406-7) which doesn't require a guide, but you will need an access permit (adult/child 600/150 CFP). You can get this at the Pape'ete *mairie* (town hall) at the **Service des Régies des Recettes** (☎ 41 58 36); enter the building from Rue des Écoles. You can also get directions to the trail here.

Inland from Hitiaa on the east coast are the **Hitiaa Lava Tubes** (Map pp406-7), elongated volcanic caverns with a river running through them. You'll need a guide (p413) to hike this extraordinary (but cold and wet) area.

TAHITI ITI

If you're looking for old-school Tahiti this should be your first stop. Tahiti Iti is the

TAHITI &
FRENCH POLYNESIA

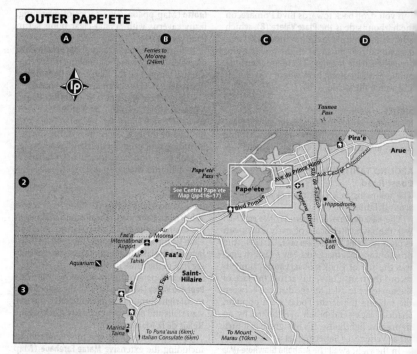

OUTER PAPE'ETE

quiet, unpretentious half of the island that attracts hikers, surfers and seekers of calm with its wild coastlines, clean lagoon and laid back pace.

The road only goes as far as Teahupoo to the south and Tautira in the north, so you can't drive around the whole island. The northcoast road from Taravao runs past steep hills and waterfalls to Tautira. The southcoast road runs past beaches and bays to Teahupoo. The size and hollowness of the wave at **Teahupoo** (Map pp406–7) have earned it an international reputation. The road stops abruptly at the Tirahi River at PK18; from here it's a two-hour walk to **Vaipoiri Cave** (Map pp406–7); another kilometre and a half along the coast from here the **Te Pari Cliffs** begin. You can hike the 8km of this coast dotted with archaeological treasures, waterfalls and caves, but only in good weather and if the swell isn't too big. A guide is essential (see opposite).

Activities

There's more to do on Tahiti than anywhere else in French Polynesia.

BEACHES

The best stretches of white sand and decent snorkelling have public entries at PK15, PK18 and PK18.5 in Puna'auia. One of Tahiti's widest beaches is at Papara's Taharuu Beach (between PK38 and PK39), which has black sand, big surf and lots of local guys hanging out and drinking beer.

On the east coast the best beach is Point Vénus (Map pp412–13; PK10), and Tahiti Iti's best black sand beaches are found in the villages of Tautira and Teahupoo.

BOAT EXCURSIONS

Probably the most fun you can have in a day on Tahiti is taking a boat excursion in Tahiti Iti. The most professional boat operator is **Teahupoo Excursions** (☎ 75 11 98; www.web.me.com /teahupooexcursion; hour/half day/full day 5000/18,000/35,000 CFP for up to six people) who run à la carte tours, or head out to the Teahupoo wave to watch surfing or to surf for 1000 CFP per person.

HIKING & CANYONING

Hiking is taking off in Tahiti, and canyoning (rappelling down waterfalls) is an

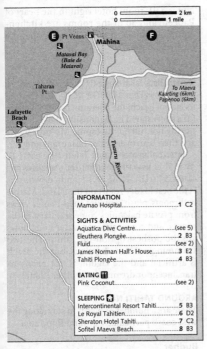

even more exhilarating way to explore the interior. There are a handful of DIY hikes around the island, particularly the **Fautaua Valley Trail** (see p411) and the trails from the **Vaipahi Spring Gardens** (p411). The best guided hiking spots are the **Hitiaa Lava Tubes** (p411) and the **Te Pari Cliffs** (opposite). For a list of guides, contact **Syndicat des Guides de Randonnées de Polynesie Francaise** (☎ 56 16 48; syndicatguides@hotmail.com).

DIVING & WHALE-WATCHING
There are some excellent diving opportunities in Tahiti, and some dive shops also lead whale-watching tours between July and October when humpbacks swim near the coasts.

Aquatica Dive Center (Map pp412-13; ☎ 53 34 96; www.aquatica-dive.com; Intercontinental Resort) Also lead whale-watching, fishing and jet ski tours.

Eleuthera Plongée (Map pp412-13; ☎ 42 49 29; www.dive-tahiti.com; Marina Taina) A big outfit who also lead whale-watching excursions.

Fluid (Map pp412-13; ☎ 85 41 46, 70 83 75; Marina Taina).

Tahiti Plongée (Map pp412-13; ☎ 41 00 62, 43 62 51; www.tahitiplongee.pf; PK7.5, Puna'auia)

SURFING
Tahiti offers some fabulous beginner breaks particularly at Papenoo and along the east coast. More advanced surfers can head to the Papara shore break and the reef breaks at Sapinus and Taapuna along the west coast, and the Tapuaeraha Pass (Big Vairao Pass) and Te Ava Iti (small Viarao Pass) at Tahiti Iti. Tahiti's most radical wave is at Hava'e Pass in Teahupoo on Tahiti Iti, where there's a big international surf contest held each May; see p477 for details.

To paddle out for your first time or hone your skills, visit **Tura'l Mataare Surf School** (Map pp406-7; ☎ 41 91 37; surfschool@mail.pf; PK 18.3; Wed, Sat & Sun) on the mountain side of the road in Pae'a. Half-day lessons including transfers and equipment are 4800 CFP.

GOLF
The **Olivier Breaud International Golf Course of Atimaono** (Map pp406-7; ☎ 57 40 32; PK 40.2, Papara; nine holes 3300 CFP) is a beautiful 18-hole par-72 course with some rather difficult par 3s.

Courses
Les Ateliers 'Te Oro' (Map pp406-7; ☎ 58 30 27; http://danse-emergence.typepad.fr, in French; Tamanu Center Puna'auia) offers two-, three- and five-day Tahitian dance workshops (from two to four hours per day) for adults and children from age 11. Prices depend on group size and the length of the course. The same school runs classes on Mo'orea as well – see the website for details.

Tahiti for Children
Travelling with children is extremely easy in Tahiti. Any kid who loves the beach will love French Polynesia, and Polynesians absolutely love children. Just outside Pape'ete's urban sprawl, the **Lagoonarium** (Map pp406-7; ☎ 43 62 90; PK11; adult/child 500/300 CFP; 9am-6pm) is a meshed-in area of lagoon with a modest underwater viewing room; it's reached through a giant (though crumbling) concrete shark's mouth. The entrance to the Lagoonarium is part of the Captain Bligh Restaurant, so if you eat at the restaurant, there's no charge to visit the Lagoonarium.

Kids will also dig the huge Galapagos tortoises at the 137-hectare **Jardin Botanique** (p411), on the far south coast of Tahiti Nui. It's also great fun exploring the walking paths, past ponds and palms, eels, crabs, ducks and chickens.

Sleeping

Central Pape'ete is not the place to stay if you're looking for tranquillity; the options on the outskirts of town offer more palm-fringed, beach-like choices.

All places listed here take credit cards.

PAPE'ETE

Cityside digs are the best places to stay if you want to enjoy the nightlife.

Budget

our pick **Fare Suisse** (off Map pp416–17; ☎ 42 00 30; www .fare-suisse.com; dm 5500 CFP, d/f 10,000/15,000 CFP; ✕ 🖳) The tiled rooms here are bright, quiet and are decorated with bamboo furniture. Beni, the dynamic owner, picks guests up free of charge at the airport, lets them store their luggage and creates a super pleasant atmosphere. Breakfast is an extra 1200 CFP.

Ahitea Lodge (off Map pp416–17; ☎ 53 13 53; pension .ahitea@mail.pf; r with breakfast from 8500 CFP; ✕ 🖳) The only budget place in town with a pool, this central place is a real bargain. Rooms are big and tiled; the cheapest ones have shared bath and no air-con. There's a comfy lounge area, communal kitchen and a garden.

Midrange

Sofitel Maeva Beach (Map pp412–13; ☎ 42 80 42; www .sofitel.com; Maeva Beach; d 16,000–20,000 CFP; ✕ 🖳 🖭) With prices that nudge it into the midrange category, this resort is one of the better deals on the island. The '70s style exterior could use a facelift, but rooms have one of the happiest (think fluorescent) colour schemes around if you can handle it. The semi man-made white-sand beach, with Mo'orea smack dab in the distance, really makes you feel you're on a tropical holiday.

Le Royal Tahitien (Map pp412–13; ☎ 50 40 40; www.hotel royaltahitien.com; r 18,000 CFP; ✕ 🖭) The circa 1975 tiki-tacky decor here is so well-kept that it's become appealingly retro. Rooms have wood panelling, olive-green carpet and orange Formica countertops, but they're clean and the staff are smiling. The grounds are studded with mango trees and plumeria, and the pool has a cool fake waterfall; there's a skinny black-sand beach in front. Local musicians perform on Friday and Saturday evenings and the place can really rock.

Hotel Tahiti Nui (Map pp416–17; ☎ 50 33 50; www.hotel tahitinui.com; r/ste 18,000/25,000 CFP; ✕ 🖳 🖭) Not yet open at the time of research, the Tahiti Nui is a 91-room hotel right in the heart of Papeete and 50 of the rooms are kitchen-equipped suites. It will have a pool and a business centre.

Top End

Sheraton Hotel Tahiti (Map pp412–13; ☎ 86 48 48; www.star woodtahiti.com; r from 33,000 CFP; ✕ 🖳 🖭) Despite its lack of beach, the Sheraton is a lovely place for a short stay. The lagoonside pool is fantastic, the hot tub has awesome Mo'orea views and there's an over-water restaurant and bar.

Intercontinental Resort Tahiti (Map pp412–13; ☎ 86 51 10; www.tahiti.interconti.com; r/bungalows from 40,000/55,000 CFP; ✕ 🖳 🖭) Hands down, this is the best luxury resort on the island. Marble bathrooms, plush canopies and Mo'orea views from private balconies come standard in the rooms, and romantic over-water bungalows are the poshest option on Tahiti. The two swimming pools are fabulous, but the beach is artificial and the lagoon is not nearly as translucent or dreamy as on other islands.

AROUND TAHITI NUI

There are a number of places to stay along the west coast, particularly around Puna'auia.

Budget

Pension Te Miti (Map pp406–7; ☎ 58 48 61; www.pensiontemiti .com; PK18.6; dm 2500 CFP, r from 6500 CFP; ✕) Run by a young, friendly French couple, this lively place has a low-key backpacker vibe. It's about 200m from a white-sand beach and prices include breakfast. There's an equipped communal kitchen, a few bicycles for guests' use and a laundry service (500 CFP); 24-hour airport transfers are available for 1500 CFP per person.

our pick **Taaroa Lodge** (Map pp406–7; ☎ 58 39 21; www .taaroalodge.com; PK18; dm 2500 CFP, r 6000 CFP, bungalow 10,000 CFP) Right on the beach and a fabulous bargain, you'll have to book way in advance to get a bed here. Breakfast is included, there are kitchen facilities and a really friendly atmosphere. The lodge is owned by Ralph Stanford, the ex-longboard surfing champion of Tahiti and France.

Midrange

Relais de la Maroto (Map pp406–7; ☎ 57 90 29; maroto@mail .pf; r 7000 CFP, bungalows from 9500 CFP) Smack in the lush heart of the island, this place has renovated but musty motel-style rooms and also a few bungalows to choose from. The restaurant here is OK but expensive. The wine cellar is exceptional and there are regular wine-tasting evenings frequented by Tahiti's elite.

Pension de la Plage (Map pp406-7; ☎ 45 56 12; www .pensiondelaplage.com; PK15.4; s/d/f 7900/8800/12,800 CFP; 🛋 🖳) Just across the road from Puna'auia's white-sand beach, this impeccably maintained place offers comfortable motel-style rooms in several garden-side buildings around a swimming pool. Each has tile floors and giant windows; some have kitchenettes. Breakfast is available for 900 CFP and dinner for 2500 CFP.

Hiti Moana Villa (Map pp406-7; ☎ 57 93 93; hitimoana villa@mail.pf; PK32; bungalows from 9000 CFP; 🛋) Spotlessly clean bungalows set around a well-tended garden make this lagoonside spot in Papara a great option. There is no beach, but there is a pontoon for swimming and a small swimming pool. Bicycles and kayaks can be rented. Airport transfers cost 1500 CFP per person each way.

Le Relais Fenua (Map pp406-7; ☎ 45 01 98; www.relais -fenua.pf; PK18.25; r from 9400 CFP; 🛋 🖳 🛋) A great option in Pa'ea, with clean and spacious rooms with TVs set around a little swimming pool. The lagoon is just across the road, and there's a few affordable eating options just around the corner. Airport transfers cost 1500 CFP and breakfast costs 1000 CFP per person.

Top End
Manava Suite Resort (Map pp406-7; ☎ 50 84 45; www.pearl resorts.com; PK 10.8; 🛋 🖳 🛋) Scheduled to open in April 2009 (check website for pricing), the Manava offers modern suites and studios all with mini kitchens. The infinity pool promises to be the biggest on Tahiti.

Le Méridien (Map pp406-7; ☎ 47 07 07; www.lemeridien .com; r from 38,000 CFP, bungalows 72,000 CFP; 🛋 🖳 🛋) Le Méridien has lovely grounds dotted with lily ponds and fronted by a natural white-sand beach with Mo'orea views – if you want a resort where you can swim in the lagoon on Tahiti, this is your best bet. The rooms are a bit disappointing, with tiled floors and aging furniture and bedspreads.

TAHITI ITI
The south coast of Tahiti Iti has some of the best sleeping options on the whole island. You'll also eat well over here.

Midrange
Pension Bonjouir (Map pp406-7; ☎ 77 89 69; www .bonjouir.com; r 7000 CFP, bungalows 11,500 CFP; 🖳)

You'll need to take the shuttle boat from the dock at PK17 in Teahupoo (2200 CFP return) or walk about 40 minutes to get to this, lush beach-side remote spot, but once you get here you may never want to leave. Accommodation is nothing fancy but has Tahitian flair. Bring mosquito repellent even though all the beds have nets. Half board is 4500 CFP and a few bungalows have their own kitchens.

our pick **Vanira Lodge** (Map pp406-7; ☎ 57 70 18; www .vaniralodge.com; d bungalows 12,500 CFP, f bungalows with kitchen 14,000 CFP; 🛋) Drive up a steep driveway on this mini plateau to enjoy vast views of the lagoon. The seven bungalows are all built from a combination of bamboo, thatch, rustic planks of wood, glass, coral and rock. Cosy nooks, handcarved furniture, airy mezzanines and al fresco kitchens are unique touches. Breakfast costs 1200 CFP, but you're on your own for other meals. Bikes and kayaks are free, but you'll want a car if you stay here.

Pension Chayan (Map pp406-7; ☎ 57 46 00; www .pensionchayantahiti.pf; PK14, Vairao; r from 15,000 CFP) Chayan has four sparkling concrete bungalows – all with minikitchens – nestled in a magnificent tropical garden complete with a spectacular waterfall and natural bathing pool. Across the road there is a small black-sand beach for swimming. The owners are friendly and super helpful.

Eating
Unless otherwise noted, the following places all accept credit cards.

PARADISE ON THE CHEAP
If your budget doesn't allow for 50,000 CFP hotel rooms and 3000 CFP lunches, don't despair – it's still possible to have a great time on Tahiti.

- **Best free sights** Le Marché de Pape'ete (p409), and Faarumai Waterfalls (p411).
- **Best free activity** Hiking around Vaipahi Spring Gardens (p411).
- **Best Cheap Eats** Breakfast on fresh pastries and lunch on baguette sandwiches from local grocery stores. For dinner get anything from a *roulotte* (food vans) on the Pape'ete waterfront (p416) or at random roadside locations around the island.

CENTRAL PAPE'ETE

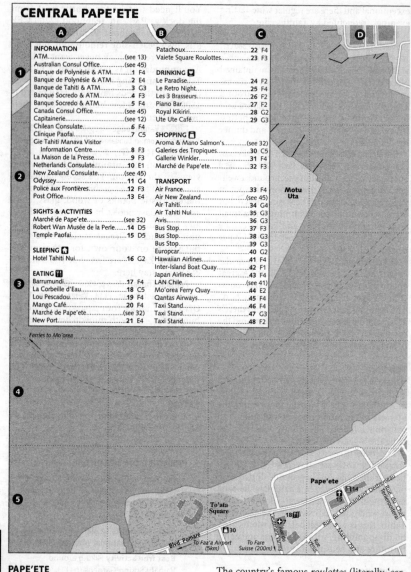

INFORMATION
ATM......................................(see 13)
Australian Consul Office..........(see 45)
Banque de Polynésie & ATM.......**1** F4
Banque de Polynésie & ATM.......**2** E4
Banque de Tahiti & ATM............**3** G3
Banque Socredo & ATM.............**4** F3
Banque Socredo & ATM.............**5** F4
Canada Consul Office...............(see 45)
Capitainerie............................(see 12)
Chilean Consulate....................**6** F4
Clinique Paofai........................**7** C5
Gie Tahiti Manava Visitor
    Information Centre...............**8** F3
La Maison de la Presse.............**9** F3
Netherlands Consulate.............**10** E1
New Zealand Consulate............(see 45)
Odyssey.................................**11** G4
Police aux Frontières...............**12** F3
Post Office.............................**13** E4

SIGHTS & ACTIVITIES
Marché de Pape'ete.................(see 32)
Robert Wan Musée de la Perle....**14** D5
Temple Paofai.........................**15** D5

SLEEPING 🛏
Hotel Tahiti Nui.......................**16** G2

EATING 🍴
Barrumundi.............................**17** F4
La Corbeille d'Eau....................**18** C5
Lou Pescadou..........................**19** F4
Mango Café.............................**20** F4
Marché de Pape'ete.................(see 32)
New Port................................**21** E4

Patachoux..............................**22** F4
Vaiete Square Roulottes...........**23** F3

DRINKING 🍷
Le Paradise.............................**24** F2
Le Retro Night.........................**25** F4
Les 3 Brasseurs.......................**26** F2
Piano Bar...............................**27** F2
Royal Kikiriri...........................**28** G2
Ute Ute Café...........................**29** G3

SHOPPING 🛍
Aroma & Mano Salmon's...........(see 32)
Galeries des Tropiques.............**30** C5
Gallerie Winkler.......................**31** F4
Marché de Pape'ete.................**32** F3

TRANSPORT
Air France..............................**33** F4
Air New Zealand......................(see 45)
Air Tahiti...............................**34** G4
Air Tahiti Nui..........................**35** G3
Avis......................................**36** G3
Bus Stop...............................**37** F3
Bus Stop...............................**38** G3
Bus Stop...............................**39** G3
Europcar...............................**40** G2
Hawaiian Airlines.....................**41** F4
Inter-Island Boat Quay.............**42** F1
Japan Airlines.........................**43** F4
LAN Chile..............................(see 41)
Mo'orea Ferry Quay.................**44** E2
Qantas Airways.......................**45** F4
Taxi Stand.............................**46** F4
Taxi Stand.............................**47** G3
Taxi Stand.............................**48** F2

Motu
Uta

Ferries to Mo'orea

Pape'ete

To'ata
Square

To Faa'a Airport
(5km)

To Fare
Suisse (200m)

Blvd Pomare

Rue du Commandant Destremeau

Rue du Chef Teriierooiterai

Rue 5 Mars 1797

Rue Venus

PAPE'ETE

Ma'a Tahiti (traditional Tahitian food) is often served as a special on Fridays at many budget and midrange places.

Budget

ourpick **Vaiete Square Roulottes** (Map pp416-17; Vaiete Square; snacks from 200 CFP, mains from 800 CFP; 🕐 dinner)

The country's famous *roulottes* (literally 'caravans' in French) are a gastronomic pleasure. These little mobile stalls sizzle, fry and grill up a storm every evening from around 6pm; things don't quiet down until well into the night. Get good thin-crust pizzas or everything and anything else from hamburgers to crêpes. Finish your meal with a Nutella-and-

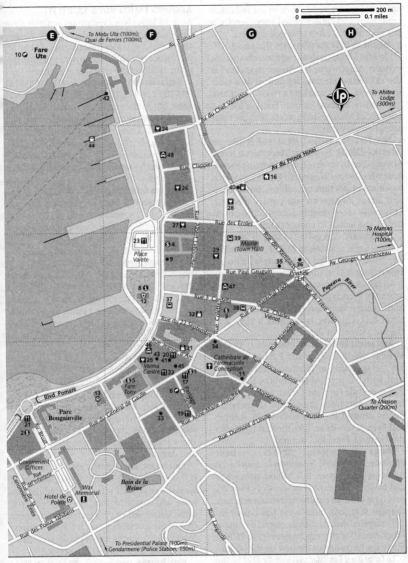

banana waffle. Live music livens the scene most weekend nights. No credit cards.

Patachoux (Map pp416-17; ☎ 83 72 82; sandwiches from 480 CFP; ☺ Mon-Sat) Takeaway sandwiches here are the deluxe version – fresh wholemeal or French bread stuffed with gourmet meats, fish and/or salads. Otherwise sit at the outdoor patio and order from a menu of salads and fresh fish with international flair. Desserts like fruit tarts, creamy French pastries and a divine chocolate fondant from the bakery window are not to be missed.

Lou Pescadou (Map pp416-17; ☎ 43 74 26; Rue Anne-Marie Javouhey; dishes 1100-2800 CFP; ☺ lunch & dinner) A Pape'ete institution, this cheery restaurant has hearty pizza and pasta dishes. It's

TAHITI & FRENCH POLYNESIA

authentic Italian, right down to the red check tablecloths and carafes of red wine. Service is fast and there are lots of veggie options.

Marché de Pape'ete (Map pp416-17; mains 1200 CFP; ☻ breakfast & lunch) Grab one of the daily specials (usually couscous or a Tahitian-style stew) at the cafeteria-style counter and sit at a table in the heat of the market to enjoy live music and plenty of local colour. Food is located upstairs of Marché de Pape'ete, and does not accept credit cards.

New Port (Map pp416-17; ☎ 42 76 52; Blvd Pomare; dishes 1400-2200 CFP; ☻ breakfast & lunch Mon-Sat) If you like or want to try raw fish in its many forms, order the 'assiette Newport' (1800 CFP) which has a small portion of sashimi, *poisson cru* and *tartar du thon* so you can try them all. Otherwise there's plenty of cooked fish, meat dishes and salads to choose from.

Barrumundi (Map pp416-17; ☎ 42 05 35; Rue du Général de Gaulle; sushi plates from 250 CFP, mains from 1500 CFP; ☻ lunch & dinner Wed-Sat, lunch only Tue) You get two restaurants in one at this place: a trendy nouveau-style sushi restaurant downstairs and a swanky French place upstairs. The excellent and creative sushi arrives via a floating conveyer belt. Upstairs, tables have a view over the busy streets of Pape'ete.

Restaurant Le Belvédère (Map pp406-7; ☎ 42 73 44; dishes 2000-5000 CFP; ☻ lunch & dinner) Fondues are the speciality at this fine-dining restaurant, which is perched 600m above the city in Pira'e, outside Pape'ete. Le Belvédère provides free transport from some of the larger hotels in and around Pape'ete at 11.45am, 4.30pm and 7pm. If you drive, take the first right after the Hamuta Total fuel station.

Mango Café (Map pp416-17; ☎ 43 25 55; Rue Jeanne d'Arc; dishes 2200-3600 CFP; ☻ lunch Mon-Fri, dinner Tue-Sat) As far as decor goes, this Miami-style white and bright restaurant is as stylish as Pape'ete gets. The Tahitian cuisine nouveau menu here changes regularly but always has lots of locally inspired dishes, such as *magret de canard* (duck breast) with fresh mangoes (3250 CFP). The wine list is one of the best on the island.

La Corbeille d'Eau (Map pp416-17; ☎ 43 77 14; Blvd Pomare; appetisers & dishes 2500-5000 CFP; ☻ lunch & dinner) There are no prices on the menu here but for the exceptional dining experience you get at this intimate French place, you'll be happy to pay whatever it costs once the bill comes. There are only a handful of tables and the focus is on the food, which is prepared by one of Tahiti's best chefs.

AROUND TAHITI NUI & TAHITI ITI

Most of Tahiti Nui's restaurant action is along the west coast not far from Pape'ete. Besides the following finer restaurants, there are plenty of tasty and inexpensive *roulottes* that open up along the roadside at night.

Restaurant Hinerava (Map pp406-7; ☎ 81 93 61; PK18, Teahupoo; dishes 1200-2000 CFP; ☻ breakfast, lunch & dinner; ✗) At the end of the road in Teahupoo, this is a surprisingly classy place serving very good food. There's a great selection of fish, meats and burger plates, *ma'a Tahiti* (2500 CFP) is available all day on Sundays and daily specials such as *mahi mahi* in vanilla sauce on other days of the week.

Western Grill (Map pp406-7; ☎ 41 30 56; PK 12.6, Puna'auia; mains 1500-2400 CFP; ☻ lunch & dinner) Tired of raw fish? Tie your pony up at this saloon, complete with a Native American statue by the door and Western kitsch a go-go, for a good 'ole American steak or burger and a beer.

Restaurant Taumatai (Map pp406-7; ☎ 57 13 59; Taravao; dishes 1500-2500 CFP; ☻ lunch & dinner Tue-Sat, lunch Sun) Grab a terrace table at this delightful little place in Taravao on the road to Tautira, serving the town's best French and Tahitian food in an elegant garden setting. The restaurant is hidden behind a stone wall, so it's a little hard to find.

Pink Coconut (Map pp412-13; ☎ 41 22 23; Marina Taina, Puna'auia; mains from 1600 CFP; ☻ lunch & dinner) We love this lively spot, right on Marina Taina among the sailboats. Dine on French-inspired fare, like delicious risotto with scallops and wild mushrooms, or a French-style shellfish platter. At night it's candle lit and on the weekends there's sometimes live music and dancing.

Restaurant Nuutere (Map pp406-7; ☎ 57 41 15; PK32.5, Paea; dishes 2000-3500 CFP; ☻ Wed-Mon) French specialities, cooked with local ingredients and some odd imported ones, like ostrich or crocodile, are served in an intimate dining room. One of the specialities here is the *korori* (pearl oyster meat) starter baked gratin-style in sea snail shells. Don't expect fast service.

Blue Banana (Map pp406-7; ☎ 41 22 24; PK11.2, Puna'auia; dishes 2000-4000 CFP; ☻ lunch & dinner Mon-Sat; ✗) Keeping on the psychedelic fruit theme, this hip, lagoonside restaurant is heavenly romantic. The roof in the main dining room retracts, revealing a starry night-sky tableau. The food is as good as the ambience – feast on innovative French dishes (small portions) and fine French vintages from the air-conditioned cellar.

our pick **Coco's Restaurant** (Map pp406–7; ☎ 58 21 08; PK16, Puna'auia; dishes 2000-4500 CFP; ✆ lunch & dinner) Dine in a gorgeous, open plantation-style house bordered by a tropical garden that's framed by coconut trees and looks out to Mo'orea. This is the sort of place that doesn't list prices on the menu, and each dish is served under a silver dome so that everyone can unveil their meal at the same time. The fine food is very French, with lots of seafood options.

Drinking

After a stay on other islands, where nightlife is just about nonexistent, Pape'ete could almost pass itself off as a city of wild abandon, though it only gets super crazy on weekends. There is very little going on after about 10pm outside of Pape'ete.

BARS & PUBS

The snazzy top-end hotels, such as the Sheraton Hotel Tahiti and the Intercontinental Resort Tahiti, all have bars where you can enjoy the ocean breezes and nibble free peanuts.

Ute Ute Café (Map pp416–17; ☎ 53 46 46) Meaning 'red hot' in Tahitian, that's exactly what this place is right now. Decor is city lounge–style red and black, and the coolest DJs and live bands play here. It also serves nouvelle cuisine (with dishes like prime rib with *porcini* mushrooms flambéed in Jack Daniels).

Les 3 Brasseurs (Map pp416–17; Blvd Pomare) This congenial brewpub has excellent microbrewed beer on tap and a constant stream of locals and tourists wanting to sample it. Cover bands perform here at the weekend, and you can also chow on some good French-style pub grub for lunch and dinner.

Le Rétro Night (Map pp416–17; ☎ 42 86 83; Blvd Pomare; ✆ lunch & dinner) It's overpriced with only so-so food, but the location, smack in the centre of Pape'ete in the Vaima Centre, is perhaps the best in town. It's full of attitude and atmosphere, and is a great place for sipping an espresso.

NIGHTCLUBS

Boulevard Pomare is the main drag for nightclubs and discos. From the Tahitian waltz to European electronic music, it's all here. Dress codes are enforced and men in shorts and flip-flops will be turned away; woman can get away with wearing as little as they like. Admission for men is between 1500 CFP and 2000 CFP (which will usually include a free drink) but women can usually

get in for free. Clubs typically close around 3am or 4am.

Le Paradise (Map pp416–17; Blvd Pomare; ✆ Wed-Sat) This is the classic, slightly kitsch Pape'ete bar/disco that attracts a mixed crowd of Polynesians and French.

Royal Kikiriri (Map pp416–17; ☎ 43 58 64; Rue Colette) A local favourite, the Royal Kikiriri showcases live music with its namesake band every night. Just about everyone gets asked to dance, so you'll soon be swaying your hips in the local foxtrot.

Piano Bar (Map pp416–17; Rue des Ecoles; admission 2000 CFP Fri & Sat) A favourite with local transvestites, this classic seedy port bar is where everyone gets their groove on. The music (techno, dance and local) isn't as important as the general atmosphere – snag a dark corner and soak it in. There's a drag show on Friday and Saturday nights at around 2am.

Entertainment

Early nights are the norm on Tahiti unless you're out shaking your hips at the bars and clubs. The only must see is a dance performance which is held several times a week in the big hotels. Brush aside images of cheesy tourist performances; these groups are professional and are enjoyed every bit as much by locals as by wide-eyed visitors. The 45-minute performances generally start at about 8pm. They are often accompanied by a buffet (around 8000 CFP), although a drink at the bar will sometimes get you in.

Shopping

There's really not much to buy in Tahiti besides Tahitian pearls (and boy are there lots of pearl shops) and a few handicrafts. Your best bet for everything from *pareu* (sarong-type garment) to woven hats, pearls, vanilla and homemade *monoï* (fragranced coconut oil) is the Marché de Pape'ete (p409). Watch out though – anything that seems to be mass produced probably is mass produced in China, Indonesia or the Philippines. Upstairs at the market you can even get tattooed at **Aroma & Mano Salmon's** (☎ Aroma 70 95 73, Mano 27 06 38; demonaroma@yahoo.com; Marché de Pape'ete).

Several art galleries show the work of Polynesian artists, including:

Galerie des Tropiques (Map pp416–17; ☎ 41 05 00; cnr Blvd Pomare & Rue Cook)

Gallerie Winkler (Map pp416–17; ☎ 42 81 77; Rue Jeanne d'Arc)

MO'OREA

pop 14,230 / area 53 sq km

Mo'orea is a tropical island paradise cliché brought to life. If you've been dreaming of holiday-brochure turquoise lagoons, white-sand beaches, vertical peaks and lush landscapes you'd be hard-pressed to find better than this gem of an island. Hovering under 20km across the 'Sea of the Moon' from its big sister, Tahiti, Mo'orea absorbs its many visitors so gracefully that its feels surprisingly nontouristy. Dine on stylishly prepared fresh seafood, lounge on the svelte strips of sand or take part in the myriad outdoor activities available. Mo'orea has something for everyone.

ORIENTATION

A road runs around the coast and two roads run into the interior; they meet and climb to the *belvédère* (lookout). Most people live in coastal villages: Vaiare is the busiest centre with its frenetic quay, but Afareaitu is the administrative centre. Tourist development is concentrated in two strips: from Maharepa down the east side of Cook's Bay (Baie de Cook) to Paopao, and around Hauru Point on the northwest corner of the island. The airport is at the northeast corner.

Beaches aren't as plentiful as you'd think; good ones are at Hauru Point and at Temae, near the airport.

The *pointe kilométrique* markers start at zero at the airport and meet at Haapiti, which is at PK24 in a clockwise direction and PK35 anticlockwise.

INFORMATION

Banque Socredo, Banque de Tahiti and Banque de Polynésie have ATMs and are clustered around the small shopping centre at Maharepa at PK6.3.

In medical emergencies your hotel should be your first port of call.

Mo'orea Hospital (☎ 56 23 23; Afareaitu)

Mo'orea visitor information centre (☎ 56 29 09; Hauru Point) This office is at Le Petit Village shopping centre.

Post offices (☼ 8am-12pm and 1:30-4pm Mon-Fri, 8am-9am Sat) At Maharepa and Papetoai (east of Hauru Point).

Restaurant Iguane Rock Café (☎ 56 17 16; Le Petit Village, Hauru Point; per hr 800 CFP; ☼ 10am-midnight) Is the best place for internet access.

TRANSPORT

Crossing the 20km separating Mo'orea from Tahiti is dead easy. It takes less than 10 minutes by plane, or 30 minutes by high-speed ferry. Once you arrive, there are plenty of places to pick up a car or scooter.

Getting There & Away

Air Moorea (☎ Tahiti 86 41 41, Mo'orea 56 10 34) flies from Faa'a airport on Tahiti to Mo'orea (from 2600 CFP) at least every half-hour. There's no need to book, just turn up. **Air Tahiti** (☎ 86 42 42) also flies to Mo'orea, but chiefly for passengers connecting to other islands in the Society group. There's usually only one to three flights a day from Bora Bora (from 18,400 CFP), Huahine (from 13,000 CFP) and Ra'iatea (from 13,000 CFP).

The **Aremiti 5** (☎ Pape'ete 42 88 88, Mo'orea 56 31 10) and the **Moorea Express** (☎ Pape'ete 82 47 47, Mo'orea 56 43 43) jet between Tahiti and Mo'orea six or more times daily between 6am and 4.30pm. The trip takes about 30 minutes; fares are 900 CFP. You can buy tickets at the ticket counter on the quay just a few minutes before departure.

Getting Around

It's best to rent a scooter, car or bicycle to get around Mo'orea: distances are long and there is no public transport. Hitching is another option, which is generally safe provided the usual precautions are taken.

Air Moorea offers a 600 CFP minibus service to any of the island's hotels after each flight. Most hotels, even budget places, offer airport transfers. Mo'orea **taxis** (☎ 56 10 18) are horribly expensive: travelling from the airport to the Beachcomber Intercontinental will cost approximately 4000 CFP.

A shuttle bus meets most of the boat arrivals (300 CFP) and runs to or from any of the Cook's Bay or Hauru Point hotels. You can hop on this bus anytime for shorter distances around the island as well. Ask at the Mo'orea visitor information centre for the schedule, or just flag the bus down if you see it. The big resorts also offer private bus services to guests for 1500 CFP each way on a fixed schedule. Car-hire operators can be found at the Vaiare boat quay, the airport, some of the major hotels and around Cook's Bay and Hauru Point. You'll pay from around 8000 CFP per day, including insurance and unlimited mileage. The main operators include:

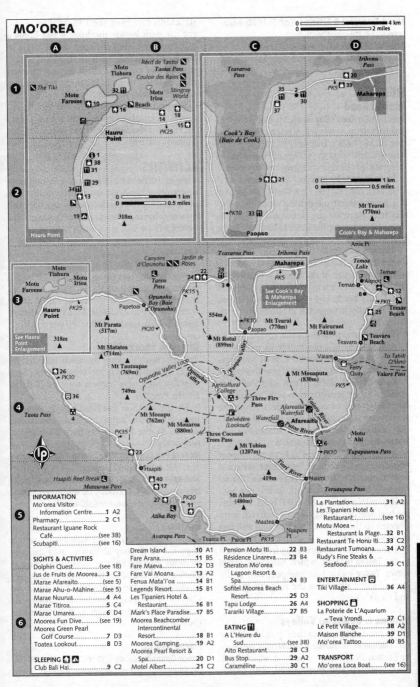

MO'OREA

TAHITI & FRENCH POLYNESIA

Albert Transport & Activities (☎ 56 19 28), which generally has the lowest prices.

Avis (☎ 56 32 61)

Europcar (☎ 56 34 00) Also rents those funny little 'fun car' buggies.

SIGHTS
Coastal Road

Spectacular **Cook's Bay**, with Mt Rotui (899m) as a backdrop, is a lovely stretch of water and one of Mo'orea's two tourist strips. At the base of Cook's Bay the village of **Paopao** has an interesting mural in its former fish market.

Jus de Fruits de Mo'orea (Fruit Juices of Mo'orea; ☎ 56 11 33; PK11; admission free; ⏰ 8.30am-4.30pm Mon-Sat) is a perfect thirst-quenching stop. The various fruit liqueurs are delicious, but a bottle of 100% pineapple juice (320 CFP) is the perfect tonic.

Opunohu Bay (Baie d'Opunohu) still feels wonderfully fresh and isolated. At the northwest corner of the island is **Hauru Point**, Mo'orea's other main tourist strip. It has a 5km sandy **beach**, one of Mo'orea's best; you have to walk through the grounds of a hotel to reach it.

The evocative **Marae Nuurua**, on the water's edge at the end of a football field, marks the start of the less developed side of Mo'orea. **Haapiti** and **Atiha Bay** are popular with surfers.

Marae Umarea, about 100m south of Chez Pauline in Afareaitu, is worth exploring. This long wall of coral boulders along the waterfront is thought to date from about AD 900 and is Mo'orea's oldest. Afareaitu's two **waterfalls** are a major attraction.

A road on the lagoon side of the airport runway extends around **Temae Lake**, which is now home to the **Moorea Green Pearl Golf Course**; however the route is cut off, so it is not possible to rejoin the main coastal road. Nearby, the best beaches on the east coast stretch from Teavaro to the airport. **Teavaro Beach** also has good snorkelling.

The island road climbs away from the coast to the **Toatea Lookout**, which has great Tahiti views. **Vaiare** has a bustling port and is the start of the walk across the ridge to Paopao and Cook's Bay.

Paopao & Opunohu Valleys

In the pre-European era the Opunohu Valley was dotted with *marae* – the largest number in French Polynesia – some of which have been restored and maintained. The oldest

structures date from the 13th century. From the car park beside the huge **Marae Titiroa** a walking track leads through dense forest to **Marae Ahu-o-Mahine**, with an imposing three-stepped *ahu* (altar). A short way up the road from Marae Titiroa is **Marae Afareaito** and an adjacent **archery platform**.

Beyond Marae Afareaito the road continues to climb steeply, winding up to the excellent **belvédère** on the slopes of Mt Tohiea (1207m).

ACTIVITIES

Your guest house can suggest a lagoon tour operator; a six-hour tour visiting the two bays, feeding the sharks, swimming with the rays and having a *motu* picnic costs around 6000 CFP.

Cycling

This is a great way to see Mo'orea's sights. Doing the 60km circuit in a day is possible (depending on the state of those thighs), although is tiring, particularly given the rather sorry state of the bikes available. Many of the hotels rent bikes for around 2000 CFP per day.

Diving & Snorkelling

You'll probably spend as much time in the water as out of it on Mo'orea. For the best snorkelling join a lagoon tour or head to Hauru Point.

To the north of the island, there is some great diving for beginners and experienced divers. All the big resorts have dive operators or try:

Moorea Fun Dive (☎ 56 40 38; www.moorea-fundive .com; PK26.7) Near Moorea Camping.

Scubapiti (☎ 56 20 38, 78 03 52; www.scubapiti.com; Les Tipaniers Hotel & Restaurant) The only dive centre that refuses to engage in controversial shark-feeding.

Hiking

Good hikes include the two-hour stretch from the ferry quay at Vaiare, over the crater ridge into the central valley, emerging at Cook's Bay. The climb from near the agricultural school in the Opunohu Valley to Three Coconut Trees Pass is spectacular – your pension will be happy to give you directions to the trailhead.

Horse Riding

Ranch Opunohu Valley (☎ 56 28 55; trips 5000 CFP; ⏰ closed Mon) offers two-hour guided horse rides into the island's interior. Call to arrange a trip.

Surfing & Kite Surfing

The most popular spot is **Haapiti** (May to October), which has the regularity and strength of a reef waves with the security of a beach wave. Other spots include **Temae** (a difficult right-hander), **Paopao (Cook's Bay)** and **Opunohu Bay**; and the expert-only left-hander at **Intercontinental Moorea Resort**.

On windy days you'll see dozens of kites whipping across the lagoon in front of the Intercontinental Moorea Resort. If you want to give it a go contact **Lakana Fly** (☎ 56 51 58, 70 96 71; two-hour course 1200 CFP; Hauru Point).

Whale- & Dolphin-Watching

You can count on finding dolphins year-round but it's the whales, who migrate to Mo'orea from July to October, who draw in the crowds. If you're lucky you'll get to swim with the mammals, but just seeing them in the water is a real thrill – trips cost 7900 CFP and kids under 12 are half price. We recommend:

Dr Michael Poole (☎ 56 23 22, 77 50 07; www.dr michaelpoole.com; ☽ Mon & Thu) A world specialist on South Pacific marine mammals.

Dolphin Quest (☎ 55 19 48; adult/child 20,000/12,000 CFP) A 'shallow-water encounter' with captive dolphins in an enclosure at the Mo'orea Beachcomber Intercontinental Resort. Snorkelling with dolphins is 19,000 CFP.

SLEEPING

Most accommodation is concentrated on the east side of Cook's Bay and around Hauru Point.

Cook's Bay to Hauru Point

Magnificent Cook's Bay does not have any beach, and so is the quieter, less touristy sister to Hauru Point.

BUDGET

our pick **Pension Motu Iti** (☎ 55 05 20; www.pension motuiti.com; dm 1700 CFP, garden/beach bungalows 10,500/12,000 CFP; ☐) One of the best value spots on Mo'orea, this place is impeccably friendly and clean. Waterfront rooms, which hover over the beach, could be considered a poor man's over-water bungalow and have views of sunrise and sunset. The dorms are airy (but not very social) and the beachside restaurant serves reasonably priced, tasty food.

Motel Albert (☎ 56 12 76; fax 56 58 58; r 5400 CFP, houses 10,500 CFP) An excellent budget choice, this place has a handful of mini-houses with terraces, as well as a row of brightly decorated rooms with terraces closed in with mosquito screens. It's on the mountainside of the road in a lush garden. All options have kitchens and there's a minimum stay of three nights.

MIDRANGE

Club Bali Hai (☎ 56 13 68; www.clubbalihai.com; d 16,000-27,000 CFP, bungalows 25,000-33,000 CFP; ☒ ☐) This stylish, breezy spot right on the bay has a swimming pool, tennis court, boat dock and restaurant. On some evenings you can have a sundowner with Muk, one of the two remaining American 'Bali Hai boys' who built French Polynesia's first over-water bungalows.

TOP END

Moorea Pearl Resort & Spa (☎ 50 84 52; www.pearl resorts.com; d 27,000-33,000 CFP, garden/beach/over-water bungalows 39,000/46,000/69,000 CFP; ☒ ☐ ☒) Occupying the site of the old Bali Hai Moorea, the infinity pool here is the island's best. The white-sand beach is smaller than those at other resorts, but the Pearl's vibe is more intimate and very classy. The restaurant has a very good reputation even among locals, but skip the buffet.

Sheraton Mo'orea Lagoon Resort & Spa (☎ 55 11 11, reservations 86 48 49; www.sheratonmoorea.com; garden/beach/over-water bungalows 38,000/60,000/91,000 CFP; ☒ ☒ ☐) The beach here is particularly splendid (with fabulous snorkelling) and the activities desk is great – both of these aspects are important since the hotel is quite isolated from the main areas of the island. Breakfast is good but otherwise skip the restaurant. Mandara Spa treatments can be enjoyed at the spa or in your room.

Hauru Point

Unlike Cook's Bay, Hauru Point has a beach. Though narrow, it's pretty spectacular with turquoise water, a few *motu* (islets) out front to swim to and good snorkelling.

Moorea Camping (☎ 56 14 47; fax 56 30 22; PK27.5; tent sites per person 1100 CFP, dm/d 1500/2500 CFP, bungalows 5000-9000 CFP) Accommodation looks like military barracks, yet the dorms are the cheapest on the island and you can cook in the waterfront kitchen and live on the beach.

Les Tipaniers Hotel & Restaurant (☎ 56 12 67; www.lestipaniers.com; bungalow with/without kitchen from 14,500/7500 CFP) It's a bustling hub of activity on this lovely knuckle of beach jutting out towards a coral-laden stretch of lagoon. Bungalows aren't going to win any architectural awards but they're big, practical (most have kitchens and one to two bedrooms) and clean. The restaurant is one of the best on Mo'orea (see opposite).

Fare Vai Moana (☎ 56 17 14; www.fare-vaimoana .com; garden/beach bungalows 15,000/22,000 CFP) This upscale, beachfront hotel is a more intimate and less expensive alternative to a resort. There are 13 very comfortable bungalows with refrigerator, mezzanine and bathroom with hot water; each accommodates up to four people, but rates are for two people.

Tapu Lodge (☎ 55 20 55; www.tapulodge.com; 3- to 4-/6-person units 15,900/26,500 CFP) These enormous, immaculate, modern units are more solid and stylish than you'll find anywhere else in this price range and have ocean views. They're close enough to the action of Hauru Point but far enough away to be very quiet.

Fenua Mata'i'oa (☎ 55 00 25; Village Tiahura; www .fenua-mataioa.com; ste 30,000-60,000 CFP; ✷ 💻 🐾) The four sophisticated and exuberantly decorated suites here are dripping with paintings, pillows, silks and antiques. The only downside is that, although the pension has lagoon access, there's no beach but the garden is lushly fabulous.

🏆 Dream Island (☎ 56 38 81; www.dream -island.com; bungalows 35,000-53,000 CFP) A three-minute boat ride from Haapiti brings you to this superbly located, exclusive, island paradise. The two houses/bungalows were built using local materials in authentic Polynesian style and are equipped with kitchens and phones.

Legends Resort (☎ 83 19 09; www.legendsresort.fr; villas 37,400-91,200 CFP; ✷ 🐾 💻) Each modern villa here has gorgeous views over the lagoon (the resort is on a hill), its own kitchen and laundry areas, plus a private Jacuzzi on the generous terrace space.

Moorea Beachcomber Intercontinental Resort (☎ 55 19 19; www.moorea.intercontinental.com; d 36,000 CFP, garden/beach/over-water bungalows 49,000/58,000/86,000 CFP; ✷ 🐾 💻) Moorwa Beachcomber is family friendly and the biggest resort on Mo'orea. While impersonal it's undeniably pretty with it's spread of spacious wooden bungalows fringing the lagoon. The spa here, Helene Spa, is the most respected on the island.

Haapiti to Temae

Mark's Place Paradise (☎ 56 43 02, 78 93 65; www .marks-place-paradise.com; camping per person 1100 CFP, dm/ bungalows from 2000/8000 CFP; 💻) The well-planted garden, creative dorm bungalows and surfy/ social atmosphere make this a great backpacker option on Mo'orea. It's away from the beach and just about everything else besides the Haapiti surf break, but bike and kayak rentals (per day 1000 CFP) make getting around less of a chore. A handful of very cool private bungalows are also available (we love the one made of stone and colourful bottles).

🏆 Tarariki Village (☎ 55 21 05; pension tarariki@mail.pf; 2-/4-person bungalow 7500/12,000 CFP, tree house 9500 CFP) Right on its own white-sand beach, this place has miniature cabins with two beds and a bathroom (cold water only), a bigger beachfront family bungalow and a Robinson Crusoe-style thatched bungalow perched in a tree. In the middle of the property is a superb *fare potee* (open dining area), which is used as a communal kitchen.

Fare Arana (☎ 56 44 03; www.farearana.com; d with/ without air-con 11,900/9900 CFP; ✷ 🐾) This hilltop place is quite stylish. The gardens have a Southeast Asian flavour while the comfortable two-storey rooms have French touches. There are magnificent views, loads of flowers and convivial staff. Good-value packages including activities are often available from the website.

Fare Maeva (☎ 56 18 10; www.faremaevamoorea.com; Temae; bungalows 10,200 CFP) This charming, isolated place is dominated by coconut trees and coral gravel. All the tidy, artistically decorated bungalows have a bathroom and kitchen, and the beach is only 200m away.

Résidence Linareva (☎ 55 05 65; www.linareva.com; 1-/2-/4-/6-person bungalows from 11,500/12,500/19,500/ 27,500 CFP; 💻) This option has a wide variety of well-furnished bungalows in a lush garden by the beach and has a great reputation. If you don't mind the isolated location and the sometimes stand-offish reception, it's a great place to stay and is gay friendly.

Sofitel Moorea Beach Resort (☎ 55 03 55; www .sofitel.com; garden/beach/over-water bungalows from 31,000/58,000/76,000 CFP; ✷ 💻 🐾) This resort is on the best beach on the island and the service is stellar. We weren't crazy about some of the 'modern touches' (bright orange tables and digitalised Gauguin bed headboards are maybe an acquired taste), but overall the hotel is elegant and relaxing.

EATING

Cook's Bay and Hauru Point are the dining epicentres. Most places close around 9pm and are open for lunch and dinner.

Maharepa & Cook's Bay

Caraméline (☎ 56 15 88; Maharepa shopping center; breakfasts from 950 CFP, lunch from 1300 CFP; 🕑 breakfast & lunch) Get all-day American-, French- or Tahitian-style breakfasts, burgers, pizzas, salads, ice-cream treats and more at this affordable and popular cafe.

Restaurant Te Honu Iti (☎ 56 19 84; mains 1900-4200 CFP; 🕑 lunch & dinner Thu-Tue) The terrace of this place sits over the water, and at night the water is lit up so that you can watch rays and fish swim below. Dine on exquisite veal osso bucco (2400 CFP), lobster (4200 CFP) or an array of other French-inspired dishes.

Rudy's Fine Steaks & Seafood (☎ 56 58 00; mains 2000-4500 CFP; 🕲) The name says it all at this new, hacienda-style eatery. Carnivores will be particularly happy as they dine in air-con bliss.

Aito Restaurant (☎ 56 45 52; mains around 2500 CFP) One of the musts on Mo'orea, the food here is French, Corsican and Tahitian and the ambience is lively, breezy and boozy. Live music is on Friday nights.

Hauru Point

The strip along Hauru Point is teeming with places to eat.

A L'Heure du Sud (sandwiches 450-600 CFP; 🕑 I0.30am-3.30pm Thu-Tue) A great variety of well-stuffed sandwiches (think: steak and barbecue sauce stuffed in a baguette) are served at this *roulotte* in front of Le Petit Village shopping centre. Cash only.

Restaurant Tumoana (☎ 56 37 60; mains 1000-2000 CFP) Expect basic, yet yummy Tahitian/French grub, and don't miss Friday and Sunday nights when there's live music and dancing.

La Plantation (☎ 56 45 10; mains 1100-3600 CFP) Lots of choice in Cajun specialities, as well as some of Mo'orea's best vegetarian dishes, are available at this classy, white-clad, jazz-infused restaurant. There's often live music on Saturdays and the wine list and service are as good as the food.

Les Tipaniers Hotel & Restaurant (☎ 56 12 67; lunch 1200-1700 CFP, dinner 1600-3600 CFP) Breakfast and dinner are served at the beachside restaurant, but it's dinner, at the less well-located but elegant roadside restaurant, that is truly to die for. Choose from dishes like filet of lamb with warm goat cheese (1950 CFP), to fresh fish of the day with a choice of mango, vanilla, sea urchin (sounds weird, tastes great) or Mediterranean tomato sauces (1880 CFP).

our pick **Bus Stop** (☎ 56 41 19; mains 1600-2000 CFP; 🕑 lunch & dinner Thu-Tue) The seared tuna with vanilla sauce (1980 CFP) was the best dish we ate on Mo'orea and the giant loaf of fresh baked bread served with it did not go to waste. The fricassee of chicken and shrimp stew with turmeric (1800 CFP) is near island-famous as are the generous, luscious desserts.

Motu Tiahura

our pick **Motu Moea – Restaurant la Plage** (☎ 74 96 96; mains 1400-3000 CFP) This place has an idyllic setting on Motu Tiahura (also known as Motu Moea). The food is fresh, tasty and fancy; fruity cocktails are also available. You can get a boat over to the *motu* (500 CFP) from Les Tipaniers Hotel & Restaurant or the Moorea Beachcomber Intercontinental Resort – or stuff your money in a zip lock and swim.

DRINKING & ENTERTAINMENT

The big hotels have bars where all are welcome to enjoy a predinner drink, and many of the restaurants listed earlier, such as Les Tipaniers, are good spots for a sunset tipple. A couple of times a week (usually Wednesday and Saturday evening), the bigger hotels organise excellent Polynesian music and dance performances by local groups.

Tiki Village (☎ 55 02 50; Tue-Sat night with/without dinner 8700/4400 CFP) A Tahitian cultural village where tourists can watch local people 'living' in the traditional way. The 60-person dance performances here are the biggest on the island. A ticket with dinner and the evening dance performance entitles you to free activities during the day also.

SHOPPING

The coastal road is littered with souvenir places. For *pareu*, T-shirts and other curios, try the Maison Blanche between Cook's Bay and Maharepa and at Cook's Bay stop at Honu Iti Boutique. Mo'orea has a number of art galleries, such as Galerie van der Heyde at Cook's Bay and La Poterie de L'Aquarium – Teva Yrondy also near Cook's Bay.

The major black-pearl specialists have outlets on Mo'orea.

Make your trip to Mo'orea even more unforgettable by getting inked at **Moorea Tattoo** (☎ 76 42 60; www.mooreatattoo.com; PK 32 Haapiti).

HUAHINE

pop 5741 / area 75 sq km

Boasting some of the best beaches in the country and a snoozy Polynesian charm, Huahine is the perfect spot to break from city blues, dump the watch and let the days flow by like the pages of a romance novel. If you do care to pick up the pace, there's a slew of activities available in the outlandishly aquamarine lagoon, a few hikes to tackle up the low, lush mountains and archaeology buffs will love Maeva, one of the most extensive complexes of pre-European *marae* in French Polynesia. With only one real resort, Huahine remains undeveloped and unpretentious, far from the hype of Bora Bora and much less expensive.

Huahine comprises two islands of fairly similar size: Huahine Nui (Big Huahine) to the north and Huahine Iti (Little Huahine) to the south. Huahine Nui is more developed, home to the bustling yet miniscule village of Fare and most of the main tourist and administrative facilities. Huahine Iti offers the island's best beaches, most azure lagoons and a serene, get-away-from-it-all atmosphere.

ORIENTATION

A 60km, mostly sealed, road follows the coast most of the way around both islands. A series of *motu* stretches along the east coast of the two islands, while around the north coast of Huahine Nui is Lake Fauna Nui. It almost cuts off the northern peninsula, where the airport is, from the rest of Huahine Nui. There are only a few beaches.

Fare, the principal town, is on the west coast of Huahine Nui. Faie and Maeva, on the east coast, and Fitii, on the west, are the other main settlements on Huahine Nui. Huahine Iti has four villages: Haapu, Parea, Tefarerii and Maroe.

INFORMATION

There's a bank opposite the quay in Fare and another on the bypass road parallel to Fare's main street. Both have ATMs. Visiting yachties can get water from Pacific Blue Adventure, on the quay. The *capitainerie* (harbour master's office) is also on the quay.

Ao Api New World (☎ 68 70 99; per hr 900 CFP) Look for this internet cafe in the same building as the visitor information centre.

Huahine visitor information centre (☎ 68 78 81; ◷ 7.30-11.30am Mon-Sat) On Fare's main street.
Medical Centre (☎ 68 82 20; ◷ 24hr) On the bypass road in Fare; it handles minor emergencies.
Post office To the north of Fare towards the airport.

TRANSPORT

There are regular flights to Huahine from surrounding islands.

Getting There & Away

Huahine's airport is 2.5km from Fare. **Air Tahiti** (☎ 68 77 02; ◷ 7.30-11.45am & 1.30-4.30pm Mon-Fri, 7.30-11.30am Sat) has an office on Fare's main street. Destinations include Pape'ete (11,000 CFP, three to five daily), Ra'iatea (6000 CFP, daily), Bora Bora (8000 CFP, daily) and Mo'orea (13000 CFP, 30 minutes, daily).

Inter-island cargo ships are another option, although less reliable. The *Vaeanu* and *Hawaiki Nui* depart from Pape'ete and stop at Huahine. For more on travelling by cargo ship, see p483.

Getting Around

Public transport on Huahine doesn't really exist. If you need a taxi, call **Moe's Taxi** (☎ 72 80 60) who speaks perfect English. From the airport it costs 500 CFP to go to Fare and 1500 CFP to go to the south of the island.

Three operators rent cars on the island:
Hertz (☎ 66 76 85; per 24hr 7500 CFP) On the main strip in Fare.
Avis-Pacificar (☎ 68 73 34; per 24hr 8500 CFP) Next to the Mobil petrol station in Fare, it also has a counter at the airport.
Europcar (☎ 68 82 59; per 24hr 9500 CFP) Near the post office, at the airport and the Relais Mahana.

For scooters, check with Europcar.

HUAHINE NUI

This 60km clockwise circuit of the larger island starts at **Fare**, the image of a sleepy South Seas port. The smells of hamburger grease and freshly caught fish linger in the sticky air and the place vibrates with the pumping reggae bass. Check out the colourful little waterside **market** and the few creative boutiques, sign up for a dive or otherwise rent a ramshackle bicycle and just pedal around.

The most extensive complex of pre-European *marae* in French Polynesia is on Huahine. **Maeva** village was the seat of royal power on the island and nearly 30 *marae* are

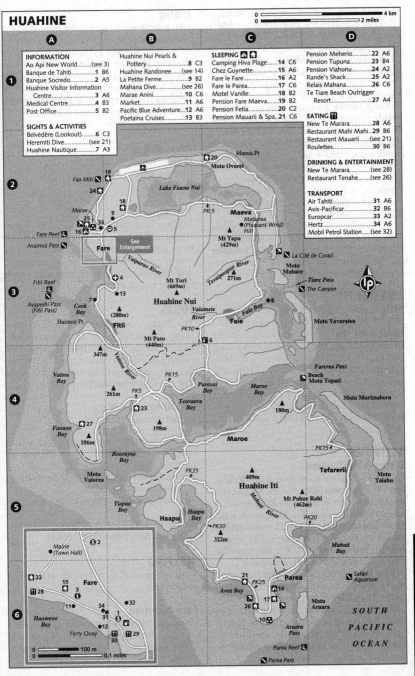

HUAHINE

0		4 km
0		2 miles

INFORMATION
Ao Api New World.........(see 3)
Banque de Tahiti.................**1** B6
Banque Socredo.................**2** A5
Huahine Visitor Information
  Centre..........................**3** A6
Medical Centre...................**4** B3
Post Office.......................**5** B2

SIGHTS & ACTIVITIES
Belvédère (Lookout).........**6** C3
Heremiti Dive................(see 21)
Huahine Nautique............**7** A3

Huahine Nui Pearls &
  Pottery.......................**8** C3
Huahine Randonee......(see 14)
La Petite Ferme.................**9** B2
Mahana Dive................(see 26)
Marae Anini...................**10** C6
Market...........................**11** A6
Pacific Blue Adventure...**12** A6
Poetaina Cruises.............**13** B3

SLEEPING
Camping Hiva Plage.......**14** C6
Chez Guynette..............**15** A6
Fare Ie Fare...................**16** A2
Fare Ie Parea.................**17** C6
Motel Vanille.................**18** B2
Pension Fare Maeva.......**19** B2
Pension Fetia.................**20** C2
Pension Mauarii & Spa...**21** C6

Pension Meherio.............**22** A6
Pension Tupuna..............**23** B4
Pension Viahonu............**24** A2
Rande's Shack................**25** A2
Relais Mahana................**26** C6
Te Tiare Beach Outrigger
  Resort........................**27** A4

EATING
New Te Marara................**28** A6
Restaurant Mahi Mahi.....**29** B6
Restaurant Mauarii......(see 21)
Roulettes......................**30** B6

DRINKING & ENTERTAINMENT
New Te Marara.............(see 28)
Restaurant Tenahe.......(see 26)

TRANSPORT
Air Tahiti......................**31** A6
Avis-Pacificar................**32** B6
Europcar.......................**33** A2
Hertz............................**34** A6
Mobil Petrol Station.....(see 32)

Manua Pt
Motu Ovarei
Faa Miti
Lake Fauna Nui
Maeva
Marae
Matairea
(Pleasant Wind)
Hill
Fare Reef
Mt Tapu
(429m)
Avamoa Pass
Fare
See Enlargement
La Cité de Corail
Vaiparao River
Motu Mahare
Tiare Pass
The Canyon
Fitii Reef
Mt Turi
(669m)
Tevaipoopoo River
271m
Huahine Nui
Avapeihi Pass
(Fitii Pass)
Cook Bay
Vaiumete River
Faie Bay
Faie
Motu Vavaratea
Huimoo Pt
Fitii
(280m)
PK10
Mt Paeo
(440m)
PK6
347m
Vaitona River
Farerea Pass
Beach
Motu Topati
PK15
Puravai Bay
Maroe Bay
Motu Murimahora
Vaitou Bay
261m
PK5
Teavaava Bay
180m
Faauoo Bay
186m
Maroe
PK15
Bourayne Bay
Motu Taiahu
Motu Vaiorea
PK35
Huahine Iti
Tefarerii
Tiapaa Bay
Haapu Bay
409m
Mt Pohue Rahi
(462m)
Haapu
Haapu Bay
PK30
322m
Mahuti River
PK20
Mahuti Bay
Safari Aquarium
Parea
Avea Bay
PK25
Motu Araara
SOUTH
PACIFIC
OCEAN
Araara Pass
Parea Reef
Parea Pass

Fare (Enlargement)
Mairie
(Town Hall)
Haamene Bay
Ferry Quay
0   100 m
0   0.1 miles

scattered along the shoreline and up Matairea (Pleasant Wind) Hill. It takes about two hours to explore the *marae* around Maeva village. Start at the defence wall on the Fare side of Maeva. From here a trail goes uphill through forest and vanilla plantations to a magnificent collection of *marae* in the bush. Watch out though since it's easy to get lost.

From Maeva the coast road turns inland beside narrow Faie Bay to the village of **Faie**. While you're in the area, don't miss a visit to **Huahine Nui Pearls & Pottery** (☎ 78 30 20; www.huahine pearlfarm.com; admission free; ☉ 10am-4pm). Peter Owen, the owner, is a potter as well as a pearl farmer and his work is shown in Pape'ete galleries and at his farm on a coral head. From Faie a ferry departs for the pearl farm every 15 minutes between 10am and 3pm.

Huahine's famous blue-eyed eels can be seen in the river immediately downstream of the bridge. It's a steep climb to the **belvédère** on the slopes of Mt Turi. The road weaves through farms before returning to Fare.

HUAHINE ITI

Start at the village of Maroe, on the south side of Maroe Bay, and head clockwise to **Marae Anini**, the community *marae* on the island's southern tip. Made of massive coral blocks, this large coastal *marae* was dedicated to 'Oro (the god of war) and Hiro (the god of thieves and sailors) and is a great stop for a picnic. Some of the best **beaches** around Huahine are found on the southern peninsula and along its western shore around Avea Bay.

ACTIVITIES
Diving & Snorkelling

Huahine has some great dive spots. **Mahana Dive** (☎ 68 76 32; www.mahanadive.com; Avea Bay), run by the exuberant, English-speaking Annie, is an excellent dive shop. On the quay in Fare, **Pacific Blue Adventure** (☎ 68 87 21; www.divehuahine .com) is another friendly centre. The newest centre is **Heremiti Dive** (☎ 27 90 57; www.heremitidive .com) at Pension Mauarii on Huahine Iti.

Fare has a pretty, sandy **beach** just north of the town. The wide, super-clear lagoon drops off quickly here, providing some fabulous snorkelling amid stunning coral and dense fish populations. Just south of Maeva, near the visitor car park at the now defunct Sofitel, you'll find **La Cité de Corail**, which offers more superb snorkelling.

Hiking

DIY hiking opportunities are limited to the *marae* walk at Maeva, the 3km trail inland to the *belvédère* and a one-hour circuit from Parea on Huahine Iti. For more serious hiking, including treks to the tops of either Mt Tapu on Huahine Nui or Mt Pohue Rahi on Huahine Iti, contact Terii at **Huahine Randonee** (☎ 73 53 45; Camping Hiva Plage; half-day hikes 4500 CFP per person including transport, water and snacks).

Horse Riding

La Petite Ferme (☎ 68 82 98; 2hr/day trip 4500/10,000 CFP), just north of Fare, offers guided horseriding trips.

Surfing

Huahine has some of the best and most consistent surf in French Polynesia, best tackled by experienced surfers. Local surfers can be very possessive, however, so be respectful, don't turn up in a group and don't even think of taking pictures.

TOURS

The Huahine lagoon is superb and includes many untouched *motu* accessible only by boat. A variety of **lagoon tours** (per person around 7500 CFP) are offered, with stops for snorkelling, swimming, fish feeding and a *motu*. Try the following outfits, both just south of Fare:
Huahine Nautique (☎ 68 83 15)
Poetania Cruises (☎ 68 89 49)

Several operators run three-hour island tours for about 5000 CFP per person; try the following:
Huahine Ecotour (☎ 68 81 69) Ask for the archaeology 'walk about,' owner Paul's speciality.
Huahine Explorer (☎ 68 87 33) Run by Viahonu pension.
Huahine Land (☎ 68 89 21; www.huahineland.com) Has a fantastic reputation and offers a bit of everything.

SLEEPING

Most accommodation options are in and around Fare

Fare & Around

The places listed here are either right in town or a few kilometres to the north or south.
Chez Guynette (☎ 68 83 75; chezguynette@mail.pf; dm 1800, s/d/t 4500/5500/6500 CFP) A Huahine in-

stitution, this is the most social place to stay in the whole country. The seven simple but comfortable rooms have fans and bathrooms (with hot water). Dorms are spacious and clean (though not at all private), there's a big communal kitchen and the terrace restaurant has the best people-watching this side of Pape'ete.

Pension Vaihonu (68 87 33; vaihonu@mail.pf; dm/huts/houses 2000/5500/8500 CFP) A rustic little place overlooking a stretch of coral and sand beach, which isn't swimmable, Vaihonu offers clean six-bed dorms with tiled floors, simple beachside huts or spacious two-storey homes with kitchens and hot-water bathrooms.

ourpick Pension Fetia (72 09 50; bungalows incl breakfast 9000-20,000 CFP) Isolated out on Motu Overei, this place is fronted by a wide white-sand beach that ends at coral formations (not good for swimming). The local wood and bamboo constructed bungalows are huge with coral gravel floors, and all have a semi-outdoor feel to them – equipped with kitchens and mosquito nets. Also has a lovely waterfront restaurant that serves meals; dinner costs 2500 CFP.

Pension Meherio (60 61 35; s/d 7900/10,000 CFP incl breakfast) One of Fare's newest options, this is a great place to stay. Room exteriors have woven bamboo, interiors have lots of colourful local fabrics, there are plenty of plant-filled common areas and you're a stone's throw from Fare's nicest beach and snorkelling. Bikes, kayaks and snorkelling gear are free for guests.

Rande's Shack (68 86 27; randesshack@mail.pf; bungalows 10,000-15,000 CFP) Great for families and a long-time surfer favourite, American expat Rande and his lovely Tahitian wife give a warm welcome and offer two great-value beachside houses with self-catering, the larger of which sleeps up to six people.

Motel Vanille (68 71 77; www.motelvanille.com; bungalows 10,500/17,300 CFP;) This pretty guest house is very popular and often fully booked. It features five local-style bungalows with bathrooms (with hot water), mosquito screens and small verandas, set around a swimming pool. Bicycles are available for guests' use. Half-board is an additional 2900 CFP per person and the restaurant here is quite good.

Pension Fare Maeva (68 75 53; www.fare-maeva.com; bungalows 12,800 CFP;) On a coral rock beach (not good for swimming), this place has 10 well-kept bungalows sleeping two to four people, all with kitchens, private bathrooms (with hot water) and mosquito screens. New rooms, under construction at the time of writing, will be smaller, less expensive versions of the bungalows. There's a room-plus-car deal at 12,000 CFP (plus taxes) per day for two people. The good Restaurant Tehina is located here around the small pool.

Fare le Fare (60 63 77; www.tahitisafari.com, in French; luxury tents 16,500 CFP) By far the most unusual sleeping option on Huahine, this fabulous find offers giant African-themed luxury safari tents. Spacious and airy, the tents are uniquely decorated and feature high ceilings, wooden floors and large beds. Right on a good swimming beach, the place has a funky, self-catering, gnarled-wood kitchen, and free snorkels, masks, kayaks and bicycles. There's also a sister setup in Parea (see p430).

Around Huahine Nui

Pension Tupuna (68 70 21; bungalows from 6500 CFP incl breakfast) On a relatively isolated private beach, the four Polynesian-style bungalows each have hot-water bathrooms and are located in a lush tropical garden bursting with all sorts of exotic trees. Mostly organic meals (dinner is 3000 CFP) are served family-style; kayaks and snorkelling equipment are free.

Te Tiare Beach Outrigger Resort (60 60 50; www.tetiarebeachresort.com; bungalows 42,000-90,000 CFP;) Huahine's one true luxury resort is as low-key, intimate and pretty as the island itself. You'll need a boat to get here and the 41 bungalows (11 of which are over the lagoon) are posh, huge and blend harmoniously into the environment. The onsite restaurant serves fine food at reasonable prices; we found the service stellar and the beach perfect for swimming. Regular boat shuttles to Fare are free for guests.

Huahine Iti

The (marginally) smaller island has several ideally situated places, as well as the most beautiful beaches and widest lagoon.

Camping Hiva Plage (68 89 50; Parea; camp sites from 1200 CFP) Run by friendly Terii Tetumu, who is also Huahine's only licensed hiking guide, this place was still being constructed at the time of writing but is in a great location on the beach near Parea.

Fare Ie Parea (☎ 60 63 77; www.tahitisafari.com, in French; luxury tents 16,500 CFP) The beach here is about on par with the Fare location, but there's an interesting *marae* (Taiharuru) on-site and it's much more quiet over this side. Manager Marguerite is charming, helpful and adds some Polynesian flair. Tents are the same style as those at Fare Ie Fare.

Pension Mauarii & Spa (☎ 68 86 49; www.mauarii.com; r/bungalows from 7000/15,500 CFP; 💻) Mauarii is on a fabulous beachside location, has loads of activities on offer, tons of character, a hippyish little spa and one of the island's best-respected restaurants – but some travellers have complained that the 'shabby chic' sacrifices comfort. There are loads of different room-and-bungalow options, all crafted from local materials and with creative touches, like oyster-shell shingles or knobbly wooden coffee tables.

Relais Mahana (☎ 68 81 54; www.relaismahana.com; r 28,000 CFP, bungalows 28,000-33,000 CFP; 💻 🌊) Totally renovated in 2007, this upscale hotel is on what's arguably the best beach on Huahine. Bungalow interiors are decorated with local art in soothing muted colours, and all bathrooms (except in the rooms) have indoor-outdoor showers in private mini-gardens. Unfortunately prices are very high for what you get and we've had a few reports about rude management.

EATING

Most of Huahine's places to eat are found near Fare. Around the rest of the island, eating options are limited to restaurants in *pensions* – some of which are fabulous – and casual *snack* eateries.

Fare & Around

The quayside *roulottes*, open from morning to night, are Huahine's best bargain for cheap eats.

Restaurant Mahi Mahi (dishes 1000-3500 CFP; ☽ breakfast & lunch) Right in downtown Fare, this surf-style eatery has a live lobster tank and a stunning mural on the wall of the namesake fish. The menu has interesting dishes like turkey curry with banana (1400 CFP), plenty of seafood, a great pastry counter, cocktails from 900 CFP and a good wine list. Yummy breakfasts are available from 900 CFP.

New Te Marara (☎ 68 70 81; dishes 1500-2000 CFP; ☽ lunch & dinner) In a great location right on the lagoon, this lively restaurant is a favour-ite local watering hole and the best place to eat around Fare. It has a beach-bar vibe and offers a meat- and seafood-based menu.

Around the Island

Once you've left Fare there aren't too many places to eat, apart from the hotels and a few scattered, inexpensive *snack* places.

our pick **Restaurant Mauarii** (☎ 68 86 49; dishes 1500-4500 CFP; ☽ lunch & dinner) Not only is this one of the few places in French Polynesia where you can consistently order *maa Tahiti* (traditional Tahitian food) à la carte, but it's also one of the only places you'll find the absolutely delectable local crab on the menu (from 3500 CFP – but worth it). The setting is in a Polynesian-style hut overlooking an expanse of turquoise water. Is located on the same grounds as Pension Maurarii.

DRINKING & ENTERTAINMENT

There are three ways to entertain yourself most nights on Huahine: curl up in bed with a bottle of Bordeaux and a trashy novel; cruise the Fare strip with your pals (blaring radio mandatory); or head to Huahine's only bar, **New Te Marara** (☎ 68 70 81). Linger over a fruity cocktail as the sun sinks low on the horizon, or get rowdy over a few pitchers with friends old and new after the dinner crowd heads home.

Otherwise Relais Mahana hosts occasional Friday night 'mini dance shows' at its **Restaurant Tenahe** (☎ 68 81 54; dance show with buffet 5100 CFP).

RA'IATEA & TAHA'A

The twin islands of Ra'iatea and Taha'a, though encircled by a common lagoon, are far from identical; from geography to history and general vibe, it's even hard to believe they're related at all! Ra'iatea is vast and mountainous with a regal past yet has never really been a hit with the tourism crowd; meanwhile shy, short Taha'a quietly sits in Ra'iatea's shadow and is drawing in an increasing number of visitors with her white-sand *motu* and lush views of Bora Bora. Neither island, however, is very touristy and both offer a glimpse of a self-reliant Polynesia and a more authentic way of life.

Transport

The airport is on Ra'iatea, and transport between the two islands is easy.

GETTING THERE & AWAY
Air

Air Tahiti (☎ 60 04 44; ⌚ 7.30am-noon & 2-5.15pm Mon-Fri, 7.30-11.15am Sat, 2.30-5.15pm Sun) has an office at the airport. The airline offers direct flights from Tahiti (12,000 CFP, eight daily), Mo'orea (13,000 CFP), Huahine (5600 CFP), Bora Bora (6300 CFP, daily) and Maupiti (6900 CFP, three weekly).

Boat

A couple of *navette* (shuttle boat) services (1000 CFP) between Uturoa, on Ra'iatea, and various stops on Taha'a – Taravana Marina, Tiva, Tapuamu, Patio and Haamene – are operated by **Enota Transport** (☎ 65 67 10). Services operate Monday to Friday and Saturday morning.

There is also a **taxi-boat service** (☎ 65 65 29) between the two islands, which operates daily between 6am and 6pm. It costs 6000 CFP to go to southern Taha'a and 12,000 CFP to go to northern Taha'a (prices are per person, with a minimum of two people). You can be picked up at the airport or any of the accessible pontoons. Advance booking (24 hours) is required.

The **Maupiti Express** (☎ 67 66 69) travels between Bora Bora, Taha'a and Ra'iatea. On Monday, Wednesday and Friday it leaves Vaitape (Bora Bora) at 7am, arrives at Taha'a at 8.15am and at Uturoa, Ra'iatea, at 8.45am. The same days it leaves Uturoa at 4pm, stops at Taha'a and arrives back at Bora Bora at 5.45pm. The one-way/return fare is 3500/4500 CFP; it costs 700 CFP to go from Ra'iatea to Taha'a.

The cargo ships *Vaeanu, Taporo VII* and *Hawaiki Nui* also make a stop at Ra'iatea. For more on travelling by cargo ship see p483.

The **Tamarii Taha'a** (☎ 65 65 29) goes to the west coast of Taha'a twice daily from the Uturoa *navette* quay (Map p434), at around 10.30am and 4.30pm. The one-hour trip to Patio on Taha'a costs 1000 CFP.

GETTING AROUND
Ra'iatea

Most accommodation places will meet you at the airport (for a fee). Otherwise, the 3km taxi trip into Uturoa costs about 1300 CFP. There's a **taxi stand** (Map p434; ☎ 66 20 60) by the market but the taxis are very expensive.

Around the island you can rent a car or hitchhike (which is never entirely safe but you're unlikely to run into trouble here).

Europcar (Map p434; ☎ 66 34 06; europcar-loc@mail.pf; Uturoa) and **Hertz** (Map p434; ☎ 66 44 88; Uturoa) hire cars for around 11,000 CFP per day.

Europcar has scooters for 6500 CFP for 24 hours; some guest houses hire bicycles. Europcar rents boats with outboards.

Taha'a

There is no public transport system on Taha'a. **Europcar** (Map p432; ☎ 65 67 00; fax 65 68 08; www .europcar.com) charges 11,000 CFP for 24 hours including unlimited mileage and insurance. It also rents bikes. You can rent a scooter on Ra'iatea and bring it across on the *navette*.

RA'IATEA
pop 12,024 / area 170 sq km

No other French Polynesian island feels as intensely mysterious as Ra'iatea. As the ancient seat of Polynesian spirituality and home to Taputapuatea, the site that many consider to be the queen of all Polynesian *marae*, this island has more than its share of *mana* (spiritual force). Perhaps this intensity comes from the dark, brooding mountains that shade the deep valleys and the country's only navigable river, or its emblem flower, the *tiare apetahi*, that simply won't grow anywhere else in the world except the Temehani Plateau. But it's also the people who have a reputation for being hardcore gossips and fiercely protective of the island's secrets. This is another side of the country – no beaches but plenty of spine-tingling exploration to take on.

Orientation

Ra'iatea's road hugs the coast that winds around the mountainous interior. The highest points are the 800m-high Temehani Plateau and 1017m Mt Tefatua (Toomaru).

The airport is at the northern tip of the island. Uturoa extends southeast of the airport. Small villages are scattered across the rest of the island.

Information

The three French Polynesian banks have branches with ATMs in Uturoa. There are two internet cafes in the *gare maritime*.

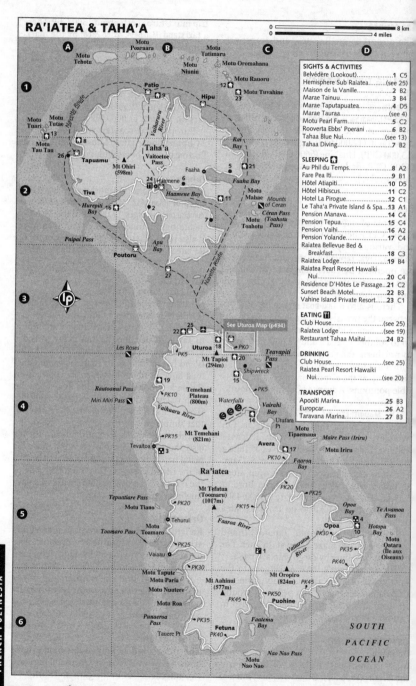

RA'IATEA & TAHA'A

0 ————— 8 km
0 ————— 4 miles

See Uturoa Map (p434)

SOUTH

PACIFIC

OCEAN

TAHITI &
FRENCH POLYNESIA

Hospital (Map p434; ☎ 60 08 01) Opposite the post office; offers emergency services.

Post office (Map p434); North of the centre, towards the airport.

Raiatea visitors information centre (Map p434; ☎ 60 07 77; inforaiatea@mail.pf; ☺ 8am-4pm Mon-Fri, 8am-3pm Sat, 9.30am-3pm Sun) In the *gare maritime* boat terminal).

Sights

We'd recommend renting a vehicle (or if you are in really good shape, a bicycle) and driving the entire 98km sealed circuit around Ra'iatea. Exploring the island this way gives a taste of its wild natural beauty, but take a picnic as there's nowhere to buy lunch.

Uturoa (Map p434), Ra'iatea's busy port, is the second-largest town in French Polynesia, and is one of those places where its utter lack of charm is actually charming. Take some time to wander around: the place provides a sample of the local flavour, plus there's some funky little shops and great deals on black pearls. The Protestant church on the north side of the town centre has a memorial stone to pioneer missionary John Williams.

Soon after you've passed the mouth of the Faaroa River, a turn-off heads to the south coast. Turn right here to climb to a **belvédère** (Map p432) with great views of Faaroa Bay.

Or turn left to reach **Marae Taputapuatea** (Map p432), which had immense importance to the ancient Polynesians. Any *marae* built on another island had to incorporate one of Taputapuatea's stones as a symbol of allegiance – even one in the Cook Islands or Hawai'i! At the very end of the cape is the smaller **Marae Tauraa**, a *tapu* enclosure with the tall 'stone of investiture' where young *ari'i* (chiefs) were enthroned.

At Tevaitoa village, on the northwestern side of the island, massive stone slabs stand in the 50m-long wall of **Marae Tainuu** (Map p432), behind the church (the church was built on the *marae*). Turn-offs lead to the Temehani Plateau on the stretch to the **Apooiti Marina** (Map p432), then the road passes the airport and returns to Uturoa.

Activities

DIVING & SNORKELLING

Ra'iatea has two diving centres: **Hemisphere Sub Raiatea** (Map p432; ☎ 66 12 49; www.diveraiatea.com), at the Apooiti Marina, and **Te Mara Nui Plongée** (Map p434; ☎ 66 11 88; www.temaranui.pf) at the marina at Uturoa. Both companies charge around 5500 CFP for a one-tank excursion, and 6000 CFP for an introductory dive. The highlight is the superb Teavapiti Pass.

Uturoa-based **Polynésie Croisière** (☎ 28 60 06; www.polynesie-croisiere.com) offer all-inclusive diving tours through the Leeward Islands on their scuba-equipped catamaran – a three-day, three-night tour costs around 82,000 CFP per person.

Ra'iatea has few beaches – a hotel or guest house pontoon is the most you can expect – but some of the reef *motu* are splendid and perfect for swimming or snorkelling. Ask at your hotel about renting a boat or joining a lagoon tour.

HIKING

Good walking opportunities include the walk up to the **Temehani Plateau** (Map p432); but you'll need a guide. Try **Eric Pelle** (☎ 66 49 54; hikes per person from 3600 CFP). The short climb up **Mt Tapioi** (Map p432); the **Three Waterfalls walk** behind Kaoha Nui Ranch; and Hotopu, Opoa and Faeratai Valleys to the south are also good walks.

YACHTING

Ra'iatea is the yacht-charter centre of French Polynesia. Bareboat charter rates vary seasonally (July to August is the high season). Cruises on a crewed yacht usually include tour programmes at the stops en route. It takes eight to 10 days to explore the Leeward Islands from Ra'iatea. For info on charter companies, see p475.

Tours

Most tours actually spend the majority of their time on Taha'a, but all companies listed here pick up from the pier in Uturoa. Tours generally involve travel by *pirogue* (local outrigger canoes) and 4WD, dividing their time between Taha'a's rugged interior and splendid lagoon. Unless stated otherwise, all tours visit a pearl and vanilla plantation, stop for snorkelling and include lunch on a *motu*.

Dave's Tours (☎ 65 62 42; tours 8000 CFP)
L'excursion Bleue (☎ 66 10 90; www.tahaa.net; tours 9500 CFP)
Tahaa Tour Excursions (☎ 65 62 18; tours 6500 CFP)

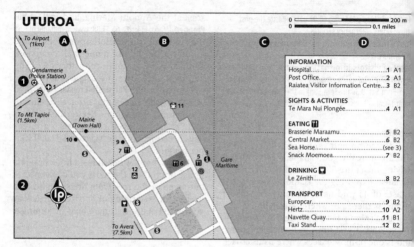

For something completely different go on a river- or sea-kayaking tour with **Lagon Aventure** (☎ 79 26 27; www.lagonaventure.com; tours from 7500 CFP).

Sleeping
UTUROA & AROUND
Both of these options are slightly out of town.

Raiatea Bellevue Bed & Breakfast (☎ 66 15 15; www.raiateabellevue-tahiti.com; r per person incl breakfast 4300 CFP; 🖥 🛋) This place is perched high above the northern side of Uturoa in a lush junglelike setting. The five tidy rooms have hot-water bathrooms, TV, refrigerator and fan, and open on to a terrace beside a small swimming pool. Airport transfers cost 1000 CFP per person. Credit cards aren't accepted.

Raiatea Pearl Resort Hawaiki Nui (☎ 60 05 00; www.pearlresorts.com; r from 20,000 CFP, bungalows 31,000-42,000 CFP; ❄ 🍴 🖥) Ra'iatea's swankiest hotel has excellent service and stylish bungalows, but sadly its location, wedged between the road and the lagoon, isn't exactly stunning. That said, there is outrageous snorkelling in front and you can paddle free kayaks out to the white-sand *motu* across the lagoon. Bikes and snorkels are available, and the bar and restaurant has a chummy, old South Seas feel to it.

EAST COAST
our pick **Pension Tepua** (☎ 66 33 00; www.tepua-raiatea.com; dm/s/d 2500/5000/7500 CFP, bungalows 10,000 CFP; 🖥 🛋) A social and pretty spot, this is one of

the best budget options in the Society Islands. The owner speaks five languages, including perfect English, and rooms are simple but clean and colourfully decorated. The dorms are spacious, and the bungalows sleep between four and six people and come with colourful Tahitian bedspreads, fridges, sinks and bathrooms. The on-site bar and restaurant (as well as a communal kitchen), TV lounge, small pool and pontoon over the lagoon add even more laidback ambience. Bike and kayak rental is available.

Pension Yolande (☎ 66 35 28; d 6000 CFP) Yolande, a charming Ra'iatea *mama*, keeps this cute-as-a-button place on a white-sand beach in ship shape. Rooms all have sunken kitchens with adjacent hot-water bathrooms. Meals are available in a small *fare* (gazebo) facing the sea (breakfast 1000 CFP and full dinner 2500 CFP), kayaks are free and airport transfers cost 1300 CFP per group one-way. No credit cards.

Pension Manava (☎ 66 28 26; www.manavapension.com; d/f 8000/9400 CFP; 🖥) This is a super friendly, well-managed place with spacious bungalows, all with kitchens, dotting a big, open garden. The huge two-bedroom family bungalow is great value for a group. The place offers free airport transfers and nightly trips to Uturoa restaurants. Credit cards aren't accepted.

Hôtel Atiapiti (☎ 66 16 65; bungalows from 13,000 CFP incl breakfast) Besides having one of the better beaches (plus snorkelling) on the island, you'll get plenty of ancient Polynesian spirtual vibes here from Taputapuatea Marae right next door. Semi open-concept bungalows are decorated with bright, artistic flair and have mini kitchens and terraces. Add 2500 CFP per person for half board at the inviting country-style restaurant. Grab a free kayak or bike to explore the area. Airport transfers are 2500 CFP per person return.

WEST COAST

This coast isn't as lush as the east coast but is the best choice for surfers and is very lagoon-oriented.

ourpick Sunset Beach Motel (☎ 66 33 47; www .raiatea.com/sunsetbeach; camp sites per person 1500 CFP; bungalow s/d/tr/q 12,000/13,300/14,500/15,600 CFP) Just the location (on an expansive coconut plantation lined by a skinny strip of white sand) alone would make this one of Ra'iatea's best options, but the bungalows – which are perhaps better described as small homes – make this one of the best deals in the islands. It's a particularly great find for families as the kitchen-equipped bungalows comfortably sleep four and kids stay for half price. Pirogues, pedal boats (which you can enjoy off the fantastic pontoon), bikes and airport transfers are free. The owners offer heaps of activities and the island's best camping is here.

Raiatea Lodge (☎ 66 20 00; www.raiateahotel.com; s/d/t/q 12,000/15,000/19,000/28,000 CFP; 🍴 💻 🛖) This is Ra'iatea's second-poshest place (after the Pearl Resort Hawaiki Nui). The colonial plantation-style building sits at the back of a coconut plantation, but you can still glimpse Bora Bora across the lagoon. Rooms have hardwood floors, big terraces and heaps of comforts and mod-cons that are usually only found at French Polynesia's swankiest resorts. The restaurant (mains from 1800 CFP) has a good reputation and the bar can get lively. Add 2200 CFP for return airport transfers. Bikes and kayaks (there's a lagoon-side pontoon) are free and English is spoken.

Eating

You'll find small *snack*-style places and a few *roulottes* dotted around the island.

UTUROA & AROUND

Uturoa has several well-stocked supermarkets, open Monday to Saturday and some on Sunday morning. A handful of *roulottes* open at night along the waterfront strip at the north end of the marina.

Central Market (Map p434; 🕑 5.30am-6pm Mon-Sat, 5am-9am Sun) Head to this small yet colourful local market for homemade *monoï* (fragrant coconut oil), flowers, and fruits and veggies.

Snack Moemoea (Map434; ☎ 66 39 84; dishes 600-1700 CFP; 🕑 breakfast & lunch) This is the most popular place in town, with a large menu offering a variety of different *poisson cru* (raw fish) options, as well as Chinese and French dishes. Those on a budget can also eat well – burgers, hot dogs and *croque-monsieur* sandwiches are all around 1000 CFP.

Brasserie Maraamu (☎ 66 46 54; dishes 1000-1800 CFP; 🕑 lunch Mon-Fri, breakfast & dinner Mon-Fri) More Chinese than Moemoea, this is another immensely popular joint serving huge plates of reasonably priced food, including a handful of tofu-based vegetarian options as well as steaks, poultry and fish. Hinano beer is on tap and breakfasts range from American eggs to Tahitian *poisson cru* and *firifiri* (doughnuts).

Sea Horse (Map434; ☎ 66 16 34; dishes 1200-2100 CFP; 🕑 closed dinner Sun) With a fabulous location looking out on the lagoon from the *gare maritime*, Sea Horse is upscale Chinese with plenty of soups and seafood on offer. It's elegant, romantic and won't break the bank.

Club House (Map p432; ☎ 66 11 66; dishes 1500-3000 CFP; 🕑 lunch & dinner) In Apooiti Marina, the setting for this place is striking – a large, airy room overlooking the marina – but its French-Polynesian cuisine doesn't quite live up to its inventive and stylish ambitions. Patrons can be picked up and dropped off for free as far as Sunset Beach Motel and Pension Manava.

AROUND THE ISLAND

Bring a picnic if you're travelling around the island as there aren't many opportunities to find a meal during the day. You can pick up baguette sandwiches at local shops around the island before around 11am.

ourpick Raiatea Lodge (☎ 60 01 00; dishes from 1800 CFP; 🕑 lunch & dinner) There's still the ever-so-common grilled tuna steak with vanilla sauce, but also specialities from around the world using local ingredients. The semi-outdoor Zen-style setting is superb and is a great place for a drink as well.

Drinking & Entertainment

It's difficult to find a reason to stay up late on Ra'iatea but try the following places:

Le Zénith (Map p434; men/women 1500 CFP/free; from 10pm Fri & Sat) On weekends Restaurant Moana, located above the Leogite Supermarket in Uturoa, metamorphoses into this disco.

Club House (Map p432; ☎ 66 11 66) A sunset drink at this place in the Apooiti Marina is mandatory. The restaurant may not serve the best food, but the mellow ambience is as fantastic as the sunset views.

Raiatea Pearl Resort Hawaiki Nui (☎ 60 05 00) The bar at this resort also offers great lagoon views, and stages weekly Polynesian dance performances – call about prices.

Shopping

Uturoa has several well-stocked souvenir outlets, as well as some unique boutiques and excellent-value pearl shops. **Hei Tattoos** (☎ 76 30 25; haiputona_haiti@yahoo.fr; Uturoa) owner Isidore Haiti specialises in Marquesan and tribal-style tattoos.

TAHA'A

pop 5003 / area 90 sq km

As sweet and pretty as its hibiscus flower shape, Taha'a is about as low-key an island as you'll find in the Society Archipelago. Most people visit on a day trip from Ra'iatea; however, if you really want to get away from it all, stop longer. The economy putters along on pearl farming and vanilla production, but tourism, particularly in the luxury sector, is adding a new dimension to the charming simplicity. There are some fabulous sleeping options on the lush, though mostly beachless island (this is where you'll find the budget choices), as well as the sandy

motu that are blessed with sunset views over the iconic Bora Bora silhouette.

A coast road encircles most of the island but traffic is very light and there is no public transport. Taha'a's easily navigable lagoon and safe yacht anchorages make it a favourite for visiting yachties.

The population is concentrated in eight main villages on the coast. The main quay is at Tapuamu, and Patio is the main town. The roads around the south and north part of the island meet at Haamene.

Taha'a's only bank is the Banque Socredo in Patio, where there's also a post office.

Around the Island

The 70km circuit of the island is quite possible as a bicycle day trip, although there are some steep sections. Starting from the Taravana Marina, the first navette stop from Ra'iatea, the road hugs the coast around Apu Bay. At the top of the bay the route leaves the coast and climbs up and over to **Haamene** village. The **Maison de la Vanille** (☎ 65 67 27) is a vanilla producer worth a visit. Pause for pictures just after **Tapuamu** when a chain of motu fringing the northern coast of the island comes into view. You'll pass through copra plantations on the way to Faaha Bay on the island's eastern side; stop on the north side of the bay and pay **Motu Pearl Farm** (☎ 65 66 67) a visit. You can take a tour and purchase loose pearls (often cheaper than from a shop). There are more pearl farms located along the coast road closer to Haamene, including **Rooverta Ebbs' Poerani** (☎ 65 60 25; admission 100 CFP), where you can watch pearl grafting. The road then winds around seemingly endless small bays before returning to the Taravana Marina.

VANILLA, VANILLA, VANILLA

Taha'a is accurately nicknamed 'the vanilla island' since three-quarters of French Polynesian vanilla (about 25 tons annually) is produced here. Several vanilla farms are open to the public; at these family-run operations you can buy vanilla pods (about 1000 CFP for a dozen) and see how it's produced.

Jacqueline Mama, a Taha'a vanilla farmer, gives these tips on buying and keeping vanilla pods: 'When you massage the bean with your fingers it should be flat. If the pod is puffed up at all it means that there is still moisture inside and your vanilla might mould when you get home. Once you buy your vanilla, keep it in an airtight place. Wrapping it tightly in plastic wrap usually does the job. If it starts to lose its sheen, you can close it in a jar with a drop of rum to revive it.'

Activities

DIVING & SNORKELLING

Taha'a has two dive centres, **Tahaa Blue Nui** (☎ 65 67 78, 60 84 00; www.bluenui.com), at Le Taha'a Private Island & Spa (right), and the independent **Tahaa Diving** (☎ 65 78 37; www.tahaa-diving.com). The dive centres on Ra'iatea also regularly use the dive sites to the east of the island by Céran Pass and will collect you from hotels in the south of Taha'a.

There are no beaches on Taha'a, and you have to go to the *motu* for swimming and snorkelling. Ask at your guest house about options for getting to the *motu*.

Tours

Many tour operators are based in Taha'a but they also offer to pick up from Ra'iatea. The places listed here are exclusive to Taha'a. Tours start at about 6500 CFP.

Poerani Tours (☎ 65 60 25)

Vaipoe Tours (☎ 65 60 83; Pension Vaipoe) Full-day lagoon tours.

Vanilla Tours (☎ 65 62 46) Ethno-botanic oriented and recommended.

Sleeping

It's wise to make reservations so that you'll be collected from the appropriate village quay, or even the airport on Ra'iatea.

THE ISLAND

Most of the following places either provide or rent bicycles to guests.

Au Phil du Temps (☎ 65 64 19; www.pension-au-phil-du-temps.com; r/bungalows per person 5300/6300 CFP) Kitted out with TVs, mosquito nets and private outside bathrooms, the local-style bungalows are just a few metres from the lagoon and are very popular and well kept. No credit cards.

Pension Vaihi (☎ 65 62 02; bungalows 7000 CFP) Head to this family guest house situated on the southern side of Hurepiti Bay for real isolation and tranquillity. The three spotless lagoonside bungalows come with bathrooms. Half/full board adds 3000/4500 CFP per person.

Hôtel Hibiscus (☎ 65 61 06; www.hibiscustahaa.com; bungalows from 10,600 CFP) This place is haphazardly run and there's a lot of drinking going on at the restaurant/bar, giving this hotel a boisterous, albeit unpredictable charm. Bungalows (some of which can sleep up to 10 people) all have bathroom, terrace and

fan and there are seven free boat moorings with dock access.

Residence D'Hôtes Le Passage (☎ 65 66 75; www.tahitilepassage.com; bungalows with full board and activities per person 18,000 CFP; 🌐 🖥 🖳) You get an all-inclusive package when you stay here (minus alcohol, which you can purchase). Cosy, stylish bungalows feel more like rooms and are clustered on a flowery hillside and linked by outdoor staircases. Meals are taken at a restaurant overlooking the sea and there's a pontoon.

Fare Pea Iti (☎ 60 81 11; www.farepeaiti.pf; bungalows 30,000–36,000 CFP; 🖳 🖳) This is a fabulously well-designed place with bungalows worthy of a shabby-chic spread in an architectural magazine; expect lots of bamboo, stone work and drapy white fabrics. Add 7300 CFP per person per day for half board – it's expensive but the food is very good. Airport transfers are 8400 CFP return.

THE MOTU

Motu digs are set in private paradises that rival (and some would say exceed) the settings of Bora Bora's better resorts.

Hotel La Pirogue (☎ 60 81 45; www.hotel-la-pirogue.com; bungalows from 27,500 CFP; 🖳) Intimate, friendly and rustic, this place appeals to couples and families looking for a bit of luxury at a less exorbitant price. The restaurant has a varied menu and good reputation (half board is an extra 6500 CFP per person).

Vahine Island Private Island Resort (☎ 65 67 38; www.vahine-island.com; bungalows 50,000–67,000 CFP; 🖳) In a to-die-for location this intimate, traveller recommended resort has nine Polynesian-style bungalows – three of which are perched over the lagoon. The bungalows are not ultra-posh. but they are lovingly decorated with bright Tahitian bedspreads and have spacious wooden terraces. Add 10,500 CFP per person per day for half board (mandatory if you plan on eating). Airport transfers cost 7200 CFP per person return.

Le Taha'a Private Island & Spa (☎ 50 84 54; www.letahaa.com; bungalows from 104,000 CFP; 🌐 🖳 🖳) French Polynesia's only Relais & Chateaux resort aims to be the most exclusive resort in the country and we think it hits the mark. If you don't have an over-water-bungalow facing either Taha'a or Bora Bora, you'll at least have your own pool. Le Taha'a is definitely a destination resort, but the place offers enough activities to keep most guests entertained for days. Reach the resort by boat (10,000 CFP per person) or via private helicopter from Bora Bora (18,000 CFP per person).

Eating & Drinking

There are shops in each village and a few *roulottes* open around the island at night, but the dining options are very limited. The *motu* resorts all have their own bars.

Restaurant Tahaa Maitai (☎ 65 70 85; dishes 1500-3000 CFP; ☽ lunch & dinner) Travellers recommend this restaurant right on Haamene Bay for both its fabulous views and its delicious cuisine. The menu features lots of fresh seafood, local fruits and vegetables and delicious French desserts. There's also a long cocktail list, making this a popular local watering hole.

BORA BORA

pop 8900 / area 47 sq km

Tell someone you're heading to Bora Bora, one of the world's most famous dream destinations, and prepare for a jealous response and cries of 'Can I come too?' Indeed, there are worse things in life than splashing about in a huge glinting turquoise swimming pool, snorkelling amid pristine coral reefs among countless tropical fish, sipping a cocktail on your private terrace, feeling the cool breeze dancing over your skin as you explore the lagoon, and sampling gourmet fare in a fancy restaurant. The good thing is that you can mix slow-paced sun-and-sand holidays with action-packed experiences. Diving, water sports and hiking are available.

Sure, this diva of an island is overpriced, but if there's one place where you shouldn't mind about savings and money, it's here. Live for the moment.

ORIENTATION

A 32km road circles the island, which is about 9km north to south and 4km across. Vaitape, on the western side, is the main settlement, looking directly out to Teavanui Pass, the only entry to the lagoon.

INFORMATION

All services are in Vaitape. You'll find branches of Banque de Tahiti, Banque de Polynésie and Banque Socredo, where you can exchange money or use the ATM. There's also a **medical centre** (☎ 67 70 77; ☽ 7.30am-3.30pm Mon, Wed & Fri) and a pharmacy.

Aloe Cafe (per hr 1600 CFP; ☽ 6am-6pm Mon-Sat) The place for internet access and wi-fi (same rates). At the back of a small shopping centre.

Bora Bora visitor information centre (☎ 67 76 36; info-bora-bora@mail.pf; ☽ 7.30am-4pm Mon-Fri) The office is on the quay at Vaitape and has pamphlets and other info. Mildly helpful.

Post office (☽ 7am-3pm Mon-Fri, 8-10am Sat) Also has internet access (with the Manaspot card, on sale at the counter).

TRANSPORT

Numerous flights head to Bora Bora on a daily basis.

Getting There & Away

AIR

Air Tahiti (☎ 67 70 35; Vaitape; ☽ 7.30-11.30am & 1.30-4.30pm Mon-Fri, 8-11am Sat) flies between Bora Bora and Tahiti (14,500 CFP, up to 10 flights daily), Huahine (7500 CFP, one to three flights daily), Mo'orea (from 18,400 CFP, one to three flights daily) and Ra'iatea (from 6300 CFP, one or two flights daily). Air Tahiti also has direct flights from Bora Bora to the Tuamotus, with a very handy flight to Rangiroa (from 23,000 CFP, daily), an onward connection to Manihi (23,400 CFP, six flights weekly) and onward connections to other atolls, including Tikehau, Fakarava and Manihi.

BOAT

Inter-island boats dock at the Farepiti quay, located 3km north of Vaitape. Two cargo ships, the **Hawaiki Nui** (☎ 54 99 54 in Pape'ete; contact@stim .pf) and the **Vaeanu** (☎ 41 25 35 in Pape'ete), make two trips a week between Pape'ete and Bora Bora (via Huahine, Ra'iatea and Taha'a). For more on travelling by cargo ship, see p483.

The **Maupiti Express 2** (☎ 67 66 69; Vaitape; www .maupitiexpress.com) runs between Bora Bora and Maupiti (3000/4000 CFP one-way/return, three times weekly) and Ra'iatea/Taha'a (3000/4000 CFP one-way/return, four times weekly). The boat departs the Vaitape quay for Maupiti at 8.30am on Tuesday, Thursday and Saturday; the return trip leaves Maupiti at 4pm on the same day. The boat departs for Ra'iatea and Taha'a at 7am on Monday, Wednesday and Friday and at 3pm on Sunday.

Getting Around

The airport is on Motu Mute at the northern edge of the lagoon; two large catamaran ferries then transfer you to the Vaitape quay (free). A regular bus service from the quay goes to the hotels at Matira Point (500 CFP).

You need to be at the quay at least 1¼ hours before your flight leaves. The top-end hotels transfer their guests directly to/from the airport; other places collect you at the quay.

There is no real public transport on Bora Bora. Car-hire agencies include: **Bora Bora Rent a Car – Avis** (☎ 67 70 03; www.avis-tahiti.com), with an agency opposite the quay in central Vaitape plus desks in several hotels; and **Fare Piti Rent-a-Car** (☎ 67 65 28), in Vaitape. Rates are around 12,000 CFP for 24 hours. Cars can be delivered directly to your hotel. These outlets also rent bikes (2000 CFP per day). Many hotels also rent bikes.

What about renting a boat? If you can get a few of you together, this is a cheaper option than the organised tours available. **La Plage** (☎ 67 68 75, 28 48 66; laplage.bora@hotmail.com), based on the beach at the Novotel, rents small 6HP or 15HP four-seater motorboats that are easy to drive; no licence is required for the 6HP boats. You can expect to pay 15,000 CFP to 20,000 CFP per day for the boat, with petrol and transfers included.

SIGHTS

Bora Bora's 32km coast road hugs the shoreline almost all the way around the island and is dotted with *marae* and WWII remnants. We describe an anticlockwise tour that starts in Vaitape; as it's flat except for the decent hill around Fitiiu Point it makes a good bicycle ride, though it's not a bad idea to join a 4WD tour (see p442) because some sights are not easy to find (due to lack of signage).

At PK6, Hotel Bora Bora at Raititi Point marks the start of the pleasant sandy stretch of **Matira Beach**. From the eastern edge of the Hotel Matira property, a walking trail (10 minutes) runs up the hill to a battery of WWII **coastal defence guns**.

The Intercontinental Bora Bora Le Moana Beach Resort is on a side road that runs out to **Matira Point** and a great public beach. The annual Hawaiki Nui inter-island canoe race ends on this beach.

At Fitiiu Point (PK15) the road climbs briefly away from the coast. Just as the road starts to climb, a track peels off to **Marae Aehuatai** at the water's edge.

The small, private **Museé de la Marine** (Marine Museum; ☎ 67 75 24; admission by donation) has an interesting collection of model ships. There are no set hours, so you'll need to call head before visiting. Just after Taihi Point a steep and often muddy track climbs to a WWII radar station situated atop Popotei Ridge and on to a lookout that's above the village of Faanui.

At the end of Tereia Point a rectangular concrete water tank marks the position of another **WWII coastal gun**. There's no path: just clamber straight up the hill for a couple of minutes. **Marae Fare-Opu** is squeezed between the road and water's edge. Two of the slabs of this paved platform are clearly marked with petroglyphs.

Faanui Bay was the site of the US military base during WWII. Note the picturesque **church**, slightly inland. On the coastal road, the **Marae Taianapa** lies on private property on the edge of a coconut plantation, just off the mountain side of the road (ask around).

ACTIVITIES

If you need to tear yourself off the beach towel or the sun-lounger, there are plenty of options to keep you active.

Diving & Snorkelling

Bora Bora provides enthralling diving for the experienced and novices alike. A few favourites include Tapu, famous for its lemon shark encounters, as well as Toopua and Toopua Iti, which feature numerous eagle rays. Outside the reef, to the north, Muri Muri (La Vallée Blanche) offers guaranteed sightings of grey sharks, turtles and barracudas, in less than 20m. A lowlight is the lack of diversity – there are only four to five sites available. See p75 for more information on diving.

An introductory or single dive costs about 8500 CFP, a two-tank dive is 14,500 CFP. There are four state-of-the-art dive shops on Bora Bora:

Bathys Diving (☎ 60 76 00; www.bathys-diving.com) At Intercontinental Resort & Thalasso Spa Bora Bora.

Bora Bora Blue Nui (☎ 67 79 07; www.bluenui.com) At Bora Bora Pearl Beach Resort.

Bora Diving Centre (☎ 67 71 84, 77 67 46; www.boradive.com) At Matira, at the Novotel Bora Bora and at Le Méridien Bora Bora.

TAHITI & FRENCH POLYNESIA

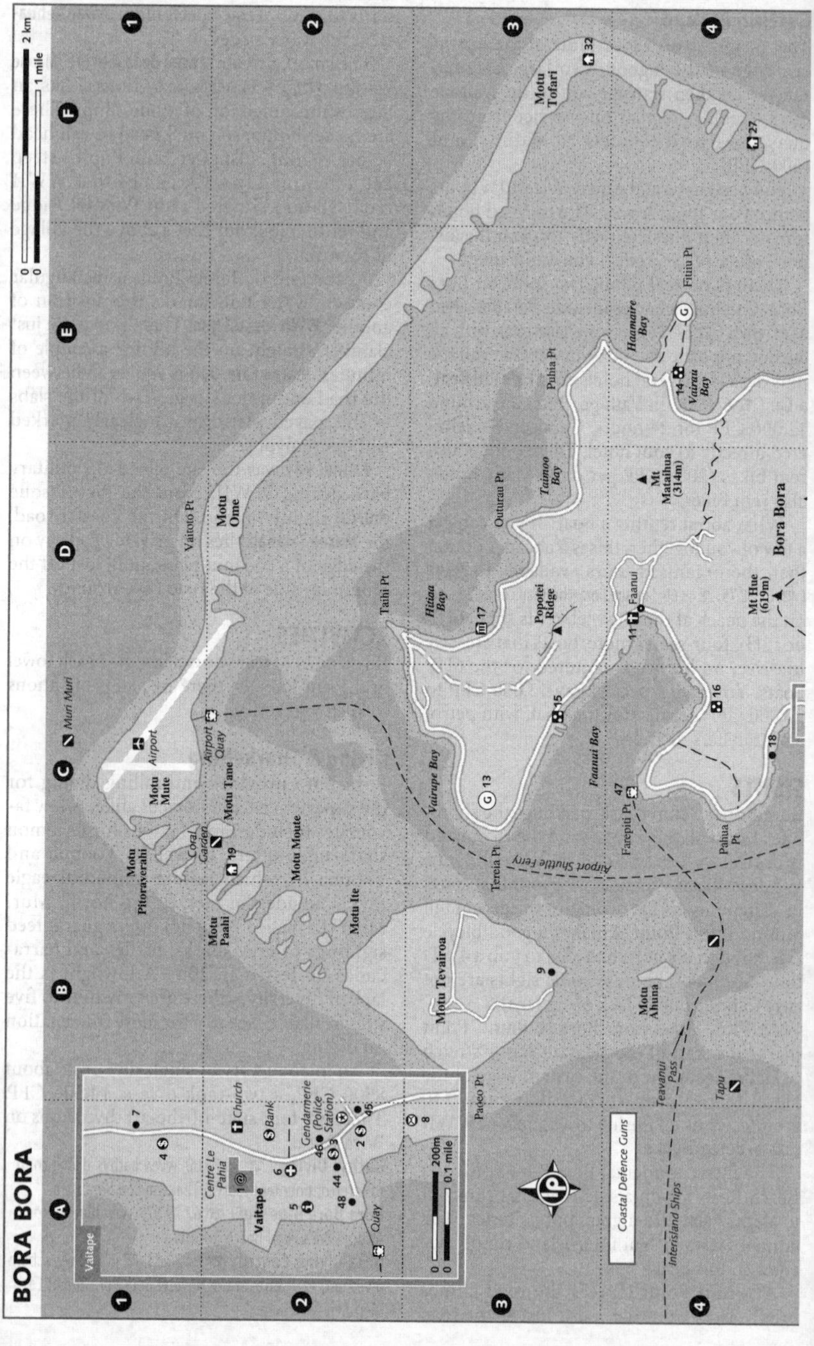

BORA BORA

0   1 mile
0   2 km

1 km

Map labels

F
E
D
C
B
A

1
2
3
4

Motu Tofari
32
27
Fitiu Pt
Haamaire Bay
14
Vaiura Bay
Pahia Pt
Taimoo Bay
Mt Maatahua (314m)
Bora Bora
Motu Ome
Vaiioto Pt
Muri Muri
Taihi Pt
Hitiaa Bay
17
Otutaui Pt
Popotei Ridge
Mt Hue (619m)
Faanui
11
Airport
Motu Mute
Airport Quay
Motu Tane
15
Faanui Bay
16
G 13
Vaurupe Bay
18
Coral Gardens
19
Motu Moute
Terreia Pt
Airport Shuttle ferry
Faopiti Pt
47
Pahia Pt
Motu Pitoraverahi
Motu Paahi
Motu Ite
Motu Tevairoa
9
Motu Ahuna
Padeo Pt
Teavanui Pass
Tapu
Interisland Ships
Coastal Defence Guns

Inset: Vaitape

Vaitape
7
4
Centre Le Pahia
Church
Bank
5
6
Gendarmerie (Police Station)
46
3
2
45
48 44
8
Quay

0   0.1 mile
0   200m

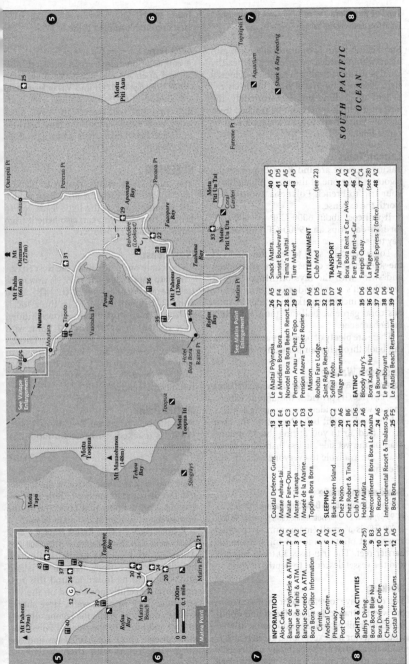

INFORMATION
Aloe Cafe	**1** A2
Banque de Polynésie & ATM	**2** A2
Banque de Tahiti & ATM	**3** A2
Banque Socredo & ATM	**4** A1
Bora Bora Visitor Information	
Centre	**5** A2
Medical Centre	**6** A2
Pharmacy	**7** A1
Post Office	**8** A3

SIGHTS & ACTIVITIES
Bathys Diving	(see 25)
Bora Bora Blue Nui	**9** B3
Bora Diving Centre	**10** D6
Church	**11** D4
Coastal Defence Guns	**12** A5

Coastal Defence Guns	**13** C3
Marae Aehua-tai	**14** E4
Marae Fare-Opu	**15** C3
Marae Taianapa	**16** C4
Musee de la Marine	**17** D3
Topdive Bora Bora	**18** C4

SLEEPING
Blue Heaven Island	**19** C2
Chez Nono	**20** A6
Chez Robert & Tina	**21** B6
Club Med	**22** D6
Hotel Matira	**23** A6
Intercontinental Bora Le Moana	
Resort	**24** A6
Intercontinental Resort & Thalasso Spa	
Bora Bora	**25** F5

Le Maitai Polynesia	**26** A5
Le Méridien Bora Bora	**27** F4
Novotel Bora Bora Beach Resort	**28** B5
Pension Anau – Chez Teipo	**29** E6
Pension Maeva – Chez Rosine	
Masson	**30** A6
Rohotu Fare Lodge	**31** D5
Saint Régis Resort	**32** F3
Sofitel Motu	**33** D7
Village Temanuata	**34** A6

EATING
Bloody Mary's	**35** D6
Bora Kaina Hut	**36** D6
La Bounty	**37** A5
Le Flamboyant	**38** D6
Le Matira Beach Restaurant	**39** A5

Snack Matira	**40** A5
Sunset Boulevard	**41** D5
Tama'a Maitai	**42** A5
Tiare Market	**43** A5

ENTERTAINMENT
Club Med	(see 22)

TRANSPORT
Air Tahiti	**44** A2
Bora Bora Rent a Car – Avis	**45** A2
Fare Piti Rent-a-Car	**46** A2
Farepiti Quay	**47** C4
La Plage	(see 28)
Maupiti Express 2 (office)	**48** A2

Topdive Bora Bora (☎ 60 50 50; www.topdive.com) On the northern edge of Vaitape.

Snorkelling is no less impressive, with gin-clear waters and a smattering of healthy coral gardens packed with rainbow-coloured fish. The area off Hotel Bora Bora has excellent snorkelling but, unfortunately, the best snorkelling spots can't be reached from shore – you'll have to take a lagoon tour or rent a boat.

Lagoon Tours
Taking a cruise around Bora Bora's idyllic lagoon will be one of the main highlights of your trip to French Polynesia and it's well worth the expense.

It will cost about 6000 CFP to 7000 CFP for half-day trips and 9000 CFP for whole-day trips.

Tours typically stop to feed the sharks at the southern edge of the lagoon, and to feed and swim with the rays off Motu Toopua (whether it's a good idea or not is debatable), and include snorkelling stops at various coral gardens. Full-day tours include a *motu* barbecue.

There are plenty of operators available. You can book through your pension or hotel.

Undersea Walks
Aqua Safari (☎ 28 87 77, 75 20 22; www.aquasafaribora .com; trips 7800 CFP) provides the unique experience of walking underwater, wearing a diver's helmet and weight belt. Pumps on the boat above feed air to you during the 35-minute 'walk on the wet side', in less than 4m of water. Walks are available to everyone over the age of eight.

Semi-submersible
For nondivers, **Bora Bora Submarine** (☎ 67 55 55, 74 99 99; www.boraborasubmarine.com; per adult 18,000-24,000 CFP) is a small (maximum six people) vessel that offers coral-viewing outside the barrier reef. The trip lasts 30 to 45 minutes and the vessel descends to depths of 35m.

Walking
You don't have to get all your thrills on or in the water. Draped in thick forest and dominated by bulky basaltic mountains, the island's interior has exceptional green treats. A guide is essential as the paths are notoriously difficult to find and to follow. **Polynesia Island**

Tours (☎ 29 66 60; half-/full-day walks 3500/6500 CFP) offers reputable guided tours.

4WD Trips
A couple of operators organise island tours aboard open 4WDs. **Tupuna Mountain Safari** (☎ 67 75 06; trips 6600 CFP) and **Vavau Adventures** (☎ 60 38 30, 72 01 21; trips 6600 CFP) run half-day trips that visit American WWII sites, along with locally important (and hard-to-find) archaeological areas and a few stops at lookouts.

SLEEPING
You could easily whittle away your life savings on deluxe hotels on Bora Bora, which are as sumptuous as the hype leads you to believe. However, you can also benefit from staying at cheaper *pensions*.

West Coast
There's only one place along the west coast.

Rohotu Fare Lodge (☎ 70 77 99; www.rohotu farelodge.com; bungalows 19,000 CFP; 🖳) Find yourself brilliantly poised in three local-style, fully equipped bungalows hidden in a verdant array of tropical flora, with cracking views over Povai Bay. There's no beach nearby, but Matira Point is an easy bike ride away. If you don't fancy cooking, there's a number of excellent restaurants nearby.

Matira Point
With the best beach on Bora Bora, Matira Point is packed with accommodation options.

BUDGET
They may lack the wow factor of the top hotels, but there are a number of little *pensions* around Matira Point that lay claim to the best sweep of beach on the main island.

Pension Maeva – Chez Rosine Masson (☎ 67 72 04; dm/d with shared bathroom 3700/7400 CFP) Amenities and privacy are fairly limited, but there's more than a touch of island atmosphere to be found around this rustic house peacefully positioned on the water's edge. The wooden walls, large shared lounge room and gorgeous lagoonside setting all add nicely to the tropical Polynesian atmosphere. There are five rooms and one dorm-style room with three beds (and no doors).

Chez Nono (☎ 67 71 38; nono.leverd@mail.pf; s/d with shared bathroom 6500/7500 CFP, bungalows 10,000-13,000 CFP) There's something of a lively atmosphere at this long-standing *pension*, partly thanks to the divine beach setting (it's right on Matira Beach) and partly due to the fact that the property is cramped, especially the house with six rooms – claustrophobic and hot – so you'll just have to put up along with your neighbours. Much better are the two round-shaped bungalows.

Chez Robert & Tina (☎ 67 72 92; pensionrobertet tina@mail.pf; d 8000-9200 CFP) The three modern, fan-cooled homes, all with shared kitchen, might not be terribly Polynesian, but the location screams Bora Bora – you're right at the tip of the point! Tip: angle for an upstairs room with balcony – the views of the lagoon will make you swoon. There's no direct beach access, but Matira Beach is just a *pareu's* throw away.

MIDRANGE
As you saunter into the midrange category, you can safely expect private bathrooms with hot water.

Novotel Bora Bora Beach Resort (☎ 60 59 50; www .novotel.com; r from 19,000 CFP; 🕱 🗔 🗷) The Novotel is a good choice if you're looking for low-key luxury, with a wide range of amenities including a Japanese restaurant, a pool right by the beach and an on-site dive centre. The 70 rooms are comfortable but lack both character and lagoon views.

Le Maitai Polynesia (☎ 60 30 00; www.hotelmaitai .com; r/bungalows from 20,000/30,000 CFP; 🕱 🗔) This option is a good deal with its nicely furnished rooms, and the over-water bungalows are the cheapest on Bora Bora. Best of all, it's close to the action. Don't get carried way – this is no exclusive experience but, at the price, it's hard to find a comparable bargain, especially if you can score promotional rates.

Hotel Matira (☎ 67 70 51, 60 58 40; www.hotel -matira.com; bungalows 22,000-37,000 CFP) Like many of the places along this stretch, the lagoon setting is spectacular, and the bungalows facing this direction are priced accordingly. They occupy a grassy property overlooking the beach. Pity about the concrete wall at the entrance, though.

Village Temanuata (☎ 67 75 61; www.temanuata .com; bungalows from 16,000 CFP) This popular venture is ideally positioned on Matira Point but only two units have full lagoon views. The rest are tightly packed together on a verdant property. It has an annexe ('Temanuata Iti') with five bungalows that are about 1km to the west.

Club Med (☎ 60 46 04; bboccrec01@clubmed.com; all-inclusive package per person from 20,000 CFP; 🕱 🗔) Club Med may equal package tours, but individual guests are welcome if there's space available (no minimum stay). It's actually a good deal when you factor in all the perks, including excursions, evening shows, activities and copious buffet-style food. Absorb the ambience either in the rambling gardens, on your sun-drenched terrace or on the fine stretch of beach.

TOP END
Intercontinental Bora Bora Le Moana Resort (☎ 60 49 00; www.tahitiresorts.intercontinental.com; bungalows from 70,000 CFP; 🕱 🗔 🗷) This option is a perfect balance between luxury, seclusion and convenience. Moana Beach spreads along the eastern side of Matira Point, a glorious stretch of beach is right out front, and there's sensational snorkelling offshore. But best of all, though you're in an exclusive resort, you don't feel cut off from the island.

East Coast
The east coast is less built-up than the rest of the island, with only a few places to choose from here.

Pension Anau – Chez Teipo (☎ 67 78 17; teipobora@ mail.pf; bungalow s/d 7200/10,500 CFP) Who said Bora Bora was out of your financial reach? This modest *pension* features four fully equipped bungalows in a well-tended garden by the lagoon. The lowlight is the lack of beach and swimming options, but free bikes greatly expand your possibilities.

The Motu
Staying on a *motu* ensures unrivalled tranquillity, a complete escape and great views of Bora Bora.

our pick Blue Heaven Island (☎ 72 42 11; www .blueheavenisland.com; bungalows 24,000 CFP) You'll be hard-pushed to make your holiday money go further than at this bijou hideaway, with five Polynesian-style bungalows deployed over several acres of coconut grove. They are simple yet functional and have solar-power and a kitchenette. Meals are available on request and include homegrown vegetables. There's a svelte china-white ribbon of beach and a

TAHITI & FRENCH POLYNESIA

fantastic coral garden just offshore. Payment is by cash only.

Sofitel Motu (☎ 60 56 00; www.sofitel.com; bungalows from 45,000 CFP; ✴ ▯) A good balance between luxury, seclusion, privacy (there are only 31 units) and convenience – situated on tiny Motu Piti Uu Uta, this Sofitel is five glorious minutes by boat from the main island, so you're not too far from the action (and you can use the facilities of the Sofitel Marara).

Le Méridien Bora Bora (☎ 60 51 51; www.lemeridien -borabora.com; bungalows from 70,000 CFP; ✴ ▯ ▩) Not your average five-star hotel, Le Méridien also features green credentials and is strongly involved in sea-turtle protection work (check out www.boraboraturtles.com), so guests have the added bonus of watching the rehabilitating turtles. The over-water bungalows and the infinity-edge swimming pool impress as well.

Saint Régis Resort (☎ 60 78 88; www.stregis.com /borabora; bungalows from 90,000 CFP; ✴ ▯ ▩) The darling of stylish travel mags, the Saint Régis is a romantic resort, extremely quiet and popular with couples. The 90 overwater and beach villas have an artistic and casual elegance that let the luxury sneak up on you. You can also book in for a beauty treatment in the serene Miri Miri spa. Its two restaurants are of very high standard.

Intercontinental Resort & Thalasso Spa Bora Bora (☎ 60 76 00; www.boraboraspa.interconti.com; bungalows from 100,000 CFP; ✴ ▯ ▩) Seen from above, the layout of the 80 over-water bungalows resembles two giant crab's claws. The wow factor continues inside, with a Starck-inspired decor. The seawater air-conditioning system is the pride of the hotel, and justifiably so: it saves 90% of the electricity consumed by a conventional cooling system of similar capacity.

EATING

Good news for gourmands: there's a wide choice of restaurants on Bora Bora, from European gourmet dining to *roulottes* and *snacks*. Nearly all the independent restaurants (excluding *snack* bars), as well as some of the resort restaurants, offer free transport to and from your hotel.

All of the luxury hotels have dance performances with buffet dinners several times a week. Expect to pay around 7500 CFP to 9500 CFP.

Most restaurants firmly shut the door at 9pm.

West Coast

In Vaitape, there's a string of cheap eateries along the main road that sell sandwiches and cool drinks. In the evening, several *roulottes* along the main road serve simple dishes.

Bloody Mary's (☎ 67 72 86; mains 1000-2700 CFP; ☾ lunch & dinner Mon-Sat) The stage is set: a backdrop featuring lots of exotic plants, a thatched roof, sand floors and coconut stools. Grilled lagoon fish and pelagics take centre stage, with a support cast of vegetables and French fries. Guest stars include meat dishes cooked the American-barbecue way. It's a concept that has been cult since 1979, so you can't go wrong.

Bora Kaina Hut (☎ 67 54 06; mains 1400-2600 CFP; ☾ lunch & dinner Wed-Mon) A great place for a *diner à deux*. The Kaina Hut exudes romantic vibes at dinner with candlelit tables, wooden furniture, sand floor and soothing soundtrack. Excellent seafood, including oysters, mussels and lagoon fish, and divine desserts, will make you weep.

our pick Sunset Boulevard (☎ 67 57 67; mains 1700-3000 CFP; ☾ dinner Tue-Sun) Everybody's got a soft spot for this snazzy eatery, where you eat on two permanently moored boats or on two decks in a tropical garden right by the lagoon. Sushi and sashimi are stand-outs, as well as skewered fish and beef.

Matira Point & Around

Snack Matira (☎ 67 71 32; mains 500-2000 CFP; ☾ lunch Tue-Sun) The decor is nonexistent at this no-frills eatery but the lagoonside location more than makes up for it. Fish, steaks, burgers and sandwiches are the order of the day.

Tama'a Maitai (☎ 60 30 00; mains 1000-2600 CFP; ☾ lunch & dinner) Part of Le Maitai Polynesia, Tama'a Maitai overlooks the beach and catches lots of breeze. No culinary acrobatics here: just keep-the-faith classics such as salads, pizzas, fish and meat dishes, as well as a few vegetarian options.

La Bounty (☎ 67 70 43; mains 1300-3000 CFP; ☾ lunch & dinner) Funky little La Bounty is festively decorated with loads of bright yellow lights and dense foliage in an open-air thatched-roof building. The menu is eclectic and inventive – salads and *spaghetti au thon frais* (spaghetti with fresh tuna) sit happily alongside flavoursome thincrust pizzas and even fondue.

Le Flamboyant (☎ 67 61 99; mains 1400-2900 CFP; ☺ lunch Thu-Sat & Mon-Tue, dinner Thu-Tue) The speci-alities on offer at this fine French-Polynesian eatery are always a treat, but the winner is the *uru* (breadfruit) gnocchi. The crumble with tropical fruits and taro ice cream will finish you off sweetly. Opt for the set menu: at 4000 CFP, it's a bargain.

our pick Le Matira Beach Restaurant (☎ 67 53 79; mains 1500-4000 CFP; ☺ lunch & dinner Fri-Wed) A very high-quality restaurant right on the beach. It's easy to be seduced by an inven-tive array of sophisticated dishes, such as *tofu de carottes et thon mariné* (carrot tofu and marinated tuna). Lunch is casual, but dinner is a romantic affair. A sweet tooth will be in seventh heaven here, with celestial desserts and ice creams.

Tiare Market (☺ 6.30am-1.30pm & 3-7pm Mon-Sat, 6.30am-1pm & 3-6.30pm Sun) Across from the Novotel Bora Bora is this well-stocked supermarket.

The Motu

Free shuttles, which generally operate until midnight, allow you to enjoy the restaurants at the luxury *motu* hotels. It's best to reserve. At dinner, expect to pay anything between 2400 CFP and 3000 CFP for a fish dish.

DRINKING & ENTERTAINMENT

Dinner and a show in one of the big hotels are about the limit of nightlife on Bora Bora; make the most of the daytime activities and have an early night.

Any of the luxury hotels will provide a cold beer or cocktail (about 1000 CFP) by the la-goon. The *motu* hotels run free shuttles until about midnight. The bar at Bloody Mary's (opposite) is popular.

Don't miss a traditional dance perform-ance by a local group in one of the luxury hotels. Some places allow you in for the price of a drink at the bar. For about 7500 CFP to 9500 CFP, you can combine the performance with a sumptuous buffet din-ner. Performances take place two or three times weekly.

Other than that, nightlife is as restrained as it is on the other islands of French Polynesia. At the time of writing, the most 'happening' place was the Club Med (☎ 60 46 04; admission 1500 CFP), which is open to non-guests at weekends for its themed evenings.

SHOPPING

Black pearl jewellery is sold in many places around Bora Bora, and you will find numerous retail shops. Apart from pearls, shopping on Bora Bora tends to mean hopping between the many galleries and boutiques that are scattered around the island, wrapping yourself in various brightly coloured *pareu* (sarongs), find-ing the perfect Marquesan woodcarving or perhaps getting yourself a traditional Marquesan-designed tattoo.

MAUPITI

So you've been to Bora Bora. You've expe-rienced the frisson of luxurious lodgings, languished on Matira Beach and eaten at upscale restaurants. Why not try something a bit different?

Bora Bora's discreet little sister, Maupiti, is one of the most ravishing islands in French Polynesia and is already being talked of as a rising star of the region. Yet it still remains a hideaway where insiders come to revel in an unblemished tropical playground and to drop out of sight in a handful of quaint *pensions,* where you can enjoy fantastic views of the shimmering aqua lagoon without even leaving your bed. Maupiti offers complete relaxation – there's only one road, and virtually no cars, just bicycles. And when you want to play, there's plenty of scope for activities on the water, such as kayaking, snorkelling and diving.

Nirvana found? You be the judge.

ORIENTATION & INFORMATION

A 10km road encircles the island. The main settlement is on the east coast.

The high island mass is surrounded by a wide but shallow lagoon fringed with five *motu,* including Motu Tuanai, where the airport is located. There's only one pass, Onoiau, to the south. Yachties, beware, as this pass is exposed to big swells and strong currents.

TRANSPORT

There is no public transport on Maupiti, and most folks reserve their *pension* and trans-port from the airport in advance.

Getting There & Away

Air Tahiti flies from Maupiti to Tahiti (15,400 CFP, 1½ hours, five flights weekly), Ra'iatea (7400 CFP, 25 minutes, three flights weekly) and Bora Bora (7000 CFP, 20 minutes, one or two flights weekly). The **Air Tahiti office** (☎ 67 15 05, 67 81 24; ◷ 8am-noon Mon-Fri) is in the village.

The **Maupiti Express 2** (☎ 67 66 69, 78 27 11; www.maupitiexpress.com) runs between Maupiti and Bora Bora on Tuesday, Thursday and Saturday (one-way/return 3000/4000 CFP). Leaving Vaitape (Bora Bora) at 8.30am, it arrives at Maupiti at 10.15am and then departs for the return trip at 4pm, arriving back at Bora Bora at 5.45pm.

Getting Around

If you've booked accommodation you'll be met at the airport, although some places charge for the trip (around 2500 CFP return).

It's simple to arrange a boat out to the *motu* from the village and vice versa. It costs 500 CFP to 1500 CFP to go from the main island to the *motu*, and between 3000 CFP and 5000 CFP for a lagoon excursion. Every *pension* on the mainland or *motu* can arrange these transfers.

Most *pensions* rent bikes for around 1000 CFP per day.

SIGHTS

Maupiti's star attractions are its five idyllic **motu**: spits of sand and crushed coral dotted with swaying palms and floating in the jade lagoon that surrounds the main island. Besides acting as quiet retreats, the *motu* also boast Maupiti's best beaches (though Tereia, on the main island, is a very serious contender).

Motu Paeao, situated at the northern end of the lagoon, is ideal for swimming and snorkelling. At low tide you can reach **Motu Auira** from Tereia Beach by wading across the lagoon. **Motu Tiapaa** has beautiful sandy white beaches and you'll find some good snorkelling on either its ocean or lagoon sides. It also is the most developed *motu*, with a handful of *pensions*. If you have a kayak you can paddle across to the completely isolated **Motu Pitihahei**, but be sure to steer way to the north of Onoiau Pass, which is very dangerous due to strong currents. The airport and a few *pensions* are

found on **Motu Tuanai**, with lovely views of the village huddled at the foot of the high island mass.

You can walk (or bike) around the island in just a few hours. Just northeast of the main quay (it's signposted), make a beeline for **Marae Vaiahu**, Maupiti's most important *marae*. This features a large coastal site covered with coral slabs and a fish box made of coral blocks.

Fringed by a placid turquoise lagoon and backed by arching coconut trees, small **Tereia Beach**, on the northern coast, could be straight off the cover of a travel brochure. It's a wonderful place to sunbathe or have friendly splash-wars in the translucent water, but it's not ideal for swimming as the lagoon is too shallow.

ACTIVITIES
Snorkelling & Lagoon Tours

Maupiti's magnificent lagoon is crystal clear, bath-warm and packed with colourful species fluttering around healthy coral gardens, which provides great **snorkelling** opportunities. The best sites are the reefs stretching north of Onoiau Pass (but beware of the currents) and Motu Paeao, as well as the 'Underwater Trail', which consists of five buoys that were installed in an area to the south of the island. Each buoy is equipped with interpretative panels.

Most guest houses have masks and snorkels you can borrow. The *pensions* also run lagoon tours with snorkelling stops (3000 CFP to 5000 CFP). Maupiti Nautique (see opposite) also offers snorkelling trips to the manta rays' cleaning station.

IMPORTANT! READ THIS...

Maupiti has no banks or ATMs, and none of the island's sleeping options take credit cards or even travellers cheques, so it's imperative you bring enough cash with you to pay for your entire stay. Plan ahead as most banks have a limit on how much cash you can get out of the ATM in one day. Half board usually includes free water, coffee and tea, but rarely beer and soft drinks.

Also beware of tricky currents when snorkelling or kayaking near Onoiau Pass (where a few of the *pensions* are).

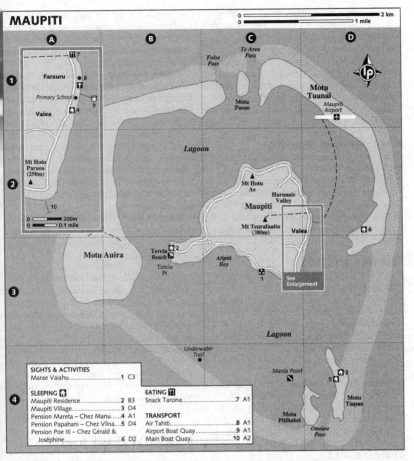

MAUPITI

| | | 0 | 2 km |
| | | 0 | 1 mile |

A **B** **C** **D**

1

Fararuu

Primary School

Vaiea

Mt Hotu
Paraoa
(250m)

0 — 200m
0 — 0.1 mile

False
Pass

Te Area
Pass

Motu
Paeao

Motu
Tuanai

Maupiti
Airport

2

Lagoon

Mt Hotu
Ae

Haranaie
Valley

Maupiti

Mt Teurafaatiu
(380m)

Vaiea

See
Enlargement

3

Motu Auira

Tereia
Beach

Tercia
Pt

Atipiti
Bay

4

Lagoon

Underwater
Trail

Manta Point

Motu
Tiapaa

Motu
Pitihahei

Onoiau
Pass

SIGHTS & ACTIVITIES
Marae Vaiahu.................................1 C3

SLEEPING
Maupiti Residence.........................2 B3
Maupiti Village..............................3 D4
Pension Mareta – Chez Manu......4 A1
Pension Papahani – Chez Vilna....5 D4
Pension Poe Iti – Chez Gérald &
   Joséphine..................................6 D2

EATING
Snack Tarona................................7 A1

TRANSPORT
Air Tahiti......................................8 A1
Airport Boat Quay........................9 A1
Main Boat Quay..........................10 A2

Diving

Diving on Maupiti started in 2008. There are outstanding dive sites outside the lagoon, including a stunning drop-off just north of the pass, but they aren't always accessible due to the strong currents and swell in the pass. See p75 for more information on diving in French Polynesia.

Another calling card for divers on Maupiti is Manta Point, which is home to a cleaning station visited by manta rays. It's in the lagoon, near the pass, and, in principle, they're here every morning.

Maupiti's sole dive operator, **Maupiti Nautique** (☎ 67 83 80; www.maupiti-nautique.com) charges 6000 CFP for single or introductory dive trips (including gear) and 11,500 CFP

for two-tank trips. An open-water course costs 40,000 CFP. The 'dive and whale-watch combination' is great value at just 11,000 CFP. Cash only.

Kayaking

Sea kayaking is another popular activity of the DIY variety. Paddling around the quiet lagoon offers the chance to discover hidden spots, search for leopard rays and manta rays, or just put down the oar, lie back and sunbathe. Most places to stay either rent or offer free sea kayaks for guests' use.

Walking

Maupiti has some good walking, including the one-hour clamber up **Mt Hotu Paraoa**

(250m), which looms high above the village. It's also a superb climb to the summit of **Mt Teurafaatiu** (380m), the island's highest point. Allow three hours for the return trip. Both are fairly arduous hikes but the 360-degree panoramas are phenomenal. Neither track is easy to follow and they are not properly waymarked, so it's best to go with a guide – contact your *pension* to secure one (about 3000 CFP).

Whale- & Dolphin-Watching

Every year during the austral winter, from mid-July to October, humpback whales frolic off Maupiti's barrier reef. Whale-watching trips are available through the local dive operator, **Maupiti Nautique** (☎ 67 83 80; www.maupiti-nautique.com). Dolphins can be spotted all year-round along the reef. A three-hour excursion costs 7000 CFP.

SLEEPING & EATING

For the full Robinson Crusoe experience, places on the *motu* are hard to beat. If island life is your top priority, stay on the main island. Better yet: combine the two options! Most people opt for half or full board at their accommodation; if you're staying on the *motu* this will likely be your only option. Several small village shops sell basic supplies.

Pension Mareta – Chez Manu (☎ 67 82 32; chez-manu@mail.pf; r with shared bathroom per person 3000 CFP) Nice prices, plain rooms and a family atmosphere make this place a viable port of call for budgeteers. Guests may use the cooking facilities for an extra 300 CFP or order a meal for about 2000 CFP.

Maupiti Village (☎ 67 80 08; Motu Tiapaa; dm/r/bungalows with full board per person 6000/7000/12,000 CFP) Digs are in three particle-board rooms with a shared outside bathroom, a bare-bones six-bed dorm or two teensy cabins with saggy mattresses. However visitors usually forgive its shortcomings for the top-notch location on the ocean side of Motu Tiapaa, affordable rates, laid-back vibes and lovely food. Kayaks are free.

Pension Poe Iti – Chez Gérald & Joséphine (☎ 74 58 76; maupitiexpress@mail.pf; Motu Tuanai; bungalows s/d 7500/8500 CFP; 🌐) This highly affable and efficient *pension* whose two big windmills attest to its commitment to preserving the environment. Four well-proportioned bungalows (hot water) are scattered in a

well-tended property right by the lagoon. Gourmet palates, you're in luck: Joséphine will treat you with tasty Polynesian dishes at dinner, including parrot fish in coconut sauce. Free kayaks.

Pension Papahani – Chez Vilna (☎ 60 15 35; pensionpapahani@hotmail.fr; Motu Tiapaa; bungalows with half board per person 9500-12,500 CFP) This *pension* is staffed by a friendly family – informality is the name of the game at this place – so you'll immediately shift down a few gears here. The five bungalows here are set in attractive tropical gardens. Try for one of the newer, slightly more expensive bungalows as the two units at the rear look a bit tired. You will also find excellent snorkelling options offshore here.

Maupiti Residence (☎ 67 82 61; maupiti.residence@mail.pf; bungalows 12,000-16,000 CFP; 🌐 💻) With a well-deserved reputation as one of the best-value *pensions* on Maupiti, this venture delivers all the hedonist essentials: two large and comfortable villas that are fully self-contained, a spiffing Tereia beach frontage and plenty of perks, including free bicycles and kayaks. And not to mention soul-stirring sunsets. Truly lovely. Credit cards are accepted.

Snack Tarona (☎ 67 82 46; dishes 900-1200 CFP; ⏰ lunch & dinner) Just north of the village, this simple eatery serves hearty portions of traditional French Polynesian dishes, such as raw fish, tuna sashimi, braised beef and pork with taro.

TUAMOTU ISLANDS

Anyone who loves the water will adore this archipelago; so you can expect wrinkly fingers and toes because there is a good chance you will be in the water more often than out. According to Darwin's theory of atoll formation, these rings of coral are the barrier reefs of volcanic islands that sank to the bottom of the Pacific millions of years ago. Today these atolls are veritable underwater playgrounds, that are teeming with sharks, healthy corals and so many fish that you could practically put an empty hook down and they'll still bite. It is a pared down way of life out here in the Tuamotu Islands and you will find only a few trees, shrubs and coconut palms that are able to thrive in the coral soils and man-made

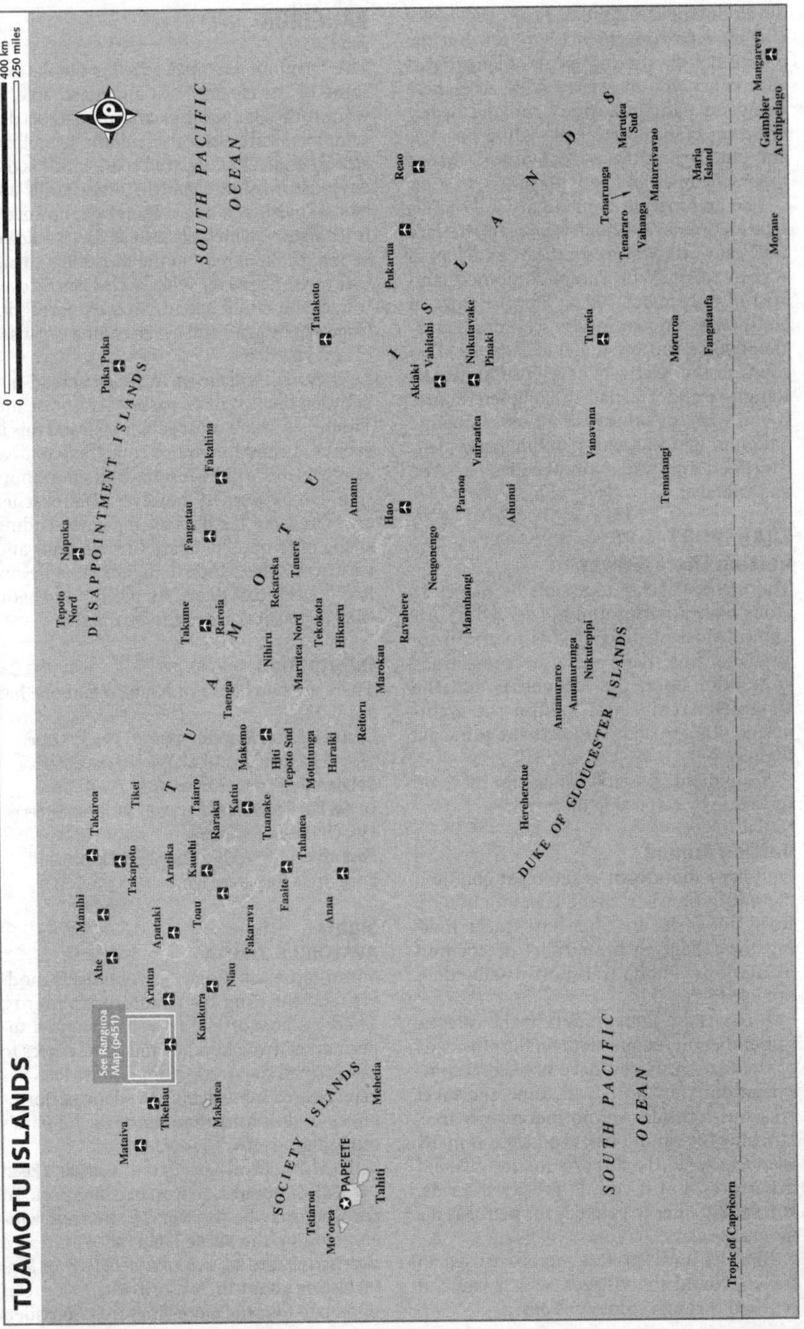

TUAMOTU ISLANDS

400 km
250 miles

0
0

SOUTH PACIFIC OCEAN

SOUTH PACIFIC OCEAN

DISAPPOINTMENT ISLANDS

DUKE OF GLOUCESTER ISLANDS

SOCIETY ISLANDS

Gambier Archipelago

T U A M O T U   A R C H I P E L A G O

See Rangiroa Map (p451)

Puka Puka

Napuka
Tepoto Nord

Mataiva
Tikehau
Makatea
Mehetia

Tetiaroa
Mo'orea
PAPEETE
Tahiti

Ahe
Manihi
Takaroa
Takapoto
Tikei

Arutua
Apataki
Aratika
Kauehi
Taiaro

Kaukura
Toau
Raraka
Katiu

Niau
Fakarava
Faaite
Tuanake
Tahanea

Anaa
Haraiki
Motutunga
Tepoto Sud
Hiti

Makemo
Taenga

Marutea Nord
Nihiru
Tekokota
Hikueru
Tanere
Rekareka

Reitoru
Raroia
Takume

Marokau
Ravahere

Hereheretue
Anuanuraro
Anuanurunga
Nukutepipi

Nengonengo
Mamuhangi
Paraoa
Ahunui
Vairaatea

Hao
Amanu

Vanavana
Tematangi

Moruroa
Fangataufa

Akiaki
Vahitahi
Nukutavake
Pinaki

Tatakoto

Pukarua
Reao

Tureia

Morane

Tenarunga
Tenararo
Vahanga
Matureivavao
Maria Island

Marutea Sud
Mangareva

Fakahina
Fangatau

Tropic of Capricorn

development is minimal. Fruit, vegetables and modern conveniences are few but the plentiful fish, smiling locals, silent nights with knock-you-out starry skies (with there being no light pollution) and the nearly blinding colours from the white beaches and blue lagoon make most visitors change their schedules and stay longer.

The archipelago is made up of 77 atolls scattered over a stretch of ocean that are 1500km northwest to southeast and 500km east to west. With a total combined land area of only about 700 sq km, the rings of coral islets known locally as *motu*, encircle 6000 sq km of sheltered lagoons. You can visit the relatively developed atolls like Rangiroa and Tikehau in complete luxury if you wish, or otherwise try out authentic Paumotu life (but with plumbing and plentiful food and water) on beauties like Ahe and Mataiva.

TRANSPORT
Getting There & Away
The archipelago is accessible by plane; 31 atolls have airstrips and are served by Air Tahiti. Most of the traffic is to and from Pape'ete, but there are also connections with Bora Bora, the Marquesas and the Gambier Archipelago. Within the archipelago, Rangiroa and Hao are the principal flight hubs.

See individual island listings for more on travelling by cargo ship or see p458.

Getting Around
Outboard motorboat is the most common method of transport in the Tuamotu Islands. Road networks are often just tracks linking the village to the airport or coconut plantations. Public transport usually does not exist.

Airports are sometimes near the villages, sometimes on remote *motu* on the other side of the lagoon. If you have booked accommodation, your hosts will come and meet you, but transfers are not necessarily free. Hitching (by car or boat) is possible as many islanders go to the airports for arrivals and departures. But if you do get given a ride, you should offer to help pay for petrol as it's quite expensive.

Bicycles and scooters are often used to travel around the villages, which you can rent out through some *pensions*.

RANGIROA
pop 3245

The Tuamotu Archipelago's 'Big Smoke' has some of the cleanest sea air imaginable, is wondrously languorous and its biggest developments are a resort, a middle school, an airport and 12km of paved road. If this is the city, just imagine what the other atolls are like! What is big about Rangiroa, however, is its lagoon, which at 1640 sq km is said to be the second largest in the world. It's so big that you can't see the other side as you fly over it and you could spend years exploring its forgotten beaches and never-ending expanses of coral gardens.

The main village of Avatoru, spread out between the two main passes (Avatouru and Tiputa), is where most people stay and this is very convenient if you've come here to dive as most sites will be just beyond your doorstep. Do be warned, however, that beaches are scarce. For landlubbers the never-ending string of remote *motu* are the real draw and trips across the lagoon to the stunning Île aux Récifs (Island of Reefs, see p451) and Lagon Bleu (opposite) are not to be missed.

Information
There are two banks in Avatoru and one has an ATM.

Centre Médical Avatoru (☎ 96 03 75; ⌚ 7:30am-12pm & 3-5:30pm Mon-Fri. 8-11am Sat) East of Avatoru.

Gendarmerie (police station; ☎ 96 73 61)

Le Kai Kai Restaurant (☎ 96 03 39; Tevaiohie; per hr 1500 CFP) Internet access.

Post offices (⌚ 7:30am-12pm & 2-4:40pm Mon-Fri, 8-9am Sat)In Avatoru and Tiputa.

Sights
AVATORU & TIPUTA
Somniferous as it may be, Avatoru is modern and bustling by Tuamotu standards. There's a post office, a few banks and a supermarket, two churches and some places to eat. A small site overlooking Tiputa Pass has been cleared for watching the daily performances of dolphins that dance in the pass's outgoing current.

To visit a pearl farm, go to **Gauguin's Pearl** (☎ 96 05 39), about 1km west of the airport. To see what may be the world's strangest winery, stop by the **Vin de Tahiti** (☎ 96 04 70; www .vindetahiti.pf; half-day tours per person 6000 CFP; ⌚ Mon-Fri) tasting room in Avatoru where you can sign up to tour the *motu* vineyards. Sébastien

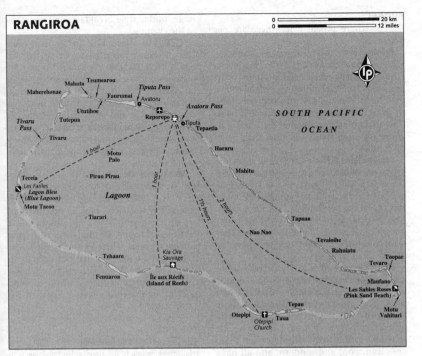

RANGIROA

Thépenier, the winery's oenologist, describes the wines as having a 'mineral flavour from the soil'.

Around the middle of the day, you could pretty safely fire a gun along the main street in Tiputa (the island's administrative centre) and not hit anyone. It's a charming little village, and you'll likely be the only visitor in town.

AROUND THE ISLAND

Lagon Bleu (Blue Lagoon) is one hour away by boat on the western edge of the atoll, close to Motu Taeoo. A string of *motu* and coral reefs have formed a shockingly blue, idyllic pool on the edge of the main reef, a lagoon within a lagoon.

Les Sables Roses (Pink Sand Beach) on the southeast edge of Rangiroa's lagoon near Motu Vahituri, 1½ to two hours from Avatoru by boat, is pretty but the shifting sands are sometimes not even visible – many travellers complain it's not worth the price to get here.

On the south side of the atoll, an hour by boat from Avatoru, **Île aux Récifs** (Island of Reefs), also known as Motu Ai Ai, lies in water dotted with *feo* (coral outcrops)

that have weathered into strange petrified silhouettes; many consider this Rangiroa's top sight.

Organised tours are really the only way to see the sights, though they rely on the weather and the number of takers. Lagoon and *motu* trips typically cost 7500 CFP to 10,000 CFP and can be arranged through your hotel.

Activities
DIVING

Rangiroa is one of the best-known dive sites in the Pacific because of its sharks. Divers enter on the ocean side and drift with the strong current into the lagoon. Contact **Paradive** (☎ 96 05 55; Reporepo), the **Raie Manta Club** (☎ 96 84 80; www.raiemantaclub.free.fr; Reporepo), **Topdive** (☎ 96 05 60; www.topdive.com; Reporepo), **Six Passengers** (☎ 96 02 60; Reporepo) or **Rangiroa Plongeé** (☎ 27 57 82; Tevaiohei). For more on diving in French Polynesia, see p75.

Sleeping

Rangiroa has lots of simple, family-run *pensions* (only a sample is listed here) and a few more luxurious places.

BUDGET

Except where noted, prices here are per person.

Pension Loyna (☎ 96 82 09; www.pensionloyna.fr.st; Avatoru; r with half board 6000-7500 CFP) This lovely, clean *pension* has cheaper rooms in the owner's home (shared bathroom); several rooms with bathroom and new two-bedroom family bungalows with bathroom are out back. The ocean is 100m away, but the warm welcome and high standards more than make up for this.

Pension Teina & Marie (☎ 96 03 94; pensionteina simone@caramail.com; Reporepo; r with half board 6500-7500 CFP, camp sites 1000 CFP) Great views of Tiputa Pass and a friendly, laidback atmosphere make this one of the best budget, no-frills options. The food is phenomenally good and non-guests can reserve in the morning if they want to eat here at night. Campers have use of bathroom facilities.

Pension Bounty (☎ 96 05 22; www.pension-bounty .com; Reporepo; r with breakfast 7500 CFP; 🖳) Located about 100m from the Kia Ora beach (the best on Avatoru), the owners at Pension Bounty go out of their way to ensure their guests have everything they need. Lodging here is in rooms rather than bungalows, but these are clean, cool and modern, and all have mosquito screens and hot water. Dinner is available (you'll need to add 3500 CFP per person), but you also have your own equipped kitchen. English, Spanish and Italian are spoken here and this place accepts credit cards.

MIDRANGE

You can pay with a credit card in most of the midrange bracket.

Pension Tuanake (☎ 96 04 45; www.sitetuanake.fr.st; Vaimate; s/d/tr with half board 10,500/16,000/21,000 CFP; 🖳) A cross between a family-run place and a hotel, Tuanake has two small bungalows for three people and two bungalows for six people. It's clean, organised, and set in a coconut plantation on the coral gravel-lined lagoon. The food is great.

Raira Lagon (☎ 96 04 23; www.raira-lagon.pf; Tevaiohie; bungalows with half board per person from 11,000 CFP; 🍴 🖳) Feeling even less family-run than Pension Tuanake but still retaining a friendly vibe, this place has 10 fan-cooled bungalows spread throughout a garden fringed by one of the better beaches in the area. The restaurant here faces the lagoon and serves large, buffet-style breakfasts and cocktails in the evening.

our pick **Le Merou Bleu** (☎ 79 16 82; www .merou-bleu.com, in French; Avatoru; s/d/tr with half board from 11,500/21,000/32,000 CFP; 🖳) An outstanding option in a magical garden setting right on Avatoru Pass in front of the surf break. Bungalows are creatively made from woven coconut thatch and other natural materials but manage to maintain a good level of comfort, with hot water, mosquito nets and lovely terraces perfect for lounging. Credit cards aren't accepted.

Tevahine Dream (☎ 93 12 75; www.tevahinedream .com; Avatoru; bungalow with half board per person 12,500 CFP, house 25,000 CFP per day for up to four people) Zen meets Polynesia with huge bungalows that are dripping with wood and drapey white fabrics. Bathrooms are mini oases with ferns and coral gravel. There's also a whole house option (with a kitchen) that can sleep up to six people. The beach is coral gravel, good for snorkelling and there's a little dipping pool up by the eating terrace and bar. No credit cards.

TOP END

our pick **Les Relais de Joséphine** (☎ 96 02 00; http:// relaisjosephine.free.fr; Reporepo; s/d/tr bungalow with half board 20,000/31,100/39,000 CFP; 🖳) The setting of this very French interpretation of the Polynesian *pension*, in full view of the dancing dolphins on Tiputa Pass, is arguably the prettiest in the Avatoru area. The Euro-Balinese design and dining on the elegant French-style food make this place feel very luxurious. Non-guests can reserve early in the day for lunch or dinner.

Novotel Rangiroa Beach Resort (☎ 86 66 66; www .novotel.com; Tevaiohie; bungalows 23,000-38,000 CFP; 🍴) Bungalows here aren't memorable but are certainly comfortable. There's not really a beach but there is a pontoon. The restaurant serves good food and has lagoon views (though we've received complaints about slow service). There are a handful of rooms designed for disabled guests.

Hotel Kia Ora (☎ 96 03 84; www.hotelkiaora.com; Reporepo; bungalows 39,000-80,000 CFP; 🍴 🖳 🏊) The biggest resort in the Tuamotus and the priciest option on Rangiroa, Kia Ora has an old-school feel to it. Bungalows are dotted around a magnificent coconut plantation situated on the best beach around Avatoru. The sister property Kia Ora Sauvage, isolated on Motu

Avearahi, is an hour by boat and only takes 10 guests at a time. The beach setting is stunning and at night, the whole place is lit by candlelight and oil lamps. Prices include full board, which is compulsory; minimum stay of two nights.

Eating

Most people take half board at their *pension*; however, if you don't eat fish, be prepared to cater for yourself. Avatoru has a few supermarkets.

Le Relley Ohotu (Reporepo; burgers 500-800 CFP, mains 1000-1500 CFP) A buzzing *snack* opposite Chez Glorine, overlooking the water. The servings are diver's sized and the fish is fresh.

Snack de la Marina (☎ 96 85 64; mains 1000-2000 CFP; ☽ closed lunch Sun) A local favourite that serves excellent, fresh food in massive portions. For dessert get hot *gaufres* (Belgian-style waffles; from 400 CFP) with a choice of sweet toppings.

Rangiroa Lagoon Grill (☎ 96 04 10; mains from 1500 CFP; ☽ closed Mon) A new, highly recommended option right on the water that serves a more classic version of French food, including lots of grilled meat dishes (as well as fish). Offers pick-up service.

Le Kai Kai Restaurant (☎ 96 03 39; Tevaiohie; lunch 350-1000 CFP, dinner mains 1300-2000 CFP; ☽ closed Wed; 🖳) French garden restaurant, with simple lunch and more elaborate dinner menus including a set option. Evening cocktails are available, and transfers from your Avatoru *pension* or hotel are free.

Getting There & Away

The airport is in the Avatoru area. **Air Tahiti** (☎ 93 11 00; ☽ 7.30am-6.30pm Mon-Sat) has an office inside the airport.

Rangiroa is connected by air to Tahiti, Bora Bora, the Marquesas and other atolls in the Tuamotus. There are several flights daily between Rangiroa and Pape'ete (from 16,400 CFP). It's also possible to fly directly from Bora Bora (from 23,700 CFP).

The *Dory*, *Mareva Nui*, *Vai-Aito*, *Saint-Xavier Maris-Stella* and *Rairoa Nui* all serve Rangiroa; the *Aranui* stops on Rangiroa on its way back from the Marquesas. For details, see p463.

Getting Around

Getting around Rangiroa is a fairly haphazard affair. The only public transport is **Ignace**
Tupahiroa (☎ 77 28 02; 500 CFP) who runs a minibus between the Tiputa and Avatoru passes several times a day (unscheduled). Hitching is another option.

A sealed road runs the 10km from Avatoru village at the western end of the string of islets to the Tiputa Pass at the eastern extremity. If you want to move about, the best option is hiring a bicycle or a scooter.

There are regular boats (1000 CFP return) that cross the pass separating the Avatoru islets from Tiputa village; taking a bicycle over costs 500 CFP extra.

If you have booked accommodation, your hosts will meet you at the airport. If your *pension* is near the airport, transfers will probably be free; places further away tend to charge (ask when you book).

Europcar (☎ 96 03 28; Avatoru; ☽ 7.30am-6pm) rents cars from 6600/8100 CFP for a half-/full-day. **JJ Location** (☎ 27 57 82; Tevaiohie) rents scooters for 1400 CFP per hour or 3600/5300 CFP for a half-/full-day and bikes for 800/1400 CFP for a half-/full-day. Otherwise, **Location Arenahio** (☎ 96 82 45; Avatoru; ☽ 7.30am-6pm Mon-Sat), hires out cars for 6200/8400 CFP for a half-/full-day; scooters are 4200/5200 CFP and bicycles 800/1400 CFP. Credit cards are accepted.

FAKARAVA

pop 699 / lagoon area 1121 sq km

Fakarava might be the second-largest atoll in the Tuamotus (after Rangiroa), but it can claim Garuae Pass, located in the north of the atoll, as the widest pass in all of French Polynesia. It also has a second pass, Tumakohua, in the far south, that the locals reckon is the most beautiful in the Tuamotus, and it's hard not to agree. The atoll's particularly diverse ecosystem has made it a Unesco-protected area.

Most islanders live in **Rotoava** village at the northeastern end, 4km east of the airport. Aside from Rangiroa's Avatoru, this is the most developed and busy town in the Tuamotus but it's still pretty quiet by most people's standards. A handful of inhabitants also live in **Tetamanu** village, on the edge of the southern pass.

Activities

Visits to pearl farms and picnics plus snorkelling on idyllic *motu* can be arranged as a half-day boat excursion from 9500 CFP per person.

Dive operators include:

Fakarava Diving Center (☎ 93 40 75; www.fakarava
-diving-center.com) At Pension Paparara.

Te Ava Nui (☎ 98 42 50, 98 43 50, 79 69 50; www.diving
fakarava.com; Rotoava)

Topdive (☎ 98 43 23, 73 38 22; www.topdive.com) At
Hôtel Maitai Dream Fakarava.

Fakarava is also on the program for several
dive-cruise operators and the *Aranui 3*.

Sleeping & Eating

Relais Marama (☎ 98 42 51; www.relais.marama.com;
campsites per person 2000 CFP, bungalow s/d 5000/9000
CFP; 🖳) A good-value, backpacker-like option with immaculate bungalows with shared
bathroom. All prices include breakfast, while
other meals you can use the communal
kitchen or go to nearby eateries. Campers
share the same facilities as the bungalows.
No credit cards.

Pension Paparara (☎ 98 42 66; www.fakarava-dive
lodge.com; s/d/tr bungalow with shared bath and half board
9500/16,800/23,700 CFP, s/d/tr bungalow with private bath
and half board 15,800/20,000/28,400 CFP) You have two
options here: one of two small but wonderfully organic 'Robinson *fare*' that are right on
the water that share a coldwater bathroom,
or more comfortable but still artistic beachside bungalows with private bathrooms.

Pension Kiria (☎ 83 41 05; pensionkiria@mail.pf; s/d
bungalows with half board 11,000/19,000 CFP) Each of the
four bungalows here is made from coconut
thatch and a variety of local materials – every
one is unique and exceptionally beautiful.
The smiles of the owners stand out even by
Paumotu standards. No credit cards.

Havaiki Pearl Guesthouse (☎ 93 40 16; www
.havaiki.com; s/d with half board 11,500/18,000 CFP; 🖳)
This is the liveliest *pension* on Fakarava and
the ambience is like a small hotel. Bungalows
are basic wooden structures, but they're all
well-decorated with local fabrics and have
good mosquito nets. The restaurant serves
meals to guests and non-guests and has loads
of options, including American-style burgers and sandwiches. English is spoken and
airport transfers cost between 1000 CFP and
2000 CFP.

Tokerau Village (☎ 98 41 09, 71 30 46; tokerauvillage@
mail.pf; bungalow s/d with half board 12,000/22,000 CFP)
Flora, the owner here, spends her days fine-
tuning the garden and making sure there's
not a speck of dust in any of the four, large,
modern wood bungalows. Each unit has a
big terrace, mosquito net, TV and sleeps up

to three people. The food is delicious, some
English is spoken and the whole place runs
on solar energy.

Hôtel Maitai Dream Fakarava (☎ 43 08 83; www.hotel
maitai.com; bungalows 27,000-38,000 CFP; 🔀 🖳) With
27 classy wooden bungalows, a restaurant and
numerous activities on offer, this is the biggest
and most luxurious option on Fakarava. The
beach is good and there's a particularly picturesque pontoon, but the hotel is understaffed
and beds lack mosquito nets.

Raimiti (☎ 55 05 65; www.raimiti.com; s/d bungalow with full board for two nights from 47,000/84,000 CFP)
Crusoe-chic and very isolated, the bungalows
on this sandy private *motu* to the west of the
atoll ooze romance. Meals are excellent, especially considering the beachside location.
Oil lamps light the scene at night and during the day; if you're not off on an organised
activity, you can walk for hours along the
empty lagoon or exterior reef. Prices include
transfers and activities.

ourpick **Snack Te Anuanua** (☎ 98 41 58; Rotoava;
mains 1200-2900 CFP) A surprisingly chic restaurant with sea views, good music and even
better food.

Getting There & Around

The airport is about 4km west of Rotoava. **Air
Tahiti** (☎ 67 70 35/85; www.airtahiti.pf) flies Pape'ete–
Fakarava daily from 16,500 CFP one-way and
Rangiroa–Fakarava every Tuesday and Friday
from 5200 CFP.

The *Saint-Xavier Maris-Stella*, *Vai-Aito* and
Mareva Nui stop at Fakarava.

From Rotoava a track goes to the southwest
of the atoll for about 40km. The guest houses
arrange boat excursions.

TIKEHAU

pop 507 / lagoon area 461 sq km

If it's endless stretches of empty white-
and pink-sand beaches you're looking for,
Tikehau should be your first stop. The atoll
is geologically different from many others in
the archipelago: its baroque bays and craggy
nooks have been whittled by the sea both into
the lagoonside shores and along the exterior
reef. The result, surrounded by the bluest of
lagoons, is better than a postcard-come-to-
life, yet the only things that seem to flock
to Tikehau are seabirds and a huge variety
of fish.

Most islanders live in **Tuherahera village**, in
the southwest of the atoll, leaving the ma-

jority of the paradisaical *motu* untouched. With regular flights and cargo ships, it's a well-stocked and well-tended place that's easy to navigate for the wide-eyed visitor. Just remember that there's no bank (and also sparse internet access), so bring lots of cash.

Sights & Activities

Scuba diving in the magnificent **Tuheiava Pass** is excellent; you're likely to see manta rays and sharks. Dive centres include **Raie Manta Club** (☎ 96 22 53; http://raiemantaclub.free.fr) at Tikehau Village, and **Tikehau Blue Nui** (☎ 96 22 40, 96 23 00; www.bluenui.com) at Tikehau Pearl Beach Resort.

Lagoon excursions allow visitors to explore the magnificent waters. Regular stops include a visit to the rocky **Motu Puarua** (Île aux Oiseaux, or Bird Island) where several species of ground-nesting birds are easily spotted. A less common but interesting stop is at **Île de Eden**, an establishment of the Church of the New Testament who have created an organic garden in the infertile sands of their superb *motu*. A last stop is usually a barbecue picnic on one of many idyllic *motu*. *Pensions* generally organise excursions, and trips cost from 7000 CFP to 7500 CFP per person.

Sleeping & Eating

All *pensions* on Tikehau are on white-sand beaches on the lagoon side of the atoll and a handful are on private *motu*. Unless otherwise noted, prices quoted are per person per day.

Pension Panau (☎ /fax 96 22 99; Tuherahera; bungalows with half board 6000 CFP) This is the least expensive place on Tikehau and the most simple, but with that million-dollar beach in front, you won't need much more than the friendly family vibe to keep you happy.

Pension Hotu (☎ /fax 96 22 89; Tuherahera; bungalows with half board 8500 CFP) On one of the nicest stretches of beach, and the farthest *pension* from the village, this friendly place has five spacious and clean bungalows that have a little more artistic flair than the others in this price bracket, with hand-painted *pareu* on the walls and cool coral and wood decoration.

Tikehau Village (☎ 96 22 86; Tuherahera; tike hauvillage@mail.pf; s/d/f bungalows with half board 15,000/22,000/33,200 CFP) The eight beachfront bungalows here are dripping with thatch, varnished local wood and coral stonework – plus the bathrooms have hot water. The shady terraces look out over white sand and turquoise lagoon bliss. The restaurant area is one of the prettiest spots around, overlooking the water with cool breezes and a social vibe – non-guests are welcome. Credit cards are accepted and English is spoken.

Ninamu (☎ 737810; www.motuninamu.com; bungalows with half-board around 20,000 CFP) Still under construction when we passed, this Australian-run place was already looking like one of the most ecoconscious places to stay in the Tuamotus. On a private white- and pink-sand *motu* just northwest of the village, the massive bungalows are built from gnarled hunks of wood, coral stonework and coconut thatch. Everything is powered by wind and solar, and toilets are self-composting. Let's hope the service is as stellar as the surrounds.

Relais Royal Tikehau (☎ 96 23 37; www.royal tikehau.com, in French; s/d with half board 16,000/24,000 CFP, s/d bungalow with half board from 20,500/30,500 CFP; 🖳) Bungalows here are big and comfy and decorated with Polynesian taste – think lots of ruffles and bright colours. The whole place, situated out on a private *motu*, is run on solar and wind power; the charming hosts speak English. It's about a 20-minute walk across some shallow waterways to the village.

** our pick** **Tikehau Pearl Beach Resort** (☎ 96 23 00; www.pearlresorts.com; bungalows 48,000-83,000 CFP; 🔲 🔲) We love this resort not only for its stunning isolated *motu* setting between endless swaths of white- and pink-sand beaches and bright blue waters, but also for its environmental and social consciousness – a huge percentage of the village is employed here and the director tries to keep energy use and impact to a minimum. There are free shuttle boats to the village five times a day. Credit cards are accepted.

Snack Chez Cindy (☎ 96 22 67; mains 700-1200 CFP; ⊙ lunch & dinner) The only snack place in town, this is a busy place serving good *poisson cru*, steak, chow mein and burgers.

Getting There & Away

The airport is about 1km east of the village. **Air Tahiti** (☎ 96 22 66) flies seven times a week between Pape'ete and Tikehau (from 16,400 CFP), direct or via Rangiroa (from 5200 CFP); several flights a week go to Bora Bora (from 23,700 CFP).

The *Mareva Nui*, *Saint-Xavier Maris-Stella* offer limited transport to Tikehau.

TAHITI & FRENCH POLYNESIA

Getting Around

The 10km track around the *motu* on which Tuherahera is situated passes the airport. Bicycles can be borrowed or hired from your hosts.

MATAIVA

pop 204 / lagoon area 25 sq km

Despite the limited tourist infrastructure, this tiny atoll offers a delightful escape. There are superb and easily accessible beaches, numerous snorkelling spots, lots of fish and one of the few noteworthy archaeological sites in the Tuamotus. Air Tahiti flights make it possible to spend a pleasant weekend here.

The structure of the Mataiva lagoon gives it an unusual appearance: the coral heads create walls 50m to 300m wide that form about 70 basins with a maximum depth of 10m. Seen from the plane it looks like a mosaic of greens.

Sights & Activities

Marae Papiro is a well-kept *marae* on the edge of a *hoa* (shallow waterway linking a lagoon to the sea), about 14km from the village. In the centre of this *marae*, you can see the stone seat from which, according to legend, the giant Tu guarded the pass against invasion. In the south, along the edge of the lagoon, there are gorgeous **beaches**.

Île aux Oiseaux (Bird Island), to the east of the lagoon, is a coral spit that's a favourite nesting place for *oio*, *tara* and red-footed boobies.

Don't miss the chance to help locals catch fish in one of the numerous **fish parks** around the lagoon and the pass. Sorted, scaled and gutted, the fish are sold in the village.

Sleeping & Eating

The three *pensions* are in the village and prices are per person per day. No credit cards.

Mataiva Village (☎ 96 32 95; campsites s/d 1500/2500 CFP, s/d bungalows with full board from 7500/14,000 CFP; ⊗) This option has clean and comfortable two-person bungalows with bathroom (cold water only), but there's not much of a beach.

ourpick **Pension Ariiheevai** (☎ 76 73 23, 96 32 50; fax 96 32 46; bungalows with full board and excursions 8000 CFP; ⊗) Six huge bungalows all on the edge of the white-sand fringed emerald lagoon are immaculately kept. The food is great and there are plenty of activities offered, including flower-garland making and picnics at Marae Papiro. Kayaks and bikes are free.

Apart from the *pensions* there's really nowhere to eat, although there are several small shops with basic food supplies.

Getting There & Away

Mataiva is 350km northeast of Tahiti and 100km west of Rangiroa.

Air Tahiti (☎ 96 32 48) runs two Pape'ete–Mataiva flights (16,400 CFP one-way) a week, and one flight to/from Rangiroa (5900 CFP one-way).

Mataiva is on the routes of the *Mareva Nui* and *Saint-Xavier Maris-Stella*.

Getting Around

A track goes almost all the way around the island, in the middle of the coconut plantation, for about 28km. The *pensions* rent bicycles for about 1000 CFP per day and organise trips to the various sites for about 3000 CFP.

MANIHI

pop 818 / lagoon area 192 sq km

Considered the birthplace of the Tahitian pearl industry, Manihi is a classically gorgeous atoll with one deep pass (Punaeroa) in the southwest and great fishing. Since pearl prices began to plummet around 2000, approximately 50 farms have gone out of business. However there are still about eight family-run and three industrial pearl farms dotted around the lagoon. Manihi is now eclipsed by its quiet neighbour Ahe in terms of numbers of pearls produced, but it's still a great place to buy the pearl of your dreams.

The atoll is 28km long and 8km wide and the best beaches and picnic spots are at the south of the lagoon. The not-very-pretty village of Turipaoa takes about five minutes to wander round.

There are a number of magnificent diving sites near the pass, including Punaeroa Pass and Le Tombant.

There's no bank, but the Manihi Pearl Beach Resort (opposite) and the local shops may be able to change money. The post office is in Turipaoa village as is the medical clinic.

Sights & Activities

The *pensions* and hotels organise pearl-farm visits, usually combined with a picnic and village excursion from around 3500 CFP.

You can dive with **Manihi Blue Nui** (☎ 96 42 17; www.bluenui.com); there's a great wall dive with excellent marine life.

Sleeping

Each of these options are on private *motu* and accept credit cards.

Pension Vainui (☎ 96 42 89; www.pensionvainui.com; full board per person 8900 CFP) Located east of the village and about a 30-minute boat ride from the airport, this all-inclusive *pension* has ageing rooms with shared bathrooms. There is not much privacy here, but the site is one of the best you'll find on the atoll and the welcome is friendly. Rates here include daily excursions; airport transfers cost 1000 CFP return.

Motel Nanihi Paradise (☎ 96 41 54; www.nanihiparadise.com; bungalows from 13,000 CFP) On a tiny *motu*, this place has clean, two-bedroom bungalows with kitchens and luminous bathrooms. Meals can be arranged.

Manihi Pearl Beach Resort (☎ 96 42 73, in Pape'ete 43 16 10; fax 96 42 72, in Pape'ete 43 17 86; beach/over-water bungalows 31,000/67,000 CFP; ☒ ☐) An exceptionally well-run resort, this place feels like a super luxurious summer camp for honeymooners. There are a slew of daily activities on offer ranging from deep-sea fishing to a free star-watching talk. Of course you could just as easily spend the day enjoying the little beach, the comfort of your plush bungalow and the very good restaurant.

Getting There & Away

The representative of **Air Tahiti** (☎ 96 43 34, ☎ 96 42 71) is in Turipaoa but on flight days will be at the airport. There are almost daily flights between Pape'ete and Manihi (19,600 CFP one-way), direct or via Ahe, Tikehau or Rangiroa (10,700 CFP one-way). There's also a twice-weekly flight to Fakarava (10,700 CFP one-way).

The *Mareva Nui* and *Saint-Xavier Maris-Stella* service Manihi and accept passengers.

Getting Around

The only track on Manihi links Motu Taugaraufara to the airport, covering a total distance of about 9km. Getting around the atoll requires, for the most part, a boat. The Manihi Pearl Beach Resort (see above) rents bicycles for around 1000 CFP per day but the road is barren and shadeless.

All sleeping options offer airport transfers, and the pensions will organise transport if you want to dive with Manihi Blue Nui dive club (see opposite).

AHE

pop 566 / lagoon area 170 sq km

Although Ahe is the biggest pearl producing atoll in the Tuamotus, its 20km long by 10km wide ring of coral is less developed than many other surrounding atolls. Still, the atoll's beauty draws in a large number of yachties and the two *pensions* here are among the best in the archipelago. It's a great place to experience the unadorned charm of the Tuamotus and to buy pearls.

The dusty, flower-filled village of Tenukupara is on the southwest side. There's no bank on the atoll.

Chez Raita (☎ 96 44 53; www.ahedream.com, in French; bungalows with half/full board per person 7500/9500 CFP) is owned by the local fireman and his family. It's a friendly and charming place on a white-sand *motu* on the east side of the atoll.

In a coconut plantation facing the lagoon, **Cocoperle Lodge** (☎ 96 44 08; www.cocoperlelodge.com; bungalows with half/full board per person from 11,000/13,000 CFP; ☐) has a hand-full of comfy ecochic bungalows. Excellent meals are served in a *fare* by the lagoon and the bar is open all day. Activities include snorkelling, kayaking and excursions to the nearby bird *motu* or to a pearl farm. The lodge is run on solar power and plans to open a dive club in 2009.

Air Tahiti flies from Pape'ete to Ahe four days weekly (19,600 CFP one-way). Twice-weekly flights to Manihi are 5900 CFP one-way.

The *Saint-Xavier Maris-Stella* and *Mareva Nui* service Ahe.

MARQUESAS ISLANDS

Whether you believe in legends or not, this archipelago looks like something from the pages of a fairy tale. Here, nature's fingers have dug deep grooves and fluted sharp edges, sculpting intricate jewels that jut up dramatically from the cobalt-blue ocean; waterfalls taller than skyscrapers trickle down vertical canyons; the ocean thrashes towering sea cliffs like a furious beast; sharp basalt pinnacles project from emerald forests; and scalloped bays are blanketed with desert arcs of white or black sand.

No wonder that over the last 170 years the Marquesas have been an escape for artists, writers, adventurers and musicians, including Paul Gauguin, Herman Melville and Jack London.

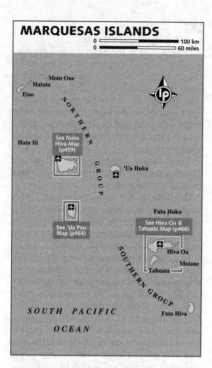

MARQUESAS ISLANDS

0 ———— 100 km
0 ———— 60 miles

Motu One
Hatutu
Eiao

NORTHERN GROUP

Hatu Iti

See Nuku Hiva Map (p459)

'Ua Huka

See 'Ua Pou Map (p464)

Fatu Huku

See Hiva Oa & Tahuata Map (p466)

Hiva Oa
Motane
Tahuata

SOUTHERN GROUP

SOUTH PACIFIC OCEAN

Fatu Hiva

IMPORTANT! READ THIS...

The Marquesas are *not* a beach destination, although there are a few enticing beaches. As appealing as these beaches may look, the reality is they are invariably infested with *nono* – a small, aggressive biting fly. Fortunately they are found almost exclusively on beaches and do not carry diseases. It's best to stay in the mountains and valleys where there are endless opportunities for hiking, horse riding, exploring the almost overwhelming number of archaeological sites or simply discovering this mysteriously wonderful culture.

It's not all about inspiring landscapes, though. The Marquesas are culturally intense and offer plenty of sites dating from pre-European times. However, they remain largely underrated. According to Pierre Ottino, French Polynesia's most respected archaeologist, 'the Marquesas can't compete with Easter Island in terms of proportions, but they boast much more diversity, with statues, gathering

places, ceremonial centres and houses, all set within varied and powerful landscapes'.

If you've got energy to burn, hiking, horseback riding, diving and snorkelling will keep you busy. An ecotourist's dream, the Marquesas represent the perfect combination of nature, culture and adventure.

Transport

The Marquesas stretch over 350km and are divided into northern and southern groups. Only six of the 15 islands are inhabited and travelling within the archipelago can be difficult.

Getting There & Away

Nuku Hiva and Hiva Oa are well connected with Tahiti, with almost daily direct flights from Pape'ete. There's also a once-weekly direct flight from Rangiroa in the Tuamotus to Nuku Hiva. Flights to 'Ua Huka via Nuku Hiva run four days a week, and 'Ua Pou has flights six days a week via Nuku Hiva or Hiva Oa.

The *Taporo IX* and *Aranui* service the Marquesas, departing from Pape'ete and travelling via the Tuamotus (Fakarava and/or Rangiroa). Note that the *Taporo IX* doesn't take passengers. For more on travelling by cargo ship, see p483.

Getting Around

The easiest and quickest way to island hop within the archipelago is by regular Air Tahiti flights, with Nuku Hiva and Hiva Oa being the hub islands. Tahuata and Fatu Hiva are only accessible by boat (both from Atuona).

You can hop on the cargo ship *Aranui* if your timing is right (ask your hosts about arrival dates).

On the islands, there's no public transport and you'll have to charter taxis to get around the islands' web of 4WD tracks (and, increasingly, surfaced roads). It is also possible to rent your own vehicle on Nuku Hiva and Hiva Oa. Chartering a speedboat is sometimes a more convenient option to travel between two villages.

NUKU HIVA

pop 2632 / area 340 sq km
This huge (the second largest in French Polynesia after Tahiti), sparsely populated island boasts a fantastic terrain, with razor-edged basaltic cliffs pounded by crashing

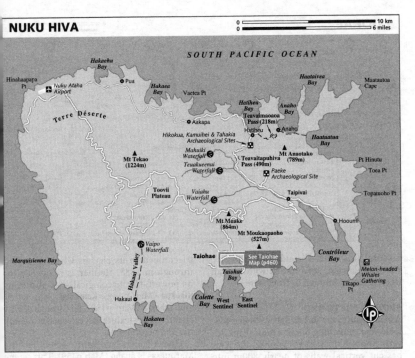

NUKU HIVA

waves, deep bays blessed with Robinson Crusoe beaches, dramatic waterfalls and timeless valleys that feel like the end of the world. The main town of Taiohae, the 'capital' of the Marquesas, has managed to hold on to that slow-down-it's-the-South-Pacific feeling.

If you've got itchy feet for active pursuits, you'll find some of the most inspirational hikes and rides in Polynesia. Snorkelling is also available – and what snorkelling! Imagine yourself swimming with a pod of melon-headed whales in the open ocean – both thrilling and unique. Culture vultures will get a buzz with plenty of archaeological sites scattered around the island.

Information

The following are in Taiohae.

Banque Socredo (Map p460; ☎ 92 03 63; ☻ 7.30-11.30am & 1.30-4pm Mon-Fri) Currency exchange, as well as two ATMs.

Hospital (Map p460; ☎ 91 20 00) Around 100m from the post office, there's a dentist here too. Each village also has basic medical services.

Moetai Marine (Map p460; ☎ 92 07 50; ☻ 8am-5pm Mon-Fri) On the quay, here you'll find internet access (per hr 900 CFP) and laundry service (1000 CFP). Also can help yachties with formalities.

Post office (Map p460; ☻ 7-11.30am & noon-3.30pm Mon-Thu, 7-11.30am & noon-2.30pm Fri) On the eastern side of the bay, has internet access (with the Manaspot card, available at the counter) and an ATM.

Tourist office (Map p460; ☎ 92 03 73; marquises@mail .pf; ☻ 7.30am-4pm Mon-Fri) Has a few brochures and can help with simple queries. See also www.marquises.pf.

Sights

TAIOHAE

The only town of any size on Nuku Hiva, **Taiohae** (Map p460) is strung along the shoe-shaped Taiohae Bay. It has a handful of sights, including the well-proportioned **Notre-Dame Cathedral of the Marquesas Islands**, the stones of which come from the archipelago's six inhabited islands. On the seafront, the **pae pae Piki Vehine** contains modern sculptures and a dozen magnificent *tiki* (sacred statues) made by local sculptors and artisans from Easter Island. The neatly restored **tohua Koueva**, a sacred place venerated by the ancient Marquesans, is about 1.5km up the Pakiu Valley on the road to Taipivai. The almost

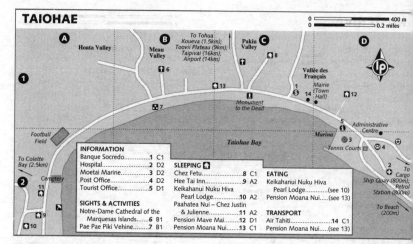

mystical hush that shrouds this extensive paved esplanade, surrounded with banyan trees, is reason enough to come here.

AROUND THE ISLAND
A real beauty, the **Hakaui Valley** (Map p459) looks like something out of a tonic drink advert. About 8km west of Taiohae, the river has cut vertical walls of nearly 800m into the basalt and the **Vaipo Waterfall** (Map p459) plunges an awesome 350m into a basin. From Taiohae, the valley can be reached by speedboat (about 30 minutes). From Hakaui Bay, where the boat anchors, allow about 2½ hours to reach the waterfall on foot, on a flat path which follows the river. A guide is required. Contact **Marquises Plaisance** (☎ 92 08 75, 73 23 48; e.bastard@mail.pf), which can arrange day trips to the waterfall from Taiohae (13,500 CFP for two people).

The reason to stop in **Taipivai** (Map p459), about 16km northeast of Taioahe, is to visit the **Paeke archaeological site** (Map p459), with two well-preserved paved platforms flanked by a set of brick-coloured *tiki*. It's on a hillside at the exit of the village on the way to Hatiheu.

From Taipivai, follow the main road 7.5km as it climbs to the 490m **Teavaitapuhiva Pass** (Map p459), from which you enjoy a dynamite view over Hatiheu Bay.

Hatiheu (Map p459) is a graceful little village dominated by a crescent of black sand, soaring peaks and colourful gardens; it's no wonder that Robert Louis Stevenson succumbed to its charms when he passed through in 1888. Hatiheu is renowned for its powerful archaeological sites, including **Hikokua** (Map p459), **Kamuihei** (Map p459) and **Tahakia** (Map p459), all located nearby Hatiheu. They feature vast esplanades (*tohua*), *tiki* and petroglyphs.

One of the best-kept secrets in the Marquesas is **Anaho** (Map p459). This serene hamlet is only accessible by speedboat (15 minutes from Hatiheu, 7000 CFP) or a little less than 1½ hours by foot from Hatiheu. It's a popular anchorage for visiting yachts and, with the only coral reef on Nuku Hiva, the bay is lagoon-like and inviting.

From Anaho, a 30-minute stroll along an easy-to-follow path to the east leads to **Haatuatua Bay** (Map p459). The reward? A crescent-shaped bay fringed with a yellow scimitar of sand, framed by lofty volcanic ridges. Pure bliss.

On the northwest, **Aakapa** (Map p459) is in a superb setting below high peaks; it can be reached by 4WD from Hatiheu.

Activities
HIKING
Hiking is *the* very best Nuku Hiva has to offer, and is a dizzying experience (literally). The catch? A guide is essential because trails are not marked. Your best bet is to contact **Marquises Rando** (☎ 92 07 13, 29 53 31; www.marquis esrando.com, in French). It's run by a professional guide who offers ultra-scenic hikes which take in some awe-inspiring viewpoints. Hikes

range from five to six hours, are suitable for all levels and cost from 6600 CFP per person.

Other excellent walking options include the hikes to the Vaipo Waterfall (opposite) and from Hatiheu to Anaho (opposite).

HORSE RIDING

Horse riding is another good way to soak up the drop-dead gorgeous scenery. In Taiohae, **Sabine Teikiteetini** (☎ 92 01 56, 25 35 13; half-day rides incl transfers 8000 CFP) is a qualified guide who can arrange lovely rides on Toovii Plateau. Rides last about three hours.

WHALE-WATCHING

Now it's time to get wet. If you've ever fancied snorkelling with a pod of melon-headed whales (*Peponocephala electra*), this is your perfect chance. These intriguing creatures congregate off the east coast in the morning. While an encounter is not exactly guaranteed, the operator claims a success rate of 70%. It's not for the faint-hearted, though; the 45-minute journey to get to the site can be a nightmare if the sea is choppy. Whalewatching excursions are run by **Marquises Plaisance** (☎ 92 08 75, 73 23 48; e.bastard@mail.pf; halfday cruise 16,000 CFP for 2 people).

Sleeping
TAIOHAE

Chez Fetu (Map p460; ☎ 92 03 66; r per person 2000 CFP) The single, rustic bungalow is acceptable if you can survive old furnishings, saggy mattresses and a few bugs. It's about 200m up a small dirt path that starts at the west side of the Kamake shop.

Paahatea Nui – Chez Justin & Julienne (Map p460; ☎ 92 00 97; paahateanui@mail.pf; r/bungalows per person incl breakfast 3200/5500 CFP) You'll be made to feel at home at this well-priced establishment, on the western side of the bay. The three rooms in the main house are well scrubbed. Want more privacy? Book one of the six bungalows set in a fragrant garden. No meals are available, except breakfast, but you can use the kitchen. There's a small beach across the road.

Pension Moana Nui (Map p460; ☎ 92 03 30; pension moananui@mail.pf; s incl breakfast/half board 6500/9000 CFP, d incl breakfast/half board 9400/15,000 CFP; 🞮 🖳) This is the perfect headquarters for the budget-conscious traveller who's not looking for fancy trimmings, though has the added appeal of a very handy location, a good restaurant and free wi-fi. The eight rooms are utilitarian but

clean and well organised, with private facilities, hot shower and daily cleaning.

Pension Mave Mai (Map p460; ☎ 92 08 10; pension -mavemai@mail.pf; s/d 8000/9000 CFP; 🞮) All eight rooms are light and well appointed, with private facilities (hot water) and air-con, as well as a kitchenette in two of the rooms. But they're not terribly Polynesian. There's an onsite restaurant (half board costs 3000 CFP).

Keikahanui Nuku Hiva Pearl Lodge (Map p460; ☎ 92 07 10; www.pearlresorts.com; bungalows d from 30,000 CFP; 🞮 🖳 🞮) Nuku Hiva's swankiest option comprises 20 Polynesian-style bungalows hidden in a sea of spruce greenery set on a hillside. The real bonus is the cracking views of Taiohae Bay. The ambience is intimate and informal, and there's a tiny swimming pool.

Hee Tai Inn (Map p460; ☎ 92 03 82; rose.corser@mail .pf; s/d 8500/10,500 CFP; 🞮 🖳) This place was only getting off the ground when we were researching, but when it does it's likely it'll be one of the most reliable hotels on Nuku Hiva, with eight well-equipped rooms. It's run by an American lady, so English-speaking visitors will feel right at home here.

AROUND THE ISLAND

Chez Yvonne – Restaurant Hinakonui (☎ 92 02 97; hinakonui@mail.pf; Hatiheu; bungalows incl breakfast s/d 5000/7000 CFP, with half board 8000/12,000 CFP) This place has a split personality. While the restaurant serves flavoursome Marquesan specialities (see p462), the five boxy bungalows are in serious need of a touch up. However, they can do the trick for one night if you need to break up your journey to Anaho.

If you've succumbed to the charms of Anaho (and no doubt you will), you can bunk down at **Kao Tiae** (☎ 92 00 08; bungalows per person with half board 5000 CFP) or nearby **Te Pua Hinako** (☎ 92 04 14; r with half board per person 4600 CFP), a coconut's throw away from the sea shore. Both are run by the same family. Absolutely no frills, but you're here for the scenery and the hush (and the delicious local food).

Eating

Pension Moana Nui (Map p460; ☎ 92 03 30; mains 1500-2900 CFP; 🕑 lunch & dinner Mon-Sat) This is where all heads turn when it comes to a well-priced meal in an attractive setting on the seafront. The eclectic menu offers something for every mood, from woodfired pizzas to fish fillet and beef dishes.

Keikahanui Nuku Hiva Pearl Lodge (Map p460; ☎ 92 07 10; mains 1300-3000 CFP; ☿ lunch & dinner) If chef Erick Lafond is still here by the time you get there, you'll be treated to top-notch fare, with quality local ingredients fused with Gallic know-how. *Espadon fumé au bois de rose* (rosewood-smoked swordfish)? Très bon! Light meals are available at lunchtime.

In Hatiheu, be sure to stop at **Chez Yvonne – Restaurant Hinakonui** (☎ 92 02 97; Hatiheu; mains 1600-3000 CFP; ☿ lunch & dinner Mon-Sat, by reservation), which has a magnificent terrace that opens directly on to the seafront. The menu brims with local flavours – think grilled lobster, goat in coconut sauce, shrimps and sweet potatoes.

Getting There & Away

Find the office for **Air Tahiti** (Map p460; ☎ 91 02 25, 92 01 45; ☿ 8am-noon & 2-4pm Mon-Fri) in the centre of Taiohae.

There are up to nine weekly flights between Pape'ete and Nuku Hiva (28,000 CFP one-way, three hours). There is also one direct flight per week from Rangiroa to Nuku Hiva, but no service going back to Rangiroa (28,000 CFP one-way, 2½ hours).

Within the Marquesas there are five to seven weekly flights from Nuku Hiva to Hiva Oa (10,600 CFP one-way), and four to six flights per week from Nuku Hiva to 'Ua Huka and 'Ua Pou (both cost 6600 CFP one-way). These flights connect with the Pape'ete flights through Nuku Hiva.

The *Aranui* (opposite) stops at Taiohae and Taipivai.

Getting Around

Slowly but surely the roads of Nuka Hiva are being paved. At the time of writing a sealed road ran from Taiohae to within a few kilometres of the airport and almost to the Teavaitapuhiva Pass.

It takes at least 1¼ hours to reach the airport from Taiohae along a winding road. Licensed 4WD taxis generally wait for each flight. Transfers to Taiohae cost 4000 CFP per person.

To get around the island, you can rent 4WDs with or without a driver. From Taiohae, the vehicle (which will take four passengers) with a driver costs around 12,000 CFP to Taipivai and 20,000 CFP to Hatiheu.

4WDs without a driver can be rented from 12,000 CFP to 16,000 CFP per day. The fol-lowing operators can deliver directly to your hotel or *pension*. Contact **Pension Moana Nui** (☎ 92 03 30; pensionmoananui@mail.pf) or **Nuku Rent A Car** (☎ 92 06 91, 73 51 67).

'UA HUKA

pop 582 / area 83 sq km

This low-key, less-visited island remains something of a 'secret' and you'll probably have it all for yourself. Here's your chance to buy carvings from master artisans, zigzag up the flanks of an extinct volcano to reach mysterious archaeological sites tucked away in the jungle, take a boat excursion to offshore islets and delve right into Marquesan life.

There are only three villages – Vaipaee, Hane and Hokatu. Be warned: the addictive peaceful atmosphere could hold you captive longer than expected.

Sights

The island's main town, **Vaipee**, is at the end of the very narrow, deep and aptly named Invisible Bay. The **museum** (admission free, donations appreciated) in the town centre displays pestles, *tiki*, sculptures, *pahu* (drums), jewellery and period photos, as well as a traditional house. The **arboretum**, halfway between Vaipaee and Hane, offers a striking contrast between the wealth of plants and the relative aridity of the island.

The number-one reason to stop in **Hane** is the **Meiaute archaeological site**, higher up in the valley. It includes three 1m-high red-tuff *tiki* that watch over a group of stone structures, *pae pae* and *me'ae*.

About 4km east of Hane, **Hokatu** is so mel-low and scenic that you may never want to leave. It lies in a sheltered bay edged with a pebble beach pounded with frothy azure seas, and offers direct views of imposing, sugar-loafed Motu Hane. On the waterfront there's a small **petroglyph museum** (admission free).

Each village also has a *fare artisanal* (craft centre) where you can stock up on elaborate woodcarvings.

Twitchers will make a beeline for the islets of **Hemeni** and **Teuaua** near the southwestern point of 'Ua Huka, where thousands of *kaveka* (sooty terns) nest year-round.

'Ua Huka has a few lovely beaches, including **Manihina Beach** and **Hatuana Beach**.

Motu Papa, a popular picnic and snorkelling spot, is just offshore from the airport, between Vaipaee and Hane.

ALL ABOARD

If there's an iconic trip in French Polynesia, it must be on the *Aranui*. For nearly 25 years, this 104m-long boat has been the umbilical cord between Tahiti and the Marquesas and a hot favourite with tourists. Its 14-day voyage, departing from Pape'ete, takes it to one or two atolls in the Tuamotus and the six inhabited islands of the Marquesas. There are 16 trips per year. It's very convenient because you get an overview of the archipelago in a relatively short time at a fraction of what you'd pay if you had to do it independently.

It's both a freighter and a passenger vessel, with four classes of accommodation, from large cabins with balcony, double bed and bathroom (€4500 to €4800 per person) to dorm-style beds with shared bathroom facilities (€2000 per person). Foreigners are not supposed to use deck class, used by islanders, but if you are just going from one island to the next and there's room, there shouldn't be a problem.

For more information, contact your travel agency or the shipowner directly at **Compagnie Polynésienne de Transport Maritime** (CPTM; ☎ 42 62 42, 43 48 89 in Papeete; www.aranui.com).

Vaikivi Petroglyphs is little-visited archaeological site on the Vaikivi Plateau that's well worth the detour, if only for the walk or horse ride to get there (see Activities, below). The petroglyphs represent an outrigger canoe, a human face and various geometric designs.

Activities

From Hane or Vaipaee, it's a memorable three-hour **walk** inland to the Vaikivi Petroglyphs, a lovely archaeological site hidden in the jungle. Ask at your *pension* for a guide; the usual cost is about 5000 CFP, with picnic included.

Horse riding trips can also be organised through your *pension*. A ride typically costs 5000 CFP for a half day or 10,000 CFP for a full day, including a guide. A fantastic ride is from Vaipaee to Hane, along the windswept coast, or from Hane to the Vaikivi Petroglyphs.

Sleeping & Eating

Excursions by boat, 4WD and horse are organised through your *pension*. Payment is by cash only.

Chez Maurice et Delphine (☎ /fax 92 60 55; Hokatu; s/d with half board 7000/14,000 CFP) An adorable *pension* with five well-arranged (but simply built) bungalows on a little knoll on the village outskirts, with sweeping views of Motu Hane. It has delightful hosts too (Maurice is an accomplished sculptor), and excellent Marquesan food. Airport transfers are 2000 CFP return.

Le Reve Marquisien (☎ 79 10 52; revemarquisien@mail.pf; Vaipaee; s/d with half board 15,000/19,000 CFP) A perfect escape hatch situated in a secluded clearing at the far end of the village, and sur-

rounded by a lush coconut grove. The four bungalows are of a high standard. So, what's wrong with this place? Nothing, but it feels a bit too isolated (it's a 2km walk down to Vaipee). Transfers are included.

Getting There & Away

There are three flights a week to Nuku Hiva (from 6600 CFP) and Pape'ete (from 31,400 CFP). There's also one direct 'Ua Huka–Atuona (Hiva Oa) return flight per week. Contact the **Air Tahiti representative** (☎ 92 60 85) in Vaipaee.

The *Aranui* (above) stops at 'Ua Huka.

Getting Around

A 13km road links Vaipaee to Hokatu via Hane. The airport is midway between Vaipaee and Hane.

The *pension* owners can take you by 4WD to visit the three villages (10,000 CFP per day).

'UA POU
pop 2110 / area 125 sq km

'Ua Pou's jewel-like natural setting will frame everything you do here, from hiking across the island to visiting secluded hamlets. A collection of 12 pointy pinnacles seem to soar like missiles from the basaltic shield. Almost constantly shrouded in swirling mist and flecked by bright sunlight, they form one of the Marquesas' most enduring images. The island also offers up a handful of powerful archaeological sites, including two *tohua* (an open-air gathering place) that were neatly restored for the Marquesas Arts Festival of 2007 hosted by 'Ua Pou.

'UA POU

Information

There's a small medical centre with a doctor and dentist in the south of Hakahau.

Banque Socredo (☎ 92 53 63; Hakahau; ⏱ 7.30am-noon & 1-3pm Mon-Fri) Currency exchange, as well as an ATM.

Post office (Hakahau; ⏱ 7-11.30am & 12.15-3pm Mon-Thu, 7-11.30am & 12.15-2pm Fri, 7-11.30am Sat) On the seafront, it also has internet access (with the Manaspot card, on sale at the counter) and an ATM.

Sights

'Ua Pou's largest settlement, **Hakahau**, has few charms, but it's blessed with a photogenic location and it's a convenient base to start your island adventures. The stone-and-timber **Catholic church** in the south of town displays noteworthy sculptures by local artisans.

Time seems to have stood still in picturesque little **Hohoi** in the southeast of the island, 13km from Hakahau. Above the village, the magnificent **tohua Mauia** comprises a huge L-shaped stone platform and numerous *pae pae* dotted around the main complex. The whole area was restored in 2007

and hosted memorable dance and cultural performances during the Marquesas Arts Festival in December 2007.

Charming **Hakahetau** in the island's northwest springs up like an oasis after driving along the dusty track. At the far end of the village, make a beeline for the grandiose **Tetahuna archaeological site**. This *tohua* was also restored in 2007. Continue higher in the valley until you reach **Manfred Cascade**, suitable for a refreshing dip.

'Ua Pou has some good beaches (though watch out for *nono*). White-sanded **Anahoa Beach** is a 25-minute scenic walk east of Hakahau. **Hakanai Bay** is a popular picnic spot; it's known as Plage aux Requins (Shark Beach).

Activities

You can **walk** along the 4WD tracks that connect the villages. For deeper exploration, it's advisable to hire a guide since it's easy to get lost. Ask at your *pension*. Recommended hikes include the cross-island path from Hakahau to Hakahetau (about three hours) and the more challenging Poumaka loop (about four hours). Both hikes afford hauntingly beautiful panoramas of the interior of the island. A full-day guided walk is about 7000 CFP for two.

Sleeping & Eating

Pension Leydj (☎ 92 53 19; Hakahetau; r incl breakfast/half board per person 3500/5500 CFP) In a plum setting on a hill at the edge of Hakahetau, this mellow *pension* offers clean, well-swept, yet impersonal rooms with shared bathrooms (cold water), at a nice price. Owner Tony is a renowned master carver and his spouse Célestine can cook some seriously good Marquesan meals.

Pension Vehine (☎ 92 50 63, 70 84 32; fax 92 53 21; Hakahau; r or bungalows incl breakfast/half board per person 4500/6500 CFP) In the centre of Hakahau, this *pension* offers two simple rooms with shared bathroom in a house or two beautifully finished bungalows in the garden.

Restaurant-Pension Pukuéé (☎ 92 50 83, 72 90 08; pukuee@mail.pf; Hakahau; r with half board per person 8600 CFP; 🖥) Reliable, friendly and fabulously situated on a hillside with swooning views of Hakahau Bay, Pukuéé offers four smallish rooms with shared bathrooms (hot water) in a wooden house surrounded by greenery. Owner Jérôme is great with excursion organisation and his wife Elisa is a real cordon bleu cook. Wi-fi is available.

Getting There & Away

There is an office for **Air Tahiti** (☎ 91 52 25; ☾ 7.30am-noon & 1.30-3.30pm Mon-Fri) in Hakahau.

There are flights six days a week on a 20-seater plane from Nuku Hiva to 'Ua Pou (6600 CFP one-way), connecting with the Pape'ete–Nuku Hiva flight (Pape'ete to 'Ua Pou costs 31,500 CFP one-way). There are also two to three weekly flights from Hiva Oa to 'Ua Pou (8200 CFP one-way).

The *Aranui* (p463) stops at Hakahau and Hakahetau.

Getting Around

One 4WD dirt track runs most of the way around the island, the only inaccessible bit being between Hakamaii and Hakatao.

The airport is at Aneou, about 10km west of Hakahau. Your hosts will come to collect you if you have booked accommodation (about 2000 CFP per person return).

Ask at your *pension* about hiring a 4WD with driver; expect to pay 15,000 CFP per day.

HIVA OA

pop 2010 / area 320 sq km

Sweet Hiva Oa. Nowhere is the Marquesas' verdant, moody beauty better captured than here. This oh-so-mellow island is a picturesque mix of lush jungle, sea-smashed coastal cliffs and lofty volcanic peaks. No wonder that French painter Paul Gauguin and singer-songwriter Jacques Brel were won over by the island's powerful landscapes and serenity and chose to live out their lives in Atuona.

Hiva Oa has something for everyone. Archaeology buffs will love it for its large pre-European sites, some of which have been extensively restored. Outdoorsy types will take on diving, walking or horseback riding. Hiva Oa is also the optimal launching pad for exploring Tahuata and Fatu Hiva.

Information

Most services are in Atuona. There's a small but well-equipped hospital behind the mayor's office.

Banque Socredo (☎ 92 73 54; ☾ 7.30-11.30am & 1.30-4pm Mon-Fri) Has foreign exchange and a 24-hour ATM.

Post office (☾ 7.30-11.30am & 1.30-4.30pm Mon-Thu, 7.30-11.30am & 1.30-3.30pm Fri, 7.30-8.30am Sat) Also has internet access (with the Manaspot card, available at the counter) and an ATM.

Tourism office (☎ 92 78 93; www.maquises-hivaoa.org.pf; ☾ 8am-noon & 1-3pm Mon-Fri) Located right in the centre, it has useful brochures and sells sketch maps of most tourist sites (100 CFP).

Sights

ATUONA & AROUND

This tidy town is a place of pilgrimage for fans of Gauguin, who lived here from 1901 to 1903, and Jacques Brel who was a resident until 1978. The refurbished **Espace Culturel Paul Gauguin** (adult/child 600/300 CFP; ☾ 8-11am & 2-5pm Mon-Thu, 7.30am-2.30pm Fri, 8-11am Sat) has digital exhibits of the painter's work. Outside, have a look at the **Maison du Jouir** (House of Pleasure), a replica of Gauguin's own house. Behind the Espace Culturel Paul Gauguin you'll find a hangar that houses the **Centre Jacques Brel** (adult/child 500/250 CFP; ☾ 8-11am & 2-3pm Mon-Thu, 7.30am-2.30pm Fri, 8-11am Sat). In the centre is Brel's plane, *Jojo*; posters tracing the musician's life adorn the walls and his music plays dreamily over the sound system.

Gauguin and Brel are buried in the small **Calvaire Cemetery**, perched on a hill overlooking Atuona.

Hidden high up in the Tahauku valley, the **Tehueto petroglyphs** are a good walk from Atuona, but it's usually quite overgrown and the path is confusing; hire a guide (ask at your *pension*).

Hiva Oa's most bizarre statue is the **Smiling Tiki**, which can be found near the road to the airport, about 10km from Atuona. About 1m in height, it stands alone in a clearing. To find it (no sign), ask for the little sketch map that's on sale at the tourism office.

AROUND THE ISLAND

Near the village of **Taaoa**, 7km southwest of Atuona, the eerie **Tohua Upeke**, with more than

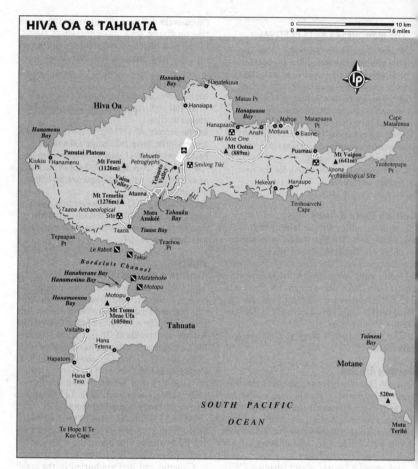

HIVA OA & TAHUATA

1000 *pae pae,* some of which are restored, is a definite must see for culture buffs.

One of the best-preserved archaeological sites in French Polynesia, the **lipona archaeological site,** lies on the outskirts of **Puamau,** a two-hour drive northeast of Atuona. Puamau itself is a delightful, timeless village that occupies a coastal plain bordered by a vast amphitheatre of mountains. In the village, **Tohua Pehe Kua** is the tomb of the valley's last chief.

It's a winding but scenic 1½-hour journey by 4WD to wild and beautiful **Hanapaaoa** from Atuona. Ask a local to take you to the **Tiki Moe One,** hidden in a forest on a hillside. One of the quirkiest statues in the Marquesas, it features a carved crown around the head. From Hanapaaoa, you can get to **Anahi** and **Nahoe,** two end-of-the-world hamlets to the west. The 4WD track snakes along the coast, offering ethereal vistas around every other bend.

Another gem of a village, Hanaiapa is cradled by striking mountains carpeted with shrubs and coconut trees. At the entrance of the village (coming from Atuona), you'll find some well-preserved **petroglyphs.**

Hanaiapa is a cul-de-sac, but you can walk to the hamlet of **Hanatekuua** – a little path follows the coastline.

Activities

HIKING

There are some truly excellent hiking possibilities on Hiva Oa. Given the lack of waymarked trail, a guide is strongly recommended (except if you stay on easy-to-follow 4WD tracks). **Alain Tricas** (☎ 20 40 90) is a competent guide with a strong environmental and cultural ethos who can customise hikes in the wildest areas of Taaoa valley. He charges 1000 CFP per hour (per person), with a maximum of 8000 CFP per day. Another professional guide is **Henry Bonno** (☎ 92 74 44).

HORSE RIDING

A network of trails leading to some of the most beautiful sites can be explored on horseback. **Hamau Ranch – Chez Paco** (☎ 92 70 57, 28 68 21; hamauranch@mail.pf; rides 7000-14,000 CFP) organises three-hour jaunts on the plateau near the airport. The ultimate is a full-day ride to Hanatekuua Bay, to the north of the island.

DIVING

Hiva Oa certainly doesn't possess dazzling tropical reefs (there's no barrier reef and no turquoise lagoon in the Marquesas), but there are many excellent diving sites along the crumpled coastline of Hiva Oa and Tahuata. See p75 for more information on dive sites.

The only dive centre in the Marquesas, **SubAtuona** (☎ 92 70 88, 27 05 24; eric.lelyonnais@wanadoo .fr; Atuona) charges 7000/13,000 CFP (minimum two divers) for a single/two-tank dive, including all gear. It also offers day trips to Tahuata that combine one dive and a tour of Tahuata's main villages (15,000 CFP per person).

BOAT EXCURSIONS TO TAHUATA

Taking a boat excursion to nearby Tahuata (p468) is well worth the expense (especially given the lack of reliable boat services to Tahuata). **SubAtuona** (☎ 92 70 88, 27 05 24; eric. lelyonnais@wanadoo.fr; Atuona; full-day tours 11,000 CFP) can arrange day trips to Tahuata, which typically stop to visit Hapatoni and Vaitahu and a picnic in Hanamenino Bay.

Sleeping

Accommodation is mainly concentrated in Atuona and its surrounding area. Unless otherwise noted, credit cards are accepted.

Temetiu Village (☎ 91 70 60; www.temetiuvillage.com; standard bungalows s/d 7000/8900 CFP, large bungalows 9200 CFP; 💻 🍸) Efficient hosts, a homely atmosphere, top-notch location and high standards of cleanliness all add up to a winning formula. Digs are in four bungalows perched on a lush hillside. There are also two older (and slightly cheaper) bungalows, but they lack the wow

factor. Other pluses include a small pool and high-quality meals.

Pension Moehau (☎ 92 72 69; www.relaismoehau.pf; s/ d incl breakfast 8100/12,000 CFP, with half board 11,100/18,200 CFP) All rooms here are scrupulously clean, amply sized and well appointed (hot water, fan and plump bedding) but avoid the ones at the back – they face the dark hill behind. Ask for an oceanside room.

Pension Kanahau – Chez Tania (☎ 91 71 31, 70 16 26; http://pensionkanahau.com; s/d 10,000/12,000 CFP; 💻) Location-wise, this *pension* plays in the same league as nearby Temetiu Village, with a flower-filled garden and stupendous views of Tahauku Bay. The four bungalows are well furnished, spacious and sparkling clean (hot water is available); two units are equipped with cooking facilities (add 1000 CFP). Except breakfast (1100 CFP), meals are not provided, but the owner drives guests to town for lunch or dinner, for free. You can pay in dollars or euros.

Hotel Hanakéé Hiva Oa Pearl Lodge (☎ 92 75 87; www.pearlresorts.com; bungalows from 23,000 CFP; ❌ 💻 🍸) Hiva Oa's upscale resort, the Hanakéé boasts 14 well-designed bungalows adorned with fancy touches and lots of tropical flowers. The location is ace, on a mound overlooking Tahauku Bay. It also has wi-fi.

Eating

In Atuona, you will find several well-stocked grocery stores.

Snack Make Make (☎ 92 74 26; mains 800-2500 CFP; ❤ lunch & dinner Mon-Sat) This place boasts an eclectic menu, from Chinese specialities, fish dishes to goat and mussels.

Snack Kaupe – Chez Kahu (☎ 92 71 61; mains 1000-1700 CFP; ❤ lunch Sun-Fri, dinner daily) Blink and you'd miss this modest place (no sign), but what a shame that'd be. Kahu, one of the best Haka Manu (Bird's Dance) dancers in the Marquesas, takes pride in his little kitchen and turns out faultlessly prepared classics, such as grilled sirloin or fish.

Restaurant Moehau (☎ 92 72 69; pizzas 1100-1700 CFP, dishes 1500-2800 CFP; ❤ lunch & dinner) It's worth stopping in one night for a pizza at this terrace restaurant (go for the fish pizza). There are also good fish and meat dishes available.

Hotel Hanakéé Hiva Oa Pearl Lodge (☎ 92 75 87; mains 1500-2800 CFP; ❤ lunch & dinner) Certainly the most suitable place for a romantic *moment à deux*. Bag a seat on the terrace and sample the excellent French-influenced cuisine.

Getting There & Away
Air Tahiti (☎ 92 70 90; ⏰ 7.30-11.30am & 1.30-4.30pm Mon-Fri) in Atuona offers daily flights (not always direct) to Pape'ete (31,200 CFP), Nuku Hiva (10,600 CFP, five to seven times a week), 'Ua Pou (8200 CFP, two to three weekly flights) and 'Ua Huka (8200 CFP, one weekly flight).

The *Aranui* stops at Hiva Oa, see boxed text, p463.

To get to Tahuata, see right. To get to Fatu Hiva, see opposite.

Getting Around
The airport is 13km from Atuona. If you have booked accommodation, your host will come and collect you for about 3500 CFP return.

Excursions by 4WD cost about 8000 CFP to Taaoa, 10,000 CFP to Hanaiapa, 17,000 CFP to Puamau and 20,000 CFP to Hanapaaoa – these prices are for the full car (four people). For information, contact *pension* owners.

Atuona Rent-a-Car (☎ 92 76 07, 72 17 17) and **Hiva Oa Location** (☎ 91 70 60, 24 65 05) rent 4WDs without driver for about 13,000 CFP per day.

TAHUATA
pop 671 / area 70 sq km
Most travellers visit Tahuata on a day tour from neighbouring Hiva Oa, which is a shame as it deserves more than a day to do it justice. There's plenty to keep you busy, from meeting master carvers in Vaitahu or Hapatoni (the two main villages), and horse-riding to working your suntan on a deserted beach or exploring the archaeological sites. Or you could just soak up the ultra-chilled atmosphere.

Bring wads of cash as there is no bank.

Sights & Activities
On the hill that dominates tiny **Vaitahu** village are a few remains of the **French fort**. The seafront stone **Catholic church** includes a wooden statue which is a masterpiece of modern Marquesan art. A small Polynesian art and history **museum** is situated in the *mairie* (town hall). Copra-drying sheds are dotted here and there, and brightly coloured traditional *vaka* (outrigger canoes)

are lined up on the shore. Some top-rate Marquesan sculptors and tattooists work in Vaitahu.

Hapatoni curves around a wide bay several kilometres south of Vaitahu by boat (15 minutes) or bridleway. It has a 19th-century royal road and a magnificent **me'ae**.

Yachties usually anchor in idyllic **Hanamoenoa Bay**. Other soul-stirring bays lined with a ribbon of white sand include **Hanahevane** and **Hanamenino**.

Divers, gear up – there's top-notch action along the coast. **Diving** is arranged through SubAtuona in Hiva Oa (see p467).

The 17km AWD track that joins Vaitahu and Motopu is ideal for **horse riding**; ask the locals about hiring horses.

Sleeping & Eating
Tahuata has only one place to stay, **Pension Amatea** (☎ 92 92 84, 76 24 90; r per person with half board 7000 CFP), in Vaitahu. The house is not terribly Polynesian, but it's a convenient spot to flop down for a few days. There are four ordinary rooms with shared bathrooms. Marguerite, the owner, can help arrange activities and also transport to and from Tahuata.

Every village has one or two small shops.

Getting There & Around
Don't rely on the communal *bonitier*, which normally runs a twice-weekly Vaitahu–Atuona ferry service (4000 CFP return, one hour each way) as it's frequently out of order. Your best bet is to contact Pension Amatea (see above), which can help arrange passage with private boats (about 15,000 CFP per boatload).

Another option is to board the *Aranui* (p463) at Hiva Oa.

If you're pushed for time, you can also take an excursion from Hiva Oa. **SubAtuona** (☎ 92 70 88, 27 05 24) charges 11,000 CFP per person for a day trip (minimum four people), which includes visits of Hapatoni, Vaitahu and a picnic on a beach at Hanamenino.

A 17km track, accessible to 4WD vehicles, crosses the island's interior to link Vaitahu with Motopu and Vaitahu with Hapatoni. It costs 15,000 CFP for a day's hire with driver.

Hapatoni is less than 15 minutes from Vaitahu by speedboat. It costs about 6000 CFP to hire a boat between Vaitahu and Hapatoni, and 7000 CFP to 10,000 CFP between Vaitahu and Hanahevane Bay.

ATU HIVA

op 687 / area 80 sq km

Congratulations – you've made it to one of the ardest-to-reach islands in French Polynesia. With no landing strip and only poorly serv-ed by the *bonitiers* from Hiva Oa (75km), atu Hiva is not a bad place to play castaway or a few days, if not weeks.

When arriving by boat, expect a visual hock: wrinkled cliffs tumble into the ocean and splendid bays, including the iconic Bay of Virgins, indent the coastline.

There are only two villages (Omoa and Hanavave), one good *pension* and one dirt track, so there are plenty of oppor-unities to move into slow gear. Oh, and it also offers the biggest petroglyphs in French Polynesia.

Bring a stash of cash as there's no bank on the island.

Sights

Omoa is famous for its two giant **petroglyphs**, in two different locations. The first site fea-ures a huge fish (probably a dorado) as well as a few small anthropomorphic designs in-scribed on big basaltic boulders. The second ite is a 20-minute walk from Chez Lionel Cantois (below) and has a clearly outlined whale incised on a big slab.

Hanavave is on the seashore, at the mouth of a steep-sided valley leading into the **Bay of Virgins**, a favourite of passing yachties. With its towering basaltic cones drenched in pur-ple at sunset, it ranks as one of the most scenic bays in the South Pacific. This phal-ic skyline was originally (and aptly) named Baie des Verges in French (Bay of Penises). Outraged, the missionaries promptly added a redeeming 'i' to make the name Baie des Vierges (Bay of Virgins).

You can walk (four hours) or ride to the Bay of Virgins from Omoa along the island's only track.

Sleeping & Eating

The only accommodation options are in Omoa.

Chez Lionel Cantois (☎ 92 81 84, 70 03 71; chez lionel@mail.pf; s/d incl breakfast 5000/6000 CFP, bungalow incl breakfast 9000 CFP; dinner 2000 CFP) Basking in familial warmth, this *pension* at the far end of Omoa has an air of *Little House on the Prairie*. The well-equipped bungalow with bathroom (hot water) in the manicured gar-den is welcoming but, if funds are short, the two rooms in the owners' house can fit the bill. Lionel is a treasure trove of local infor-mation and can take you virtually anywhere on the island, while his wife Bernadette pre-pares delicious Marquesan meals.

Chez Norma Ropati (☎ 92 80 13; r per person with half board 4200 CFP) An acceptable fallback, with four boxy and rather darkish rooms with shared bathroom.

Getting There & Away

Fatu Hiva is the most difficult island to get to in the Marquesas. The easiest option is the communal *bonitier* (pray it's not out of service), which usually runs on Tuesday from Hanavave and Omoa to Atuona (same day return), costing 4000 CFP one-way. The crossing takes anything between three to five hours. You can also find out if charters are being organised during your stay and you may be able to share the costs. Another op-tion is to hop on the *Aranui* (p463) when it stops at Atuona, Omoa or Hanavave.

Getting Around

The only dirt road is 17km long and links Hanavave with Omoa, but it's quicker (and cheaper) to hire a speedboat to travel be-tween the two villages (about 7000 CFP per boat).

AUSTRAL ISLANDS

Fly south towards the Tropic of Capricorn to find the blustery Austral Archipelago where it's cool enough to grow peaches yet warm enough for bananas, coconut palms and turquoise, coral-laden lagoons. While it's the perfect climate for hiking and outdoor activities, the nights can get downright chilly – be sure to pack warm socks and a jumper! On these outrageously fertile islands you'll find some of the most authentic Polynesian culture in all of French Polynesia, including a hearty local cuisine – scarcely touched by French and Chinese spices – and a thriving pandanus weaving industry.

With the Bora Bora–like lagoon of Raivavae, the limestone caves and whale watching on Rurutu, and the fertile plains and white-sand beaches of Tubuai, these would surely be some of French Polynesia's

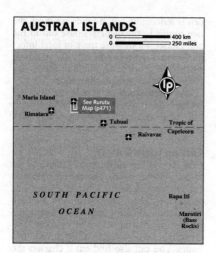

premier destinations if they weren't so isolated and expensive to get to.

Transport

Air Tahiti flies to Rururu and Tubuai about five times a week. One-way fares are Tahiti–Rururu from 19,000 CFP, Tahiti–Tubuai from 21,000 CFP, Tahiti–Raivavae from 24,000 CFP, Rururu–Tubuai from 9500 CFP and Tubuai–Raivavae from 9500 CFP. Rimatara had completed building an airstrip at the time of writing, but no flights had yet been scheduled. Getting to Rapa Iti, over 1000km south of Tahiti, is a real high-sea adventure.

The cargo ship *Tuhaa Pae II* does three trips a month to the Australs and accepts passengers. For more on travelling by cargo ship, see p483.

RURURU
pop 2089 / area 36 sq km

Vertical limestone cliffs pockmarked with caves line Rururu's coast, while the volcanic interior is a fertile, mind-bogglingly abundant jungle. The island is a *makatea*, a geologic phenomenon where a coral atoll has been thrust from the sea by volcanic activity to wall in the island it once encircled. While there's very little fringing reef, there are plenty of white-sand beaches and bright-blue swimming areas close to shore. From July to October migrating humpbacks draw in admirers from around the globe who come to see the mammals in some of the clearest waters on the planet.

Of the three main villages, Moerai is th largest. It is 4km south of the airport and ha the cargo-ship dock, a post office with inter net connection, a Banque Socredo with a ATM and a few small shops. About one-thir of the scenic 36km road around the islan is sealed.

Sights & Activities

Turning right out of the main village o Moerai, you'll find a large roadside cavern with stalactites and stalagmites called **Tan Uapoto**. Traditionally this cave was used t both salt (for preservation) and divide whal meat among the islanders. Just beyond th cave there's a whale-watching platform. O the northwest side of the island, there's sign-posted track that leads inland to **Ana Ae Cave**, the most stunning cavern on the islan with plenty of oozy stalagmites and stalac tites. Today the locals have also dubbed the Mitterand Cave since President Françoi Mitterand visited here in 1990.

Raie Manta Club (☎ 96 85 60, 72 31 45; raieman club@mail.pf; half day 10,000 CFP) has been offerin very professional whale-watching tours fo over nine years. They also offer exploratio dives around the coast.

All *pensions* offer worthwhile half-da **island tours** for around 3500 CFP.

For **horse-riding**, contact Viriamu at Pensio Teautamatea (see below). Superb trips, suit able for all levels, pass some stunning view points in the island's interior (5000 CFP fo a half day).

The island's interior is perfect for **walking** A network of tracks criss-cross the Tetuanu Plateau (200m), leading to the peaks of Mt Taatioe (389m), Manureva (385m) and Teap (359m). You can also walk the cross-islan road between Moerai and Avera.

Sleeping & Eating

Unless otherwise mentioned, credit cards are accepted.

Pension Teautamatea (☎ 93 02 93; teautamatea@ mail.pf; s/d/tr/q with half board 8300/13,000/17,700/22,40 CFP; 🖳) Run by a British-Rururu couple, the cosy rooms here are artistically decorated in a Polynesian-meets-European-country-side chic. It's in a stunning setting in front of Marae Tararoa and just across the road from one of Rururu's best beaches. No credit cards.

RURUTU

Manôtel (☎ 93 02 26; manotel@mail.pf; s/d/tr bungalow with half board per person 11,100/15,600/20,200 CFP; 🖳) The exceptionally well-run Manôtel has very pretty and stylish bungalows with fan, good bathroom and particularly inviting terraces; it's across the road from a long stretch of white beach. The garden is blooming with colours and the owner runs some of the best island tours around.

Rurutu Lodge (☎ 94 02 15, 79 09 01; rurutulodge@mail .pf; bungalow s/d/tr with half board from 11,000/17,200/21,200 CFP; 🖳) This is the closest thing you'll find to a hotel in the Australs, run by the Raie Manta diving club. You won't get much of a connection with the locals here, but it's pleasantly designed and has flower-filled gardens and a lovely beach. There are occasional Saturday night buffet and dance performances (3000 CFP).

Tiare Hinano (☎ 77 55 24; mains from 900 CFP; ⏰ 10.30am-8.30pm Mon-Sat) A Chinese chef straight from China whips up good, authentically Eastern grub, as well as local favourites.

Getting Around

Most *pensions* rent bicycles for about 1000 CFP to 1600 CFP a day. Manôtel (see left) also rents a 4WD for 9000 CFP for eight hours.

TUBUAI

pop 1979 / area 45 sq km

Tubuai is flatter than most French Polynesian high islands, and its stretches of fertile plains, mixed with the ideal climate, have made it the fruit bowl and veggie bin for all of French Polynesia; it's also the administrative centre of the Austral Archipelago. The lagoon is as blue as Raivavae's but is consistently windy (an average of 300 days per year!); while less picturesque it's more inviting for wind sports.

Mataura, about 4km east of the airport, is the main village and has a post office with a public internet post, a **Banque Socredo** (⏰ 7-11.30am & 1.30-4pm Mon-Fri) with an ATM outside, a basic hospital and a supermarket.

Over 200 *marae* have been found in Tubuai and the few that have been cleared are among the most fascinating in the country. **Raitoru** and **Haunarei Marae** are two connected *marae* that were for birthing and umbilical cord cutting ceremonies respectively. At **Vaitauarii** are the remains of a site dedicated to tattooing Tubuai royalty. *Marae* tours, offered by either of the two *pensions* below, cost 2500 CFP.

For sleeping we recommend **Raroata Dream** (☎ 95 07 12; maletdoom@mail.pf; r with half/full board per person 4400/6600 CFP; 🖳), which is the home of Wilson Doom, the president of the local kitesurfing club. Wilson's cousin Heinui runs the much bigger and more private **Pension Vaiteanui** (☎ 93 22 40; bodinm@mail.pf; s/d with half board 7600/10,300 CFP; 🖳) which has basic but comfortable rooms.

Air Tahiti flies to Tubuai five times a week and the *Tuhaa Pae II* also stops by here.

RAIVAVAE

pop 1049 / area 16 sq km

This is a paradise not only because of the sweeping blue lagoon, idyllic white-sand *motu* or the mountainous interior dominated by square-topped Mt Hiro (437m), but also because of the ultra-warm Polynesian welcome and extraordinary glimpse into a traditional way of life. Amazingly, though considered one of the great beauties of the South Pacific, the island receives only a trickle of tourists.

The quay is at Rairua, as well as a post office (with a public internet post), medical clinic and *gendarmerie* (police station). You'll also find little stores everywhere along the coast road.

Most of Raivavae's *marae* have been destroyed to create taro fields, used as foundations for houses or simply been forgotten in the bush. **Marae Mauna-Oto** on the east coast is one of the few that has been cleared and is also known as the 'princess *marae*' because of the tomb near the entrance that some people believe belongs to a Raiavavae princess. Another well-maintained *marae*, **Marae Pou Pou**, can be found about 1km from the Vaiuru entrance of the cross-island road.

Raivavae is most famous for its two giant stone *tiki*, now in museums on Tahiti (see p411). The only remaining **tiki** stands neglected and overgrown in a private garden just to the west of Mahanatoa.

All *pensions* offer excursions to *motu* (2500 CFP to 6000 CFP), Mt Hiro (2500 CFP) plus a free tour of the island by car and free bike use for stays of more than three days. You can also count on fantastic local-style meals, but you'll get laughed at if you ask about credit cards. Offering three clean coconut-thatched bungalows on one of Raivavae's best beaches, American/Polynesian-run **Tama Resort** (☎ /fax 95 42 52; s/d/tr with half board 8500/13,000/17,000 CFP, s/ d/tr with full board 10,000/16,000/22,000 CFP) is a solid option. Well-kept **Chez Linda et Nelson** (☎ 95 44 25; pensionchezlinda@hotmail.fr; Rairua; r with half board s/d 7000/10,000 CFP, bungalows with half board s/d 10,000/12,500 CFP) has three Polynesian-style bungalows and three rooms with shared bathrooms in the uncommonly nice owner's house.

Tuhaa Pae II sails by about twice a month.

THE GAMBIER ARCHIPELAGO

All the makings of an island holiday paradise can be found in the Gambier Archipelago, but it's so far away (1700km southeast from Tahiti) and expensive to get to that it remains one of the least developed regions in French Polynesia. The geology here is unique: one reef, complete with sandy *motu*, encircles a small archipelago of lush high islands dotting a blue lagoon that's as clear as air. Adding to the allure, the Gambier is the cradle of Polynesian Catholicism and houses some of the most eerie and interesting post-European structures in the country. It's also famous for its lustrous and colourful pearls.

Gambier Archipelago time is one hour ahead of Tahiti time. Rikitea, the town of Mangareva, has shops and a post office but no bank.

TRANSPORT
Air Tahiti (☎ 97 82 65) flies to the Gambier Archipelago from Pape'ete (57,000 CFP return) about once a week.

From Tahiti, the cargo ship *Nuku Hau* sails via the eastern Tuamotus to the Gambier Archipelago once a month. For more on travelling by cargo ship, see p458.

The airport is on Motu Totegegie, on the northeastern side of the lagoon. A communal ferry from Mangareva meets every flight; the journey takes 45 minutes and costs 500 CFP.

Pension owners can organise island tours by boat and visits to the major sites and pearl farms. On Mangareva there is a small network of walking tracks. It's possible to bike the 23km around the island, but sections are very steep.

SIGHTS & ACTIVITIES
In the upper part of Rikitea stands the white-washed **Cathédrale Saint-Michel** (Cathedral of St Michael), built between 1839 and 1848, which was Laval's (the French missionary) most ambitious project. While still imposing (the building can accommodate 1200 people – more than the population of the island today), the church was closed at the time of research and was scheduled for a US$2 million restoration. Jaques Sauvage, the 88-year-old guardian, has the key and sometimes lets people inside – ask through your *pension* or at the *gendarmerie*.

Other Laval constructions include the **Rouru Convent** which once housed 60 Mangarevan nuns, although it's said Laval would hide every woman on the island in the convent whenever a whaling ship docked. On the outer islands you'll find the 1868 **Église Saint-Gabriel** (Church of St Gabriel) on Taravai; the 1839 **Église Saint-Raphaël** (Church of St Raphael) on Aukena and the majestic 1841 **Église Nôtre-Dame-de-la-Paix** (Our Lady of Peace Church) on Akamaru.

To check out Mangareva's mother-of-pearl carvings, head to the **Camika CED** (carving school; ☎ 97 82 89; Rikitea; ☯ 8am-3pm Mon-Fri) near Cathédrale Saint-Michel, where you can watch as students engrave shells. Finished products, including small pendants and barrettes, start at around 4000 CFP.

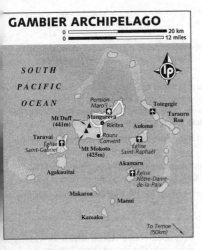

GAMBIER ARCHIPELAGO

SLEEPING & EATING

Only Pension Maro'i takes credit cards on Mangareva, so you'll need to bring plenty of cash.

Pension Maro'i (☎ 97 84 62; btqhinarau@hotmail .com; bungalows with breakfast 9500 CFP; lunch or dinner 2200 CFP) Mangareva's newest option has four immaculate bungalows laid out on a grassy, fruit tree–studded lawn lined with a white beach. It's on the opposite side of the island from Rikitea.

Chez Bianca & Benoît (☎ /fax 97 83 76; Rikitea; s/d with half board 10,000/16,500 CFP; bungalow s/d with half board 17,000/22,000 CFP; ☽ closed Jun) Big bungalows sleep three to four people, and have bamboo woven walls and decks with views over Rikitea and the lagoon. It has a central location with dynamic owners and good food.

Pizzatomic (☎ 97 83 09; Rikitea; pizzas from 1000 CFP; ☽ 5.15-9pm Fri-Sun) Next door to the now bulldozed fallout shelter, get glowing hot pizzas to eat in or take away.

TAHITI & FRENCH POLYNESIA DIRECTORY

ACCOMMODATION

Although the brochures show exotic overwater bungalows, French Polynesia has everything from camping and hostel dormitories to five-star accommodation. However, in all categories, the balance between price and quality can be discouraging. Expect it to be expensive (p478) and enjoy the fabulous locations, if not the rooms and service.

Air-conditioning is often not supplied, even in some quite expensive places, but the night breeze means you can usually live without it. Many cheaper places don't supply towels or soap.

Credit cards are welcome at luxury resorts, and many midrange places accept them; however budget places rarely do. The prices quoted in this chapter include taxes, but many places will quote you pretax prices and the add-ons might horrify you. We have rounded prices to the nearest 100 CFP, so use quoted prices as a guide only. The *taxe de séjour* (accommodation tax) is charged per person per night and can really add up for families.

Camping & Hostels

Camping options aren't common in French Polynesia, but beyond the handful of places that are set up for campers, guest houses will sometimes allow you to pitch your tent and use their facilities; you'll pay anywhere from 1200 CFP to 2500 CFP per person. Camping is possible on Tahiti, Mo'orea, Huahine, Ra'iatea, Bora Bora, Maupiti, Rangiroa, Tikehau and Mataiva. You may need to rethink camping if it's raining too hard. Also make sure your tent is mosquito-proof or lather yourself in repellent. Some guest houses have dorm beds ranging from 2000 CFP to 3500 CFP per person per night.

Hotels

A hotel that is neither a resort nor a *pension* is a rare beast in French Polynesia. Anything in the top-end price category is a resort, while midrange and budget offerings are most often *pensions*. There are a few business-oriented hotels in Pape'ete that are not enticing to anyone on a real holiday (think no beach, no garden and lots of traffic), but a few places on the more touristy islands that cater to holiday makers are lovely. You'll typically pay from around 10,000 CFP to 40,000 CFP per night for a bungalow.

Pensions

Pensions are a godsend for travellers who baulk at the prices (and gloss) of the big hotels. These little establishments, generally a family affairs, are great places to meet

---

PRACTICALITIES

■ *Tahiti Beach Press* is the weekly English-language tourist paper that includes some local news coverage. If you read French, there are two Tahitian dailies: *Les Nouvelles de Tahiti* and *La Dépêche de Tahiti*.

■ There are about 10 independent radio stations that broadcast music programs with news flashes in French and Tahitian, along with the occasional interview. Among the best-known stations are Tiare FM (the pioneer nongovernment radio station), Radio Bleue, Radio Maohi, Te Reo o Tefana (a pro-independence station), Radio 1, NRJ and RFO-Radio Polynésie.

■ The video format in French Polynesia is Secam, but videos made for tourists are generally also available in PAL and NTSC.

■ French Polynesia uses 220V, 60Hz electricity, although some deluxe hotels may have 110V supply for electric shavers. Sockets are French-style, requiring a plug with two round pins.

■ French Polynesia follows the international metric system. See the Quick Reference, inside the front cover, for conversions.

---

locals and other travellers. At the lower end of the scale, brace yourself for cold showers, lumpy pillows and thin walls, but lap up the charm, interesting discussions and artistic touches that are often part and parcel of the experience. Upmarket *pensions* can be private, have lots of amenities and be downright luxurious.

Many *pensions*, particularly on islands where there are few to no other eating options available, offer half board (or *demi-pension*), which means breakfast and dinner. It can cost anything from 4000 CFP to 6000 CFP per person per day, although prices vary widely from island to island. Young children usually stay for free, and children up to about 12 usually pay half price.

Think ahead in terms of money as many *pensions* do not take credit cards.

Resorts

If you are ever going to pamper yourself silly, French Polynesia is a great place to do it. The sumptuous luxury hotels often manage to blend their opulent bungalows into the natural setting. Some of the top hotels are on isolated *motu* and can only be reached by boat. Four- and five-star hotels are found on Tahiti, Mo'orea, Bora Bora, Huahine, Ra'iatea, Tikehau, Taha'a, Rangiroa, Hiva Oa, Manihi and Nuku Hiva. You can expect restaurants, bars, swimming pool, a shop or two and a well-organised activities desk. Most of the bigger hotels put on a Polynesian dance performance, often with buffet meal, a few times a week. Glass-

bottomed coffee tables, which look straight down into the lagoon, have become standard features of the over-water bungalows. The prices are just as dazzling: expect to pay from 45,000 CFP to 250,000 CFP a night, not including meals.

ACTIVITIES

French Polynesia offers a range of leisure activities. Scuba diving and snorkelling are the main activities, but sailing is also very popular. Increasing numbers of surfers are sampling the islands' excellent reef-breaks, while the jagged relief of the high islands makes for some superb walking and horse riding.

Cycling

On many islands it is possible to rent bicycles, which is the perfect way to get around. The rough roads leading into the interior are great for mountain biking, should you decide to bring one with you from home.

Diving & Snorkelling

French Polynesia is a diver's dream. The warm, bright waters, the lack of plankton (which ensures water clarity) and the myriad tropical fish will entice you from the shore. Conditions are close to perfect: visibility often reaches 40m and the water's a bath-like 29°C in summer and 26°C in winter, with only 1°C of variation down to 45m. Forget the wetsuit and fly free. Most dives are only a five- to 15-minute boat trip from the shore.

There are about 25 professional dive centres in French Polynesia. They open year-round. All are at least level 1 on the French CMAS scale, and most have at least one Professional Association of Dive Instructors (PADI) registered instructor. Operators are listed under Activities in island sections earlier in this chapter. A single dive typically costs 6000 CFP to 8500 CFP.

An excellent website is www.polynesia-diving.com. For more on diving in Tahiti and French Polynesia, see p75.

The coral reefs and coral outcrops that are dotted around the lagoons are perfect for snorkelling. You can join a lagoon tour by boat, hire an outboard-powered boat or just grab your gear and head out to explore the lagoon yourself.

Hiking

The high islands offer superb walks, but the tracks are sometimes unmarked and are hard to follow: a guide is often necessary. Tahiti and Mo'orea are the main islands for walking, but there are also good walks on Ra'iatea, Bora Bora, Maupiti, Raivavae and Nuku Hiva. The ideal time for hiking is May to October. During the rainy season (November to April), the paths can be dangerous and even impassable.

Horse Riding

There are equestrian centres on Tahiti, Mo'orea, Huahine and Bora Bora in the Society Islands. Most places offer short jaunts and longer excursions that explore the island interiors. Horses are an important part of life in the Marquesas, and there are various places to rent them, with or without a guide; you can also horse ride on Rurutu in the Australs.

Surfing

Polynesia was the birthplace of *horue* (surfing), and in recent years there has been a major resurgence of local interest. Tahiti in particular has surf shops, board shapers and a local surfing scene. The island is home to Teahupoo, one of the most powerful waves in the world, and the home of the Billabong Pro competition held each year. Tahiti, Mo'orea and Huahine are the three main islands for surfing, but Rangiroa and Tikehau in the Tuamotus also have some good surfing spots.

In general, there are good conditions on the north and east coasts from November to April and on the west and south coasts for the other half of the year. However these distinctions are really theoretical: in practice it is the direction of the swells that makes a spot good at any given time.

Access to the shore breaks is generally easy from the coast roads. You may need to find a boat to take you out to the reef-breaks, or resign yourself to a lot of paddling.

For more information on surfing in French Polynesia, check out www.surfing tahiti.com.

Like surfers anywhere else, French Polynesians can be very possessive of *their* waves. If you want to enjoy the surf, observe all the usual surfing etiquette: give way to local surfers, smile and say hello and, on the outer islands don't take pictures.

You certainly don't need a wetsuit in the warm waters of French Polynesia, but a T-shirt or Lycra vest will protect you from the sun. The local surf shops all have body-board equipment, as well as a variety of (expensive) surfboards.

On Tahiti, the **Tura'l Mataare Surf School** (Map pp406-7; ☎ 41 91 37; surfschool@mail.pf; PK18.3) offers half-day lessons including transfers and equipment for 4800 CFP. The courses are run by a qualified instructor and include equipment, transport to the different surfing spots and insurance.

Yachting

Hiring a yacht is a great way to explore French Polynesia, and you can choose from a bareboat charter (which you sail yourself) or a cabin on a fully crewed luxury boat. Ra'iatea is the main yachting base in French Polynesia, although there are a number of yacht-charter operations around the islands. Cruises on a crewed yacht will usually include tour programs at the stops en route. Dive cruises are also possible.

The following companies offer cruises and charter boats:

Atara Royal (☎ 79 22 40; www.motoryachtchartertahiti.com) Luxury, dive-equipped motor cruiser based in Ra'iatea visits the Leeward, Tuamotu and Marquesas archipelagos.

Aqua Polynésie (☎ 73 47 31; www.aquapolynesie.com) Luxurious 14m catamarans with crewed cruises around the Leeward Islands and the Tuamotus, and a boat specially equipped for dive cruises.

Archipels Croisières (☎ 56 36 39; www.archipels.com) Reasonably priced crewed cruises to the Leeward Islands and the Tuamotus on deluxe 18m catamarans.

L'Escapade (☎ 72 85 31; www.escapade-voile.com) Sail on a 14m monohull to Tetiaroa, the Society and Tuamotu Islands from Tahiti.

MoeMoea Nui (☎ 70 74 04; www.marquise-croisiere .com) Cruise the Marquesas with this Nuku Hiva–based 14m catamaran.

Polynésie Croisière (☎ 28 60 06; www.polynesie -croisiere.com) Scuba-specialist catamarans based on Ra'iatea offer a host of cruises to the Leeward Islands.

Sun Sail (☎ 60 04 85; www.sunsail.com) Offers bareboat charters, hire with skipper and/or host, and cabin charter from Ra'iatea. About 20 boats of a variety of types are available for hire.

Tahiti Yacht Charter (☎ 45 04 00; www.tahitiyacht charter.com) Catamarans and monohulls; bareboat charter or hire with skipper and host. Cruises are possible in all the archipelagos.

The Moorings (☎ 66 35 93; www.moorings.com) Twenty different options, including bareboat charters, hire with skipper and host, or cabin charters. It's based at Apooiti Marina at Ra'iatea.

BUSINESS HOURS

Banks are usually open between 9am and noon and 2pm and 5pm Monday to Friday. Shops and offices normally open around 7.30am, close for lunch between 11.30am and 1.30pm and then shut around 5pm Monday through Friday. On Saturday, shops are typically open between 7.30am and 11.30am; almost everything (except a few grocery stores and boutiques on more touristy islands) is closed on Sunday. Restaurant hours vary according to the type of food served and the clientele. Most places open around 10.30am and stay open until about 11pm. We have not listed business hours in our reviews unless they differ from these standard hours. See p629 for public holidays in the region.

CHILDREN

Fire the babysitter and bring the kids: French Polynesia is a great destination to explore with children. There are no major health concerns, the climate is good and the food is easy to navigate. Most locals have a number of children themselves and will not be troubled by a screaming child at the next table, should the treasure be throwing a tantrum over dinner. Children are very much a part of public life in Polynesia.

Practicalities

Sunscreen and nappies are readily availabl in French Polynesia, but are very expensiv (1700 CFP for 38 nappies!). The drinkin water is safe in Pape'ete, on Bora Bora an on Tubuai, but you may like to buy bottle water anyway (or even better, bring you own water filter); on the other islands yo will all be dependent on bottled water.

There are medical facilities everywhere in Polynesia. Mamao Hospital in Pape'ete has a modern paediatric department.

You will have priority when boarding Air Tahiti aircraft. A Carte Famille (Family Card), which costs 2000 CFP, entitles you to significant reductions on some flights (see p482 for details). At hotels and guest houses, children under 12 generally are charged only 50% of the adult rate; very young children usually stay for free.

CONSULATES

Given that French Polynesia is not an independent country, there are no foreign embassies, only consulates, and many countries are represented in Pape'ete by honorary consuls.

The following honourary consuls and diplomatic representatives are all on Tahiti. Many are just single representatives and do not have official offices, so you'll have to call them.

Australia (Map pp416-17; ☎ 46 88 53; service@mobil .pf; BP 9068, Pape'ete)

Austria, Switzerland & Leichtenstein (☎ 43 91 14; paulmaetztahiti@mail.pf; Rue Cannonière Zélée, Pape'ete BP 4560, Pape'ete)

Canada (Map pp416-17; ☎ 46 88 53; service@mobil.pf; BP 9068, Pape'ete)

Chile, Brazil, Paraguay, Argentina & Bolivia (Map pp416-17; ☎ 43 89 19; c.chilepapeete@mail.pf; BP 952, Pape'ete)

China (☎ 45 61 79; BP 4495, Pape'ete)

Denmark (☎ 54 04 54; c.girard@groupavocats.pf; BP 548, Pape'ete)

Germany (☎ 42 99 94; BP 452, Pira'e)

Great Britain (☎ 70 63 82; BP 50009 Pira'e)

Italy (off Map pp412-13; ☎ 43 45 01; consolato _polinesia@yahoo.fr; BP 380 412, Tamanu)

Israel (☎ 42 41 00; consulisrael@mail.pf; BP 37, Pape'ete)

Japan (☎ 45 45 45; nippon@mail.pf; BP 342, Pape'ete)

Korea (☎ 43 64 75; bbaudry@mail.pf; BP 2061, Pape'ete)

Netherlands (Map pp416-17; ☎ 42 49 37; htt@mail.pf; Mobil Bldg, Fare Ute, Pape'ete BP 2804, Pape'ete)

New Zealand (Map pp416-17; ☎ 54 07 40; nzcgnou@offratel.nc; c/- Air New Zealand, Vaima Centre, Pape'ete BP 73, Pape'ete)

Norway (☎ 42 89 72; amitahiti@mail.pf; BP 274, Pape'ete)

Spain (☎ 77 85 40; mlpromotion@mail.pf; BP 186, Pape'ete)

Sweden (☎ 47 54 75; jacques.solari@sopadep.pf; BP 1617, Pape'ete)

United States (Map pp406-7; ☎ 42 65 35; usconsul@mail.pf; US Info, Centre Temanu, Puna'auia BP 10765, Paea)

FESTIVALS & EVENTS

January

Chinese New Year Usually falling between late January and mid-February, the New Year is ushered in with dancing, martial arts displays and fireworks.

February

Tahiti Nui Marathon One thousand runners gather on Mo'orea for this long-established fundraising event along a flat course past spectacular scenery.

March

Arrival of the First Missionaries On 5 March the landing of the first LMS missionaries is re-enacted at Point Vénus on Tahiti Nui. Celebrations are held at Protestant churches on Tahiti and Mo'orea and in Tipaerui and Afareaitu.

April/May

Beauty Contests Many contests are held ahead of the Miss Tahiti and Miss Heiva i Tahiti contests in June (Mr Tahiti contests are also held).

Billabong Tahiti Pro Surfing Tournament Three days of international-level surfing in the big waves of Teahupoo (Tahiti).

June/July

Miss Tahiti & Miss Heiva i Tahiti contests Winners of beauty contests around the archipelago in the last 12 months gather in Pape'ete to vie for the chance to represent French Polynesia around the world. Miss Heiva reigns for the month-long Heiva celebrations.

Tahiti International Golf Open This four-day event is held on Tahiti in late June or early July.

July/August

Heiva i Tahiti (www.tahiti-heiva.org) This major Polynesian festival, held in Pape'ete, includes traditional demonstrations throughout July. Mini-Heiva events take place on other islands in August.

September

Annual Flower Show In Parc Bougainville, Pape'ete.

October

Carnival Late in the month there are parades throughout the islands with floats decked with flowers.

November

Hawaiki Nui Canoe Race The major sporting event of the year.

All Saints' Day Graves are cleaned and decorated in an explosion of flowers; families sing hymns in candlelit cemeteries on 1 November.

December

Tiare Tahiti Days The national flower is celebrated on 1 and 2 December.

Marquesas Arts Festival A major arts festival at 'Ua Pou, celebrating Marquesan identity.

GAY & LESBIAN TRAVELLERS

French laws concerning homosexuality prevail in French Polynesia, which means there is no legal discrimination against homosexual activity. Homophobia in French Polynesia is uncommon, although open displays of affection in public should be avoided. French Polynesia does feel remarkably heterosexual, given the preponderance of honeymooning couples, but you will meet lots of very camp *mahu* working in restaurants and hotels.

For gay package tours, check out http://tahiti-tourisme.com/specials/tahitigayvacations.asp and for the best transvestite action head to the **Piano Bar** in Pape'ete (p419).

Te Anuanua o Te Fenua (Gay, Lesbian & Bisexual Association of French Polynesia; ☎ 77 31 11) was formed in 1997 and is based on Tahiti.

INTERNET ACCESS

Internet cafes are getting more popular – although the ones on the smaller islands often have only ancient computers. Most top-end hotels offer internet access to their guests, and access is fairly straightforward on Tahiti, Mo'orea, Bora Bora, Huahine, Rangiroa and Ra'iatea. You'll generally pay about 9000 CFP per hour.

If you're toting your own computer through the Society, Marquesas or Austral Islands, you should consider buying a prepaid **Mana Pass** (available at post offices in 1-/3-/10-hour denominations for 990/2000/5300 CFP) that allows you to access the internet at 'Mana Spots' (wi-fi zones) located in post offices and at some hotels, restaurants and public areas. Check the website www.manaspot.pf for current locations.

INTERNET RESOURCES

Useful generalist English-language sites include:

Haere Mai (www.haere-mai.pf) Lists small hotels and family *pensions*.

Island Adventures (www.english.islandsadventures .com) Air Tahiti's site with great-value air and lodging packages in small hotel and *pensions* throughout the country.

LonelyPlanet.com (www.lonelyplanet.com) Provides summaries on travelling to most places on earth, including the all-important Forum bulletin board, where you can ask questions of travellers who've been to Tahiti recently.

Tahiti Explorer (www.tahitiexplorer.com) Discounts on lodging, customised honeymoon packages and destination descriptions.

Tahitipresse (www.tahitipresse.pf) Up-to-the-minute news.

Tahiti Tourisme (www.tahiti-tourisme.com) Official Tahiti tourism website in English.

MONEY

The unit of currency in French Polynesia is the Cour de Franc Pacifique (CFP), referred to in English as 'the Pacific Franc'. There are coins of one, two, five, 10, 20, 50 and 100 CFP; and notes of 500, 1000, 5000 and 10,000 CFP. The CFP is pegged to the euro. For exchange rates, see the Quick Reference page, inside the front cover.

There are fairly hefty bank charges for changing money and travellers cheques in French Polynesia. You generally pay at least 500 CFP commission on travellers cheques and to exchange cash, although exchange rates do vary from bank to bank. Given the cost of living in French Polynesia and the low crime rate, you are better off exchanging larger sums of money (that is, making fewer transactions) than smaller amounts.

TELEPHONE

Public phone boxes are found even in surprisingly remote locations, and all use the same phonecards. Phonecards can be bought from post offices, newsagencies, shops and some supermarkets. They are available in 1000, 2000 and 5000 CFP denominations.

There are no area codes in French Polynesia. Local phone calls cost 34 CFP for four minutes at normal tariff rates.

Mobile phone services operate on 900 GSM and SIM cards are available for 5000 CFP at post offices on main islands bearing a 'Vini' sign. This price includes one hour of local minutes. Additional minutes can be purchased from 1000 CFP, also at the post office (Tahiti is your best bet as outer islands tend to run out of these 'top up' cards). Many foreign mobile services have coverage in Tahiti, but roaming fees are usually quite high.

TIME

Tahiti (and neighbouring islands) is 10 hours behind GMT. The Marquesas are half an hour ahead of Tahiti, but check flight schedules carefully: Air Tahiti departures and arrivals for the Marquesas may operate to Tahiti time. Gambier Archipelago time is one hour ahead of Tahiti time.

TOURIST INFORMATION IN TAHITI & FRENCH POLYNESIA

The main tourist office is the **Gie Tahiti Manava Visitor Information Centre** (☎ 50 57 00; tahiti-tourisme.com; Fare Manihini, Blvd Pomare; ⊙ 7.30am-5pm Mon-Fri, 8am-noon Sat & public holidays), which is located in the centre of Pape'ete. This office has information about the whole of French Polynesia. The more touristy islands generally have some sort of tourist office or counter, but they vary widely in usefulness and dependability.

For information before you leave home, contact **Tahiti Tourisme** (☎ 50 57 00; www.tahiti-tourisme.com). Information about Tahiti Tourisme office locations and phone numbers around the world, as well as a slew of international websites, can be found on the website.

HOW MUCH?

- **Night in an over-water bungalow:** from US$500

- **Burger, fries and a Coke at a roulotte (food van):** 1500 CFP

- **Five-island airpass:** 26,500 CFP

- **Dinner for two at a midrange restaurant:** 7000 CFP

- **Simple bungalow with fan:** 6000 CFP to 10,000 CFP per night

- **1L petrol:** 1.50 CFP

- **1L bottled water:** 120 CFP

- **Bottle of Hinano:** 200 CFP

- **Souvenir T-shirt:** 2000 CFP

- **Plate of poisson cru:** 1200 CFP

VISAS

Everyone needs a passport to visit French Polynesia. The regulations are much the same as for France: if you need a visa to visit France, then you'll need one to visit French Polynesia. Anyone from an EU country can stay for up to three months without a visa, as can Australians and citizens of a number of other non-EU European countries, including Switzerland.

Citizens of Argentina, Canada, Chile, Japan, Mexico, New Zealand (NZ), USA and some European countries can stay for up to one month without a visa. Other nationalities need a visa, which can be applied for at French diplomatic missions. Visa regulations for French Polynesia can change at short notice, so check with a travel agent shortly before departing.

Apart from permanent residents and French citizens, all visitors to French Polynesia need to have an onward or return ticket.

Visa Extensions

For those who are awarded three months on arrival it can be trickier still to get a longer extension. EU citizens are the exception to this rule and can apply for a residence permit (renewable every three months), but getting permission to work legally can be a real headache.

For visa extensions try at the **Police aux Frontières** (Map pp416-17; Frontier Police; ☎ 42 40 74; pafport@mail.pf; ⏱ airport office 8am-noon & 2-5pm Mon-Fri, Pape'ete office 7.30am-noon & 2-5pm Mon-Fri), at Faa'a airport and next to the Manava Visitors Bureau in Pape'ete, at least one week before the visa or exemption expires. Dress nice and smile big. An extension costs 3500 CFP.

Stays by foreign visitors may not exceed three months. For longer periods, you must apply to the French consular authorities in your own country for a residence permit; you cannot lodge your application from French Polynesia unless you have a sponsor or get married.

Yacht Formalities

In addition to presenting the certificate of ownership of the vessel, sailors are subject to the same passport and visa requirements as travellers arriving by air or by cruise ship. Unless you have a return air ticket, you are required to provide a banking guarantee of repatriation equivalent to the price of an airline ticket to your country of origin.

Yachties must advise the **Police aux Frontières** (Map pp416-17; Frontier Police; ⏱ 7.30am-noon & 2-5pm Mon-Fri), which is situated next to the visitor information centre in Pape'ete, of their final departure. If your first port of call is not Pape'ete, it must be a port with a *gendarmerie* (police station): Afareaitu (Mo'orea), Uturoa (Ra'iatea), Fare (Huahine), Vaitape (Bora Bora), Taiohae (Nuku Hiva, Marquesas), Hakahau ('Ua Pou, Marquesas), Atuona (Hiva Oa, Marquesas), Mataura (Tubuai, Australs), Moerai (Rurutu, Australs), Rairua (Raivavae, Australs), Avatoru (Rangiroa, Tuamotus) or Rikitea (Mangareva, Gambiers). The *gendarmerie* must be advised of each arrival and departure, and of any change of crew.

Before arriving at the port of Pape'ete, announce your arrival on channel 12. You can anchor at the quay or the beach, but there are no reserved places. Next, you'll need to report to the **Capitainerie** (Map pp416-17; Harbour Master's Office; ⏱ 7-11.30am & 1-4pm Mon-Thu, 7-11.30am & 1-3pm Fri), in the same building as the Police aux Frontières, and complete an arrival declaration.

VOLUNTEERING

Generally, volunteering opportunities in French Polynesia are set up for residents or long-term visitors. Still you could contact the following organisations to find out if they need a hand and/or to make a donation.

Fenua Animalia (☎ 42 34 23; www.fenua-animalia .org) Tahiti's much-needed animal protection organisation is gaining momentum and doing a great job.

Te Honu Tea (☎ 57 97 32; www.tehonutea.fr, in French) Actively studies and protects sea turtles and their habitat.

WOMEN TRAVELLERS

French Polynesia is a great place for solo women to explore. Local women are very much a part of public life in the region, and it's not unusual to see Polynesian women out drinking beer together or walking alone, so you'll probably feel pretty comfortable following suit.

TRANSPORT IN TAHITI & FRENCH POLYNESIA

GETTING THERE & AWAY

Air

Faa'a International Airport (Map pp412-13; PPT; ☎ 86 60 61; www.tahiti-aeroport.pf), on Tahiti, is the only international airport in French Polynesia. It's on the outskirts of Pape'ete, about 5km west of the capital. International check-in desks are at the east end of the terminal.

A number of international airlines serve French Polynesia. Airline offices in Pape'ete include:

Aircalin (Air Caledonie International, airline code SB; ☎ 85 09 04; www.aircalin.nc; Faa'a International Airport)

Air France (airline code AF; ☎ 47 47 47; www.air france.com; Rue Georges Legarde; hub Orly Airport, Paris) Code-share with Air Tahiti Nui.

Air New Zealand (airline code NZ; ☎ 54 07 47; www .airnz.com; Vaima Centre) Code-share with Air Tahiti Nui.

Air Tahiti Nui (airline code TN; ☎ 45 55 55; www .airtahiti.com; Pont de L'Est)

Hawaiian Airlines (airline code HA; ☎ 42 15 00; www.hawaiianair.com)

Japan Airlines (airline code JL; ☎ 50 70 65; jal@ southpacificrepresentation.pf; Vaima Centre; hub Narita International Airport, Tokyo) Code-share with Air Tahiti Nui.

Lan Chile (airline code LA; ☎ 42 64 55; www.lan.com; Vaima Centre)

Qantas Airways (airline code QF; ☎ 43 06 65; www .qantas.com; Vaima Centre; hub Kingsford Smith Airport, Sydney) Code-share with Air Tahiti Nui.

Flights go to Tahiti direct from Los Angeles, New York, Honolulu, Sydney, Auckland, Osaka, Tokyo, Easter Island (with connections to Santiago, Chile) and New Caledonia. The interior airline, **Air Tahiti** (Map pp416-17; ☎ 86 42 42; www.airtahiti.pf), has flights once a week to the Cook Islands. Tahiti is a popular stop on round-the-world (RTW) tickets (see p636) and is included in several air passes (see p636).

There is no departure tax within French Polynesia.

ASIA

Air Tahiti Nui operates flights between Japan (Tokyo and Osaka) and Pape'ete. Return flights from Tokyo start at US$1900. From other parts of Asia, the simplest connection is via Australia or NZ.

A good travel agent in Japan is **No. 1 Travel** (☎ 03-3205 6073; www.no1-travel.com).

AUSTRALIA & NEW ZEALAND

There are direct flights to both Auckland and Sydney. Fares increase considerably in the high season (June to September and over Christmas). From Sydney, expect to pay from AU$1050/1500 for a return trip in the low/high season with either Qantas or Air New Zealand.

As in Australia, fares from NZ increase during the high season. From Auckland, return fares start at NZ$850/1250 in the low/high season. Both Air New Zealand and Qantas/Air Tahiti Nui offer connecting flights from Pape'ete to LA.

OTHER PACIFIC ISLANDS

There are regular connections between French Polynesia and NZ, New Caledonia, the Cook Islands and Hawai'i. Island hopping around the Pacific is not difficult, but because some flights only operate once a week or every few days you may be faced with some scheduling problems if your time is limited.

SOUTH AMERICA

LAN operates flights between Santiago (Chile) and Pape'ete; one flight a week has a stopover on Easter Island. Return fares cost from US$2200.

UK & CONTINENTAL EUROPE

Air New Zealand (from London and Frankfurt), Air France and Air Tahiti Nui have flights to Pape'ete via LA. Return fares from Paris and Frankfurt start at around €1800; return fares from London start at around £1400 in the low season. From other destinations in Europe the easiest option is to travel to one of these cities and connect with flights to Pape'ete.

Recommended travel agencies are:

Anyway (☎ 08 92 89 38 92; www.anyway.fr; France)

Expedia (www.expedia.com) Worldwide agencies great for Europe originating flights

Flightbookers (☎ 0870 010 7000; www.ebookers .com; UK)

STA Travel (☎ 01805 456; www.statravel.de; UK)

Trailfinders (☎ 0845 058 5858; www.trailfinders .co.uk; UK)

Travel Bag (☎ 0870 890 1456; www.travelbag.co.uk; UK)

PACKAGE-TOUR PARADISE

French Polynesia lends itself to the package tour. Given the high price of flights to the region, and the often astronomical price of accommodation once there, a package tour can work out to be a financial godsend. On the downside, package tours don't give much leeway to explore. Although most tours offer the opportunity to visit more than one island, you will have to prebook one hotel for each destination before departure.

There are a variety of tour packages available from travel agents in all Western countries, and a number of online booking agents also offer special flight and hotel deals. If you want more than just a straightforward combo package, a good travel agent is essential – they can negotiate better prices at the larger hotels, handle Air Tahiti bookings for your domestic flights and have your schedule finalised before you arrive. In addition to the traditional travel operators, there are agencies that specialise in diving tours. These packages typically include flights, accommodation, diving fee and diving tours.

A great list of packages available from several different agencies with departures from around the world are available on the Air Tahiti Nui (www.airtahitinui.com) website.

Tahiti specialists in the USA include **Tahiti Legends** (☎ 800 200 1214; www.tahitilegends.com) and **Tahiti Vacations** (☎ 800 553 3477; www.tahitivacation.com). Packages for seven nights start at US$1900 on Mo'orea and US$2600 on Bora Bora.

In Australia, **Hideaway Holidays** (☎ 02-9743 0253; www.hideawayholidays.com.au) offers heaps of flight-and-accommodation deals to Tahiti. Seven-night packages from Sydney to Tahiti start at AU$2300.

In the UK, **Audley Travel** (☎ 01993 838 830; www.audleytravel.com) arranges packages to French Polynesia. Ten-day packages start at £2400 to Tahiti and £3000 to Bora Bora.

For stays in family *pensions* or small hotels, you can book packages from www.easytahiti.com and www.islandsadventures.com.

USA & CANADA

Coming from the USA, you can fly direct from LA, New York or Honolulu to Pape'ete. Air New Zealand and Air Tahiti Nui serve this route, and Air France flights from Paris to Pape'ete go via LA. Return fares from LA to Pape'ete range from around US$900 to US$1800. If you are starting your trip in Honolulu, return fares from Honolulu to Pape'ete start from US$1050 in the low season (January to May) and US$2250 in the high season (November to December).

There are no direct flights from Canada, so you will need to go via Honolulu or the west coast of the USA. Return fares from Vancouver via LA start from C$2500 in the low season.

If you want to book your flight and hotel as a package, see above for more information. The following agencies are recommended for online bookings:

Orbitz (www.orbitz.com)
Travelocity (www.travelocity.com)

Sea

Travelling to French Polynesia by yacht is entirely feasible: you can often pick up crewing positions from North America, Australia or NZ, or in the islands; ask at yacht clubs in San Diego, LA, San Francisco, Honolulu, Sydney, Cairns or Auckland.

It takes about a month to sail from the US west coast to Hawai'i and another month south from there to the Marquesas; with stops, another month takes you west to Tahiti and the Society Islands. Then it's another long leg southwest to Australia or NZ.

For yacht formalities while in French Polynesian waters, see p479.

GETTING AROUND

Getting around French Polynesia is half the fun. Travelling between islands involves flights or boat travel and, thanks to French Government financial support, travel to the larger and more densely populated islands is relatively easy and reasonably priced, though getting to the remote islands can be harder.

Air

With the exception of a few charter operations, flying within French Polynesia means **Air Tahiti** (☎ 86 42 42; www.airtahiti.pf) and its associate, **Air Moorea** (☎ 86 41 41; www.airmoorea.com). Air Tahiti flies to 41 islands in all five of the major island groups. Window seats on its modern fleet of high-wing turboprop aircraft offer great views, but for the nervous flyer these flights can be rather hair-raising. Air Moorea is the secondary airline, operating smaller aircraft between Tahiti and Mo'orea.

Flight frequencies ebb and flow with the seasons, and in the July–August peak season, extra flights are scheduled. Air Tahiti publishes a useful flight schedule booklet (available from the airport domestic check-in counter), which is essential reading for anyone planning a complex trip around the islands. If you are making reservations from afar, you can reserve online and pay by credit card.

Note that Air Tahiti and Air Tahiti Nui are different airlines; Air Tahiti Nui is the international carrier, while Air Tahiti operates domestic flights only.

AIR PASSES

Several passes allow you to save on visiting multiple islands: all require you begin your trip in Pape'ete and limit the number of transits through Pape'ete. You are only allowed one stopover on each island but you can transit on an island as long as the flight number does not change. Stopping at an island to change flights counts as a stopover.

Passes are valid for 28 days and all flights (except between Pape'ete and Mo'orea) must be booked at the beginning. You can fly either Air Tahiti or Air Moorea on the Pape'ete to Mo'orea sector. Once you've taken the first flight, the routing cannot be changed and the fare is nonrefundable. There may be restrictions on which 'colour' flights you can use.

The passes include *Passe Découverte* (Discovery Pass: four Society Islands; adult/child 26,500/16,600 CFP); *Passe Bora Bora* (all six Society Islands; 36,200/21,500 CFP); *Passe Bora Tuamotu* (add three islands in the Tuamotus; 51,200/29,000 CFP); and *Passe Lagons* (Lagoons Pass: Mo'orea, Rangiroa, Tikehau, Manihi and Fakarava; 40,700/23,700 CFP). Add the Marquesas (Nuku Hiva and Hiva Oa) to any other pass for 48,700/27,700 CFP or the Australs (Rurutu, Raivavae, Rimatara and Tubuai) for 28,500/17,600 CFP.

Limited flights (blue or white) are offered through a *Passe Bleu Découverte* (Blue Discovery Pass: Mo'orea, Huahine and Ra'iatea; 21,700 CFP) and a *Passe Bleu* (Blue

Pass: add Bora Bora; 27,700 CFP). There are no children's fares and Mo'orea must be your last visit.

REDUCED-FARE CARDS

Air Tahiti offers several cards that let you buy tickets at reduced prices, depending on whether the flight is classified as blue, white or red.

If you're aged under 25, a *Carte Jeunes* (Youth Card), and if you're over 60 a *Carte Marama* (Third Age Card), gives you up to 50% reductions (depending on the colour of the flight) and costs 1000 CFP. A *Carte Famille* (Family Card) gives adults up to 50% and children up to 75% discount. It costs 2000 CFP. You need a passport and photos and for the Family Card the kids' birth certificates.

These cards are issued on the spot, only in Pape'ete.

Bicycle

French Polynesia is an ideal region to explore by bike. Distances are manageable, the coast roads are generally flat, traffic is light (outside Pape'ete) and you can travel at your own pace. You can ride around many of the islands in a morning or afternoon. Bicycles can often be rented for about 1500 CFP per day, and many guest houses have bicycles for their guests, sometimes for free, though you might be riding an old rattler. A mountain bike is ideal for some of the rougher roads and it's even worth bringing your trusty steed with you; they're accepted on all the inter-island ships.

Boat

Boat travel within the Society group isn't as easy as you'd hope, unless you're only going to Mo'orea or taking a cruise or sailboat. A number of companies shuttle back and forth between Tahiti and Mo'orea each day; other routes between the islands are less frequent but served at least twice a week by cargo vessels. A passenger-only vessel to serve the Society Islands is planned for 2011.

In the other archipelagos, travel by boat is more difficult. If you are short on time and keen to travel beyond the Society Islands, you may need to consider flying at least some of the way.

You can generally catch a ride on one of the cargo ships, known as *goélettes* (schooners), that transport goods between islands. Island hopping by cargo ship is probably the most gritty immerse-yourself-in-the-local-culture experience you're likely to have in French Polynesia. Nowadays most cargo-ship passengers are required to have berths on the deck or cabins (some with air-con), but these are very basic. If you get seasick, be prepared to get really seasick. Plus, the ships run to uncertain schedules. But then again, if you wanted to get off the beaten track, you were looking for adventure anyway!

Bonitiers (large wooden boats) do many of the runs around islands or to nearby islands in the Marquesas.

CRUISE SHIP

At the other end of the spectrum from rudimentary cargo ships are luxury cruise ships operating in the Society Islands. These vessels are incredibly stylish and comfortable and offer shore excursions at each stop.

Managed by **Bora Bora Pearl Cruises** (☎ 43 43 03; www.boraborapearlcruises.com), the *Haumana* is a magnificent 36m catamaran that accommodates up to 60 people and does three- or four-day cruises between Bora Bora, Ra'iatea and Taha'a. The *Tia Moana* and *Tu Moana*, both also managed by Bora Bora Pearl Cruises, offer seven-day cruises in the Society Islands.

You may see the enormous *Paul Gauguin* (seven-day voyages) anchored in Pape'ete. They depart Pape'ete to visit the Society Islands and sometimes an atoll or two in the Tuamotus.

For a more intimate cruising experience, **Archipels Croisieres** (☎ 55 36 39; www.archilpels .com) have five eight-person catamarans that cruise the Society Islands and Tuamotus. It's a full-service experience with all meals and activities.

See the Tahiti Tourisme website (www .tahiti-tourisme.com) for more information about cruising.

FERRY & CARGO SHIP

It takes between 30 minutes and an hour to travel between Tahiti and Mo'orea, depending on which company you go with. The car ferries, such as those run by Mo'orea Ferry, are slower than the high-speed ferries, which take only passengers, motorcycles and bicycles. See the Mo'orea section (p420) for more information about ferries to/from Mo'orea.

Vaeanu (☎ 41 25 35) operates the Pape'ete–Huahine–Ra'iatea–Taha'a–Bora Bora round trip, leaving Pape'ete on Tuesday and Thursday at 5pm. It sets out from Bora Bora on Wednesday and Friday. The Huahine and Ra'iatea arrivals are in the middle of the night (most guest house owners will not pick you up). Reservations are advisable and the one-way tariff to any of the islands to/from Pape'ete is 2000 CFP. The office is at the Motu Uta port area in Pape'ete, near the *Aranui* office; take *le truck* No 3 from the *mairie* (town hall).

Hawaiki Nui (☎ 54 99 54) also travels the Society Islands circuit on a similar schedule and has two departures a week (Tuesday and Thursday at 4pm; deck/cabin per person 2000/5500 CFP).

The **Maupiti Express** (☎ 67 66 69) makes regular trips between Bora Bora and Maupiti (one-way 3500 CFP) and Bora Bora to Taha'a and Ra'iatea (one-way 3500 CFP). The boat departs the Vaitape quay in Bora Bora for Maupiti at 8.30am on Tuesday, Thursday and Saturday; the return trip leaves Maupiti at 4pm on the same day. Tickets can be purchased at the quay.

About 10 ships operate through the Tuamotus; routes and fares vary, so it's best to check with the offices for the individual ships. They include the **Saint-Xavier Maris-Stella** (☎ 42 23 58), **Nuku Hau** (☎ 45 23 24), **Mareva Nui** (☎ 42 25 53), and the **Kura Ora II** and **Kura Ora III** (☎ 45 55 45). Expect to pay around 7000 CFP for a one-way trip to Rangiroa and up to around 11,000 CFP for further out atolls.

The **Aranui** (☎ 42 62 40; www.aranui.com) is a veritable institution, taking freight and passengers on 16 trips a year from Pape'ete (see boxed text, p463). The only other cargo ship, the **Taporo IX**, won't take passengers.

Services to the Australs are limited; the **Tuhaa Pae II** (☎ 50 96 09, 41 36 06; snathp@mail.pf) leaves Pape'ete for the Australs three times a month. It stops at Rurutu and Tubuai on every trip, Rimatara and Raivavae twice a month, Rapa once every two months and Maria Island in the Gambiers very occasionally. You can choose between berths and air-con cabins. From Pape'ete to Rurutu, Rimatara or Tubuai a berth/air-con cabin costs 6000/8200 CFP; to Raivavae it costs 8500/12,000 CFP. Three meals add another 3100 CFP per day.

The **Nuku Hau** (☎ 45 23 24) sails to the Gambier Archipelago via the Tuamotus (10,000 CFP per person deck-class, plus 1950 CFP for three meals a day).

YACHT

French Polynesia is an enormously popular yachting destination. See p475) for more information.

Bus

French Polynesia doesn't have much of a public transport system, and Tahiti is the only island where public transport is even an option. The colourful, old *le trucks* (trucks with bench seats in the back for passengers) have been almost entirely replaced now by a less personable, but more modern fleet of proper air-con buses. Buses stop at designated spots (marked with a blue clock) and supposedly run on a schedule – although times are hardly regular.

Car & Scooter

If you want to explore the larger islands of the Society group at your own pace, it is well worth renting a car.

DRIVING LICENCE

Car-hire agencies in French Polynesia only ask to see your national driving licence, so an international driving licence is unnecessary.

HIRE

There are many different car-hire agencies on the more touristy islands, but the prices really don't vary much. For a small car, expect to pay between 7000 CFP and 11,000 CFP per day, which includes unlimited kilometres and insurance. Most places also rent vehicles for four- and eight-hour periods at reduced rates. If you only plan to hire a car for one day, eight hours is more than enough time to check out even the largest islands.

At certain times of year (July, August and New Year's Eve), it's wise to book vehicles a few days in advance; on the smaller islands it's best to always book ahead as the number of cars are limited. You'll need a credit card, of course.

On Tahiti you will find the major international car-hire agencies such as Avis, Budget, Europcar and Hertz. On other islands such as Mo'orea, Huahine, Ra'iatea and Bora Bora, as well as on Rangiroa in the Tuamotus, the market is divided up between Avis and Europcar. Smaller local agencies exist on some islands, but the rates are almost as high.

You can hire a car on Rurutu in the Australs, but on the Marquesas, rental vehicles are mainly 4WDs complete with a driver. Rental without a driver is possible only on Atuona (Hiva Oa) and Taiohae (Nuku Hiva).

Avis and Europcar both hire scooters on a number of islands. It's a good way of getting around the small islands; however, bear in mind you won't be wearing protective gear, so this is probably not the place to learn to ride a scooter. You'll pay around 6500 CFP a day. After numerous accidents there are no scooters for hire on Tahiti.

ROAD RULES

Driving is on the right-hand side in French Polynesia. Although the accident statistics are pretty grim, driving in French Polynesia is not difficult, and the traffic is light almost everywhere apart from the busy coastal strip around Pape'ete on Tahiti. However, the overtaking habits of locals can sometimes get the heart rate up. Beware of drunk drivers at night, and of pedestrians and children who may not be used to traffic, particularly in more remote locations.

Tokelau

For those with an insatiable desire to get as far off the beaten track as is humanly possible, it must be comforting to know that places like Tokelau still exist. In a world where travel has become easy and accessible to the masses, travelling to Tokelau still requires a degree of dedication that dissuades all but the most committed visitors.

It takes upwards of 24 hours to reach Tokelau by boat from its nearest neighbour, Samoa, and you can forget about flying – there's no airstrip. Once you're there, the ship that brought you is your only means of getting between the nation's three atolls: it takes nine hours to travel between the two most distant ones. This ship will be your only ticket home, so you'll have to be prepared to stay for at least five days until its ready to leave – or wait for the next one in a couple of weeks.

It's largely due to this remoteness that the indigenous culture has been preserved on Tokelau to a far greater degree than elsewhere in the Pacific. Each of the three atolls – Atafu, Fakaofo and Nukunonu – is a ribbon of tiny *motu* (islands) surrounding a lagoon. They're home to a small population of hardy souls who live an almost subsistence lifestyle in very crowded conditions.

And here's the reward. Tokelau survives on a culture of sharing and cooperation, so if you're prepared to muck in, you'll quickly find yourself adopted into the lives of these contagiously happy people. Your old life will seem very far away indeed.

HIGHLIGHTS

- Descend beneath the clear waters of any of the lagoons for memorable snorkelling or diving (p491)
- Pitch your tent on an uninhabited speck of an island for a genuine castaway experience (p490)
- Boogie down with the locals at a community disco (p488)
- Take on the old ladies at bingo (p488)
- Head out fishing with the experts (p491)

TOKELAU

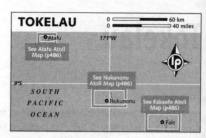

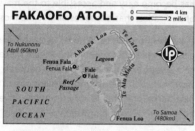

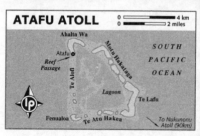

CLIMATE & WHEN TO GO

Sitting just south of the equator, Tokelau is truly tropical, with an average temperature of 28°C and heavy but irregular rainfall. It's at the northern limit of the South Pacific cyclone zone, so tropical storms are rare but certainly not unknown – the most recent was Cyclone Percy in 2005.

The best months to travel to Tokelau are from April to October. Between November and January, ships are usually full of scholarship students and other Tokelauans living abroad, returning to spend Christmas with their families. December to March is cyclone season, when the trip from Samoa could be rough.

HISTORY

Tokelau's atolls have been populated by Polynesians for about 1000 years, but it wasn't until the 18th century that 'Tokelau' came to exist. A series of wars at this time united these previously fiercely independent atolls. At the end of the wars, Fakaofo had conquered Atafu and Nukunonu, bringing them under the rule of the god Tui Tokelau and creating the first united entity of Tokelau.

Soon afterwards, Tokelau came to the attention of English and US ships sailing the. Whalers frequented the atolls in the 1820s, and in the middle of the 19th century missionary groups began devoting time to evangelising the Tokelauans. From the 1840s to the 1860s, first Catholic, then Protestant missionaries from Samoa converted the people of the three atolls to Christianity.

Conversion was a mixed blessing. The French missionary Pierre Bataillon transported 500 reluctant Tokelauans to Wallis Island in the 1850s because he feared they would otherwise die of starvation. Then Peruvian slave traders seized about 250 people – half of the atolls' population – in the 1860s. The combined effect of the transportation, slaving and disease reduced Tokelau's population from 1000 to only 200. Desperate to save the remaining people, Tokelauans pleaded with the UK for protection as a British colony, and in 1889 Tokelau was annexed to the Gilbert & Ellice Islands Protectorate (see p538).

In the early 20th century, large numbers of Tokelauans left their homes to work the

STATE OF INDEPENDENCE

With colonisation now largely relegated to the dustbin of history, the movement towards independence for territories such as Tokelau has gained momentum. The Tokelauan chiefs, the village councils, the United Nations and the NZ government are all determined that Tokelau should have self-government (in free association with NZ, like the Cook Islands and Niue). The only problem is that the Tokelauan people keep voting against it. Referenda held in 2006 and 2007 failed to achieve the two-thirds majority required for it to pass, although the last one came very close, with 64.4% of the people in favour.

Despite this, government and administration has been increasingly shifted from NZ to Tokelau in the last few decades. When the Tokelauan people finally decide to go it alone, they'll find a constitution, national flag, national anthem and national symbol ready and waiting for them.

phosphate mines of Banaba (Ocean Island) in the Gilbert Islands. After New Zealand (NZ) took over responsibility for Tokelau in 1925, the flow of emigration shifted to Western Samoa (then also an NZ territory). Following Samoa's independence in 1962, many Tokelauans relocated to NZ.

Tokelau's local government comprises three village councils called the *taupulega* – one on each atoll – made up of the heads of family, regardless of gender. Every three years, each atoll elects a *pulenuku* (village mayor) and a *faipule* (atoll representative), who form the Tokelau Executive Council. Annually, the position of Tokelau's *ulu o Tokelau* (head of government) rotates among the three atolls until the following election. Delegates from each atoll are also elected every three years to serve with the *pulenuku* and *faipule* on Tokelau's 21-member parliament, the General Fono. The number of delegates from each atoll is determined by population density, thus ensuring a representative government based on the varying size of each village.

In early 2005, Tokelau was hit not only by Cyclone Percy but also by a spring tide that inundated the villages of Fakaofo and Nukunonu. Homes were under a metre of seawater, and important crops such as coconuts and bananas were hard hit by the winds. Nobody was seriously injured, but the damage was extensive.

Recent improvements in infrastructure have included the creation of a reliable telephone system and direct internet services.

THE CULTURE

Tokelau's isolation from the rest of the world, as well as NZ's hands-off approach to its administration, has resulted in *faka*

Tokelau (the Tokelauan way) being well preserved. However, the large numbers of Tokelauans living abroad has resulted in an ever-increasing awareness of the benefits of modern *palagi* (Western) culture – whether perceived or real.

Judith Huntsman and Antony Hooper's enormous *Tokelau: A Historical Ethnography* is *the* definitive text, telling you all you ever wanted to know about Tokelau and its people. With Allan Thomas and Ineleo Tuia, Huntsman has also compiled an interesting collection of tales called *Songs and Stories of Tokelau: An Introduction to the Cultural Heritage*.

Lifestyle

Partly because of the difficulty of travel between the atolls, Tokelau society is still compartmentalised into the three atolls and their (mainly) single village. The one name describes both the atoll and the village (for example, Atafu Atoll/Atafu Village). *Maopoopo* (village unity) is paramount in Tokelau. Beyond that, each village is divided into two *faitu* – or sides – on a roughly territorial basis. The two sides compete enthusiastically in fishing, action songs, dancing, sports and, most importantly, *kilikiti* (village cricket).

The elderly are awarded enormous respect in Tokelau. Each *kau kaiga* (family group) is led by the *matai*, with the three *taupulega* (village councils of elders and *matai*) ordering daily life. Elders are expected to contribute to the community, both through attendance at the *taupulega* and by encouraging younger workers at their tasks.

Each village *taupulega* administers the *aumaga* (village workforce), which gathers fish, harvests crops and maintains village buildings. Almost all males over school age, except for public servants, join the *aumaga*. The female equivalent is the *komiti a fafine* (women's committee), whose job it is to ensure village cleanliness and health.

Under Tokelau's system of *inati* (sharing), resources are divided between families according to need. The *inati* system developed over the centuries out of necessity: in an environment where resources were so scarce, community cooperation was vital. Individualism is not a virtue in these circumstances, nor is it really an option.

Inati still operates – each day, the village's catch of fish is laid out on the beach and apportioned by the *taupulega* – but it is under increasing pressure from the cash economy. Steps have been taken to ensure that employed Tokelauans, mainly public servants, do not receive unfair benefits through this principle of sharing. There are only a dozen police officers in Tokelau and no imprisonment system. In Tokelau's closely knit society, punishment takes the form of public rebukes, fines or labour.

Modern Tokelauan society survives due to foreign aid from NZ, which pumps in NZ$13 million per year (or NZ$8900 per head), swamping the gross domestic product of NZ$2.6 million. Most revenue comes from fishing licence fees, copra, handicrafts and stamps; interest from an international trust fund complements these earnings. Tokelau's isolation adds to the country's financial woes – telecommunications and transport cost 25% of the yearly budget. All medical supplies, equipment and many foodstuffs are imported.

The public service is the main source of regular income for Tokelauans; these jobs are rotated among villagers and a village tax is imposed on wages. The other major source of income is from the *aumaga*. Payment for *aumaga* work, which was traditionally unpaid, provides an income for young Tokelauans who would otherwise have to look for work overseas. Remittances from Tokelauan relatives living away from home is another source of income.

While each atoll has a hospital, it's a fact of life for Tokelauans that any serious health problem can easily be life threatening – medical supplies are difficult to come by, and specialist care is days away in Samoa.

Entertainment on the islands is limited to community discos on the three atolls. Expect lots of 'cold stuff' (beer), loud music and dancing. Although gambling for money is illegal, weekly bingo games are extremely popular with women. Prizes include boxes of washing powder and bottles of shampoo.

Population

Tokelauans are Polynesian, closely related to Tuvaluans, Samoans and Cook Islanders. The liberal sprinkling of European surnames is the legacy of some enthusiastic whalers and beachcombers of the late 19th century.

Tokelau's islands are cramped beyond belief, even though emigration has relieved some of the population pressure. Tokelauans are crowded into four small villages. Atafu and Nukunonu both have only one village, perched on each atoll's main motu. Around 400 people live on Fakaofo's tiny (4-hectare) Fale Island; in fact, Fale's population density is one of the highest in the Pacific, and is such that the island's numerous *puaka* (domestic pigs) have been squeezed out to reside on the reef rather than on land. Fakaofo's second islet, Fenua Fala, has a smaller cluster of homes with a hospital, school and church.

Land shortages have long forced emigration from Tokelau, and most of the country's people live overseas, predominantly in Samoa, NZ and Australia. Almost 6500 Tokelauans live in NZ – four times as many as in Tokelau itself. They have maintained affinity and allegiance with their familial atolls and actively retain the language and culture of their homeland.

SPORT

Tokelauans play similar sports to Samoa and NZ; rugby, netball and *kilikiti* (the Polynesian form of cricket) are popular. When playing *kilikiti*, each side fields as many players as are available – on crowded Tokelau that means 50 per side is not uncommon. A shot into the ocean or lagoon is a confirmed 'six'.

RELIGION

Tokelau is a staunchly Christian country – the percentage of the population that does not belong to one of the two main churches is tiny. Sunday is devoted almost entirely to church activities, with time off for a large meal and a midday snooze. If you attend church while in Tokelau, the community will better accept you – and it will give you something to do on Sunday. Work and many activities are forbidden on Atafu and Fakaofo on Sunday; Nukunonu is less strict.

Tokelau's religious composition reflects the arrival of Samoan missionaries of different denominations during the 19th century: Atafu is almost completely Protestant, Nukunonu is largely Catholic, and Fakaofo, where Catholic and Protestant missionaries arrived almost simultaneously, is split between the two faiths. Interdenominational tension is all but unknown on Fakaofo, as it would run contrary to the supreme concept of *maopoopo*.

Prior to the arrival of Christianity, Tokelauans worshipped the god Tui Tokelau – personified in a slab of coral that stands in the *fale fono* on Fakaofo. The usual pantheon of Polynesian gods was also acknowledged in Tokelau.

LANGUAGE

Tokelauan is a Polynesian language, closely related to Tuvaluan and Samoan. Because of frequent contact with NZ, most Tokelauans speak some English.

Tokelauan pronunciation is similar to other Polynesian languages, except that 'f' is pronounced as a soft 'wh', and 'g' is pronounced 'ng' (a soft sound) as in Samoan.

Tokelauan basics

Hello.	*Malo ni* or *Talofa*
Goodbye.	*Tofa.*
How are you?	*Ea mai koe?*
I'm well.	*Ko au e lelei.*
Please.	*Fakamolemole.*
Thank you.	*Fakafetai.*
Yes.	*Io.*
No.	*Heai.*

ENVIRONMENT

Tokelau may not have an environment to worry about in another few decades – climate change and the associated rise in sea level are the two biggest environmental issues pressing this atoll nation (see boxed text, right).

More immediate environmental concerns include the overexploitation of some fish and other marine species, as well as its (albeit tiny) forest resources. Due to the country's very limited acreage, waste disposal is also a big problem, as is the improper disposal of chemicals.

On a more positive note, Tokelau has set the goal of being completely self-sufficient in its energy needs through sustainable sources. A pilot programme in solar energy genera-

---

THE END?

Consisting only of low-lying coral atolls rising to a maximum of 5m, Tokelau faces great risk from global warming. It is predicted that all three atolls will be uninhabitable by the end of the 21st century, though some estimates give only another 30 years. While some Tokelauans regard these predictions as overly dramatic, others foresee the end of their 1000-year-old history. See p70 for more on the issue of global warming.

---

tion on Fakaofo has been such a success that they're considering extending it to the other atolls.

Geography

Tokelau's three small atolls lie roughly in a line, 480km north of their nearest neighbour and main link with the outside world, Samoa. The three atolls are separated not only from the rest of the world but also from each other – it is 92km between Nukunonu and Atafu, and 64km between Nukunonu and Fakaofo.

The trio are classic coral atolls: thin necklaces of small islets surrounding central lagoons. The low-lying islands have a maximum elevation of only 5m above sea level, and the land area is tiny, amounting to only 12.2 sq km across the three atolls. None of the 128 islets are more than 200m wide.

Ecology

Like all coral atolls, Tokelau's soil is thin and infertile, and holds water poorly. Coconut and pandanus are the most common plant species; *kanava* is a tree popularly used for timber. Bananas, pawpaw, taro, breadfruit and other staple food crops grow on the islands. Migratory seabirds are common visitors to the atolls; otherwise, fauna consists of rats, lizards, poultry and the reef-exiled pigs.

FOOD & DRINK

The traditional method of cooking in Tokelau is the *umu* (earth oven), which will be familiar to anyone who has spent some time in the Pacific; they're most popular on Fakaofo. However, most households cook on kerosene stoves. The traditional diet of fish, *kumala* (sweet potato), breadfruit, taro, pigs and fowl is supplemented

TOKELAU

TOKELAU, AT LAST *Rowland Burley*

It took me nearly two years to get to Tokelau, but it was well worth the wait.

The first problem was communicating with TALO in laid-back Samoa. Emails would sometimes remain unanswered for weeks at a time, and their replies were often sparse at best. But eventually a sailing schedule materialised for the supply ships that make the eight-day trip from Apia around the islands, and I arranged my leave to coincide with one of them. As the months passed, I confirmed the departure date regularly but then, when it was far too late to alter my holiday plans, the sailing was moved forward by several days. I'd just have to wait till next year.

Over the following months, I went through the same painstaking process of finding the ship schedule and booking my leave – although this time I left several days clear both before and after the trip, in case the date changed again. And, of course, change it did, but this time by a whole week! Faced with having to wait another whole year, I eventually managed to scrounge some extra leave, and I was finally set to go.

In Apia, the folk at TALO couldn't have been nicer, and they reassured me that the ship really was still going, although I didn't actually believe it until we pulled away from the wharf. The 24 hours it took to get to Nukunonu would have been fine if the good ship *MV Lady Naomi* had been just a little more stable, but once we arrived, it was just perfect. I spent a whole week exploring the three atolls, with no vehicles and no tourists – the real Polynesia at last.

Rowland Burley is an inveterate traveller who has been to all the world's countries and most of its territories and island groups. Tokelau was one of the very last places he needed to visit, leaving only a couple of remote Pacific and Indian Ocean atolls before he can claim having been everywhere.

---

by the processed foods that are brought in roughly every 12 days by cargo ship. Canned meat, also a mainstay of the Pacific, is in plentiful supply.

If you're staying with one of the accommodation establishments detailed on right, or with a local family, your food needs will be looked after. Processed food (and other supplies) can be bought from the small village-owned co-op stores on each atoll. Supplies of fresh fish, vegetables and drinking coconuts should be negotiated with someone from the *taupulega*.

As on all coral atolls, fresh water is scarce. The porous coral soil drains quickly, so despite the heavy rainfall there are few groundwater reserves except on Fakaofo. Instead, rainwater is collected from roofs into rainwater tanks. Tank water tends to taste somewhat brackish, perhaps explaining the preference for 'cold stuff' (beer).

Make sure you have permission before grabbing a coconut to drink from – such resources are limited in Tokelau.

Beer, invariably Samoan, is sold at the co-op stores on Fakaofo and Nukunonu; its sale is strictly rationed on more-traditional Atafu. Tokelau's isolation means that supplies of *hostuff* ('hot stuff'; spirits) and beer can be unreliable. *Kaleve*, made from fermented coconut sap, is also drunk.

TOKELAU DIRECTORY

ACCOMMODATION

Accommodation on Tokelau must be arranged before arrival through the **Tokelau Apia Liaison Office** (TALO; ☎ 685-20822; hei_perez@hotmail.com; PO Box 865, Apia; ☺ 8am-5pm Mon-Fri) in Samoa. Official places to stay are very limited; you may be able to arrange accommodation in a private home but it won't be easy without contacts. Facilities are basic – all that is provided is a bed and meals.

Nukunonu has a relative goldmine of options, with *three* places to stay. The newest and most comfortable is **Te Mahina** (☎ 4190; zak-p@lesamoa.net; per person NZ$50), which even has some en suite rooms (NZ$30 extra). **Luana Liki Hotel** (☎ 4140; hei_perez@hotmail.com; per person NZ$50) is a wonderfully friendly place with nine rooms. It is owned by retired teachers Luciano and Juliana Perez, and they will happily organise lagoon outings and snorkelling expeditions inside and outside the reef. The other alternative is one of the three self-catering rooms on the top floor of the **Fale Fono** (main administration building; ☎ 4139; per person NZ$50), but visiting officials often use them.

Atafu has one small **accommodation house** (☎ 2146; fax 2108; per person NZ$50), which is run by master fisherman Feleti Lopa.

On Fakaofo there are no official places to stay, although TALO might be able to arrange something should you have the urge to stay there.

If village life is proving a bit too claustrophobic and you have a tent, consider moving out to one of the remote uninhabited islets for a quiet retreat. Remember that every single island in Tokelau, big or small, is owned by either a family or a village, and it's important to get permission to visit before you go.

ACTIVITIES

Diving and **snorkelling** both inside and outside the atolls' lagoons is fantastic. There is almost nothing in the way of search and rescue facilities, though, so diving outside the reef should be undertaken with maximum caution. Talk to the locals to find out where the safest diving spots can be found. The nearest compression chamber is so far away (Fiji) that it might as well be on Mars.

Ask the local men if you can accompany them on **fishing** trips, but be aware that they are working and won't always be able to accommodate your wishes.

INTERNET RESOURCES

Fakaofo (www.fakaofo.tk) Specific information about Fakaofo.

Lonely Planet (www.lonelyplanet.com/tokelau) Tokelau profile.

New Zealand Ministry of Foreign Affairs (www .mfat.govt.nz/Countries/Pacific/Tokelau.php) NZ government site, with lots of useful information.

Council for the Ongoing Government of Tokelau (www.tokelau.org.nz) Official government portal.

MONEY

The NZ dollar is the official currency, though Samoan tala will sometimes be accepted (for exchange rates see the Quick Reference page). There are no banks in Tokelau but you can change foreign currency through the Department of Finance on each atoll.

TELEPHONE

Tokelau was connected with the international phone system only in 1994 and has the international dialling code ☎ 690. There are no area codes – all local numbers have four digits.

TIME

Tokelau is 11 hours behind GMT.

VISAS

The Tokelau Apia Liaison Office (see opposite) in Samoa issues one-month visitor permits for NZ$20 (a one- or two-week permit is the same price, so you may as well apply for a month). Accommodation needs to be arranged through TALO prior to arrival in Tokelau, and a return ticket to Samoa must be booked. Also, consent must be given by the village *taupulega*.

TRANSPORT IN TOKELAU

GETTING THERE & AWAY

Getting to Tokelau is not something you do on a whim – planning, waiting and keeping your fingers crossed all carry equal weight. And make sure you've got sea legs – there's no airstrip on Tokelau so the only way to get there is by boat or yacht.

Boat

Several ships service Tokelau from Apia in Samoa, with one departure every 12 days or so (usually there are two or three sailings per month). The Tokelau Administration owns a cargo ship, MV *Tokelau*, which makes the trip to Tokelau every two or three weeks. In addition, there are larger, dual-purpose passenger/cargo vessels that are hired to make the round trip every month or so. MV *Tokelau* is short on bunks but is said to be more stable in high seas and to have better food (all meals are included in the fares).

Bookings on these ships are made through the Tokelau Apia Liaison Office (see opposite) in Samoa. Allow plenty of time to process your booking, and be aware that tourists are a lower priority than locals. Also be aware that the annual sailing schedule changes occasionally, but usually only by a day or so.

The trip to Fakaofo (the closest atoll to Samoa) takes between 24 and 26 hours, although by 2010 a new vessel will cut the journey down to 15 hours. Travellers have a choice between cabin fare (NZ$528 return) and deck fare (NZ$286); children's tickets are half price. In either case there will be plenty of company on the voyage – you'll be travelling with a boatload of Tokelauans from Samoa and NZ returning home to see their families. The round trip from Apia to Tokelau and back takes from five to eight days. There is no harbour on any of the atolls. The ship waits offshore while passengers and cargo are transferred via small boats and dinghies – a hair-raising experience if seas are heavy.

Yacht

Seek advice about the voyage to Tokelau from someone who has been there, and see p641 for more information about sailing in the Pacific.

Tokelau's atolls are low-lying and make difficult visual targets. There are no harbours and anchoring offshore is not easy, especially in an offshore wind. The sea floor drops off sharply outside the coral reef, and the water is too deep for most anchor chains. There is one anchorage beyond the reefs at each atoll, but leave a crew member aboard in case the anchor doesn't hold. The channels blasted through the coral are shallow and are intended for dinghies only.

If you're heading to Tokelau on your own yacht, you will still need to apply for a visitor permit (see p491).

GETTING AROUND

Inter-island travel is possible only on the ships that leave Apia for Tokelau (p491). These ships usually visit all three atolls twice on each voyage. Sailing time is four hours between Fakaofo and Nukunonu, and five hours between Nukunonu and Atafu. Travel between the small islands on an atoll is usually done in a small aluminium dinghy, or by wading if the tide is low enough.

There are only a handful of vehicles in Tokelau.

Tonga

Say goodbye to tourist hype – you're now in the Kingdom of Tonga, the never-colonised South Pacific 'paradise' that is now in a highly anticipated period of change. This remote kingdom of 171 islands and 100,000 people, where what King Tupou IV said went, now has a new king and the promise of democracy.

This is a country that survives on international aid and remittances sent from Tongans living overseas. There doesn't seem much incentive to do a lot! You may get the impression that most Tongans would prefer visitors just to put their holiday money straight into the national coffers and get back on the aircraft without leaving the airport; expats seem determined to build a tourist industry, but the locals just don't seem to care. In some ways, it's incredibly refreshing and in others incredibly frustrating. You won't have to try to gain a cultural experience – it's all around. Where else can you ask for directions in a country's capital and be told told: 'It's the first place past the mango tree'?

There's no doubting the natural beauty of Tonga – from the picture-postcard beaches you'd expect to find in the South Pacific, to the rainforests and soaring cliffs of 'Eua, to the protected waterways of sensational Vava'u and the magnificent underwater world throughout the islands. Travellers choose the pace of their adventure in Tonga, mixing slow-paced sun-and-sand holidays with unique and intrepid experiences. Throw away any preconceived ideas, slow down to the pace of the locals, and you'll love the place. Expect too much and you'll likely go away frustrated.

HIGHLIGHTS

- Swim with the **humpback whales** (p523) that come to breed in Tonga's waters every year, or simply watch them in awe.

- Kayak among the spectacular turquoise waterways, islands and deserted beaches of **Vava'u** (p516).

- Explore **Niuafo'ou** (Tin Can Island; p529), the remote island in the Niuas that resembles a doughnut floating in the sea.

- Hike through **'Eua's** (p510) virgin tropical rainforests to the edge of dramatic cliffs and delve into limestone caves.

- Marvel at the imposing **Ha'amonga Trilithon** (p508), the 'Stonehenge of the South Pacific' constructed to track the changing seasons.

★ Niuafo'ou

★ Vava'u

Ha'amonga Trilithon ★
★ 'Eua

TONGA

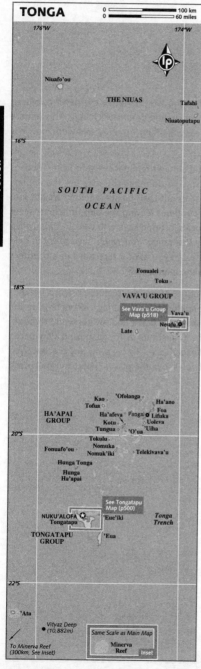

CLIMATE & WHEN TO GO

'Tonga' means south, and the kingdom is cooler and less humid than islands closer to the equator. The climate varies little across the island groups. Vava'u and the Niuas are warmer and wetter than Tongatapu, and 'Eua is cooler. May to October is the best time to visit; the wet season is November to April. Cyclone season is also from November to April, but most cyclones occur between January and March and not many hit Tonga.

COSTS & MONEY

Tonga is still one of the least expensive Pacific destinations, but prices have been shooting up in recent years. Without including inter-island transport, strict budgeters could get by on T$50 a day each. Based on twin-share accommodation, midrange travellers enjoying a few activities should budget on around T$120 a day each, while top-end travellers would need a daily minimum of around T$250 each.

HISTORY

Tonga has a rich mythological tradition, and many ancient legends relate to the islands' creation. One tells that the Tongan islands were fished out of the sea by the mighty Polynesian god Tangaloa. Another story has Tonga plucked from the ocean by the demigod Maui, a temperamental hero well known throughout the Pacific.

The earliest date confirmed by radiocarbon testing for settlement of the Tongan group is around 1100 BC. On Tongatapu, the Lapita people had their first capital at Toloa, near present-day Fua'amotu International Airport. Archaeological excavations in the village of Hihifo in Ha'apai unearthed Lapita pottery, which has carbon-dated settlement of this area to more than 3000 years ago. Islands of the Vava'u Group have been settled for around 2000 years.

The first king of Tonga, known as the Tu'i Tonga, was 'Aho'eitu. He came to power some time in the middle of the 10th century AD and was the first in a line of almost 40 men to hold the title.

During the 400 years after the first Tu'i Tonga, the Tongans were aggressive colonisers, extending their empire over eastern Fiji, Niue and northward as far as the Samoas and Tokelau.

THE 'FRIENDLY ISLANDS' – A MISNOMER?

On Captain James Cook's third voyage, he spent from April to July 1777 in the Tongan islands. While visiting Lifuka in the Ha'apai group, Cook and his men were treated to lavish feasting and entertainment by chief Finau, inspiring Cook to name his South Seas paradise the Friendly Islands.

Later it was learned that the celebration had been part of a conspiracy to raid the two ships *Resolution* and *Discovery* for their plainly visible wealth. The entertainment had been planned in order to gather the Englishmen in one spot so that they could be quickly killed and their ships looted. There was, however, a last-minute dispute between Finau and his nobles, and the operation was abandoned. Cook never learned how narrowly they had escaped – if he had, he may have changed his name for the 'friendly islands'.

European Arrival

The first European arrivals in Tonga were Dutch explorers Willem Schouten and Jacob le Maire, who discovered the Niuas group in 1616.

Tongatapu's first European visitor was Dutchman Abel Tasman, who spent a few days trading with islanders and named the island Amsterdam in 1643. The next European contact came with James Cook, who became close friends with the 30th Tu'i Tonga, Fatafehi Paulaho.

In 1643 Abel Tasman was also the first European to visit the Ha'apai group. Vava'u remained undiscovered by Europeans until Don Francisco Antonio Mourelle of Spain showed up in 1781, making it one of the last South Pacific islands to be contacted by Europeans.

House of Tupou

In 1831 missionaries baptised the ruling Tu'i Tonga, who took the Christian name George. As King George Tupou I, he united Tonga and, with the help of the first prime minister, Reverend Shirley Baker, came up with a flag, a state seal and a national anthem, and then began drafting a constitution, passed in

1875. It included a bill of rights, a format for legislative and judicial procedures, laws for succession to the throne and a section on land tenure. It is also responsible for Tonga's heavily Christian laws today.

The second king, George Tupou II, who took over in 1893, lacked the charisma, character and fearlessness of his predecessor; he signed a Treaty of Friendship with Britain in 1900, placing Tonga under British protection and giving Britain control over Tonga's foreign affairs.

He died at the age of 45 in 1918, and his 18-year-old daughter Salote became queen of Tonga. Queen Salote's primary concerns for her country were medicine and education. With intelligence and compassion she made friends for Tonga throughout the world and was greatly loved by her subjects and foreigners alike. Her legendary attendance at Queen Elizabeth's coronation in 1953 won many hearts as she took part in the procession bareheaded in an open carriage through London, smiling resolutely at the crowds despite pouring rain.

Her son, King Taufa'ahau Tupou IV, took over as ruler of Tonga on his mother's death in 1965. He has several notable accomplishments to his credit, including the re-establishment of full sovereignty for Tonga on 4 June 1970, and Tonga's admission to the Commonwealth of Nations and to the UN. In his later years, however, he made a number of questionable economic decisions, including selling Tongan passports and appointing an American 'court jester' who oversaw the loss of T$50 million in funds. An imposing figure who was renowned as the world's heaviest monarch, the 210kg king became a health role model for Tongans when he shed over 75kg in weight! He was 88 when he died in September 2006.

TONGA FAST FACTS

Capital city (and island) Nuku'alofa (Tongatapu)
Population 101,000
Land area 718 sq km
Number of islands 171
International telephone code ☎ 676
Currency Tongan *pa'anga* (T$)
Languages Tongan and English
Greeting *Malo e lelei* (hello)
Website www.tongaholiday.com

TONGA

A NEW KING! – A NEW DEMOCRACY?

King George Tupou V, following in the footsteps of his father, was crowned in a lavish ceremony on 1 August 2008. While most Tongans were happy to see the new king crowned and would never suggest abolishing the royal family, many would like to see an end to the nepotism, wasteful follies and corruption, and to have more of a say in the affairs of the country. And the new king agrees.

'The sovereign of the only Polynesian kingdom ... is voluntarily surrendering his powers to meet the democratic aspirations of many of his people,' said the Lord Chamberlain in a statement before the coronation. The people 'favour a more representative, elected parliament. The king agrees with them.'

Although Tonga is a constitutional monarchy, the monarch has had near-absolute power, appointing the Prime Minister and a 12-man 'cabinet for life'. Those 12 members have been permanent representatives in the 30-seat legislative assembly. The king's 30 nobles choose nine additional representatives, and the electorate chooses nine more.

But things are going to change. The King plans to 'guide his country through a period of political and economic reform for the 21st century ... His majesty wishes to ensure that the monarchy is fully prepared for elections in 2010 under a revised voting system granting the majority voice in parliament to the people.'

Time will tell whether the monocled bachelor, a graduate of Oxford and Sandhurst, the British military academy, is true to his word. While an estimated 40 per cent of Tongans live below the poverty line, the equivalent of a third of Tonga's yearly aid budget was spent on his coronation! For the official word from the top, check out www.palaceoffice.govt.to.

In the last years of his life, the king resisted growing democracy calls, peaking in a 2005 strike by public servants that lasted for months and resulted in huge growth in pro-democracy sentiment. Two months after the king's death, riots in Nuku'alofa killed eight, destroyed much of the business district, shocked the world and saw Australian and New Zealand (NZ) troops in the supposedly peaceful Pacific paradise. Nuku'alofa still bears the scars.

THE CULTURE

Tonga is a largely homogenous, church- and family-oriented society. Although on the whole Tongans are open and extremely hospitable, due to cultural nuances many foreigners feel a bit at arm's length. Patience is a virtue and Tongan time is a flexible entity.

Respectful dress is considered important in Tonga. Despite the increasing Western influence, modest dress is expected, though this code is a little more relaxed in Nuku'alofa and to a lesser extent Neiafu. Swimsuits should be worn only in resorts or on very isolated beaches; Tongans swim fully dressed. Tongan law prohibits appearing in a public place without a shirt.

You'll often see Tongans wearing distinctive pandanus mats called ta'ovala. In place of a ta'ovala, women often wear a kiekie, a decorative waistband of woven strips of pandanus. Men frequently wear a wraparound skirt known as a tupenu and women an anklelength vala (skirt) and kofu (tunic).

The concept of keeping 'face' is extremely strong in Tonga. Causing someone to lose face is a very serious social transgression, so if something does not meet your expectations, don't start waving and shouting about it.

Population

Tongans make up the vast majority of people in Tonga. There are a few palangi (Westerners) expats and a small but significant population of Chinese immigrants.

Tonga's total resident population is around 101,000. Tongatapu has more than 65% of the total population, with around 30% in Nuku'alofa (the island's and the nation's capital).

Despite steady emigration, only Ha'apai and the Niuas suffer from falling populations. Estimates suggest there are as many Tongans living abroad as there are in the kingdom, mostly in NZ, Australia and the US. Tonga's economy is highly dependent on remittances sent by Tongans living overseas; however, support from overseas relatives is decreasing as the next generation of expat Tongans become more detached from their homeland.

FAKALEITI

One of the most distinctive features of Tongan culture are *fakaleiti*, a modern continuation of an ancient Polynesian tradition, known as *fa'afafine* in Samoa and *mahu* or *rae rae* in French Polynesia.

The term *fakaleiti* is made up of the prefix *faka-* (in the manner of) and *-leiti* from the English word *lady*. Traditionally, if a Tongan woman had too many sons and not enough daughters she would need one of the sons to assist with 'woman's work' such as cooking and housecleaning. This child would then be brought up as a daughter. These days, becoming a *fakaleiti* can also be a lifestyle choice. There is little stigma attached to *fakaleiti*, and they mix easily with the rest of society, often being admired for their style.

On Tongatapu, the Tonga Leitis' Association is an active group – note that members prefer to call themselves simply *leiti* (ladies). The association sponsors several popular, well-attended events, including the international Miss Galaxy competition in early July, which attracts *fakaleiti* and transvestites from several countries.

RELIGION

Tonga is, on the surface at least, a very religious country. Ninety-nine per cent of the country identifies itself as being of Christian faith. The Free Wesleyan Church (which is the royal family's church of choice) claims the largest number of adherents, followed by the (Methodist) Free Church of Tonga, the Church of England, the Roman Catholics, Seventh Day Adventists and the wealthy and increasingly prominent Mormons.

Many Tongans still believe in the spirits, taboos, superstitions, medical charms and gods of pre-Christian Polynesia. One such belief is that if a family member is suffering a bad illness, it is because the bones of their ancestors have been disturbed. Many will return to old family burial sites, dig up remains and rebury old relatives to remedy their own ill health.

ARTS

Tongans enjoy a fine reputation for their craftsmanship in woodcarving throughout the Pacific and many excellent examples can be bought in stores, markets or from the roadside. The Tongan gods Tangaloa and Hikuleo are popular subjects. See p56 for more about Pacific carving.

The enormous Ha'amonga 'a Maui trilithon (p508) on Tongatapu is one of the most impressive carved stone structures in Polynesia.

Dance

The most frequently performed traditional dance in Tonga is called the *lakalaka*. The *tau'olunga*, a female solo dance, is the most beautiful and graceful of all Tongan dances. The most popular male dance is the *kailao* – the war dance.

Literature

Tonga Islands: William Mariner's Account by Dr John Martin (see the boxed text, p512 for more on William Mariner) and *Tales of the Tikongs* by Epeli Hau'ofa should be mandatory companion reading for anyone who's visiting Tonga. The former provides

THE SUNDAY EXPERIENCE

It is important to remember that Tonga comes to a screeching halt at midnight each Saturday night for 24 hours – Friday is the night if you want to party until the wee hours. Sunday is a day of rest and it is enshrined in Tongan law that it is illegal to work. There are no international or domestic flights; shops are closed; the streets are empty; sports are prohibited; and Tongans are going to church, feasting and resting. The tourism industry is starting to make inroads, though, and you'll find some restaurants are open.

No visitor should miss the amazing cultural experience of attending a church service in Tonga. The singing is unbelievable, whether you're at the Centenary Chapel in Nuku'alofa (p502) or in a small village church on a remote island.

BEST EATS & DRINKS

The Tongan diet consists mostly of root vegetables, coconut products, taro, fresh fruit, pork, chicken and fish, with little seasoning. Tonga's seafood is easy to come by and delicious; *ika lahi* (marinated raw fish) must be tried at least once.

Royal Coffee (www.royalcoffee.to) is tasty and made from locally grown beans. Likewise, **Ikale** (www.royalbeer.to) is the locally brewed beer. Don't go home without tasting kava!

Following are Lonely Planet's top Tongan dining experiences:

- Try a Tongan feast. The Oholei Beach & Hina Cave Feast & Show (p508) on Tongatapu is superb.
- Local foodies in Nuku'alofa rave about top-notch Luna Rossa (p507).
- Friends Café (p507) in Nuku'alofa has great food, Royal Coffee and a breezy atmosphere (everyone tries it at least once).
- Pay a visit to Mariners Café (p515) in Pangai. After a week in Ha'apai, you'll never savour a pizza in quite the same way.
- Hang out at Aquarium Café (p524) in Neiafu enjoying the tasty tapas, Ikale beer and the superb Port of Refuge views.

---

a fascinating historical background on many sights throughout the islands, while the latter is a collection of wry, satirical vignettes on life in 'Tiko' that gives the visitor an insight into the modern Tongan way of life.

Friendly Isles: A Tale of Tonga, *'Utulei, My Tongan Home* and *The Tongan Past*, by Vava'u resident Patricia Ledyard Matheson, are all books that relate anecdotes of Tongan life.

Queen Salote of Tonga, written by Elizabeth Wood-Ellem, is a warm account of the queen's life.

Island Kingdom: Tonga Ancient and Modern by Ian Campbell provides a very readable history of Tonga. With a clever play on the title, *Island Kingdom Strikes Back*, by Kalafi Moala, covers the more recent history (corruption, skulduggery and illegal arrest) in the kingdom.

Tapa

Tapa is Tonga's most renowned craft. Along with pandanus weavings, tapa is considered part of the *koloa* (wealth) of Tongan families. See p55 for further information.

LANGUAGE

Tongan is a Polynesian language similar to Samoan. Because of the conquering exploits of ancient Tongans, similar languages are spoken on Wallis Island and Niue. In Nuku'alofa at least, almost everyone can speak English, though a few basic Tongan words are always appreciated.

Tongan Basics

Hello.	Malo e lelei.
Goodbye.	'Alu a.
How are you?	Fefe hake?
I'm well (thanks).	Sai pe (malo).
Please.	Faka molemole.
Thank you (very much).	Malo (aupito).
Yes.	'Io.
No.	Ikai.

ENVIRONMENT

The Kingdom of Tonga is made up of 171 islands, scattered across 700,000 sq km of ocean. Geographically Tonga is composed of four major island groups, which are, from south to north: Tongatapu, Ha'apai, Vava'u and the Niuas.

Tonga sits on the eastern edge of the Indo-Australian plate, which has the Pacific tectonic plate sliding under it from the east, creating the Tonga Trench. This 2000km-long oceanic valley that stretches from Tonga to NZ is one of the deepest in the world – if Mt Everest was placed in the deepest part of the Tonga Trench, there would still be over 2km of water on top of it! Tonga is also moving southeast at 20mm a year, meaning that the region is a particularly volatile area for volcanic and earthquake activity.

cology

Tonga's national flower is the *heilala*. The most common plant you will see in Tonga is the coconut palm.

Dolphins and migrating humpback whales swim in the waters around Tonga. The humpbacks come from June to October and can often be seen offshore from the major islands.

The only land mammal native to Tonga is the flying fox (fruit bat).

Tonga has surprisingly few birds, but of interest are the *henga* (blue-crowned lorikeet); the *koki* (red shining parrot) of 'Eua; and the *malau* (megapode or incubator bird), originally found only on the island of Niuafo'ou, but also introduced in recent years to Late island to the west of Vava'u.

National Parks

Tonga has eight officially protected areas, including five national marine parks and reserves, one national historic park (the 23-hectare Ha'amonga Trilithon Reserve), the 449-hectare 'Eua National Park and the Mt Talau National Park in Vava'u. There are plans to declare Tofua and Kao in Ha'apai as national parks. The whole of Ha'apai is a designated conservation area.

TONGATAPU

pop 69,000 / area 260 sq km

Tongatapu (Sacred South) island is the landing and launching pad for most activity in Tonga. Most of the island's population lives in Nuku'alofa (Abode of Love) and its villages.

Tongatapu faces the islands of Fafá and Pangaimotu, and is partially bordered by Fanga 'Uta Lagoon. Outside of Nuku'alofa, the island is comprised of plots of agricultural land, small villages and plenty of churches.

Most archaeological sights – such as Lapaha and Ha'amonga 'a Maui Trilithon – are found on Tongatapu's eastern side, which also features caves, calm sandy coves, and the airport. To the west is the wilder surf coast and the Mapu'a Vaca blowholes.

INFORMATION
Bookshops
Friendly Islands Bookshop (Map pp504-5; ☎ 23787; Taufa'ahau Rd & Salote Rd) The only bookshop of any

consequence in Tonga was burnt down in the 2006 riots. Now with two stores, but a less comprehensive selection of newspapers and magazines, paperbacks, travel titles and books about Tonga.

Internet Access
Nuku'alofa has many internet cafes. Tops are the following:

Café Escape (Map pp504-5; ☎ 21212; Taufa'ahau Rd; per 15min T$2)

Friends Tourist Centre (Map pp504-5; ☎ 26323; Taufa'ahau Rd; per 15min T$2)

Medical Services
Vaiola Hospital (Map pp504-5; ☎ 23200; Taufa'ahau Rd) Recommended only for emergencies and after-hours needs.

Village Mission Pharmacy (Map pp504-5; ☎ 27522; vmissp@hotmail.com; 'Unga Rd; ☽ 8.30am-5pm Mon-Fri, 9am-noon Sat) There is a doctor either here or at its sister clinic, the Village Mission Clinic (☎ 29052) in Ha'ateiho, 5km south of Nuku'alofa. The central pharmacy is well stocked with sunscreen, insect repellent, contact-lens solution, baby formula, Gastrolyte, earplugs and the like.

Money
ANZ (Map pp504-5; ☎ 24944; www.anz.com/tonga; ☽ 9am-4pm Mon-Fri 9am-noon Sat) ANZ has two branches and six ATMs in Nuku'alofa.

MBF (Map pp504-5; ☎ 24600; Taufa'ahau Rd; ☽ 9am-4pm Mon-Fri)

Westpac Bank of Tonga (Map pp504-5; ☎ 23933; ☽ 9am-4pm Mon-Fri, 9am-noon Sat) Three branches and five ATMs in Nuku'alofa.

Post
Post office (Map pp504-5; ☎ 21700; cnr Taufa'ahau & Salote Rds; ☽ 8.30am-4pm Mon-Fri) This office has a poste restante window next to the main entrance; address to: Post Restante, GPO, Nuku'alofa, Kingdom of Tonga. Ask specifically for any larger parcels. International post cleared 2pm Monday and Friday.

Tourist Information
Friends Tourist Centre (Map pp504-5; ☎ 26323; www.friendstonga.com; Taufa'ahau Rd; ☽ 8am-10pm Mon-Fri, 8am-7.30pm Sat) A switched-on tour-booking office with plenty of details on what's happening around the kingdom.

Tonga Visitors Bureau (TVB; Map pp504-5; ☎ 25334; www.tongaholiday.com; Vuna Rd; ☽ 8.30am-4.30pm Mon-Fri, 9am-12.30pm Sat & holidays) The government-run institution with information on Tonga.

TONGA

TONGATAPU

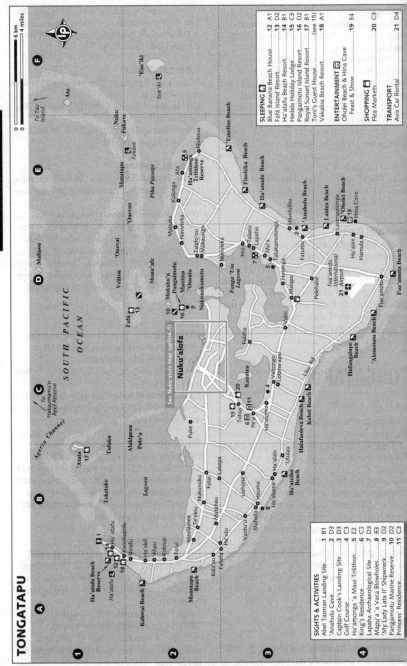

0 ————— 6 km
0 ————— 4 miles

SIGHTS & ACTIVITIES
Abel Tasman Landing Site......................1	B1
'Anahulu Cave...2	D3
Captain Cook's Landing Site..................3	D3
Golf Course...4	C3
Ha'amonga 'a Maui Trilithon................5	E2
King's Residence....................................6	C3
Lapaha Archaeological Site....................7	D3
Mapu'a 'a Vaca Blowholes....................8	B3
'My Lady Lata II' Shipwreck.................9	D2
Pangaimotu Marine Reserve.................10	D2
Princess' Residence..............................11	C3

SLEEPING
Blue Banana Beach House.....................12	A1
Fafá Island Resort.................................13	D2
Ha'atafu Beach Resort..........................14	B1
Heilala Holiday Lodge............................15	C3
Pangaimotu Island Resort.....................16	D2
Royal Sunset Island Resort....................17	B1
Toni's Guest House..................(see 15)	
Vakaloa Beach Resort...........................18	A1

ENTERTAINMENT
Oholei Beach & Hina Cave Feast & Show...............................19	E4

SHOPPING
Flea Markets..20	C3

TRANSPORT
Avis Car Rental......................................21	D4

Travel Agencies

The following agencies make bookings for local tours in addition to selling international flights:

Tsave Taufonua (Map pp504-5; ☎ 23052; www ufonua.com; Fund Management Bldg, Taufa'ahau Rd) Books ny tours and domestic package holidays to all island groups.

Jones Travel & Tours (Map pp504-5; ☎ 23423; jtl fice@travel.emjones.to; cnr Taufa'ahau & Wellington Rds)

Teta Tours (Map pp504-5; ☎ 23690; www.tetatours nga.to; cnr Wellington & Railway Rds)

GETTING THERE & AWAY

See p534 for information on transport between Tongatapu and other countries.

Air

Fua'amotu International Airport is 21km southeast and a 30-minute drive from Nuku'alofa. **Chathams Pacific** (Map pp504-5; ☎ 23192; www.chathamspacific.com) services 'Eua, Ha'apai and Vava'u from the domestic terminal. Transfers between the international and domestic terminals cost T$5 for a taxi.

Offices in Nuku'alofa of airlines connecting Tongatapu with other Pacific destinations:

Air New Zealand (Map pp504-5; ☎ 23192; www airnz.co.nz; Vuna Rd) The Air NZ Travel Centre is down on he waterfront.

Air Pacific (Map pp504-5; ☎ 23423; www.airpacific com; cnr Taufa'ahau & Wellington Rds) Contact Jones Travel & Tours.

Pacific Blue (Map pp504-5; ☎ 24566; www.virgin lue.com.au; cnr Salote & Fatafehi Rds)

Boat

MV 'Olovaha connects Tongatapu with Ha'apai, Vava'u and the Niuas. Other vessels provide frequent services between Tongatapu and 'Eua. See p535 for details of schedules and fares.

GETTING AROUND

To/From the Airport

Taxis meet all incoming flights, charging T$40 between the airport and Nuku'alofa. Many hotels and guest houses arrange transfers from the airport if you pre-book (some for free), or there are shuttles that will take you into town for T$10 to T$20 per person.

Bicycle

Some guest houses have bicycles for guest use.

Niko's Bicycle Rental (Map pp504-5; Waterfront, Vuna Rd; half-/full-day bicycle hire T$8/15) is next to the International Dateline Hotel.

Boat

The offshore island resorts all provide boat transport.

Bus

Buses are run privately. There are no public buses and no fixed timetables. Nuku'alofa's two bus terminals are on Vuna Rd. Buses to outlying areas of Tongatapu depart from the western terminal (close to Vuna Wharf; Map pp504–5), while Nuku'alofa buses leave from the eastern terminal (opposite the TVB; Map pp504–5). Fares range from 70 *seniti* to T$1.70. Bus services run from about 8am to 5pm, and there are no buses on Sunday.

In urban areas, bus stops are marked with a small sign reading 'Pasi'. Elsewhere, flag down a bus by waving.

Car & Minibus

Car- and minibus-hire companies generally offer unlimited kilometres included in their rates, and some offer special rates for weekends or long-term rental. Legally, you must get a Tongan driving licence from the police before heading out. Contact Fab and Sunshine by telephone, as they will deliver rental cars to you. Companies include the following:

Avis (Map pp504-5; ☎ 21179, airport 35224; www .avis.com; Fund Management Bldg, Taufa'ahau Rd) From T$80 per day.

Fab Rentals (☎ 23077; rogerlee@kalianet.to; Salote Rd, Maufanga) Cars and vans for T$50 to T$60 per day, including insurance and door-to-door service.

Sunshine Rental Cars (☎ /fax 23848; sunshinerental cars@yahoo.com; Lopaukamea, Nuku'alofa) Cars from T$50 per day.

Taxi

Taxis charge a minimum fare of T$3 for the first kilometre and 70c for each additional kilometre. Ask for the fare to your destination before you agree to pay or get in. Taxis have a 'T' on the licence plate and are not permitted to operate on Sunday, but some guest houses know secret Sunday taxi suppliers. Taxi companies include the following:

Atelaite Taxi (☎ 23919)
Holiday Taxi (☎ 25655)
Wellington Taxi (☎ 24744)

TONGA

TONGATAPU IN...

Two Days

Find your bearings on a circumnavigational **island tour** (opposite), exploring archaeological marvels, caves and seaside cemeteries, witnessing the blowholes in action and getting acquainted with Tongatapu's western beaches. Alight in Nuku'alofa to soak up the sunset tones over the waterfront, then dine on superb seafood around at **Luna Rossa** (p507) by the lagoon. On day two, join the bustle and explore the wares at **Talamahu Market** (below). Take a break with a Royal Coffee at **Friends Café** (p507), before perusing the capital's sights on foot. Later, join the tasty feast and entertaining show at **Oholei Beach & Hina Cave** (p508).

Four Days

Follow the two-day itinerary, then head over by plane or ferry to **'Eua** (p510) to hike in its dramatic landscape and soak up impressive ocean views, particularly during whale season. Or head for Tongatapu's **outer islands** (p510) for beachside frolics and navel gazing. Spend a night on one of these islands, then after a lazy morning, return to Nuku'alofa and wander down to the **Billfish Bar & Restaurant** (p507) for an Ikale beer (or two!) and enjoy good food in relaxed surroundings.

NUKU'ALOFA
pop 23,000

Nuku'alofa is the kingdom's seat of government and home of the royal family. While it may not fulfil a vision of Pacific paradise, Tonga's 'big smoke' (sometimes referred to as 'dirty nuke') still has a little charm and promise if you blow the dust from its surface and ignore the scars of the 2006 riots. Its broad waterfront strip provides magnificent views across the bay to beautiful coral islands (just a boat ride away); there's a bustling market and, enviable quality dining options for a place its size; and you'll still find the occasional chicken roaming in the main street.

Sights
ROYAL PALACE
Surrounded by large lawns and Norfolk pines, the white Victorian-style Royal Palace, erected in 1867, is a symbol of Tonga to the rest of the world. The palace grounds are not open to visitors but you can get a good view from the waterfront area on the west side.

ROYAL TOMBS
The Mala'ekula, the large parklike area opposite the basilica, has been the resting place of the royals since 1893. It's off limits to the public but you can peer through the crested perimeter fence.

CHURCHES
Royal watchers/rubberneckers (regardless of denomination) head to the 1952 **Centenary Chapel** (Wellington Rd) to catch a glimpse of members of the royal family at a Sunday service and to hear the magnificent, booming singing of the congregation. Dress well.

Nuku'alofa's most distinctive structure is the **Basilica of St Anthony of Padua** (Taufa'ahau Rd), opposite the Royal Tombs. It has a beautiful interior of stained glass, wooden beams and hand-crafted furnishings.

St Mary's Cathedral (Vuna Rd), near Faua Jetty, is worth visiting for its beautiful rose gardens, stained glass and vaulted ceiling.

TALAMAHU MARKET
One of Nuku'alofa's most interesting sights is **Talamahu** (Salote Rd; ⏰ early morning-4.30pm Mon-Sat), the kingdom's main fresh-produce hub. You'll find produce in handmade woven frond baskets, branches of bananas, colourful pyramids of weighed-out produce and a few food stands – plus excellent Tongan arts and crafts. A hive of activity, particularly on Saturday mornings.

TONGAN NATIONAL CENTRE
The centre was closed at the time of research, but there were assurances it would be re-opening before long. It would be a major feat to spend any time in Tonga without having some sort of cultural experience, but a visit to the **Tongan National Centre** (☎ 23022; Taufa'ahau Rd, Vaiola; admission free; ⏰ 9am-4pm Mon-Fri) is a good spot to start. The museum contains historical artefacts and cultural items still in use today. **Cultural tours** (adult/child T$15/8; ⏰ tours 2pm Mon-

ri) include demonstrations of tapa making, weaving and basketry, traditional dancing and carving.

Activities

DIVING & SNORKELLING

Around the Tongatapu Group subaquatic adventures range from snorkelling around the wreck off Pangaimotu and the excellent Makaha'a Reef to diving 'Eua's unique sea caves.

Deep Blue Diving (☎ 26203; www.deepbluediving to; Faua Jetty) offers a number of diving options, its major drawcards being 'Eua's enormous sea caves and the beautiful uninhabited islands north of Tongatapu. It also has Deep Blue Lodge, providing accommodation five minutes' walk from central Nuku'alofa. Introductory dives cost T$170; two-tank dives inner/outer reef T$180/300.

Royal Sunset Island Resort (Map p500; ☎ 21254; www.royalsunset.biz) on 'Atata is close to a host of dive sites. It offers one-/two-tank dives for T$90/168; packages for five/10 dives T$580/1,060. No introductory dives or PADI certification.

FISHING

Deep Blue Diving (☎ 26203; www.deepbluediving.to; Faua Jetty) offers bottom fishing for a half-/full day for T$575/800, trawling for a half-/full day for T$690/1100 for up to four people.

Royal Sunset Island Resort (Map p500; ☎ 21254; www.royalsunset.biz) offers half-/full-day game fishing for T$642.50/987.50 (maximum four anglers).

GOLF

Take a swing at Tonga's only **golf course** (Map p500; ☎ 8704194), a relaxed nine-hole affair at 'Atele on the way to the airport. Green fees are T$20/30 for nine/18 holes with rental gear included. Nothing stuffy here – singlet and jandals are fine.

SAILING

Head out for a sail with **Seastar Yacht Charters** (☎ 22800; www.seastar.to) for day or overnight cruising. Look at the website for all the options.

SURFING

Tongatapu's northwest coast, off Ha'atafu Beach, is renowned for its surf. Steve Burling at **Ha'atafu Beach Resort** (Map p500; ☎ 41088; www.surfingtonga.com; Ha'atafu) knows it all from 28 years surfing in Tonga. Check out his informative website.

WHALE-WATCHING

Whale-watching can be arranged through Deep Blue Diving and Royal Sunset Island Resort (see left).

Tours

Tongatapu's main sights can be comfortably covered in a day tour of the island. Most tour operators require a minimum of four people.
Supa Tours (☎ 16450; phlatohi@kalianet.to) Big John runs Tongatapu island tours (T$75 per person for two people, T$40 per person for four people). Plenty of time for lunch and swimming along the way. Arrange a meeting point when you call.
Toni's Tours (☎ 21049, 48720; www.geocities.com /tmatthias2000) Toni's popular island tours (T$40) run daily (minimum three people). Take food and drinks, swimming gear and good shoes.

Sleeping

Houses and flats for rent are listed at the TVB and on the bulletin board at Friends Tourist Centre. Prices start around T$400/500 per month for a furnished apartment/house; elegance will set you back upwards of T$850 per month. Self-contained apartments in Nuku'alofa:
Captain Cook Vacation Apartments (☎ 25600; info@captaincook.to; Vuna Rd; d apt T$150, extra person T$25; ☒) Two-bedroom apartments on the waterfront. Long stay discounts.
Lagoon Lodge (☎ 26515; lagoon.lodge@kalianet.to; 'Umusi; 1-/2-bed apt from T$165/260) Bright, lagoonside apartments. You'll need to take a taxi or hire a car. Long stay discounts.
Marketonga (☎ 75623; www.marketonga.to) Deals in furnished rental properties.

BUDGET

Midrange options, including Ali Baba's Guest House and Heilala Holiday Lodge, also offer excellent budget rooms.
Toni's Guest House (Map p500; ☎ 21049, 48720; www .geocities.com/tmatthias2000; Tofua; dm T$15-20) Toni's is an expanding budget favourite, virtually overtaking the neighbourhood in Tofoa, 3km south of Nuku'alofa. It's renowned for regular kava sessions, popular tours and brightly coloured buildings. Toni's offers a shuttle service to/from town for T$1 and airport transfers for T$10.

TONGA

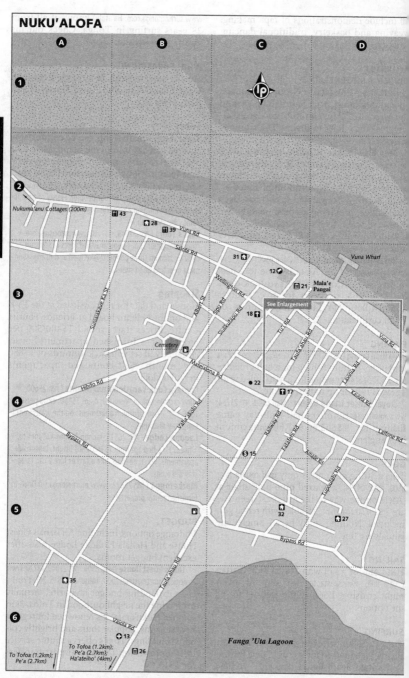

NUKU'ALOFA

Nukuma'anu Cottages (200m)

Vuna Rd

Salote Rd

Wellington Rd

Albert St

Sipu Rd

Siulikutapu Rd

Vuna Wharf

Mala'e Pangai

See Enlargement

Tui Rd

Taufa'ahau Rd

Vuna Rd

Laumia Rd

Kanela Rd

Cemetery

Mateialona Rd

Hihifo Rd

Vaha'akolo Rd

Railway Rd

Fatafehi Rd

Amalie Rd

Laifone Rd

Bypass Rd

Tupoulahi Rd

Taufa'ahau Rd

Bypass Rd

Vaiola Rd

Fanga 'Uta Lagoon

To Tofoa (1.2km);
Pe'a (2.7km)

To Tofoa (1.2km);
Pe'a (2.7km);
Ha'ateiho' (4km)

43

28

39

31

12

21

18

17

22

15

32

27

35

13

26

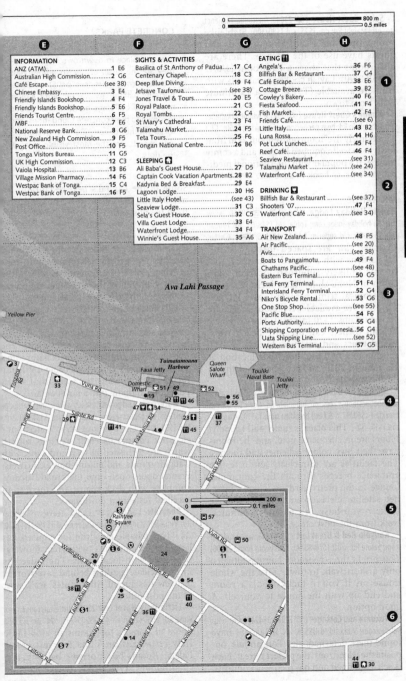

INFORMATION
ANZ (ATM).....................................1 E6
Australian High Commission.........2 G6
Café Escape.............................(see 38)
Chinese Embassy............................3 E4
Friendly Islands Bookshop..............4 F4
Friendly Islands Bookshop..............5 E6
Friends Tourist Centre.....................6 F5
MBF...7 E6
National Reserve Bank....................8 G6
New Zealand High Commission......9 F5
Post Office...................................10 F5
Tonga Visitors Bureau...................11 G5
UK High Commission....................12 G5
Vaiola Hospital.............................13 B6
Village Mission Pharmacy.............14 B6
Westpac Bank of Tonga................15 C4
Westpac Bank of Tonga................16 F5

SIGHTS & ACTIVITIES
Basilica of St Anthony of Padua.....17 C4
Centenary Chapel..........................18 C3
Deep Blue Diving..........................19 F4
Jetsave Taufonua.....................(see 38)
Jones Travel & Tours.....................20 E5
Royal Palace.................................21 C3
Royal Tombs.................................22 C4
St Mary's Cathedral......................23 F4
Talamahu Market..........................24 F4
Teta Tours....................................25 F6
Tongan National Centre................26 B6

SLEEPING
Ali Baba's Guest House..................27 D5
Captain Cook Vacation Apartments..28 B2
Kadynia Bed & Breakfast...............29 E4
Lagoon Lodge...............................30 H6
Little Italy Hotel.......................(see 43)
Seaview Lodge..............................31 C3
Sela's Guest House........................32 C5
Villa Guest Lodge.........................33 E4
Waterfront Lodge..........................34 F4
Winnie's Guest House...................35 A6

EATING
Angela's.......................................36 F6
Billfish Bar & Restaurant...............37 G4
Café Escape..................................38 E6
Cottage Breeze.............................39 B2
Cowley's Bakery............................40 F6
Fiesta Seafood...............................41 F4
Fish Market...................................42 F4
Friends Café............................(see 6)
Little Italy....................................43 B2
Luna Rossa...................................44 H6
Pot Luck Lunches..........................45 F4
Reef Café......................................46 F4
Seaview Restaurant...................(see 31)
Talamahu Market.....................(see 24)
Waterfront Café.......................(see 34)

DRINKING
Billfish Bar & Restaurant ....(see 37)
Shooters '07.................................47 F4
Waterfront Café ....(see 34)

TRANSPORT
Air New Zealand...........................48 F5
Air Pacific.................................(see 20)
Avis...(see 38)
Boats to Pangaimotu.....................49 F4
Chathams Pacific......................(see 48)
Eastern Bus Terminal.....................50 G5
'Eua Ferry Terminal.......................51 F6
Interisland Ferry Terminal..............52 G4
Niko's Bicycle Rental.....................53 G6
One Stop Shop.........................(see 55)
Pacific Blue..................................54 F6
Ports Authority.............................55 G4
Shipping Corporation of Polynesia..56 G4
Uata Shipping Line...................(see 52)
Western Bus Terminal...................57 G5

TONGA

Sela's Guest House (☎ 25040; mettonga@kalianet .to; off Fatafehi Rd; dm T$25, s/d T$80/100) Stablelike rooms open off a central courtyard, and guests have use of the kitchen. There are also rooms that share a bathroom (s/d/tr T$35/60/90). Lavish cooked breakfasts with fruit are available (T$15). It's a 15-minute walk from town.

Winnie's Guest House (☎ 25215; winnies@kalianet .to; Vaha'akolo Rd; beds per person incl breakfast T$50; 🖳) This homely five-room house about 2km from town has a well-equipped kitchen and a comfy lounge. It's popular with international medical students, so book in advance.

MIDRANGE

Heilala Holiday Lodge (Map p500; ☎ 29910; www .heilala-holiday-lodge.com; Tofua; s/d T$48/68, s/d Tongan fale T$68/95, s/d superior fale T$115/145; 🖳) Cute, thatched *fale* are spaced through tropical gardens with a shaded swimming pool in this unlikely suburban location, 3km south of Nuku'alofa. Rates include a toast and tropical trims breakfast, and kitchen facilities are available. Delicious meals are served (mains T$20 to T$28). The extremely helpful owners can organise beach trips, island tours and car hire. Heilala will be moving to a beautiful beachside location at Ha'atafu in 2010, so keep abreast of things on the website.

our pick **Ali Baba's Guest House** (☎ 25154; www .alibabaguesthouse.com; off Tupoulahi Rd, Ngele'ia; s/d incl breakfast T$60/80, d & f incl breakfast from T$110, extra person T$10; 🖳) This place is funky and friendly. Floors are in chequered gold, and the rooms have their own colour schemes and themes. The facilities are ultraclean, and a festive ambience breezes through the communal lounge to the pretty gardens. There's internet, satellite television and a book exchange to keep you busy. It's about 15 minutes' walk from the post office.

Kadynia Bed & Breakfast (☎ 46018; www.kadynia .com; Salote Rd; s/d/f T$70/80/90, 3-bedroom house T$200) This bright three-bedroom house is situated only a short walk to town. Take the whole house or, if you're lucky, book a room and end up with the house to yourself. A good option.

Nukuma'anu Cottages (☎ 22186, 15424; www.tonga holiday.com; Vuna Rd; d US$78; 🌐) Readers have found these detached, airy Tongan *fale*, opposite the waterfront, the perfect retreat. Each is self-contained and has plenty of comforts.

Some of the capital's best restaurants are nearby, and it's a short drive or good stroll from the post office.

TOP END

Establishments in this category have cable/ satellite TV, private telephones and some of Nuku'alofa's best restaurants attached to them. While all of these options are on the waterfront, there is no real beach here.

Villa Guest Lodge (☎ 24998; www.tongavilla.com; Vuna Rd; s/d/tr incl breakfast NZ$104/127/152; 🌐 🖳) An elegant and attractive lodge that is centrally located and close to good restaurants. The five double rooms have compact bathrooms. There's a huge lounge with cable TV and a broad balcony facing the waterfront – just perfect for dipping into a novel or two.

Waterfront Lodge (☎ 24692; www.waterfront-lodge .com; Vuna Rd; garden/seaview d incl breakfast T$184/200, extra bed T$50; 🌐) The boutique-style Waterfront's elegance colours its eight spacious rooms, which are furnished in teak and cane, with Gauguin prints and marine-blue bed covers. French doors open onto the broad balcony, complete with deck chairs; and there is an excellent restaurant downstairs.

Seaview Lodge (☎ 23709; seaview@kalianet .to; Vuna Rd; standard/garden/seaview d T$195/235/270; 🌐) This reliable favourite for regulars has large balconied rooms (with great showers) decorated with local crafts. The lodge sits in immaculate gardens behind rave-worthy Seaview Restaurant, 10 minutes' walk west of the post office.

Little Italy Hotel (☎ 25053; littleitalytonga.com; Vuna Rd; pool/ocean view r T$205/235; 🌐 🖳) Two floors of Tonga's top rooms sit atop Little Italy restaurant on Vuna Rd west of the Palace. Rooms boast private balcony, air-conditioning, coffee maker, refrigerator and free wireless internet access. There's even a radio in the shower!

Eating

Nuku'alofa's decent spread of cafes and restaurants are mostly stretched along the waterfront, Vuna Rd, and on or nearby the main drag, Taufa'ahau Rd.

Tongan cuisine can be sampled at island-style buffets and feasts (see p508).

CAFES

Friends Café (☎ 22390; Taufa'ahau Rd; breakfast from T$5, mains T$9.50-20; ☼ breakfast, lunch & dinner Mon-Fri, breakfast & lunch Sat) With a breezy charm and dependably good food, Friends, on the opposite corner from the post office in the centre of town, is deservedly popular with visitors and locals alike. Everything from panini to seafood chowder to stacked burgers.

Café Escape (☎ 21212; Taufa'ahau Rd; breakfast T$5-16, mains T$8-16; ☼ breakfast, lunch & dinner Mon-Fri, to 4.30pm Sat) Slick little Café Escape could be anywhere but provides a refined, air-con oasis and infuses the tropics into its mixed menu. Locals claim it has the best coffee in Tonga.

Reef Café (☎ 26777; Vuna Rd; breakfast T$5-16, mains T$8-20; ☼ breakfast Mon-Sat, lunch & dinner) With the attraction of being open on Sunday for lunch and dinner, the Reef has a certain ambience down at the domestic wharf. Casual and well-priced dining from a changing blackboard menu.

RESTAURANTS

Pot Luck Lunches (☎ 25091; off Salote Rd; lunch T$4-6; ☼ lunch Mon-Fri) Take pot luck on the one set meal prepared in the training restaurant at 'Ahopanilolo College behind St Mary's Cathedral.

Angela's (☎ 23930; Wellington Rd; mains T$8-25 ☼ lunch & dinner) Gets the nod for top Chinese restaurant in town. Good value. It's licensed and takeaways are available.

Billfish Bar & Restaurant (☎ 24084; Vuna Rd; meals T$10-32; ☼ lunch & dinner Mon-Sat) This is the closest you'll get to pub-style meals – and they're great. Choose from burgers, mountainous chicken stir-fry, Thai fish curry, ultrafresh fish and chips, NZ steaks and garlic prawns. There's often live music; see p508.

Little Italy (☎ 25053; Vuna Rd; pizza & pasta T$14-20; ☼ lunch & dinner Mon-Sat) The Alps meet the Pacific in this Tonganified trattoria where pizzas, pastas and homemade Italian desserts plump up the menu. A local favourite since

1996, now with two floors of hotel rooms on top!

Cottage Breeze (☎ 28940; Vuna Rd; mains T$16-30; ☼ lunch & dinner Tue-Sun) Earning a glowing reputation, this place on Vuna Rd to the west of the palace offers consistently good food and service. Everything from pork ribs to seafood grills.

Fiesta Seafood (☎ 56062; Salote Rd; T$15-30; ☼ lunch & dinner Mon-Sat) Reasonably priced fresh seafood – the soup is superb – back on Salote Rd. Licensed and open until 11pm daily.

Waterfront Café (☎ 24692; www.waterfront-lodge.com; Vuna Rd; mains T$20-40; ☼ breakfast, lunch & dinner Mon-Sat) Soak up the stylishly breezy mood and follow sundowners with reasonable meals of pasta (with truffle sauce), fish parcels, scotch-fillet steak, lobster and seafood.

Seaview Restaurant (☎ 23709; Vuna Rd; mains T$30-45; ☼ dinner Mon-Fri) Seaview has long been on the lips of seafood-loving locals and expats. Specialises in seafood and steak down Vuna Rd west of the Palace. Bookings recommended.

our pick **Luna Rossa Restaurant** (☎ 26324; www.lunarossarestaurant.net; Lagoon Lodge; mains T$18-39; ☼ dinner Mon-Fri; ☒) You'll need a car or taxi to get here – owner Marco's place in town was burnt down in the riots – but it will be worth it for sophisticates. This is intimate fine dining on authentic Italian cuisine, with the bonus of ultrafresh and well-prepared seafood. The food is complemented by excellent service and good wines. Turn up on the right day and you could be sitting next to royalty!

SELF-CATERING

Talamahu Market (Salote Rd; ☼ early morning-4.30pm Mon-Sat) Fruit and vegetables are sold by the pyramid (around T$2 to T$3) or woven frond basket (for root crops and coconuts) with prices generally marked. The fish market on Tuimatamoana Harbour starts when boats come in around 5am Monday to Saturday.

Cowley's Bakery (The Bread Bin; ☎ 26019; Salote Rd; baked goods 50 seniti-T$2; ☼ 6am-10pm Mon-Sat, noon-midnight Sun) Does a brisk trade in baked goods including meat pies, pull-apart savoury breads, muffins, doughnuts and lurid pineapple-iced cupcakes.

Drinking

Tongans drink with enthusiasm and Nuku'alofa has a spirited bar scene, ranging from upmarket to unashamedly seedy. Friday

TONGA

is the big night, as everywhere closes at midnight on Saturday.

Inquire locally about recommended kava circles (which you may be invited to join). Ordinarily a male-only affair, both men and women are welcome around the kava bowl at Toni's Guest House (p503).

A few popular venues line the waterfront on Vuna Rd.

Billfish Bar & Restaurant (☎ 24084; Vuna Rd; ✆ 9am-2am Mon-Thu, 9am-4am Fri, 5pm-11.59pm Sat) The most popular bar in town, this relaxed open-air place (with decent food; see p507) regularly has live music.

Waterfront Café (☎ 21004; Vuna Rd; ✆ 10am-late) An upmarket watering hole. Sip on sundowner champagne cocktails, margaritas and daiquiris or a cool beer, and sink into the rattan chairs at this colonial-style bar-restaurant.

Shooters '07 (☎ 28701; Vuna Rd; ✆ 10am-late Mon-Fri, to midnight Sat) This place serves it all, from simple meals to beers and cocktails. There's a big screen for sporting events plus a dance floor and pool tables. Has the potential to get a bit rough if you stay past your bedtime.

Entertainment

ourpick **Oholei Beach & Hina Cave Feast & Show** (Map p500; ☎ 11733; simana.kami@bigpond.com; T$45 buffet & show; ✆ 7pm). While other such shows have gone downhill of late, this one has spectacularly resurfaced after a break of a couple of decades. The evening starts with entertainment on sandy Oholei Beach, followed by a tasty Tongan feast. The highlight, though, is the dancing in Hina Cave: professionally and enthusiastically done. Transfers from accommodation throughout Tongatapu to this southeast coast location are included.

Shopping

Tongan arts, crafts and carvings are sold on both floors of the Talamahu Market (p502) and in various shops along Taufa'ahau Rd.

Join the locals and rifle through the stalls at the **flea markets** (Map p500; Taufa'ahau & Vuna Rds; ✆ Sat morning) to find some old weavings and mats, and a change to the traveller's wardrobe: secondhand clothes, presoftened Hawaiian shirts.

AROUND THE ISLAND

Tongatapu features beaches, caves, blowholes and coral reefs, as well as some of the most

extensive excavated archaeological sites in the Pacific. As buses are sporadic and taxis expensive, the best way to see the sights is by island tour (see p503) or rental car.

Eastern Tongatapu

East of Nuku'alofa, between Tofoa and Pe'a, you'll pass the **royal residences** of the Princess, adorned with white tigers and cannon, and the King, an austere European-style hill-top palace, opposite.

A cairn above a mangrove inlet near Holonga village marks **Captain Cook's landing site**.

MU'A (LAPAHA)

The Mu'a area contains the richest concentration of archaeological remnants in Tonga. In AD 1200 the 11th Tu'i Tonga, Tu'itatui, moved the royal capital from Heketa (near present-day Niutoua) to Lapaha, now known as Mu'a. There are 28 royal stone tombs (*langi*) in the area (15 of which are monumental), built with enormous limestone slabs. These were carried by canoes either from nearby Pangaimotu, Motutapu and other parts of Tongatapu, or possibly from as far away as Ha'apai.

Turn towards the sea on the dirt road just north of the Catholic church to reach a grassy area with two monumental mounds. This is Tonga's most imposing ancient burial site. The structure closest to the main road is the **Paepae 'o Tele'a** (Platform of Tele'a), a pyramid-like stone memorial. Tele'a was a Tu'i Tonga who reigned during the 16th century. The other, the **Langi Namoala**, has a fine example of a *fonualoto* (vault for a corpse) on top – thought to be the burial site of a female chief.

To the northeast is the **'Esi'aikona**, an elevated platform used as a rest area by the chief and his family.

HA'AMONGA 'A MAUI TRILITHON

The South Pacific's equivalent of Stonehenge, the Ha'amonga 'a Maui (Maui's Burden) **trilithon** near Niutoua, is one of ancient Polynesia's most intriguing monuments. Archaeologists and oral history credit its construction to Tu'itatui, the 11th Tu'i Tonga. The structure consists of three large coralline stones, each weighing about 40 tonnes, arranged into a trilithic gate; it's preserved in the national historic reserve.

It is now widely accepted that the trilithon had a similar function to Britain's Stonehenge: to track the changing seasons. Vegetation in line with the arms of the double-V design between the trilithon and the sea was cleared in 1967, and on the winter solstice the sun was seen to rise and set in perfect alignment with the clearings. On the summer solstice, the sun rose and set along the two other arms.

A walking track winds northward past several *langi* (known as the *Langi Heketa*), including **'Esi Makafakinanga**, supposedly Tu'itatui's backrest. Such chiefly backrests were common in Polynesia, and apparently Tu'itatui used this one as a shield against attack from behind while he watched construction.

Take the infrequent Niutoua bus (T$1) and get off about 1km before Niutoua; the driver can indicate the spot.

'ANAHULU CAVE

Tonga's most famous cave is an overloved, slightly eerie place full of stalactites and stalagmites blackened from the soot of flamingfrond torches and too much traffic. The cool, refreshing pool is a popular swimming spot. Bring a torch.

Buses run to tidy Haveluliku (or Fatumu just to the south) once or twice a day (T$1.50), or walk 3km from Mu'a.

Western Tongatapu

Tongatapu's west side is considered the island's 'scenic side'. A series of coves divided by rocky outcrops slope gently into clear pools on the southern coast, providing excellent swimming at high tide and an opportunity for observing the variety of marine life trapped at low tide. **Keleti Beach** and **Halafuoleva Beach** make good spots. The outer reef consists of a line of terraces and blowholes that shoot like geysers when the waves hit them at high tide. Do not swim too close to the blowholes – there's a powerful vortex that can suck you under. Taxis from Nuku'alofa cost around T$20 each way.

MAPU'A 'A VACA BLOWHOLES

On an especially good day at Mapu'a 'a Vaca (Chief's Whistles), hundreds of blowholes spurt at once. They are best viewed on a windy day with a strong swell, when the water, forced up through natural vents in the coralline limestone, can shoot 30m into the air. The blowholes stretch 5km along the south coast, near the village of Houma.

To get there by public transport, take a bus from Nuku'alofa to Houma and walk 1km south to the parking area above the blowholes.

HA'ATAFU BEACH RESERVE

On the sunset side of the island, the Ha'atafu Beach Reserve encompasses Ha'atafu's clean, sandy beach and surrounding reef. There's protected swimming and reasonable snorkelling at high tide in the broad lagoon, and the reef-breaks offer some of the best surfing in Tonga (suitable for more experienced surfers). If your timing is good, you may see whales swimming outside the reef from the beach (June to November).

The Hihifo bus passes all western Tongatapu's resorts; one-way fares from Nuku'alofa cost T$1.50. A taxi costs T$25 to T$30.

SLEEPING & EATING

Some of the resorts at Ha'atafu are looking decidedly run down. The following should meet expectations.

Ha'atafu Beach Resort (☎ 41088; www.surfing tonga.com; dm A$55, garden/beachfront fale per person A$65/75, child 2-12yr A$40) Mainly catering to all-inclusive surfing holidays, this lovely family-run set-up is as laid-back and peaceful as you'd expect. Paths connect thatched-roof bungalows to clean, shared facilities and the dining room. Rates here include full breakfast and buffet dinner. Facilities including snorkelling gear and paddle skis are for guest-use only. Its owner, Steve, is a Tonga surfing guru.

our pick Blue Banana Beach House (☎ 41575; www.bluebananastudios.com; d or tw per night/week small fale A$80/500, big fale A$130/860, minimum 3 nights) Looking for an attractive, secluded, self-contained studio cabin nestled among trees on the beach edge all to yourself? The beautifully decorated Blue Banana *fale* provide the beauty of an offshore island with the convenience of the mainland. Bring supplies or dine over the road at Vakaloa Beach Resort.

Vakaloa Beach Resort (☎ 41234; www.vakaloa beachresort.to; garden/ocean view fale T$220/280) Under new ownership, the Vakaloa is sprucing up. The restaurant can seat 200 and is open to nonguests and for functions. The rooms are tidy, clean and well furnished. A good upmarket choice at Ha'atafu Beach.

TONGA

OFFSHORE ISLANDS & REEFS
Pangaimotu

Only 10 minutes by boat from Nuku'alofa, Pangaimotu is the closest island resort.

Pangaimotu Island Resort (☎ 15762; pangaimotu _island@yahoo.com.au; tent site/hire T$10/5, dm T$35, s/d 1st night T$60/90, subsequent nights T$50/80) overlooks the water and Nuku'alofa and has five rustic, thatched *fale*. This place receives mixed reviews. If you're after a bit of comfort, stay somewhere else. There's good snorkelling in the marine reserve and around the half-submerged wreck of *My Lady Lata II* near the landing site. Snorkelling gear and fins (T$5 each) are available.

Sunday trips to Pangaimotu leave from the domestic wharf at Nuku'alofa at 10am, 11am, noon and 1pm, returning at 3pm, 4pm, 5pm and 6pm. From Monday to Saturday the boat leaves at 10am and 11am, returning at 4pm and 5pm. The trip (adult/child return T$15/6) takes about 10 minutes.

Fafá Island

The most elegant of Tongatapu's island resorts is **Fafá Island Resort** (☎ 22800; www.fafa.to; d & tw superior fale US$212, deluxe fale US$280, half-/full board US$59/70), set on a magnificent beach. The traditional-style *fale* are perfect in their simplicity, with tall wood-shingle roofs and walls of woven palm leaves; private garden bathrooms have solar hot water. The restaurant serves Euro–Asian–Tongan dishes featuring plenty of local seafood; it also hosts a weekly culture show and feast.

Day trips to Fafá (T$57.50 including lunch) depart Faua Jetty at 11am and return at 4.30pm daily. One-way airport/Nuku'alofa to island transfers cost US$25/12.

'Atata

'Atata, 10km from Tongatapu, has lovely beaches, a small fishing village at its northern end and the **Royal Sunset Island Resort** (☎ 21254; www.royalsunset.biz; bungalow d east side T$250, west side T$330, superior T$350, half-/full board T$94/106; 🏊). Beachfront bungalows have a private bathroom, ceiling fan, fridge and tea- and coffee-making facilities. The resort's Polynesian-style restaurant–bar is an incredible structure supported by immense wooden beams. Snorkelling, diving (see p503) and fishing are possible. Standards have slipped in the past decade, but new owners are refurbishing and renovating.

Sunday day trips including lunch and boa transfers (45 minutes) cost T$62. The boa leaves Tuimatamoana Harbour at 10am and returns at 4pm.

'Eua
pop 5000 / area 87 sq km

Rugged 'Eua is a slice of natural paradise all its own. Known as 'the forgotten island', it is 40km southeast of Tongatapu, and geologically the oldest island in Tonga and one of the oldest in the Pacific. With its own species of plants, trees and the endemic red shining parrot, 'Eua has a growing awareness of itself as a unique ecotourism destination.

SIGHTS & ACTIVITIES

The ocean crashes over rocks on 'Eua's shore, providing few safe swimming beaches, though wading in rock pools at the right tide is an option.

Northern 'Eua

'Eua's northern tip is relatively inaccessible, but has some impressive features, including **Kahana Spring** and the nearby dramatic cliff-top **viewpoints**, from where you can scramble down to isolated **Fangutave Beach**. From there it's possible to hike through the rainforest to some spectacular hidden **caves**. The tracks can be difficult to find, so seek local advice or, better still, go with a local guide (see opposite).

Central 'Eua

The eastern part of central 'Eua is covered with Tonga's greatest extent of natural rainforest, with dense junglelike growth, giant tree ferns and vines and enormous, ancient banyan trees. The 'Eua National Park and 'Eua Plantation Forest cover much of the area, which is underlaid with eroded limestone, causing a Swiss-cheese landscape of caves and sinkholes. Pick up a map of trails from the Hideaway (opposite).

Central 'Eua's highlights are the **Hafu Pool**; the dramatic **Lauua & Lokupo lookouts** overlooking the park, beach and pounding ocean; and the **'Ana Kuma** (Rat's Cave), where those who brave the unnerving drop into it are rewarded by spectacular views.

Southern 'Eua

Southern 'Eua's **Lakufa'anga** area contains the island's finest geological features. The area's most prominent site is the **Rock Garden**, a collection of bizarrely shaped eroded coral slabs surrounded by a grassy meadow with wild horses. Close by is the **Liangahu'o 'a Maui**, a giant limestone arch. Across the arch is the **Bowl of Cliffs**, an impressive half-circle of cliffs between which the sea churns like a flushing toilet bowl.

TOURS

Hideaway (below) is a well-organised operator running various tours and the island's top accommodation. It assists guests to plan unguided hikes and runs guided walks to 'Eua's prime sites that include guide, transport and lunch – there are four options. Check out the website. It also runs whale-watching boat trips (T$100 per person – minimum of 3 people). If you're really lucky, you'll also be able to see whales from your room or the bar. 4WD tours head to parts of rugged 'Eua that are inaccessible any other way. It also rents out bicycles for T$15 per day.

Contact Deep Blue Diving (p503) to experience Tonga's largest sea caves, just off 'Eua, in visibility of over 60m all year round. One is likened to a cathedral.

SLEEPING

All accommodation on 'Eua is of the budget variety.

ourpick Hideaway (☎ 50255; www.kalianet.to/hideawayeua; Tufuvai village; camping T$12, s/d/tr/q incl breakfast T$55/70/85/100) This is the first choice for most travellers to 'Eua. Its viewing platform, built over the rocky shore, makes for fantastic sunset viewing and whale-watching (June to November). Comfortable motel-style rooms have good, hot showers. Rates include continental breakfast and transfers, and are cheaper in the November-to-May off-season. Dinner is available for T$20.

Taina's Place (☎ 50186; Telefoni Rd; camping per tent T$15, tent hire T$15, cabin s/d T$25/35) Five cute houses are arranged in gardens near the forest. Bathroom facilities are nearby, and the communal lounge/kitchen area is an easy spot to relax in.

Deep Resort (☎ 50421; moanas@kalianet.to; Tufuvai village; dm T$25, s/d incl breakfast T$45/60) Three newish and roomy log-look cabins in an unbeatable position on Tufuvai Beach. It provides transfers and also does meals.

EATING

Cooked meals are available at all accommodation places, for guests and nonguests (book by noon). The most popular is the Hideaway's ocean-view bar–restaurant (dinner T$18 to T$20), while the Deep Resort's Tongan-style bar–restaurant (meals T$7.50 to T$20) is a charming spot to sit and soak up afternoon beverages and crashing surf. Taina's expansive dinner spreads (T$15 to T$18) include Tongan specialities such as '*ota ika* (raw fish in coconut milk).

GETTING THERE & AROUND

On a calm day there is nothing to the two-hour ferry trip between 'Eua and Tongatapu (T$28 one way), but it can get very rough. The ferry leaves Nuku'alofa daily (except Sunday) at 12.30pm, but the return ferry is at the rather nasty hour of 5am!

Chathams Pacific (www.chathamspacific.com) makes the 10-minute flight from Tongatapu to 'Eua's Kaufana Airport (one way T$67) twice daily.

Accommodation hosts will pick you up at the wharf or airport. Bike and horse hire can be arranged at Hideaway (bike/horse T$15/30 per day).

Minerva Reef

This reef, awash most of the time, is Tonga's southernmost extremity. It lies 350km southwest of Tongatapu and serves as a rest point for yachts travelling from Tonga to NZ.

HA'APAI GROUP

pop 8200 / area 110 sq km

Virtually untouched and one of Tonga's best-kept secrets, the Ha'apai islands are sprinkled across the kingdom's central waters. With 62 islands, 45 of which are uninhabited, Ha'apai appears like the idyllic South Pacific paradise: palm-fringed islands, vibrant reefs, deserted white beaches and even a couple of massive volcanoes. There may not be a lot in the way of tourist facilities here, but for more adventurous travellers searching for a special South Seas experience, Ha'apai is the place to head to. It's a sleepy, seductive place, located well off the beaten track – and you get the feeling the locals would prefer to keep it that way. Only a scattering of tourists visit each year.

TONGA

WILLIAM MARINER

Thanks to a series of serendipitous incidents, the world has an extensive account of the customs, language, religion and politics of pre-Christian Tonga.

In February 1805 15-year-old William Charles Mariner went to sea on the privateer *Port-au-Prince*. The voyage took the ship across the Atlantic, around Cape Horn, up the west coast of South America, to the Sandwich (Hawaiian) Islands and finally into Tonga's Ha'apai Group. The crew anchored at the northern end of Lifuka and was immediately welcomed with yams and barbecued pork. Their reception seemed friendly enough (see p495), but on 1 December 1806 an attack was launched while 300 Tongans were aboard the ship. The British, sorely outnumbered, decided to destroy the ship, its crew and its attackers rather than allow it to be taken.

Young Mariner was captured and escorted ashore. Finau 'Ulukalala I, the reigning chief of Ha'apai, assumed that Mariner was the captain's son and ordered the young man's life to be spared.

Meanwhile, the *Port-au-Prince*, which hadn't been destroyed, was dragged ashore, raided and burned. The conflagration heated the cannons sufficiently to cause them to fire, creating panic among the Tongans. Mariner pantomimed an explanation of the phenomenon, initiating a rapport with the Tongans that would carry him through the next four years.

Mariner was taken under the wing of Finau and became privy to most of the goings-on in Tongan politics. He learned the language well and travelled with the chief, observing and absorbing the finer points of Tongan ceremony and protocol. He was given the name Toki 'Ukamea (Iron Axe), and Finau appointed one of his royal wives, Mafi Hape, to be Mariner's adoptive mother.

After the death of Finau, the king's son permitted young William to leave Tonga on a passing English vessel. Back in England, were it not for a chance meeting with an amateur anthropologist, Dr John Martin, his unique Tongan experiences might have been lost. Martin, fascinated with Mariner's tale, suggested collaboration on a book, and the result, *An Account of the Natives of the Tonga Islands,* is a masterpiece of Pacific literature.

History

Archaeological excavations in the southern Lifuka island reveal settlement dating back over 3000 years. The first European to turn up was Abel Tasman in 1643. Later, several notable events in Tongan history took place in Ha'apai. Captain Cook narrowly escaped the cooking pot in 1777 (see p495), the mutiny on the *Bounty* occurred offshore in 1789 (see p516), the *Port-au-Prince* was ransacked in 1806 (see above), and in 1831 Ha'apai was the first island group to be converted to Christianity following the baptism of its ruler Taufa'ahau. He took the name of Siaosi (George) after the King of England, and adopted the surname of Tupou. His wife was baptised Salote after Queen Charlotte. As King George Tupou I he united Tonga and established the royal line that continues through to the present day. King George Tupou V was crowned on 1 August 2008 (see p496).

Activities

Sandy, deserted beaches and uninhabited islands may be all you need for a perfect trip to Ha'apai, but remember to bring your own sunscreen and insect repellent. At the time of research neither was available in Pangai.

Ocean Blue Adventures (☎ 69639; www.tonga-dive .com) is based between Matafonua Lodge and Sandy Beach Resort at the northern tip of Foa. Formerly known as Happy Ha'apai Divers, this company operates **diving, snorkelling, whale-watching, sea kayaking** and **sailing** trips. There are plenty of options, so check out the website. Whale-watching trips (six hours) run from June to November for US$110 (minimum of 4). Diving costs are: introductory dive $US85; single/two-tank dive $US60/95; six-/10-dive package $US270/425; PADI open-water course $US495.

Fins n Flukes (☎ 13549, 13261; www.finsnflukes.com), based in Pangai on Lifuka, is due to open its doors for **diving, snorkelling** and **whale-watching** tours. This will be a good option for those staying in Pangai. Diving costs are: introductory dive T$160; two-tank dive T$140; six-/10-dive package T$560/900; PADI open-water course T$950. Snorkelling trips cost from T$40.

Friendly Islands Kayak Company (p522), although based in Vava'u, also offers organised kayaking in Ha'apai.

Getting There & Away

AIR

Ha'apai's Pilolevu Airport is 3km north of Pangai on Lifuka. The island's main road passes right through the middle of the runway, meaning that the road is closed when aircraft are arriving or departing. **Chathams Pacific** (☎ 28000; www.chathamspacific.com) flies daily (except Sunday) between Ha'apai and Tongatapu, and twice a week between Ha'apai and Vava'u. See p535 for details.

BOAT

MV 'Olovaha stops weekly at Pangai on Lifuka on both its northbound and southbound runs between Tongatapu and Vava'u. See p535 for ferry details. There are periods, however, when it just doesn't show up.

There are marginally protected anchorages along the lee shores of Lifuka, Foa, Ha'ano, Uoleva, Ha'afeva, Nomuka and Nomuka'iki.

Getting Around

TO/FROM THE AIRPORT & WHARF

Taxis charge T$7 between the airport and Pangai on Lifuka. If you arrive at the airport and there are no taxis, ask someone heading into town for a lift. Head to Mariner's Café (p515) and sort yourself out there.

The Foa Island resorts (p515) will arrange transfers for you – make sure to ask about this when you book.

There is a sporadic bus service between Pangai and the airport turn-off that costs T$1 – do not rely on this to get you to your flight on time, though. Take a taxi if you want to make your departing flight.

BICYCLE

Lifuka and Foa are flat, and a bicycle is a great option for exploring. Ask at Mariner's Café (p515) for up-to-date information about where to rent one. Expect to pay T$15 per day.

BOAT

The TVB in Lifuka may assist in arranging boat transport around the islands – though you may be told to ask at Mariner's Café!

BUS

A sporadic bus service operates between Hihifo, south of Pangai on Lifuka, and Faleloa on Foa roughly between 8am and 4pm weekdays and 8am and noon Saturday. The trip from Pangai to Faleloa costs T$1. There's a bus stop on the corner of Holopeka and Fau Rds. There is no schedule, and the bus goes either when it's full or the driver gets the urge.

TAXI

Several taxis operate in Pangai, but sometimes the drivers go to NZ to work as fruitpickers – so taxi services are sporadic too! Ask at Mariner's Café or at your guest house.

LIFUKA GROUP

Most visitors to Ha'apai stay within the Lifuka group of islands found along the eastern barrier reef of Ha'apai. Almost all accommodation and services are located within the Lifuka group with most of the action based on Lifuka island. Its capital, Pangai, is the centre of Ha'apai's limited activity.

Lifuka

Pangai, Lifuka's main town, has basic services but struggles to be described as attractive. Highlight of the week is the ferry arrival from Tongatapu and its subsequent unpacking. On hot afternoons the wharf is a writhing mass of drenched, cooling-down kids.

INFORMATION

The town water supply in Ha'apai should be used only for washing and bathing. Drink only bottled or rain water.

Friendly Islands Bookshop (☎ 60198; Holopeka Rd) Stocks a few titles on Tonga, magazines and film and fishing supplies.

Niu'ui Hospital (☎ 60201; Hihifo) Basic facilities. The pharmacy is open 8.30am to 4.30pm.

Post office (cnr Waterfront & Palace Rds) Mail can be sent c/o Post Office, Pangai, Ha'apai. The Customs & Inland Revenue office is also based here.

Tonga Visitors Bureau (TVB; ☎ 60733; www.tonga holiday.com; Holopeka Rd; ⏱ 8.30am-12.30pm & 1.30-4.30pm Mon-Fri) A sometimes helpful office that posts tide timetables and may assist with accommodation bookings, boat charter or other queries.

Westpac Bank of Tonga (☎ 60933; Holopeka Rd; ⏱ 9am-12.30pm & 1.30-3.30pm Mon-Fri) Exchanges foreign currencies (cash and travellers cheques), gives cash advances on Visa and MasterCard and also deals with MoneyGram cash transfers. There is no ATM.

SIGHTS

The best way to get around the sights is by rental bicycle; ask at Mariner's Café (p515).

TONGA

Shirley Baker Monument & European Cemetery

About 800m north of Pangai, the grave and monument of Reverend Shirley Baker, Tonga's first prime minister and adviser to King George Tupou I, stands amid the graves of various 19th- and early-20th-century German and English traders and missionaries. A Tongan cemetery, with decorated sand and coral mounds, is directly opposite.

Hihifo's Archaeological Sites

Hihifo, the village south of Pangai, hides some archaeological relics seemingly of more interest to rooting pigs than anyone else. Hidden behind a low wire fence in a grove of ironwood is **Olovehi Tomb** (Loto Kolo Rd), the burial ground for people holding the noble title of Tuita.

About 1.2km south of Pangai, a turning towards the east leads to the circular **Velata Mound Fortress**, a type of ring ditch fortification found throughout Tonga, Fiji and Samoa.

Southern Lifuka

From Hihifo, the road continues to **Hulu'ipaonga Point**, with its sweep of white beach. About 200m short of the point is **Hulu'ipaongo Tomb**, the burial site of the Mata'uvave line of chiefs.

SLEEPING

Accommodation options on Lifuka are basic, with shared facilities. Expect an early rise – Lifuka's rooster population is boisterous.

Fonongava'inga (Langilangi) Guesthouse (☎ 60038; vimahi@kalianet.to; Palace Rd, Pangai; s/d/tr T$15/25/45) The broad verandah and homely, light-filled communal lounge make this place worth the few minutes' walk from the centre of town. Langilangi enjoys teaching local crafts to guests. Most guests head to Mariner's Café for meals. Kitchen use is available for T$3 per day.

'Evaloni's Guesthouse (☎ 60029; Loto Kolo Rd, Pangai; s/d T$25/35, d with private bathroom from T$75) A ramshackle range of fan-cooled rooms downstairs and two spacious rooms upstairs, 'Evaloni's has a tapa-lined veranda on which to shoot some pool. Order meals in advance (breakfast/dinner T$15/25) or, better, head to nearby Mariner's Café.

Fifita Guesthouse (☎ 60213; marinerstonga@yahoo.co.uk; Fau Rd, Pangai; s/d incl breakfast T$30/45, f with sitting room T$65) Fifita's central location beside Mariner's Café and just a short walk from the wharf makes it a popular accomodation choice. It's basic but friendly, with plenty of travel banter exchanged in the communal kitchen.

Lindsay Guesthouse (☎ 60107; cnr Loto Kolo & Tuita Rds, Pangai; s/d/f incl breakfast T$30/40/55) A clean and friendly spot, with a broad veranda and communal sitting room and kitchen. The scent of baking bread wafts across the lawn from the bakery. Bikes (T$15) are available for guests. Breakfast is T$6 to T$10, dinner T$15 to T$20.

Billy's Place (☎ 60336; s/d fale incl breakfast T$55/65, larger fale T$65/75, self-contained fale T$100, minimum 2-night stay) Both Billy and his place are looking a bit tired, but if you're okay with isolation and want to have a whole west-side beach to yourself, this place is a good option. There are secluded bungalows with clean, shared facilities and kitchen use for T$5 per day. Northeast of Pangai, it's a 10-minute 1.5km bike ride (free bikes are available for guests) or a T$5 taxi ride to town.

EATING

The only option for eating out in Pangai is Mariner's Café (opposite).

Matuku-ae-tau Bakery (Lindsay Guesthouse, cnr Loto Kolo & Tuita Rds; ☼ 8am-5pm Mon-Sat, 5-8pm Sun) The bakery's two ovens keep the island in bread, jam-filled rolls and *keki* (which are similar to doughnuts). There's a mad rush on Sunday afternoon.

The multicoloured *fale koloa* around the town sell their own selection of groceries, but they can't be called supermarkets. Pickings are often slim at **Pangai Market** (cnr Waterfront & Palace Rd; ☼ 9am-5pm Mon-Sat); head down early in the day for fresh produce.

SHOPPING

Women's Island Development Handicraft Shop (☎ 60478; Loto Kolo Rd) Local women sell their tapa, cards and various woven items made from pandanus leaves here.

Foa

To the north of Lifuka and connected by a potholed causeway, Foa is a heavily wooded island. Houmale'eia Beach, on the northern tip, is the best beach on the 'Ha'apai mainland', with sandy water access, sublime views of Nukunamo and some beautiful snorkelling.

HEAD TO MARINER'S CAFÉ

Ha'apai is a superb place to visit, and there are a couple of ways to do it.

For those who come to dive, snorkel, whale-watch or sit on the beach as part of a relaxing holiday and want a bit of comfort, book yourself into one of the Foa Island resorts – up-market Sandy Beach Resort or the more affordable Matafonua Lodge (see below).

For adventurous types who are out exploring, your initial arrival on Ha'apai may be a bit of a surprise, whether you arrive by plane or ferry. Simply put, there isn't much here. If you were trying to get away from it all, you've succeeded!

Best advice is to head straight to **Mariner's Café** (☎ 60374; VHF Channel 16; marinerstonga@yahoo .co.uk; Fau Rd; meals & snacks T$6.50-25; ☙ breakfast, lunch & dinner Mon-Sat, dinner Sun). You won't fully appreciate the lure of this place, named for William Mariner (p512), until you've spent some time on Ha'apai's shores. This relaxed social mecca is Lifuka's only real restaurant and bar and has a good range of tasty and fresh dishes. Run by Craig and Magda, it's a good place to come for advice. Sit down with a beer or coffee and absorb some local knowledge before heading out for adventure. Internet access is available for T$3 for 30 minutes.

SLEEPING

Both the sleeping options are right next to activity operators Ocean Blue Adventures (see p512) at the northern tip of the island.

Matafonua Lodge (☎ 69766; www.matafonua.com; fale d & tw NZ$120) These uncluttered, elevated *fale* have water views over foreshore foliage. Purpose-built as a dive resort in 2006, Matafonua offers freshwater showers in well-designed shared facilities. Kids are welcome. A kiosk-style café-bar with reasonable prices overlooks Nukunamo island, and the sandy swimming beach is superb. Rental kayaks and bicycles are available for hire.

Sandy Beach Resort (☎ 60600; www.sandy beachresort.de; s/d €90/140) Long regarded as one of Tonga's best resorts, Sandy Beach's 12 comfortable bungalows are oriented for sunset views over the magnificent white-sand Houmale'eia Beach. Rates include airport transfers. Breakfast/dinner costs €$11/33.

GETTING THERE & AROUND

A sporadic bus service from Pangai stops at Faleloa (T$1 one way), a 30-minute walk from the resorts and Houmale'eia Beach. By bicycle from Pangai it takes around one hour; the taxi fare is about T$30.

Nukunamo

The small enticing picture-postcard island viewed from the tip of Foa is Nukunamo, an uninhabited island with a shining white beach covered with beautiful shells. At low tide you can snorkel to Nukunamo over the life-filled coral heads between the islands. Only confident swimmers should attempt this, and

only with local advice, as the currents through the pass can be powerful. Talk to Matafonua Lodge before you go as there is talk that the island, owned by the Princess, may soon have 'off limits' status.

Ha'ano

Cultural travellers will get a good dose of traditional Tongan life on the strikingly clean and friendly island of Ha'ano that lies to the north of Foa and Nukunamo.

At the time of research, Kiwi Greig Thorby was about to open his **Fualu Bay Resort** (☎ 65902; www.fualubayresort.com), with a focus on fishing, halfway up the western side of the island. As well as *fale* accommodation, the resort will have a restaurant and bar plus camping facilities. Greig will be able to provide boat transfers to Ha'ano from Faleloa on Foa Island.

Alternatively, paddle a kayak across from Foa (see p512 to hire a kayak from Ocean Blue Adventures).

Uoleva

If you're looking to really get away from it all, Uoleva, to the south of Lifuka, is the place to come for it. It provides a real South Seas experience with little to do other than swim, snorkel and fish.

SLEEPING

Uoleva's very basic accommodation has unbeatable, absolute beachfront positions on a broad, white-sand beach on the northwest coast. There is no electricity or running water on this virtually uninhabited island. Both places receive rave reviews from intrepid travellers, but not-such-rave reviews from those expecting too much in the way of facilities. Bring your own drinks, some food and mosquito repellent; inform owners in advance if you want meals.

Taiana's Beach Resort (☎ 60612; s/d/f fale T$18/25/45) Ponder the stars and lapping waves at this absolute beach-bum paradise. Tapalined *fale* have mats over sandy floors and enclosed sitting areas.

Captain Cook Hideaway (☎ 60014, 8791144; s/d cabins T$18/25) Located 200m south of Taiana's, this place has basic beachfront cabins. Savour the peace and solitude. Meals are available (breakfast/lunch/dinner T$10/15/20).

GETTING THERE & AROUND

You can walk/wade between the southern tip of Lifuka and the northern tip of Uoleva at low tide, but check out the tide chart at the TVB and get local advice before you attempt it. Wear something to protect your feet and use your common sense – even locals have drowned crossing here. It takes 45 minutes to walk from Pangai to the southern tip of Lifuka (taxi T$8), around 20 minutes between the islands (1.5km), and a further hour or so to reach Uoleva's 'resorts'. Both places offer boat transfers for guests from Pangai (ask at the TVB).

'Uiha

The conservative and traditional island of 'Uiha, to the south of Uoleva, is a friendly place with two villages: 'Uiha, with a wharf, and Felemea, about 1.5km south.

In the centre of 'Uiha village is a large, elevated burial ground containing several **royal tombs**. The burial ground of the Tongan royal family was on 'Uiha until the move to Nuku'alofa. At the village church are two **cannon**, souvenirs taken from a Peruvian blackbirding (slaving) ship that was attacked and destroyed by the locals in 1863.

You'll get a good introduction to village life at **'Esi-'o-Ma'afu Homestay** (☎ 60605, 60438; VHF Channel 16; fale s/d T$20/25), a friendly, welcoming place right on the beach at Felemea. Shared facilities are clean, and there's a small kitchen (T$3) or, with notice, the owners will prepare delicious Tongan food. Talk to the TVB in Pangai about bookings and boat transport.

Tofua & Kao

Seventy kilometres west of Lifuka are pyramidal Kao (1046m) and its smoking partner, Tofua (507m). On a good day they are visible from Lifuka.

Tofua is a flat-topped volcanic island that, like Niuafo'ou in the Niuas, is shaped like a huge floating doughnut. It rather entices the intrepid traveller to climb up and peer in. At the bottom of the crater is a beautiful, 250m-deep crystal-clear lake that is 38m above sea level. The crater rim is a tough one-hour climb from the Hokala landing site on the northern side of the island. A seaplane service that used to land in the crater lake was unfortunately discontinued due to a lack of customers.

Just offshore is where the infamous mutiny on the *Bounty* occurred (see p246). On 28 April 1789, Captain Bligh and 18 loyal seamen landed on Tofua after being set adrift. Islanders clubbed quartermaster John Newton to death. Bligh and the rest escaped and embarked on a 6500km journey to Timor in an open boat, desperately short of water, having not discovered Tofua's large freshwater lake.

The four-hour hike up uninhabited Kao, 4km north of Tofua, is not recommended without a guide. The 1046m volcano is the highest point in Tonga, but there is no marked track and the vegetation is dense.

Reaching Tofua or Kao is not easy without your own boat. Talk to the TVB in Pangai or contact Greig at Fualu Bay Resort (p515) if you are keen.

VAVA'U GROUP

pop 17,000 / area 119 sq km

Shaped like a giant jellyfish with its tentacles dangling south, Vava'u is picturesque at every turn. Those tentacles are made up of spectacular islands (61 in all!) intertwined with turquoise waterways and encircling reefs that have created one of the most popular sheltered cruising grounds on the planet. To really experience it you have to get out on the water. Regarded as one of the world's great sailing locations, Vava'u is the holiday activity destination of Tonga: charter sailing, sea kayaking, mountain biking, hiking, game fishing, surfing, diving and even swimming with whales are all possible

DISAPPEARING ISLAND: FONUAFO'OU

The Ha'apai group is home to Tonga's only disappearing island. From 1781 to 1865 there were repeated reports of a shoal 72km northwest of Tongatapu and 60km west of Nomuka in the south of the Ha'apai group. In 1885 an island 50m high and 2km long was confirmed and, amid great excitement, Tonga planted its flag and claimed it as Fonuafo'ou, meaning 'New Land'.

Then in 1894 Fonuafo'ou went missing! Two years later it reappeared 320m high before disappearing again. In 1927 it re-emerged and in 1930 was measured at 130m high and 2.5km long! By 1949 there was again no trace of Fonuafo'ou, which had once more been eroded by the sea. Fonuafo'ou came back again, but at last report this geographical freak had once more submerged.

If the 'New Land' does come back, unless you are on a yacht, your best chance of spotting it is on a ferry returning to Tongatapu from the Niuas.

here. Stay in town or head out to one of the islands to enjoy the stunning scenery and activities that Vava'u offers in abundance.

History

Vava'u is believed to have been settled for around 2000 years. The capital of Neiafu looks out onto Port of Refuge, christened by Don Francisco Antonio Mourelle of Spain who sighted Vava'u on 4 March 1781 while en route from Manila to Mexico. Mourelle claimed the new-found paradise, one of the last South Pacific islands to be contacted by Europeans, for Spain.

William Mariner (see p512) spent time here during Finau 'Ulukala I of Ha'apai's conquest of Vava'u in 1808. Later, on the death of 'Ulukala III, King George Tupou I added Vava'u to his realm when he formed a united Tonga in 1845.

Climate

Vava'u enjoys a tropical climate with average daily temperatures of 29°C in January and 24°C in June. The weather is warm and generally sunny throughout the year. June to October is the main tourist season with visitors turning up to see the whales. In November to April the weather is more humid and thunderstorms are more frequent, but the water is warmer for swimming and there is still excellent visibility for diving and quieter winds for sailing. Traditionally this is cyclone season in the South Pacific, but only one cyclone has touched down in Vava'u in the last 16 years.

Information

For online information on what's happening in Vava'u, check out www.vavau.to.

Getting There & Away

AIR

Lupepau'u Airport is a 15-minute drive north of Neiafu. **Chathams Pacific** Airport (☎ 71403) Neiafu (Map p520; ☎ 71480; www.chathamspacific.com; Fatafehi Rd) flies daily between Tongatapu and Vava'u, and twice weekly between Ha'apai and Vava'u.

BOAT

See p535 for inter-island ferry information. The ferry offices are at Neiafu's main wharf.

Getting Around

TO/FROM THE AIRPORT

Some accommodation, including island resorts, offer airport transfers for a price. The Paradise International Hotel bus meets incoming flights and is free/T$20 for guests/ nonguests. Taxis charge T$20 for the airport–Neiafu trip.

BICYCLE

Vava'u is hilly, but fairly manageable by bicycle. Adventure Backpackers (p523) rents out good bikes (half-/full day T$13/20), and Friendly Islands Kayak Company (p522) runs mountain-bike tours.

BOAT

For details, see p521.

BUS

Buses run from Sailoame and 'Utakalongalu Markets to most parts of Vava'u and its connected islands, leaving when full. They usually make the run into town in the morning and return in the afternoon, so they're not very convenient for day trips from town.

TONGA

VAVA'U GROUP

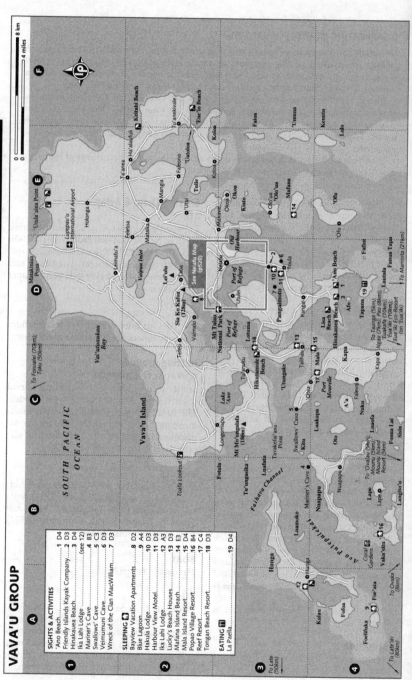

SIGHTS & ACTIVITIES
'Ano Beach..1 D4
Friendly Islands Kayak Company....2 D3
Hinakauea Beach...............................3 D4
Ika Lahi Lodge............................(see 12)
Mariner's Cave..................................4 B3
Swallows' Cave..................................5 C3
Veimumuni Cave...............................6 D3
Wreck of the Clan MacWilliam.......7 D3

SLEEPING
Bayview Vacation Apartments.........8 D2
Blue Lagoon.......................................9 A4
Hakula Lodge...................................10 D3
Harbour View Motel.......................11 D3
Ika Lahi Lodge.................................12 A3
Lucky's Beach Houses.....................13 D3
Mafana Island Beach......................14 E3
Mala Island Resort..........................15 D4
Popao Village Resort......................16 B4
Reef Resort......................................17 C4
Tongan Beach Resort......................18 D3

EATING
La Paella..19 D4

CAR & SCOOTER

Tongan licences are available for T$17 from the police station (see right).

Pasifika Rentals (Map p520; ☎ 12698) has a few rental cars for T$60 to T$80 per day. Call ahead or get the TVB to arrange one for you.

Vava'u Scooter Rental (Map p520; ☎ 71331; Fatafehi Rd), run by Lotu, has scooters for T$45 (9am to 4pm) or T$56 (24 hours).

There are an incredible number of cars in Vava'u with broken or cracked windscreens. Do not park your rental vehicle under a coconut tree – and when driving, watch out for pigs.

TAXI

Taxis charge T$5 around Neiafu, and T$20 to the airport, 'Ano and Hinakauea Beaches, and Talihau village.

NEIAFU

pop 5900

Overlooking Port of Refuge, surely one of the world's most amazing and protected harbours, Neiafu may or may not appeal. Home to a surprising number of good restaurants and bars along the waterfront, the town itself is more than a tad ramshackle and rundown. Four hundred to 500 visiting yachts turn up each year between May and October, and with a steady flow of visitors flying in during the same period (many who are here to swim with the whales), the busy season sees the small town transformed into a hive of activity. Things quieten in the summer, though. On Sundays Neiafu is mostly quiet, aside from the vibrant and uplifting singing emanating from numerous churches.

Information

Vava'u has its own eclectic English radio station: PIG FM, at 89.3FM. Greg, the Canadian who runs it, plays what he likes – expect Zappa, Sinatra and George Michael in the same song set! A yachties' information net is on VHF Channel 6 at 8.30am Monday to Saturday.

INTERNET ACCESS

Aquarium Café (☎ 70493; Fatafehi Rd; per 15min T$3; ☯ 8am-11pm) An excellent option open all day.

Café Tropicana (☎ 71322; Fatafehi Rd; per 15min T$3; ☯ 6.30am-6pm Mon-Sat)

MEDICAL SERVICES

Prince Wellington Ngu Hospital (☎ 70201; Mateialona Rd; ☯ 24hr) For emergencies.

Vava'u Pharmacy & Health Centre (☎ 70213; paharmacy@kalianetvav.to; opposite Tonga Visitors Bureau ☯ 8.30am-4pm Mon, Tue, Thu & Fri, 8.30-11.30am Sat) NZ-trained doctor, pharmacist and physio. Also retails health products.

MONEY

The Westpac Bank of Tonga, ANZ, Western Union and MBF, all on Fatafehi Rd, change cash and travellers cheques. All open until around 11.30am on Saturday. Westpac and ANZ have 24-hour ATMs.

POLICE

Police station (Map p520; ☎ 922, 70236; Tu'i Rd; ☯ 8.30am-4.30pm Mon & Tue, to 12.30pm Wed-Fri)

POST

Post office (☎ 70002; Fatafehi Rd; ☯ 8.30am-4pm) North of 'Utukalongalu market. Poste restante mail (c/o General Delivery, Post Office, Neiafu, Vava'u).

TOURIST INFORMATION

Tonga Visitors Bureau (TVB; ☎ 70115; VHF Channel 16; Fatafehi Rd; ☯ 8.30am-4.30pm Mon-Fri) A well-stocked office with helpful staff happy to assist with bookings and accommodation reservations.

Vava'u Adventures (☎ 70493; www.vavauadventures .com) Runs an activity booking service from its base at Aquarium Café. Email ahead for information and bookings.

Sights

Taking in the Port of Refuge view of yachts bobbing at their moorings from a cafe or bar may be the only sight you need to see in Neiafu.

Standing high above Port of Refuge, on Fatafehi Rd, colonial-style **St Joseph's Cathedral** is Neiafu's most prominent building. The stretch of road along the waterfront cliff below the cathedral is **Hala Lupe** (Way of Doves), named for the mournful singing of the female prisoners (convicted of adultery by the church) who constructed it.

Turning left in front of the cathedral will take you down to **Old Harbour** and boat access to the eastern islands.

The flat-topped mountain dominating Port of Refuge, 131m **Mt Talau** (Mo'unga Talau), is protected in the **Mt Talau National Park**. From the centre of Neiafu, travel west along Tapueluelu Rd for around 2km, until the road narrows

TONGA

NEIAFU

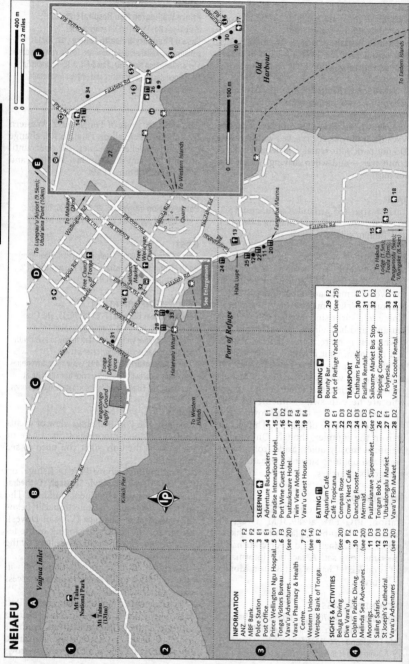

INFORMATION
ANZ	1 F2
MBF Bank	2 F2
Police Station	3 E1
Post Office	4 E1
Prince Wellington Ngu Hospital	5 D1
Tonga Visitors Bureau	6 F3
Vava'u Adventures	(see 20)
Vava'u Pharmacy & Health Centre	7 F2
Western Union	(see 14)
Westpac Bank of Tonga	8 F2

SIGHTS & ACTIVITIES
Beluga Diving	(see 20)
Dive Vava'u	9 F2
Dolphin Pacific Diving	10 F3
Melinda Sea Adventures	(see 20)
Moorings	11 D3
Sailing Safaris	12 D3
St Joseph's Cathedral	13 D3
Vava'u Adventures	(see 20)

SLEEPING
Adventure Backpackers	14 E1
Paradise International Hotel	15 D4
Port Wine Guest House	16 D2
Puataukanave Hotel	17 F3
Twin View Motel	18 E4
Vava'u Guest House	19 E4

EATING
Aquarium Café	20 D3
Café Tropicana	21 E1
Compass Rose	22 D3
Crow's Nest Café	23 D3
Dancing Rooster	24 D3
Mermaid	25 D3
Puataukanave Supermarket	(see 17)
Tongan Bob's	26 F2
'Utukalongalu Market	27 E1
Vava'u Fish Market	28 D2

DRINKING
Bounty Bar	29 F2
Port of Refuge Yacht Club	(see 25)

TRANSPORT
Chathams Pacific	30 F3
Pasifika Rentals	31 C1
Salloame Market Bus Stop	32 D2
Shipping Corporation of Polynesia	33 D2
Vava'u Scooter Rental	34 F1

TONGA

CHANGE IS IN THE WIND

Not much changes fast in Tonga except businesses in Vava'u. These start up, close down, and change ownership and/or management at a frantic pace. It seems that many come to these islands with a South Pacific dream, buy or start a business, stick at it for a while, then decide that it wasn't for them after all. It has been said that 'for every beach in Tonga, a *palangi's* dreams lie buried in the sands'. One bar in Neiafu has apparently changed hands five times in the last six years! During research, at the end of the tourist season, it seemed that every second business was up for sale. Keep this in mind if things turn out differently from the description in this book – and send us some feedback.

into a bush track. When it begins to descend, a side track turns off to the right and leads steeply up to the summit, where you get a great view.

Activities

DIVING & SNORKELLING

Vava'u's dive sites range from hard and soft coral gardens and encrusted wrecks to vast sea caves and other geological marvels. There is a wide variety of diving for all levels and abilities.

Dive Vava'u (☎ 70492; www.divevavau.com) operates from down on the waterfront below Tongan Bob's. An introductory dive costs T$250, including training and two reef dives, equipment and instruction; a two-tank dive trip is T$170; five-/10-day packages cost T$750/1350; PADI open-water courses cost T$750. It also has a whale-watching licence.

Dolphin Pacific Diving (☎ 70292; VHF Channel 71; www.dolphinpacificdiving.com) prides itself on being a relaxed, friendly operation. It's on the waterfront beside Puataukanave Motel and offers introductory dives for T$240; a two-tank dive including a light lunch and all equipment hire for T$200; six-/10-dive packages for T$540/875; PADI open-water qualification for T$675/1200 for one/two people. It also does a lot of television work for whale-watching and offers a full-day trip for T$270.

Beluga Diving (☎ 70327; VHF Channel 16; www.belugadivingvavau.com), on the waterfront next to Moorings, offers introductory dives for US$100; two-tank dives at two different sites for US$95; five days diving plus wreck dive for US$450; PADI open-water course for US$350. It also runs whale-watching tours for US$170 including lunch.

Most boat tours and some whale-watching trips include a little snorkelling into Mariner's and Swallows' Caves or over coral gardens.

Operators will run snorkelling trips out of season for around T$80. A good snorkelling day trip would be to head out to Mala Island Resort (p526) for lunch and snorkel from its beach to the beautiful Japanese Gardens nearby.

For more on diving in the Vava'u Group, see p78.

FISHING

Vava'u is regarded as one of the best game-fishing destinations in the Pacific and a prime site for catching marlin.

Hakula Sport Fishing Charters (☎ 70872; www.fishtonga.com), operated by Hakula Lodge (p523), has day charters for A$1200 for up to six anglers.

Target One (☎ 70647; www.visitvavau.com/target1) has various options. Email for rates.

Ika Lahi Lodge (Map p518; ☎ 70611; ww.tongafishing.com), based on Hunga Island, charters for NZ$1400 per full day, for a maximum of four anglers.

KARTING

Vava'u Adventures (☎ 70493; www.vavauadventures.com), operating out of Aquarium Café (see p524), runs exciting three-hour guided kart tours of Vava'u where you can take it all in while driving your own one- or two-seater kart (US$80/135).

SAILING & BOATING

This is the perfect way to experience Vava'u: cruising the islands and stopping off to snorkel and wander beaches at will.

Moorings (☎ 70016; VHF Channel 72; www.tongasailing.com) charters out catamarans and monohulls ranging from 12m to 15m, which sleep up to 10 passengers. Prices vary according to the season. Check the website for details.

Melinda Sea Adventures (☎ 70975; VHF Channel 16; www.sailtonga.com) operates the traditionally rigged gaff ketch *Melinda*, a beautiful sight under sail in Vava'u. Fully crewed, minimum three-day charters. Rates depend on the season and number of passengers. Whale-watching trips are also available.

Sailing Safaris (☎ 70650; VHF Channel 68; www.sailing safaris.com) has a host of options, including whale-watching, bareboat and skippered charters. It also runs five-day live-aboard sailing courses for US$900 per person.

Vava'u Adventures (☎ 70493; www.vavauadventures .com) hires out sailing dinghies from US$10 per hour. Ask at Aquarium Café.

SEA KAYAKING

Island resorts and beachside accommodation places generally provide kayaks for guest use.

The ecofriendly **Friendly Islands Kayak Company** (Map p518; ☎ 70173; VHF Channel 71; www .fikco.com) has been revealing some of Tonga's magic to kayaking adventurers on its camping and paddling expeditions around Vava'u (and Ha'apai) since 1991. It provides truly unique experiences (and supplies excellent equipment) on five-/nine-/11-day packages (with four/six/eight days of guided kayaking) for US$900/1790/2130. The action-packed Vava'u Adventure Week (US$1620) includes sea kayaking, whale-watching, mountain biking and sailing or diving. There's a friendly local Tongan guide on every trip, providing a great way to become friends with and learn about the life of the locals. A real Tongan experience.

SURFING

Vava'u's reef surfing gets the thumbs up from Kurt Carlson at **Vava'u Surf & Adventure Tours** (☎ 71075; www.talihaubeach.com) – check out his website and contact him for details. His trips have received rave reviews.

WHALE-WATCHING

Vava'u has become one of the world's top whale-watching destinations, particularly due to the opportunity to swim with humpbacks. The activity is not without controversy (see opposite), and **Whales Alive** (www.whalesalive .org.au) is an organisation devoted to the whales' protection.

There are 13 commercial whale-watching licences in Vava'u, all with similar prices, so you have plenty of options. The whales are generally around from June to late October.

Ecologically sensitive **Whale Discoveries** (☎ 70173; VHF Channel 71; www.whalediscoveries.com) watches rather than swims with the whales, but provides snorkelling gear for use elsewhere on its day trips (US$160 including drinks).

Diving operators (see p521) often fit whale-watching between dives.

YACHT RACES

On a balmy Friday afternoon you can't beat knocking back an Ikale or rum and watching a relaxed yacht race around Port of Refuge. If you want to become 'rail meat' (crew), turn up to the Port of Refuge Yacht Club (at the Mermaid, p524) when the skippers meet at around 4pm between May and the end of October. Spectators can watch from the bar at the 5pm race start. There's a ton of fun to be had afterwards.

Tours

Many operators also run day boat excursions that typically include Swallows' and Mariner's Caves, picnicking on an uninhabited island and snorkelling at an offshore reef. The presence of humpback whales (June to November) is a special bonus.

Soki's Island Tours (contact the TVB) runs tailored boat tours (T$80, minimum three people) that can include snorkelling and fishing.

Sleeping

There's a good range of accommodation around Neiafu and its causeway-connected islands (see also p526). Bookings are advised between May and November.

Check the notice boards of Adventure Backpackers (opposite), Café Tropicana (p524) and the Mermaid (p524) for details on rentals. **Bayview Vacation Apartments** (Map p518; ☎ 70724; bayviewtonga.com), just beyond the Vaipua Inlet causeway, has well-furnished apartments starting at US$300 per week.

BUDGET

Bathrooms are shared unless otherwise noted at the following places.

Vava'u Guest House (☎ 70300; kiwifish@kalianet.to; Fatafehi Rd; s/d T$20/30, fale s/d $45/60) Located 1.5km south of Neiafu and opposite the Paradise International Hotel, the backpacker building down the front is passable, but the four *fale* behind are excellent value. Tongan-run and friendly.

WHALE ENCOUNTERS

Tonga is an important breeding ground for humpback whales, which migrate to Tongan waters between June and November; it's one of the best places in the world to see these magnificent creatures. They can be seen bearing young in the calm reef-protected ocean, caring for new calves (conceived here 11 months earlier), and engaging in elaborate mating rituals.

Humpbacks are dubbed 'singing whales' because the males sing during courtship routines, and the low notes of their 'songs' can reach 185 decibels and carry 100km through the open ocean. They are also known for their dramatic antics in the water. They 'breach' (throw themselves completely out of the water), 'spyhop' (stand vertically upright above the water's surface), 'barrel roll' (splash the water with their long pectoral fins) and perform other remarkable acrobatic feats.

As Tonga's whale-watching industry has grown, so has concern over its possible impact. At the centre of the debate is the practice of swimming with whales, which some say disturbs the mothers and calves just when they are most vulnerable – and may force them to abandon the area before they are ready. Whale-watching operators should take their cue from the whales: if they seem disturbed and want to get away from the boat, then they should not be pursued.

Humpback populations around the world have declined rapidly over the past 200 years, from 150,000 in the early 1800s to an estimated 12,000 today. The same predictable migration habits that once made the giants easy prey for whalers nowadays make them easy finds for whale-watchers.

Adventure Backpackers (☎ 70955; visitvavau.com /backpackers; Fatafehi Rd; dm T$25, s/d from T$75/85) This central, modern hostel in the middle of Neiafu makes a handy base to spring into Vava'u's myriad activities and nightlife. Fan-cooled rooms are bright, clean and secure, and there's a shared kitchen and communal area and a sun-soaked terrace.

Port Wine Guest House (☎ 70479; portwine@kalianet .to; Ha'amea Rd; s/d T$35/60) Kindly Tongan granny Lu'isa's place is just back from town in Neiafu. Relax on the verandah at her homely, four-room guest house after a hard day's adventure. Guests can use the well-stocked kitchen and fill water bottles from the tank. The roosters crow early!

MIDRANGE

Puataukanave Hotel (☎ 71002; puashotel@kalianetvav .to; Fatafehi Rd;) This massive Tongan-run place on the town waterfront has a huge range of options from 'deluxe' with kitchen and balcony (single/double T$240/270) to backpacker rooms (single/double T$40/52). The latter are a good deal. Send an e-mail and assess your options.

Twin View Motel (☎ 70597; tongaonline.de; 2-bedroom unit from US$55) Next to Vava'u Guest House, 1.5km south of town, this place has six very good two-bedroom motel units with kitchen that are both spacious and tastefully decorated. Run by the efficient Natu, there should be a restaurant and bar up and run-

ning by the time this book is published. Airport transfers cost T$25 per trip.

Harbour View Motel (Map p518; ☎ 70687; www .harbourviewresort.com; s/d T$150, 2-bedroom unit T$200) Set in tropical gardens south of Neiafu, this place has detached cabins, each with kitchenette and veranda. It's a relaxed, family-oriented place run by expat Kiwis. You can swim off the wharf below the resort. Taxis cost T$10 from Neiafu, T$30 from the airport.

TOP END

Paradise International Hotel (☎ 70211; www .tongahost.com; Fatafehi Rd; island/garden/harbour view d US$79/99/119;) With spacious gardens overlooking the harbour 1.5km south of town, this hotel has 48 standard (if dated) hotel rooms, a swimming pool (T$5 for nonguests) and a decent restaurant. Airport transfers for guests are free.

Hakula Lodge (Map p518; ☎ 70872; VHF Channel 71; www.fishtonga.com; s/d/tr A$200/225/275;) The most attractive and atmospheric of Neiafu's accommodation options, Hakula Lodge consists of two units opening onto a full-length veranda overlooking Port of Refuge. Guests can head down the tropical garden path to swim off the private jetty, from where the owners' whale-watching and fishing trips depart (see p521). It's located 2km south of Neiafu.

Eating & Drinking

Neiafu has a swathe of dining options, most of which double as bars. The choice is constantly expanding.

CAFES & RESTAURANTS

Crow's Nest Café (crowsnestcafe@gmail.com; ⏱ 6.30am-3pm Mon-Sat) A 'garden café' and 'boutique bakery', Crow's Nest is down next to the fish market. The royal family loves their bread, and locals flock to the 2pm to 3pm 'happy hour' when what's left of the day's baking goes out the door at bargain prices. Very popular with yachties.

Mermaid (☎ 70730; VHF Channel 16; breakfast & light meals T$4-16, mains T$25-36; ⏱ breakfast, lunch & dinner) Home of the Port of Refuge Yacht Club and the first port of call for many – the first beer is free for arriving yachties – Mermaid overhangs the water. Yachties tie up tenders to the pontoon while others wind through a pirate-like lair from the road above to one of Neiafu's most popular spots. The extensive menu attracts plenty of repeat diners for bulging tortillas, juicy grills and the popular seafood dishes. Happy hour flows from 4pm to 6pm.

Compass Rose (☎ 71167; Fatafehi Rd; lunch T$8-15, mains T$18-30; ⏱ lunch & dinner Mon-Sat) Perched on the edge of Hala Lupe, with elevated views over Port of Refuge, this Canadian-run place offers relaxed elegance, good food and bar facilities.

our pick **Aquarium Café** (☎ 70493; Fatafehi Rd; breakfast T$8-16, meals T$9-16; ⏱ breakfast, lunch & dinner; 🖳) A great one-stop shop, you can get it all here at Aquarium with tasty tapas, a fully stocked bar, internet for T$3 per 15 minutes, and an activity booking service. There are superb views out over the harbour from the deck and excellent service from American owners Ben, Lisa and their staff. Top spot in town – you can tell because all the locals and the yachties are here!

Café Tropicana (☎ 71322; Fatafehi Rd; breakfast T$8-16, meals T$11-16; ⏱ 6.30am-6pm Mon-Sat; 🖳) Nab a table in the cool interior or slouch into a deck-chair on the harbour-view terrace at this central cafe next to Adventure Backpackers. Tasty options range from sandwiches (around T$6) and burgers to Tongan dishes. Pies, cookies and cakes line the front cabinet. Kiwi Lisa runs a laid-back place.

Tongan Bob's (Kovana Rd; mains T$16-20; ⏱ noon-late Mon-Fri) As laid-back as it comes. Head to Tongan Bob's (run by Matt the Aussie) fo everything you could ask for – a sand floo to sink your toes into and tasty Mexican sta ples. Tuesday is $2 tacos night, Wednesda is *fakaleiti* night (see p497) and Thursda features the pub quiz. There's a big screer for sporting events.

Dancing Rooster (☎ 70886; Fatafehi Rd; mains T$24-42; ⏱ lunch & dinner Mon-Sat) Descend the stairs to the tropical garden overlooking Port o Refuge and dine on dishes served with fi nesse from the Swiss chef. Portions are gen erous, and options include rich local fish soup and lobster cooked any which way.

La Paella (Map p518; ☎ 16310; VHF Channel 10; din ner & entertainment T$70) Adventurous diners will have to make an effort to get here, but it's good! Tapana Island's Spanish-run La Paella restaurant gets rave reviews for its plentiful paella and lively entertainment. You'll need to take a taxi to 'Ano Beach for $20 – book ahead and La Paella will pick you up by boat from there.

our pick **Bounty Bar** (☎ 70576; Fatafehi Rd; ⏱ Mon-Sat) A lively place in the middle of town, Bounty Bar has ice-cold beer and stunning sunset views from its covered ter race overlooking the waterfront. The food is excellent – try the pan-fried snapper – with everything on the menu under T$20.

TONGAN FEASTS

Joining a Tongan feast is the best way to ex perience Tongan food – much of which is cooked in an *'umu* – and get a good dose of traditional Tongan music and dance at the same time. Contact the TVB or your accom modation for current feasts. Expect to pay around T$40.

SELF-CATERING

Neiafu's three supermarkets stock a reason able range. **Puatukanave Supermarket** (☎ 70644; Fatafehi Rd), affectionately known as 'Pua', has refrigerated chocolate as well as wine, beer and spirits.

The best place for fresh produce is **'Utukalongalu Market** (⏱ 8.30am-4.30pm Mon-Thu, 8.30am-midnight Fri, 7am-noon Sat), close to Halaevalu Wharf. The freshest fish can be found at the **Vava'u Fish Market** (Halaevalu Wharf; ⏱ 8.30am-4.30pm Mon-Fri, to noon or 1pm Sat).

On Sunday afternoon, just follow your nose through town to the bakeries.

LOCAL VOICES: TALKING WITH OFA & KAVA *Craig McLachlan*

This is the first time I have ever done my Lonely Planet research by sea kayak! I took part in a Friendly Islands Kayaks (see p522) five-day trip and greatly enjoyed paddling up to island resorts to check them out for this edition of *South Pacific*. The guides were two locals from Pangaimotu village, Ofa and Kava, who were happy to split the group, one accompanying me on my research while the other led the regular clients.

Ofa is a tall, solidly built 26-year-old Bob Marley lookalike who has been kayak-guiding for four seasons. He has dreadlocks that hang halfway down his back, knows his stuff, and works hard to keep his clients happy. Ofa is a general all-round happy guy – he is unmarried and loves his kava!

Kava is 30, tall and angular, a caring and considerate guy who loves his job and will do anything for his clients – including climbing coconut trees whenever asked to knock down drinking nuts. He then swiftly and expertly chops them open with a machete. Kava is married with a two-year old son he loves dearly.

Here's what the guys had to say about the new king, their off-season and their favourite eating and drinking spots in Vava'u.

'I like the Tongan system [of government]. We have no need to change. People are happy here. It is only Tongans who live overseas making lots of money telling their relatives in Tonga about democracy that makes people unhappy here. I am happy with the old system and our new king,' said Kava. Ofa agreed but, unmarried, he had different plans for the off-season.

'I will stay in my village and drink kava every night and sleep all day. I'll do some work in my relative's plantation if I run out of money...but I don't want to.'

Kava plans to go to Nuku'alofa to earn money. He wants to get a new house for his family. (Later I visited the village to meet Kava's family and participate in a kava session. I was stunned at the poor living conditions his family endures. Kava has worked on the inter-island ferry and on cargo ships to Australia and NZ.)

Both guys also agreed when I asked them about their favourite eating and drinking hangouts in Vava'u. 'It's too expensive for Tongans to eat in *palangi* restaurants in Neiafu. We don't make much money. The only time we eat out is on the last night of the kayak trip when there is a trip party.'

Same for going out drinking. 'It's too expensive. I stay in the village and drink kava. On Fridays and Saturdays my friends and I buy cheap rum, get drunk in the village then go to Tongan Bob's in Neiafu,' said Ofa.

'Tongan Bob's is the best drinking spot, is it?' I asked.

'Yes,' said Ofa, 'there are lots of single *palangi* girls. I can have a different girlfriend every night! Hee hee hee!' he giggled, revealing a grin that I'm sure would make him extremely popular with female visitors. Kava is at pains to point out that he stays home with his family.

One more thing the guys agree on: '*Palangi* complain that their Tongan workers don't work hard enough – but they're wrong. Tongans will work harder if they are treated better.'

AROUND VAVA'U
Sia Ko Kafoa

Vava'u Island is nearly bisected by the Vaipua Inlet, which separates the Neiafu area from western Vava'u. The two sides of the island are connected by a causeway and a road climbs to the village of Taoa (meaning 'Spear') on the western shore. Behind Taoa are the twin hills of Lei'ulu, used as a burial ground, and Sia Ko Kafoa. On the summit is an *'esi*, a mound used as a rest area by chiefs and nobles and a place where young virgins were presented to amorous chiefs.

'Utula'aina Point

'Utula'aina Point, surrounded by steep cliffs above a turbulent sea in the island's north, provides perhaps the most spectacular views on Vava'u Island. To get there, head north from Holonga village. Look out for whales between June and November. There's also a steep track leading to a secluded beach 50m before the trailhead.

Toula & Veimumuni Cave

Near the southern point of Vava'u Island is Toula village. From Toula, turn east (it's signposted) following the path uphill past a cemetery. As you begin to descend to the beach, you'll see Veimumuni Cave in the bluff. Inside it are an appealing freshwater spring and swimming hole.

Pangaimotu & 'Utungake

'Ano and **Hinakauea Beaches**, near the southern end of Pangaimotu, are beautiful and very quiet, with sheltered turquoise water, abundant vegetation, good snorkelling and a safe anchorage. Directly across from 'Ano is Tapana Island, home to La Paella (see p524) restaurant. A boat will pick you up at 'Ano Beach with a prior booking.

The long, thin island of 'Utungake is connected by a causeway to Pangaimotu. Just past the causeway, **Tongan Beach Resort** (☎ 70380; VHF Channel 71; www.thetongan.com; high season d & tw T$400, half/full board T$88/110) on Hikutamole Beach is a relaxed place looking out onto the main channel into Port of Refuge. It has recently renovated rooms, a lovely sand-floor *fale* bar and beachfront restaurant. There are lots of packages to choose from on the website.

Overlooking the water at Talihau Beach at the tip of 'Utungake, **Lucky's Beach Houses** (☎ 71075; www.talihaubeach.com; fale T$60, beach house T$120), run by Kurt and Lynn, has two houses and two *fale* right by the water. Guests can launch a kayak off the beach to explore the islands and paddle over to nearby Mala. Dinner is available (from T$20). Kurt knows all there is to know about surfing in Vava'u.

SOUTHERN VAVA'U ISLANDS

If you study the map on p518 you will see that Vava'u has an incredible number of islands and waterways to the south. Visitors can either head out to one of the growing number of island resorts, or take it all in by boat or on a multiday kayak tour.

Mala

Just south of 'Utungake, the small island of Mala is only a few minutes by boat from the road end. It has a sandy swimming beach and a popular resort. The **Japanese Gardens** is a beautiful snorkelling spot between Mala and Kapa, though a strong current flows between these two islands and 'Utungake. Beware of a legendary cannibal god who reputedly lives on Mala and is said to capture and devour passing boaters.

Mala Island Resort (☎ 71304, 8835766; VHF Channel 16; www.malaisland.com; s/d bungalow US$69/99; 🐾) is an upbeat, welcoming place with magnificent views run by Americans Shawn and Karie. The tapa-lined bungalows have creaky wooden floors and plenty of charm. There's a big screen for sports events and a popular Sunday barbecue. A taxi from town costs T$20 to Talihau Beach, and the resort's boat can meet you there. Low-season rates available.

Kapa

Kapa island's main attraction, **Swallows' Cave** ('Anapekepeka), cuts into a cliff on the west side of the island. It's actually inhabited by hundreds of swiftlets, and the exceptional underwater visibility makes it great for snorkelling. The water is crystal clear despite the floor of the cave being 18m below the surface, and the only access is by boat.

Kapa is also home to Vava'u's newest hotspot, **Reef Resort** (☎ 59276, 8867898; VHF Channel 71; www.reeferesortvavau.com; r T$400, full board T$120; 🐾). This place receives top reviews despite having been open only a short time. With a perfect beachfront location, spacious clean rooms and accommodating owners, things look bright at Reef Resort. Return airport transfers cost T$100 per person.

Hunga & Fofoa

A large, sheltered lagoon formed by Hunga, Kalau and Fofoa offers excellent anchorage and impressive **snorkelling**.

Ika Lahi Lodge (Map p518; ☎ 70611; www.tongafishing .com; tw NZ$250, full board NZ$150) is a fishing-focused resort (*ika lahi* means 'big fish, many fish'). It's handily close to the deep ocean and has four guest units with balconies and plenty of interest for nonfishing partners. Check out the website for options.

Foe'ata & Foelifuka

The island of Foe'ata, immediately south of Hunga, offers glorious white **beaches** and good **snorkelling**. There is an anchorage on the north side of Foelifuka, beside Foe'ata.

The ecolodge-cum–eccentric dream **Blue Lagoon** (☎ 71300; VHF Channel 16; www.foiata-island .com; fale d T$270, half-/full board T$86.25/97.75) enjoys an idyllic beach position on Foe'ata. Each of the six large *fale* is uniquely constructed in its immediate environment from local materials, and the food is some of Vava'u's best. Transfers cost T$130.

uapapu

uapapu is best known for **Mariner's Cave**, a idden cave at its northern end. An interest-1g phenomenon of this cave, caused by the welling sea, is the fog that forms every few seconds, only to disappear again just as fast. he main entrance is a couple of metres below 1e surface and the tunnel is about 4m long; se the swell to pull you towards it, then exit rhen the swell pushes you out. Snorkelling ear is recommended.

'aka'eitu

The small, hilly island of Vaka'eitu has se-1uded beaches on each side, a secure over-1ight anchorage and some of Vava'u's best norkelling in the nearby **coral gardens**.

'aunga, Ngau & Pau

ust south of Kapa, the inviting and sporadi-ally inhabited islands of Taunga and Ngau 1ave idyllic **beaches** with fine **snorkelling** and ;ood anchorages. At low tide you can walk rom Ngau along a slender ribbon of sand to he uninhabited island of Pau. This is the real leserted Pacific island stuff of your dreams.

'Eua'iki & 'Euakafa

The small raised island of 'Eue'iki has easy ooat access to the stunning white **beach**, and a **coral garden** off the southern shore. You can circumnavigate the island in around 45 min-1tes at low tide.

A sandy beach rings the north side of unin-habited 'Euakafa. From its eastern end a trail leads through the forest and mango trees to the summit (100m) and the overgrown tomb of Talafaiva.

Mark Belvedere's **'Eua'iki Island Eco-Resort** (☎ 12935; www.tongaislandresort.com; d fale US$195, full board per person T$80), previously known as Treasure Island, is in a magical setting on 'Eua'iki island. Its thatched bar–restaurant perches on a white, sandy beach, and solid *fale* with water-view balconies are spaced along the beachfront. There are deep chan-nels on both sides of the island that the whales use, and if you're lucky, you may find them frolicking right in front of you as you eat breakfast. Meals generally feature fish (the day's catch) or meat, and may be available to yachties if booked ahead. Mark is a special-ist in the maritime history of the Pacific and makes your visit an educational experience by explaining the seafaring migration of the Pacific. Check out www.kaliafoundation.org for information on the Polynesian seafaring tradition. Return boat transfers cost T$60 to Neiafu, T$80 to the airport.

Mounu & 'Ovalau

A short distance southeast of Vaka'eitu are Mounu and 'Ovalau, two more of the perfect islands Vava'u has in abundance.

Mounu Island Resort (☎ 70747; VHF Channel 77; www.mounuisland.com) consists of ecofriendly wooden *fale* spaced around the island for privacy. The resort has developed a glowing reputation as a place to get away from it all and relax. Whale-watching tours are run by the owners. Email for prices.

EASTERN VAVA'U ISLANDS

Vava'u's eastern islands are best reached from Neiafu's Old Harbour.

Mafana

At the time of research, budget accommoda-tion catering for backpackers and adventur-ous ecofriendly travellers was being set up at **Mafana Island Beach** (☎ 74834; www.mafanaisland beach.com), 15 minutes by boat from the Old Harbour. Camping will cost T$20 (with own tent), single/double T$50/80 in tepees on a beautiful secluded beach. There will also be a bar and kitchen facilities, and daytrippers will be welcome.

'Ofu, Kenutu & Lolo

'Ofu is a friendly island and well worth a day's exploration. Its surrounding waters are the primary habitat of the prized but endangered *'ofu* shell – buying them will only encourage their collection.

The small, uninhabited island of Kenutu, just east of 'Ofu, has superb **beaches**, and coral patches south of the island offer good **snorkelling** and **diving**. There's an anchor-age on the western side. The reef between Kenutu and Lolo islands, immediately south, is very dramatic.

THE NIUAS

Tongan tradition remains very much alive on these three small volcanic islands in Tonga's extreme northern reaches which are as close to Samoa as they are to Vava'u. These were the first Tongan islands to be seen by Europeans (Schouten and Le Maire in 1616); it may seem like little has changed in the ensuing four centuries. The main islands of Niuatoputapu and Niuafo'ou are set about 100km apart.

Any trip to the Niuas should be approached with flexibility in mind as weather conditions often cause delays and cancellations of services. The closest most people will ever get to the remote Niuas (meaning 'Rich in Coconuts') is picking up a first-day cover of Niuafo'ou's decorative postage stamps (see opposite).

Getting There & Away

AIR

At the time of research, there were no flights to the Niuas, but **Chathams Pacific** (☎ 23192; www.chathamspacific.com) was planning to have weekly flights starting in the near future. As part of its licence to operate in Tonga it needs to provide flights to the Niuas; check the website for updates. Both Niuatoputapu and Niuafo'ou have landing strips.

BOAT

MV 'Olovaha is supposed to make a return trip from Vava'u to Niuatoputapu and Niuafo'ou, then back to Vava'u once a month, but the unpredictable schedule is reliant on the weather, the state of the vessel, and government subsidies. Inquire at the TVB in Tongatapu.

Due to its volcanic nature, Niuafo'ou lacks a decent anchorage or landing site, leaving access reliant on the mercy of the wind and waves. The arrival of the 'Olovaha is a highlight, and the precarious loading and unloading of goods is a fascinating spectacle.

Most visitors to Niuatoputapu arrive on private yachts. Be extremely careful on approaching the island. The word is that marker and range sites are inaccurate.

NIUATOPUTAPU

pop 1400 / area 18 sq km

Niuatoputapu (Very Sacred Coconut) has a squashed sombrero shape made up of a steep and narrow central ridge 130m high and surrounding coastal plains. Much of this is plantation land, with many archaeological sites hidden in the undergrowth.

The north coast is bounded by a series of reefs, but there is a passage through to Falehau Wharf; yachts anchor just northwest of here. The air strip is near the southern tip of the island.

Information

Sleepy Hihifo is the Niuas' 'capital' ar home to a police station, a post office ar a small store. Cash and travellers chequ can be changed at the Treasury, though sometimes runs out of cash so it's advisab to bring pa'anga with you.

Check out www.niuatoputapu.info f more information.

Sights & Activities

The island is surrounded by magnifice white beaches of remarkable diversity ar is easily circumnavigated in seven to eig hours (11km).

Boat trips, including to the nearby volcan island of Tafahi, can be negotiated with loc fishermen. There's good **diving** outside th reef, but no diving equipment is available o the island.

NIUTOUA SPRING

The cool, sparkling pool of Niutoua Sprir flows through a crack in the rock just we of Hihifo. It's great for a swim. If you inter to bathe at Niutoua, bear in mind that th spectacle of palangi swimming will quick draw an audience. Swim in baggy clothes wi a minimum of exposed skin.

BEACHES & SWIMMING

The most beautiful beaches are on th northwest side of the main island and o **Hunganga**, home to Palm Tree Island Resor Near Hihifo, a maze of shallow waterway wind between the islets of Nukuseila Tafuna, Tavili and Hunganga. At low tid you can walk anywhere in the area by wa ing through a few centimetres of water. / high tide, the passages (especially betwee Niuatoputapu and Hunganga) are excelle for swimming.

Sleeping & Eating

Kalolaine Guesthouse (☎ 85021; s/d T$20/25) War hospitality awaits in this Hihifo village hom with a spacious lounge and neat room Guests can use the kitchen or book mea in advance.

Palm Tree Island Resort (☎ 85090; www.palmtr islandresort.com; s/d T$180/240, half-/full board T$40/6 The four beachfront fale on the Hungang islet provide a comfortable base for explora tion or navel gazing. Each has private facili ties and impressive views; cycles, kayaks an norkelling equipment are provided. Meals eature lots of fresh fish and organic fruit and egetables. There's a dinghy shuttle to Hihifo r you can walk across at low tide.

Excellent campsites are located on the west of Hihifo and the beach along the island's south coast, though you need to get permission first.

Bring your own food to the island as only imited groceries are available.

TAFAHI
pop 150 / area 3.4 sq km
Nine kilometres north of Niuatoputapu is the perfect cone of the extinct volcano Tafahi (656m). On the right tide you can cross to Tafahi (40 minutes) in the morning and return in the afternoon. It's a 3½-hour return walk to the summit from where, on a good day, you can see Samoa! You'll have to negotiate boat transfers with a local fisherman. Tafahi is reputed to produce the best kava in the kingdom.

NIUAFO'OU
pop 735 / area 49 sq km
Remote Niuafo'ou, about 100km west of Niuatoputapu, resembles a doughnut floating in the sea. It is a collapsed volcanic cone thought to have once topped 1300m in height. Today, the highest point on the caldera is at 210m, and the enclosed lake is nearly 5km wide and 23m above sea level. During the past 150 years, Niuafo'ou has experienced 10 major volcanic eruptions. After a particularly nasty one in 1946, the government evacuated the 1300 residents to 'Eua island, and Niuafo'ou was uninhabited until 200 homesick locals returned in 1958.

Niuafo'ou has no coral reef and no sandy beaches, just open ocean surrounds. The islanders speak a notably different dialect from Tonga's other islands (it's closer to Samoan), and its fiercely loyal residents have a reputation for toughness.

Information
Boil all lake water before drinking; locals are generally happy to fill your water bottles from their rainwater tanks when asked.

Money can be changed at the Treasury.

Sights & Activities
A track leads right around the doughnut-shaped volcanic cone (taking approximately six hours) and its splendid freshwater lake, **Vai Lahi** (Big Lake), which nearly fills the island's large and mysterious crater. Along the southern and western shores is a vast, barren moonscape of **lava flows**. On the northern shore, mounds of volcanic slag, lava tubes, vents and craters are accessible from the main road. Beneath this flow is the buried village of **'Angaha**.

Keep an eye out for Niuafo'ou's most unusual inhabitants, the **megapode birds**, which use the warm volcanic soil to incubate their eggs.

Sleeping
There are numerous excellent campsites on the crater (especially on the lake shores), although you should ask for permission, and camping will draw a lot of attention and curiosity. A handful of village houses offer guest rooms; contact the TVB in Tongatapu for details. Many local people would be happy to take you in for the night; a gift would be appreciated in return.

There are several small shops scattered through the villages, but it would be wise to bring plenty of food with you.

TONGA

TIN CAN ISLAND
Niuafo'ou is the 'Tin Can Island' legendary for its unique postal service. In days of old, since there was no anchorage or landing site, mail and supplies for residents were sealed up in a biscuit tin and tossed overboard from a passing supply ship. A strong swimmer from the island would then retrieve the parcel. Outbound mail was tied to the end of metre-long sticks, and the swimmer would carry them balanced overhead out to the waiting ship. This method persisted until 1931, when the mail swimmer was taken by a shark.

In keeping with its postal tradition, special Niuafo'ou postage stamps, first issued by the Tongan government in 1983, are prized by collectors.

TONGA DIRECTORY

ACCOMMODATION

Camping

Camping is generally discouraged in Tonga, and is illegal in Ha'apai and Vava'u unless it's part of a guided trip. Camping trips to uninhabited islands in Ha'apai and Vava'u are easily arranged and thoroughly recommended. A few places to stay allow camping.

Guesthouses

In Tongatapu and Vava'u it is easy to find clean, well-run guest houses, many of which will have cooking facilities. In Ha'apai cooking facilities are the norm, but the room standard is on the whole a lot lower. Generally, expect cold showers. The average budget price is between T$30 and T$40 for a bed, a little more for a private bathroom.

Hotels & Resorts

'Resort' is an extremely loose term in Tonga and you may find some 'resorts' don't meet your image of what a resort should be. If you find that prices are surprisingly cheap, don't expect much in the way of facilities. Even if prices are expensive, don't expect too much and check the website if they have one. There is boutique-style accommodation with plenty of comforts in Tongatapu and its nearby islands, on Foa in Ha'apai and throughout the Vava'u group. Many of these are quite eclectic, with an eco bent.

ACTIVITIES

Caving

'Eua has the most dramatic caves in Tonga and plenty of sinkholes to delve into and emerge from on the roots of giant banyan trees. A visit to water-accessible caves is requisite on Vava'u, while the freshwater pool in 'Anahulu Cave on Tongatapu is a popular swimming spot.

Cycling

Flat terrain and generally slow driving make Tongatapu and Lifuka (Ha'apai) ideal places for cycling. Bicycles can be hired on Tongatapu, 'Eua, Ha'apai and Vava'u.

Diving & Snorkelling

Great visibility, comfortable water temperatures and sheltered waters create magnificent conditions for diving and snorkelling. Professional dive outfits operate out of Vava'u, Ha'apai and Tongatapu. See p78 for a spotlight on some of Tonga's dive sites.

Fishing

Vava'u has some of the best game fishing in the Pacific and hosts Tonga's International Billfish Tournament in September. Tongatapu and Ha'apai also have a handful of professional fishing charters.

Hiking

'Eua's national park and plantation forest provide a varied terrain with some of the South Pacific's best hiking (and no snakes or poisonous spiders). Other good hiking venues include the Niuas, Kao and volcanic Tofua in Ha'apai and various islands in the Vava'u group.

Kayaking

Kayaking around Vava'u and Ha'apai rates among the top adventure activities in the world, with a mix of reefs, beaches, whales, uninhabited islands and cultural interactions in villages.

Sailing

Vava'u's idyllic, sheltered islands make for a stunning sailing destination that is well known among yachties. May to November is the most popular sailing season. Operators are at pains to point out that while November to April is officially the cyclone season, cyclones are few and far between and there is excellent yachting to be had in summer. There are various yacht charter options in Vava'u, Ha'apai and Tongatapu.

Surfing

Tongatapu's western waters, particularly at Ha'atafu Beach, offer excellent surfing. Surfers can access reef breaks by boat in Vava'u.

Whale-watching

Due to the incredible opportunity to swim with humpback whales in Tonga, the kingdom is one the world's top whale-watching destinations between June and November, when whales come to mate and bear their young. Vava'u is the main centre for whale-watching, but there are also operators in Tongatapu, Ha'apai and 'Eua. See p523 for more information.

BUSINESS HOURS

Business hours are flexible, but usually run from 9am to 4.30pm, with most shops open 8.30am

PRACTICALITIES

■ The weekly *Tonga Chronicle* is the official newspaper of the Tongan government and runs an insert in English. The only English-language newspaper for sale is the *New Zealander*, a weekly published in Australia for New Zealanders.

■ Tune into English programming on **Radio New Zealand International** (www.rnzi.com) at 15720kHz, 9885kHz, 9870kHz and 17675kHz; **Radio Australia** (www.abc.net.au/ra), with short-wave frequencies including 5995kHz, 12080kHz, 15515kHz, broadcast at Nuku'alofa 103FM and 101.7FM; and **BBC World Service** (www.bbc.co.uk/worldservice), no direct service – refer to the East Asia schedule online. See each website for details on shortwave and satellite radio frequencies and listening via the internet.

■ Satellite TV is increasingly available in Tonga, while local TV is heavily religious and has three stations – two local plus one US Christian.

■ Tonga has both the PAL system (Australasia and most of Western Europe) and the NTSC system (North America and Japan).

■ Power in Tonga is 240V AC, 50Hz. Three-pronged plugs used in NZ and Australia are OK here.

■ Tonga uses the metric system. See the Quick Reference page for conversions.

to 5pm Monday to Friday (some close for an hour at lunch), and 9am to noon on Saturday.

Cafe-style eateries open early and restaurants are typically open from lunchtime until around 10.30pm, but those that double as bars can stay open until as late as 2am. Everything closes at midnight on Saturday, and only those restaurants/bars that have accommodation are officially allowed to open on Sunday, though there are exceptions.

See p532 for public holidays that will affect opening hours.

CHILDREN

Tonga is a great place to travel with children, and there's plenty to keep them happy: swimming, snorkelling, beachcombing, cycling, kayaking, short boat trips, and visits to interesting sights and cultural events (especially Tongan feasts).

Accommodation with a beach or swimming pool may be all the entertainment you need. Some hotels allow children to stay free, others have a reduced children's rate, and a few do not accept children at all. Inquire whether your accommodation can arrange baby-sitting, if required, as the small size and island location of some may make this difficult.

The larger supermarkets in Nuku'alofa and Neiafu are well stocked, and disposable nappies (diapers) and UHT and powdered milk are widely available, but sunscreen and insect repellent can be hard to find outside of Nuku'alofa.

It's worth picking up some children's snorkelling gear before arriving in Tonga. You'll need to bring your own child car seat and check that it clips into seatbelts.

DANGERS & ANNOYANCES

Tonga is a safe country to visit. There has been a rise in thefts in recent years, though these rarely occur against the person. Any attacks on *palangi* usually go hand in hand with late nights and alcohol. Brawls are common in bars – keep tuned for trouble.

There are a lot of dogs roaming around Tonga: most are either friendly or will keep their distance, but a few (especially when they're in packs) are aggressive. Pretending to throw a stone often discourages them.

In Nuku'alofa, cases of taxi drivers taking new arrivals to the wrong guest houses are common, so make sure you get dropped where you asked to be dropped.

Despite official word to the contrary, one sip of water out of the tap may convince you that town water supplies are not fit to drink. Rainwater or bottled water make better alternatives.

EMBASSIES & CONSULATES

The following foreign diplomatic representatives are found in Nuku'alofa:

Australia (Map pp504–5; ☎ 23244; www.tonga .embassy.gov.au; Salote Rd) High Commission.

Canada Limited consular services available at the Australian High Commission.

China (Map pp504–5; ☎ 24554; fax 24595; Vuna Rd) Embassy.

EU (☎ 23820; eutonga@kalianet.to; Taufa'ahau Rd) European Commission.

Germany (☎ 23477; fax 23154; Taufa'ahau Rd) Honorary Consulate.

NZ (Map pp504–5; ☎ 23122; nzhcnuk@kalianet.to; Taufa'ahau Rd) High Commission.

UK (Map pp504–5; ☎ 24395; britcomt@kalianet.to; Vuna Rd) High Commission.

US (Peace Corps; ☎ 25466, Ministry of Foreign Affairs 23600; National Reserve Bank) Nearest US Embassy is in Suva, Fiji.

FESTIVALS & EVENTS

Tongan families need little excuse for a feast, and each island group has an annual festival featuring music and dance. The biggest is Tongatapu's week-long **Heilala Festival**, held in July. There are parades, dance and sporting competitions, arts and music. The **Miss Galaxy Pageant**, also held in Nuku'alofa in July, is the flamboyant and fun international *fakaleiti* (see the boxed text, p497) competition, and is always sold out.

GAY & LESBIAN TRAVELLERS

As in most of Polynesia, homosexuality is an accepted fact of life in Tonga and you'll see plenty of gay men around, including those following the fine old Polynesian tradition of *fakaleiti* (see the boxed text, p497). Whatever lesbian population exists is much more under cover. Public displays of sexual affection are frowned upon, whether gay or straight.

HOLIDAYS

In addition to New Year's Day, Easter, Anzac Day, Christmas Day and Boxing Day (see p629 for dates), public holidays in Tonga include the following:

Prince Tupouto'a's Birthday 4 May
Emancipation Day 4 June
Birthday of the Heir to the Crown of Tonga 12 July
Official Birthday of the King of Tonga 1 August
Constitution Day 4 November
King George I Day 4 December

INTERNET ACCESS

Internet cafes on Tongatapu and Vava'u charge around T$5 per hour. Access is limited in other island groups. Many mid- to top-range accommodation houses have wireless and/or computers available for guest use, depending upon the location.

INTERNET RESOURCES

The website of the **Tonga Visitors Bureau** (www.tongaholiday.com) is a good starting point for travel information. **Matangi Tonga** (Wind of Tonga; www.matangitonga.to) is like an online newspaper and has the best coverage of Tongan news and issues. Also good is www.planet-tonga.com.

MONEY
Credit Cards

Credit cards are accepted at many tourist facilities, with Visa and MasterCard the most common, but these often attract a 4% to 5% fee on transactions. There are ATMs with Visa, MasterCard and Cirrus facilities in Tongatapu and Vava'u. Western Union has offices throughout Tonga, and MoneyGram is represented by the Westpac Bank of Tonga.

Currency

Notes come in denominations of one, two, five, 10, 20 and 50 *pa'anga* (T$). Coins come in denominations of one, five, 10, 20 and 50 *seniti*.

Country	Unit	Pa'anga
Australia	A$1	T$1.42
Canada	C$1	T$1.75
CFP zone	100 CFP	T$2.50
euro zone	€1	T$2.90
Fiji	F$1	T$1.25
Japan	¥100	T$2.40
NZ	NZ$1	T$1.25
Samoa	ST1	85 *seniti*
Solomon Islands	S$1	33 *seniti*
UK	£1	T$3.50
US	US$1	T$2.20
Vanuatu	100Vt	T$2.05

HOW MUCH?

- Cup of coffee: T$3 to T$4
- Drinking coconut: T$1
- Bicycle hire: T$15
- Lobster meal: T$35
- Whale-watching trip: T$250
- 1L unleaded petrol: T$3
- 1.5L bottled water: T$2.50
- 355mL bottle of Ikale beer: T$7
- Souvenir T-shirt: T$30
- Sipi (mutton) curry: T$8

TONGA TIME

Sit down, put your thinking cap on, and ponder this. When it is midday in Tonga on Sunday and everyone is obeying the law and doing nothing, it is exactly the same time (midday) in Samoa, only it's Saturday. Sort of makes sense, right? Everyone has heard of the International Date Line (IDL), right? But if Samoa and Tonga are on opposite sides of the IDL, how can the time be the same? Shouldn't they be in different time zones?

Looking at a map you'll notice that the IDL isn't exactly straight. In fact it has some major kinks. The theory was good at the 1884 International Meridian Conference in Washington when it was decided to put the imaginary IDL at the meridian of 180 degrees longitude, exactly halfway around the world from the Greenwich meridian (0 degrees) – but it was also agreed that the IDL 'should not interfere with the use of standard or local time where desirable'.

Fiji didn't want to be split into two different days, it wasn't desirable for the Aleutian Islands to be a day ahead of Alaska – and the Tongan King didn't want to be a day behind South Pacific heavyweights Australia and NZ. So the line was drawn arbitrarily east of Tonga. To make things really confusing, in 1892 American traders persuaded the Samoan king to adopt the American date, resulting in a further kink in the IDL – meaning that Samoa and Tonga are in the same time zone, only on different sides of the IDL.

Moneychangers

Australian, US, NZ and Fijian dollars plus British sterling are most easily exchanged in Tonga, but yen and euros are also widely accepted. Travellers cheques receive the best exchange rates, and all major brands are accepted.

TELEPHONE

Tonga's international telephone code is ☎ 676. There are no local area codes. The emergency phone number is ☎ 911; the international operator is ☎ 913; directory enquiry is ☎ 910.

Public pay phones are located throughout Tonga. You can use phonecards to make local and overseas calls. Phonecards are readily available in denominations of T$5, T$10 and T$20.

Mobile-phone users can get SIM cards in Tongatapu through **UCall** (☎ 0800 222; www.tcc.to; Salote Rd) or **Digicel** (☎ 0800 3444; www.digiceltonga.com; Taufa'ahau Rd). Mobiles need to be GSM 800/900 compatible and must be unlocked from your local operator. Alternatively, Digicel will sell you a phone for T$50 that includes T$5 credit. Mobile coverage is pretty good throughout Tonga.

TIME

Tonga is 20 minutes east of the 180th meridian, placing it 13 hours ahead of Greenwich Mean Time. Due to an odd kink in the International Date Line (see above), however, noon in Tonga is 3pm the previous day in Los Angeles, 11pm the previous day in London and 9am the same day in Sydney. When NZ is on summer daylight saving time, Tonga and NZ share the same time; the rest of the year NZ is one hour behind.

TIPPING

Tongans do not expect tips, though you won't cause any offence by rewarding special service with one. You may see *fakapale* (gifts of money) given to performers at cultural events as a sign of appreciation. Spectators stick small bills to the well-oiled arms and shoulders of the dancers.

TOURIST INFORMATION

The **Tonga Visitors Bureau** (TVB; ☎ 25334; www.tongaholiday.com) has offices in Nuku'alofa, Ha'apai and Vava'u.

VISAS

Most countries' citizens are granted a 31-day visitors visa on arrival upon presentation of a passport with at least six months' validity and an onward ticket. Those intending to fly in and depart Tongan waters by yacht require a letter of authority from one of Tonga's diplomatic missions overseas or the immigration division.

One-month extensions are granted at the immigration departments in Nuku'alofa, Ha'apai and Vava'u for up to six months. You'll need one passport photo for each extension (T$46) and a photocopy of your onward ticket.

TRANSPORT IN TONGA

GETTING THERE & AWAY

Air

From Fiji, Samoa, Los Angeles, Australia and NZ, access to Tonga is straightforward. Auckland (NZ) and Nadi (Fiji) are the most convenient connecting points. For overseas airline details, see p635. Flights are often full between December and February. The cheapest flights are booked early and online.

Air New Zealand (Map pp504-5; ☎ 23192; www .airnewzealand.com; Air NZ Travel Centre, Vuna Rd)

Air Pacific (Map pp504-5; ☎ 23422; www.airpacific .com; cnr Taufa'ahau & Wellington Rds)

Pacific Blue (Map pp504-5; ☎ 24566; www.flypacific blue.com; cnr Salote & Fatafehi Rds)

ASIA

Air Pacific operates direct flights from Tokyo to Nadi (Fiji), which connect with flights to Tonga (Nuku'alofa). Air New Zealand has flights from Tokyo, Osaka, Singapore and Hong Kong to Auckland, with onward flights to the Tonga. Qantas and countless other airlines have flights from Asian cities to Sydney, from where Pacific Blue has flights to Tonga.

AUSTRALIA & NZ

Air New Zealand and Pacific Blue operate flights between Auckland and Tonga.

From Australia, Pacific Blue has flights between Tonga and Sydney, with connections to other Australian cities. Air Pacific flights from Brisbane and Sydney to Nadi (Fiji) connect with flights to Tonga. Alternatively, fly via Auckland to Tonga with Air NZ.

CANADA & USA

Los Angeles and Honolulu are the two major gateway cities for travel between the US (and Canada) and the South Pacific.

From Los Angeles you can fly to Tonga via Samoa on Air New Zealand, or via Auckland. Alternatively, take the Air Pacific (code sharing with Qantas) or Air New Zealand flights direct from Los Angeles to Nadi, then connect to Nuku'alofa.

EUROPE

Europeans usually fly to the South Pacific via LA, Sydney or Auckland, then direct (or via Fiji) to Nuku'alofa. Air New Zealand flies from London

or Frankfurt to Los Angeles, with connecti from Los Angeles to the South Pacific.

PACIFIC

Nadi and Auckland are the region's t major air transport hubs. Nadi is a 1 hour hop from Tonga, and Auckland i 2½-hour flight.

Air Pacific flies between Nuku'alofa a Nadi, while Air New Zealand flies betwe Nuku'alofa and Apia.

Various air passes connect Tonga with t other Pacific islands. See p636 for more air passes.

Sea

Trans-Pacific yachts come to Tonga on t trade winds from Samoa, the Cook Islan or French Polynesia. Others arrive fro NZ. Ports of entry for yachts are Nuku'alo (Tongatapu), Neiafu (Vava'u), Pang (Ha'apai), Falehau (Niuatoputapu) and Fu (Niuafo'ou). As of January 2008, all vesse calling on Tonga must give customs 24-ho advance notice of arrival.

Day sailing within the island groups is n restricted, but a Coastal Clearance Permit required when moving between groups serve by customs offices. Be sure to pay harbo dues as the receipt will be requested in th next port. Contact customs on arrival at th next island group. When travelling betwee Nuku'alofa and Vava'u, you can request th the Coastal Clearance includes Ha'apai you're intending to stop there.

In Nuku'alofa, pay harbour dues on depa ture at the **Ports Authority** (Map pp504-5; ☎ 2316 marports@kalianet.to; Queen Salote Wharf; ⏰ 8.30am-12.30p & 1.30-4.30pm Mon-Fri). Customs is based in the **On Stop Shop** (Map pp504-5; ☎ 23967; Queen Salote Wha ⏰ 8.30am-12.30pm & 1.30-4.30pm Mon-Fri). The custom clearance fee in Tonga is T$50. In Vava'u, pu up at the southern end of Neiafu Wharf an contact the **boarding officers** (☎ 70053; ⏰ 8.30ar 12.30pm & 1.30-4.30pm Mon-Fri). In Ha'apai, check i with the customs officer at the treasury office

To summon the harbour master and fo emergencies in Tonga use VHF Channel 16

GETTING AROUND
To/From the Airport

Shuttles and taxis meet incoming flights o Tongatapu and Vava'u, and taxis may mee flights in Ha'apai. Many places to stay wr organise airport transfers for guests.

ir

lying is by far the easiest, fastest and most omfortable way to get around Tonga. At the ime of research, all domestic flights were being perated by the very efficient **Chathams Pacific** (Map p504-5; ☎ 23192; www.chathamspacific.com; Air NZ Travel entre, Vuna Rd). Bookings can be made and paid for online. Flights are scheduled to work in with arriving and departing international flights from Tongatapu's Fua'amotu International Airport. Direct flights between Tongatapu and Vava'u one-way T$232; 50 minutes), and Tongatapu nd Ha'apai (one way T$144, 45 minutes) operate at least once daily. Ha'apai and Vava'u (one vay T$134, 40 minutes) are connected three imes a week. Tongatapu and 'Eua (one way T$67, 15 minutes) are connected twice daily. Flights from Tongatapu to the Niuas should be running by the time this book is published. There are no flights on Sundays.

Boat

INTER-ISLAND FERRY

Depending on many factors, passenger freighters travel between the main island groups, and trips range from almost pleasurable cruising with sightseeing and whale-watching en route to barfing hell-rides kept afloat with plenty of midnight prayers. In either event, consider it a cultural experience. The TVB website (www.tongaholidays.com) lists ferry schedules (prone to delay, alteration and cancellation), which must be rechecked prior to intended travel. Economy (deck class) fares are listed here (children aged under 12 pay 50%).

The main carrier is MV *'Olovaha*, run by the **Shipping Corporation of Polynesia** (Map pp504-5; ☎ 23853; www.scptonga.com; Queen Salote Wharf, Nuku'alofa). This rusty tub has the unpleasant nickname of 'the orange vomit' and does weekly runs from Tongatapu (Nuku'alofa) to Ha'apai (Lifuka; T$68, 11½ hours) and Vava'u (Neiafu; T$88, 19 hours). Every couple of months it goes to the Niuas (T$103 from Tongatapu), but it is rarely able to land at Niuafo'ou. It's advisable to buy only a one-way ticket as many passengers swear they will never get back on it once they've completed their outbound journey.

MV *Pulupaki*, run by **Uata Shipping Line** (Walter Line; Map pp504-5; ☎ 23855; uataline@kalianet.to; Queen Salote Wharf, Nuku'alofa), is a lot quicker but wasn't operating at the time of research. It had been relocated to Fiji and no-one knew if it was coming back.

There are services daily (except Sunday) between Tongatapu and 'Eua on **MV Ikale** (☎ 23855) or **MV Alaimoana** (☎ 21326; 'Unga Rd). Boats depart Nuku'alofa's Tuimatamoana Harbour on alternate days at 12.30pm for the two-hour crossing, returning from 'Eua's Nafanua Wharf around 5am the next morning. The generally simple crossing can get rough. One-way costs T$28.

OTHER VESSELS

Smaller islands off the main ferry routes in all island groups can be reached by smaller boats.

Car

Rental cars are available on Tongatapu and Vava'u. You must organise a Tongan driving licence from the police, for which your only test will be to simultaneously produce your home driving licence, your passport and T$17 cash. Hiring a car or van with a driver is another option

People drive very slowly on the left-hand side of the road in Tonga. The speed limit is 40km/h in villages and 65km/h elsewhere and, except for a few budding organ donors on Tongatapu, it is faithfully observed.

When driving, watch out for children, dogs, chickens and pigs; and don't park under coconut trees – you will be liable for the broken windscreen.

Local Transport

BUS

Buses run on Tongatapu, and in a more limited capacity on Vava'u and its causeway-linked islands, and Lifuka and Foa in the Ha'apai Group. Fares range from 50 *seniti* to T$1.70 depending upon the island and the distance travelled. Don't expect to get where you're going in a hurry.

TAXI

Taxis can be recognised by a 'T' in front of the numbers on the licence plate. There are plenty of taxis on Tongatapu and Vava'u, a few on Lifuka and one on 'Eua. Don't be surprised if it's not an 'official' taxi that picks you up – chances are, if you ask someone to organise a taxi, it will be their husband, brother or nephew who comes to get you. Just pay the going rate.

Passengers should always ask the rate before getting in the taxi, and a smart move is to ask for the going rate at your accommodation before you leave so you've got a ballpark figure. Around town is usually T$5.

TONGA

Tuvalu

Tell people that you're going to Tuvalu and the most common response you'll get is 'where?' One of the smallest and most remote countries on earth, the five atolls and four islands of this tropical nation don't make it onto most people's travel agendas. Approaching the islands by plane, the view below is mesmerising – after endless miles of dull ocean, a dazzling smear of turquoise and green appears, ringed with coral and studded with tiny, palm topped islets, bobbing vulnerably in the surrounding waters. The landmass of Fongafale, Tuvalu's main island is so startlingly narrow that as the plane nears the airstrip it seems as if it's about to tip into the ocean.

You'll likely spend the most time in Tuvalu's capital, Funafuti Atoll, and its administrative centre Fongafale. The pace of life is so laid-back here that it's easy to slip into a tropical coma, and that's part of Tuvalu's appeal. Activities could include slowly strolling round the town, joining the locals at the airstrip to watch for an arriving plane, or floating in the calm waters of the Funafuti lagoon at sunrise or sunset. Feeling more energetic? Hire a motorcycle and join the local boy-racers zipping up and down the country's only tarmac road; or arrange a trip around the insanely beautiful Funafuti Conservation area for a Robinson Crusoe experience extraordinaire. Plenty of time on your hands? Take a cargo boat to the outer islands for about as unspoiled a taste of the South Pacific as you're going to get.

It's environmental concerns rather than paradise pursuits that have focused international attention on Tuvalu, however. The tiny island nation lacks sufficient resources to deal with a mounting pile of waste, suffers from population pressures (on Fongafale), and is one of the world's lowest lying nations. Rising sea levels mean that Tuvalu might become the first country on earth to be extinguished because of global warming.

HIGHLIGHTS

- Realise the desert island fantasy of your wildest dreams and explore the clear waters and deserted islets of the stunning **Funafuti Conservation Area** (p547).

- Experience traditional life on a remote island with the few remaining families of **Funafala islet** (p546).

- Join the locals for a sunset or early morning dip in the luminous waters of the **Funafuti lagoon** (p545).

- Take in a unique performance of Tuvalu's national dance, **fatele** (p541).

- Hire a bicycle and explore the length of **Fongafale** (p546).

Funafuti ★

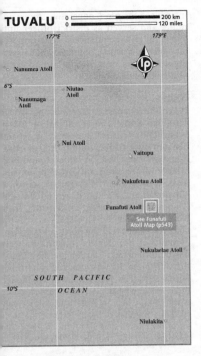

TUVALU

0   200 km
0   120 miles

177°E   179°E

Nanumea Atoll

6°S

Nanumaga Atoll   Niutao Atoll

Nui Atoll

Vaitupu

Nukufetau Atoll

Funafuti Atoll

See Funafuti Atoll Map (p543)

Nukulaelae Atoll

SOUTH PACIFIC

10°S   OCEAN

Niulakita

CLIMATE & WHEN TO GO

In warm, tropical Tuvalu the temperature rarely falls below 28°C or rises above 31°C, but the country receives a fair amount of rainfall, up to 3500mm a year in the south (including Funafuti). The rains are for the most part brief and heavy and the rainy season lasts from November to February. From May to October winds are light and from the southeast (the trade winds), changing to west-northwest during the November to April 'cyclone season'. While outside the tropical cyclone belt, Tuvalu had dealt with the occasional tempest.

COSTS & MONEY

The legal currency of Tuvalu is the Australian dollar, but there are also Tuvaluan 5c, 10c, 20c, 50c and $1 coins. See the Quick Reference page for exchange rates. There isn't much accommodation on Tuvalu so you won't find a huge range of prices. A basic double room with a shared bathroom should set you back about A$40 to A$50. Slightly up the scale, an en suite double in a comfortable guest house costs around A$70. A double room with private bath and air-con costs from A$110 to A$160. Food on Tuvalu is inexpensive. You'll pay A$1 to A$2 for a street snack and A$6 or 7 for a meal in a restaurant, or up to A$16 if you choose something fancy such as lobster.

HISTORY
In the Beginning

Although Tuvalu (too-*vah*-loo) is made up of nine islands, its name actually means 'Cluster of Eight'. The *ninth* and southernmost island, Niulakita, has been inhabited only since the mid-20th century.

Tuvalu's story begins some 2000 years ago when Polynesians, mostly from Samoa via Tokelau, but also from Tonga and Uvea (Wallis Island), settled here. The northern islands, especially Nui, were also settled by Micronesians from Kiribati (formerly the Gilbert Islands).

Power rested in the hands of *aliki,* powerful chiefs and leaders of Tuvaluan society. Under each *aliki* was a regimented social strata in which everyone had their place. Each *sologa* (family) had a particular speciality or community responsibility – for example building, fishing, dancing or healing – and it was *tapu* (taboo) to leak this hereditary information to other families. Land was the most valuable asset and was passed down through the male side of the family, with communal lands set aside to support and maintain those in need.

Outside Influences

Records state that Spanish explorers were the first outsiders to spot the islands in 1568, but proper European contact didn't occur until 1781, when Spaniard Francisco Antonio Mourelle landed at Niutao. American explorer De Peyster came to the islands in 1819, naming Funafuti 'Ellice's Island', after his friend Edward Ellice, an English politician.

TUVALU

TUVALU FACTS

Capital Funafuti Atoll; the administrative centre is Fongafale islet

Population 12,000

Land area 26 sq km

Number of islands Nine

International telephone code ☎ 688

Currency Australian dollar (A$)

Languages Tuvaluan, Gilbertese and English

Greeting *Talofa* (Tuvaluan)

Website www.timelesstuvalu.com

From the 1820s onwards the fabric of traditional Tuvaluan society began to change as whalers and other traders came the islands, bringing with them money, alcohol and new tools and goods. The *mana* (power) of the *aliki* (chiefs) disappeared as people lost respect for their leaders' often drunk and disorderly behaviour. The majority of *palagi* (pah-lung-ee; Westerners) lived peacefully alongside the Tuvaluans, but many earned a reputation of dishonesty and possessiveness; an opinion that for many was solidified when 'blackbirders' (slavers) raided the southern islands in 1863, looking for labourers to work in the harsh Peruvian guano mines. They persuaded the islanders to board their ship by promising knowledge of Christianity and succeeded in taking 250 people from Nukulaelae, and 171 from Funafuti. They never returned.

Tuvaluan culture took an even greater hit with the arrival of Samoan missionaries from the London Missionary Society (LMS) in 1865. In time they supplanted traditional religion with Christianity, and began to dominate the *aliki* and take over their positions of authority and privilege. Use of the men's narrow, woven pandanus loincloth was suppressed. Pastors, who regarded it as sexually stimulating and 'evil', banned the quick, rhythmic dancing of the *fakanau* (traditional fast-paced dance).

Colonialism

Tuvalu fell into the hands of Great Britain in 1886, when the imperial powers of Britain and Germany each claimed a 'sphere of influence' in the western and central Pacific. Tuvalu fell within the British 'sphere', and in 1892 was incorporated into the Gilbert & Ellice Islands Protectorate. Thus Kiribati and Tuvalu (and later Tokelau), although ethnically and culturally different, were arbitrarily joined. Between 1900 and 1979 the British Phosphate Company (BPC) mine on Ocean Island (now Banaba, in today's Kiribati) employed an average of 200 Tuvaluans at any given time, on two-year work contracts. Others worked on the BPC phosphate mines in Nauru.

Laws imposed on the colony became increasingly strict and paternalistic. Donald Gilbert Kennedy, a New Zealand schoolteacher who arrived in 1923, established an authoritarian boarding school. He also introduced the *fusi* (cooperative stores) and radio, and served as district officer until 1939. In 1930 regulations were imposed on dancing, feasting, domestic animals and night fishing – even sleeping in an eating house attracted a fine.

WWII

When the Japanese invaded during WWII, Tuvaluan workers were trapped on Ocean Island and Nauru. Concerned by Japan's plans to push further south, the US established an army base on Funafuti and built a large airfield and anti-aircraft bunkers here, as well as airfields further north at Nukufetau and Nanumea. More than 6000 Americans were based in Tuvalu, from where they bombed Japanese bases in the Gilberts, Nauru and the Marshall Islands.

Many of Fongafale's inhabitants were moved to Funafala islet for the duration of the war. Funafuti was attacked nine times during 1943. Few people were killed, though there was one particularly lucky break on 23 April 1943, when an American soldier persuaded a number of locals to leave the shelter of the church and go to the dugouts. Ten minutes later the church was bombed.

Postwar & Independence

In the aftermath of WWII, a fair number of islanders used their war compensation money to migrate. People of Nanumaga shifted to Tonga and the Carolines; others moved from Vaitupu to Kioa in Fiji. The colony headquarters was set up at Tarawa in the Gilberts, and many Tuvaluans went there for work or study.

BEST EATS

The fresh fish here is delicious but, surprisingly, many of Tuvalu's restaurants are rather heavy on the Chinese food, and you'll find menus laden with sweet and sour pork and fried noodles. There are a few restaurants that serve tasty local specialities though, such as fish in taro and coconut cream, or *palusami* – fish or meat, coconut and onion rolled up in taro. Curried chicken or fish rotis are sold as a street snack. In Fongafale try Hala Vai Seafood restaurant (p548) for Tuvaluan fish dishes or Filamona (p548) for filling curries and stir-fries.

HOW THE ISLANDS FORMED

The Traditional Version

Tuvalu's islands were created by *Te Pusi* (the Eel) and *Te Ali* (the Flounder). Carrying home a heavy rock, a friendly competition of strength turned into a fight and *Te Pusi* used his magic powers to turn *Te Ali* flat, like the islands of Tuvalu, and made himself round like the coconut trees. *Te Pusi* threw the black, white and blue rock into the air – and there it stayed. With a magic spell it fell down but a blue part remained above to form the sky. *Te Pusi* threw it up again, and its black side faced down, forming night. With another spell the rock fell down on its white side and formed day. *Te Pusi* broke the rest of the rock into eight pieces, forming the eight islands of Tuvalu. With a final spell he threw the remaining pieces of blue stone and formed the sea.

The Scientific Version

After his Pacific voyages between 1835 and 1836, Charles Darwin proposed that coral atolls were built on slowly sinking volcanoes, while at the same time the crater edge was being built up by new deposits of coral. The subsidence theory explained why coral rock was found at depths far greater than the 40m at which coral polyps can survive (see p66). His theory was controversial at the time – others believed that reefs grew on underwater platforms raised by volcanic action.

Darwin proposed that a coral atoll be drilled for samples, and Tuvalu achieved scientific fame when the Royal Society of London funded expeditions to Funafuti. In 1898, after three 'boring' expeditions (see p545), scientists managed to obtain atoll core samples from 340m below the surface. When analysed, they showed traces of shallow water organisms, thus supporting Darwin's hypothesis. Not until 1952, on Enewetak in the Marshall Islands, was it possible to drill to a depth of 1290m (right through the coral structure) and actually reach volcanic rock.

The union of the Gilbert and Ellice islands was an unnatural construct that stemmed from British rule, so when the Gilberts began to clamour for independence from the UK in the mid-1960s, Ellice Islanders began fighting for their own separate independence, afraid that their more populous neighbours would have greater political clout. In response to UN calls for decolonisation, the first House of Representatives was established in 1967. The Gilberts were allotted 18 seats, the Ellice Islands just five, but the Ellice Islanders retained a disproportionate hold on civil service positions.

In a 1974 referendum, Ellice Islanders voted overwhelmingly for separation from the Gilberts and in 1975, in preparation for independence, the islands became a British dependency with its own government. Between 1975 and 1976 Ellice Islanders departed Tarawa en mass for their homeland; on 1 October 1978 the Ellice Islands became the independent nation of Tuvalu. Britain's Queen Elizabeth II is the head of state, represented by a governor general.

The new, independent nation became heavily dependent on foreign aid, which helped construct the hospital (1978), the deep-water wharf and cargo storage facilities (1981), and the hotel (1993). In 1987 Australia, NZ and the UK together contributed A$24.7 million for a Tuvalu Trust Fund, which has today grown to a market value of some A$100 million. Aside from aid money, hard-working Tuvaluan men send money back from work on cargo ships at sea, and licences issued to the big Asian fishing fleets bring in a healthy stream of cash. And then there's dot tv.

Every country has a 'top-level domain', the two letters that identify it on the internet. Lucky Tuvalu didn't get tu, it got tv. In the late 1990s, when the Tuvaluan government realised how much TV companies would pay for an address like CNN.tv or BBC.tv, it set up the .tv Corp, and in 2002 it sold the rights to VeriSign for a 15-year term at US$45 million.

THE CULTURE
The National Psyche

Family life is the cornerstone of Tuvaluan society. Lifestyles are simple and revolve around family, friends and conversation. Tuvaluans are less outgoing than in other Pacific countries (no cries of '*bula*' to every passing foreigner here) and smiles are less evident than the local equivalent of eyebrows raised in greeting, so practise raising your own in return.

Although many Tuvaluans have lived abroad for work or study, their bond with their homeland remains strong; most are passionate about preserving island lifestyle and culture while still learning from positive influences from abroad. While some locals we spoke to were worried about the effect of rising sea levels (one older man told us about the days when the beach on Fongafale was wide enough to play ball games – today you can barely walk along it) and preserving Tuvaluan culture in the event of a mass migration, many are in denial about the seriousness of the threat to the islands. A mostly Christian population, many prefer to believe in the power of God than in the wrath of nature.

Lifestyle

The traditional Tuvaluan home is an open *fale,* which have coral floors or raised wooden platforms. It's only on the more remote islands that you'll see homes like this, however. On Funafuti most homes are built in the Western style. People usually have little furniture apart from woven mats. Every few blocks there is a thatched *maneapa,* often used for song and dance practice and card games, as well as for more formal community gatherings and church services; each of the outer island groups has its own *maneapa* in Funafuti. Protocol governs the *maneapa*; for example, no one should walk in the inner circle, and the support poles have symbolic significance, with the sitting place at each reserved for important people. Sit barefooted and cross-legged, and avoid walking in front of people.

While much traditional culture has been retained, the family unit is being broken down as people are attracted to the cash economy on Funafuti, and many young men are trained as crew to work on cargo ships at sea. It is difficult to live by traditional subsistence fishing and agriculture in the high-density areas. Most families eat significant amounts of high-calorie, fatty imported food, and alcohol consumption is on the rise. As you'll notice soon after arriving, obesity is a major problem here, as are related illnesses such as diabetes. Average life expectancy remains relatively high, though, with women living to 65 and men to 62.

Population

Over 93% of the 9500 Tuvaluans registere in the last census are of Polynesian origin and over 40% of them live on densely popu lated Funafuti, which currently has some 40 people per square kilometre over its tiny lan area. At the current growth rate of 1.7% pe year, the population is expected to double i 40 years, and 36% are under the age of 15.

SPORT

While in Tuvalu, try to watch, or better sti join in, a game of Tuvalu's unique sport, t ano. Almost completely incomprehensible t a first-timer, it's great fun and one of the fe games that men and women play together.

To play te ano you need two round balls about 12cm in diameter and woven from dried pandanus leaves. Two opposing team face each other about 7m apart in five o six parallel rows of about six people, an nominate their *alovaka* (captain) and *tin pukepuke* (catcher), who stand in front o each team.

Team members hit the ball to each othe with the aim of eventually reaching th catcher. Only the catcher can throw the bal back to the captain to hit back to the othe team. To keep the game lively, two balls are used simultaneously. When either ball fall to the ground the other team scores a point and the first to 10 points wins the game.

RELIGION

Tuvaluans are overwhelmingly Christian with most (90% of the population) belonging to the Protestant *Ekalesia Kelisiano o Tuvalu,* which is derived from the LMS. Seventh Day Adventists, Baha'i and Brethren Assembly each account for another 2% of the population, and there's a very small mosque for the tiny community of Muslim converts.

ARTS
Dance

Discos are the dances of choice for many young people. Though such dances are referred to by many older folks (and in many guidebooks) as 'twists', the young men we spoke to told us that this was outdated and should be referred to as 'clubbing' if you don't want to lose your street cred! Traditional dancing is still practised and familiar to all, forming a central part of family and community events.

> ## FATELE
>
> Describing a *fatele* as a session of community music, singing and dancing omits the most important element – its competitiveness. At opposite ends of the *maneapa* (meeting house), each village 'side' encircles a square wooden 'drum' on a metal cabin-cracker tin.
>
> Singers, male and female, sit cross-legged around the drummers, who start gently and build, the tempo getting faster and faster, louder and louder until it peaks in a thumping, crashing crescendo. The singing follows suit, starting softly and harmoniously and building to a full-throated melange of harmonies and counterharmonies. *Fatele* means 'to multiply', hinting at that steadily increasing speed.
>
> To one side of the musicians and singers are the dancers, often a group of very substantial dames with flower *fous* wreathing their heads and brown grass skirts. An occasional male dancer jumps up to do a little warriorlike, bent-leg knee-knocking, but essentially it's left to the women to sway statuesquely, concluding their dance with a defiant swirl that communicates a veiled challenge to their rivals across the room who will then try to outdo them.
>
> The other side tries to.

Handicrafts

Traditional handicrafts include ornamental stars, woven pandanus balls, model *fale* and canoes, shell necklaces, hairclasps, brightly coloured dancing skirts and woven fans of varied design. Utilitarian items include baskets and trays, carved fish hooks and coconut-fibre rope. Woven pandanus mats (sleeping, floor and ceremonial) are highly valued. The creation of ceremonial mats is often competitive, producing imaginative, brightly coloured designs. Sitting mats take up to a week to make, while sleeping mats can take five to 10 weeks.

The local I-Kiribati population make and sell hand-smocked *tibuta*, traditional women's tops from Kiribati.

Literature

The Cruise of the Janet Nichol in the South Seas, by Fanny Stevenson (who is the wife of Robert Louis Stevenson) includes her impressions of Tuvalu in 1890; you should be able to find excerpts on the internet or otherwise get a secondhand copy at the major online bookstores. *A South Seas Spell* (1975), by British journalist June Knox-Mawer, recounts the author's stay in the 1960s with Tuvaluans on Kioa, in Fiji, and Funafuti. *Where the Hell is Tuvalu?* (2000), by Philip Ells, is the comic tale of a young lawyer's two-year volunteer stint as 'the People's Lawyer' in Tuvalu. *Treasure Islands: Sailing the South Seas in the Wake of Fanny and Robert Louis Stevenson* (2005) by Pamela Stephenson is more 'dear diary' than storytelling, but she

visits and describes some of the less-visited outer islands.

The library on Funafuti has a decent Pacific collection and a small treasure-trove of dusty books on Tuvalu. The oldest (and most fragile) of these is *Funafuti or Three Months on a Coral Atoll* (1899), by Caroline Martha Edgeworth David, wife of the scientist who proved Darwin's theory of atoll formation on Funafuti (see the boxed text, p539); it's of its colonial time, but her personal battle coming to terms with a strange environment and culture will be familiar to many readers.

The books mentioned below are in the library on Fongafale, but may be hard to find elsewhere.

The Material Culture of Tuvalu (1961), by Gerd Koch, concentrates on the atolls of Niutao and Nanumaga. *Tuvalu: A History* (1983) was written by a team of Tuvaluans and provides an interesting local view of colonial and WWII history. *Strategic Atolls: Tuvalu and the Second World War* (1994), by Peter McQuarrie, is a good account, with photographs, of the islands in WWII.

Time & Tide: The Islands of Tuvalu (2001), by Peter Bennetts and Tony Wheeler, is a Lonely Planet photographic book about the islands.

LANGUAGE

English is widely spoken. Tuvaluan is a Polynesian language related to Tokelauan. Tuvaluan uses an 'l' sound where some Polynesian languages use an 'r' sound, so the name for a chief (*ariki* in the Cook Islands) is *aliki* in Tuvalu. When missionaries put the language into written form they used Samoan orthography so, as in Samoa, the letter 'g' is used for the soft 'ng' sound.

Tuvaluan basics

Hello.	*Talofa.*
Goodbye.	*Tofa.*
How are you?	*E a koe?*
I'm well.	*Malosi.*
Please.	*Fakamolemole.*
Thank you.	*Fakafetai.*
Yes.	*Io* or *Ao*
No.	*Ikai.*

ENVIRONMENT
Geography
Tuvalu's five coral atolls and four islands spread over 800km of ocean. Funafuti, the capital, is about 1100km north of Fiji, and the northern islands are about 250km south of Kiribati. With a total land area of only 26 sq km, Tuvalu is one of the world's smallest countries; the highest land is a mere 5m above sea level.

Ecology
Tuvalu's infertile atoll soils support coconut palms, pandanus, salt-tolerant ferns and some atoll scrub. There are about 50 endemic plant species, and cultivated plants include banana, taro and breadfruit. Vegetation has an important role in foreshore protection but degradation is quite severe. Large tree species traditionally used for canoes and building are becoming rare.

Marine life is diverse, with dolphins and manta rays commonly seen in Funafuti lagoon. Green turtles breed in Tuvalu, and hawksbills and leatherbacks are sometimes seen. There are breeding colonies of seabirds in the conservation area (p547), and in town you'll see fairy terns hovering low on the shoreline, and some waders at the water's edge. There are no native land mammals, but rats, dogs, cats and pigs have been introduced as has the ubiquitous cane toad.

As an atoll nation, the major long-term ecological threat to Tuvalu comes from global warming (see p70) and rising sea levels. In 2002, the Tuvaluan government even threatened to sue the United States and Australia for failing to back the Kyoto Protocol. As well as shoreline erosion, water bubbles up through the porous coral on which the islands are based, and causes widespread salt contamination of areas used to grow staple crops. Over the past few years 'king tides', the biggest swells of the year, have been higher than ever. If sea levels continue to rise as predicted, the islands could be wiped off the face of the earth.

Several television companies have made documentaries about Tuvalu's environmental plight, including PBS's *That Sinking Feeling*; *Trouble in Paradise*, an international documentary made in 2004; and locally made *Te Malosiga O Fenua: The Strength of the Island*.

What will happen to the population if Tuvalu does start to go under? The government has been in talks with Australia, which has twice rejected Tuvalu's pleas to open a migration channel. New Zealand currently accepts 75 migrants a year and has said it will absorb Tuvalu's population if it comes to that.

Population pressures and changing lifestyles also present a problem. Tiny 2.8 sq km Fongafale islet, only about a third of which is habitable, is crammed with some 4500 people. Large areas are taken up by the airfield and by enormous 'borrow pits', where material was excavated or 'borrowed' for its construction during WWII. These borrow pits end up filled with waste, due to a lack of adequate garbage disposal and the reliance on imported packaged food. People are being encouraged to separate their garbage and use organic waste for compost and for growing vegetables. This in turn would help reduce the dependence, if only a little, on imported food.

As a visitor, you can help by arriving with as little plastic as possible, taking it out again with you when you go, and minimising your throw-away rubbish while in-country.

FUNAFUTI ATOLL

pop 4500 / area 2.8 sq km

Tuvalu's capital and the only place in the country where tourists can change money, make international phone calls or use the internet, Funafuti (foo-*nah*-foo-ti) Atoll is a necklace of islands, 24km long and 18km wide, with a stunning lagoon to one side, and wild, open ocean to the other. Fongafale (also

FUNAFUTI ATOLL

spelt Fogafale or Fagafale) is Tuvalu's answer
to a metropolis, the seat of government, and
the largest islet in Funafuti Atoll. Funafuti's
must-sees include the sublime marine conservation area to the west and Funafala islet to
the south, which is lined with talcum powder
beaches and has basic accommodation right
by the water.

ORIENTATION
Fongafale, a thin, boomerang-shaped slice
of land, is only 12km long with the South
Pacific Ocean on the east and the protected
lagoon on the west. The airstrip runs from
northeast to southwest on the widest part
of the island, with the village and administrative centre of Vaiaku on the lagoon side.
The deep-water wharf is 1.7km north of the
hospital. Four hundred metres at its widest
point and 10m at the thinnest, the main
road that runs along its length is at times
half the islet's length.

INFORMATION
The following are all located in Vaiaku.

Internet Access
Coconut Wireless (50m north of Motualu Internet Bar; 9am-7pm Mon-Fri, 10am-10pm Sat, 2pm-7pm Sun; 5c a minute).
Motualo Internet Bar (50m north of the Library & National Archive; 9am-10pm Mon-Sat, 2pm-10pm Sun; 5c a minute).

There's also an internet café opposite the post office and next to DHL.

Media
Department of Community Affairs (20 172; Ministry of Home Affairs, Government Offices) Produces local documentaries.
Tuvalu Media Corporation (20 138; opposite Vaiaku Lagi Hotel) Publishes the monthly newsletter and broadcasts Radio Tuvalu. You can listen in daily from 6.30-8am, 11.30-1pm & 6.30-10pm.

Medical Services
Princess Margaret Hospital (20 480, 20 749) At the northern end of town. The pharmacy may not have a wide selection of drugs, so bring any medical supplies you need.

Money
National Bank of Tuvalu (NBT; 20 803; 10am-2pm Mon-Thu, 9am-1pm Fri) Opposite the airport building.

Post
Post Office (8am-noon & 1.30-3pm Mon-Fri) The post office is on the ground floor of the gleaming government offices. At the south end of Te Auala o Fongafale.

Tourist Information
Tuvalu receives few tourists – of the thousand or so foreign visitors who journey to the
country every year, only around 10 per cent
are tourists. There is no visitor information
centre on Funafuti.
Funafuti Town Council (Kaupule Funafuti; 20 489, 20 422) Arranges boats to the conservation area.
Government tourist information (20 055; fax 20 722; www.timelesstuvalu.com; Ministry of Finance, Economic Planning & Industries, top fl, Government Offices)

Travel Agencies
Tuvalu Travel Office (20737; travel@tuvalu.tv) At the airport; deals with ticketing and reconfirmation of flights.

TRANSPORT
Getting There & Away
AIR
Australian and EU aid helped build Funafuti
International Airport's small wooden air-
port building in 1993. Both Air Fiji and Air
Pacific have regular flights between Suva and
Funafuti (see p553).

There are no domestic flights between
Funafuti and the outer islands.

BOAT
Funafuti lagoon has two reef passages that are
large enough for ships to enter, and it also has
a deep-water wharf north of Vaiaku. There are

TUVALU

TUVALU

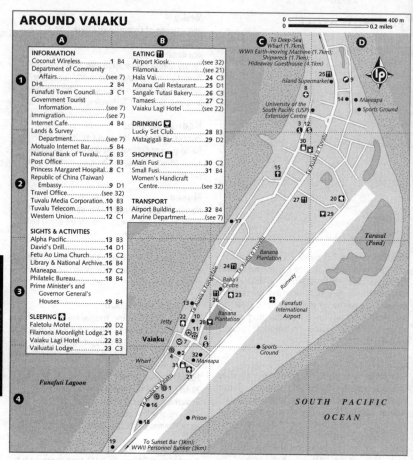

AROUND VAIAKU

0 .... 400 m
0 .... 0.2 miles

INFORMATION
Coconut Wireless................1 B4
Department of Community
  Affairs.........................(see 7)
DHL...................................2 B4
Funafuti Town Council......3 C1
Government Tourist
  Information...................(see 7)
Immigration.....................(see 7)
Internet Cafe......................4 B4
Lands & Survey
  Department...................(see 7)
Motualo Internet Bar...........5 B4
National Bank of Tuvalu......6 B3
Post Office..........................7 B3
Princess Margaret Hospital..8 C1
Republic of China (Taiwan)
  Embassy...........................9 D1
Travel Office.....................(see 32)
Tuvalu Media Corporation..10 B3
Tuvalu Telecom................11 B3
Western Union...................12 C1

SIGHTS & ACTIVITIES
Alpha Pacific......................13 B3
David's Drill.......................14 D1
Fetu Ao Lima Church.........15 C2
Library & National Archive..16 B4
Maneapa...........................17 B4
Philatelic Bureau................18 B4
Prime Minister's and
  Governor General's
  Houses............................19 B4

SLEEPING
Faletolu Motel...................20 D2
Filamona Moonlight Lodge..21 B4
Vaiaku Lagi Hotel.............22 B3
Vailuatai Lodge.................23 C3

EATING
Airport Kiosk...................(see 32)
Filamona..........................(see 21)
Hala Vai............................24 C3
Moana Gali Restaurant.....25 D1
Sangale Tutasi Bakery.......26 C3
Tamaesi............................27 C2
Vaiaku Lagi Hotel.............(see 22)

DRINKING
Lucky Set Club..................28 B3
Matagigali Bar...................29 D2

SHOPPING
Main Fusi..........................30 C2
Small Fusi.........................31 B4
Women's Handicraft
  Centre...........................(see 32)

TRANSPORT
Airport Building.................32 B4
Marine Department............(see 7)

To Deep-Sea
Wharf (1.7km);
WWII Earth-moving Machine (1.7km);
Shipwreck (1.7km);
Hideaway Guesthouse (4.1km)

Island Supermarket

University of the
South Pacific (USP)
Extension Centre

Maneapa
Sports Ground

Tarasal
(Pond)

Banana
Plantation

Baha'i
Centre

Runway

Funafuti
International
Airport

Banana
Plantation

Jetty

Vaiaku

Maneapa

Wharf

Funafuti Lagoon

Sports
Ground

SOUTH PACIFIC
OCEAN

Prison

To Sunset Bar (3km);
WWII Personnel Bunker (3km)

occasional boat services to Fiji from Tuvalu. For further information, see p553.

Getting Around
The stifling heat means that walking further than Vaiaku isn't really an option. The easiest way to get around Fongafale is to hire a motorcycle.

BICYCLE
Your accommodation should be able to arrange a bicycle for you to hire, but be prepared to sweat.

BOAT
The easiest way to see the lagoon and some of the smaller islets is with the Funafuti Town

Council (see p543). The council's boat costs around A$150 for several hours. They can provide life jackets and snorkelling gear if you ask in advance, although it may not be in the best condition. You could try to find another local boat to take you, but if you want to visit the conservation area this could well work out to be more expensive as you will still have to pay a fee to the Town Council.

BUS
Fongafale has a minibus service that runs the length of the town from 6.30am to 7pm (50c) with a limited service to the Fetu Ao Lima Church on Sundays. During the week, there are buses that go as far as the northern end of the island (60c) and are timed

to leave early in the morning and return at about 4pm to coincide with school hours.

CAR & MOTORCYCLE

It's not usually possible to hire a car, although you could try asking around. Far better to hire a motorcycle. Your accommodation will be able to sort out hire for you (we rented a moped belonging to the hotel receptionist's mother). This should cost around A$10 per day.

TAXI

Taxis costs around A$5 from the hotel to the deep-water wharf, and A$3 from the hotel to the southern end of the islet near the governor general's residence. There are many private taxi operators; ask at your accommodation.

FONGAFALE ISLET
Sights & Activities

The best thing about a visit to Fongafale is simply soaking up the slow-paced island way of life. Take a stroll around town or hop on a bike or motorcycle to explore the islet from top to toe.

Tuvalu's **airstrip** is where all the action takes place; people play ball games on the runway's tarmac in the late afternoons, young men race up and down it on their motorcycles, and on steamy summer nights, you'll sometimes catch the bizarre sight of families dragging their sleeping mats and pillows out to spend the night on the tarmac (in the stifling heat it's the best place to catch the island's breezes), before returning to their houses at dawn.

It's also good fun to hang around the outskirts of the airstrip at flight departure and arrival times, which are a major event. People gather around the sidelines or in the *maneapa* next to the airport building to welcome and say goodbye to friends and relatives or just to check out the new arrivals. The fire engine sounds its siren to clear the runway, and as the plane arrives you'll see locals farewelling and garlanding friends and family.

Towards the southern end of the runway are the neighbouring **prime minister's and governor general's houses**. From the road you can see a very beautiful traditionally built **maneapa** on the lagoon side of the compound garden, the only one remaining on Fongafale; ask someone for permission to go closer and check out its intricate construction and thatching.

The tiny, crumbling building might not look like much, but Tuvalu's **Library and National Archive** (☎ 20 128; ◷ 8am-12.30 & 1.30-4pm Mon-Fri, 10am-noon Sat) holds an impressive selection of magazines, books, journals and encyclopedias about the Pacific, a small selection of works on Tuvalu and a range of fiction from Shakespeare to Mills & Boon; even if there's nothing there that takes your fancy it's worth a visit just to feel the cool blast of the air-con – welcome respite from the heat outside.

Next door is the **Philatelic Bureau** (☎ 20 224; ◷ 8am-12.30pm & 1.30-4pm Mon-Fri). They sell collectors editions of sought-after Tuvaluan stamps as well as regular stamps (adorned with everything from Pope Benedict to Gaugin) and a few postcards. The ladies working at the bureau are very welcoming and always pleased to chat. They told us that most of the stamps are printed in Great Britain before being sent to the bureau in Tuvalu. Here they spend much of their time answering requests from abroad, packaging the stamps in collectors packs and selling them on to Europe and the United States.

In the morning and at sunset you'll see plenty of locals cooling off in the gorgeous waters of the **Funafuti lagoon**, the perfect way to start and end the day. The concrete jetty just south of Vaiaku Lagi Hotel is the best spot to enter, and at dusk you'll be joined by local school kids who use the jetty as a jumping-off point and will be happy to show you their underwater skills. There's no live coral near the shore, but if you have a snorkel handy there are enough brightly coloured reef fish to keep you happy. Modesty is key – women should swim in long shorts and T-shirts, and men in long shorts. You may be able to hire **kayaks** from the hotel.

In 1896 Australian Professor Edgeworth David led the first of three coral-drilling expeditions to Funafuti to investigate Darwin's theory of atoll formation (see boxed text on p539). If you're stuck for things to do you could look for the memorial to this expedition, **David's Drill**. Situated at the northern end of town, it's commemorated by a concrete base and an inscription, surrounding the drill hole. You'll have to look very hard through the undergrowth to see it, and you could ask the locals all day without finding anyone who has heard of it.

Fongafale holds on to a few relics from its involvement in WWII. At the islet's southern end, hidden in the scrub in an old **personnel**

bunker and near the deep-water wharf, an enormous **earth-moving machine**, still bearing its American maker's plate, is quietly rusting away. The **wreck** on the lagoon shore beyond the wharf is a fishing boat, destroyed during Cyclone Bebe in 1972.

FONGAFALE BY BICYCLE
Heading South

Start at the airport and head south along the runway road. Stop at the **prime minister's and governor general's houses** (p545) – if you're lucky you might find someone to show you around the grounds. Keep on heading south, out of town, and soak up the stilted houses, domestic holdings, children playing in the street and other elements of island life that surround you. Try and ignore the garbage-filled borrow pits and focus on the awesome view of the sea, through the palm trees, on both your right and left hand sides. Continue to the end of the road – perhaps 3km from the airport – follow the bush track and emerge at the end of Fongafale, where ocean and lagoon meet. It's an astonishing view – crashing waves on one side and a ring of islets circling the calm lagoon on the other. Heading back, stop at the **Sunset Bar** (p548) for a cold drink – if you can find anyone there, that is.

Returning, veer left off the runway road onto Vaiaku Rd; pass the **Philatelic Bureau** (p545) and step into the welcoming coolness of the **library** (p545) for a well-deserved rest and a browse through the racks. Stay on this road back to the airport.

Heading North

From the airport, cycle along the road adjacent to the runway and watch the young men racing up and down on their motorcycles (try and race them – you won't win). Turn left at the **Matagigali Bar** (p548) (stopping for fortification if necessary) and pass over the main road to the **Fetu Ao Lima Church**, rebuilt on the site of the church destroyed in WWII. Passing the area around the *fusi* and hospital, you'll end up on the main (and only) road heading north. Look out for the massive WWII **earth-moving machine** (above) on the right side of the road, and check out the action at the deep-water wharf and the **wreck** (above) in the lagoon.

Beyond the wharf you can cycle on for another 4km or so to the northern end of Fongafale, past a landfill. You'll pass quiet households, a couple of guest houses and beach picnic spots, and can collapse gratefully at the kiosk beside the secondary school for a drink.

On the way home, turn left after the Island Supermarket and at the bend on the road, opposite a *maneapa*, you can hunt for the **David's Drill** (p545) site at ground level. Weave your way back to the *fusi* if you need to shop, or head back to where you started for a drink and some sustenance at **Filamona** (p548).

AROUND FUNAFUTI

It would be a shame to visit Tuvalu without experiencing the **Funafuti Conservation Area** (opposite), about a half-hour motorboat ride across the lagoon. If you book through the town council, it should cost you around A$150 for a return boat trip (maximum 12 people), including time on one or two of the islets and perhaps some snorkelling. The length of time you'll be out and where you'll go largely depends on the weather. There's an A$50 fee per camera for those taking photographs; commercial photographers pay more. This might seem expensive, but the conservation area badly needs the revenue. Safety equipment on the boat is likely to be limited, but if you ask in advance they can arrange to bring along some snorkel gear for you; there is no diving.

Just outside the northern boundary of the conservation area is the islet of **Tepuka**, where you'll find some pretty beaches and decent snorkelling. There are some WWII relics in the centre (you'll need directions to find them). Ask around for private boat operators to take you out there (try the Alpha Pacific office near the Media Centre; ☎ 20 900); you'll pay around A$100 for a return trip.

At the southern end of the atoll is the islet of **Funafala**. During WWII, when the Americans took over Fongafale, the villagers were relocated here. The majority moved back after the war but a small community remained, although today there are fewer than ten families. People have moved away from Funafala, the locals told us, to find better work opportunities and schooling for their children. The islet feels remote and traditional, and is the kind of place where you can while away the hours chatting to the locals and drinking toddy in the *maneapa*. On the day we visited, we heard tales of WWII and a Funafuti lagoon

FUNAFUTI CONSERVATION AREA

Close your eyes and conjure up the most perfect, pint-sized desert island possible. That's right. Blinding white sand, brochure-ready turquoise sea, a thicket of native forest filled with twittering seabirds... Multiply by five and you've got the Funafuti Conservation Area – five eye-wateringly beautiful islets strung out like beads along the western side of the atoll. No-one lives on these islets and, with the consent of the landowners, they are a protected zone – a strict no fishing, no hunting, no gathering area. Green turtles nest on the beaches, and though much of the coral close to shore has suffered from bleaching, there are still scores of brightly coloured reef fish calling out for you to don a mask and snorkel. Once ashore you'll have the islands to yourself – perfect for making like Tom Hanks in *Castaway*.

Until 2005 there were six islets, but tiny Tepuka Savilivili was wiped out by a massive storm – an unpleasant preview of what might happen to Tuvalu as global warming progresses.

The conservation area, initiated in 1996, covers 33 sq km of lagoon, reef, channel, ocean and island habitats. It's open to visitors for snorkelling, walking, picnicking and birdwatching.

filled with war ships. Funafala is about one hour by boat from Vaiaku (see p544); the Town Council's boat will cost A$100 return but double this if you're staying overnight (see right), as it will have to make two return trips.

Amatuku is an islet about 10km north of Vaiaku. A boys' mission school was started here in the late 1890s, before being transferred to Vaitupu. The relatively isolated Tuvalu Maritime Training Institute was established here in 1979 in order to simulate ship operations. About 60 Tuvaluans are admitted to train as seamen each year, and have a good reputation with international shipping companies. Most send their wages back to their families, and their remittances are an important part of Tuvalu's economy.

SLEEPING

There's a small but adequate selection of accommodation on Fongafale that includes a hotel, a lodge, a motel and some family-run guest houses. There's also a basic guesthouse on Funafala islet.

It's usually cheaper to stay in a family-run guest house, although they may or may not have room depending how many members of the family are visiting at the time. If you don't mind sacrificing your privacy, staying with a family is a great way to get a more developed sense of Tuvaluans' day-to-day lives. Expect to pay around A$40 for a single room with fan, shared bathroom and kitchen. In town try **Vailuatai Lodge** (☎ 20664; funafutit@ yahoo.com; opposite the Baha'i Centre); ask locally for other possibilities.

Hideaway Guesthouse (☎ 20 365; tufha@tuvalu .tv; s/d with fan A$35/45, apt A$60; ✷) This place is a little way out of town and facilities are simple, but the owners are very welcoming. The accommodation is mostly reserved for volunteers and long stayers, but it's worth checking as they might have room for you to stay for a couple of nights. You can catch a minibus to the deep-water wharf and walk the 2.5km to the guesthouse; on weekdays there is a morning and late afternoon bus service to the door. Better still, hire a scooter. There's no sign, so look for the fence and satellite dish of the Taiwanese ambassador's house. The guesthouse is next door.

Funafuti Town Council can arrange simple beach house accommodation out of town. Ask for details.

Funafala Islet Guesthouse (☎ 20365; tufha@tuvalu .tv; s/d with fan A$40/50; ✷) Wonderfully located on the beach on Funafala, this tiny place has two single beds, louvre windows and solar electricity, but no mosquito screens. It's next to a *maneapa* where guests can sleep and catch the sea breeze on scorching nights, and has a toilet block and water tank. Take your own food (as there are no shops) and a couple of good books. You'll need to book in person and pay in advance at Funafuti Town Council.

Filamona Moonlight Lodge (☎ 20 983; s/d incl breakfast A$60/70; ✷) The most conveniently located lodgings in Vaiaku, right next to the *maneapa* by the airport and perfectly placed for watching the main event. This family-run lodge has a dorm and several doubles. There's a communal lounge with TV, a basic self-catering kitchen, a verandah upstairs overlooking the runway and an on-site restaurant and bar on

TUVALU

the ground floor that is a popular meeting place for locals.

Fale Tolu Motel (☎ 20 545; faletolu@gmail.com; s/d with air-con A$80/110; 🐼) At the northern end of the runway, just across from the Matagigali Bar, this is a new place with three big, sparse, air-conditioned rooms with fridge and TV.

ourpick Vaiaku Lagi Hotel (☎ 20 500; fax 20 503; s/d A$110/160; 🐼) It's not the hotel facilities that make Tuvalu's only hotel the pick of the bunch – the staff is indifferent and the rooms are pretty basic for the price with sporadic hot water, malfunctioning telephones and two choices of mattress (rock hard or spongy) – it's the location. Sitting on the edge of the lagoon, some 100m northwest of the airport, rooms have small balconies with outstanding views over the water. You'll soon forget about the hotel's downsides when you're sitting on your balcony watching an impossibly brilliant sunset. At the back of the hotel is a jetty that's perfect for plopping into the lagoon for a morning dip.

EATING

Most restaurants on Tuvalu are good value, many of them selling cheap, filling plates of Chinese-style food. Restaurants sometimes suffer from shortages when shipments don't arrive. At the time of research there was a lack of rice on the island, and one restaurant was even closed because of it!

Tamaesi (meals A$4-8; 🕑 breakfast, lunch & dinner) Pull up a plastic pew for a massive portion of fried noodles, noodle soup or a stir-fry. You'll find that half the stuff on the menu isn't available, though, and they don't exactly believe in service with a smile. Takeaways are available.

Filamona (meals A$5-7; 🕑 lunch & dinner) Attached to the lodge of the same name, this is one of the nicest places to eat in Fongafale with a large open, breeze-filled bar and restaurant overlooking the runway, comfortable chairs, a fridge full of cold beer and a hearty warm welcome. Dishes include stir-fries and curried mutton, and there are regular blackboard specials.

Moana Gali Restaurant (meals from A$6) Basic place beside the Island Supermarket. The Chinese cook reputedly cooks good simple food to order. People rave about the fresh fish soup. The place was closed at the time of research. As the owner, who also runs the supermarket, explained, there had been problems with shipments, and he couldn't run his restaurant without any rice.

Vaiaku Lagi Hotel (meals A$6-14; 🕑 breakfast, lunch & dinner) As with most of the restaurants on Tuvalu, most of the menu here consists of Chinese-style stir fries and rice, although there are sometimes some good fresh fish options. Fried rice and omelettes are pretty much all there is for vegetarians. There's a great raised outside terrace here, with tables facing the lagoon. A great place for a leisurely lunch.

ourpick Hala Vai Seafood Restaurant (☎ 20 562 meals A$7-16; 🕑 lunch & dinner) This basic place has just four wooden tables but is regularly touted by the locals as the best place in town. It's a convivial place with substantial portions of mostly Chinese food, but the menu also includes some South Pacific favourites such as pork with taro. There are great fish dishes here, and on rare occasions they have lobster.

Sangale Tutasi Bakery, just north of the airport, makes good bread. There is also a **kiosk** at the airport where you can sit and watch the plane depart while chewing on a sandwich, roti or sweet pastries. Rotis can be bought from **roadside sellers** throughout town.

DRINKING

Thursday to Saturday is party night on Fongafale, when the old timers go to 'twists' (discos) and the youngsters go 'clubbing' at the rough-and-ready **Matagigali Bar** (🕑 8pm till late) and **Lucky Set Club** (🕑 8pm till late). Tuvaluan men are not afraid to knock back the beers; women visitors should take care if going out alone, and steer clear of revealing clothing.

Out of town, **Sunset Bar** is good for a sundowner if you're passing by. It may be closed if no custom or appear to be closed so it's always worth knocking to find out.

SHOPPING

Fongafale has few shops.

Women's Handicraft Centre (Airport Bldg; 🕑 8am-noon & 2-4pm Mon-Fri & for flights) This place sometimes has only shell necklaces and cane baskets, but occasionally it stocks good-quality items of traditional design in natural materials.

Local craftswomen also have stalls set up near the Funafuti airport and sell brightly coloured, less labour-intensive items made especially for Tuvalu's small number of travellers. See p541 for more on handicrafts.

The *fusis*, or island cooperative stores, sell a selection of basic groceries and, if a ship's been in recently, a few cold-stored vegetables.

OUTER ISLANDS

A trip to be made only if you've plenty of time to spare, Tuvalu's beautiful and remote outer islands have very little infrastructure for visitors. The only way to reach them is by government cargo ships *Nivaga II* and *Manu Folau* (see p553). The boats do a round trip lasting several days to each of the three island groups – the northern group comprises Nanumea Atoll, Niutao Atoll, Nanumaga Atoll and Nui Atoll; the central group is Vaitupu, Nukufetau Atoll and Fongafale islet; and the southern group comprises Nukulaelae Atoll and Niulakita. The ships call in at each island for the best part of a day to unload and load supplies and passengers. So if you're prepared to spend your nights on board ship, you can explore the islands during the daytime. If you choose to get off the boat and plan to stay, be warned; it might be some weeks before the next transport arrives! Give advance warning of your arrival and come prepared to be pretty much self-sufficient.

NUKUFETAU ATOLL
pop 590 / area 3 sq km

This atoll is the closest to Funafuti, about 100km to the northwest. Locally known as 'the island of the civil servants', because so many government workers come from here, it is also known for the (literally) fast-talking locals.

During WWII large cargo ships and warships anchored in the lagoon, and two runways were built on Motulalo islet. The shattered remnants of a B24 Liberator bomber can be found among the palm trees, some distance north of the main runway. The island started the first primary school in Tuvalu, and the annual Founding Day on 11 February is a major celebration.

The **council guesthouse** (☎ 36 005; A\$45) is right beside the primary school and has two bedrooms.

VAITUPU
pop 1590 / area 5.6 sq km

Vaitupu has the largest land area in Tuvalu; even so, in 1947, some families migrated from the overcrowded island to the island of Kioa in Fiji.

Motufoua, the first of Tuvalu's two secondary schools, is located here, and there are over 600 boarders between the ages of 13 and 21. In March 2000 a terrible dormitory fire killed 18 teenage girls and their warden (the dormitory doors were locked and windows barred). *Vaitupu: An Account of Life on a Remote Polynesian Atoll* (1999), by John Chalkley, is an illustrated memoir of the author's time teaching on Vaitupu in the 1970s; you'll find it in the library on Fongafale.

You can walk almost all the way around the densely vegetated island, wading across the shallow entrances to the two lagoons at low tide. Just south of the harbour in the village are the foundations of early trader Heinrich Nitz's house. His gravestone (the actual grave is further along the road) reveals that he was born in Stralsund, Germany, in 1839 and died on Vaitupu in 1906. Many islanders are descendants of Nitz.

The **council guest house** (☎ 30 005; r A\$50) is behind the church and *maneapa*, close to the harbour. You can get meals here, and the quantities are huge. The *fusi* is right by the harbour.

The Funafuti–Vaitupu boat trip takes eight or nine hours. Passengers are transferred to a small boat and shuttled into the harbour, which is too small for larger boats.

NUI ATOLL
pop 550 / area 2.8 sq km

Nui Atoll has 11 main islets along the eastern side of its lagoon. There are many white-sand **beaches**, framed with strips of green, and at low tide it is possible to walk between them. Kiribati is also spoken here as some of the people are of Micronesian descent. Contact the **local island council** (☎ 23 005) if you want to stay at the guest house.

NANUMAGA ATOLL
pop 590 / area 2.8 sq km

Nanumaga (nah-noo-*mah*-nga) Atoll is oval-shaped with two landlocked lagoons and a narrow fringing reef. The two island sides, Tonga and Tokelau, reflect the islanders' origins and are further subdivided into five clans. Respect for the elders suffered in 1979 when they spent almost all of the atoll's funds purchasing poor land in Texas! Contact the **island council** (☎ 33 005) about their **guest house** (r A\$60).

NIUTAO ATOLL
pop 660 / area 2.5 sq km

In 1949 Niutao Atoll acquired the island of Niulakita in the country's south, and families

---

MAROONED IN TUVALU *Tony Wheeler*

It's comparatively easy to fly to Funafuti, the main island of the Tuvalu group, but very few visitors get any further. The passenger-cargo ship *Nivaga II*, which runs around the islands, is irregular and unreliable (quite apart from being bloody uncomfortable), and yachties, who might be tempted to drop by some of the islands, are put off by the poor anchorages. In two visits to Tuvalu I managed to visit eight of the nine islands, although along the way there was a spell as a castaway and the prime minister died.

Photographer Peter Bennetts was the catalyst for this misadventure. Concerned about the dangers of global warming and rising sea levels, he'd convinced the Tuvaluan government to support a project to produce a photographic book about the islands and the dangers they faced. He convinced me to come along to write the text. The government's role was transport: we would go along on the patrol boat *Te Mataili*, which would drop us off at various islands on the group. In Funafuti Peter and I met the prime minister, Ionatana Ionatana, and we signed the contract for Lonely Planet to produce the book which eventually emerged as *Time & Tide*. The next day we sailed south to Nukulaelae, and that evening the prime minister had a heart attack and dropped dead. It set the tone for the whole project because back in Funafuti bad weather set in, the patrol ship couldn't leave base and, after a few days of hanging around, Peter and I retreated to Australia.

A couple of months later we returned to Funafuti for a second try, but this time the patrol boat wasn't available. We hitched a ride on the government fishing boat *Manaui*, which took us to Vaitupu along with a film crew from *National Geographic*. A couple of days later the *Manaui* landed us at Nukufetau, then continued to Funafuti to drop the film crew off, promising to return to pick us up 48 hours later. It didn't. The fishing boat, it transpired, had suffered some sort of major mechanical failure, which, doubly unfortunately, coincided with a major electronic failure in the phone connection with Nukufetau. Day after day passed while we pondered what an extended stay in the small settlement would be like. 'Don't worry,' the islanders counselled. 'The *Nivaga II* usually drops by every three months, if it hasn't broken down and got stuck in Fiji for six months.'

Fortunately we didn't have to wait that long. A week later the patrol boat was patrolling again, picked us up and took us to all but one of the other islands. I'm not planning a return trip to tick Nui, the missing island, off my list.

---

were settled there to relieve overpopulation on this small home atoll. The people, known for their traditional handicrafts, retain some traditional beliefs, and until 1982 they had among them a woman who had inherited the power to make rain. Niutao has a **council guest house** (☎ 28 005; r A$60).

NANUMEA ATOLL
pop 660 / area 3.9 sq km

Nanumea is Tuvalu's northernmost atoll and the closest to Kiribati. It is also one of the most beautiful, with a **fresh-water pond** (unusual for atolls) and a large **church** blessed with stained-glass windows and a tall steeple that rises above the coconut palms. It suffered several Japanese attacks during WWII. Plane **wrecks** and a half disintegrated cargo ship near the main settlement serve as reminders. The old runway took up a sixth of the land area, and its construction involved felling almost

half of the existing coconut trees. Contact the **island council** (☎ 26 005) about the guest house.

NUKULAELAE ATOLL
pop 400 / area 1.8 sq km

About 120km southeast of Funafuti, Tuvalu's easternmost atoll has two main islets, Niuoku and Tumuiloto, on the eastern side of the lagoon, but the population all live on Fangaua on the western side. Blackbirders kidnapped two-thirds of its population in 1863 and forced them to work as slaves in Peruvian mines. Today, the people from Nukulaelae have a reputation for their dancing and singing.

There is a pre-Christian **archaeological site** of small standing-stone 'platforms' situated about halfway along Niuoku. It's known as a *faleatau* (house of God), and bears similarities to others in eastern Polynesia. Located near the southern end of

Tumuiloto, a memorial and a small chapel marks the shipwreck arrival site of Elekana, the Cook Islander credited with introducing Christianity to Tuvalu.

Visitors can stay at the island council **guesthouse** (☎ 35 005; r $A60). There are no channels into the lagoon, and transfers ashore from larger ships can be tricky.

NIULAKITA
pop 35 / area 400 sq m

Tuvalu's ninth and southernmost landmass is the tiny coral island of Niulakita. It is at a little higher elevation than the other islands, with fertile soils and lush vegetation. It has white-sand **beaches** within a closed-ring reef, and a pretty church. Niulakita was not considered part of the eight islands of old Tuvalu, as it never had a permanent population. It had various foreign 'owners' and in the late 19th century was exploited for its guano; later, it was a copra plantation. In 1949 it was taken over by the people of Niutao, and now supports a shifting population of families from Niutao who stay for a year or two and are then replaced by others.

There is no guest house but you could try to arrange to stay with one of the local families; contact the **island council** (☎ 21 022). A small channel has been blasted in the surrounding reef to allow access to the beach, but it's usually a hairy ride in through the waves.

TUVALU DIRECTORY

ACCOMMODATION

There's only one hotel on Funafuti (p548), which is pretty basic for the price, as well as a motel, a lodge and some reasonably priced guest houses. The majority of the outer islands have basic council guest houses. Tax is included in the room rates given in this chapter. See p537 for details on budgets.

ACTIVITIES

The best thing to do in Tuvalu? Slow down and enjoy the wonderfully laid-back island lifestyle. If you're looking for action, you won't find it here, but you can swim in the lagoon, cycle, tool around on a motorbike, snorkel (best to take your own gear) or take a trip to the conservation area. You cannot dive on Tuvalu.

BUSINESS HOURS

Government offices are open weekdays from 8am to 12.30pm and 1.30pm to 4pm. Therefore it's probably best not to make appointments between noon and 2pm. Government offices, NGOs and banks close on public holidays (see p629 for a list of public holidays in the Pacific), but not all places do. You'll usually find at least one place to eat, and even *fusi* open on Sunday after church.

CHILDREN

Tuvaluans welcome children as all Pacific countries do. Child-specific activities and entertainment are pretty much non-existent, so be prepared to make your own or to join in locally with, for example, dance or singing practice.

EMBASSIES & CONSULATES
Tuvaluan Embassies & Consulates

Tuvalu's diplomatic representation abroad consists of one high commission: **Fiji** (☎ 679-330 1355; fax 679-330 1023; 16 Gorrie St, PO Box 14449, Suva) as well a handful of honorary consulates including **Australia** (☎ 61 2 9299 8997; fax 61 2 9299 8978; Suite 7, Ana House, 301 George St, Sydney) and the **United Kingdom** (☎ /fax 44 20 8879 0985; fax 679-330 1023; 230 Worple Rd, London SW20 8RH)

Embassies & Consulates in Tuvalu

The only resident embassy in Tuvalu is that of the **Republic of China (Taiwan)** (☎ 20 278). Other major nations that have a South Pacific interest handle Tuvalu from their embassy in Suva in Fiji (see p168 for further information).

PRACTICALITIES

- The Tuvalu Media Corporation on Funafuti publishes *Tuvalu Echoes*, a monthly national newsletter in English and Tuvaluan.

- Radio Tuvalu on FM 94.8 has several daily programmes in Tuvaluan, with fill-in from the BBC World Service.

- Appliances run on Australian-style plugs with three flat pins.

- Tuvalu uses the metric system (see the Quick Reference page for conversions).

FESTIVALS & EVENTS

In addition to New Year's, Easter, Christmas and Boxing Day (see p629), Tuvalu celebrates:

Funafuti Youth Day 11 February
Commonwealth Day March
Bomb Day (Japanese bombing Funafuti) 23 April
Gospel Day Second Monday in May
Queen's Birthday Early June
Children's Day Early August
Independence Day Early October
Hurricane Day (1972 Cyclone Bebe) 21 October
Prince Charles' Birthday Early November

These days generally involve some sort of ceremonial and church service, followed by evening sports and dancing.

INTERNET ACCESS

There are three internet cafés in Funafuti. The national server is often down, and even when it isn't the service is pretty slow. If you're emailing someone in Tuvalu, be patient; it can take a long time to get a response.

INTERNET RESOURCES

Jane's Oceania Pages (www.janeresture.com) A wide-ranging and interesting website about Oceania, with links to specific countries. It's maintained by Jane Resture, descendant of one of the earliest traders and settlers in Tuvalu.
Timeless Tuvalu (www.timelesstuvalu.com) This government-run site has information on sights, activities and accommodation on Tuvalu as well as a number of useful links.
Tuvalu Online (www.tuvaluislands.com) An excellent site with interesting links. It has photos, news headlines, archives and general information about the country.

MONEY

You're strongly advised to take enough Australian cash with you to cover your trip – there are no ATMs or credit-card facilities available on Tuvalu. See the Quick Reference page for exchange rates.

There is only one bank in Tuvalu, the National Bank of Tuvalu on Funafuti (see p543). There are several major currencies, plus Fijian dollars, that are accepted for exchange; the rate for cash is better than travellers cheques, but neither rate is great. Note that there's a commission payable on travellers cheques.

There is a **Western Union** (☎ 20622; www.western union.com) branch in Funafuti that accepts money transfers, but the lines are often down

---

HOW MUCH?

- **Apple:** A$1.50
- **Postcard:** A$1
- **Folding bicycle:** A$100
- **Mask & snorkel:** A$30
- **Plain shell necklace:** A$2, or free when checking out
- **1.5L drinking water:** A$2.30
- **1L petrol:** A$2.50
- **Can VB beer:** A$2.50
- **Souvenir T-shirt:** A$20
- **Take-away roti:** A$1

---

so don't count on being able to receive money from home.

A 10% government tax on accommodation is included in prices listed in this chapter. Tipping isn't expected.

TELEPHONE

Tuvalu's international telephone code is ☎ 688.

The Tuvalu Telecom building is next door to the police station. There's a small telephone office here with several booths from which to make (very expensive) international calls. The mobile phone system was introduced in 2005, but at the time of writing the system had been down for over a year and it wasn't possible to use mobiles. There are no public phone boxes. The hotel has telephones in all its rooms but, due to a technical fault, they had been out of commission for more than six months at the time of research.

TOURIST INFORMATION

There is no visitor information centre in Tuvalu.

Government tourist information (☎ 20 055; fax 20 722; www.timelesstuvalu.com; Ministry of Finance, Economic Planning & Industries, top fl, Government Offices)

TIME

Tuvalu is 12 hours ahead of Greenwich Mean Time (GMT). When it's noon in Tuvalu, it's noon the same day in Fiji, 10am the same day in Sydney and 2pm the previous day in Hawai'i.

VISAS

Visitors do not require a visa and are granted a one-month entry permit on arrival. You need a valid passport and a return ticket – and a valid yellow-fever certificate if you have come from an infected area. Visa extensions, available at **Immigration** (☎ 20 729; Government Offices), are granted for a maximum of three months.

TRANSPORT IN TUVALU

GETTING THERE & AWAY
Air

Tuvalu's small international airport is on Funafuti.

Air Fiji (☎ 679-331 3666; www.airfiji.com.fj) flies from Suva to Funafuti (from F$1400 return) on Monday and Thursday.

Air Pacific (☎ 20 737; www.airpacific.com) ploughs the Suva-to-Funafuti route on Tuesdays and Thursdays (from F$950 return; 2hr 20 min). For more details about airlines see p640.

DEPARTURE TAX

An international departure tax of A$30 applies to all visitors over 12 years old.

Sea

If you have plenty of time on your hands and a flexible schedule (timetables are erratic and irregular) it's possible to get to Tuvalu by boat from Fiji. MVs *Nivaga II* and *Manu Folau*, both government-owned cargo/passenger ships, travel to Suva, Fiji, every three months or so (the trip takes about four days). One-way fares are around A$80/340 for deck/double cabin, with meals. **Pacific Agencies** (☎ 679-331 5444; info@pacship.com.fj) is the agent for MV *Nivaga II* and *Manu Folau* in Suva. The **Marine Department** (☎ 20 055; Government Offices) handles schedules and bookings in Funafuti.

The cargo boat *Nei Matagare* makes trips several times a year between Tuvalu and Fiji. **Williams & Goslings** (☎ 679-331 2633; www.wgfiji.com.fj) are its Suva agents.

GETTING AROUND
Air

There is no domestic airline in Tuvalu.

Boat

All inter-island transport is by boat. Only Funafuti and Nukufetau have reef passages large enough for ships to enter their lagoons and only Funafuti has a real dock. This means ships must load and unload into a small boat, which can be hazardous in rough seas – not for those who aren't confident swimmers.

MVs *Nivaga II* and *Manu Folau* typically visit each of the outer islands once every three or four weeks. The southern trip takes three or four days, and the northern trip about a week. It's not the most comfortable trip – livestock as well as people are crammed into the decks, and the toilets are often in a dire state. Taking plenty of drinking water with you is a must, and taking your own food is not a bad idea either; shipboard meals tend to be corned beef and rice, or rice and corned beef. A return trip to the northern/southern islands costs around A$260/200 for 1st class without food, and A$115/90 for deck class without food.

For bookings and schedule confirmation, contact the **Marine Services Office** (☎ 20 055; Government Offices) in Funafuti. Schedules are unreliable as the boats may be off for maintenance or detouring to pick up VIPs.

Yachts have to check in at Funafuti for immigration and customs clearance on arrival and before leaving Tuvalu. There are no mooring fees nor other formalities, but you must moor outside the conservation area. Entering the lagoon can be risky, however, and island hopping can be difficult, dangerous and expensive.

Car & Motorcycle

There is no organised car hire. Motorcycles and mopeds are the most popular means of land transport, and are available for rent on Funafuti for a daily rate of A$10; you may be asked to produce your home licence. Driving is on the left side of the road.

Local Transport

The capital, Fongafale, has a minibus and taxi service.

554

Vanuatu

The Happiest Country in the World? Yes, Vanuatu was given that gong in 2007, and there's nothing quite as glorious as a holiday among an entire nation of happy people. The locals smile at you as they pass. Hop on a bus and have a conversation. Need an answer and ask anyone for a polite attentive reply. Add to that the scented balmy breezes, gourmet food and several best-in-the-world experiences that very few people know about: a luxury liner shipwrecked in clear diveable water; accessible active volcanoes; a banyan tree the size of a soccer field; pounding waterfalls; an ancient living culture with extraordinary ceremonies; picture-perfect beaches and an underwater paradise for snorkellers and scuba divers.

Port Vila, the national capital, buzzes at the centre of Vanuatu's tourist trade, all colonial and cool, with a view for every restaurant, and hotel beds that float you out over lagoons. If you've come on a package deal, you're just starting your adventure. Stay on when it ends to try out the sporty options, such as abseiling down a waterfall, parasailing over Vila's glorious harbour, horse riding along a beach or acting like Robinson Crusoe on any of the tiny offshore islands.

The outer islands have amazing highlights. Tanna, Espiritu Santo (known as Santo), Erromango, Malekula, Ambae, Ambrym, Pentecost. They are as mysterious and exotic as their names and offer diving, trekking, wild horses, dugongs, colourful lakes, impenetrable jungles, magic, dance and land diving. But it's the happiness, the way you feel safe, the knowledge that the locals love their country and want you to enjoy its pleasures, that really strike you about Vanuatu. Ni-Vanuatu (ni-Van) people aren't after the tourist dollar. There's no bargaining, no hawkers, no pressure to buy. It is so refreshing.

HIGHLIGHTS

- Feeling Cupid's arrow during a romantic tropical dinner complete with a glorious sunset and stunning harbour views in **Port Vila** (p574)
- Camping in the surreal caldera of an active volcano surrounded by the jungle, cane forests, lava beds and ash planes of **Mt Marum** (p590) on Ambrym
- Swimming through an underwater world of luxury liners, coral gardens and encrusted caves off **Luganville** (p598)
- Connecting with people's savagery and mysticism at cannibal sites and spirit caves around the **Dog's Head** (p587) on Malekula
- Talking to the gods of thunder and hear their thunderous replies punctuated with brilliant volcanic fireworks at **Mt Yasur** (p581) on Tanna

CLIMATE & WHEN TO GO

Vanuatu's climate varies from wet tropical in the north (over 4000mm of rainfall a year) to subtropical in the south (less than 2000mm), with dry rain-shadow areas in between. The dry season, from May to October, is cruising time: sparkling days and pleasantly cool evenings. This is Vanuatu at its glorious best; festivals and sporting contests are held, beaches call. For walking, the cooler period from June to August is better. Speaking of cool, it's advisable to take some warm clothing year-round.

November to April is the wet season, with higher temperatures, heavier rains and mosquitoes. December to March is cyclone time. Vanuatu averages 2.5 cyclones a year.

Temperatures in Luganville and Port Vila range from 27°C in July to 30°C in January. Winter nights in Vila can drop to below 12°C from June to August.

COSTS & MONEY

Vanuatu's vatu (Vt) goes a long way, especially once you move away from the big resorts. Budget accommodation may cost only 1800Vt including meals. And a meal could be lobster, or it could be a few SAO biscuits on a rough day. Also, be patient if your expected bungalow blew away, you've been forgotten, or rats ate the only mattress. This is homemade accommodation in a tropical jungle, but hey, it's great.

If you're paying between 7000Vt and 18,000Vt a night, your midrange accommodation will be delightful, and anything over 20,000Vt you'll be totally looked after in a top-end tropical paradise. Try each category for your share of adventure, a chance to live a little on the edge, plus some serious pampering.

HISTORY

In July 2004, an archaeological dig at Teouma, near Port Vila, unearthed Lapita pottery and the skeletal remains of nine Lapita people, chickens and pigs, dating back 3200 years. The site continues to provide archaeologists with insights into the beliefs and rituals of these first people to settle, establish crops and have domestic animals. Lapita people are the ancestors of all Polynesian people, from Tahiti to Hawaii to New Zealand. They had crossed the sea from the Solomon Islands.

Between the 11th and 15th centuries AD, many Polynesians arrived from the central Pacific in sailing canoes holding up to 50 people, live animals, and gardens growing in the boats. Vanuatu's traditions tell of cultural heroes arriving around this time from islands to the east, bringing with them new skills and customs.

Ancient Vanuatu

The people lived in clan-based villages, each with its own language because villages were separated by impassable mountains and rocky coastlines. Everyone lived in the shadow of their ancestors' spirits. Some spirits were benevolent, but others were hostile; famines, cyclones, enemy attack and other misfortunes could result if they became displeased. Magic was the main defence against angry spirits.

Inter-island trade networks were established using large sailing canoes. Otherwise, villagers regarded their neighbours with deep suspicion. Skirmishes between villages were frequent, and usually the victor captured a male or two. It gave a chief great status to present a victim, ready for the pot, to chiefs of other villages. The victims' relatives would mount reprisals, so hostilities continued indefinitely.

Alongside this, the culture was steeped in agriculture. Yam cultivation decided the cycle of the year, and months were named after yams.

European Explorers

The first Europeans to visit Vanuatu, in May 1606, were on a Spanish expedition led by Pedro Fernández de Quirós, who was convinced that Santo was the fabled *terra australis incognita*. It was not until May 1768 that Louis-Antoine de Bougainville sailed between Malekula and Santo, proving that Vanuatu's largest island was not *terra australis*.

James Cook arrived on 16 July 1774, on his second Pacific expedition. He drew the first charts of the region and named places he visited, including Tanna, Erromango, Ambrym and the Shepherd Islands.

In 1789, shortly after the famous mutiny on the *Bounty*, William Bligh sailed through the northern Banks group in his longboat. He sighted several previously unrecorded islands, and returned three years later to confirm his discoveries.

VANUATU

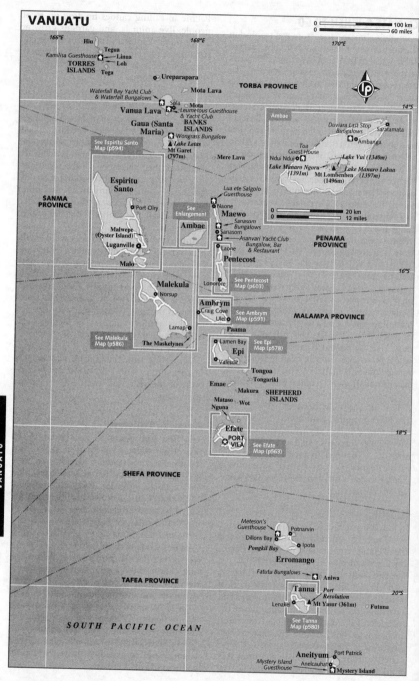

VANUATU

| | | | 100 km |
| | | | 60 miles |

166°E · 168°E · 170°E

Hiu
Tegua
Kamilisa Guesthouse · Linua
TORRES Loh
ISLANDS Toga

Ureparapara

TORBA PROVINCE

Mota Lava
14°S

Waterfall Bay Yacht Club
& Waterfall Bungalows · Sola
Mota
Vanua Lava *Leumerous Guesthouse*
& Yacht Club

Gaua (Santa **BANKS**
Maria) **ISLANDS**
Wongrass Bungalow
▲*Lake Letas*
Mt Garet · Mere Lava
(797m)

SANMA
PROVINCE

See Espiritu Santo
Map (p594)

Espiritu
Santo
Port Olry

Malwepe
(Oyster Island)
Luganville

Malo

Ambae

Duviara Last Stop
Bungalows · Saratamata
Toa
Guest House · Ambanga
Ndui Ndui
Lake Vui (1340m)
Lake Manaro Ngoru *Lake Manaro Lakua*
(1391m) Mt Lombenben *(1397m)*
(1496m)

0 · 20 km
0 · 12 miles

Lua ete Salgolo
Guesthouse
Naone
See
Enlargement **Maewo**
Ambae *Sanasom*
Bungalows
Sanasom
Asanvari Yacht Club
Laone *Bungalow, Bar*
& Restaurant

PENAMA
PROVINCE

Pentecost

Lonorore
See Pentecost
Map (p603)
16°S

Malekula
Norsup

Ambrym
Craig Cove
Ulei See Ambrym
Map (p591)

MALAMPA PROVINCE

Lamap · **Paama**

See Malekula
Map (p586) **The Maskelynes**

Lamen Bay See Epi
Epi Map (p578)
Valesdir

Tongoa
Tongariki

Emae **SHEPHERD**
Makura **ISLANDS**
Mataso Wot
Nguna

Efate
PORT
VILA
See Efate
Map (p563)
18°S

SHEFA PROVINCE

Meteson's
Guesthouse Potnarvin
Dillons Bay
Ipota
Pongkil Bay
Erromango

TAFEA PROVINCE

Fatutu Bungalows Aniwa

Port
Resolution
Tanna
Lenakel Mt Yasur (361m) Futuna
20°S
See Tanna
Map (p580)

SOUTH PACIFIC OCEAN

Aneityum Port Patrick
Mystery Island Anelcauhat
Guesthouse **Mystery Island**

VANUATU

> **VANUATU FACTS**
>
> **Capital city (and island)** Port Vila (Efate)
> **Population** 206,000
> **Land area** 12,200 sq km
> **International telephone code** ☎ 678
> **Currency** Vatu (Vt)
> **Languages** Bislama, English, French and more than 100 local languages
> **Greeting** *Alo* (Bislama)
> **Website** www.vanuatutourism.com

Missionaries & Traders

The first Christian missionary on the scene was the Reverend John Williams from the London Missionary Society (LMS). In 1839 he stepped ashore on Erromango, and was promptly eaten. After this inauspicious beginning the church decided to send Polynesian teachers from Samoa, hoping they would be more acceptable. However, a number of them were also killed or died of malaria.

In 1848 the Reverend John Geddie arrived on Aneityum and made it the headquarters for the Presbyterian mission in Vanuatu, the major Christian denomination on the southern islands. The Anglican Diocese of Melanesia followed in 1860 and became influential in the northern islands; Catholicism arrived in 1887.

Meanwhile, traders heard about the sandalwood trees on Erromango. There was great demand for the wood in China, where it was used for incense. Islanders traded tree trunks for guns, tobacco, or men from enemy villages to be eaten at ceremonies. The best study of the turbulent times of the 19th-century sandalwood trade is Dorothy Shinberg's *They Came for Sandalwood*.

Blackbirding developed as cheap labour was needed for the sugar-cane industries, coconut plantations and nickel mines of nearby countries. Blackbirders kidnapped shiploads of ni-Vanuatu (ni-Van; Vanuatu people) but the missionaries stepped in, campaigning relentlessly until the practice was banned.

European Settlement

The first European settler was a cattle rancher who arrived in 1854. Others followed, lured by the chance to produce cotton during the US Civil War. Intense rivalry existed between the French and English. Brawls were commonplace, as were clashes between settlers and ni-Vanuatu, who resented the loss of their land.

As elsewhere in the Pacific, the local inhabitants were decimated by European diseases. Some say Vanuatu's population was about one million in the early 19th century, but in 1935 only 41,000 ni-Vanuatu remained.

Condominium

In 1906, seeing the Germans becoming influential in the region, the British and French governments, in an awkward moment of togetherness, established the Anglo-French Condominium of the New Hebrides. Vanuatu would be ruled equally by the two colonial powers.

Cynics called the Condominium 'the Pandemonium', as the dual administration produced a bizarre duplication of authorities. Road rules were an issue, as the English drove on the left, the French on the right. Anglo-French rivalry reached new extremes of farce, as the height of each flag up each ministerial flagpole was measured every morning. At least the food was edible in the French jail.

To Kill a Bird with Two Stones by Jeremy MacClancy is available at the Vanuatu Cultural Centre (p567) in Vila. It's an excellent history from Vanuatu's earliest beginnings through the Condominium period (the 'two stones' of the title).

WWII

US forces arrived in Vanuatu in early 1942 and constructed bases, first at Havannah Harbour and Port Vila on Efate, then in southeastern Santo. With Japan's defeat in 1945, the US forces withdrew, leaving behind huge quantities of equipment. Some was sold, the remainder dumped into the sea near Luganville on Santo, at Million Dollar Point.

Cargo cults appeared on several islands as ni-Van sought to secure the kind of wealth they'd seen in the camps – they believed that if they acted like Europeans, then 'cargo' would come their way.

Independence

Land ownership had become Vanuatu's major political issue by the mid-1960s. It was the spark that spurred the country to seek independence.

At this time white settlers 'owned' about 30% of the country's land area. A movement based on *kastom* (custom; rules relating to traditional beliefs) called the Nagriamel sprang up under the leadership of the charismatic Jimmy Stevens. Operating from Santo, its aims were to protect ni-Vanuatu claims to their traditional land. By the late 1960s, Nagriamel had expanded to other islands in northern Vanuatu.

Another great leader, Father Walter Lini, formed the New Hebrides National Party in 1971. It was later called the Vanua'aku Party. His book *Beyond Pandemonium: From New Hebrides to Vanuatu* tells of the lead-up to his country's independence.

The Condominium authorities agreed to hold the country's first general election in November 1979. The Vanua'aku Party were clear winners. Independence was fixed for mid-1980.

Serious threats of secession were being made on Santo and Tanna in early 1980; late in May matters came to a head. An insurrection on Tanna split the island between government supporters and rebels. On Santo, secessionists seized Luganville and hoisted the flag of the Independent Republic of Vemarana. Several other northern islands proclaimed their own secessions during June. They merged and announced a Provisional Government of the Northern Islands, under Jimmy Stevens.

Order was not restored until the new government brought in soldiers from Papua New Guinea following independence on 30 July, after which the secessionist ringleaders were arrested and the rebellion collapsed.

New Nation

Since independence, the ni-Vanuatu government's desire has been for development that benefits everyone equally, while preserving customs and traditions. There were years with too many political parties, much infighting and some high-profile scandals. Now, President Kalkot Matas Kelekele and Prime Minister Ham Lini have led a quiet revolution in the higher ranks. Kelekele's book *New Hebrides: The Road to Independence* includes contributions from young ni-Van writers and provides a broad look at the issues the country faces.

In 2005 Vanuatu qualified for the **US Millennium Challenge** (www.mca.gov), a grant available to countries that show they will use it for sustainable economic growth. It was the only South Pacific country to be selected.

The US$40 million has been used to replac airfields on Pentecost and Ambae, and seal th road around Efate. Increased markets for or ganically grown produce are assisting Vanuatu economic upturn. Other encouraging eco nomic trends are the millions of vatu earne by 1200 ni-Van workers under New Zealand' Registered Seasonal Employer (RSE) scheme the impressive strides in the tourism industry the rising interest in copra, the demand fo Vanuatu beef, which consistently outstrips sup ply, and the increased variety of Vanuatu crop now allowed into New Zealand.

THE CULTURE

Vanuatu's culture and customs vary widely Dances, funerals, weddings, initiations, sys tems of authority, artistic styles, and animal and crop husbandry all differ from island to island. Yet there are common themes, par ticularly the obligation to pay for all services rendered and the finality of any area labelled *tabu,* which means 'sacred' as well as 'forbidden'. If a part of a traditional ceremony, a section of beach, a cave, anywhere at all, is *tabu,* it must be respected.

The lavishly illustrated *Arts of Vanuatu,* edited by Joel Bonnemaison et al, is a fabulous introduction to the diversity of Vanuatu's culture, connecting historic and contemporary influences.

The National Psyche

Ownership of ancestral land, sea and reefs, and everything that comes from them, is fundamental to ni-Vanuatu life. It is held by ni-Van for the future, and the rhythm of the seasons dictates how those resources are used. They viewed with horror the European way of using the land; disputes over use and ownership are still serious issues. Always carry at least 500Vt with you as you never know when you'll have to pay a fee for swimming, fishing, or looking at or walking on a property. This is despite the fact that ni-Van are very hospitable and generous. It is a matter of respect for the value of the resource.

Everyone has a role to play in society. Each village is run by a chief who acts as a justice of the peace and as a delegate for the village. His word is law. Even politicians must do what the chief says when visiting his home villages.

When Mother Nature provides for all of your needs, society has to develop new hallenges. In many areas, chiefs achieve heir rank through *nimangki* (grade-taking) ceremonies, which include a lavish feast. Villagers who eat at the feast are then indebted to the chief, becoming a party of supporters who look to him for leadership and guidance. Each step up the village social adder is accompanied by the ritual killing of pigs, so only men who have acquired enough pigs can hope to reach society's highest levels.

A young man needs a wife to care for his pigs, but he cannot look for a wife until he has built himself a house.

Lifestyle

The centre of village life is the *nakamal*, a men's clubhouse and clan museum, where men meet to discuss village and national issues. A traditional *nakamal* is always strictly *tabu* to women, and tourists may still be barred from entering in *kastom*-oriented areas. Women, too, have a meeting house, where they produce goods for sale, such as woven sections of roof.

Women spend many hours in the family garden and watching over the husband's pigs, while men tend their cash crops, fish, hunt, build boats, carve artefacts and discuss village matters. While the women prepare the evening meal, the men talk in the *nakamal* and drink kava.

There are strict rules in every village regarding dress. Islanders do not wear scant or revealing clothing, and women's thighs are always covered.

Overall, the most pressing problem for all ni-Van families is finding the money to pay their children's school fees each quarter.

Population

Vanuatu's population is almost entirely ni-Vanuatu (Melanesian, although some islands have a strong Polynesian heritage). There are a few Europeans, Asians and other Pacific islanders.

Mostly everyone lives in rural areas, in villages of fewer than 50 people, along narrow coastal strips or on tiny offshore islets. There is a drift into towns, particularly Vila, by ni-Vanuatu in search of work.

ARTS

The population is spread over 83 islands, and Vanuatu's art and traditions vary from

---

LAPITA UNEARTHED

Decorative Lapita pottery, with its fine geometric patterns, has been found throughout the Pacific, as the Lapita people were sea-farers. The site at Teouma is the oldest cemetery to be found in the Pacific. For cultural reasons the heads of those buried had been placed in large Lapita pots, some still almost intact. Some bones at the dig site show the existence of turtles as large as those in the Galapagos.

If you're staying out on Tranquillity Island (Moso; p576) ask about the old Lapita cooking site the owners found when they were building the new bungalow. The site even included a shell axe.

---

island to island; this diversity contributes to the country's unique cultural identity.

The most common subject matters in ni-Vanuatu arts are the human form and traditional interpretations of what ancestral figures looked like. The most important artefacts are made for *nimangki* (grade-taking ceremonies). A Sydney exhibition of these unique figures, masks and drums in 2008 caused a sensation throughout the international art world. Nothing like these figures had been seen before.

The Vanuatu Cultural Centre in Port Vila (p567) is an excellent place to learn more about art and culture in Vanuatu.

Carvings

While wood is the main carved material, objects are also made from tree fern, stone and coral. Serious carving is almost entirely created for ceremonies, while items for sale to tourists are usually small copies of the real thing.

The best carvings come from northern Ambrym. Items to look out for:

- carved bows and arrows, and traditional ceremonial spears
- war clubs made to designs attributed to ancestral cultural heroes
- pig-killing clubs shaped like mattocks, with two stylised faces carved on either side
- large platters and bowls in which yams and kava are pounded, or in which laplap (Vanuatu's national dish) is also served

VANUATU

- model canoes, some with figureheads, others with sails made from dried pandanus leaves
- statues made from tree ferns, representing ancestral figures
- *tamtam* (the slit-gong drums with faces carved above the slit).

Cinema

Wan Smol Bag Theatre in Vila has produced several excellent videos that are for sale around Vila. They're about sensitive issues, as in *Pacific Star,* a musical comedy about the chaos caused when tourists arrive on a remote Pacific island. It's a total romp. More serious is *Vanua-Tai of Land and Sea,* about turtle conservation, and *Mr Right Guy,* about a young girl in a nightclub.

Dances & Ceremonies

Traditional dances in Vanuatu require constant rehearsals. The timing is exquisite and the movements regimented; everyone turns, leaps and stomps together. Thus harmony and cooperation develop between people and villages. There are two major styles of dance: impersonation and participation. Impersonation dances require more rehearsal, as each dancer pretends to be an ancestor or legendary figure and wears an elaborate mask or headdress, such as in the Rom dances of Ambrym (see p593). In participatory dances, several people – or even several villages – take part to enact traditional themes such as hunting, war and death, as in the Toka dances of Tanna.

Literature

James Michener's novel *Tales of the South Pacific* depicts life in Santo when US forces were garrisoned there during WWII. *Beach-masters* by Thea Astley has interesting parallels with the 1980 Santo rebellion. Gwendoline Page's *Coconuts and Coral* is a detailed and often amusing account of life in the New Hebrides during the 1960s. They're guaranteed to put you in the mood for your visit to Vanuatu.

The Talking Tree by Fepai Kolia is a poetry book that takes a stark look at ni-Van life. *The Story of the Eel & Other Stories* are delightful myths and local legends from Uripiv Island. And don't miss the set of illustrated legends: *nabanga pikinini* adapted by Pauline Grindley. They're on sale at Vanuatu Cultural Centre in Port Vila (p567) and they're gorgeous.

Music

String bands developed during WWII, when ni-Van heard the US soldiers playing blue grass. The singing is done with a pinched throat, forming a high-pitched lyrical note. Musicians are getting recognition, and sound studios and training rooms are being established on many islands. You're bound to hear the big hit *Jewel in a Crown* by the Nauten Boys of Tanna, who sing a mix of reggae, country and rock, with an off beat that is a typical Toka dance rhythm. Vanuatu is the jewel.

Vanuatu's *tamtam* (slit drums) are logs with hollowed-out slits and carved human faces (up to five, one above the other) set above the drum part. *Tamtam* are the largest free-standing musical instruments in the world.

Painting & Sand Drawing

Petroglyphs and rock paintings are the country's most ancient forms of pictorial art. The former are common and widespread, although their meanings have been lost and their main significance these days is to archaeologists. Several islands have caves where the walls are decorated with hand stencils and simple paintings of animals.

Styles of painting include bark art; body painting is part of traditional ceremonies.

Ni-Van create beautiful sand drawings, making many delicate loops and circles without raising their fingers, to leave messages or illustrate local legends, songs or ceremonies. The most elaborate and picturesque versions are made in Ambrym. Drawings may be public or sacred, and they have World Heritage status.

Traditional Dress

In *kastom*-oriented parts of Tanna and Pentecost, men still wear *namba* (penis sheaths) every day, while women dress in grass skirts. On Santo, the men wear *mal mal* (loincloths), while some women wear an apron of leaves. In southern Malekula, women of the Small Nambas people traditionally wear raffia skirts woven from banana-tree fibres.

In other parts of Vanuatu, grass skirts are fashioned from the bark of the *burao* (wild hibiscus). Once it's stripped, the bark is placed in sea water, dried, measured into lengths and, if necessary, dyed.

JOHN NICHOLLS

Vanuatu is a very green destination. What initiatives keep it this way? Vanuatu is as Captain Cook found it, green and bountiful. And now he wouldn't worry about being eaten as everyone feeds themselves well from their highly productive land. The main thing that protects this ecological wonderland is that people walk everywhere. Initiatives include the tribal chiefs' periodic taboos on fishing and shell-collecting; Moso Island's turtle hatchery; the Epi island guest house micro-hydropower; and Bokissa island's rainwater catchment and desalination facilities.

Do local businesses have programs? Our diesel-generated power grid is being replaced by wind power, and more vehicles are using Vanuatu's own coconut diesel. This means employment as well as less gasoline imports. Fewer coconut crabs are killed for restaurants; we're fighting the aquarium fish and live-coral trade; and addressing the 'reuse or recycle' issue. We are also encouraging the uptake of carbon offsets. We're the first 'happiest nation in the world'; why not the first carbon-neutral destination?

I hear Vanuatu Hotels is sponsoring the annual Vanuatu Green Award. Yes, tourism operators mustn't see sustainable practice as a hindrance. Objective and correct information has to be openly discussed. The Green Award also recognises the quiet achievers, who challenge communal lethargy.

You tell me even the best plans can go wrong. Oh dear. On Tanna we set up a convalescent habitat for any turtles speared by villagers, buying them before they were eaten. It felt good to save so many turtles. Then we discovered we'd spawned a turtle-spearing industry. They were being speared to sell back to us!

www.vanuatu-hotel.vu

However, most ni-Van wear traditional dress only to attend ceremonies, when elaborate headgear is also worn. Masks are usually made from tree-fern material and represent the faces of demons and ancestral spirits. Others are constructed out of clay reinforced with coconut fibres and layered onto a wickerwork frame.

Painted tree-fern face masks in southern Malekula are decorated with feathers and carved pigs' tusks.

Weaving

Baskets and mats are made throughout the country, as are traps for fish, shellfish and birds. Weaving is done mostly by women, using pandanus leaves and *burao* stalks. Wicker, coconut leaves and rattan are used when a more robust item is required.

LANGUAGE

Bislama, a form of pidgin English, is Vanuatu's national language. English and French are also widely spoken, and schools teach in French or English. But Vanuatu also has the greatest number of different local languages per capita in the world with about 120 still spoken. It's extraordinary to meet young people who are illiterate (schooling costs heaps) yet can speak a dozen languages fluently.

Bislama basics

Hello.	*Alo.*
Hello. (to a group).	*Alo olgeta.*
Good morning.	*Gud morning.*
Good night.	*Gud naet.*
Goodbye/See you.	*Bae/mi lukem yu.*
How are you?	*Olsem wanem?*
Good thanks.	*I gud man tankyu tumas.*
Thank you.	*Tankyu tumas.*
Yes.	*Olraet.*
No thank you.	*No. I olraet tankyu tumas.*
Do you speak English?	*Yu tok tok Engglis?*
Sorry, I don't understand.	*Sore, mi no save.*
My name is…	*Nem blong mi…*

ENVIRONMENT

Vanuatu lies squarely on the Pacific Ring of Fire, so it gets frequent earth tremors, and rises or subsides by up to 2cm per year in some areas. There are nine active volcanoes (seven on land), and fumaroles and thermal springs are found throughout the archipelago.

Animals

Cats, dogs, cattle, horses, pigs and goats were all introduced to Vanuatu and have since gone wild. Rats are the bane of village life and do much damage to the copra industry.

Native land mammals are restricted to four flying-fox species and eight bat species. Marine life includes more than 300 species

VANUATU

BEST EATS

Thanks largely to its French influence, Port Vila is well known in the Pacific for its international cuisine. The main supermarkets all carry a good range of local and imported food and drink, but look around the restaurants for an exquisite dining experience with a mix of picturesque surroundings, rippling water and fantastic flavour treats.

- For Tahitian fish salad in a great alfresco atmosphere try Waterfront Bar & Grill (p574).
- Try Tilly's (p574) for romantic waterside dining.
- For perfect balance in flavours and textures head to Mangoes Restaurant (p574).
- Tamanu on the Beach Resort & Restaurant (p575) has oh-so-delicious local prawns.
- For a magnificent steak topped with Roquefort cheese visit L'Houstalet (p574).

Outside Vila and the resorts on Tanna and Santo, a restaurant is a small room where women serve one meal all day, flavoured with fresh herbs and coconut. Larger villages have tiny stores selling guitar strings, tinned mackerel and biscuits, but there's excellent bread everywhere. Most places have markets, so if you're cooking, look for *Island Edibles* by Judy MacDonnell so you'll know what to buy.

of coral and 450 species of reef fish. The country's largest mammal is the dugong, the world's only herbivorous marine mammal.

Of Vanuatu's 121 bird species, 55 can be found on Santo, including all seven of the country's endemics. One very interesting species is the mound-building, fowl-like megapode (*namalao* in Bislama) that uses the warm volcanic soils to incubate its eggs.

There are 19 native lizards, all small skinks and geckos, and one land snake, the harmless Pacific boa, which grows to 2.5m. While the yellow-bellied and banded sea snakes are extremely venomous, their small mouths and teeth aren't suitable for savaging humans.

The saltwater (or estuarine) crocodiles that live in Vanua Lava have probably swum down from the Solomon Islands after losing their bearings during cyclones.

Plants

About 75% of the country is covered by natural vegetation, including rainforest and rain-shadow grasslands. Cyclones tear at the jungle regularly, renewing it. Logging and subsistence farming hacks into a bit, but much of the country is a botanical wonderland.

The lord of most forests is the banyan, whose crown can be 70m or more across. Forests of mighty kauri trees are found on Erromango, while cloudforests dripping with moss and moisture are a magnificent feature of many highland areas.

Vanuatu has around 20 species of palm, of which 14 are endemic. Orchids festoon the trees in many areas; there are 158 orchid species.

Less enchanting are the introduced weeds such as Lantana and the widespread 'mile-a-minute' vine (see also the boxed text, p601).

Conservation Areas

There are four official conservation areas in Vanuatu: Vatthe (p602) and Loru (p601) on Santo, the kauri reserve (p585) on Erromango, and the cloudforest area around Lake Manaro on Ambae (p604). For information on these areas, it is best to contact the **Environment Unit** (Map p566; ☎ 25302; Georges Pompidou Bldg) in Port Vila, or its **Luganville office** (☎ 36153).

Local chiefs and *kastom* landholders often proclaim conservation areas as a means of protecting some valuable resource, such as turtles or coconut crabs, from overexploitation.

EFATE

pop 45,000 / area 915 sq km

This is Vanuatu's heart, a central island that buzzes with activities – tourist, commercial, industrial and educational. Its varied coastline offers bays and inlets, islands and islets, cliffs and crevices. Efate is the tourists' soft option, unlike the other islands, where

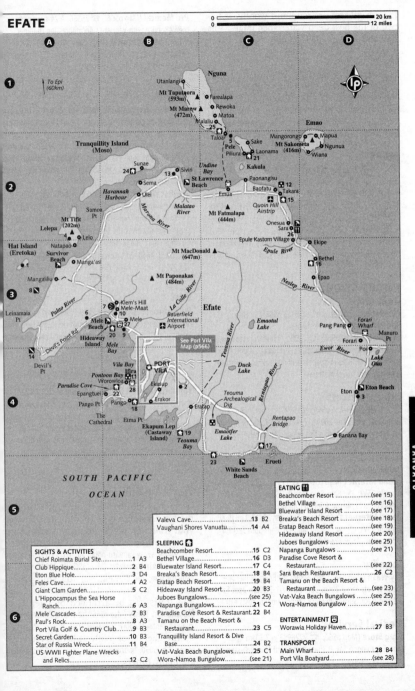

EFATE

0 — 20 km
0 — 12 miles

SOUTH PACIFIC OCEAN

VANUATU

SIGHTS & ACTIVITIES
Chief Roimata Burial Site	1 A3
Club Hippique	2 B4
Eton Blue Hole	3 D4
Feles Cave	4 A2
Giant Clam Garden	5 C2
L'Hippocampus the Sea Horse Ranch	6 A3
Mele Cascades	7 B3
Paul's Rock	8 A3
Port Vila Golf & Country Club	9 B3
Secret Garden	10 B3
Star of Russia Wreck	11 B4
US WWII Fighter Plane Wrecks and Relics	12 C2
Valeva Cave	13 B2
Vaughani Shores Vanuatu	14 A4

SLEEPING
Beachcomber Resort	15 C2
Bethel Village	16 D3
Bluewater Island Resort	17 C4
Breaka's Beach Resort	18 B4
Eratap Beach Resort	19 B4
Hideaway Island Resort	20 B3
Juboes Bungalows	(see 21)
Napanga Bungalows	21 C2
Paradise Cove Resort & Restaurant	22 B4
Tamanu on the Beach Resort & Restaurant	23 C5
Tranquillity Island Resort & Dive Base	24 B2
Vat-Vaka Beach Bungalows	25 C2
Wora-Namoa Bungalow	(see 21)

EATING
Beachcomber Resort	(see 15)
Bethel Village	(see 16)
Bluewater Island Resort	(see 17)
Breaka's Beach Resort	(see 18)
Eratap Beach Resort	(see 19)
Hideaway Island Resort	(see 20)
Juboes Bungalows	(see 21)
Napanga Bungalows	(see 21)
Paradise Cove Resort & Restaurant	(see 22)
Sara Beach Restaurant	26 C2
Tamanu on the Beach Resort & Restaurant	(see 23)
Vat-Vaka Beach Bungalows	(see 25)
Wora-Namoa Bungalow	(see 21)

ENTERTAINMENT
Worawia Holiday Haven	27 B3

TRANSPORT
Main Wharf	28 B4
Port Vila Boatyard	(see 28)

the adventures are wild and woolly. It has two of the best deep-water anchorages, Vila Bay and Havannah Harbour, as well as the principal airport, and the national capital, Port Vila.

Port Vila – the face of Vanuatu, better known around the world than Efate or even Vanuatu itself – is a pretty town, albeit dusty and wobbly, with a great climate, spectacular views, gorgeous hotels and restaurants, and an exciting range of activities and events.

MAPS

The **Drug Store** (☎ 22789; ⏲ 7.30am-6pm Mon-Fri, to noon Sat, 8.30am-noon Sun) in Port Vila sells the 1:200,000 map of Vanuatu published by South Pacific Maps. The **Vanuatu Tourism Office** (VTO; ☎ 22813; www.vanuatutourism.com; Lini Hwy; ⏲ 7.30am-4.30pm Mon-Fri, 8am-noon Sun) has free maps of Efate and Port Vila, and **Jasons** (www.jasons .com/guides/South-Pacific/) free map of Vanuatu is in most hotels.

INFORMATION
Bookshops

Centrepoint supermarket (Map p566; Lini Hwy) French magazines and newspapers.

Stop Press (Map p566; ☎ 22232, Nambatu; stoppress@ vanuatu.com.vu; Au Bon Marché; ⏲ 6am-7.30pm) Australian and British newspapers and magazines, paperbacks, reference and travel material.

Internet Access

Cyber Village (Map p566; ☎ 27728; cyber@vatu.com; Nambatu; per 15min 200Vt; ⏲ 6.30am-7.30pm) An attractive complex with a fish pond, cafe (meals 950Vt to 1700Vt) and 24-hour access to a prepaid hotspot. There are showers for tourists and cheap international phone calls (per minute 40Vt).

Island Internet (Map p566; ☎ 7751165; Lini Hwy; per min 15Vt; ⏲ 8am-5pm Mon-Fri, 9am-noon Sat) Fast connections in air-conditioned comfort.

Naviti Internet Cafe (Map p566; ☎ 27813; Lini Hwy; per min 15Vt; ⏲ 8am-8pm Mon-Fri, 8am-5pm Sat) For when other places are closed.

Laundry

Ezy Wash (Map p566; ☎ 24386; rue Bouganville; one load 1000Vt; ⏲ 7.30am-5pm Mon-Fri, 7.30am-2pm Sat, 8.30am-noon Sun) Very quick service. Ironing costs extra.

Medical Services

Drug Store (Map p566; ☎ 22789; ⏲ 7.30am-6pm Mon-Fri, to noon Sat, 8.30am-noon Sun) This well-stocked pharmacy is tops.

Pro Medical (Map p566; ☎ 25566) A 24-hour paramedic service with Vanuatu's decompression chamber.

Vila Central Hospital (Map p566; ☎ 22100) Has a dentist, private practitioners and a dispensary; it's open for outpatients during business hours.

Money

You'll need cash in vatu for everything, including accommodation, mostly everywhere away from Port Vila. Foreign exchange is provided by **ANZ** (Map p566; ☎ 22536; Lini Hwy ⏲ 8am-3pm Mon-Fri) and **Westpac** (Map p566; ☎ 22084; Lini Hwy; ⏲ 8.30am-4pm Mon-Fri). They both have ATMs.

Goodies Money Exchange (Map p566; ☎ 23445; goodies@vanuatu.net.vu; cnr Lini Hwy & rue Pasteur; ⏲ 8am-5.30pm Mon-Fri, 8am-4pm Sat, 8.30am-noon Sun) Generally gives the best rates. Check out the great carvings while you're there.

National Bank of Vanuatu (NBV; Map p566; ☎ 22201; rue de Paris) Can also handle foreign exchange.

Post

Post office (Map p566; ☎ 22000; Lini Hwy) Poste restante, stamp counter, internet facilities (25Vt per minute), card-operated phones outside, and private phone and fax booths inside.

Tourist Information

Vanuatu Tourism Office (VTO; Map p566; ☎ 22813; www.vanuatutourism.com; Lini Hwy; ⏲ 7.30am-4.30pm Mon-Fri, 8am-noon Sun) Free maps and information about accommodation, activities, tours and the outer islands. The website shows accommodation options with direct links for booking, tour operators, events calendar and much more.

Travel Agencies

It's a good idea to use local agencies so that the tourist dollar goes to Vanuatu. Arrange your itinerary, flights, tours and accommodation online with Silvana of **Vanuatu Hotels** (☎ 24444; www.vanuatu-hotels.vu) in Port Vila, or contact **Air Vanuatu** (Map p566 ☎ 23848; www.air vanuatu.com; rue de Paris, Vila) for your international and domestic flights. Transfers and tours can be arranged by Glenda of **Melanesian Tours** (Map p566; ☎ 26847, 7772729; www .melanesiantours.com) up the hill from Poppy's on the Lagoon or Willy at **Horizon Tours** (Map p566; ☎ 25050; horizon@vanuatu.com.vu). And there are many others.

PORT VILA

EFATE IN...

Two Days

Spend your first day wandering around. Take our walking tour (p570), go out to one of the resort islands (p568) and visit Mele Cascades (p568). At about 6pm, head to a kava bar for a shell or two, then go outside the city, to Tamanu perhaps, for dinner.

Next morning, join a day tour out on a yacht (p568). When you return, try a Melanesian feast at Ekasup Cultural Village (p568).

Four Days

With two more days, some scuba diving (p568), and an ecotour (p571) with Pascal are unmissable. Use the afternoons to visit the cultural centre (p567) and the Secret Garden (p568) for an insight into local history and culture. Eat at a restaurant with entertainment, such as Flaming Bull Steakhouse (p574), then cross the road for some action at Rumours (p575). On the last night, dine at a restaurant with great ambience, such as Roxy's (p574) or Sunset Bungalows (p573).

One Week

You have three more days? Great. Take a tour around the island (p571) and include a night on Nguna or Epi to experience village life. Spend another day on fun activities (p568) and your last day back in town, shopping at the markets (p567).

The VTO website lists overseas travel agencies specialising in Vanuatu. See p571 for local tour operators offering trips around Efate and to outer islands.

TRANSPORT
Getting There & Around

See Transport in Vanuatu p609 for details of airline and shipping services to and from Vila.

TO/FROM THE AIRPORT

Airport shuttle buses cost 400Vt per person to/from Vila, and taxis offer rates from 600Vt to 1000Vt (shared). If you don't have much luggage, you can catch a minibus (100Vt) from outside the domestic terminal.

CAR & MOTORCYCLE

Vila's car-hire companies include **Avis** (Map p566; ☎ 22570; Olympic Bldg), **Budget** (Map p566; ☎ 23170; Nambatu) and **Discount Rentals** (Map p566; ☎ 23242, 24475; Nambatu). A four-seater vehicle for town/island use costs from 6000/8500Vt (including VAT and insurance) a day.

On Wheels (Map p566; ☎ 22775, 7741591; buggy funrental@vanuatu.com.vu; Nambatu; ⏰ 7.30am-5.30pm) rents a Willys jeep (8000Vt), motorbikes (7000Vt) and scooters (4000Vt) as well as cars.

Scooters can be hired through **Vanuatu Islands Travel Centre** (Map p566; ☎ 7747000, 7741000; ⏰ 8am-5pm Mon-Sat, 9am-3pm Sun). A single seater costs per half/full day 3500/5500Vt.

MINIBUS & TAXI

The main roads are usually thick with minibuses between 6am and 7.30pm. Fares are a uniform 100Vt in town. To travel further afield to, say, Hideaway Island costs 200Vt. There are also many taxis offering a competitive service (see p610).

Vila's main taxi stand is beside the market.

PORT VILA
pop 38,000

Climbing steep hillsides around horseshoe-shaped Vila Bay, Port Vila offers stunning views around every crooked corner. It was declared the seat of the newly proclaimed Condominium government in 1906, so it has some charming colonial buildings. With its faded French atmosphere and beautiful harbour, Vila is one of the South Pacific's most attractive towns. It's also delightfully jaded, with its broken footpaths, strings of bargain basement shops and unhurried rhythm as smiling people check out the many cafes and restaurants.

Orientation

Vila's main shopping precinct follows the shoreline for about 1km, so it's easily explored

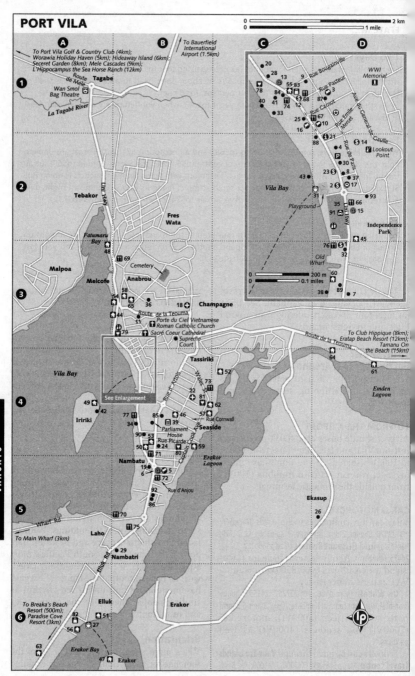

PORT VILA

0 — 2 km
0 — 1 mile

A
To Port Vila Golf & Country Club (4km);
Worawia Holiday Haven (5km); Hideaway Island (6km);
Seceret Garden (8km); Mele Cascades (9km);
L'Hippocampus the Sea Horse Ranch (12km)

B
To Bauerfield
International
Airport (1.5km)

Tagabe
Route de Mele
Wan Smol Bag Theatre
La Tagabé River

C

20
28
78
84
13
55 83
9
41
68
12
40
33
25
16
67 10
88
43
31
Vila Bay
Playground
35
91
76
32
Old Wharf
38
89
7
60
23
2

D
WWI Memorial
Rue Bougainville
Rue Pasteur
Rue Carnot
Rue Emile Mercet
Ave du Cénéral de Gaulle
Rue de Paris
Lint Hwy
14
Lookout Point
30
37
17
93
66
15
Independence Park
45

Tebakor
Lim Hwy
Fres Wata
Fatumaru Bay
48
69
Malpoa
Cemetery
Melcofe
Anabrou
58
64
65
18
Champagne
44
11
Route de la Teouma
Porte du Ciel
Roman Catholic Church
Sacré Coeur Cathedral
79
Supreme Court

Vila Bay
See Enlargement

Tassiriki
52
Route de la Teouma
64
To Club Hippique (8km);
Eratap Beach Resort (12km);
Tamanu On
the Beach (15km)
61
Emden Lagoon

49
42
Iririki
77
34
85
22
73
81
62
46
39
Rue Cornwall
Seaside
57
Parliament House
Rue Picarde
90
53
24
59
50
71
80
Erakor Lagoon
Nambatu
19
6
5
72

92
86
Rue d'Anjou
Ekasup
26

70
Wharf Rd
75
Laho
To Main Wharf (3km)

29
Nambatri

To Breaka's Beach
Resort (500m);
Paradise Cove
Resort (3km)
Elluk
82
51
56
27
63
Erakor Bay
47
Erakor
Erakor

VANUATU

on foot. Lini Hwy, the main street, winds parallel to the waterfront. Rue Carnot and rue de Paris are known as Chinatown. You'll find anything here, from Japanese stereos to straw hats, Chinese cigarettes and balls of wool.

During WWII, US forces established radar stations known as Numbers One, Two and Three. Number Two and Number Three have been preserved in Bislama; Nambatu and Nambatri are now among Vila's plushest residential areas. 'Nambawan' is Independence Park.

Sights
VANUATU CULTURAL CENTRE
This excellent **museum**, **library** and **cultural centre** (Map p566; ☎ 22129; www.vanuatuculture.org; off rue

d'Artois; adult/child 500/100Vt; 🕐 9am-4.30pm Mon-Fri, to noon Sat) is home to a well-displayed selection of traditional artefacts, including such items as *tamtam*, massive outrigger canoes, ceremonial headdresses and examples of Lapita and Wusi pottery. There are photographic displays, and you can watch videos about traditional ceremonies and legends.

MARKETS
Vila's colourful **outdoor market** (Map p566) is open round the clock from Monday morning to noon on Saturday with women from all over the island wearing beautiful island dresses selling their fruit and vegetables. Along the harbour wall past the playground is the **Nambawan Market** (Map p566), just as colourful, where

VANUATU

the women will braid your hair and sell you jewellery, woodcarving, souvenirs and clothes. Midway, but across Lini Hwy, is **Hebrida Market Place** (Map p566). This fun place is jam-packed with hand-painted clothes, hand-made souvenirs, woven bags, mats, carvings and women with sewing machines, ready to make to order an island dress or two.

IRIRIKI, ERAKOR & HIDEAWAY ISLAND

These gorgeous islands have white-sand or coral beaches and lovely resorts accessible by 24-hour ferries – **Iririki ferry** (1500Vt, redeemable at the resort) leaves from Vila's waterfront; **Erakor ferry** (free) docks just south of Le Lagon; **Hideaway ferry** (island entry 1000Vt) putts out from Mele Beach. Go out for a dream time: walk around the islands; enjoy the fabulous restaurants, bars and massage centres; hire kayaks, catamarans or snorkelling gear from the water sports centres; kick up your heels at a feast night or seafood buffet; settle in for the happy hours.

MELE CASCADES

You see the **cascades** (Map p563; adult/child 1000/500Vt; 9am-4.30pm) as you drive along the road towards Klem's Hill. Shaded by rainforest, pool after pool of stunningly clear aquamarine water have formed below a 35m waterfall. A little path with guide ropes wobbles up to the top. There are toilets and change rooms at the entrance. Go out by bus, or take a guided tour with **Evergreen** (Map p566; 23050; www.evergreen.com.vu; tours 2600Vt; 9am & 2pm) with drinks and tropical fruit included.

SECRET GARDEN

This **outdoor cultural centre** and **nature reserve** (Map p563; 26222; adult/child 800/400Vt; 9am-4.30pm) is fascinating: snake feeding; a cannibal house; gruesome stories and photos; exotic plants. See and touch a coconut crab or a bright green banded iguana, and see bungalows built in the different traditional styles. The historical and cultural anecdotes are a great read. There's an island feast night (3000Vt) on Thursday.

EKASUP CULTURAL VILLAGE

Futuna islanders demonstrate and talk about their traditional lifestyle at their *kastom* village (Map p566; book with Nafonu Tatoka Tours, p571). Original local music and *kastom* dancing show off the colourful

costumes. The **feast nights** (24217; adult/chi 3100/1550Vt; 5pm Fri) include shells of kava fun entertainment and interesting food. Yo need to book by the day before.

Activities

ABSEILING & PARASAILING

The team at **Edge Abseiling** (7753153; www.edgevanuatu.com; abseiling 8000Vt; 10am Mon, Wed Fri) takes you down the Mele Cascades like one wild shower-bath. **Port Vila Parasailing** (25696, 7772702; www.portvilaparasailing.com; s/tandem 8000/6000Vt) takes you out over the sparkling waters. Like wow!

BOAT TRIPS

Blue Semi Submarine (7743144; adult/child/family 2500/1800/7000Vt; half-hourly 7.30am-4pm) See the sea-floor from a deep viewing chamber. Leaves from Nambawan Market.

IslanDreams Kayaking (Map p566; 7754954, 7752952; islandreams@bigpond.com; adult/child 5000/2500Vt; 9am & 2pm) Head out to a coral reef from pretty Mele Bay watching marine life pass under your sea kayak's glass bottom.

Meridian Charters Sunset Cruise (Map p566; 25595, 7743352; adult/child/family 4000/2000/9500Vt; 5-7pm Tue-Sun) *Caraid*, a handsome 20m motor yacht, sails from Le Café du Village. French wines and cheeses; very romantic.

Vanuatu Jet (Map p566; 26426; www.vanuatujet.com; 30 min adult/child 5000/3500Vt) Sideways slides, fishtails – hang on tight. It's available for high-speed transfers too.

BOAT TRIPS WITH SNORKELLING & DIVING

Coongoola Day Cruise (Map p566; 25020; www.southpacdivecruise.com.vu; adult/child/diver 8900/4400/10,300Vt) Sail to Tranquillity Island on *Lady of the Sea*, once the mother ship for the Sydney–Hobart yacht race. Picnic on the beach, visit the turtle sanctuary, dive or snorkel – you'll love it all.

Sailaway Cruises (Map p566; 25155, 23802; www.sailawayvanuatu.com; adult/diver 8500/11,000Vt) Fab day with a small group on the *Golden Wing*, a 12.6m trimaran. Includes snorkelling and diving around Hat Island and Paul's Rock, top spots for healthy coral and colourful fish, and lunch on Survivor Beach (of TV fame).

FLYING

Port Vila's harbour makes a magnificent backdrop to a short sight-seeing tour, but, hey, take off to rainforests, lagoons, volcanoes – just keep flying.

Vanuatu Seaplanes (Map p566; ☎ 22591, 7742619; www.vanuatuseaplanes.com; flights from 6500Vt) Choose your own adventure; space for four passengers.

Vanuatu Helicopters (Map p566; ☎ 25022, 7744106; www.vanuatuhelicopters.com; waterfront/canyon/volcano 2000/20,000/135,000Vt) Adventure, romance, elegance, this offers it all.

GAME & REEF FISHING

Vanuatu's waters and the available choices (game and reef, liveaboard, remote island) mean your time on the deep blue will be memorable (shared half-/whole-day trips start at around per person 10,000/15,000Vt).

Crusoe Fishing Adventures (Map p566; ☎ 22439, 7745490; www.crusoefishing.com.vu) Boats include *Horizon*, a spacious Capricorn Classic 12.6m cruiser, with the latest hi-tech equipment set up for day trips or liveaboards.

Wild Blue Fishing ((Map p566; ☎ 22398, 7743288; www.fishing.com.vu) Shimano tackle on a 10.2m Blackwatch or 9m Reefmaster. Offers great packages including accommodation on an island.

Lelepa Island Fishing Charter (☎ 23144, 7742714; www.lelepatours.com; half/full day 39,000/48,000Vt; ⏱ 5am Sun-Fri) Locals take you where the big fish are in a 7.5m Banana Boat with Shimano tackle.

HORSE RIDING

Clip through the rainforest, ride along the beach; go bareback into the sea; take a sunset trail; sit at the bar while the kids ride a pony; have a picnic; ride to a village. All sorts of adventures from 11am to 5.30pm except Monday, one hour/full day from 3400/9000Vt):

Club Hippique (Map p563; ☎ 23347; chap@vanuatu .com.vu) By the lagoon with tube rides and kayaks as well.

L'Hippocampus the Sea Horse Ranch (Map p563; ☎ 25152, 7740102; lhippocampus@vanuatu.com.vu) On a farm by Mele Bay, think best horse, best beach or rainforest, best experience.

SCUBA DIVING

Efate's dive sites include wrecks, coral reefs, deep drop-offs, thermal vents, caverns and swim-throughs, such as the Cathedral, a warren of underwater holes, stipples and tunnels; Paul's Rock, with sheer walls of coral down an extinct submarine volcano; and the *Star of Russia*, an iron-hulled schooner with masts and hull still intact, home to thousands of colourful fish. For the brightest coral, try the offshore-island or boat dives.

Introductory dives start from 5500Vt; double dives for certified divers from 8500Vt and gear hire from 1200Vt. Bus and/or boat trips and meals add extra. All operators offer Professional Association of Diving Instructors (PADI) courses, costing from 28,500Vt:

Big Blue Vanuatu (Map p566; ☎ 27518, 7744054; www.bigbluevanuatu.com; 8am-4pm) Mike and Maggie have been dive instructors for years. They also offer snorkel adventures.

Hideaway Island (Map p563; ☎ 22963; www.hide away.com.vu) Beside a marine sanctuary with a new dive manager and new equipment.

Nautilus Water sports (Map p566; ☎ 22398; www .nautilus.com.vu; Lini Hwy) Great resources: five-star PADI dive centre, dive boat and skills pool. Some dive packages include on-site accommodation.

Tranquillity Island Dive Base (Map p563; ☎ 25020, 27211; www.southpacdivecruise.com.vu) A range of packages from a day trip to ones including accommodation on the island (see p576).

Vaughani Shores Vanuatu (Map p563; ☎ 29273, 7773326; www.divevanuatu.org) Head to Devils Point for boat dives and deep offshore exploring with a marine ecology expert, B&B accommodation (single/double for 9000/14,000Vt), hammocks and meals for both divers and nondivers.

SPORTING CENTRES & CLUBS

Port Vila Tennis Club (Cercle Sportif; Map p566; ☎ 22437; Rte du Stade; activities from Vt500) Has five hard courts, two squash courts, gym, beach volleyball and aerobics and yoga classes.

Port Vila Golf & Country Club (Map p563; ☎ 22564; www.vanuatu.com.vu/~pvgcc/; Rte de Mele) A challenging course with palm-tree and ocean-front hazards, and an excellent 19th hole overlooking Mele Bay. Visitors very welcome: 3000Vt for 18 holes, 1500Vt for club and buggy hire, 1000Vt for a caddie.

SWIMMING & SURFING

Beaches are unexpectedly hard to find. Catch a bus to the following:

Devil's Point Rd (Map p563) All along here is whitesand beach.

Breaka's Beach Resort (Map p563) Good surfing and swimming right along to Pango Point.

Erakor Island (Map p563) Intermediate surfing out at the point.

Eratap Beach Resort (Map p563) Swim here, or canoe across to Eratap Island to surf.

WALKING, CYCLING & BUGGYING

Pascal Guillet of **EcoTours** (☎ 25299, 7745596; www .vanuatu-ecotour.com.vu; half-day tours from 2900Vt) leads you through lush gardens, down cascades, into rock pools and along riverbanks. Cycling tours are grand adventures through villages, across rivers, and up mountain tops; there's a bike tour to Tanna; and you can hire bikes (per day 2500Vt). Book as far in advance as possible.

Have a blast on a **Buggy Run** (Map p566; ☎ 22775, 7741591; buggyfunrental@vanuatu.com.vu; scenic/jungle/rainforest rides 5000/6500/16,000Vt). Your guide buggy leads kids between six and 106 on wicked trails.

Port Vila Walking Tour

Start with breakfast on the waterfront at **Nambawan Café & Juice Bar** (**1**; p574), stop to watch the **pétanque game** (**2**), then cross Lini Hwy and go two blocks north to rue

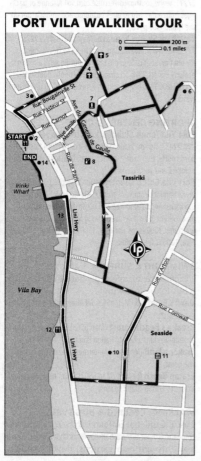

PORT VILA WALKING TOUR

Bougainville. Turn right and start the gentle stroll (well, steep slog, so it's lucky you're fit) up the hill past the lovely **Government Building** (**3**) to the splendid **Sacré Coeur Cathedral** (**4**). Turn right up behind the cathedral. Hidden on your left is charming **Porte du Ciel** (**5**), a little Vietnamese Roman Catholic church. Go uphill again at the next corner, following the road through the French sector until you come to the gloriously pink **Court House** (**6**). You can go inside to see fabulous timber doors and a sweeping staircase. Head back downhill to the **WWI Memorial** (**7**) and rest on the bench while you admire the stunning view. Back on your feet, go down rue Emile Mercet, turn into Ave du General de Gaulle, and along to **Lookout Point** (**8**) then continue past **Independence Park** (**9**). At the T-junction, go east to the roundabout at rue d'Artois, turn right and follow rue d'Artois for a block. Note **Parliament House** (**10**) on your right. Turn left and then left again. This stunning building is the **Vanuatu Cultural Centre** (**11**; p567). Wander around its museum, a small, friendly place, where you'll get some fascinating insights into the local culture.

Back outside, head towards the ocean, down to Lini Hwy and there, just downhill, is long-time favourite **Waterfront Bar & Grill** (**12**; p574), a top spot for a drink. Edge your way along the sea wall deciding which yacht you'd like to sail away on, then walk down Lini Hwy to the glorious **outdoor market** (**13**; p567). Continue along the sea wall to **Nambawan Market** (**14**; p567) to fossick for local souvenirs.

Vanuatu for Children

Vila markets (p567) are adventure worlds. Give your kids some coins and watch them shop. In between is a playground and the **Wet n Wild** (1hr/all-day pass 1000/2500Vt; ☺ 9.30am-4.30pm) extravaganza with floating trampolines, walkways and slides. Next to it are submarine boats (p568), where you watch the fish.

Catch a bus to anywhere. Kids love the buses. Or catch a bus to the **Fun Factory**

WALK FACTS

Start Nambawan Café & Juice Bar
Finish Nambawan Market
Distance 3km
Duration Three hours including museum browse

28256; over/under age 3 1000/600Vt; 7.30am-5pm
ue-Fri, 7am-5.30pm Sat & Sun) and have a cof-
ee while they shoot rubber balls from a
pace craft.

Erakor (p568) is a top spot. There's a ferry
ride across, and your ankle biters can build
castles in wet sand, surrounded by starfish.

Mele Cascades (p568) and the Secret
Garden are kid magnets (p568). You'll just
die as they climb up through a waterfall, but
they'll be rapt. If they're old enough for kayaks
and snorkelling, head out to Hideaway Island
(p568) for the **Marine Park Adventure** (family pass
4950Vt): feed fish, snorkel along a trail, tour in
a glass-bottom boat, lunch in the restaurant.
Fantastic value.

Go to Tanna. The flight is such an adventure, and Mt Yasur Volcano will absolutely
fascinate them. They'll talk of little else for
months. And if it's school holidays, book into
Santo's Turtle Bay (p601) for a week so your
children can do the circus workshops while
you scuba dive.

Tours

There are stacks of tours, from half-day to
five-day ones. Around Efate tours include
swimming at Eton Blue Hole, visiting WWII
relics, river cruises and fire-walking. Take
a sunset cruise, a helicopter flight, a glass-
bottom boat glide or an evening extravaganza of feasting and dancing at a cultural
village. Try birdwatching or river kayaking.
Visit Efate's small offshore islands for superb
beaches and great coral reefs. Get grounded
on an overnight tour to an island bungalow.

Best of all, have a grand adventure to the
outer islands: to Tanna's or Ambrym's volcanoes, to Santo's magnificent shipwreck, to
Epi's dugongs, to Malekula's cannibal sites.
Some operators offering a range of tours:
Island Holiday Tours (Map p566; 26426, 7750740;
www.islandholidaytours.com; Lini Hwy)
Real Adventure Tours (Map p566; 22743; www
.adventurevanuatu.vu; Adventure Centre)
Vanuatu Discovery (Map p566; 23167; vandiscovery@
vanuatu.com.vu; Lini Hwy)
Vanuatu Namba1 Tours (Map p566; 27936,
7774247; Nambawan Market)

Specialised tours:
Lelepa Island Day Tours (23144, 7742714; www
.lelepatours.com; adult 7800Vt; 8amSun-Fri) A family
adventure including fishing from a 7m Banana Boat.
Nafonu Tatoka Tours (24217, 7746734; www

.vanuatutourism.com/ekasup.htm; adult/child
3850/1900Vt; 9am & 2pm Mon-Fri, 9am Sat) A stunning cultural experience at Ekasup Village (p568).
Roimata Cultural Tours (26949, 5447025,
5440695; roimata@vanuatuculture.org; adult 6000Vt;
9am Mon-Sat) Tour starts at Vanuatu Cultural Centre
and includes a feast on the beach. See p576.
Island Expert Tours (7756648, 7752271; pele
islandtours@vanuatu.com.vu; adult/child 7800/3600Vt;
8.30am pickup) Esly runs day tours to Pele (p577).

The **VTO** (www.vanuatutourism.com/vanuatu/cms/en/
activities/tours.html) lists more operators; ask exactly
what your tour includes when you book.

Sleeping

There's stacks of accommodation in Vila and
surrounds. Many places offer free accommodation for children under 12, so always ask.
Most rooms have a fridge.

BUDGET

Note that Hideaway and Erakor Island resorts
(p572 and p573, respectively) also offer budget
accommodation.

Vila Hibiscus Motel (Map p566; 28289; vilahibiscus
motel@vanuatu.com.vu; dm/s/d 1500/2500/3600Vt, unit/apt
from 4900/5500Vt) The price is right, the gardens
lovely, the atmosphere cheerful and the family
apartments are splendid self-contained affairs.
There's shared kitchen and bathroom facilities
for the rooms, and it's an easy walk into town.

Treetops Lodge & Bungalows (Map p566; 22944,
7742944; swedcons@vanuatu.com.vu; Elluk Rd; B&B dm/s/d
from 2000/4000/5000Vt;) It's relaxed, rustic and
rusty with a great dining/living area set up
on the verandah (if Karl your host is around,
listen to his tales about Vanuatu's glorious
history). Up the steps, a gorgeous bungalow
(7500Vt) with a mezzanine is indeed in the
tree tops.

City Lodge (Map p566; 26826; citylodge@van
uatu.com.vu; s/d 3800/4700Vt, r with air-con 5800Vt;)
Location, location. If you're busy in the city,
you'll find it's ideal to stay here. Besides, the
minimalist rooms are bright and new.

Room With a View (Map p566; 23703, 7751327;
www.vanuatutourism.com; cnr Renee Pujol & rte de la Teouma;
PO Box 889; s/d/tr B&B 4000/5500/6500Vt) This lovely
colonial building just a few minutes from the
centre has a balcony with the best views – the
perfect place to eat your excellent breakfast,
then just sit and chat because you meet a fascinating range of people. Borrow the mountain
bikes for free.

VANUATU

KARL WALDEBACK

What is the background to Vanuatu becoming the World's Happiest Country? Back in 1906, the French wanted to annex Vanuatu to New Caledonia; the British wanted to prevent the French from gaining anything, anywhere. So the Condominium was born, a silly thing: two mighty powers governing a tiny traditional archipelago, using both French and English law. However, through the infighting between these administrative parties the ni-Van were largely left alone and the recipe for a complete mess-up became the foundations for a Westminster-style democracy and the most successful and least corrupt country in the South Pacific.

But didn't independence end in rebellion? Another curse turned blessing. The British wanted out and the French wanted to hold on, because their nationals owned all the valuable land. This conflict meant everyone became either French or English, no matter where they lived. Vanuatu became the only Melanesian country where the locals identified themselves with a country rather than an island, language or tribe.

And these days? Real civil war is not remotely likely, as Vanuatu's population comes from 132 different-language (not dialect) 'nations', where 96 of those ancient languages are still spoken every day. The further split by the French/English division means there could never be a powerful enough disruptive group based on ethnicity. Vanuatu is thus blessed by its diversity and colonial incompetence.

Karl Waldeback runs Treetops Lodge & Bungalows in Port Vila

MIDRANGE

Coconut Palms Resort (Map p566; ☎ 23696; www.coco nutpalms.vu; rue Cornwall; B&B dm/d/tw 5250/9600/9600Vt, B&B r/apt with air-con 13,600/16,1350Vt 🔀 💻 🗐) Welcome to the place with everything. Full range of interesting rooms and the communal areas are excellent: spacious dining room, sports bar, lounge bar, sparkling big pool, kitchen and barbecue area. Rates include breakfast, and for the tropical feel, enjoy your lunch and dinner in the gazebo by the pool.

Olympic Hotel (Map p566; ☎ 22464; olympichotel@ vanuatu.com.vu; Lini Hwy; PO Box 1537; deluxe/studio/apt 7300/8100/10,100Vt; 🔀) The Olympic's rooms are quietly comfortable and spacious, sleep three and have views over the main streets and harbour, and it's so good to be in the centre of town. Lounge around on the grand patio with wi-fi connection.

Kaiviti Village Motel (Map p566; ☎ 24684; www.kaiviti motel.com; studio/apt 8400/13,500Vt; 🔀 🗐) Newly updated, the rooms are looking good and the location is just right. Enjoy a drink at the poolside bar while the kids splash up a storm in the pool.

ourpick **Hideaway Island Resort** (Map p563; ☎ 22963; www.hideaway.com.vu; tw 8800Vt, bungalows d/tr/q 21,300/26,3000/31,300Vt; 🔀 🗐) On the edge of a marine sanctuary, this place buzzes with divers and snorkellers. The rooms with shared facilities open onto a wide verandah; there's no communal kitchen but who'd cook with Bruce's fish curry available at the restaurant?

There's a blackboard menu, with mains from 500Vt to 1500Vt. The bungalows are cheerfully bright, and kids stay for free. Join in the Melanesian feast (2400Vt), try the kayaks and catamaran, swim, play volleyball, eat fish curry. Budget dorm beds are also available for 3400Vt.

Tradewinds Resort (Map p566; ☎ 27018; www .tradewinds.com.vu; PO Box 1687; studio/2-/4-bedroom apt 12,000/18,000/25,000Vt; 🔀 🗐) Self-contained Western-style apartments catch the trade winds for tropical comfort. It's a home-away-from-home and great for families. Cute pool too, beside the barbecue.

Moorings Hotel (Map p566; ☎ 26800; www.moorings vanuatu.com/; Lini Hwy; d/family 12,400/14,500Vt; 🔀 🗐) Shiny new, on the waterfront and around a large pool, this popular new place has everything including Rumours Nightclub and Moos Bar & Grill (open from 7am till 9.30pm).

Seachange Lodge (Map p566; ☎ 26551; www.sea change.com; PO Box 5101; Lini Hwy; studio/cottage/lodge/chalet d 12,500/14,900/18,200/23,200Vt; 🔀 🗐) Orchids line your path as you meander down to your waterside spot, with kayaks awaiting and recliner chairs offering. But take yourself inside because the rooms are designer-special.

Pacific Lagoon Apartments (Map p566; ☎ 23860; www.members.optusnet.com.au/pla32; Pango Rd; PO Box 827; 4-person garden/lagoon apt 13,500/16,000Vt) Set in a large grassy area fronting the lagoon, this is perfect for families. Attractive two-bedroom apartments have sunny bathrooms,

---

NO PITTER-PATTER

These three totally gorgeous child-free places are way too romantic for the pitter-patter of tiny feet. Absorb the ambience in rambling gardens, on a sun-drenched balcony, in a lazing pool or paddling on the lagoon. Their restaurants offer fine waterside dining (lunch and dinner) using Vanuatu's freshest organic best, and main meals range from 1500Vt to 5500Vt.

Vila Chaumières (Map p566; ☎ 22866; vilchaum@vanuatu.com.vu; s/d/tr 12,600/12,600/15,700Vt; 🄫 🖳) Garden bungalows, lagoon-side rooms and a little palm-fringed beach. Come down to the restaurant, out over the water, and feed the fish before dining in the soft light.

Breaka's Beach Resort (Map p563; ☎ 23670; www.breakas.com; garden/beachfront bungalow 22,400/29,800Vt; 🐉) Traditional bungalows styled to delight any eye. Surf out the front, visit nearby Pango caves, play bocce, tennis, table tennis. Or relax, have a massage and dine alfresco. Ask about the family villas (set up for kids) next door, costing from 47,000Vt to 76,500Vt.

Sunset Bungalows (Map p566; ☎ 29968; www.sunset-bungalows.com; superior/ste bungalows 28,700/35,000Vt; 🄫 🐉) Cool timber floors swish out to become over-water balconies. A little waterfall tinkles into the European-style pool. Take a kayak out on the lagoon then indulge yourself at the beautiful restaurant, where you might order a half-lobster drizzled with chilli.

---

comfortable lounges and shiny kitchens. There are kayaks, barbecues, babysitting and a laundry service.

Poppy's on the Lagoon (Map p566; ☎ 23425; www.poppys.com.vu; studio/bungalow/ste/cottage 14,500/17,000/22,000/36,000Vt; 🄫 🖳 🐉) A delightful spot with kayaks and canoes, massages, babysitting, movies and games. Accommodation is self-contained plus the cafe serves home-cooked meals. Ask your hosts, Peter and Jo, about their overnight Tanna safari (21,000Vt).

TOP END

Le Lagon (Map p566; ☎ 22313; www.lelagonvanuatu.vu; B&B d/bungalow/ste from 19,200/28,100/52,000Vt; 🄫 🐉) Grand old-style accommodation amid spreading lawns, restaurants, lagoon, water sports centre, swimming pools, tennis courts and golf course. There's a kids' club and free stays for children under 13. Ask about package deals that include meals and drinks.

our pick Chantilly's on the Bay (Map p566; ☎ 27079; www.chantillysonthebay.com; Lini Hwy; PO Box 279; studio/apt/sunlover d 21,500/24,000/26,000Vt; 🄫 🐉) A sparkling boutique hotel sitting prettily on Fatumaru Bay with its own jetty. Rooms have balconies, the famous bay views and a kitchenette. Be decadent and ask for the sunlover apartment with extended deck. Children are welcome; babysitters are available.

Paradise Cove Resort & Restaurant (Map p563; ☎ 22701; www.paradisecoveresort.net; 1-/2-bedroom bungalows 21,600/26,600Vt; 🐉) Self-contained, spacious bungalows with every luxury, like a little kitchen, too nice to use. Snorkel gear is

available, and diving is on offer if you're certified, because you're out near Pango Point, a top spot for coral and fish. The restaurant offers an international menu (mains 1300Vt to 2500Vt, open all day) and serves breakfast until early afternoon.

Erakor Island Resort (Map p566; ☎ 26983; www.erakor.vu; PO Box 24; superior/deluxe/family bungalows 25,500/28,800/30,600Vt; 🖳) Walk along a lantern-lit path to your own bit of waterfront on this 6.5-hectare island. There's catamarans, outrigger canoes, snorkel gear etc (for hire or free for guests), or try the Get Wet Water sports: scuba diving and fishing. The lodge has spacious bunk rooms and a large kitchen; no matter what your budget you can enjoy Erakor. Budget dorm beds are also available for 3000Vt.

There are so many places offering a full range of facilities in lovely grounds, with prices ranging from 12,000Vt to 90,000Vt for a double with breakfast and all mod cons. Here's a few of them; go to www.vanuatutourism.com, www.vanuatu-hotels.vu or www.vanuatu.net.vu/directory to find more. **Iririki Island Resort** (Map p566; ☎ 23388; www.iririki.com/) now has child-free/child-welcome sections; **Le Meridien** (Map p566; ☎ 22040; www.lemeridien.com/vanuatu) has a casino; **Eratap Beach Resort** (Map p563; ☎ 5545007; www.eratap.com) is Vanuatu's newest boutique resort and it's gorgeous. The **Sebel** (Map p566; ☎ 28882; www.mirvachotels.com/sebel-vanuatu) is doing attractive things inside Vila's eyesore building; the **Melanesian** (Map p566; ☎ 22150; www.melanesianportvila.com) is ageing gracefully; and charming

VANUATU

Fatumaru Lodge (Map p566; ☎ 23456; www.fatumaru .com), lovely as ever, has a new swimming pool. See their websites for the bigger picture and package-deal details.

Eating

Dining out in Vila means great food, friendly staff and glorious views. The following is just a taste.

RESTAURANTS

Nambawan Café & Juice Bar (Map p566; ☎ 25264; mains 480-1950Vt; ☺ 6.30am-8pm) The place to hang out, this outside eatery on the harbour has free wi-fi, a simple menu, and, oh joy, free film nights on Wednesday and Sunday. The night lights of the harbour behind the screen plus pizzas and beer in front equals top night.

Harbour View Chinese Restaurant (Map p566; ☎ 23668; mains 980-2900Vt; ☺ lunch & dinner) The views are spectacular and the banquets get raves. Eat in the spacious restaurant or out on the deck. If you don't like Chinese, try the sizzle plates.

Flaming Bull Steakhouse (Map p566; ☎ 27716; mains 1000-1600Vt; ☺ noon-11pm) The steak here is tops. Add the congenial atmosphere and you will keep coming back. Local bands play love songs for you.

Kanpai (Map p566; ☎ 26687; mains 1000-2500Vt; ☺ lunch & dinner) Look out over the town as you enjoy perfectly cooked Japanese dishes as well as sushi and sashimi. The lunch boxes offer a taste treat, and they're served into the evening.

Mangoes Restaurant (Map p566; ☎ 24923; mains 1200-2500Vt; ☺ 7am-late) The chef here is a hero, cooking everything to perfection using the best seafood and other local produce, then adding his special touch. Even your children will lick their plates.

L'Houstalet (Map p566; ☎ 22303; meals 1300-2700Vt; ☺ lunch & dinner) Famous for its flying fox and wild pigeon, L'Houstalet offers much more: great atmosphere, exciting food, including swords of flaming prawns, and takeaway pizza or pasta (from 800Vt) if you prefer.

Roxy's on the Lagoon (Map p566; ☎ 26983; mains 1450-2250Vt; ☺ 7.30am-10pm) Absorb the magic of the lagoon while the chef cooks meals to please. It has an extensive menu; check out the special nights, such as ladies' night when the fair sex are given a glass of wine.

El Gecko (Map p566; ☎ 25597; mains 1500-3000Vt ☺ 6.30am-9.30pm Mon-Sat) It's relaxed courtyard dining with well-priced food, an extensive menu from steak to coconut crab (off the menu now, hopefully), quick service and waiters who're like old friends.

Waterfront Bar & Grill (Map p566; ☎ 23490; mains 1650-2900Vt; ☺ 9am-midnight) The in place for yachties and renowned for its ribs, but really, you can't go past the seafood dishes.

Chill (Map p566; ☎ 22578; mains 1800-4900Vt; ☺ 11am-late) Top location, upstairs, next to the market and looking over the harbour. It's a fun place with excellent food; the 990Vt lunch special is a treat if you're not too hungry.

Tilly's (Map p566; ☎ 27079; mains 2100-2800Vt; ☺ 7am-10pm) Downstairs between the pool and the harbour, at Chantilly's on the Bay. Sit back, relax in these lovely surroundings, and enjoy totally excellent fine dining, French, fusion or simply a piece of fish cooked just right.

QUICK EATS

Seaview Takeaway (Map p566; ☎ 27207; takeaway 250-590Vt; ☺ 7am-9.30pm) The place for chicken 'n' chips, with tables and chairs set right on the sea wall.

Au Péché Mignon (Map p566; ☎ 27271; Lini Hwy; meals 500-1300Vt; ☺ 6am-6pm) A very French patisserie that spills out onto the street. Quiches, pizza slices, salads and coffee to set you on your way.

Seafoods (Map p566; ☎ 23795; Nambatu; meals 550-1000Vt; ☺ 8am-8pm Mon-Sat, 10am-8pm Sun) 'See Food and Eat It' the sign says. Top-quality seafood takeaway, cooked while you wait.

Café Deli (Map p566; ☎ 27500; Lini Hwy; meals 550-1400Vt; ☺ 7.30am-6pm Mon-Fri, 7.30am-2pm Sat; ☒) Interesting salads, ready-cooked meals such as spiced chicken and house-made pies and pastries are served in air-conditioned comfort.

La Casa (Map p566; ☎ 26969; Nambatu; meals 1300-2200Vt; ☺ lunch & dinner Mon-Sat, dinner Sun) Great pizzas (1450Vt, takeaway) and family-friendly restaurant. There's English comfort food and French delicacies, which makes for an interesting menu.

Drinking

Vila has a few atmospheric bars and an abundance of kava bars where the bamboo walls and earth floors create their own atmosphere.

Hemisphere (Map p566; ☎ 28882; www.mirvachotels .com/sebel-vanuatu; ☺ 5-11.30pm Mon-Sat) An elegant bar on the rooftop of the Sebel. Everyone comes to happy hour from 5pm Friday. It's amazingly good and includes complimentary canapés.

Office Pub (Map p566; noon-midnight Tue-Sat, 5pm-midnight Sun-Mon) The town's only true pub has a cosy atmosphere: booths, wooden sculptures and an old English bar where people chat and listen to live music.

Waterfront Bar & Grill (Map p566; 23490; 11am-late) Live music plays well into the night here and everyone just kicks back, enjoying the ambience.

Anchor Inn (Map p566; 11am-8.30pm Sun-Thu, 11am-12.30am Fri-Sat) A great beer garden that buzzes, especially when international sports are on. It doesn't serve food, except on Friday, the 'Free BBQ' night. It's home to the Vanuatu Cruising Yacht Club (24634; www.vanuatu cruisingyachtclub.org), so you'll hear all the yachtie goss.

Rumours (Map p566; 26800; Moorings Hotel, Lini Hwy; 8pm-late Tue-Sat) The town's tourist nightclub with a great sound system, live bands in the garden, Foxtel showing all sports and free entry except for special events.

The sunset **kava cup** (small/large 50/100Vt), served in a coconut shell or plastic bowl, is a ritual. Try it out at Ron's Nakamal (in Nambatu) or Seaside Kava Strip (behind the hospital).

Entertainment
Many places offer feasts (almost all on Thursday night so make sure you're in town that night), which include kava tasting, string bands and *kastom* dancers. Try **Solo's Feast 'n' Fun Night** (adult/child 2800/1300Vt; 5pm Thu), held at **Worawia Holiday Haven** (Map p563; 25498; www.resort-vanuatu.com/worawia.htm). The Solomons from the local village prepare traditional food in a ground oven, unfolding and explaining the dishes while you try the kava. Then join in the dancing.

Shopping
When you've bought up the markets you'll find a number of shops selling duty-free products on Lini Hwy. They're reasonable for alcohol, perfume, fine china and jewellery, but not so great on electrical goods.

L'atelier (Map p566; Hebrida Market Place) The perfect place for wooden carvings and handicrafts.

Philippe Metois Photography (Map p566; Lini Hwy) Vanuatu captured at its best – unframed prints start at 1250Vt, framed at 10,000Vt.

Diana Tam Gallery (Map p566; 23038; www.diana tam.info; Pango Rd; 1.30-5pm Mon-Fri, 2-4pm Sat) Diana's stunning oil paintings, prints and glassware. See examples on the website.

AROUND EFATE
The road north mainly follows the coast, passing coconut plantations, cattle stations and rocky inlets. There are superb views from Klem's Hill, 200m above sea level.

Stores are scarce outside Vila. Most people live off their own garden produce, which you can sample at roadside stalls – just leave your money in the box.

If you are hiring a car, fill up before you go. There are no petrol stations.

White Sands Beach
East of Vila, past Teouma River (Efate's largest), a right-hand turn takes you down to the coastal road where the Pacific Ocean is fringed with screw-trunked pandanus palms. If you feel like swimming be careful of currents.

You'll find five luxurious French-colonial cottages with little love-nest porches at **Tamanu on the Beach Resort & Restaurant** (27279, 7743454; www.tamanu.vu; B&B d planters/beachfront 16,500/19,000Vt;). Use the bikes, then swim in rock pools. Chef Heriaud has built the restaurant's great reputation for fine dining (mains from 1050Vt to 4800Vt); arrive by helicopter for a major experience. It's right on the beach and open for breakfast, lunch and dinner.

Rentapao River
The modern bungalows at **Bluewater Island Resort** (27588; www.bluewaterisland.com; B&B d/family 12,000/14,000Vt;) wrap around a blue lagoon. The resort has kayaks (rainforest river paddle 3900Vt), snorkel gear and sports facilities.

If you're game, you can swim with massive fish/turtles (3900/3900Vt) in the resort's open-air **aquarium** (entry adult/child 850/450Vt); feed beautiful reef sharks by hand (adult/child 2000/1000Vt) then kick back at a Melanesian feast (adult/child 3900/1900Vt). Do the lot (rainforest kayaking, swims with fish and turtles, feeding and feasting) for only 10,000Vt.

Eton
Continue around the east coast to **Eton Blue Hole** (entry 300Vt), a lovely garden with picnic tables, toilets and change rooms. Slither

CHIEF ROIMATA

This 16th-century paramount chief, revered throughout Vanuatu for bringing an end to local wars, died at a feast in Feles Cave. In honour, his body was transported to Hat Island, a large grave dug and up to 300 members of his community buried with his body, to accompany him to the hereafter. The story, passed down through the generations, led a French archaeologist to the gravesite. In July 2008, Chief Roimata Domain (the gravesite, Feles cave and his place of residence) were given World Heritage listing. See Roimata Cultural Tours p571 for tour information.

down the bank into the blue, blue water for fun swimming and canoeing.

Another pretty picnic area 2km along the coast is **Eton Beach** (entry 300Vt), famous for its gurgling river and white-sand beach.

Bethel

Stop for lunch or stop for ages because time waits for you here. **Bethel Village** (☎ 25161, 5410035; www.bethelvanuatu.com; r 4500Vt) is a range of attractive bungalows in a garden in front of the local village. Watch weaving, learn about herbs, take village walks and eat in the traditional restaurant, which is open for breakfast (500Vt), lunch and dinner (both 1200Vt).

Sara Beach

Sara Beach Restaurant (☎ 23191; lunch buffet adult/child 1000/500Vt; ☽ lunch) has an idyllic setting on Sara Beach, a local string band playing in the corner, and an excellent spread of local food such as yam in coconut milk and chicken with fresh herbs and carrots.

Takara

The waters out from Takara, with the prevailing southeast winds, offer ideal conditions for **kitesurfing**. Ring ☎ 23576 for daily weather reports.

Two **US WWII fighter planes** lie in the shallows near **Baofatu**. They ran out of fuel coming in to land at Quoin Hill. Erik will take you out in a canoe to see them, and show you the **Matanawora WWII Relics** (☎ 27693). Alternatively, ask him about an eco-adventure boat ride out to Emao for walking and snorkelling.

Allen Noppert runs the great **Beachcomber Resort** (☎ 23576; beachc@vanuatu.com.vu; Takara; lodge s/d 4400/6800Vt; bungalows from dm/s/d 3000/5300/9000Vt; ☒), which has a hot mineral pool alongside a cold swimming pool – hydrotherapy fun. You can also buy local artists' work here. The Western-style bungalows sprawl along the shoreline, some of which are self-contained. The atrium restaurant (mains 1300Vt to 2100Vt; open from 7.30am till late) has its own hot pool – swim to your plate of nibbles.

Emua Wharf

Boats (☎ 27113, 29995) leave from here for Nguna (3000Vt), Pele (2000Vt) and Kakula (1500Vt) and should be arranged in advance, unless you're arriving by transport truck.

A taxi to Emua from Vila costs 6000Vt.

Siviri

At Undine Bay is white-sand **St Lawrence Beach** (300Vt), isolated and inviting, fringed with palm trees. Nearby is pretty Siviri known for its fragrant flowers. Explore **Valeva Cave** (admission 100Vt) in a kayak (1000Vt). It has chambers, tunnels and an underground lake. The villagers will show you the massive limestone boulder that was somehow moved by people, and the strange footprints engraved in the rock floor.

West Coast Offshore Islands

Three very different islands offer an interesting range of activities. **Tranquillity (Moso) Island** has a turtle sanctuary, dive base and rustic resort; **Lelepa** has spectacular Feles Cave, cave drawings and fishing adventures; **Hat (Eretoka) Island** is the burial ground of Chief Roimata, a sacred place. The coral reefs around here are bright, healthy and include unforgettable Paul's Rock (for diving these waters see p568).

At **Tranquillity Island Resort** (☎ 25020, 22560; www.tranquillitydive.com; s fare/lodge 20,400/23,200Vt; d fare/lodge 34,000/38,800Vt), rates include transfers, meals, kayaks, snorkel gear, two days on this rambling island, a traditional bungalow for some atmosphere and a little luxury thrown in.

There are day tours to Lelepa (p571) and Tranquillity Island (p568).

VANUATU

NGUNA & PELE
pop 1200 each

These little islands have several pretty traditional villages, just a short hop from Vila. Locals have built bungalows, set up tours and invite you to experience island life. Villages run successfully here, they say, because of standards established by New Zealand missionary Peter Milne. Both islands are part of a marine-protected area (www.marineprotectedarea.com.vu) and offer excellent snorkelling.

Sights & Activities

Nguna has a long **white-sand beach** and a labelled **snorkel trail** through exotic coral gardens. Pele has a **Giant Clam Garden**, inspired by the one at the Maskelynes.

Guided hikes (guides 1000Vt) take you through village gardens to mountain peaks and lakes. Utanlangi, by a sheltered cove, is the best place from which to climb Nguna's extinct volcano **Mt Taputaora** (593m); the climb is long and arduous, but you'll be rewarded with superb panoramas over the Shepherd Islands and much of Efate.

Great fun is going in an outrigger canoe to watch the villagers **turtle tagging**. Sponsor your own turtle, name it, and see it back into the ocean.

Visit Nguna's magnificent **nakamal**, built more than 200 years ago. It has huge log supports and a soaring roof, one of the very last of its kind.

Sleeping & Eating

our pick **Wora-Namoa Bungalow** (☎ 28777, 7760020; Pele; B&B adult/child 3000/1500Vt) Maurice manages this grand beach bungalow, made from local timbers and decorated with hand-dyed materials. It was built by Aussie kids as a school project and offers a complete village experience (Melanesian meals are 350Vt).

Juboes Bungalows (☎ 22219; Nguna; s incl meals 3000Vt) Emma Tasong has a spacious Western-style guest house with a kitchen across from two bungalows that share outside facilities. They're all in a garden a few steps from the sea. Near Taloa.

Two options on Pele are:

Napanga Bungalows (☎ 27113, 5418410; Pele; s/family incl meals 3000/9000Vt) Kenneth has two colourful bungalows on the cutest little bay in Pele. Sit on a deck chair and watch for dugong while you sip juice from a coconut. He's a good cook too.

Vat-Vaka Beach Bungalows (☎ 22463, 29995; www.vatvaka.com; Nguna; s/d incl meals 3500/6000Vt) These bungalows are a world away from the mainland. They nestle into a beachfront garden, lanterns are supplied for light, and the flush toilet in the outhouse is almost cute. Ask for Yoan Jay. Near Taloa.

Getting There & Around

Kalsong's transport truck leaves from the Hua Chinese Store in Vila, some time between 11.30am and 12.30pm Monday to Saturday (500Vt). Ask people to point it out or ring him (☎ 7757410). The truck connects with a boat to the Nguna (500Vt). Two other trucks should leave between 12.30pm and 2pm. See Emua Wharf (opposite) for private taxi and boat details. Return trips are at 6am.

Island Expert Tours runs day tours to Pele (see p571).

EPI

pop 5000 / area 444 sq km

Epi is a fascinating island, just a hop, skip and jump from Efate. It's an adventure island, where you become part of the village structure. Listen to the local lads pounding the kava ready for you to drink in the dusky *nakamal*; chat to the ladies of the village as they prepare their ground ovens and wrap

---

CUTE DUGONGS

Bondas has been going to sea for months at a time, but if he's around you can snorkel near him, watching his fat little snout swishing around on the ocean floor as he separates out his food. He'll roll over to get a better look at you and float up to have his tummy rubbed. The experience is extraordinary – you realise in one mind-blowing moment what conservation is all about. Dugongs inhabit warm tropical and subtropical coastal waters. But, worldwide, populations are declining due to overhunting, drowning in fishing nets, pollution and loss of food resources. In fact, dugong are considered vulnerable to extinction. Fortunately, by being so cute, they've turned themselves into a major tourist attraction. Hopefully, this will help protect them.

VANUATU

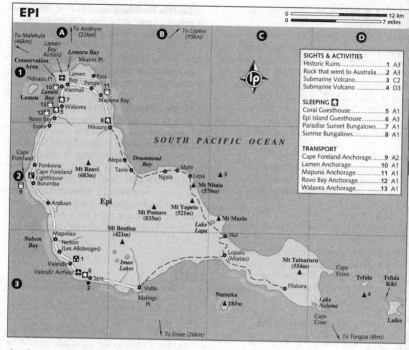

EPI

| | 0 | 12 km |
| | 0 | 7 miles |

SIGHTS & ACTIVITIES
Historic Ruins.........................1 A3
Rock that went to Australia....2 A3
Submarine Volcano.................3 C2
Submarine Volcano.................4 D3

SLEEPING
Coral Guesthouse...................5 A1
Epi Island Guesthouse............6 A1
Paradise Sunset Bungalows....7 A1
Sunrise Bungalows.................8 A1

TRANSPORT
Cape Foreland Anchorage.......9 A2
Lamen Anchorage..................10 A1
Mapuna Anchorage...............11 A1
Rovo Bay Anchorage.............12 A1
Walavea Anchorage..............13 A1

SOUTH PACIFIC OCEAN

the *laplap* in banana leaves; walk along beaches, to gardens, waterfalls and the conservation area where megapodes and turtles lay their eggs. Go snorkelling, pig hunting, horse riding, or look for whales and dolphins. Swim with young Bondas the dugong if he's back in town, then watch and listen to the submarine volcanoes bubbling off the east coast.

TRANSPORT
Getting There & Around
Air Vanuatu (☎ 23848) flies from Vila to Valesdir on Monday, Wednesday and Friday, and to Lamen Bay on Tuesday and Saturday. Landing at Lamen Bay is stunning as the plane comes in low over coral reefs and crystal-clear turquoise water.

Fresh Cargo (☎ 7760660) calls into Epi twice a week; see p610. There are several good anchorages in north Epi: Lamen Bay, Mapuna Bay, Rovo Bay, Walavea and Cape Foreland. All can be unsuitable depending on the wind direction.

A good plan when visiting Epi is to fly to Lamen Bay, make your way down the west coast by truck (7500Vt) and then fly out of Valesdir (or vice versa). Epi's roads are basic, and there are only walking tracks in the east.

SIGHTS & ACTIVITIES
Lamen Bay is home to massive **sea turtles** and several **dugong**, hopefully including Bondas (see boxed text, p577: he'll let you hang around and rub his tum – not vigorously, as his spiky coat will rip your fingers off). Ask your host about borrowing snorkel gear.

Sea kayaks and **outrigger canoes** are available (500Vt), or try your hand at **reef fishing** from a local fishing boat (1000Vt). **Spear fishing** is especially good at night; the locals will take you out. If you're into **game fishing** there's trawling (half/full day 9000/18,000Vt) or deep-sea fishing (8000Vt per day). Ask your host to arrange any of these activities.

Down south, **Valesdir** includes the Valesdir plantation, which produces copra and beef cattle. There are **historic ruins** of a mansion here. In the 1920s, Valesdir had its own coinage; one coin was marked 'five centimes' on one side

> **BON ANNÉE**
>
> All through January, to welcome the new year, villagers prepare flower-embedded posts and set out together to walk as far as they can, dancing along, stopping at each village they pass to sing songs and chant, 'Happy, Happy, Bon Année'. Then they dust their listeners with talcum powder and set off to the next village.

and 'six pence' on the other. For many years, there was a grand race day near the airstrip. Horses came from all over the Pacific.

In the tiny bay is the **rock that went to Australia**. This rock had a boy sitting on it when the boy disappeared. When he returned two years later he had some clothes, a leg of bullock and tales about a trip to Australia.

The cliffs are steep and the jungle dense behind the plantations. To the east are two **submarine volcanoes** that steam or bubble, and give the evening sky a deep scarlet glow.

SLEEPING & EATING

Coral Guesthouse (☎ 28301; david.naunga@tvl.net.vu; Lamen Bay; s/d 1500/3000Vt) Aisen will look after you and arrange your adventures at these attractive bungalows set along a grassy beachfront. Meals are 1000Vt per day.

Sunrise Bungalows (☎ 28230; Nikaura; s with meals 2800Vt) The eastern end of the road (3500Vt by truck) brings you to these charming little bungalows in the foothills of Mt Renvi. They're by a marine sanctuary with excellent coral.

our pick Paradise Sunset Bungalows (☎ 28230; Lamen Bay; B&B 3000Vt) A relaxed and friendly place 15 minutes from the airfield. The rooms and shared facilities are basic, but the food and the bay views are lovely. Tasso has snorkel gear, bikes and outriggers, and will arrange tours to Laman Island, gardens and local crafts. A truck to the airstrip is 300Vt. The large restaurant (buffet 500Vt; open breakfast, lunch and dinner) is often full of yachties, which makes for a fun evening.

Epi Island Guesthouse (☎ /fax 28225; www.epi -island-guesthouse.com; Valesdir; adult/child incl meals 10,000/5000Vt) An arty lodge powered by a micro-hydro turbine and winner of the Green Award 2008. It has a central room full of fascinating bits such as 1865–75 Enfield guns once owned by blackbirders, a library and games. Sleep in a beach hut if you like, but be back for the ex-

cellent meals that Alix whips up. Babysitting is available.

If you can make up a group, enjoy an island feast with the local string band and *kastom* dancing.

There are a few small stores selling limited groceries, a fish shop behind the bungalows, a cold room selling ice cream and meat, and a bakery in Lamen Bay.

TANNA

pop 33,000 / area 565 sq km

The Tannese are passionate about their island – and you will be, too. There are lush undisturbed rainforests, heady night-perfumed flowers, coffee plantations, plains where wild horses run with their foals, mountains, hot springs and waterfalls. Presiding over it all is fuming, furious Mt Yasur, the world's most accessible volcano. The local chiefs have formed marine and wildlife sanctuaries, and there are gardening, surfing, cycling, walking or volcano enthusiasts everywhere. Note that there are very serious quarantine controls – the island has no nasty bugs, so everything's grown without insecticides, herbicides or pesticides, and the locals want to keep it that way. Christianity, cargo cult and *kastom* are important, and all natural phenomena have a fourth dimension of spirituality and mystique.

When the volcano has finished working its magic on you, there are horses to ride, forests to trek through, waterfalls to stand under and a kilometre-deep drop-off tumbling with coral to snorkel along. Meet *kastom* villagers wearing *namba* and grass skirts, watch age-old festivals or just laze on a tropical island beach and watch the sun set.

ORIENTATION

Isangel is the administrative centre of the Tafea province. The name Tafea comes from the five populated islands in the province: Tanna, Aneityum, Futuna, Erromango and Aniwa.

Spectacular South Beach Rd is its own amusement park ride, with stunning ocean and cliff views at every turn. Make sure you've reached the end before dusk, as you'll never find the broken road sections in your headlights.

VANUATU

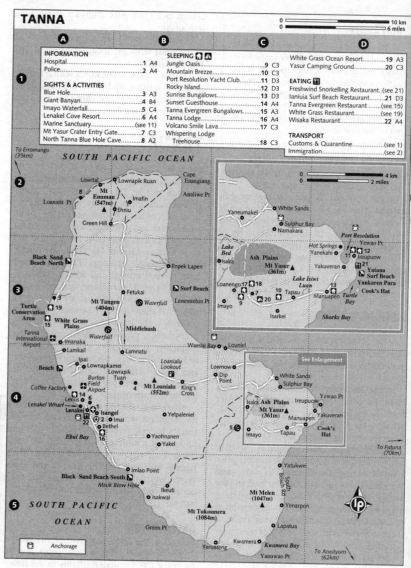

TANNA

INFORMATION
Hospital	1 A4
Police	2 A4

SIGHTS & ACTIVITIES
Blue Hole	3 A3
Giant Banyan	4 B4
Imayo Waterfall	5 C4
Lenakel Cove Resort	6 A4
Marine Sanctuary	(see 11)
Mt Yasur Crater Entry Gate	7 C3
North Tanna Blue Hole Cave	8 A2

SLEEPING
Jungle Oasis	9 C3
Mountain Brezze	10 C3
Port Resolution Yacht Club	11 D3
Rocky Island	12 D3
Sunrise Bungalows	13 D3
Sunset Guesthouse	14 A4
Tanna Evergreen Bungalows	15 A3
Tanna Lodge	16 A4
Volcano Smile Lava	17 C3
Whispering Lodge Treehouse	18 C3

White Grass Ocean Resort	19 A3
Yasur Camping Ground	20 C3

EATING
Freshwind Snorkelling Restaurant	(see 21)
Ianiua Surf Beach Restaurant	21 D3
Tanna Evergreen Restaurant	(see 15)
White Grass Restaurant	(see 19)
Wisaka Restaurant	22 A4

TRANSPORT
Customs & Quarantine	(see 1)
Immigration	(see 2)

Tanna's centre is a fertile, dense forest, aptly called Middlebush, with coconut, coffee, vegetables and fruit grown here for export. Kava is a major cash crop.

East Tanna is a tourist highlight, with Mt Yasur, Sharks Bay and Port Resolution within hiking, horse riding or cycling distance of each other.

INFORMATION
You'll need to take enough cash (vatu) for your whole time here as you can change travellers cheques only at the NBV in Isangel and credit cards are accepted only at the large resorts.

Ambulance (☎ 88659)
Emergencies (☎ 112)

THE NEKOWIAR & TOKA CEREMONY

About every three years, come August, a great restlessness spreads across Tanna. The men scour the bush and villages for pigs and kava, counting, calculating. Finally one of the chiefs announces that his village will host the Nekowiar. Hooray! Romance is in the air. It will be a three-day extravaganza of song, dance and feasting during which the leaders of neighbouring villages organise marriages. Negotiations for the marriages continue for months afterwards.

Preparations for the Nekowiar are exhaustive. Three complex dances are practised, and beauty magic takes over. Men, women, boys and girls use powders mixed with coconut oil to colour their faces a deep red, with black and yellow stripes.

Finally, as many as 2000 people assemble while the hosts display around 100 live, squealing pigs, tied by the feet and suspended on poles.

The ceremony begins with the host village's young men dancing an invitation to the women. They respond with the Napen-Napen, a spectacular dance that represents their toil in the fields, and continues throughout the first night.

The male guests watch and wait for dawn, when they dance the Toka, a pounding, colourful dance that shows scenes of daily life. The Toka reaches its climax that night. If the Toka dancers make a circle around a woman, she's tossed up and down between them. During this stage a man may have sex with any woman who is willing.

On the third day the chief of the host village produces the *kweriya*, a 3m bamboo pole with white and black feathers wound around it and hawks' feathers on top. It announces that the Nao – the host village's dance – is to begin. This men's dance enacts events such as hunting and wrestling.

The climax is in the afternoon. Pigs, kava roots, woven mats, grass skirts and massive quantities of *laplap* (Vanuatu's national dish) are brought out. The pigs are ceremonially clubbed and cooked, and a huge feast begins.

If you get a chance to attend, go for it. You may need to camp out, like the villagers. It costs 8000Vt to watch, plus 10,000Vt to video it.

Hospital (☎ 88659) At Lenakel.

Internet access (per min 25Vt; Lenakel ☯ 7-11.30am & 1.30-5pm) At Lorakau Computer School next to the market.

Police (☎ 88658) At Isangel.

TRANSPORT
Getting There & Around

Air Vanuatu's rather swish ATR42 flies between Vila and Tanna every morning. Another very little plane makes twice-weekly flights, landing also at Aniwa, Aneityum, Futuna and Erromango. Taxis (Hilux utes) and the local bus meet each incoming flight. The fare to Lenakel is 1000/200Vt by taxi/bus.

You can get package deals in Vila that typically include air fares, transfers, accommodation, meals and visits to Mt Yasur and a *kastom* village (from 37,000Vt).

There are ports of entry at Port Resolution and Lenakel, and anchorages at Sulphur Bay and Waesisi Bay. **Immigration** (☎ 88658) is at the police station in Isangel. **Customs & Quarantine** (☯ 7.30-11.30am & 1.30-4.30pm) is in Lenakel, opposite Lenakel Wharf. The customs officer goes to Port Resolution once a week.

All the major attractions are linked by roads (a term used loosely to describe connected bumps and bogs) to Lenakel, the capital.

Everyone wants to head across the island, but the road is a ripper so transfers cost from 2000Vt to 6000Vt, depending on whether other tourists are sharing. This fearsomely expensive charter will quickly fill up with locals so there's plenty of people to push if you get stuck. Besides, the trip is an adventure with wonderful views.

MT YASUR

This **active volcano** (admission 2250Vt) is so accessible that 4WD vehicles can get to within 150m of the crater rim.

Mt Yasur's ash-laden smoke has smothered the vegetation, reducing the landscape to an alien prehistoric desert, with the gaunt shapes of surviving pandanus palms adding to the surrealistic view. The track from the entry gate then enters a gully on the southern slopes. Tree ferns crowd in on either side, a lush contrast to the desolation of the plains.

The level of activity within Yasur fluctuates between dangerous and relatively calm,

VANUATU

MERIAN NUMAKE

You are a role model for all ni-Vanuatu in the tourism industry. How did you get to this point? All these years we've had hardships and challenges, but we never gave up or looked down on ourselves because we knew to benefit the island's population. I encourage all locals to work really hard to achieve their goal, since we have proved it ourselves. We are now graded as a resort; we have won the Vanuatu Tourism Awards for 2006 and 2008.

How did you start? In 1996 when the airport was starting, Sam and I thought we should build a bungalow since we have the land very close to it. After two years of clearing and construction, we had four small basic bungalows with shared facilities. Building materials were our trees cut down for timbers, our coconut leaves, our coral and sand.

It's come a long way since then. As years went by I was looking for bigger visions, so in 2003 I built three ocean-views with en suites, then a family cottage. In 2006 I built a honeymoon suite, which is very luxurious and upmarket. Then a magnificent overwater restaurant and bar.

What are your plans now? We are building five ocean bungalows because international flights from Noumea to Tanna will start in June 2009.

Merian Numake owns and runs Tanna Evergreen Bungalows in west Tanna

but when it's hot it's hot. Along the path to the crater rim, there are whiffs of sulphur and whooshing, roaring noises. Ahead is a silhouette of people on the rim, golden fireworks behind them. Then you're looking into a dark central crater where three vents take turns to spit rockets of red-molten rock and smoke. The ground trembles and a fountain of fiery magma shoots up and spreads against the sky. All turns quiet, except for the thudding of boulders as big as trucks somersaulting down into the vast campfire.

Just when you're getting used to it, there's a gasp and a bang, the ground shakes, and lumps of red-hot magma shoot high overhead. Black smoke boils upwards in a dense column, lightning flashes inside the crater, and magma splashes in the central vent and subsides again.

Some visitors find Yasur terrifying; it's definitely unforgettable.

Don't go up to the rim when the volcano is reaching levels 3 and 4. And buy some special singed cards to post at **Volcano Post** (www.vanuatupost.vu), the world's only postbox on top of a volcano.

To horse ride up the volcano, book at Jungle Oasis (p584) or Mountain Brezze (p584) in east Tanna.

WEST TANNA

Visible from the aeroplane as you come in to land are the coral reefs and rock pools of the west coast. The main town is **Lenakel**, which has mains electricity, some stores, excellent bakeries, and colourful markets on Monday

and Thursday afternoon, and Friday. The kava bars provide a meeting place. (Tanna's kava is potent, probably the strongest in the country.)

Sights & Activities

All experiences start with **Mt Yasur volcano**. Tours leave from the west in mid-afternoon and return for dinner at about 8pm. If you're not on a package from Port Vila, your host will arrange your tour.

Visit **Yakel** or **Ipai**, where you see village life that hasn't changed in centuries, or Imai, a small Jon Frum settlement (see opposite). There's *kastom* dancing, colourful *namba* and grass skirts, *laplap* and artefacts. People gather nightly under a huge banyan at Yakel to drink kava, and dancing nights occur on a regular basis.

Horses and guides are available at **Lenakel Cove Resort** (☎ 88860; www.tafea-tourism.com/lencove .htm; village/banyan tour 2000/3500Vt); jungle trails take you past villages to a **giant banyan** as big as a soccer field. It's near Lowrapik Tuan.

Sea kayaks are available at several resorts. **Guided walks** take you through rainforests and coffee plantations, among the wild horses, along stunning coastlines and under two grand waterfalls. And there's a two-day **trek** around the top of Tanna.

There's excellent **snorkelling** right along the west coast, with the reef face cascading down covered in coral, in and out of its pocketed volcanic surface. A **Blue Hole** just north of White Grass Ocean Resort is like a fish nursery with coral wall decorations.

Surfing at the black-sand beach north of Louniel is fun. Boogie boards are available, or try riding the local outrigger canoes – that'll test your balance.

North Tanna Blue Hole Cave is a fishing-boat trip away. Duck-dive and come up in a stunning grotto, where the turquoise water is lit from a hole in the cave roof.

Sleeping & Eating

Accommodation in the west enjoys 24-hour electricity. These are a few of the excellent options.

our pick **Tanna Evergreen Bungalows** (☎ 88774; www.tevergreenresort-tours.vu; PO Box 9; B&B budget s/d 3500/5500Vt, garden s/d/q 4500/6500/9000Vt, camping 1000Vt; ▢) Sam and Merian's bungalows hide in the lush gardens; some are en suite, others ocean-views or both. The honeymoon bungalow is so romantic. Snorkel at the end of the garden along the drop-off. Stunning coral and fish. Snorkel gear, babysitting, laundry, massage, glass-bottomed kayaks, tours – it's all here. Don't miss the Magic Tour (4800Vt).

Sunset Guesthouse (☎ 88683; sunsettanna@yahoo .co.nz; s/d B&B 3000/5000Vt, with bathroom 3500/6000Vt) Traditional bungalows have little verandahs looking out over rock pools. They're just two minutes' walk from Lenakel. Helen will look after you, arrange tours and cook lunch (500Vt) and dinner (1500Vt).

White Grass Ocean Resort (☎ 88688; www.white grassvanuatu.com.vu; PO Box 5; s/d/tr/family B&B 16,500/23,100 /28,000/27,500Vt; ▢ ▣) A cosy resort where bungalows look out onto tiny rocky inlets, which are linked with timber bridges. There's a bar, hammocks, tennis, *pétanque* (boule) and a three-hole golf course. Snorkel gear, mountain bikes, kayaks and golf clubs are available.

Tanna Lodge (☎ 30061, 5479707; tannalodge@vanuatu .com.vu; d from 30,500Vt; ▣ ▢) Big, bold and beautiful, with thatched roofs that sweep over timber verandahs and staircases. The restaurant, bar, lounge and sunken deck are fun areas, then head off to your villa in a private spot by the sheltered bay. There's a hot pool and two large bat caves in case you're going batty with tropical delight. Rates include breakfast.

Wisaka Restaurant (☎ 88968; Lenakel; meals 300Vt; ☽ breakfast, lunch & dinner Mon-Fri) A friendly little place where a dish like fish with vegetables in coconut milk is prepared then served till it's gone, so it's pot luck really.

White Grass Restaurant (meals 800-2500Vt; ☽ lunch & dinner) In lovely surroundings, overlooking the ocean – a spread of light and colour at sunset, and reliably good food.

Tanna Evergreen Restaurant (meals 1000-2100Vt; ☽ 6am-11pm) The new deck sweeps out to show fab views, the meals are always a treat and it's fun chatting to other guests.

EAST TANNA

In the east, some places have electricity available in the evenings. There's a little store in Port Resolution with handicrafts, fruit and vegetables.

THE JON FRUM MOVEMENT

Magic is a central force in ni-Vanuatu lives. So in 1936, when Jon Frum came from the sea at Green Point and announced himself to some kava drinkers, they could see that he was the brother of the god of Mt Tukosmera. He told the men that if the Europeans left Tanna, there would be an abundance of wealth. They spread the word. It was the beginning of a neopagan uprising, with followers doing things the missionaries had banned, such as traditional dancing – but not cannibalism, fortunately.

When US troops arrived a few years later, many Tannese went to Efate and Santo to work for them. There they met African American soldiers, who were colourful, with theatrical uniforms, decorations, badges, belts and hats. The African Americans had huge quantities of transport equipment, radios, Coca-Cola and cigarettes. But most of all, they were generous and friendly, treating the ni-Van as equals. Here was the wealth and way of life the ni-Van had been told about – Jon Frum must be American, they decided.

Some supporters made radio aerials out of tin cans and wire to contact Jon Frum. Others built an airfield in the bush and constructed wooden aircraft to entice his cargo planes to land. Still others erected wharves where his ships could berth. Small red crosses were placed all over Tanna and remain a feature in Jon Frum villages, where flags are raised each evening to this god of their collective imagination.

VANUATU

Sights & Activities

Mt Yasur volcano dominates the landscape as you travel east across the ash plains. There are many tours up to see the old man, and all tours can be arranged through your host.

Horses are available at Jungle Oasis (right) and Mountain Brezze (right). Head across the ash plains, up the volcano, and down to Port Resolution and Sharks Bay.

The impressive **Imayo Waterfall** lies deep in the rainforest. The trek takes three hours each way – for experienced bushwalkers. Ask your host about guides.

Sharks Bay attracts dozens of yellow reef sharks. Stand on the cliff top to watch them (admission 500Vt), then walk along the stunning coastline.

SULPHUR BAY

This **Jon Frum Village** (admission 500Vt), built around a square ceremonial ground, used to be the cult's major centre (see p583). The church to one side houses the movement's most sacred red cross. Beside it, an unpainted post dedicated to Christ is used to heal backaches.

Dances are held on the ceremonial ground on Friday nights, when songs of praise are sung to the tunes of American battle hymns.

PORT RESOLUTION

Tanna's best anchorage is this beautiful bay with its magnificent cliffs. The village has pretty bungalows and wide flower-lined paths leading up to the Yacht Club and to a **marine sanctuary** at Yewao Point where you can snorkel in the calm water just before the coral reef finishes.

Another path reaches an attractive **white-sand beach** at Ireupuow, and the last path brings you to a top **surf beach**, with deep swells along 2.5km to Yankaren Para (watch your board; make sure it travels on the same plane as you).

Sleeping & Eating

Yasur Camping Ground (☎ 88646, 5470496; PO Box 195; tent & site B&B s/d/family 1000/1500/1700Vt) Charlie and family have set up a campsite and restaurant (meals from 500Vt). BYO tent and it will cost even less. Return transfers to airport/volcano are 4000/1000Vt, but stay a while for ashboarding, *kastom* dancing, cultural tours, trekking and a total return to nature, right at the gate to old Yasur.

Jungle Oasis (☎ 88676, 5448228; www.vanuatu-hotels.vu/Jungle_Oasis; bungalows s/d 3200/4000Vt, guest house d/family 5000/6000Vt, camping 1000Vt) Kelson also has a tree house that is set amid the more grounded bungalows and guest house. But he's off to be a politician so his family is holding the fort. Rates include breakfast; there are meals available in the dining room (dinner 1200Vt).

Rocky Island (☎ 88061, 7774247; rockyislandbungalows_tanna@yahoo.com.au; Ireupuow; s/d B&B 1500/2000Vt) Romp on your private beach, a flower-lined stroll from Port Resolution village. Wahe Philippe is your manager; local ladies serve *kaikai* (meals) in the little restaurant for 700Vt.

Sunrise Bungalows (☎ 88050; www.sunrisebungalows.netfast.org; Turtle Bay; s/d B&B 2000/3000Vt, family bungalow with bathroom 5000Vt) Wild-cane bungalows teeter amid jungle and cliff, with the ocean just below. Isaac is your host, and an excellent one at that. Ask about camping up on a hill with volcano views. Volcano tours are 4450Vt; your tropical breakfast is served in a spacious restaurant; lunch and dinner are 1000Vt.

Mountain Brezze (☎ 88019, 5412140; mountainbrezze@gmail.com; PO Box 85; s incl meals 2500Vt) This is a peaceful spot, even with old Yasur roaring. Spacious bungalows are set in an unusual, meandering garden, and a nearby cave has been turned into a natural sauna (250Vt). Ask for Joseph. In the grounds is Saddleback Horseriding offering two-hour/day rides for 2000/3000Vt.

Whispering Lodge Treehouse (☎ 88000, 5417737; B&B 2500Vt) Tree houses are all the rage in east Tanna. If you don't sleepwalk, you might like to try this place, which is way up high with glorious views, but dead scary.

Volcano Smile Lava (☎ 88899, 88000; adventure@vanuatu.com.vu; s/d incl breakfast & lunch 2500/5000Vt) This newcomer with the strange name is all-out to please. Bungalows are tiny but there are mosquito nets, good flush toilets and dinner for 1000Vt.

Port Resolution Yacht Club (☎ 88791, 5416989; www.portresolution.com.vu; PO Box 877; B&B s/d/tr 3200/4800/5300Vt, camping 1500Vt) Up on a bluff, each bungalow has a view of the bay. Werry turns on the electricity in the evenings, and there's warm showers. The dining room (meals from 500Vt to 1200Vt) has cold beer.

Freshwind Snorkelling Restaurant (☎ 88791; Port Resolution; dishes 450Vt; ☙ by arrangement) Village

SOME OTHER SOUTHERN ISLANDS

Mystery Island

'Welcome to Paradise,' the pilot will say as you clamber out of his tiny plane onto Aneityum's grass airstrip on Mystery Island. And it's true: this beautiful sandy islet off Aneityum is surrounded by a broad sandbank and dazzling coral in an azure sea, just like in the movies. Garden paths crisscross the island, many leading to little thatched loos. **Snorkelling** is fantastic off the end of the airstrip, as the island is a marine sanctuary. Aneityum people believe Mystery Island is the home of ghosts, so no one will live there.

Cross to **Anelcauhat**, Aneityum's main village, to see fascinating ruins of whaling-industry equipment, missionary Geddie's church and old irrigation channels. Take stunning walks from Anelcauhat to picturesque **Port Patrick**, impressive **Inwan Leleghei Waterfall** or to the top of **Inrerow Atahein** (853m), an extinct volcano.

Mystery Island Guesthouse (☎ 88888, 88896; beds 2500Vt) has colourful bungalows and a central kitchen with gas refrigerator. You need to bring your own food, although someone will row across from Aneityum each day to see if you need anything. Cruise ships call about every six weeks (hence the little loos). Otherwise you'll probably have this paradise to yourself; book the whole island for 8000Vt, just to make sure!

Erromango

The 'land of mangoes' is mountainous, with almost all the people living in two main villages on its rugged coast. Each village has a fertile eco-garden, where taro, tomato, corn and sweet potato thrive among huge mango, coconut and pawpaw trees.

Dillons Bay is Erromango's largest settlement, with a huge crystal-clear **swimming hole** formed by the Williams River as it turns to the sea. Sandalwood trees still grow in the rainforest, and a rock shows the outline of Williams, the first missionary here. They laid his short, stout body on this rock and chipped around it prior to cooking it.

Guided walks from Dillons Bay include trips to the **kauri reserve**, to see the ancient 40m-high trees, and a three-day walk down south and across to Ipota. There's magnificent scenery as you drop in and out of deep, fjordlike valleys, pass taro gardens, carve through tropical rainforests and trek down a 300m-high escarpment to scenic **Pongkil Bay**. Then you follow the coastal cliffs to a final steep descent to **South River**, situated beside a picturesque estuary. Boulder-hop and ford South River as you follow it to the Ipota road. A guide will cost you about 1500Vt per day, plus food.

At the mouth of the Williams River, **Meteson's Guesthouse** (☎ 88792, 88993; s/d B&B 4200/5600Vt) has been extended to sleep 10. Chief William arranges fishing trips and guides for treks. Meals are 350Vt.

Aniwa

This island is set around beautiful, clear-blue Itcharo Lagoon, with 1.5km of white-sand beach, coconut palms, marine sanctuary, great snorkelling, gorgeous coral and stacks of fish. The very cute **Fatutu Bungalows** (☎ 88059, 7754383; spsp@vanuatu.com.vu; bungalow 4000Vt) are 10m from the beach. There's a flush toilet and lots of balmy tropical weather. Melanesian meals (600Vt) are available, plus cold drinks.

ladies produce island dishes, served on the beach, and cold drinks. Just like a picnic.

Ianiuia Surf Beach Restaurant (☎ 88061; Port Resolution; 3-course buffet 1000Vt; ☺ by arrangement) Chef Lea serves a range of chicken or vegetable dishes using local produce, fresh herbs and flair. You can camp in the grounds (700Vt with breakfast).

MALEKULA

pop 25,000 / area 2023 sq km

Shaped like a sitting dog, Malekula has two highland areas connected by 'the dog's neck'. The uplands are extremely rugged and inhospitable, rising to over 800m and crisscrossed by narrow valleys.

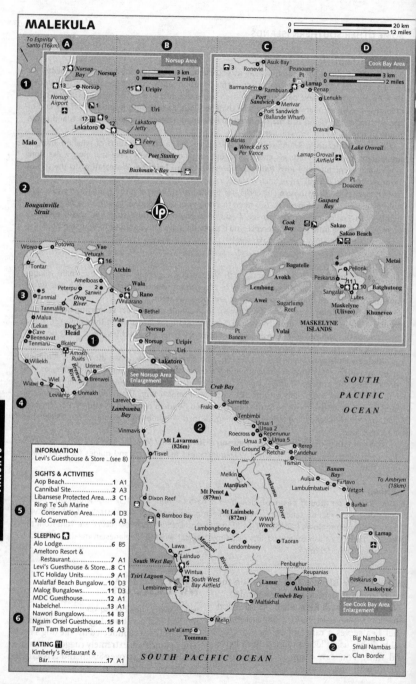

MALEKULA

Norsup Area

Cook Bay Area

INFORMATION

Levi's Guesthouse & Store ..(see 8)

SIGHTS & ACTIVITIES

Aop Beach	1	A1
Cannibal Site	2	A3
Libansese Protected Area	3	C1
Ringi Te Suh Marine Conservation Area	4	D3
Yalo Cavern	5	A3

SLEEPING

Alo Lodge	6	B5
Ameltoro Resort & Restaurant	7	A1
Levi's Guesthouse & Store	8	C1
LTC Holiday Units	9	A1
Malaflaf Beach Bungalow	10	D3
Malog Bungalows	11	D3
MDC Guesthouse	12	A1
Nabelchel	13	A1
Nawori Bungalows	14	B3
Ngaim Orsel Guesthouse	15	B1
Tam Tam Bungalows	16	A3

EATING

| Kimberly's Restaurant & Bar | 17 | A1 |

Big Nambas
Small Nambas
Clan Border

VANUATU

Two of Malekula's major cultural groups are the Big Nambas and Small Nambas, named because of the size of the men's *namba* (penis sheath). Small Nambas men wear only one leaf of dried fibre wound around the penis and tucked into a bark belt. Their semi-*kastom* communities are built around *tamtam*, ready to beat a rhythm, and a dance area.

Big Nambas men wind large purple pandanus fibres around their penis, securing the loose ends in a thick bark belt and leaving the testicles exposed. They had such an awesome warlike reputation that no foreigner dared venture into their territory. Even police expeditions, which came to punish them for killing traders, were ambushed and dispersed. They kept a stone fireplace where unwelcome outsiders were ritually cooked and eaten. You can see cannibal sites at Unmet and near Sanwir.

Big Nambas *erpnavet* (grade-taking) ceremonies are preceded by lengthy rehearsals. The men cover themselves in charcoal and coconut oil, tie nut rattles around their ankles and wear feathers in their hair. At the highest level, a man has the powerful characteristics of a hawk, and a hawk dance is performed by a spirit man. The outfit, the movement and the spirit are stunning and unforgettable.

INFORMATION

There are no ATMs and all places accept only cash. The NBV in Lakatoro will change travellers cheques and Australian dollars, but you can't access cash through your accounts, so take heaps of vatu.

The **tourism officer** (☎ 48491; malampatourism@ gmail.com) is based at the council offices in Lakatoro and can help with any aspect of tourism in the province. There's a **hospital** (☎ 48410) at Norsup, on the northeast coast.

There's no malaria in Malekula's mountainous central regions, whereas the coast is infested with it.

TRANSPORT
Getting There & Around

Every day **Air Vanuatu** (☎ 23748, 23878) flies to Norsup out of Santo or Vila, and lands at Lamap-Orovail airfield on Tuesday and Saturday. Some planes fly to South West Bay unless it's under water, and a loop links Norsup with Ambrym, Paama and Epi.

A chartered speedboat ride from Wala in northern Malekula to Luganville on Santo costs around 20,000Vt.

A roads runs from Norsup around the north coast, another down the east coast to Lamap. The roads are rough and rutted and ford many river beds, so in the wet season they are often closed.

It costs 300/100Vt by taxi/minibus from Norsup airport into Lakatoro, but at weekends there aren't many around. Boats often arrive at Litslits south of Lakatoro in the early evening, and a taxi then is also unlikely, so try to hitch if you see a vehicle. Otherwise you may have to walk, which is not easy in the dark.

A **truck** (☎ 48594) operates along the east coast between Lakatoro and Lamap (1000Vt) on week days, leaving Lamap at 5am and returning from Lakatoro at 1pm. At weekends you need to charter the truck (16,000Vt). Trucks/ taxis run more frequently between Lakatoro and Veturah in the north (200/900Vt).

Most public transport leaves Lakatoro from the MDC General Store.

All inhabited islands are linked to the mainland by speedboats or canoes. Ask at local stores if you wish to hire one.

THE DOG'S HEAD
Sights & Activities

Take your bloodthirsty self on a demanding half-day return walk to the Big Nambas **cannibal site** deep in the forest behind Sanwir – it's complete with a stone fireplace, stone tables where corpses were dismembered, and many bones.

The **overnight trek** across the rugged 'dog's head' takes you from Sanwir to Malua, on the west coast – return by transport at 5am. This trek has been documented by the Australian Heritage Foundation as it combines natural and cultural treasures with magnificent scenery, caves, waterfalls and *kastom* villages.

Kastom dancing tours go to Rano or Amelboas to see Small Nambas dances; to Unmet and Mae to see Big Nambas. Other tours go to the spectacular **Yalo Cavern** near Tanmial and the islets of Wala and Vao.

Sleeping & Eating

Tam Tam Bungalows (☎ 48926; Veturah; s/d 1500/3000Vt) The bungalows are linked by flower-lined paths around rock pools of coral. Owner Jean-Michel has bikes and snorkel gear; a speedboat and spear fishing can be arranged. There's power until 9pm, a store selling crafts, and a *nakamal* for drinking kava. Meals are 500Vt.

our pick **Nawori Bungalows** (☎ 5415564; Wala Mainland; B&B 2500Vt) Etienne hosted the film crew for the *Last One Standing* TV series so his bungalows are quite swish, with a generator, flush toilet and mosquito nets. Bring food with you, or ask his wife Enny to cook for you.

EAST MALEKULA

Norsup's commercial activities revolve around Plantations Réunies de Vanuatu (PRV), whose coconut plantations border the town. Just beyond the airport terminal is sandy **Aop Beach**, with palms and turquoise water making it a pretty spot to wait for your plane. A long stretch of beautiful coral reef stretches southwards from Aop Beach to Litslits, the main port for this area.

Lakatoro

Set on two levels divided by a steep slope, this attractive place with many shady trees is Malampa province's administrative capital. On the top level are the **Council Offices** (☎ 48491) and the **Cultural Centre** (☎ 48651), which has fascinating exhibits and photos. On the bottom level, at the northern end of town, are the LTC Co-op, NBV bank, post office, bakery and Air Vanuatu office. The southern end has the MDC General Store and market. Ask here about hiring fishing boats or taking a boat out to Uripiv and Uri islands.

Tours to Small and Big Nambas cultural villages and to cannibal sites can be arranged through your hosts (around 4000Vt shared for a truck plus entry fees per person 2500Vt), or ask about treks around the Dog's Head.

Lakatoro has mains electricity.

SLEEPING & EATING

Nabelchel (☎ 48899; Norsup; B&B 2500Vt) Near the airport, these bungalows share a pleasant central sitting area. Meals can be supplied (500Vt), but it's wise to take some food in case nobody is around.

MDC Guesthouse (☎ 7755874; Lakatoro; r with fan/air-con 2500/5000Vt; ✷) At the southern end of town, this is actually a motel (two storeys!) with spacious rooms and shared kitchen and facilities. Your host is Trelly.

Ameltoro Resort & Restaurant (☎ 48431, 7742724; Lakatoro; B&B 3000Vt) Cute egg-shaped bungalows and a gorgeous restaurant where Rona cooks a French-influenced meal (by arrangement, from 500Vt) for you.

LTC Holiday Units (☎ 48554, 7755643; apt fan/air-con 6500/8500Vt) Niawin manages eight self-contained, one-bedroom Western-style units set in grassland.

Kimberly's Restaurant & Bar (Lakatoro; meals 250-400Vt; ☯ 7am-9pm Mon-Sat) A little place opposite the LTC Co-op with colourful tablecloths and resident geckos for luck. The drinks are cold, Kimberly's cooking is excellent and the locals are always ready to chat.

Uripiv & Uri

These islands have **marine reserves** proclaimed by the chief. They have everything for snorkellers: beautiful coral, colourful fish, and turtles. The sanctuary at Uri protects the mangroves and reef, and you'll see colourful giant clams.

Kalki runs the very friendly **Ngaim Orsel Guesthouse** (☎ 48564; Uripiv; PO Box 62; B&B 2000Vt) set in an old *natsaro* (dance area) filled with exotic plants. There's a bungalow, a library and a quaint house with three bedrooms, kitchen, lounge and electricity when needed. He's a good cook (meals 500Vt) and will arrange trips to the marine reserve (1200Vt for canoe, guide and fees) or an island feast with a string band (3000Vt) for a group.

You can get to Uripiv and Uri by speedboat from the Lakatoro jetty. Plenty of boats go across between 4pm and 4.30pm (200Vt) or charter a speedboat for 2000Vt.

THE SOUTHEAST COAST

Pankumu River is Vanuatu's longest watercourse outside Santo. The river has repeatedly changed course, leaving a large wetland of oxbows and bayous. It is a great spot for birdwatching. The chestnut-bellied kingfisher is widely distributed on the island, as is the emerald dove or *sot leg* (in Bislama).

Libansese Protected Area

This **forest and beach area** at Asuk Bay is totally beautiful, with a backdrop of mountains and a wide river overhung with tropical trees and vines. You expect to see crocodiles but there's only eels and fish, and lots of birds overhead. **Bongman James** (☎ 5449352) takes you up the river by boat (s/d 1500/3000Vt); he'll meet you at the bus stop in Ronevie, or collect you by boat from Levi's Store in Lamap (s/d 2000/3000Vt one way across the inlet to Asuk Bay). Afterwards, you can snorkel in the **marine sanctuary** (admission 200Vt).

THE MANBUSH WALK

A fantastic walk starts from the bush track, heading inland from the road, about 200m north of the Pankumu River at **Retchar**. Drive up to Red Ground, behind Unua 5, then it's a 10km, two-hour walk along the Pankumu as it narrows into winding channels, isolated pools and a series of minor cascades. There's a chance the villagers from **Melkin** have cleared a trail. Melkin has the head *nakamal* for the Small Nambas, but you can't look at it. There are dancing grounds, *tamtam*, drums and stone carvings. It's *kastom*, right in the centre of ManBush, where everyone also attends Bible studies every day. You can spend the night in the **Women's Club** (1000Vt).

The walk continues next day with a seriously gruelling six-hour climb to **Lambongbong** (the locals carried a generator in from Melkin so stop complaining), an old trading centre where you could exchange goods for pigs. Up here, villagers still make fire by rubbing sticks together. It's so beautiful that it's seriously worth the agony. There are *kastom* dances (5000Vt) and guides to take you to caves, waterfalls and a conservation area (per person 500Vt). Then there's an easier six-hour walk over mountains and past waterfalls to **South West Bay**, where you can fly to Lamap or go north by boat.

You need to be fit, and you must have a guide as weather conditions constantly change the track. See www.malekulahikingtrail.blogspot.com/or http://malekulahiking.googlepages.com/lamaptourism for more information.

Port Sandwich

Malekula's safest **anchorage** was named after the Earl of Sandwich, a British prime minister, and is favoured by touring yachts. At the wharf, a small golden beach may tempt you in for a swim. Don't do it! Don't even paddle. This is the worst place for shark attacks.

Lamap

Lamap is where you organise taxis and speedboats. The truck for Lakatoro (1000Vt) leaves each weekday at 5am. Book with Lewis at Levi's store (☎ 48594).

The **Roman Catholic mission** is a large, modern church with interesting wall paintings modelled on traditional sand-drawing designs. A three-day **art festival** rotates around the area every two years celebrating local culture, song and *kastom* dances. Contact the **Tourism Officer** (malampatourism@gmail.com) for details.

If you're stuck in Lamap overnight, the very basic **Levi's Guesthouse** (☎ 48594; beds 1200Vt), behind Levi's Store, has six beds in three rooms and a large kitchen (self-catering; there's some canned food and biscuits in the store). There's electricity in the evening. One-way transfers from Lamap airfield are 500Vt.

THE MASKELYNES

The road from Lamap ends at a sandy beach, **Point Douceur** (1500Vt) where canoes and speedboats head out to the Maskelynes (3000Vt). It's a 20-minute walk from the airport through coconut plantations.

The Maskelynes are just gorgeous. Most islands have coral reefs with excellent **diving** and **snorkelling**, especially at Sakao Beach. But be *very* careful of strong currents between the islands. Some of the islands are very rugged; others have patches of mangrove-lined coast or sandy beaches. The main island, **Maskelyne (Uliveo)**, is a friendly, busy place; watch the villagers make canoes, weave, string necklaces and hunt for edible sea creatures when the tide is out. You're welcome at the kava bars, and you can hire outrigger canoes for free (1000Vt with a guide).

Take a tour to **Ringi Te Suh Marine Conservation Area** (2000Vt), a 100-hectare reef protected by the villagers of Pellonk. You can snorkel over the beautiful giant clams and picnic on an artificial island.

Take a **Mangrove Discovery Tour** (1000Vt) to learn about this ecologically rich resource or a half-day **fishing expedition** (11,000Vt) to catch yellow-fin tuna; or go by outrigger to an island to see **kastom dances** (5000Vt).

Sleeping & Eating

our pick **Malog Bungalows** (☎ 48514, 5428221; www.positiveearth.com; Peskarus; s/d incl meals 4000/8000Vt, camping 500Vt) Kalo has three traditional rooms on the shore between the mangroves, with shared flush toilets and showers plus generator lighting till 9pm. He'll take you in an outrigger to a reef for beginners' snorkelling; it's shallow, clear, still and pretty. Dine in the large tropical pagoda; ask about specialities,

VANUATU

such as just-caught lobster or mud crab (they cost only a bit more).

Malaflaf Beach Bungalow (☎ 48458; Lutes; s/d incl meals 3000/4000Vt) Ambong has built two-bedroom bungalows with their own sandy beach on a crystal-clear lagoon with a coral reef. Further along is the cookhouse, where your host creates local meals that you can eat on the beach while watching the sunset.

SOUTH WEST BAY

The ancient traditions of the Small Nambas people are well preserved in southwestern Malekula. *Nakamal* and dancing grounds are being opened to tourists, and grade-taking is on the increase.

Wintua

This village looks out over South West Bay from behind forested hills. You can do a day walk into the hills to three mainly *kastom* villages (5000Vt for a *kastom* dance). Enquire at Alo Lodge. There's safe **swimming** off the western end of the airstrip, and a canoe trip to the **fish nursery** at Tsiri Lagoon is available. A three-hour **waterfall walk** takes you through rainforest to a deep plunge pool, the home of large eels.

Alo Lodge (☎ 48829; B&B s/d 3500/5000Vt) has four bedrooms with new beds, and a verandah covered in grand artwork. Owner George Thompson arranges transport, guides, deep-sea fishing and tours out of Wintua.

AMBRYM

pop 13,500 / area 680 sq km

Ambrym (called the Black Island because of its volcanic soils) has amazing twin volcanoes, Mt Marum and Mt Benbow, which keep volcanologists all over the world on the alert. Other attractions include Vanuatu's best tree-fern carvings and *tamtam*; Rom dances of northern and western Ambrym; and Lake Fanteng Conservation Reserve.

Magic in Vanuatu is strongest on the islands with active volcanoes, and Ambrym is considered the country's sorcery centre. Sorcerers (*man blong majik* or *man blong posen*) are feared and despised. Many ni-Van have seen too many unexplained happenings and would treat anyone who was found practising black magic severely. Tourists can visit villages that feature tra-

ditional magic, but magic for tourists is no considered black.

Ambrym is also the island for sand draw ings, with 180 sand designs, each referring to specific object, legend, dance or creature.

FESTIVALS

North Ambrym loves a good festival Accommodation (1500Vt) is organised for tourists, crafts are for sale and stalls are heaped with food. For details, check with the **Vanuatu Cultural Centre** (☎ 22129; vks@vanuatu.com.vu) in Por Vila, **Mayumi** (☎ 37365; mayumi@WrecksToRainforest .com) on Santo, or **Chief Sekor** (☎ 48444, 48631) in Olal.

There are three main festivals, each an annual extravaganza of cultural demonstrations, ceremonies, fashion shows, Rom dances, magic, and cooking lessons with guides and explanations in English and French:

Fanla Art Festival July, in Fanla.

North Ambrym Magic Festival July, in Olal.

Back to My Roots Festival August, in Olal.

TRANSPORT
Getting There & Around

Air Vanuatu (☎ 23748) calls in to both of Ambrym's airports (Craig Cove and Ulei) on flights out of both Vila and Luganville on Tuesday and Saturday, and many tour companies in Vila (p571) offer volcano adventure flights to Ambrym.

The best anchorages are at Craig Cove and Sanesup in the south (Port Vatu is OK in good weather), and Buwoma Bay, Ranvetlam, Ranon and Nobul in the north.

If you aren't concerned about deep ocean swells and fierce currents, you can go with Douglas of Solomon Douglas Bungalows (see p593) by speedboat from north Ambrym to Pangi in southwest Pentecost (13,000Vt).

Some 4WD trucks (which you can wave down) grind their way along the rutted road that connects Craig Cove with Maranata in the south. Others go from Ulei to Endu on the east coast and around the northern tip.

Speedboats travel between Craig Cove and Ranvetlam (12,000Vt one way). Ask your bungalow host to arrange transport.

VOLCANOES

The dark, brooding outlines of Mt Benbow and Mt Marum are about a kilometre apart, shrouded in smoke and cloud but dominating the vast, grey ash plain that lies within

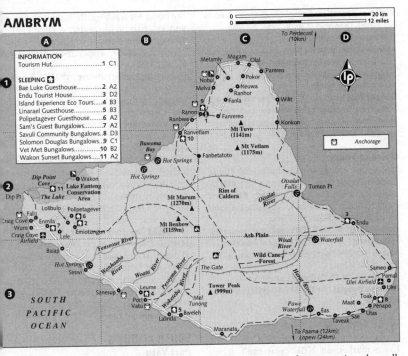

AMBRYM

INFORMATION
Tourism Hut..............................1 C1

SLEEPING
Bae Luke Guesthouse...............2 A2
Endu Tourist House..................3 D2
Island Experience Eco Tours....4 B3
Linarael Guesthouse.................5 B3
Polipetagever Guesthouse........6 A2
Sam's Guest Bungalows...........7 A2
Savuli Community Bungalows...8 D3
Solomon Douglas Bungalows...9 C1
Vet Met Bungalows................10 B2
Wakon Sunset Bungalows.....11 A2

the old caldera. At night, the sky above them glows red.

White smoke pours from Mt Benbow's vents, but its central crater was plugged by a landslide. It's not certain how long it will be before it blows the plug. Look over the smoky gullet of Mt Marum and see the red-hot magma boiling way below like a satanic pot of tomato soup. She spews molten rock and dense black smoke from her vents. Both volcanoes are closely monitored, and evacuation plans are always ready.

To go up you have to be fit and used to walking on steep terrain, and you need a good guide (see p592) to hack your way through jungle, cross glassy strips of old lava, push through wild bamboo forest and trudge along steamy gorges. And when you reach the caldera the hard work starts.

There's no shade, just wave after wave of barren grey ridges. Skin protection and plenty of drinking water are essential. There's a dry slippery crust around both volcanoes so your boots need to be strong enough to kick toe holes. Ankle support is also necessary as there's some boulder

hopping. Between the mountains, the walk over the razor-backed ridge gets very narrow and snakes nastily upwards, while vents all around spurt acrid smoke. Mother Nature does her best to be daunting.

Access Points

The best idea is to go up one way and down another (different guides will meet you on the caldera). Trek prices depend on the distance travelled by truck (up to 5000Vt return), local fees (1500Vt per person), whether you stay overnight and how many guides you use (2000Vt per person). The sacred custom of the north is that there's no fishing, hunting or other activities from September to December – the yam-planting season. Volcano trips are available only from the south during these months.

The four routes (three via Craig Cove airport, route four via Ulei airport) are as follows:

Emiotungun or Polipetagever Truck it to the road's end, then walk along sand cliffs with no major slopes. If you come back this way, go direct with the truck to the hot pools at Baiap. Very relaxing!

VANUATU

Ranon or Ranvetlam A complete experience – truck to Fanbetatoto, three hours of jungle, views, ash plain – return or continue down south.

Lalinda or Port Vatu The slopes are fierce, but this way is the quickest: a truck trip, then a three-hour slog from the end of the road. The sudden break from forest to ash plain is stunningly beautiful.

Endu or Toak From Endu, it's a four-hour trek to the ash plain, across Wisal River, and back through a wild cane forest. From Toak, you camp on the ash plane, returning along black-sand beaches and pools.

Volcano Tours

Your tour guides usually have gear (tents, sleeping bags, hard hats, gloves, gas masks) should you want to hire anything. Ask if you need to bring your own food. Some options:

Apia (☎ 48450) Operates out of Endu.

Dolven Bong (☎ 5412929) Operates out of Emiotungun.

Isaiah Bong (☎ 48405) Operates out of Ranvetlam.

Joseph (☎ 23167; vandiscovery@vanuatu.com.vu) Operates out of Toak.

Sam David (☎ 48620) Operates out of Craig Cove.

Solomon Douglas (☎ 5412615, 5412896) Operates out of Ranon.

WEST AMBRYM

Ambrym's commercial centre, Craig Cove, has a market, an NBV (you can't access cash so bring plenty of vatu), and a co-op that sells fresh bread, canned food, alcohol and hardware.

Sights & Activities

Volcano tours run out of Craig Cove, Emiotungun and Polipetagever.

Emiotungun has lovely old **carvings** in the *nasara* (namakal) (entry 300Vt). Polipetagever villagers perform **Rom dances** (5500Vt), **magic shows** (500Vt), **sand drawing** (500Vt) and **string band concerts** (300Vt). Or take a historical tour for 1500Vt.

Lake Fanteng Conservation Area (local fee 500Vt) at Dip Point is a beautiful spot, with many wild ducks and more than 30 bird species.

Sleeping

There's often a bit of a food shortage on Ambrym. Your host may provide some meals, but it's best to take food and offer it as a gift if you don't need it.

Wakon Sunset Bungalows (☎ 48547; www.positive earth.org/bungalows/malampa/wakon.htm; Dip Point; s/d 1000/2000Vt, camping 1000Vt) Chief Jessy's bungalow has two bedrooms, a bush kitchen, and

the ocean for washing. Be Robinson Cruso snorkel, fish or birdwatch – Lake Fanten Conservation Reserve is 10 minutes away Meals are 200Vt, a speedboat from Crai Cove 1200Vt.

Polipetagever Guesthouse (☎ 48852; jbongsavei gmail.com; Polipetagever; s/d incl meals 1500/3000Vt) Th quaint guesthouse is built from forest timbe that's been planed with axes and tied wit vines (you don't want to know about the pi toilet). Transfers to the airport–volcano roa end are 3000/2500Vt return.

Sam's Guest Bungalows (☎ 48620, 48874; Craig Cove s/d/family incl meals 2500/4500/7000Vt) Small bungalows and bathrooms are behind Sam's family compound so you can enjoy family and village life. You'll find Sam at the airfield; he arranges tours and transport.

our pick **Bae Luke Guesthouse** (☎ 5414778, 5414803; Emiotungun; tr incl meals 4000Vt) This Western-style house by a friendly village has a gas-fired kitchen and inside toilet. Oh, the luxury. Moses arranges volcano tours (truck 5000Vt return shared, entry 1500Vt, guide 2000Vt) and has tents (500Vt) if you prefer to overnight up there.

SOUTH AMBRYM
Port Vatu

our pick **Island Experience Eco Tours** (☎ 5446190; tassojohn@yahoo.com; s/d 2000/3500Vt), run by John Tasso, is in Port Vatu. Stay in the guest bungalow (meals 300Vt to 800Vt) and build a house using vines and *natangura* leaves (1500Vt); go fishing (1500Vt) or wild pig hunting (2000Vt); and take Tasso's overnight volcano tour (4300Vt including tent and entry fee, BYO food). A taxi is 7000Vt from Craig Cove.

Lalinda

The chief at Lalinda is the *kastom* owner of the southern access to the volcanoes (entry fee 1000Vt). Problem is, the village is divided by church affiliations. If you come by truck, take your driver's advice about where to go; the Seventh Day Adventist faction have built a new entry road that is quite superior but possibly blocked.

Linarael Guesthouse (☎ 48854; beds 1000Vt) sleeps six people and has a kitchen; water is available nearby and there's a loo down a path. The locals will cook dinner (500Vt), and there's a baker ready to bake for your journey!

THE ROM DANCE

Ambrym's most striking traditional ceremony, the Rom dance, combines *maghe* (grade-taking) elements with magic. When a man wishes to move up in the village structure, he must find someone who owns the design of a mask and ask to buy it, with pigs and cash. The owner makes his *nakamal* (men's clubhouse) *tabu* (taboo), and the buyer comes to discuss the purchase and learn the rules determining the colours and shapes of the mask. Once the design has been bought, the buyer invites men to pay to enter this *nakamal* where they practise the dance for days, cooking the food the buyer has provided. Finally there's a feast, and next morning the dancers perform wearing the extraordinary costume: a tall, conical, brightly painted banana-fibre mask and a thick cloak of banana leaves.

Only those men who paid to enter the *nakamal* will have seen the Rom costume being made. Anyone who disobeyed this *tabu* would be fined a pig and have their backs whipped with *nanggalat* (a native plant that burns your skin for days) or wild cane. Wild cane also marks the entrance to the *tabu* area. Be careful!

Costumes are burnt following the dance, to ensure that the spirit of the dance doesn't stay to make trouble in the village. Most tourists see only a pretend dance.

EAST AMBRYM

Ulei recently opened as an entry point to the volcanoes. Toak, near the airfield, is a large village where you'll see very traditional sand drawing, magic, *kastom* stories, dances, caves and waterfalls. Taxis can be hired here.

New and gorgeous **Savuli Community Bungalows** (☎ 48786, 23167; Toak; s incl meals 3000Vt), made of stone and bamboo, is set along the black-sand beach; ask for Jeppy (transfers 1500Vt shared). Overnight volcano treks including tents and camp-fire–cooked meals are 6500Vt.

Endu is a pretty village further north along the coast. **Endu Tourist House** (☎ 48450; s 1000Vt) is in a garden with rock pools to play in. Ask for Apia or Chief Moses. Meals are 500Vt and transfers from the airport are 1700Vt. Tours include an extraordinary waterfall walk and Rom dances. The volcanoes are a four-hour trek away (5000Vt).

NORTH AMBRYM

Most of Ambrym's northern coast has high volcanic cliffs rising straight out of the sea. The **motorboat journey** north from Craig Cove burbles past sheer angled cliffs, *namaruh* forests, rock caves, hot pools, coral reefs, turtles, dolphins and wild ducks.

The **tourism hut** (☎ 30050) in Ranon is open most days, certainly when boats are in the bay. The best **Rom dances and magic** (admission 3000Vt) can be seen inland at Ranhor and Fanla. An **island feast** can be prepared for a group.

Chief Joseph at Ranvetlam is the *kastom* owner of the northern approach to the volcanoes; the guides also live in this village.

A return boat-ride between Ranon and Ranvetlam is 2000Vt, or to Olal it's 6000Vt.

Sleeping

Solomon Douglas Bungalows (☎ 5412615, 5412896; Ranon; B&B 3000Vt) Stay in traditional bungalows on the beach or up the cliff where there are stunning views. Meals are 600Vt. Douglas has a truck for visits to Fanla, tours to Rom dances and volcano truck-and-treks. He does speedboat transfers to/from Craig Cove (12,000Vt); ask him to stop while you snorkel along the coral-bedecked shoreline, or bask in the hot springs.

Vet Met Bungalows (☎ 48687; www.positive earth.org/vetmet/; Ranvetlam; s/d incl meals 5500/7500Vt) Brightly painted bungalows and a lovely dining area all on a peaceful cliff where you can walk down to a rocky bay. Owner Isaiah Bong arranges volcano tours, provides tents and organises Rom dances at neighbouring villages.

ESPIRITU SANTO

pop 33,000 / area 3677 sq km

Great news. Santo has its long-promised big bright international airport, and planes now fly direct from Brisbane and Sydney. Furthermore, the locals have responded with grand developments to welcome the new tourists. Shops are painted, streets are beautified (well, there's only really one street but

ESPIRITU SANTO

0 — 20 km
0 — 12 miles

it's looking good), accommodation is polished. So divers, here to see the healthy reefs and the world's best wreck, as elegant as the *Titanic;* adventurers here to conquer impenetrable jungle and extraordinary caves; and those who just want stunning blue holes, white-sand beaches and azure water, come enjoy. The island awaits you.

Santo's people live mainly on the southern and eastern coastal strips. Fanafo, north of Luganville, was where, in 1963, charismatic Jimmy Stevens formed the Nagriamel movement. Then, on 27 May 1980, eight weeks before national independence, he and his supporters staged a coup known as the Coconut Rebellion. Armed mainly with bows and arrows, they occupied Luganville and proclaimed Santo's independence, calling their new country Vemarana. However, the new nation collapsed with Stevens' arrest on 1 September.

Inland, villages are isolated and the locals totally self-sufficient, even dressing in clothes woven from the leaves of the jungle. Southwest Santo has Vanuatu's highest mountains: Mt Tabwemasana (1879m), Mt Kotamtam (1747m), Mt Tawaloala (1742m) and Santo

Peak (1704m). About 5000 people live in tiny villages that interrupt these thickly wooded mountains tumbling abruptly into the sea. As *kastom* demands, there are important *nimangki* ceremonies throughout the villages.

INFORMATION

In Luganville, Patrick Vurobaravu, at the **VTO** (Map p597; ☎ 36984; vtosanto@tourism.vu; Main St; ⏱ 7.30am-4.30pm), will answer all your queries as will Dave Cross at **Beachfront Resort** (Map p597; ☎ 36881), president of Espiritu Santo Tourism Association. Their websites are also helpful: www.vanuatutourism.com and www.espiritusan totourism.com.

Shopping is small-town style, but there's a range of boutique clothes and accessories along with the diving gear at **Santo Island Dive & Fishing** (Map p597; ☎ 37742; Main St). The pharmacy at the hospital and two small chemist shops in Luganville sell a range of deodorants. Bring anything more serious with you. Luganville is the only town outside Vila with commercial banking facilities, all on the main street.

Ambulance (Map p597; ☎ 36112)
ANZ Bank (Map p597; ☎ 36711; ⏱ 8am-3pm Mon-Fri) Has an ATM.
Club de Sanma (Map p597; ☎ 36039; Main St; ⏱ 9am-midnight) The money exchange here offers good rates.
Computer Net (Map p597; ☎ 37773; admin@comput .net; per min 25Vt) The fastest connections. Also prints photos (600Vt per page).
NBV (Map p597; ☎ 36441; ⏱ 8am-3pm Mon-Fri)
Northern District Hospital (Map p597; ☎ 36345) Perched above the town in Le Plateau.
Police (Map p597; ☎ 36222)
Post office (Map p597; ⏱ 8.30am-4pm Mon-Fri) There's a cardphone outside.
Westpac Bank (Map p597; ☎ 36625; ⏱ 8am-4pm Mon-Fri)

There's a **shop** (Map p594; ☎ 7742798) with groceries and internet access at Lapita Plantation on Aore Island's western corner.

TRANSPORT
Getting There & Around
AIR

Pekoa International Airport is big, bright and brand new. It welcomes international flights from Brisbane and Sydney, and there are at least two return flights daily to Vila. It's also the feeder airport for Vanuatu's northern islands. Contact Air Vanuatu at its **town office** (Map p597; ☎ 36421; Main St) and **airport office** (☎ 36506).

VANUATU

FROM JUNGLE TO CITY TO DIVING MECCA

Segond Channel was the Allies' base during WWII. For three years to September 1945, more than half a million military personnel, mainly Americans, were stationed here waiting to head into battle in the Pacific. There were sometimes 100 ships moored off Luganville.

Roads were laid. There were 40 cinemas, four military hospitals, five airfields, a torpedo boat base, jetties and market gardens. Quonset huts were erected for use as offices, workshops and servicemen's accommodation. More than 10,000 ni-Van came to work for the troops. To them, the servicemen seemed fabulously wealthy and generous.

Unfortunately, USS *President Coolidge*, a luxury liner turned troopship, hit a friendly mine and became the world's largest accessible and diveable shipwreck.

After the war, the USA offered the Condominium government the surplus equipment but they didn't respond, so the lot was dumped. Everything from bulldozers, aeroplane engines and jeeps to crates of Coca-Cola went into the sea at what is now Million Dollar Point. The coral-encrusted equipment makes the point a popular diving and snorkelling spot.

Santo's other commercial strip is northwest, at Lajmoli; if your flight goes that way, sit on the inland side to see the awesome central mountains.

BOAT

Luganville has **Customs** (Map p597; ☎ 36854, 36225), quarantine and **Immigration** (Map p597; ☎ 36724) facilities for yachts at or near the Main Wharf. Segond Channel, with its sandy bottom, is the town's main anchorage but Aore Island is the safest: 40m deep and away from the southeasterlies that hit the mainland.

The **Maritime College** (Map p594; ☎ 36547, 5536547; marico@vanuatu.com.vu) has a marine repair workshop and also charters its 21m *Euphrosyne II* (150,000Vt for 24 hours). It's a sturdy boat with two decks, bunk rooms, skipper and crew. Great for a group of up to 20 wanting an outer-island adventure.

CAR

Santo has unsealed roads connecting Luganville with the southwest, north and east coasts; elsewhere travel by boat or walk. Hire cars at **Apex Motors & Car Rental** (Map p597; ☎ 36061; www.apex-hotel.vu), where an around-town five-seater costs 7500Vt per day plus tax and insurance. **Santo 4WD Rental** (Map p597; ☎ 37259; www.santo4wd.com; from per day 11,000Vt) also hires scooters from 4000Vt.

MINIBUS & TAXI

A minibus will pass you every minute in Luganville between 7am and 5.30pm. Hail one and you'll be dropped at your destination. Around Luganville is 100Vt; 200Vt from the airport.

A minibus runs up the east coast from Luganville to Port Olry (600Vt) on week days, leaving Unity Shell Garage in Luganville at about 4pm. To return, stand by the roadside in Port Olry before 6.30am.

Cute colourful taxis and public-transport trucks zip around Luganville. After 5.30pm, the market is the best place to find them, or ring Johnny (☎ 5447698) or Estello (☎ 7742178).

LUGANVILLE
pop 12,200

Vanuatu's northern capital has a wide main street that sprawls along several kilometres of waterfront with interesting views at every corner, two main parks and dozens of dusty (albeit freshly painted in spots) shops. The town has that tropical feel, as though something is about to happen. You think you belong even if you're only here a week.

The **Luganville–Aore swim** (www.pacificswims.com) is making it big on the grand-ocean-swims scene. It's a 2.6km swim in pretty tough ocean, held every year in June. People from Fiji, NZ and Australia battle against the locals.

Sights

There are lots of WWII remains (Map p597) in town, such as the corrugated-iron **Quonset huts** at Main Wharf and near Unity Park, and the rusting **steel sea walls** that are evidence of busier times. **Million Dollar Point** (admission 500Vt per car) shows its coral-encrusted machinery to snorkellers and divers.

Most people have never seen the elusive Lysepsep people, but spend time in the impenetrable mountains of Central Santo, and you may find them watching you. About 1m

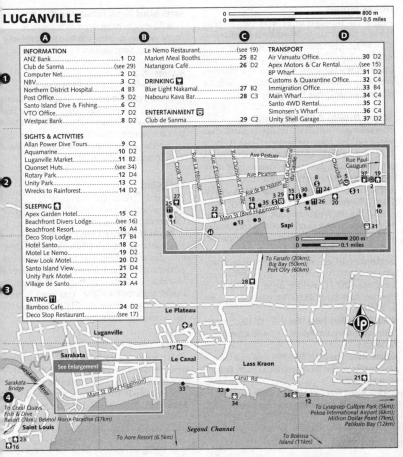

LUGANVILLE

INFORMATION	
ANZ Bank	1 D2
Club de Sanma	(see 29)
Computer Net	2 D2
NBV	3 C2
Northern District Hospital	4 B3
Post Office	5 D2
Santo Island Dive & Fishing	6 C2
VTO Office	7 D2
Westpac Bank	8 D2

SIGHTS & ACTIVITIES	
Allan Power Dive Tours	9 C2
Aquamarine	10 D2
Luganville Market	11 B2
Quonset Huts	(see 34)
Rotary Park	12 D4
Unity Park	13 C2
Wrecks to Rainforest	14 D2

SLEEPING	
Apex Garden Hotel	15 C2
Beachfront Divers Lodge	(see 16)
Beachfront Resort	16 A4
Deco Stop Lodge	17 B4
Hotel Santo	18 C2
Motel Le Nemo	19 D2
New Look Motel	20 D2
Santo Island View	21 D4
Unity Park Motel	22 C2
Village de Santo	23 A4

EATING	
Bamboo Cafe	24 D2
Deco Stop Restaurant	(see 17)

Le Nemo Restaurant	(see 19)
Market Meal Booths	25 B2
Natangora Café	26 D2

DRINKING	
Blue Light Nakamal	27 B2
Nabouru Kava Bar	28 C3

ENTERTAINMENT	
Club de Sanma	29 C2

TRANSPORT	
Air Vanuatu Office	30 D2
Apex Motors & Car Rental	(see 15)
BP Wharf	31 D2
Customs & Quarantine Office	32 C4
Immigration Office	33 B4
Main Wharf	34 C4
Santo 4WD Rental	35 C2
Simonsen's Wharf	36 C4
Unity Shell Garage	37 D2

all, they grow their hair very long and use it as a screen. The **Lysepsep Culture Park** (Map p594; ☎ 7754491) shows many of their unusual customs. You need to book a group, at least a day before, and check that you'll see the dances.

Villagers come from all over to sell their produce at the **Luganville Market** (Map p597; Main St; ⏱ 24hr), near the Sarakata Bridge.

Unity Park (Map p597) spreads along the waterfront to the market. It has a kids' playground and lovely shady trees. **Rotary Park** (Map p597) has barbecues.

Activities
GAME & REEF FISHING
Head out to the deep blue, game fishing with **Seascape Charters** (Map p594; ☎ 37379; www.vanuatu seascape.com; half/full day 65,000/90,000Vt) in a 7.5m Shark Cat (maximum of six people). The catch is tagged and returned, or given to a village. A fun day with barbecue, snorkelling and a little fishing is 40,000Vt.

Santo Island Dive & Fishing (Map p597; ☎ 7758080; www.santodive.com; half/full day 19,000/29,000Vt) stays closer to shore for reef fishing, snorkelling and a picnic lunch.

GOLF
The **Santo Golf Club** (Map p594; ⏱ Sat & Sun) at Palikulo Bay welcomes visitors, but you need your own clubs. The course runs along the seafront with fine views of Aese Island and Palikulo Point; there's a tournament on the last Sunday of every month.

VANUATU

HORSE RIDING

Beginners through to experts can arrange horse riding through **Belmol Horse Paradise** (Map p594; ☎ 36823; belmolhorse@yahoo.co.nz; half day 7000Vt) near Wailapa. Clippity-clop among coconut palms, into lagoons, up onto the plateau, round up some sleek Santo cattle or choose a full day's ride (price negotiable).

SCUBA DIVING & SNORKELLING

Snorkelling is excellent, totally brilliant. But you shouldn't come to Santo without trying a dive. The coral's bright and healthy, the wrecks are world class, prices are fantastic and dive operators extremely professional. Look at their websites for some amazing images, such as MV *Henry Bonneaud*, one of the world's top night dives; USS *President Coolidge*, lying in 21m to 67m of water; and Tutuba Point, a spectacular drift dive with brilliant corals and marine life.

There are boat and offshore dives for beginners to gurus. An intro dive costs about 10,000Vt; double dives offshore/boat are 8200/12,600Vt; diver certification courses cost from 38,000Vt; equipment hire is 1500Vt.

Allan Power Dive Tours (Map p597; ☎ 36822; www .allan-power-santo.com; Main St, Luganville) A favourite for 38 years.

Aquamarine (Map p597; ☎ 36196; www.aquamarine santo.com; Luganville) Big and popular. Sit on the deck to study your notes.

Bokissa Island Dive (Map p594; ☎ 30030; www.bokissa .com) Especially for guests of Bokissa Eco Island Resort (p600).

Santo Island Dive & Fishing (Map p597; ☎ 775808 7758082; www.santodive.com; Main St, Luganville) Choose your own adventure with this small, professional operator. Great picnic lunch too.

SWIMMING

The best place for swimming near Luganvill is at the beach in front of Beachfront Resor where you're most welcome. There's a beac on the way to Palikulo Point (about 1200V by taxi return). But for gorgeous beaches go up the east coast to Champagne Beach and Lonnoc Beach.

TREKKING

Favourite treks are through the Vatthe Conservation Area (p602) and the Loru Conservation Area (p601).

Wrecks to Rainforest (Map p597; ☎ 7754491; www .wreckstorainforest.com; treks per day from 6000Vt) runs a four-day trek taking you through rainforest, gardens, along and across Wailapa River to Marakae. A three-day trek to Funaspef includes Millennium Cave. You sleep in traditional villages where the MalMal people still use Stone-Age equipment.

Tours

There are many operators with minivans or taxis ready with tours (from 2000/4000Vt per half/full day). A typical day trip includes a visit to Champagne Beach and Matevulu Blue Hole. Discuss where you

---

MATT YATES

Matt, I hear you've been a circus performer for many years. I've been performing and teaching for 20 years taking shows around the world, running Lunar Circus in Western Australia (WA) and hosting the WA Circus Festival. Our show is a comedy/acrobatic show, 'contemporary circus'; no animals but plenty of funny antics and gravity-defying acts.

What has brought you to Santo? My partner Patricia has had a life-long romance with the Pacific and planned for us to teach circus and do shows in Port Vila. Then we came to Santo for a holiday and fell in love with it. When we found Turtle Bay we could not help but dream about the things we could do here.

Do ni-Van children attend your workshops as well? Yes, absolutely. Our Sunday workshop is mostly local kids. They're great acrobats; they have amazing strength and body awareness. They don't spend time in front of TV; they're out all day playing and working. You see little kids carrying bundles of leaves that are bigger than themselves and holding massive bush knives!

How has the first six months in business turned out? Well, it's been an adventure. Harder than we thought, but dreaming is always easier. It's great to see that we have created something very beautiful. Our guests have nothing but good things to say. We like to make people's stay memorable, to give them that tropical-adventure holiday that people come for.

Matt Yates runs Turtle Bay Resort and Lunar Circus Vanuatu

will go: some cultural highlights are a real fizzer, some guides can't access Champagne Beach, some places require long bus trips. Tailored tours offer hiking, WWII relics, culture, nature.

An absolute must-do is Millennium Cave (p601), high in the hills inland from Luganville. Another is RiriRiri River & Blue Hole, a grotto of tree ferns overhanging a white-sand and crystal-blue pool. Tour operators include:

Heritage Tours (☎ 36862, 7740968) Speak to Tim.

Little Paradise of Port Olry (☎ 3766, 37606, 7743776; PO Box 115) Ask for Tarcisius.

Paradise Tours (☎ 7747159) Luke has been running tours for years.

Santo Destination Tours (☎ 7758001) Ask for Kenery.

Santo Island Tours (☎ 36601, 7742151) Kenneth has a good range.

Santo Safari Tours (☎ 7742178; erickwilliams54@ yahoo.com) Erick is new to the game and enthusiastic.

Wrecks to Rainforest (Map p597; ☎ 37365; www .wreckstorainforest.com) Local tours, adventure treks, Leweton tribal tour and package tours to other islands.

Sleeping

These are just a few of the places in and around Luganville. Check websites such as www.vanuatutourism.com and www.vanuatu -hotels.vu for more.

BUDGET

Unity Park Motel (Map p597; ☎ 36052; locm@vanuatu .com.vu; Main St; s/tw/tr/q 1500/2400/2700/3600Vt; r with bathroom 2700Vt; ✖) Upstairs are lovely airy rooms (ask for a front one with air-con for 3900Vt). Downstairs is more basic. The shared kitchen and bathroom are spacious, and there's a laundry. You can relax in the rotunda in the garden.

our pick Beachfront Divers Lodge (Map p597; ☎ 36881; www.thebeachfrontresort.com; dm with fan/air-con from 2500/3000Vt; ✖) Custom-built for divers, with secure wash facilities, these sparkling, spacious dorm rooms open onto a central court and barbecue area. The kitchen is inspiring. You can camp in the grounds, and restaurant meals are totally affordable.

New Look Motel (Map p597; ☎ 36440; newlook@van uatu.com.vu; Main St; s/d/tr 2820/3940/3940Vt) Above the store, with large communal areas on the rooftop, mean you meet lots of people. Ask for a room with verandah and views of the harbour.

Santo Island View (Map p597; ☎ 36494; www.santo islandview.com; PO Box 40; s/d/ste from 2900/4500/8000Vt;

□ ☎) Hike up the hill, or hop on a bus, because this place is great. The balconies have coastal views (ask for a front room), the gardens are pretty and there's a new swimming pool. The bar serves some snacks from 500Vt.

Motel Le Nemo (Map p597; ☎ 37991; www.motel-le -nemo-santo.vu; r with fan/air-con/balcony 4500/6500/8500Vt; ✖) A good price in a good position, with Western-style motel rooms along a corridor and the restaurant downstairs to keep you happily wining and dining.

Apex Garden Hotel & Restaurant (Map p597; ☎ 36061; www.apex-hotel.vu; Main St; s/d from 4900/5500Vt, ste from 13,900Vt; ✖) In the centre of town, it's good value with comfortable rooms and a large beer garden under cover. The Chinese restaurant is open for all meals (mains 1100Vt to 2100Vt).

MIDRANGE

Beachfront Resort (Map p597; ☎ 36881; www.thebeach frontresort.com; s/d/tr from 4500/6500/11,000Vt, family apt 10,000Vt; ✖) An oh-so-friendly, low-key spot featuring modern bungalows with kitchenettes. Walk across the lawn to an excellent black-sand beach. It's the best place to swim, even if you aren't staying. Talk to resort manager Dave Cross (☎ 7743911) about tourist activities.

Deco Stop Lodge (Map p597; ☎ 36175; www.decostop .com.vu; B&B dm/unit 4500/11,500Vt; ☎) High on the ridge behind Luganville overlooking Segond Channel, Deco Stop has a huge deck floating around a grand swimming pool. The friendly new owners, Ben and Kim, ensure a great social atmosphere. Many rooms are set up with secure wash areas for divers' gear. Transfers are 1200Vt.

our pick Hotel Santo (Map p597; ☎ 36250; hotel santo@vanuatu.com.vu; s/d 6000/7800Vt, upstairs s/d/tr 12,000/13,200/14,500Vt; ✖ ☎) The place to see and be seen is this retro '70s hotel, with its fabulous huge *tamtam* in the foyer. Sit out on the patio with a G&T and watch life come your way. Spacious rooms open onto the pool area; more luxurious rooms are upstairs. Guests can hire hotel cars. The restaurant (meals 900Vt to 1600Vt; open breakfast, lunch and dinner) has an extensive menu that combines Western and local foods.

Coral Quays Fish & Dive Resort (Map p594; ☎ 36257; www.coralquays.com; B&B s/d from 9500/9800Vt; ✖ ☎) Eighteen attractive bungalows with soaring ceilings sit in a tropical garden. Use the private jetty to snorkel or dive over coral gardens and the *Tui Twaite* shipwreck, 800m away. A secure wash and dry room, kayaks, bikes and snorkel gear are available, or have a massage (2000/3500Vt for 30/60 minutes). A minibus/taxi from town costs 100/600Vt.

Village de Santo (Map p597; ☎ 36123; www.villagede santo.com; d 14,000Vt; ☒) Swish new self-contained family units nestle around a pool and little shop. It's very close to the beach and a stroll into town. Luxury living for a family; enjoy.

TOP END

Aore Resort (Map p594; ☎ 36705, 36703; www.aore resort.com; B&B s/d/tr from 16,540/20,360/25,590Vt; ☐ ☒) Spacious bungalows, grassy slopes to the water, snorkel gear, kayaks and mountain bikes (visitors can hire them). All good, and the restaurant (mains 1400Vt to 2000Vt; open all meals) is a grand area. The ferry leaves from BP Wharf (2500Vt return); ask for the schedule when you book. Nonguests can hang out at the resort for 1000Vt a day.

our pick **Bokissa Eco Island Resort** (Map p594; ☎ 30030; www.bokissa.com; d 34,000Vt; ☒ ☐ ☒) Fluffy-white-towel luxurious with bunga-lows 10 footsteps away from astounding snorkelling over plate corals piled high, branches of soft coral, and anemones with their Nemos. It's a busy dive base (six-dive package 53,000Vt), and nondivers can kayak up a river, walk, turtle-watch and swim in the pool with a swim-up bar. Transfers (7500Vt return) leave from Simonsen's Wharf. Check the website for regular specials.

Eating

Market Meal Booths (Map p597; meals 350Vt; ☺ 7.30am-10pm) Sit at a bright little table and a cheery lady appears at the booth window with a glass of red cordial. There's a choice of dishes, but steak's the best. You can watch it being cooked, fresh herbs added, delicious.

Bamboo Cafe (Map p597; mains 450-850Vt; ☺ 9.30am-9.30pm) Bench tables under a grand traditional roof give this little cafe a happy atmosphere. The chef is very good – check out the cakes! Ask about the special nights, with feasts, bar-becue and kava.

Natangora Café (Map p597; ☎ 36811; Main St; meals 450-1250Vt; ☺ 7.30am-4.30pm Mon-Fri, 8am-1pm Sat) Specialises in breakfast, house-roasted coffee, hamburgers and salads. The alfresco setting and reasonable prices make it popular with locals, expats and tourists alike.

Le Nemo Restaurant (Map p597; ☎ 37991; mains 800-3500Vt; ☺ breakfast, lunch & dinner Tue-Sun) Chef Mouroux serves fine French dishes, like, oh joy, his French onion soup, his *Iles flotante*. If he has moved on, find where he is; this is dining not to be missed.

Deco Stop Restaurant (Map p597; ☎ 36175; mains 1500Vt; ☺ 7am-9pm) You're on top of the world, sitting around the beautiful pool, gazing way out over the channel, and choosing from an excellent menu.

Coral Quays Restaurant (Map p594; ☎ 36257; mains 1700-2700Vt; ☺ breakfast, lunch & dinner) The chef is famous for her gourmet food served on a wide verandah with local-timber tables. Try the sunset platter. Ask about transport if you're coming for dinner.

Drinking & Entertainment

The entertainment scene is pretty light on in Luganville. Deco Stop Lodge (p599) is your best bet. Kava bars are open from 6pm till 10pm – look for a red or green light.

Club de Sanma (Map p597; ☎ 36039; clubdesanma@ vanuatu.com.vu; ☺ 10am-midnight) Squeeze onto the balcony for a beer (shame about the pokies inside); happy hour starts at 5.30pm, and TV screens show international sports. Friday, the jazz and blues night, kicks on till 3am.

Nabouru Kava Bar (Map p597; Kava strip) has a pleasant sitting area in a pretty garden, in a strip of kava bars. In town, **Blue Light Nakamal** (Map p597; Main St) is opposite the market.

THE EAST COAST ROAD

There are so many places to stay as you head north that you could take forever.

First is Splash Extreme, due to open late in 2009. Certainly worth asking about it.

Next is **Barrier Beach** where very new and very modern **Moyyen House by the Sea** (☎ 30026; www.moyyan.com; B&B d 28,000Vt) is cool dark tim-ber and glass over white sand and blue water. Moyyen's sparkling restaurant is open for lunch and dinner (mains 3000Vt).

Further along you'll see a turnoff to **Oyster Island** (Malwepe). Summon the boat by banging on the gas cylinder, then kick back with a drink and a meal on the sweep of deck. Chef Tasso cooks up a storm (mains 950Vt to 2500Vt; open lunch and dinner). You must try the oysters because, guess what, there's a stack of oysters.

On the island, stay at **our pick** **Oyster Island Resort** (☎ /fax 36283; www.oysterislandresort.com; B&B d/family 6500/10,000Vt). Lie in your cute dumpling of a luxury bungalow, gaze through rosewood-framed windows onto a serene waterfront and dream about the deep-water and lobster fishing and blue-hole canoeing you're about to enjoy.

Back on the mainland, stop at **Matevulu Blue Hole** (Santo's largest) as you must take a plunge here. It's something unique, looking through crystal at your pretty blue legs. Climb up the old tree for a dive. Scuba-diving photography is interesting here, as the blue filter produces unusual effects.

Another 2km north is the home of **Lunar Circus Vanuatu** (☎ 37966; www.turtlebayresort.vu), where Matt and Patricia hold shows and weekly circus classes (weeklong children's school holiday workshop is 20,000Vt). Such a buzz (see boxed text, p598).

our pick **Turtle Bay Resort** (☎ 37988; www.turtlebayresort.vu; dm/d/family 2000/8000/9000Vt; 🖳) is lovely and old and has been revived. Dorm rooms are bright and cheery, private units look fantastic, there's deck chairs by the water, canoes and bikes, a long timber bar, private verandahs, lush gardens and a weekly cinema night. Holiday territory. Call in for a meal (dinner mains from 1100Vt to 1900Vt) and ask about the circus dates. Covering 220 hectares, **Loru Conservation Area** (admission 500Vt) contains one of the last patches of lowland forest remaining on Santo's east coast. There are several excellent **nature walks**, many **coconut crabs** and a **bat cave**, which the villagers use as a cyclone shelter. If you've come without a guide, ask for one at Kole 1 village. For more details, see www.positiveearth.org.

In a beautiful coastal setting is lovely **Lonnoc Beach**, all white and turquoise, with stunning views of **Elephant Island**. A **guide** (500Vt) from Lonnoc village will take you to visit local gardens, to Hog Harbour or to swim at a blue hole. Go out in a canoe to fish or see turtles, or take a half-day **boat trip** (1000Vt) to Elephant Island.

Each traditional bungalow at **Lonnoc Beach Bungalows & Restaurant** (☎ 36141, 5416456; PO Box 293; B&B s/d 3380/5600Vt) has a cute porch, but there's electricity only in the restaurant. Spend your evenings at the bar, or take a kerosene lamp down to the beach. Tough choice. The restaurant (mains 400Vt to 1200Vt) is open from 6.30am till 9pm and serves local and Western meals and cold drinks.

The road past Lonnoc Beach ends at **Champagne Beach** where photographers love to take photos. It's an easy 10-minute saunter across, and you're likely to have the horseshoe of fine white sand and turquoise water to yourself (entry 500Vt per adult and child).

Keep heading north to **Port Olry**, a fishing village where you can snorkel, learn basket weaving, walk to a deserted island (well, it's an island some of the time), bush walk and stay at **Little Paradise of Port Olry** (☎ 37661, 7743776; B&B s/d 2000/2500Vt) bungalow. Ask for Tine Viney or Tarcisius.

Getting There & Away

There's a daily minibus service along the east coast (see p596). Taxis cost about 2000Vt (shared) to Oyster Island, 4000Vt to Lonnoc Beach.

THE CENTRAL ROAD
Millennium Cave

Trek and trudge through the jungle, across creeks, along bamboo bridges and through cascades to this massive cave, 20m wide and 50m high. Climb down a bamboo ladder, and through a rocky pool dodging cascades and little bats, then out into the sunlight and into icy water to zap down the rapids on a kid's blow-up floaty thingy past amazing towering rocks, gorgeous rainforest and waterfalls. Scramble out all wet and shivery to climb back up to your bus. It's a totally awesome experience.

VANUATU

FIGHTING TOGETHER

Crown of thorns starfish have washed down onto Vanuatu's precious coral gardens. All dive operators and volunteers are working together, removing the destructive pests. Big Blue Dive devised the most effective removal process. You ease the starfish off the coral with a hooked wire and flick it into a bag. Full bags are taken ashore and the very smelly starfish buried. Thousands have been removed. See www.tellusconsultants.com/Thread/ACANTH.HTM.

New Zealand volunteers (www.forestandbird.org.nz) are trying to remove the *Merremia peltata*, or big-leaf vine, which strangles Vanuatu's tall trees. To date, it involves cutting the runners, which are perhaps 30m long with many branches, and putting poison on the cuts. There has to be a quicker way. See the vine on www.hear.org/pier/species/merremia_peltata.htm for more.

Big Bay Highway

This 28km road takes you to Malao village on Big Bay, past the magnificent panorama of the rugged **Cumberland Ranges** as you wind down to the fast-flowing Lape River. The river is often ankle-deep over the causeway – there are some large swimming holes and a picnic spot on the western bank. It's best to hire a car with a driver because he'll know the roads. There are no signposts, mostly everyone gets lost, and there are freaky parts, like at the edge of a high scarp where you enter the Vatthe Conservation Area. The track is one way, steep and drops off sharply so there's nowhere to pull over. Honk your horn as you descend to warn traffic coming up.

Vatthe Conservation Area

This **protected area** (www.positiveearth.org /bungalows/SANMA/vatthe_ca.htm) covers about 2720 hectares, stretching along the coast from north of Matantas to the Jordan River (one of Vanuatu's largest rivers), and inland to the top of a 400m-high limestone scarp. It is Vanuatu's only extensive alluvial and limestone forest and is on a list for World Heritage nomination. Special treats are the **forest walks** (guides per half/full day 1000/1500Vt) or you could take a two-day trek to the highest point on the scarp. The forests are dominated by tall trees, many with large buttress roots, including strandline forest, swamp forest, coral limestone forest, savannah and River Jordan riparian vegetation.

Then there's **birdwatching**: see most of Vanuatu's native land and freshwater bird species, including the endangered Santa Cruz ground-dove, the mound building megapode and the chestnut-bellied kingfisher.

Tours can be arranged through the information centre, on the left as you arrive. Ask here for Chief Solomon or Puriti, who have **Bay of Illusions Yacht Club** (☎ 7767279, 5414352; knr.baereleo@vanuatu.com.vu; B&B 2200Vt) with two new bungalows near the beach at **Matantas**. Camping is also available (toilets provided). Tasty Western meals are 1000Vt to 1400Vt, but bring your own food as well.

A truck to Matantas from Luganville costs 9000Vt (one way), but the daily minibus to Sara Village leaves Unity Shell Petrol Station, Luganville, at 3pm (500Vt), then a truck on to Matantas is only another 2000Vt. If you're staying at Lonnoc, ask Wendy to arrange a day trip for you.

PENTECOST

pop 15,500 / area 438 sq km

Pentecost has the *naghol* (land diving), the most remarkable custom in all of Melanesia, where men make spectacular leaps of courage from high towers as a gift to the gods, to ensure a bountiful yam harvest. Pentecost also has great scenery, significant waterfalls and lots of festivals and ceremonies. Mostly everyone lives along the west coast, which has

---

THE LAND DIVERS OF PENTECOST

The men of Pentecost spend many weeks building towers by binding tree trunks, saplings and branches to a tall tree with vines. The towers are the shape of a man up to 35m high. The tower sighs as it bends in the wind; you'll sigh, as you see the men make their spectacular leaps to ensure a successful harvest.

Each diver carefully selects his own liana vines, then an experienced elder checks to ensure that it's strong and elastic enough. The soil in front of the tower is cleared of rocks, then loosened. Fathers teach their young sons to dive from their shoulders. Boys practise diving from boulders into the sea. At age eight they are circumcised; then they can make their first jump.

Between 10 and 20 males per village will dive. Each man prepares in turn while his friends tie his vines. The women sing and dance below. As he raises his hands he tells the crowd his most intimate thoughts; the people stop their singing and dancing, and stand quietly – these could be his last words.

Finally the diver claps his hands, crosses his arms and leans forward. In slow motion, falling, he arches his back. The platform breaks away. Snap. The vines abruptly stop him. Only his hair will touch the soil, to fertilise the yam crop. The crowd roars its appreciation, dancing, stomping and whistling in tribute.

It is such a celebration. The colour and sounds add to the atmosphere: men wearing small red-dyed *namba*, clearly visible from so high above; women wearing white grass skirts made from wild hibiscus, spinning and twirling – a sea of swirling white grass.

high rainfall, attributed to local rainmakers. ceptical Westerners say it's high because the land's mountainous spine catches the southasterlies, causing precipitation.

Penama Day is celebrated on 15 September, vith *kastom* dances and feasts. Dances are reat fun with feathers, exotic headgear and ange-seed anklets that make rhythmic rattles. small red pandanus mats are worn and are lso used as currency, as presents at births or unerals and when grades are taken.

TRANSPORT

Lonorore airfield, down south, is very new and very long, and aircraft can now land n any weather, a great relief to travellers. **Air Vanuatu** (☎ 23748) flies in five times a week, and four times to Sara airfield in the north. You can drive along the west coast road, a set of ruts hanging onto cliff faces (30,000Vt), if your nerves and fingernails are made of steel.

Pentecost has good protection from the southeastern trade winds along the west coast, with many anchorages and landing places. Panas and Loltong are popular.

NORTH PENTECOST

Just 1km northwest of Sara airfield at **Nazareth** is Lini Memorial College, where Vanuatu's first prime minister is buried. There are also stores, an NBV bank and a market. If you need to stay overnight, there's the **Ezekiel Bonga Guesthouse** (☎ 38388; Nazareth; beds 1800Vt) above a shop, with a squat toilet down through the village (neat arrangement, especially on a wet night). It's self-catering.

Loltong Restaurant (meals 300Vt), 10km south in the island's principal administrative centre, sells island-style meals, kava and handicrafts. Loltong has an excellent anchorage, and you can hire taxis here.

A bit further south, John runs **Bangaware Bungalow** (☎ 38126; www.pentecostisland.net/bangaware; Nambwarangiut; s 1500Vt), attractive traditional accommodation with a water-seal toilet along a path. The bungalow is beside a marine reserve that's great for **snorkelling**.

SOUTH PENTECOST

A sandy beach extends 12km from just before Lonorore airfield south to Ranputor. Coconut plantations occupy the narrow plains between mountains and sea. The south is the home of the *naghol*, and you can witness this amazing

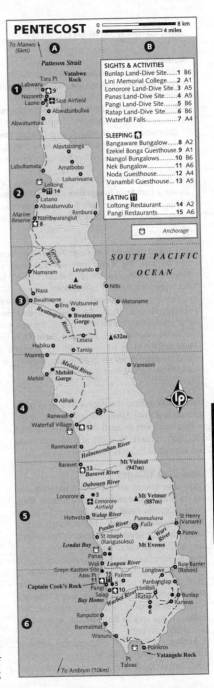

VANUATU

SOME OTHER NORTHERN ISLANDS

Ambae

Ambae has **Mt Lombenben** (1496m) on the rim of a semiactive volcano that rumbles dynamically. A cone rose out of blue **Lake Manaro Lakua**, one of its famous crater lakes, in 2005, creating world news, then went back down. Hot and lime-green **Lake Vui** also sends volcanologists into a frenzy whenever it boils. **Lake Manaro Ngoru**, the third crater lake, is dry with a central cold-water spring. All in a blanket of mist amid the finest cloudforest in Vanuatu.

Located down south, the colourful **Toa Guesthouse** (☎ 38405; Ndui Ndui; dm/s/tw 1500/2000/3500Vt) has traditional bungalows. It's a six-hour slog up through the cloudforest, then an amazing night camping by the lakes. Jeffrey has tents, or you could bring your own. Transfers are 2000Vt, and meals cost 500Vt.

Lake access from the north is a four-hour trek along a maintained road. Stay at comfortable **Duviara Last Stop Bungalows** (☎ 36436; dpvuhu@yahoo.com; Ambanga; s 1500Vt), in the cloudforest, where workshops are run. It recently won the Commonwealth silver medal for conservation. Guides and entry fees cost 1000Vt each, transfers 5000Vt, meals 800Vt.

Maewo

The 'Island of Water' has rivers, hot springs, deep cold pools, magnificent waterfalls and water-taro terraces. **Big Water waterfall** is thought of as the Eighth Wonder of the World. **Lua ete Salgolo Guesthouse** (☎ 38342; Naone; s 1500Vt) is a cute little place from where you can explore Big Water. Ask for Paul or Hamileon.

Down south, at **Sanasom**, is magnificent **Hole of the Moon cave** and **Malangauliuli**, a cave with spectacular petroglyphs. Chief Jonah, kastom owner of the cave, runs the **Sanasom Bungalows** (☎ 38353; Sanasom; s incl meals 3500Vt). Transport from Naone is around 5000Vt.

At the southern tip, **Asanvari Yacht Club Bungalow, Bar & Restaurant** (☎ 38239; Asanvari; beds 1000Vt) sits on a picture-perfect bay near a 30m waterfall. Chief Nelson arranges cave tours and transport from north Pentecost (6000Vt), a 10km trip across violent seas. Meals (500Vt to 950Vt) are served from 7.30am to 7pm.

celebration during the naghol season at most weekends during April, May and June.

For transport around the south, ring **John** (☎ 38444) or **Jonas** (☎ 38308). A truck ride from the airport to Salap is 4000Vt.

Land-Dive Villages

Land-dive towers are erected in **Lonorore** and on the hills between **Panas** and nearby **Wali**. Further south, **Pangi** and **Salap** spread along the stony shore of Bay Homo. Pangi is the tourist hub of south Pentecost. It has a kava bar, ANZ bank, clinic and John's store where you can hire taxis and speedboats.

Across the island from Salap is **Ranwas**, a charming village perched on a high ridge with distant views of the sea. From here a slippery path heads north to Bunlap and Baie Barrier. **Ratap**, on the way to Ranwas, has very traditional land diving.

Bunlap (☎ 38834) is a large, full-kastom village on a steep hillside, again with very traditional land diving, two ceremonial dancing areas ringed with coral stones, and traditional leaf houses built so low that their roofs almost touch the ground.

SIGHTS & ACTIVITIES

Luke Fargo, in Pangi, can arrange a tour to the **land diving** (☎ 38444, 38120; entry 8000Vt) but many tourists come on day trips from Vila. **Packages** (www.vanuatutourism.com/vanuatu/cms/en/culture/nagol2008.tml; 1 day/overnight from 35,000/42,000Vt) are available. The VTO (p564) in Efate can provide a dive program, and Efate's Vanuatu Cultural Centre (p567) has information on the very traditional diving at Bunlap.

If you're very fit, you're able to **hike** from Salap to Bunlap, spend a night at Bunlap, then return along the 4WD road straight across the bottom of the island. Walking conditions are difficult and strenuous; ask in the village for a guide. You can't follow a map. Paths and roads change constantly because of jungle growth, earth movements and weather.

Gaua (Santa Maria)

Gaua offers spectacular hikes, including a two-day test around the island's three major sights: pretty **Lake Letas**, one of the largest freshwater lakes in the Pacific; Mt Garet (797m), a semiactive volcano; and fabulous **Siri Falls**. Wind and climb up to the lake and canoe across to the volcano, a sulphurous mess that seeps orange into the lake. It's well worth the effort. Then it's a vicious trek down to the falls, 120m of roaring power pummelling to the sea.

Stay at the thatched two-bedroom **Wongrass Bungalow** (☎ 38504; s incl meals 3500Vt), near the airport. Charles will arrange tours to the crater lake (3500Vt), or water music at a *kastom* museum built meticulously by traditional methods (7000Vt).

Vanua Lava

Sola, the island's capital, is the centre for excellent walks, such as the glorious day's walk via Mosina across the plateau overlooking Vureas Bay, through water-taro gardens, over streams and rapids to **Waterfall Bay**, where spectacular **Sasara Falls** tumbles over the cliff into the bay. A speedboat from Sola to Waterfall Bay costs around 18,000Vt return.

In Sola, stay at **Leumerous Guesthouse** (☎ 38556, 38823; Sola; s incl meals 2500Vt, camping 500Vt) where thatched bungalows sit along a garden path. On the beach is the **Leumerous Yachtclub** (meals 300/900Vt), everybody's favourite spot. Enjoy breakfast, lunch or dinner with yachties and locals.

At Waterfall Bay, only minutes from the falls, is **Waterfall Bay Yacht Club** (☎ 38550; meals 400Vt) in a grand bungalow with artefacts and handicrafts for sale. Stay overnight at **Waterfall Bungalows** (incl meals 3000Vt). The rumbling waterfall will lull you to sleep.

Torres Islands

Dazzling **white-sand beaches** are the rule, with good **surfing**, especially when the trade winds are blowing. There's excellent **snorkelling** on most islands: **Linua**, which is unpopulated except for the tourist accommodation; **Loh**, across a tidal sandbank; **Tegua** and **Hiu** to the north; and **Toga** where most of the people live. Everyone gets around in outrigger canoes. The delightful **Kamilisa Guesthouse** (☎ 38573, 38565; Linua; s incl meals 2900Vt) is in a delicate rainforest, right on the lagoon. Butterfly lovers will find this place amazing.

Take **adventure walks** to waterfalls and bananas and the stone ruins of a feasting hall, where 100 people were killed by the eel spirit. Other tours include visits to villages to see *kastom* dances. Or walk up a river with your host and help him catch river prawns. How fresh will they be! **Swimming** and **snorkelling** are safe in Bay Homo because of the reef.

North of the airstrip is magnificent **Waterfall Falls**, tumbling down behind Waterfall Village into pretty rock pools.

From Salap to Bunlap costs 8000Vt return by speedboat or truck.

SLEEPING & EATING

Nangol Bungalows (☎ 38444, ☎ /fax 38448; www.rekvanuatu.com; s/d incl meals 5600/9000Vt, camping 500Vt) Chief Willy has sadly passed away but his sons re managing Nangol, just south of Salap. It has a relaxing setting by the bay with several spacious bungalows and good shared facilities. An island feast with a local string band can be arranged for a group.

Nek Bungalow (☎ 38012, 38357; Pangi; s incl meals 3000Vt) A well-maintained bungalow of bamboo and sago palm on the beach near the store and restaurants. It can sleep eight people. Ask for Clement and he'll look after you!

Noda Guesthouse (☎ 38141, 38303; www.pentecostisland.net/noda; Waterfall Village; s incl meals 2500Vt) A great place to stay while you play in the cascades. The house has four bedrooms and electricity in the evenings, and Chief Zachari is a gracious host.

Vanambil Guesthouse (☎ 38308; Baravet; B&B 3000Vt) A short drive north of the airstrip, the guest house has four rooms, all screened, and a pleasant garden setting. Jonas arranges landdiving, snorkel, waterfall and cave tours.

Sara and Alice have **restaurants** (☎ 38120; meals 200-300Vt; ⏱ 6am-9pm Mon-Fri) in Pangi. Both women cook the one dish and stay open till it's all sold. No knowing what your next meal will be, but it will be fresh and tasty. Transport from Lonorore airfield to Pangi by truck or boat is 4000Vt.

VANUATU

VANUATU DIRECTORY

ACCOMMODATION

There's only one camping ground around Vanuatu, and that's situated near the volcano on Tanna. But many bungalow owners will let you use their grounds for a minimal fee. You'll need to ask the local chief for permission if you want to pitch your tent anywhere else.

Guest house or bungalow? A guest house is often a concrete building with a kitchen. Bungalows are usually thatched cubby houses with pandanus-leaf walls, set in gorgeous surroundings. They both cost between around 1800Vt and 10,000Vt, which may include meals served in a separate hut (bathrooms and toilet are also separate). But as these are humid tropical islands covered with jungle, you will need to be prepared for the unexpected, so bring emergency food, toilet paper, earplugs and torch.

There's an impressive selection of resorts and hotels in and around Vila, and there are a few on Santo and Tanna. Many lovely hotel rooms cost under 7000Vt, while luxury resorts start at around 18,000Vt per double.

In this chapter budget accommodation is under 7000Vt; midrange refers to accommodation between 7000Vt and 20,000Vt; and top end is over 20,000Vt.

ACTIVITIES

It's easy to be very lazy in Vanuatu, but it's also difficult to ignore the excellent diving, snorkelling, hiking, horse riding, fishing, sailing and extreme sports. You'll find you're easily immersed in the country's culture and natural environment.

Diving

Vanuatu's scuba sites include several world-class dives (see p79). Vila has a great range of underwater topography and a Corsair WWII fighter plane wreck near Pele, amid fan corals and healthy reefs, while Santo has USS *President Coolidge* among others. *The Lady and the President,* by Peter Stone, covers the tragedy of war and delights of scuba diving.

For details of dive operators, see the text in the Efate (p569) and Santo (p598) sections.

Fishing

World-standard game fishing, river fishing and spear fishing are on offer in Vanuatu; if it lives in water you can enjoy chasing it, with string and a bent pin or the latest hi-tech gear. Always check who owns the water, though, and pay them first. See p569 and p597 for operators.

Hiking

The country has many fine walks, including strenuous two- to five-day hikes on

Erromango, Ambrym, Santo, Pentecost, Vanua Lava, Gaua and Malekula. You can organise walks yourself (guides cost between 1000Vt and 3000Vt a day) or through your host or a tour operator. Don't set out alone with a map – sorry, all roads change dramatically during cyclones and mudslides or disappear under a metre-high layer of vine. Without a local guide you'll quickly be up you know where.

Always wear long pants in the jungle to protect yourself from stinging plants. Sandals and runners are not suitable for jungle treks or volcano climbs.

Swimming

Although the swimming close to Vila is not brilliant, further afield there are glorious beaches: white-sand, black-sand, volcanic rock or coral. Sharks, stonefish and strong currents are a danger in some areas. Always seek local advice before plunging in.

Yachting

Charter a cruising trimaran with skipper and crew:

Sailaway Cruises (☎ 23802, 25155; www.adventure vanuatu.com; Port Vila) Has a 12.5m trimaran, *Golden Wing* (75,000Vt per 24 hours).

Bali Hai Charters (☎ 5422126; dennyswan@hotmail .com; PO Box 1011) Has a 11m trimaran, *Witchitit* (60,000Vt per 24 hours).

BUSINESS HOURS

Government offices are generally open from Monday to Friday from 7.30am to 11.30am, and 1.30pm to 4.30pm, sometimes on Saturday morning as well. Shops trade from 7.30am to around 6pm; only some close for the midday siesta. Saturday shopping finishes at 11.30am, although Chinese stores remain open all weekend.

CHILDREN

Children will enjoy the freedom of being in this laid-back environment. Encourage them to read *Vanuatu & New Caledonia* by Carol Jones before you go. It's a cheerful book, set out as postcards with lots of maps and photos.

EMBASSIES & CONSULATES
Vanuatu's Diplomatic Representatives

Vanuatu does not have embassies or consulates overseas. Honorary consuls:

Australia NSW (☎ 02-9597 4046); Victoria (☎ 03-9642 8888; australia_vanuatu@dfat.gov.au)
France (☎ 01 40 53 82 25; ambafra@vanuatu.com.vu)

Contact details for other consuls can be obtained from the **Foreign Affairs Department** (☎ 22347; www.vanuatugovernment.gov.vu; Port Vila).

Embassies & Consulates in Vanuatu

All the diplomatic representations to Vanuatu are in Vila.

Australia (Map p566; ☎ 22777; www.vanuatu.embassy .gov.au; KPMG House, rue Pasteur) High commission.
China (Map p566; ☎ 24877; rue d'Auvergne) Embassy.
France (Map p566; ☎ 22353; fax 22695; Lini Hwy) Embassy.
New Zealand (Map p566; ☎ 22933; kiwi@vanuatu.vu; Lini Hwy) High commission.

FESTIVALS & EVENTS

There are so many festivals and activities; these are examples only:

Jon Frum Day Prayers and flowers are offered in the church at Sulphur Bay on Tanna, followed by a flag-raising ceremony and military parade, where men march with bamboo rifles. 15 February.
Yam Festival Dancing and feasting in the villages to praise the harvest. April.
Naghol A spectacular land-diving ritual held in several villages on Pentecost. Weekends April to July.
Island Relays Join a team to race around Efate, or across Tanna to Mt Yasur volcano. June and July.
Ocean Swims In Vila and Luganville. Mid-June.
Horse-Racing Carnivals Port Vila Race Day is big: eight races including the Vanuatu Cup. Tanna races are held at old Burton airport and on the Mt Yasur ash plains, an awesome sight. July to September.
Independence Day Every village has a celebration. Vila has the widest range of activities: sporting events, military parade, fun stalls at Independence Park; canoe and yacht races in the bay; string-band competitions; *kastom* dancing. 30 July.
Agriculture Show See animals, art and lots of food stalls. Mid-August.
Circumcision Ceremonies Dancing, colourful costumes, face and body paint, and a grand feast celebrate the rite of passage of a boy. Tourists are welcome to watch, but take note of where you're allowed to walk. August to September.
Nekowiar and Toka Ceremony A three-day extravaganza of dancing and feasting on Tanna, while villages cement relationships and arrange marriages. The place and date is only announced close to the time. September and October every three years.
Fest'Napuan A major outdoor music concert with big-name local bands and international guests. November.

VANUATU

Two vaguely useful calendars can be found at www.vanuatutourism.com/vanuatu /cms/en/activities/calendar2007.html and www.south-pacific.travel/spto/export/sites /spto/destinations/vanuatu/calendar.shtml.

INTERNET ACCESS

You can access the internet in Vila, Luganville and Lenakel, but you'll have on-line withdrawal on the other islands.

INTERNET RESOURCES

Rocket Guide to Vanuatu (www.vanuatu-vacations .com) Up-to-date info on everything.

South Pacific Travel Organisation (www.spto.org /spto/cms/destinations/vanuatu) Fairly comprehensive listings.

Vanuatu A to Z (www.vanuatuatoz.com) All you wanted to know, but it has aged a bit.

Vanuatu Hotel Directory (www.vanuatu-hotels.vu) Local online booking service, with information about the country and useful links.

Vanuatu Travel (www.vanuatutravel.com.au) Updated fairly often.

Volcano Live (www.volcanolive.com) The latest on Vanuatu volcanoes.

VTO (www.vanuatutourism.com) Stacks of information and links to local agents and online booking services.

Wantok Environment Centre (www.positiveearth .org) Great for outer island bungalows and ecotourism projects. You've got to love the section on Vanuatu's birds complete with their call-sounds.

Wikipedia (www.en.wikipedia.org/wiki/History_of _Vanuatu) In-depth information on all aspects of Vanuatu's history.

MONEY

Vanuatu currency is the vatu (Vt), which floats against a basket of currencies including the US dollar, so it is reasonably stable.

The three commercial banks in Vanuatu are ANZ, Westpac and the local NBV. All have their offices in central Vila and branches in Luganville. ANZ has two ATMs in Vila, one in Luganville and one at each international airport; Westpac has one in Vila.

Duty-free shops, restaurants and hotels in Vila generally accept credit cards, or cash and travellers cheques in Australian or US dollars. There are also private moneychangers in Vila and Luganville.

Take plenty of vatu everywhere outside Vila and Luganville as you won't be able to change

---

HOW MUCH?

- **Local newspaper:** 100Vt
- **Hair extensions:** 15,000Vt
- **Waterfront 600 sq metre block:** 6.5 million vatu
- **Hand-carved outrigger canoe:** 3000Vt
- **Car hire:** town/island use 5500/7000Vt
- **1L petrol:** 168Vt
- **1L bottled water:** 120Vt
- **Bottle of Tusker beer:** 350-450Vt
- **Souvenir T-shirt:** 1800Vt
- **Quarter chicken, fries and salad:** 520Vt

---

foreign currencies or access any accounts, not even over the counter at a bank.

TELEPHONE & FAX

There are no area codes in Vanuatu.

International Calls

The code for international calls out of Vanuatu is ☎ 00. Vanuatu's incoming code is ☎ 678.

Calls to Australia, NZ, New Caledonia and Fiji cost 133/108Vt per minute peak/off-peak; calls further afield are 216/168Vt. Peak times are 6am to 6pm Monday to Friday.

Many larger hotels have IDD phones, but you cannot make international reverse-charge calls from Vanuatu.

Mobile Phones

Vanuatu is on GSM digital and has two networks: **Telecom Vanuatu** (Map p566; www.smile.com .vu), and **Digicel** (Map p566; www.digicelvanuatu.com); both these have offices in Vila. Almost the entire country is now covered. Buy a smile SIM card package (3000Vt including 2500Vt of calls), or a Digicel phone with card for 2000Vt. You can buy top-up cards everywhere. Local calls cost 30Vt for a minute.

Phonecards & Fax

All public phones need a phonecard, and there are six available, from 450Vt to 2700Vt. It's best to always keep some with you, so stock up in Vila or Luganville (they make excellent gifts if you buy too many).

Local and international fax facilities are available at Vila's post office and the Telecom Vanuatu office in Luganville. The cheapest time (off-peak) to make a domestic call is between 6pm and 6am Monday to Friday and all weekend.

TIME
Vanuatu time is GMT/UMT plus 11 hours. Noon in Vila is 1am in London, 6pm in Los Angeles and 1pm in Auckland.

TOURIST INFORMATION
The **VTO** (Map p566; ☎ 22813; www.vanuatutourism.com; Lini Hwy; ☼ 7.30am-4.30pm Mon-Fri, 8am-noon Sun) has a very informative website and includes details of Vanuatu's overseas representatives.

VISAS
Every visitor must have a passport valid for a further four months and an onward ticket. Entry visas are not required for nationals of the British Commonwealth and EU. Check at www.vanuatutourism.com/visa _info.htm to see whether you need one. You're allowed an initial stay of up to 30 days, extended one month at a time for up to four months.

Nonexempt visitors should contact the **Principal Immigration Officer** (☎ 22354; PMB 092, Port Vila) to organise their visa application (2500Vt fee). This must be finalised *before* you arrive.

Visa extensions require leaving your passport and onward ticket with the immigration department in Vila or Luganville for about three days.

TRANSPORT IN VANUATU

GETTING THERE & AWAY
Air
The following airlines have regular scheduled flights to Vanuatu.
Air Pacific (Map p566; ☎ 22836; www.airpacific.com; South Pacific Travel, Lini Hwy, Port Vila)
Air Vanuatu (Map p566; ☎ 23848; www.airvanuatu.com; rue de Paris, Port Vila)
Aircalin (Map p566; ☎ 22019; www.aircalin.nc; Lini Hwy, Port Vila)
Pacific Blue (Map p566; ☎ 22836; www.flypacificblue.com; South Pacific Travel, Lini Hwy, Port Vila)

Both Air Vanuatu and Pacific Blue operate direct flights from Brisbane and Sydney to Port Vila. Return fares from Brisbane/Sydney start from A$600/800.

Air Vanuatu also has direct flights from Melbourne (from A$800) and Auckland (from NZ$800) to Vila, plus flights via Nadi (Fiji), Honiara (Solomon Islands) and Noumea (New Caledonia). And, oh joy, it now has direct flights to Espiritu Santo from Brisbane and Sydney.

Air Pacific and Aircalin have flights from Nadi and Noumea. For other Pacific islands you need to get connecting flights in NZ, Fiji or New Caledonia.
Qantas Airways (www.qantas.com.au) Acts as sales agent for Air Vanuatu outside Australia, NZ, Fiji and New Caledonia (Air Vanuatu has its own offices in those countries).
South Pacific Travel (Map p566; ☎ 22836; spts@vanuatu.com.vu;, Lini Hwy, Port Vila; ☼ 8am-5pm Mon-Fri, 8-11am Sat) in Vila is an agent for Pacific Blue, Air Pacific and Air Vanuatu.

AIRPORTS
Efate's Bauerfield International Airport has an ANZ ATM, an NBV branch for currency exchange, a cafe and duty-free shopping. If you haven't organised accommodation, **Vanuatu Standby Accommodation** (www.vanuatustandbyaccommodation.com), located in a booth at the airport, can arrange it on the spot, and its website is full of information and useful links.

Santo's Pekoa International Airport has an ANZ ATM, cafe and duty-free shop.

Sea
MV Havannah (☎ 25225, 29967; carvanuatu@vanuatu.com.vu) sails out of Noumea for Vila, Malekula and Santo about every six weeks (adult/child 13,000/9500Vt). Vila to Santo or Lakatoro costs 6000Vt. Ask for Frank Maki.

Vila hosts P&O's *Pacific Sky* and *Pacific Princess* about once or twice a fortnight. **South Sea Shipping** (Map p566; ☎ 22205; southsea@vanuatu.com.vu) in Vila is the agent.

The best source of general information on yachting matters is **Yachting World Vanuatu** (Map p566; ☎ /fax 23273, VHF16; www.yachtingworld-vanuatu.com; Lini Hwy). It has a sea-wall tie up and diesel dock; it'll arrange customs and quarantine inspections to your buoy; there's hot showers, wi-fi and the Waterfront Bar & Grill is next door.

VANUATU

The authorised ports of entry for touring yachts are Vila, Luganville (Santo), Lenakel (Tanna) or Sola (Vanua Lava). There are hefty fines if you make landfall in or depart from Vanuatu until customs and immigration have been cleared. The landing fee is 7000Vt for the first 30 days and 100Vt per day thereafter. Quarantine clearance is 3000Vt.

Port Vila Boatyard (Map p563; ☎ 23417; www.port vilaboatyard.com) has many amenities and facilities in sheltered Pontoon Bay.

GETTING AROUND
Air
Air Vanuatu's domestic wing offers scheduled flights to 28 airfields using its fleet of 20-seat Twin Otters, a 44-seat ATR and a tiny nine-seat Islander. While the service is generally reliable, it's best not to arrange connecting flights on the same day. You can download the flight schedule from www.airvanuatu .com, and book Santo and Tanna flights on-line. Email requests for flights to other islands then purchase tickets at **Air Vanuatu office** (Map p566; ☎ 23848; www.airvanuatu.com; rue de Paris, Vila; ⏱ 7.30am-5pm Mon-Fri) or the **Luganville office** (Map p597; ☎ 36421; Main St, Luganville). Show your international flight ticket with Air Vanuatu/Pacific Blue to receive a 20/10% discount. Children to age 12/students receive a 50/25% discount (take your student card).

It pays to book well in advance, and you must reconfirm your flights.

Unity Airlines (Map p566; ☎ 24475, 23242; www .unity-airlines.com; Nambawan, Port Vila; ⏱ 7.30am-5pm Mon-Fri, 8am-noon Sat & Sun) flies tour groups to outer islands and is available for charter.

Boat
CANOE & SPEEDBOAT
When ni-Vanuatu talk of speedboats, they mean outboard-powered dinghies. Canoes are dugout craft with outriggers, paddle-powered Speedboat prices are high, so it's best to wait fo a scheduled service rather than charter.

PASSENGER BOAT
Fresh Cargo (Map p566; ☎ 7760660, 5553670; freshcarg vanuatu@gmail.com) carries 70 people in a substan tial catamaran. It heads north from Port Vil on Efate to Epi (4500Vt), Malekula (6500Vt and Santo (7500Vt) twice a week and is avail able for charter.

Bus & Taxi
Minibuses with a red 'B' on their number plates operate in Vila, Luganville and north east Malekula. They don't run fixed routes bu zoom to your destination. Flag them down b' the roadside.

Taxis in Vila and Luganville are mostly sedans, but elsewhere they're 4WD truck with a red 'T' on their number plates. Charges depend on distance, but also on the state o the road. Ask your driver for a price. It wil be honest and reasonable. A short trip in Vila might cost 400Vt, but a day charter will cos between 8000Vt and 12,000Vt. Local taxi meet flights at island airstrips, but may no be around on Sunday, public holidays or when there's no fuel on the island.

Car & Motorcycle
You can hire cars, 4WDs and scooters in Vila (p565) and Luganville (p596). The minimum age for renting a car is 23; for a scooter it's 17 provided you've held a valid driving licence for over a year. You don't need an International Driving Licence.

There's a speed limit of 50km/h in Vila and Luganville, but out of town you'll be doing about 5km/h because of the impossible road. Vehicles drive on the right; seatbelts are not compulsory.

Wallis & Futuna

Wallis and who? No it's not Gromet. These two little-known volcanic specks lie smack in the centre of Polynesia/Melanesia far from the modern world and its claymation comedies. Wallis and Futuna's French-funded economy allows islanders to drive flashy 4WDs to and from their taro fields and enjoy satellite TV at night after a beer or some kava, but the culture and its intricate *coutume* (customs) have remained remarkably intact. Catholicism, however, is deeply intertwined with every part of daily life.

The population is equal parts proud and protective of their way of life and, as long as the airfares and cost of living stay as high as they are (this place makes Tahiti seem cheap), it's not likely to receive heaps of honeymooners or package tourists any time soon. Movements for independence are few: the hospitals, schools and highly paid government jobs are all welcome enough additions that the people don't mind putting up with a few handfuls of French expats.

Wallis and Futuna, which lie 230km away from each other, are linked through French colonialism, period. Wallis has ancestral connections with Tonga, while Futuna traces its roots to Samoa. This is evident in the languages, which are quite different, although mutually comprehensible, as well as the Samoan-like tapa designs of the Futunans and the Tongan-influenced designs found on Wallis. The two islands remain competitive with each other, but Wallis, being more populous and the centre of government, retains the upper hand.

HIGHLIGHTS

- Visit Wallis' paradisaical lagoon islets like **Île Fenua Fo'ou** (p617)
- Gaze down the steep walls of Wallis' **Lake Lalolalo** (p617)
- Find shards of Lapita pottery in the king's path at **To'oga Toto** (p617) on Wallis
- Marvel at the imposing tower and graceful tapa decorations at **Pierre Chanel Church** (p619) on Futuna
- Laze around on a perfect, empty beach on **Alofi** (p618)

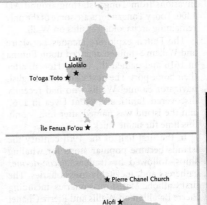

WALLIS & FUTUNA

CLIMATE & WHEN TO GO

It's not surprising that tropical Wallis and Futuna are markedly hot and humid. The sweatiest months are between November and March, while more temperate weather can be expected from April to October. Rain is likely at least 260 days of the year; Wallis averages an impressive 3m of rainfall a year, while Futuna gets a lush 4m on average. Both islands experience occasional cyclones (the season is May to October). The most destructive recorded cyclone was Raja, which ravaged the islands in 1986. For Pacific climate charts, see p627.

COSTS & MONEY

Wallis and Futuna use the Cour de Franc Pacifique (CFP), which is tied to the euro. There is only one ATM in the country and two banks. Costs are high, so be prepared to spend a minimum of around 14,000 CFP per day, excluding car hire or activities. All lodging choices fall into what could be considered 'midrange,' (between 10,000 and 16,000 CFP); there are no budget or top-end options. For more details, see p621.

HISTORY

Wallis and Futuna were populated when the great Lapita settlement wave moved across the Pacific between 1500 BC and 500 BC. Objects found on Futuna have been dated to 800 BC, although it's probable there are even older sites. Later Futuna came under the influence of Samoa, while Wallis suffered repeated invasions from Tonga, starting around AD 1400. Today Tongan forts are some of the only remaining archaeological sites on Wallis.

The Dutch explorers Jacques Le Maire and Willem Schouten chanced upon Futuna in 1616 and named the island Hoorn, after their home port. The next visitor, the English navigator Samuel Wallis who had recently discovered Tahiti, arrived at Uvea in 1767 and the island was named after him – only this time the name stuck,

In the first half of the 19th century the islands became popular stops for whaling ships, followed by traders, bêche-de-mer gatherers and, inevitably, missionaries. The first Catholic Marist missionaries, including Pierre Bataillon on Wallis and Pierre Chanel on Futuna, arrived in 1837. Chanel was murdered in 1841 by King Niuluki, an action that

WALLIS & FUTUNA FACTS

Capital city (and island) Mata'Utu (Wallis)
Population 13,480
Land area 247 sq km
International telephone code 681
Currency Cour de Franc Pacifique (CFP)
Languages Wallisian, Futunan and French
Greeting Malo (Wallisian), Maro (Futunan), Bonjour (French)
Website www.outre-mer.gouv.fr/?-wallis-et-futuna.html, in French

was to make Pierre Chanel the Pacific's first saint (see boxed text, opposite). In the second half of the century France gradually began to assume control of the islands, officially taking control over the years 1886 to 1888.

Things remained quiet until WWII when Wallis and Futuna was the only French colony to side with the collaborationist Vichy government, despite pressure from New Caledonia. The arrival of war in the Pacific ended that phase and in May 1942 the 5000 Wallisians suddenly found 2000 American forces coming ashore. Airstrips were built – the one at Hihifo is still in use today. At its peak there were 6000 Americans on Wallis and their presence deeply influenced traditional culture.

Wallis and Futuna officially became a French Territoire d'Outre-Mer (Overseas Territory) on 29th July 1961. These days there appears to be little local sentiment in favour of independence from France.

THE CULTURE
The National Psyche

Despite French presence and devout Catholicism, Wallis and Futuna are still very steeped in local tradition. Day-to-day life is dictated by a rigid social and class structure. The ruling class, the aliki, make all the decisions and hold most of the important jobs. The king is elected from one of the upper-class families by the aliki, and as long as he (or she as is sometimes the case on Wallis but never on Futuna) manages to represent the other classes in a satisfactory manner and share the wealth, they will win continued support. Because there are several royal, aliki families the power has always remained balanced, shifting to a new king and/or family when popular demand asked for a change. This remains true on Futuna (where there are two ings ruling two separate kingdoms), but the power structure on Wallis, where there are three major clans, is suffering.

Many islanders thought that King (Lavelua) Tomasi Kulimoetoke, who passed away in July 2007 after being in power for a record 48 years, had abused his position by making it near impossible for him to be ousted. When the Lavelua's named successor Kapiliele Faupala was made king in early 2008 after a six-month mourning period, tensions between the three clans intensified as the power remained with the same clan. Now there is talk of breaking up Wallis into three kingdoms, where each clan would each elect their own king.

The conflict in Wallis has not left Futuna unscathed. Only accessible via air from Wallis, when flights are cut Futuna becomes completely isolated from the world (as they often become in times of political turmoil on Wallis or in the event of cyclones and tropical depressions). A new airstrip on Futuna that was completed in late 2008 and can theoretically welcome international flights might bring an end to this isolation, but no international services have been planned yet.

Lifestyle

On Futuna you can still see the men meeting nightly in *fale fono* (village halls), dressed in *pareu* (a sarong-style garment) and having a cup of kava or three with their mates. While the men are drinking kava, the women stay in the house and play bingo. The days are hot and quiet, usually marked by working in the taro fields, fishing and napping, while early evening is an active time for playing rugby and *kirikiti* (the local game of cricket; see boxed text, p300). Most people still live in traditional *fale*, which are oblong, open-aired structures with woven roofs. Nowadays some families keep a modern house, but most will still sleep in their cool and breezy *fale*.

It's rare to see traditional *fale* on Wallis (except for in the village of Vailala) and kava drinking has been replaced almost entirely with beer drinking. Still, the lifestyle roots itself in family and tradition; people do not socialise much outside of their own extended families.

Population

The islands have a combined population of approximately 13,480, down 10% between 2003 and 2008, as many islanders left to find more opportunities overseas; most people who leave are of childbearing age, so birth rates on the islands have sharply declined. It's estimated that over 20,000 Wallisians and Futunans live in New Caledonia.

As well as the indigenous population, about 800 expats, mainly French, live on Wallis and 100 on Futuna.

RELIGION

Wallis and Futuna is very Catholic. A Sunday church service, usually at around 7am, is well worth going along to: lots of colour, lots of flowers and wonderful singing.

A huge number of often impressively large churches are found around the two islands, and even uninhabited Alofi and the small islands around the Wallis lagoon have chapels and oratories.

ST PIERRE CHANEL OF OCEANIA *Errol Hunt*

Pierre Louis Marie Chanel was born into a French peasant family in 1802, and trained as a priest. He embarked for the Pacific islands with the newly formed Catholic Society of Mary (Marist) in 1836 and, the following year, was the first missionary to set foot on Futuna. The ruling king, Niuluki, welcomed him.

As the missionaries gained converts and thus eroded the traditional power structure of the island, Niuluki became less keen on the newcomers. When Niuluki's own son asked to be baptised, the king issued an edict that the missionaries cease their activities. On 28 April 1841 a band of warriors, probably condoned by Niuluki, attacked Pierre Chanel and killed him.

Despite this (or perhaps because of it) the island soon became fully Catholic as other Marist priests took up the challenge.

Pierre Chanel was declared venerable in 1857, beatified in 1889 and finally canonised as the patron saint of Oceania in 1954. He is also recognised as the first martyr to lay his life down for Oceania (Rev John Williams had been dead for two years at this stage, but he was a Protestant – and that doesn't count).

BEST EATS

There aren't many eating options on these islands, but what's available is excellent. The only way to try the local pork-, fish- and taro-based cuisine is to get invited to someone's home or a celebration – that's unlikely (outsiders are rarely invited into islander's homes, let alone their parties) unless you're sticking around for a long time.

- Wade in the warm lagoon, enjoy the live music (on weekends) and eat masterfully prepared fresh fish at **Chez Patricia** (Wallis; p618).

- At **Somalama Park Hôtel restaurant** (Futuna; p620), way out in the middle of nowhere, a chef from China whips up fantastic northern Chinese-style food using the freshest ingredients.

Because of the strong religious devotion, dress in the islands is very conservative: both sexes keep their legs covered to the knees and women's dress is usually an ankle-length *pareu* with a matching loose-fitting blouse that reaches the elbows.

ARTS
Beautiful tapa (cloth made from the bark of mulberry and breadfruit trees) featuring traditional motifs is produced on both islands. Futuna tapa, called *siapo*, is marked with predominantly geometric patterns, whereas Wallis tapa, known as *gatu*, depicts land-and-sea designs (see p55).

Majestically large *tano'a*, the multilegged wooden bowls used for making kava, are carved on Futuna. Local woodcarving artists of note include Mika Initia, Suve Suva and Soane Hoatau.

The year's big event is on the eve of 14 July when a competition is held involving traditional dancers from several villages. The ancient *soamako* (war dances) are particularly impressive.

LANGUAGE
Virtually no English is spoken on Wallis and even less on Futuna, so being able to speak some French really helps.

Reflecting the historical connections of the islands, Wallisian is very similar to Tongan, and Futunan is similar to Samoan. See Language in

the Samoa (p302) and Tonga (p498) chapter for pronunciation tips, and Language in New Caledonia (p178) for French basics.

Wallisian basics
Hello (in the morning).	Malo te ma'uli.
Hello (later).	Malo te kataki.
Goodbye (to someone who is leaving).	'Alu la.
Goodbye (if you are leaving).	Nofo la.
How are you?	'E lelei pe?
I'm well.	Ei, 'e lelei pe.
Thank you.	Malo te ofa.
Yes.	Ei.
No.	Oho.

Futunan basics
Hello (in the morning).	Malo le ma'uli.
Hello (later).	Malo le kataki.
Goodbye (to someone who is leaving).	'Ano la.
Goodbye (if you are leaving).	Nofo la.
How are you?	E ke malie fa'i?
I'm well.	Lo, e kau malie fa'i.
Thank you.	Malo.
Yes.	Lo.
No.	E'ai.

ENVIRONMENT
The group consists of three major islands and about 20 islets, approximately 300km west of Samoa and 600km northeast of Fiji.

Wallis is a strikingly flat volcanic creation highlighted by several crater lakes. The highest bump on the landscape is Mt Lulu Fakahega (145m). Wallis' shallow lagoon can only be entered by one of four passes, the Honikulu Pass. About 15 small islets – some volcanic stumps, others classic sandy *motu* (islands) – are dotted around the lagoon.

Futuna and neighbouring Alofi lie 230km to the southwest of Wallis. The result of geological upheavals, they're much more mountainous than Wallis. Futuna's highest point is Mt Puke (524m); on Alofi it's Mt Kolofau (417m). Fringing reefs embrace both islands, while in places the mountainous interior plunges straight into the sea.

Both Wallis and Futuna sit close to the meeting point of the Pacific and the Indo-Australian continental plates and are subject to earthquake activity, most recently in the disastrous quake of 1993.

Deforestation has left only a fraction of the original forests intact (15% on Wallis, 30% on Futuna), but many of the once deforested areas are now covered by secondary growth or agricultural plantations. The problem is not ue to the use of wood as the main fuel source. he deforested, steep slopes of Futuna are articularly prone to erosion, and increased un-off poses a threat to coral reefs and vital sheries. On Alofi most of the tropical jungle ill stands.

WALLIS ISLAND

op 9,080 / area 77.9 sq km

Vhat Wallis lacks in lofty emerald peaks and early white beaches it makes up for with s outrageously clear-blue lagoon, weird rater lakes and extensive archaeological tes tucked back in the bush. It's a big, flat ingle of a place, where shiny 4WDs navi- ate the tangle of roads and traditional life is played out behind plain, modern cement walls. Head out to the lagoon where each fringing islet is dripping with empty beaches and visited only occasionally by smiling fish- erman or picnicking families. Put on a mask and snorkel to explore the abundant corals and swarms of fish and you'll fall completely *amoureux* for this place.

INFORMATION

Banque de Wallis et Futuna (BWF; ☎ 72 09 71; Fenuarama shopping centre, Mata'Utu; ☷ 8-11.30am & 1.30-4pm Mon-Fri)

Gendarmerie (☎ 72 29 17; Mata'Utu) Police.

Hospital de Sia (☎ 72 07 00; Mata'Utu)

K Prim (Uvea Sharp shopping centre, Mata'Utu; ☷ 7.30-11.30am & 2-5pm Mon-Fri) Internet and coffee.

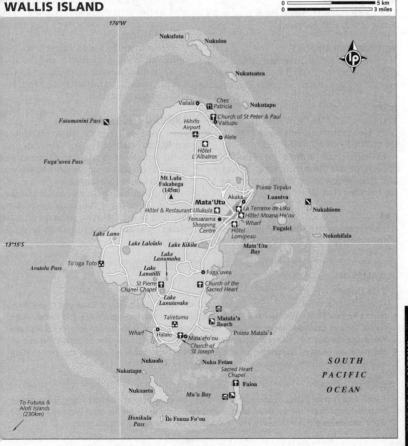

WALLIS ISLAND

176°W

Nukufotu · Nukuloa

Nukuteatea

Vailala · Chez Patricia · Nukutapu
Church of St Peter & Paul
Hihifo Airport · Vaitupu
Alele
Hôtel L'Albatros

Fatumanini Pass

Fuga'uvea Pass

Mt Lulu Fakahega (145m)
Pointe Tepako
Akaka · Luaniva
Mata'Utu · La Terrasse de Liku
Hôtel & Restaurant Ulukula · Hôtel Moana Ho'ou
Fenuarama Shopping Centre · Wharf
Hôtel Lomipeau · Fugalei
Nukuhione
Nukuhifala

Lake Lano

Lake Lalolalo · Lake Kikila
13°15'S
Lake Lanumaha
Mata'Utu Bay
To'oga Toto
Avatolu Pass · Lake Lanutilli
St Pierre Chanel Chapel · Faga'uvea
Church of the Sacred Heart
Lake Lanutavake
Talietumu · Matala'a Beach
Wharf · Halalo · Mala'efo'ou · Pointe Matala'a
Church of St Joseph

Nukuofo · Nuku Fetau
Nukutapu · Sacred Heart Chapel
Nukuaeta · Faiaoa
Mu'a Bay

To Futuna & Alofi Islands (230km)

SOUTH PACIFIC OCEAN

Honikulu Pass · Île Fenua Fo'ou

0 ——— 5 km
0 ——— 3 miles

WALLIS & FUTUNA

The shopping centre is on the road towards the Fenuarama shopping centre.

Post office (☎ 72 08 00; Mata'Utu; ☺ 7.30am-3.30pm Mon-Thu, to 1.30pm Fri)

Wallis Voyage (☎ 72 27 87; fax 72 27 28) A travel agency across from Hôtel Lomipeau.

TRANSPORT
Getting There & Away
AIR

The only airline serving Wallis and Futuna is **Aircalin** (☎ 72 00 00).

BOAT

There is no regular passenger transport by sea, but a ferry to link Wallis with Futuna was in the planning stages at the time of writing.

Getting Around

There's no public transport on Wallis, so it's a case of hire wheels or walk.

TO/FROM THE AIRPORT

Hihifo airport is 6km from Mata'Utu. Hotels offer transfers for 1500 CFP each way, but if you are stuck, someone will offer you a ride.

BOAT

Taxi boats to the southern islets are available from Halalo through **Foto Fenua** (☎ 72 12 37) for 1000 CFP to 2000 CFP return.

In Vailala, ask around for Vitolio (no phone); he can drop you off at Nukufotu and then pick you up again according to the tides for 1000 CFP.

CAR

Car hire costs around 8000 CFP per day; there are no scooters or bicycles for hire on Wallis.

Unless otherwise noted, all rental agencie are in Mata'Utu.

Multi Service (☎ 72 27 52; Hihifo airport)
Pacific Auto Location (☎ 72 28 32; fax 72 29 33)
Pacific Dihn Motoka (☎ 72 26 57)
Plaisir du Fenua (☎ 72 02 27)

MATA'UTU
pop 1191

Mata'Utu is the country's sprawling adminis trative and business centre – it's a long, hot walk from anywhere to anywhere, so, unsurprisingly no one walks anywhere. There are no street names, and no tourist information source.

The waterfront is dominated by **Our Lady of Good Hope Cathedral**, looking across the open green to the lagoon. The Maltese cross centred between the two towers is the royal insignia of Wallis. The adjacent **King's Palace**, with its two-storey verandas running all the way around, almost looks like an Australian country residence.

Across from the King's Palace is the post office, while the gendarmerie and the Uvea Sharp and Fenuarama shopping centres are straight up the road inland about 500m, 1km and 1.5km respectively.

AROUND THE ISLAND

For a good look over the whole island, head for **Mt Lulu Fakahega** (145m). You can drive to the top, where there's a small abandoned chapel. Footpaths meander down to the west coast road from the summit.

The 35km island-circuit road is unsealed and at times fairly rough. It never actu- ally runs along the coast, although in a few places there are detours that run along the water's edge.

WALLIS IN...

Two Days

Your first day in Wallis can be spent exploring by car. You'll need a local to show you to the hard-to-find **To'oga Toto** (opposite) and **Talietumu** (opposite) archaeological sites, and **Lanutavake** (opposite) and **Lalolalo** (opposite) crater lakes. Finish the day with sunset views from **Mt Lulu Fakahega** (below) and dinner at **Chez Patricia** (p618). The next day can be leisurely spent on the northern islets of **Nukufotu** (opposite) and **Nukuloa** (opposite) visiting the bird-nesting grounds, hiking and swimming.

Four Days

Spend your first two days as above and then take an excursion on your third day, either diving or picnicking around the southern islets, with **Evasion Bleue** (opposite). Your last day should be spent **snorkelling** (opposite) with the rays and turtles around the eastern islets.

In Mala'efo'ou, the **Church of St Joseph** is the oldest church on the island. It has a beautiful interior covered in a kaleidoscope of decorations. Many of them are inspired by traditional land-and-sea tapa designs. Other impressively grand churches can be found in nearly every village.

An unmarked side road leads to the impressive **Talietumu** archaeological site. This huge and beautifully restored site was a fortified Tongan settlement, dating from around AD 1450. The fortress wall apparently runs for several kilometres in each direction, although much of it has been destroyed and other parts engulfed by the jungle. The stone paved roads in and around the site were used only by the king, whose feet were not allowed to touch the ground.

In the southwest of the island, the striking, lush **Lake Lanutavake** is situated just off the road.

Lake Lalolalo is the most spectacular of the Wallis crater lakes. The eerie lake is an almost perfect circle, with sheer rocky cliffs falling 30m down to the inky, 80m-deep lake waters. Tropical birds are often seen gliding effortlessly across the lake and it is taboo to clear the jungle here, making this some of the best preserved primary forest on the island. It's said that the American forces dumped equipment into the lake at the end of WWII.

Back along the coast is **To'oga Toto**, an immense, nearly hidden ruin of a Tongan fort. The name is translated as 'the blood of Tongans', referring to bloody battles that were fought here; an alternative name for the area is the *marais sanglant* ('swamp of blood'), since the marshy water reflects a red hue through the many tropical chestnut trees. It's a trek to get here and another to tramp through all the vines and jungle to actually see the site, but it's worth it if only to find the scattered shards of Lapita pottery (see p612) in the stone-paved king's path.

Continue to the northern end of the island to the tranquil coastal villages around **Vailala**.

AROUND THE LAGOON

The calm, turquoise waters and impressive variety of islets of Wallis' lagoon are as much a reason to visit this island as the sights of the interior. Located in the south, **Faioa** probably has the finest beaches, while **Île Fenua Fo'ou** (more commonly referred to as 'the pass') has plenty of *fale* camping space. You can spend the day fishing, snorkelling or just lounging on the beach of crystalline sands, then be swept to sleep by one of the world's most spectacular night skies. Though don't forget to bring plenty of fresh water since there's none on the islet. Located just opposite, **Nukuaeta** is the only islet with fresh water and was once a leper colony. The unique flora of this small island makes this a fascinating place to visit.

In the north, the Unesco-protected **Nukufotu** is a nesting ground for marine birds and you can walk from here to the neighbouring islet of **Nukuloa**. Climb up the high rocks for breathtaking views of the lagoon.

The islets to the east offer the best **snorkelling** and are frequented by turtles and rays.

ACTIVITIES

Te U Hauhaulele (☎ 72 12 37), the local diving club of Wallis, can arrange dives. The president changes yearly, so there is no fixed phone but you can contact the number listed for information.

Evasion Bleue (☎ 72 13 68; www.wallis-and -futuna-islands.com) is a dive centre (including lake and night dives) that also provides taxi-boat service to islets in the lagoon (from 1500 CFP to 3000 CFP) and lagoon excursions. This is really the only tourist-geared outfit in the country and should be your first stop when looking for activities.

WALLIS FOR CHILDREN

Anywhere out on islets of the lagoon is a fantastic adventure for kids. There is no end of sandy beaches, warm water and colourful fish.

L'Association de Vakalä (☎ 72 29 67; www .vakala.net; boat rental/class 2000/4000 CFP) is a sailing school near Akaka, but visitors can stop by for a sail or hire a kayak to boat out to the eastern *motu*.

Les Enfants du Lagon (☎ 72 13 68; www.wallis-and -futuna-islands.com), created by Evasion Bleue, is a group who works with local children to protect sea turtles. When we visited the group were raising 60 baby hawksbills and one green turtle in an enclosure. Contact Evasion Bleue (above) to have a look, join the kids or lend a hand.

SLEEPING

Hôtel & Restaurant Ulukula (☎ 72 23 85; small/big room 8000/9100 CFP) Near the Fenuarama shopping centre, this is Wallis' newest hotel, still under construction at the time of research. It's not on the water but it will have a swimming pool.

Hôtel Moana Ho'ou (☎ 72 21 35; moana-hoou@mail .wf; s/d incl breakfast 8500/12,500 CFP; ☒) In a lovely waterfront location in Mata'Utu, this is a quiet option, although rooms aren't as bright or modern as Lomipeau's.

Hôtel Lomipeau (☎ 72 20 21; hotel.lomipeau@wallis .co.nz; s/d incl breakfast 12,500/14,500 CFP; ☒ ☒) Centrally located in Mata'Utu, this standard hotel-style place has great views of the lagoon, but the funny noises coming from the old plumbing pipes might keep you awake. Staff is friendly

Hôtel L'Albatros (☎ 72 20 99; fax 72 18 27; s/d 13,750/17,000 CFP; ☒ ☒) It's near the airport but away from Mata'Utu, which makes getting out and about even more of a chore. Bungalows, however, are clean, modern and overlook the pool.

EATING & DRINKING

Aside from a few restaurants, simple snack bars dot the island. There's a supermarket in the Fenuarama shopping centre.

Chez Patricia (☎ 72 21 38; mains 1500-1900 CFP; ☒ lunch & dinner) A waterfront, out-of-the-way spot in Vailala, this Wallisian-decorated eatery is a stylish choice for a great meal.

Le Récif (☎ 72 20 21; mains 1850-2350 CFP; ☒ breakfast, lunch & dinner) This restaurant at Hôtel Lomipeau has an extensive menu, good service and a bright setting, but it's overpriced for the small portions.

La Terrasse de Liku (☎ 72 27 37; mains 2000-2500 CFP; ☒ lunch & dinner) Near town and on the waterfront, locals dig this place, but expats complain that it lacks fresh, local ingredients.

FUTUNA & ALOFI

Futuna: pop 4400 / area 64 sq km
Alofi: pop 0 / area 51 sq km
Loaded with flowers, sparkling beaches, traditional houses and vistas over Pacific blue, Futuna is storybook Polynesian pretty. Yet since the islanders here have firmly decided not to develop tourism in order to preserve

their lifestyle, it's a particularly difficult place to get around. Finding someone to hire you a car can take all day, bikes are unheard of, it's too hot to walk and people drive by and laugh at you if you try to hitchhike. While the islanders are unflinchingly nice, you do get the sense that they're just putting up with you until you go home. And it makes sense: this is a paradise anyone would want to keep to themselves. It's divided into two kingdoms, Alo and Sigave, which today live in peaceful if not competitive harmony with each other.

Uninhabited Alofi, with its tropical forest and beach, is just as gorgeous and more wild. A strait less than 2km wide separates the two islands.

LEAVA
pop 950
Everything of note is concentrated in Leava, Futuna's major centre, on the south coast. There are a couple of supermarkets, the island's administrative headquarters (there's even a library) and a wharf. It's all along one road, so you can't get lost.

Information
Banque de Wallis et Futuna (☎ 72 36 40) Has very irregular opening hours and no ATM.
Gendarmerie (☎ 72 32 17; ☒ 7.30-11.30am & 2-5pm)
Hospital de Kaleveleve (☎ 72 33 29)
Internet (☎ 72 31 20; Somalama Park Hôtel; per day 1000 CFP) Unlimited internet access per day.
Post office (☎ 72 08 00; ☒ 7.30am-2pm Mon-Fri) The only public telephone on the island is located here; you can buy phonecards inside.
SB Travel Futuna (☎ 72 32 04; sbtravel@mail.wf) Handles all Aircalin flights and can book flights and hotels for Futuna.

Sights
It's a 33km circuit around Futuna, but with speed bumps on the good roads and potholes on the bad ones it'll take at least 1½ hours to go round. This route starts at Leava and travels counterclockwise.

Grand **Leava Church** has a fine ceiling with carved wooden men that support the rafters with an outstretched arm; if you look closely you'll notice that each little man is completely unique. Like much Futuna carving, the woodwork was done using a chainsaw.

The road leads up to a plateau with fantastic views over a forest of coconut palms

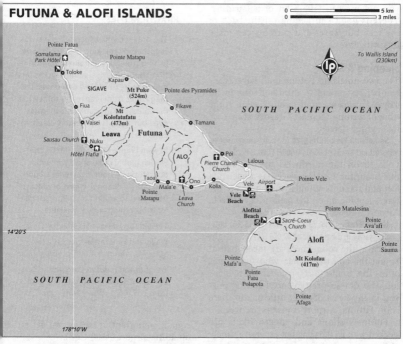

FUTUNA & ALOFI ISLANDS

and fruit trees and out to the idyllic shores of Alofi. Continuing to the descent to the eastern side of the island, the view gets even better with the rolling jungle, crystal coastline and **traditional fale villages**. Passing the first of many quiet villages of beautifully constructed traditional houses, you reach the famous, towering **Pierre Chanel Church** (called Petelo Sanele in Futunan). The exterior is in need of a new coat of paint, but the interior, which has enough pews to seat several hundred worshippers, is painstakingly decorated throughout with white and brown tapa. The chapel includes relics of the saint, including some of his clothes and the war club said to have dispatched him.

After the village of Poi, the sealed road ends and it gets pretty bumpy until Pointe Fatua in the north of the island. There's an uninhabited stretch from Fikave to Kapau where you'll pass the lava rock formations of **Pointe des Pyramides**, and it's about here that you start to pray to St Chanel that your rent-a-wreck doesn't break down. The paved road begins again right before Somalama Park Hôtel.

Heading south back towards Leava, **Sausau Church** is a colourful, three-towered confection that would fit right in at Disneyland. It was built in just eight months after its predecessor was destroyed in the catastrophic 1993 earthquake.

No road crosses the interior, but there is a network of footpaths winding up into the central hills. With enough time you might even find a way up **Mt Puke** (524m).

Boats run across to uninhabited **Alofi** from Vele beach (for the whole boat 4000 CFP, 15 minutes), beside the airport. Alofi has an idyllic beach, clear water and plenty of shady trees, and people often come from Futuna to tend gardens and check on their pigs. There's a series of open, solar-powered *fale* for overnight accommodation, but people usually just stay for the day. Alofi even has a small **church** – Sacré Coeur.

Activities

The *pensions* (guest houses) claim that they offer excursions from around 10,000 CFP, but getting them to actually take you on one can take a bit of persuading. There is good snorkelling off the back of the reef, but waves and currents can make this dangerous.

Sleeping & Eating

The two hotels on Futuna both have excellent bar-restaurants. A third hotel run by SB Travel Futuna was under construction at the time of writing (contact Gregory at lalovi@mail.wf for details).

Somalama Park Hôtel (☎ 72 31 20; somalama@mail.wf; s/d/t incl breakfast 9000/10,000/11,000 CFP; ❄ ▢) Located on the northwest tip of Futuna, this beautiful, isolated place has a hacienda feel and the only sounds you'll hear are the waves lapping up on the palm-fringed beach. Airport transfers are 1500 CFP.

Hôtel Fiafia (☎ 72 32 45; fax 72 35 56; hotel_fiafia@yahoo.fr; d incl breakfast 12,000 CFP; ❄) Right in Leava, the rooms here are nicer than at Somalama and the owner, who sometimes offers free island tours, is much more helpful. The not-so-pretty central setting puts you in the heart of what little action there is on Futuna. Airport transfers are free.

Futuna's shops and supermarkets are stocked with an amazing but expensive variety of imported goods. Snack bars come and go.

Getting There & Around

There are flights with **Aircalin** (☎ 72 00 05; sbtravel@mail.wf) to/from Wallis 11 times weekly (one-way 13,500 CFP), but flights are cancelled when there are north-blowing winds stronger than 10 knots (common between November and March but can happen any time of year). Futuna's airstrip is 12.5km from Leava and was paved in 2008, so it can now potentially welcome international flights – but none had been planned at the time of writing.

The two hotels can try to arrange car hire, which is usually 9000 CFP per day for a dilapidated Suzuki. Finding a bicycle to hire is near impossible.

WALLIS & FUTUNA DIRECTORY

ACCOMMODATION

The few hotels are rarely full. Nevertheless, booking ahead secures you a room, but,

equally important, it means you get picked up at the airport (1500 CFP).

All the hotels are comfortable with air-con and private bathrooms, but are impersonal and have no particular style. Prices range from 7000 CFP for a single room to 15,000 CFP for a two-person bungalow; a French-style breakfast is included. The exceedingly polite and formal service you'll find everywhere is a bit disorienting for such a wild and natural destination.

ACTIVITIES

The lagoon is the place to be for nearly every activity on Wallis (see p617), while there are a few hiking opportunities on Futuna. Especially on Wallis, if you ask around, you should be able to find a local to take you out fishing.

Snorkellers should head for the reef fringes; the best being around the eastern islets of Wallis, Vele beach on Futuna and around the lagoon on Alofi.

French or not, one of the most popular sports on Wallis is *kirikiti*, the Polynesian version of cricket (see boxed text, p300).

BUSINESS HOURS

Shops are open Monday to Friday from 7.30am to 11.30am and 1.30pm to 5pm, and many open on weekends, but they tend to shut for a long, lazy lunch.

CHILDREN

Wallis and Futuna is very family oriented, so you'll fit right in if you have children. The shops are well stocked with baby supplies, although they are quite expensive.

EMBASSIES & CONSULATES

There are no overseas diplomatic representatives and since Wallis and Futuna is a French territory, French embassies abroad represent the islands.

FESTIVALS & EVENTS

Most holidays and festivals are the French dates also celebrated in New Caledonia and Tahiti and French Polynesia (see p477). In addition to this, 29 July commemorates the day when Wallis and Futuna became a French territory; St Pierre Chanel Day is 28 April.

INTERNET ACCESS

There's an internet cafe, K Prim, in the Uvea Sharp shopping centre near the Fenuarama shopping centre in Mata'Utu. On Futuna, guests can use the terminal at Somalama Park Hôtel.

INTERNET RESOURCES

Pacific Magazine (www.pacificmagazine.net) For news in English.

rfo.fr (http://wallisfutuna.rfo.fr, in French) For RFO TV programming and written articles.

MONEY

As in Tahiti and French Polynesia and New Caledonia, the Cour de Franc Pacifique (CFP) is the local currency, tied to the euro. For exchange rates, see the Quick Reference inside this book's front cover. It's wise to bring some CFP with you – there's no bank at the Wallis airport.

The Banque de Wallis et Futuna (BWF) branch in the Fenuarama shopping centre in Mata'Utu can advance cash to Visa and MasterCard holders. It will change foreign currency, but exacts a horrific 1000 CFP commission on each travellers cheque exchange.

Credit cards are accepted in most hotels and at car-hire agencies, but not in most shops.

HOW MUCH?

- **Pareu:** 3500 CFP
- **Shell necklace:** 300 CFP
- **Imported pear:** 100 CFP
- **Kava bowl:** 10,000 CFP
- **Tapa handbag:** 6000 CFP
- **1L petrol:** 160 CFP
- **1L bottled water:** 200 CFP
- **Bottle of Foster's lager:** 240 CFP
- **Souvenir T-shirt:** 1200 CFP
- **1kg of mangoes:** 300 CFP

ATMs

The country's only ATM is located at the Banque de Wallis et Futuna branch, which is found at the Fenuarama shopping centre. It tends to run out of cash on Friday night and doesn't get refilled till Monday morning.

Tipping

There's no need to tip and your server might not understand the gesture.

TELEPHONE
Mobile Phones

For the time being this country is a cellular-free zone.

Phonecards

Public phones require a telecard (1000, 3000 or 5000 CFP), which can be bought at post offices. In Futuna the only public phone is outside the post office in Leava. On Wallis there are several cardphones, including one at the Hôtel Lomipeau and at the post office in Mata'Utu.

TIME

Wallis and Futuna is just west of the International Date Line and 12 hours ahead of GMT.

VISAS

Visa regulations are the same as for France's other Pacific territories; refer to the Embassies & Consulates section in the Tahiti & French Polynesia (p476) or New Caledonia (p222) chapters for diplomatic representation.

TRANSPORT IN WALLIS & FUTUNA

GETTING THERE & AWAY
Air
There are flights with **Aircalin** (www.aircalin .nc, in French) three times weekly to/from New Caledonia (return in low/high season 58,500/80,000 CFP); two of the flights return to Noumea (New Caledonia) via Nadi in Fiji. For local Aircalin contact details, see below.

None of the South Pacific air passes include Wallis and Futuna.

Sea
There are no regular ferries nor cruise ships docking.

Yachts don't visit Wallis that often, despite its welcoming lagoon. Because there is not much room around the Mata'Utu wharf, yachts are encouraged to moor near the petroleum wharf at Halalo in the south of Wallis.

GETTING AROUND
Air
There are 11 flights weekly between the islands with **Aircalin** (☎ in Wallis 72 00 00, in Futuna 72

32 04; www.airca lin.nc, in French), at least once dail (return from 24,800 CFP). It is best to boo in advance.

Boat
Transfers to the islets of Wallis are availab from 1000 CFP to 2000 CFP return, but a subject to island time and the tides. For mo details, see p616. Contact local fishermen get a lift to Alofi from Futuna (return 400 CFP). See p618 for more details.

Car
There is no public transport on either of th islands; if you want to get anywhere, you have to hire a car (per day around 10,00 CFP). On Futuna hiring a car is an out-o someone's house affair; no one will ask fo a driving permit or have considered any in surance issues. On Wallis things are mo professional and you will need to show you permit (any kind will do), and insurance va ies from agency to agency. On both island driving is on the right-hand side and ther are no enforced rules of the road. For car-hi agency details, see p616 for Wallis and p62 for Futuna.

No one hires out motorcycles, scooters bicycles.

South Pacific Directory

CONTENTS

This South Pacific Directory covers region-wide information but for country-specific information, see the Directory section for each country chapter. Some subjects are covered in both directories; for example, accommodation options in the region are given in this directory, but specific accommodation prices are covered in the country directories. When seeking information, consult both directories and note the cross-references.

ACCOMMODATION

There's accommodation in the South Pacific to suit most budgets – from no-frills *fales* (houses) and village homestays to luxury resorts and live-aboard cruisers – though not all countries have offerings that cover the whole spectrum. Some countries have outstanding luxury options but few budget choices, while other countries don't have any five-star accommodation. This really depends on the maturity of the country's tourist industry – Fiji and French Polynesia, for example, have good accommodation options, but in places that get far fewer tourists the choices are usually limited. For detailed information see Accommodation in the country chapter directories.

Where there's sufficient choice we've listed accommodation in three price categories (budget, midrange and top end) and listed by budget order. Budget accommodation may include campgrounds, homestays, hostels and cheap hotels. Midrange options can take the form of hotels and motels, as well as guest houses and fully furnished houses for weekly rental. Plush hotels and resorts dominate the top-end options, but keep in mind the word 'resort' is used loosely in some countries and isn't always synonymous with luxury.

The best accommodation is often fully booked and may be more expensive during peak tourist times – see When to Go, p26. A few countries, such as Tokelau, Pitcairn Island and theoretically the Cook Islands require accommodation to be booked before arrival, but most don't. In more expensive countries like New Caledonia and French Polynesia, package tours that include accommodation are well worth investigating and can offer substantial savings. See p640 for more details.

Camping

Pacific islands generally have lots of outdoors space and camping can be a good way to save money in expensive places like Tahiti and New Caledonia. But campgrounds in this region don't come with amenities blocks, games rooms or state-of-the-art cooking facilities. You'll be lucky to find one or two like that in the whole huge region. Here we're talking coconut palms, thatched shelters, pit toilets, campfires, and the buzz of mosquitoes and a long slice of heavenly beach. In a few countries, an occasional hotel will allow you to pitch your tent.

However, not many countries cater for campers – the only places with any facilities are French Polynesia, New Caledonia, Easter Island, Fiji and Vanuatu. Tonga has some facilities, but like most Melanesian countries camping is not customary. Playing host to travellers is an important Melanesian tradition and usually you'd be invited to sleep in a home, school building or even a police station – to decline and pitch a tent would cause offence. Check the individual country chapters for more information.

If you want to camp somewhere other than a designated camping area, it's important to seek permission from customary landowners. And try to leave no trace of your visit – carry out everything you carry in.

Guest Houses & Hostels

Backpacker hostels aren't common in the region, but budget travellers can opt for local guest houses that have similar facilities – shared rooms, showers and kitchen facilities. Guest houses are often patronised by locals, as well as church and aid workers, and are usually a more grassroots experience than most city hotels. There are often rules about smoking and drinking, and some have evening curfews. Guest houses appear in several countries but the term is variously defined – expect anything from a hostel to a midrange hotel.

New Caledonia has the Pacific's sole hostel affiliated with **Hostelling International** (www.hi hostels.com), though many countries have no hostels. Fiji, Samoa and the Cook Islands are all countries where hostels are a more common accommodation alternative. French Polynesia also has hostel-style digs on its larger islands. The following websites are a good resource for hostels and other budget accommodation:
Hostel Planet (www.hostelplanet.com)
Hostels.com (www.hostels.com)
Hostelz (www.hostelz.com)

Hotels

What qualifies as a hotel in the Pacific varies enormously from top-end luxury pads to cheap city digs pitched towards locals, and thus all budgets are covered. What you get for what you pay is determined by the country: lower those expectations for the more expensive destinations, while enjoy the complimentary extras (such as breakfast and maybe dinner) that are common in cheaper countries.

Cheap hotels offer very basic rooms, and may have dorm facilities as well. In some countries, the budget end of the spectrum is bolstered by hostels and guest houses (see above). Rooms with kitchenettes are a fabulous way to save money, especially for families or groups. Many budget accommodation options will not accept credit cards.

Midrange and top-end hotels generally offer the mod cons: air-con, tea- and coffee-making facilities, a restaurant, bar and swimming pool.

There's usually internet access available (even only from the office) and they may offer garde and beachfront bungalows, or a room in th main building. Rooms within a hotel can var in size, facilities and outlook as well as price s ask to see a few. Most hotels in this range can b contacted and booked via websites, and mos accept credit cards.

Organised Village Stays

Many small communities in the Pacific offe village stays and they can be a terrific way o experiencing traditional village life. Usuall this will be a rural community, and it's a grea way to spend some of your tourist dollar with local people and a good alternative t the gloss of hotels and resorts. This kind o accommodation has taken off in some coun tries in recent years – a Pacific version of th B&B (though you may have to take all meal with your hosts, not just breakfast). Reserv village stays either directly through the villag or through the local tourist office, and keep your expectations at ground level – a thatche hut with mats on the floor, pit toilet and col shower are as flash as some come.

Rental Accommodation

Rentals can be good for families or group who want to stay in a place for a week or more They're not always the cheapest option, bu you can save on meals by making good use o the kitchen. However, short-term rentals ar not that common in the Pacific. Rarotonga (p269) has the best range.

Resorts

The best of the top-end resorts in the Pacifi are as good as they come. Luxurious over water bungalows lapped by pristine azure wa ters, glass-bottomed coffee tables that double as an ever-changing looking glass into th underwater world, white-sand beaches tha you may have to yourself – if you've got th budget you can have it all and more in th South Pacific. French Polynesia is often re garded as the best of the best (see the boxe text, p166), but if that's just a tad too pricey options abound in other countries.

Many couples come to the Pacific fo their wedding and honeymoon, and a luxurious tropical island resort is pretty darn romantic.

Pacific resorts are a wide and varied lot. The internet has become a huge marketing too for resorts right across the Pacific, but resort websites can be very 'advertorial' in content and aren't always true indicators of what to expect – if you want details and specifics, quiz travel agents, ring or email resorts and use the recommendations in this guidebook. Many resorts have slim margins on room rates but make a packet on extras (meals, drinks, activities etc). Depending on the country, resorts on the mainland may offer better facilities in terms of entertainment, dining and tours and will be closer to towns, while those on offshore islands might have better beaches. You might prefer a resort that offers lots of activities and opportunities to see the country and meet locals, or one on a secluded palm-fringed islet in the ocean that has beautiful decor and an exclusive stretch of beach.

Resorts are almost always much cheaper if prebooked before you leave home as a package tour, and include meals, airfares and airport transfers (see p640). Internet rates are always cheaper than walk-in 'rack rates'.

Staying in Villages

Pacific Islanders are famous for their hospitality. Particularly in countries and areas that have few formal tourist facilities, you'll almost certainly be offered accommodation in someone's home or in a communal village space. This can be a wonderful and intimate experience of local culture and lifestyle but it's important to remember your manners. While invitations can confer a degree of honour on the host family, even the most welcome guest will eventually strain a family's resources and after a few days it may be considerate to move on even if there's been no request for you to do so. Express your gratitude when leaving by offering a gift in exchange for the chance to stay in the village – don't call it 'payment' or it may be refused. It may well be refused anyway, but do your best to leave something behind. Cash mightn't always be accepted, but kava or shop goods (such as rice or canned meat) could be. Gifting alcohol may be inappropriate but you'll know after you've stayed with a community. Something as simple as buying a soccer ball from a local store can be nice to leave behind for the village kids or memento from home is always gratefully received.

ACTIVITIES

Millions of square kilometres of warm briny tropical water, pristine lagoons and long stretches of beach are the most obvious attraction for travellers in the Pacific and almost everyone comes to this region to get wet – scuba diving, snorkelling, surfing, swimming, sea kayaking and sailing are all popular, and the fishing is among the world's best. But there's more to the Pacific than watery pursuits. Opportunities abound for hiking, cycling, horse riding, birding and whale-watching, as well as visiting archaeological or sacred sites and WWII relics. Caving is big in the Cook Islands (p290) and Tonga (p530).

The Pacific is a devoutly Christian region and Sunday is solemnly observed as a day of rest – some activities in some parts might be regarded as disrespectful. But most areas that are accustomed to the ways of tourists are pretty relaxed about their pursuits whatever day it happens to be. Attending a Sunday church service to listen to the beautiful singing is for many a highlight of their Pacific travels.

Diving

The Pacific offers scuba divers some of the world's best diving. For full details on dive sites, conditions, centres and courses, see the South Pacific Diving chapter (p73). Dive shop details are listed in the individual country chapters.

Fishing

For many anglers the South Pacific is a dream destination, with both its great sport fishing and excellent big-game fishing. Common catches include yellowfin and skipjack tuna, wahoo, barracuda, sailfish, and blue, black and striped marlin.

For more information on fishing opportunities, see the following chapters: New Caledonia (p220), Rarotonga & Cook Islands (p264), Samoa (p330), Solomon Islands (p390), Tonga (p530) and Vanuatu (p606).

Hiking

The higher Pacific islands offer terrific opportunities to walk through magnificent forested interiors, climb mountains and even live volcanoes. Since many walking tracks cross land under customary ownership, ask around before heading off – you may need to seek permission or possibly pay a small fee. Some of the walks mentioned in this guide require the services of a local guide.

Countries that offer substantial hiking opportunities are Fiji (p167), French Polynesia (p475), New Caledonia (p220), Samoa (p331), Tonga (p530) and the Cook Islands (p264). Bushwalking in the heat has the potential to be a truly miserable or even dangerous experience. Take sun protection, insect repellent and plenty of water. It's often best to do your hiking in the cool of the early morning.

Sailing

For information about taking your own yacht into the Pacific or getting a berth on someone else's see p641. All Pacific countries have yacht clubs and they're a good first port of call for information about yacht rental. For details of yacht clubs and yacht rentals in the individual country chapters, check under 'Boat' in the Getting Around sections and under 'Activities' in the Directory section. Many people charter yachts in French Polynesia, with or without a crew (see p475).

Surfing

Polynesians invented surfing and the first recorded observations of boardriding were made in Hawai'i and Tahiti in the 1770s. Nevertheless, surfing in many other Pacific islands is still in its infancy. Surfers come in droves to French Polynesia (p475) that hosts the Billabong Tahiti Pro, one of the glamour events on the pro surfing world tour (www .aspworldtour.com) at Teahupoo. Fiji (p167) too is popular with surfers. Increasingly, however, surfers are seeking the uncrowded waves of the Pacific islands and finding them in the Solomon Islands (p390), Samoa (p331), the Cooks Islands (p265), Vanuatu (p584) and Tonga (p509).

There are few easy-going beach breaks in the Pacific, so surfers need to be intermediate at least, and should always seek local advice before heading out. Since waves break outside lagoon reefs the paddle out can be long. Coral reefs are very unforgiving if you get that take-off wrong. Few islands have surfboards for sale, so surfers must come equipped, but the rewards of surfing virgin waves in warm crystal-clear water are incredible.

There are a few tour operators that specialise in surfing holidays in the South Pacific, including **South Pacific Surfing Holidays** (☎ USA 0208 123 8622, 02 8005 1232 in Australia; www.surfing -pacific.com) and **World Surfaris** (☎ 617 5444 4011; www.worldsurfaris.com).

Water Sports

The shallow lagoon waters of the Pacifi offer amazing opportunities for snorkel lers. Some of the best snorkelling spots i the Pacific include Taveuni's Somosom Strait (p158) and Kadavu's Great Astrolab Reef (p164) in Fiji, Motu Nui (p92) i Easter Island, around the Loyalty Island (p206) and Île aux Canards (p186) in Nev Caledonia, Tikehau's lagoon (p454) in th Tuamotus and Bora Bora (p439) in Frencl Polynesia, Matapa Chasm in Niue (p234 and Rarotonga's lagoon (p265) in the Cooks Perhaps the best of the lot is off Uepi Islan (p378) in the Solomons magnificent Marov Lagoon where reef sharks, giant clams an countless fish and corals are dizzying i their abundance.

Sea kayaking is popular, and kayak tour are offered in a handful of countries, includin Fiji (p167), Tonga (p522) and Samoa (p331)

Kite surfers have discovered the wonders o Aitutaki's superb lagoon in the Cook Island (see p275).

Some countries also offer opportunities t windsurf and jet ski.

Whale-Watching

Migrating humpback whales spend mucl of the second half of the year in Pacific wa ters, and several countries, including Nev Caledonia (p221), the Cooks (p266) an Rururtu (p470) in French Polynesia, offer ex cellent opportunities to view them. Tonga of fers great whale-watching experiences (p522) as well as opportunities for even closer experi ences – see the boxed text on p523.

BUSINESS HOURS

Most family businesses in the Pacific hav fairly relaxed opening hours – grocery store may open early in the morning and stay ope until late. Banks have more formal openin hours: 9.30am to 3pm Monday to Friday i average, but depending on the country the may close even earlier. Some banks ope on Saturday morning, but they're an excep tion to the rule. In general, businesses an government offices open from 9am to 4pn or 5pm Monday to Friday, but in countrie with French ties (New Caledonia and Frencl Polynesia, for example), they get going a early as 7.30am. Many businesses will shu at lunch for an hour (or two in those French connection countries). For more informa

on on opening hours, see Business Hours
the country chapter directories. We don't
st opening hours in this guide unless they
ffer significantly from the norm.

HILDREN

ew regions in the world are family-friendly
the South Pacific. With endless sunshine,
ndy beaches, swimming and snorkelling
ere's plenty to keep kids active and in-
rested. Kids need reminding to cover up
gainst sunburn in most Pacific countries as
e relentless sun is the biggest danger they're
kely to face. Tourism in some places is better
t up for kids than others – Fiji, Vanuatu and
e Cooks cater well for families.

Family is profoundly important in Pacific
ltures and children are highly prized. Child-
aring is a communal responsibility – you
ight be wondering where your toddler has
ot to when he/she turns up carried on the hip
f a motherly eight-year-old village girl. Kids
re quickly absorbed into games with local
ildren and fun has no language barrier.

Some hotels and resorts have no-children
licies (especially under 12s) but then others
t kids stay for free – always ask when book-
g. Some tours and activities are discounted
r kids.

Kids have to understand that touching coral
d marine life is a definite no-no. Coral can
e easily damaged and a few species of fish
d shellfish can give a nasty sting (see boxed
xt, p650).

racticalities

ake sure your children's vaccinations (p644)
e up to date – certain malarial prophylactics
e not suitable for very small children, so
nsult you doctor. Carry a copy of your chil-
ren's health and vaccination records which
e important if they fall ill. Make sure your
avel insurance covers your children as well
the countries you plan to visit. High UV
nscreen is widely available in major towns
ut not always in more remote areas. A hat
d lightweight clothing that covers the whole
dy will provide protection against sunburn
d insect bites. Children need constant rehy-
ration in hot climates – Gastrolite can help
revent dehydration and mask unpleasant-
sting water. If your child is sensitive to the
cal water, boil drinking water or buy bottled
ater. Also see the Medical Checklist (p644)
r more on what to bring from home.

Very small children can be carried in a
backpack or baby sling, but strollers might
be more hassle than they're worth – often
the paths are rough and unsealed, and
strollers are hopeless on the beach and in
crowded buses.

Pharmacies and stores in larger towns
have supplies of disposable nappies (diapers), infant formula and long-life milk,
but don't assume you can buy these in more
remote regions.

Hotels and resorts that cater to children
usually have portable cots and perhaps
even a highchair, but it pays to check this
in advance. Highchairs are not common
in restaurants. Breastfeeding in public is
usually OK.

CLIMATE CHARTS

Consult the following charts while you're
planning your trip.

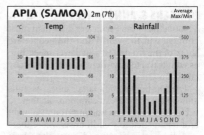

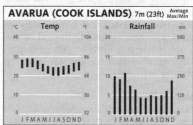

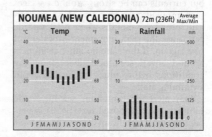

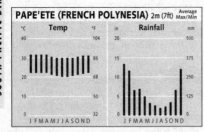

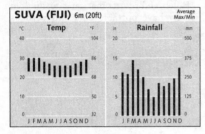

mobile (though not aggressive) and has lon
venomous spines that cause extremely pair
ful wounds. Most other beasties – such as se
urchins, stonefish and cone shells – sit placidl
on the seafloor. The simple rule is look bu
don't touch – reef shoes (or old runners) ca
be useful. Stings and bites are extremely rar

Shark attacks too are extremely rare an
swimming inside a reef offers protectior
Blacktip reef sharks look menacing and ca
grow to 2m long – sometimes swimming i
groups (shivers) in shallow waters – but ar
harmless unless provoked.

Mosquitoes

Malaria exists in western regions of the Sou
Pacific – particularly the Solomons an
Vanuatu – but even where mosquitoes don
carry malaria their bites can cause discomfo
and, in some cases, dengue fever (p647
Mosquitoes are less of a problem around th
coast where sea breezes keep them away, bu
inland they can be a pest. For more informa
tion see the boxed text, p648.

Theft

Petty crime does exist and thefts from hir
cars and beach bags do occur. Look after you
valuables and keep them out of sight. The mo
important things to guard are your passpor
papers, tickets and money – in that order. Kee
these with you at all times – you'll know im
mediately if they do go missing. Conceale
money belts are a hassle. An ordinary walle
is better for money, while keep your docu
ments and passport with you in a daypac
or bag and remain vigilant about its securit
(stow document photocopies separately i
your luggage). Valuables are normally safe in
locked hotel room if you're heading out for th
day, but tuck them out of sight. Many Pacifi
cultures have relaxed attitudes to propert
but it's best not to leave expensive gear lyin
around. Most hotels have safes or secure place
for valuables.

DISABLED TRAVELLERS

Unfortunately, Pacific countries generall
have very poor facilities for disabled trave
lers. Wheelchair users will find getting aroun
a real problem since small domestic airplane
have steps and narrow doors, and shippin
services may not have ramp access. Som
bigger international resorts offer rooms wit
disabled access, but it's not common. Tha

DANGERS & ANNOYANCES

The islands of the Pacific are safer than most
countries in the world and the people are
some of the friendliest you'll ever meet. But,
as with travel to anywhere, it pays to exercise
common sense.

Even in the Pacific's larger cities, assaults
and violent crime are uncommon, but they do
occur. Be aware when walking around at night
and try to stick to well-lit areas where there
are others around – avoid situations where
you might be vulnerable.

Grazes, coral cuts and even insect bites can
quickly become infected in tropical climes.
Treat any lesions liberally with antiseptic.
Have great respect for the sun and keep
yourself hydrated.

Marine Hazards

Many Pacific islands have sheltered lagoons
that offer safe swimming and snorkelling,
but currents can be strong around passages
that empty into the open sea. These are typically near river mouths where a falling tide
can cause the swift movement of water out
of a lagoon. If there are no other swimmers
around, always seek local advice about the
conditions before plunging in and avoid
swimming alone.

Stay alert for venomous sea life – the
Lionfish (see the boxed text, p650) is perhaps the most significant of these because it's

said, Pacific cultures look after their old, disabled and infirm as integrated members of the community – they have no special schools or aged-care facilities. So islander people won't simply look away when you're needing help to get into a taxi or up some stairs, they'll call helpers, pitch in and assist people with disabilities.

Get in touch with your national support organisation (preferably the 'travel officer' if there is one) and enquire about the countries you plan to visit.

EMBASSIES & CONSULATES

The Directory sections of the individual country chapters list the addresses and contact details of embassies and consulates.

As a visitor you are bound by the laws of the country you're visiting and the embassy of the country of which you're a citizen is powerless to intervene. So if you've committed a crime in another country, embassy staff will show no sympathy, even where such actions are legal in your home country. The onus is on the visitor to a country to be aware of and adhere to local laws.

However, if you are in a dire emergency you might get some assistance – if your passport has been stolen your embassy will help you get a new one. In other genuine emergencies you might get some assistance once all other avenues have been exhausted. A crime committed against you would be a matter for the local police. Stolen money, tickets or valuables are normally covered by insurance and your embassy would (reasonably) expect you to have travel insurance. Your embassy may be able to help you seek assistance elsewhere with other local-government agencies. But it will normally only evacuate citizens in the event of a major natural disaster, war or sudden civil upheaval, such as a violent coup where all citizens of its country are affected.

GAY & LESBIAN TRAVELLERS

Attitudes towards homosexuality in the Pacific are multilayered and complex. Due to the conservative influence of the Christian church homosexuality is, on one level, regarded as unnatural, and some religious and community leaders can get vociferous in their opposition to it. Yet in Polynesia there are long traditions of male cross-dressing and transgenderism that are usually, though not always, associated with homosexuality – see the boxed texts on p497 and p402 for more information. Melanesian countries tend to be less tolerant of homosexuality, but this stance has noticeably softened over the last decade or so.

There are very few clubs or other facilities for gays and lesbians in the Pacific, except in French Polynesia (p477).

Male homosexuality is technically illegal (although this is rarely enforced) in many Pacific countries, including the Cooks, Fiji, Niue, the Solomons, Tokelau and Tonga. Female homosexuality only gets an official mention in Samoa, where it is also illegal. In the more liberal French colonies of New Caledonia and French Polynesia, homosexuality is legal. Excessive public displays of affection – both heterosexual and homosexual – are frowned upon in most Pacific societies.

HOLIDAYS

Most Western holidays are observed in the Pacific islands. 'Festivals & Events' in the country Directory sections list extra national holidays.

Easter includes Good Friday, Holy Saturday, Easter Sunday and Easter Monday. Many Catholic countries observe the Ascension 40 days after Easter Sunday. Whit Sunday (Pentecost) is seven weeks after Easter. The Assumption is celebrated on 15 August.

American Samoa celebrates Martin Luther King Day, Presidents' Day, US Independence Day, Labor Day, Columbus Day, Veterans' Day and Thanksgiving. French territories celebrate Labour Day, Bastille Day, All Saints' Day and Armistice Day.

Countries associated with New Zealand and Australia (Cook Islands, Niue, Samoa and Tonga) often celebrate Anzac Day. If a public holiday falls on a weekend, the holiday is often taken on the preceding Friday or following Monday.

The following is a list of some standard Western public holidays:

New Year's Day 1 January
Martin Luther King Day Third Monday in January
Presidents' Day Third Monday in February
Easter March/April
Anzac Day 25 April
Labour Day 1 May
Whit Sunday & Monday May/June (Pentecost)
US Independence Day 4 July
Bastille Day 14 July
Assumption Day 15 August

Columbus Day 2nd Monday in October
All Saints' Day 1 November
Veterans' (Armistice) Day 11 November
Thanksgiving Fourth Thursday in November
Christmas Day 25 December
Boxing Day 26 December

INSURANCE

Travel insurance that covers theft, loss and medical problems is almost essential. There's a wide variety of policies available, and those handled by STA Travel and other student travel organisations are usually good value. There's strong competition among travel insurers, most of which have websites where you can take out policies online – shop around and compare like with like. See the Health chapter (p644) for details on medical insurance.

Some policies exclude 'dangerous activities', which can include scuba diving, motorcycling and even hiking. A locally acquired motorcycle licence is not valid under some policies. See p643 for more details on car and motorcycle insurance.

INTERNET ACCESS

In theory there are various ways you can connect to the internet while travelling in the South Pacific. The major international internet service providers (ISPs), such as AOL (www.aol.com), CompuServe (www.compuserve.com) and IBM Net (www.ibm.com), have very few local dial-in nodes in the South Pacific, so they're not really an option.

However, public internet facilities are the way to go. Wi-fi–enabled laptop users will find increasing numbers of wi-fi hotspots in major tourist and urban centres. Prepaid wi-fi is easy to use and inexpensive. Many upper-end hotels offer wi-fi or LAN-based internet access for laptop users (often for free) and have resident computers for others. And with the proliferation of internet cafes, travellers without their own computers are never far from internet access.

See the Directory of the individual country chapters for information about internet access in that country.

MONEY

The South Pacific has some very exotic-sounding currencies – Vanuatu's vata, Samoa's tala and the Tongan pa'anga. However, some of the countries of the South Pacific use US, Australian or NZ dollars, while the Pacific franc (the Cour de Franc Pacifique, or CFP) is legal tender in the French territories of New Caledonia and French Polynesia. The 'Money' sections of the individual country Directories has all the practical information you need for countries you're visiting, including what currencies are used there.

Exchange rates can fluctuate substantially, however we've printed the exchange rates at the time of going to press on the Quick Reference page inside of the front cover. See also the Getting Started chapter (p27) that gives a rundown on local costs. **Oanda** (www.oanda.com) is a useful website for up-to-date currency exchange rates.

Be aware that using money in foreign countries costs. Whether it's fees for buying and cashing travellers cheques, exchanging hard currency, withdrawing money from overseas ATMs or international-currency fees charged for overseas credit-card transactions. These days with internet banking its much easier to transfer money between account while you're away from home.

When taking money overseas it's best not to put all your eggs in one basket; instead give yourself a few options. A combination of credit and/or cash card, travellers cheques and a stash of cash gives you options to fall back on if an ATM swallows your card or the banks in an area are closed.

ATMs & Credit Cards

Withdrawing cash against your home bank or credit account from Cirrus, Maestro and Visa-enabled ATMs is the easiest way of getting money in Pacific countries.

Credit cards allow you to pay for expensive items (eg airline tickets) without carrying lots of cash around, and you get the best exchange rate (often lower than the advertised rate) on transactions. They also allow you to withdraw cash at selected banks and from the many ATMs that are linked up internationally. However if an ATM swallows your card that was issued outside the Pacific, it can be a major headache. Most major credit cards can withdraw cash from Cirrus, Maestro and Visa-enabled ATMs, but it's always prudent to check with your bank. ATMs are common in major Pacific centres, but unknown in the outer islands or rural areas.

Cash cards, which you use at home to withdraw money directly from your bank account or savings account, can be used in the Pacific at ATMs linked to international networks.

Charge cards such as American Express (Amex) have offices in many countries that will replace a lost card within 24 hours. However, Amex offices in this part of the Pacific are limited to Australia, French Polynesia, New Caledonia and NZ. Charge cards are not widely accepted off the beaten track.

Another option is Visa TravelMoney, a prepaid travel card that gives 24-hour access to your funds in local currency via Visa ATMs. The card is pin-protected and its value is stored on the system, not on the card. So if you lose your card, your money's safe. Many banks are offering this type of product too; however, most issue these cards in major currencies only.

Be warned: fraudulent shopkeepers have been known to quickly make several imprints of your credit card when you're not looking, and then copy your signature from the one that you authorise. Try not to let your card out of sight, and always check your statements upon your return.

Bargaining

Bargaining is not practised in any Pacific country and it may also offend. While it is becoming more common in tourist shops and markets in major cities, village people will take their goods home rather than accept a lower price than what's asked. Protracted haggling is considered extremely rude. The one exception is Fiji where Indo-Fijians expect to bargain and will initiate it.

Cash

Nothing beats cash for convenience…or risk. If you lose it, it's gone forever and very few travel insurers will come to your rescue. Those that will limit the amount to somewhere around US$300.

For tips on carrying your money safely, see Theft (p628).

Moneychangers

Fees, commissions and buy/sell exchange rates mean that every time you change money you lose. If you're travelling to three Pacific countries, buy all three currencies before you leave home rather than changing one for another. Even big city bank branches in your home country may not hold cash in the Pacific currency you're after but can usually order it in for you. Banks and moneychangers in major Pacific gateway cities, like Auckland, Brisbane,

LA and Honolulu, are more likely to have bills in obscure Pacific currencies.

The Cook Islands dollar is the only currency that cannot be changed outside the country – all other Pacific currencies are fully convertible, but you may have trouble exchanging some of the lesser-known ones at small banks. Currencies of countries with high inflation have poor exchange rates. To redeem anything like its face value, it's best to get rid of any cash in Pacific currencies before you leave the region.

Most airports and big hotels have banking facilities that are open outside normal office hours, sometimes on a 24-hour basis. The best exchange rates are offered at banks. Exchange bureaus generally offer worse rates or charge higher commissions. Hotels are almost always the worst places for exchanging money. American Express and Thomas Cook usually don't charge a commission for changing their own travellers cheques, but may offer a less favourable rate than banks.

Tipping

Attitudes to tipping vary in the Pacific but, in general, tipping is not expected. In Polynesian countries leaving tip is fine if you feel so disposed; however, in Melanesian countries it's more complicated. In traditional Melanesian societies a gift places obligation on the receiver to reciprocate somehow, and this can cause confusion and embarrassment when you're just trying to say thanks to the lady who cleans your hotel room – particularly if you're about to leave. You can always ask. Tipping is becoming more common in cities like American Samoa's Pago Pago or French Polynesia's Pape'ete.

Travellers Cheques

The only reason for carrying travellers cheques rather than cash is the security they offer from loss and theft, but they're losing popularity as more travellers withdraw money from ATMs.

American Express and Thomas Cook travellers cheques are widely accepted and have efficient replacement policies. If you're going to remote places, stick to American Express since small local banks may not accept other brands.

When you change cheques ask about fees and commissions as well as the exchange rate. There may be a per-cheque service fee, a flat transaction fee or a fee charged as a percentage of the total transaction. Some banks charge fees (often exorbitant) to change cheques and not cash. Others do the reverse. Since some banks and money-changers charge a per-cheque fee, get your cheques in large denominations.

Keep a record of cheque numbers – without them replacing lost cheques will be a slow process.

Value-added Tax

Value-added tax (VAT), known as TVA *(taxe sur la valeur ajoutée)* in French-speaking countries, is levied in some Pacific nations such as French Polynesia, New Caledonia, the Cook Islands and Fiji. It's added too the price of goods and services, including hotel and restaurant bills, and is usually included in the prices quoted. Throughout this guide, all prices listed include VAT unless otherwise stated.

POST

Email and the rise of internet cafes has largely done away with snail mail. Postage costs vary from country to country, as does post office efficiency: the 'slowest post' award must go to Pitcairn Island – expect three months for letters either way.

Major post offices still provide poste-restante services. Ask people writing to you to print your name, underline your surname and mark the envelope 'Poste Restante (General Delivery)' with the name of the city and country. Your passport may be required for identification when collecting mail and a fee may be charged. Check under your first name as well as your surname. Post offices usually hold letters for a month.

If you're arriving by yacht, letters should have the name of the vessel included somewhere in the address. Mail is normally filed under the name of the vessel rather than by surname.

TELEPHONE
Mobile Phones

Your mobile telephone carrier may have global-roaming agreements with local providers in the South Pacific, but the costs of calling home can be staggering. Mobile coverage in some South Pacific countries is limited to major urban areas. See the individual country chapters for more information on how you can get mobile phone coverage.

TELEPHONE CODES

Country	ITC (☎)	IAC (☎)
American Samoa	684	00
Cook Islands	682	00
Easter Island	56-32	00
Fiji	679	05
French Polynesia	689	00
New Caledonia	687	00
Niue	683	00
Pitcairn Island	872	00
Samoa	685	00
Solomon Islands	677	00
Tokelau	690	00
Tonga	676	00
Tuvalu	688	00
Vanuatu	678	00
Wallis & Futuna	681	19

ITC – International Telephone Code (to call into that country)
IAC – International Access Code (to call internationally from that country)

Other country codes include: Australia ☎ 61, Canada ☎ 1, France ☎ 33, Germany ☎ 49, Hong Kong ☎ 852, Indonesia ☎ 62, Japan ☎ 81, Malaysia ☎ 60, New Zealand ☎ 64, Papua New Guinea ☎ 675, Singapore ☎ 65, South Africa ☎ 27, UK ☎ 44, USA ☎ 1.

Phone Codes

For international calls, you can dial directly from most countries in the South Pacific to almost anywhere in the world. This is usually cheaper than going through the operator. To call abroad you simply dial the international access code (IAC) for the country you are calling from (most commonly ☎ 00 in the Pacific, but see the table, above), then the international telephone code (ITC) for the country you are calling (also see the table, above) the local area code (if there is one, and usually dropping the leading zero if there is one) and finally the number. If, for example, you are in the Cook Islands (IAC ☎ 00) and you want to make a call to the USA (ITC ☎ 1), San Francisco (area code ☎ 212), number ☎ 123 4567, then you dial ☎ 00-1-212-123 4567. To call from Fiji (IAC ☎ 05) to Australia (ITC ☎ 61), Sydney (area code ☎ 02), number ☎ 1234 5678, then you dial ☎ 05-61-2-1234 5678 (dropping the zero from Sydney's area code). There are no area codes in any of the countries of the South Pacific.

Phonecards

Public telephones can be rare in Pacific countries, but it's usually not too hard to find a shop owner who will let you use their phone for a local call. Some top-end hotels charge pretty steeply for the privilege of using their phones. Phonecards are used in various Pacific countries – even Pitcairn Island, with just one public telephone, has its own phonecards. Refer to 'Telephone' in the Directory of the individual countries for more details.

TIME

Local time relative to Greenwich Mean Time (GMT, which is the same as Coordinated Universal Time – UTC) is specified in the Practicalities boxed text in the Directory of each of the country chapters. Most Pacific islands don't use daylight saving time, except for Vanuatu and Pitcairn Island in the summer. It's worth checking your airline tickets and itinerary very carefully if a country on your route is either starting or finishing daylight saving.

The International Date Line splits the South Pacific region in half and makes time zones complicated – flying east across the International Date Line will have you arriving at your destination before you left. Crossing from east to west, you will lose a day. The International Date Line runs along the 180-degree longitude, detouring 800km to the east around Fiji and Tonga, and 3600km to the east to accommodate all of Kiribati in one day.

Times that are valid at midday in Fiji:

Country	Time
American Samoa	1pm, previous day
Cook Islands	2pm, previous day
Easter Island	6pm, previous day
Gambier Archipelago	3pm, previous day
Marquesas Islands	2.30pm, previous day
New Caledonia	11am, same day
Niue	1pm, previous day
Pitcairn Island	3.30pm, previous day
Samoa	1pm, previous day
Society Islands	2pm, previous day
Solomon Islands	11am, same day
Tahiti	2pm, previous day
Tokelau	2pm, previous day
Tonga	1pm, same day
Tuvalu	Midday, same day
Vanuatu	11am, same day
Wallis & Futuna	Midday, same day

Some international hours at the same time:

Country	Time
Berlin	1am, same day
Honolulu	2pm, previous day
London	Midnight, same day
Los Angeles	4pm, previous day
New Zealand	Midday, same day
New York	7pm, previous day
Paris	1am, same day
Singapore	8am, same day
Sydney	10am, same day
Tokyo	9am, same day

TOURIST INFORMATION

The quality and quantity of tourist information varies from one Pacific country to another. But thanks to the internet, even the most remote islands, like Tokelau for example, now have websites. See 'Tourist Information' in the Directory section of individual country chapters for more details.

The **South Pacific Tourism Organisation** (SPTO; ☎ 679-330 4177; www.spto.org) is an intergovernmental organisation that fosters regional cooperation in the development and promotion of tourism in the Pacific. The SPTO serves as a tourist office for a few countries; however, it doesn't offer a lot in the way of services to independent travellers.

VISAS

More often than not in the Pacific, you will get a visa or tourist permit at the airport or port on arrival, but not always – see Visas in the Directory sections of the country chapters for more details. It's worth checking with the embassies or consulates of the countries you plan to visit before travelling as visa requirements can change.

With just a valid passport, you can visit most Pacific countries for up to three months, provided you have an onward or return ticket and 'sufficient means of support'.

VOLUNTEERING

Volunteering is a great way to get to know a country and do something worthwhile as well as have an adventure. Many volunteers find their work to be profoundly rewarding, and there's a strong movement among travellers towards making a contribution to the countries they visit. There are all sorts of volunteering organisations – some require long-term commitments from people who have experience or tertiary qualifications in specific fields, while others are more based around the notion of short-term working-holidays on community projects.

Volunteer organisations active in the Pacific region include:

Australian Volunteers International (☎ 03-9279 1788; www.australianvolunteers.com; PO Box 350, Fitzroy, Vic 3065, Australia)

Global Volunteers (☎ 1 800 487 1074; www.global volunteers.org; 375 E Little Canada Rd, St Paul, Minnesota, 55117-1628, USA)

Madventurer (☎ 0845 121 1996; www.madventurer .com; 1 Pink Lane, Newcastle on Tyne, NE1 5DW, UK)

Projects Abroad (☎ 21 674 4449; www.projects -abroad.org; 4th Fl, Letterstedt House, Newlands on Main, cnr of Campground, Cape Town 7700, South Africa) With offices worldwide.

UN Volunteers (☎ 228-815 20 00; www.unv.org; Postfach 260 111, D-53153, Bonn, Germany)

US Peace Corps (☎ 1 800 424 8580; www.peacecorps .gov; 1111, 20th St NW, Washington DC 20526, USA)

Voluntary Service Overseas (VSO; ☎ 020-8780 7200; www.vso.org.uk; 317 Putney Bridge Rd, London SW15 2PN, UK) There are also offices in Canada, Ireland and the Netherlands.

Volunteer Service Abroad (VSA; ☎ 04-472 5759; www.vsa.org.nz; PO Box 12-246, Wellington, New Zealand)

World Wildlife Fund (WWF; Secretariat ☎ 22 346 91 11; www.panda.org; Ave du Mont-Blanc 27 1196, Gland, Switzerland) With offices worldwide.

WORK

Generally it's hard to get a work visa for Pacific countries. To find out the rules and regulations regarding work in a particular country, contact the relevant embassy, consulate or immigration office, or check their website.

Transport in the South Pacific

This chapter has the practical information about travel to and around the island states of the South Pacific. For the detailed nuts and bolts of travelling within Pacific countries, see the Transport section of the individual country chapters. Flights and tours can be booked online at www.lonelyplanet.com/bookings.

GETTING THERE & AWAY

AIR

Due to vast expanses of open ocean and the relatively small numbers of travellers visiting the region, just getting to the South Pacific can be expensive. The main gateways are the US, Australia, New Zealand (NZ) and Japan, and large international airlines fly routes between these countries that link a number of South Pacific destinations. There are also several smaller local airlines that only service the Pacific region. For a list of the airlines

THINGS CHANGE

The information in this chapter is particularly vulnerable to change. Check directly with the airline or a travel agent to make sure you understand how a fare (and ticket you may buy) works, and be aware of the security requirements for international travel. Shop carefully. The details given in this chapter should be regarded as pointers and are not a substitute for your own careful, up-to-date research.

that can get you into the region, see the following Airlines section. For a list of airlines that will get you around once you are in the region, see p640. Also check the Transport section of individual country chapters for specific schedule information.

Airlines

You can join the mailing lists of most airlines which offer last-minute deals on flights that can be very attractive.

Air France (☎ in France 08 20 82 08 20; www.airfrance.com) Flies from Paris to New Caledonia and French Polynesia, and from Japan to New Caledonia.

Air New Zealand (☎ in NZ 0800 737 000; www.airnz.co.nz) Flies between NZ, the USA and Japan with connections to most Pacific countries.

Air Niugini (☎ 675-327 3444; www.airniugini.com.pg) Flies to Port Moresby from Australia and Asian gateways, and connects PNG with the Solomon Islands.

Air Pacific (☎ 679-672 0888; www.airpacific.com) Flies between Fiji, Japan, Australia, NZ and the US (LA and Honolulu), with connections to New Caledonia, Samoa, Tonga, Vanuatu and the Solomon Islands.

Air Tahiti Nui (☎ 689-46 02 02; www.airtahitinui.com) Flies between French Polynesia, the USA, France, Australia, NZ and Japan.

Air Vanuatu (☎ 678-23480; www.airvanuatu.com) Flies to Australia, NZ, Fiji, New Caledonia and the Solomon Islands.

Aircalin (☎ 687-26 55 00; www.aircalin.nc) Flies from New Caledonia to Australia, NZ, Japan, Indonesia, Singapore, Thailand, Vanuatu, Fiji and French Polynesia. It is the only airline that flies to Wallis and Futuna.

Hawaiian Airlines (☎ in Hawai'i 808-838 3700; www.hawaiianair.com) Connects mainland US cities through Honolulu to American Samoa and Tahiti (French Polynesia).

Japan Airlines (☎ in Japan 0120 25 5931; www.jal.co.jp) Flies from Japan to French Polynesia.

Korean Air (☎ 850-2-2667 0386; www.koreanair.com) Flies from South Korea to Fiji.

LAN Chile (☎ 56-2-526 2000; www.lan.com) Flies between Chile and French Polynesia, with stops at Easter Island.

Our Airline (☎ 674-444 3746; www.ourairline.com.au) Formerly Air Nauru, flies between Australia, Solomon Islands and Nauru.

Pacific Blue (☎ 61-7-3295 2284; www.flypacificblue.com) Offshoot of Virgin Blue flying from Australia and NZ to the Cook Islands, Fiji, Tonga, Samoa, Vanuatu, PNG and the Solomons.

Polynesian Blue (☎ 685-22172; www.polynesianblue .com) Partnership between Virgin Blue and the Samoan government. Flies from Australia and NZ to Samoa.

Qantas (☎ in Australia 13 13 13; www.qantas.com) Code-shares with some Pacific airlines, flying from Australia, NZ and the US to New Caledonia, Vanuatu, Tahiti (French Polynesia) and Fiji.

Solomon Airlines (☎ 677-20031; www.flysolomons .com) Connects the Solomons to Australia, Fiji and Vanuatu.

United (☎ in the US 1 800 538 2929; www.united.com) Flies or code-shares with Star Alliance partners from the US and Japan to the Cook Islands, French Polynesia, Fiji, and Samoa.

Tickets

South Pacific destinations tend to be relatively expensive to get to, and flying between Pacific islands is costly too. Because transport to and between Pacific islands is almost exclusively done by plane, you need to have it planned up front. Many people come to the Pacific as a stopover on a round-the-world (RTW) ticket, or you might consider an air pass (see right) that allows stops on several Pacific islands.

Don't automatically discount tours and packages from travel agents that include flights, transfers and accommodation because agents buy fares and accommodation wholesale and can bundle packages together at very competitive prices. Also consider specialist diving-tour agencies and other activity-based tours. These packages typically include flights and accommodation, plus any activity fees and tours.

The travel sections of daily newspapers often advertise discount fares. Be wary of deals that seem too good to be true and check the bona fides of vendors you're unfamiliar with. On the whole, travel agents can't compete on price with internet booking sites but they offer packages, advice and extended services that can be worth the extra money.

For long-term travel there are plenty of discount tickets valid for 12 months, allowing multiple stopovers with open dates.

The (return) airfares quoted in this book should be used as a guide only. Airport taxes, surcharges and the like are not included in these fares and they can quickly add up to hundreds of dollars. See p638 for indicative airfares under regional headings to the major gateway cities – Honolulu (Hawai'i), Pape'ete (French Polynesia), Nadi (Fiji), Sydney (Australia) and Auckland (NZ) – from where you'll be able to pick up connecting flights to the South Pacific's island destinations.

Full-time students and people under 26 who can show a valid International Student Identity Card (ISIC) may have access to better deals than other travellers – they may not always be cheaper fares but could include more flexibility to change flights and/or routes.

INTERCONTINENTAL TICKETS

Choose between RTW fares or Circle Pacific tickets to get you to and around the Pacific.

Round-the-world Tickets

Various airline alliances offer RTW tickets, which give travellers an almost endless variety of possible airline and destination combinations.

RTWs can be excellent value; expect to pay from US$3000, AU$3500, €2000 or UK£1350. Star Alliance (a code-sharing group of airlines that includes Air NZ) and OneWorld (including Qantas) offer some of the best RTWs for the South Pacific region.

Fiji is the most popular destination for travellers on RTWs, but Samoa, French Polynesia, Tonga and the Cook Islands can all be visited as part of a RTW.

Circle Pacific Tickets

Circle Pacific fares are similar to a RTW ticket except that they're used for travel only between Pacific Rim countries – the USA, South Pacific, South America, Southeast Asia, NZ and Australia. They can be great value if you're combining a Pacific journey with destinations in Australasia and the Americas. As with RTW tickets, there are advance-purchase restrictions, as well as limits on how many stopovers you can make. Fares are based on mileage.

For an idea of price, you should expect to pay about US$4000 for a fare which includes Los Angeles–Tahiti (Pape'ete)–Cook Islands (Rarotonga)–Auckland–Brisbane–Singapore–Los Angeles. Air New Zealand and its Star Alliance (www.staralliance.com) partners sell this product, as does Qantas and the One World (www.oneworld.com) affiliates.

AIR PASSES

Inter-country flights in the Pacific can be prohibitively expensive. A good way to travel to a handful of countries is by using

CLIMATE CHANGE & TRAVEL

Climate change is a serious threat to the ecosystems that humans rely upon, and air travel is the fastest-growing contributor to the problem. Lonely Planet regards travel, overall, as a global benefit, but believes we all have a responsibility to limit our personal impact on global warming.

Flying & Climate Change

Pretty much every form of motor travel generates carbon dioxide (the main cause of human-induced climate change) but planes are far and away the worst offenders, not just because of the sheer distances they allow us to travel, but because they release greenhouse gases high into the atmosphere. The statistics are frightening: two people taking a return flight between Europe and the US will contribute as much to climate change as an average household's gas and electricity consumption over a whole year.

Carbon Offset Schemes

Climatecare.org and other websites use 'carbon calculators' that allow jetsetters to offset the greenhouse gases they are responsible for with contributions to energy-saving projects and other climate-friendly initiatives in the developing world – including projects in India, Honduras, Kazakhstan and Uganda.

Lonely Planet, together with Rough Guides and other concerned partners in the travel industry, supports the carbon offset scheme run by climatecare.org. Lonely Planet offsets all of its staff and author travel.

For more information check out our website: lonelyplanet.com.

an air pass. Some passes are arranged by airlines, while others are put together by travel agents. Seating availability for heavily discounted fares can be quite limited, so book early. Note that most air passes have to be bought well in advance, and many must be purchased before travel to the South Pacific commences. Air passes come and go with some frequency, so seek up-to-date information from airlines and travel agents.

In addition to air passes offered by airlines and their affiliates, travel agencies and wholesalers combine air sectors into interesting combinations. Air Brokers International (www.airbrokers.com), World Travellers' Club (www.around-the-world.com) and Travelscene (www.travelscene.com), for example, offer excellent circle-Pacific fares out of the US.

Boomerang Pass

The Boomerang Pass sold by Qantas (www.qantas.com) can be used to travel between Australia, NZ and the southwest Pacific islands of Fiji, Vanuatu, Tonga, Samoa, New Caledonia and the Solomon Islands on airlines that Qantas code-shares with (Air Pacific and Air Vanuatu). It costs AU$160 to AU$360 per sector, depending on mileage. The pass must be purchased before or in conjunction with travel to Australia, NZ and the southwest Pacific. It's not available to residents of Australia, NZ or the southwest Pacific.

Circle Asia & South West Pacific

This air pass is sold by One World (www.oneworld.com) alliance flyers (Qantas and others) and allows travel beginning and terminating in Australia, NZ and several Asian countries to include one or more stopovers in the southwest Pacific, including Tonga, Vanuatu, Fiji and New Caledonia. Routes must also take in both northeast and southeast Asia. The base fare is routed through Sydney–Tokyo–Hong Kong–Perth–Sydney costs AU$2300, to which additional stopovers in the southwest Pacific may be added for AU$200 per country.

Oceanie Pass

This **Aircalin** (www.aircalin.com) pass is sold to passengers residing outside the South Pacific (including Australia and NZ). A minimum of two sectors costing from US$160 to US$340 per sector must be purchased before departure in conjunction with any long-haul ticket into the region. It offers connections to New Caledonia, Vanuatu, Fiji, French Polynesia, NZ and Australia.

ONLINE BOOKING AGENCIES

A selection of online booking agencies is listed here, together with the country or region in which the website is based.

Air Brokers International (www.airbrokers.com; USA)

CheapTickets (www.cheaptickets.com; USA)

ebookers.com (www.ebookers.com; UK, Continental Europe)

Expedia.ca (www.expedia.ca; Canada)

Expedia.com (www.expedia.com; USA, UK, France, Netherlands)

House of Travel (www.houseoftravel.co.nz; NZ)

JustFares (www.justfares.com; USA)

My Travel (www.mytravel.com; UK)

Orbitz (www.orbitz.com; USA)

travel.com.au (www.travel.com.au; Australia)

Travelocity.ca (www.travelocity.ca; Canada)

Webjet (www.webjet.com.au; Australia)

World Travellers' Club (www.around-the-world.com; USA)

Asia

Flying from Japan, there are direct flights to Fiji, French Polynesia and New Caledonia. There are also direct flights from South Korea to Fiji and New Caledonia. Travellers from other Asian destinations will find it easiest to fly to Australia or NZ and connect there with onward flights to the South Pacific. Most Asian countries offer fairly competitive airfare deals – Bangkok, Singapore and Hong Kong are some of the best places to shop around for discount tickets.

JAPAN & SOUTH KOREA

Recommended agencies in Japan include **STA Travel** (☎ 03-5391 2922; www.statravel.co.jp) and **No 1 Travel** (☎ 03-3205 6073; www.no1-travel.com). In Seoul try **STA Travel** (☎ 02 733 9494; www.statra vel.co.kr).

From Japan, return fares to Nadi (Fiji) are around ¥161,000 and to Pape'ete (Tahiti) from ¥176,000. Fares from South Korea to Fiji start from US$1400.

Australasia

Although being close to Australia and NZ, the South Pacific is still reasonably expensive to get to from Australasia. This is partly because there's not a lot of competition on these routes and they're generally flown by small national airlines. There's not much difference between seasonal fares, except during the Christmas holiday period when fares increase considerably.

Brisbane and Sydney on Australia's east coast have excellent connecting flights to Melanesia (Solomons, Vanuatu, Fiji and New Caledonia), while Auckland is the main gateway into Polynesia (Cook Islands, Samoa, Tonga and French Polynesia).

Australia's east coast and NZ are both included in the routing of several air passes (see p636).

AUSTRALIA

Some travel agents specialise in discount South Pacific air tickets, and some, particularly smaller ones, advertise cheap air fares in the travel sections of weekend newspapers, such as the *Age* (in Melbourne) and the *Sydney Morning Herald*.

Travel agencies that specialise in South Pacific holidays include **Hideaway Holidays** (☎ 02-8799 2500; www.hideawayholidays.com.au), **Talpacific Holidays** (☎ 02-9262 6318; www.talpacific .com), **Pacific Holidays** (☎ 02-9080 1600; www.pacific holidays.com.au) and **Pacific Traveller** (☎ 03-8662 7399; www.pacifictra veller.com.au).

Return fares from east-coast capitals to Fiji cost from AU$650/900 in the low/high season, to French Polynesia AU$1200/1600 and to Vanuatu AU$700/1000. Virgin's Polynesian Blue and Pacific Blue airlines are cheaper than the big-name airlines like Qantas and Air New Zealand.

NEW ZEALAND

The *New Zealand Herald* has a travel section in which travel agents advertise fares. Both **Go Holidays** (☎ 09-914 4700; www.goholidays .co.nz) and **Air New Zealand** (☎ 0800 737 000; www.airnewzealand.co.nz) offer a range of fares and packages from NZ to most South Pacific destinations.

You can get year-round return fares to Fiji from about NZ$800 and return fares to the Cook Islands from NZ$600. To French Polynesia, return fares start from about NZ$1200.

Europe

There are many flights from most major European cities to LA, Honolulu, Sydney and Auckland, from where connecting flights into the South Pacific are frequent. London, Paris and Frankfurt have the most flight options, but there's not much variation in fares between these cities. Flights from Europe via Japan and South Korea are shorter, but there are only direct connections with New Caledonia, Fiji and French Polynesia.

The South Pacific is almost exactly on the other side of the globe from Europe, so a RTW ticket (see p636) is probably the most economical way to get into the region. Low season for travel from Europe is both January to June and October to November. High season is July to September and during the Christmas and New Year period.

CONTINENTAL EUROPE

In Germany, **Adventure Travel** (☎ 0911 979 95 55; www.adventure-holidays.com) and **Art of Travel** (☎ 089-21 10 76-13; www.artoftravel.de, in German) specialise in South Pacific travel.

In the Netherlands, try **Wereldcontact** (☎ 0343 530 530; www.wereldcontact.nl) and **Pacific Island Travel** (☎ 020-626 13 25; www.pacificislandtravel .com) for flight/accommodation deals.

Travel agencies in France that specialise in South Pacific travel include **Nouvelles Frontières** (☎ 08 25 00 07 47; www.nouvelles-frontieres .fr), **Ultramarina** (☎ 08 25 02 98 02; www.ultramarina .com) and **OTU Voyages** (☎ 08 20 81 78 17; www.ot u.fr).

From Paris and Frankfurt, low-season return fares to Pape'ete (Tahiti) start from €1400, while fares to Nadi (Fiji) start from €1200. There are cheap fares from major European cities to Honolulu from €1000 and about €1100 to Australia.

UK

Discount air travel is big business in London. Advertisements for many travel agencies appear in the travel pages of the weekend broadsheet newspapers, as well as *Time Out*, the *Evening Standard* and in the free magazine *TNT*.

Recommended travel agencies that offer good South Pacific products include **All Ways Pacific** (☎ 01494 432747; www.all-ways .co.uk), **Trailfinders** (☎ 0845 058 5858; www.trail finders.co.uk) and **Travelbag** (☎ 0800 082 5000; www.travel bag.co.uk).

From the UK, flights via LA are generally the easiest – and often the cheapest – option for travel to the South Pacific. Air New Zealand or Qantas flights from London to Australia or NZ often allow for stopovers in the South Pacific. Flights from London via Seoul and Tokyo are another possibility.

Return fares from London to Nadi (Fiji) and Rarotonga (Cook Islands) start from £900/1200 in the low/high season, and flights to Pape'ete (Tahiti) cost from £1300/1600.

Travelling to Honolulu costs from £700, and Sydney and Auckland fares start from about £750.

North America

The gateway cities for travel into the South Pacific are LA and Honolulu from where there are direct flights to the Cooks, Fiji, French Polynesia and Samoa. There are also numerous flights to Australia and NZ from where you can connect to other Pacific destinations. From Canada, most flights to the South Pacific will travel via LA and/or Honolulu.

The air passes mentioned on p636 offer excellent value for travellers from North America.

In general, travel to South Pacific is cheapest in the June-to-August period, while November and December are the most expensive months.

CANADA

The *Toronto Globe & Mail*, *Toronto Star*, *Montreal Gazette* and *Vancouver Sun* are good places to start looking for cheap fares. **Goway** (☎ 800 387 8850; www.goway.com) is a Toronto-based travel agency specialising in trips to the South Pacific.

Flying from Vancouver to Honolulu, year-round return fares start at around C$500, or C$700 from Toronto. Fares from Vancouver to Nadi (Fiji) start from C$1700/2200 in the low/high season, or C$2000/3000 to Pape'ete (Tahiti). From Toronto and Ottawa, return low season fares to Nadi start from C$2200 and C$2500 to Pape'ete.

USA

Discount travel agencies in the US can be found through the *Yellow Pages* or major newspapers. The *Los Angeles Times*, *New York Times*, *San Francisco Examiner* and *Chicago Tribune* have weekly travel sections with ads and information.

US travel agents who specialise in the South Pacific region include **Newmans Vacations** (☎ 800 342 1956; www.newmansvacations .com), **Pacific for Less** (☎ 808 875 7589; www.pacific -for-less.com) and **South Seas Adventures** (☎ 800 576 7327; www.south-seas- adventures.com).

Year-round fares to Honolulu start from around US$300 from LA and US$450 from New York. From LA, low/high season fares start from US$1100/1400 to Pape'ete and

Nadi. From New York and other east-coast cities, return low/high season fares start from US$1500/2500 to Pape'ete (Tahiti) and US$1400/1900 to Nadi (Fiji).

Air New Zealand flights from LA to Australia and NZ often include one free stopover in the Cook Islands, Fiji, Samoa, Tahiti or Tonga. In the low/high season, expect to pay around US$1300/1700 for a return fare to Auckland, including this stopover.

South America

LAN (www.lan.com) operates flights between Santiago and Pape'ete, and one flight a week stops on Easter Island. For more information on fares and schedules, contact LAN or **Sertur** (☎ 02-335 0395; www.sertur.cl, in Spanish) in Santiago, an affiliate of STA Travel. From Santiago, return fares to Pape'ete cost from US$1800.

SEA

Cruise ships are an expensive way of seeing the South Pacific – they only ever call into the major tourist islands and rarely stay longer than a few hours.

Inter-island shipping routes connect many remote islands within South Pacific countries that are not serviced by airplane. Cargo vessels, some of which carry passengers, travel between some far-flung island groups and the main trading island of the country they belong to, while other ships carry cargo across international borders.

The South Pacific is a favourite playground for yachties and many people tour the region aboard their own sailing vessel (or someone else's).

These options are detailed in the Getting Around section on opposite.

TOURS

It's worth considering the many and various packages offered by travel agents and airlines – these can be off-the-shelf or tailored to your requirements. Tours – that can include flights, airport transfers, accommodation, meals and activities – can be very cost effective, and often work best for families, wedding parties and groups travelling together. Lone travellers and couples too should compare the cost and convenience of joining a tour or buying a package trip. It's quite possible to book a package and extend your stay with independent

travel – visitor permits issued on arrival in most Pacific countries are good for 31 days and most countries allow extensions of at least three months.

GETTING AROUND

AIR

Flying in light aircraft is the primary way of getting between the islands within South Pacific countries. While the international routes to/from Pacific capitals are flown in big Boeings and Airbuses, the domestic sectors are flown by De Havilland Twin Otters, Embraer Bandeirantes, Brit Norman Islanders, Saab 340s and other small prop planes – don't expect cabin crew and complimentary meals. These small aircraft often land on grass airstrips on remote islands, where the airport terminal is just a tin shed and a guy with a two-way radio. Some inter-island flights might operate just once or twice a week and may be heavily booked, so don't assume you can make travel arrangements on the spot. Details of domestic air travel are given in the Transport section of individual country chapters.

The most cost-effective way of travelling to more than one or two South Pacific nations is by buying an air pass. There are several international and domestic air passes available which can make air travel more affordable, although residents of the Pacific–Australasia region are ineligible for most international air passes. See p636 for information on international air passes.

Airlines in South Pacific

The following airlines fly between several South Pacific countries. Check the Transport section of the individual country chapters for schedules and fares.

Air Fiji (☎ 679-331 3666; www.airfiji.com.fj) Flies between Fiji and Tuvalu.

Air Pacific (☎ 679-672 0888; www.airpacific.com) Flies from Fiji, the Solomon Islands, Samoa, Tonga and Vanuatu.

Air Tahiti (☎ 689 86 40 23; www.airtahiti.aero) Flies between French Polynesia and the Cook Islands.

Air Vanuatu (☎ 678-23848; www.airvanuatu.com) Flies from Vanuatu to Fiji, New Caledonia and the Solomon Islands.

Aircalin (☎ 687-26 55 00; www.aircalin.nc) Flies from New Caledonia to Fiji, French Polynesia, Vanuatu, and Wallis and Futuna.

Inter-Island Airways (☎ 684-699 5700; www.inter islandair.com) Flies between American Samoa, Samoa and Tonga.

Polynesian Airlines (☎ 685-22172; www.polynesian airlines.com) Flies between Samoa and American Samoa.

Solomon Airlines (☎ 667-20031; www.solomonair lines.com.au) Flies from the Solomon Islands to Vanuatu and Fiji.

BOAT

There are a few possibilities for those romantics taken with the idea of travelling the Pacific by sea. It's certainly much slower than flying, not necessarily any cheaper and, with such vast distances of open ocean, you'd want to have plenty of good reading material. However, if this just adds to the appeal, then this could be the route for you. For information about yacht chartering or sailing on board a tall ship, see right.

Cargo Ship & Ferry

Cargo and dual-purpose cargo/passenger ships ply between the following countries: Tuvalu and Fiji, Vanuatu and New Caledonia, Samoa and Tokelau, Samoa and the Cook Islands. There's also a car ferry operating between Samoa and American Samoa. See 'Getting There & Away' in the Transport section of the individual country chapters for more detailed information on these services. Pitcairn Island and Tokelau, rely on cargo ships for connection to the outside world. See the 'Getting There & Away' section in those chapters for details. Travel agents don't book cargo-ship travel. You can either book through a freighter agent or directly with a shipping company.

Cruise Ship

Cruise ships will never be the cheapest, or the fastest way, from A to Z but they're usually pretty luxurious. Cruise-ship fares vary enormously, but generally prices go upwards from US$200 per day. Major port-of-calls are Noumea (New Caledonia), Port Vila (Vanuatu), Rarotonga (Cook Islands) and Pape'ete, Mo'orea and Bora Bora (all in French Polynesia). Melanesian cruises usually depart from Australia's east coast, mostly from Sydney and Brisbane. Other cruises depart from the US west-coast ports like Seattle, San Francisco, LA or Honolulu.

Travel agents, or the cruise companies themselves, need to be contacted well in advance if you are planning on taking a South Pacific cruise. A few companies include:

Crystal Cruises (www.crystalcruises.com)
Discovery World Cruises (www.discoveryworldcruises.com)
P&O (www.pocruises.com)
Phoenix Reisen Cruises (www.phoenixreisen.com)
Princess Cruises (www.princess.com)
ResidenSea (www.residensea.com)
Saga Cruises (www.sagacruises.com)

Yacht

Between May and October, the harbours of the South Pacific swarm with cruising yachts from around the world. Almost invariably, yachts follow the favourable westerly winds from the Americas towards Asia, Australia or NZ.

Popular routes from the US west coast take in Hawai'i and Palmyra Atoll before following the traditional path through Samoa and American Samoa, Tonga, Fiji and NZ. From the Atlantic and Caribbean, yachties access the South Pacific via Panama, the Galápagos Islands, the Marquesas, the Society Islands and the Tuamotus. Possible stops include Suwarrow (northern Cook Islands), Rarotonga and Niue.

The cyclone season begins in November and most yachties try to be well on their way to NZ by the early part of that month.

The yachting community is quite friendly and yachties are a good source of information about world weather patterns, navigation and maritime geography. They're also worth approaching to ask about day charters, diving and sailing lessons.

CREWING

Yachties are often looking for crew, and for those who'd like a bit of adventure, this can be a great opportunity. Most of the time, crew members will only be asked to take a turn on watch – to scan the horizon for cargo ships, stray containers and the odd reef – and possibly to cook or clean up the boat. In port, crew may be required to dive and scrape the bottom, paint or make repairs. In most cases, sailing experience is not necessary and crew members can learn as they go. Most yachties charge crew around US$20 per day for food and supplies.

If you'd like to find a crewing berth on a yacht, try to find one that has wind-vane steering, since the tedious job of standing at the wheel staring at a compass all day and

RESPONSIBLE YACHTING

- Don't add to the unsightly (and ecologically hazardous) trash floating up on island beaches by allowing rubbish to fall into the sea, even if you are nowhere near an island. Rubbish can float a long way!

- Many harbours are fished for food. So unless you have holding tanks or on-board sewerage treatment, use on-shore toilet facilities when you are in harbour.

- Never anchor on coral, or allow your anchor to drag through live coral.

- When in public view, observe the local customs regarding dress. Don't lounge about the deck topless on Sunday, for example!

all night is likely to go to the crew members of the lowest status (that's you). Comfort is also greatly increased on yachts that have a furling jib, a dodger to keep out the weather, a toilet and shower. Yachts rigged for racing are usually more manageable than simple liveaboards. As a general rule, about 3m of length for each person aboard affords relatively uncrowded conditions.

If you're trying to find a berth on someone else's yacht (or trying to find crew for your own boat), ask at local yacht clubs and look at noticeboards at marinas and yacht clubs. In the US, Honolulu and the west coast – San Francisco, Newport Beach and San Diego – are the places to start looking. Australia's northeastern seaboard is good and so are Auckland, Whangarei and the Bay of Islands in NZ. In the South Pacific, ask around in Pape'ete, Pago Pago, Apia, Nuku'alofa, Noumea or Port Vila.

Some companies that organise sailing trips around the South Pacific are:

Ocean Voyages (www.oceanvoyages.com) Organises yacht charters in the South Pacific. It's possible to charter a whole boat or book a berth on a yacht sailing a particular route. A charter is about the only way to get to some remote islands and atolls if you don't have your own yacht.

Tallship Soren Larsen (www.sorenlarsen.co.nz) This 45m tallship sails from Auckland to various South Pacific countries between March and November. It's possible to join the crew in Auckland or at any of the ports on its trip. Count on about NZ$220 per day.

RED TAPE

You must enter a country at an official 'port of entry' (usually the capital). If this means sailing past a dozen beautiful outlying islands on the way to an appointment with an official in a dull capital city, bad luck. Ports of entry are listed in the Transport section of the country chapters.

When you arrive, hoist your yellow quarantine flag (Q flag) and wait for the appropriate local official to contact you. Often, you are expected to alert them by VHF radio (usually on channel 16). Some countries charge visiting yachties entrance fees. Ask customs officials at the port of entry about requirements for visiting other islands in the country. Bear in mind that you are legally responsible for your crew's actions as well as your own.

LOCAL TRANSPORT
Bicycle

On flat South Pacific islands, riding a bicycle can be an excellent way to get around. For specific information, such as bike rental, see 'Getting Around' in the Transport section of the individual country chapters. Most rental bikes won't come with a helmet or lock unless you ask for them. Watch for poor road surfaces, and check your travel insurance for disclaimers about hazardous activities. If you're bringing your own bike into the country, ask the airline about costs and rules regarding dismantling and packing the bike.

Boat

Within a country, ferries and/or cargo boats are often the only way to get to some of the outer islands. See 'Getting Around' in the Transport section of individual country chapters for details about inter-island travel within a country.

Bus

Large and populous islands will usually have some kind of bus service. However, Pacific island public transport is rarely described as ruthlessly efficient. Buses are often privately (or sometimes family) owned. It is not unusual for owner-drivers to set their own schedules, and if there aren't many people travelling on a particular day, the buses may just stop altogether. Build flexibility into your plans.

Car & Motorcycle

Larger islands and tourist destinations will usually have some car- or motorcycle-hire companies – see Transport in the individual country chapters for more details.

Driving in some Pacific countries is on the righthand side of the road, while it's on the left in others. Countries that are part of the British Commonwealth drive on the left. Take extra care when you're driving on the 'wrong' side of the road and when crossing the road on foot.

Roads in rural areas may be no more than dirt tracks used mostly for foot traffic. Be careful of people or animals on the road and drive especially carefully near villages. Road conditions can be dreadful in undeveloped areas and worse if there's been recent cyclone or flood damage.

When you rent a car, ask about petrol availability if you're heading off the main routes, and make sure you get the insurance rules and conditions explained. Check your own travel insurance policy too; some do not cover unsealed roads or riding a motorcycle.

Prior to travelling, check whether you need an International Driving Permit to drive in the countries you are visiting.

Hitching

In some Pacific countries hitching is an accepted way of getting where you're going, and is practised by locals and tourists alike. In others it's not the local custom and only tourists are seen trying it. It is possible anywhere, however, and can be quite an efficient way to get around.

The main difficulty on a Pacific island is that rides won't be very long, perhaps only from one village to the next, and it could take you a while to go a longer distance. Hitching can be a great way to meet locals and is an option for getting around when the buses aren't running. You might be expected to pay a small fee for a ride, so offer what you think the ride is worth – although offers of payment will often be refused.

Keep in mind that hitching is never entirely safe. If you do choose to hitch, it is safer to travel in pairs.

TOURS

Many travellers now seek activity-based holidays, and several of these types of trips are packaged into organised tours. Local companies often specialise in activity-based tours – see the Tours sections in the individual country chapters.

Health Dr Michael Sorokin

With sensible precautions and behaviour, the health risk to travellers to the Pacific region is low. Mosquito-transmitted disease is the main problem. The Solomon Islands and Vanuatu share the one serious health hazard: malaria (the Solomons also has saltwater crocodiles). Elsewhere the main danger is from mosquito-borne dengue fever. The region is completely rabies-free.

BEFORE YOU GO

Prevention is the key to staying healthy while abroad. A little planning before departure, particularly for pre-existing illnesses, will save trouble later. See your dentist before a long trip, carry a spare pair of contact lenses and glasses, and take your optical prescription with you. Bring medications in their original, clearly labelled containers. A signed and dated letter from your physician describing your medical conditions and medications, including generic names, is also a good idea. If carrying syringes or needles, be sure to have a physician's letter documenting their medical necessity or obtain a prepared pack from a travel health clinic.

INSURANCE

If your health insurance does not cover you for medical expenses abroad, consider supplemental insurance. Check the Travel Services section of the Lonely Planet website at www .lonelyplanet.com/bookings/insurance.do for more information. Find out in advance if your insurance plan will make payments directly to providers or reimburse you later for overseas health expenditures. In many countries, doctors expect payment in cash.

For Americans, check whether your health plan covers expenses in countries associated with the US – American Samoa, Federated States of Micronesia, Guam, Marshall Islands, Northern Mariana Islands and Palau. If you are an EU citizen, you have the same rights in French Polynesia, New Caledonia, and Wallis and Futuna as you do in France, but remember to obtain the European Health Insurance Card (EHIC) before leaving home.

It is still best to have private health insurance cover. New Zealanders may have free access to public but not private facilities in the Cook Islands. Serious illness or injury may require evacuation, such as from Tuvalu to Fiji, or even from those countries with 'good' health facilities to a major regional centre, such as from Suva to Auckland. Make sure that your health insurance has provision for evacuation. Under these circumstances, hospitals will accept direct payment from major international insurers, but for all other health-related costs cash upfront is the usual requirement.

RECOMMENDED VACCINATIONS

The World Health Organization (WHO) recommends that all travellers be covered for diphtheria, tetanus, measles, mumps, rubella and polio, regardless of their destination. Since most vaccines don't produce immunity until at least two weeks after they're given, visit a physician at least six weeks before departure. A recent influenza vaccination is always a good idea when travelling. If you have not had chicken pox (varicella), consider being vaccinated.

MEDICAL CHECKLIST

It is a very good idea to carry a medical and first-aid kit with you in case of minor illness or injury. Following is a list of items you should consider packing:

- Antibiotics (prescription only), eg ciprofloxacin (Ciproxin) or norfloxacin (Utinor, Noroxin)
- Antibiotic plus steroid eardrops (prescription only), eg Sofradex, Kenacort otic
- Antidiarrhoeal drugs (eg loperamide)
- Acetaminophen (paracetamol) or aspirin*
- Anti-inflammatory drugs (eg ibuprofen)
- Antihistamines (for hay fever and allergic reactions)
- Antibacterial ointment (prescription only; eg Bactroban) for cuts and abrasions
- Antimalarial pills
- Antigiardia tablets (prescription only; eg tinidazole)
- Steroid cream or hydrocortisone cream (for allergic rashes)
- Bandages, gauze, gauze rolls, waterproof dressings
- Adhesive or paper tape
- Scissors, safety pins, tweezers#
- Thermometer
- Pocket knife#
- DEET-containing insect repellent for the skin
- Permethrin-containing insect spray for clothing, tents and bed nets
- Sun block
- Oral rehydration salts (eg Gastrolyte, Diarolyte, Replyte)
- Iodine tablets (for water purification)
- Syringes and sterile needles, and intravenous fluids if travelling in very remote areas

*Aspirin should not be used for fever; it can cause bleeding in cases of dengue fever
#Not in carry-on luggage

If you are travelling more than 24 hours away from a town area, consider taking a self-diagnostic kit that can identify, from a finger prick, malaria in the blood (applies only to Solomons and Vanuatu).

INTERNET RESOURCES

There is a wealth of travel-health advice on the internet. For further information, the Lonely Planet website (www.lonelyplanet. com) is a good place to start. The WHO publishes a superb book called *International Travel and Health*, revised annually and available online at www.who.int/ith at no cost. Other websites of general interest are **MD Travel Health** (www.mdtravelhealth.com), which provides complete travel-health recommendations for every country and is updated daily, also available at no cost; the **Centers for Disease Control and Prevention** (www.cdc.gov); **Fit for Travel** (www.fitfortravel.scot.nhs.uk), which has up-to-date information about outbreaks and is very user-friendly; and www.traveldoctor. com.au, a similar Australian site.

It's also a good idea to consult your government's travel-health website before departure, if one is available:
Australia (www.dfat.gov.au/travel)
Canada (www.hc-sc.gc.ca/pphb-dgspsp/tmp-pmv /pub_e.html)
UK (www.doh.gov.uk/traveladvice/index.htm)
USA (www.cdc.gov/travel)

REQUIRED & RECOMMENDED VACCINATIONS

If you have been in a designated yellow fever country within the previous six days, you need an International Certificate of Vaccination against yellow fever for entry into American Samoa, Fiji, New Caledonia, Niue, Pitcairn, Samoa, Solomon Islands and Tonga.

Palau may require evidence of vaccination against cholera if you have arrived from a currently infected country.

For all countries in the region, vaccinations are recommended for hepatitis A, hepatitis B and typhoid fever.

It is recommended that some visitors are vaccinated against Japanese B encephalitis.

Side Effects of Vaccinations

All vaccinations can produce slight soreness and redness at the inoculation site, and a mild fever with muscle aches over the first 24 hours. These side effects are less likely with hepatitis A inoculations and a little more common with hepatitis B and typhoid inoculations. Yellow-fever vaccine is dangerous for anyone with an egg allergy, and in about 5% of cases causes a flu-like illness any time within a week of vaccination.

FURTHER READING

Good options for further reading include *Travel with Children*, by Cathy Lanigan, and *Healthy Travel Australia, New Zealand and the Pacific*, by Dr Isabelle Young.

IN TRANSIT

DEEP VEIN THROMBOSIS (DVT)

Blood clots may form in the legs during plane flights, chiefly because of prolonged immobility. The longer the flight, the greater the risk. The chief symptom of DVT is swelling or pain of the foot, ankle or calf, usually but not always on just one side. When a blood clot travels to the lungs, it may cause chest pain and breathing difficulties. Travellers with any of these symptoms should immediately seek medical attention.

To prevent the development of DVT on long flights, you should walk about the cabin, contract the leg muscles while sitting, drink plenty of fluids, and avoid alcohol and tobacco. There is no good evidence that aspirin prevents DVT.

JET LAG & MOTION SICKNESS

To avoid jet lag (common when crossing more than five time zones), try drinking plenty of nonalchoholic fluids and eating light meals. Upon arrival, get exposure to natural sunlight and readjust your schedule (for meals, sleep and so on) as soon as possible.

Antihistamines such as dimenhydrinate (Dramamine), meclizine (Antivert, Bonine) or promethazine (Avomine) are usually the first choice for treating motion sickness, but they are more effective in prevention than in treatment. A herbal alternative is ginger.

IN THE SOUTH PACIFIC

AVAILABILITY & COST OF HEALTH CARE

The quality of health care varies over the region and within each country. Health facilities range from 'good' in Fiji, French Polynesia and American Samoa; 'reasonable' in the Cook Islands, New Caledonia, Samoa, Solomon Islands, Tonga and Vanuatu; and 'basic' in the other countries. These are all small countries with limited budgets, so even 'good' does not necessarily equate to the facilities you could expect in a well-developed country.

Having 'good' health services means that the country has readily available doctors in private practice and standard hospital and laboratory facilities with consultants in the major specialties – internal medicine, obstetrics/gynaecology, orthopaedics, ophthalmology, paediatrics, pathology, psychiatry and general surgery. Private dentists, opticians and pharmacies are also available. French Polynesia has very good military medical facilities, but the private sector is so well developed that civilians will not normally have access to these.

In countries where facilities are 'reasonable', specialised services may be limited or available periodically, but private general practitioners, dentists and pharmacies are present.

'Basic' services refers to the presence of nurses, midwives and a few doctors, limited government dental services, unreliable pharmaceutical supplies and hospitals far removed from Western standards.

Even in the countries with more developed facilities, the further you get from main cities the more basic the services. In secondary centres and outer islands, the quality of service is generally lower – not necessarily because of staffing but because of lower-quality diagnostic and treatment facilities. Small hospitals, health centres and clinics are situated conveniently throughout the region, but staffing and facilities will vary. Intergovernmental or church-mission aid and doctors may well be present in some of these facilities.

Private consultation and private hospital fees are approximately equivalent to Australian costs. Government-provided service fees vary from modest to negligible, but waiting times can be very long. Direct payment is required everywhere except where a specific arrangement is made, such as in the case of evacuation or where a prolonged hospital stay is necessary; your insurer will need to be contacted by you. Although most of the larger hospitals are coming into line in accepting credit cards, there will be difficulty with the more remote small hospitals. Also, most private practitioners are reluctant to acceptable this form of payment, except for the larger private doctor groups in American Samoa, Fiji and Tahiti. Even these still prefer cash, and not all credit cards are accepted – check with the relevant company beforehand. If a credit card is not accepted, you should be able to arrange cash on credit through the local banking system; however, in more remote areas, such as Tokelau and Futuna, you won't find a bank. Keeping a few hundred dollars in travellers cheques is a wise move.

Most commonly used medications are available in countries with good or reasonable health care. Where only basic care is available, even aspirin and antiseptics may be hard to come by. Private pharmacies are not allowed by law to dispense listed drugs without prescription from a locally registered practitioner, but many will do so for travellers if shown the container. While the container should preferably specify the generic name of the drug, this has become much less of a problem with the use of internet search engines.

Commonly used drugs, including oral contraceptives and antibiotics, are available in the main centres, where there are private pharmacies, but do not expect large supplies. Oral contraceptives are obtainable without prescription in Fiji, as is the 'morning after' pill. Asthma inhalers and most anti-inflammatories are over-the-counter preparations in the Samoas, Fiji and Tahiti. Even in the 'good' countries it is best to have a sufficient supply of a regularly taken drug as a particular brand may not be available and sometimes quantities can be limited. This applies particularly to psychotropic drugs, such as antidepressants, antipsychotics, anti-epileptics and mood elevators.

Insulin is available even in smaller centres, but you cannot guarantee getting a particular brand, combination or preferred administration method. If you have been prescribed the very latest oral antidiabetic or antihypertensive, make sure you have enough for the duration of your travel.

Except in the remote poorly staffed clinics, the standard of medical and dental care is generally quite good even if facilities are not sophisticated. The overall risk of illness for a normally healthy person is low; the most common problems are diarrhoeal upsets, viral sore throats, and ear and skin infections, all of which can mostly be treated with self-medication. For serious symptoms, such as sustained fever or chest or abdominal pains, it is best to go to the nearest clinic or private practitioner in the first instance.

Tampons and pads are readily available in main centres but do not rely on getting them if you travel to one of the outer islands. Dengue fever, especially in the first three months of pregnancy, poses a hazard because of fever, but otherwise there is no reason why a normal pregnancy should prevent travel to the region (except perhaps to the Solomon Islands and parts of Vanuatu, because of malaria; see p648). However, on general principles immunisation in the first three months of pregnancy is not recommended, and Japanese B encephalitis or yellow fever vaccines should not be given.

For young children, it is again dengue fever that could be a problem. The disease tends to come in epidemics, mainly in the hotter, wetter months, so it should be possible to plan holidays accordingly. In tropical climates dehydration develops very quickly when a fever and/or diarrhoea and vomiting occur.

INFECTIOUS DISEASES
Dengue Fever
Risk All countries, especially in the hotter, wetter months
Dengue fever is spread through the bite of the mosquito. It causes a feverish illness with headache and severe muscle pains similar to those experienced with a bad, prolonged attack of influenza. There might also be a fine rash. Mosquito bites should be avoided whenever possible – be obsessive about the use of insect repellents (see boxed text, p648). Self-treatment includes paracetamol, fluids and rest. Danger signs are prolonged vomiting, blood in the vomit and/or a blotchy dark red rash.

Eosinophilic Meningitis
Risk Cook Islands, French Polynesia, Fiji, Tonga
A strange illness manifested by scattered abnormal skin sensations, fever and sometimes by the meningitis symptoms (headache, vomiting, confusion, stiffness of the neck and spine), which give it its name. Eosinophilic meningitis is caused by a microscopic parasite – the rat lungworm – that contaminates raw food. There is no proven specific treatment, but symptoms may require hospitalisation. For prevention, pay strict attention to advice on food and drink.

Hepatitis A
Risk All countries
Hepatitis A is a viral disease causing liver inflammation. Fever, debility and jaundice (yellow colouration of the skin and eyes, together with dark urine) occur and recovery is slow. Most people recover completely over time,

but the virus can be dangerous to people with other forms of liver disease, the elderly and sometimes to pregnant women towards the end of pregnancy. It is spread by contaminated food or water. Self-treatment consists of rest, a low-fat diet and avoidance of alcohol. The vaccine is close to 100% protective.

Hepatitis B
Risk All countries
Like hepatitis A, hepatitis B is a viral disease causing liver inflammation, but the problem is more serious and the virus frequently goes on to cause chronic liver disease and even cancer. It is spread, like HIV, by mixing bodily fluids as in sexual intercourse, by contaminated needles and by accidental blood contamination. Treatment is complex and specialised, but vaccination is highly effective.

Hepatitis C
Risk Incidence is uncertain within the region but must be assumed to be present
Hepatitis C is a viral disease similar to hepatitis B. It causes liver inflammation that can go on to become chronic liver disease or result in a symptomless carrier state. The virus is spread almost entirely by blood contamination from shared needles or contaminated needles used for tattooing or body piercing. Treatment is complex and specialised. There is no vaccine available.

HIV/AIDS
Risk All countries
The incidence of HIV infection is on the rise in the whole Pacific region. Government reports usually underestimate the size of the problem, so when international conference discussions say that the incidence is reaching epidemic proportions you can take it that the danger posed by unprotected sex is huge; condoms are essential. If you require an injection for anything, check that a new needle is being used or have your own supply.

Japanese B Encephalitis
Reported outbreaks Incidence is uncertain in the region but must be assumed to be present
Japanese B encephalitis is a serious viral disease transmitted by mosquitoes. Early symptoms are flu-like and this is usually as far as the infection goes, but sometimes the illness proceeds to cause brain fever (encephalitis), which has a high death rate. There is

no specific treatment. Effective vaccination is available – it involves three inoculations over a month and is expensive. Allergic and sensitivity reactions to the vaccine, though rare, can occur. Vaccination is usually recommended for anyone staying more than a few weeks and/or going to work in villages.

Leptospirosis
Risk American Samoa, Fiji, French Polynesia, possibly elsewhere
Also known as Weil's disease, leptospirosis produces fever, headache, jaundice and, later, kidney failure. It is caused by a spirochaete organism found in water contaminated by rat urine. The organism penetrates skin, so swimming in flooded areas is a risk practice. If diagnosed early, the disease is cured with penicillin.

Malaria
Risk Solomon Islands (except the outlying atolls and Honiara), Vanuatu (except Port Vila and Futuna, Tongoa, Aneityum and Mystery Islands)
Malaria is a parasite infection transmitted by infected anopheles mosquitoes. While these mosquitoes are regarded as night feeders, they can emerge when light intensity is low (eg in

overcast conditions under the jungle canopy or the interior of dark huts). In the Solomon Islands and Vanuatu, both malignant (falciparum) and less threatening but relapsing forms are present. Since no vaccine is available, travellers must rely on mosquito-bite prevention (including tropical insect repellents, knockdown insecticides and, where necessary, bed nets impregnated with permethrin – see boxed text, opposite) and taking antimalarial drugs before, during and after risk exposure. No antimalarial is 100% effective.

Malaria causes a variety of symptoms but the essence of the disease is fever. In a malarial zone it is best to assume that fever is due to malaria unless blood tests rule it out. This applies to up to a few months after leaving the area as well. Malaria is curable if diagnosed early.

Tuberculosis
Risk Tuvalu

The scourge of the 19th century, tuberculosis has not been eliminated in the region and there is something of a resurgence where HIV/AIDS is prevalent. It is spread by droplet infection from an infected person and is a risk for household contacts or healthcare workers but not for transient travellers. Vaccination with the related BCG organism has been abandoned by US authorities, and other countries recommend it only for special cases. The best protection against tuberculosis is a healthy diet and lifestyle.

Typhoid Fever
Risk Sporadic in all countries

Typhoid fever is a bacterial infection acquired from contaminated food and/or water. The germ can be transmitted by food handlers and flies, and can be present in inadequately cooked shellfish. It causes fever, debility and late-onset diarrhoea. If left untreated , it can produce delirium and is occasionally fatal, but the infection is curable with antibiotics. Vaccination is moderately effective, but care with eating and drinking is equally important.

Yaws
Risk Solomon Islands

Yaws is a bacterial infection that causes multiple skin ulcers. It was thought to have been eliminated, but there has been a recent resurgence. Infection is conveyed by direct contact. Treatment with penicillin produces a dramatic cure.

TRAVELLER'S DIARRHOEA
Diarrhoea (ie frequent, loose bowel movements) is caused by viruses, bacteria or parasites present in contaminated food or water. In temperate climates the cause is usually viral; in the tropics, bacteria or parasites are more usual. If you develop diarrhoea, be sure to drink plenty of fluids, preferably an oral rehydration solution (eg Diarolyte, Gastrolyte, Replyte). A few loose stools don't require treatment, but if you start having more than four or five stools a day, you should take an antibiotic (usually a quinolone drug) and an antidiarrhoeal agent (such as Loperamide). If diarrhoea is bloody, persists for more than 72 hours or is accompanied by fever, shaking, chills or severe abdominal pain, seek medical attention.

Giardiasis
A parasite present in contaminated water, giardia produces bloating and a foul-smelling and persistent although not 'explosive' diarrhoea. One dose (four tablets) of tinidazole usually cures the infection.

ENVIRONMENTAL HAZARDS
Threats to health from animals and insects are rare indeed, but travellers need to be aware of them.

Bites & Stings
Saltwater crocodile attacks, though rare, are well recorded in the Solomon Islands. Crocodiles can swim into tidal rivers; heed local warnings.

JELLYFISH
Watch out for the whip-like stings of the blue-coloured Indo-Pacific man-of-war. If you see these floating in the water or stranded on the beach, it is wise not to go in the water. The sting is very painful and is best treated with vinegar or ice packs. Do not use alcohol.

POISONOUS CONE SHELLS
Poisonous cone shells abound along shallow coral reefs. Avoid handling them. Stings mainly cause local reactions, but nausea, faintness, palpitations or difficulty in breathing are signs that flag the need for medical attention.

SEA SNAKES
As in all tropical waters, sea snakes may be seen around coral reefs. Unprovoked, sea

HEALTH

snakes are extremely unlikely to attack and their fangs will not penetrate a wet suit.

Coral Ear

Coral ear is a common name for inflammation of the ear canal. It has nothing to do with coral, and is caused by water entering the canal activating any fungal spores that may be lying around and predisposing the area to bacterial infection and inflammation. Inflammation usually starts after swimming but can be reactivated by water dripping into the ear canal after a shower, especially if long, wet hair lies over the ear opening.

Apparently trivial, it can be very, very painful and can spoil a holiday. Apart from diarrhoea, it is the most common reason for travellers to consult a doctor. Self-treatment with an antibiotic plus steroid eardrop preparation is very effective. Stay out of the water until pain and itching have gone.

Coral Cuts

Cuts and abrasions from dead coral cause no more trouble than similar injuries from any other sort of rock, but live coral can cause prolonged infection. Never touch coral. If you do happen to cut yourself on live coral, you will need to treat the wound immediately. Get out of the water as soon as possible, clean the wound thoroughly, getting out all the little bits of coral, apply an antiseptic and cover with a waterproof dressing. Once you've done this, you can then get back in the water if you want to.

Diving Hazards

Because the region has wonderful opportunities for scuba diving, it is easy to get overexcited and neglect strict depth and time precautions. Few dives are very deep, but the temptation to spend longer than safe amounts of time at relatively shallow depths is great and is probably the main cause of decompression illness (the 'bends') in the region. Early pains may not be severe and may be attributed to other causes, but any muscle or joint pain after scuba diving must be suspect.

At the time of writing, privately run compression chambers can be found in Fiji, Tahiti and Vanuatu, but transport to a chamber can be difficult. Supply of oxygen to the chambers is sometimes a problem. Novice divers must be especially careful. Even experienced divers should check with organisations like Divers' Alert Network (DAN; www.diversalert network.org) about the current site and status of compression chambers, and insurance to cover costs.

VENOMOUS MARINE LIFE

Probably the most dangerous thing you'll have to worry about when snorkelling over a reef is sunburn. However, there are several venomous critters worth mentioning in case of a chance encounter.

The well-camouflaged stonefish spends much of its time on the seafloor pretending to be a weed-covered rock. If you tread on a stonefish's sharp, extremely venomous dorsal spines, you'll find that the pain is immediate and incapacitating. Bathing the wound in hot water reduces the pain and the effects of the venom, but medical attention should be sought urgently.

The lionfish, a relative of the stonefish, is a strikingly banded brown-and-white fish with large, graceful dorsal fins containing venomous spines. Lionfish are obvious when they're swimming around, but they can also hide under ledges.

Then there's the cone shell, several species of which have highly toxic venom. The bad ones have a venomous proboscis – a rapidly extendible, dartlike stinging device that can reach any part of the shell's outer surface. Cone shell venom can be fatal. Stings should be immobilised with a tight pressure bandage (not a tourniquet) and splint. Get medical attention immediately.

Avoid contact with jellyfish, which have stinging tentacles; seek local advice. Dousing in vinegar will deactivate any stingers that have not 'fired'. Calamine lotion, antihistamines and analgesics may reduce the reaction and relieve the pain. Other stinging sea creatures include flame or stinging coral and sea urchins.

Generally speaking, the best way to avoid contact with any of the above while you're in the water is to look but don't touch. Shoes with strong soles will provide protection from stonefish, but reef walking damages the reef, so you shouldn't be doing it anyway – regard the stonefish as an environmental protection officer.

> ### DRINKING WATER
>
> To prevent diarrhoea, avoid tap water unless it has been boiled, filtered or chemically disinfected (with iodine tablets), and steer clear of ice. This is a sensible overall precaution, but the municipal water supply in capital cities in the region can be trusted.

Food & Water

The municipal water supply in capital cities and other large towns in the region can be trusted, but elsewhere avoid untreated tap water. In some areas the only fresh water available may be rainwater collected in tanks and this should be boiled. Steer clear of ice. Only eat fresh fruits or vegetables if cooked or peeled; be wary of dairy products that might contain unpasteurised milk. Eat food that is heated right through and avoid buffet-style meals. Food in restaurants frequented by locals is not necessarily safe, but most resort hotels have good standards of hygiene, although individual food handlers can carry infection. Food that comes to you piping hot is likely to be safe. Be wary of salads. If you are preparing your own salads from market produce, make sure that each piece and leaf is thoroughly washed with water that is safe. Be adventurous by all means, but expect to suffer the consequences if you succumb to temptation and try raw fish or crustaceans as eaten by some locals.

FISH POISONING

Ciguatera is a form of poisoning that affects otherwise safe and edible fish unpredictably. Poisoning is characterised by stomach upsets, itching, faintness, slow pulse and bizarre inverted sensations – cold feeling hot and vice versa. Ciguatera has been reported in many carnivorous reef fish, including red snapper, barracuda and even Spanish mackerel; in French Polynesia it is quite frequent in the smaller reef fish. There is no safe test to determine whether a fish is poisonous or not and, although local knowledge is not entirely reliable, it is reasonable to eat what the locals are eating. Fish caught after times of reef destruction, such as after a major hurricane, are more likely to be poisonous. Deep-sea tuna is perfectly safe.

Treatment consists of rehydration and if the pulse is very slow, medication may be needed. Healthy adults will make a complete recovery, although disturbed sensation may persist for some weeks – sometimes much longer.

Heat

The region lies within the tropics, so it is hot and for the most part humid.

Heat exhaustion is actually a state of dehydration associated, to a greater or lesser extent, with salt loss. Natural heat loss is through sweating and so it is easy to become dehydrated without realising it. Thirst is a late sign. Heat exhaustion is prevented by drinking at least 2L to 3L of water per day – more if actively exercising. Salt-replacement solutions are useful, as muscle weakness and cramps are due to salt and water loss and can be made worse by drinking water alone. The powders used for treating dehydration due to diarrhoea are just as effective when dehydration is due to heat exhaustion. Apart from commercial solutions, a reasonable drink consists of a good pinch of salt to a pint (half-litre) of water. Salt tablets can result in too much salt being taken, and can cause headaches and confusion.

HEAT STROKE

When the cooling effect of sweating fails, heat stroke ensues. This is an emergency condition characterised not only by muscle weakness and exhaustion but also by mental confusion. Skin will be hot and dry. If this occurs, 'put the fire out' by cooling the body with water on the outside and, if possible, with cold drinks for the inside. Seek medical help for follow-up.

Sunburn

Exposure to the ultraviolet rays of the sun causes burning of the skin with accompanying pain and misery and the long-term danger of skin cancer. The time of highest risk is between 11am and 3pm – remember that cloud cover does not block out UV rays. Sunburn is likely to be a particular problem for those taking doxycycline as an antimalarial. The Australian 'slip, slop, slap' slogan is a useful mantra: slip on a shirt, slop on sunscreen and slap on a hat. Treat sunburn as you would any other burn – cool, wet dressings are best. Severe swelling may respond to a cortisone cream.

TRADITIONAL MEDICINE

The Pacific region has been settled for thousands of years and systems of treatment involving local herbs, roots and leaves have evolved over the centuries, with each region or village having its own traditional healers. Some of these folk remedies undoubtedly have effective ingredients, and governments and research institutions are currently actively investigating many of them. Extravagant claims (eg AIDS cures, aphrodisiacs) can be ignored, and it is best to avoid the more exotic compounds made with animal ingredients. Tree-bark concoctions for fever are similar to aspirin in their effects. Chinese herbs are available in all of the main towns.

Kava (see boxed text, p61) is a concoctio made from the root of *Piper methysticum* and has sedative and muscle relaxant prop erties. When taken in concentrated forn (eg tablets) or when mixed with alcoho it has been linked with liver damage, bu mild 'tourist' social drinking will cause little harm other than indigestion. Kava is drunl throughout the region, most commonly i Fiji, New Caledonia, the Samoan islands Tonga and Vanuatu.

Betel-nut chewing is common in the Solomon Islands. It has an astringent effec in the mouth, but claims about other healin properties remain unproven. Prolonged user are predisposed to mouth cancers.

Glossary

aiga – see *kainga* (Samoa)
ainga – see *kainga*
ava – see *kava* (Samoa)
ahima'a – earth/stone oven
ahu – raised altar or chiefly backrest found on ancient *marae* (Polynesia)
aitu – spirit, ghost (Polynesia)
aliki – see *ariki*
ali'i – see *ariki*
ari'i – see *ariki*
ariki – paramount chief; members of a noble family
atoll – low-lying island built up from successive deposits of coral
atua – god or gods (Polynesia)
aualuma – society of unmarried women (western Polynesia)
aumaga – see *aumanga* (Samoa and Tokelau)
aumanga – society of untitled men who do most of the fishing and farming (Polynesia)
Austronesians – people or languages from Indonesia, Malaysia and the Pacific islands

babai – large plant resembling taro, commonly eaten in Kiribati
bai – traditional men's meeting house (Palau)
barrier reef – a long, narrow coral reef lying off shore and separated from the land by a lagoon of deep water that shelters the land from the sea; see also *fringing reef*
bêche-de-mer – lethargic, bottom-dwelling sea creature
beka – see *peka* (Fiji)
bigman – chief (Solomons, Vanuatu)
bilibili – bamboo raft (Fiji)
bilo – vessel made from half a coconut shell and used for drinking *kava* (Fiji)
biu – treehouse for initiated boys (Solomon Islands)
blackbirding – a 19th-century recruitment scheme little removed from outright slavery
bonito – blue-fin tuna
borrow pits – pits dug out to provide landfill (Tuvalu)
bougna – traditional *Kanak* meal of yam, *taro* and sweet potatoes with chicken, fish or crustaceans, wrapped in banana leaves and cooked in coconut milk in an earth oven (New Caledonia)
bringue – family event with friends (French Polynesia)
bula – Fijian greeting
burao – wild hibiscus tree
bure – thatched dwelling (Fiji)

cagou – New Caledonia's national bird
Caldoche – white people born in New Caledonia whose ancestral ties go back to the convicts or the early French settlers
cargo cults – religious movements whose followers hope for the imminent delivery of vast quantities of modern wealth (cargo), from either supernatural forces or the inhabitants of faraway countries
case – traditional *Kanak* house (New Caledonia); see also *grande case*
CFP – Cour de franc Pacifique (also called the Pacific franc); the local currency in all three of France's Pacific territories
Chamorro – the indigenous people of the Mariana Islands including Guam
chef – customary leader of a clan (New Caledonia)

dalo – see *taro* (Fiji)
dapal – a women's meeting house in Yap
drua – double-hulled canoe (Fiji)

'ei – necklace (Cook Islands)

fa'a – see *faka*
fa'afafine – see *fakaleiti* (Samoa)
fafine – see *vahine*
faka – according to (a culture's) customs and tradition, eg *fa'a Samoa* or *faka Pasifika*
fakaleiti – man who dresses and lives as a woman (Tonga)
fale – house with thatched roof and open sides, but often used to mean any building
fale fono – meeting house, village hall or parliament building
fale umu – kitchen huts
faluw – a Yapese meeting house for men
fanua – see *fenua* (Samoa)
fare – see *fale*
fatele – traditional music and dance performance (Tuvalu)
fenua – land
fiafia – dance performance (Samoa)
fono – governing council (Polynesian)
FSM – Federated States of Micronesia
fusi – cooperative stores (Tuvalu)

gîte – group of bungalows used for tourist accommodation (French territories)
grade-taking – process by which Melanesian men progress through a series of castes, proving their worth through feasts and gifts; see *nimangki*

grande case – big house where tribal chiefs meet; see also *case*

heilala – Tonga's national flower
honu – turtle (French Polynesia)
horue – surfing (French Polynesia)
hôtel de ville – see *mairie*

i'a – see *ika*
ika – fish
inati – sharing (Tokelau)

kahlek – night fishing using burning torches to attract flying fish into hand-held nets (FSM)
kai – food
kaiga – see *kainga*
kainga – extended family (Polynesia)
kaleve – see *kaokioki* (Tokelau)
kaloama – juvenile goatfish (Niue)
Kanak – indigenous New Caledonians
kanaka – people (Polynesia)
kaokioki – beer-like fermented coconut drink
kastom – custom; rules relating to traditional beliefs (Solomons, Vanuatu)
kastom ownership – traditional ownership of land, objects or reef
katuali – black-and-grey-striped sea kraits (Niue)
kava – mud-coloured, mildly intoxicating drink made from the roots of the *Piper methysticum* plant
kikau – thatch-roofed
kilikiti – see *kirikiti*
kirikiti – cricket with many players on each side (French Polynesia, Samoa, Tokelau, Tuvalu, and Wallis and Futuna)
korkor – a Marshallese dugout fishing canoe made from a breadfruit log
koutu – ancient open-air royal courtyard (Cook Islands)
kuli – see *kuri*
kumala – see *kumara*
kumara – sweet potato
kuri – dogs

la coutume – custom (New Caledonia); see *kastom*
lanai – a Hawaiian word commonly used in Micronesia to refer to a veranda
Lapita – ancestors of the Polynesians
laplap – Vanuatu national dish
latte stones – the stone foundation pillars used to support ancient Chamorro buildings in the Marianas; the shafts and capstones were carved from limestone quarries
lava-lava – sarong-type garment; wide piece of cloth worn as a skirt by women and men
lei – see *'ei*
LMS – London Missionary Society
lovo – traditional feast (Fiji)

mahimahi – dolphin fish
mahu – see *fakaleiti* (French Polynesia)
maire – aromatic leaf (Cook Islands)
mairie – town hall (French Polynesia, New Caledonia)
makatea – geological term for a raised coral island; cora coastal plain around an island
mal mal – *T-piece* of cotton on *tapa* cloth worn by male dancers (Vanuatu)
malae – see *marae*
malo – Polynesian greeting
man blong majik/posen – sorcerers
mana – personal spiritual power
maneaba – traditional community meeting house (Kiribati)
maneapa – community meeting house (Tuvalu)
manu – birds
Maohi – see *Maori*
Maori – indigenous people (Cook Islands, Society Islands)
marae – community village green (western Polynesia); pre-Christian sacred site (eastern Polynesia); ceremonial meeting ground (Cook Islands)
masi – bark cloth with designs printed in black and rust (Fiji)
matai – senior male, political representative of a family (Samoa, Tokelau and Tuvalu)
mataiapo – see *matai* (Cook Islands)
me'ae – see *marae*
meke – dance performance that enacts stories and legends (Fiji)
Melanesia – islands of the western Pacific comprising Papua New Guinea, Solomon Islands, Vanuatu, New Caledonia and Fiji; the name is Greek for 'black islands'
Métro – someone from France (New Caledonia)
Micronesia – islands of the northwestern Pacific, including Palau, Northern Mariana Islands, Guam, FSM, Marshall Islands, Nauru and Kiribati; the name is Greek for 'small islands'
mission dress – see *muu-muu*
moa – chicken
moai – large stone statues (Easter Island)
Mother Hubbard – see *muu-muu*
motu – island, islet
muu-muu – long, loose-fitting dress introduced to the Pacific by the missionaries
mwaramwars – headwreaths of flowers and fragrant leaves (FSM)

naghol – land-diving ritual (Vanuatu)
nakamal – men's clubhouse (New Caledonia, Vanuatu)
namalao – fowl-like megapode
namba – traditional sheath (Vanuatu)
natsaro – traditional dancing ground (Vanuatu)
nguzunguzu – carved wooden canoe figurehead (Solomons)

imangki – status and power earned by *grade-taking* (Vanuatu)

iu – coconut

i-Vanuatu – people from Vanuatu

oni – age-defying juice (French Polynesia)

ono – small gnats, sandflies (French Polynesia)

uku – village (Polynesian)

u'u – see *nuku*

mung – a perfumed love potion (FSM)

no – barracuda

ka – raw fish marinated in coconut milk and lime juice (Niue)

a'anga – the currency of Tonga

ADI – Professional Association of Dive Instructors

ae pae – paved floor of a *marae*

akalolo – marijuana (French Polynesia)

alagi – see *palangi*

alangi – white person, westerner (Polynesia)

apuans – ancient people who are among the ancestors of modern Melanesians

areo – see *pareu*

areu – *lava-lava* (Cook Islands, French Polynesia, New Caledonia and Vanuatu)

arpa – see *pareu*

e'a – see *peka* (Samoa)

ebai – a Yapese community meeting house

eka – bat, small bird

elagic – creatures living in the upper waters of the open ocean

ilou – *Kanak* dance, performed for important ceremonies or events

olynesia – the huge triangle of ocean and islands bounded by Hawai'i, New Zealand and Easter Island; includes the Cook Islands, French Polynesia, Niue, Pitcairn Island, Samoa, American Samoa, Tokelau, Tonga, Tuvalu, and Wallis and Futuna; the name is Greek for 'many islands'

olynesian Outliers – the islands of eastern Melanesia and southern Micronesia that are populated by Polynesians

opaa – Westerner (French Polynesia)

ua'a – see *puaka*

uaka – pig (Polynesia)

ukao – topknot

ulenuku – head man, village mayor (Polynesia)

ulenu'u – see *pulenuku*

urse seine – large net generally used between two boats that is drawn around a school of fish, especially tuna; boats that use this method are called *purse seiners*

Quonset hut – WWII military storage shed made from corrugated iron

a'atira – see *rangatira* (Tahiti)

ae rae – see *fakaleiti* (French Polynesia)

ragatira – see *rangatira* (Samoa)

rai – Yapese stone money (FSM)

rangatira – chief, nobility (Polynesia)

ratu – chief (Fiji)

RFO – Radio France Outre-Mer

rori – see *bêche-de-mer* (French Polynesia)

sa – sacred, forbidden; holy day, holy time (Samoa and Tuvalu)

sakau – see *kava*

Saudeleur – tyrannical royal dynasty that ruled ancient Pohnpei

scrab faol – see *skrab dak*

seka – narcotic ceremonial drink similar to *kava* (FSM)

sevusevu – presentation of a gift to a village chief and, by extension, to the ancestral gods and spirits (Fiji)

siapo – *tapa* (Samoa)

skrab dak – megapode bird (Solomon Islands)

snack – cheap café (French Territories)

SPF – South Pacific Forum

SPTO – South Pacific Tourism Organisation

sulu – see *lava-lava* (Fiji and Tuvalu)

swim-through – hole or tunnel large enough to swim through

tabu – see *tapu*

tagimoucia – national flower of Fiji

tahua – see *tufanga* (Tahiti)

tamaaraa – traditional-style feast

tamtam – slit-gong, slit-drum; made from carved logs with a hollowed-out section (Vanuatu)

tanata – people (Polynesia)

tangata – see *tanata*

tano'a – multi-legged wooden bowl used for mixing *kava* (Wallis and Futuna)

ta'ovala – distinctive woven pandanus mats worn around the waist in Tonga

tapa – see *masi*

tapu – sacred, prohibited

taro – plant with green heart-shaped leaves, cultivated for both its leaf and edible rootstock

tatau – tattoo

taulasea – traditional healer (Samoa)

taupo – ceremonial virgin (Samoa)

taupou – title bestowed by high-ranking chief upon a young woman of his family (Polynesia)

taupulega – village council of elders and *matai* (Tokelau)

thu – a loincloth worn by Yapese males and by outer island Chuukese

tifaifai – see *tivaevae* (French Polynesia)

tiki – carved human figure (Polynesia)

tivaevae – colourful intricately sewn appliqué works (Cook Islands)

tokosra – paramount chief (FSM)

to'ona'i – Sunday lunch (Samoa)

T-piece – small piece of cloth covering only the groin area (Solomons, Vanuatu)
trepang – bêche-de-mer
tu' – see *tui* (Tonga)
tuba– see *kaokioki* (Yap, FSM)
tufanga – priest, expert (Polynesia)
tufuga – see *tufanga* (Samoa)
tui – paramount king (central Pacific)
tumunu – hollowed-out coconut-tree stump used to brew bush-beer; also bush-beer drinking sessions

uga – coconut crab
ulihega – bait fish (Niue)
'umala – see *kumara*

umete – wooden dishes (French Polynesia)
umu – earth oven
umukai – feast of foods cooked in an *umu*
USP – University of the South Pacific

va'a – see *vaka*
vahine – woman (Polynesia)
vaka – canoe
vale – see *fale* (Fiji)

wantok – one talk; the western Melanesian concept that all those who speak your language are allies (Solomon Islands)

yaqona – see *kava* (Fiji)

The Authors

ROWAN MCKINNON

Coordinating Author, Getting Started, Itineraries, Environment, Raratonga & the Cook Islands, Directory, Transport

Rowan – lapsed rock muso and freelance writer – has travelled many times in the South Pacific. He caught the bug as a kid growing up on Nauru before the family settled in bayside Melbourne. He's travelled to Papua New Guinea a dozen times, learning the subtle ways of Melanesian culture and collecting Melanesian art. He's seen shark-callers in the Solomons, drunk kava in Vanuatu and travelled to Fiji, Kiribati and Tuvalu. For this book Rowan went east to come to grips with Polynesia and the brilliant Cook Islands.

My Favourite Trip

I love the untamed Solomons where too few tourists go – the islands and lagoons of Western Province (p375) are as beautiful as anywhere I've seen. My partner and I took our two-year-old daughter up to the wilds of northern Malaita (p383) and that was an adventure. Tanna (p579) in Vanuatu is another highlight and seeing Mt Yasur is breathtaking. Fiji's Mamanucas (p135) are wonderful and the lagoons of Tuvalu (p536) are crystal clear. The Cook Islands really blew me away – Rarotonga (p256) is so laid back and physically beautiful with every creature comfort you could ask for; Aitutaki's lagoon (p273) is more stunning than you can imagine; and makatea islands and atolls are endlessly interesting. I'd happily spend a fortnight surfing in 'Upolu (p302) in Samoa or Tahiti (p413) and island hop through the Marquesas (p457).

BRETT ATKINSON

Niue

Brett's latest visit to Niue was his third opportunity to experience the mandatory relaxation of one of the world's smallest nations. From his base in Auckland, New Zealand, Brett's travelled to and written about many Pacific island countries, but the quirky and idiosyncratic Niue remains his favourite. This time round, he signed up for yet another palm-tree trimmed Niuean driver's licence, caught up with old acquaintances for Sunday afternoon drinks at the Washaway Café, and experienced the humbling thrill of snorkeling with a humpback whale and her calf. For ongoing Pacific island thrills, Brett throws his support behind the increasingly multicultural rugby teams of the Auckland Blues and the All Blacks.

LONELY PLANET AUTHORS

Why is our travel information the best in the world? It's simple: our authors are passionate, dedicated travellers. They don't take freebies in exchange for positive coverage so you can be sure the advice you're given is impartial. They travel widely to all the popular spots, and off the beaten track. They don't research using just the internet or phone. They discover new places not included in any other guidebook. They personally visit thousands of hotels, restaurants, palaces, trails, galleries, temples and more. They speak with dozens of locals every day to make sure you get the kind of insider knowledge only a local could tell you. They take pride in getting all the details right, and in telling how it is. Think you can do it? Find out how at **lonelyplanet.com**.

THE AUTHORS

CELESTE BRASH
Food & Drink, Pitcairn Islan
Tahiti & French Polynesia, Wallis & Futur

Celeste first visited French Polynesia in 1991 and moved to the country perm nently in 1995. Her first five years were spent on a remote atoll *sans* plumbing airstrip, but now she calls the modern island of Tahiti home. Her award winnin travel stories have appeared in *Travelers' Tales* books and her travel articles ha appeared in major US publications, including the *LA Times* and *Islands* magazin She's written over a dozen Lonely Planet guides on destinations around th world but considers the South Pacific her speciality.

JEAN-BERNARD CARILLET
Diving, Easter Islan
Solomon Islands, Tahiti & French Polynesi

A Paris-based journalist and photographer, Jean-Bernard is a die-hard Sout Pacific lover, a diving instructor and a Polynesian dance aficionado. He ha travelled the length and breadth of the South Sea for nearly 15 years now this assignment was his 10th trip to the South Pacific – from the Solomor and Vanuatu to Easter Island and Fiji. Jean-Bernard is also an expert on Frenc Polynesia, about which he has written numerous articles and guides.

He's contributed to many Lonely Planet titles, both in French and English, and has coordinated their dive guide *Tahiti & French Polynesia*.

PETER DRAGICEVICH
Samoa, American Samoa, Tokela

Growing up in one of the main Polynesian pockets of the world's bigges Polynesian city, Peter's been surrounded by Pasifika sights and sounds fc as long as he can remember – from the soaring Samoan choirs at his chilc hood church to the scintillating drummers that welcome his favourite rugb league team onto the field. Although his professional writing career has le him all over the world, Peter has now returned to West Auckland, wher there's always a ready supply of taro at the local shops and he can swa around in a lava-lava all day whenever the mood takes him. This is the 12t book he's coauthored for Lonely Planet.

JOCELYN HAREWOOD
New Caledonia, Vanuat

Jocelyn has been writing for Lonely Planet for the past seven years an this is her third research trip to Vanuatu, where there are more delightfu features to discover at each return. But her visit to New Caledonia was first, so she's perfectly placed to tell everybody that this is a great plac for an adventure or an idyllic laze-about. And it doesn't matter if you don' speak French. When Jocelyn's not working on a book, she plays with he grandchildren, for research of course.

NANA LUCKHAM   Tuvalu

Nana's first taste of the South Pacific was a two-week stopover in Fiji, where she won a dance competition and took part in many kava ceremonies. This time around she was delighted to explore the quieter side of the region and get to know the remote and even more laid back Tuvalu. Nana has worked full-time as a travel writer for the past three years, after time spent as a UN Press Officer in New York and Geneva and an editor in London. She has contributed to several other guidebooks, including Lonely Planet's guide to Fiji, and when not on the road she lives in the exotic wilds of southwest London.

CRAIG MCLACHLAN   Tonga

An island-addict from way back, Craig has covered islands from those of Greece to Okinawa to Tonga for Lonely Planet. His first foray to Tonga was as a teenager when his father, an architect, designed a resort island in the kingdom and he was introduced to his first kava session. He's never looked back! A Kiwi, Craig runs an outdoor activity company in Queenstown, New Zealand in the southern hemisphere summer, then hits the road for Lonely Planet in the off-season. He has an MBA from the University of Hawaii, speaks fluent Japanese, is a 25-year karate practitioner and has written several books. Check out his website at www.craigmclachlan.com. Craig highly recommends Tongan *Ikale* beer.

DEAN STARNES   Fiji

Dean was an impressionable six years old when he first travelled to Fiji. The week he spent bobbing above the Mamanuca reefs with a leaky mask and a pair of floaties ignited a passion for travel that has since taken him around the world and to over 85 countries. With several visits to Fiji now under his weight belt, Dean knew it was time to come home when he started preferring kava to beer. He now lives in Auckland where he alternates between writing for Lonely Planet, freelancing as a graphic designer and shirking responsibilities. His book, *Roam; the Art of Travel* and his website, www.deanstarnes. com, feature photography and stories about his wayfaring ways.

CONTRIBUTING AUTHOR

George Dunford wrote the Directory, History and Culture chapters. Completing an honours degree in history at the Australian National University saw George studying several units in Pacific history and later working with the Pacific Manuscript Bureau. He has also written historical material on Captain Cook's journals for the National Library of Australia's award-winning Endeavour CD-ROM. He has contributed to several books for Lonely Planet, including *New Zealand* and *Southeast Asia on a Shoestring*, and has worked as a freelance writer.

Michael Sorokin wrote the Health chapter, and has extensive experience working as a physician and GP in the Pacific Islands, South Africa, the UK and rural South Australia. He was awarded the Order of Fiji in recognition of his services to health care in Fiji. .

Behind the Scenes

Lonely Planet's 1st edition of South Pacific was coordinated by Errol Hunt in 2000. The 2nd and 3rd editions were coordinated by Geert Cole and Leanne Logan.

This new edition was coordinated by longtime Melanesian wanderer Rowan McKinnon. Heading out around the islands were Rowan, Brett Atkinson, Celeste Brash, Jean-Bernard Carillet, Peter Dragicevich, Jocelyn Harewood, Nana Luckham, Craig McLachlan and Dean Starnes.

Other material was supplied by George Dunford (Destination, History and The Culture), Tony Horwitz (Captain James Cook box in the History chapter), Errol Hunt (Maui's Fish box in Culture and St Pierre Chanel of Oceania box in Wallis & Futuna chapter), Clement Paligaru (Indo-Fijian History & Culture box in the Fiji chapter), Martin Robinson (Fa'alavelave box in American Samoa), former Tuvaluan prime minister Saufatu Sopoanga (Climate Change & Global Warming box in the Environment chapter), Dr Michael Sorokin (Health chapter), Tony Wheeler (Lost on Niue box in the Niue chapter and Marooned in Tuvalu box in the Tuvalu chapter) and global wanderer Rowland Burley (Tokelau, at Last box in the Tokelau chapter).

THIS BOOK

Commissioning Editors Judith Bamber, Errol Hunt
Coordinating Editor Trent Holden
Coordinating Cartographer Brendan Streager
Coordinating Layout Designer Jessica Rose
Managing Editor Geoff Howard
Managing Cartographer Alison Lyall
Managing Layout Designer Sally Darmody
Assisting Editors Susie Ashworth, Andrea Dobbin, Kate Evans, Cathryn Game, Jocelyn Hargrave, Piers Kelly, Kristin Odijk, Donna Wheeler
Assisting Cartographers Ildiko Bogdanovits, Mick Garrett
Cover Designer Pepi Bluck
Project Managers Chris Girdler, Glenn van der Knijff
Thanks to Shahara Ahmed, Imogen Bannister, Valeska Canas, Nicholas Colicchia, David Connolly, Quentin Frayne, Emma Gilmour, Carol Jackson, Laura Jane, Lisa Knights, Averil Robertson, Suzannah Shwer, Dianne Schallmeiner, Jeanette Wall

THANKS
ROWAN MCKINNON

A heartfelt thanks to Gayna Malone and Nooroa Ruaine, Lydia Nga, Queen Manarangi Tutai and Des Clark. To Parua Tavioni, many thanks for the morning tea. Thanks also to Marshall Humphries, Papa

---

THE LONELY PLANET STORY

Fresh from an epic journey across Europe, Asia and Australia in 1972, Tony and Maureen Wheeler sat at their kitchen table stapling together notes. The first Lonely Planet guidebook, *Across Asia on the Cheap*, was born.

Travellers snapped up the guides. Inspired by their success, the Wheelers began publishing books to Southeast Asia, India and beyond. Demand was prodigious, and the Wheelers expanded the business rapidly to keep up. Over the years, Lonely Planet extended its coverage to every country and into the virtual world via lonelyplanet.com and the Thorn Tree message board.

As Lonely Planet became a globally loved brand, Tony and Maureen received several offers for the company. But it wasn't until 2007 that they found a partner whom they trusted to remain true to the company's principles of travelling widely, treading lightly and giving sustainably. In October of that year, BBC Worldwide acquired a 75% share in the company, pledging to uphold Lonely Planet's commitment to independent travel, trustworthy advice and editorial independence.

Today, Lonely Planet has offices in Melbourne, London and Oakland, with over 500 staff members and 300 authors. Tony and Maureen are still actively involved with Lonely Planet. They're travelling more often than ever, and they're devoting their spare time to charitable projects. And the company is still driven by the philosophy of *Across Asia on the Cheap*: 'All you've got to do is decide to go and the hardest part is over. So go!'

Paiere Mokoroa, Roger Malcolm, Richard the English amateur physicist. Thanks to Lance for the genuine Chinese-made Rolex Oyster Perpetual Superlative Chronometer, and to Wendy thanks for help and advice with the broken leg. A gracious thanks to the many nameless Cook Islanders who saw me hobbling and stopped to offer me a lift. Thanks to Herman Melville for *Moby Dick* that I took to bed at night, and thanks too to Tito on Mangaia, Paka Worthington, Carey Winterflood and Liz Raizis. Yachtsman Fredrik Fransson, thank you for the sailing itinerary, and good on you too Jenny Blake.

It was a great privilege to work with commissioning editor Judith Bamber, head carto David Connolly and an outstanding team of authors – to Brett Atkinson, Celeste Brash, Jean-Bernard Carillet, Peter Dragicevich, George Dunford, Jocelyn Harwood, Nana Luckman, Craig McLachlan and Dean Starnes, thanks for the sustained effort and great work.

To my family, as always, thanks for the big commitment and sacrifice from the whole crew – Jane, Lewis, Eadie, Lauren and Wesley.

BRETT ATKINSON
On Niue, a big *'fakaaue lahi to Ida'*, Tanya, and the team at the Niue Tourism Office, Robyn, Joe and Willy for the Hash House beers, and Stafford for the conversation, company, and occasional conspiracy theory. At Lonely Planet thanks to Judith Bamber for choosing to go the extra mile and commission one of the smaller LP gigs, and to Rowan McKinnon for his grace and humour as coordinating author. In Auckland, love and special thanks to Carol, and to Mum and Dad for their unwavering and unconditional support.

CELESTE BRASH
Most thanks to my kids Jasmine and Tevai and my husband Josh for putting up with my absences. In French Polynesia thanks to Joel House, Edwin and Jacqueline, Ben and Hinano, Lily and Ralph and family, Mateo Pakaiti and Jacques Sauvage, Cathy Campbell and especially to JB Carillet for all-time collaboration. On Wallis and Futuna thanks to Pascal Nicomette and Gregory at SB Travel Futuna. For Pitcairn, big thanks to the whole crew of the *Braveheart* and the Jolly family, Simon and Shirley Young, Jaqui Christian, Brenda Christian, Jay and Carol Warren and Melanie Tankard. And of course thanks to the Lonely Planet inhouse gang, especially Judith Bamber and David Connolly.

JEAN-BERNARD CARILLET
Heaps of thanks to Lonely Planet's Judith for her trust. In French Polynesia, a heartfelt *'mauruuru roa'* goes out to Yan & Vai and *fetii*, who are my family and guardian angels. A big thanks also to all diving staff (and colleagues) and to all the people who helped out and made this trip so enlightening, including Verly, Maire, Moearii, Eric, Jean-Christophe, Ronald, Laurent, Fred, Helene, Pierre, Yves, Jean-Yves and Alex, among others. In Easter Island thanks to Sergio Rapu, Enrique Tucki, Lionel, Jérôme, Antoine and Sabrina. In the Sols, I'm grateful to Franck, Don, Kerrie, Chris, Karen and Sunga, among others. Rowan, coordinating author extraordinaire, deserves the thumbs up for his courage and perseverance. And how could I forget my daughter Eva, who shared some of my Polynesian adventures and gives direction to my otherwise roving life.

PETER DRAGICEVICH
'Fa'afatai tele' to all the people that helped make this the most enjoyable Lonely Planet assignment I've yet undertaken. Thanks to Cindy (of Samoa) Filo and Edward Cowley for setting me up with the best Apia support team I could have wished for. To Shaddow Fau, Russell Jobling and Ivy Warner: thank you for welcoming me into your hearts and showing me such a great time in your beautiful country. I can't wait to return. Thanks also to Aniva and Bob and their family and staff for making me feel so at home – despite my Lonely Planet sneakiness.

JOCELYN HAREWOOD
Returning to Vanuatu is such a pleasure. Everybody makes me feel like a long-lost friend, and the enthusiasm everyone feels for their country is contagious. This latest research trip was one delightful expedition due to the help of John and Silvana Nicholls, Peter Whitelaw and Karl Waldeback. Thanks so much. How would I manage without you? Everybody in the tourism business helped with their knowledge and insights. The outer islands were shown to me by the bungalow and hotel owners. Locals like Dave, Matt and Mal in Espiritu Santo, Kalo in the Maskelynes, Chief Charles of Gaua, Kelson, Merian and Hugh on Tanna, Sam and John in Ambrym, islanders everywhere. *Tankyu tumas.* Finally thanks to my daughter Juliet, who brought Charlotte and Amelia along with me for a few days to uncover the best spots for kids.

Hey, everybody in New Caledonia, thanks for sharing the laughter as we broached the English–French language divide. Together we discovered your country by communicating with hands and eyes and a great mix of words. Fantastic. The people in the Office du Tourisme gave me a wealth of information, books and brochures, DVDs, CDs, glossy folders and pamphlets. Thanks especially to Jacques Houssard and Alain Bonneaud. This beautiful land you helped me get around lived up to its reputation and I can't wait to return. Special thanks to Tione who wrote about New Caledonia for the last edition and passed on loads of news, to Anne for helping out stacks, and to Rick, Noelie, Jean-Christophe, Florente, Auguste and Richard for telling me all about this land you all love.

NANA LUCKHAM

Many thanks to Judith Bamber for letting me take on the gig and to Rowan McKinnon for enthusiastic coordinating authorness. Thanks also to everyone who helped out my research and answered my questions in Tuvalu, especially the staff of the Funafuti town council for an amazing trip around the Marine Conservation Area and the ladies at the Philatelic Bureau for the chat and the free stamps. And to Ben Swift, thanks as always for keeping me company on the road; and for the lagoonside marriage proposal.

CRAIG MCLACHLAN

A huge 'malo aupito' to my exceptionally beautiful wife Yuriko and our boys Riki and Ben for putting up with the huge mess of books, notes and pamphlets on Tonga in our living room. I promise I'll tidy it all up soon! And a hearty cheers to all those who helped me when I was on the road – and on the water in Vava'u – especially to Kava and Ofa.

DEAN STARNES

Fiji is a friendly place and I owe a large 'vinaka vakalevu' (and probably a few Fiji Bitters) to all the people who helped me out while I was on the road. I'm particularly grateful to Chris Keehn, Peter Kohler and Martin Garea-Balado for their invaluable advice on yacht-crewing and to Fabia Lonnquist, Janelle Morey, and Anna Scanlan for their insights into Suva. This book is far richer for the expertise lent by Céline Cottille, Iliana Lagi Naigulevu, Laurent Bloc'h, Julika Bourget, Jonathan Prasad, Helen Sykes and Vasemaca Rakabu Driso.

It wouldn't be right not to acknowledge the legacy of work from previous editions and the help and assistance from fellow author Nana Luckman, commissioning editor Judith Bamber and managing cartographer David Connolly.

My warmest thanks however, are reserved for my wife Debbie and my mum. The former not only had to spend a wet New Zealand winter alone, but supported me tirelessly through the write-up period and the later, for her willingness to proofread some grammatically challenged first drafts.

OUR READERS

Many thanks to the travellers who used the last edition and wrote to us with helpful hints, useful advice and interesting anecdotes:

Mike Abbott, Margriet Katoen, George Maylam, Jan Gert Notenbomer, Jessica & Henry Wadsworth.

ACKNOWLEDGMENTS

Many thanks to the following for the use of their content:

Globe on title page ©Mountain High Maps 1993 Digital Wisdom, Inc.

Internal photographs: p13 (#2) Ross Barnett; p6, p15 (#1) Jean-Bernard Carillet; p13 (#8) Grant Dixon; p8, p9 (#1), p14 Peter Hendrie; p10, p11 (#9, #10) Paul Kennedy; p12, p16 Casey Mahaney; p9 (#3) Will Salter; p15 (#10) Leonard Zell.

SEND US YOUR FEEDBACK

We love to hear from travellers – your comments keep us on our toes and help make our books better. Our well-travelled team reads every word on what you loved or loathed about this book. Although we cannot reply individually to postal submissions, we always guarantee that your feedback goes straight to the appropriate authors, in time for the next edition. Each person who sends us information is thanked in the next edition – and the most useful submissions are rewarded with a free book.

To send us your updates – and find out about Lonely Planet events, newsletters and travel news – visit our award-winning website: **lonelyplanet.com/contact**.

Note: we may edit, reproduce and incorporate your comments in Lonely Planet products such as guidebooks, websites and digital products, so let us know if you don't want your comments reproduced or your name acknowledged. For a copy of our privacy policy visit lonelyplanet.com/privacy.

Index

INDEX

GreenDex

TRAVELLING SUSTAINABLY

The problems of waste management and nature conservation are critical to the futures of all countries in the South Pacific, and many of our readers are looking to minimise the ecological impact of their travel. The following attractions, tours, and accommodation and eating venues have been selected by this guidebook's authors because they have active sustainable-tourism policies. Some hotels and accommodation places have committed to water- and waste-recycling programs, and some are constructed of ecofriendly materials and have minimal impacts on the lands they inhabit. Some are involved in conservation or environmental education, and many are owned and operated by local and indigenous operators and train other locals in tourism and hospitality – thereby preserving and fostering local culture and livelihoods.

There are as yet no Pacific-wide eco-accreditation schemes and so these selections are necessarily subjective and potentially contentious, but our authors believe these operators act in a way that is consistent with the ethos and ethic of sustainable tourism.

Lonely Planet is committed to supporting sustainable tourism. If you think we've omitted someone who should be listed here, or disagree with our choices, email us at talk2us@lonelyplanet.com.au. For more on sustainable travel, see www.lonelyplanet.com.au/responsibletravel.

684

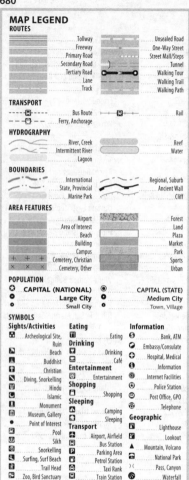

LONELY PLANET OFFICES

Australia
Head Office
Locked Bag 1, Footscray, Victoria 3011
☎ 03 8379 8000, fax 03 8379 8111
talk2us@lonelyplanet.com.au

USA
150 Linden St, Oakland, CA 94607
☎ 510 250 6400, toll free 800 275 8555
fax 510 893 8572
info@lonelyplanet.com

UK
2nd fl, 186 City Rd,
London EC1V 2NT
☎ 020 7106 2100, fax 020 7106 2101
go@lonelyplanet.co.uk

Published by Lonely Planet Publications Pty Ltd
ABN 36 005 607 983

© Lonely Planet Publications Pty Ltd 2009

© photographers as indicated 2009

Cover photograph: Close-up of frangipani flowers, Ile des Pins, South Province, New Caledonia, Jean-Bernard Carillet/Lonely Planet Images. Many of the images in this guide are available for licensing from Lonely Planet Images: www.lonelyplanetimages.com.

Printed by Fabulous Printers Pte Ltd
Printed in Singapore.